STATE RANKINGS
2004

A Statistical View of the 50 United States

Kathleen O'Leary Morgan and Scott Morgan, Editors

Morgan Quitno Press
© Copyright 2004, All Rights Reserved
512 East 9th Street, P.O. Box 1656
Lawrence, KS 66044-8656
USA
800-457-0742 or 785-841-3534
www.statestats.com

Fifteenth Edition

State Rankings 2004 sells for $54.95 ($6.00 shipping) and is only available in paper binding. For those who prefer ranking information tailored to a particular state, we also offer *State Perspectives*, state-specific reports for each of the 50 states. These individual guides provide information on a state's data and rank for each of the categories featured in the national *State Rankings* volume. *Perspectives* sell for $19.00 or $9.50 if ordered with *State Rankings*. We also publish a monthly *State Statistical Trends* ($299 a year). If crime statistics are your interest, please ask about our annual *Crime State Rankings* ($54.95 paper). If you are interested in city and metropolitan crime data, we offer *City Crime Rankings* ($42.95 paper). If you are interested in health statistics for states, please ask about our annual *Health Care State Rankings* ($54.95 paper). Also available is the first edition of our *Education State Rankings*. This view of K-12 education at the state level is $49.95. All of our data sets are also available on CD in pdf format as well as various database formats. These sell for $100 each. Shipping and handling is $6.00 per order. For information, please visit our website at www.statestats.com.

Fifteenth Edition
Printed in the United States of America
March 2004

PREFACE

From education to transportation, taxes to housing, agriculture to government finance, *State Rankings 2004* provides a giant collection of easy-to-understand statistics about life and government in your state. Find out how much tax revenue your state government collects. Learn what your state pays its teachers. Discover how much grain is harvested and milk is produced in your state. From basic state facts to interesting trivia, *State Rankings* features the most user-friendly, up-to-date collection of state information possible. In all, more than 550 tables of state statistics are provided.

Important Notes About *State Rankings 2004*

Our mission in publishing *State Rankings* is to translate complicated and often convoluted statistics into meaningful, easy-to-understand state comparisons. Each year, we review our books, update the majority of tables add a few new ones and remove others that no longer are pertinent. In this 2004 edition of *State Rankings,* you'll find 569 tables of state comparisons.

While there are a number of changes in this newly revised edition of *State Rankings,* its organization and other popular features remain the same. Source information and footnotes clearly are shown at the bottom of each page, while national totals, rates and percentages are prominently displayed at the top of each table. Every other line is shaded in gray for easier reading. Numerous information-finding tools are provided: a thorough table of contents, table listings at the beginning of each chapter, a detailed index and a chapter thumb index. In addition, a roster of sources, with addresses, phone numbers and Internet websites is found in the back of the book.

The numbers shown in *State Rankings* require no additional calculations to convert them from millions, thousands, etc. All states are ranked on a high to low basis, with any ties among the states listed alphabetically for a given ranking. Negative numbers are shown in parentheses "( )." For tables displaying national totals (as opposed to rates, per capita, etc.) a separate column is included that shows what percent of the national total each individual state's total represents. This column is headed by "% of USA." This percentage figure is particularly interesting when compared with a state's share of the nation's population for a particular year.

For basic information about states, check out the "State Fast Facts" section. Here you'll learn that Vermont, South Dakota, Pennsylvania and Minnesota apparently hired the same songwriter. Their state songs are "Hail, Vermont," "Hail, South Dakota," "Hail, Pennsylvania," and "Hail, Minnesota." In addition, find out which state is the lucky winner of our annual "Most Livable State Award."

For those of you needing information for just one state, we once again are offering our *State Perspective* series of publications. These 26-page comb bound reports feature data and ranking information for an individual state, pulled from the national *State Rankings 2004* book. (For example *New York in Perspective* features information about the state of New York only.) They serve as great timesavers for researchers who do not want to page through the entire *State Rankings* volume searching for information for their particular state. Purchased individually, *State Perspectives* sell for $19. When purchased with a copy of *State Rankings 2004,* these handy, quick reference guides are just $9.50.

Other Books From Morgan Quitno Press

In addition to *State Rankings 2004,* our company offers four other rankings reference books. *Education State Rankings* is our newest state reference book. Now in its second edition, this volume compares states in teachers' salaries, class sizes, graduation rates and more than 400 other categories relating to preK-12 education. *Health Care State Rankings 2004* provides an in-depth view of health care by state. Included in this 540-page annual volume are statistics on health care facilities, providers, insurance and finance, incidence of disease, mortality, physical fitness, natality and reproductive health. An annual compilation of state crime data is featured in *Crime State Rankings.* In its 11th edition for 2004, this reference volume examines state law enforcement personnel and expenditures, juvenile crime, corrections, arrests and offenses. Our *City Crime Rankings* reference book compares U.S. metropolitan areas and cities of 75,000+ population in all major crime categories. Numbers of crimes, crime rates and crime trends over one and five years are presented for all major crime categories reported by the FBI (features 2002 data.) The data in all our reference books also are available on CD-ROM. These feature a searchable PDF version of each book as well as the raw data in .dbf, Excel and ASCII formats.

State Statistical Trends is our popular monthly journal that compares changes in life and government for the 50 United States. Each 100-page monthly issue examines a different subject and provides a collection of tables, graphics and commentary showing state multi-year trends. For further information about *Trends* or any of our other publications, check out our website at www.statestats.com or give us a call toll-free at 1-800-457-0742.

Finally, we sincerely appreciate the assistance of those people who help to make this book possible year after year. To the librarians, government statisticians and other information keepers we extend a huge "thank you."

Special thanks goes to Joe and Joan Williams of Elmwood, Nebraska, the original editors and creators of *State Rankings.* Nearly 40 years ago, the Williams had the foresight to see the need for a straightforward, user-friendly book of state statistics. It has been our great honor to carry on their mission of creating books of statistics that all of us can understand and use.

We hope you find this newly revised volume interesting and useful. We always enjoy hearing comments from our readers, so please do not hesitate to give us a call, send us an e-mail or drop us a note with your suggestions.

-THE EDITORS

WHICH STATE IS THE MOST LIVABLE?

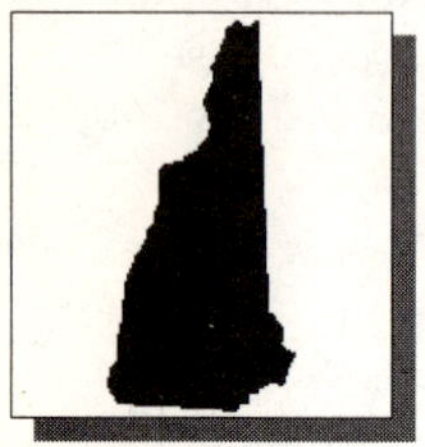

It's not that we do not like Minnesota. But the editors take great pleasure in welcoming New Hampshire as the winner of Morgan Quitno's 14th annual Most Livable State Award.

Since 1996, Minnesota has dominated our annual competition. But this year, New Hampshire slipped past Minnesota by the smallest of margins and has earned the top honor.

The competition was fierce. Both states did well in nearly every category with only a few exceptions (average temperature, for example.)

At the bottom of the rankings, Mississippi comes in at #50 for the sixth year in a row.

For 14 years now, Morgan Quitno Press has issued its Most Livable State Award. With the publication of each year's new edition of *State Rankings*, we reexamine our collection of data and select the factors that reflect a state's basic quality of life.

The 2004 award is based on 44 factors ranging from median household income to crime rate, sunny days to infant mortality rate. For this year's award, two factors were dropped: a state cost of living index that is no longer published and the divorce rate.

Another three factors were added: personal bankruptcy rate, rate of public libraries and percent of female-headed families with children living in poverty.

Unique among the various rankings of states, our Most Livable State Award does not focus on any one category of data. Instead it takes into account a broad range of economic, educational, health-oriented, public safety and environmental statistics.

The Most Livable State Award is one of five such designations announced each year by Morgan Quitno. The Safest City/Metro Area Award is based on statistics from our *City Crime Rankings* volume. The Most Dangerous and Safest State designations are announced with our *Crime State Rankings* volume. The Healthiest State Award is based on factors derived from *Health Care State Rankings* and the Smartest State Award is based on our newest book, *Education State Rankings*.

While we strive to make our books as objective as possible, these awards give us the opportunity to choose the factors we think tell an interesting story about life in the 50 United States. Congratulations (and thank you) to the citizens of New Hampshire.

\- THE EDITORS

Negative Factors
1. Percent Change in Number of Crimes: 2001 to 2002 (Table 27)
2. Crime Rate (Table 28)
3. State Prisoner Incarceration Rate (Table 62)
4. Personal Bankruptcy Rate (Table 102)
5. Pupil-Teacher Ratio in Public Elementary and Secondary Schools (Table 122)
6. Rate of Public Libraries and Branches in 2001 (Table 152)
7. Unemployment Rate (Table 171)
8. Percent of Nonfarm Employees in Government (Table 185)
9. Electricity Prices (Table 204)
10. Hazardous Waste Sites on the National Priority List per 10,000 Square Miles (Table 218)
11. State & Local Taxes as a Percent of Personal Income (Table 291)
12. Per Capita State and Local Government Debt Outstanding (Table 303)
13. Percent of Population Not Covered by Health Insurance (Table 359)
14. Births of Low Birthweight as a Percent of All Births (Table 375)
15. Teenage Birth Rate (Table 376)
16. Infant Mortality Rate (Table 382)
17. Age-Adjusted Death Rate by Suicide (Table 399)
18. Population per Square Mile (Table 437)
19. Poverty Rate (Table 499)
20. Percent of Female-Headed Families with Children Living in Poverty in 2002 (Table 503
21. State and Local Government Spending for Welfare Programs as a Percent of All Spending (Table 506)
22. Percent of Households Receiving Food Stamps (Table 531)
23. Deficient Bridges as a Percent of Total Bridges (Table 547)
24. Highway Fatality Rate (Table 550)
25. Fatalities in Alcohol-Related Crashes as a Percent of All Highway Fatalities (Table 557)

Positive Factors
26. Per Capita Gross State Product (Table 93)
27. Percent Change in Per Capita Gross State Product: 1997 to 2001 (Adjusted to Constant 1996 Dollars) (Table 94)
28. Per Capita Personal Income (Table 97)
29. Change in Per Capita Personal Income: 2001 to 2002 (Table 98)
30. Median Household Income (Table 100)
31. Public High School Graduation Rate (Table 126)
32. Percent of Population Graduated from High School (Table 127)
33. Expenditures for Education as a Percent of All State and Local Government Expenditures (Table 137)
34. Percent of Population With a Bachelor's Degree or More (Table 150)
35. Books in Public Libraries Per Capita (Table 153)
36. Per Capita State Art Agencies' Legislative Appropriations (Table 154)
37. Average Weekly Earnings of Production Workers on Manufacturing Payrolls (Table 161)
38. Job Growth: 2002 to 2003 (Table 176)
39. Normal Daily Mean Temperature (Table 232)
40. Percent of Days That Are Sunny (Table 233)
41. Homeownership Rate (Table 424)
42. Domestic Migration of Population: 2002 to 2003 (Table 481)
43. Marriage Rate (Table 487)
44. Percent of Eligible Population Reported Voting (Table 498)

The 2004 Most Livable State Award:

New Hampshire Grabs the Top Spot

<u>ALPHA ORDER</u>

RANK	STATE	LIVABILITY RATING	03 RANK	CHANGE
47	Alabama	19.25	47	0
31	Alaska	24.18	32	1
38	Arizona	21.55	45	7
44	Arkansas	20.07	44	0
36	California	21.82	38	2
23	Colorado	26.84	19	-4
9	Connecticut	30.41	11	2
18	Delaware	27.59	18	0
37	Florida	21.64	39	2
35	Georgia	22.70	34	-1
32	Hawaii	23.93	41	9
17	Idaho	28.00	20	3
26	Illinois	25.02	30	4
20	Indiana	27.00	22	2
4	Iowa	30.80	2	-2
11	Kansas	29.52	6	-5
42	Kentucky	20.50	37	-5
49	Louisiana	17.91	49	0
12	Maine	28.93	16	4
14	Maryland	28.73	14	0
16	Massachusetts	28.16	9	-7
34	Michigan	23.82	28	-6
2	Minnesota	34.48	1	-1
50	Mississippi	16.70	50	0
20	Missouri	27.00	25	5
27	Montana	24.68	21	-6
8	Nebraska	30.43	4	-4
30	Nevada	24.23	31	1
1	New Hampshire	34.50	3	2
5	New Jersey	30.68	12	7
41	New Mexico	20.66	40	-1
33	New York	23.91	33	0
45	North Carolina	19.93	42	-3
15	North Dakota	28.66	17	2
29	Ohio	24.48	29	0
40	Oklahoma	20.77	34	-6
27	Oregon	24.68	24	-3
22	Pennsylvania	26.89	27	5
24	Rhode Island	25.75	26	2
48	South Carolina	19.16	43	-5
10	South Dakota	29.82	8	-2
46	Tennessee	19.64	48	2
39	Texas	21.18	36	-3
19	Utah	27.52	13	-6
3	Vermont	32.61	7	4
7	Virginia	30.48	5	-2
25	Washington	25.11	23	-2
43	West Virginia	20.48	46	3
13	Wisconsin	28.84	10	-3
6	Wyoming	30.50	14	8

<u>RANK ORDER</u>

RANK	STATE	LIVABILITY RATING	03 RANK	CHANGE
1	New Hampshire	34.50	3	2
2	Minnesota	34.48	1	-1
3	Vermont	32.61	7	4
4	Iowa	30.80	2	-2
5	New Jersey	30.68	12	7
6	Wyoming	30.50	14	8
7	Virginia	30.48	5	-2
8	Nebraska	30.43	4	-4
9	Connecticut	30.41	11	2
10	South Dakota	29.82	8	-2
11	Kansas	29.52	6	-5
12	Maine	28.93	16	4
13	Wisconsin	28.84	10	-3
14	Maryland	28.73	14	0
15	North Dakota	28.66	17	2
16	Massachusetts	28.16	9	-7
17	Idaho	28.00	20	3
18	Delaware	27.59	18	0
19	Utah	27.52	13	-6
20	Indiana	27.00	22	2
20	Missouri	27.00	25	5
22	Pennsylvania	26.89	27	5
23	Colorado	26.84	19	-4
24	Rhode Island	25.75	26	2
25	Washington	25.11	23	-2
26	Illinois	25.02	30	4
27	Montana	24.68	21	-6
27	Oregon	24.68	24	-3
29	Ohio	24.48	29	0
30	Nevada	24.23	31	1
31	Alaska	24.18	32	1
32	Hawaii	23.93	41	9
33	New York	23.91	33	0
34	Michigan	23.82	28	-6
35	Georgia	22.70	34	-1
36	California	21.82	38	2
37	Florida	21.64	39	2
38	Arizona	21.55	45	7
39	Texas	21.18	36	-3
40	Oklahoma	20.77	34	-6
41	New Mexico	20.66	40	-1
42	Kentucky	20.50	37	-5
43	West Virginia	20.48	46	3
44	Arkansas	20.07	44	0
45	North Carolina	19.93	42	-3
46	Tennessee	19.64	48	2
47	Alabama	19.25	47	0
48	South Carolina	19.16	43	-5
49	Louisiana	17.91	49	0
50	Mississippi	16.70	50	0

METHODOLOGY: To determine a state's "Livability Rating," each state's rankings for 43 categories were averaged. The scale is 1 to 50, the higher the number, the better. Data used are for the most recent year in which comparable numbers are available from most states. All factors were given equal weight. States with no data available for a given category were ranked based only on the remaining factors. In our book, data are listed from highest to lowest. However, for purposes of this award, we inverted rankings for those factors we determined to be "positive." Thus the state with the highest median income in the book (ranking 1st) would be given a number 50 ranking for this award.

STATE FAST FACTS

STATE	NICKNAME	CAPITAL	POPULATION*	AREA**
Alabama	Heart of Dixie	Montgomery	4,500,752	52,237
Alaska	The Last Frontier	Juneau	648,818	615,230
Arizona	Grand Canyon State	Phoenix	5,580,811	114,006
Arkansas	The Natural State	Little Rock	2,725,714	53,182
California	Golden State	Sacramento	35,484,453	158,869
Colorado	Centennial State	Denver	4,550,688	104,100
Connecticut	Constitution State	Hartford	3,483,372	5,544
Delaware	First State	Dover	817,491	2,396
Florida	Sunshine State	Tallahassee	17,019,068	59,928
Georgia	Peach State	Atlanta	8,684,715	58,977
Hawaii	Aloha State	Honolulu	1,257,608	6,459
Idaho	Gem State	Boise	1,366,332	83,574
Illinois	Land of Lincoln	Springfield	12,653,544	57,918
Indiana	Hoosier State	Indianapolis	6,195,643	36,420
Iowa	Hawkeye State	Des Moines	2,944,062	56,276
Kansas	Sunflower State	Topeka	2,723,507	82,282
Kentucky	Bluegrass State	Frankfort	4,117,827	40,411
Louisiana	Pelican State	Baton Rouge	4,496,334	49,651
Maine	Pine Tree State	Augusta	1,305,728	33,741
Maryland	Free State	Annapolis	5,508,909	12,297
Massachusetts	Bay State	Boston	6,433,422	9,241
Michigan	Great Lake State	Lansing	10,079,985	96,705
Minnesota	North Star State	St. Paul	5,059,375	86,943
Mississippi	Magnolia State	Jackson	2,881,281	48,286
Missouri	Show Me State	Jefferson City	5,704,484	69,709
Montana	Treasure State	Helena	917,621	147,046
Nebraska	Cornhusker State	Lincoln	1,739,291	77,358
Nevada	Sagebrush State	Carson City	2,241,154	110,567
New Hampshire	Granite State	Concord	1,287,687	9,283
New Jersey	Garden State	Trenton	8,638,396	8,215
New Mexico	Land of Enchantment	Santa Fe	1,874,614	121,598
New York	Empire State	Albany	19,190,115	53,989
North Carolina	Tar Heel State	Raleigh	8,407,248	52,672
North Dakota	Peace Garden State	Bismarck	633,837	70,704
Ohio	Buckeye State	Columbus	11,435,798	44,828
Oklahoma	Sooner State	Oklahoma City	3,511,532	69,903
Oregon	Beaver State	Salem	3,559,596	97,132
Pennsylvania	Keystone State	Harrisburg	12,365,455	46,058
Rhode Island	Ocean State	Providence	1,076,164	1,231
South Carolina	Palmetto State	Columbia	4,147,152	31,189
South Dakota	Mount Rushmore State	Pierre	764,309	77,121
Tennessee	Volunteer State	Nashville	5,841,748	42,146
Texas	Lone Star State	Austin	22,118,509	267,277
Utah	Beehive State	Salt Lake City	2,351,467	84,904
Vermont	Green Mountain State	Montpelier	619,107	9,615
Virginia	Old Dominion	Richmond	7,386,330	42,326
Washington	Evergreen State	Olympia	6,131,445	70,637
West Virginia	Mountain State	Charleston	1,810,354	24,231
Wisconsin	Badger State	Madison	5,472,299	65,499
Wyoming	Equality State	Cheyenne	501,242	97,818

*2003 Census resident population estimates.

**Total of land and water area in square miles.

STATE SONG	STATE FLOWER	STATE TREE	STATE BIRD
Alabama	Camellia	Southern Pine	Yellowhammer
Alaska's Flag	Forget-Me-Not	Sitka Spruce	Willow Ptarmigan
Arizona	Saguaro Cactus Blossom	Palo Verde	Cactus Wren
Arkansas	Apple Blossom	Pine	Mockingbird
I Love You, California	Golden Poppy	California Redwood	California Valley Quail
Where the Columbines Grow	Rocky Mountain Columbine	Colorado Blue Spruce	Lark Bunting
Yankee Doodle Dandy	Mountain Laurel	White Oak	American Robin
Our Delaware	Peach Blossom	American Holly	Blue Hen Chicken
Swanee River	Orange Blossom	Sabal Palmetto Palm	Mockingbird
Georgia On My Mind	Cherokee Rose	Live Oak	Brown Thrasher
Hawaii Ponoi	Yellow Hibiscus	Candlenut	Nene
Here We Have Idaho	Syringa	White Pine	Mountain Bluebird
Illinois	Purple Violet	White Oak	Cardinal
On the Banks of the Wabash, Far Away	Peony	Tulip Poplar	Cardinal
The Song of Iowa	Wild Rose	Oak	Eastern Goldfinch
Home on the Range	Sunflower	Cottonwood	Western Meadowlark
My Old Kentucky Home	Goldenrod	Tulip Tree	Cardinal
Give Me Louisiana	Magnolia	Cypress	Eastern Brown Pelican
State of Maine Song	White Pine Cone and Tassel	Eastern White Pine	Chickadee
Maryland, My Maryland	Black-eyed Susan	White Oak	Baltimore Oriole
All Hail to Massachusetts	Mayflower	American Elm	Chickadee
Michigan, My Michigan	Apple Blossom	White Pine	Robin
Hail! Minnesota	Pink and White Lady's Slipper	Red Pine	Common Loon
Go, Mississippi!	Magnolia	Magnolia	Mockingbird
Missouri Waltz	Hawthorn	Dogwood	Bluebird
Montana	Bitterroot	Ponderosa Pine	Western Meadowlark
Beautiful Nebraska	Goldenrod	Cottonwood	Western Meadowlark
Home Means Nevada	Sagebrush	Single-Leaf Pinon	Mountain Bluebird
Old New Hampshire	Purple Lilac	White Birch	Purple Finch
Ode to New Jersey	Purple Violet	Red Oak	Eastern Goldfinch
O Fair New Mexico	Yucca	Pinon	Roadrunner
I Love New York	Rose	Sugar Maple	Bluebird
The Old North State	Dogwood	Pine	Cardinal
North Dakota Hymn	Wild Prairie Rose	American Elm	Western Meadowlark
Beautiful Ohio	Scarlet Carnation	Buckeye	Cardinal
Oklahoma!	Mistletoe	Redbud	Scissortailed Flycatcher
Oregon, My Oregon	Oregon Grape	Douglas Fir	Western Meadowlark
Hail! Pennsylvania	Mountain Laurel	Hemlock	Ruffed Grouse
Rhode Island	Violet	Red Maple	Rhode Island Red
Carolina	Yellow Jessamine	Palmetto	Carolina Wren
Hail, South Dakota	Pasque Flower	Black Hills Spruce	Ringnecked Pheasant
The Tennessee Waltz	Iris	Tulip Poplar	Mockingbird
Texas, Our Texas	Bluebonnet	Pecan	Mockingbird
Utah, We Love Thee	Sego Lily	Blue Spruce	Seagull
Hail, Vermont	Red Clover	Sugar Maple	Hermit Thrush
Carry Me Back to Old Virginia	Dogwood	Dogwood	Cardinal
Washington, My Home	Western Rhododendron	Western Hemlock	Willow Goldfinch
The West Virginia Hills; This Is My West Virginia; and West Virginia, My Home, Sweet Home	Big Rhododendron	Sugar Maple	Cardinal
On Wisconsin!	Wood Violet	Sugar Maple	Robin
Wyoming	Indian Paintbrush	Cottonwood	Meadowlark

TABLE OF CONTENTS

TABLE OF CONTENTS (continued)

III. Defense

IV. Economy

TABLE OF CONTENTS (continued)

V. Education

VI. Employment and Labor

TABLE OF CONTENTS (continued)

VII. Energy and Environment

VIII. Geography

TABLE OF CONTENTS (continued)

IX. Government Finance: Federal

X. Government Finance: State and Local

TABLE OF CONTENTS (continued)

TABLE OF CONTENTS (continued)

XI. Health

TABLE OF CONTENTS (continued)

XIV. Social Welfare

TABLE OF CONTENTS (continued)

XV. Transportation

XVI. Sources

XVII. Index

Date Each State Admitted to Statehood*

<table>
<tr><td colspan="3"><u>ALPHA ORDER</u></td><td colspan="3"><u>RANK ORDER</u></td></tr>
<tr><th>RANK</th><th>STATE</th><th>DATE OF ADMISSION</th><th>RANK</th><th>STATE</th><th>DATE OF ADMISSION</th></tr>
<tr><td>22</td><td>Alabama</td><td>December 14, 1819</td><td>1</td><td>Delaware</td><td>December 7, 1787</td></tr>
<tr><td>49</td><td>Alaska</td><td>January 3, 1959</td><td>2</td><td>Pennsylvania</td><td>December 12, 1787</td></tr>
<tr><td>48</td><td>Arizona</td><td>February 14, 1912</td><td>3</td><td>New Jersey</td><td>December 18, 1787</td></tr>
<tr><td>25</td><td>Arkansas</td><td>June 15, 1836</td><td>4</td><td>Georgia</td><td>January 2, 1788</td></tr>
<tr><td>31</td><td>California</td><td>September 9, 1850</td><td>5</td><td>Connecticut</td><td>January 9, 1788</td></tr>
<tr><td>38</td><td>Colorado</td><td>August 1, 1876</td><td>6</td><td>Massachusetts</td><td>February 6, 1788</td></tr>
<tr><td>5</td><td>Connecticut</td><td>January 9, 1788</td><td>7</td><td>Maryland</td><td>April 28, 1788</td></tr>
<tr><td>1</td><td>Delaware</td><td>December 7, 1787</td><td>8</td><td>South Carolina</td><td>May 23, 1788</td></tr>
<tr><td>27</td><td>Florida</td><td>March 3, 1845</td><td>9</td><td>New Hampshire</td><td>June 21, 1788</td></tr>
<tr><td>4</td><td>Georgia</td><td>January 2, 1788</td><td>10</td><td>Virginia</td><td>June 26, 1788</td></tr>
<tr><td>50</td><td>Hawaii</td><td>August 21, 1959</td><td>11</td><td>New York</td><td>July 26, 1788</td></tr>
<tr><td>43</td><td>Idaho</td><td>July 3, 1890</td><td>12</td><td>North Carolina</td><td>November 21, 1789</td></tr>
<tr><td>21</td><td>Illinois</td><td>December 3, 1818</td><td>13</td><td>Rhode Island</td><td>May 29, 1790</td></tr>
<tr><td>19</td><td>Indiana</td><td>December 11, 1816</td><td>14</td><td>Vermont</td><td>March 4, 1791</td></tr>
<tr><td>29</td><td>Iowa</td><td>December 28, 1846</td><td>15</td><td>Kentucky</td><td>June 1, 1792</td></tr>
<tr><td>34</td><td>Kansas</td><td>January 29, 1861</td><td>16</td><td>Tennessee</td><td>June 1, 1796</td></tr>
<tr><td>15</td><td>Kentucky</td><td>June 1, 1792</td><td>17</td><td>Ohio</td><td>March 1, 1803</td></tr>
<tr><td>18</td><td>Louisiana</td><td>April 30, 1812</td><td>18</td><td>Louisiana</td><td>April 30, 1812</td></tr>
<tr><td>23</td><td>Maine</td><td>March 15, 1820</td><td>19</td><td>Indiana</td><td>December 11, 1816</td></tr>
<tr><td>7</td><td>Maryland</td><td>April 28, 1788</td><td>20</td><td>Mississippi</td><td>December 10, 1817</td></tr>
<tr><td>6</td><td>Massachusetts</td><td>February 6, 1788</td><td>21</td><td>Illinois</td><td>December 3, 1818</td></tr>
<tr><td>26</td><td>Michigan</td><td>January 26, 1837</td><td>22</td><td>Alabama</td><td>December 14, 1819</td></tr>
<tr><td>32</td><td>Minnesota</td><td>May 11, 1858</td><td>23</td><td>Maine</td><td>March 15, 1820</td></tr>
<tr><td>20</td><td>Mississippi</td><td>December 10, 1817</td><td>24</td><td>Missouri</td><td>August 10, 1821</td></tr>
<tr><td>24</td><td>Missouri</td><td>August 10, 1821</td><td>25</td><td>Arkansas</td><td>June 15, 1836</td></tr>
<tr><td>41</td><td>Montana</td><td>November 8, 1889</td><td>26</td><td>Michigan</td><td>January 26, 1837</td></tr>
<tr><td>37</td><td>Nebraska</td><td>March 1, 1867</td><td>27</td><td>Florida</td><td>March 3, 1845</td></tr>
<tr><td>36</td><td>Nevada</td><td>October 31, 1864</td><td>28</td><td>Texas</td><td>December 29, 1845</td></tr>
<tr><td>9</td><td>New Hampshire</td><td>June 21, 1788</td><td>29</td><td>Iowa</td><td>December 28, 1846</td></tr>
<tr><td>3</td><td>New Jersey</td><td>December 18, 1787</td><td>30</td><td>Wisconsin</td><td>May 29, 1848</td></tr>
<tr><td>47</td><td>New Mexico</td><td>January 6, 1912</td><td>31</td><td>California</td><td>September 9, 1850</td></tr>
<tr><td>11</td><td>New York</td><td>July 26, 1788</td><td>32</td><td>Minnesota</td><td>May 11, 1858</td></tr>
<tr><td>12</td><td>North Carolina</td><td>November 21, 1789</td><td>33</td><td>Oregon</td><td>February 14, 1859</td></tr>
<tr><td>39</td><td>North Dakota</td><td>November 2, 1889</td><td>34</td><td>Kansas</td><td>January 29, 1861</td></tr>
<tr><td>17</td><td>Ohio</td><td>March 1, 1803</td><td>35</td><td>West Virginia</td><td>June 20, 1863</td></tr>
<tr><td>46</td><td>Oklahoma</td><td>November 16, 1907</td><td>36</td><td>Nevada</td><td>October 31, 1864</td></tr>
<tr><td>33</td><td>Oregon</td><td>February 14, 1859</td><td>37</td><td>Nebraska</td><td>March 1, 1867</td></tr>
<tr><td>2</td><td>Pennsylvania</td><td>December 12, 1787</td><td>38</td><td>Colorado</td><td>August 1, 1876</td></tr>
<tr><td>13</td><td>Rhode Island</td><td>May 29, 1790</td><td>39</td><td>North Dakota</td><td>November 2, 1889</td></tr>
<tr><td>8</td><td>South Carolina</td><td>May 23, 1788</td><td>39</td><td>South Dakota</td><td>November 2, 1889</td></tr>
<tr><td>39</td><td>South Dakota</td><td>November 2, 1889</td><td>41</td><td>Montana</td><td>November 8, 1889</td></tr>
<tr><td>16</td><td>Tennessee</td><td>June 1, 1796</td><td>42</td><td>Washington</td><td>November 11, 1889</td></tr>
<tr><td>28</td><td>Texas</td><td>December 29, 1845</td><td>43</td><td>Idaho</td><td>July 3, 1890</td></tr>
<tr><td>45</td><td>Utah</td><td>January 4, 1896</td><td>44</td><td>Wyoming</td><td>July 10, 1890</td></tr>
<tr><td>14</td><td>Vermont</td><td>March 4, 1791</td><td>45</td><td>Utah</td><td>January 4, 1896</td></tr>
<tr><td>10</td><td>Virginia</td><td>June 26, 1788</td><td>46</td><td>Oklahoma</td><td>November 16, 1907</td></tr>
<tr><td>42</td><td>Washington</td><td>November 11, 1889</td><td>47</td><td>New Mexico</td><td>January 6, 1912</td></tr>
<tr><td>35</td><td>West Virginia</td><td>June 20, 1863</td><td>48</td><td>Arizona</td><td>February 14, 1912</td></tr>
<tr><td>30</td><td>Wisconsin</td><td>May 29, 1848</td><td>49</td><td>Alaska</td><td>January 3, 1959</td></tr>
<tr><td>44</td><td>Wyoming</td><td>July 10, 1890</td><td>50</td><td>Hawaii</td><td>August 21, 1959</td></tr>
</table>

Source: U.S. Bureau of the Census
  "1980 Census of Population" (vol. 1, part A, PC80-1-A)
First thirteen states show date of ratification of Constitution.

I. AGRICULTURE

Number of Farms in 2002

National Total = 2,158,090 Farms*

<u>ALPHA ORDER</u>

RANK	STATE	FARMS	% of USA
21	Alabama	47,000	2.2%
50	Alaska	590	0.0%
40	Arizona	7,300	0.3%
20	Arkansas	48,500	2.2%
7	California	84,000	3.9%
28	Colorado	30,000	1.4%
45	Connecticut	3,900	0.2%
48	Delaware	2,400	0.1%
22	Florida	44,000	2.0%
18	Georgia	50,000	2.3%
44	Hawaii	5,300	0.2%
33	Idaho	24,000	1.1%
11	Illinois	76,000	3.5%
12	Indiana	63,000	2.9%
3	Iowa	92,500	4.3%
12	Kansas	63,000	2.9%
5	Kentucky	89,000	4.1%
30	Louisiana	29,000	1.3%
41	Maine	6,700	0.3%
37	Maryland	12,200	0.6%
43	Massachusetts	6,000	0.3%
16	Michigan	52,000	2.4%
8	Minnesota	79,000	3.7%
23	Mississippi	43,000	2.0%
2	Missouri	107,000	5.0%
31	Montana	28,000	1.3%
16	Nebraska	52,000	2.4%
47	Nevada	3,000	0.1%
46	New Hampshire	3,100	0.1%
38	New Jersey	9,600	0.4%
35	New Mexico	15,000	0.7%
26	New York	37,000	1.7%
15	North Carolina	56,000	2.6%
28	North Dakota	30,000	1.4%
9	Ohio	78,000	3.6%
6	Oklahoma	87,000	4.0%
24	Oregon	41,000	1.9%
14	Pennsylvania	59,000	2.7%
49	Rhode Island	700	0.0%
32	South Carolina	24,500	1.1%
27	South Dakota	32,500	1.5%
4	Tennessee	90,000	4.2%
1	Texas	230,000	10.7%
35	Utah	15,000	0.7%
42	Vermont	6,600	0.3%
19	Virginia	49,000	2.3%
25	Washington	39,000	1.8%
34	West Virginia	20,500	0.9%
10	Wisconsin	77,000	3.6%
39	Wyoming	9,200	0.4%

<u>RANK ORDER</u>

RANK	STATE	FARMS	% of USA
1	Texas	230,000	10.7%
2	Missouri	107,000	5.0%
3	Iowa	92,500	4.3%
4	Tennessee	90,000	4.2%
5	Kentucky	89,000	4.1%
6	Oklahoma	87,000	4.0%
7	California	84,000	3.9%
8	Minnesota	79,000	3.7%
9	Ohio	78,000	3.6%
10	Wisconsin	77,000	3.6%
11	Illinois	76,000	3.5%
12	Indiana	63,000	2.9%
12	Kansas	63,000	2.9%
14	Pennsylvania	59,000	2.7%
15	North Carolina	56,000	2.6%
16	Michigan	52,000	2.4%
16	Nebraska	52,000	2.4%
18	Georgia	50,000	2.3%
19	Virginia	49,000	2.3%
20	Arkansas	48,500	2.2%
21	Alabama	47,000	2.2%
22	Florida	44,000	2.0%
23	Mississippi	43,000	2.0%
24	Oregon	41,000	1.9%
25	Washington	39,000	1.8%
26	New York	37,000	1.7%
27	South Dakota	32,500	1.5%
28	Colorado	30,000	1.4%
28	North Dakota	30,000	1.4%
30	Louisiana	29,000	1.3%
31	Montana	28,000	1.3%
32	South Carolina	24,500	1.1%
33	Idaho	24,000	1.1%
34	West Virginia	20,500	0.9%
35	New Mexico	15,000	0.7%
35	Utah	15,000	0.7%
37	Maryland	12,200	0.6%
38	New Jersey	9,600	0.4%
39	Wyoming	9,200	0.4%
40	Arizona	7,300	0.3%
41	Maine	6,700	0.3%
42	Vermont	6,600	0.3%
43	Massachusetts	6,000	0.3%
44	Hawaii	5,300	0.2%
45	Connecticut	3,900	0.2%
46	New Hampshire	3,100	0.1%
47	Nevada	3,000	0.1%
48	Delaware	2,400	0.1%
49	Rhode Island	700	0.0%
50	Alaska	590	0.0%
	District of Columbia	0	0.0%

Source: U.S. Department of Agriculture, National Agricultural Statistics Service
"Farms and Land in Farms" (http://usda.mannlib.cornell.edu/reports/nassr/other/zfl-bb/fmno0203.pdf)
**A farm is any establishment from which $1,000 or more of agricultural products were sold or would normally be sold during the year. This includes places with five or more horses, except horses in boarding stables or racetracks.*

Land in Farms in 2002

National Total = 941,480,000 Acres*

ALPHA ORDER

RANK	STATE	ACRES	% of USA
32	Alabama	8,900,000	0.9%
44	Alaska	920,000	0.1%
16	Arizona	26,500,000	2.8%
22	Arkansas	14,600,000	1.6%
14	California	27,700,000	2.9%
11	Colorado	31,300,000	3.3%
49	Connecticut	360,000	0.0%
46	Delaware	560,000	0.1%
30	Florida	10,200,000	1.1%
27	Georgia	11,000,000	1.2%
41	Hawaii	1,440,000	0.2%
24	Idaho	11,900,000	1.3%
14	Illinois	27,700,000	2.9%
20	Indiana	15,400,000	1.6%
10	Iowa	32,600,000	3.5%
3	Kansas	47,400,000	5.0%
23	Kentucky	13,600,000	1.4%
34	Louisiana	8,050,000	0.9%
43	Maine	1,260,000	0.1%
40	Maryland	2,100,000	0.2%
46	Massachusetts	560,000	0.1%
29	Michigan	10,400,000	1.1%
13	Minnesota	28,400,000	3.0%
27	Mississippi	11,000,000	1.2%
12	Missouri	29,800,000	3.2%
2	Montana	56,700,000	6.0%
4	Nebraska	46,400,000	4.9%
37	Nevada	6,800,000	0.7%
48	New Hampshire	410,000	0.0%
45	New Jersey	820,000	0.1%
5	New Mexico	44,000,000	4.7%
36	New York	7,600,000	0.8%
31	North Carolina	9,100,000	1.0%
7	North Dakota	39,400,000	4.2%
21	Ohio	14,700,000	1.6%
9	Oklahoma	34,000,000	3.6%
17	Oregon	17,200,000	1.8%
35	Pennsylvania	7,700,000	0.8%
50	Rhode Island	60,000	0.0%
38	South Carolina	4,800,000	0.5%
5	South Dakota	44,000,000	4.7%
25	Tennessee	11,700,000	1.2%
1	Texas	131,000,000	13.9%
26	Utah	11,600,000	1.2%
42	Vermont	1,340,000	0.1%
33	Virginia	8,700,000	0.9%
19	Washington	15,700,000	1.7%
39	West Virginia	3,600,000	0.4%
18	Wisconsin	15,900,000	1.7%
8	Wyoming	34,600,000	3.7%

RANK ORDER

RANK	STATE	ACRES	% of USA
1	Texas	131,000,000	13.9%
2	Montana	56,700,000	6.0%
3	Kansas	47,400,000	5.0%
4	Nebraska	46,400,000	4.9%
5	New Mexico	44,000,000	4.7%
5	South Dakota	44,000,000	4.7%
7	North Dakota	39,400,000	4.2%
8	Wyoming	34,600,000	3.7%
9	Oklahoma	34,000,000	3.6%
10	Iowa	32,600,000	3.5%
11	Colorado	31,300,000	3.3%
12	Missouri	29,800,000	3.2%
13	Minnesota	28,400,000	3.0%
14	California	27,700,000	2.9%
14	Illinois	27,700,000	2.9%
16	Arizona	26,500,000	2.8%
17	Oregon	17,200,000	1.8%
18	Wisconsin	15,900,000	1.7%
19	Washington	15,700,000	1.7%
20	Indiana	15,400,000	1.6%
21	Ohio	14,700,000	1.6%
22	Arkansas	14,600,000	1.6%
23	Kentucky	13,600,000	1.4%
24	Idaho	11,900,000	1.3%
25	Tennessee	11,700,000	1.2%
26	Utah	11,600,000	1.2%
27	Georgia	11,000,000	1.2%
27	Mississippi	11,000,000	1.2%
29	Michigan	10,400,000	1.1%
30	Florida	10,200,000	1.1%
31	North Carolina	9,100,000	1.0%
32	Alabama	8,900,000	0.9%
33	Virginia	8,700,000	0.9%
34	Louisiana	8,050,000	0.9%
35	Pennsylvania	7,700,000	0.8%
36	New York	7,600,000	0.8%
37	Nevada	6,800,000	0.7%
38	South Carolina	4,800,000	0.5%
39	West Virginia	3,600,000	0.4%
40	Maryland	2,100,000	0.2%
41	Hawaii	1,440,000	0.2%
42	Vermont	1,340,000	0.1%
43	Maine	1,260,000	0.1%
44	Alaska	920,000	0.1%
45	New Jersey	820,000	0.1%
46	Delaware	560,000	0.1%
46	Massachusetts	560,000	0.1%
48	New Hampshire	410,000	0.0%
49	Connecticut	360,000	0.0%
50	Rhode Island	60,000	0.0%
	District of Columbia	0	0.0%

Source: U.S. Department of Agriculture, National Agricultural Statistics Service
"Farms and Land in Farms" (http://usda.mannlib.cornell.edu/reports/nassr/other/zfl-bb/fmno0203.pdf)
**A farm is any establishment from which $1,000 or more of agricultural products were sold or would normally be sold during the year. This includes places with five or more horses, except horses in boarding stables or racetracks.*

Average Number of Acres per Farm in 2002

National Average = 436 Acres*

<u>ALPHA ORDER</u>

RANK	STATE	ACRES
36	Alabama	189
6	Alaska	1,559
2	Arizona	3,630
22	Arkansas	301
21	California	330
9	Colorado	1,043
48	Connecticut	92
28	Delaware	233
29	Florida	232
30	Georgia	220
25	Hawaii	272
14	Idaho	496
18	Illinois	364
27	Indiana	244
20	Iowa	352
12	Kansas	752
43	Kentucky	153
24	Louisiana	278
37	Maine	188
41	Maryland	172
47	Massachusetts	93
34	Michigan	200
19	Minnesota	359
26	Mississippi	256
23	Missouri	279
5	Montana	2,025
10	Nebraska	892
4	Nevada	2,267
44	New Hampshire	132
50	New Jersey	85
3	New Mexico	2,933
32	New York	205
42	North Carolina	163
8	North Dakota	1,313
37	Ohio	188
17	Oklahoma	391
15	Oregon	420
45	Pennsylvania	131
49	Rhode Island	86
35	South Carolina	196
7	South Dakota	1,354
46	Tennessee	130
13	Texas	570
11	Utah	773
33	Vermont	203
39	Virginia	178
16	Washington	403
40	West Virginia	176
31	Wisconsin	206
1	Wyoming	3,761

<u>RANK ORDER</u>

RANK	STATE	ACRES
1	Wyoming	3,761
2	Arizona	3,630
3	New Mexico	2,933
4	Nevada	2,267
5	Montana	2,025
6	Alaska	1,559
7	South Dakota	1,354
8	North Dakota	1,313
9	Colorado	1,043
10	Nebraska	892
11	Utah	773
12	Kansas	752
13	Texas	570
14	Idaho	496
15	Oregon	420
16	Washington	403
17	Oklahoma	391
18	Illinois	364
19	Minnesota	359
20	Iowa	352
21	California	330
22	Arkansas	301
23	Missouri	279
24	Louisiana	278
25	Hawaii	272
26	Mississippi	256
27	Indiana	244
28	Delaware	233
29	Florida	232
30	Georgia	220
31	Wisconsin	206
32	New York	205
33	Vermont	203
34	Michigan	200
35	South Carolina	196
36	Alabama	189
37	Maine	188
37	Ohio	188
39	Virginia	178
40	West Virginia	176
41	Maryland	172
42	North Carolina	163
43	Kentucky	153
44	New Hampshire	132
45	Pennsylvania	131
46	Tennessee	130
47	Massachusetts	93
48	Connecticut	92
49	Rhode Island	86
50	New Jersey	85
	District of Columbia**	NA

Source: U.S. Department of Agriculture, National Agricultural Statistics Service
    "Farms and Land in Farms" (http://usda.mannlib.cornell.edu/reports/nassr/other/zfl-bb/fmno0203.pdf)
*A farm is any establishment from which $1,000 or more of agricultural products were sold or would normally be sold during the year. This includes places with five or more horses, except horses in boarding stables or racetracks.
**Not applicable.

Average per Acre Value of Farmland and Buildings in 2003

National Average = $1,270 per Acre*

ALPHA ORDER

RANK	STATE	PER ACRE VALUE
21	Alabama	$2,000
NA	Alaska**	NA
26	Arizona	1,600
29	Arkansas	1,470
6	California	3,200
41	Colorado	730
2	Connecticut	7,700
6	Delaware	3,200
10	Florida	3,000
17	Georgia	2,500
NA	Hawaii**	NA
34	Idaho	1,280
12	Illinois	2,770
13	Indiana	2,750
20	Iowa	2,050
42	Kansas	620
21	Kentucky	2,000
32	Louisiana	1,350
31	Maine	1,450
5	Maryland	4,200
2	Massachusetts	7,700
14	Michigan	2,700
28	Minnesota	1,550
32	Mississippi	1,350
26	Missouri	1,600
46	Montana	400
38	Nebraska	800
43	Nevada	480
14	New Hampshire	2,700
1	New Jersey	8,500
48	New Mexico	230
25	New York	1,650
8	North Carolina	3,100
45	North Dakota	460
11	Ohio	2,800
40	Oklahoma	740
36	Oregon	1,150
8	Pennsylvania	3,100
2	Rhode Island	7,700
24	South Carolina	1,800
44	South Dakota	470
17	Tennessee	2,500
39	Texas	750
37	Utah	1,100
21	Vermont	2,000
16	Virginia	2,630
35	Washington	1,270
29	West Virginia	1,470
19	Wisconsin	2,300
47	Wyoming	300

RANK ORDER

RANK	STATE	PER ACRE VALUE
1	New Jersey	$8,500
2	Connecticut	7,700
2	Massachusetts	7,700
2	Rhode Island	7,700
5	Maryland	4,200
6	California	3,200
6	Delaware	3,200
8	North Carolina	3,100
8	Pennsylvania	3,100
10	Florida	3,000
11	Ohio	2,800
12	Illinois	2,770
13	Indiana	2,750
14	Michigan	2,700
14	New Hampshire	2,700
16	Virginia	2,630
17	Georgia	2,500
17	Tennessee	2,500
19	Wisconsin	2,300
20	Iowa	2,050
21	Alabama	2,000
21	Kentucky	2,000
21	Vermont	2,000
24	South Carolina	1,800
25	New York	1,650
26	Arizona	1,600
26	Missouri	1,600
28	Minnesota	1,550
29	Arkansas	1,470
29	West Virginia	1,470
31	Maine	1,450
32	Louisiana	1,350
32	Mississippi	1,350
34	Idaho	1,280
35	Washington	1,270
36	Oregon	1,150
37	Utah	1,100
38	Nebraska	800
39	Texas	750
40	Oklahoma	740
41	Colorado	730
42	Kansas	620
43	Nevada	480
44	South Dakota	470
45	North Dakota	460
46	Montana	400
47	Wyoming	300
48	New Mexico	230
NA	Alaska**	NA
NA	Hawaii**	NA
	District of Columbia**	NA

Source: U.S. Department of Agriculture, Economic Research Service
   "Agricultural Land Values" (http://usda.mannlib.cornell.edu/reports/nassr/other/plr-bbl)
As of January 1, 2003. Value of farmland and buildings in nominal dollars.
***Not applicable or available.*

Percent Change in Average per Acre Value of Farmland: 2002 to 2003

National Percent Change = 5.0% Increase*

<u>ALPHA ORDER</u>

RANK	STATE	PERCENT CHANGE
20	Alabama	5.3
NA	Alaska**	NA
20	Arizona	5.3
5	Arkansas	7.3
41	California	3.2
45	Colorado	2.8
19	Connecticut	5.5
2	Delaware	8.5
7	Florida	7.1
1	Georgia	8.7
NA	Hawaii**	NA
41	Idaho	3.2
27	Illinois	4.9
17	Indiana	5.8
39	Iowa	3.5
48	Kansas	0.0
3	Kentucky	8.1
43	Louisiana	3.1
38	Maine	3.6
26	Maryland	5.0
9	Massachusetts	6.9
4	Michigan	8.0
9	Minnesota	6.9
35	Mississippi	3.8
20	Missouri	5.3
34	Montana	3.9
29	Nebraska	4.6
47	Nevada	2.1
35	New Hampshire	3.8
15	New Jersey	6.3
46	New Mexico	2.2
43	New York	3.1
9	North Carolina	6.9
30	North Dakota	4.5
37	Ohio	3.7
32	Oklahoma	4.2
30	Oregon	4.5
25	Pennsylvania	5.1
9	Rhode Island	6.9
16	South Carolina	5.9
13	South Dakota	6.8
14	Tennessee	6.4
32	Texas	4.2
28	Utah	4.8
20	Vermont	5.3
18	Virginia	5.6
40	Washington	3.3
5	West Virginia	7.3
8	Wisconsin	7.0
20	Wyoming	5.3

<u>RANK ORDER</u>

RANK	STATE	PERCENT CHANGE
1	Georgia	8.7
2	Delaware	8.5
3	Kentucky	8.1
4	Michigan	8.0
5	Arkansas	7.3
5	West Virginia	7.3
7	Florida	7.1
8	Wisconsin	7.0
9	Massachusetts	6.9
9	Minnesota	6.9
9	North Carolina	6.9
9	Rhode Island	6.9
13	South Dakota	6.8
14	Tennessee	6.4
15	New Jersey	6.3
16	South Carolina	5.9
17	Indiana	5.8
18	Virginia	5.6
19	Connecticut	5.5
20	Alabama	5.3
20	Arizona	5.3
20	Missouri	5.3
20	Vermont	5.3
20	Wyoming	5.3
25	Pennsylvania	5.1
26	Maryland	5.0
27	Illinois	4.9
28	Utah	4.8
29	Nebraska	4.6
30	North Dakota	4.5
30	Oregon	4.5
32	Oklahoma	4.2
32	Texas	4.2
34	Montana	3.9
35	Mississippi	3.8
35	New Hampshire	3.8
37	Ohio	3.7
38	Maine	3.6
39	Iowa	3.5
40	Washington	3.3
41	California	3.2
41	Idaho	3.2
43	Louisiana	3.1
43	New York	3.1
45	Colorado	2.8
46	New Mexico	2.2
47	Nevada	2.1
48	Kansas	0.0
NA	Alaska**	NA
NA	Hawaii**	NA
	District of Columbia**	NA

Source: U.S. Department of Agriculture, Economic Research Service
   "Agricultural Land Values" (http://usda.mannlib.cornell.edu/reports/nassr/other/plr-bb/)
*As of January 1, 2003. Value of farmland and buildings in nominal dollars.
**Not applicable or available.

Net Farm Income in 2002

National Total = $35,323,130,000*

ALPHA ORDER

RANK	STATE	FARM INCOME	% of USA
9	Alabama	$1,199,560,934	3.4%
47	Alaska	20,113,254	0.1%
7	Arizona	1,462,236,049	4.1%
12	Arkansas	815,668,482	2.3%
1	California	5,197,239,148	14.7%
15	Colorado	711,149,746	2.0%
40	Connecticut	99,869,601	0.3%
44	Delaware	81,868,231	0.2%
3	Florida	2,667,272,100	7.6%
5	Georgia	1,698,536,294	4.8%
42	Hawaii	97,686,817	0.3%
8	Idaho	1,255,546,711	3.6%
17	Illinois	642,007,989	1.8%
38	Indiana	107,756,549	0.3%
4	Iowa	1,766,834,573	5.0%
27	Kansas	375,516,471	1.1%
14	Kentucky	744,373,343	2.1%
32	Louisiana	231,515,405	0.7%
45	Maine	46,757,497	0.1%
35	Maryland	194,827,483	0.6%
46	Massachusetts	36,810,207	0.1%
37	Michigan	167,315,199	0.5%
24	Minnesota	462,198,804	1.3%
26	Mississippi	401,418,091	1.1%
25	Missouri	450,995,864	1.3%
33	Montana	215,619,085	0.6%
10	Nebraska	980,474,947	2.8%
43	Nevada	92,816,129	0.3%
50	New Hampshire	5,280,870	0.0%
34	New Jersey	198,336,224	0.6%
16	New Mexico	677,532,089	1.9%
21	New York	567,612,105	1.6%
6	North Carolina	1,660,513,879	4.7%
20	North Dakota	604,945,202	1.7%
31	Ohio	267,949,677	0.8%
13	Oklahoma	758,037,400	2.1%
28	Oregon	359,876,553	1.0%
19	Pennsylvania	610,966,576	1.7%
49	Rhode Island	5,795,995	0.0%
36	South Carolina	177,907,511	0.5%
22	South Dakota	558,670,463	1.6%
29	Tennessee	339,217,572	1.0%
2	Texas	3,686,460,497	10.4%
30	Utah	290,510,344	0.8%
39	Vermont	105,401,763	0.3%
23	Virginia	507,954,779	1.4%
11	Washington	969,129,560	2.7%
48	West Virginia	7,356,755	0.0%
18	Wisconsin	640,127,516	1.8%
41	Wyoming	99,568,386	0.3%

RANK ORDER

RANK	STATE	FARM INCOME	% of USA
1	California	$5,197,239,148	14.7%
2	Texas	3,686,460,497	10.4%
3	Florida	2,667,272,100	7.6%
4	Iowa	1,766,834,573	5.0%
5	Georgia	1,698,536,294	4.8%
6	North Carolina	1,660,513,879	4.7%
7	Arizona	1,462,236,049	4.1%
8	Idaho	1,255,546,711	3.6%
9	Alabama	1,199,560,934	3.4%
10	Nebraska	980,474,947	2.8%
11	Washington	969,129,560	2.7%
12	Arkansas	815,668,482	2.3%
13	Oklahoma	758,037,400	2.1%
14	Kentucky	744,373,343	2.1%
15	Colorado	711,149,746	2.0%
16	New Mexico	677,532,089	1.9%
17	Illinois	642,007,989	1.8%
18	Wisconsin	640,127,516	1.8%
19	Pennsylvania	610,966,576	1.7%
20	North Dakota	604,945,202	1.7%
21	New York	567,612,105	1.6%
22	South Dakota	558,670,463	1.6%
23	Virginia	507,954,779	1.4%
24	Minnesota	462,198,804	1.3%
25	Missouri	450,995,864	1.3%
26	Mississippi	401,418,091	1.1%
27	Kansas	375,516,471	1.1%
28	Oregon	359,876,553	1.0%
29	Tennessee	339,217,572	1.0%
30	Utah	290,510,344	0.8%
31	Ohio	267,949,677	0.8%
32	Louisiana	231,515,405	0.7%
33	Montana	215,619,085	0.6%
34	New Jersey	198,336,224	0.6%
35	Maryland	194,827,483	0.6%
36	South Carolina	177,907,511	0.5%
37	Michigan	167,315,199	0.5%
38	Indiana	107,756,549	0.3%
39	Vermont	105,401,763	0.3%
40	Connecticut	99,869,601	0.3%
41	Wyoming	99,568,386	0.3%
42	Hawaii	97,686,817	0.3%
43	Nevada	92,816,129	0.3%
44	Delaware	81,868,231	0.2%
45	Maine	46,757,497	0.1%
46	Massachusetts	36,810,207	0.1%
47	Alaska	20,113,254	0.1%
48	West Virginia	7,356,755	0.0%
49	Rhode Island	5,795,995	0.0%
50	New Hampshire	5,280,870	0.0%
	District of Columbia	0	0.0%

Source: U.S. Department of Agriculture, Economic Research Service
"Net Farm Income for States: 1990-2002"

*Net farm income is a measure of the net value of production in a given year. It is determined by subtracting total production expenses from gross farm income.

Net Farm Income per Operation in 2002

National Average = $16,368 per Operation

ALPHA ORDER

RANK	STATE	PER OPERATION
12	Alabama	$25,523
7	Alaska	34,090
1	Arizona	200,306
22	Arkansas	16,818
2	California	61,872
14	Colorado	23,705
11	Connecticut	25,608
6	Delaware	34,112
3	Florida	60,620
8	Georgia	33,971
20	Hawaii	18,431
4	Idaho	52,314
33	Illinois	8,447
48	Indiana	1,710
18	Iowa	19,101
42	Kansas	5,961
34	Kentucky	8,364
37	Louisiana	7,983
40	Maine	6,979
25	Maryland	15,969
41	Massachusetts	6,135
47	Michigan	3,218
43	Minnesota	5,851
30	Mississippi	9,335
44	Missouri	4,215
38	Montana	7,701
19	Nebraska	18,855
9	Nevada	30,939
49	New Hampshire	1,704
15	New Jersey	20,660
5	New Mexico	45,169
26	New York	15,341
10	North Carolina	29,652
16	North Dakota	20,165
46	Ohio	3,435
32	Oklahoma	8,713
31	Oregon	8,777
29	Pennsylvania	10,355
36	Rhode Island	8,280
39	South Carolina	7,262
21	South Dakota	17,190
45	Tennessee	3,769
23	Texas	16,028
17	Utah	19,367
24	Vermont	15,970
28	Virginia	10,366
13	Washington	24,849
50	West Virginia	359
35	Wisconsin	8,313
27	Wyoming	10,823

RANK ORDER

RANK	STATE	PER OPERATION
1	Arizona	$200,306
2	California	61,872
3	Florida	60,620
4	Idaho	52,314
5	New Mexico	45,169
6	Delaware	34,112
7	Alaska	34,090
8	Georgia	33,971
9	Nevada	30,939
10	North Carolina	29,652
11	Connecticut	25,608
12	Alabama	25,523
13	Washington	24,849
14	Colorado	23,705
15	New Jersey	20,660
16	North Dakota	20,165
17	Utah	19,367
18	Iowa	19,101
19	Nebraska	18,855
20	Hawaii	18,431
21	South Dakota	17,190
22	Arkansas	16,818
23	Texas	16,028
24	Vermont	15,970
25	Maryland	15,969
26	New York	15,341
27	Wyoming	10,823
28	Virginia	10,366
29	Pennsylvania	10,355
30	Mississippi	9,335
31	Oregon	8,777
32	Oklahoma	8,713
33	Illinois	8,447
34	Kentucky	8,364
35	Wisconsin	8,313
36	Rhode Island	8,280
37	Louisiana	7,983
38	Montana	7,701
39	South Carolina	7,262
40	Maine	6,979
41	Massachusetts	6,135
42	Kansas	5,961
43	Minnesota	5,851
44	Missouri	4,215
45	Tennessee	3,769
46	Ohio	3,435
47	Michigan	3,218
48	Indiana	1,710
49	New Hampshire	1,704
50	West Virginia	359
	District of Columbia*	NA

Source: U.S. Department of Agriculture, Economic Research Service
    "Net Farm Income for States: 1990-2002"
*Not applicable.

Net Farm Income per Acre in 2002

National Average = $38 per Acre

<u>ALPHA ORDER</u>

RANK	STATE	PER ACRE
8	Alabama	$135
33	Alaska	22
20	Arizona	55
19	Arkansas	56
4	California	188
31	Colorado	23
1	Connecticut	277
7	Delaware	146
2	Florida	261
6	Georgia	154
15	Hawaii	68
9	Idaho	106
31	Illinois	23
47	Indiana	7
22	Iowa	54
46	Kansas	8
20	Kentucky	55
27	Louisiana	29
24	Maine	37
11	Maryland	93
16	Massachusetts	66
38	Michigan	16
38	Minnesota	16
26	Mississippi	36
40	Missouri	15
48	Montana	4
35	Nebraska	21
43	Nevada	14
44	New Hampshire	13
3	New Jersey	242
40	New Mexico	15
14	New York	75
5	North Carolina	182
40	North Dakota	15
37	Ohio	18
33	Oklahoma	22
35	Oregon	21
12	Pennsylvania	79
10	Rhode Island	97
24	South Carolina	37
44	South Dakota	13
27	Tennessee	29
29	Texas	28
30	Utah	25
12	Vermont	79
18	Virginia	58
17	Washington	62
50	West Virginia	2
23	Wisconsin	40
49	Wyoming	3

<u>RANK ORDER</u>

RANK	STATE	PER ACRE
1	Connecticut	$277
2	Florida	261
3	New Jersey	242
4	California	188
5	North Carolina	182
6	Georgia	154
7	Delaware	146
8	Alabama	135
9	Idaho	106
10	Rhode Island	97
11	Maryland	93
12	Pennsylvania	79
12	Vermont	79
14	New York	75
15	Hawaii	68
16	Massachusetts	66
17	Washington	62
18	Virginia	58
19	Arkansas	56
20	Arizona	55
20	Kentucky	55
22	Iowa	54
23	Wisconsin	40
24	Maine	37
24	South Carolina	37
26	Mississippi	36
27	Louisiana	29
27	Tennessee	29
29	Texas	28
30	Utah	25
31	Colorado	23
31	Illinois	23
33	Alaska	22
33	Oklahoma	22
35	Nebraska	21
35	Oregon	21
37	Ohio	18
38	Michigan	16
38	Minnesota	16
40	Missouri	15
40	New Mexico	15
40	North Dakota	15
43	Nevada	14
44	New Hampshire	13
44	South Dakota	13
46	Kansas	8
47	Indiana	7
48	Montana	4
49	Wyoming	3
50	West Virginia	2
	District of Columbia*	NA

Source: U.S. Department of Agriculture, Economic Research Service
"Net Farm Income for States: 1990-2002"
Not applicable.

Farm Income: Cash Receipts from Commodities in 2002

National Total = $192,947,507,000*

ALPHA ORDER

RANK ORDER

RANK	STATE	FARM INCOME	% of USA		RANK	STATE	FARM INCOME	% of USA
29	Alabama	$2,962,089,000	1.5%		1	California	$26,106,640,000	13.5%
49	Alaska	50,679,000	0.0%		2	Texas	12,664,912,000	6.6%
27	Arizona	2,997,195,000	1.6%		3	Iowa	10,833,860,000	5.6%
14	Arkansas	4,526,611,000	2.3%		4	Nebraska	9,588,658,000	5.0%
1	California	26,106,640,000	13.5%		5	Kansas	7,861,794,000	4.1%
12	Colorado	4,880,517,000	2.5%		6	Illinois	7,486,125,000	3.9%
43	Connecticut	468,489,000	0.2%		7	Minnesota	7,478,126,000	3.9%
40	Delaware	723,513,000	0.4%		8	Florida	6,848,253,000	3.5%
8	Florida	6,848,253,000	3.5%		9	North Carolina	6,602,899,000	3.4%
15	Georgia	4,472,045,000	2.3%		10	Wisconsin	5,318,908,000	2.8%
41	Hawaii	509,143,000	0.3%		11	Washington	5,208,955,000	2.7%
19	Idaho	3,933,672,000	2.0%		12	Colorado	4,880,517,000	2.5%
6	Illinois	7,486,125,000	3.9%		13	Indiana	4,799,545,000	2.5%
13	Indiana	4,799,545,000	2.5%		14	Arkansas	4,526,611,000	2.3%
3	Iowa	10,833,860,000	5.6%		15	Georgia	4,472,045,000	2.3%
5	Kansas	7,861,794,000	4.1%		16	Missouri	4,401,882,000	2.3%
24	Kentucky	3,111,713,000	1.6%		17	Ohio	4,276,038,000	2.2%
33	Louisiana	1,773,423,000	0.9%		18	Pennsylvania	4,042,439,000	2.1%
44	Maine	442,394,000	0.2%		19	Idaho	3,933,672,000	2.0%
36	Maryland	1,431,766,000	0.7%		20	South Dakota	3,779,495,000	2.0%
45	Massachusetts	380,274,000	0.2%		21	Oklahoma	3,730,952,000	1.9%
22	Michigan	3,390,072,000	1.8%		22	Michigan	3,390,072,000	1.8%
7	Minnesota	7,478,126,000	3.9%		23	North Dakota	3,222,630,000	1.7%
28	Mississippi	2,962,343,000	1.5%		24	Kentucky	3,111,713,000	1.6%
16	Missouri	4,401,882,000	2.3%		25	New York	3,104,484,000	1.6%
34	Montana	1,687,481,000	0.9%		26	Oregon	3,102,265,000	1.6%
4	Nebraska	9,588,658,000	5.0%		27	Arizona	2,997,195,000	1.6%
47	Nevada	366,242,000	0.2%		28	Mississippi	2,962,343,000	1.5%
48	New Hampshire	147,573,000	0.1%		29	Alabama	2,962,089,000	1.5%
39	New Jersey	855,727,000	0.4%		30	Virginia	2,172,890,000	1.1%
32	New Mexico	1,956,978,000	1.0%		31	Tennessee	1,999,858,000	1.0%
25	New York	3,104,484,000	1.6%		32	New Mexico	1,956,978,000	1.0%
9	North Carolina	6,602,899,000	3.4%		33	Louisiana	1,773,423,000	0.9%
23	North Dakota	3,222,630,000	1.7%		34	Montana	1,687,481,000	0.9%
17	Ohio	4,276,038,000	2.2%		35	South Carolina	1,452,079,000	0.8%
21	Oklahoma	3,730,952,000	1.9%		36	Maryland	1,431,766,000	0.7%
26	Oregon	3,102,265,000	1.6%		37	Utah	1,057,178,000	0.5%
18	Pennsylvania	4,042,439,000	2.1%		38	Wyoming	875,784,000	0.5%
50	Rhode Island	46,087,000	0.0%		39	New Jersey	855,727,000	0.4%
35	South Carolina	1,452,079,000	0.8%		40	Delaware	723,513,000	0.4%
20	South Dakota	3,779,495,000	2.0%		41	Hawaii	509,143,000	0.3%
31	Tennessee	1,999,858,000	1.0%		42	Vermont	476,352,000	0.2%
2	Texas	12,664,912,000	6.6%		43	Connecticut	468,489,000	0.2%
37	Utah	1,057,178,000	0.5%		44	Maine	442,394,000	0.2%
42	Vermont	476,352,000	0.2%		45	Massachusetts	380,274,000	0.2%
30	Virginia	2,172,890,000	1.1%		46	West Virginia	378,486,000	0.2%
11	Washington	5,208,955,000	2.7%		47	Nevada	366,242,000	0.2%
46	West Virginia	378,486,000	0.2%		48	New Hampshire	147,573,000	0.1%
10	Wisconsin	5,318,908,000	2.8%		49	Alaska	50,679,000	0.0%
38	Wyoming	875,784,000	0.5%		50	Rhode Island	46,087,000	0.0%
						District of Columbia	0	0.0%

Source: U.S. Department of Agriculture, Economic Research Service
"Farm Marketings"
Commodities include crops and livestock.

Farm Income: Crops in 2002

National Total = $99,467,672,000

ALPHA ORDER

RANK	STATE	FARM INCOME	% of USA
36	Alabama	$583,811,000	0.6%
50	Alaska	22,773,000	0.0%
18	Arizona	1,903,139,000	1.9%
21	Arkansas	1,574,866,000	1.6%
1	California	19,865,008,000	20.0%
23	Colorado	1,378,928,000	1.4%
39	Connecticut	314,125,000	0.3%
43	Delaware	177,184,000	0.2%
4	Florida	5,609,028,000	5.6%
20	Georgia	1,582,309,000	1.6%
38	Hawaii	424,354,000	0.4%
17	Idaho	1,935,141,000	1.9%
2	Illinois	5,923,828,000	6.0%
9	Indiana	3,248,526,000	3.3%
3	Iowa	5,759,106,000	5.8%
12	Kansas	2,536,465,000	2.6%
27	Kentucky	1,151,034,000	1.2%
26	Louisiana	1,159,374,000	1.2%
42	Maine	211,923,000	0.2%
35	Maryland	621,423,000	0.6%
40	Massachusetts	297,024,000	0.3%
15	Michigan	2,130,372,000	2.1%
6	Minnesota	3,833,272,000	3.9%
29	Mississippi	1,012,645,000	1.0%
16	Missouri	2,099,829,000	2.1%
32	Montana	701,983,000	0.7%
7	Nebraska	3,764,363,000	3.8%
44	Nevada	155,085,000	0.2%
46	New Hampshire	91,297,000	0.1%
34	New Jersey	663,118,000	0.7%
37	New Mexico	574,926,000	0.6%
25	New York	1,234,324,000	1.2%
10	North Carolina	2,658,886,000	2.7%
13	North Dakota	2,498,974,000	2.5%
11	Ohio	2,645,811,000	2.7%
30	Oklahoma	837,492,000	0.8%
14	Oregon	2,294,134,000	2.3%
24	Pennsylvania	1,360,038,000	1.4%
49	Rhode Island	39,787,000	0.0%
33	South Carolina	691,852,000	0.7%
19	South Dakota	1,719,982,000	1.7%
28	Tennessee	1,086,785,000	1.1%
5	Texas	4,577,242,000	4.6%
41	Utah	249,426,000	0.3%
48	Vermont	76,178,000	0.1%
31	Virginia	721,763,000	0.7%
8	Washington	3,713,638,000	3.7%
47	West Virginia	78,289,000	0.1%
22	Wisconsin	1,550,606,000	1.6%
45	Wyoming	126,213,000	0.1%

RANK ORDER

RANK	STATE	FARM INCOME	% of USA
1	California	$19,865,008,000	20.0%
2	Illinois	5,923,828,000	6.0%
3	Iowa	5,759,106,000	5.8%
4	Florida	5,609,028,000	5.6%
5	Texas	4,577,242,000	4.6%
6	Minnesota	3,833,272,000	3.9%
7	Nebraska	3,764,363,000	3.8%
8	Washington	3,713,638,000	3.7%
9	Indiana	3,248,526,000	3.3%
10	North Carolina	2,658,886,000	2.7%
11	Ohio	2,645,811,000	2.7%
12	Kansas	2,536,465,000	2.6%
13	North Dakota	2,498,974,000	2.5%
14	Oregon	2,294,134,000	2.3%
15	Michigan	2,130,372,000	2.1%
16	Missouri	2,099,829,000	2.1%
17	Idaho	1,935,141,000	1.9%
18	Arizona	1,903,139,000	1.9%
19	South Dakota	1,719,982,000	1.7%
20	Georgia	1,582,309,000	1.6%
21	Arkansas	1,574,866,000	1.6%
22	Wisconsin	1,550,606,000	1.6%
23	Colorado	1,378,928,000	1.4%
24	Pennsylvania	1,360,038,000	1.4%
25	New York	1,234,324,000	1.2%
26	Louisiana	1,159,374,000	1.2%
27	Kentucky	1,151,034,000	1.2%
28	Tennessee	1,086,785,000	1.1%
29	Mississippi	1,012,645,000	1.0%
30	Oklahoma	837,492,000	0.8%
31	Virginia	721,763,000	0.7%
32	Montana	701,983,000	0.7%
33	South Carolina	691,852,000	0.7%
34	New Jersey	663,118,000	0.7%
35	Maryland	621,423,000	0.6%
36	Alabama	583,811,000	0.6%
37	New Mexico	574,926,000	0.6%
38	Hawaii	424,354,000	0.4%
39	Connecticut	314,125,000	0.3%
40	Massachusetts	297,024,000	0.3%
41	Utah	249,426,000	0.3%
42	Maine	211,923,000	0.2%
43	Delaware	177,184,000	0.2%
44	Nevada	155,085,000	0.2%
45	Wyoming	126,213,000	0.1%
46	New Hampshire	91,297,000	0.1%
47	West Virginia	78,289,000	0.1%
48	Vermont	76,178,000	0.1%
49	Rhode Island	39,787,000	0.0%
50	Alaska	22,773,000	0.0%
	District of Columbia	0	0.0%

Source: U.S. Department of Agriculture, Economic Research Service
"Farm Marketings"

Farm Income: Livestock in 2002

National Total = $93,479,835,000*

<u>ALPHA ORDER</u>

RANK	STATE	FARM INCOME	% of USA
14	Alabama	$2,378,278,000	2.5%
49	Alaska	27,906,000	0.0%
29	Arizona	1,094,056,000	1.2%
10	Arkansas	2,951,745,000	3.2%
2	California	6,241,632,000	6.7%
9	Colorado	3,501,589,000	3.7%
45	Connecticut	154,364,000	0.2%
39	Delaware	546,329,000	0.6%
28	Florida	1,239,225,000	1.3%
12	Georgia	2,889,736,000	3.1%
46	Hawaii	84,789,000	0.1%
17	Idaho	1,998,531,000	2.1%
22	Illinois	1,562,297,000	1.7%
23	Indiana	1,551,019,000	1.7%
5	Iowa	5,074,754,000	5.4%
4	Kansas	5,325,329,000	5.7%
18	Kentucky	1,960,679,000	2.1%
38	Louisiana	614,049,000	0.7%
42	Maine	230,471,000	0.2%
32	Maryland	810,343,000	0.9%
47	Massachusetts	83,250,000	0.1%
27	Michigan	1,259,700,000	1.3%
8	Minnesota	3,644,854,000	3.9%
19	Mississippi	1,949,698,000	2.1%
15	Missouri	2,302,053,000	2.5%
30	Montana	985,498,000	1.1%
3	Nebraska	5,824,295,000	6.2%
43	Nevada	211,157,000	0.2%
48	New Hampshire	56,276,000	0.1%
44	New Jersey	192,609,000	0.2%
26	New Mexico	1,382,052,000	1.5%
20	New York	1,870,160,000	2.0%
6	North Carolina	3,944,013,000	4.2%
37	North Dakota	723,656,000	0.8%
21	Ohio	1,630,227,000	1.7%
11	Oklahoma	2,893,460,000	3.1%
33	Oregon	808,131,000	0.9%
13	Pennsylvania	2,682,401,000	2.9%
50	Rhode Island	6,300,000	0.0%
35	South Carolina	760,227,000	0.8%
16	South Dakota	2,059,513,000	2.2%
31	Tennessee	913,073,000	1.0%
1	Texas	8,087,670,000	8.7%
34	Utah	807,752,000	0.9%
40	Vermont	400,174,000	0.4%
25	Virginia	1,451,127,000	1.6%
24	Washington	1,495,317,000	1.6%
41	West Virginia	300,197,000	0.3%
7	Wisconsin	3,768,302,000	4.0%
36	Wyoming	749,571,000	0.8%

<u>RANK ORDER</u>

RANK	STATE	FARM INCOME	% of USA
1	Texas	$8,087,670,000	8.7%
2	California	6,241,632,000	6.7%
3	Nebraska	5,824,295,000	6.2%
4	Kansas	5,325,329,000	5.7%
5	Iowa	5,074,754,000	5.4%
6	North Carolina	3,944,013,000	4.2%
7	Wisconsin	3,768,302,000	4.0%
8	Minnesota	3,644,854,000	3.9%
9	Colorado	3,501,589,000	3.7%
10	Arkansas	2,951,745,000	3.2%
11	Oklahoma	2,893,460,000	3.1%
12	Georgia	2,889,736,000	3.1%
13	Pennsylvania	2,682,401,000	2.9%
14	Alabama	2,378,278,000	2.5%
15	Missouri	2,302,053,000	2.5%
16	South Dakota	2,059,513,000	2.2%
17	Idaho	1,998,531,000	2.1%
18	Kentucky	1,960,679,000	2.1%
19	Mississippi	1,949,698,000	2.1%
20	New York	1,870,160,000	2.0%
21	Ohio	1,630,227,000	1.7%
22	Illinois	1,562,297,000	1.7%
23	Indiana	1,551,019,000	1.7%
24	Washington	1,495,317,000	1.6%
25	Virginia	1,451,127,000	1.6%
26	New Mexico	1,382,052,000	1.5%
27	Michigan	1,259,700,000	1.3%
28	Florida	1,239,225,000	1.3%
29	Arizona	1,094,056,000	1.2%
30	Montana	985,498,000	1.1%
31	Tennessee	913,073,000	1.0%
32	Maryland	810,343,000	0.9%
33	Oregon	808,131,000	0.9%
34	Utah	807,752,000	0.9%
35	South Carolina	760,227,000	0.8%
36	Wyoming	749,571,000	0.8%
37	North Dakota	723,656,000	0.8%
38	Louisiana	614,049,000	0.7%
39	Delaware	546,329,000	0.6%
40	Vermont	400,174,000	0.4%
41	West Virginia	300,197,000	0.3%
42	Maine	230,471,000	0.2%
43	Nevada	211,157,000	0.2%
44	New Jersey	192,609,000	0.2%
45	Connecticut	154,364,000	0.2%
46	Hawaii	84,789,000	0.1%
47	Massachusetts	83,250,000	0.1%
48	New Hampshire	56,276,000	0.1%
49	Alaska	27,906,000	0.0%
50	Rhode Island	6,300,000	0.0%
	District of Columbia	0	0.0%

Source: U.S. Department of Agriculture, Economic Research Service
"Farm Marketings"
Includes livestock products.

Farm Income: Government Payments in 2002

National Total = $10,961,465,000*

ALPHA ORDER					RANK ORDER			
RANK	STATE	PAYMENTS	% of USA		RANK	STATE	PAYMENTS	% of USA
18	Alabama	$262,147,846	2.4%		1	Texas	$986,215,648	9.0%
48	Alaska	1,828,906	0.0%		2	Iowa	737,106,591	6.7%
34	Arizona	68,925,916	0.6%		3	Georgia	652,788,731	6.0%
9	Arkansas	446,552,798	4.1%		4	Illinois	612,706,426	5.6%
8	California	451,494,915	4.1%		5	Nebraska	485,090,659	4.4%
24	Colorado	188,413,519	1.7%		6	Minnesota	480,482,533	4.4%
46	Connecticut	4,916,466	0.0%		7	Kansas	452,680,461	4.1%
41	Delaware	11,863,468	0.1%		8	California	451,494,915	4.1%
31	Florida	81,466,540	0.7%		9	Arkansas	446,552,798	4.1%
3	Georgia	652,788,731	6.0%		10	Missouri	397,291,671	3.6%
49	Hawaii	1,801,933	0.0%		11	North Dakota	381,658,005	3.5%
25	Idaho	163,322,433	1.5%		12	Indiana	332,781,811	3.0%
4	Illinois	612,706,426	5.6%		13	Wisconsin	330,604,219	3.0%
12	Indiana	332,781,811	3.0%		14	Oklahoma	308,822,353	2.8%
2	Iowa	737,106,591	6.7%		15	South Dakota	281,255,574	2.6%
7	Kansas	452,680,461	4.1%		16	Ohio	278,967,436	2.5%
28	Kentucky	137,901,414	1.3%		17	North Carolina	268,132,212	2.4%
20	Louisiana	251,735,443	2.3%		18	Alabama	262,147,846	2.4%
40	Maine	13,751,551	0.1%		19	Montana	259,095,501	2.4%
36	Maryland	48,337,940	0.4%		20	Louisiana	251,735,443	2.3%
44	Massachusetts	6,204,328	0.1%		21	Mississippi	249,758,155	2.3%
23	Michigan	188,512,974	1.7%		22	Washington	214,137,716	2.0%
6	Minnesota	480,482,533	4.4%		23	Michigan	188,512,974	1.7%
21	Mississippi	249,758,155	2.3%		24	Colorado	188,413,519	1.7%
10	Missouri	397,291,671	3.6%		25	Idaho	163,322,433	1.5%
19	Montana	259,095,501	2.4%		26	New York	158,173,511	1.4%
5	Nebraska	485,090,659	4.4%		27	Virginia	153,790,489	1.4%
42	Nevada	11,121,146	0.1%		28	Kentucky	137,901,414	1.3%
47	New Hampshire	3,895,082	0.0%		29	Pennsylvania	129,113,184	1.2%
43	New Jersey	6,433,775	0.1%		30	Tennessee	107,178,427	1.0%
33	New Mexico	72,996,412	0.7%		31	Florida	81,466,540	0.7%
26	New York	158,173,511	1.4%		32	Oregon	80,290,017	0.7%
17	North Carolina	268,132,212	2.4%		33	New Mexico	72,996,412	0.7%
11	North Dakota	381,658,005	3.5%		34	Arizona	68,925,916	0.6%
16	Ohio	278,967,436	2.5%		35	South Carolina	64,019,171	0.6%
14	Oklahoma	308,822,353	2.8%		36	Maryland	48,337,940	0.4%
32	Oregon	80,290,017	0.7%		37	Wyoming	47,260,274	0.4%
29	Pennsylvania	129,113,184	1.2%		38	Utah	45,718,910	0.4%
50	Rhode Island	696,540	0.0%		39	Vermont	36,340,808	0.3%
35	South Carolina	64,019,171	0.6%		40	Maine	13,751,551	0.1%
15	South Dakota	281,255,574	2.6%		41	Delaware	11,863,468	0.1%
30	Tennessee	107,178,427	1.0%		42	Nevada	11,121,146	0.1%
1	Texas	986,215,648	9.0%		43	New Jersey	6,433,775	0.1%
38	Utah	45,718,910	0.4%		44	Massachusetts	6,204,328	0.1%
39	Vermont	36,340,808	0.3%		45	West Virginia	5,683,089	0.1%
27	Virginia	153,790,489	1.4%		46	Connecticut	4,916,466	0.0%
22	Washington	214,137,716	2.0%		47	New Hampshire	3,895,082	0.0%
45	West Virginia	5,683,089	0.1%		48	Alaska	1,828,906	0.0%
13	Wisconsin	330,604,219	3.0%		49	Hawaii	1,801,933	0.0%
37	Wyoming	47,260,274	0.4%		50	Rhode Island	696,540	0.0%
						District of Columbia	0	0.0%

Source: U.S. Department of Agriculture, Economic Research Service
"Farm Marketings"
**Government payments made directly to farmers in cash.*

"

Acres Planted in 2003

National Total = 325,335,000 Acres*

<u>ALPHA ORDER</u>

RANK	STATE	ACRES	% of USA
31	Alabama	2,049,000	0.6%
NA	Alaska**	NA	NA
38	Arizona	716,000	0.2%
15	Arkansas	7,996,000	2.5%
21	California	4,653,000	1.4%
17	Colorado	6,297,000	1.9%
46	Connecticut	92,000	0.0%
41	Delaware	444,000	0.1%
36	Florida	1,064,000	0.3%
26	Georgia	3,807,000	1.2%
48	Hawaii	22,000	0.0%
22	Idaho	4,443,000	1.4%
3	Illinois	23,342,000	7.2%
10	Indiana	12,193,000	3.7%
1	Iowa	24,841,000	7.6%
4	Kansas	23,237,000	7.1%
18	Kentucky	5,504,000	1.7%
27	Louisiana	3,455,000	1.1%
44	Maine	281,000	0.1%
34	Maryland	1,332,000	0.4%
45	Massachusetts	114,000	0.0%
16	Michigan	6,610,000	2.0%
6	Minnesota	20,031,000	6.2%
23	Mississippi	4,310,000	1.3%
9	Missouri	13,940,000	4.3%
13	Montana	9,100,000	2.8%
7	Nebraska	19,156,000	5.9%
40	Nevada	469,000	0.1%
47	New Hampshire	70,000	0.0%
43	New Jersey	328,000	0.1%
35	New Mexico	1,166,000	0.4%
28	New York	3,301,000	1.0%
20	North Carolina	4,751,000	1.5%
5	North Dakota	21,964,000	6.8%
12	Ohio	10,109,000	3.1%
11	Oklahoma	10,777,000	3.3%
30	Oregon	2,471,000	0.8%
24	Pennsylvania	3,978,000	1.2%
49	Rhode Island	11,000	0.0%
33	South Carolina	1,556,000	0.5%
8	South Dakota	17,487,000	5.4%
19	Tennessee	4,959,000	1.5%
2	Texas	24,126,000	7.4%
37	Utah	1,047,000	0.3%
42	Vermont	331,000	0.1%
29	Virginia	2,700,000	0.8%
25	Washington	3,890,000	1.2%
39	West Virginia	622,000	0.2%
14	Wisconsin	8,381,000	2.6%
32	Wyoming	1,668,000	0.5%

<u>RANK ORDER</u>

RANK	STATE	ACRES	% of USA
1	Iowa	24,841,000	7.6%
2	Texas	24,126,000	7.4%
3	Illinois	23,342,000	7.2%
4	Kansas	23,237,000	7.1%
5	North Dakota	21,964,000	6.8%
6	Minnesota	20,031,000	6.2%
7	Nebraska	19,156,000	5.9%
8	South Dakota	17,487,000	5.4%
9	Missouri	13,940,000	4.3%
10	Indiana	12,193,000	3.7%
11	Oklahoma	10,777,000	3.3%
12	Ohio	10,109,000	3.1%
13	Montana	9,100,000	2.8%
14	Wisconsin	8,381,000	2.6%
15	Arkansas	7,996,000	2.5%
16	Michigan	6,610,000	2.0%
17	Colorado	6,297,000	1.9%
18	Kentucky	5,504,000	1.7%
19	Tennessee	4,959,000	1.5%
20	North Carolina	4,751,000	1.5%
21	California	4,653,000	1.4%
22	Idaho	4,443,000	1.4%
23	Mississippi	4,310,000	1.3%
24	Pennsylvania	3,978,000	1.2%
25	Washington	3,890,000	1.2%
26	Georgia	3,807,000	1.2%
27	Louisiana	3,455,000	1.1%
28	New York	3,301,000	1.0%
29	Virginia	2,700,000	0.8%
30	Oregon	2,471,000	0.8%
31	Alabama	2,049,000	0.6%
32	Wyoming	1,668,000	0.5%
33	South Carolina	1,556,000	0.5%
34	Maryland	1,332,000	0.4%
35	New Mexico	1,166,000	0.4%
36	Florida	1,064,000	0.3%
37	Utah	1,047,000	0.3%
38	Arizona	716,000	0.2%
39	West Virginia	622,000	0.2%
40	Nevada	469,000	0.1%
41	Delaware	444,000	0.1%
42	Vermont	331,000	0.1%
43	New Jersey	328,000	0.1%
44	Maine	281,000	0.1%
45	Massachusetts	114,000	0.0%
46	Connecticut	92,000	0.0%
47	New Hampshire	70,000	0.0%
48	Hawaii	22,000	0.0%
49	Rhode Island	11,000	0.0%
NA	Alaska**	NA	NA
	District of Columbia**	NA	NA

Source: U.S. Department of Agriculture, National Agricultural Statistics Service
"Crop Production, 2003 Summary" (Cr Pr 2-1 (04), January 2004)
(http://usda.mannlib.cornell.edu/reports/nassr/field/pcp-bban/)
**Estimated totals.*
***No acreage or not available.*

Acres Harvested in 2003

National Total = 307,171,000 Acres*

ALPHA ORDER

RANK	STATE	ACRES	% of USA
31	Alabama	1,931,000	0.6%
NA	Alaska**	NA	NA
38	Arizona	711,000	0.2%
15	Arkansas	7,771,000	2.5%
23	California	4,060,000	1.3%
17	Colorado	5,557,000	1.8%
46	Connecticut	90,000	0.0%
41	Delaware	432,000	0.1%
35	Florida	1,033,000	0.3%
27	Georgia	3,330,000	1.1%
48	Hawaii	22,000	0.0%
22	Idaho	4,238,000	1.4%
2	Illinois	23,165,000	7.5%
10	Indiana	11,993,000	3.9%
1	Iowa	24,629,000	8.0%
3	Kansas	21,843,000	7.1%
18	Kentucky	5,332,000	1.7%
26	Louisiana	3,386,000	1.1%
44	Maine	276,000	0.1%
34	Maryland	1,295,000	0.4%
45	Massachusetts	111,000	0.0%
16	Michigan	6,483,000	2.1%
5	Minnesota	19,679,000	6.4%
21	Mississippi	4,243,000	1.4%
9	Missouri	13,742,000	4.5%
12	Montana	8,494,000	2.8%
7	Nebraska	18,560,000	6.0%
40	Nevada	462,000	0.2%
47	New Hampshire	69,000	0.0%
43	New Jersey	319,000	0.1%
37	New Mexico	721,000	0.2%
28	New York	3,234,000	1.1%
20	North Carolina	4,439,000	1.4%
4	North Dakota	21,237,000	6.9%
11	Ohio	9,947,000	3.2%
13	Oklahoma	8,457,000	2.8%
30	Oregon	2,383,000	0.8%
24	Pennsylvania	3,850,000	1.3%
49	Rhode Island	11,000	0.0%
33	South Carolina	1,469,000	0.5%
8	South Dakota	16,685,000	5.4%
19	Tennessee	4,706,000	1.5%
6	Texas	18,765,000	6.1%
36	Utah	936,000	0.3%
42	Vermont	323,000	0.1%
29	Virginia	2,589,000	0.8%
25	Washington	3,804,000	1.2%
39	West Virginia	614,000	0.2%
14	Wisconsin	8,023,000	2.6%
32	Wyoming	1,596,000	0.5%

RANK ORDER

RANK	STATE	ACRES	% of USA
1	Iowa	24,629,000	8.0%
2	Illinois	23,165,000	7.5%
3	Kansas	21,843,000	7.1%
4	North Dakota	21,237,000	6.9%
5	Minnesota	19,679,000	6.4%
6	Texas	18,765,000	6.1%
7	Nebraska	18,560,000	6.0%
8	South Dakota	16,685,000	5.4%
9	Missouri	13,742,000	4.5%
10	Indiana	11,993,000	3.9%
11	Ohio	9,947,000	3.2%
12	Montana	8,494,000	2.8%
13	Oklahoma	8,457,000	2.8%
14	Wisconsin	8,023,000	2.6%
15	Arkansas	7,771,000	2.5%
16	Michigan	6,483,000	2.1%
17	Colorado	5,557,000	1.8%
18	Kentucky	5,332,000	1.7%
19	Tennessee	4,706,000	1.5%
20	North Carolina	4,439,000	1.4%
21	Mississippi	4,243,000	1.4%
22	Idaho	4,238,000	1.4%
23	California	4,060,000	1.3%
24	Pennsylvania	3,850,000	1.3%
25	Washington	3,804,000	1.2%
26	Louisiana	3,386,000	1.1%
27	Georgia	3,330,000	1.1%
28	New York	3,234,000	1.1%
29	Virginia	2,589,000	0.8%
30	Oregon	2,383,000	0.8%
31	Alabama	1,931,000	0.6%
32	Wyoming	1,596,000	0.5%
33	South Carolina	1,469,000	0.5%
34	Maryland	1,295,000	0.4%
35	Florida	1,033,000	0.3%
36	Utah	936,000	0.3%
37	New Mexico	721,000	0.2%
38	Arizona	711,000	0.2%
39	West Virginia	614,000	0.2%
40	Nevada	462,000	0.2%
41	Delaware	432,000	0.1%
42	Vermont	323,000	0.1%
43	New Jersey	319,000	0.1%
44	Maine	276,000	0.1%
45	Massachusetts	111,000	0.0%
46	Connecticut	90,000	0.0%
47	New Hampshire	69,000	0.0%
48	Hawaii	22,000	0.0%
49	Rhode Island	11,000	0.0%
NA	Alaska**	NA	NA
	District of Columbia**	NA	NA

Source: U.S. Department of Agriculture, National Agricultural Statistics Service
"Crop Production, 2003 Summary" (Cr Pr 2-1 (04), January 2004)
(http://usda.mannlib.cornell.edu/reports/nassr/field/pcp-bban/)

*Estimated totals.

**No acreage or not available.

Acres Harvested: Corn in 2003

National Total = 78,736,000 Acres*

ALPHA ORDER

RANK	STATE	ACRES	% of USA
29	Alabama	220,000	0.3%
NA	Alaska**	NA	NA
42	Arizona	47,000	0.1%
25	Arkansas	365,000	0.5%
21	California	520,000	0.7%
16	Colorado	1,080,000	1.4%
43	Connecticut	30,000	0.0%
31	Delaware	170,000	0.2%
37	Florida	75,000	0.1%
26	Georgia	340,000	0.4%
NA	Hawaii**	NA	NA
30	Idaho	190,000	0.2%
2	Illinois	11,200,000	14.2%
5	Indiana	5,600,000	7.1%
1	Iowa	12,400,000	15.7%
9	Kansas	2,900,000	3.7%
15	Kentucky	1,170,000	1.5%
21	Louisiana	520,000	0.7%
44	Maine	28,000	0.0%
23	Maryland	480,000	0.6%
45	Massachusetts	20,000	0.0%
11	Michigan	2,300,000	2.9%
4	Minnesota	7,200,000	9.1%
20	Mississippi	550,000	0.7%
9	Missouri	2,900,000	3.7%
38	Montana	65,000	0.1%
3	Nebraska	8,100,000	10.3%
47	Nevada	4,000	0.0%
46	New Hampshire	15,000	0.0%
36	New Jersey	80,000	0.1%
32	New Mexico	130,000	0.2%
17	New York	1,000,000	1.3%
18	North Carolina	740,000	0.9%
13	North Dakota	1,450,000	1.8%
8	Ohio	3,300,000	4.2%
28	Oklahoma	230,000	0.3%
40	Oregon	51,000	0.1%
13	Pennsylvania	1,450,000	1.8%
48	Rhode Island	2,000	0.0%
27	South Carolina	240,000	0.3%
6	South Dakota	4,400,000	5.6%
19	Tennessee	710,000	0.9%
12	Texas	1,830,000	2.3%
39	Utah	55,000	0.1%
34	Vermont	96,000	0.1%
24	Virginia	470,000	0.6%
32	Washington	130,000	0.2%
41	West Virginia	48,000	0.1%
7	Wisconsin	3,750,000	4.8%
35	Wyoming	85,000	0.1%

RANK ORDER

RANK	STATE	ACRES	% of USA
1	Iowa	12,400,000	15.7%
2	Illinois	11,200,000	14.2%
3	Nebraska	8,100,000	10.3%
4	Minnesota	7,200,000	9.1%
5	Indiana	5,600,000	7.1%
6	South Dakota	4,400,000	5.6%
7	Wisconsin	3,750,000	4.8%
8	Ohio	3,300,000	4.2%
9	Kansas	2,900,000	3.7%
9	Missouri	2,900,000	3.7%
11	Michigan	2,300,000	2.9%
12	Texas	1,830,000	2.3%
13	North Dakota	1,450,000	1.8%
13	Pennsylvania	1,450,000	1.8%
15	Kentucky	1,170,000	1.5%
16	Colorado	1,080,000	1.4%
17	New York	1,000,000	1.3%
18	North Carolina	740,000	0.9%
19	Tennessee	710,000	0.9%
20	Mississippi	550,000	0.7%
21	California	520,000	0.7%
21	Louisiana	520,000	0.7%
23	Maryland	480,000	0.6%
24	Virginia	470,000	0.6%
25	Arkansas	365,000	0.5%
26	Georgia	340,000	0.4%
27	South Carolina	240,000	0.3%
28	Oklahoma	230,000	0.3%
29	Alabama	220,000	0.3%
30	Idaho	190,000	0.2%
31	Delaware	170,000	0.2%
32	New Mexico	130,000	0.2%
32	Washington	130,000	0.2%
34	Vermont	96,000	0.1%
35	Wyoming	85,000	0.1%
36	New Jersey	80,000	0.1%
37	Florida	75,000	0.1%
38	Montana	65,000	0.1%
39	Utah	55,000	0.1%
40	Oregon	51,000	0.1%
41	West Virginia	48,000	0.1%
42	Arizona	47,000	0.1%
43	Connecticut	30,000	0.0%
44	Maine	28,000	0.0%
45	Massachusetts	20,000	0.0%
46	New Hampshire	15,000	0.0%
47	Nevada	4,000	0.0%
48	Rhode Island	2,000	0.0%
NA	Alaska**	NA	NA
NA	Hawaii**	NA	NA
	District of Columbia**	NA	NA

Source: U.S. Department of Agriculture, National Agricultural Statistics Service
   "Crop Production, 2003 Summary" (Cr Pr 2-1 (04), January 2004)
      (http://usda.mannlib.cornell.edu/reports/nassr/field/pcp-bban/)
Estimated totals. Acres harvested for all purposes. There were 71,139,000 acres harvested for grain.
**No acreage or not available.*

Acres Harvested: Soybeans in 2003

National Total = 72,321,000 Acres*

<u>ALPHA ORDER</u>

RANK	STATE	ACRES	% of USA
27	Alabama	160,000	0.2%
NA	Alaska**	NA	NA
NA	Arizona**	NA	NA
10	Arkansas	2,890,000	4.0%
NA	California**	NA	NA
NA	Colorado**	NA	NA
NA	Connecticut**	NA	NA
26	Delaware	178,000	0.2%
31	Florida	12,000	0.0%
24	Georgia	180,000	0.2%
NA	Hawaii**	NA	NA
NA	Idaho**	NA	NA
2	Illinois	10,250,000	14.2%
4	Indiana	5,350,000	7.4%
1	Iowa	10,550,000	14.6%
11	Kansas	2,480,000	3.4%
16	Kentucky	1,240,000	1.7%
18	Louisiana	740,000	1.0%
NA	Maine**	NA	NA
20	Maryland	430,000	0.6%
NA	Massachusetts**	NA	NA
12	Michigan	1,990,000	2.8%
3	Minnesota	7,400,000	10.2%
14	Mississippi	1,430,000	2.0%
5	Missouri	4,940,000	6.8%
NA	Montana**	NA	NA
6	Nebraska	4,490,000	6.2%
NA	Nevada**	NA	NA
NA	New Hampshire**	NA	NA
29	New Jersey	88,000	0.1%
NA	New Mexico**	NA	NA
28	New York	138,000	0.2%
15	North Carolina	1,400,000	1.9%
9	North Dakota	3,030,000	4.2%
7	Ohio	4,280,000	5.9%
23	Oklahoma	245,000	0.3%
NA	Oregon**	NA	NA
22	Pennsylvania	375,000	0.5%
NA	Rhode Island**	NA	NA
21	South Carolina	420,000	0.6%
8	South Dakota	4,190,000	5.8%
17	Tennessee	1,120,000	1.5%
24	Texas	180,000	0.2%
NA	Utah**	NA	NA
NA	Vermont**	NA	NA
19	Virginia	480,000	0.7%
NA	Washington**	NA	NA
30	West Virginia	15,000	0.0%
13	Wisconsin	1,650,000	2.3%
NA	Wyoming**	NA	NA

<u>RANK ORDER</u>

RANK	STATE	ACRES	% of USA
1	Iowa	10,550,000	14.6%
2	Illinois	10,250,000	14.2%
3	Minnesota	7,400,000	10.2%
4	Indiana	5,350,000	7.4%
5	Missouri	4,940,000	6.8%
6	Nebraska	4,490,000	6.2%
7	Ohio	4,280,000	5.9%
8	South Dakota	4,190,000	5.8%
9	North Dakota	3,030,000	4.2%
10	Arkansas	2,890,000	4.0%
11	Kansas	2,480,000	3.4%
12	Michigan	1,990,000	2.8%
13	Wisconsin	1,650,000	2.3%
14	Mississippi	1,430,000	2.0%
15	North Carolina	1,400,000	1.9%
16	Kentucky	1,240,000	1.7%
17	Tennessee	1,120,000	1.5%
18	Louisiana	740,000	1.0%
19	Virginia	480,000	0.7%
20	Maryland	430,000	0.6%
21	South Carolina	420,000	0.6%
22	Pennsylvania	375,000	0.5%
23	Oklahoma	245,000	0.3%
24	Georgia	180,000	0.2%
24	Texas	180,000	0.2%
26	Delaware	178,000	0.2%
27	Alabama	160,000	0.2%
28	New York	138,000	0.2%
29	New Jersey	88,000	0.1%
30	West Virginia	15,000	0.0%
31	Florida	12,000	0.0%
NA	Alaska**	NA	NA
NA	Arizona**	NA	NA
NA	California**	NA	NA
NA	Colorado**	NA	NA
NA	Connecticut**	NA	NA
NA	Hawaii**	NA	NA
NA	Idaho**	NA	NA
NA	Maine**	NA	NA
NA	Massachusetts**	NA	NA
NA	Montana**	NA	NA
NA	Nevada**	NA	NA
NA	New Hampshire**	NA	NA
NA	New Mexico**	NA	NA
NA	Oregon**	NA	NA
NA	Rhode Island**	NA	NA
NA	Utah**	NA	NA
NA	Vermont**	NA	NA
NA	Washington**	NA	NA
NA	Wyoming**	NA	NA
	District of Columbia**	NA	NA

Source: U.S. Department of Agriculture, National Agricultural Statistics Service
"Crop Production, 2003 Summary" (Cr Pr 2-1 (04), January 2004)
(http://usda.mannlib.cornell.edu/reports/nassr/field/pcp-bban/)
**Estimated totals.*
***No acreage or not available.*

Acres Harvested: Wheat in 2003

National Total = 52,839,000 Acres*

ALPHA ORDER

RANK	STATE	ACRES	% of USA
36	Alabama	75,000	0.1%
NA	Alaska**	NA	NA
35	Arizona	119,000	0.2%
17	Arkansas	570,000	1.1%
18	California	485,000	0.9%
8	Colorado	2,229,000	4.2%
NA	Connecticut**	NA	NA
37	Delaware	47,000	0.1%
40	Florida	12,000	0.0%
23	Georgia	230,000	0.4%
NA	Hawaii**	NA	NA
11	Idaho	1,170,000	2.2%
15	Illinois	810,000	1.5%
19	Indiana	430,000	0.8%
39	Iowa	19,000	0.0%
1	Kansas	10,000,000	18.9%
21	Kentucky	330,000	0.6%
30	Louisiana	140,000	0.3%
NA	Maine**	NA	NA
29	Maryland	145,000	0.3%
NA	Massachusetts**	NA	NA
16	Michigan	660,000	1.2%
9	Minnesota	1,825,000	3.5%
33	Mississippi	125,000	0.2%
14	Missouri	870,000	1.6%
3	Montana	5,050,000	9.6%
10	Nebraska	1,820,000	3.4%
41	Nevada	7,000	0.0%
NA	New Hampshire**	NA	NA
38	New Jersey	26,000	0.0%
30	New Mexico	140,000	0.3%
34	New York	120,000	0.2%
20	North Carolina	410,000	0.8%
2	North Dakota	8,500,000	16.1%
13	Ohio	1,000,000	1.9%
4	Oklahoma	4,600,000	8.7%
12	Oregon	1,080,000	2.0%
26	Pennsylvania	165,000	0.3%
NA	Rhode Island**	NA	NA
24	South Carolina	185,000	0.4%
6	South Dakota	2,747,000	5.2%
22	Tennessee	270,000	0.5%
5	Texas	3,450,000	6.5%
32	Utah	135,000	0.3%
NA	Vermont**	NA	NA
27	Virginia	160,000	0.3%
7	Washington	2,345,000	4.4%
41	West Virginia	7,000	0.0%
25	Wisconsin	180,000	0.3%
28	Wyoming	151,000	0.3%

RANK ORDER

RANK	STATE	ACRES	% of USA
1	Kansas	10,000,000	18.9%
2	North Dakota	8,500,000	16.1%
3	Montana	5,050,000	9.6%
4	Oklahoma	4,600,000	8.7%
5	Texas	3,450,000	6.5%
6	South Dakota	2,747,000	5.2%
7	Washington	2,345,000	4.4%
8	Colorado	2,229,000	4.2%
9	Minnesota	1,825,000	3.5%
10	Nebraska	1,820,000	3.4%
11	Idaho	1,170,000	2.2%
12	Oregon	1,080,000	2.0%
13	Ohio	1,000,000	1.9%
14	Missouri	870,000	1.6%
15	Illinois	810,000	1.5%
16	Michigan	660,000	1.2%
17	Arkansas	570,000	1.1%
18	California	485,000	0.9%
19	Indiana	430,000	0.8%
20	North Carolina	410,000	0.8%
21	Kentucky	330,000	0.6%
22	Tennessee	270,000	0.5%
23	Georgia	230,000	0.4%
24	South Carolina	185,000	0.4%
25	Wisconsin	180,000	0.3%
26	Pennsylvania	165,000	0.3%
27	Virginia	160,000	0.3%
28	Wyoming	151,000	0.3%
29	Maryland	145,000	0.3%
30	Louisiana	140,000	0.3%
30	New Mexico	140,000	0.3%
32	Utah	135,000	0.3%
33	Mississippi	125,000	0.2%
34	New York	120,000	0.2%
35	Arizona	119,000	0.2%
36	Alabama	75,000	0.1%
37	Delaware	47,000	0.1%
38	New Jersey	26,000	0.0%
39	Iowa	19,000	0.0%
40	Florida	12,000	0.0%
41	Nevada	7,000	0.0%
41	West Virginia	7,000	0.0%
NA	Alaska**	NA	NA
NA	Connecticut**	NA	NA
NA	Hawaii**	NA	NA
NA	Maine**	NA	NA
NA	Massachusetts**	NA	NA
NA	New Hampshire**	NA	NA
NA	Rhode Island**	NA	NA
NA	Vermont**	NA	NA
	District of Columbia**	NA	NA

Source: U.S. Department of Agriculture, National Agricultural Statistics Service
"Crop Production, 2003 Summary" (Cr Pr 2-1 (04), January 2004)
(http://usda.mannlib.cornell.edu/reports/nassr/field/pcp-bban/)
Estimated totals.
*No acreage or not available.

Cattle on Farms in 2004

National Total = 94,882,000 Cattle*

ALPHA ORDER

RANK	STATE	CATTLE	% of USA
25	Alabama	1,360,000	1.4%
49	Alaska	12,500	0.0%
34	Arizona	850,000	0.9%
16	Arkansas	1,900,000	2.0%
4	California	5,200,000	5.5%
10	Colorado	2,400,000	2.5%
44	Connecticut	54,000	0.1%
48	Delaware	25,000	0.0%
18	Florida	1,740,000	1.8%
27	Georgia	1,250,000	1.3%
42	Hawaii	156,000	0.2%
15	Idaho	2,010,000	2.1%
26	Illinois	1,310,000	1.4%
36	Indiana	830,000	0.9%
8	Iowa	3,450,000	3.6%
2	Kansas	6,650,000	7.0%
13	Kentucky	2,320,000	2.4%
34	Louisiana	850,000	0.9%
43	Maine	91,000	0.1%
41	Maryland	235,000	0.2%
45	Massachusetts	48,000	0.1%
30	Michigan	1,030,000	1.1%
10	Minnesota	2,400,000	2.5%
31	Mississippi	1,020,000	1.1%
6	Missouri	4,350,000	4.6%
10	Montana	2,400,000	2.5%
3	Nebraska	6,250,000	6.6%
37	Nevada	510,000	0.5%
47	New Hampshire	39,000	0.0%
46	New Jersey	46,000	0.0%
21	New Mexico	1,510,000	1.6%
23	New York	1,420,000	1.5%
32	North Carolina	880,000	0.9%
17	North Dakota	1,750,000	1.8%
28	Ohio	1,230,000	1.3%
5	Oklahoma	5,100,000	5.4%
22	Oregon	1,440,000	1.5%
19	Pennsylvania	1,640,000	1.7%
50	Rhode Island	5,500	0.0%
38	South Carolina	425,000	0.4%
7	South Dakota	3,650,000	3.8%
14	Tennessee	2,210,000	2.3%
1	Texas	13,900,000	14.6%
33	Utah	860,000	0.9%
40	Vermont	285,000	0.3%
20	Virginia	1,540,000	1.6%
29	Washington	1,120,000	1.2%
39	West Virginia	380,000	0.4%
9	Wisconsin	3,350,000	3.5%
24	Wyoming	1,400,000	1.5%

RANK ORDER

RANK	STATE	CATTLE	% of USA
1	Texas	13,900,000	14.6%
2	Kansas	6,650,000	7.0%
3	Nebraska	6,250,000	6.6%
4	California	5,200,000	5.5%
5	Oklahoma	5,100,000	5.4%
6	Missouri	4,350,000	4.6%
7	South Dakota	3,650,000	3.8%
8	Iowa	3,450,000	3.6%
9	Wisconsin	3,350,000	3.5%
10	Colorado	2,400,000	2.5%
10	Minnesota	2,400,000	2.5%
10	Montana	2,400,000	2.5%
13	Kentucky	2,320,000	2.4%
14	Tennessee	2,210,000	2.3%
15	Idaho	2,010,000	2.1%
16	Arkansas	1,900,000	2.0%
17	North Dakota	1,750,000	1.8%
18	Florida	1,740,000	1.8%
19	Pennsylvania	1,640,000	1.7%
20	Virginia	1,540,000	1.6%
21	New Mexico	1,510,000	1.6%
22	Oregon	1,440,000	1.5%
23	New York	1,420,000	1.5%
24	Wyoming	1,400,000	1.5%
25	Alabama	1,360,000	1.4%
26	Illinois	1,310,000	1.4%
27	Georgia	1,250,000	1.3%
28	Ohio	1,230,000	1.3%
29	Washington	1,120,000	1.2%
30	Michigan	1,030,000	1.1%
31	Mississippi	1,020,000	1.1%
32	North Carolina	880,000	0.9%
33	Utah	860,000	0.9%
34	Arizona	850,000	0.9%
34	Louisiana	850,000	0.9%
36	Indiana	830,000	0.9%
37	Nevada	510,000	0.5%
38	South Carolina	425,000	0.4%
39	West Virginia	380,000	0.4%
40	Vermont	285,000	0.3%
41	Maryland	235,000	0.2%
42	Hawaii	156,000	0.2%
43	Maine	91,000	0.1%
44	Connecticut	54,000	0.1%
45	Massachusetts	48,000	0.1%
46	New Jersey	46,000	0.0%
47	New Hampshire	39,000	0.0%
48	Delaware	25,000	0.0%
49	Alaska	12,500	0.0%
50	Rhode Island	5,500	0.0%
	District of Columbia	0	0.0%

Source: U.S. Department of Agriculture, National Agricultural Statistics Service
"Cattle" (http://usda.mannlib.cornell.edu/reports/nassr/livestock/pct-bb/)
As of January 1, 2004.

Milk Cows on Farms in 2002

National Total = 9,114,000 Milk Cows*

ALPHA ORDER

RANK	STATE	MILK COWS	% of USA
39	Alabama	21,000	0.2%
50	Alaska	1,100	0.0%
17	Arizona	140,000	1.5%
35	Arkansas	35,000	0.4%
1	California	1,589,000	17.4%
25	Colorado	92,000	1.0%
37	Connecticut	25,000	0.3%
46	Delaware	9,000	0.1%
13	Florida	153,000	1.7%
28	Georgia	86,000	0.9%
47	Hawaii	7,500	0.1%
6	Idaho	366,000	4.0%
20	Illinois	116,000	1.3%
13	Indiana	153,000	1.7%
12	Iowa	210,000	2.3%
23	Kansas	93,000	1.0%
18	Kentucky	128,000	1.4%
32	Louisiana	54,000	0.6%
34	Maine	38,000	0.4%
29	Maryland	82,000	0.9%
39	Massachusetts	21,000	0.2%
8	Michigan	303,000	3.3%
5	Minnesota	510,000	5.6%
35	Mississippi	35,000	0.4%
16	Missouri	145,000	1.6%
42	Montana	19,000	0.2%
30	Nebraska	72,000	0.8%
37	Nevada	25,000	0.3%
43	New Hampshire	18,000	0.2%
45	New Jersey	14,000	0.2%
9	New Mexico	268,000	2.9%
3	New York	672,000	7.4%
31	North Carolina	67,000	0.7%
33	North Dakota	46,000	0.5%
10	Ohio	260,000	2.9%
27	Oklahoma	89,000	1.0%
22	Oregon	95,000	1.0%
4	Pennsylvania	599,000	6.6%
49	Rhode Island	1,400	0.0%
39	South Carolina	21,000	0.2%
21	South Dakota	99,000	1.1%
25	Tennessee	92,000	1.0%
7	Texas	325,000	3.6%
23	Utah	93,000	1.0%
13	Vermont	153,000	1.7%
19	Virginia	118,000	1.3%
11	Washington	247,000	2.7%
44	West Virginia	16,000	0.2%
2	Wisconsin	1,292,000	14.2%
48	Wyoming	4,500	0.0%

RANK ORDER

RANK	STATE	MILK COWS	% of USA
1	California	1,589,000	17.4%
2	Wisconsin	1,292,000	14.2%
3	New York	672,000	7.4%
4	Pennsylvania	599,000	6.6%
5	Minnesota	510,000	5.6%
6	Idaho	366,000	4.0%
7	Texas	325,000	3.6%
8	Michigan	303,000	3.3%
9	New Mexico	268,000	2.9%
10	Ohio	260,000	2.9%
11	Washington	247,000	2.7%
12	Iowa	210,000	2.3%
13	Florida	153,000	1.7%
13	Indiana	153,000	1.7%
13	Vermont	153,000	1.7%
16	Missouri	145,000	1.6%
17	Arizona	140,000	1.5%
18	Kentucky	128,000	1.4%
19	Virginia	118,000	1.3%
20	Illinois	116,000	1.3%
21	South Dakota	99,000	1.1%
22	Oregon	95,000	1.0%
23	Kansas	93,000	1.0%
23	Utah	93,000	1.0%
25	Colorado	92,000	1.0%
25	Tennessee	92,000	1.0%
27	Oklahoma	89,000	1.0%
28	Georgia	86,000	0.9%
29	Maryland	82,000	0.9%
30	Nebraska	72,000	0.8%
31	North Carolina	67,000	0.7%
32	Louisiana	54,000	0.6%
33	North Dakota	46,000	0.5%
34	Maine	38,000	0.4%
35	Arkansas	35,000	0.4%
35	Mississippi	35,000	0.4%
37	Connecticut	25,000	0.3%
37	Nevada	25,000	0.3%
39	Alabama	21,000	0.2%
39	Massachusetts	21,000	0.2%
39	South Carolina	21,000	0.2%
42	Montana	19,000	0.2%
43	New Hampshire	18,000	0.2%
44	West Virginia	16,000	0.2%
45	New Jersey	14,000	0.2%
46	Delaware	9,000	0.1%
47	Hawaii	7,500	0.1%
48	Wyoming	4,500	0.0%
49	Rhode Island	1,400	0.0%
50	Alaska	1,100	0.0%
	District of Columbia	0	0.0%

Source: U.S. Department of Agriculture, National Agricultural Statistics Service
"Milk Production, Disposition and Income 2002 Summary" (April 2003)
(http://usda.mannlib.cornell.edu/reports/nassr/dairy/pmp-bbml/)
**Average number during year. Excludes heifers not yet fresh.*

Milk Production in 2002

National Total = 165,497,000,000 Pounds of Milk*

ALPHA ORDER

RANK	STATE	POUNDS	% of USA
43	Alabama	300,000,000	0.2%
50	Alaska	14,360,000	0.0%
13	Arizona	3,073,000,000	1.9%
38	Arkansas	432,000,000	0.3%
1	California	33,217,000,000	20.1%
18	Colorado	1,970,000,000	1.2%
37	Connecticut	456,000,000	0.3%
46	Delaware	150,000,000	0.1%
16	Florida	2,411,000,000	1.5%
26	Georgia	1,433,000,000	0.9%
47	Hawaii	105,800,000	0.1%
6	Idaho	7,757,000,000	4.7%
17	Illinois	2,020,000,000	1.2%
15	Indiana	2,567,000,000	1.6%
12	Iowa	3,785,000,000	2.3%
24	Kansas	1,610,000,000	1.0%
22	Kentucky	1,660,000,000	1.0%
34	Louisiana	632,000,000	0.4%
32	Maine	654,000,000	0.4%
28	Maryland	1,294,000,000	0.8%
40	Massachusetts	357,000,000	0.2%
7	Michigan	5,870,000,000	3.5%
5	Minnesota	8,812,000,000	5.3%
35	Mississippi	497,000,000	0.3%
19	Missouri	1,949,000,000	1.2%
41	Montana	346,000,000	0.2%
30	Nebraska	1,166,000,000	0.7%
36	Nevada	485,000,000	0.3%
42	New Hampshire	322,000,000	0.2%
45	New Jersey	233,000,000	0.1%
8	New Mexico	5,561,000,000	3.4%
3	New York	11,780,000,000	7.1%
31	North Carolina	1,154,000,000	0.7%
33	North Dakota	644,000,000	0.4%
11	Ohio	4,295,000,000	2.6%
29	Oklahoma	1,293,000,000	0.8%
21	Oregon	1,717,000,000	1.0%
4	Pennsylvania	10,849,000,000	6.6%
49	Rhode Island	23,200,000	0.0%
39	South Carolina	367,000,000	0.2%
25	South Dakota	1,580,000,000	1.0%
27	Tennessee	1,335,000,000	0.8%
10	Texas	5,106,000,000	3.1%
23	Utah	1,635,000,000	1.0%
14	Vermont	2,669,000,000	1.6%
20	Virginia	1,885,000,000	1.1%
9	Washington	5,514,000,000	3.3%
44	West Virginia	249,000,000	0.2%
2	Wisconsin	22,199,000,000	13.4%
48	Wyoming	63,000,000	0.0%

RANK ORDER

RANK	STATE	POUNDS	% of USA
1	California	33,217,000,000	20.1%
2	Wisconsin	22,199,000,000	13.4%
3	New York	11,780,000,000	7.1%
4	Pennsylvania	10,849,000,000	6.6%
5	Minnesota	8,812,000,000	5.3%
6	Idaho	7,757,000,000	4.7%
7	Michigan	5,870,000,000	3.5%
8	New Mexico	5,561,000,000	3.4%
9	Washington	5,514,000,000	3.3%
10	Texas	5,106,000,000	3.1%
11	Ohio	4,295,000,000	2.6%
12	Iowa	3,785,000,000	2.3%
13	Arizona	3,073,000,000	1.9%
14	Vermont	2,669,000,000	1.6%
15	Indiana	2,567,000,000	1.6%
16	Florida	2,411,000,000	1.5%
17	Illinois	2,020,000,000	1.2%
18	Colorado	1,970,000,000	1.2%
19	Missouri	1,949,000,000	1.2%
20	Virginia	1,885,000,000	1.1%
21	Oregon	1,717,000,000	1.0%
22	Kentucky	1,660,000,000	1.0%
23	Utah	1,635,000,000	1.0%
24	Kansas	1,610,000,000	1.0%
25	South Dakota	1,580,000,000	1.0%
26	Georgia	1,433,000,000	0.9%
27	Tennessee	1,335,000,000	0.8%
28	Maryland	1,294,000,000	0.8%
29	Oklahoma	1,293,000,000	0.8%
30	Nebraska	1,166,000,000	0.7%
31	North Carolina	1,154,000,000	0.7%
32	Maine	654,000,000	0.4%
33	North Dakota	644,000,000	0.4%
34	Louisiana	632,000,000	0.4%
35	Mississippi	497,000,000	0.3%
36	Nevada	485,000,000	0.3%
37	Connecticut	456,000,000	0.3%
38	Arkansas	432,000,000	0.3%
39	South Carolina	367,000,000	0.2%
40	Massachusetts	357,000,000	0.2%
41	Montana	346,000,000	0.2%
42	New Hampshire	322,000,000	0.2%
43	Alabama	300,000,000	0.2%
44	West Virginia	249,000,000	0.2%
45	New Jersey	233,000,000	0.1%
46	Delaware	150,000,000	0.1%
47	Hawaii	105,800,000	0.1%
48	Wyoming	63,000,000	0.0%
49	Rhode Island	23,200,000	0.0%
50	Alaska	14,360,000	0.0%
	District of Columbia**	NA	NA

Source: U.S. Department of Agriculture, National Agricultural Statistics Service
"Milk Production, Disposition and Income 2002 Summary" (April 2003)
(http://usda.mannlib.cornell.edu/reports/nassr/dairy/pmp-bbm/)
**Excludes milk sucked by calves.*

Milk Production per Milk Cow in 2002

National Average = 18,159 Pounds of Milk per Cow*

<u>ALPHA ORDER</u>

RANK	STATE	POUNDS
41	Alabama	14,286
47	Alaska	13,055
2	Arizona	21,950
49	Arkansas	12,343
5	California	20,904
3	Colorado	21,413
9	Connecticut	18,240
27	Delaware	16,667
36	Florida	15,758
28	Georgia	16,663
43	Hawaii	14,107
4	Idaho	21,194
19	Illinois	17,414
26	Indiana	16,778
13	Iowa	18,024
20	Kansas	17,312
48	Kentucky	12,969
50	Louisiana	11,704
23	Maine	17,211
35	Maryland	15,780
25	Massachusetts	17,000
8	Michigan	19,373
21	Minnesota	17,278
42	Mississippi	14,200
46	Missouri	13,441
10	Montana	18,211
32	Nebraska	16,194
7	Nevada	19,400
14	New Hampshire	17,889
29	New Jersey	16,643
6	New Mexico	20,750
16	New York	17,530
22	North Carolina	17,224
44	North Dakota	14,000
31	Ohio	16,519
39	Oklahoma	14,528
12	Oregon	18,074
11	Pennsylvania	18,112
30	Rhode Island	16,571
17	South Carolina	17,476
34	South Dakota	15,960
40	Tennessee	14,511
37	Texas	15,711
15	Utah	17,581
18	Vermont	17,444
33	Virginia	15,975
1	Washington	22,324
38	West Virginia	15,563
24	Wisconsin	17,182
44	Wyoming	14,000

<u>RANK ORDER</u>

RANK	STATE	POUNDS
1	Washington	22,324
2	Arizona	21,950
3	Colorado	21,413
4	Idaho	21,194
5	California	20,904
6	New Mexico	20,750
7	Nevada	19,400
8	Michigan	19,373
9	Connecticut	18,240
10	Montana	18,211
11	Pennsylvania	18,112
12	Oregon	18,074
13	Iowa	18,024
14	New Hampshire	17,889
15	Utah	17,581
16	New York	17,530
17	South Carolina	17,476
18	Vermont	17,444
19	Illinois	17,414
20	Kansas	17,312
21	Minnesota	17,278
22	North Carolina	17,224
23	Maine	17,211
24	Wisconsin	17,182
25	Massachusetts	17,000
26	Indiana	16,778
27	Delaware	16,667
28	Georgia	16,663
29	New Jersey	16,643
30	Rhode Island	16,571
31	Ohio	16,519
32	Nebraska	16,194
33	Virginia	15,975
34	South Dakota	15,960
35	Maryland	15,780
36	Florida	15,758
37	Texas	15,711
38	West Virginia	15,563
39	Oklahoma	14,528
40	Tennessee	14,511
41	Alabama	14,286
42	Mississippi	14,200
43	Hawaii	14,107
44	North Dakota	14,000
44	Wyoming	14,000
46	Missouri	13,441
47	Alaska	13,055
48	Kentucky	12,969
49	Arkansas	12,343
50	Louisiana	11,704

District of Columbia   0

Source: U.S. Department of Agriculture, National Agricultural Statistics Service
   "Milk Production, Disposition and Income 2002 Summary" (April 2003)
   (http://usda.mannlib.cornell.edu/reports/nassr/dairy/pmp-bbml/)
**Excludes milk sucked by calves.*
***Not applicable.*

Hogs and Pigs on Farms in 2003

National Total = 60,040,000 Hogs and Pigs*

ALPHA ORDER

RANK	STATE	HOGS AND PIGS	% of USA
26	Alabama	165,000	0.3%
50	Alaska	1,500	0.0%
29	Arizona	127,000	0.2%
20	Arkansas	310,000	0.5%
28	California	135,000	0.2%
15	Colorado	770,000	1.3%
45	Connecticut	3,800	0.0%
39	Delaware	18,000	0.0%
33	Florida	30,000	0.0%
23	Georgia	295,000	0.5%
37	Hawaii	23,000	0.0%
35	Idaho	26,000	0.0%
4	Illinois	3,950,000	6.6%
5	Indiana	3,100,000	5.2%
1	Iowa	15,800,000	26.3%
9	Kansas	1,630,000	2.7%
18	Kentucky	380,000	0.6%
38	Louisiana	20,000	0.0%
43	Maine	6,500	0.0%
32	Maryland	40,000	0.1%
40	Massachusetts	14,500	0.0%
13	Michigan	950,000	1.6%
3	Minnesota	6,400,000	10.7%
21	Mississippi	305,000	0.5%
6	Missouri	2,950,000	4.9%
25	Montana	170,000	0.3%
7	Nebraska	2,900,000	4.8%
44	Nevada	5,000	0.0%
46	New Hampshire	2,900	0.0%
41	New Jersey	12,000	0.0%
48	New Mexico	2,500	0.0%
31	New York	73,000	0.1%
2	North Carolina	9,900,000	16.5%
27	North Dakota	150,000	0.2%
10	Ohio	1,520,000	2.5%
8	Oklahoma	2,340,000	3.9%
34	Oregon	27,000	0.0%
12	Pennsylvania	1,100,000	1.8%
47	Rhode Island	2,600	0.0%
22	South Carolina	300,000	0.5%
11	South Dakota	1,260,000	2.1%
24	Tennessee	215,000	0.4%
14	Texas	930,000	1.5%
16	Utah	660,000	1.1%
49	Vermont	2,100	0.0%
19	Virginia	370,000	0.6%
36	Washington	24,000	0.0%
42	West Virginia	10,000	0.0%
17	Wisconsin	490,000	0.8%
30	Wyoming	124,000	0.2%

RANK ORDER

RANK	STATE	HOGS AND PIGS	% of USA
1	Iowa	15,800,000	26.3%
2	North Carolina	9,900,000	16.5%
3	Minnesota	6,400,000	10.7%
4	Illinois	3,950,000	6.6%
5	Indiana	3,100,000	5.2%
6	Missouri	2,950,000	4.9%
7	Nebraska	2,900,000	4.8%
8	Oklahoma	2,340,000	3.9%
9	Kansas	1,630,000	2.7%
10	Ohio	1,520,000	2.5%
11	South Dakota	1,260,000	2.1%
12	Pennsylvania	1,100,000	1.8%
13	Michigan	950,000	1.6%
14	Texas	930,000	1.5%
15	Colorado	770,000	1.3%
16	Utah	660,000	1.1%
17	Wisconsin	490,000	0.8%
18	Kentucky	380,000	0.6%
19	Virginia	370,000	0.6%
20	Arkansas	310,000	0.5%
21	Mississippi	305,000	0.5%
22	South Carolina	300,000	0.5%
23	Georgia	295,000	0.5%
24	Tennessee	215,000	0.4%
25	Montana	170,000	0.3%
26	Alabama	165,000	0.3%
27	North Dakota	150,000	0.2%
28	California	135,000	0.2%
29	Arizona	127,000	0.2%
30	Wyoming	124,000	0.2%
31	New York	73,000	0.1%
32	Maryland	40,000	0.1%
33	Florida	30,000	0.0%
34	Oregon	27,000	0.0%
35	Idaho	26,000	0.0%
36	Washington	24,000	0.0%
37	Hawaii	23,000	0.0%
38	Louisiana	20,000	0.0%
39	Delaware	18,000	0.0%
40	Massachusetts	14,500	0.0%
41	New Jersey	12,000	0.0%
42	West Virginia	10,000	0.0%
43	Maine	6,500	0.0%
44	Nevada	5,000	0.0%
45	Connecticut	3,800	0.0%
46	New Hampshire	2,900	0.0%
47	Rhode Island	2,600	0.0%
48	New Mexico	2,500	0.0%
49	Vermont	2,100	0.0%
50	Alaska	1,500	0.0%
	District of Columbia	0	0.0%

Source: U.S. Department of Agriculture, National Agricultural Statistics Service
"Hogs and Pigs" (http://usda.mannlib.cornell.edu/reports/nassr/livestock/php-bb/)
As of December 1, 2003.

Chickens in 2002 (Leading States Only)

National Total = 8,590,180,000 Chickens*

ALPHA ORDER

RANK	STATE	CHICKENS	% of USA
3	Alabama	1,051,300,000	12.2%
NA	Alaska***	NA	NA
NA	Arizona***	NA	NA
2	Arkansas	1,186,300,000	13.8%
NA	California**	NA	NA
NA	Colorado***	NA	NA
NA	Connecticut***	NA	NA
10	Delaware	257,400,000	3.0%
15	Florida	114,700,000	1.3%
1	Georgia	1,290,500,000	15.0%
22	Hawaii	880,000	0.0%
NA	Idaho***	NA	NA
NA	Illinois***	NA	NA
NA	Indiana**	NA	NA
NA	Iowa**	NA	NA
NA	Kansas***	NA	NA
8	Kentucky	269,900,000	3.1%
NA	Louisiana**	NA	NA
NA	Maine***	NA	NA
7	Maryland	292,900,000	3.4%
NA	Massachusetts***	NA	NA
NA	Michigan***	NA	NA
17	Minnesota	44,200,000	0.5%
4	Mississippi	769,500,000	9.0%
NA	Missouri**	NA	NA
NA	Montana***	NA	NA
20	Nebraska	3,700,000	0.0%
NA	Nevada***	NA	NA
NA	New Hampshire***	NA	NA
NA	New Jersey***	NA	NA
NA	New Mexico***	NA	NA
21	New York	2,400,000	0.0%
5	North Carolina	735,200,000	8.6%
NA	North Dakota***	NA	NA
18	Ohio	39,000,000	0.5%
11	Oklahoma	232,800,000	2.7%
NA	Oregon**	NA	NA
14	Pennsylvania	133,200,000	1.6%
NA	Rhode Island***	NA	NA
12	South Carolina	192,900,000	2.2%
NA	South Dakota***	NA	NA
13	Tennessee	186,400,000	2.2%
6	Texas	588,100,000	6.8%
NA	Utah***	NA	NA
NA	Vermont***	NA	NA
9	Virginia	265,500,000	3.1%
NA	Washington**	NA	NA
16	West Virginia	89,700,000	1.0%
19	Wisconsin	33,800,000	0.4%
NA	Wyoming***	NA	NA

RANK ORDER

RANK	STATE	CHICKENS	% of USA
1	Georgia	1,290,500,000	15.0%
2	Arkansas	1,186,300,000	13.8%
3	Alabama	1,051,300,000	12.2%
4	Mississippi	769,500,000	9.0%
5	North Carolina	735,200,000	8.6%
6	Texas	588,100,000	6.8%
7	Maryland	292,900,000	3.4%
8	Kentucky	269,900,000	3.1%
9	Virginia	265,500,000	3.1%
10	Delaware	257,400,000	3.0%
11	Oklahoma	232,800,000	2.7%
12	South Carolina	192,900,000	2.2%
13	Tennessee	186,400,000	2.2%
14	Pennsylvania	133,200,000	1.6%
15	Florida	114,700,000	1.3%
16	West Virginia	89,700,000	1.0%
17	Minnesota	44,200,000	0.5%
18	Ohio	39,000,000	0.5%
19	Wisconsin	33,800,000	0.4%
20	Nebraska	3,700,000	0.0%
21	New York	2,400,000	0.0%
22	Hawaii	880,000	0.0%
NA	Alaska***	NA	NA
NA	Arizona***	NA	NA
NA	California**	NA	NA
NA	Colorado***	NA	NA
NA	Connecticut***	NA	NA
NA	Idaho***	NA	NA
NA	Illinois***	NA	NA
NA	Indiana**	NA	NA
NA	Iowa**	NA	NA
NA	Kansas***	NA	NA
NA	Louisiana**	NA	NA
NA	Maine***	NA	NA
NA	Massachusetts***	NA	NA
NA	Michigan***	NA	NA
NA	Missouri**	NA	NA
NA	Montana***	NA	NA
NA	Nevada***	NA	NA
NA	New Hampshire***	NA	NA
NA	New Jersey***	NA	NA
NA	New Mexico***	NA	NA
NA	North Dakota***	NA	NA
NA	Oregon**	NA	NA
NA	Rhode Island***	NA	NA
NA	South Dakota***	NA	NA
NA	Utah***	NA	NA
NA	Vermont***	NA	NA
NA	Washington**	NA	NA
NA	Wyoming***	NA	NA
	District of Columbia	0	0.0%

Source: U.S. Department of Agriculture, National Agricultural Statistics Service
   "Poultry - Production and Value 2002 Summary"
      (http://usda.mannlib.cornell.edu/reports/nassr/poultry/pbh-bbp/)
*Broilers. Total includes numbers for states not shown separately but excludes states producing less than 500,000 birds. **These states produced a combined total of 809,900,000 chickens. They are combined to avoid disclosing individual operations. National total does not include chickens used for egg production. ***Not available.*

Eggs Produced in 2002

National Total = 86,698,000,000 Eggs

ALPHA ORDER

RANK	STATE	EGGS	% of USA
13	Alabama	2,281,000,000	2.6%
NA	Alaska*	NA	NA
NA	Arizona*	NA	NA
8	Arkansas	3,329,000,000	3.8%
4	California	6,124,000,000	7.1%
22	Colorado	1,008,000,000	1.2%
28	Connecticut	855,000,000	1.0%
34	Delaware	347,000,000	0.4%
11	Florida	2,731,000,000	3.2%
6	Georgia	4,961,000,000	5.7%
38	Hawaii	117,500,000	0.1%
37	Idaho	242,000,000	0.3%
27	Illinois	893,000,000	1.0%
5	Indiana	5,973,000,000	6.9%
1	Iowa	9,910,000,000	11.4%
NA	Kansas*	NA	NA
24	Kentucky	921,000,000	1.1%
33	Louisiana	494,000,000	0.6%
21	Maine	1,079,000,000	1.2%
25	Maryland	894,000,000	1.0%
40	Massachusetts	80,000,000	0.1%
15	Michigan	1,771,000,000	2.0%
9	Minnesota	3,124,000,000	3.6%
16	Mississippi	1,588,000,000	1.8%
14	Missouri	1,837,000,000	2.1%
39	Montana	104,000,000	0.1%
10	Nebraska	2,977,000,000	3.4%
NA	Nevada*	NA	NA
42	New Hampshire	46,000,000	0.1%
32	New Jersey	533,000,000	0.6%
NA	New Mexico*	NA	NA
20	New York	1,100,000,000	1.3%
12	North Carolina	2,518,000,000	2.9%
NA	North Dakota*	NA	NA
2	Ohio	7,940,000,000	9.2%
23	Oklahoma	951,000,000	1.1%
29	Oregon	760,000,000	0.9%
3	Pennsylvania	6,520,000,000	7.5%
NA	Rhode Island*	NA	NA
17	South Carolina	1,380,000,000	1.6%
31	South Dakota	568,000,000	0.7%
35	Tennessee	300,000,000	0.3%
7	Texas	4,774,000,000	5.5%
25	Utah	894,000,000	1.0%
41	Vermont	59,000,000	0.1%
30	Virginia	734,000,000	0.8%
18	Washington	1,369,000,000	1.6%
36	West Virginia	261,000,000	0.3%
19	Wisconsin	1,158,000,000	1.3%
43	Wyoming	3,600,000	0.0%

RANK ORDER

RANK	STATE	EGGS	% of USA
1	Iowa	9,910,000,000	11.4%
2	Ohio	7,940,000,000	9.2%
3	Pennsylvania	6,520,000,000	7.5%
4	California	6,124,000,000	7.1%
5	Indiana	5,973,000,000	6.9%
6	Georgia	4,961,000,000	5.7%
7	Texas	4,774,000,000	5.5%
8	Arkansas	3,329,000,000	3.8%
9	Minnesota	3,124,000,000	3.6%
10	Nebraska	2,977,000,000	3.4%
11	Florida	2,731,000,000	3.2%
12	North Carolina	2,518,000,000	2.9%
13	Alabama	2,281,000,000	2.6%
14	Missouri	1,837,000,000	2.1%
15	Michigan	1,771,000,000	2.0%
16	Mississippi	1,588,000,000	1.8%
17	South Carolina	1,380,000,000	1.6%
18	Washington	1,369,000,000	1.6%
19	Wisconsin	1,158,000,000	1.3%
20	New York	1,100,000,000	1.3%
21	Maine	1,079,000,000	1.2%
22	Colorado	1,008,000,000	1.2%
23	Oklahoma	951,000,000	1.1%
24	Kentucky	921,000,000	1.1%
25	Maryland	894,000,000	1.0%
25	Utah	894,000,000	1.0%
27	Illinois	893,000,000	1.0%
28	Connecticut	855,000,000	1.0%
29	Oregon	760,000,000	0.9%
30	Virginia	734,000,000	0.8%
31	South Dakota	568,000,000	0.7%
32	New Jersey	533,000,000	0.6%
33	Louisiana	494,000,000	0.6%
34	Delaware	347,000,000	0.4%
35	Tennessee	300,000,000	0.3%
36	West Virginia	261,000,000	0.3%
37	Idaho	242,000,000	0.3%
38	Hawaii	117,500,000	0.1%
39	Montana	104,000,000	0.1%
40	Massachusetts	80,000,000	0.1%
41	Vermont	59,000,000	0.1%
42	New Hampshire	46,000,000	0.1%
43	Wyoming	3,600,000	0.0%
NA	Alaska*	NA	NA
NA	Arizona*	NA	NA
NA	Kansas*	NA	NA
NA	Nevada*	NA	NA
NA	New Mexico*	NA	NA
NA	North Dakota*	NA	NA
NA	Rhode Island*	NA	NA
	District of Columbia	0	0.0%

Source: U.S. Department of Agriculture, National Agricultural Statistics Service
   "Poultry - Production and Value 2002 Summary"
    (http://usda.mannlib.cornell.edu/reports/nassr/poultry/pbh-bbp/)
**These states produced a combined 1,189,000,000 eggs. They are combined to avoid disclosing individual operations.*

II. CRIME AND LAW ENFORCEMENT

Crimes in 2002

National Total = 11,877,218 Crimes*

ALPHA ORDER

RANK	STATE	CRIMES	% of USA
21	Alabama	200,331	1.7%
46	Alaska	27,745	0.2%
11	Arizona	348,467	2.9%
30	Arkansas	112,672	0.9%
1	California	1,384,872	11.7%
23	Colorado	195,936	1.6%
32	Connecticut	103,719	0.9%
44	Delaware	31,803	0.3%
3	Florida	905,957	7.6%
9	Georgia	385,830	3.2%
37	Hawaii	75,238	0.6%
40	Idaho	42,547	0.4%
5	Illinois	506,086	4.3%
17	Indiana	230,966	1.9%
34	Iowa	101,265	0.9%
31	Kansas	110,997	0.9%
29	Kentucky	118,799	1.0%
19	Louisiana	228,528	1.9%
42	Maine	34,381	0.3%
16	Maryland	259,120	2.2%
22	Massachusetts	198,890	1.7%
8	Michigan	389,366	3.3%
24	Minnesota	177,454	1.5%
28	Mississippi	119,442	1.0%
14	Missouri	261,077	2.2%
43	Montana	31,948	0.3%
38	Nebraska	73,606	0.6%
35	Nevada	97,752	0.8%
45	New Hampshire	28,306	0.2%
15	New Jersey	259,789	2.2%
36	New Mexico	94,196	0.8%
4	New York	537,121	4.5%
7	North Carolina	392,826	3.3%
50	North Dakota	15,258	0.1%
6	Ohio	469,104	3.9%
27	Oklahoma	165,715	1.4%
26	Oregon	171,443	1.4%
10	Pennsylvania	350,446	3.0%
41	Rhode Island	38,393	0.3%
20	South Carolina	217,569	1.8%
48	South Dakota	17,342	0.1%
13	Tennessee	290,961	2.4%
2	Texas	1,130,292	9.5%
33	Utah	103,129	0.9%
49	Vermont	15,600	0.1%
18	Virginia	229,039	1.9%
12	Washington	309,931	2.6%
39	West Virginia	45,320	0.4%
25	Wisconsin	176,987	1.5%
47	Wyoming	17,858	0.2%

RANK ORDER

RANK	STATE	CRIMES	% of USA
1	California	1,384,872	11.7%
2	Texas	1,130,292	9.5%
3	Florida	905,957	7.6%
4	New York	537,121	4.5%
5	Illinois	506,086	4.3%
6	Ohio	469,104	3.9%
7	North Carolina	392,826	3.3%
8	Michigan	389,366	3.3%
9	Georgia	385,830	3.2%
10	Pennsylvania	350,446	3.0%
11	Arizona	348,467	2.9%
12	Washington	309,931	2.6%
13	Tennessee	290,961	2.4%
14	Missouri	261,077	2.2%
15	New Jersey	259,789	2.2%
16	Maryland	259,120	2.2%
17	Indiana	230,966	1.9%
18	Virginia	229,039	1.9%
19	Louisiana	228,528	1.9%
20	South Carolina	217,569	1.8%
21	Alabama	200,331	1.7%
22	Massachusetts	198,890	1.7%
23	Colorado	195,936	1.6%
24	Minnesota	177,454	1.5%
25	Wisconsin	176,987	1.5%
26	Oregon	171,443	1.4%
27	Oklahoma	165,715	1.4%
28	Mississippi	119,442	1.0%
29	Kentucky	118,799	1.0%
30	Arkansas	112,672	0.9%
31	Kansas	110,997	0.9%
32	Connecticut	103,719	0.9%
33	Utah	103,129	0.9%
34	Iowa	101,265	0.9%
35	Nevada	97,752	0.8%
36	New Mexico	94,196	0.8%
37	Hawaii	75,238	0.6%
38	Nebraska	73,606	0.6%
39	West Virginia	45,320	0.4%
40	Idaho	42,547	0.4%
41	Rhode Island	38,393	0.3%
42	Maine	34,381	0.3%
43	Montana	31,948	0.3%
44	Delaware	31,803	0.3%
45	New Hampshire	28,306	0.2%
46	Alaska	27,745	0.2%
47	Wyoming	17,858	0.2%
48	South Dakota	17,342	0.1%
49	Vermont	15,600	0.1%
50	North Dakota	15,258	0.1%
	District of Columbia	45,799	0.4%

Source: Federal Bureau of Investigation
   "Crime in the United States 2002" (Uniform Crime Reports, October 27, 2003)
Includes murder, rape, robbery, aggravated assault, burglary, larceny-theft and motor vehicle theft.

Percent Change in Number of Crimes: 2001 to 2002

National Percent Change = 0.0% Change*

ALPHA ORDER

RANK	STATE	PERCENT CHANGE
8	Alabama	3.9
9	Alaska	3.2
3	Arizona	8.0
14	Arkansas	1.2
11	California	2.8
5	Colorado	5.1
39	Connecticut	(2.9)
29	Delaware	(1.4)
24	Florida	(0.8)
27	Georgia	(1.0)
1	Hawaii	14.1
11	Idaho	2.8
32	Illinois	(1.5)
29	Indiana	(1.4)
6	Iowa	4.9
48	Kansas	(4.7)
15	Kentucky	0.8
45	Louisiana	(4.1)
22	Maine	(0.6)
26	Maryland	(0.9)
16	Massachusetts	0.6
47	Michigan	(4.5)
20	Minnesota	(0.4)
19	Mississippi	(0.1)
39	Missouri	(2.9)
46	Montana	(4.2)
24	Nebraska	(0.8)
2	Nevada	8.8
41	New Hampshire	(3.2)
49	New Jersey	(5.1)
42	New Mexico	(3.3)
43	New York	(3.4)
38	North Carolina	(2.8)
21	North Dakota	(0.5)
28	Ohio	(1.3)
7	Oklahoma	4.0
37	Oregon	(2.1)
44	Pennsylvania	(3.7)
33	Rhode Island	(1.6)
23	South Carolina	(0.7)
35	South Dakota	(1.7)
33	Tennessee	(1.6)
10	Texas	2.9
4	Utah	7.1
50	Vermont	(8.1)
18	Virginia	0.3
17	Washington	0.5
35	West Virginia	(1.7)
29	Wisconsin	(1.4)
13	Wyoming	2.7

RANK ORDER

RANK	STATE	PERCENT CHANGE
1	Hawaii	14.1
2	Nevada	8.8
3	Arizona	8.0
4	Utah	7.1
5	Colorado	5.1
6	Iowa	4.9
7	Oklahoma	4.0
8	Alabama	3.9
9	Alaska	3.2
10	Texas	2.9
11	California	2.8
11	Idaho	2.8
13	Wyoming	2.7
14	Arkansas	1.2
15	Kentucky	0.8
16	Massachusetts	0.6
17	Washington	0.5
18	Virginia	0.3
19	Mississippi	(0.1)
20	Minnesota	(0.4)
21	North Dakota	(0.5)
22	Maine	(0.6)
23	South Carolina	(0.7)
24	Florida	(0.8)
24	Nebraska	(0.8)
26	Maryland	(0.9)
27	Georgia	(1.0)
28	Ohio	(1.3)
29	Delaware	(1.4)
29	Indiana	(1.4)
29	Wisconsin	(1.4)
32	Illinois	(1.5)
33	Rhode Island	(1.6)
33	Tennessee	(1.6)
35	South Dakota	(1.7)
35	West Virginia	(1.7)
37	Oregon	(2.1)
38	North Carolina	(2.8)
39	Connecticut	(2.9)
39	Missouri	(2.9)
41	New Hampshire	(3.2)
42	New Mexico	(3.3)
43	New York	(3.4)
44	Pennsylvania	(3.7)
45	Louisiana	(4.1)
46	Montana	(4.2)
47	Michigan	(4.5)
48	Kansas	(4.7)
49	New Jersey	(5.1)
50	Vermont	(8.1)
	District of Columbia	3.1

Source: Federal Bureau of Investigation
   "Crime in the United States 2002" (Uniform Crime Reports, October 27, 2003)
*Includes murder, rape, robbery, aggravated assault, burglary, larceny-theft and motor vehicle theft.

Crime Rate in 2002

National Rate = 4,118.8 Crimes per 100,000 Population*

<u>ALPHA ORDER</u>

RANK	STATE	RATE
17	Alabama	4,465.2
20	Alaska	4,309.7
1	Arizona	6,386.3
23	Arkansas	4,157.5
27	California	3,943.7
19	Colorado	4,347.8
41	Connecticut	2,997.2
28	Delaware	3,939.0
3	Florida	5,420.6
15	Georgia	4,507.2
2	Hawaii	6,043.7
37	Idaho	3,172.5
26	Illinois	4,016.4
30	Indiana	3,750.0
35	Iowa	3,448.2
25	Kansas	4,087.0
42	Kentucky	2,902.6
7	Louisiana	5,098.1
45	Maine	2,656.0
11	Maryland	4,747.4
39	Massachusetts	3,094.2
29	Michigan	3,874.1
33	Minnesota	3,535.1
22	Mississippi	4,159.2
14	Missouri	4,602.4
34	Montana	3,512.9
21	Nebraska	4,256.7
16	Nevada	4,497.5
50	New Hampshire	2,220.0
40	New Jersey	3,024.2
8	New Mexico	5,077.8
44	New York	2,803.7
13	North Carolina	4,721.4
48	North Dakota	2,406.2
24	Ohio	4,107.3
12	Oklahoma	4,743.2
10	Oregon	4,868.4
43	Pennsylvania	2,841.0
31	Rhode Island	3,589.1
4	South Carolina	5,297.3
49	South Dakota	2,278.7
9	Tennessee	5,018.9
5	Texas	5,189.6
18	Utah	4,452.4
46	Vermont	2,530.0
38	Virginia	3,140.3
6	Washington	5,106.8
47	West Virginia	2,515.2
36	Wisconsin	3,252.7
32	Wyoming	3,580.9

<u>RANK ORDER</u>

RANK	STATE	RATE
1	Arizona	6,386.3
2	Hawaii	6,043.7
3	Florida	5,420.6
4	South Carolina	5,297.3
5	Texas	5,189.6
6	Washington	5,106.8
7	Louisiana	5,098.1
8	New Mexico	5,077.8
9	Tennessee	5,018.9
10	Oregon	4,868.4
11	Maryland	4,747.4
12	Oklahoma	4,743.2
13	North Carolina	4,721.4
14	Missouri	4,602.4
15	Georgia	4,507.2
16	Nevada	4,497.5
17	Alabama	4,465.2
18	Utah	4,452.4
19	Colorado	4,347.8
20	Alaska	4,309.7
21	Nebraska	4,256.7
22	Mississippi	4,159.2
23	Arkansas	4,157.5
24	Ohio	4,107.3
25	Kansas	4,087.0
26	Illinois	4,016.4
27	California	3,943.7
28	Delaware	3,939.0
29	Michigan	3,874.1
30	Indiana	3,750.0
31	Rhode Island	3,589.1
32	Wyoming	3,580.9
33	Minnesota	3,535.1
34	Montana	3,512.9
35	Iowa	3,448.2
36	Wisconsin	3,252.7
37	Idaho	3,172.5
38	Virginia	3,140.3
39	Massachusetts	3,094.2
40	New Jersey	3,024.2
41	Connecticut	2,997.2
42	Kentucky	2,902.6
43	Pennsylvania	2,841.0
44	New York	2,803.7
45	Maine	2,656.0
46	Vermont	2,530.0
47	West Virginia	2,515.2
48	North Dakota	2,406.2
49	South Dakota	2,278.7
50	New Hampshire	2,220.0
	District of Columbia	8,022.3

Source: Federal Bureau of Investigation
    "Crime in the United States 2002" (Uniform Crime Reports, October 27, 2003)
Includes murder, rape, robbery, aggravated assault, burglary, larceny-theft and motor vehicle theft.

Percent Change in Crime Rate: 2001 to 2002

National Percent Change = 1.1% Decrease*

<u>ALPHA ORDER</u>

RANK	STATE	PERCENT CHANGE
6	Alabama	3.5
10	Alaska	1.5
3	Arizona	5.1
14	Arkansas	0.7
11	California	1.3
7	Colorado	3.4
39	Connecticut	(3.6)
35	Delaware	(2.8)
35	Florida	(2.8)
34	Georgia	(2.7)
1	Hawaii	12.5
12	Idaho	1.2
30	Illinois	(2.2)
27	Indiana	(1.9)
5	Iowa	4.8
48	Kansas	(5.2)
15	Kentucky	0.2
43	Louisiana	(4.4)
23	Maine	(1.4)
31	Maryland	(2.3)
15	Massachusetts	0.2
47	Michigan	(4.9)
20	Minnesota	(1.1)
18	Mississippi	(0.6)
37	Missouri	(3.5)
46	Montana	(4.7)
22	Nebraska	(1.3)
4	Nevada	5.0
43	New Hampshire	(4.4)
49	New Jersey	(5.9)
45	New Mexico	(4.5)
40	New York	(3.8)
42	North Carolina	(4.2)
17	North Dakota	(0.1)
24	Ohio	(1.5)
8	Oklahoma	3.2
37	Oregon	(3.5)
41	Pennsylvania	(3.9)
33	Rhode Island	(2.5)
25	South Carolina	(1.8)
29	South Dakota	(2.1)
32	Tennessee	(2.4)
13	Texas	0.9
2	Utah	5.3
50	Vermont	(8.7)
20	Virginia	(1.1)
19	Washington	(0.8)
25	West Virginia	(1.8)
28	Wisconsin	(2.0)
9	Wyoming	1.7

<u>RANK ORDER</u>

RANK	STATE	PERCENT CHANGE
1	Hawaii	12.5
2	Utah	5.3
3	Arizona	5.1
4	Nevada	5.0
5	Iowa	4.8
6	Alabama	3.5
7	Colorado	3.4
8	Oklahoma	3.2
9	Wyoming	1.7
10	Alaska	1.5
11	California	1.3
12	Idaho	1.2
13	Texas	0.9
14	Arkansas	0.7
15	Kentucky	0.2
15	Massachusetts	0.2
17	North Dakota	(0.1)
18	Mississippi	(0.6)
19	Washington	(0.8)
20	Minnesota	(1.1)
20	Virginia	(1.1)
22	Nebraska	(1.3)
23	Maine	(1.4)
24	Ohio	(1.5)
25	South Carolina	(1.8)
25	West Virginia	(1.8)
27	Indiana	(1.9)
28	Wisconsin	(2.0)
29	South Dakota	(2.1)
30	Illinois	(2.2)
31	Maryland	(2.3)
32	Tennessee	(2.4)
33	Rhode Island	(2.5)
34	Georgia	(2.7)
35	Delaware	(2.8)
35	Florida	(2.8)
37	Missouri	(3.5)
37	Oregon	(3.5)
39	Connecticut	(3.6)
40	New York	(3.8)
41	Pennsylvania	(3.9)
42	North Carolina	(4.2)
43	Louisiana	(4.4)
43	New Hampshire	(4.4)
45	New Mexico	(4.5)
46	Montana	(4.7)
47	Michigan	(4.9)
48	Kansas	(5.2)
49	New Jersey	(5.9)
50	Vermont	(8.7)
	District of Columbia	3.6

Source: Federal Bureau of Investigation
"Crime in the United States 2002" (Uniform Crime Reports, October 27, 2003)
Includes murder, rape, robbery, aggravated assault, burglary, larceny-theft and motor vehicle theft.

Violent Crimes in 2002

National Total = 1,426,325 Violent Crimes*

<u>ALPHA ORDER</u>

RANK	STATE	CRIMES	% of USA
22	Alabama	19,931	1.4%
40	Alaska	3,627	0.3%
17	Arizona	30,171	2.1%
29	Arkansas	11,501	0.8%
1	California	208,388	14.6%
24	Colorado	15,882	1.1%
31	Connecticut	10,767	0.8%
38	Delaware	4,836	0.3%
2	Florida	128,721	9.0%
11	Georgia	39,271	2.8%
42	Hawaii	3,262	0.2%
41	Idaho	3,419	0.2%
5	Illinois	78,214	5.5%
19	Indiana	22,001	1.5%
35	Iowa	8,388	0.6%
33	Kansas	10,229	0.7%
30	Kentucky	11,418	0.8%
18	Louisiana	29,690	2.1%
46	Maine	1,396	0.1%
8	Maryland	42,015	2.9%
15	Massachusetts	31,137	2.2%
6	Michigan	54,306	3.8%
27	Minnesota	13,428	0.9%
34	Mississippi	9,858	0.7%
16	Missouri	30,557	2.1%
43	Montana	3,197	0.2%
37	Nebraska	5,428	0.4%
25	Nevada	13,856	1.0%
45	New Hampshire	2,056	0.1%
14	New Jersey	32,168	2.3%
26	New Mexico	13,719	1.0%
4	New York	95,030	6.7%
12	North Carolina	39,118	2.7%
50	North Dakota	496	0.0%
10	Ohio	40,128	2.8%
23	Oklahoma	17,587	1.2%
32	Oregon	10,298	0.7%
7	Pennsylvania	49,578	3.5%
44	Rhode Island	3,051	0.2%
13	South Carolina	33,761	2.4%
48	South Dakota	1,350	0.1%
9	Tennessee	41,562	2.9%
3	Texas	126,018	8.8%
36	Utah	5,488	0.4%
49	Vermont	658	0.0%
20	Virginia	21,256	1.5%
21	Washington	20,964	1.5%
39	West Virginia	4,221	0.3%
28	Wisconsin	12,238	0.9%
47	Wyoming	1,364	0.1%

<u>RANK ORDER</u>

RANK	STATE	CRIMES	% of USA
1	California	208,388	14.6%
2	Florida	128,721	9.0%
3	Texas	126,018	8.8%
4	New York	95,030	6.7%
5	Illinois	78,214	5.5%
6	Michigan	54,306	3.8%
7	Pennsylvania	49,578	3.5%
8	Maryland	42,015	2.9%
9	Tennessee	41,562	2.9%
10	Ohio	40,128	2.8%
11	Georgia	39,271	2.8%
12	North Carolina	39,118	2.7%
13	South Carolina	33,761	2.4%
14	New Jersey	32,168	2.3%
15	Massachusetts	31,137	2.2%
16	Missouri	30,557	2.1%
17	Arizona	30,171	2.1%
18	Louisiana	29,690	2.1%
19	Indiana	22,001	1.5%
20	Virginia	21,256	1.5%
21	Washington	20,964	1.5%
22	Alabama	19,931	1.4%
23	Oklahoma	17,587	1.2%
24	Colorado	15,882	1.1%
25	Nevada	13,856	1.0%
26	New Mexico	13,719	1.0%
27	Minnesota	13,428	0.9%
28	Wisconsin	12,238	0.9%
29	Arkansas	11,501	0.8%
30	Kentucky	11,418	0.8%
31	Connecticut	10,767	0.8%
32	Oregon	10,298	0.7%
33	Kansas	10,229	0.7%
34	Mississippi	9,858	0.7%
35	Iowa	8,388	0.6%
36	Utah	5,488	0.4%
37	Nebraska	5,428	0.4%
38	Delaware	4,836	0.3%
39	West Virginia	4,221	0.3%
40	Alaska	3,627	0.3%
41	Idaho	3,419	0.2%
42	Hawaii	3,262	0.2%
43	Montana	3,197	0.2%
44	Rhode Island	3,051	0.2%
45	New Hampshire	2,056	0.1%
46	Maine	1,396	0.1%
47	Wyoming	1,364	0.1%
48	South Dakota	1,350	0.1%
49	Vermont	658	0.0%
50	North Dakota	496	0.0%
	District of Columbia	9,322	0.7%

Source: Federal Bureau of Investigation
"Crime in the United States 2002" (Uniform Crime Reports, October 27, 2003)
**Violent crimes are offenses of murder, forcible rape, robbery and aggravated assault.*

Percent Change in Number of Violent Crimes: 2001 to 2002

National Percent Change = 0.9% Decrease*

ALPHA ORDER

RANK	STATE	PERCENT CHANGE
16	Alabama	1.8
37	Alaska	(2.9)
7	Arizona	5.2
45	Arkansas	(5.7)
33	California	(2.1)
12	Colorado	2.5
48	Connecticut	(6.3)
23	Delaware	(0.7)
27	Florida	(1.5)
46	Georgia	(5.8)
8	Hawaii	4.7
6	Idaho	6.5
25	Illinois	(1.3)
39	Indiana	(3.2)
5	Iowa	6.6
47	Kansas	(6.2)
3	Kentucky	8.6
39	Louisiana	(3.2)
34	Maine	(2.7)
22	Maryland	(0.2)
16	Massachusetts	1.8
31	Michigan	(2.0)
13	Minnesota	2.2
27	Mississippi	(1.5)
19	Missouri	0.3
19	Montana	0.3
9	Nebraska	4.1
2	Nevada	12.1
44	New Hampshire	(4.1)
35	New Jersey	(2.8)
43	New Mexico	(4.0)
38	New York	(3.1)
41	North Carolina	(3.3)
30	North Dakota	(1.8)
19	Ohio	0.3
24	Oklahoma	(0.8)
41	Oregon	(3.3)
29	Pennsylvania	(1.7)
49	Rhode Island	(6.9)
15	South Carolina	2.0
1	South Dakota	15.3
35	Tennessee	(2.8)
11	Texas	3.2
10	Utah	3.3
13	Vermont	2.2
18	Virginia	1.5
26	Washington	(1.4)
50	West Virginia	(16.2)
31	Wisconsin	(2.0)
4	Wyoming	7.2

RANK ORDER

RANK	STATE	PERCENT CHANGE
1	South Dakota	15.3
2	Nevada	12.1
3	Kentucky	8.6
4	Wyoming	7.2
5	Iowa	6.6
6	Idaho	6.5
7	Arizona	5.2
8	Hawaii	4.7
9	Nebraska	4.1
10	Utah	3.3
11	Texas	3.2
12	Colorado	2.5
13	Minnesota	2.2
13	Vermont	2.2
15	South Carolina	2.0
16	Alabama	1.8
16	Massachusetts	1.8
18	Virginia	1.5
19	Missouri	0.3
19	Montana	0.3
19	Ohio	0.3
22	Maryland	(0.2)
23	Delaware	(0.7)
24	Oklahoma	(0.8)
25	Illinois	(1.3)
26	Washington	(1.4)
27	Florida	(1.5)
27	Mississippi	(1.5)
29	Pennsylvania	(1.7)
30	North Dakota	(1.8)
31	Michigan	(2.0)
31	Wisconsin	(2.0)
33	California	(2.1)
34	Maine	(2.7)
35	New Jersey	(2.8)
35	Tennessee	(2.8)
37	Alaska	(2.9)
38	New York	(3.1)
39	Indiana	(3.2)
39	Louisiana	(3.2)
41	North Carolina	(3.3)
41	Oregon	(3.3)
43	New Mexico	(4.0)
44	New Hampshire	(4.1)
45	Arkansas	(5.7)
46	Georgia	(5.8)
47	Kansas	(6.2)
48	Connecticut	(6.3)
49	Rhode Island	(6.9)
50	West Virginia	(16.2)
	District of Columbia	1.4

Source: Federal Bureau of Investigation
   "Crime in the United States 2002" (Uniform Crime Reports, October 27, 2003)
**Violent crimes are offenses of murder, forcible rape, robbery and aggravated assault.*

Violent Crime Rate in 2002

National Rate = 494.6 Violent Crimes per 100,000 Population*

<u>ALPHA ORDER</u>

RANK	STATE	RATE
21	Alabama	444.2
12	Alaska	563.4
13	Arizona	552.9
22	Arkansas	424.4
10	California	593.4
27	Colorado	352.4
33	Connecticut	311.1
9	Delaware	599.0
2	Florida	770.2
20	Georgia	458.8
41	Hawaii	262.0
42	Idaho	254.9
8	Illinois	620.7
26	Indiana	357.2
36	Iowa	285.6
24	Kansas	376.6
38	Kentucky	279.0
6	Louisiana	662.3
48	Maine	107.8
3	Maryland	769.8
18	Massachusetts	484.4
14	Michigan	540.3
40	Minnesota	267.5
31	Mississippi	343.3
15	Missouri	538.7
28	Montana	351.5
32	Nebraska	313.9
7	Nevada	637.5
47	New Hampshire	161.2
25	New Jersey	374.5
4	New Mexico	739.5
17	New York	496.0
19	North Carolina	470.2
50	North Dakota	78.2
29	Ohio	351.3
16	Oklahoma	503.4
34	Oregon	292.4
23	Pennsylvania	401.9
37	Rhode Island	285.2
1	South Carolina	822.0
46	South Dakota	177.4
5	Tennessee	716.9
11	Texas	578.6
43	Utah	236.9
49	Vermont	106.7
35	Virginia	291.4
30	Washington	345.4
44	West Virginia	234.3
45	Wisconsin	224.9
39	Wyoming	273.5

<u>RANK ORDER</u>

RANK	STATE	RATE
1	South Carolina	822.0
2	Florida	770.2
3	Maryland	769.8
4	New Mexico	739.5
5	Tennessee	716.9
6	Louisiana	662.3
7	Nevada	637.5
8	Illinois	620.7
9	Delaware	599.0
10	California	593.4
11	Texas	578.6
12	Alaska	563.4
13	Arizona	552.9
14	Michigan	540.3
15	Missouri	538.7
16	Oklahoma	503.4
17	New York	496.0
18	Massachusetts	484.4
19	North Carolina	470.2
20	Georgia	458.8
21	Alabama	444.2
22	Arkansas	424.4
23	Pennsylvania	401.9
24	Kansas	376.6
25	New Jersey	374.5
26	Indiana	357.2
27	Colorado	352.4
28	Montana	351.5
29	Ohio	351.3
30	Washington	345.4
31	Mississippi	343.3
32	Nebraska	313.9
33	Connecticut	311.1
34	Oregon	292.4
35	Virginia	291.4
36	Iowa	285.6
37	Rhode Island	285.2
38	Kentucky	279.0
39	Wyoming	273.5
40	Minnesota	267.5
41	Hawaii	262.0
42	Idaho	254.9
43	Utah	236.9
44	West Virginia	234.3
45	Wisconsin	224.9
46	South Dakota	177.4
47	New Hampshire	161.2
48	Maine	107.8
49	Vermont	106.7
50	North Dakota	78.2

District of Columbia   1,632.9

Source: Federal Bureau of Investigation
"Crime in the United States 2002" (Uniform Crime Reports, October 27, 2003)
*Violent crimes are offenses of murder, forcible rape, robbery and aggravated assault.

Percent Change in Violent Crime Rate: 2001 to 2002

National Percent Change = 2.0% Decrease*

<u>ALPHA ORDER</u>

RANK	STATE	PERCENT CHANGE
12	Alabama	1.4
40	Alaska	(4.4)
9	Arizona	2.3
45	Arkansas	(6.2)
33	California	(3.5)
16	Colorado	0.8
47	Connecticut	(7.0)
27	Delaware	(2.0)
33	Florida	(3.5)
48	Georgia	(7.5)
8	Hawaii	3.1
6	Idaho	4.8
27	Illinois	(2.0)
38	Indiana	(3.7)
4	Iowa	6.5
46	Kansas	(6.7)
3	Kentucky	8.0
33	Louisiana	(3.5)
33	Maine	(3.5)
23	Maryland	(1.5)
12	Massachusetts	1.4
29	Michigan	(2.4)
12	Minnesota	1.4
25	Mississippi	(1.9)
21	Missouri	(0.3)
20	Montana	(0.1)
7	Nebraska	3.6
2	Nevada	8.2
44	New Hampshire	(5.3)
38	New Jersey	(3.7)
43	New Mexico	(5.2)
32	New York	(3.4)
42	North Carolina	(4.7)
22	North Dakota	(1.4)
19	Ohio	0.0
23	Oklahoma	(1.5)
41	Oregon	(4.6)
25	Pennsylvania	(1.9)
49	Rhode Island	(7.8)
16	South Carolina	0.8
1	South Dakota	14.9
37	Tennessee	(3.6)
15	Texas	1.2
10	Utah	1.6
10	Vermont	1.6
18	Virginia	0.2
30	Washington	(2.6)
50	West Virginia	(16.2)
30	Wisconsin	(2.6)
5	Wyoming	6.2

<u>RANK ORDER</u>

RANK	STATE	PERCENT CHANGE
1	South Dakota	14.9
2	Nevada	8.2
3	Kentucky	8.0
4	Iowa	6.5
5	Wyoming	6.2
6	Idaho	4.8
7	Nebraska	3.6
8	Hawaii	3.1
9	Arizona	2.3
10	Utah	1.6
10	Vermont	1.6
12	Alabama	1.4
12	Massachusetts	1.4
12	Minnesota	1.4
15	Texas	1.2
16	Colorado	0.8
16	South Carolina	0.8
18	Virginia	0.2
19	Ohio	0.0
20	Montana	(0.1)
21	Missouri	(0.3)
22	North Dakota	(1.4)
23	Maryland	(1.5)
23	Oklahoma	(1.5)
25	Mississippi	(1.9)
25	Pennsylvania	(1.9)
27	Delaware	(2.0)
27	Illinois	(2.0)
29	Michigan	(2.4)
30	Washington	(2.6)
30	Wisconsin	(2.6)
32	New York	(3.4)
33	California	(3.5)
33	Florida	(3.5)
33	Louisiana	(3.5)
33	Maine	(3.5)
37	Tennessee	(3.6)
38	Indiana	(3.7)
38	New Jersey	(3.7)
40	Alaska	(4.4)
41	Oregon	(4.6)
42	North Carolina	(4.7)
43	New Mexico	(5.2)
44	New Hampshire	(5.3)
45	Arkansas	(6.2)
46	Kansas	(6.7)
47	Connecticut	(7.0)
48	Georgia	(7.5)
49	Rhode Island	(7.8)
50	West Virginia	(16.2)
	District of Columbia	1.9

Source: Federal Bureau of Investigation
    "Crime in the United States 2002" (Uniform Crime Reports, October 27, 2003)
*Violent crimes are offenses of murder, forcible rape, robbery and aggravated assault.

Murders in 2002

National Total = 16,204 Murders*

<u>ALPHA ORDER</u>

RANK	STATE	MURDERS	% of USA
19	Alabama	303	1.9%
41	Alaska	33	0.2%
15	Arizona	387	2.4%
30	Arkansas	142	0.9%
1	California	2,395	14.8%
25	Colorado	179	1.1%
32	Connecticut	80	0.5%
42	Delaware	26	0.2%
4	Florida	911	5.6%
8	Georgia	606	3.7%
43	Hawaii	24	0.1%
40	Idaho	36	0.2%
3	Illinois	949	5.9%
16	Indiana	362	2.2%
38	Iowa	44	0.3%
33	Kansas	78	0.5%
22	Kentucky	184	1.1%
9	Louisiana	593	3.7%
46	Maine	14	0.1%
12	Maryland	513	3.2%
26	Massachusetts	173	1.1%
6	Michigan	678	4.2%
31	Minnesota	112	0.7%
21	Mississippi	264	1.6%
18	Missouri	331	2.0%
44	Montana	16	0.1%
36	Nebraska	48	0.3%
24	Nevada	181	1.1%
48	New Hampshire	12	0.1%
17	New Jersey	337	2.1%
29	New Mexico	152	0.9%
5	New York	909	5.6%
10	North Carolina	548	3.4%
50	North Dakota	5	0.0%
11	Ohio	526	3.2%
27	Oklahoma	163	1.0%
34	Oregon	72	0.4%
7	Pennsylvania	624	3.9%
39	Rhode Island	41	0.3%
20	South Carolina	298	1.8%
49	South Dakota	11	0.1%
13	Tennessee	420	2.6%
2	Texas	1,302	8.0%
37	Utah	47	0.3%
47	Vermont	13	0.1%
14	Virginia	388	2.4%
22	Washington	184	1.1%
35	West Virginia	57	0.4%
28	Wisconsin	154	1.0%
45	Wyoming	15	0.1%

<u>RANK ORDER</u>

RANK	STATE	MURDERS	% of USA
1	California	2,395	14.8%
2	Texas	1,302	8.0%
3	Illinois	949	5.9%
4	Florida	911	5.6%
5	New York	909	5.6%
6	Michigan	678	4.2%
7	Pennsylvania	624	3.9%
8	Georgia	606	3.7%
9	Louisiana	593	3.7%
10	North Carolina	548	3.4%
11	Ohio	526	3.2%
12	Maryland	513	3.2%
13	Tennessee	420	2.6%
14	Virginia	388	2.4%
15	Arizona	387	2.4%
16	Indiana	362	2.2%
17	New Jersey	337	2.1%
18	Missouri	331	2.0%
19	Alabama	303	1.9%
20	South Carolina	298	1.8%
21	Mississippi	264	1.6%
22	Kentucky	184	1.1%
22	Washington	184	1.1%
24	Nevada	181	1.1%
25	Colorado	179	1.1%
26	Massachusetts	173	1.1%
27	Oklahoma	163	1.0%
28	Wisconsin	154	1.0%
29	New Mexico	152	0.9%
30	Arkansas	142	0.9%
31	Minnesota	112	0.7%
32	Connecticut	80	0.5%
33	Kansas	78	0.5%
34	Oregon	72	0.4%
35	West Virginia	57	0.4%
36	Nebraska	48	0.3%
37	Utah	47	0.3%
38	Iowa	44	0.3%
39	Rhode Island	41	0.3%
40	Idaho	36	0.2%
41	Alaska	33	0.2%
42	Delaware	26	0.2%
43	Hawaii	24	0.1%
44	Montana	16	0.1%
45	Wyoming	15	0.1%
46	Maine	14	0.1%
47	Vermont	13	0.1%
48	New Hampshire	12	0.1%
49	South Dakota	11	0.1%
50	North Dakota	5	0.0%
	District of Columbia	264	1.6%

Source: Federal Bureau of Investigation
   "Crime in the United States 2002" (Uniform Crime Reports, October 27, 2003)
Includes nonnegligent manslaughter.

Percent Change in Number of Murders: 2001 to 2002

National Percent Change = 1.0% Increase*

<u>ALPHA ORDER</u>

RANK	STATE	PERCENT CHANGE
43	Alabama	(20.1)
41	Alaska	(15.4)
27	Arizona	(3.3)
29	Arkansas	(4.1)
14	California	8.6
11	Colorado	13.3
44	Connecticut	(23.8)
12	Delaware	13.0
18	Florida	4.2
21	Georgia	1.3
45	Hawaii	(25.0)
7	Idaho	20.0
28	Illinois	(3.4)
38	Indiana	(12.3)
37	Iowa	(12.0)
40	Kansas	(15.2)
20	Kentucky	1.7
8	Louisiana	18.4
46	Maine	(26.3)
10	Maryland	15.0
6	Massachusetts	21.0
22	Michigan	0.9
32	Minnesota	(5.9)
33	Mississippi	(6.4)
35	Missouri	(11.0)
50	Montana	(52.9)
13	Nebraska	11.6
23	Nevada	0.6
48	New Hampshire	(29.4)
24	New Jersey	0.3
4	New Mexico	53.5
31	New York	(5.3)
15	North Carolina	8.5
47	North Dakota	(28.6)
9	Ohio	16.4
36	Oklahoma	(11.9)
39	Oregon	(14.3)
29	Pennsylvania	(4.1)
17	Rhode Island	5.1
34	South Carolina	(9.7)
3	South Dakota	57.1
25	Tennessee	(0.7)
26	Texas	(2.3)
49	Utah	(29.9)
1	Vermont	85.7
16	Virginia	6.6
19	Washington	2.8
5	West Virginia	42.5
42	Wisconsin	(19.8)
2	Wyoming	66.7

<u>RANK ORDER</u>

RANK	STATE	PERCENT CHANGE
1	Vermont	85.7
2	Wyoming	66.7
3	South Dakota	57.1
4	New Mexico	53.5
5	West Virginia	42.5
6	Massachusetts	21.0
7	Idaho	20.0
8	Louisiana	18.4
9	Ohio	16.4
10	Maryland	15.0
11	Colorado	13.3
12	Delaware	13.0
13	Nebraska	11.6
14	California	8.6
15	North Carolina	8.5
16	Virginia	6.6
17	Rhode Island	5.1
18	Florida	4.2
19	Washington	2.8
20	Kentucky	1.7
21	Georgia	1.3
22	Michigan	0.9
23	Nevada	0.6
24	New Jersey	0.3
25	Tennessee	(0.7)
26	Texas	(2.3)
27	Arizona	(3.3)
28	Illinois	(3.4)
29	Arkansas	(4.1)
29	Pennsylvania	(4.1)
31	New York	(5.3)
32	Minnesota	(5.9)
33	Mississippi	(6.4)
34	South Carolina	(9.7)
35	Missouri	(11.0)
36	Oklahoma	(11.9)
37	Iowa	(12.0)
38	Indiana	(12.3)
39	Oregon	(14.3)
40	Kansas	(15.2)
41	Alaska	(15.4)
42	Wisconsin	(19.8)
43	Alabama	(20.1)
44	Connecticut	(23.8)
45	Hawaii	(25.0)
46	Maine	(26.3)
47	North Dakota	(28.6)
48	New Hampshire	(29.4)
49	Utah	(29.9)
50	Montana	(52.9)
	District of Columbia	14.3

Source: Federal Bureau of Investigation
"Crime in the United States 2002" (Uniform Crime Reports, October 27, 2003)
**Includes nonnegligent manslaughter.*

Murder Rate in 2002

National Rate = 5.6 Murders per 100,000 Population*

ALPHA ORDER

RANK	STATE	RATE
11	Alabama	6.8
21	Alaska	5.1
9	Arizona	7.1
20	Arkansas	5.2
11	California	6.8
27	Colorado	4.0
39	Connecticut	2.3
30	Delaware	3.2
18	Florida	5.5
9	Georgia	7.1
44	Hawaii	1.9
37	Idaho	2.7
6	Illinois	7.5
16	Indiana	5.9
46	Iowa	1.5
34	Kansas	2.9
26	Kentucky	4.5
1	Louisiana	13.2
48	Maine	1.1
2	Maryland	9.4
37	Massachusetts	2.7
13	Michigan	6.7
40	Minnesota	2.2
3	Mississippi	9.2
17	Missouri	5.8
45	Montana	1.8
35	Nebraska	2.8
4	Nevada	8.3
49	New Hampshire	0.9
28	New Jersey	3.9
5	New Mexico	8.2
23	New York	4.7
14	North Carolina	6.6
50	North Dakota	0.8
25	Ohio	4.6
23	Oklahoma	4.7
42	Oregon	2.0
21	Pennsylvania	5.1
29	Rhode Island	3.8
7	South Carolina	7.3
47	South Dakota	1.4
8	Tennessee	7.2
15	Texas	6.0
42	Utah	2.0
41	Vermont	2.1
19	Virginia	5.3
32	Washington	3.0
30	West Virginia	3.2
35	Wisconsin	2.8
32	Wyoming	3.0

RANK ORDER

RANK	STATE	RATE
1	Louisiana	13.2
2	Maryland	9.4
3	Mississippi	9.2
4	Nevada	8.3
5	New Mexico	8.2
6	Illinois	7.5
7	South Carolina	7.3
8	Tennessee	7.2
9	Arizona	7.1
9	Georgia	7.1
11	Alabama	6.8
11	California	6.8
13	Michigan	6.7
14	North Carolina	6.6
15	Texas	6.0
16	Indiana	5.9
17	Missouri	5.8
18	Florida	5.5
19	Virginia	5.3
20	Arkansas	5.2
21	Alaska	5.1
21	Pennsylvania	5.1
23	New York	4.7
23	Oklahoma	4.7
25	Ohio	4.6
26	Kentucky	4.5
27	Colorado	4.0
28	New Jersey	3.9
29	Rhode Island	3.8
30	Delaware	3.2
30	West Virginia	3.2
32	Washington	3.0
32	Wyoming	3.0
34	Kansas	2.9
35	Nebraska	2.8
35	Wisconsin	2.8
37	Idaho	2.7
37	Massachusetts	2.7
39	Connecticut	2.3
40	Minnesota	2.2
41	Vermont	2.1
42	Oregon	2.0
42	Utah	2.0
44	Hawaii	1.9
45	Montana	1.8
46	Iowa	1.5
47	South Dakota	1.4
48	Maine	1.1
49	New Hampshire	0.9
50	North Dakota	0.8

| | District of Columbia | 46.2 |

Source: Federal Bureau of Investigation
   "Crime in the United States 2002" (Uniform Crime Reports, October 27, 2003)
*Includes nonnegligent manslaughter.

Murders with Firearms in 2002

National Total = 9,369 Murders*

<u>ALPHA ORDER</u>

RANK	STATE	MURDERS	% of USA
19	Alabama	186	2.0%
38	Alaska	18	0.2%
11	Arizona	290	3.1%
24	Arkansas	103	1.1%
1	California	1,737	18.5%
22	Colorado	108	1.2%
31	Connecticut	45	0.5%
40	Delaware	17	0.2%
NA	Florida**	NA	NA
8	Georgia	415	4.4%
41	Hawaii	10	0.1%
38	Idaho	18	0.2%
4	Illinois*	481	5.1%
16	Indiana	206	2.2%
36	Iowa	22	0.2%
34	Kansas	27	0.3%
30	Kentucky	53	0.6%
7	Louisiana	431	4.6%
45	Maine	6	0.1%
10	Maryland	301	3.2%
27	Massachusetts	80	0.9%
5	Michigan	463	4.9%
29	Minnesota	60	0.6%
20	Mississippi	117	1.2%
15	Missouri	229	2.4%
47	Montana	4	0.0%
44	Nebraska	7	0.1%
21	Nevada	109	1.2%
43	New Hampshire	8	0.1%
17	New Jersey	205	2.2%
28	New Mexico	66	0.7%
3	New York	506	5.4%
9	North Carolina	367	3.9%
49	North Dakota	2	0.0%
12	Ohio	289	3.1%
26	Oklahoma	85	0.9%
32	Oregon	40	0.4%
6	Pennsylvania	434	4.6%
35	Rhode Island	26	0.3%
18	South Carolina	200	2.1%
48	South Dakota	3	0.0%
13	Tennessee	276	2.9%
2	Texas	795	8.5%
36	Utah	22	0.2%
41	Vermont	10	0.1%
14	Virginia	257	2.7%
25	Washington	87	0.9%
33	West Virginia	34	0.4%
22	Wisconsin	108	1.2%
45	Wyoming	6	0.1%

<u>RANK ORDER</u>

RANK	STATE	MURDERS	% of USA
1	California	1,737	18.5%
2	Texas	795	8.5%
3	New York	506	5.4%
4	Illinois*	481	5.1%
5	Michigan	463	4.9%
6	Pennsylvania	434	4.6%
7	Louisiana	431	4.6%
8	Georgia	415	4.4%
9	North Carolina	367	3.9%
10	Maryland	301	3.2%
11	Arizona	290	3.1%
12	Ohio	289	3.1%
13	Tennessee	276	2.9%
14	Virginia	257	2.7%
15	Missouri	229	2.4%
16	Indiana	206	2.2%
17	New Jersey	205	2.2%
18	South Carolina	200	2.1%
19	Alabama	186	2.0%
20	Mississippi	117	1.2%
21	Nevada	109	1.2%
22	Colorado	108	1.2%
22	Wisconsin	108	1.2%
24	Arkansas	103	1.1%
25	Washington	87	0.9%
26	Oklahoma	85	0.9%
27	Massachusetts	80	0.9%
28	New Mexico	66	0.7%
29	Minnesota	60	0.6%
30	Kentucky	53	0.6%
31	Connecticut	45	0.5%
32	Oregon	40	0.4%
33	West Virginia	34	0.4%
34	Kansas	27	0.3%
35	Rhode Island	26	0.3%
36	Iowa	22	0.2%
36	Utah	22	0.2%
38	Alaska	18	0.2%
38	Idaho	18	0.2%
40	Delaware	17	0.2%
41	Hawaii	10	0.1%
41	Vermont	10	0.1%
43	New Hampshire	8	0.1%
44	Nebraska	7	0.1%
45	Maine	6	0.1%
45	Wyoming	6	0.1%
47	Montana	4	0.0%
48	South Dakota	3	0.0%
49	North Dakota	2	0.0%
NA	Florida**	NA	NA
	District of Columbia**	NA	NA

Source: Federal Bureau of Investigation
   "Crime in the United States 2002" (Uniform Crime Reports, October 27, 2003)
**Of the 14,054 murders in 2002 for which supplemental data were received by the F.B.I. There were an additional 2,150 murders for which the type of murder weapon was not reported to the F.B.I. Includes nonnegligent manslaughter. Numbers are for reporting jurisdictions only. Illinois' figure is for Chicago only.*
***Not available.*

Percent of Murders Involving Firearms in 2002

National Percent = 66.7% of Murders*

<u>ALPHA ORDER</u>

RANK	STATE	PERCENT
20	Alabama	65.0
33	Alaska	54.5
4	Arizona	75.9
5	Arkansas	75.2
8	California	72.5
19	Colorado	65.1
31	Connecticut	60.0
2	Delaware	77.3
NA	Florida**	NA
11	Georgia	72.3
44	Hawaii	43.5
37	Idaho	50.0
6	Illinois*	74.2
23	Indiana	63.8
37	Iowa	50.0
47	Kansas	40.3
21	Kentucky	64.6
1	Louisiana	77.5
45	Maine	42.9
18	Maryland	65.4
39	Massachusetts	49.4
13	Michigan	68.5
35	Minnesota	53.6
24	Mississippi	63.6
12	Missouri	69.2
42	Montana	44.4
43	Nebraska	43.8
26	Nevada	61.9
7	New Hampshire	72.7
29	New Jersey	61.2
34	New Mexico	54.1
32	New York	58.8
14	North Carolina	68.3
48	North Dakota	40.0
30	Ohio	60.7
36	Oklahoma	52.1
27	Oregon	61.5
8	Pennsylvania	72.5
25	Rhode Island	63.4
15	South Carolina	68.0
49	South Dakota	33.3
17	Tennessee	66.7
28	Texas	61.3
41	Utah	46.8
3	Vermont	76.9
16	Virginia	67.5
40	Washington	48.1
22	West Virginia	64.2
8	Wisconsin	72.5
45	Wyoming	42.9

<u>RANK ORDER</u>

RANK	STATE	PERCENT
1	Louisiana	77.5
2	Delaware	77.3
3	Vermont	76.9
4	Arizona	75.9
5	Arkansas	75.2
6	Illinois*	74.2
7	New Hampshire	72.7
8	California	72.5
8	Pennsylvania	72.5
8	Wisconsin	72.5
11	Georgia	72.3
12	Missouri	69.2
13	Michigan	68.5
14	North Carolina	68.3
15	South Carolina	68.0
16	Virginia	67.5
17	Tennessee	66.7
18	Maryland	65.4
19	Colorado	65.1
20	Alabama	65.0
21	Kentucky	64.6
22	West Virginia	64.2
23	Indiana	63.8
24	Mississippi	63.6
25	Rhode Island	63.4
26	Nevada	61.9
27	Oregon	61.5
28	Texas	61.3
29	New Jersey	61.2
30	Ohio	60.7
31	Connecticut	60.0
32	New York	58.8
33	Alaska	54.5
34	New Mexico	54.1
35	Minnesota	53.6
36	Oklahoma	52.1
37	Idaho	50.0
37	Iowa	50.0
39	Massachusetts	49.4
40	Washington	48.1
41	Utah	46.8
42	Montana	44.4
43	Nebraska	43.8
44	Hawaii	43.5
45	Maine	42.9
45	Wyoming	42.9
47	Kansas	40.3
48	North Dakota	40.0
49	South Dakota	33.3
NA	Florida**	NA
	District of Columbia**	NA

Source: Morgan Quitno Press using data from Federal Bureau of Investigation
"Crime in the United States 2002" (Uniform Crime Reports, October 27, 2003)
Of the 14,054 murders in 2002 for which supplemental data were received by the F.B.I. There were an additional 2,150 murders for which the type of murder weapon was not reported to the F.B.I. Murder includes nonnegligent manslaughter. Illinois' percentage is for Chicago only.
**Not available.*

Rapes in 2002

National Total = 95,136 Rapes*

<u>ALPHA ORDER</u>

RANK	STATE	RAPES	% of USA
19	Alabama	1,664	1.7%
37	Alaska	511	0.5%
20	Arizona	1,608	1.7%
35	Arkansas	754	0.8%
1	California	10,198	10.7%
14	Colorado	2,066	2.2%
36	Connecticut	730	0.8%
45	Delaware	358	0.4%
3	Florida	6,753	7.1%
13	Georgia	2,108	2.2%
43	Hawaii	372	0.4%
38	Idaho	497	0.5%
6	Illinois	4,298	4.5%
16	Indiana	1,843	1.9%
34	Iowa	797	0.8%
30	Kansas	1,035	1.1%
29	Kentucky	1,088	1.1%
22	Louisiana	1,529	1.6%
42	Maine	377	0.4%
24	Maryland	1,370	1.4%
18	Massachusetts	1,777	1.9%
4	Michigan	5,364	5.6%
11	Minnesota	2,273	2.4%
28	Mississippi	1,127	1.2%
23	Missouri	1,465	1.5%
47	Montana	237	0.2%
39	Nebraska	464	0.5%
33	Nevada	928	1.0%
40	New Hampshire	446	0.5%
25	New Jersey	1,347	1.4%
31	New Mexico	1,027	1.1%
7	New York	3,885	4.1%
12	North Carolina	2,196	2.3%
48	North Dakota	163	0.2%
5	Ohio	4,809	5.1%
21	Oklahoma	1,573	1.7%
26	Oregon	1,238	1.3%
8	Pennsylvania	3,731	3.9%
41	Rhode Island	395	0.4%
15	South Carolina	1,959	2.1%
44	South Dakota	361	0.4%
10	Tennessee	2,290	2.4%
2	Texas	8,508	8.9%
32	Utah	943	1.0%
50	Vermont	126	0.1%
17	Virginia	1,839	1.9%
9	Washington	2,734	2.9%
46	West Virginia	328	0.3%
27	Wisconsin	1,237	1.3%
49	Wyoming	148	0.2%

<u>RANK ORDER</u>

RANK	STATE	RAPES	% of USA
1	California	10,198	10.7%
2	Texas	8,508	8.9%
3	Florida	6,753	7.1%
4	Michigan	5,364	5.6%
5	Ohio	4,809	5.1%
6	Illinois	4,298	4.5%
7	New York	3,885	4.1%
8	Pennsylvania	3,731	3.9%
9	Washington	2,734	2.9%
10	Tennessee	2,290	2.4%
11	Minnesota	2,273	2.4%
12	North Carolina	2,196	2.3%
13	Georgia	2,108	2.2%
14	Colorado	2,066	2.2%
15	South Carolina	1,959	2.1%
16	Indiana	1,843	1.9%
17	Virginia	1,839	1.9%
18	Massachusetts	1,777	1.9%
19	Alabama	1,664	1.7%
20	Arizona	1,608	1.7%
21	Oklahoma	1,573	1.7%
22	Louisiana	1,529	1.6%
23	Missouri	1,465	1.5%
24	Maryland	1,370	1.4%
25	New Jersey	1,347	1.4%
26	Oregon	1,238	1.3%
27	Wisconsin	1,237	1.3%
28	Mississippi	1,127	1.2%
29	Kentucky	1,088	1.1%
30	Kansas	1,035	1.1%
31	New Mexico	1,027	1.1%
32	Utah	943	1.0%
33	Nevada	928	1.0%
34	Iowa	797	0.8%
35	Arkansas	754	0.8%
36	Connecticut	730	0.8%
37	Alaska	511	0.5%
38	Idaho	497	0.5%
39	Nebraska	464	0.5%
40	New Hampshire	446	0.5%
41	Rhode Island	395	0.4%
42	Maine	377	0.4%
43	Hawaii	372	0.4%
44	South Dakota	361	0.4%
45	Delaware	358	0.4%
46	West Virginia	328	0.3%
47	Montana	237	0.2%
48	North Dakota	163	0.2%
49	Wyoming	148	0.2%
50	Vermont	126	0.1%
	District of Columbia	262	0.3%

Source: Federal Bureau of Investigation
   "Crime in the United States 2002" (Uniform Crime Reports, October 27, 2003)
**Forcible rape is the carnal knowledge of a female forcibly and against her will. Assaults or attempts to commit rape by force or threat of force are included. However, statutory rape without force and other sex offenses are excluded.*

Percent Change in Number of Rapes: 2001 to 2002

National Percent Change = 4.7% Increase*

<u>ALPHA ORDER</u>

RANK	STATE	PERCENT CHANGE
3	Alabama	21.5
36	Alaska	2.0
20	Arizona	5.9
50	Arkansas	(15.5)
35	California	2.4
19	Colorado	7.0
8	Connecticut	14.2
49	Delaware	(14.8)
38	Florida	1.7
43	Georgia	(3.3)
48	Hawaii	(9.0)
6	Idaho	16.9
18	Illinois	7.2
17	Indiana	7.4
2	Iowa	22.8
11	Kansas	9.5
32	Kentucky	3.5
12	Louisiana	9.0
7	Maine	15.6
47	Maryland	(5.5)
45	Massachusetts	(4.3)
37	Michigan	1.9
38	Minnesota	1.7
41	Mississippi	(1.7)
20	Missouri	5.9
1	Montana	26.1
14	Nebraska	7.7
28	Nevada	5.1
42	New Hampshire	(2.6)
24	New Jersey	5.4
4	New Mexico	20.8
10	New York	9.6
24	North Carolina	5.4
40	North Dakota	(0.6)
14	Ohio	7.7
20	Oklahoma	5.9
23	Oregon	5.5
16	Pennsylvania	7.6
46	Rhode Island	(5.0)
9	South Carolina	10.7
33	South Dakota	2.8
29	Tennessee	4.3
30	Texas	4.1
26	Utah	5.2
5	Vermont	17.8
31	Virginia	3.9
26	Washington	5.2
34	West Virginia	2.5
13	Wisconsin	8.3
43	Wyoming	(3.3)

<u>RANK ORDER</u>

RANK	STATE	PERCENT CHANGE
1	Montana	26.1
2	Iowa	22.8
3	Alabama	21.5
4	New Mexico	20.8
5	Vermont	17.8
6	Idaho	16.9
7	Maine	15.6
8	Connecticut	14.2
9	South Carolina	10.7
10	New York	9.6
11	Kansas	9.5
12	Louisiana	9.0
13	Wisconsin	8.3
14	Nebraska	7.7
14	Ohio	7.7
16	Pennsylvania	7.6
17	Indiana	7.4
18	Illinois	7.2
19	Colorado	7.0
20	Arizona	5.9
20	Missouri	5.9
20	Oklahoma	5.9
23	Oregon	5.5
24	New Jersey	5.4
24	North Carolina	5.4
26	Utah	5.2
26	Washington	5.2
28	Nevada	5.1
29	Tennessee	4.3
30	Texas	4.1
31	Virginia	3.9
32	Kentucky	3.5
33	South Dakota	2.8
34	West Virginia	2.5
35	California	2.4
36	Alaska	2.0
37	Michigan	1.9
38	Florida	1.7
38	Minnesota	1.7
40	North Dakota	(0.6)
41	Mississippi	(1.7)
42	New Hampshire	(2.6)
43	Georgia	(3.3)
43	Wyoming	(3.3)
45	Massachusetts	(4.3)
46	Rhode Island	(5.0)
47	Maryland	(5.5)
48	Hawaii	(9.0)
49	Delaware	(14.8)
50	Arkansas	(15.5)
	District of Columbia	44.8

Source: Federal Bureau of Investigation
"Crime in the United States 2002" (Uniform Crime Reports, October 27, 2003)
Forcible rape is the carnal knowledge of a female forcibly and against her will. Assaults or attempts to commit rape by force or threat of force are included. However, statutory rape without force and other sex offenses are excluded.

Rape Rate in 2002

National Rate = 33.0 Rapes per 100,000 Population*

<u>ALPHA ORDER</u>

RANK	STATE	RATE
19	Alabama	37.1
1	Alaska	79.4
30	Arizona	29.5
33	Arkansas	27.8
32	California	29.0
6	Colorado	45.8
46	Connecticut	21.1
10	Delaware	44.3
14	Florida	40.4
44	Georgia	24.6
27	Hawaii	29.9
19	Idaho	37.1
24	Illinois	34.1
27	Indiana	29.9
35	Iowa	27.1
18	Kansas	38.1
37	Kentucky	26.6
24	Louisiana	34.1
31	Maine	29.1
43	Maryland	25.1
34	Massachusetts	27.6
3	Michigan	53.4
7	Minnesota	45.3
16	Mississippi	39.2
40	Missouri	25.8
39	Montana	26.1
36	Nebraska	26.8
11	Nevada	42.7
23	New Hampshire	35.0
50	New Jersey	15.7
2	New Mexico	55.4
48	New York	20.3
38	North Carolina	26.4
41	North Dakota	25.7
12	Ohio	42.1
8	Oklahoma	45.0
22	Oregon	35.2
26	Pennsylvania	30.2
21	Rhode Island	36.9
4	South Carolina	47.7
5	South Dakota	47.4
15	Tennessee	39.5
17	Texas	39.1
13	Utah	40.7
47	Vermont	20.4
42	Virginia	25.2
8	Washington	45.0
49	West Virginia	18.2
45	Wisconsin	22.7
29	Wyoming	29.7

<u>RANK ORDER</u>

RANK	STATE	RATE
1	Alaska	79.4
2	New Mexico	55.4
3	Michigan	53.4
4	South Carolina	47.7
5	South Dakota	47.4
6	Colorado	45.8
7	Minnesota	45.3
8	Oklahoma	45.0
8	Washington	45.0
10	Delaware	44.3
11	Nevada	42.7
12	Ohio	42.1
13	Utah	40.7
14	Florida	40.4
15	Tennessee	39.5
16	Mississippi	39.2
17	Texas	39.1
18	Kansas	38.1
19	Alabama	37.1
19	Idaho	37.1
21	Rhode Island	36.9
22	Oregon	35.2
23	New Hampshire	35.0
24	Illinois	34.1
24	Louisiana	34.1
26	Pennsylvania	30.2
27	Hawaii	29.9
27	Indiana	29.9
29	Wyoming	29.7
30	Arizona	29.5
31	Maine	29.1
32	California	29.0
33	Arkansas	27.8
34	Massachusetts	27.6
35	Iowa	27.1
36	Nebraska	26.8
37	Kentucky	26.6
38	North Carolina	26.4
39	Montana	26.1
40	Missouri	25.8
41	North Dakota	25.7
42	Virginia	25.2
43	Maryland	25.1
44	Georgia	24.6
45	Wisconsin	22.7
46	Connecticut	21.1
47	Vermont	20.4
48	New York	20.3
49	West Virginia	18.2
50	New Jersey	15.7
	District of Columbia	45.9

Source: Federal Bureau of Investigation
   "Crime in the United States 2002" (Uniform Crime Reports, October 27, 2003)
*Forcible rape is the carnal knowledge of a female forcibly and against her will. Assaults or attempts to commit rape by force or threat of force are included. However, statutory rape without force and other sex offenses are excluded.

Robberies in 2002

National Total = 420,637 Robberies*

<u>ALPHA ORDER</u>

RANK	STATE	ROBBERIES	% of USA
20	Alabama	5,962	1.4%
42	Alaska	489	0.1%
14	Arizona	8,000	1.9%
32	Arkansas	2,524	0.6%
1	California	64,968	15.4%
27	Colorado	3,579	0.9%
25	Connecticut	4,060	1.0%
38	Delaware	1,154	0.3%
4	Florida	32,581	7.7%
9	Georgia	13,432	3.2%
36	Hawaii	1,210	0.3%
46	Idaho	240	0.1%
5	Illinois	25,272	6.0%
19	Indiana	6,612	1.6%
37	Iowa	1,169	0.3%
34	Kansas	2,165	0.5%
29	Kentucky	3,063	0.7%
16	Louisiana	7,123	1.7%
45	Maine	270	0.1%
10	Maryland	13,417	3.2%
15	Massachusetts	7,169	1.7%
12	Michigan	11,847	2.8%
26	Minnesota	3,937	0.9%
28	Mississippi	3,356	0.8%
17	Missouri	7,024	1.7%
44	Montana	283	0.1%
35	Nebraska	1,359	0.3%
23	Nevada	5,118	1.2%
43	New Hampshire	413	0.1%
8	New Jersey	13,905	3.3%
33	New Mexico	2,206	0.5%
3	New York	36,653	8.7%
11	North Carolina	12,205	2.9%
50	North Dakota	58	0.0%
6	Ohio	17,871	4.2%
30	Oklahoma	2,966	0.7%
31	Oregon	2,742	0.7%
7	Pennsylvania	17,163	4.1%
40	Rhode Island	916	0.2%
22	South Carolina	5,774	1.4%
47	South Dakota	117	0.0%
13	Tennessee	9,413	2.2%
2	Texas	37,580	8.9%
39	Utah	1,140	0.3%
49	Vermont	77	0.0%
18	Virginia	6,961	1.7%
21	Washington	5,797	1.4%
41	West Virginia	657	0.2%
24	Wisconsin	4,713	1.1%
48	Wyoming	93	0.0%

<u>RANK ORDER</u>

RANK	STATE	ROBBERIES	% of USA
1	California	64,968	15.4%
2	Texas	37,580	8.9%
3	New York	36,653	8.7%
4	Florida	32,581	7.7%
5	Illinois	25,272	6.0%
6	Ohio	17,871	4.2%
7	Pennsylvania	17,163	4.1%
8	New Jersey	13,905	3.3%
9	Georgia	13,432	3.2%
10	Maryland	13,417	3.2%
11	North Carolina	12,205	2.9%
12	Michigan	11,847	2.8%
13	Tennessee	9,413	2.2%
14	Arizona	8,000	1.9%
15	Massachusetts	7,169	1.7%
16	Louisiana	7,123	1.7%
17	Missouri	7,024	1.7%
18	Virginia	6,961	1.7%
19	Indiana	6,612	1.6%
20	Alabama	5,962	1.4%
21	Washington	5,797	1.4%
22	South Carolina	5,774	1.4%
23	Nevada	5,118	1.2%
24	Wisconsin	4,713	1.1%
25	Connecticut	4,060	1.0%
26	Minnesota	3,937	0.9%
27	Colorado	3,579	0.9%
28	Mississippi	3,356	0.8%
29	Kentucky	3,063	0.7%
30	Oklahoma	2,966	0.7%
31	Oregon	2,742	0.7%
32	Arkansas	2,524	0.6%
33	New Mexico	2,206	0.5%
34	Kansas	2,165	0.5%
35	Nebraska	1,359	0.3%
36	Hawaii	1,210	0.3%
37	Iowa	1,169	0.3%
38	Delaware	1,154	0.3%
39	Utah	1,140	0.3%
40	Rhode Island	916	0.2%
41	West Virginia	657	0.2%
42	Alaska	489	0.1%
43	New Hampshire	413	0.1%
44	Montana	283	0.1%
45	Maine	270	0.1%
46	Idaho	240	0.1%
47	South Dakota	117	0.0%
48	Wyoming	93	0.0%
49	Vermont	77	0.0%
50	North Dakota	58	0.0%
	District of Columbia	3,834	0.9%

Source: Federal Bureau of Investigation
   "Crime in the United States 2002" (Uniform Crime Reports, October 27, 2003)
**Robbery is the taking or attempting to take anything of value by force or threat of force.*

Percent Change in Number of Robberies: 2001 to 2002

National Percent Change = 0.7% Decrease*

ALPHA ORDER				RANK ORDER		
RANK	STATE	PERCENT CHANGE		RANK	STATE	PERCENT CHANGE
8	Alabama	6.8		1	Montana	23.0
35	Alaska	(4.9)		2	Nebraska	20.5
47	Arizona	(9.8)		3	Arkansas	15.7
3	Arkansas	15.7		4	South Dakota	13.6
21	California	0.5		5	Massachusetts	10.7
20	Colorado	0.7		5	Wyoming	10.7
31	Connecticut	(2.9)		7	Oklahoma	8.0
23	Delaware	(0.2)		8	Alabama	6.8
26	Florida	(0.9)		9	Texas	6.3
37	Georgia	(6.7)		10	Wisconsin	6.1
11	Hawaii	6.0		11	Hawaii	6.0
29	Idaho	(2.0)		12	Minnesota	4.8
18	Illinois	1.4		13	Ohio	3.9
41	Indiana	(7.8)		14	Nevada	3.8
19	Iowa	1.3		15	Maine	2.3
48	Kansas	(10.6)		16	Mississippi	1.9
36	Kentucky	(6.3)		17	Virginia	1.5
45	Louisiana	(9.4)		18	Illinois	1.4
15	Maine	2.3		19	Iowa	1.3
25	Maryland	(0.8)		20	Colorado	0.7
5	Massachusetts	10.7		21	California	0.5
44	Michigan	(8.4)		22	New York	0.3
12	Minnesota	4.8		23	Delaware	(0.2)
16	Mississippi	1.9		24	Oregon	(0.3)
46	Missouri	(9.6)		25	Maryland	(0.8)
1	Montana	23.0		26	Florida	(0.9)
2	Nebraska	20.5		27	New Jersey	(1.5)
14	Nevada	3.8		28	Pennsylvania	(1.9)
40	New Hampshire	(7.2)		29	Idaho	(2.0)
27	New Jersey	(1.5)		30	Washington	(2.3)
49	New Mexico	(18.1)		31	Connecticut	(2.9)
22	New York	0.3		32	North Dakota	(3.3)
43	North Carolina	(8.3)		33	South Carolina	(3.6)
32	North Dakota	(3.3)		34	Utah	(4.8)
13	Ohio	3.9		35	Alaska	(4.9)
7	Oklahoma	8.0		36	Kentucky	(6.3)
24	Oregon	(0.3)		37	Georgia	(6.7)
28	Pennsylvania	(1.9)		38	Rhode Island	(7.1)
38	Rhode Island	(7.1)		38	West Virginia	(7.1)
33	South Carolina	(3.6)		40	New Hampshire	(7.2)
4	South Dakota	13.6		41	Indiana	(7.8)
42	Tennessee	(7.9)		42	Tennessee	(7.9)
9	Texas	6.3		43	North Carolina	(8.3)
34	Utah	(4.8)		44	Michigan	(8.4)
50	Vermont	(28.0)		45	Louisiana	(9.4)
17	Virginia	1.5		46	Missouri	(9.6)
30	Washington	(2.3)		47	Arizona	(9.8)
38	West Virginia	(7.1)		48	Kansas	(10.6)
10	Wisconsin	6.1		49	New Mexico	(18.1)
5	Wyoming	10.7		50	Vermont	(28.0)
					District of Columbia	1.4

Source: Federal Bureau of Investigation
"Crime in the United States 2002" (Uniform Crime Reports, October 27, 2003)
*Robbery is the taking or attempting to take anything of value by force or threat of force.

Robbery Rate in 2002

National Rate = 145.9 Robberies per 100,000 Population*

ALPHA ORDER

RANK	STATE	RATE
18	Alabama	132.9
38	Alaska	76.0
14	Arizona	146.6
29	Arkansas	93.1
6	California	185.0
34	Colorado	79.4
22	Connecticut	117.3
15	Delaware	142.9
4	Florida	194.9
11	Georgia	156.9
26	Hawaii	97.2
47	Idaho	17.9
3	Illinois	200.6
25	Indiana	107.4
41	Iowa	39.8
33	Kansas	79.7
39	Kentucky	74.8
10	Louisiana	158.9
45	Maine	20.9
1	Maryland	245.8
24	Massachusetts	111.5
21	Michigan	117.9
36	Minnesota	78.4
23	Mississippi	116.9
19	Missouri	123.8
44	Montana	31.1
35	Nebraska	78.6
2	Nevada	235.5
43	New Hampshire	32.4
9	New Jersey	161.9
20	New Mexico	118.9
5	New York	191.3
13	North Carolina	146.7
50	North Dakota	9.1
12	Ohio	156.5
32	Oklahoma	84.9
37	Oregon	77.9
17	Pennsylvania	139.1
31	Rhode Island	85.6
16	South Carolina	140.6
48	South Dakota	15.4
8	Tennessee	162.4
7	Texas	172.5
40	Utah	49.2
49	Vermont	12.5
28	Virginia	95.4
27	Washington	95.5
42	West Virginia	36.5
30	Wisconsin	86.6
46	Wyoming	18.6

RANK ORDER

RANK	STATE	RATE
1	Maryland	245.8
2	Nevada	235.5
3	Illinois	200.6
4	Florida	194.9
5	New York	191.3
6	California	185.0
7	Texas	172.5
8	Tennessee	162.4
9	New Jersey	161.9
10	Louisiana	158.9
11	Georgia	156.9
12	Ohio	156.5
13	North Carolina	146.7
14	Arizona	146.6
15	Delaware	142.9
16	South Carolina	140.6
17	Pennsylvania	139.1
18	Alabama	132.9
19	Missouri	123.8
20	New Mexico	118.9
21	Michigan	117.9
22	Connecticut	117.3
23	Mississippi	116.9
24	Massachusetts	111.5
25	Indiana	107.4
26	Hawaii	97.2
27	Washington	95.5
28	Virginia	95.4
29	Arkansas	93.1
30	Wisconsin	86.6
31	Rhode Island	85.6
32	Oklahoma	84.9
33	Kansas	79.7
34	Colorado	79.4
35	Nebraska	78.6
36	Minnesota	78.4
37	Oregon	77.9
38	Alaska	76.0
39	Kentucky	74.8
40	Utah	49.2
41	Iowa	39.8
42	West Virginia	36.5
43	New Hampshire	32.4
44	Montana	31.1
45	Maine	20.9
46	Wyoming	18.6
47	Idaho	17.9
48	South Dakota	15.4
49	Vermont	12.5
50	North Dakota	9.1
	District of Columbia	671.6

Source: Federal Bureau of Investigation
   "Crime in the United States 2002" (Uniform Crime Reports, October 27, 2003)
*Robbery is the taking or attempting to take anything of value by force or threat of force.

Aggravated Assaults in 2002

National Total = 894,348 Aggravated Assaults*

ALPHA ORDER

RANK	STATE	ASSAULTS	% of USA
23	Alabama	12,002	1.3%
42	Alaska	2,594	0.3%
16	Arizona	20,176	2.3%
26	Arkansas	8,081	0.9%
1	California	130,827	14.6%
25	Colorado	10,058	1.1%
34	Connecticut	5,897	0.7%
38	Delaware	3,298	0.4%
2	Florida	88,476	9.9%
12	Georgia	23,125	2.6%
44	Hawaii	1,656	0.2%
41	Idaho	2,646	0.3%
5	Illinois	47,695	5.3%
19	Indiana	13,184	1.5%
31	Iowa	6,378	0.7%
30	Kansas	6,951	0.8%
29	Kentucky	7,083	0.8%
15	Louisiana	20,445	2.3%
48	Maine	735	0.1%
9	Maryland	26,715	3.0%
13	Massachusetts	22,018	2.5%
6	Michigan	36,417	4.1%
28	Minnesota	7,106	0.8%
35	Mississippi	5,111	0.6%
14	Missouri	21,737	2.4%
40	Montana	2,661	0.3%
36	Nebraska	3,557	0.4%
27	Nevada	7,629	0.9%
45	New Hampshire	1,185	0.1%
18	New Jersey	16,579	1.9%
24	New Mexico	10,334	1.2%
4	New York	53,583	6.0%
11	North Carolina	24,169	2.7%
50	North Dakota	270	0.0%
17	Ohio	16,922	1.9%
20	Oklahoma	12,885	1.4%
32	Oregon	6,246	0.7%
8	Pennsylvania	28,060	3.1%
43	Rhode Island	1,699	0.2%
10	South Carolina	25,730	2.9%
47	South Dakota	861	0.1%
7	Tennessee	29,439	3.3%
3	Texas	78,628	8.8%
37	Utah	3,358	0.4%
49	Vermont	442	0.0%
22	Virginia	12,068	1.3%
21	Washington	12,249	1.4%
39	West Virginia	3,179	0.4%
33	Wisconsin	6,134	0.7%
46	Wyoming	1,108	0.1%

RANK ORDER

RANK	STATE	ASSAULTS	% of USA
1	California	130,827	14.6%
2	Florida	88,476	9.9%
3	Texas	78,628	8.8%
4	New York	53,583	6.0%
5	Illinois	47,695	5.3%
6	Michigan	36,417	4.1%
7	Tennessee	29,439	3.3%
8	Pennsylvania	28,060	3.1%
9	Maryland	26,715	3.0%
10	South Carolina	25,730	2.9%
11	North Carolina	24,169	2.7%
12	Georgia	23,125	2.6%
13	Massachusetts	22,018	2.5%
14	Missouri	21,737	2.4%
15	Louisiana	20,445	2.3%
16	Arizona	20,176	2.3%
17	Ohio	16,922	1.9%
18	New Jersey	16,579	1.9%
19	Indiana	13,184	1.5%
20	Oklahoma	12,885	1.4%
21	Washington	12,249	1.4%
22	Virginia	12,068	1.3%
23	Alabama	12,002	1.3%
24	New Mexico	10,334	1.2%
25	Colorado	10,058	1.1%
26	Arkansas	8,081	0.9%
27	Nevada	7,629	0.9%
28	Minnesota	7,106	0.8%
29	Kentucky	7,083	0.8%
30	Kansas	6,951	0.8%
31	Iowa	6,378	0.7%
32	Oregon	6,246	0.7%
33	Wisconsin	6,134	0.7%
34	Connecticut	5,897	0.7%
35	Mississippi	5,111	0.6%
36	Nebraska	3,557	0.4%
37	Utah	3,358	0.4%
38	Delaware	3,298	0.4%
39	West Virginia	3,179	0.4%
40	Montana	2,661	0.3%
41	Idaho	2,646	0.3%
42	Alaska	2,594	0.3%
43	Rhode Island	1,699	0.2%
44	Hawaii	1,656	0.2%
45	New Hampshire	1,185	0.1%
46	Wyoming	1,108	0.1%
47	South Dakota	861	0.1%
48	Maine	735	0.1%
49	Vermont	442	0.0%
50	North Dakota	270	0.0%
	District of Columbia	4,962	0.6%

Source: Federal Bureau of Investigation
   "Crime in the United States 2002" (Uniform Crime Reports, October 27, 2003)
*Aggravated assault is an attack for the purpose of inflicting severe bodily injury.

Percent Change in Number of Aggravated Assaults: 2001 to 2002

National Percent Change = 1.6% Decrease*

<u>ALPHA ORDER</u>

RANK	STATE	PERCENT CHANGE
26	Alabama	(2.0)
33	Alaska	(3.2)
4	Arizona	12.8
47	Arkansas	(9.9)
38	California	(3.9)
13	Colorado	2.1
48	Connecticut	(10.2)
17	Delaware	0.9
27	Florida	(2.1)
41	Georgia	(5.6)
5	Hawaii	8.0
9	Idaho	5.4
36	Illinois	(3.3)
25	Indiana	(1.9)
8	Iowa	6.1
44	Kansas	(6.7)
3	Kentucky	17.9
28	Louisiana	(2.2)
49	Maine	(11.0)
18	Maryland	0.2
19	Massachusetts	(0.4)
19	Michigan	(0.4)
15	Minnesota	1.1
36	Mississippi	(3.3)
11	Missouri	3.8
31	Montana	(2.7)
21	Nebraska	(1.5)
2	Nevada	19.9
33	New Hampshire	(3.2)
39	New Jersey	(4.6)
32	New Mexico	(2.9)
42	New York	(5.9)
23	North Carolina	(1.6)
21	North Dakota	(1.5)
40	Ohio	(5.5)
33	Oklahoma	(3.2)
43	Oregon	(6.0)
30	Pennsylvania	(2.6)
45	Rhode Island	(7.5)
12	South Carolina	2.8
1	South Dakota	21.3
24	Tennessee	(1.7)
14	Texas	1.7
7	Utah	6.5
10	Vermont	4.5
16	Virginia	1.0
29	Washington	(2.4)
50	West Virginia	(19.9)
46	Wisconsin	(8.6)
5	Wyoming	8.0

<u>RANK ORDER</u>

RANK	STATE	PERCENT CHANGE
1	South Dakota	21.3
2	Nevada	19.9
3	Kentucky	17.9
4	Arizona	12.8
5	Hawaii	8.0
5	Wyoming	8.0
7	Utah	6.5
8	Iowa	6.1
9	Idaho	5.4
10	Vermont	4.5
11	Missouri	3.8
12	South Carolina	2.8
13	Colorado	2.1
14	Texas	1.7
15	Minnesota	1.1
16	Virginia	1.0
17	Delaware	0.9
18	Maryland	0.2
19	Massachusetts	(0.4)
19	Michigan	(0.4)
21	Nebraska	(1.5)
21	North Dakota	(1.5)
23	North Carolina	(1.6)
24	Tennessee	(1.7)
25	Indiana	(1.9)
26	Alabama	(2.0)
27	Florida	(2.1)
28	Louisiana	(2.2)
29	Washington	(2.4)
30	Pennsylvania	(2.6)
31	Montana	(2.7)
32	New Mexico	(2.9)
33	Alaska	(3.2)
33	New Hampshire	(3.2)
33	Oklahoma	(3.2)
36	Illinois	(3.3)
36	Mississippi	(3.3)
38	California	(3.9)
39	New Jersey	(4.6)
40	Ohio	(5.5)
41	Georgia	(5.6)
42	New York	(5.9)
43	Oregon	(6.0)
44	Kansas	(6.7)
45	Rhode Island	(7.5)
46	Wisconsin	(8.6)
47	Arkansas	(9.9)
48	Connecticut	(10.2)
49	Maine	(11.0)
50	West Virginia	(19.9)
	District of Columbia	(0.8)

Source: Federal Bureau of Investigation
  "Crime in the United States 2002" (Uniform Crime Reports, October 27, 2003)
*Aggravated assault is an attack for the purpose of inflicting severe bodily injury.

Aggravated Assault Rate in 2002

National Rate = 310.1 Aggravated Assaults per 100,000 Population*

ALPHA ORDER

RANK	STATE	RATE
23	Alabama	267.5
8	Alaska	402.9
12	Arizona	369.8
18	Arkansas	298.2
11	California	372.6
26	Colorado	223.2
38	Connecticut	170.4
7	Delaware	408.5
3	Florida	529.4
22	Georgia	270.1
44	Hawaii	133.0
32	Idaho	197.3
10	Illinois	378.5
29	Indiana	214.1
28	Iowa	217.2
24	Kansas	255.9
37	Kentucky	173.1
6	Louisiana	456.1
49	Maine	56.8
5	Maryland	489.5
17	Massachusetts	342.5
14	Michigan	362.3
43	Minnesota	141.6
34	Mississippi	178.0
9	Missouri	383.2
19	Montana	292.6
30	Nebraska	205.7
16	Nevada	351.0
47	New Hampshire	92.9
33	New Jersey	193.0
2	New Mexico	557.1
21	New York	279.7
20	North Carolina	290.5
50	North Dakota	42.6
41	Ohio	148.2
13	Oklahoma	368.8
35	Oregon	177.4
25	Pennsylvania	227.5
40	Rhode Island	158.8
1	South Carolina	626.5
45	South Dakota	113.1
4	Tennessee	507.8
15	Texas	361.0
42	Utah	145.0
48	Vermont	71.7
39	Virginia	165.5
31	Washington	201.8
36	West Virginia	176.4
46	Wisconsin	112.7
27	Wyoming	222.2

RANK ORDER

RANK	STATE	RATE
1	South Carolina	626.5
2	New Mexico	557.1
3	Florida	529.4
4	Tennessee	507.8
5	Maryland	489.5
6	Louisiana	456.1
7	Delaware	408.5
8	Alaska	402.9
9	Missouri	383.2
10	Illinois	378.5
11	California	372.6
12	Arizona	369.8
13	Oklahoma	368.8
14	Michigan	362.3
15	Texas	361.0
16	Nevada	351.0
17	Massachusetts	342.5
18	Arkansas	298.2
19	Montana	292.6
20	North Carolina	290.5
21	New York	279.7
22	Georgia	270.1
23	Alabama	267.5
24	Kansas	255.9
25	Pennsylvania	227.5
26	Colorado	223.2
27	Wyoming	222.2
28	Iowa	217.2
29	Indiana	214.1
30	Nebraska	205.7
31	Washington	201.8
32	Idaho	197.3
33	New Jersey	193.0
34	Mississippi	178.0
35	Oregon	177.4
36	West Virginia	176.4
37	Kentucky	173.1
38	Connecticut	170.4
39	Virginia	165.5
40	Rhode Island	158.8
41	Ohio	148.2
42	Utah	145.0
43	Minnesota	141.6
44	Hawaii	133.0
45	South Dakota	113.1
46	Wisconsin	112.7
47	New Hampshire	92.9
48	Vermont	71.7
49	Maine	56.8
50	North Dakota	42.6
	District of Columbia	869.2

Source: Federal Bureau of Investigation
"Crime in the United States 2002" (Uniform Crime Reports, October 27, 2003)
**Aggravated assault is an attack for the purpose of inflicting severe bodily injury.*

Property Crimes in 2002

National Total = 10,450,893 Property Crimes*

<u>ALPHA ORDER</u>

RANK	STATE	CRIMES	% of USA
21	Alabama	180,400	1.7%
46	Alaska	24,118	0.2%
10	Arizona	318,296	3.0%
30	Arkansas	101,171	1.0%
1	California	1,176,484	11.3%
22	Colorado	180,054	1.7%
33	Connecticut	92,952	0.9%
44	Delaware	26,967	0.3%
3	Florida	777,236	7.4%
8	Georgia	346,559	3.3%
37	Hawaii	71,976	0.7%
40	Idaho	39,128	0.4%
6	Illinois	427,872	4.1%
17	Indiana	208,965	2.0%
34	Iowa	92,877	0.9%
31	Kansas	100,768	1.0%
29	Kentucky	107,381	1.0%
19	Louisiana	198,838	1.9%
42	Maine	32,985	0.3%
16	Maryland	217,105	2.1%
23	Massachusetts	167,753	1.6%
9	Michigan	335,060	3.2%
25	Minnesota	164,026	1.6%
28	Mississippi	109,584	1.0%
14	Missouri	230,520	2.2%
43	Montana	28,751	0.3%
38	Nebraska	68,178	0.7%
35	Nevada	83,896	0.8%
45	New Hampshire	26,250	0.3%
15	New Jersey	227,621	2.2%
36	New Mexico	80,477	0.8%
4	New York	442,091	4.2%
7	North Carolina	353,708	3.4%
50	North Dakota	14,762	0.1%
5	Ohio	428,976	4.1%
27	Oklahoma	148,128	1.4%
26	Oregon	161,145	1.5%
11	Pennsylvania	300,868	2.9%
41	Rhode Island	35,342	0.3%
20	South Carolina	183,808	1.8%
48	South Dakota	15,992	0.2%
13	Tennessee	249,399	2.4%
2	Texas	1,004,274	9.6%
32	Utah	97,641	0.9%
49	Vermont	14,942	0.1%
18	Virginia	207,783	2.0%
12	Washington	288,967	2.8%
39	West Virginia	41,099	0.4%
24	Wisconsin	164,749	1.6%
47	Wyoming	16,494	0.2%

<u>RANK ORDER</u>

RANK	STATE	CRIMES	% of USA
1	California	1,176,484	11.3%
2	Texas	1,004,274	9.6%
3	Florida	777,236	7.4%
4	New York	442,091	4.2%
5	Ohio	428,976	4.1%
6	Illinois	427,872	4.1%
7	North Carolina	353,708	3.4%
8	Georgia	346,559	3.3%
9	Michigan	335,060	3.2%
10	Arizona	318,296	3.0%
11	Pennsylvania	300,868	2.9%
12	Washington	288,967	2.8%
13	Tennessee	249,399	2.4%
14	Missouri	230,520	2.2%
15	New Jersey	227,621	2.2%
16	Maryland	217,105	2.1%
17	Indiana	208,965	2.0%
18	Virginia	207,783	2.0%
19	Louisiana	198,838	1.9%
20	South Carolina	183,808	1.8%
21	Alabama	180,400	1.7%
22	Colorado	180,054	1.7%
23	Massachusetts	167,753	1.6%
24	Wisconsin	164,749	1.6%
25	Minnesota	164,026	1.6%
26	Oregon	161,145	1.5%
27	Oklahoma	148,128	1.4%
28	Mississippi	109,584	1.0%
29	Kentucky	107,381	1.0%
30	Arkansas	101,171	1.0%
31	Kansas	100,768	1.0%
32	Utah	97,641	0.9%
33	Connecticut	92,952	0.9%
34	Iowa	92,877	0.9%
35	Nevada	83,896	0.8%
36	New Mexico	80,477	0.8%
37	Hawaii	71,976	0.7%
38	Nebraska	68,178	0.7%
39	West Virginia	41,099	0.4%
40	Idaho	39,128	0.4%
41	Rhode Island	35,342	0.3%
42	Maine	32,985	0.3%
43	Montana	28,751	0.3%
44	Delaware	26,967	0.3%
45	New Hampshire	26,250	0.3%
46	Alaska	24,118	0.2%
47	Wyoming	16,494	0.2%
48	South Dakota	15,992	0.2%
49	Vermont	14,942	0.1%
50	North Dakota	14,762	0.1%
	District of Columbia	36,477	0.3%

Source: Federal Bureau of Investigation
"Crime in the United States 2002" (Uniform Crime Reports, October 27, 2003)
**Property crimes are offenses of burglary, larceny-theft and motor vehicle theft.*

Percent Change in Number of Property Crimes: 2001 to 2002

National Percent Change = 0.1% Increase*

ALPHA ORDER				RANK ORDER		
RANK	STATE	PERCENT CHANGE		RANK	STATE	PERCENT CHANGE
8	Alabama	4.1		1	Hawaii	14.6
8	Alaska	4.1		2	Arizona	8.3
2	Arizona	8.3		2	Nevada	8.3
14	Arkansas	2.1		4	Utah	7.3
10	California	3.7		5	Colorado	5.4
5	Colorado	5.4		6	Iowa	4.8
37	Connecticut	(2.5)		7	Oklahoma	4.6
34	Delaware	(1.6)		8	Alabama	4.1
25	Florida	(0.7)		8	Alaska	4.1
21	Georgia	(0.4)		10	California	3.7
1	Hawaii	14.6		11	Texas	2.8
12	Idaho	2.5		12	Idaho	2.5
34	Illinois	(1.6)		13	Wyoming	2.3
29	Indiana	(1.2)		14	Arkansas	2.1
6	Iowa	4.8		15	Washington	0.6
46	Kansas	(4.5)		16	Massachusetts	0.4
18	Kentucky	0.0		17	Virginia	0.1
45	Louisiana	(4.3)		18	Kentucky	0.0
22	Maine	(0.5)		18	Mississippi	0.0
26	Maryland	(1.1)		18	West Virginia	0.0
16	Massachusetts	0.4		21	Georgia	(0.4)
48	Michigan	(4.9)		22	Maine	(0.5)
24	Minnesota	(0.6)		22	North Dakota	(0.5)
18	Mississippi	0.0		24	Minnesota	(0.6)
42	Missouri	(3.3)		25	Florida	(0.7)
47	Montana	(4.7)		26	Maryland	(1.1)
26	Nebraska	(1.1)		26	Nebraska	(1.1)
2	Nevada	8.3		26	Rhode Island	(1.1)
40	New Hampshire	(3.1)		29	Indiana	(1.2)
49	New Jersey	(5.4)		29	South Carolina	(1.2)
41	New Mexico	(3.2)		31	Wisconsin	(1.3)
43	New York	(3.5)		32	Ohio	(1.4)
38	North Carolina	(2.8)		32	Tennessee	(1.4)
22	North Dakota	(0.5)		34	Delaware	(1.6)
32	Ohio	(1.4)		34	Illinois	(1.6)
7	Oklahoma	4.6		36	Oregon	(2.1)
36	Oregon	(2.1)		37	Connecticut	(2.5)
44	Pennsylvania	(4.0)		38	North Carolina	(2.8)
26	Rhode Island	(1.1)		39	South Dakota	(2.9)
29	South Carolina	(1.2)		40	New Hampshire	(3.1)
39	South Dakota	(2.9)		41	New Mexico	(3.2)
32	Tennessee	(1.4)		42	Missouri	(3.3)
11	Texas	2.8		43	New York	(3.5)
4	Utah	7.3		44	Pennsylvania	(4.0)
50	Vermont	(8.5)		45	Louisiana	(4.3)
17	Virginia	0.1		46	Kansas	(4.5)
15	Washington	0.6		47	Montana	(4.7)
18	West Virginia	0.0		48	Michigan	(4.9)
31	Wisconsin	(1.3)		49	New Jersey	(5.4)
13	Wyoming	2.3		50	Vermont	(8.5)
					District of Columbia	3.5

Source: Federal Bureau of Investigation
   "Crime in the United States 2002" (Uniform Crime Reports, October 27, 2003)
*Property crimes are offenses of burglary, larceny-theft and motor vehicle theft.

Property Crime Rate in 2002

National Rate = 3,624.1 Property Crimes per 100,000 Population*

ALPHA ORDER

RANK	STATE	RATE
16	Alabama	4,020.9
23	Alaska	3,746.3
1	Arizona	5,833.4
24	Arkansas	3,733.1
28	California	3,350.3
17	Colorado	3,995.4
39	Connecticut	2,686.1
29	Delaware	3,340.0
4	Florida	4,650.4
15	Georgia	4,048.4
2	Hawaii	5,781.7
37	Idaho	2,917.5
26	Illinois	3,395.6
27	Indiana	3,392.8
34	Iowa	3,162.6
25	Kansas	3,710.3
41	Kentucky	2,623.6
8	Louisiana	4,435.7
43	Maine	2,548.2
18	Maryland	3,977.6
42	Massachusetts	2,609.8
30	Michigan	3,333.8
33	Minnesota	3,267.6
21	Mississippi	3,815.9
14	Missouri	4,063.8
35	Montana	3,161.4
19	Nebraska	3,942.8
20	Nevada	3,860.0
50	New Hampshire	2,058.7
40	New Jersey	2,649.7
9	New Mexico	4,338.2
47	New York	2,307.7
11	North Carolina	4,251.2
46	North Dakota	2,328.0
22	Ohio	3,755.9
12	Oklahoma	4,239.8
6	Oregon	4,576.0
44	Pennsylvania	2,439.1
32	Rhode Island	3,303.8
7	South Carolina	4,475.3
49	South Dakota	2,101.3
10	Tennessee	4,302.0
5	Texas	4,611.0
13	Utah	4,215.5
45	Vermont	2,423.3
38	Virginia	2,848.9
3	Washington	4,761.4
48	West Virginia	2,280.9
36	Wisconsin	3,027.8
31	Wyoming	3,307.4

RANK ORDER

RANK	STATE	RATE
1	Arizona	5,833.4
2	Hawaii	5,781.7
3	Washington	4,761.4
4	Florida	4,650.4
5	Texas	4,611.0
6	Oregon	4,576.0
7	South Carolina	4,475.3
8	Louisiana	4,435.7
9	New Mexico	4,338.2
10	Tennessee	4,302.0
11	North Carolina	4,251.2
12	Oklahoma	4,239.8
13	Utah	4,215.5
14	Missouri	4,063.8
15	Georgia	4,048.4
16	Alabama	4,020.9
17	Colorado	3,995.4
18	Maryland	3,977.6
19	Nebraska	3,942.8
20	Nevada	3,860.0
21	Mississippi	3,815.9
22	Ohio	3,755.9
23	Alaska	3,746.3
24	Arkansas	3,733.1
25	Kansas	3,710.3
26	Illinois	3,395.6
27	Indiana	3,392.8
28	California	3,350.3
29	Delaware	3,340.0
30	Michigan	3,333.8
31	Wyoming	3,307.4
32	Rhode Island	3,303.8
33	Minnesota	3,267.6
34	Iowa	3,162.6
35	Montana	3,161.4
36	Wisconsin	3,027.8
37	Idaho	2,917.5
38	Virginia	2,848.9
39	Connecticut	2,686.1
40	New Jersey	2,649.7
41	Kentucky	2,623.6
42	Massachusetts	2,609.8
43	Maine	2,548.2
44	Pennsylvania	2,439.1
45	Vermont	2,423.3
46	North Dakota	2,328.0
47	New York	2,307.7
48	West Virginia	2,280.9
49	South Dakota	2,101.3
50	New Hampshire	2,058.7
	District of Columbia	6,389.4

Source: Federal Bureau of Investigation
   "Crime in the United States 2002" (Uniform Crime Reports, October 27, 2003)
*Property crimes are offenses of burglary, larceny-theft and motor vehicle theft.

Percent Change in Property Crime Rate: 2001 to 2002

National Percent Change = 0.9% Decrease*

<u>ALPHA ORDER</u>

RANK	STATE	PERCENT CHANGE
7	Alabama	3.7
9	Alaska	2.5
3	Arizona	5.3
11	Arkansas	1.5
10	California	2.2
8	Colorado	3.6
36	Connecticut	(3.2)
35	Delaware	(2.9)
34	Florida	(2.7)
29	Georgia	(2.2)
1	Hawaii	12.9
13	Idaho	0.9
29	Illinois	(2.2)
24	Indiana	(1.7)
4	Iowa	4.6
46	Kansas	(5.0)
19	Kentucky	(0.6)
45	Louisiana	(4.5)
22	Maine	(1.3)
33	Maryland	(2.4)
15	Massachusetts	0.0
48	Michigan	(5.3)
22	Minnesota	(1.3)
18	Mississippi	(0.4)
40	Missouri	(3.9)
47	Montana	(5.1)
24	Nebraska	(1.7)
5	Nevada	4.5
42	New Hampshire	(4.3)
49	New Jersey	(6.2)
44	New Mexico	(4.4)
39	New York	(3.8)
41	North Carolina	(4.1)
17	North Dakota	(0.1)
24	Ohio	(1.7)
6	Oklahoma	3.8
38	Oregon	(3.4)
42	Pennsylvania	(4.3)
28	Rhode Island	(2.0)
32	South Carolina	(2.3)
37	South Dakota	(3.3)
29	Tennessee	(2.2)
13	Texas	0.9
2	Utah	5.6
50	Vermont	(9.1)
21	Virginia	(1.2)
19	Washington	(0.6)
15	West Virginia	0.0
27	Wisconsin	(1.9)
12	Wyoming	1.3

<u>RANK ORDER</u>

RANK	STATE	PERCENT CHANGE
1	Hawaii	12.9
2	Utah	5.6
3	Arizona	5.3
4	Iowa	4.6
5	Nevada	4.5
6	Oklahoma	3.8
7	Alabama	3.7
8	Colorado	3.6
9	Alaska	2.5
10	California	2.2
11	Arkansas	1.5
12	Wyoming	1.3
13	Idaho	0.9
13	Texas	0.9
15	Massachusetts	0.0
15	West Virginia	0.0
17	North Dakota	(0.1)
18	Mississippi	(0.4)
19	Kentucky	(0.6)
19	Washington	(0.6)
21	Virginia	(1.2)
22	Maine	(1.3)
22	Minnesota	(1.3)
24	Indiana	(1.7)
24	Nebraska	(1.7)
24	Ohio	(1.7)
27	Wisconsin	(1.9)
28	Rhode Island	(2.0)
29	Georgia	(2.2)
29	Illinois	(2.2)
29	Tennessee	(2.2)
32	South Carolina	(2.3)
33	Maryland	(2.4)
34	Florida	(2.7)
35	Delaware	(2.9)
36	Connecticut	(3.2)
37	South Dakota	(3.3)
38	Oregon	(3.4)
39	New York	(3.8)
40	Missouri	(3.9)
41	North Carolina	(4.1)
42	New Hampshire	(4.3)
42	Pennsylvania	(4.3)
44	New Mexico	(4.4)
45	Louisiana	(4.5)
46	Kansas	(5.0)
47	Montana	(5.1)
48	Michigan	(5.3)
49	New Jersey	(6.2)
50	Vermont	(9.1)

	District of Columbia	4.1

Source: Federal Bureau of Investigation
   "Crime in the United States 2002" (Uniform Crime Reports, October 27, 2003)
*Property crimes are offenses of burglary, larceny-theft and motor vehicle theft.

Burglaries in 2002

National Total = 2,151,875 Burglaries*

ALPHA ORDER

RANK	STATE	BURGLARIES	% of USA
19	Alabama	42,578	2.0%
45	Alaska	3,908	0.2%
11	Arizona	59,087	2.7%
30	Arkansas	23,229	1.1%
1	California	238,428	11.1%
24	Colorado	31,678	1.5%
35	Connecticut	17,088	0.8%
43	Delaware	5,355	0.2%
3	Florida	177,242	8.2%
8	Georgia	73,932	3.4%
37	Hawaii	12,722	0.6%
40	Idaho	7,441	0.3%
6	Illinois	81,123	3.8%
18	Indiana	42,605	2.0%
34	Iowa	18,643	0.9%
31	Kansas	19,679	0.9%
28	Kentucky	27,855	1.3%
14	Louisiana	45,350	2.1%
41	Maine	6,965	0.3%
20	Maryland	39,765	1.8%
22	Massachusetts	33,243	1.5%
9	Michigan	70,970	3.3%
26	Minnesota	28,034	1.3%
25	Mississippi	29,593	1.4%
17	Missouri	42,721	2.0%
47	Montana	3,289	0.2%
38	Nebraska	10,329	0.5%
33	Nevada	18,951	0.9%
44	New Hampshire	4,838	0.2%
15	New Jersey	43,898	2.0%
32	New Mexico	19,634	0.9%
7	New York	76,700	3.6%
4	North Carolina	99,535	4.6%
50	North Dakota	2,243	0.1%
5	Ohio	99,164	4.6%
21	Oklahoma	35,171	1.6%
29	Oregon	25,696	1.2%
12	Pennsylvania	55,610	2.6%
42	Rhode Island	6,415	0.3%
16	South Carolina	43,745	2.0%
48	South Dakota	3,034	0.1%
10	Tennessee	61,248	2.8%
2	Texas	212,602	9.9%
36	Utah	15,124	0.7%
46	Vermont	3,489	0.2%
23	Virginia	31,757	1.5%
13	Washington	54,948	2.6%
39	West Virginia	9,677	0.4%
27	Wisconsin	27,926	1.3%
49	Wyoming	2,448	0.1%

RANK ORDER

RANK	STATE	BURGLARIES	% of USA
1	California	238,428	11.1%
2	Texas	212,602	9.9%
3	Florida	177,242	8.2%
4	North Carolina	99,535	4.6%
5	Ohio	99,164	4.6%
6	Illinois	81,123	3.8%
7	New York	76,700	3.6%
8	Georgia	73,932	3.4%
9	Michigan	70,970	3.3%
10	Tennessee	61,248	2.8%
11	Arizona	59,087	2.7%
12	Pennsylvania	55,610	2.6%
13	Washington	54,948	2.6%
14	Louisiana	45,350	2.1%
15	New Jersey	43,898	2.0%
16	South Carolina	43,745	2.0%
17	Missouri	42,721	2.0%
18	Indiana	42,605	2.0%
19	Alabama	42,578	2.0%
20	Maryland	39,765	1.8%
21	Oklahoma	35,171	1.6%
22	Massachusetts	33,243	1.5%
23	Virginia	31,757	1.5%
24	Colorado	31,678	1.5%
25	Mississippi	29,593	1.4%
26	Minnesota	28,034	1.3%
27	Wisconsin	27,926	1.3%
28	Kentucky	27,855	1.3%
29	Oregon	25,696	1.2%
30	Arkansas	23,229	1.1%
31	Kansas	19,679	0.9%
32	New Mexico	19,634	0.9%
33	Nevada	18,951	0.9%
34	Iowa	18,643	0.9%
35	Connecticut	17,088	0.8%
36	Utah	15,124	0.7%
37	Hawaii	12,722	0.6%
38	Nebraska	10,329	0.5%
39	West Virginia	9,677	0.4%
40	Idaho	7,441	0.3%
41	Maine	6,965	0.3%
42	Rhode Island	6,415	0.3%
43	Delaware	5,355	0.2%
44	New Hampshire	4,838	0.2%
45	Alaska	3,908	0.2%
46	Vermont	3,489	0.2%
47	Montana	3,289	0.2%
48	South Dakota	3,034	0.1%
49	Wyoming	2,448	0.1%
50	North Dakota	2,243	0.1%
	District of Columbia	5,170	0.2%

Source: Federal Bureau of Investigation
   "Crime in the United States 2002" (Uniform Crime Reports, October 27, 2003)
*Burglary is the unlawful entry of a structure to commit a felony or theft. Attempts are included.

Percent Change in Number of Burglaries: 2001 to 2002

National Percent Change = 1.7% Increase*

ALPHA ORDER

RANK	STATE	PERCENT CHANGE
10	Alabama	4.8
27	Alaska	1.6
7	Arizona	7.8
11	Arkansas	4.7
20	California	2.6
2	Colorado	11.0
33	Connecticut	(0.4)
12	Delaware	4.1
30	Florida	0.7
18	Georgia	3.0
1	Hawaii	14.0
37	Idaho	(0.9)
22	Illinois	2.5
33	Indiana	(0.4)
4	Iowa	10.4
45	Kansas	(4.1)
17	Kentucky	3.3
43	Louisiana	(2.4)
28	Maine	1.0
46	Maryland	(4.3)
22	Massachusetts	2.5
40	Michigan	(1.5)
5	Minnesota	10.0
36	Mississippi	(0.8)
35	Missouri	(0.6)
50	Montana	(10.4)
9	Nebraska	5.8
8	Nevada	7.0
38	New Hampshire	(1.0)
49	New Jersey	(6.2)
32	New Mexico	0.4
47	New York	(4.6)
42	North Carolina	(2.3)
15	North Dakota	3.6
24	Ohio	2.3
26	Oklahoma	1.7
44	Oregon	(3.6)
24	Pennsylvania	2.3
48	Rhode Island	(6.0)
19	South Carolina	2.7
41	South Dakota	(1.7)
20	Tennessee	2.6
13	Texas	4.0
6	Utah	9.6
3	Vermont	10.8
31	Virginia	0.5
15	Washington	3.6
29	West Virginia	0.8
14	Wisconsin	3.7
39	Wyoming	(1.3)

RANK ORDER

RANK	STATE	PERCENT CHANGE
1	Hawaii	14.0
2	Colorado	11.0
3	Vermont	10.8
4	Iowa	10.4
5	Minnesota	10.0
6	Utah	9.6
7	Arizona	7.8
8	Nevada	7.0
9	Nebraska	5.8
10	Alabama	4.8
11	Arkansas	4.7
12	Delaware	4.1
13	Texas	4.0
14	Wisconsin	3.7
15	North Dakota	3.6
15	Washington	3.6
17	Kentucky	3.3
18	Georgia	3.0
19	South Carolina	2.7
20	California	2.6
20	Tennessee	2.6
22	Illinois	2.5
22	Massachusetts	2.5
24	Ohio	2.3
24	Pennsylvania	2.3
26	Oklahoma	1.7
27	Alaska	1.6
28	Maine	1.0
29	West Virginia	0.8
30	Florida	0.7
31	Virginia	0.5
32	New Mexico	0.4
33	Connecticut	(0.4)
33	Indiana	(0.4)
35	Missouri	(0.6)
36	Mississippi	(0.8)
37	Idaho	(0.9)
38	New Hampshire	(1.0)
39	Wyoming	(1.3)
40	Michigan	(1.5)
41	South Dakota	(1.7)
42	North Carolina	(2.3)
43	Louisiana	(2.4)
44	Oregon	(3.6)
45	Kansas	(4.1)
46	Maryland	(4.3)
47	New York	(4.6)
48	Rhode Island	(6.0)
49	New Jersey	(6.2)
50	Montana	(10.4)

District of Columbia	4.5

Burglary Rate in 2002

National Rate = 746.2 Burglaries per 100,000 Population*

<u>ALPHA ORDER</u>

RANK	STATE	RATE
12	Alabama	949.0
31	Alaska	607.0
2	Arizona	1,082.9
17	Arkansas	857.1
26	California	679.0
23	Colorado	702.9
42	Connecticut	493.8
27	Delaware	663.3
4	Florida	1,060.5
16	Georgia	863.7
8	Hawaii	1,021.9
36	Idaho	554.8
29	Illinois	643.8
24	Indiana	691.7
30	Iowa	634.8
21	Kansas	724.6
25	Kentucky	680.6
9	Louisiana	1,011.7
37	Maine	538.1
20	Maryland	728.5
39	Massachusetts	517.2
22	Michigan	706.1
35	Minnesota	558.5
7	Mississippi	1,030.5
18	Missouri	753.1
49	Montana	361.6
33	Nebraska	597.3
14	Nevada	871.9
48	New Hampshire	379.4
41	New Jersey	511.0
5	New Mexico	1,058.4
46	New York	400.4
1	North Carolina	1,196.3
50	North Dakota	353.7
15	Ohio	868.2
10	Oklahoma	1,006.7
19	Oregon	729.7
44	Pennsylvania	450.8
32	Rhode Island	599.7
3	South Carolina	1,065.1
47	South Dakota	398.7
6	Tennessee	1,056.5
11	Texas	976.1
28	Utah	653.0
34	Vermont	565.9
45	Virginia	435.4
13	Washington	905.4
38	West Virginia	537.1
40	Wisconsin	513.2
43	Wyoming	490.9

<u>RANK ORDER</u>

RANK	STATE	RATE
1	North Carolina	1,196.3
2	Arizona	1,082.9
3	South Carolina	1,065.1
4	Florida	1,060.5
5	New Mexico	1,058.4
6	Tennessee	1,056.5
7	Mississippi	1,030.5
8	Hawaii	1,021.9
9	Louisiana	1,011.7
10	Oklahoma	1,006.7
11	Texas	976.1
12	Alabama	949.0
13	Washington	905.4
14	Nevada	871.9
15	Ohio	868.2
16	Georgia	863.7
17	Arkansas	857.1
18	Missouri	753.1
19	Oregon	729.7
20	Maryland	728.5
21	Kansas	724.6
22	Michigan	706.1
23	Colorado	702.9
24	Indiana	691.7
25	Kentucky	680.6
26	California	679.0
27	Delaware	663.3
28	Utah	653.0
29	Illinois	643.8
30	Iowa	634.8
31	Alaska	607.0
32	Rhode Island	599.7
33	Nebraska	597.3
34	Vermont	565.9
35	Minnesota	558.5
36	Idaho	554.8
37	Maine	538.1
38	West Virginia	537.1
39	Massachusetts	517.2
40	Wisconsin	513.2
41	New Jersey	511.0
42	Connecticut	493.8
43	Wyoming	490.9
44	Pennsylvania	450.8
45	Virginia	435.4
46	New York	400.4
47	South Dakota	398.7
48	New Hampshire	379.4
49	Montana	361.6
50	North Dakota	353.7
	District of Columbia	905.6

Source: Federal Bureau of Investigation
"Crime in the United States 2002" (Uniform Crime Reports, October 27, 2003)
**Burglary is the unlawful entry of a structure to commit a felony or theft. Attempts are included.*

Larcenies and Thefts in 2002

National Total = 7,052,922 Larcenies and Thefts*

ALPHA ORDER

RANK	STATE	THEFTS	% of USA
21	Alabama	123,932	1.8%
46	Alaska	17,739	0.3%
11	Arizona	201,541	2.9%
30	Arkansas	71,129	1.0%
1	California	715,692	10.1%
20	Colorado	125,193	1.8%
34	Connecticut	64,292	0.9%
45	Delaware	18,555	0.3%
3	Florida	511,478	7.3%
7	Georgia	234,591	3.3%
37	Hawaii	49,344	0.7%
39	Idaho	29,060	0.4%
5	Illinois	301,892	4.3%
17	Indiana	146,073	2.1%
33	Iowa	68,411	1.0%
29	Kansas	73,877	1.0%
31	Kentucky	70,776	1.0%
19	Louisiana	133,302	1.9%
41	Maine	24,591	0.3%
18	Maryland	143,320	2.0%
26	Massachusetts	107,922	1.5%
9	Michigan	214,367	3.0%
24	Minnesota	122,150	1.7%
32	Mississippi	70,468	1.0%
14	Missouri	159,921	2.3%
43	Montana	23,679	0.3%
36	Nebraska	51,440	0.7%
38	Nevada	47,459	0.7%
44	New Hampshire	19,468	0.3%
16	New Jersey	147,984	2.1%
35	New Mexico	53,406	0.8%
4	New York	318,025	4.5%
8	North Carolina	229,307	3.3%
49	North Dakota	11,501	0.2%
6	Ohio	287,045	4.1%
27	Oklahoma	100,185	1.4%
25	Oregon	118,925	1.7%
10	Pennsylvania	212,441	3.0%
42	Rhode Island	24,051	0.3%
23	South Carolina	123,196	1.7%
48	South Dakota	12,139	0.2%
13	Tennessee	161,610	2.3%
2	Texas	688,992	9.8%
28	Utah	74,795	1.1%
50	Vermont	10,684	0.2%
15	Virginia	157,548	2.2%
12	Washington	193,526	2.7%
40	West Virginia	27,524	0.4%
22	Wisconsin	123,365	1.7%
47	Wyoming	13,303	0.2%

RANK ORDER

RANK	STATE	THEFTS	% of USA
1	California	715,692	10.1%
2	Texas	688,992	9.8%
3	Florida	511,478	7.3%
4	New York	318,025	4.5%
5	Illinois	301,892	4.3%
6	Ohio	287,045	4.1%
7	Georgia	234,591	3.3%
8	North Carolina	229,307	3.3%
9	Michigan	214,367	3.0%
10	Pennsylvania	212,441	3.0%
11	Arizona	201,541	2.9%
12	Washington	193,526	2.7%
13	Tennessee	161,610	2.3%
14	Missouri	159,921	2.3%
15	Virginia	157,548	2.2%
16	New Jersey	147,984	2.1%
17	Indiana	146,073	2.1%
18	Maryland	143,320	2.0%
19	Louisiana	133,302	1.9%
20	Colorado	125,193	1.8%
21	Alabama	123,932	1.8%
22	Wisconsin	123,365	1.7%
23	South Carolina	123,196	1.7%
24	Minnesota	122,150	1.7%
25	Oregon	118,925	1.7%
26	Massachusetts	107,922	1.5%
27	Oklahoma	100,185	1.4%
28	Utah	74,795	1.1%
29	Kansas	73,877	1.0%
30	Arkansas	71,129	1.0%
31	Kentucky	70,776	1.0%
32	Mississippi	70,468	1.0%
33	Iowa	68,411	1.0%
34	Connecticut	64,292	0.9%
35	New Mexico	53,406	0.8%
36	Nebraska	51,440	0.7%
37	Hawaii	49,344	0.7%
38	Nevada	47,459	0.7%
39	Idaho	29,060	0.4%
40	West Virginia	27,524	0.4%
41	Maine	24,591	0.3%
42	Rhode Island	24,051	0.3%
43	Montana	23,679	0.3%
44	New Hampshire	19,468	0.3%
45	Delaware	18,555	0.3%
46	Alaska	17,739	0.3%
47	Wyoming	13,303	0.2%
48	South Dakota	12,139	0.2%
49	North Dakota	11,501	0.2%
50	Vermont	10,684	0.2%
	District of Columbia	21,708	0.3%

Source: Federal Bureau of Investigation
   "Crime in the United States 2002" (Uniform Crime Reports, October 27, 2003)
*Larceny and theft is the unlawful taking of property without use of force, violence or fraud. Attempts are included.
Motor vehicle thefts are excluded.

Percent Change in Number of Larcenies and Thefts: 2001 to 2002

National Percent Change = 0.6% Decrease*

<u>ALPHA ORDER</u>

RANK	STATE	PERCENT CHANGE
7	Alabama	3.3
3	Alaska	6.3
2	Arizona	7.9
14	Arkansas	2.2
13	California	2.6
9	Colorado	3.2
31	Connecticut	(2.2)
45	Delaware	(4.7)
24	Florida	(1.0)
26	Georgia	(1.6)
1	Hawaii	9.8
12	Idaho	2.7
26	Illinois	(1.6)
21	Indiana	(0.8)
7	Iowa	3.3
41	Kansas	(4.1)
23	Kentucky	(0.9)
43	Louisiana	(4.5)
19	Maine	0.0
28	Maryland	(1.8)
15	Massachusetts	1.0
49	Michigan	(5.4)
29	Minnesota	(1.9)
18	Mississippi	0.2
43	Missouri	(4.5)
41	Montana	(4.1)
32	Nebraska	(2.4)
6	Nevada	5.3
35	New Hampshire	(3.0)
47	New Jersey	(5.2)
48	New Mexico	(5.3)
39	New York	(3.4)
37	North Carolina	(3.3)
20	North Dakota	(0.7)
35	Ohio	(3.0)
4	Oklahoma	6.0
37	Oregon	(3.3)
46	Pennsylvania	(4.9)
16	Rhode Island	0.7
34	South Carolina	(2.8)
39	South Dakota	(3.4)
30	Tennessee	(2.1)
10	Texas	2.9
5	Utah	5.8
50	Vermont	(14.0)
17	Virginia	0.3
21	Washington	(0.8)
33	West Virginia	(2.6)
25	Wisconsin	(1.5)
11	Wyoming	2.8

<u>RANK ORDER</u>

RANK	STATE	PERCENT CHANGE
1	Hawaii	9.8
2	Arizona	7.9
3	Alaska	6.3
4	Oklahoma	6.0
5	Utah	5.8
6	Nevada	5.3
7	Alabama	3.3
7	Iowa	3.3
9	Colorado	3.2
10	Texas	2.9
11	Wyoming	2.8
12	Idaho	2.7
13	California	2.6
14	Arkansas	2.2
15	Massachusetts	1.0
16	Rhode Island	0.7
17	Virginia	0.3
18	Mississippi	0.2
19	Maine	0.0
20	North Dakota	(0.7)
21	Indiana	(0.8)
21	Washington	(0.8)
23	Kentucky	(0.9)
24	Florida	(1.0)
25	Wisconsin	(1.5)
26	Georgia	(1.6)
26	Illinois	(1.6)
28	Maryland	(1.8)
29	Minnesota	(1.9)
30	Tennessee	(2.1)
31	Connecticut	(2.2)
32	Nebraska	(2.4)
33	West Virginia	(2.6)
34	South Carolina	(2.8)
35	New Hampshire	(3.0)
35	Ohio	(3.0)
37	North Carolina	(3.3)
37	Oregon	(3.3)
39	New York	(3.4)
39	South Dakota	(3.4)
41	Kansas	(4.1)
41	Montana	(4.1)
43	Louisiana	(4.5)
43	Missouri	(4.5)
45	Delaware	(4.7)
46	Pennsylvania	(4.9)
47	New Jersey	(5.2)
48	New Mexico	(5.3)
49	Michigan	(5.4)
50	Vermont	(14.0)

| | District of Columbia | (2.7) |

Source: Federal Bureau of Investigation
   "Crime in the United States 2002" (Uniform Crime Reports, October 27, 2003)
*Larceny and theft is the unlawful taking of property without use of force, violence or fraud. Attempts are included.
Motor vehicle thefts are excluded.

Larceny and Theft Rate in 2002

National Rate = 2,445.8 Larcenies and Thefts per 100,000 Population*

<u>ALPHA ORDER</u>

RANK	STATE	RATE
16	Alabama	2,762.3
18	Alaska	2,755.4
2	Arizona	3,693.6
23	Arkansas	2,624.6
38	California	2,038.1
15	Colorado	2,778.0
40	Connecticut	1,857.9
31	Delaware	2,298.2
7	Florida	3,060.3
19	Georgia	2,740.4
1	Hawaii	3,963.7
35	Idaho	2,166.8
28	Illinois	2,395.9
29	Indiana	2,371.7
30	Iowa	2,329.5
20	Kansas	2,720.2
43	Kentucky	1,729.2
10	Louisiana	2,973.7
39	Maine	1,899.7
22	Maryland	2,625.8
46	Massachusetts	1,679.0
37	Michigan	2,132.9
27	Minnesota	2,433.4
26	Mississippi	2,453.8
13	Missouri	2,819.2
24	Montana	2,603.7
9	Nebraska	2,974.8
34	Nevada	2,183.5
50	New Hampshire	1,526.8
44	New Jersey	1,722.7
11	New Mexico	2,878.9
47	New York	1,660.1
17	North Carolina	2,756.0
41	North Dakota	1,813.7
25	Ohio	2,513.3
12	Oklahoma	2,867.6
3	Oregon	3,377.1
45	Pennsylvania	1,722.2
33	Rhode Island	2,248.3
8	South Carolina	2,999.5
48	South Dakota	1,595.0
14	Tennessee	2,787.7
6	Texas	3,163.4
4	Utah	3,229.1
42	Vermont	1,732.8
36	Virginia	2,160.1
5	Washington	3,188.8
49	West Virginia	1,527.5
32	Wisconsin	2,267.2
21	Wyoming	2,667.5

<u>RANK ORDER</u>

RANK	STATE	RATE
1	Hawaii	3,963.7
2	Arizona	3,693.6
3	Oregon	3,377.1
4	Utah	3,229.1
5	Washington	3,188.8
6	Texas	3,163.4
7	Florida	3,060.3
8	South Carolina	2,999.5
9	Nebraska	2,974.8
10	Louisiana	2,973.7
11	New Mexico	2,878.9
12	Oklahoma	2,867.6
13	Missouri	2,819.2
14	Tennessee	2,787.7
15	Colorado	2,778.0
16	Alabama	2,762.3
17	North Carolina	2,756.0
18	Alaska	2,755.4
19	Georgia	2,740.4
20	Kansas	2,720.2
21	Wyoming	2,667.5
22	Maryland	2,625.8
23	Arkansas	2,624.6
24	Montana	2,603.7
25	Ohio	2,513.3
26	Mississippi	2,453.8
27	Minnesota	2,433.4
28	Illinois	2,395.9
29	Indiana	2,371.7
30	Iowa	2,329.5
31	Delaware	2,298.2
32	Wisconsin	2,267.2
33	Rhode Island	2,248.3
34	Nevada	2,183.5
35	Idaho	2,166.8
36	Virginia	2,160.1
37	Michigan	2,132.9
38	California	2,038.1
39	Maine	1,899.7
40	Connecticut	1,857.9
41	North Dakota	1,813.7
42	Vermont	1,732.8
43	Kentucky	1,729.2
44	New Jersey	1,722.7
45	Pennsylvania	1,722.2
46	Massachusetts	1,679.0
47	New York	1,660.1
48	South Dakota	1,595.0
49	West Virginia	1,527.5
50	New Hampshire	1,526.8

| | District of Columbia | 3,802.4 |

Source: Federal Bureau of Investigation
   "Crime in the United States 2002" (Uniform Crime Reports, October 27, 2003)
Larceny and theft is the unlawful taking of property without use of force, violence or fraud. Attempts are included. Motor vehicle thefts are excluded.

Motor Vehicle Thefts in 2002

National Total = 1,246,096 Motor Vehicle Thefts*

<u>ALPHA ORDER</u>

RANK	STATE	THEFTS	% of USA
25	Alabama	13,890	1.1%
43	Alaska	2,471	0.2%
4	Arizona	57,668	4.6%
36	Arkansas	6,813	0.5%
1	California	222,364	17.8%
18	Colorado	23,183	1.9%
29	Connecticut	11,572	0.9%
41	Delaware	3,057	0.2%
3	Florida	88,516	7.1%
10	Georgia	38,036	3.1%
30	Hawaii	9,910	0.8%
42	Idaho	2,627	0.2%
7	Illinois	44,857	3.6%
19	Indiana	20,287	1.6%
38	Iowa	5,823	0.5%
35	Kansas	7,212	0.6%
32	Kentucky	8,750	0.7%
20	Louisiana	20,186	1.6%
46	Maine	1,429	0.1%
12	Maryland	34,020	2.7%
15	Massachusetts	26,588	2.1%
5	Michigan	49,723	4.0%
26	Minnesota	13,842	1.1%
31	Mississippi	9,523	0.8%
14	Missouri	27,878	2.2%
45	Montana	1,783	0.1%
37	Nebraska	6,409	0.5%
22	Nevada	17,486	1.4%
44	New Hampshire	1,944	0.2%
11	New Jersey	35,739	2.9%
34	New Mexico	7,437	0.6%
6	New York	47,366	3.8%
17	North Carolina	24,866	2.0%
47	North Dakota	1,018	0.1%
8	Ohio	42,767	3.4%
28	Oklahoma	12,772	1.0%
24	Oregon	16,524	1.3%
13	Pennsylvania	32,817	2.6%
39	Rhode Island	4,876	0.4%
23	South Carolina	16,867	1.4%
48	South Dakota	819	0.1%
16	Tennessee	26,541	2.1%
2	Texas	102,680	8.2%
33	Utah	7,722	0.6%
49	Vermont	769	0.1%
21	Virginia	18,478	1.5%
9	Washington	40,493	3.2%
40	West Virginia	3,898	0.3%
27	Wisconsin	13,458	1.1%
50	Wyoming	743	0.1%

<u>RANK ORDER</u>

RANK	STATE	THEFTS	% of USA
1	California	222,364	17.8%
2	Texas	102,680	8.2%
3	Florida	88,516	7.1%
4	Arizona	57,668	4.6%
5	Michigan	49,723	4.0%
6	New York	47,366	3.8%
7	Illinois	44,857	3.6%
8	Ohio	42,767	3.4%
9	Washington	40,493	3.2%
10	Georgia	38,036	3.1%
11	New Jersey	35,739	2.9%
12	Maryland	34,020	2.7%
13	Pennsylvania	32,817	2.6%
14	Missouri	27,878	2.2%
15	Massachusetts	26,588	2.1%
16	Tennessee	26,541	2.1%
17	North Carolina	24,866	2.0%
18	Colorado	23,183	1.9%
19	Indiana	20,287	1.6%
20	Louisiana	20,186	1.6%
21	Virginia	18,478	1.5%
22	Nevada	17,486	1.4%
23	South Carolina	16,867	1.4%
24	Oregon	16,524	1.3%
25	Alabama	13,890	1.1%
26	Minnesota	13,842	1.1%
27	Wisconsin	13,458	1.1%
28	Oklahoma	12,772	1.0%
29	Connecticut	11,572	0.9%
30	Hawaii	9,910	0.8%
31	Mississippi	9,523	0.8%
32	Kentucky	8,750	0.7%
33	Utah	7,722	0.6%
34	New Mexico	7,437	0.6%
35	Kansas	7,212	0.6%
36	Arkansas	6,813	0.5%
37	Nebraska	6,409	0.5%
38	Iowa	5,823	0.5%
39	Rhode Island	4,876	0.4%
40	West Virginia	3,898	0.3%
41	Delaware	3,057	0.2%
42	Idaho	2,627	0.2%
43	Alaska	2,471	0.2%
44	New Hampshire	1,944	0.2%
45	Montana	1,783	0.1%
46	Maine	1,429	0.1%
47	North Dakota	1,018	0.1%
48	South Dakota	819	0.1%
49	Vermont	769	0.1%
50	Wyoming	743	0.1%
	District of Columbia	9,599	0.8%

Source: Federal Bureau of Investigation
"Crime in the United States 2002" (Uniform Crime Reports, October 27, 2003)
Includes the theft or attempted theft of a self-propelled vehicle. Excludes motorboats, construction equipment, airplanes and farming equipment.

Percent Change in Number of Motor Vehicle Thefts: 2001 to 2002

National Percent Change = 1.4% Increase*

ALPHA ORDER

RANK	STATE	PERCENT CHANGE
8	Alabama	10.1
36	Alaska	(5.6)
6	Arizona	10.5
41	Arkansas	(6.9)
11	California	8.9
7	Colorado	10.4
40	Connecticut	(6.5)
9	Delaware	10.0
28	Florida	(1.6)
20	Georgia	1.2
1	Hawaii	47.0
9	Idaho	10.0
45	Illinois	(8.0)
36	Indiana	(5.6)
14	Iowa	5.8
49	Kansas	(9.7)
32	Kentucky	(2.2)
41	Louisiana	(6.9)
50	Maine	(14.5)
13	Maryland	6.2
34	Massachusetts	(4.5)
43	Michigan	(7.2)
44	Minnesota	(7.9)
23	Mississippi	0.5
26	Missouri	(0.5)
31	Montana	(2.1)
27	Nebraska	(1.2)
3	Nevada	18.9
48	New Hampshire	(9.2)
35	New Jersey	(5.2)
15	New Mexico	4.2
29	New York	(1.9)
22	North Carolina	0.9
39	North Dakota	(6.3)
19	Ohio	1.3
17	Oklahoma	1.6
5	Oregon	11.3
46	Pennsylvania	(8.1)
33	Rhode Island	(3.3)
21	South Carolina	1.0
23	South Dakota	0.5
38	Tennessee	(6.1)
25	Texas	0.0
4	Utah	18.6
18	Vermont	1.5
29	Virginia	(1.9)
16	Washington	3.6
2	West Virginia	21.2
47	Wisconsin	(8.6)
12	Wyoming	6.8

RANK ORDER

RANK	STATE	PERCENT CHANGE
1	Hawaii	47.0
2	West Virginia	21.2
3	Nevada	18.9
4	Utah	18.6
5	Oregon	11.3
6	Arizona	10.5
7	Colorado	10.4
8	Alabama	10.1
9	Delaware	10.0
9	Idaho	10.0
11	California	8.9
12	Wyoming	6.8
13	Maryland	6.2
14	Iowa	5.8
15	New Mexico	4.2
16	Washington	3.6
17	Oklahoma	1.6
18	Vermont	1.5
19	Ohio	1.3
20	Georgia	1.2
21	South Carolina	1.0
22	North Carolina	0.9
23	Mississippi	0.5
23	South Dakota	0.5
25	Texas	0.0
26	Missouri	(0.5)
27	Nebraska	(1.2)
28	Florida	(1.6)
29	New York	(1.9)
29	Virginia	(1.9)
31	Montana	(2.1)
32	Kentucky	(2.2)
33	Rhode Island	(3.3)
34	Massachusetts	(4.5)
35	New Jersey	(5.2)
36	Alaska	(5.6)
36	Indiana	(5.6)
38	Tennessee	(6.1)
39	North Dakota	(6.3)
40	Connecticut	(6.5)
41	Arkansas	(6.9)
41	Louisiana	(6.9)
43	Michigan	(7.2)
44	Minnesota	(7.9)
45	Illinois	(8.0)
46	Pennsylvania	(8.1)
47	Wisconsin	(8.6)
48	New Hampshire	(9.2)
49	Kansas	(9.7)
50	Maine	(14.5)

| | District of Columbia | 20.4 |

Source: Federal Bureau of Investigation
   "Crime in the United States 2002" (Uniform Crime Reports, October 27, 2003)
**Includes the theft or attempted theft of a self-propelled vehicle. Excludes motorboats, construction equipment, airplanes and farming equipment.*

Motor Vehicle Theft Rate in 2002

National Rate = 432.1 Motor Vehicle Thefts per 100,000 Population*

ALPHA ORDER

RANK	STATE	RATE
31	Alabama	309.6
21	Alaska	383.8
1	Arizona	1,056.9
37	Arkansas	251.4
5	California	633.2
8	Colorado	514.4
27	Connecticut	334.4
22	Delaware	378.6
7	Florida	529.6
16	Georgia	444.3
3	Hawaii	796.0
44	Idaho	195.9
26	Illinois	356.0
30	Indiana	329.4
42	Iowa	198.3
35	Kansas	265.5
41	Kentucky	213.8
15	Louisiana	450.3
49	Maine	110.4
6	Maryland	623.3
18	Massachusetts	413.6
9	Michigan	494.7
33	Minnesota	275.8
29	Mississippi	331.6
10	Missouri	491.5
43	Montana	196.1
24	Nebraska	370.6
2	Nevada	804.5
46	New Hampshire	152.5
17	New Jersey	416.0
20	New Mexico	400.9
39	New York	247.2
32	North Carolina	298.9
45	North Dakota	160.5
23	Ohio	374.5
25	Oklahoma	365.6
12	Oregon	469.2
34	Pennsylvania	266.0
14	Rhode Island	455.8
19	South Carolina	410.7
50	South Dakota	107.6
13	Tennessee	457.8
11	Texas	471.4
28	Utah	333.4
48	Vermont	124.7
36	Virginia	253.3
4	Washington	667.2
40	West Virginia	216.3
38	Wisconsin	247.3
47	Wyoming	149.0

RANK ORDER

RANK	STATE	RATE
1	Arizona	1,056.9
2	Nevada	804.5
3	Hawaii	796.0
4	Washington	667.2
5	California	633.2
6	Maryland	623.3
7	Florida	529.6
8	Colorado	514.4
9	Michigan	494.7
10	Missouri	491.5
11	Texas	471.4
12	Oregon	469.2
13	Tennessee	457.8
14	Rhode Island	455.8
15	Louisiana	450.3
16	Georgia	444.3
17	New Jersey	416.0
18	Massachusetts	413.6
19	South Carolina	410.7
20	New Mexico	400.9
21	Alaska	383.8
22	Delaware	378.6
23	Ohio	374.5
24	Nebraska	370.6
25	Oklahoma	365.6
26	Illinois	356.0
27	Connecticut	334.4
28	Utah	333.4
29	Mississippi	331.6
30	Indiana	329.4
31	Alabama	309.6
32	North Carolina	298.9
33	Minnesota	275.8
34	Pennsylvania	266.0
35	Kansas	265.5
36	Virginia	253.3
37	Arkansas	251.4
38	Wisconsin	247.3
39	New York	247.2
40	West Virginia	216.3
41	Kentucky	213.8
42	Iowa	198.3
43	Montana	196.1
44	Idaho	195.9
45	North Dakota	160.5
46	New Hampshire	152.5
47	Wyoming	149.0
48	Vermont	124.7
49	Maine	110.4
50	South Dakota	107.6

District of Columbia	1,681.4

Source: Federal Bureau of Investigation
"Crime in the United States 2002" (Uniform Crime Reports, October 27, 2003)
*Includes the theft or attempted theft of a self-propelled vehicle. Excludes motorboats, construction equipment, airplanes and farming equipment.

Prisoners in State Correctional Institutions: Year End 2002

National Total = 1,277,127 State Prisoners*

ALPHA ORDER

RANK	STATE	PRISONERS	% of USA
15	Alabama	27,947	2.2%
41	Alaska	4,398	0.3%
14	Arizona	29,359	2.3%
28	Arkansas	13,090	1.0%
1	California	162,317	12.7%
25	Colorado	18,833	1.5%
24	Connecticut	20,720	1.6%
35	Delaware	6,778	0.5%
3	Florida	75,210	5.9%
6	Georgia	47,445	3.7%
39	Hawaii	5,423	0.4%
36	Idaho	6,204	0.5%
8	Illinois	42,693	3.3%
23	Indiana	21,611	1.7%
33	Iowa	8,398	0.7%
32	Kansas	8,935	0.7%
27	Kentucky	15,933	1.2%
10	Louisiana	35,736	2.8%
47	Maine	1,900	0.1%
18	Maryland	24,162	1.9%
31	Massachusetts	10,329	0.8%
5	Michigan	50,591	4.0%
34	Minnesota	7,129	0.6%
21	Mississippi	22,705	1.8%
13	Missouri	30,099	2.4%
44	Montana	3,290	0.3%
42	Nebraska	4,058	0.3%
30	Nevada	10,478	0.8%
46	New Hampshire	2,451	0.2%
16	New Jersey	27,891	2.2%
37	New Mexico	5,989	0.5%
4	New York	67,065	5.3%
12	North Carolina	32,803	2.6%
50	North Dakota	1,112	0.1%
7	Ohio	45,646	3.6%
20	Oklahoma	23,385	1.8%
29	Oregon	12,086	0.9%
9	Pennsylvania	40,168	3.1%
43	Rhode Island	3,520	0.3%
19	South Carolina	23,715	1.9%
45	South Dakota	2,898	0.2%
17	Tennessee	24,989	2.0%
2	Texas	162,003	12.7%
38	Utah	5,567	0.4%
48	Vermont	1,863	0.1%
11	Virginia	33,729	2.6%
26	Washington	16,062	1.3%
40	West Virginia	4,544	0.4%
22	Wisconsin	22,133	1.7%
49	Wyoming	1,737	0.1%

RANK ORDER

RANK	STATE	PRISONERS	% of USA
1	California	162,317	12.7%
2	Texas	162,003	12.7%
3	Florida	75,210	5.9%
4	New York	67,065	5.3%
5	Michigan	50,591	4.0%
6	Georgia	47,445	3.7%
7	Ohio	45,646	3.6%
8	Illinois	42,693	3.3%
9	Pennsylvania	40,168	3.1%
10	Louisiana	35,736	2.8%
11	Virginia	33,729	2.6%
12	North Carolina	32,803	2.6%
13	Missouri	30,099	2.4%
14	Arizona	29,359	2.3%
15	Alabama	27,947	2.2%
16	New Jersey	27,891	2.2%
17	Tennessee	24,989	2.0%
18	Maryland	24,162	1.9%
19	South Carolina	23,715	1.9%
20	Oklahoma	23,385	1.8%
21	Mississippi	22,705	1.8%
22	Wisconsin	22,133	1.7%
23	Indiana	21,611	1.7%
24	Connecticut	20,720	1.6%
25	Colorado	18,833	1.5%
26	Washington	16,062	1.3%
27	Kentucky	15,933	1.2%
28	Arkansas	13,090	1.0%
29	Oregon	12,086	0.9%
30	Nevada	10,478	0.8%
31	Massachusetts	10,329	0.8%
32	Kansas	8,935	0.7%
33	Iowa	8,398	0.7%
34	Minnesota	7,129	0.6%
35	Delaware	6,778	0.5%
36	Idaho	6,204	0.5%
37	New Mexico	5,989	0.5%
38	Utah	5,567	0.4%
39	Hawaii	5,423	0.4%
40	West Virginia	4,544	0.4%
41	Alaska	4,398	0.3%
42	Nebraska	4,058	0.3%
43	Rhode Island	3,520	0.3%
44	Montana	3,290	0.3%
45	South Dakota	2,898	0.2%
46	New Hampshire	2,451	0.2%
47	Maine	1,900	0.1%
48	Vermont	1,863	0.1%
49	Wyoming	1,737	0.1%
50	North Dakota	1,112	0.1%
	District of Columbia**	NA	NA

*Source: U.S. Department of Justice, Bureau of Justice Statistics
"Prisoners in 2002" (July 2003, NCJ-200248)*

Advance figures as of December 31, 2002. Totals reflect all prisoners, including those sentenced to a year or less and those unsentenced. National total does not include 163,528 prisoners under federal jurisdiction. State and federal prisoners combined total 1,440,655.

***Responsibility for sentenced felons in D.C. was transferred to the Federal Bureau of Prisons in 2001.*

State Prisoner Incarceration Rate in 2002

National Rate = 427 State Prisoners per 100,000 Population*

ALPHA ORDER

RANK	STATE	RATE
5	Alabama	612
23	Alaska	396
9	Arizona	513
12	Arkansas	479
16	California	452
20	Colorado	415
21	Connecticut	405
15	Delaware	453
17	Florida	450
7	Georgia	552
38	Hawaii	308
13	Idaho	461
33	Illinois	336
28	Indiana	348
39	Iowa	284
34	Kansas	327
25	Kentucky	380
1	Louisiana	794
49	Maine	141
19	Maryland	425
42	Massachusetts	234
10	Michigan	501
49	Minnesota	141
2	Mississippi	743
8	Missouri	529
27	Montana	361
44	Nebraska	228
11	Nevada	483
46	New Hampshire	192
36	New Jersey	322
37	New Mexico	309
30	New York	346
31	North Carolina	345
48	North Dakota	161
22	Ohio	398
4	Oklahoma	667
32	Oregon	342
35	Pennsylvania	325
47	Rhode Island	191
6	South Carolina	555
26	South Dakota	378
18	Tennessee	430
3	Texas	692
43	Utah	233
45	Vermont	214
14	Virginia	460
40	Washington	261
41	West Virginia	250
24	Wisconsin	391
28	Wyoming	348

RANK ORDER

RANK	STATE	RATE
1	Louisiana	794
2	Mississippi	743
3	Texas	692
4	Oklahoma	667
5	Alabama	612
6	South Carolina	555
7	Georgia	552
8	Missouri	529
9	Arizona	513
10	Michigan	501
11	Nevada	483
12	Arkansas	479
13	Idaho	461
14	Virginia	460
15	Delaware	453
16	California	452
17	Florida	450
18	Tennessee	430
19	Maryland	425
20	Colorado	415
21	Connecticut	405
22	Ohio	398
23	Alaska	396
24	Wisconsin	391
25	Kentucky	380
26	South Dakota	378
27	Montana	361
28	Indiana	348
28	Wyoming	348
30	New York	346
31	North Carolina	345
32	Oregon	342
33	Illinois	336
34	Kansas	327
35	Pennsylvania	325
36	New Jersey	322
37	New Mexico	309
38	Hawaii	308
39	Iowa	284
40	Washington	261
41	West Virginia	250
42	Massachusetts	234
43	Utah	233
44	Nebraska	228
45	Vermont	214
46	New Hampshire	192
47	Rhode Island	191
48	North Dakota	161
49	Maine	141
49	Minnesota	141

District of Columbia** NA

Source: U.S. Department of Justice, Bureau of Justice Statistics
"Prisoners in 2002" (July 2003, NCJ-200248)

As of December 31, 2002. Includes only inmates sentenced to more than one year. Does not include federal incarceration rate of 49 prisoners per 100,000 population. State and federal combined incarceration rate is 476 prisoners per 100,000 population.

**Responsibility for sentenced felons in D.C. was transferred to the Federal Bureau of Prisons in 2001.*

Percent Change in Number of State Prisoners: 2001 to 2002

National Percent Change = 2.4% Increase*

ALPHA ORDER

RANK	STATE	PERCENT CHANGE
19	Alabama	4.5
50	Alaska	(3.8)
9	Arizona	6.0
22	Arkansas	3.9
36	California	1.8
3	Colorado	7.9
3	Connecticut	7.9
48	Delaware	(3.2)
22	Florida	3.9
27	Georgia	3.3
42	Hawaii	(0.1)
25	Idaho	3.7
49	Illinois	(3.7)
29	Indiana	3.1
15	Iowa	5.5
21	Kansas	4.2
27	Kentucky	3.3
43	Louisiana	(0.2)
1	Maine	11.5
37	Maryland	1.7
47	Massachusetts	(2.4)
26	Michigan	3.6
3	Minnesota	7.9
12	Mississippi	5.8
18	Missouri	4.7
46	Montana	(1.1)
29	Nebraska	3.1
35	Nevada	2.4
34	New Hampshire	2.5
45	New Jersey	(0.9)
13	New Mexico	5.7
44	New York	(0.7)
37	North Carolina	1.7
40	North Dakota	0.1
39	Ohio	0.8
33	Oklahoma	2.7
11	Oregon	5.9
15	Pennsylvania	5.5
2	Rhode Island	8.6
17	South Carolina	5.0
22	South Dakota	3.9
14	Tennessee	5.6
41	Texas	0.0
20	Utah	4.3
7	Vermont	7.0
8	Virginia	6.5
9	Washington	6.0
6	West Virginia	7.8
32	Wisconsin	3.0
29	Wyoming	3.1

RANK ORDER

RANK	STATE	PERCENT CHANGE
1	Maine	11.5
2	Rhode Island	8.6
3	Colorado	7.9
3	Connecticut	7.9
3	Minnesota	7.9
6	West Virginia	7.8
7	Vermont	7.0
8	Virginia	6.5
9	Arizona	6.0
9	Washington	6.0
11	Oregon	5.9
12	Mississippi	5.8
13	New Mexico	5.7
14	Tennessee	5.6
15	Iowa	5.5
15	Pennsylvania	5.5
17	South Carolina	5.0
18	Missouri	4.7
19	Alabama	4.5
20	Utah	4.3
21	Kansas	4.2
22	Arkansas	3.9
22	Florida	3.9
22	South Dakota	3.9
25	Idaho	3.7
26	Michigan	3.6
27	Georgia	3.3
27	Kentucky	3.3
29	Indiana	3.1
29	Nebraska	3.1
29	Wyoming	3.1
32	Wisconsin	3.0
33	Oklahoma	2.7
34	New Hampshire	2.5
35	Nevada	2.4
36	California	1.8
37	Maryland	1.7
37	North Carolina	1.7
39	Ohio	0.8
40	North Dakota	0.1
41	Texas	0.0
42	Hawaii	(0.1)
43	Louisiana	(0.2)
44	New York	(0.7)
45	New Jersey	(0.9)
46	Montana	(1.1)
47	Massachusetts	(2.4)
48	Delaware	(3.2)
49	Illinois	(3.7)
50	Alaska	(3.8)
	District of Columbia**	NA

Source: U.S. Department of Justice, Bureau of Justice Statistics
"Prisoners in 2002" (July 2003, NCJ-200248)
From December 31, 2001 to December 31, 2002. Includes inmates sentenced to more than one year and those sentenced to a year or less or with no sentence. The percent change in number of prisoners under federal jurisdiction during the same period was an 4.2% increase. The combined state and federal increase was 2.6%.
**Responsibility for sentenced felons in D.C. was transferred to the Federal Bureau of Prisons in 2001.*

Prisoners Under Sentence of Death in 2002

National Total = 3,533 State Prisoners*

ALPHA ORDER

RANK	STATE	PRISONERS	% of USA
7	Alabama	191	5.4%
NA	Alaska**	NA	NA
9	Arizona	120	3.4%
18	Arkansas	40	1.1%
1	California	614	17.4%
32	Colorado	5	0.1%
29	Connecticut	7	0.2%
25	Delaware	14	0.4%
3	Florida	366	10.4%
10	Georgia	112	3.2%
NA	Hawaii**	NA	NA
23	Idaho	20	0.6%
8	Illinois	159	4.5%
19	Indiana	36	1.0%
NA	Iowa**	NA	NA
32	Kansas	5	0.1%
19	Kentucky	36	1.0%
13	Louisiana	86	2.4%
NA	Maine**	NA	NA
24	Maryland	15	0.4%
NA	Massachusetts**	NA	NA
NA	Michigan**	NA	NA
NA	Minnesota**	NA	NA
16	Mississippi	66	1.9%
16	Missouri	66	1.9%
31	Montana	6	0.2%
29	Nebraska	7	0.2%
14	Nevada	83	2.3%
38	New Hampshire	0	0.0%
25	New Jersey	14	0.4%
36	New Mexico	2	0.1%
32	New York	5	0.1%
5	North Carolina	206	5.8%
NA	North Dakota**	NA	NA
6	Ohio	205	5.8%
10	Oklahoma	112	3.2%
21	Oregon	26	0.7%
4	Pennsylvania	241	6.8%
NA	Rhode Island**	NA	NA
15	South Carolina	72	2.0%
32	South Dakota	5	0.1%
12	Tennessee	95	2.7%
2	Texas	450	12.7%
27	Utah	11	0.3%
NA	Vermont**	NA	NA
22	Virginia	23	0.7%
28	Washington	10	0.3%
NA	West Virginia**	NA	NA
NA	Wisconsin**	NA	NA
36	Wyoming	2	0.1%

RANK ORDER

RANK	STATE	PRISONERS	% of USA
1	California	614	17.4%
2	Texas	450	12.7%
3	Florida	366	10.4%
4	Pennsylvania	241	6.8%
5	North Carolina	206	5.8%
6	Ohio	205	5.8%
7	Alabama	191	5.4%
8	Illinois	159	4.5%
9	Arizona	120	3.4%
10	Georgia	112	3.2%
10	Oklahoma	112	3.2%
12	Tennessee	95	2.7%
13	Louisiana	86	2.4%
14	Nevada	83	2.3%
15	South Carolina	72	2.0%
16	Mississippi	66	1.9%
16	Missouri	66	1.9%
18	Arkansas	40	1.1%
19	Indiana	36	1.0%
19	Kentucky	36	1.0%
21	Oregon	26	0.7%
22	Virginia	23	0.7%
23	Idaho	20	0.6%
24	Maryland	15	0.4%
25	Delaware	14	0.4%
25	New Jersey	14	0.4%
27	Utah	11	0.3%
28	Washington	10	0.3%
29	Connecticut	7	0.2%
29	Nebraska	7	0.2%
31	Montana	6	0.2%
32	Colorado	5	0.1%
32	Kansas	5	0.1%
32	New York	5	0.1%
32	South Dakota	5	0.1%
36	New Mexico	2	0.1%
36	Wyoming	2	0.1%
38	New Hampshire	0	0.0%
NA	Alaska**	NA	NA
NA	Hawaii**	NA	NA
NA	Iowa**	NA	NA
NA	Maine**	NA	NA
NA	Massachusetts**	NA	NA
NA	Michigan**	NA	NA
NA	Minnesota**	NA	NA
NA	North Dakota**	NA	NA
NA	Rhode Island**	NA	NA
NA	Vermont**	NA	NA
NA	West Virginia**	NA	NA
NA	Wisconsin**	NA	NA
	District of Columbia**	NA	NA

*Source: U.S. Department of Justice, Bureau of Justice Statistics
"Capital Punishment 2002" (Bulletin, November 2003, NCJ-201848)*

*As of December 31, 2002. Does not include 24 federal prisoners under sentence of death. There were 71 executions in 2002.

**No death penalty as of 12/31/02.

Full-Time Sworn Officers in Law Enforcement Agencies in 2000

National Total = 708,022 Officers*

<u>ALPHA ORDER</u>

RANK	STATE	OFFICERS	% of USA
21	Alabama	10,655	1.5%
48	Alaska	1,348	0.2%
20	Arizona	11,533	1.6%
32	Arkansas	6,157	0.9%
1	California	73,662	10.4%
22	Colorado	10,309	1.5%
26	Connecticut	8,327	1.2%
44	Delaware	1,774	0.3%
5	Florida	39,452	5.6%
10	Georgia	21,173	3.0%
39	Hawaii	2,914	0.4%
40	Idaho	2,749	0.4%
4	Illinois	39,847	5.6%
19	Indiana	11,900	1.7%
33	Iowa	5,333	0.8%
29	Kansas	6,563	0.9%
28	Kentucky	7,144	1.0%
13	Louisiana	18,548	2.6%
43	Maine	2,367	0.3%
15	Maryland	15,221	2.1%
14	Massachusetts	18,082	2.6%
9	Michigan	21,673	3.1%
25	Minnesota	8,606	1.2%
30	Mississippi	6,562	0.9%
17	Missouri	13,630	1.9%
45	Montana	1,760	0.2%
37	Nebraska	3,486	0.5%
34	Nevada	5,252	0.7%
42	New Hampshire	2,542	0.4%
6	New Jersey	29,062	4.1%
35	New Mexico	4,456	0.6%
2	New York	72,853	10.3%
12	North Carolina	18,903	2.7%
49	North Dakota	1,293	0.2%
8	Ohio	25,082	3.5%
27	Oklahoma	7,622	1.1%
31	Oregon	6,496	0.9%
7	Pennsylvania	26,373	3.7%
41	Rhode Island	2,688	0.4%
24	South Carolina	9,741	1.4%
46	South Dakota	1,708	0.2%
16	Tennessee	14,494	2.0%
3	Texas	51,478	7.3%
36	Utah	4,179	0.6%
50	Vermont	1,034	0.1%
11	Virginia	20,254	2.9%
23	Washington	9,910	1.4%
38	West Virginia	3,150	0.4%
18	Wisconsin	13,237	1.9%
47	Wyoming	1,477	0.2%

<u>RANK ORDER</u>

RANK	STATE	OFFICERS	% of USA
1	California	73,662	10.4%
2	New York	72,853	10.3%
3	Texas	51,478	7.3%
4	Illinois	39,847	5.6%
5	Florida	39,452	5.6%
6	New Jersey	29,062	4.1%
7	Pennsylvania	26,373	3.7%
8	Ohio	25,082	3.5%
9	Michigan	21,673	3.1%
10	Georgia	21,173	3.0%
11	Virginia	20,254	2.9%
12	North Carolina	18,903	2.7%
13	Louisiana	18,548	2.6%
14	Massachusetts	18,082	2.6%
15	Maryland	15,221	2.1%
16	Tennessee	14,494	2.0%
17	Missouri	13,630	1.9%
18	Wisconsin	13,237	1.9%
19	Indiana	11,900	1.7%
20	Arizona	11,533	1.6%
21	Alabama	10,655	1.5%
22	Colorado	10,309	1.5%
23	Washington	9,910	1.4%
24	South Carolina	9,741	1.4%
25	Minnesota	8,606	1.2%
26	Connecticut	8,327	1.2%
27	Oklahoma	7,622	1.1%
28	Kentucky	7,144	1.0%
29	Kansas	6,563	0.9%
30	Mississippi	6,562	0.9%
31	Oregon	6,496	0.9%
32	Arkansas	6,157	0.9%
33	Iowa	5,333	0.8%
34	Nevada	5,252	0.7%
35	New Mexico	4,456	0.6%
36	Utah	4,179	0.6%
37	Nebraska	3,486	0.5%
38	West Virginia	3,150	0.4%
39	Hawaii	2,914	0.4%
40	Idaho	2,749	0.4%
41	Rhode Island	2,688	0.4%
42	New Hampshire	2,542	0.4%
43	Maine	2,367	0.3%
44	Delaware	1,774	0.3%
45	Montana	1,760	0.2%
46	South Dakota	1,708	0.2%
47	Wyoming	1,477	0.2%
48	Alaska	1,348	0.2%
49	North Dakota	1,293	0.2%
50	Vermont	1,034	0.1%
	District of Columbia	3,963	0.6%

Source: U.S. Department of Justice, Bureau of Justice Statistics
"Census of State and Local Law Enforcement Agencies, 2000" (Bulletin, October 2002, NCJ 194066)
**Includes state and local police, sheriffs' departments and special police agencies.*

Rate of Full-Time Sworn Officers in Law Enforcement Agencies in 2000

National Rate = 252 Officers per 100,000 Population*

<u>ALPHA ORDER</u>

RANK	STATE	RATE
22	Alabama	240
34	Alaska	215
29	Arizona	225
26	Arkansas	230
33	California	217
22	Colorado	240
16	Connecticut	245
27	Delaware	226
13	Florida	247
10	Georgia	259
21	Hawaii	241
36	Idaho	212
4	Illinois	321
40	Indiana	196
45	Iowa	182
18	Kansas	244
46	Kentucky	177
1	Louisiana	415
44	Maine	186
6	Maryland	287
8	Massachusetts	285
32	Michigan	218
47	Minnesota	175
25	Mississippi	231
18	Missouri	244
41	Montana	195
38	Nebraska	204
9	Nevada	263
37	New Hampshire	206
3	New Jersey	345
16	New Mexico	245
2	New York	384
24	North Carolina	235
39	North Dakota	201
30	Ohio	221
30	Oklahoma	221
42	Oregon	190
34	Pennsylvania	215
11	Rhode Island	256
20	South Carolina	243
27	South Dakota	226
12	Tennessee	255
13	Texas	247
43	Utah	187
49	Vermont	170
7	Virginia	286
50	Washington	168
48	West Virginia	174
13	Wisconsin	247
5	Wyoming	299

<u>RANK ORDER</u>

RANK	STATE	RATE
1	Louisiana	415
2	New York	384
3	New Jersey	345
4	Illinois	321
5	Wyoming	299
6	Maryland	287
7	Virginia	286
8	Massachusetts	285
9	Nevada	263
10	Georgia	259
11	Rhode Island	256
12	Tennessee	255
13	Florida	247
13	Texas	247
13	Wisconsin	247
16	Connecticut	245
16	New Mexico	245
18	Kansas	244
18	Missouri	244
20	South Carolina	243
21	Hawaii	241
22	Alabama	240
22	Colorado	240
24	North Carolina	235
25	Mississippi	231
26	Arkansas	230
27	Delaware	226
27	South Dakota	226
29	Arizona	225
30	Ohio	221
30	Oklahoma	221
32	Michigan	218
33	California	217
34	Alaska	215
34	Pennsylvania	215
36	Idaho	212
37	New Hampshire	206
38	Nebraska	204
39	North Dakota	201
40	Indiana	196
41	Montana	195
42	Oregon	190
43	Utah	187
44	Maine	186
45	Iowa	182
46	Kentucky	177
47	Minnesota	175
48	West Virginia	174
49	Vermont	170
50	Washington	168
	District of Columbia	693

Source: U.S. Department of Justice, Bureau of Justice Statistics
   "Census of State and Local Law Enforcement Agencies, 2000" (Bulletin, October 2002, NCJ 194066)
*Includes state and local police, sheriffs' departments and special police agencies.

State and Local Government Expenditures for Police Protection in 2000

National Total = $56,798,071,000*

<u>ALPHA ORDER</u>

RANK	STATE	EXPENDITURES	% of USA
26	Alabama	$655,951,000	1.2%
42	Alaska	176,972,000	0.3%
16	Arizona	1,096,134,000	1.9%
36	Arkansas	351,795,000	0.6%
1	California	8,703,685,000	15.3%
22	Colorado	830,063,000	1.5%
25	Connecticut	681,914,000	1.2%
44	Delaware	166,302,000	0.3%
3	Florida	3,738,392,000	6.6%
12	Georgia	1,279,240,000	2.3%
38	Hawaii	221,899,000	0.4%
40	Idaho	207,380,000	0.4%
5	Illinois	3,053,337,000	5.4%
21	Indiana	842,818,000	1.5%
32	Iowa	426,865,000	0.8%
31	Kansas	429,773,000	0.8%
30	Kentucky	488,139,000	0.9%
23	Louisiana	829,333,000	1.5%
45	Maine	163,824,000	0.3%
15	Maryland	1,120,192,000	2.0%
10	Massachusetts	1,478,778,000	2.6%
9	Michigan	1,792,535,000	3.2%
20	Minnesota	873,741,000	1.5%
33	Mississippi	403,888,000	0.7%
19	Missouri	885,498,000	1.6%
46	Montana	135,806,000	0.2%
37	Nebraska	235,245,000	0.4%
28	Nevada	539,187,000	0.9%
41	New Hampshire	187,070,000	0.3%
6	New Jersey	2,231,315,000	3.9%
34	New Mexico	382,185,000	0.7%
2	New York	5,716,952,000	10.1%
11	North Carolina	1,381,315,000	2.4%
50	North Dakota	68,182,000	0.1%
8	Ohio	2,124,836,000	3.7%
29	Oklahoma	518,334,000	0.9%
24	Oregon	695,999,000	1.2%
7	Pennsylvania	2,220,991,000	3.9%
39	Rhode Island	211,195,000	0.4%
27	South Carolina	653,266,000	1.2%
48	South Dakota	88,020,000	0.2%
18	Tennessee	940,212,000	1.7%
4	Texas	3,204,048,000	5.6%
35	Utah	380,972,000	0.7%
49	Vermont	77,900,000	0.1%
13	Virginia	1,175,518,000	2.1%
17	Washington	1,007,208,000	1.8%
43	West Virginia	171,146,000	0.3%
14	Wisconsin	1,124,272,000	2.0%
47	Wyoming	98,946,000	0.2%

<u>RANK ORDER</u>

RANK	STATE	EXPENDITURES	% of USA
1	California	$8,703,685,000	15.3%
2	New York	5,716,952,000	10.1%
3	Florida	3,738,392,000	6.6%
4	Texas	3,204,048,000	5.6%
5	Illinois	3,053,337,000	5.4%
6	New Jersey	2,231,315,000	3.9%
7	Pennsylvania	2,220,991,000	3.9%
8	Ohio	2,124,836,000	3.7%
9	Michigan	1,792,535,000	3.2%
10	Massachusetts	1,478,778,000	2.6%
11	North Carolina	1,381,315,000	2.4%
12	Georgia	1,279,240,000	2.3%
13	Virginia	1,175,518,000	2.1%
14	Wisconsin	1,124,272,000	2.0%
15	Maryland	1,120,192,000	2.0%
16	Arizona	1,096,134,000	1.9%
17	Washington	1,007,208,000	1.8%
18	Tennessee	940,212,000	1.7%
19	Missouri	885,498,000	1.6%
20	Minnesota	873,741,000	1.5%
21	Indiana	842,818,000	1.5%
22	Colorado	830,063,000	1.5%
23	Louisiana	829,333,000	1.5%
24	Oregon	695,999,000	1.2%
25	Connecticut	681,914,000	1.2%
26	Alabama	655,951,000	1.2%
27	South Carolina	653,266,000	1.2%
28	Nevada	539,187,000	0.9%
29	Oklahoma	518,334,000	0.9%
30	Kentucky	488,139,000	0.9%
31	Kansas	429,773,000	0.8%
32	Iowa	426,865,000	0.8%
33	Mississippi	403,888,000	0.7%
34	New Mexico	382,185,000	0.7%
35	Utah	380,972,000	0.7%
36	Arkansas	351,795,000	0.6%
37	Nebraska	235,245,000	0.4%
38	Hawaii	221,899,000	0.4%
39	Rhode Island	211,195,000	0.4%
40	Idaho	207,380,000	0.4%
41	New Hampshire	187,070,000	0.3%
42	Alaska	176,972,000	0.3%
43	West Virginia	171,146,000	0.3%
44	Delaware	166,302,000	0.3%
45	Maine	163,824,000	0.3%
46	Montana	135,806,000	0.2%
47	Wyoming	98,946,000	0.2%
48	South Dakota	88,020,000	0.2%
49	Vermont	77,900,000	0.1%
50	North Dakota	68,182,000	0.1%
	District of Columbia	329,503,000	0.6%

Source: U.S. Bureau of the Census, Governments Division
   "State and Local Government Finances: 1999-00" (http://www.census.gov/govs/www/estimate00.html)
*Direct general expenditures.

Per Capita State & Local Government Expenditures for Police Protection: 2000

National Per Capita = $201*

<u>ALPHA ORDER</u>

RANK	STATE	PER CAPITA
39	Alabama	$147
2	Alaska	282
9	Arizona	212
44	Arkansas	131
5	California	256
18	Colorado	192
16	Connecticut	200
10	Delaware	211
7	Florida	233
34	Georgia	155
21	Hawaii	183
31	Idaho	160
6	Illinois	245
42	Indiana	138
40	Iowa	146
31	Kansas	160
47	Kentucky	121
20	Louisiana	186
45	Maine	128
10	Maryland	211
8	Massachusetts	232
23	Michigan	180
24	Minnesota	177
41	Mississippi	142
33	Missouri	158
37	Montana	150
43	Nebraska	137
3	Nevada	267
36	New Hampshire	151
4	New Jersey	265
12	New Mexico	210
1	New York	301
25	North Carolina	171
49	North Dakota	106
19	Ohio	187
37	Oklahoma	150
14	Oregon	203
22	Pennsylvania	181
15	Rhode Island	201
30	South Carolina	162
48	South Dakota	116
28	Tennessee	165
35	Texas	153
26	Utah	170
45	Vermont	128
28	Virginia	165
26	Washington	170
50	West Virginia	95
13	Wisconsin	209
16	Wyoming	200

<u>RANK ORDER</u>

RANK	STATE	PER CAPITA
1	New York	$301
2	Alaska	282
3	Nevada	267
4	New Jersey	265
5	California	256
6	Illinois	245
7	Florida	233
8	Massachusetts	232
9	Arizona	212
10	Delaware	211
10	Maryland	211
12	New Mexico	210
13	Wisconsin	209
14	Oregon	203
15	Rhode Island	201
16	Connecticut	200
16	Wyoming	200
18	Colorado	192
19	Ohio	187
20	Louisiana	186
21	Hawaii	183
22	Pennsylvania	181
23	Michigan	180
24	Minnesota	177
25	North Carolina	171
26	Utah	170
26	Washington	170
28	Tennessee	165
28	Virginia	165
30	South Carolina	162
31	Idaho	160
31	Kansas	160
33	Missouri	158
34	Georgia	155
35	Texas	153
36	New Hampshire	151
37	Montana	150
37	Oklahoma	150
39	Alabama	147
40	Iowa	146
41	Mississippi	142
42	Indiana	138
43	Nebraska	137
44	Arkansas	131
45	Maine	128
45	Vermont	128
47	Kentucky	121
48	South Dakota	116
49	North Dakota	106
50	West Virginia	95

	District of Columbia	576

Source: Morgan Quitno Press using data from U.S. Bureau of the Census, Governments Division
   "State and Local Government Finances: 1999-00" (http://www.census.gov/govs/www/estimate00.html)
*Direct general expenditures.

State and Local Government Expenditures for Corrections in 2000

National Total = $48,805,439,000*

ALPHA ORDER

RANK	STATE	EXPENDITURES	% of USA
30	Alabama	$404,284,000	0.8%
41	Alaska	174,989,000	0.4%
16	Arizona	955,000,000	2.0%
33	Arkansas	327,770,000	0.7%
1	California	7,170,388,000	14.7%
17	Colorado	820,339,000	1.7%
27	Connecticut	553,905,000	1.1%
38	Delaware	228,076,000	0.5%
4	Florida	3,272,673,000	6.7%
10	Georgia	1,375,497,000	2.8%
42	Hawaii	154,622,000	0.3%
39	Idaho	191,101,000	0.4%
8	Illinois	1,762,571,000	3.6%
21	Indiana	726,912,000	1.5%
35	Iowa	297,568,000	0.6%
32	Kansas	349,255,000	0.7%
23	Kentucky	610,565,000	1.3%
19	Louisiana	779,845,000	1.6%
45	Maine	123,304,000	0.3%
13	Maryland	1,103,902,000	2.3%
18	Massachusetts	794,586,000	1.6%
7	Michigan	1,852,720,000	3.8%
25	Minnesota	591,083,000	1.2%
36	Mississippi	291,839,000	0.6%
22	Missouri	672,333,000	1.4%
44	Montana	124,733,000	0.3%
37	Nebraska	231,457,000	0.5%
29	Nevada	471,493,000	1.0%
46	New Hampshire	115,184,000	0.2%
9	New Jersey	1,480,255,000	3.0%
34	New Mexico	315,419,000	0.6%
2	New York	4,392,230,000	9.0%
12	North Carolina	1,158,568,000	2.4%
50	North Dakota	40,430,000	0.1%
6	Ohio	1,937,408,000	4.0%
28	Oklahoma	511,322,000	1.0%
20	Oregon	747,312,000	1.5%
5	Pennsylvania	2,221,971,000	4.6%
43	Rhode Island	139,225,000	0.3%
26	South Carolina	558,521,000	1.1%
48	South Dakota	81,081,000	0.2%
24	Tennessee	604,026,000	1.2%
3	Texas	3,755,643,000	7.7%
31	Utah	351,415,000	0.7%
49	Vermont	66,304,000	0.1%
11	Virginia	1,246,135,000	2.6%
14	Washington	1,053,373,000	2.2%
40	West Virginia	184,132,000	0.4%
15	Wisconsin	1,029,820,000	2.1%
47	Wyoming	98,351,000	0.2%

RANK ORDER

RANK	STATE	EXPENDITURES	% of USA
1	California	$7,170,388,000	14.7%
2	New York	4,392,230,000	9.0%
3	Texas	3,755,643,000	7.7%
4	Florida	3,272,673,000	6.7%
5	Pennsylvania	2,221,971,000	4.6%
6	Ohio	1,937,408,000	4.0%
7	Michigan	1,852,720,000	3.8%
8	Illinois	1,762,571,000	3.6%
9	New Jersey	1,480,255,000	3.0%
10	Georgia	1,375,497,000	2.8%
11	Virginia	1,246,135,000	2.6%
12	North Carolina	1,158,568,000	2.4%
13	Maryland	1,103,902,000	2.3%
14	Washington	1,053,373,000	2.2%
15	Wisconsin	1,029,820,000	2.1%
16	Arizona	955,000,000	2.0%
17	Colorado	820,339,000	1.7%
18	Massachusetts	794,586,000	1.6%
19	Louisiana	779,845,000	1.6%
20	Oregon	747,312,000	1.5%
21	Indiana	726,912,000	1.5%
22	Missouri	672,333,000	1.4%
23	Kentucky	610,565,000	1.3%
24	Tennessee	604,026,000	1.2%
25	Minnesota	591,083,000	1.2%
26	South Carolina	558,521,000	1.1%
27	Connecticut	553,905,000	1.1%
28	Oklahoma	511,322,000	1.0%
29	Nevada	471,493,000	1.0%
30	Alabama	404,284,000	0.8%
31	Utah	351,415,000	0.7%
32	Kansas	349,255,000	0.7%
33	Arkansas	327,770,000	0.7%
34	New Mexico	315,419,000	0.6%
35	Iowa	297,568,000	0.6%
36	Mississippi	291,839,000	0.6%
37	Nebraska	231,457,000	0.5%
38	Delaware	228,076,000	0.5%
39	Idaho	191,101,000	0.4%
40	West Virginia	184,132,000	0.4%
41	Alaska	174,989,000	0.4%
42	Hawaii	154,622,000	0.3%
43	Rhode Island	139,225,000	0.3%
44	Montana	124,733,000	0.3%
45	Maine	123,304,000	0.3%
46	New Hampshire	115,184,000	0.2%
47	Wyoming	98,351,000	0.2%
48	South Dakota	81,081,000	0.2%
49	Vermont	66,304,000	0.1%
50	North Dakota	40,430,000	0.1%
	District of Columbia	304,504,000	0.6%

Source: U.S. Bureau of the Census, Governments Division
"State and Local Government Finances: 1999-00" (http://www.census.gov/govs/www/estimate00.html)
**Direct general expenditures.*

Per Capita State and Local Government Expenditures for Corrections in 2000

National Per Capita = $173*

<u>ALPHA ORDER</u>

RANK	STATE	PER CAPITA
49	Alabama	$91
2	Alaska	279
13	Arizona	185
37	Arkansas	122
6	California	211
11	Colorado	190
23	Connecticut	162
1	Delaware	290
8	Florida	204
22	Georgia	167
35	Hawaii	128
27	Idaho	147
29	Illinois	142
40	Indiana	119
44	Iowa	102
34	Kansas	130
25	Kentucky	151
19	Louisiana	174
47	Maine	97
7	Maryland	208
36	Massachusetts	125
12	Michigan	186
38	Minnesota	120
44	Mississippi	102
38	Missouri	120
31	Montana	138
32	Nebraska	135
3	Nevada	234
48	New Hampshire	93
17	New Jersey	176
20	New Mexico	173
4	New York	231
28	North Carolina	143
50	North Dakota	63
21	Ohio	170
26	Oklahoma	148
5	Oregon	218
14	Pennsylvania	181
33	Rhode Island	133
30	South Carolina	139
42	South Dakota	107
43	Tennessee	106
15	Texas	179
24	Utah	157
41	Vermont	109
18	Virginia	175
16	Washington	178
44	West Virginia	102
10	Wisconsin	192
9	Wyoming	199

<u>RANK ORDER</u>

RANK	STATE	PER CAPITA
1	Delaware	$290
2	Alaska	279
3	Nevada	234
4	New York	231
5	Oregon	218
6	California	211
7	Maryland	208
8	Florida	204
9	Wyoming	199
10	Wisconsin	192
11	Colorado	190
12	Michigan	186
13	Arizona	185
14	Pennsylvania	181
15	Texas	179
16	Washington	178
17	New Jersey	176
18	Virginia	175
19	Louisiana	174
20	New Mexico	173
21	Ohio	170
22	Georgia	167
23	Connecticut	162
24	Utah	157
25	Kentucky	151
26	Oklahoma	148
27	Idaho	147
28	North Carolina	143
29	Illinois	142
30	South Carolina	139
31	Montana	138
32	Nebraska	135
33	Rhode Island	133
34	Kansas	130
35	Hawaii	128
36	Massachusetts	125
37	Arkansas	122
38	Minnesota	120
38	Missouri	120
40	Indiana	119
41	Vermont	109
42	South Dakota	107
43	Tennessee	106
44	Iowa	102
44	Mississippi	102
44	West Virginia	102
47	Maine	97
48	New Hampshire	93
49	Alabama	91
50	North Dakota	63

| | District of Columbia | 533 |

Source: Morgan Quitno Press using data from U.S. Bureau of the Census, Governments Division
"State and Local Government Finances: 1999-00" (http://www.census.gov/govs/www/estimate00.html)
*Direct general expenditures.

III. DEFENSE

U.S. Department of Defense Domestic Expenditures in 2002

National Total = $276,281,367,000*

<u>ALPHA ORDER</u>

RANK	STATE	EXPENDITURES	% of USA
9	Alabama	$7,432,145,000	2.7%
33	Alaska	1,978,698,000	0.7%
7	Arizona	8,946,782,000	3.2%
35	Arkansas	1,715,989,000	0.6%
1	California	36,567,588,000	13.2%
17	Colorado	5,341,905,000	1.9%
14	Connecticut	6,260,559,000	2.3%
47	Delaware	521,134,000	0.2%
4	Florida	14,727,019,000	5.3%
5	Georgia	11,335,549,000	4.1%
21	Hawaii	4,293,459,000	1.6%
44	Idaho	603,073,000	0.2%
19	Illinois	4,509,221,000	1.6%
27	Indiana	2,947,481,000	1.1%
42	Iowa	924,232,000	0.3%
30	Kansas	2,489,466,000	0.9%
20	Kentucky	4,322,458,000	1.6%
25	Louisiana	3,286,132,000	1.2%
34	Maine	1,770,957,000	0.6%
6	Maryland	10,836,070,000	3.9%
15	Massachusetts	6,022,125,000	2.2%
26	Michigan	3,243,056,000	1.2%
31	Minnesota	2,097,325,000	0.8%
24	Mississippi	3,797,930,000	1.4%
8	Missouri	7,522,744,000	2.7%
49	Montana	470,438,000	0.2%
39	Nebraska	1,060,309,000	0.4%
37	Nevada	1,266,138,000	0.5%
41	New Hampshire	936,639,000	0.3%
18	New Jersey	5,094,791,000	1.8%
32	New Mexico	2,016,378,000	0.7%
13	New York	6,644,252,000	2.4%
12	North Carolina	6,734,295,000	2.4%
43	North Dakota	607,672,000	0.2%
16	Ohio	5,946,252,000	2.2%
22	Oklahoma	4,146,617,000	1.5%
38	Oregon	1,062,852,000	0.4%
11	Pennsylvania	7,218,929,000	2.6%
40	Rhode Island	960,877,000	0.3%
23	South Carolina	3,817,164,000	1.4%
48	South Dakota	475,969,000	0.2%
29	Tennessee	2,599,656,000	0.9%
3	Texas	23,280,700,000	8.4%
28	Utah	2,796,609,000	1.0%
46	Vermont	524,724,000	0.2%
2	Virginia	31,234,545,000	11.3%
10	Washington	7,221,635,000	2.6%
45	West Virginia	552,977,000	0.2%
36	Wisconsin	1,641,101,000	0.6%
50	Wyoming	336,016,000	0.1%

<u>RANK ORDER</u>

RANK	STATE	EXPENDITURES	% of USA
1	California	$36,567,588,000	13.2%
2	Virginia	31,234,545,000	11.3%
3	Texas	23,280,700,000	8.4%
4	Florida	14,727,019,000	5.3%
5	Georgia	11,335,549,000	4.1%
6	Maryland	10,836,070,000	3.9%
7	Arizona	8,946,782,000	3.2%
8	Missouri	7,522,744,000	2.7%
9	Alabama	7,432,145,000	2.7%
10	Washington	7,221,635,000	2.6%
11	Pennsylvania	7,218,929,000	2.6%
12	North Carolina	6,734,295,000	2.4%
13	New York	6,644,252,000	2.4%
14	Connecticut	6,260,559,000	2.3%
15	Massachusetts	6,022,125,000	2.2%
16	Ohio	5,946,252,000	2.2%
17	Colorado	5,341,905,000	1.9%
18	New Jersey	5,094,791,000	1.8%
19	Illinois	4,509,221,000	1.6%
20	Kentucky	4,322,458,000	1.6%
21	Hawaii	4,293,459,000	1.6%
22	Oklahoma	4,146,617,000	1.5%
23	South Carolina	3,817,164,000	1.4%
24	Mississippi	3,797,930,000	1.4%
25	Louisiana	3,286,132,000	1.2%
26	Michigan	3,243,056,000	1.2%
27	Indiana	2,947,481,000	1.1%
28	Utah	2,796,609,000	1.0%
29	Tennessee	2,599,656,000	0.9%
30	Kansas	2,489,466,000	0.9%
31	Minnesota	2,097,325,000	0.8%
32	New Mexico	2,016,378,000	0.7%
33	Alaska	1,978,698,000	0.7%
34	Maine	1,770,957,000	0.6%
35	Arkansas	1,715,989,000	0.6%
36	Wisconsin	1,641,101,000	0.6%
37	Nevada	1,266,138,000	0.5%
38	Oregon	1,062,852,000	0.4%
39	Nebraska	1,060,309,000	0.4%
40	Rhode Island	960,877,000	0.3%
41	New Hampshire	936,639,000	0.3%
42	Iowa	924,232,000	0.3%
43	North Dakota	607,672,000	0.2%
44	Idaho	603,073,000	0.2%
45	West Virginia	552,977,000	0.2%
46	Vermont	524,724,000	0.2%
47	Delaware	521,134,000	0.2%
48	South Dakota	475,969,000	0.2%
49	Montana	470,438,000	0.2%
50	Wyoming	336,016,000	0.1%
	District of Columbia	4,140,735,000	1.5%

Source: U.S. Department of Defense
  "Atlas/Data Abstract for the United States" (http://www.dior.whs.mil/mmid/l03/fy02/ATLAS_2002.pdf)
**Expenditures for payroll, grants and prime contracts ($25,000 or more) for civil and military functions. Does not include payroll, contracts or grants to U.S. territories and other countries.*

Per Capita U.S. Department of Defense Domestic Expenditures in 2002

National Per Capita = $959*

<u>ALPHA ORDER</u>

RANK	STATE	PER CAPITA
6	Alabama	$1,659
3	Alaska	3,085
7	Arizona	1,644
32	Arkansas	634
19	California	1,045
15	Colorado	1,187
5	Connecticut	1,810
31	Delaware	647
25	Florida	882
9	Georgia	1,327
2	Hawaii	3,461
41	Idaho	449
44	Illinois	358
40	Indiana	479
47	Iowa	315
23	Kansas	918
18	Kentucky	1,057
29	Louisiana	734
8	Maine	1,368
4	Maryland	1,988
21	Massachusetts	938
46	Michigan	323
43	Minnesota	417
11	Mississippi	1,325
9	Missouri	1,327
39	Montana	517
34	Nebraska	614
37	Nevada	584
28	New Hampshire	735
35	New Jersey	594
16	New Mexico	1,089
45	New York	347
27	North Carolina	811
20	North Dakota	959
38	Ohio	521
14	Oklahoma	1,188
49	Oregon	302
36	Pennsylvania	586
24	Rhode Island	899
22	South Carolina	930
33	South Dakota	626
41	Tennessee	449
17	Texas	1,071
12	Utah	1,206
26	Vermont	851
1	Virginia	4,286
13	Washington	1,190
48	West Virginia	306
49	Wisconsin	302
30	Wyoming	674

<u>RANK ORDER</u>

RANK	STATE	PER CAPITA
1	Virginia	$4,286
2	Hawaii	3,461
3	Alaska	3,085
4	Maryland	1,988
5	Connecticut	1,810
6	Alabama	1,659
7	Arizona	1,644
8	Maine	1,368
9	Georgia	1,327
9	Missouri	1,327
11	Mississippi	1,325
12	Utah	1,206
13	Washington	1,190
14	Oklahoma	1,188
15	Colorado	1,187
16	New Mexico	1,089
17	Texas	1,071
18	Kentucky	1,057
19	California	1,045
20	North Dakota	959
21	Massachusetts	938
22	South Carolina	930
23	Kansas	918
24	Rhode Island	899
25	Florida	882
26	Vermont	851
27	North Carolina	811
28	New Hampshire	735
29	Louisiana	734
30	Wyoming	674
31	Delaware	647
32	Arkansas	634
33	South Dakota	626
34	Nebraska	614
35	New Jersey	594
36	Pennsylvania	586
37	Nevada	584
38	Ohio	521
39	Montana	517
40	Indiana	479
41	Idaho	449
41	Tennessee	449
43	Minnesota	417
44	Illinois	358
45	New York	347
46	Michigan	323
47	Iowa	315
48	West Virginia	306
49	Oregon	302
49	Wisconsin	302
	District of Columbia	7,275

Source: Morgan Quitno Press using data from U.S. Department of Defense
"Atlas/Data Abstract for the United States" (http://www.dior.whs.mil/mmid/l03/fy02/ATLAS_2002.pdf)
*Expenditures for payroll, grants and prime contracts ($25,000 or more) for civil and military functions. Does not include payroll, contracts or grants to U.S. territories and other countries.

U.S. Department of Defense Total Contracts in 2002

National Total = $158,737,415,000*

ALPHA ORDER

RANK	STATE	CONTRACTS	% of USA
11	Alabama	$4,671,560,000	2.9%
34	Alaska	911,379,000	0.6%
5	Arizona	6,685,404,000	4.2%
35	Arkansas	833,141,000	0.5%
1	California	23,816,177,000	15.0%
17	Colorado	2,623,565,000	1.7%
9	Connecticut	5,638,585,000	3.6%
48	Delaware	135,060,000	0.1%
4	Florida	7,072,528,000	4.5%
7	Georgia	5,814,189,000	3.7%
28	Hawaii	1,433,119,000	0.9%
47	Idaho	160,697,000	0.1%
21	Illinois	2,005,762,000	1.3%
22	Indiana	1,860,428,000	1.2%
38	Iowa	552,234,000	0.3%
30	Kansas	1,222,935,000	0.8%
19	Kentucky	2,268,260,000	1.4%
23	Louisiana	1,682,812,000	1.1%
32	Maine	1,107,663,000	0.7%
6	Maryland	6,505,462,000	4.1%
10	Massachusetts	4,928,676,000	3.1%
20	Michigan	2,179,870,000	1.4%
25	Minnesota	1,528,525,000	1.0%
18	Mississippi	2,271,530,000	1.4%
8	Missouri	5,755,990,000	3.6%
49	Montana	128,624,000	0.1%
43	Nebraska	306,122,000	0.2%
42	Nevada	359,262,000	0.2%
37	New Hampshire	605,698,000	0.4%
14	New Jersey	3,452,131,000	2.2%
36	New Mexico	823,396,000	0.5%
13	New York	4,434,731,000	2.8%
26	North Carolina	1,520,130,000	1.0%
44	North Dakota	206,758,000	0.1%
15	Ohio	3,444,496,000	2.2%
24	Oklahoma	1,572,682,000	1.0%
39	Oregon	404,145,000	0.3%
12	Pennsylvania	4,570,861,000	2.9%
41	Rhode Island	364,616,000	0.2%
31	South Carolina	1,138,083,000	0.7%
45	South Dakota	190,931,000	0.1%
29	Tennessee	1,304,693,000	0.8%
3	Texas	13,699,670,000	8.6%
27	Utah	1,509,359,000	1.0%
40	Vermont	383,948,000	0.2%
2	Virginia	18,128,348,000	11.4%
16	Washington	2,789,477,000	1.8%
46	West Virginia	169,542,000	0.1%
33	Wisconsin	1,064,759,000	0.7%
50	Wyoming	79,204,000	0.0%

RANK ORDER

RANK	STATE	CONTRACTS	% of USA
1	California	$23,816,177,000	15.0%
2	Virginia	18,128,348,000	11.4%
3	Texas	13,699,670,000	8.6%
4	Florida	7,072,528,000	4.5%
5	Arizona	6,685,404,000	4.2%
6	Maryland	6,505,462,000	4.1%
7	Georgia	5,814,189,000	3.7%
8	Missouri	5,755,990,000	3.6%
9	Connecticut	5,638,585,000	3.6%
10	Massachusetts	4,928,676,000	3.1%
11	Alabama	4,671,560,000	2.9%
12	Pennsylvania	4,570,861,000	2.9%
13	New York	4,434,731,000	2.8%
14	New Jersey	3,452,131,000	2.2%
15	Ohio	3,444,496,000	2.2%
16	Washington	2,789,477,000	1.8%
17	Colorado	2,623,565,000	1.7%
18	Mississippi	2,271,530,000	1.4%
19	Kentucky	2,268,260,000	1.4%
20	Michigan	2,179,870,000	1.4%
21	Illinois	2,005,762,000	1.3%
22	Indiana	1,860,428,000	1.2%
23	Louisiana	1,682,812,000	1.1%
24	Oklahoma	1,572,682,000	1.0%
25	Minnesota	1,528,525,000	1.0%
26	North Carolina	1,520,130,000	1.0%
27	Utah	1,509,359,000	1.0%
28	Hawaii	1,433,119,000	0.9%
29	Tennessee	1,304,693,000	0.8%
30	Kansas	1,222,935,000	0.8%
31	South Carolina	1,138,083,000	0.7%
32	Maine	1,107,663,000	0.7%
33	Wisconsin	1,064,759,000	0.7%
34	Alaska	911,379,000	0.6%
35	Arkansas	833,141,000	0.5%
36	New Mexico	823,396,000	0.5%
37	New Hampshire	605,698,000	0.4%
38	Iowa	552,234,000	0.3%
39	Oregon	404,145,000	0.3%
40	Vermont	383,948,000	0.2%
41	Rhode Island	364,616,000	0.2%
42	Nevada	359,262,000	0.2%
43	Nebraska	306,122,000	0.2%
44	North Dakota	206,758,000	0.1%
45	South Dakota	190,931,000	0.1%
46	West Virginia	169,542,000	0.1%
47	Idaho	160,697,000	0.1%
48	Delaware	135,060,000	0.1%
49	Montana	128,624,000	0.1%
50	Wyoming	79,204,000	0.0%
	District of Columbia	2,420,198,000	1.5%

Source: U.S. Department of Defense
   "Atlas/Data Abstract for the United States" (http://www.dior.whs.mil/mmid/l03/fy02/ATLAS_2002.pdf)
*Includes prime contracts ($25,000 or more) for civil and military functions. Does not include contracts to U.S. territories and other countries.

Per Capita U.S. Department of Defense Total Contracts in 2002

National Per Capita = $551*

<u>ALPHA ORDER</u>

RANK	STATE	PER CAPITA
7	Alabama	$1,043
3	Alaska	1,421
4	Arizona	1,229
30	Arkansas	308
12	California	680
17	Colorado	583
2	Connecticut	1,630
43	Delaware	168
24	Florida	424
12	Georgia	680
6	Hawaii	1,155
48	Idaho	120
45	Illinois	159
32	Indiana	302
40	Iowa	188
21	Kansas	451
18	Kentucky	555
26	Louisiana	376
9	Maine	855
5	Maryland	1,194
11	Massachusetts	767
38	Michigan	217
31	Minnesota	304
10	Mississippi	792
8	Missouri	1,015
47	Montana	141
42	Nebraska	177
44	Nevada	166
19	New Hampshire	475
25	New Jersey	403
23	New Mexico	445
36	New York	232
41	North Carolina	183
29	North Dakota	326
32	Ohio	302
21	Oklahoma	451
49	Oregon	115
27	Pennsylvania	371
28	Rhode Island	341
34	South Carolina	277
35	South Dakota	251
37	Tennessee	225
15	Texas	630
14	Utah	651
16	Vermont	623
1	Virginia	2,487
20	Washington	460
50	West Virginia	94
39	Wisconsin	196
45	Wyoming	159

<u>RANK ORDER</u>

RANK	STATE	PER CAPITA
1	Virginia	$2,487
2	Connecticut	1,630
3	Alaska	1,421
4	Arizona	1,229
5	Maryland	1,194
6	Hawaii	1,155
7	Alabama	1,043
8	Missouri	1,015
9	Maine	855
10	Mississippi	792
11	Massachusetts	767
12	California	680
12	Georgia	680
14	Utah	651
15	Texas	630
16	Vermont	623
17	Colorado	583
18	Kentucky	555
19	New Hampshire	475
20	Washington	460
21	Kansas	451
21	Oklahoma	451
23	New Mexico	445
24	Florida	424
25	New Jersey	403
26	Louisiana	376
27	Pennsylvania	371
28	Rhode Island	341
29	North Dakota	326
30	Arkansas	308
31	Minnesota	304
32	Indiana	302
32	Ohio	302
34	South Carolina	277
35	South Dakota	251
36	New York	232
37	Tennessee	225
38	Michigan	217
39	Wisconsin	196
40	Iowa	188
41	North Carolina	183
42	Nebraska	177
43	Delaware	168
44	Nevada	166
45	Illinois	159
45	Wyoming	159
47	Montana	141
48	Idaho	120
49	Oregon	115
50	West Virginia	94
	District of Columbia	4,252

Source: Morgan Quitno Press using data from U.S. Department of Defense
"Atlas/Data Abstract for the United States" (http://www.dior.whs.mil/mmid/I03/fy02/ATLAS_2002.pdf)
**Expenditures for payroll, grants and prime contracts ($25,000 or more) for civil and military functions. Does not include payroll, contracts or grants to U.S. territories and other countries.*

U.S. Department of Defense Contracts for Military Functions in 2002

National Total = $155,326,763,000*

ALPHA ORDER

RANK	STATE	CONTRACTS	% of USA
11	Alabama	$4,545,057,000	2.9%
34	Alaska	881,273,000	0.6%
5	Arizona	6,662,478,000	4.3%
36	Arkansas	731,199,000	0.5%
1	California	23,632,846,000	15.2%
17	Colorado	2,597,630,000	1.7%
8	Connecticut	5,630,341,000	3.6%
47	Delaware	123,763,000	0.1%
4	Florida	6,858,018,000	4.4%
7	Georgia	5,746,684,000	3.7%
26	Hawaii	1,426,334,000	0.9%
46	Idaho	150,141,000	0.1%
21	Illinois	1,890,128,000	1.2%
22	Indiana	1,830,444,000	1.2%
38	Iowa	530,107,000	0.3%
30	Kansas	1,195,247,000	0.8%
18	Kentucky	2,192,394,000	1.4%
27	Louisiana	1,414,167,000	0.9%
32	Maine	1,096,423,000	0.7%
6	Maryland	6,426,655,000	4.1%
10	Massachusetts	4,844,317,000	3.1%
19	Michigan	2,150,141,000	1.4%
25	Minnesota	1,486,795,000	1.0%
20	Mississippi	2,149,950,000	1.4%
9	Missouri	5,615,874,000	3.6%
48	Montana	117,053,000	0.1%
43	Nebraska	290,608,000	0.2%
41	Nevada	337,822,000	0.2%
37	New Hampshire	592,226,000	0.4%
15	New Jersey	3,244,870,000	2.1%
35	New Mexico	791,265,000	0.5%
13	New York	4,274,010,000	2.8%
28	North Carolina	1,409,554,000	0.9%
45	North Dakota	175,051,000	0.1%
14	Ohio	3,396,417,000	2.2%
23	Oklahoma	1,544,286,000	1.0%
42	Oregon	304,451,000	0.2%
12	Pennsylvania	4,469,056,000	2.9%
40	Rhode Island	361,279,000	0.2%
31	South Carolina	1,104,365,000	0.7%
44	South Dakota	181,231,000	0.1%
29	Tennessee	1,249,635,000	0.8%
3	Texas	13,513,486,000	8.7%
24	Utah	1,501,763,000	1.0%
39	Vermont	379,301,000	0.2%
2	Virginia	18,031,694,000	11.6%
16	Washington	2,706,404,000	1.7%
49	West Virginia	104,054,000	0.1%
33	Wisconsin	1,041,986,000	0.7%
50	Wyoming	78,547,000	0.1%

RANK ORDER

RANK	STATE	CONTRACTS	% of USA
1	California	$23,632,846,000	15.2%
2	Virginia	18,031,694,000	11.6%
3	Texas	13,513,486,000	8.7%
4	Florida	6,858,018,000	4.4%
5	Arizona	6,662,478,000	4.3%
6	Maryland	6,426,655,000	4.1%
7	Georgia	5,746,684,000	3.7%
8	Connecticut	5,630,341,000	3.6%
9	Missouri	5,615,874,000	3.6%
10	Massachusetts	4,844,317,000	3.1%
11	Alabama	4,545,057,000	2.9%
12	Pennsylvania	4,469,056,000	2.9%
13	New York	4,274,010,000	2.8%
14	Ohio	3,396,417,000	2.2%
15	New Jersey	3,244,870,000	2.1%
16	Washington	2,706,404,000	1.7%
17	Colorado	2,597,630,000	1.7%
18	Kentucky	2,192,394,000	1.4%
19	Michigan	2,150,141,000	1.4%
20	Mississippi	2,149,950,000	1.4%
21	Illinois	1,890,128,000	1.2%
22	Indiana	1,830,444,000	1.2%
23	Oklahoma	1,544,286,000	1.0%
24	Utah	1,501,763,000	1.0%
25	Minnesota	1,486,795,000	1.0%
26	Hawaii	1,426,334,000	0.9%
27	Louisiana	1,414,167,000	0.9%
28	North Carolina	1,409,554,000	0.9%
29	Tennessee	1,249,635,000	0.8%
30	Kansas	1,195,247,000	0.8%
31	South Carolina	1,104,365,000	0.7%
32	Maine	1,096,423,000	0.7%
33	Wisconsin	1,041,986,000	0.7%
34	Alaska	881,273,000	0.6%
35	New Mexico	791,265,000	0.5%
36	Arkansas	731,199,000	0.5%
37	New Hampshire	592,226,000	0.4%
38	Iowa	530,107,000	0.3%
39	Vermont	379,301,000	0.2%
40	Rhode Island	361,279,000	0.2%
41	Nevada	337,822,000	0.2%
42	Oregon	304,451,000	0.2%
43	Nebraska	290,608,000	0.2%
44	South Dakota	181,231,000	0.1%
45	North Dakota	175,051,000	0.1%
46	Idaho	150,141,000	0.1%
47	Delaware	123,763,000	0.1%
48	Montana	117,053,000	0.1%
49	West Virginia	104,054,000	0.1%
50	Wyoming	78,547,000	0.1%
	District of Columbia	2,317,943,000	1.5%

U.S. Department of Defense Contracts for Civil Functions in 2002

National Total = $3,410,652,000*

ALPHA ORDER

RANK	STATE	CONTRACTS	% of USA
8	Alabama	$126,503,000	3.7%
28	Alaska	30,106,000	0.9%
34	Arizona	22,926,000	0.7%
12	Arkansas	101,942,000	3.0%
5	California	183,331,000	5.4%
33	Colorado	25,935,000	0.8%
45	Connecticut	8,244,000	0.2%
41	Delaware	11,297,000	0.3%
2	Florida	214,510,000	6.3%
20	Georgia	67,505,000	2.0%
47	Hawaii	6,785,000	0.2%
43	Idaho	10,556,000	0.3%
10	Illinois	115,634,000	3.4%
29	Indiana	29,984,000	0.9%
36	Iowa	22,127,000	0.6%
32	Kansas	27,688,000	0.8%
19	Kentucky	75,866,000	2.2%
1	Louisiana	268,645,000	7.9%
42	Maine	11,240,000	0.3%
18	Maryland	78,807,000	2.3%
16	Massachusetts	84,359,000	2.5%
30	Michigan	29,729,000	0.9%
24	Minnesota	41,730,000	1.2%
9	Mississippi	121,580,000	3.6%
7	Missouri	140,116,000	4.1%
40	Montana	11,571,000	0.3%
38	Nebraska	15,514,000	0.5%
37	Nevada	21,440,000	0.6%
39	New Hampshire	13,472,000	0.4%
3	New Jersey	207,261,000	6.1%
26	New Mexico	32,131,000	0.9%
6	New York	160,721,000	4.7%
11	North Carolina	110,576,000	3.2%
27	North Dakota	31,707,000	0.9%
23	Ohio	48,079,000	1.4%
31	Oklahoma	28,396,000	0.8%
14	Oregon	99,694,000	2.9%
13	Pennsylvania	101,805,000	3.0%
49	Rhode Island	3,337,000	0.1%
25	South Carolina	33,718,000	1.0%
44	South Dakota	9,700,000	0.3%
22	Tennessee	55,058,000	1.6%
4	Texas	186,184,000	5.5%
46	Utah	7,596,000	0.2%
48	Vermont	4,647,000	0.1%
15	Virginia	96,654,000	2.8%
17	Washington	83,073,000	2.4%
21	West Virginia	65,488,000	1.9%
35	Wisconsin	22,773,000	0.7%
50	Wyoming	657,000	0.0%

RANK ORDER

RANK	STATE	CONTRACTS	% of USA
1	Louisiana	$268,645,000	7.9%
2	Florida	214,510,000	6.3%
3	New Jersey	207,261,000	6.1%
4	Texas	186,184,000	5.5%
5	California	183,331,000	5.4%
6	New York	160,721,000	4.7%
7	Missouri	140,116,000	4.1%
8	Alabama	126,503,000	3.7%
9	Mississippi	121,580,000	3.6%
10	Illinois	115,634,000	3.4%
11	North Carolina	110,576,000	3.2%
12	Arkansas	101,942,000	3.0%
13	Pennsylvania	101,805,000	3.0%
14	Oregon	99,694,000	2.9%
15	Virginia	96,654,000	2.8%
16	Massachusetts	84,359,000	2.5%
17	Washington	83,073,000	2.4%
18	Maryland	78,807,000	2.3%
19	Kentucky	75,866,000	2.2%
20	Georgia	67,505,000	2.0%
21	West Virginia	65,488,000	1.9%
22	Tennessee	55,058,000	1.6%
23	Ohio	48,079,000	1.4%
24	Minnesota	41,730,000	1.2%
25	South Carolina	33,718,000	1.0%
26	New Mexico	32,131,000	0.9%
27	North Dakota	31,707,000	0.9%
28	Alaska	30,106,000	0.9%
29	Indiana	29,984,000	0.9%
30	Michigan	29,729,000	0.9%
31	Oklahoma	28,396,000	0.8%
32	Kansas	27,688,000	0.8%
33	Colorado	25,935,000	0.8%
34	Arizona	22,926,000	0.7%
35	Wisconsin	22,773,000	0.7%
36	Iowa	22,127,000	0.6%
37	Nevada	21,440,000	0.6%
38	Nebraska	15,514,000	0.5%
39	New Hampshire	13,472,000	0.4%
40	Montana	11,571,000	0.3%
41	Delaware	11,297,000	0.3%
42	Maine	11,240,000	0.3%
43	Idaho	10,556,000	0.3%
44	South Dakota	9,700,000	0.3%
45	Connecticut	8,244,000	0.2%
46	Utah	7,596,000	0.2%
47	Hawaii	6,785,000	0.2%
48	Vermont	4,647,000	0.1%
49	Rhode Island	3,337,000	0.1%
50	Wyoming	657,000	0.0%
	District of Columbia	102,255,000	3.0%

Source: U.S. Department of Defense
"Atlas/Data Abstract for the United States" (http://www.dior.whs.mil/mmid/l03/fy02/ATLAS_2002.pdf)
**Includes prime contracts ($25,000 or more). Does not include contracts to U.S. territories and other countries.*

U.S. Department of Defense Domestic Personnel in 2002

National Total = 2,810,943 Personnel*

<u>ALPHA ORDER</u>

RANK	STATE	PERSONNEL	% of USA
16	Alabama	61,389	2.2%
33	Alaska	25,815	0.9%
21	Arizona	48,667	1.7%
34	Arkansas	24,717	0.9%
1	California	274,471	9.8%
17	Colorado	60,752	2.2%
39	Connecticut	16,923	0.6%
45	Delaware	11,452	0.4%
5	Florida	135,050	4.8%
6	Georgia	134,517	4.8%
15	Hawaii	62,597	2.2%
44	Idaho	12,592	0.4%
11	Illinois	75,413	2.7%
27	Indiana	34,134	1.2%
37	Iowa	17,749	0.6%
24	Kansas	36,899	1.3%
18	Kentucky	59,696	2.1%
20	Louisiana	51,138	1.8%
40	Maine	15,681	0.6%
8	Maryland	88,458	3.1%
29	Massachusetts	31,542	1.1%
25	Michigan	35,738	1.3%
31	Minnesota	26,084	0.9%
22	Mississippi	43,801	1.6%
19	Missouri	52,823	1.9%
46	Montana	10,724	0.4%
35	Nebraska	19,917	0.7%
38	Nevada	17,129	0.6%
49	New Hampshire	6,566	0.2%
23	New Jersey	43,054	1.5%
32	New Mexico	25,918	0.9%
9	New York	79,436	2.8%
4	North Carolina	142,801	5.1%
41	North Dakota	14,688	0.5%
13	Ohio	69,333	2.5%
14	Oklahoma	65,992	2.3%
36	Oregon	18,243	0.6%
10	Pennsylvania	77,352	2.8%
43	Rhode Island	13,057	0.5%
12	South Carolina	71,382	2.5%
47	South Dakota	10,430	0.4%
26	Tennessee	34,271	1.2%
2	Texas	232,020	8.3%
28	Utah	33,680	1.2%
50	Vermont	5,358	0.2%
3	Virginia	206,827	7.4%
7	Washington	90,276	3.2%
42	West Virginia	13,326	0.5%
30	Wisconsin	26,184	0.9%
48	Wyoming	7,731	0.3%

<u>RANK ORDER</u>

RANK	STATE	PERSONNEL	% of USA
1	California	274,471	9.8%
2	Texas	232,020	8.3%
3	Virginia	206,827	7.4%
4	North Carolina	142,801	5.1%
5	Florida	135,050	4.8%
6	Georgia	134,517	4.8%
7	Washington	90,276	3.2%
8	Maryland	88,458	3.1%
9	New York	79,436	2.8%
10	Pennsylvania	77,352	2.8%
11	Illinois	75,413	2.7%
12	South Carolina	71,382	2.5%
13	Ohio	69,333	2.5%
14	Oklahoma	65,992	2.3%
15	Hawaii	62,597	2.2%
16	Alabama	61,389	2.2%
17	Colorado	60,752	2.2%
18	Kentucky	59,696	2.1%
19	Missouri	52,823	1.9%
20	Louisiana	51,138	1.8%
21	Arizona	48,667	1.7%
22	Mississippi	43,801	1.6%
23	New Jersey	43,054	1.5%
24	Kansas	36,899	1.3%
25	Michigan	35,738	1.3%
26	Tennessee	34,271	1.2%
27	Indiana	34,134	1.2%
28	Utah	33,680	1.2%
29	Massachusetts	31,542	1.1%
30	Wisconsin	26,184	0.9%
31	Minnesota	26,084	0.9%
32	New Mexico	25,918	0.9%
33	Alaska	25,815	0.9%
34	Arkansas	24,717	0.9%
35	Nebraska	19,917	0.7%
36	Oregon	18,243	0.6%
37	Iowa	17,749	0.6%
38	Nevada	17,129	0.6%
39	Connecticut	16,923	0.6%
40	Maine	15,681	0.6%
41	North Dakota	14,688	0.5%
42	West Virginia	13,326	0.5%
43	Rhode Island	13,057	0.5%
44	Idaho	12,592	0.4%
45	Delaware	11,452	0.4%
46	Montana	10,724	0.4%
47	South Dakota	10,430	0.4%
48	Wyoming	7,731	0.3%
49	New Hampshire	6,566	0.2%
50	Vermont	5,358	0.2%
	District of Columbia	37,161	1.3%

Source: U.S. Department of Defense

   "Atlas/Data Abstract for the United States" (http://www.dior.whs.mil/mmid/l03/fy02/ATLAS_2002.pdf)

**Includes Active Duty Military, Civilian and Reserve and National Guard personnel. Does not include personnel in U.S. territories or in other countries.*

U.S. Department of Defense Active Duty Military Personnel in 2002

National Total = 1,045,077 Personnel*

<u>ALPHA ORDER</u>

RANK	STATE	PERSONNEL	% of USA
22	Alabama	11,354	1.1%
19	Alaska	15,906	1.5%
15	Arizona	22,448	2.1%
30	Arkansas	4,855	0.5%
1	California	123,948	11.9%
12	Colorado	29,733	2.8%
32	Connecticut	4,239	0.4%
33	Delaware	3,899	0.4%
6	Florida	55,815	5.3%
5	Georgia	64,392	6.2%
9	Hawaii	34,608	3.3%
31	Idaho	4,251	0.4%
13	Illinois	25,036	2.4%
43	Indiana	1,041	0.1%
48	Iowa	447	0.0%
20	Kansas	15,819	1.5%
10	Kentucky	34,081	3.3%
17	Louisiana	16,541	1.6%
39	Maine	2,689	0.3%
11	Maryland	30,928	3.0%
41	Massachusetts	2,427	0.2%
42	Michigan	1,173	0.1%
45	Minnesota	702	0.1%
21	Mississippi	14,005	1.3%
18	Missouri	16,119	1.5%
34	Montana	3,512	0.3%
25	Nebraska	7,793	0.7%
24	Nevada	8,461	0.8%
49	New Hampshire	326	0.0%
28	New Jersey	6,306	0.6%
23	New Mexico	11,254	1.1%
16	New York	20,882	2.0%
3	North Carolina	94,296	9.0%
26	North Dakota	7,465	0.7%
27	Ohio	6,899	0.7%
14	Oklahoma	23,664	2.3%
44	Oregon	705	0.1%
37	Pennsylvania	3,098	0.3%
38	Rhode Island	2,974	0.3%
8	South Carolina	37,943	3.6%
35	South Dakota	3,350	0.3%
40	Tennessee	2,554	0.2%
2	Texas	115,100	11.0%
29	Utah	5,447	0.5%
50	Vermont	61	0.0%
4	Virginia	90,851	8.7%
7	Washington	38,521	3.7%
46	West Virginia	558	0.1%
47	Wisconsin	532	0.1%
36	Wyoming	3,292	0.3%

<u>RANK ORDER</u>

RANK	STATE	PERSONNEL	% of USA
1	California	123,948	11.9%
2	Texas	115,100	11.0%
3	North Carolina	94,296	9.0%
4	Virginia	90,851	8.7%
5	Georgia	64,392	6.2%
6	Florida	55,815	5.3%
7	Washington	38,521	3.7%
8	South Carolina	37,943	3.6%
9	Hawaii	34,608	3.3%
10	Kentucky	34,081	3.3%
11	Maryland	30,928	3.0%
12	Colorado	29,733	2.8%
13	Illinois	25,036	2.4%
14	Oklahoma	23,664	2.3%
15	Arizona	22,448	2.1%
16	New York	20,882	2.0%
17	Louisiana	16,541	1.6%
18	Missouri	16,119	1.5%
19	Alaska	15,906	1.5%
20	Kansas	15,819	1.5%
21	Mississippi	14,005	1.3%
22	Alabama	11,354	1.1%
23	New Mexico	11,254	1.1%
24	Nevada	8,461	0.8%
25	Nebraska	7,793	0.7%
26	North Dakota	7,465	0.7%
27	Ohio	6,899	0.7%
28	New Jersey	6,306	0.6%
29	Utah	5,447	0.5%
30	Arkansas	4,855	0.5%
31	Idaho	4,251	0.4%
32	Connecticut	4,239	0.4%
33	Delaware	3,899	0.4%
34	Montana	3,512	0.3%
35	South Dakota	3,350	0.3%
36	Wyoming	3,292	0.3%
37	Pennsylvania	3,098	0.3%
38	Rhode Island	2,974	0.3%
39	Maine	2,689	0.3%
40	Tennessee	2,554	0.2%
41	Massachusetts	2,427	0.2%
42	Michigan	1,173	0.1%
43	Indiana	1,041	0.1%
44	Oregon	705	0.1%
45	Minnesota	702	0.1%
46	West Virginia	558	0.1%
47	Wisconsin	532	0.1%
48	Iowa	447	0.0%
49	New Hampshire	326	0.0%
50	Vermont	61	0.0%
	District of Columbia	12,767	1.2%

Source: U.S. Department of Defense
"Atlas/Data Abstract for the United States" (http://www.dior.whs.mil/mmid/l03/fy02/ATLAS_2002.pdf)
**Does not include active duty personnel in U.S. territories, in other countries or others undistributed.*

U.S. Department of Defense Domestic Civilian Personnel in 2002

National Total = 628,028 Personnel*

ALPHA ORDER

RANK	STATE	PERSONNEL	% of USA
11	Alabama	20,474	3.3%
33	Alaska	4,204	0.7%
24	Arizona	8,290	1.3%
34	Arkansas	3,686	0.6%
2	California	58,076	9.2%
18	Colorado	10,183	1.6%
39	Connecticut	2,497	0.4%
45	Delaware	1,429	0.2%
6	Florida	27,144	4.3%
5	Georgia	31,167	5.0%
12	Hawaii	16,508	2.6%
44	Idaho	1,472	0.2%
16	Illinois	12,780	2.0%
22	Indiana	8,719	1.4%
43	Iowa	1,546	0.2%
30	Kansas	5,603	0.9%
23	Kentucky	8,348	1.3%
26	Louisiana	7,440	1.2%
29	Maine	5,791	0.9%
4	Maryland	32,090	5.1%
27	Massachusetts	6,829	1.1%
25	Michigan	8,038	1.3%
38	Minnesota	2,576	0.4%
21	Mississippi	9,289	1.5%
20	Missouri	9,330	1.5%
47	Montana	1,187	0.2%
35	Nebraska	3,365	0.5%
40	Nevada	2,072	0.3%
48	New Hampshire	1,051	0.2%
15	New Jersey	13,943	2.2%
28	New Mexico	6,704	1.1%
17	New York	11,220	1.8%
13	North Carolina	16,444	2.6%
42	North Dakota	1,621	0.3%
9	Ohio	22,080	3.5%
10	Oklahoma	21,972	3.5%
36	Oregon	3,121	0.5%
7	Pennsylvania	24,920	4.0%
32	Rhode Island	4,346	0.7%
19	South Carolina	9,370	1.5%
46	South Dakota	1,219	0.2%
31	Tennessee	5,496	0.9%
3	Texas	37,238	5.9%
14	Utah	14,725	2.3%
50	Vermont	567	0.1%
1	Virginia	77,119	12.3%
8	Washington	23,259	3.7%
41	West Virginia	1,783	0.3%
37	Wisconsin	3,074	0.5%
49	Wyoming	1,004	0.2%

RANK ORDER

RANK	STATE	PERSONNEL	% of USA
1	Virginia	77,119	12.3%
2	California	58,076	9.2%
3	Texas	37,238	5.9%
4	Maryland	32,090	5.1%
5	Georgia	31,167	5.0%
6	Florida	27,144	4.3%
7	Pennsylvania	24,920	4.0%
8	Washington	23,259	3.7%
9	Ohio	22,080	3.5%
10	Oklahoma	21,972	3.5%
11	Alabama	20,474	3.3%
12	Hawaii	16,508	2.6%
13	North Carolina	16,444	2.6%
14	Utah	14,725	2.3%
15	New Jersey	13,943	2.2%
16	Illinois	12,780	2.0%
17	New York	11,220	1.8%
18	Colorado	10,183	1.6%
19	South Carolina	9,370	1.5%
20	Missouri	9,330	1.5%
21	Mississippi	9,289	1.5%
22	Indiana	8,719	1.4%
23	Kentucky	8,348	1.3%
24	Arizona	8,290	1.3%
25	Michigan	8,038	1.3%
26	Louisiana	7,440	1.2%
27	Massachusetts	6,829	1.1%
28	New Mexico	6,704	1.1%
29	Maine	5,791	0.9%
30	Kansas	5,603	0.9%
31	Tennessee	5,496	0.9%
32	Rhode Island	4,346	0.7%
33	Alaska	4,204	0.7%
34	Arkansas	3,686	0.6%
35	Nebraska	3,365	0.5%
36	Oregon	3,121	0.5%
37	Wisconsin	3,074	0.5%
38	Minnesota	2,576	0.4%
39	Connecticut	2,497	0.4%
40	Nevada	2,072	0.3%
41	West Virginia	1,783	0.3%
42	North Dakota	1,621	0.3%
43	Iowa	1,546	0.2%
44	Idaho	1,472	0.2%
45	Delaware	1,429	0.2%
46	South Dakota	1,219	0.2%
47	Montana	1,187	0.2%
48	New Hampshire	1,051	0.2%
49	Wyoming	1,004	0.2%
50	Vermont	567	0.1%
	District of Columbia	15,640	2.5%

Source: U.S. Department of Defense
"Atlas/Data Abstract for the United States" (http://www.dior.whs.mil/mmid/l03/fy02/ATLAS_2002.pdf)
Does not include civilian personnel in U.S. territories or civilian personnel in other countries. Includes military and civil functions.

U.S. Department of Defense Reserve and National Guard Personnel in 2002

National Total = 1,137,838 Personnel*

ALPHA ORDER

RANK	STATE	PERSONNEL	% of USA
11	Alabama	29,561	2.6%
46	Alaska	5,705	0.5%
27	Arizona	17,929	1.6%
29	Arkansas	16,176	1.4%
1	California	92,447	8.1%
24	Colorado	20,836	1.8%
36	Connecticut	10,187	0.9%
42	Delaware	6,124	0.5%
3	Florida	52,091	4.6%
7	Georgia	38,958	3.4%
34	Hawaii	11,481	1.0%
40	Idaho	6,869	0.6%
9	Illinois	37,597	3.3%
18	Indiana	24,374	2.1%
30	Iowa	15,756	1.4%
31	Kansas	15,477	1.4%
28	Kentucky	17,267	1.5%
14	Louisiana	27,157	2.4%
39	Maine	7,201	0.6%
17	Maryland	25,440	2.2%
23	Massachusetts	22,286	2.0%
15	Michigan	26,527	2.3%
20	Minnesota	22,806	2.0%
25	Mississippi	20,507	1.8%
13	Missouri	27,374	2.4%
43	Montana	6,025	0.5%
37	Nebraska	8,759	0.8%
41	Nevada	6,596	0.6%
48	New Hampshire	5,189	0.5%
21	New Jersey	22,805	2.0%
38	New Mexico	7,960	0.7%
5	New York	47,334	4.2%
10	North Carolina	32,061	2.8%
47	North Dakota	5,602	0.5%
6	Ohio	40,354	3.5%
26	Oklahoma	20,356	1.8%
32	Oregon	14,417	1.3%
4	Pennsylvania	49,334	4.3%
45	Rhode Island	5,737	0.5%
19	South Carolina	24,069	2.1%
44	South Dakota	5,861	0.5%
16	Tennessee	26,221	2.3%
2	Texas	79,682	7.0%
33	Utah	13,508	1.2%
49	Vermont	4,730	0.4%
8	Virginia	38,857	3.4%
12	Washington	28,496	2.5%
35	West Virginia	10,985	1.0%
22	Wisconsin	22,578	2.0%
50	Wyoming	3,435	0.3%

RANK ORDER

RANK	STATE	PERSONNEL	% of USA
1	California	92,447	8.1%
2	Texas	79,682	7.0%
3	Florida	52,091	4.6%
4	Pennsylvania	49,334	4.3%
5	New York	47,334	4.2%
6	Ohio	40,354	3.5%
7	Georgia	38,958	3.4%
8	Virginia	38,857	3.4%
9	Illinois	37,597	3.3%
10	North Carolina	32,061	2.8%
11	Alabama	29,561	2.6%
12	Washington	28,496	2.5%
13	Missouri	27,374	2.4%
14	Louisiana	27,157	2.4%
15	Michigan	26,527	2.3%
16	Tennessee	26,221	2.3%
17	Maryland	25,440	2.2%
18	Indiana	24,374	2.1%
19	South Carolina	24,069	2.1%
20	Minnesota	22,806	2.0%
21	New Jersey	22,805	2.0%
22	Wisconsin	22,578	2.0%
23	Massachusetts	22,286	2.0%
24	Colorado	20,836	1.8%
25	Mississippi	20,507	1.8%
26	Oklahoma	20,356	1.8%
27	Arizona	17,929	1.6%
28	Kentucky	17,267	1.5%
29	Arkansas	16,176	1.4%
30	Iowa	15,756	1.4%
31	Kansas	15,477	1.4%
32	Oregon	14,417	1.3%
33	Utah	13,508	1.2%
34	Hawaii	11,481	1.0%
35	West Virginia	10,985	1.0%
36	Connecticut	10,187	0.9%
37	Nebraska	8,759	0.8%
38	New Mexico	7,960	0.7%
39	Maine	7,201	0.6%
40	Idaho	6,869	0.6%
41	Nevada	6,596	0.6%
42	Delaware	6,124	0.5%
43	Montana	6,025	0.5%
44	South Dakota	5,861	0.5%
45	Rhode Island	5,737	0.5%
46	Alaska	5,705	0.5%
47	North Dakota	5,602	0.5%
48	New Hampshire	5,189	0.5%
49	Vermont	4,730	0.4%
50	Wyoming	3,435	0.3%
	District of Columbia	8,754	0.8%

Source: U.S. Department of Defense
   "Atlas/Data Abstract for the United States" (http://www.dior.whs.mil/mmid/l03/fy02/ATLAS_2002.pdf)
*Does not include reserve and national guard personnel in U.S. territories.

U.S. Department of Defense Total Compensation in 2002

National Total = $114,950,056,000*

<u>ALPHA ORDER</u>

RANK	STATE	TOTAL PAY	% of USA
10	Alabama	$2,714,478,000	2.4%
29	Alaska	1,044,376,000	0.9%
17	Arizona	2,187,684,000	1.9%
33	Arkansas	848,525,000	0.7%
2	California	12,389,975,000	10.8%
11	Colorado	2,686,331,000	2.3%
37	Connecticut	581,052,000	0.5%
43	Delaware	370,597,000	0.3%
4	Florida	7,545,843,000	6.6%
5	Georgia	5,494,660,000	4.8%
9	Hawaii	2,842,371,000	2.5%
41	Idaho	424,501,000	0.4%
16	Illinois	2,437,665,000	2.1%
28	Indiana	1,052,263,000	0.9%
45	Iowa	331,487,000	0.3%
26	Kansas	1,243,767,000	1.1%
19	Kentucky	2,034,428,000	1.8%
22	Louisiana	1,530,774,000	1.3%
35	Maine	658,632,000	0.6%
8	Maryland	4,219,937,000	3.7%
31	Massachusetts	942,402,000	0.8%
30	Michigan	1,011,905,000	0.9%
40	Minnesota	526,232,000	0.5%
23	Mississippi	1,518,240,000	1.3%
20	Missouri	1,749,732,000	1.5%
46	Montana	322,022,000	0.3%
34	Nebraska	729,654,000	0.6%
32	Nevada	904,882,000	0.8%
47	New Hampshire	291,671,000	0.3%
21	New Jersey	1,579,586,000	1.4%
27	New Mexico	1,161,017,000	1.0%
18	New York	2,075,117,000	1.8%
6	North Carolina	5,163,465,000	4.5%
42	North Dakota	389,682,000	0.3%
15	Ohio	2,469,274,000	2.1%
13	Oklahoma	2,553,211,000	2.2%
36	Oregon	642,383,000	0.6%
14	Pennsylvania	2,488,636,000	2.2%
38	Rhode Island	573,191,000	0.5%
12	South Carolina	2,634,884,000	2.3%
48	South Dakota	276,280,000	0.2%
24	Tennessee	1,281,800,000	1.1%
3	Texas	9,414,371,000	8.2%
25	Utah	1,262,729,000	1.1%
50	Vermont	128,436,000	0.1%
1	Virginia	13,038,690,000	11.3%
7	Washington	4,381,655,000	3.8%
44	West Virginia	335,143,000	0.3%
39	Wisconsin	532,458,000	0.5%
49	Wyoming	255,570,000	0.2%

<u>RANK ORDER</u>

RANK	STATE	TOTAL PAY	% of USA
1	Virginia	$13,038,690,000	11.3%
2	California	12,389,975,000	10.8%
3	Texas	9,414,371,000	8.2%
4	Florida	7,545,843,000	6.6%
5	Georgia	5,494,660,000	4.8%
6	North Carolina	5,163,465,000	4.5%
7	Washington	4,381,655,000	3.8%
8	Maryland	4,219,937,000	3.7%
9	Hawaii	2,842,371,000	2.5%
10	Alabama	2,714,478,000	2.4%
11	Colorado	2,686,331,000	2.3%
12	South Carolina	2,634,884,000	2.3%
13	Oklahoma	2,553,211,000	2.2%
14	Pennsylvania	2,488,636,000	2.2%
15	Ohio	2,469,274,000	2.1%
16	Illinois	2,437,665,000	2.1%
17	Arizona	2,187,684,000	1.9%
18	New York	2,075,117,000	1.8%
19	Kentucky	2,034,428,000	1.8%
20	Missouri	1,749,732,000	1.5%
21	New Jersey	1,579,586,000	1.4%
22	Louisiana	1,530,774,000	1.3%
23	Mississippi	1,518,240,000	1.3%
24	Tennessee	1,281,800,000	1.1%
25	Utah	1,262,729,000	1.1%
26	Kansas	1,243,767,000	1.1%
27	New Mexico	1,161,017,000	1.0%
28	Indiana	1,052,263,000	0.9%
29	Alaska	1,044,376,000	0.9%
30	Michigan	1,011,905,000	0.9%
31	Massachusetts	942,402,000	0.8%
32	Nevada	904,882,000	0.8%
33	Arkansas	848,525,000	0.7%
34	Nebraska	729,654,000	0.6%
35	Maine	658,632,000	0.6%
36	Oregon	642,383,000	0.6%
37	Connecticut	581,052,000	0.5%
38	Rhode Island	573,191,000	0.5%
39	Wisconsin	532,458,000	0.5%
40	Minnesota	526,232,000	0.5%
41	Idaho	424,501,000	0.4%
42	North Dakota	389,682,000	0.3%
43	Delaware	370,597,000	0.3%
44	West Virginia	335,143,000	0.3%
45	Iowa	331,487,000	0.3%
46	Montana	322,022,000	0.3%
47	New Hampshire	291,671,000	0.3%
48	South Dakota	276,280,000	0.2%
49	Wyoming	255,570,000	0.2%
50	Vermont	128,436,000	0.1%
	District of Columbia	1,676,392,000	1.5%

Source: U.S. Department of Defense
"Atlas/Data Abstract for the United States" (http://www.dior.whs.mil/mmid/I03/fy02/ATLAS_2002.pdf)
**Includes Civilian Pay, Military Active Duty Pay, Reserve and National Guard Pay and Retired Military Pay. Based on location of recipient. Does not include recipients in U.S. territories and other countries.*

U.S. Department of Defense Military Active Duty Pay in 2002

National Total = $40,944,590,000*

ALPHA ORDER

RANK	STATE	PAYROLL	% of USA
22	Alabama	$455,373,000	1.1%
17	Alaska	636,055,000	1.6%
16	Arizona	750,741,000	1.8%
31	Arkansas	173,847,000	0.4%
2	California	5,064,724,000	12.4%
12	Colorado	1,119,988,000	2.7%
28	Connecticut	222,554,000	0.5%
35	Delaware	129,759,000	0.3%
6	Florida	2,333,505,000	5.7%
5	Georgia	2,376,954,000	5.8%
8	Hawaii	1,507,585,000	3.7%
33	Idaho	139,018,000	0.3%
13	Illinois	1,031,724,000	2.5%
43	Indiana	44,901,000	0.1%
49	Iowa	22,930,000	0.1%
19	Kansas	561,818,000	1.4%
9	Kentucky	1,198,470,000	2.9%
18	Louisiana	583,299,000	1.4%
41	Maine	98,688,000	0.2%
10	Maryland	1,190,006,000	2.9%
36	Massachusetts	114,897,000	0.3%
42	Michigan	54,706,000	0.1%
45	Minnesota	35,858,000	0.1%
21	Mississippi	517,261,000	1.3%
20	Missouri	547,752,000	1.3%
39	Montana	106,260,000	0.3%
26	Nebraska	291,247,000	0.7%
25	Nevada	296,570,000	0.7%
46	New Hampshire	33,092,000	0.1%
27	New Jersey	253,428,000	0.6%
23	New Mexico	378,453,000	0.9%
15	New York	776,377,000	1.9%
4	North Carolina	2,982,152,000	7.3%
29	North Dakota	216,975,000	0.5%
24	Ohio	313,266,000	0.8%
14	Oklahoma	847,911,000	2.1%
44	Oregon	41,108,000	0.1%
34	Pennsylvania	138,663,000	0.3%
32	Rhode Island	145,543,000	0.4%
11	South Carolina	1,187,059,000	2.9%
40	South Dakota	100,135,000	0.2%
37	Tennessee	109,228,000	0.3%
3	Texas	3,922,698,000	9.6%
30	Utah	184,357,000	0.5%
50	Vermont	6,459,000	0.0%
1	Virginia	5,245,614,000	12.8%
7	Washington	1,745,807,000	4.3%
48	West Virginia	26,090,000	0.1%
47	Wisconsin	32,611,000	0.1%
38	Wyoming	109,010,000	0.3%

RANK ORDER

RANK	STATE	PAYROLL	% of USA
1	Virginia	$5,245,614,000	12.8%
2	California	5,064,724,000	12.4%
3	Texas	3,922,698,000	9.6%
4	North Carolina	2,982,152,000	7.3%
5	Georgia	2,376,954,000	5.8%
6	Florida	2,333,505,000	5.7%
7	Washington	1,745,807,000	4.3%
8	Hawaii	1,507,585,000	3.7%
9	Kentucky	1,198,470,000	2.9%
10	Maryland	1,190,006,000	2.9%
11	South Carolina	1,187,059,000	2.9%
12	Colorado	1,119,988,000	2.7%
13	Illinois	1,031,724,000	2.5%
14	Oklahoma	847,911,000	2.1%
15	New York	776,377,000	1.9%
16	Arizona	750,741,000	1.8%
17	Alaska	636,055,000	1.6%
18	Louisiana	583,299,000	1.4%
19	Kansas	561,818,000	1.4%
20	Missouri	547,752,000	1.3%
21	Mississippi	517,261,000	1.3%
22	Alabama	455,373,000	1.1%
23	New Mexico	378,453,000	0.9%
24	Ohio	313,266,000	0.8%
25	Nevada	296,570,000	0.7%
26	Nebraska	291,247,000	0.7%
27	New Jersey	253,428,000	0.6%
28	Connecticut	222,554,000	0.5%
29	North Dakota	216,975,000	0.5%
30	Utah	184,357,000	0.5%
31	Arkansas	173,847,000	0.4%
32	Rhode Island	145,543,000	0.4%
33	Idaho	139,018,000	0.3%
34	Pennsylvania	138,663,000	0.3%
35	Delaware	129,759,000	0.3%
36	Massachusetts	114,897,000	0.3%
37	Tennessee	109,228,000	0.3%
38	Wyoming	109,010,000	0.3%
39	Montana	106,260,000	0.3%
40	South Dakota	100,135,000	0.2%
41	Maine	98,688,000	0.2%
42	Michigan	54,706,000	0.1%
43	Indiana	44,901,000	0.1%
44	Oregon	41,108,000	0.1%
45	Minnesota	35,858,000	0.1%
46	New Hampshire	33,092,000	0.1%
47	Wisconsin	32,611,000	0.1%
48	West Virginia	26,090,000	0.1%
49	Iowa	22,930,000	0.1%
50	Vermont	6,459,000	0.0%
	District of Columbia	542,064,000	1.3%

Source: U.S. Department of Defense
"Atlas/Data Abstract for the United States" (http://www.dior.whs.mil/mmid/l03/fy02/ATLAS_2002.pdf)
**Based on location of recipient. Does not include recipients in U.S. territories and other countries.*

U.S. Department of Defense Civilian Pay in 2002

National Total = $32,805,448,000*

<u>ALPHA ORDER</u>

RANK	STATE	PAYROLL	% of USA
10	Alabama	$1,155,442,000	3.5%
33	Alaska	236,026,000	0.7%
24	Arizona	398,829,000	1.2%
35	Arkansas	155,771,000	0.5%
2	California	3,232,460,000	9.9%
18	Colorado	498,696,000	1.5%
38	Connecticut	117,020,000	0.4%
44	Delaware	61,135,000	0.2%
6	Florida	1,352,074,000	4.1%
5	Georgia	1,444,244,000	4.4%
12	Hawaii	968,122,000	3.0%
45	Idaho	57,288,000	0.2%
16	Illinois	657,801,000	2.0%
20	Indiana	450,694,000	1.4%
43	Iowa	62,982,000	0.2%
31	Kansas	241,748,000	0.7%
26	Kentucky	343,037,000	1.0%
29	Louisiana	326,518,000	1.0%
28	Maine	329,329,000	1.0%
3	Maryland	1,924,334,000	5.9%
25	Massachusetts	346,632,000	1.1%
19	Michigan	460,212,000	1.4%
39	Minnesota	108,876,000	0.3%
21	Mississippi	429,912,000	1.3%
23	Missouri	412,694,000	1.3%
46	Montana	49,371,000	0.2%
34	Nebraska	157,647,000	0.5%
40	Nevada	91,376,000	0.3%
48	New Hampshire	47,222,000	0.1%
13	New Jersey	860,794,000	2.6%
27	New Mexico	341,843,000	1.0%
17	New York	521,090,000	1.6%
14	North Carolina	715,551,000	2.2%
42	North Dakota	65,481,000	0.2%
8	Ohio	1,238,537,000	3.8%
11	Oklahoma	1,034,426,000	3.2%
36	Oregon	152,271,000	0.5%
7	Pennsylvania	1,311,582,000	4.0%
30	Rhode Island	276,286,000	0.8%
22	South Carolina	420,209,000	1.3%
47	South Dakota	48,386,000	0.1%
32	Tennessee	240,111,000	0.7%
4	Texas	1,730,988,000	5.3%
15	Utah	712,147,000	2.2%
50	Vermont	16,109,000	0.0%
1	Virginia	4,527,016,000	13.8%
9	Washington	1,231,532,000	3.8%
41	West Virginia	75,721,000	0.2%
37	Wisconsin	118,410,000	0.4%
49	Wyoming	38,706,000	0.1%

<u>RANK ORDER</u>

RANK	STATE	PAYROLL	% of USA
1	Virginia	$4,527,016,000	13.8%
2	California	3,232,460,000	9.9%
3	Maryland	1,924,334,000	5.9%
4	Texas	1,730,988,000	5.3%
5	Georgia	1,444,244,000	4.4%
6	Florida	1,352,074,000	4.1%
7	Pennsylvania	1,311,582,000	4.0%
8	Ohio	1,238,537,000	3.8%
9	Washington	1,231,532,000	3.8%
10	Alabama	1,155,442,000	3.5%
11	Oklahoma	1,034,426,000	3.2%
12	Hawaii	968,122,000	3.0%
13	New Jersey	860,794,000	2.6%
14	North Carolina	715,551,000	2.2%
15	Utah	712,147,000	2.2%
16	Illinois	657,801,000	2.0%
17	New York	521,090,000	1.6%
18	Colorado	498,696,000	1.5%
19	Michigan	460,212,000	1.4%
20	Indiana	450,694,000	1.4%
21	Mississippi	429,912,000	1.3%
22	South Carolina	420,209,000	1.3%
23	Missouri	412,694,000	1.3%
24	Arizona	398,829,000	1.2%
25	Massachusetts	346,632,000	1.1%
26	Kentucky	343,037,000	1.0%
27	New Mexico	341,843,000	1.0%
28	Maine	329,329,000	1.0%
29	Louisiana	326,518,000	1.0%
30	Rhode Island	276,286,000	0.8%
31	Kansas	241,748,000	0.7%
32	Tennessee	240,111,000	0.7%
33	Alaska	236,026,000	0.7%
34	Nebraska	157,647,000	0.5%
35	Arkansas	155,771,000	0.5%
36	Oregon	152,271,000	0.5%
37	Wisconsin	118,410,000	0.4%
38	Connecticut	117,020,000	0.4%
39	Minnesota	108,876,000	0.3%
40	Nevada	91,376,000	0.3%
41	West Virginia	75,721,000	0.2%
42	North Dakota	65,481,000	0.2%
43	Iowa	62,982,000	0.2%
44	Delaware	61,135,000	0.2%
45	Idaho	57,288,000	0.2%
46	Montana	49,371,000	0.2%
47	South Dakota	48,386,000	0.1%
48	New Hampshire	47,222,000	0.1%
49	Wyoming	38,706,000	0.1%
50	Vermont	16,109,000	0.0%
	District of Columbia	1,010,760,000	3.1%

Source: U.S. Department of Defense
"Atlas/Data Abstract for the United States" (http://www.dior.whs.mil/mmid/I03/fy02/ATLAS_2002.pdf)
*Based on location of recipient. Does not include recipients in U.S. territories and other countries.

U.S. Department of Defense Reserve and National Guard Pay in 2002

National Total = $7,522,906,000*

ALPHA ORDER

RANK	STATE	PAYROLL	% of USA
10	Alabama	$228,951,000	3.0%
45	Alaska	45,440,000	0.6%
35	Arizona	86,440,000	1.1%
28	Arkansas	122,554,000	1.6%
1	California	461,672,000	6.1%
27	Colorado	127,966,000	1.7%
36	Connecticut	66,379,000	0.9%
37	Delaware	62,392,000	0.8%
5	Florida	286,164,000	3.8%
6	Georgia	285,903,000	3.8%
34	Hawaii	91,652,000	1.2%
46	Idaho	42,512,000	0.6%
11	Illinois	217,003,000	2.9%
9	Indiana	237,558,000	3.2%
31	Iowa	101,631,000	1.4%
30	Kansas	103,786,000	1.4%
29	Kentucky	121,488,000	1.6%
15	Louisiana	181,751,000	2.4%
41	Maine	50,088,000	0.7%
12	Maryland	202,838,000	2.7%
18	Massachusetts	173,245,000	2.3%
25	Michigan	134,373,000	1.8%
20	Minnesota	157,278,000	2.1%
19	Mississippi	171,836,000	2.3%
8	Missouri	252,516,000	3.4%
43	Montana	47,442,000	0.6%
38	Nebraska	56,515,000	0.8%
49	Nevada	37,855,000	0.5%
47	New Hampshire	38,324,000	0.5%
24	New Jersey	140,512,000	1.9%
42	New Mexico	48,577,000	0.6%
4	New York	300,580,000	4.0%
16	North Carolina	177,611,000	2.4%
40	North Dakota	51,130,000	0.7%
7	Ohio	267,190,000	3.6%
23	Oklahoma	144,421,000	1.9%
32	Oregon	100,834,000	1.3%
3	Pennsylvania	317,064,000	4.2%
44	Rhode Island	46,722,000	0.6%
26	South Carolina	133,955,000	1.8%
48	South Dakota	37,978,000	0.5%
14	Tennessee	189,245,000	2.5%
2	Texas	457,001,000	6.1%
21	Utah	150,105,000	2.0%
39	Vermont	53,577,000	0.7%
13	Virginia	193,735,000	2.6%
17	Washington	176,810,000	2.4%
33	West Virginia	94,184,000	1.3%
22	Wisconsin	146,046,000	1.9%
50	Wyoming	36,315,000	0.5%

RANK ORDER

RANK	STATE	PAYROLL	% of USA
1	California	$461,672,000	6.1%
2	Texas	457,001,000	6.1%
3	Pennsylvania	317,064,000	4.2%
4	New York	300,580,000	4.0%
5	Florida	286,164,000	3.8%
6	Georgia	285,903,000	3.8%
7	Ohio	267,190,000	3.6%
8	Missouri	252,516,000	3.4%
9	Indiana	237,558,000	3.2%
10	Alabama	228,951,000	3.0%
11	Illinois	217,003,000	2.9%
12	Maryland	202,838,000	2.7%
13	Virginia	193,735,000	2.6%
14	Tennessee	189,245,000	2.5%
15	Louisiana	181,751,000	2.4%
16	North Carolina	177,611,000	2.4%
17	Washington	176,810,000	2.4%
18	Massachusetts	173,245,000	2.3%
19	Mississippi	171,836,000	2.3%
20	Minnesota	157,278,000	2.1%
21	Utah	150,105,000	2.0%
22	Wisconsin	146,046,000	1.9%
23	Oklahoma	144,421,000	1.9%
24	New Jersey	140,512,000	1.9%
25	Michigan	134,373,000	1.8%
26	South Carolina	133,955,000	1.8%
27	Colorado	127,966,000	1.7%
28	Arkansas	122,554,000	1.6%
29	Kentucky	121,488,000	1.6%
30	Kansas	103,786,000	1.4%
31	Iowa	101,631,000	1.4%
32	Oregon	100,834,000	1.3%
33	West Virginia	94,184,000	1.3%
34	Hawaii	91,652,000	1.2%
35	Arizona	86,440,000	1.1%
36	Connecticut	66,379,000	0.9%
37	Delaware	62,392,000	0.8%
38	Nebraska	56,515,000	0.8%
39	Vermont	53,577,000	0.7%
40	North Dakota	51,130,000	0.7%
41	Maine	50,088,000	0.7%
42	New Mexico	48,577,000	0.6%
43	Montana	47,442,000	0.6%
44	Rhode Island	46,722,000	0.6%
45	Alaska	45,440,000	0.6%
46	Idaho	42,512,000	0.6%
47	New Hampshire	38,324,000	0.5%
48	South Dakota	37,978,000	0.5%
49	Nevada	37,855,000	0.5%
50	Wyoming	36,315,000	0.5%
	District of Columbia	65,762,000	0.9%

Source: U.S. Department of Defense
"Atlas/Data Abstract for the United States" (http://www.dior.whs.mil/mmid/l03/fy02/ATLAS_2002.pdf)
**Based on location of recipient. Does not include recipients in U.S. territories and other countries.*

U.S. Department of Defense Retired Military Pay in 2002

National Total = $33,677,112,000*

ALPHA ORDER

RANK	STATE	PAYROLL	% of USA
12	Alabama	$874,712,000	2.6%
43	Alaska	126,855,000	0.4%
8	Arizona	951,674,000	2.8%
23	Arkansas	396,353,000	1.2%
1	California	3,631,119,000	10.8%
9	Colorado	939,681,000	2.8%
39	Connecticut	175,099,000	0.5%
45	Delaware	117,311,000	0.3%
2	Florida	3,574,100,000	10.6%
5	Georgia	1,387,559,000	4.1%
32	Hawaii	275,012,000	0.8%
37	Idaho	185,683,000	0.6%
17	Illinois	531,137,000	1.6%
30	Indiana	319,110,000	0.9%
41	Iowa	143,944,000	0.4%
28	Kansas	336,415,000	1.0%
25	Kentucky	371,433,000	1.1%
21	Louisiana	439,206,000	1.3%
38	Maine	180,527,000	0.5%
10	Maryland	902,759,000	2.7%
31	Massachusetts	307,628,000	0.9%
26	Michigan	362,614,000	1.1%
35	Minnesota	224,220,000	0.7%
22	Mississippi	399,231,000	1.2%
16	Missouri	536,770,000	1.6%
44	Montana	118,949,000	0.4%
34	Nebraska	224,245,000	0.7%
19	Nevada	479,081,000	1.4%
40	New Hampshire	173,033,000	0.5%
29	New Jersey	324,852,000	1.0%
24	New Mexico	392,144,000	1.2%
20	New York	477,070,000	1.4%
6	North Carolina	1,288,151,000	3.8%
49	North Dakota	56,096,000	0.2%
15	Ohio	650,281,000	1.9%
18	Oklahoma	526,453,000	1.6%
27	Oregon	348,170,000	1.0%
14	Pennsylvania	721,327,000	2.1%
46	Rhode Island	104,640,000	0.3%
11	South Carolina	893,661,000	2.7%
47	South Dakota	89,781,000	0.3%
13	Tennessee	743,216,000	2.2%
3	Texas	3,303,684,000	9.8%
36	Utah	216,120,000	0.6%
50	Vermont	52,291,000	0.2%
4	Virginia	3,072,325,000	9.1%
7	Washington	1,227,506,000	3.6%
42	West Virginia	139,148,000	0.4%
33	Wisconsin	235,391,000	0.7%
48	Wyoming	71,539,000	0.2%

RANK ORDER

RANK	STATE	PAYROLL	% of USA
1	California	$3,631,119,000	10.8%
2	Florida	3,574,100,000	10.6%
3	Texas	3,303,684,000	9.8%
4	Virginia	3,072,325,000	9.1%
5	Georgia	1,387,559,000	4.1%
6	North Carolina	1,288,151,000	3.8%
7	Washington	1,227,506,000	3.6%
8	Arizona	951,674,000	2.8%
9	Colorado	939,681,000	2.8%
10	Maryland	902,759,000	2.7%
11	South Carolina	893,661,000	2.7%
12	Alabama	874,712,000	2.6%
13	Tennessee	743,216,000	2.2%
14	Pennsylvania	721,327,000	2.1%
15	Ohio	650,281,000	1.9%
16	Missouri	536,770,000	1.6%
17	Illinois	531,137,000	1.6%
18	Oklahoma	526,453,000	1.6%
19	Nevada	479,081,000	1.4%
20	New York	477,070,000	1.4%
21	Louisiana	439,206,000	1.3%
22	Mississippi	399,231,000	1.2%
23	Arkansas	396,353,000	1.2%
24	New Mexico	392,144,000	1.2%
25	Kentucky	371,433,000	1.1%
26	Michigan	362,614,000	1.1%
27	Oregon	348,170,000	1.0%
28	Kansas	336,415,000	1.0%
29	New Jersey	324,852,000	1.0%
30	Indiana	319,110,000	0.9%
31	Massachusetts	307,628,000	0.9%
32	Hawaii	275,012,000	0.8%
33	Wisconsin	235,391,000	0.7%
34	Nebraska	224,245,000	0.7%
35	Minnesota	224,220,000	0.7%
36	Utah	216,120,000	0.6%
37	Idaho	185,683,000	0.6%
38	Maine	180,527,000	0.5%
39	Connecticut	175,099,000	0.5%
40	New Hampshire	173,033,000	0.5%
41	Iowa	143,944,000	0.4%
42	West Virginia	139,148,000	0.4%
43	Alaska	126,855,000	0.4%
44	Montana	118,949,000	0.4%
45	Delaware	117,311,000	0.3%
46	Rhode Island	104,640,000	0.3%
47	South Dakota	89,781,000	0.3%
48	Wyoming	71,539,000	0.2%
49	North Dakota	56,096,000	0.2%
50	Vermont	52,291,000	0.2%
	District of Columbia	57,806,000	0.2%

Source: U.S. Department of Defense
"Atlas/Data Abstract for the United States" (http://www.dior.whs.mil/mmid/l03/fy02/ATLAS_2002.pdf)
**Based on location of recipient. Does not include recipients in U.S. territories and other countries.*

Veterans in 2002

National Total = 25,618,000 Veterans*

ALPHA ORDER

RANK	STATE	VETERANS	% of USA
23	Alabama	436,000	1.7%
47	Alaska	68,000	0.3%
16	Arizona	564,000	2.2%
31	Arkansas	277,000	1.1%
1	California	2,392,000	9.3%
22	Colorado	438,000	1.7%
29	Connecticut	289,000	1.1%
45	Delaware	82,000	0.3%
2	Florida	1,846,000	7.2%
11	Georgia	753,000	2.9%
42	Hawaii	116,000	0.5%
40	Idaho	137,000	0.5%
7	Illinois	945,000	3.7%
15	Indiana	566,000	2.2%
30	Iowa	281,000	1.1%
32	Kansas	257,000	1.0%
27	Kentucky	371,000	1.4%
25	Louisiana	379,000	1.5%
39	Maine	148,000	0.6%
19	Maryland	495,000	1.9%
18	Massachusetts	524,000	2.0%
8	Michigan	865,000	3.4%
21	Minnesota	447,000	1.7%
33	Mississippi	245,000	1.0%
14	Missouri	571,000	2.2%
43	Montana	106,000	0.4%
37	Nebraska	168,000	0.7%
34	Nevada	241,000	0.9%
41	New Hampshire	133,000	0.5%
13	New Jersey	628,000	2.5%
36	New Mexico	187,000	0.7%
4	New York	1,254,000	4.9%
9	North Carolina	779,000	3.0%
49	North Dakota	59,000	0.2%
6	Ohio	1,086,000	4.2%
28	Oklahoma	365,000	1.4%
26	Oregon	376,000	1.5%
5	Pennsylvania	1,210,000	4.7%
44	Rhode Island	96,000	0.4%
24	South Carolina	415,000	1.6%
46	South Dakota	78,000	0.3%
17	Tennessee	550,000	2.1%
3	Texas	1,701,000	6.6%
38	Utah	159,000	0.6%
48	Vermont	60,000	0.2%
10	Virginia	764,000	3.0%
12	Washington	649,000	2.5%
35	West Virginia	195,000	0.8%
19	Wisconsin	495,000	1.9%
50	Wyoming	57,000	0.2%

RANK ORDER

RANK	STATE	VETERANS	% of USA
1	California	2,392,000	9.3%
2	Florida	1,846,000	7.2%
3	Texas	1,701,000	6.6%
4	New York	1,254,000	4.9%
5	Pennsylvania	1,210,000	4.7%
6	Ohio	1,086,000	4.2%
7	Illinois	945,000	3.7%
8	Michigan	865,000	3.4%
9	North Carolina	779,000	3.0%
10	Virginia	764,000	3.0%
11	Georgia	753,000	2.9%
12	Washington	649,000	2.5%
13	New Jersey	628,000	2.5%
14	Missouri	571,000	2.2%
15	Indiana	566,000	2.2%
16	Arizona	564,000	2.2%
17	Tennessee	550,000	2.1%
18	Massachusetts	524,000	2.0%
19	Maryland	495,000	1.9%
19	Wisconsin	495,000	1.9%
21	Minnesota	447,000	1.7%
22	Colorado	438,000	1.7%
23	Alabama	436,000	1.7%
24	South Carolina	415,000	1.6%
25	Louisiana	379,000	1.5%
26	Oregon	376,000	1.5%
27	Kentucky	371,000	1.4%
28	Oklahoma	365,000	1.4%
29	Connecticut	289,000	1.1%
30	Iowa	281,000	1.1%
31	Arkansas	277,000	1.1%
32	Kansas	257,000	1.0%
33	Mississippi	245,000	1.0%
34	Nevada	241,000	0.9%
35	West Virginia	195,000	0.8%
36	New Mexico	187,000	0.7%
37	Nebraska	168,000	0.7%
38	Utah	159,000	0.6%
39	Maine	148,000	0.6%
40	Idaho	137,000	0.5%
41	New Hampshire	133,000	0.5%
42	Hawaii	116,000	0.5%
43	Montana	106,000	0.4%
44	Rhode Island	96,000	0.4%
45	Delaware	82,000	0.3%
46	South Dakota	78,000	0.3%
47	Alaska	68,000	0.3%
48	Vermont	60,000	0.2%
49	North Dakota	59,000	0.2%
50	Wyoming	57,000	0.2%
	District of Columbia	41,000	0.2%

Source: U.S. Department of Veterans Affairs, Assistant Secretary for Policy and Planning
"Estimate and Projection of the Veterans Populations"
As of September 30, 2002. National total includes 272,000 veterans in U.S. territories and overseas.

Veterans per 1,000 Population 18 and Older in 2002

National Rate = 117 Veterans*

ALPHA ORDER

RANK	STATE	VETERANS
23	Alabama	129
2	Alaska	151
7	Arizona	142
17	Arkansas	136
49	California	93
21	Colorado	131
43	Connecticut	112
19	Delaware	133
6	Florida	144
36	Georgia	120
32	Hawaii	122
9	Idaho	141
46	Illinois	101
31	Indiana	124
27	Iowa	126
25	Kansas	127
38	Kentucky	117
42	Louisiana	115
5	Maine	146
33	Maryland	121
45	Massachusetts	106
39	Michigan	116
37	Minnesota	119
39	Mississippi	116
18	Missouri	134
1	Montana	153
22	Nebraska	130
2	Nevada	151
13	New Hampshire	138
48	New Jersey	97
13	New Mexico	138
50	New York	86
29	North Carolina	125
33	North Dakota	121
25	Ohio	127
11	Oklahoma	139
9	Oregon	141
24	Pennsylvania	128
39	Rhode Island	116
19	South Carolina	133
13	South Dakota	138
29	Tennessee	125
44	Texas	108
47	Utah	99
27	Vermont	126
11	Virginia	139
7	Washington	142
13	West Virginia	138
33	Wisconsin	121
2	Wyoming	151

RANK ORDER

RANK	STATE	VETERANS
1	Montana	153
2	Alaska	151
2	Nevada	151
2	Wyoming	151
5	Maine	146
6	Florida	144
7	Arizona	142
7	Washington	142
9	Idaho	141
9	Oregon	141
11	Oklahoma	139
11	Virginia	139
13	New Hampshire	138
13	New Mexico	138
13	South Dakota	138
13	West Virginia	138
17	Arkansas	136
18	Missouri	134
19	Delaware	133
19	South Carolina	133
21	Colorado	131
22	Nebraska	130
23	Alabama	129
24	Pennsylvania	128
25	Kansas	127
25	Ohio	127
27	Iowa	126
27	Vermont	126
29	North Carolina	125
29	Tennessee	125
31	Indiana	124
32	Hawaii	122
33	Maryland	121
33	North Dakota	121
33	Wisconsin	121
36	Georgia	120
37	Minnesota	119
38	Kentucky	117
39	Michigan	116
39	Mississippi	116
39	Rhode Island	116
42	Louisiana	115
43	Connecticut	112
44	Texas	108
45	Massachusetts	106
46	Illinois	101
47	Utah	99
48	New Jersey	97
49	California	93
50	New York	86
	District of Columbia	89

Source: Morgan Quitno Press using data from U.S. Department of Veterans Affairs
   "Estimate and Projection of the Veterans Populations"
*As of September 30, 2002. National rate does not include veterans or population in U.S. territories and overseas.
Calculated using 2002 population estimates for 18 and older.

Homeland Security Grants in 2003

National Total = $2,043,979,000*

ALPHA ORDER

RANK	STATE	GRANTS	% of USA
23	Alabama	$34,505,000	1.7%
47	Alaska	18,225,000	0.9%
19	Arizona	38,617,000	1.9%
33	Arkansas	26,980,000	1.3%
1	California	164,279,000	8.0%
22	Colorado	34,592,000	1.7%
29	Connecticut	30,157,000	1.5%
45	Delaware	18,917,000	0.9%
4	Florida	86,307,000	4.2%
10	Georgia	51,767,000	2.5%
42	Hawaii	20,772,000	1.0%
39	Idaho	21,177,000	1.0%
5	Illinois	68,884,000	3.4%
14	Indiana	41,592,000	2.0%
30	Iowa	27,939,000	1.4%
32	Kansas	27,006,000	1.3%
26	Kentucky	32,841,000	1.6%
24	Louisiana	34,487,000	1.7%
40	Maine	20,981,000	1.0%
18	Maryland	38,622,000	1.9%
13	Massachusetts	42,730,000	2.1%
8	Michigan	58,080,000	2.8%
21	Minnesota	36,766,000	1.8%
31	Mississippi	27,666,000	1.4%
17	Missouri	39,532,000	1.9%
44	Montana	19,352,000	0.9%
38	Nebraska	22,823,000	1.1%
35	Nevada	24,708,000	1.2%
41	New Hampshire	20,897,000	1.0%
9	New Jersey	51,892,000	2.5%
36	New Mexico	23,356,000	1.1%
3	New York	96,664,000	4.7%
11	North Carolina	50,747,000	2.5%
48	North Dakota	18,183,000	0.9%
7	Ohio	63,888,000	3.1%
28	Oklahoma	30,298,000	1.5%
27	Oregon	30,417,000	1.5%
6	Pennsylvania	67,760,000	3.3%
43	Rhode Island	20,029,000	1.0%
25	South Carolina	32,898,000	1.6%
46	South Dakota	18,723,000	0.9%
16	Tennessee	40,057,000	2.0%
2	Texas	107,777,000	5.3%
34	Utah	25,311,000	1.2%
49	Vermont	18,110,000	0.9%
12	Virginia	46,400,000	2.3%
15	Washington	41,211,000	2.0%
37	West Virginia	23,133,000	1.1%
20	Wisconsin	38,549,000	1.9%
50	Wyoming	17,611,000	0.9%

RANK ORDER

RANK	STATE	GRANTS	% of USA
1	California	$164,279,000	8.0%
2	Texas	107,777,000	5.3%
3	New York	96,664,000	4.7%
4	Florida	86,307,000	4.2%
5	Illinois	68,884,000	3.4%
6	Pennsylvania	67,760,000	3.3%
7	Ohio	63,888,000	3.1%
8	Michigan	58,080,000	2.8%
9	New Jersey	51,892,000	2.5%
10	Georgia	51,767,000	2.5%
11	North Carolina	50,747,000	2.5%
12	Virginia	46,400,000	2.3%
13	Massachusetts	42,730,000	2.1%
14	Indiana	41,592,000	2.0%
15	Washington	41,211,000	2.0%
16	Tennessee	40,057,000	2.0%
17	Missouri	39,532,000	1.9%
18	Maryland	38,622,000	1.9%
19	Arizona	38,617,000	1.9%
20	Wisconsin	38,549,000	1.9%
21	Minnesota	36,766,000	1.8%
22	Colorado	34,592,000	1.7%
23	Alabama	34,505,000	1.7%
24	Louisiana	34,487,000	1.7%
25	South Carolina	32,898,000	1.6%
26	Kentucky	32,841,000	1.6%
27	Oregon	30,417,000	1.5%
28	Oklahoma	30,298,000	1.5%
29	Connecticut	30,157,000	1.5%
30	Iowa	27,939,000	1.4%
31	Mississippi	27,666,000	1.4%
32	Kansas	27,006,000	1.3%
33	Arkansas	26,980,000	1.3%
34	Utah	25,311,000	1.2%
35	Nevada	24,708,000	1.2%
36	New Mexico	23,356,000	1.1%
37	West Virginia	23,133,000	1.1%
38	Nebraska	22,823,000	1.1%
39	Idaho	21,177,000	1.0%
40	Maine	20,981,000	1.0%
41	New Hampshire	20,897,000	1.0%
42	Hawaii	20,772,000	1.0%
43	Rhode Island	20,029,000	1.0%
44	Montana	19,352,000	0.9%
45	Delaware	18,917,000	0.9%
46	South Dakota	18,723,000	0.9%
47	Alaska	18,225,000	0.9%
48	North Dakota	18,183,000	0.9%
49	Vermont	18,110,000	0.9%
50	Wyoming	17,611,000	0.9%
	District of Columbia	17,917,000	0.9%

Source: U.S. Department of Homeland Security, Office of Domestic Preparedness
 " FY 2003 ODP Grants" (www.dhs.gov)
For fiscal year 2003. These grants are provided to enhance the capability of state and local agencies to prevent and respond to incidents of terrorism involving the use of chemical, biological, radiological, nuclear or explosive (CBRNE) weapons. Funding is being provided for the purchase of specialized equipment, exercises, training, and planning costs associated with updating and implementing each state's Homeland Security Strategy (SHSS).

Per Capita Homeland Security Grants in 2003

National Per Capita = $6.99*

ALPHA ORDER

RANK	STATE	PER CAPITA
27	Alabama	$7.70
4	Alaska	28.41
31	Arizona	7.10
18	Arkansas	9.97
50	California	4.69
29	Colorado	7.69
22	Connecticut	8.72
6	Delaware	23.47
47	Florida	5.17
41	Georgia	6.06
9	Hawaii	16.74
12	Idaho	15.77
46	Illinois	5.47
37	Indiana	6.76
21	Iowa	9.52
19	Kansas	9.96
25	Kentucky	8.03
27	Louisiana	7.70
11	Maine	16.20
32	Maryland	7.09
38	Massachusetts	6.65
43	Michigan	5.78
30	Minnesota	7.32
20	Mississippi	9.65
34	Missouri	6.97
7	Montana	21.26
13	Nebraska	13.21
16	Nevada	11.40
10	New Hampshire	16.40
42	New Jersey	6.05
15	New Mexico	12.61
48	New York	5.05
40	North Carolina	6.11
3	North Dakota	28.68
44	Ohio	5.60
23	Oklahoma	8.68
24	Oregon	8.64
45	Pennsylvania	5.50
8	Rhode Island	18.75
26	South Carolina	8.02
5	South Dakota	24.62
35	Tennessee	6.92
49	Texas	4.96
17	Utah	10.92
2	Vermont	29.38
39	Virginia	6.37
36	Washington	6.79
14	West Virginia	12.82
32	Wisconsin	7.09
1	Wyoming	35.30

RANK ORDER

RANK	STATE	PER CAPITA
1	Wyoming	$35.30
2	Vermont	29.38
3	North Dakota	28.68
4	Alaska	28.41
5	South Dakota	24.62
6	Delaware	23.47
7	Montana	21.26
8	Rhode Island	18.75
9	Hawaii	16.74
10	New Hampshire	16.40
11	Maine	16.20
12	Idaho	15.77
13	Nebraska	13.21
14	West Virginia	12.82
15	New Mexico	12.61
16	Nevada	11.40
17	Utah	10.92
18	Arkansas	9.97
19	Kansas	9.96
20	Mississippi	9.65
21	Iowa	9.52
22	Connecticut	8.72
23	Oklahoma	8.68
24	Oregon	8.64
25	Kentucky	8.03
26	South Carolina	8.02
27	Alabama	7.70
27	Louisiana	7.70
29	Colorado	7.69
30	Minnesota	7.32
31	Arizona	7.10
32	Maryland	7.09
32	Wisconsin	7.09
34	Missouri	6.97
35	Tennessee	6.92
36	Washington	6.79
37	Indiana	6.76
38	Massachusetts	6.65
39	Virginia	6.37
40	North Carolina	6.11
41	Georgia	6.06
42	New Jersey	6.05
43	Michigan	5.78
44	Ohio	5.60
45	Pennsylvania	5.50
46	Illinois	5.47
47	Florida	5.17
48	New York	5.05
49	Texas	4.96
50	California	4.69
	District of Columbia	31.48

*Source: Morgan Quitno Press using data from U.S. Department of Homeland Security, Office of Domestic Preparedness
" FY 2003 ODP Grants" (www.dhs.gov)*

For fiscal year 2003. These grants are provided to enhance the capability of state and local agencies to prevent and respond to incidents of terrorism involving the use of chemical, biological, radiological, nuclear or explosive (CBRNE) weapons. Funding is being provided for the purchase of specialized equipment, exercises, training, and planning costs associated with updating and implementing each state's Homeland Security Strategy (SHSS).

Gross State Product in 2001

National Total = $10,137,190,000,000*

ALPHA ORDER

RANK	STATE	G.S.P.	% of USA
25	Alabama	$121,490,000,000	1.2%
45	Alaska	28,581,000,000	0.3%
23	Arizona	160,687,000,000	1.6%
34	Arkansas	67,913,000,000	0.7%
1	California	1,359,265,000,000	13.4%
21	Colorado	173,772,000,000	1.7%
22	Connecticut	166,165,000,000	1.6%
41	Delaware	40,509,000,000	0.4%
4	Florida	491,488,000,000	4.8%
10	Georgia	299,874,000,000	3.0%
39	Hawaii	43,710,000,000	0.4%
44	Idaho	36,905,000,000	0.4%
5	Illinois	475,541,000,000	4.7%
16	Indiana	189,919,000,000	1.9%
30	Iowa	90,942,000,000	0.9%
31	Kansas	87,196,000,000	0.9%
26	Kentucky	120,266,000,000	1.2%
24	Louisiana	148,697,000,000	1.5%
42	Maine	37,449,000,000	0.4%
15	Maryland	195,007,000,000	1.9%
11	Massachusetts	287,802,000,000	2.8%
9	Michigan	320,470,000,000	3.2%
17	Minnesota	188,050,000,000	1.9%
35	Mississippi	67,125,000,000	0.7%
19	Missouri	181,493,000,000	1.8%
47	Montana	22,635,000,000	0.2%
36	Nebraska	56,967,000,000	0.6%
32	Nevada	79,220,000,000	0.8%
38	New Hampshire	47,183,000,000	0.5%
8	New Jersey	365,388,000,000	3.6%
37	New Mexico	55,426,000,000	0.5%
2	New York	826,488,000,000	8.2%
12	North Carolina	275,615,000,000	2.7%
50	North Dakota	19,005,000,000	0.2%
7	Ohio	373,708,000,000	3.7%
29	Oklahoma	93,855,000,000	0.9%
27	Oregon	120,055,000,000	1.2%
6	Pennsylvania	408,373,000,000	4.0%
43	Rhode Island	36,939,000,000	0.4%
28	South Carolina	115,204,000,000	1.1%
46	South Dakota	24,251,000,000	0.2%
18	Tennessee	182,515,000,000	1.8%
3	Texas	763,874,000,000	7.5%
33	Utah	70,409,000,000	0.7%
49	Vermont	19,149,000,000	0.2%
13	Virginia	273,070,000,000	2.7%
14	Washington	222,950,000,000	2.2%
40	West Virginia	42,368,000,000	0.4%
20	Wisconsin	177,354,000,000	1.7%
48	Wyoming	20,418,000,000	0.2%

RANK ORDER

RANK	STATE	G.S.P.	% of USA
1	California	$1,359,265,000,000	13.4%
2	New York	826,488,000,000	8.2%
3	Texas	763,874,000,000	7.5%
4	Florida	491,488,000,000	4.8%
5	Illinois	475,541,000,000	4.7%
6	Pennsylvania	408,373,000,000	4.0%
7	Ohio	373,708,000,000	3.7%
8	New Jersey	365,388,000,000	3.6%
9	Michigan	320,470,000,000	3.2%
10	Georgia	299,874,000,000	3.0%
11	Massachusetts	287,802,000,000	2.8%
12	North Carolina	275,615,000,000	2.7%
13	Virginia	273,070,000,000	2.7%
14	Washington	222,950,000,000	2.2%
15	Maryland	195,007,000,000	1.9%
16	Indiana	189,919,000,000	1.9%
17	Minnesota	188,050,000,000	1.9%
18	Tennessee	182,515,000,000	1.8%
19	Missouri	181,493,000,000	1.8%
20	Wisconsin	177,354,000,000	1.7%
21	Colorado	173,772,000,000	1.7%
22	Connecticut	166,165,000,000	1.6%
23	Arizona	160,687,000,000	1.6%
24	Louisiana	148,697,000,000	1.5%
25	Alabama	121,490,000,000	1.2%
26	Kentucky	120,266,000,000	1.2%
27	Oregon	120,055,000,000	1.2%
28	South Carolina	115,204,000,000	1.1%
29	Oklahoma	93,855,000,000	0.9%
30	Iowa	90,942,000,000	0.9%
31	Kansas	87,196,000,000	0.9%
32	Nevada	79,220,000,000	0.8%
33	Utah	70,409,000,000	0.7%
34	Arkansas	67,913,000,000	0.7%
35	Mississippi	67,125,000,000	0.7%
36	Nebraska	56,967,000,000	0.6%
37	New Mexico	55,426,000,000	0.5%
38	New Hampshire	47,183,000,000	0.5%
39	Hawaii	43,710,000,000	0.4%
40	West Virginia	42,368,000,000	0.4%
41	Delaware	40,509,000,000	0.4%
42	Maine	37,449,000,000	0.4%
43	Rhode Island	36,939,000,000	0.4%
44	Idaho	36,905,000,000	0.4%
45	Alaska	28,581,000,000	0.3%
46	South Dakota	24,251,000,000	0.2%
47	Montana	22,635,000,000	0.2%
48	Wyoming	20,418,000,000	0.2%
49	Vermont	19,149,000,000	0.2%
50	North Dakota	19,005,000,000	0.2%
	District of Columbia	64,459,000,000	0.6%

Source: U.S. Department of Commerce, Bureau of Economic Analysis
"Gross State Product Data" (http://www.bea.doc.gov/bea/regional/data.htm)
**G.S.P. is the market value of goods and services produced by the labor and property located in a state. It is the state counterpart to the nation's Gross Domestic Product.*

Percent Change in Gross State Product: 1997 to 2001
(Adjusted to Constant 1996 Dollars)
National Percent Change = 15.3% Increase*

ALPHA ORDER

RANK	STATE	PERCENT CHANGE
40	Alabama	9.1
50	Alaska	(6.0)
2	Arizona	27.3
42	Arkansas	8.7
5	California	22.4
4	Colorado	25.1
22	Connecticut	15.4
9	Delaware	18.6
16	Florida	16.8
11	Georgia	18.1
49	Hawaii	3.1
3	Idaho	25.6
32	Illinois	12.0
35	Indiana	10.6
45	Iowa	6.7
33	Kansas	11.9
37	Kentucky	9.8
47	Louisiana	3.8
26	Maine	13.6
21	Maryland	15.7
7	Massachusetts	20.9
44	Michigan	7.8
18	Minnesota	16.6
46	Mississippi	6.5
40	Missouri	9.1
34	Montana	11.2
39	Nebraska	9.5
7	Nevada	20.9
6	New Hampshire	21.9
27	New Jersey	13.2
23	New Mexico	15.3
14	New York	17.7
29	North Carolina	12.9
31	North Dakota	12.3
43	Ohio	8.5
36	Oklahoma	10.0
1	Oregon	28.6
37	Pennsylvania	9.8
19	Rhode Island	16.3
28	South Carolina	13.0
13	South Dakota	17.8
30	Tennessee	12.8
16	Texas	16.8
10	Utah	18.4
12	Vermont	17.9
20	Virginia	16.2
15	Washington	17.6
48	West Virginia	3.6
25	Wisconsin	13.9
24	Wyoming	14.2

RANK ORDER

RANK	STATE	PERCENT CHANGE
1	Oregon	28.6
2	Arizona	27.3
3	Idaho	25.6
4	Colorado	25.1
5	California	22.4
6	New Hampshire	21.9
7	Massachusetts	20.9
7	Nevada	20.9
9	Delaware	18.6
10	Utah	18.4
11	Georgia	18.1
12	Vermont	17.9
13	South Dakota	17.8
14	New York	17.7
15	Washington	17.6
16	Florida	16.8
16	Texas	16.8
18	Minnesota	16.6
19	Rhode Island	16.3
20	Virginia	16.2
21	Maryland	15.7
22	Connecticut	15.4
23	New Mexico	15.3
24	Wyoming	14.2
25	Wisconsin	13.9
26	Maine	13.6
27	New Jersey	13.2
28	South Carolina	13.0
29	North Carolina	12.9
30	Tennessee	12.8
31	North Dakota	12.3
32	Illinois	12.0
33	Kansas	11.9
34	Montana	11.2
35	Indiana	10.6
36	Oklahoma	10.0
37	Kentucky	9.8
37	Pennsylvania	9.8
39	Nebraska	9.5
40	Alabama	9.1
40	Missouri	9.1
42	Arkansas	8.7
43	Ohio	8.5
44	Michigan	7.8
45	Iowa	6.7
46	Mississippi	6.5
47	Louisiana	3.8
48	West Virginia	3.6
49	Hawaii	3.1
50	Alaska	(6.0)
	District of Columbia	13.8

Source: Morgan Quitno Press using data from U.S. Department of Commerce, Bureau of Economic Analysis
"Gross State Product Data" (http://www.bea.doc.gov/bea/regional/data.htm)

*G.S.P. is the market value of goods and services produced by the labor and property located in a state. It is the state counterpart to the nation's Gross Domestic Product. Adjusted for inflation using chained 1996 dollars.

Average Annual Change in Gross State Product: 1997 to 2001
(Adjusted to Constant 1996 Dollars)
National Annual Percent Change = 2.9% Increase*

ALPHA ORDER

RANK ORDER

RANK	STATE	PERCENT CHANGE		RANK	STATE	PERCENT CHANGE
39	Alabama	1.8		1	Oregon	5.2
50	Alaska	(1.2)		2	Arizona	4.9
2	Arizona	4.9		3	Idaho	4.7
42	Arkansas	1.7		4	Colorado	4.6
5	California	4.1		5	California	4.1
4	Colorado	4.6		6	New Hampshire	4.0
22	Connecticut	2.9		7	Massachusetts	3.9
9	Delaware	3.5		7	Nevada	3.9
16	Florida	3.2		9	Delaware	3.5
10	Georgia	3.4		10	Georgia	3.4
49	Hawaii	0.6		10	Utah	3.4
3	Idaho	4.7		10	Vermont	3.4
31	Illinois	2.3		13	New York	3.3
35	Indiana	2.0		13	South Dakota	3.3
45	Iowa	1.3		13	Washington	3.3
31	Kansas	2.3		16	Florida	3.2
36	Kentucky	1.9		16	Texas	3.2
47	Louisiana	0.8		18	Minnesota	3.1
25	Maine	2.6		18	Rhode Island	3.1
20	Maryland	3.0		20	Maryland	3.0
7	Massachusetts	3.9		20	Virginia	3.0
44	Michigan	1.5		22	Connecticut	2.9
18	Minnesota	3.1		22	New Mexico	2.9
45	Mississippi	1.3		24	Wyoming	2.7
39	Missouri	1.8		25	Maine	2.6
34	Montana	2.2		25	Wisconsin	2.6
39	Nebraska	1.8		27	New Jersey	2.5
7	Nevada	3.9		27	North Carolina	2.5
6	New Hampshire	4.0		27	South Carolina	2.5
27	New Jersey	2.5		30	Tennessee	2.4
22	New Mexico	2.9		31	Illinois	2.3
13	New York	3.3		31	Kansas	2.3
27	North Carolina	2.5		31	North Dakota	2.3
31	North Dakota	2.3		34	Montana	2.2
43	Ohio	1.6		35	Indiana	2.0
36	Oklahoma	1.9		36	Kentucky	1.9
1	Oregon	5.2		36	Oklahoma	1.9
36	Pennsylvania	1.9		36	Pennsylvania	1.9
18	Rhode Island	3.1		39	Alabama	1.8
27	South Carolina	2.5		39	Missouri	1.8
13	South Dakota	3.3		39	Nebraska	1.8
30	Tennessee	2.4		42	Arkansas	1.7
16	Texas	3.2		43	Ohio	1.6
10	Utah	3.4		44	Michigan	1.5
10	Vermont	3.4		45	Iowa	1.3
20	Virginia	3.0		45	Mississippi	1.3
13	Washington	3.3		47	Louisiana	0.8
48	West Virginia	0.7		48	West Virginia	0.7
25	Wisconsin	2.6		49	Hawaii	0.6
24	Wyoming	2.7		50	Alaska	(1.2)

District of Columbia 2.6

Source: Morgan Quitno Press using data from U.S. Department of Commerce, Bureau of Economic Analysis
"Gross State Product Data" (http://www.bea.doc.gov/bea/regional/data.htm)
*G.S.P. is the market value of goods and services produced by the labor and property located in a state. It is the
state counterpart to the nation's Gross Domestic Product. Adjusted for inflation using chained 1996 dollars.

Per Capita Gross State Product in 2001

National Per Capita = $35,557*

<u>ALPHA ORDER</u>

RANK	STATE	PER CAPITA
45	Alabama	$27,201
3	Alaska	45,175
37	Arizona	30,332
47	Arkansas	25,227
8	California	39,361
9	Colorado	39,237
2	Connecticut	48,409
1	Delaware	50,918
39	Florida	30,051
18	Georgia	35,721
19	Hawaii	35,681
44	Idaho	27,931
10	Illinois	37,991
35	Indiana	31,000
34	Iowa	31,015
28	Kansas	32,289
41	Kentucky	29,569
23	Louisiana	33,295
42	Maine	29,150
16	Maryland	36,224
4	Massachusetts	44,970
30	Michigan	32,030
13	Minnesota	37,722
50	Mississippi	23,489
29	Missouri	32,201
48	Montana	24,985
25	Nebraska	33,140
12	Nevada	37,820
14	New Hampshire	37,477
6	New Jersey	42,966
38	New Mexico	30,302
5	New York	43,329
22	North Carolina	33,631
40	North Dakota	29,869
26	Ohio	32,822
46	Oklahoma	27,070
21	Oregon	34,572
24	Pennsylvania	33,205
20	Rhode Island	34,881
43	South Carolina	28,377
31	South Dakota	31,987
32	Tennessee	31,765
17	Texas	35,794
36	Utah	30,887
33	Vermont	31,242
11	Virginia	37,965
15	Washington	37,203
49	West Virginia	23,516
27	Wisconsin	32,812
7	Wyoming	41,355

<u>RANK ORDER</u>

RANK	STATE	PER CAPITA
1	Delaware	$50,918
2	Connecticut	48,409
3	Alaska	45,175
4	Massachusetts	44,970
5	New York	43,329
6	New Jersey	42,966
7	Wyoming	41,355
8	California	39,361
9	Colorado	39,237
10	Illinois	37,991
11	Virginia	37,965
12	Nevada	37,820
13	Minnesota	37,722
14	New Hampshire	37,477
15	Washington	37,203
16	Maryland	36,224
17	Texas	35,794
18	Georgia	35,721
19	Hawaii	35,681
20	Rhode Island	34,881
21	Oregon	34,572
22	North Carolina	33,631
23	Louisiana	33,295
24	Pennsylvania	33,205
25	Nebraska	33,140
26	Ohio	32,822
27	Wisconsin	32,812
28	Kansas	32,289
29	Missouri	32,201
30	Michigan	32,030
31	South Dakota	31,987
32	Tennessee	31,765
33	Vermont	31,242
34	Iowa	31,015
35	Indiana	31,000
36	Utah	30,887
37	Arizona	30,332
38	New Mexico	30,302
39	Florida	30,051
40	North Dakota	29,869
41	Kentucky	29,569
42	Maine	29,150
43	South Carolina	28,377
44	Idaho	27,931
45	Alabama	27,201
46	Oklahoma	27,070
47	Arkansas	25,227
48	Montana	24,985
49	West Virginia	23,516
50	Mississippi	23,489
	District of Columbia	112,550

*Source: Morgan Quitno Press using data from U.S. Department of Commerce, Bureau of Economic Analysis
    "Gross State Product Data" (http://www.bea.doc.gov/bea/regional/data.htm)*
*G.S.P. is the market value of goods and services produced by the labor and property located in a state. It is the
state counterpart to the nation's Gross Domestic Product.*

Percent Change in Per Capita Gross State Product: 1997 to 2001
(Adjusted to Constant 1996 Dollars)
National Percent Change = 8.3% Increase*

ALPHA ORDER

RANK	STATE	PERCENT CHANGE
32	Alabama	5.6
50	Alaska	(9.5)
19	Arizona	9.4
45	Arkansas	1.9
4	California	14.2
12	Colorado	9.9
14	Connecticut	9.8
15	Delaware	9.6
40	Florida	4.9
37	Georgia	5.4
48	Hawaii	0.1
3	Idaho	15.1
25	Illinois	7.5
30	Indiana	6.0
43	Iowa	3.8
22	Kansas	8.4
34	Kentucky	5.5
47	Louisiana	1.1
11	Maine	10.1
18	Maryland	9.5
2	Massachusetts	15.6
37	Michigan	5.4
15	Minnesota	9.6
46	Mississippi	1.8
41	Missouri	4.7
24	Montana	7.9
34	Nebraska	5.5
49	Nevada	(3.3)
5	New Hampshire	13.6
28	New Jersey	7.2
21	New Mexico	8.7
9	New York	12.0
44	North Carolina	2.4
8	North Dakota	13.1
29	Ohio	6.8
39	Oklahoma	5.2
1	Oregon	20.1
26	Pennsylvania	7.3
22	Rhode Island	8.4
34	South Carolina	5.5
6	South Dakota	13.5
32	Tennessee	5.6
30	Texas	6.0
26	Utah	7.3
7	Vermont	13.3
20	Virginia	8.8
12	Washington	9.9
42	West Virginia	4.4
15	Wisconsin	9.6
10	Wyoming	11.0

RANK ORDER

RANK	STATE	PERCENT CHANGE
1	Oregon	20.1
2	Massachusetts	15.6
3	Idaho	15.1
4	California	14.2
5	New Hampshire	13.6
6	South Dakota	13.5
7	Vermont	13.3
8	North Dakota	13.1
9	New York	12.0
10	Wyoming	11.0
11	Maine	10.1
12	Colorado	9.9
12	Washington	9.9
14	Connecticut	9.8
15	Delaware	9.6
15	Minnesota	9.6
15	Wisconsin	9.6
18	Maryland	9.5
19	Arizona	9.4
20	Virginia	8.8
21	New Mexico	8.7
22	Kansas	8.4
22	Rhode Island	8.4
24	Montana	7.9
25	Illinois	7.5
26	Pennsylvania	7.3
26	Utah	7.3
28	New Jersey	7.2
29	Ohio	6.8
30	Indiana	6.0
30	Texas	6.0
32	Alabama	5.6
32	Tennessee	5.6
34	Kentucky	5.5
34	Nebraska	5.5
34	South Carolina	5.5
37	Georgia	5.4
37	Michigan	5.4
39	Oklahoma	5.2
40	Florida	4.9
41	Missouri	4.7
42	West Virginia	4.4
43	Iowa	3.8
44	North Carolina	2.4
45	Arkansas	1.9
46	Mississippi	1.8
47	Louisiana	1.1
48	Hawaii	0.1
49	Nevada	(3.3)
50	Alaska	(9.5)

District of Columbia — 5.1

Source: Morgan Quitno Press using data from U.S. Department of Commerce, Bureau of Economic Analysis
  "Gross State Product Data" (http://www.bea.doc.gov/bea/regional/data.htm)
*G.S.P. is the market value of goods and services produced by the labor and property located in a state. It is the state counterpart to the nation's Gross Domestic Product. Adjusted for inflation using chained 1996 dollars.

Personal Income in 2002

National Total = $8,891,093,018,000*

<u>ALPHA ORDER</u>

RANK	STATE	INCOME	% of USA
25	Alabama	$112,592,496,000	1.3%
46	Alaska	20,467,016,000	0.2%
23	Arizona	142,724,553,000	1.6%
34	Arkansas	63,462,631,000	0.7%
1	California	1,155,247,009,000	13.0%
21	Colorado	149,481,393,000	1.7%
22	Connecticut	148,211,074,000	1.7%
44	Delaware	26,084,196,000	0.3%
4	Florida	494,026,543,000	5.6%
11	Georgia	245,707,269,000	2.8%
40	Hawaii	37,396,811,000	0.4%
42	Idaho	33,584,820,000	0.4%
5	Illinois	419,857,924,000	4.7%
16	Indiana	173,889,313,000	2.0%
30	Iowa	82,642,149,000	0.9%
31	Kansas	78,321,786,000	0.9%
26	Kentucky	105,013,179,000	1.2%
24	Louisiana	113,724,773,000	1.3%
41	Maine	35,990,793,000	0.4%
15	Maryland	197,155,994,000	2.2%
10	Massachusetts	250,965,602,000	2.8%
9	Michigan	303,745,428,000	3.4%
17	Minnesota	170,142,288,000	1.9%
33	Mississippi	64,241,535,000	0.7%
18	Missouri	163,602,657,000	1.8%
45	Montana	22,650,394,000	0.3%
36	Nebraska	51,086,474,000	0.6%
32	Nevada	65,571,339,000	0.7%
38	New Hampshire	43,703,213,000	0.5%
7	New Jersey	339,889,425,000	3.8%
37	New Mexico	44,351,507,000	0.5%
2	New York	684,070,084,000	7.7%
13	North Carolina	229,356,208,000	2.6%
49	North Dakota	16,846,443,000	0.2%
8	Ohio	334,832,201,000	3.8%
29	Oklahoma	87,818,043,000	1.0%
28	Oregon	100,480,909,000	1.1%
6	Pennsylvania	390,560,364,000	4.4%
43	Rhode Island	33,276,448,000	0.4%
27	South Carolina	104,301,623,000	1.2%
47	South Dakota	20,316,033,000	0.2%
20	Tennessee	158,717,070,000	1.8%
3	Texas	618,559,907,000	7.0%
35	Utah	55,953,179,000	0.6%
48	Vermont	18,167,477,000	0.2%
12	Virginia	238,325,281,000	2.7%
14	Washington	198,221,310,000	2.2%
39	West Virginia	42,574,654,000	0.5%
19	Wisconsin	163,216,142,000	1.8%
50	Wyoming	15,207,667,000	0.2%

<u>RANK ORDER</u>

RANK	STATE	INCOME	% of USA
1	California	$1,155,247,009,000	13.0%
2	New York	684,070,084,000	7.7%
3	Texas	618,559,907,000	7.0%
4	Florida	494,026,543,000	5.6%
5	Illinois	419,857,924,000	4.7%
6	Pennsylvania	390,560,364,000	4.4%
7	New Jersey	339,889,425,000	3.8%
8	Ohio	334,832,201,000	3.8%
9	Michigan	303,745,428,000	3.4%
10	Massachusetts	250,965,602,000	2.8%
11	Georgia	245,707,269,000	2.8%
12	Virginia	238,325,281,000	2.7%
13	North Carolina	229,356,208,000	2.6%
14	Washington	198,221,310,000	2.2%
15	Maryland	197,155,994,000	2.2%
16	Indiana	173,889,313,000	2.0%
17	Minnesota	170,142,288,000	1.9%
18	Missouri	163,602,657,000	1.8%
19	Wisconsin	163,216,142,000	1.8%
20	Tennessee	158,717,070,000	1.8%
21	Colorado	149,481,393,000	1.7%
22	Connecticut	148,211,074,000	1.7%
23	Arizona	142,724,553,000	1.6%
24	Louisiana	113,724,773,000	1.3%
25	Alabama	112,592,496,000	1.3%
26	Kentucky	105,013,179,000	1.2%
27	South Carolina	104,301,623,000	1.2%
28	Oregon	100,480,909,000	1.1%
29	Oklahoma	87,818,043,000	1.0%
30	Iowa	82,642,149,000	0.9%
31	Kansas	78,321,786,000	0.9%
32	Nevada	65,571,339,000	0.7%
33	Mississippi	64,241,535,000	0.7%
34	Arkansas	63,462,631,000	0.7%
35	Utah	55,953,179,000	0.6%
36	Nebraska	51,086,474,000	0.6%
37	New Mexico	44,351,507,000	0.5%
38	New Hampshire	43,703,213,000	0.5%
39	West Virginia	42,574,654,000	0.5%
40	Hawaii	37,396,811,000	0.4%
41	Maine	35,990,793,000	0.4%
42	Idaho	33,584,820,000	0.4%
43	Rhode Island	33,276,448,000	0.4%
44	Delaware	26,084,196,000	0.3%
45	Montana	22,650,394,000	0.3%
46	Alaska	20,467,016,000	0.2%
47	South Dakota	20,316,033,000	0.2%
48	Vermont	18,167,477,000	0.2%
49	North Dakota	16,846,443,000	0.2%
50	Wyoming	15,207,667,000	0.2%
	District of Columbia	24,760,391,000	0.3%

Source: U.S. Department of Commerce, Bureau of Economic Analysis
"Annual State Personal Income" (http://www.bea.doc.gov/bea/regional/spil)
**The national total shown here is the sum of the state estimates. It differs from the national income and product accounts (NIPA) estimate of personal income because it omits the earnings of federal civilian and military personnel stationed abroad and of U.S. residents employed abroad temporarily by private U.S. firms.*

Change in Personal Income: 2001 to 2002

National Percent Change = 2.5% Increase

<u>ALPHA ORDER</u>

RANK	STATE	PERCENT CHANGE
28	Alabama	2.9
4	Alaska	4.1
8	Arizona	3.9
16	Arkansas	3.5
38	California	2.2
48	Colorado	0.8
42	Connecticut	1.8
42	Delaware	1.8
8	Florida	3.9
32	Georgia	2.5
1	Hawaii	5.0
10	Idaho	3.8
45	Illinois	1.6
25	Indiana	3.1
16	Iowa	3.5
41	Kansas	1.9
14	Kentucky	3.7
6	Louisiana	4.0
3	Maine	4.3
10	Maryland	3.8
47	Massachusetts	0.9
32	Michigan	2.5
23	Minnesota	3.3
14	Mississippi	3.7
30	Missouri	2.8
6	Montana	4.0
28	Nebraska	2.9
10	Nevada	3.8
38	New Hampshire	2.2
18	New Jersey	3.4
2	New Mexico	4.9
50	New York	(0.1)
37	North Carolina	2.3
31	North Dakota	2.6
35	Ohio	2.4
46	Oklahoma	1.5
32	Oregon	2.5
24	Pennsylvania	3.2
10	Rhode Island	3.8
18	South Carolina	3.4
48	South Dakota	0.8
27	Tennessee	3.0
44	Texas	1.7
38	Utah	2.2
25	Vermont	3.1
35	Virginia	2.4
18	Washington	3.4
18	West Virginia	3.4
18	Wisconsin	3.4
4	Wyoming	4.1

<u>RANK ORDER</u>

RANK	STATE	PERCENT CHANGE
1	Hawaii	5.0
2	New Mexico	4.9
3	Maine	4.3
4	Alaska	4.1
4	Wyoming	4.1
6	Louisiana	4.0
6	Montana	4.0
8	Arizona	3.9
8	Florida	3.9
10	Idaho	3.8
10	Maryland	3.8
10	Nevada	3.8
10	Rhode Island	3.8
14	Kentucky	3.7
14	Mississippi	3.7
16	Arkansas	3.5
16	Iowa	3.5
18	New Jersey	3.4
18	South Carolina	3.4
18	Washington	3.4
18	West Virginia	3.4
18	Wisconsin	3.4
23	Minnesota	3.3
24	Pennsylvania	3.2
25	Indiana	3.1
25	Vermont	3.1
27	Tennessee	3.0
28	Alabama	2.9
28	Nebraska	2.9
30	Missouri	2.8
31	North Dakota	2.6
32	Georgia	2.5
32	Michigan	2.5
32	Oregon	2.5
35	Ohio	2.4
35	Virginia	2.4
37	North Carolina	2.3
38	California	2.2
38	New Hampshire	2.2
38	Utah	2.2
41	Kansas	1.9
42	Connecticut	1.8
42	Delaware	1.8
44	Texas	1.7
45	Illinois	1.6
46	Oklahoma	1.5
47	Massachusetts	0.9
48	Colorado	0.8
48	South Dakota	0.8
50	New York	(0.1)
	District of Columbia	6.4

Source: Morgan Quitno Press using data from U.S. Department of Commerce, Bureau of Economic Analysis
"Annual State Personal Income" (http://www.bea.doc.gov/bea/regional/spi/)

Per Capita Personal Income in 2002

National Per Capita = $30,832*

ALPHA ORDER

RANK	STATE	PER CAPITA
43	Alabama	$25,096
14	Alaska	31,792
38	Arizona	26,157
49	Arkansas	23,417
10	California	32,898
9	Colorado	33,170
1	Connecticut	42,829
13	Delaware	32,307
22	Florida	29,559
28	Georgia	28,703
20	Hawaii	30,040
44	Idaho	25,042
8	Illinois	33,320
31	Indiana	28,233
32	Iowa	28,141
27	Kansas	28,838
39	Kentucky	25,657
41	Louisiana	25,370
33	Maine	27,804
4	Maryland	36,121
3	Massachusetts	39,044
18	Michigan	30,222
7	Minnesota	33,895
50	Mississippi	22,370
26	Missouri	28,841
45	Montana	24,906
23	Nebraska	29,544
19	Nevada	30,169
6	New Hampshire	34,276
2	New Jersey	39,567
47	New Mexico	23,908
5	New York	35,708
34	North Carolina	27,566
37	North Dakota	26,567
25	Ohio	29,317
42	Oklahoma	25,136
29	Oregon	28,533
15	Pennsylvania	31,663
16	Rhode Island	31,107
40	South Carolina	25,395
36	South Dakota	26,694
35	Tennessee	27,378
30	Texas	28,401
46	Utah	24,157
24	Vermont	29,464
11	Virginia	32,676
12	Washington	32,661
48	West Virginia	23,628
21	Wisconsin	29,996
17	Wyoming	30,494

RANK ORDER

RANK	STATE	PER CAPITA
1	Connecticut	$42,829
2	New Jersey	39,567
3	Massachusetts	39,044
4	Maryland	36,121
5	New York	35,708
6	New Hampshire	34,276
7	Minnesota	33,895
8	Illinois	33,320
9	Colorado	33,170
10	California	32,898
11	Virginia	32,676
12	Washington	32,661
13	Delaware	32,307
14	Alaska	31,792
15	Pennsylvania	31,663
16	Rhode Island	31,107
17	Wyoming	30,494
18	Michigan	30,222
19	Nevada	30,169
20	Hawaii	30,040
21	Wisconsin	29,996
22	Florida	29,559
23	Nebraska	29,544
24	Vermont	29,464
25	Ohio	29,317
26	Missouri	28,841
27	Kansas	28,838
28	Georgia	28,703
29	Oregon	28,533
30	Texas	28,401
31	Indiana	28,233
32	Iowa	28,141
33	Maine	27,804
34	North Carolina	27,566
35	Tennessee	27,378
36	South Dakota	26,694
37	North Dakota	26,567
38	Arizona	26,157
39	Kentucky	25,657
40	South Carolina	25,395
41	Louisiana	25,370
42	Oklahoma	25,136
43	Alabama	25,096
44	Idaho	25,042
45	Montana	24,906
46	Utah	24,157
47	New Mexico	23,908
48	West Virginia	23,628
49	Arkansas	23,417
50	Mississippi	22,370
	District of Columbia	43,371

Source: U.S. Department of Commerce, Bureau of Economic Analysis
"Annual State Personal Income" (http://www.bea.doc.gov/bea/regional/spi/)
**The national figure is based on the sum of the state estimates. It differs from the national income and product accounts (NIPA) estimate of personal income because it omits the earnings of federal civilian and military personnel stationed abroad and of U.S. residents employed abroad temporarily by private U.S. firms.*

Change in Per Capita Personal Income: 2001 to 2002

National Percent Change = 1.4% Increase

<u>ALPHA ORDER</u>

RANK	STATE	PERCENT CHANGE
17	Alabama	2.5
17	Alaska	2.5
33	Arizona	1.1
13	Arkansas	2.9
41	California	0.7
50	Colorado	(0.9)
33	Connecticut	1.1
46	Delaware	0.4
31	Florida	1.8
42	Georgia	0.6
4	Hawaii	3.5
24	Idaho	2.2
36	Illinois	1.0
16	Indiana	2.6
6	Iowa	3.4
32	Kansas	1.4
9	Kentucky	3.1
1	Louisiana	3.7
4	Maine	3.5
21	Maryland	2.4
43	Massachusetts	0.5
30	Michigan	2.0
17	Minnesota	2.5
8	Mississippi	3.3
24	Missouri	2.2
2	Montana	3.6
21	Nebraska	2.4
47	Nevada	0.1
38	New Hampshire	0.9
21	New Jersey	2.4
2	New Mexico	3.6
49	New York	(0.5)
38	North Carolina	0.9
11	North Dakota	3.0
24	Ohio	2.2
40	Oklahoma	0.8
33	Oregon	1.1
11	Pennsylvania	3.0
14	Rhode Island	2.8
24	South Carolina	2.2
43	South Dakota	0.5
28	Tennessee	2.1
48	Texas	(0.2)
43	Utah	0.5
17	Vermont	2.5
36	Virginia	1.0
28	Washington	2.1
6	West Virginia	3.4
15	Wisconsin	2.7
9	Wyoming	3.1

<u>RANK ORDER</u>

RANK	STATE	PERCENT CHANGE
1	Louisiana	3.7
2	Montana	3.6
2	New Mexico	3.6
4	Hawaii	3.5
4	Maine	3.5
6	Iowa	3.4
6	West Virginia	3.4
8	Mississippi	3.3
9	Kentucky	3.1
9	Wyoming	3.1
11	North Dakota	3.0
11	Pennsylvania	3.0
13	Arkansas	2.9
14	Rhode Island	2.8
15	Wisconsin	2.7
16	Indiana	2.6
17	Alabama	2.5
17	Alaska	2.5
17	Minnesota	2.5
17	Vermont	2.5
21	Maryland	2.4
21	Nebraska	2.4
21	New Jersey	2.4
24	Idaho	2.2
24	Missouri	2.2
24	Ohio	2.2
24	South Carolina	2.2
28	Tennessee	2.1
28	Washington	2.1
30	Michigan	2.0
31	Florida	1.8
32	Kansas	1.4
33	Arizona	1.1
33	Connecticut	1.1
33	Oregon	1.1
36	Illinois	1.0
36	Virginia	1.0
38	New Hampshire	0.9
38	North Carolina	0.9
40	Oklahoma	0.8
41	California	0.7
42	Georgia	0.6
43	Massachusetts	0.5
43	South Dakota	0.5
43	Utah	0.5
46	Delaware	0.4
47	Nevada	0.1
48	Texas	(0.2)
49	New York	(0.5)
50	Colorado	(0.9)

	District of Columbia	7.0

Source: Morgan Quitno Press using data from U.S. Department of Commerce, Bureau of Economic Analysis
"Annual State Personal Income" (http://www.bea.doc.gov/bea/regional/spi/)

Per Capita Disposable Personal Income in 2002

National Per Capita = $26,974*

<u>ALPHA ORDER</u>

RANK	STATE	PER CAPITA
42	Alabama	$22,504
11	Alaska	28,381
38	Arizona	23,240
49	Arkansas	20,970
13	California	28,286
9	Colorado	28,773
1	Connecticut	35,982
14	Delaware	28,021
22	Florida	26,207
29	Georgia	25,221
18	Hawaii	26,716
44	Idaho	22,325
8	Illinois	29,052
31	Indiana	24,983
30	Iowa	25,083
28	Kansas	25,393
41	Kentucky	22,650
39	Louisiana	22,866
34	Maine	24,503
4	Maryland	30,990
3	Massachusetts	33,179
20	Michigan	26,541
7	Minnesota	29,297
50	Mississippi	20,408
26	Missouri	25,552
45	Montana	22,251
23	Nebraska	26,137
19	Nevada	26,636
6	New Hampshire	30,285
2	New Jersey	34,109
46	New Mexico	21,429
5	New York	30,443
36	North Carolina	24,250
37	North Dakota	24,048
25	Ohio	25,600
43	Oklahoma	22,376
33	Oregon	24,782
15	Pennsylvania	27,804
16	Rhode Island	27,384
40	South Carolina	22,704
35	South Dakota	24,263
32	Tennessee	24,891
27	Texas	25,527
47	Utah	21,289
24	Vermont	26,066
12	Virginia	28,336
10	Washington	28,703
48	West Virginia	21,223
21	Wisconsin	26,336
17	Wyoming	26,734

<u>RANK ORDER</u>

RANK	STATE	PER CAPITA
1	Connecticut	$35,982
2	New Jersey	34,109
3	Massachusetts	33,179
4	Maryland	30,990
5	New York	30,443
6	New Hampshire	30,285
7	Minnesota	29,297
8	Illinois	29,052
9	Colorado	28,773
10	Washington	28,703
11	Alaska	28,381
12	Virginia	28,336
13	California	28,286
14	Delaware	28,021
15	Pennsylvania	27,804
16	Rhode Island	27,384
17	Wyoming	26,734
18	Hawaii	26,716
19	Nevada	26,636
20	Michigan	26,541
21	Wisconsin	26,336
22	Florida	26,207
23	Nebraska	26,137
24	Vermont	26,066
25	Ohio	25,600
26	Missouri	25,552
27	Texas	25,527
28	Kansas	25,393
29	Georgia	25,221
30	Iowa	25,083
31	Indiana	24,983
32	Tennessee	24,891
33	Oregon	24,782
34	Maine	24,503
35	South Dakota	24,263
36	North Carolina	24,250
37	North Dakota	24,048
38	Arizona	23,240
39	Louisiana	22,866
40	South Carolina	22,704
41	Kentucky	22,650
42	Alabama	22,504
43	Oklahoma	22,376
44	Idaho	22,325
45	Montana	22,251
46	New Mexico	21,429
47	Utah	21,289
48	West Virginia	21,223
49	Arkansas	20,970
50	Mississippi	20,408
	District of Columbia	36,888

Source: U.S. Department of Commerce, Bureau of Economic Analysis
"Annual State Personal Income" (http://www.bea.doc.gov/bea/regional/spi/)
**Disposable personal income is personal income less personal tax and nontax payments. It is the income available to persons for spending or saving.*

Median Household Income in 2002

National Median = $43,052*

<u>ALPHA ORDER</u>

RANK	STATE	INCOME
41	Alabama	$36,771
2	Alaska	55,412
31	Arizona	41,554
49	Arkansas	32,423
13	California	48,113
11	Colorado	49,617
5	Connecticut	53,325
7	Delaware	50,878
36	Florida	38,533
24	Georgia	43,316
10	Hawaii	49,775
35	Idaho	38,613
16	Illinois	45,906
30	Indiana	41,581
29	Iowa	41,827
26	Kansas	42,523
39	Kentucky	37,893
47	Louisiana	33,312
40	Maine	37,654
1	Maryland	55,912
8	Massachusetts	50,587
17	Michigan	45,335
3	Minnesota	54,931
48	Mississippi	32,447
20	Missouri	43,955
46	Montana	33,900
22	Nebraska	43,566
15	Nevada	46,289
4	New Hampshire	53,549
6	New Jersey	53,266
45	New Mexico	35,251
27	New York	42,432
38	North Carolina	38,432
42	North Dakota	36,717
23	Ohio	43,332
44	Oklahoma	35,500
25	Oregon	42,704
21	Pennsylvania	43,577
18	Rhode Island	44,311
37	South Carolina	38,460
34	South Dakota	38,755
43	Tennessee	36,329
32	Texas	40,659
12	Utah	48,537
28	Vermont	41,929
9	Virginia	49,974
19	Washington	44,252
50	West Virginia	30,072
14	Wisconsin	46,351
33	Wyoming	40,499

<u>RANK ORDER</u>

RANK	STATE	INCOME
1	Maryland	$55,912
2	Alaska	55,412
3	Minnesota	54,931
4	New Hampshire	53,549
5	Connecticut	53,325
6	New Jersey	53,266
7	Delaware	50,878
8	Massachusetts	50,587
9	Virginia	49,974
10	Hawaii	49,775
11	Colorado	49,617
12	Utah	48,537
13	California	48,113
14	Wisconsin	46,351
15	Nevada	46,289
16	Illinois	45,906
17	Michigan	45,335
18	Rhode Island	44,311
19	Washington	44,252
20	Missouri	43,955
21	Pennsylvania	43,577
22	Nebraska	43,566
23	Ohio	43,332
24	Georgia	43,316
25	Oregon	42,704
26	Kansas	42,523
27	New York	42,432
28	Vermont	41,929
29	Iowa	41,827
30	Indiana	41,581
31	Arizona	41,554
32	Texas	40,659
33	Wyoming	40,499
34	South Dakota	38,755
35	Idaho	38,613
36	Florida	38,533
37	South Carolina	38,460
38	North Carolina	38,432
39	Kentucky	37,893
40	Maine	37,654
41	Alabama	36,771
42	North Dakota	36,717
43	Tennessee	36,329
44	Oklahoma	35,500
45	New Mexico	35,251
46	Montana	33,900
47	Louisiana	33,312
48	Mississippi	32,447
49	Arkansas	32,423
50	West Virginia	30,072
	District of Columbia	41,313

Source: U.S. Bureau of the Census
"Income in the United States: 2002" (http://www.census.gov/prod/2003pubs/p60-221.pdf)
**Three-year average: 2000-2002.*

Bankruptcy Filings in 2003

National Total = 1,661,996 Bankruptcies*

ALPHA ORDER

RANK	STATE	BANKRUPTCIES	% of USA
14	Alabama	42,360	2.5%
50	Alaska	1,541	0.1%
19	Arizona	31,994	1.9%
26	Arkansas	24,346	1.5%
1	California	146,130	8.8%
25	Colorado	25,243	1.5%
35	Connecticut	12,272	0.7%
44	Delaware	3,978	0.2%
2	Florida	95,478	5.7%
6	Georgia	79,985	4.8%
45	Hawaii	3,908	0.2%
38	Idaho	9,630	0.6%
5	Illinois	86,802	5.2%
11	Indiana	55,605	3.3%
34	Iowa	12,577	0.8%
33	Kansas	16,177	1.0%
20	Kentucky	29,659	1.8%
21	Louisiana	29,164	1.8%
41	Maine	4,593	0.3%
18	Maryland	35,173	2.1%
31	Massachusetts	18,174	1.1%
9	Michigan	62,305	3.7%
30	Minnesota	20,483	1.2%
27	Mississippi	22,856	1.4%
17	Missouri	38,000	2.3%
43	Montana	4,345	0.3%
39	Nebraska	8,555	0.5%
29	Nevada	20,689	1.2%
42	New Hampshire	4,390	0.3%
13	New Jersey	42,921	2.6%
37	New Mexico	9,967	0.6%
7	New York	75,349	4.5%
16	North Carolina	38,811	2.3%
48	North Dakota	2,276	0.1%
4	Ohio	87,833	5.3%
23	Oklahoma	26,737	1.6%
24	Oregon	25,723	1.5%
10	Pennsylvania	58,493	3.5%
40	Rhode Island	4,712	0.3%
32	South Carolina	16,335	1.0%
46	South Dakota	2,867	0.2%
8	Tennessee	65,974	4.0%
3	Texas	89,469	5.4%
28	Utah	22,444	1.4%
49	Vermont	1,919	0.1%
12	Virginia	43,842	2.6%
15	Washington	40,907	2.5%
36	West Virginia	11,102	0.7%
22	Wisconsin	28,415	1.7%
47	Wyoming	2,513	0.2%

RANK ORDER

RANK	STATE	BANKRUPTCIES	% of USA
1	California	146,130	8.8%
2	Florida	95,478	5.7%
3	Texas	89,469	5.4%
4	Ohio	87,833	5.3%
5	Illinois	86,802	5.2%
6	Georgia	79,985	4.8%
7	New York	75,349	4.5%
8	Tennessee	65,974	4.0%
9	Michigan	62,305	3.7%
10	Pennsylvania	58,493	3.5%
11	Indiana	55,605	3.3%
12	Virginia	43,842	2.6%
13	New Jersey	42,921	2.6%
14	Alabama	42,360	2.5%
15	Washington	40,907	2.5%
16	North Carolina	38,811	2.3%
17	Missouri	38,000	2.3%
18	Maryland	35,173	2.1%
19	Arizona	31,994	1.9%
20	Kentucky	29,659	1.8%
21	Louisiana	29,164	1.8%
22	Wisconsin	28,415	1.7%
23	Oklahoma	26,737	1.6%
24	Oregon	25,723	1.5%
25	Colorado	25,243	1.5%
26	Arkansas	24,346	1.5%
27	Mississippi	22,856	1.4%
28	Utah	22,444	1.4%
29	Nevada	20,689	1.2%
30	Minnesota	20,483	1.2%
31	Massachusetts	18,174	1.1%
32	South Carolina	16,335	1.0%
33	Kansas	16,177	1.0%
34	Iowa	12,577	0.8%
35	Connecticut	12,272	0.7%
36	West Virginia	11,102	0.7%
37	New Mexico	9,967	0.6%
38	Idaho	9,630	0.6%
39	Nebraska	8,555	0.5%
40	Rhode Island	4,712	0.3%
41	Maine	4,593	0.3%
42	New Hampshire	4,390	0.3%
43	Montana	4,345	0.3%
44	Delaware	3,978	0.2%
45	Hawaii	3,908	0.2%
46	South Dakota	2,867	0.2%
47	Wyoming	2,513	0.2%
48	North Dakota	2,276	0.1%
49	Vermont	1,919	0.1%
50	Alaska	1,541	0.1%
	District of Columbia	2,381	0.1%

Source: Morgan Quitno Press using data from Administrative Office of the U.S. Courts
    "Table F-2, U.S. Bankruptcy Courts"
*For 12 months through September 2003. Includes business (36,183) and Non-Business (1,625,813) filings.
Includes all chapters of bankruptcy. National total includes 14,594 bankruptcies in U.S. territories.

Personal Bankruptcy Rate in 2003

National Rate = 554 Personal Bankruptcies per 100,000 Population*

ALPHA ORDER

RANK	STATE	RATE
2	Alabama	934
50	Alaska	218
23	Arizona	559
7	Arkansas	878
37	California	399
25	Colorado	543
43	Connecticut	347
35	Delaware	419
24	Florida	551
5	Georgia	904
47	Hawaii	306
12	Idaho	687
13	Illinois	678
6	Indiana	887
36	Iowa	416
21	Kansas	583
11	Kentucky	710
17	Louisiana	637
44	Maine	344
18	Maryland	624
49	Massachusetts	276
19	Michigan	611
41	Minnesota	378
8	Mississippi	783
15	Missouri	659
32	Montana	462
30	Nebraska	478
4	Nevada	909
46	New Hampshire	326
28	New Jersey	489
28	New Mexico	489
40	New York	382
33	North Carolina	455
45	North Dakota	341
9	Ohio	755
10	Oklahoma	744
14	Oregon	674
31	Pennsylvania	464
34	Rhode Island	434
38	South Carolina	391
42	South Dakota	359
1	Tennessee	1,119
39	Texas	390
3	Utah	933
48	Vermont	296
22	Virginia	581
16	Washington	656
20	West Virginia	596
26	Wisconsin	506
27	Wyoming	492

RANK ORDER

RANK	STATE	RATE
1	Tennessee	1,119
2	Alabama	934
3	Utah	933
4	Nevada	909
5	Georgia	904
6	Indiana	887
7	Arkansas	878
8	Mississippi	783
9	Ohio	755
10	Oklahoma	744
11	Kentucky	710
12	Idaho	687
13	Illinois	678
14	Oregon	674
15	Missouri	659
16	Washington	656
17	Louisiana	637
18	Maryland	624
19	Michigan	611
20	West Virginia	596
21	Kansas	583
22	Virginia	581
23	Arizona	559
24	Florida	551
25	Colorado	543
26	Wisconsin	506
27	Wyoming	492
28	New Jersey	489
28	New Mexico	489
30	Nebraska	478
31	Pennsylvania	464
32	Montana	462
33	North Carolina	455
34	Rhode Island	434
35	Delaware	419
36	Iowa	416
37	California	399
38	South Carolina	391
39	Texas	390
40	New York	382
41	Minnesota	378
42	South Dakota	359
43	Connecticut	347
44	Maine	344
45	North Dakota	341
46	New Hampshire	326
47	Hawaii	306
48	Vermont	296
49	Massachusetts	276
50	Alaska	218

District of Columbia   412

Source: Morgan Quitno Press using data from Administrative Office of the U.S. Courts
"Table F-2, U.S. Bankruptcy Courts"

*For 12 months through September 2003. National rate does not include bankruptcies or population in U.S. territories. Includes all nonbusiness bankruptcies.

Percent Change in Personal Bankruptcy Rate: 2002 to 2003

National Percent Change = 4.4% Increase*

<u>ALPHA ORDER</u>

RANK	STATE	PERCENT CHANGE
46	Alabama	1.2
35	Alaska	4.2
16	Arizona	7.7
42	Arkansas	3.4
48	California	(2.5)
1	Colorado	18.2
32	Connecticut	4.4
28	Delaware	5.0
41	Florida	3.6
24	Georgia	5.6
50	Hawaii	(12.9)
14	Idaho	8.0
25	Illinois	5.4
38	Indiana	3.9
22	Iowa	6.5
13	Kansas	8.1
11	Kentucky	8.8
17	Louisiana	7.5
38	Maine	3.9
47	Maryland	(1.1)
31	Massachusetts	4.5
3	Michigan	12.0
26	Minnesota	5.1
44	Mississippi	2.0
7	Missouri	10.8
19	Montana	7.0
7	Nebraska	10.8
29	Nevada	4.8
11	New Hampshire	8.8
30	New Jersey	4.7
17	New Mexico	7.5
35	New York	4.2
20	North Carolina	6.7
9	North Dakota	9.7
5	Ohio	11.4
10	Oklahoma	9.1
32	Oregon	4.4
20	Pennsylvania	6.7
49	Rhode Island	(4.0)
40	South Carolina	3.7
15	South Dakota	7.8
32	Tennessee	4.4
4	Texas	11.8
45	Utah	1.4
26	Vermont	5.1
43	Virginia	2.4
35	Washington	4.2
23	West Virginia	6.1
2	Wisconsin	12.3
6	Wyoming	11.0

<u>RANK ORDER</u>

RANK	STATE	PERCENT CHANGE
1	Colorado	18.2
2	Wisconsin	12.3
3	Michigan	12.0
4	Texas	11.8
5	Ohio	11.4
6	Wyoming	11.0
7	Missouri	10.8
7	Nebraska	10.8
9	North Dakota	9.7
10	Oklahoma	9.1
11	Kentucky	8.8
11	New Hampshire	8.8
13	Kansas	8.1
14	Idaho	8.0
15	South Dakota	7.8
16	Arizona	7.7
17	Louisiana	7.5
17	New Mexico	7.5
19	Montana	7.0
20	North Carolina	6.7
20	Pennsylvania	6.7
22	Iowa	6.5
23	West Virginia	6.1
24	Georgia	5.6
25	Illinois	5.4
26	Minnesota	5.1
26	Vermont	5.1
28	Delaware	5.0
29	Nevada	4.8
30	New Jersey	4.7
31	Massachusetts	4.5
32	Connecticut	4.4
32	Oregon	4.4
32	Tennessee	4.4
35	Alaska	4.2
35	New York	4.2
35	Washington	4.2
38	Indiana	3.9
38	Maine	3.9
40	South Carolina	3.7
41	Florida	3.6
42	Arkansas	3.4
43	Virginia	2.4
44	Mississippi	2.0
45	Utah	1.4
46	Alabama	1.2
47	Maryland	(1.1)
48	California	(2.5)
49	Rhode Island	(4.0)
50	Hawaii	(12.9)
	District of Columbia	(4.9)

Source: Morgan Quitno Press using data from Administrative Office of the U.S. Courts
   "Table F-2, U.S. Bankruptcy Courts"

Twelve months ending in December 2002 to 12 months ending in September 2003. National rate does not include bankruptcies or population in U.S. territories. Includes all nonbusiness bankruptcies.

Total Tax Burden in 2003

National Percent = 30.0% of Income*

<table>
<tr><td colspan="3"><u>ALPHA ORDER</u></td><td colspan="3"><u>RANK ORDER</u></td></tr>
<tr><th>RANK</th><th>STATE</th><th>PERCENT</th><th>RANK</th><th>STATE</th><th>PERCENT</th></tr>
<tr><td>47</td><td>Alabama</td><td>26.3</td><td>1</td><td>Connecticut</td><td>35.4</td></tr>
<tr><td>50</td><td>Alaska</td><td>24.6</td><td>2</td><td>Massachusetts</td><td>33.6</td></tr>
<tr><td>16</td><td>Arizona</td><td>29.4</td><td>3</td><td>California</td><td>32.7</td></tr>
<tr><td>39</td><td>Arkansas</td><td>27.2</td><td>3</td><td>New York</td><td>32.7</td></tr>
<tr><td>3</td><td>California</td><td>32.7</td><td>5</td><td>New Jersey</td><td>32.3</td></tr>
<tr><td>11</td><td>Colorado</td><td>30.5</td><td>6</td><td>Washington</td><td>32.1</td></tr>
<tr><td>1</td><td>Connecticut</td><td>35.4</td><td>7</td><td>Minnesota</td><td>31.2</td></tr>
<tr><td>39</td><td>Delaware</td><td>27.2</td><td>8</td><td>Rhode Island</td><td>31.1</td></tr>
<tr><td>21</td><td>Florida</td><td>29.0</td><td>9</td><td>Maine</td><td>30.8</td></tr>
<tr><td>19</td><td>Georgia</td><td>29.2</td><td>10</td><td>Wyoming</td><td>30.7</td></tr>
<tr><td>29</td><td>Hawaii</td><td>28.4</td><td>11</td><td>Colorado</td><td>30.5</td></tr>
<tr><td>24</td><td>Idaho</td><td>28.7</td><td>12</td><td>Illinois</td><td>30.3</td></tr>
<tr><td>12</td><td>Illinois</td><td>30.3</td><td>13</td><td>Nevada</td><td>30.2</td></tr>
<tr><td>27</td><td>Indiana</td><td>28.5</td><td>14</td><td>Wisconsin</td><td>30.0</td></tr>
<tr><td>35</td><td>Iowa</td><td>27.7</td><td>15</td><td>Vermont</td><td>29.5</td></tr>
<tr><td>29</td><td>Kansas</td><td>28.4</td><td>16</td><td>Arizona</td><td>29.4</td></tr>
<tr><td>37</td><td>Kentucky</td><td>27.3</td><td>16</td><td>Maryland</td><td>29.4</td></tr>
<tr><td>43</td><td>Louisiana</td><td>26.7</td><td>18</td><td>Michigan</td><td>29.3</td></tr>
<tr><td>9</td><td>Maine</td><td>30.8</td><td>19</td><td>Georgia</td><td>29.2</td></tr>
<tr><td>16</td><td>Maryland</td><td>29.4</td><td>20</td><td>Utah</td><td>29.1</td></tr>
<tr><td>2</td><td>Massachusetts</td><td>33.6</td><td>21</td><td>Florida</td><td>29.0</td></tr>
<tr><td>18</td><td>Michigan</td><td>29.3</td><td>21</td><td>Virginia</td><td>29.0</td></tr>
<tr><td>7</td><td>Minnesota</td><td>31.2</td><td>23</td><td>New Hampshire</td><td>28.8</td></tr>
<tr><td>43</td><td>Mississippi</td><td>26.7</td><td>24</td><td>Idaho</td><td>28.7</td></tr>
<tr><td>34</td><td>Missouri</td><td>28.0</td><td>24</td><td>Ohio</td><td>28.7</td></tr>
<tr><td>37</td><td>Montana</td><td>27.3</td><td>26</td><td>Pennsylvania</td><td>28.6</td></tr>
<tr><td>33</td><td>Nebraska</td><td>28.2</td><td>27</td><td>Indiana</td><td>28.5</td></tr>
<tr><td>13</td><td>Nevada</td><td>30.2</td><td>27</td><td>Oregon</td><td>28.5</td></tr>
<tr><td>23</td><td>New Hampshire</td><td>28.8</td><td>29</td><td>Hawaii</td><td>28.4</td></tr>
<tr><td>5</td><td>New Jersey</td><td>32.3</td><td>29</td><td>Kansas</td><td>28.4</td></tr>
<tr><td>49</td><td>New Mexico</td><td>25.6</td><td>29</td><td>Texas</td><td>28.4</td></tr>
<tr><td>3</td><td>New York</td><td>32.7</td><td>32</td><td>North Carolina</td><td>28.3</td></tr>
<tr><td>32</td><td>North Carolina</td><td>28.3</td><td>33</td><td>Nebraska</td><td>28.2</td></tr>
<tr><td>35</td><td>North Dakota</td><td>27.7</td><td>34</td><td>Missouri</td><td>28.0</td></tr>
<tr><td>24</td><td>Ohio</td><td>28.7</td><td>35</td><td>Iowa</td><td>27.7</td></tr>
<tr><td>45</td><td>Oklahoma</td><td>26.5</td><td>35</td><td>North Dakota</td><td>27.7</td></tr>
<tr><td>27</td><td>Oregon</td><td>28.5</td><td>37</td><td>Kentucky</td><td>27.3</td></tr>
<tr><td>26</td><td>Pennsylvania</td><td>28.6</td><td>37</td><td>Montana</td><td>27.3</td></tr>
<tr><td>8</td><td>Rhode Island</td><td>31.1</td><td>39</td><td>Arkansas</td><td>27.2</td></tr>
<tr><td>41</td><td>South Carolina</td><td>27.1</td><td>39</td><td>Delaware</td><td>27.2</td></tr>
<tr><td>41</td><td>South Dakota</td><td>27.1</td><td>41</td><td>South Carolina</td><td>27.1</td></tr>
<tr><td>47</td><td>Tennessee</td><td>26.3</td><td>41</td><td>South Dakota</td><td>27.1</td></tr>
<tr><td>29</td><td>Texas</td><td>28.4</td><td>43</td><td>Louisiana</td><td>26.7</td></tr>
<tr><td>20</td><td>Utah</td><td>29.1</td><td>43</td><td>Mississippi</td><td>26.7</td></tr>
<tr><td>15</td><td>Vermont</td><td>29.5</td><td>45</td><td>Oklahoma</td><td>26.5</td></tr>
<tr><td>21</td><td>Virginia</td><td>29.0</td><td>45</td><td>West Virginia</td><td>26.5</td></tr>
<tr><td>6</td><td>Washington</td><td>32.1</td><td>47</td><td>Alabama</td><td>26.3</td></tr>
<tr><td>45</td><td>West Virginia</td><td>26.5</td><td>47</td><td>Tennessee</td><td>26.3</td></tr>
<tr><td>14</td><td>Wisconsin</td><td>30.0</td><td>49</td><td>New Mexico</td><td>25.6</td></tr>
<tr><td>10</td><td>Wyoming</td><td>30.7</td><td>50</td><td>Alaska</td><td>24.6</td></tr>
<tr><td></td><td></td><td></td><td></td><td>District of Columbia</td><td>34.8</td></tr>
</table>

Source: The Tax Foundation
"Comparing the Total Tax Burden in Each State" (http://www.taxfoundation.org/statelocal03.html)
Federal, state and local government taxes as a percent of income.

State Business Tax Climate Index 2002

National Average Score = 5.97*

ALPHA ORDER				RANK ORDER		
RANK	**STATE**	**SCORE**		**RANK**	**STATE**	**SCORE**
15	Alabama	6.58		1	Wyoming	8.30
5	Alaska	7.64		2	New Hampshire	8.05
17	Arizona	6.46		3	Nevada	7.91
48	Arkansas	4.43		4	Colorado	7.69
49	California	4.36		5	Alaska	7.64
4	Colorado	7.69		6	South Dakota	7.63
37	Connecticut	5.11		7	Florida	7.41
15	Delaware	6.58		8	Washington	7.37
7	Florida	7.41		9	Oregon	7.20
25	Georgia	5.83		10	Indiana	7.04
45	Hawaii	4.73		10	Tennessee	7.04
32	Idaho	5.43		12	Massachusetts	6.90
14	Illinois	6.71		13	Texas	6.75
10	Indiana	7.04		14	Illinois	6.71
38	Iowa	5.10		15	Alabama	6.58
36	Kansas	5.20		15	Delaware	6.58
35	Kentucky	5.37		17	Arizona	6.46
41	Louisiana	4.87		18	Michigan	6.39
43	Maine	4.83		19	Pennsylvania	6.38
31	Maryland	5.53		20	Vermont	6.36
12	Massachusetts	6.90		20	Virginia	6.36
18	Michigan	6.39		22	Montana	6.33
42	Minnesota	4.84		23	Missouri	5.89
50	Mississippi	3.97		24	North Carolina	5.85
23	Missouri	5.89		25	Georgia	5.83
22	Montana	6.33		26	South Carolina	5.81
46	Nebraska	4.67		27	Oklahoma	5.80
3	Nevada	7.91		28	Wisconsin	5.69
2	New Hampshire	8.05		29	New Mexico	5.58
40	New Jersey	5.09		30	Rhode Island	5.55
29	New Mexico	5.58		31	Maryland	5.53
44	New York	4.80		32	Idaho	5.43
24	North Carolina	5.85		32	North Dakota	5.43
32	North Dakota	5.43		34	Utah	5.40
47	Ohio	4.45		35	Kentucky	5.37
27	Oklahoma	5.80		36	Kansas	5.20
9	Oregon	7.20		37	Connecticut	5.11
19	Pennsylvania	6.38		38	Iowa	5.10
30	Rhode Island	5.55		38	West Virginia	5.10
26	South Carolina	5.81		40	New Jersey	5.09
6	South Dakota	7.63		41	Louisiana	4.87
10	Tennessee	7.04		42	Minnesota	4.84
13	Texas	6.75		43	Maine	4.83
34	Utah	5.40		44	New York	4.80
20	Vermont	6.36		45	Hawaii	4.73
20	Virginia	6.36		46	Nebraska	4.67
8	Washington	7.37		47	Ohio	4.45
38	West Virginia	5.10		48	Arkansas	4.43
28	Wisconsin	5.69		49	California	4.36
1	Wyoming	8.30		50	Mississippi	3.97
					District of Columbia	4.55

Source: The Tax Foundation
"State Business Tax Climate Index" (http://www.taxfoundation.org/bp41.pdf)
This index looks at levels of taxation and complexity of compliance to compare the states on how "business friendly" each state is compared to the others. The scale for each factor considered is one to ten, with ten being the "best."

Fortune 500 Companies in 2003

National Total = 500 Companies*

<u>ALPHA ORDER</u>

RANK	STATE	COMPANIES	% of USA
20	Alabama	6	1.2%
40	Alaska	0	0.0%
29	Arizona	3	0.6%
24	Arkansas	5	1.0%
1	California	53	10.6%
20	Colorado	6	1.2%
11	Connecticut	14	2.8%
31	Delaware	2	0.4%
16	Florida	11	2.2%
11	Georgia	14	2.8%
40	Hawaii	0	0.0%
29	Idaho	3	0.6%
4	Illinois	35	7.0%
20	Indiana	6	1.2%
31	Iowa	2	0.4%
31	Kansas	2	0.4%
24	Kentucky	5	1.0%
31	Louisiana	2	0.4%
40	Maine	0	0.0%
19	Maryland	7	1.4%
14	Massachusetts	13	2.6%
7	Michigan	25	5.0%
9	Minnesota	18	3.6%
40	Mississippi	0	0.0%
15	Missouri	12	2.4%
40	Montana	0	0.0%
24	Nebraska	5	1.0%
27	Nevada	4	0.8%
36	New Hampshire	1	0.2%
8	New Jersey	22	4.4%
40	New Mexico	0	0.0%
2	New York	52	10.4%
11	North Carolina	14	2.8%
40	North Dakota	0	0.0%
5	Ohio	28	5.6%
27	Oklahoma	4	0.8%
36	Oregon	1	0.2%
6	Pennsylvania	27	5.4%
31	Rhode Island	2	0.4%
36	South Carolina	1	0.2%
40	South Dakota	0	0.0%
20	Tennessee	6	1.2%
3	Texas	45	9.0%
36	Utah	1	0.2%
40	Vermont	0	0.0%
9	Virginia	18	3.6%
16	Washington	11	2.2%
40	West Virginia	0	0.0%
16	Wisconsin	11	2.2%
40	Wyoming	0	0.0%

<u>RANK ORDER</u>

RANK	STATE	COMPANIES	% of USA
1	California	53	10.6%
2	New York	52	10.4%
3	Texas	45	9.0%
4	Illinois	35	7.0%
5	Ohio	28	5.6%
6	Pennsylvania	27	5.4%
7	Michigan	25	5.0%
8	New Jersey	22	4.4%
9	Minnesota	18	3.6%
9	Virginia	18	3.6%
11	Connecticut	14	2.8%
11	Georgia	14	2.8%
11	North Carolina	14	2.8%
14	Massachusetts	13	2.6%
15	Missouri	12	2.4%
16	Florida	11	2.2%
16	Washington	11	2.2%
16	Wisconsin	11	2.2%
19	Maryland	7	1.4%
20	Alabama	6	1.2%
20	Colorado	6	1.2%
20	Indiana	6	1.2%
20	Tennessee	6	1.2%
24	Arkansas	5	1.0%
24	Kentucky	5	1.0%
24	Nebraska	5	1.0%
27	Nevada	4	0.8%
27	Oklahoma	4	0.8%
29	Arizona	3	0.6%
29	Idaho	3	0.6%
31	Delaware	2	0.4%
31	Iowa	2	0.4%
31	Kansas	2	0.4%
31	Louisiana	2	0.4%
31	Rhode Island	2	0.4%
36	New Hampshire	1	0.2%
36	Oregon	1	0.2%
36	South Carolina	1	0.2%
36	Utah	1	0.2%
40	Alaska	0	0.0%
40	Hawaii	0	0.0%
40	Maine	0	0.0%
40	Mississippi	0	0.0%
40	Montana	0	0.0%
40	New Mexico	0	0.0%
40	North Dakota	0	0.0%
40	South Dakota	0	0.0%
40	Vermont	0	0.0%
40	West Virginia	0	0.0%
40	Wyoming	0	0.0%
	District of Columbia	3	0.6%

Source: Fortune Magazine

  "Fortune 5 Hundred Ranked Within States" (April 14, 2003)
By state where each company's headquarters is located.

Employer Firms in 2002

National Total = 5,595,200 Firms*

ALPHA ORDER

RANK	STATE	FIRMS	% of USA
28	Alabama	85,895	1.5%
50	Alaska	16,511	0.3%
22	Arizona	107,894	1.9%
32	Arkansas	60,668	1.1%
1	California	1,022,192	18.3%
15	Colorado	140,704	2.5%
24	Connecticut	96,677	1.7%
45	Delaware	25,097	0.4%
3	Florida	413,476	7.4%
11	Georgia	194,062	3.5%
44	Hawaii	28,800	0.5%
38	Idaho	40,633	0.7%
5	Illinois	278,839	5.0%
19	Indiana	124,673	2.2%
30	Iowa	68,466	1.2%
31	Kansas	67,757	1.2%
27	Kentucky	87,589	1.6%
25	Louisiana	93,989	1.7%
40	Maine	39,180	0.7%
16	Maryland	133,536	2.4%
13	Massachusetts	173,896	3.1%
9	Michigan	211,567	3.8%
17	Minnesota	131,646	2.4%
34	Mississippi	53,409	1.0%
18	Missouri	129,777	2.3%
42	Montana	33,339	0.6%
36	Nebraska	45,342	0.8%
35	Nevada	47,340	0.8%
39	New Hampshire	39,211	0.7%
6	New Jersey	274,966	4.9%
37	New Mexico	42,066	0.8%
2	New York	474,425	8.5%
12	North Carolina	178,560	3.2%
49	North Dakota	18,639	0.3%
8	Ohio	230,705	4.1%
29	Oklahoma	75,250	1.3%
23	Oregon	100,726	1.8%
7	Pennsylvania	268,723	4.8%
43	Rhode Island	32,295	0.6%
26	South Carolina	89,634	1.6%
46	South Dakota	22,803	0.4%
21	Tennessee	108,928	1.9%
4	Texas	394,303	7.0%
33	Utah	56,346	1.0%
47	Vermont	20,755	0.4%
14	Virginia	165,185	3.0%
10	Washington	200,909	3.6%
41	West Virginia	37,364	0.7%
20	Wisconsin	122,249	2.2%
48	Wyoming	19,339	0.3%

RANK ORDER

RANK	STATE	FIRMS	% of USA
1	California	1,022,192	18.3%
2	New York	474,425	8.5%
3	Florida	413,476	7.4%
4	Texas	394,303	7.0%
5	Illinois	278,839	5.0%
6	New Jersey	274,966	4.9%
7	Pennsylvania	268,723	4.8%
8	Ohio	230,705	4.1%
9	Michigan	211,567	3.8%
10	Washington	200,909	3.6%
11	Georgia	194,062	3.5%
12	North Carolina	178,560	3.2%
13	Massachusetts	173,896	3.1%
14	Virginia	165,185	3.0%
15	Colorado	140,704	2.5%
16	Maryland	133,536	2.4%
17	Minnesota	131,646	2.4%
18	Missouri	129,777	2.3%
19	Indiana	124,673	2.2%
20	Wisconsin	122,249	2.2%
21	Tennessee	108,928	1.9%
22	Arizona	107,894	1.9%
23	Oregon	100,726	1.8%
24	Connecticut	96,677	1.7%
25	Louisiana	93,989	1.7%
26	South Carolina	89,634	1.6%
27	Kentucky	87,589	1.6%
28	Alabama	85,895	1.5%
29	Oklahoma	75,250	1.3%
30	Iowa	68,466	1.2%
31	Kansas	67,757	1.2%
32	Arkansas	60,668	1.1%
33	Utah	56,346	1.0%
34	Mississippi	53,409	1.0%
35	Nevada	47,340	0.8%
36	Nebraska	45,342	0.8%
37	New Mexico	42,066	0.8%
38	Idaho	40,633	0.7%
39	New Hampshire	39,211	0.7%
40	Maine	39,180	0.7%
41	West Virginia	37,364	0.7%
42	Montana	33,339	0.6%
43	Rhode Island	32,295	0.6%
44	Hawaii	28,800	0.5%
45	Delaware	25,097	0.4%
46	South Dakota	22,803	0.4%
47	Vermont	20,755	0.4%
48	Wyoming	19,339	0.3%
49	North Dakota	18,639	0.3%
50	Alaska	16,511	0.3%
	District of Columbia	26,503	0.5%

Source: U.S. Small Business Administration
"Small Business Economic Indicators 2002" (http://www.sba.gov/advo/stats/sbei02.pdf)
**State totals do not add to the U.S. figure as firms can be in more than one state.*

Percent Change in Number of Employer Firms: 2001 to 2002

National Percent Change = 0.6% Decrease*

<u>ALPHA ORDER</u>

RANK	STATE	PERCENT CHANGE
35	Alabama	(0.1)
22	Alaska	0.7
12	Arizona	1.1
9	Arkansas	1.5
2	California	3.7
7	Colorado	1.7
36	Connecticut	(0.2)
39	Delaware	(0.4)
1	Florida	5.3
22	Georgia	0.7
18	Hawaii	0.8
27	Idaho	0.4
37	Illinois	(0.3)
39	Indiana	(0.4)
37	Iowa	(0.3)
18	Kansas	0.8
43	Kentucky	(0.6)
48	Louisiana	(1.9)
22	Maine	0.7
12	Maryland	1.1
4	Massachusetts	2.3
42	Michigan	(0.5)
15	Minnesota	1.0
30	Mississippi	0.2
29	Missouri	0.3
10	Montana	1.4
22	Nebraska	0.7
5	Nevada	2.2
45	New Hampshire	(0.8)
46	New Jersey	(0.9)
12	New Mexico	1.1
30	New York	0.2
6	North Carolina	1.8
26	North Dakota	0.5
44	Ohio	(0.7)
34	Oklahoma	0.1
18	Oregon	0.8
11	Pennsylvania	1.2
49	Rhode Island	(2.2)
27	South Carolina	0.4
30	South Dakota	0.2
39	Tennessee	(0.4)
15	Texas	1.0
3	Utah	3.5
50	Vermont	(2.3)
7	Virginia	1.7
18	Washington	0.8
47	West Virginia	(1.2)
30	Wisconsin	0.2
15	Wyoming	1.0

<u>RANK ORDER</u>

RANK	STATE	PERCENT CHANGE
1	Florida	5.3
2	California	3.7
3	Utah	3.5
4	Massachusetts	2.3
5	Nevada	2.2
6	North Carolina	1.8
7	Colorado	1.7
7	Virginia	1.7
9	Arkansas	1.5
10	Montana	1.4
11	Pennsylvania	1.2
12	Arizona	1.1
12	Maryland	1.1
12	New Mexico	1.1
15	Minnesota	1.0
15	Texas	1.0
15	Wyoming	1.0
18	Hawaii	0.8
18	Kansas	0.8
18	Oregon	0.8
18	Washington	0.8
22	Alaska	0.7
22	Georgia	0.7
22	Maine	0.7
22	Nebraska	0.7
26	North Dakota	0.5
27	Idaho	0.4
27	South Carolina	0.4
29	Missouri	0.3
30	Mississippi	0.2
30	New York	0.2
30	South Dakota	0.2
30	Wisconsin	0.2
34	Oklahoma	0.1
35	Alabama	(0.1)
36	Connecticut	(0.2)
37	Illinois	(0.3)
37	Iowa	(0.3)
39	Delaware	(0.4)
39	Indiana	(0.4)
39	Tennessee	(0.4)
42	Michigan	(0.5)
43	Kentucky	(0.6)
44	Ohio	(0.7)
45	New Hampshire	(0.8)
46	New Jersey	(0.9)
47	West Virginia	(1.2)
48	Louisiana	(1.9)
49	Rhode Island	(2.2)
50	Vermont	(2.3)
	District of Columbia	0.7

Source: U.S. Small Business Administration
"Small Business Economic Indicators 2002" (http://www.sba.gov/advo/stats/sbei02.pdf)
**Firms can be in more than one state.*

New Employer Firms in 2002

National Total = 550,100 New Firms*

<u>ALPHA ORDER</u>

RANK	STATE	FIRMS	% of USA
27	Alabama	9,599	1.7%
48	Alaska	2,270	0.4%
19	Arizona	14,291	2.6%
35	Arkansas	5,381	1.0%
1	California	130,840	23.8%
10	Colorado	25,290	4.6%
29	Connecticut	8,726	1.6%
45	Delaware	3,223	0.6%
2	Florida	72,720	13.2%
8	Georgia	28,756	5.2%
44	Hawaii	3,555	0.6%
37	Idaho	5,039	0.9%
9	Illinois	27,342	5.0%
21	Indiana	13,530	2.5%
34	Iowa	5,660	1.0%
32	Kansas	6,703	1.2%
31	Kentucky	8,526	1.5%
26	Louisiana	9,810	1.8%
39	Maine	4,428	0.8%
16	Maryland	20,576	3.7%
14	Massachusetts	21,725	3.9%
12	Michigan	22,799	4.1%
20	Minnesota	13,683	2.5%
33	Mississippi	6,256	1.1%
17	Missouri	16,337	3.0%
43	Montana	3,569	0.6%
40	Nebraska	4,372	0.8%
28	Nevada	8,826	1.6%
38	New Hampshire	4,562	0.8%
7	New Jersey	29,916	5.4%
36	New Mexico	5,281	1.0%
3	New York	59,571	10.8%
11	North Carolina	22,950	4.2%
50	North Dakota	1,356	0.2%
13	Ohio	22,379	4.1%
30	Oklahoma	8,702	1.6%
22	Oregon	13,160	2.4%
6	Pennsylvania	31,939	5.8%
42	Rhode Island	3,597	0.7%
25	South Carolina	10,266	1.9%
49	South Dakota	1,389	0.3%
18	Tennessee	15,982	2.9%
4	Texas	54,009	9.8%
24	Utah	10,431	1.9%
46	Vermont	2,331	0.4%
15	Virginia	21,438	3.9%
5	Washington	37,562	6.8%
41	West Virginia	3,944	0.7%
23	Wisconsin	12,172	2.2%
47	Wyoming	2,275	0.4%

<u>RANK ORDER</u>

RANK	STATE	FIRMS	% of USA
1	California	130,840	23.8%
2	Florida	72,720	13.2%
3	New York	59,571	10.8%
4	Texas	54,009	9.8%
5	Washington	37,562	6.8%
6	Pennsylvania	31,939	5.8%
7	New Jersey	29,916	5.4%
8	Georgia	28,756	5.2%
9	Illinois	27,342	5.0%
10	Colorado	25,290	4.6%
11	North Carolina	22,950	4.2%
12	Michigan	22,799	4.1%
13	Ohio	22,379	4.1%
14	Massachusetts	21,725	3.9%
15	Virginia	21,438	3.9%
16	Maryland	20,576	3.7%
17	Missouri	16,337	3.0%
18	Tennessee	15,982	2.9%
19	Arizona	14,291	2.6%
20	Minnesota	13,683	2.5%
21	Indiana	13,530	2.5%
22	Oregon	13,160	2.4%
23	Wisconsin	12,172	2.2%
24	Utah	10,431	1.9%
25	South Carolina	10,266	1.9%
26	Louisiana	9,810	1.8%
27	Alabama	9,599	1.7%
28	Nevada	8,826	1.6%
29	Connecticut	8,726	1.6%
30	Oklahoma	8,702	1.6%
31	Kentucky	8,526	1.5%
32	Kansas	6,703	1.2%
33	Mississippi	6,256	1.1%
34	Iowa	5,660	1.0%
35	Arkansas	5,381	1.0%
36	New Mexico	5,281	1.0%
37	Idaho	5,039	0.9%
38	New Hampshire	4,562	0.8%
39	Maine	4,428	0.8%
40	Nebraska	4,372	0.8%
41	West Virginia	3,944	0.7%
42	Rhode Island	3,597	0.7%
43	Montana	3,569	0.6%
44	Hawaii	3,555	0.6%
45	Delaware	3,223	0.6%
46	Vermont	2,331	0.4%
47	Wyoming	2,275	0.4%
48	Alaska	2,270	0.4%
49	South Dakota	1,389	0.3%
50	North Dakota	1,356	0.2%
	District of Columbia	4,157	0.8%

Source: U.S. Small Business Administration
"Small Business Economic Indicators 2002" (http://www.sba.gov/advo/stats/sbei02.pdf)
**State totals do not add to the U.S. figure as firms can be in more than one state.*

Rate of New Employer Firms in 2002

National Rate = 9.8% of Existing Firms*

<table>
<tr><td colspan="3"><u>ALPHA ORDER</u></td><td colspan="3"><u>RANK ORDER</u></td></tr>
<tr><td>RANK</td><td>STATE</td><td>RATE</td><td>RANK</td><td>STATE</td><td>RATE</td></tr>
<tr><td>30</td><td>Alabama</td><td>11.2</td><td>1</td><td>Utah</td><td>19.2</td></tr>
<tr><td>9</td><td>Alaska</td><td>13.8</td><td>2</td><td>Nevada</td><td>19.0</td></tr>
<tr><td>11</td><td>Arizona</td><td>13.4</td><td>3</td><td>Washington</td><td>18.9</td></tr>
<tr><td>46</td><td>Arkansas</td><td>9.0</td><td>4</td><td>Florida</td><td>18.5</td></tr>
<tr><td>12</td><td>California</td><td>13.3</td><td>5</td><td>Colorado</td><td>18.3</td></tr>
<tr><td>5</td><td>Colorado</td><td>18.3</td><td>6</td><td>Maryland</td><td>15.6</td></tr>
<tr><td>46</td><td>Connecticut</td><td>9.0</td><td>7</td><td>Georgia</td><td>14.9</td></tr>
<tr><td>16</td><td>Delaware</td><td>12.8</td><td>8</td><td>Tennessee</td><td>14.6</td></tr>
<tr><td>4</td><td>Florida</td><td>18.5</td><td>9</td><td>Alaska</td><td>13.8</td></tr>
<tr><td>7</td><td>Georgia</td><td>14.9</td><td>9</td><td>Texas</td><td>13.8</td></tr>
<tr><td>22</td><td>Hawaii</td><td>12.4</td><td>11</td><td>Arizona</td><td>13.4</td></tr>
<tr><td>21</td><td>Idaho</td><td>12.5</td><td>12</td><td>California</td><td>13.3</td></tr>
<tr><td>42</td><td>Illinois</td><td>9.8</td><td>13</td><td>Oregon</td><td>13.2</td></tr>
<tr><td>34</td><td>Indiana</td><td>10.8</td><td>13</td><td>Virginia</td><td>13.2</td></tr>
<tr><td>48</td><td>Iowa</td><td>8.2</td><td>15</td><td>North Carolina</td><td>13.1</td></tr>
<tr><td>40</td><td>Kansas</td><td>10.0</td><td>16</td><td>Delaware</td><td>12.8</td></tr>
<tr><td>43</td><td>Kentucky</td><td>9.7</td><td>16</td><td>Massachusetts</td><td>12.8</td></tr>
<tr><td>39</td><td>Louisiana</td><td>10.2</td><td>18</td><td>New Mexico</td><td>12.7</td></tr>
<tr><td>29</td><td>Maine</td><td>11.4</td><td>19</td><td>Missouri</td><td>12.6</td></tr>
<tr><td>6</td><td>Maryland</td><td>15.6</td><td>19</td><td>New York</td><td>12.6</td></tr>
<tr><td>16</td><td>Massachusetts</td><td>12.8</td><td>21</td><td>Idaho</td><td>12.5</td></tr>
<tr><td>36</td><td>Michigan</td><td>10.7</td><td>22</td><td>Hawaii</td><td>12.4</td></tr>
<tr><td>37</td><td>Minnesota</td><td>10.5</td><td>23</td><td>Pennsylvania</td><td>12.0</td></tr>
<tr><td>25</td><td>Mississippi</td><td>11.7</td><td>24</td><td>Wyoming</td><td>11.9</td></tr>
<tr><td>19</td><td>Missouri</td><td>12.6</td><td>25</td><td>Mississippi</td><td>11.7</td></tr>
<tr><td>32</td><td>Montana</td><td>10.9</td><td>26</td><td>Oklahoma</td><td>11.6</td></tr>
<tr><td>43</td><td>Nebraska</td><td>9.7</td><td>27</td><td>New Hampshire</td><td>11.5</td></tr>
<tr><td>2</td><td>Nevada</td><td>19.0</td><td>27</td><td>South Carolina</td><td>11.5</td></tr>
<tr><td>27</td><td>New Hampshire</td><td>11.5</td><td>29</td><td>Maine</td><td>11.4</td></tr>
<tr><td>34</td><td>New Jersey</td><td>10.8</td><td>30</td><td>Alabama</td><td>11.2</td></tr>
<tr><td>18</td><td>New Mexico</td><td>12.7</td><td>31</td><td>Vermont</td><td>11.0</td></tr>
<tr><td>19</td><td>New York</td><td>12.6</td><td>32</td><td>Montana</td><td>10.9</td></tr>
<tr><td>15</td><td>North Carolina</td><td>13.1</td><td>32</td><td>Rhode Island</td><td>10.9</td></tr>
<tr><td>49</td><td>North Dakota</td><td>7.3</td><td>34</td><td>Indiana</td><td>10.8</td></tr>
<tr><td>45</td><td>Ohio</td><td>9.6</td><td>34</td><td>New Jersey</td><td>10.8</td></tr>
<tr><td>26</td><td>Oklahoma</td><td>11.6</td><td>36</td><td>Michigan</td><td>10.7</td></tr>
<tr><td>13</td><td>Oregon</td><td>13.2</td><td>37</td><td>Minnesota</td><td>10.5</td></tr>
<tr><td>23</td><td>Pennsylvania</td><td>12.0</td><td>38</td><td>West Virginia</td><td>10.4</td></tr>
<tr><td>32</td><td>Rhode Island</td><td>10.9</td><td>39</td><td>Louisiana</td><td>10.2</td></tr>
<tr><td>27</td><td>South Carolina</td><td>11.5</td><td>40</td><td>Kansas</td><td>10.0</td></tr>
<tr><td>50</td><td>South Dakota</td><td>6.1</td><td>40</td><td>Wisconsin</td><td>10.0</td></tr>
<tr><td>8</td><td>Tennessee</td><td>14.6</td><td>42</td><td>Illinois</td><td>9.8</td></tr>
<tr><td>9</td><td>Texas</td><td>13.8</td><td>43</td><td>Kentucky</td><td>9.7</td></tr>
<tr><td>1</td><td>Utah</td><td>19.2</td><td>43</td><td>Nebraska</td><td>9.7</td></tr>
<tr><td>31</td><td>Vermont</td><td>11.0</td><td>45</td><td>Ohio</td><td>9.6</td></tr>
<tr><td>13</td><td>Virginia</td><td>13.2</td><td>46</td><td>Arkansas</td><td>9.0</td></tr>
<tr><td>3</td><td>Washington</td><td>18.9</td><td>46</td><td>Connecticut</td><td>9.0</td></tr>
<tr><td>38</td><td>West Virginia</td><td>10.4</td><td>48</td><td>Iowa</td><td>8.2</td></tr>
<tr><td>40</td><td>Wisconsin</td><td>10.0</td><td>49</td><td>North Dakota</td><td>7.3</td></tr>
<tr><td>24</td><td>Wyoming</td><td>11.9</td><td>50</td><td>South Dakota</td><td>6.1</td></tr>
<tr><td></td><td></td><td></td><td></td><td>District of Columbia</td><td>15.8</td></tr>
</table>

Source: U.S. Small Business Administration
"Small Business Economic Indicators 2002" (http://www.sba.gov/advo/stats/sbei02.pdf)
Firms can be in more than one state. Rate figure represents the number of employer firms started in 2002 as a percent of existing firms at the beginning of 2002.

Employer Firm Terminations in 2002

National Total = 584,500 Terminations*

<u>ALPHA ORDER</u>

RANK	STATE	FIRMS	% of USA
24	Alabama	12,103	2.1%
48	Alaska	2,541	0.4%
17	Arizona	17,642	3.0%
42	Arkansas	4,491	0.8%
1	California	156,858	26.8%
29	Colorado	10,332	1.8%
27	Connecticut	11,383	1.9%
45	Delaware	3,891	0.7%
4	Florida	52,241	8.9%
9	Georgia	31,479	5.4%
44	Hawaii	3,994	0.7%
35	Idaho	7,040	1.2%
7	Illinois	32,093	5.5%
19	Indiana	16,156	2.8%
33	Iowa	7,480	1.3%
36	Kansas	6,876	1.2%
25	Kentucky	11,614	2.0%
21	Louisiana	14,416	2.5%
40	Maine	5,042	0.9%
14	Maryland	20,927	3.6%
15	Massachusetts	20,532	3.5%
10	Michigan	26,975	4.6%
23	Minnesota	12,851	2.2%
34	Mississippi	7,160	1.2%
13	Missouri	21,653	3.7%
43	Montana	4,445	0.8%
39	Nebraska	5,234	0.9%
31	Nevada	8,667	1.5%
38	New Hampshire	5,418	0.9%
8	New Jersey	31,571	5.4%
32	New Mexico	7,949	1.4%
2	New York	63,631	10.9%
12	North Carolina	22,184	3.8%
50	North Dakota	1,893	0.3%
11	Ohio	24,269	4.2%
30	Oklahoma	8,923	1.5%
20	Oregon	14,793	2.5%
6	Pennsylvania	35,859	6.1%
41	Rhode Island	4,981	0.9%
26	South Carolina	11,491	2.0%
49	South Dakota	2,098	0.4%
18	Tennessee	16,514	2.8%
3	Texas	58,114	9.9%
28	Utah	11,272	1.9%
46	Vermont	3,501	0.6%
16	Virginia	20,305	3.5%
5	Washington	40,782	7.0%
37	West Virginia	5,595	1.0%
22	Wisconsin	13,651	2.3%
47	Wyoming	2,895	0.5%

<u>RANK ORDER</u>

RANK	STATE	FIRMS	% of USA
1	California	156,858	26.8%
2	New York	63,631	10.9%
3	Texas	58,114	9.9%
4	Florida	52,241	8.9%
5	Washington	40,782	7.0%
6	Pennsylvania	35,859	6.1%
7	Illinois	32,093	5.5%
8	New Jersey	31,571	5.4%
9	Georgia	31,479	5.4%
10	Michigan	26,975	4.6%
11	Ohio	24,269	4.2%
12	North Carolina	22,184	3.8%
13	Missouri	21,653	3.7%
14	Maryland	20,927	3.6%
15	Massachusetts	20,532	3.5%
16	Virginia	20,305	3.5%
17	Arizona	17,642	3.0%
18	Tennessee	16,514	2.8%
19	Indiana	16,156	2.8%
20	Oregon	14,793	2.5%
21	Louisiana	14,416	2.5%
22	Wisconsin	13,651	2.3%
23	Minnesota	12,851	2.2%
24	Alabama	12,103	2.1%
25	Kentucky	11,614	2.0%
26	South Carolina	11,491	2.0%
27	Connecticut	11,383	1.9%
28	Utah	11,272	1.9%
29	Colorado	10,332	1.8%
30	Oklahoma	8,923	1.5%
31	Nevada	8,667	1.5%
32	New Mexico	7,949	1.4%
33	Iowa	7,480	1.3%
34	Mississippi	7,160	1.2%
35	Idaho	7,040	1.2%
36	Kansas	6,876	1.2%
37	West Virginia	5,595	1.0%
38	New Hampshire	5,418	0.9%
39	Nebraska	5,234	0.9%
40	Maine	5,042	0.9%
41	Rhode Island	4,981	0.9%
42	Arkansas	4,491	0.8%
43	Montana	4,445	0.8%
44	Hawaii	3,994	0.7%
45	Delaware	3,891	0.7%
46	Vermont	3,501	0.6%
47	Wyoming	2,895	0.5%
48	Alaska	2,541	0.4%
49	South Dakota	2,098	0.4%
50	North Dakota	1,893	0.3%
	District of Columbia	3,973	0.7%

Source: U.S. Small Business Administration
"Small Business Economic Indicators 2002" (http://www.sba.gov/advo/stats/sbei02.pdf)
**State totals do not add to the U.S. figure as firms can be in more than one state.*

Rate of Employer Firm Terminations in 2002

National Rate = 10.4% of Existing Firms*

ALPHA ORDER

RANK	STATE	RATE
21	Alabama	14.1
12	Alaska	15.5
7	Arizona	16.5
49	Arkansas	7.5
10	California	15.9
49	Colorado	7.5
38	Connecticut	11.7
13	Delaware	15.4
28	Florida	13.3
9	Georgia	16.3
22	Hawaii	14.0
5	Idaho	17.4
40	Illinois	11.5
31	Indiana	12.9
43	Iowa	10.9
45	Kansas	10.2
29	Kentucky	13.2
17	Louisiana	15.0
30	Maine	13.0
11	Maryland	15.8
36	Massachusetts	12.1
33	Michigan	12.7
47	Minnesota	9.9
26	Mississippi	13.4
6	Missouri	16.7
24	Montana	13.5
39	Nebraska	11.6
4	Nevada	18.7
23	New Hampshire	13.7
41	New Jersey	11.4
3	New Mexico	19.1
26	New York	13.4
34	North Carolina	12.6
45	North Dakota	10.2
44	Ohio	10.4
37	Oklahoma	11.9
19	Oregon	14.8
24	Pennsylvania	13.5
14	Rhode Island	15.1
31	South Carolina	12.9
48	South Dakota	9.2
14	Tennessee	15.1
18	Texas	14.9
1	Utah	20.7
7	Vermont	16.5
35	Virginia	12.5
2	Washington	20.5
19	West Virginia	14.8
42	Wisconsin	11.2
14	Wyoming	15.1

RANK ORDER

RANK	STATE	RATE
1	Utah	20.7
2	Washington	20.5
3	New Mexico	19.1
4	Nevada	18.7
5	Idaho	17.4
6	Missouri	16.7
7	Arizona	16.5
7	Vermont	16.5
9	Georgia	16.3
10	California	15.9
11	Maryland	15.8
12	Alaska	15.5
13	Delaware	15.4
14	Rhode Island	15.1
14	Tennessee	15.1
14	Wyoming	15.1
17	Louisiana	15.0
18	Texas	14.9
19	Oregon	14.8
19	West Virginia	14.8
21	Alabama	14.1
22	Hawaii	14.0
23	New Hampshire	13.7
24	Montana	13.5
24	Pennsylvania	13.5
26	Mississippi	13.4
26	New York	13.4
28	Florida	13.3
29	Kentucky	13.2
30	Maine	13.0
31	Indiana	12.9
31	South Carolina	12.9
33	Michigan	12.7
34	North Carolina	12.6
35	Virginia	12.5
36	Massachusetts	12.1
37	Oklahoma	11.9
38	Connecticut	11.7
39	Nebraska	11.6
40	Illinois	11.5
41	New Jersey	11.4
42	Wisconsin	11.2
43	Iowa	10.9
44	Ohio	10.4
45	Kansas	10.2
45	North Dakota	10.2
47	Minnesota	9.9
48	South Dakota	9.2
49	Arkansas	7.5
49	Colorado	7.5
	District of Columbia	15.1

Source: U.S. Small Business Administration
"Small Business Economic Indicators 2002" (http://www.sba.gov/advo/stats/sbei02.pdf)
**Firms can be in more than one state. Firms with paid employees ceasing operations in 2002 as a percent of employer firms existing in 2001. Some state terminations result in successor firms which are not listed as new firms, thus making terminations higher than formations for most states.*

V. EDUCATION

School-Age Population as a Percent of Total Population in 2002

National Percent = 18.5% of Population is School-Age*

ALPHA ORDER

RANK	STATE	PERCENT
31	Alabama	18.0
1	Alaska	22.2
7	Arizona	19.4
27	Arkansas	18.2
6	California	19.7
23	Colorado	18.4
15	Connecticut	18.8
43	Delaware	17.1
44	Florida	17.0
12	Georgia	18.9
44	Hawaii	17.0
3	Idaho	20.2
15	Illinois	18.8
12	Indiana	18.9
37	Iowa	17.6
17	Kansas	18.7
48	Kentucky	16.6
8	Louisiana	19.2
49	Maine	16.5
18	Maryland	18.6
46	Massachusetts	16.7
10	Michigan	19.0
18	Minnesota	18.6
8	Mississippi	19.2
27	Missouri	18.2
31	Montana	18.0
18	Nebraska	18.6
12	Nevada	18.9
23	New Hampshire	18.4
27	New Jersey	18.2
5	New Mexico	19.9
35	New York	17.7
34	North Carolina	17.8
40	North Dakota	17.4
21	Ohio	18.5
27	Oklahoma	18.2
33	Oregon	17.9
40	Pennsylvania	17.4
46	Rhode Island	16.7
40	South Carolina	17.4
10	South Dakota	19.0
37	Tennessee	17.6
4	Texas	20.1
2	Utah	21.3
39	Vermont	17.5
35	Virginia	17.7
23	Washington	18.4
50	West Virginia	16.2
23	Wisconsin	18.4
21	Wyoming	18.5

RANK ORDER

RANK	STATE	PERCENT
1	Alaska	22.2
2	Utah	21.3
3	Idaho	20.2
4	Texas	20.1
5	New Mexico	19.9
6	California	19.7
7	Arizona	19.4
8	Louisiana	19.2
8	Mississippi	19.2
10	Michigan	19.0
10	South Dakota	19.0
12	Georgia	18.9
12	Indiana	18.9
12	Nevada	18.9
15	Connecticut	18.8
15	Illinois	18.8
17	Kansas	18.7
18	Maryland	18.6
18	Minnesota	18.6
18	Nebraska	18.6
21	Ohio	18.5
21	Wyoming	18.5
23	Colorado	18.4
23	New Hampshire	18.4
23	Washington	18.4
23	Wisconsin	18.4
27	Arkansas	18.2
27	Missouri	18.2
27	New Jersey	18.2
27	Oklahoma	18.2
31	Alabama	18.0
31	Montana	18.0
33	Oregon	17.9
34	North Carolina	17.8
35	New York	17.7
35	Virginia	17.7
37	Iowa	17.6
37	Tennessee	17.6
39	Vermont	17.5
40	North Dakota	17.4
40	Pennsylvania	17.4
40	South Carolina	17.4
43	Delaware	17.1
44	Florida	17.0
44	Hawaii	17.0
46	Massachusetts	16.7
46	Rhode Island	16.7
48	Kentucky	16.6
49	Maine	16.5
50	West Virginia	16.2
	District of Columbia	13.7

Regular Public Elementary and Secondary School Districts in 2002

National Total = 14,559 Districts*

ALPHA ORDER

RANK	STATE	DISTRICTS	% of USA
35	Alabama	128	0.9%
43	Alaska	53	0.4%
17	Arizona	323	2.2%
18	Arkansas	312	2.1%
2	California	986	6.8%
27	Colorado	178	1.2%
31	Connecticut	166	1.1%
48	Delaware	19	0.1%
40	Florida	67	0.5%
26	Georgia	180	1.2%
50	Hawaii	1	0.0%
37	Idaho	114	0.8%
3	Illinois	893	6.1%
21	Indiana	294	2.0%
15	Iowa	371	2.5%
19	Kansas	304	2.1%
29	Kentucky	176	1.2%
41	Louisiana	66	0.5%
23	Maine	282	1.9%
47	Maryland	24	0.2%
16	Massachusetts	350	2.4%
8	Michigan	554	3.8%
14	Minnesota	417	2.9%
32	Mississippi	152	1.0%
10	Missouri	524	3.6%
12	Montana	452	3.1%
7	Nebraska	555	3.8%
49	Nevada	17	0.1%
27	New Hampshire	178	1.2%
6	New Jersey	603	4.1%
38	New Mexico	89	0.6%
4	New York	703	4.8%
36	North Carolina	121	0.8%
24	North Dakota	222	1.5%
5	Ohio	662	4.5%
9	Oklahoma	543	3.7%
25	Oregon	198	1.4%
11	Pennsylvania	501	3.4%
46	Rhode Island	36	0.2%
38	South Carolina	89	0.6%
29	South Dakota	176	1.2%
33	Tennessee	138	0.9%
1	Texas	1,040	7.1%
45	Utah	40	0.3%
22	Vermont	292	2.0%
34	Virginia	137	0.9%
20	Washington	296	2.0%
42	West Virginia	55	0.4%
13	Wisconsin	433	3.0%
44	Wyoming	48	0.3%

RANK ORDER

RANK	STATE	DISTRICTS	% of USA
1	Texas	1,040	7.1%
2	California	986	6.8%
3	Illinois	893	6.1%
4	New York	703	4.8%
5	Ohio	662	4.5%
6	New Jersey	603	4.1%
7	Nebraska	555	3.8%
8	Michigan	554	3.8%
9	Oklahoma	543	3.7%
10	Missouri	524	3.6%
11	Pennsylvania	501	3.4%
12	Montana	452	3.1%
13	Wisconsin	433	3.0%
14	Minnesota	417	2.9%
15	Iowa	371	2.5%
16	Massachusetts	350	2.4%
17	Arizona	323	2.2%
18	Arkansas	312	2.1%
19	Kansas	304	2.1%
20	Washington	296	2.0%
21	Indiana	294	2.0%
22	Vermont	292	2.0%
23	Maine	282	1.9%
24	North Dakota	222	1.5%
25	Oregon	198	1.4%
26	Georgia	180	1.2%
27	Colorado	178	1.2%
27	New Hampshire	178	1.2%
29	Kentucky	176	1.2%
29	South Dakota	176	1.2%
31	Connecticut	166	1.1%
32	Mississippi	152	1.0%
33	Tennessee	138	0.9%
34	Virginia	137	0.9%
35	Alabama	128	0.9%
36	North Carolina	121	0.8%
37	Idaho	114	0.8%
38	New Mexico	89	0.6%
38	South Carolina	89	0.6%
40	Florida	67	0.5%
41	Louisiana	66	0.5%
42	West Virginia	55	0.4%
43	Alaska	53	0.4%
44	Wyoming	48	0.3%
45	Utah	40	0.3%
46	Rhode Island	36	0.2%
47	Maryland	24	0.2%
48	Delaware	19	0.1%
49	Nevada	17	0.1%
50	Hawaii	1	0.0%
	District of Columbia	1	0.0%

Source: U.S. Department of Education, National Center for Education Statistics
   "Overview of Public Elementary and Secondary Schools and Districts: School Year 2001-2002" (NCES 2003-411)
For school year 2001-2002. Regular school districts are agencies responsible for providing free public education for school-age children residing within their jurisdiction. Included in these figures are 102 districts that reported having no students. This can occur when a small district has no pupils or contracts with another district to educate the students under its jurisdiction.

Public Elementary and Secondary Schools in 2002

National Total = 91,380 Schools*

<u>ALPHA ORDER</u>

RANK	STATE	SCHOOLS	% of USA
27	Alabama	1,381	1.5%
44	Alaska	506	0.6%
20	Arizona	1,742	1.9%
31	Arkansas	1,129	1.2%
1	California	8,914	9.8%
21	Colorado	1,630	1.8%
32	Connecticut	1,073	1.2%
50	Delaware	197	0.2%
7	Florida	3,314	3.6%
15	Georgia	1,969	2.2%
49	Hawaii	279	0.3%
41	Idaho	654	0.7%
4	Illinois	4,292	4.7%
16	Indiana	1,891	2.1%
23	Iowa	1,519	1.7%
25	Kansas	1,423	1.6%
26	Kentucky	1,387	1.5%
24	Louisiana	1,509	1.7%
40	Maine	681	0.7%
28	Maryland	1,340	1.5%
17	Massachusetts	1,889	2.1%
6	Michigan	3,782	4.1%
14	Minnesota	2,119	2.3%
34	Mississippi	886	1.0%
10	Missouri	2,274	2.5%
35	Montana	870	1.0%
29	Nebraska	1,280	1.4%
43	Nevada	517	0.6%
45	New Hampshire	472	0.5%
9	New Jersey	2,410	2.6%
36	New Mexico	792	0.9%
3	New York	4,298	4.7%
11	North Carolina	2,223	2.4%
42	North Dakota	529	0.6%
5	Ohio	3,826	4.2%
19	Oklahoma	1,814	2.0%
30	Oregon	1,273	1.4%
8	Pennsylvania	3,185	3.5%
48	Rhode Island	326	0.4%
33	South Carolina	1,053	1.2%
39	South Dakota	749	0.8%
22	Tennessee	1,610	1.8%
2	Texas	7,646	8.4%
37	Utah	791	0.9%
47	Vermont	359	0.4%
18	Virginia	1,839	2.0%
13	Washington	2,170	2.4%
38	West Virginia	784	0.9%
12	Wisconsin	2,208	2.4%
46	Wyoming	383	0.4%

<u>RANK ORDER</u>

RANK	STATE	SCHOOLS	% of USA
1	California	8,914	9.8%
2	Texas	7,646	8.4%
3	New York	4,298	4.7%
4	Illinois	4,292	4.7%
5	Ohio	3,826	4.2%
6	Michigan	3,782	4.1%
7	Florida	3,314	3.6%
8	Pennsylvania	3,185	3.5%
9	New Jersey	2,410	2.6%
10	Missouri	2,274	2.5%
11	North Carolina	2,223	2.4%
12	Wisconsin	2,208	2.4%
13	Washington	2,170	2.4%
14	Minnesota	2,119	2.3%
15	Georgia	1,969	2.2%
16	Indiana	1,891	2.1%
17	Massachusetts	1,889	2.1%
18	Virginia	1,839	2.0%
19	Oklahoma	1,814	2.0%
20	Arizona	1,742	1.9%
21	Colorado	1,630	1.8%
22	Tennessee	1,610	1.8%
23	Iowa	1,519	1.7%
24	Louisiana	1,509	1.7%
25	Kansas	1,423	1.6%
26	Kentucky	1,387	1.5%
27	Alabama	1,381	1.5%
28	Maryland	1,340	1.5%
29	Nebraska	1,280	1.4%
30	Oregon	1,273	1.4%
31	Arkansas	1,129	1.2%
32	Connecticut	1,073	1.2%
33	South Carolina	1,053	1.2%
34	Mississippi	886	1.0%
35	Montana	870	1.0%
36	New Mexico	792	0.9%
37	Utah	791	0.9%
38	West Virginia	784	0.9%
39	South Dakota	749	0.8%
40	Maine	681	0.7%
41	Idaho	654	0.7%
42	North Dakota	529	0.6%
43	Nevada	517	0.6%
44	Alaska	506	0.6%
45	New Hampshire	472	0.5%
46	Wyoming	383	0.4%
47	Vermont	359	0.4%
48	Rhode Island	326	0.4%
49	Hawaii	279	0.3%
50	Delaware	197	0.2%
	District of Columbia	193	0.2%

Source: U.S. Department of Education, National Center for Education Statistics
"Overview of Public Elementary and Secondary Schools and Districts: School Year 2001-2002" (NCES 2003-411)
*For school year 2001-2002. Schools having membership.

Private Elementary and Secondary Schools in 2000

National Total = 27,223 Private Schools*

ALPHA ORDER

RANK	STATE	SCHOOLS	% of USA
22	Alabama	374	1.4%
48	Alaska	69	0.3%
28	Arizona	276	1.0%
33	Arkansas	192	0.7%
1	California	3,318	12.2%
26	Colorado	339	1.2%
24	Connecticut	348	1.3%
42	Delaware	96	0.4%
4	Florida	1,545	5.7%
14	Georgia	592	2.2%
39	Hawaii	130	0.5%
43	Idaho	94	0.3%
5	Illinois	1,354	5.0%
13	Indiana	677	2.5%
29	Iowa	265	1.0%
30	Kansas	237	0.9%
23	Kentucky	368	1.4%
21	Louisiana	434	1.6%
38	Maine	139	0.5%
11	Maryland	701	2.6%
12	Massachusetts	694	2.5%
7	Michigan	1,012	3.7%
19	Minnesota	530	1.9%
32	Mississippi	207	0.8%
17	Missouri	576	2.1%
44	Montana	90	0.3%
30	Nebraska	237	0.9%
46	Nevada	80	0.3%
36	New Hampshire	171	0.6%
10	New Jersey	905	3.3%
34	New Mexico	182	0.7%
2	New York	1,981	7.3%
15	North Carolina	588	2.2%
49	North Dakota	55	0.2%
9	Ohio	974	3.6%
35	Oklahoma	179	0.7%
25	Oregon	347	1.3%
3	Pennsylvania	1,964	7.2%
40	Rhode Island	127	0.5%
27	South Carolina	326	1.2%
45	South Dakota	83	0.3%
18	Tennessee	533	2.0%
6	Texas	1,281	4.7%
47	Utah	78	0.3%
41	Vermont	122	0.4%
16	Virginia	582	2.1%
20	Washington	494	1.8%
37	West Virginia	151	0.6%
8	Wisconsin	991	3.6%
50	Wyoming	41	0.2%

RANK ORDER

RANK	STATE	SCHOOLS	% of USA
1	California	3,318	12.2%
2	New York	1,981	7.3%
3	Pennsylvania	1,964	7.2%
4	Florida	1,545	5.7%
5	Illinois	1,354	5.0%
6	Texas	1,281	4.7%
7	Michigan	1,012	3.7%
8	Wisconsin	991	3.6%
9	Ohio	974	3.6%
10	New Jersey	905	3.3%
11	Maryland	701	2.6%
12	Massachusetts	694	2.5%
13	Indiana	677	2.5%
14	Georgia	592	2.2%
15	North Carolina	588	2.2%
16	Virginia	582	2.1%
17	Missouri	576	2.1%
18	Tennessee	533	2.0%
19	Minnesota	530	1.9%
20	Washington	494	1.8%
21	Louisiana	434	1.6%
22	Alabama	374	1.4%
23	Kentucky	368	1.4%
24	Connecticut	348	1.3%
25	Oregon	347	1.3%
26	Colorado	339	1.2%
27	South Carolina	326	1.2%
28	Arizona	276	1.0%
29	Iowa	265	1.0%
30	Kansas	237	0.9%
30	Nebraska	237	0.9%
32	Mississippi	207	0.8%
33	Arkansas	192	0.7%
34	New Mexico	182	0.7%
35	Oklahoma	179	0.7%
36	New Hampshire	171	0.6%
37	West Virginia	151	0.6%
38	Maine	139	0.5%
39	Hawaii	130	0.5%
40	Rhode Island	127	0.5%
41	Vermont	122	0.4%
42	Delaware	96	0.4%
43	Idaho	94	0.3%
44	Montana	90	0.3%
45	South Dakota	83	0.3%
46	Nevada	80	0.3%
47	Utah	78	0.3%
48	Alaska	69	0.3%
49	North Dakota	55	0.2%
50	Wyoming	41	0.2%
	District of Columbia	89	0.3%

Source: U.S. Department of Education, Office of Educational Research and Improvement
"Private School Universe Survey, 1999-2000" (NCES 2001330, August 2001)
Estimate for 1999-2000.

Percent of Elementary/Secondary School Students in Private Schools in 2000

National Percent = 9.7% of Students*

ALPHA ORDER

RANK	STATE	PERCENT
27	Alabama	8.9
46	Alaska	4.3
45	Arizona	4.5
40	Arkansas	5.3
22	California	9.2
36	Colorado	6.5
15	Connecticut	11.3
1	Delaware	15.9
16	Florida	10.8
32	Georgia	7.4
4	Hawaii	14.8
47	Idaho	3.8
10	Illinois	12.7
22	Indiana	9.2
25	Iowa	9.1
28	Kansas	8.2
18	Kentucky	10.3
3	Louisiana	15.3
29	Maine	7.9
5	Maryland	14.4
12	Massachusetts	12.0
21	Michigan	9.3
20	Minnesota	9.7
26	Mississippi	9.0
14	Missouri	11.6
43	Montana	5.0
11	Nebraska	12.6
47	Nevada	3.8
19	New Hampshire	10.0
9	New Jersey	13.0
38	New Mexico	6.1
6	New York	13.8
35	North Carolina	6.8
39	North Dakota	5.9
13	Ohio	11.9
44	Oklahoma	4.8
33	Oregon	7.3
2	Pennsylvania	15.5
8	Rhode Island	13.4
31	South Carolina	7.5
37	South Dakota	6.2
22	Tennessee	9.2
40	Texas	5.3
49	Utah	2.5
17	Vermont	10.7
30	Virginia	7.8
34	Washington	6.9
40	West Virginia	5.3
7	Wisconsin	13.6
50	Wyoming	2.3

RANK ORDER

RANK	STATE	PERCENT
1	Delaware	15.9
2	Pennsylvania	15.5
3	Louisiana	15.3
4	Hawaii	14.8
5	Maryland	14.4
6	New York	13.8
7	Wisconsin	13.6
8	Rhode Island	13.4
9	New Jersey	13.0
10	Illinois	12.7
11	Nebraska	12.6
12	Massachusetts	12.0
13	Ohio	11.9
14	Missouri	11.6
15	Connecticut	11.3
16	Florida	10.8
17	Vermont	10.7
18	Kentucky	10.3
19	New Hampshire	10.0
20	Minnesota	9.7
21	Michigan	9.3
22	California	9.2
22	Indiana	9.2
22	Tennessee	9.2
25	Iowa	9.1
26	Mississippi	9.0
27	Alabama	8.9
28	Kansas	8.2
29	Maine	7.9
30	Virginia	7.8
31	South Carolina	7.5
32	Georgia	7.4
33	Oregon	7.3
34	Washington	6.9
35	North Carolina	6.8
36	Colorado	6.5
37	South Dakota	6.2
38	New Mexico	6.1
39	North Dakota	5.9
40	Arkansas	5.3
40	Texas	5.3
40	West Virginia	5.3
43	Montana	5.0
44	Oklahoma	4.8
45	Arizona	4.5
46	Alaska	4.3
47	Idaho	3.8
47	Nevada	3.8
49	Utah	2.5
50	Wyoming	2.3

District of Columbia	20.2

Source: Morgan Quitno Press using data from U.S. Dept. of Education, Office of Educational Research and Improvement
"Private School Universe Survey, 1999-2000" (NCES 2001330, August 2001)
*Estimate for 1999-2000.

Estimated Enrollment in Public Elementary and Secondary Schools in 2003

National Total = 47,792,369 Students*

ALPHA ORDER

RANK	STATE	STUDENTS	% of USA
24	Alabama	721,633	1.5%
45	Alaska	134,024	0.3%
16	Arizona	940,433	2.0%
34	Arkansas	445,229	0.9%
1	California	6,250,095	13.1%
22	Colorado	751,862	1.6%
28	Connecticut	575,760	1.2%
47	Delaware	116,274	0.2%
4	Florida	2,533,628	5.3%
9	Georgia	1,496,012	3.1%
42	Hawaii	183,829	0.4%
39	Idaho	248,509	0.5%
5	Illinois	2,089,633	4.4%
14	Indiana	995,195	2.1%
31	Iowa	482,210	1.0%
33	Kansas	469,634	1.0%
26	Kentucky	629,020	1.3%
23	Louisiana	729,516	1.5%
41	Maine	203,708	0.4%
20	Maryland	866,743	1.8%
15	Massachusetts	987,986	2.1%
8	Michigan	1,730,544	3.6%
21	Minnesota	856,863	1.8%
30	Mississippi	491,623	1.0%
18	Missouri	894,029	1.9%
44	Montana	149,574	0.3%
37	Nebraska	283,924	0.6%
35	Nevada	369,498	0.8%
40	New Hampshire	207,628	0.4%
10	New Jersey	1,365,344	2.9%
36	New Mexico	320,986	0.7%
3	New York	2,845,000	6.0%
11	North Carolina	1,345,889	2.8%
48	North Dakota	103,013	0.2%
7	Ohio	1,791,223	3.7%
27	Oklahoma	624,176	1.3%
29	Oregon	554,071	1.2%
6	Pennsylvania	1,817,200	3.8%
43	Rhode Island	157,996	0.3%
25	South Carolina	671,508	1.4%
46	South Dakota	125,441	0.3%
17	Tennessee	910,364	1.9%
2	Texas	4,223,192	8.8%
32	Utah	480,736	1.0%
49	Vermont	99,475	0.2%
12	Virginia	1,176,557	2.5%
13	Washington	1,029,131	2.2%
38	West Virginia	281,591	0.6%
19	Wisconsin	881,231	1.8%
50	Wyoming	86,108	0.2%

RANK ORDER

RANK	STATE	STUDENTS	% of USA
1	California	6,250,095	13.1%
2	Texas	4,223,192	8.8%
3	New York	2,845,000	6.0%
4	Florida	2,533,628	5.3%
5	Illinois	2,089,633	4.4%
6	Pennsylvania	1,817,200	3.8%
7	Ohio	1,791,223	3.7%
8	Michigan	1,730,544	3.6%
9	Georgia	1,496,012	3.1%
10	New Jersey	1,365,344	2.9%
11	North Carolina	1,345,889	2.8%
12	Virginia	1,176,557	2.5%
13	Washington	1,029,131	2.2%
14	Indiana	995,195	2.1%
15	Massachusetts	987,986	2.1%
16	Arizona	940,433	2.0%
17	Tennessee	910,364	1.9%
18	Missouri	894,029	1.9%
19	Wisconsin	881,231	1.8%
20	Maryland	866,743	1.8%
21	Minnesota	856,863	1.8%
22	Colorado	751,862	1.6%
23	Louisiana	729,516	1.5%
24	Alabama	721,633	1.5%
25	South Carolina	671,508	1.4%
26	Kentucky	629,020	1.3%
27	Oklahoma	624,176	1.3%
28	Connecticut	575,760	1.2%
29	Oregon	554,071	1.2%
30	Mississippi	491,623	1.0%
31	Iowa	482,210	1.0%
32	Utah	480,736	1.0%
33	Kansas	469,634	1.0%
34	Arkansas	445,229	0.9%
35	Nevada	369,498	0.8%
36	New Mexico	320,986	0.7%
37	Nebraska	283,924	0.6%
38	West Virginia	281,591	0.6%
39	Idaho	248,509	0.5%
40	New Hampshire	207,628	0.4%
41	Maine	203,708	0.4%
42	Hawaii	183,829	0.4%
43	Rhode Island	157,996	0.3%
44	Montana	149,574	0.3%
45	Alaska	134,024	0.3%
46	South Dakota	125,441	0.3%
47	Delaware	116,274	0.2%
48	North Dakota	103,013	0.2%
49	Vermont	99,475	0.2%
50	Wyoming	86,108	0.2%
	District of Columbia	67,522	0.1%

Source: National Education Association, Washington, D.C.
"Rankings & Estimates, May 2003" (Copyright © 2003, NEA, used with permission)
Estimates for school year 2002-2003.

Average Class Size in Public Elementary Schools in 2000

National Average = 21.2 Students per Class*

ALPHA ORDER

RANK	STATE	STUDENTS
40	Alabama	18.7
15	Alaska	22.0
1	Arizona	24.5
33	Arkansas	19.8
8	California	22.7
5	Colorado	23.2
29	Connecticut	20.0
25	Delaware	20.6
6	Florida	23.1
34	Georgia	19.7
6	Hawaii	23.1
14	Idaho	22.1
10	Illinois	22.3
18	Indiana	21.4
28	Iowa	20.1
43	Kansas	18.4
22	Kentucky	20.8
38	Louisiana	18.9
47	Maine	18.0
12	Maryland	22.2
19	Massachusetts	21.0
15	Michigan	22.0
15	Minnesota	22.0
27	Mississippi	20.4
20	Missouri	20.9
44	Montana	18.2
50	Nebraska	17.5
24	Nevada	20.7
29	New Hampshire	20.0
26	New Jersey	20.5
32	New Mexico	19.9
10	New York	22.3
20	North Carolina	20.9
49	North Dakota	17.8
8	Ohio	22.7
41	Oklahoma	18.6
2	Oregon	23.9
12	Pennsylvania	22.2
29	Rhode Island	20.0
48	South Carolina	17.9
39	South Dakota	18.8
34	Tennessee	19.7
42	Texas	18.5
4	Utah	23.7
45	Vermont	18.1
36	Virginia	19.4
2	Washington	23.9
36	West Virginia	19.4
22	Wisconsin	20.8
45	Wyoming	18.1

RANK ORDER

RANK	STATE	STUDENTS
1	Arizona	24.5
2	Oregon	23.9
2	Washington	23.9
4	Utah	23.7
5	Colorado	23.2
6	Florida	23.1
6	Hawaii	23.1
8	California	22.7
8	Ohio	22.7
10	Illinois	22.3
10	New York	22.3
12	Maryland	22.2
12	Pennsylvania	22.2
14	Idaho	22.1
15	Alaska	22.0
15	Michigan	22.0
15	Minnesota	22.0
18	Indiana	21.4
19	Massachusetts	21.0
20	Missouri	20.9
20	North Carolina	20.9
22	Kentucky	20.8
22	Wisconsin	20.8
24	Nevada	20.7
25	Delaware	20.6
26	New Jersey	20.5
27	Mississippi	20.4
28	Iowa	20.1
29	Connecticut	20.0
29	New Hampshire	20.0
29	Rhode Island	20.0
32	New Mexico	19.9
33	Arkansas	19.8
34	Georgia	19.7
34	Tennessee	19.7
36	Virginia	19.4
36	West Virginia	19.4
38	Louisiana	18.9
39	South Dakota	18.8
40	Alabama	18.7
41	Oklahoma	18.6
42	Texas	18.5
43	Kansas	18.4
44	Montana	18.2
45	Vermont	18.1
45	Wyoming	18.1
47	Maine	18.0
48	South Carolina	17.9
49	North Dakota	17.8
50	Nebraska	17.5
	District of Columbia	21.7

Source: U.S. Department of Education, National Center for Education Statistics
    "Schools and Staffing Survey, 1999-2000" (NCES 2002-313)
*For school year 1999-2000.

Average Class Size in Public Secondary Schools in 2000

National Average = 23.4 Students per Class*

ALPHA ORDER

RANK	STATE	STUDENTS
29	Alabama	22.1
13	Alaska	23.9
6	Arizona	25.6
43	Arkansas	20.6
1	California	28.1
12	Colorado	24.0
45	Connecticut	20.1
18	Delaware	23.2
2	Florida	27.3
14	Georgia	23.7
11	Hawaii	24.1
25	Idaho	22.8
15	Illinois	23.6
21	Indiana	23.0
39	Iowa	21.0
41	Kansas	20.8
21	Kentucky	23.0
24	Louisiana	22.9
50	Maine	18.5
10	Maryland	24.9
39	Massachusetts	21.0
9	Michigan	25.1
7	Minnesota	25.5
30	Mississippi	22.0
38	Missouri	21.1
47	Montana	19.5
36	Nebraska	21.2
4	Nevada	27.0
33	New Hampshire	21.4
36	New Jersey	21.2
17	New Mexico	23.4
18	New York	23.2
31	North Carolina	21.7
49	North Dakota	18.9
21	Ohio	23.0
32	Oklahoma	21.5
8	Oregon	25.4
26	Pennsylvania	22.4
41	Rhode Island	20.8
27	South Carolina	22.2
48	South Dakota	19.4
16	Tennessee	23.5
27	Texas	22.2
3	Utah	27.1
46	Vermont	20.0
33	Virginia	21.4
5	Washington	26.6
35	West Virginia	21.3
18	Wisconsin	23.2
44	Wyoming	20.5

RANK ORDER

RANK	STATE	STUDENTS
1	California	28.1
2	Florida	27.3
3	Utah	27.1
4	Nevada	27.0
5	Washington	26.6
6	Arizona	25.6
7	Minnesota	25.5
8	Oregon	25.4
9	Michigan	25.1
10	Maryland	24.9
11	Hawaii	24.1
12	Colorado	24.0
13	Alaska	23.9
14	Georgia	23.7
15	Illinois	23.6
16	Tennessee	23.5
17	New Mexico	23.4
18	Delaware	23.2
18	New York	23.2
18	Wisconsin	23.2
21	Indiana	23.0
21	Kentucky	23.0
21	Ohio	23.0
24	Louisiana	22.9
25	Idaho	22.8
26	Pennsylvania	22.4
27	South Carolina	22.2
27	Texas	22.2
29	Alabama	22.1
30	Mississippi	22.0
31	North Carolina	21.7
32	Oklahoma	21.5
33	New Hampshire	21.4
33	Virginia	21.4
35	West Virginia	21.3
36	Nebraska	21.2
36	New Jersey	21.2
38	Missouri	21.1
39	Iowa	21.0
39	Massachusetts	21.0
41	Kansas	20.8
41	Rhode Island	20.8
43	Arkansas	20.6
44	Wyoming	20.5
45	Connecticut	20.1
46	Vermont	20.0
47	Montana	19.5
48	South Dakota	19.4
49	North Dakota	18.9
50	Maine	18.5
	District of Columbia	20.8

Source: U.S. Department of Education, National Center for Education Statistics
"Schools and Staffing Survey, 1999-2000" (NCES 2002-313)
For school year 1999-2000.

Estimated Public Elementary and Secondary School Teachers in 2003

National Total = 3,043,975 Teachers*

ALPHA ORDER

RANK	STATE	TEACHERS	% of USA
22	Alabama	46,549	1.5%
47	Alaska	8,052	0.3%
25	Arizona	45,102	1.5%
31	Arkansas	31,771	1.0%
1	California	314,992	10.3%
24	Colorado	45,196	1.5%
26	Connecticut	42,000	1.4%
49	Delaware	7,661	0.3%
4	Florida	141,028	4.6%
10	Georgia	95,875	3.1%
43	Hawaii	11,154	0.4%
41	Idaho	13,848	0.5%
5	Illinois	134,519	4.4%
14	Indiana	60,542	2.0%
29	Iowa	34,334	1.1%
30	Kansas	32,581	1.1%
28	Kentucky	38,736	1.3%
21	Louisiana	50,255	1.7%
39	Maine	16,161	0.5%
19	Maryland	55,543	1.8%
18	Massachusetts	56,000	1.8%
9	Michigan	102,033	3.4%
17	Minnesota	56,542	1.9%
32	Mississippi	30,569	1.0%
13	Missouri	67,400	2.2%
44	Montana	10,463	0.3%
36	Nebraska	20,703	0.7%
38	Nevada	19,459	0.6%
40	New Hampshire	14,975	0.5%
8	New Jersey	103,068	3.4%
35	New Mexico	21,258	0.7%
3	New York	226,000	7.4%
12	North Carolina	86,129	2.8%
48	North Dakota	7,745	0.3%
6	Ohio	122,054	4.0%
27	Oklahoma	40,550	1.3%
33	Oregon	28,967	1.0%
7	Pennsylvania	118,650	3.9%
42	Rhode Island	13,372	0.4%
23	South Carolina	45,598	1.5%
45	South Dakota	9,018	0.3%
16	Tennessee	58,315	1.9%
2	Texas	289,680	9.5%
34	Utah	23,144	0.8%
46	Vermont	8,768	0.3%
11	Virginia	93,069	3.1%
20	Washington	52,960	1.7%
37	West Virginia	19,925	0.7%
15	Wisconsin	60,270	2.0%
50	Wyoming	6,622	0.2%

RANK ORDER

RANK	STATE	TEACHERS	% of USA
1	California	314,992	10.3%
2	Texas	289,680	9.5%
3	New York	226,000	7.4%
4	Florida	141,028	4.6%
5	Illinois	134,519	4.4%
6	Ohio	122,054	4.0%
7	Pennsylvania	118,650	3.9%
8	New Jersey	103,068	3.4%
9	Michigan	102,033	3.4%
10	Georgia	95,875	3.1%
11	Virginia	93,069	3.1%
12	North Carolina	86,129	2.8%
13	Missouri	67,400	2.2%
14	Indiana	60,542	2.0%
15	Wisconsin	60,270	2.0%
16	Tennessee	58,315	1.9%
17	Minnesota	56,542	1.9%
18	Massachusetts	56,000	1.8%
19	Maryland	55,543	1.8%
20	Washington	52,960	1.7%
21	Louisiana	50,255	1.7%
22	Alabama	46,549	1.5%
23	South Carolina	45,598	1.5%
24	Colorado	45,196	1.5%
25	Arizona	45,102	1.5%
26	Connecticut	42,000	1.4%
27	Oklahoma	40,550	1.3%
28	Kentucky	38,736	1.3%
29	Iowa	34,334	1.1%
30	Kansas	32,581	1.1%
31	Arkansas	31,771	1.0%
32	Mississippi	30,569	1.0%
33	Oregon	28,967	1.0%
34	Utah	23,144	0.8%
35	New Mexico	21,258	0.7%
36	Nebraska	20,703	0.7%
37	West Virginia	19,925	0.7%
38	Nevada	19,459	0.6%
39	Maine	16,161	0.5%
40	New Hampshire	14,975	0.5%
41	Idaho	13,848	0.5%
42	Rhode Island	13,372	0.4%
43	Hawaii	11,154	0.4%
44	Montana	10,463	0.3%
45	South Dakota	9,018	0.3%
46	Vermont	8,768	0.3%
47	Alaska	8,052	0.3%
48	North Dakota	7,745	0.3%
49	Delaware	7,661	0.3%
50	Wyoming	6,622	0.2%
	District of Columbia	4,769	0.2%

Source: National Education Association, Washington, D.C.
"Rankings & Estimates, May 2003" (Copyright © 2003, NEA, used with permission)
Estimates for school year 2002-2003.

Estimated Pupil-Teacher Ratio in
Public Elementary and Secondary Schools in 2003
National Ratio = 15.7 Pupils per Teacher*

<u>ALPHA ORDER</u>

RANK	STATE	RATIO
21	Alabama	15.5
11	Alaska	16.6
1	Arizona	20.9
36	Arkansas	14.0
3	California	19.8
11	Colorado	16.6
40	Connecticut	13.7
25	Delaware	15.2
7	Florida	18.0
17	Georgia	15.6
13	Hawaii	16.5
8	Idaho	17.9
21	Illinois	15.5
14	Indiana	16.4
36	Iowa	14.0
33	Kansas	14.4
15	Kentucky	16.2
32	Louisiana	14.5
46	Maine	12.6
17	Maryland	15.6
9	Massachusetts	17.6
10	Michigan	17.0
25	Minnesota	15.2
16	Mississippi	16.1
42	Missouri	13.3
34	Montana	14.3
40	Nebraska	13.7
6	Nevada	19.0
38	New Hampshire	13.9
44	New Jersey	13.2
27	New Mexico	15.1
46	New York	12.6
17	North Carolina	15.6
42	North Dakota	13.3
28	Ohio	14.7
23	Oklahoma	15.4
5	Oregon	19.1
24	Pennsylvania	15.3
49	Rhode Island	11.8
28	South Carolina	14.7
38	South Dakota	13.9
17	Tennessee	15.6
30	Texas	14.6
2	Utah	20.8
50	Vermont	11.3
46	Virginia	12.6
4	Washington	19.4
35	West Virginia	14.1
30	Wisconsin	14.6
45	Wyoming	13.0

<u>RANK ORDER</u>

RANK	STATE	RATIO
1	Arizona	20.9
2	Utah	20.8
3	California	19.8
4	Washington	19.4
5	Oregon	19.1
6	Nevada	19.0
7	Florida	18.0
8	Idaho	17.9
9	Massachusetts	17.6
10	Michigan	17.0
11	Alaska	16.6
11	Colorado	16.6
13	Hawaii	16.5
14	Indiana	16.4
15	Kentucky	16.2
16	Mississippi	16.1
17	Georgia	15.6
17	Maryland	15.6
17	North Carolina	15.6
17	Tennessee	15.6
21	Alabama	15.5
21	Illinois	15.5
23	Oklahoma	15.4
24	Pennsylvania	15.3
25	Delaware	15.2
25	Minnesota	15.2
27	New Mexico	15.1
28	Ohio	14.7
28	South Carolina	14.7
30	Texas	14.6
30	Wisconsin	14.6
32	Louisiana	14.5
33	Kansas	14.4
34	Montana	14.3
35	West Virginia	14.1
36	Arkansas	14.0
36	Iowa	14.0
38	New Hampshire	13.9
38	South Dakota	13.9
40	Connecticut	13.7
40	Nebraska	13.7
42	Missouri	13.3
42	North Dakota	13.3
44	New Jersey	13.2
45	Wyoming	13.0
46	Maine	12.6
46	New York	12.6
46	Virginia	12.6
49	Rhode Island	11.8
50	Vermont	11.3
	District of Columbia	14.2

Source: Morgan Quitno Press using data from National Education Association, Washington, D.C.
"Rankings & Estimates, May 2003" (Copyright © 2003, NEA, used with permission)
*Estimates for school year 2002-2003.

Estimated Average Salary of Teachers in 2003

National Average = $45,822*

<u>ALPHA ORDER</u>

RANK	STATE	SALARY
38	Alabama	$38,246
11	Alaska	49,685
27	Arizona	40,894
43	Arkansas	37,753
1	California	56,283
26	Colorado	41,275
2	Connecticut	54,362
10	Delaware	50,772
32	Florida	39,465
14	Georgia	45,533
18	Hawaii	44,464
29	Idaho	40,148
8	Illinois	51,289
16	Indiana	45,097
34	Iowa	38,921
39	Kansas	38,123
33	Kentucky	38,981
44	Louisiana	36,878
40	Maine	38,121
12	Maryland	49,677
6	Massachusetts	52,043
4	Michigan	54,071
22	Minnesota	42,833
48	Mississippi	34,555
35	Missouri	38,826
46	Montana	35,754
41	Nebraska	37,896
23	Nevada	41,795
28	New Hampshire	40,519
3	New Jersey	54,166
45	New Mexico	36,687
5	New York	52,600
20	North Carolina	43,076
49	North Dakota	33,210
15	Ohio	45,452
47	Oklahoma	34,854
13	Oregon	47,600
7	Pennsylvania	51,800
9	Rhode Island	51,076
25	South Carolina	41,279
50	South Dakota	32,416
31	Tennessee	39,677
30	Texas	40,001
37	Utah	38,413
24	Vermont	41,603
19	Virginia	43,152
17	Washington	44,949
36	West Virginia	38,508
21	Wisconsin	42,871
42	Wyoming	37,876

<u>RANK ORDER</u>

RANK	STATE	SALARY
1	California	$56,283
2	Connecticut	54,362
3	New Jersey	54,166
4	Michigan	54,071
5	New York	52,600
6	Massachusetts	52,043
7	Pennsylvania	51,800
8	Illinois	51,289
9	Rhode Island	51,076
10	Delaware	50,772
11	Alaska	49,685
12	Maryland	49,677
13	Oregon	47,600
14	Georgia	45,533
15	Ohio	45,452
16	Indiana	45,097
17	Washington	44,949
18	Hawaii	44,464
19	Virginia	43,152
20	North Carolina	43,076
21	Wisconsin	42,871
22	Minnesota	42,833
23	Nevada	41,795
24	Vermont	41,603
25	South Carolina	41,279
26	Colorado	41,275
27	Arizona	40,894
28	New Hampshire	40,519
29	Idaho	40,148
30	Texas	40,001
31	Tennessee	39,677
32	Florida	39,465
33	Kentucky	38,981
34	Iowa	38,921
35	Missouri	38,826
36	West Virginia	38,508
37	Utah	38,413
38	Alabama	38,246
39	Kansas	38,123
40	Maine	38,121
41	Nebraska	37,896
42	Wyoming	37,876
43	Arkansas	37,753
44	Louisiana	36,878
45	New Mexico	36,687
46	Montana	35,754
47	Oklahoma	34,854
48	Mississippi	34,555
49	North Dakota	33,210
50	South Dakota	32,416
	District of Columbia	50,763

Source: National Education Association, Washington, D.C.
   "Rankings & Estimates, May 2003" (Copyright © 2003, NEA, used with permission)
Estimates for school year 2002-2003.

Average Teacher's Salary as a Percent of Average Annual Wages in 2002

National Average = 121.6% of Average Annual Wages*

ALPHA ORDER

RANK	STATE	PERCENT
41	Alabama	106.8
6	Alaska	152.4
4	Arizona	153.7
15	Arkansas	140.2
2	California	174.4
5	Colorado	152.5
9	Connecticut	144.2
18	Delaware	135.3
37	Florida	108.6
7	Georgia	148.6
11	Hawaii	143.3
29	Idaho	116.5
49	Illinois	85.4
16	Indiana	135.6
10	Iowa	144.0
24	Kansas	123.6
21	Kentucky	132.4
26	Louisiana	118.8
42	Maine	104.2
8	Maryland	147.7
39	Massachusetts	107.3
1	Michigan	186.7
45	Minnesota	93.9
30	Mississippi	116.4
34	Missouri	111.1
47	Montana	89.9
28	Nebraska	116.7
36	Nevada	108.8
25	New Hampshire	120.8
3	New Jersey	156.3
43	New Mexico	100.5
22	New York	125.5
13	North Carolina	141.7
44	North Dakota	99.4
12	Ohio	142.8
46	Oklahoma	93.3
31	Oregon	116.1
19	Pennsylvania	133.1
23	Rhode Island	125.4
16	South Carolina	135.6
38	South Dakota	108.0
50	Tennessee	83.1
48	Texas	86.8
27	Utah	117.5
19	Vermont	133.1
35	Virginia	109.4
14	Washington	140.6
32	West Virginia	113.0
40	Wisconsin	107.2
33	Wyoming	112.4

RANK ORDER

RANK	STATE	PERCENT
1	Michigan	186.7
2	California	174.4
3	New Jersey	156.3
4	Arizona	153.7
5	Colorado	152.5
6	Alaska	152.4
7	Georgia	148.6
8	Maryland	147.7
9	Connecticut	144.2
10	Iowa	144.0
11	Hawaii	143.3
12	Ohio	142.8
13	North Carolina	141.7
14	Washington	140.6
15	Arkansas	140.2
16	Indiana	135.6
16	South Carolina	135.6
18	Delaware	135.3
19	Pennsylvania	133.1
19	Vermont	133.1
21	Kentucky	132.4
22	New York	125.5
23	Rhode Island	125.4
24	Kansas	123.6
25	New Hampshire	120.8
26	Louisiana	118.8
27	Utah	117.5
28	Nebraska	116.7
29	Idaho	116.5
30	Mississippi	116.4
31	Oregon	116.1
32	West Virginia	113.0
33	Wyoming	112.4
34	Missouri	111.1
35	Virginia	109.4
36	Nevada	108.8
37	Florida	108.6
38	South Dakota	108.0
39	Massachusetts	107.3
40	Wisconsin	107.2
41	Alabama	106.8
42	Maine	104.2
43	New Mexico	100.5
44	North Dakota	99.4
45	Minnesota	93.9
46	Oklahoma	93.3
47	Montana	89.9
48	Texas	86.8
49	Illinois	85.4
50	Tennessee	83.1

District of Columbia	167.1

Estimated Public High School Graduates in 2003

National Total = 2,643,066 Graduates*

ALPHA ORDER

RANK	STATE	GRADUATES	% of USA
25	Alabama	37,421	1.4%
48	Alaska	7,011	0.3%
20	Arizona	48,957	1.9%
33	Arkansas	27,212	1.0%
1	California	341,463	12.9%
21	Colorado	41,973	1.6%
29	Connecticut	32,490	1.2%
49	Delaware	6,508	0.2%
5	Florida	117,624	4.5%
10	Georgia	72,565	2.7%
42	Hawaii	11,165	0.4%
38	Idaho	16,000	0.6%
6	Illinois	114,733	4.3%
16	Indiana	57,269	2.2%
27	Iowa	33,430	1.3%
32	Kansas	29,707	1.1%
26	Kentucky	36,163	1.4%
24	Louisiana	37,939	1.4%
41	Maine	12,820	0.5%
18	Maryland	52,864	2.0%
19	Massachusetts	52,337	2.0%
9	Michigan	78,111	3.0%
14	Minnesota	60,100	2.3%
34	Mississippi	24,500	0.9%
17	Missouri	53,828	2.0%
43	Montana	10,896	0.4%
35	Nebraska	19,080	0.7%
39	Nevada	15,500	0.6%
40	New Hampshire	13,013	0.5%
8	New Jersey	79,689	3.0%
36	New Mexico	17,868	0.7%
3	New York	143,707	5.4%
12	North Carolina	63,278	2.4%
46	North Dakota	8,016	0.3%
7	Ohio	111,327	4.2%
23	Oklahoma	37,995	1.4%
30	Oregon	31,508	1.2%
4	Pennsylvania	117,991	4.5%
45	Rhode Island	8,659	0.3%
28	South Carolina	33,000	1.2%
44	South Dakota	8,815	0.3%
22	Tennessee	41,160	1.6%
2	Texas	223,288	8.4%
31	Utah	30,755	1.2%
47	Vermont	7,012	0.3%
11	Virginia	68,270	2.6%
13	Washington	62,171	2.4%
37	West Virginia	17,202	0.7%
15	Wisconsin	60,022	2.3%
50	Wyoming	5,921	0.2%

RANK ORDER

RANK	STATE	GRADUATES	% of USA
1	California	341,463	12.9%
2	Texas	223,288	8.4%
3	New York	143,707	5.4%
4	Pennsylvania	117,991	4.5%
5	Florida	117,624	4.5%
6	Illinois	114,733	4.3%
7	Ohio	111,327	4.2%
8	New Jersey	79,689	3.0%
9	Michigan	78,111	3.0%
10	Georgia	72,565	2.7%
11	Virginia	68,270	2.6%
12	North Carolina	63,278	2.4%
13	Washington	62,171	2.4%
14	Minnesota	60,100	2.3%
15	Wisconsin	60,022	2.3%
16	Indiana	57,269	2.2%
17	Missouri	53,828	2.0%
18	Maryland	52,864	2.0%
19	Massachusetts	52,337	2.0%
20	Arizona	48,957	1.9%
21	Colorado	41,973	1.6%
22	Tennessee	41,160	1.6%
23	Oklahoma	37,995	1.4%
24	Louisiana	37,939	1.4%
25	Alabama	37,421	1.4%
26	Kentucky	36,163	1.4%
27	Iowa	33,430	1.3%
28	South Carolina	33,000	1.2%
29	Connecticut	32,490	1.2%
30	Oregon	31,508	1.2%
31	Utah	30,755	1.2%
32	Kansas	29,707	1.1%
33	Arkansas	27,212	1.0%
34	Mississippi	24,500	0.9%
35	Nebraska	19,080	0.7%
36	New Mexico	17,868	0.7%
37	West Virginia	17,202	0.7%
38	Idaho	16,000	0.6%
39	Nevada	15,500	0.6%
40	New Hampshire	13,013	0.5%
41	Maine	12,820	0.5%
42	Hawaii	11,165	0.4%
43	Montana	10,896	0.4%
44	South Dakota	8,815	0.3%
45	Rhode Island	8,659	0.3%
46	North Dakota	8,016	0.3%
47	Vermont	7,012	0.3%
48	Alaska	7,011	0.3%
49	Delaware	6,508	0.2%
50	Wyoming	5,921	0.2%
	District of Columbia	2,733	0.1%

Source: National Education Association, Washington, D.C.
"Rankings & Estimates" (Copyright © 2002, NEA, used with permission)
*Estimates for school year 2002-03.

Estimated Public High School Graduation Rate in 2003

National Rate = 67.2% Graduated*

<u>ALPHA ORDER</u>

RANK	STATE	PERCENT
40	Alabama	61.2
42	Alaska	60.6
26	Arizona	71.3
18	Arkansas	74.2
29	California	70.8
24	Colorado	71.5
19	Connecticut	73.9
35	Delaware	64.1
49	Florida	52.6
44	Georgia	57.9
25	Hawaii	71.4
8	Idaho	79.8
31	Illinois	69.7
30	Indiana	70.7
5	Iowa	80.8
16	Kansas	74.9
36	Kentucky	63.8
43	Louisiana	59.4
14	Maine	75.3
15	Maryland	75.1
34	Massachusetts	67.3
45	Michigan	57.5
3	Minnesota	84.4
38	Mississippi	62.2
28	Missouri	71.0
6	Montana	80.5
11	Nebraska	76.7
37	Nevada	63.0
17	New Hampshire	74.3
1	New Jersey	89.3
41	New Mexico	61.0
46	New York	56.8
46	North Carolina	56.8
4	North Dakota	82.8
27	Ohio	71.1
13	Oklahoma	75.6
32	Oregon	69.1
10	Pennsylvania	76.9
33	Rhode Island	69.0
50	South Carolina	52.5
9	South Dakota	78.4
48	Tennessee	55.1
39	Texas	62.1
2	Utah	85.5
7	Vermont	80.2
22	Virginia	71.9
23	Washington	71.8
21	West Virginia	72.0
12	Wisconsin	76.0
20	Wyoming	73.5

<u>RANK ORDER</u>

RANK	STATE	PERCENT
1	New Jersey	89.3
2	Utah	85.5
3	Minnesota	84.4
4	North Dakota	82.8
5	Iowa	80.8
6	Montana	80.5
7	Vermont	80.2
8	Idaho	79.8
9	South Dakota	78.4
10	Pennsylvania	76.9
11	Nebraska	76.7
12	Wisconsin	76.0
13	Oklahoma	75.6
14	Maine	75.3
15	Maryland	75.1
16	Kansas	74.9
17	New Hampshire	74.3
18	Arkansas	74.2
19	Connecticut	73.9
20	Wyoming	73.5
21	West Virginia	72.0
22	Virginia	71.9
23	Washington	71.8
24	Colorado	71.5
25	Hawaii	71.4
26	Arizona	71.3
27	Ohio	71.1
28	Missouri	71.0
29	California	70.8
30	Indiana	70.7
31	Illinois	69.7
32	Oregon	69.1
33	Rhode Island	69.0
34	Massachusetts	67.3
35	Delaware	64.1
36	Kentucky	63.8
37	Nevada	63.0
38	Mississippi	62.2
39	Texas	62.1
40	Alabama	61.2
41	New Mexico	61.0
42	Alaska	60.6
43	Louisiana	59.4
44	Georgia	57.9
45	Michigan	57.5
46	New York	56.8
46	North Carolina	56.8
48	Tennessee	55.1
49	Florida	52.6
50	South Carolina	52.5
	District of Columbia	51.7

*Source: Morgan Quitno Press using data from U.S. Department of Education, National Center for Education Statistics
"Public School Student, Staff and Graduate Counts by State: School Year 2001-2002" (NCES 2003-358)*
*Calculated by comparing estimated number of public high school graduates in 2003 with 9th grade enrollment in
Fall 1999. Data exclude ungraded pupils and have not been adjusted for interstate migration or switching to private
schools.*

Percent of Population Graduated from High School in 2002

National Percent = 84.1%*

<u>ALPHA ORDER</u>

RANK	STATE	PERCENT
47	Alabama	78.9
1	Alaska	92.2
34	Arizona	84.6
39	Arkansas	81.0
41	California	80.2
17	Colorado	87.6
14	Connecticut	88.0
11	Delaware	88.5
36	Florida	83.3
37	Georgia	82.9
15	Hawaii	87.9
23	Idaho	86.8
29	Illinois	85.9
32	Indiana	85.3
12	Iowa	88.3
18	Kansas	87.5
40	Kentucky	80.8
48	Louisiana	78.8
20	Maine	87.4
18	Maryland	87.5
26	Massachusetts	86.5
26	Michigan	86.5
1	Minnesota	92.2
46	Mississippi	79.1
13	Missouri	88.1
8	Montana	89.7
7	Nebraska	89.8
31	Nevada	85.8
6	New Hampshire	90.2
29	New Jersey	85.9
38	New Mexico	81.6
35	New York	83.7
43	North Carolina	80.1
10	North Dakota	89.0
22	Ohio	87.3
33	Oklahoma	85.1
16	Oregon	87.7
28	Pennsylvania	86.1
43	Rhode Island	80.1
41	South Carolina	80.2
9	South Dakota	89.2
43	Tennessee	80.1
50	Texas	78.1
4	Utah	91.0
20	Vermont	87.4
25	Virginia	86.7
5	Washington	90.4
49	West Virginia	78.5
23	Wisconsin	86.8
3	Wyoming	91.6

<u>RANK ORDER</u>

RANK	STATE	PERCENT
1	Alaska	92.2
1	Minnesota	92.2
3	Wyoming	91.6
4	Utah	91.0
5	Washington	90.4
6	New Hampshire	90.2
7	Nebraska	89.8
8	Montana	89.7
9	South Dakota	89.2
10	North Dakota	89.0
11	Delaware	88.5
12	Iowa	88.3
13	Missouri	88.1
14	Connecticut	88.0
15	Hawaii	87.9
16	Oregon	87.7
17	Colorado	87.6
18	Kansas	87.5
18	Maryland	87.5
20	Maine	87.4
20	Vermont	87.4
22	Ohio	87.3
23	Idaho	86.8
23	Wisconsin	86.8
25	Virginia	86.7
26	Massachusetts	86.5
26	Michigan	86.5
28	Pennsylvania	86.1
29	Illinois	85.9
29	New Jersey	85.9
31	Nevada	85.8
32	Indiana	85.3
33	Oklahoma	85.1
34	Arizona	84.6
35	New York	83.7
36	Florida	83.3
37	Georgia	82.9
38	New Mexico	81.6
39	Arkansas	81.0
40	Kentucky	80.8
41	California	80.2
41	South Carolina	80.2
43	North Carolina	80.1
43	Rhode Island	80.1
43	Tennessee	80.1
46	Mississippi	79.1
47	Alabama	78.9
48	Louisiana	78.8
49	West Virginia	78.5
50	Texas	78.1
	District of Columbia	83.5

Source: U.S. Bureau of the Census
"Educational Attainment in the United States: March 2002"
(http://www.census.gov/population/socdemo/education/ppl-169/tab13.pdf)
**Persons age 25 and older.*

High School Drop Out Rate in 2001

National Median = 4.2%*

<table>
<tr><td colspan="3"><u>ALPHA ORDER</u></td><td colspan="3"><u>RANK ORDER</u></td></tr>
<tr><td>RANK</td><td>STATE</td><td>RATE</td><td>RANK</td><td>STATE</td><td>RATE</td></tr>
<tr><td>27</td><td>Alabama</td><td>4.1</td><td>1</td><td>Arizona</td><td>10.9</td></tr>
<tr><td>3</td><td>Alaska</td><td>8.2</td><td>2</td><td>Louisiana</td><td>8.3</td></tr>
<tr><td>1</td><td>Arizona</td><td>10.9</td><td>3</td><td>Alaska</td><td>8.2</td></tr>
<tr><td>11</td><td>Arkansas</td><td>5.3</td><td>4</td><td>Georgia</td><td>7.2</td></tr>
<tr><td>NA</td><td>California**</td><td>NA</td><td>5</td><td>Wyoming</td><td>6.4</td></tr>
<tr><td>NA</td><td>Colorado**</td><td>NA</td><td>6</td><td>North Carolina</td><td>6.3</td></tr>
<tr><td>41</td><td>Connecticut</td><td>3.0</td><td>7</td><td>Illinois</td><td>6.0</td></tr>
<tr><td>22</td><td>Delaware</td><td>4.2</td><td>8</td><td>Hawaii</td><td>5.7</td></tr>
<tr><td>20</td><td>Florida</td><td>4.4</td><td>9</td><td>Idaho</td><td>5.6</td></tr>
<tr><td>4</td><td>Georgia</td><td>7.2</td><td>10</td><td>New Hampshire</td><td>5.4</td></tr>
<tr><td>8</td><td>Hawaii</td><td>5.7</td><td>11</td><td>Arkansas</td><td>5.3</td></tr>
<tr><td>9</td><td>Idaho</td><td>5.6</td><td>11</td><td>New Mexico</td><td>5.3</td></tr>
<tr><td>7</td><td>Illinois</td><td>6.0</td><td>11</td><td>Oregon</td><td>5.3</td></tr>
<tr><td>NA</td><td>Indiana**</td><td>NA</td><td>14</td><td>Nevada</td><td>5.2</td></tr>
<tr><td>43</td><td>Iowa</td><td>2.7</td><td>14</td><td>Oklahoma</td><td>5.2</td></tr>
<tr><td>39</td><td>Kansas</td><td>3.2</td><td>16</td><td>Rhode Island</td><td>5.0</td></tr>
<tr><td>18</td><td>Kentucky</td><td>4.6</td><td>17</td><td>Vermont</td><td>4.7</td></tr>
<tr><td>2</td><td>Louisiana</td><td>8.3</td><td>18</td><td>Kentucky</td><td>4.6</td></tr>
<tr><td>40</td><td>Maine</td><td>3.1</td><td>18</td><td>Mississippi</td><td>4.6</td></tr>
<tr><td>27</td><td>Maryland</td><td>4.1</td><td>20</td><td>Florida</td><td>4.4</td></tr>
<tr><td>37</td><td>Massachusetts</td><td>3.4</td><td>21</td><td>Tennessee</td><td>4.3</td></tr>
<tr><td>NA</td><td>Michigan**</td><td>NA</td><td>22</td><td>Delaware</td><td>4.2</td></tr>
<tr><td>29</td><td>Minnesota</td><td>4.0</td><td>22</td><td>Missouri</td><td>4.2</td></tr>
<tr><td>18</td><td>Mississippi</td><td>4.6</td><td>22</td><td>Montana</td><td>4.2</td></tr>
<tr><td>22</td><td>Missouri</td><td>4.2</td><td>22</td><td>Texas</td><td>4.2</td></tr>
<tr><td>22</td><td>Montana</td><td>4.2</td><td>22</td><td>West Virginia</td><td>4.2</td></tr>
<tr><td>29</td><td>Nebraska</td><td>4.0</td><td>27</td><td>Alabama</td><td>4.1</td></tr>
<tr><td>14</td><td>Nevada</td><td>5.2</td><td>27</td><td>Maryland</td><td>4.1</td></tr>
<tr><td>10</td><td>New Hampshire</td><td>5.4</td><td>29</td><td>Minnesota</td><td>4.0</td></tr>
<tr><td>42</td><td>New Jersey</td><td>2.8</td><td>29</td><td>Nebraska</td><td>4.0</td></tr>
<tr><td>11</td><td>New Mexico</td><td>5.3</td><td>31</td><td>Ohio</td><td>3.9</td></tr>
<tr><td>33</td><td>New York</td><td>3.8</td><td>31</td><td>South Dakota</td><td>3.9</td></tr>
<tr><td>6</td><td>North Carolina</td><td>6.3</td><td>33</td><td>New York</td><td>3.8</td></tr>
<tr><td>45</td><td>North Dakota</td><td>2.2</td><td>34</td><td>Utah</td><td>3.7</td></tr>
<tr><td>31</td><td>Ohio</td><td>3.9</td><td>35</td><td>Pennsylvania</td><td>3.6</td></tr>
<tr><td>14</td><td>Oklahoma</td><td>5.2</td><td>36</td><td>Virginia</td><td>3.5</td></tr>
<tr><td>11</td><td>Oregon</td><td>5.3</td><td>37</td><td>Massachusetts</td><td>3.4</td></tr>
<tr><td>35</td><td>Pennsylvania</td><td>3.6</td><td>38</td><td>South Carolina</td><td>3.3</td></tr>
<tr><td>16</td><td>Rhode Island</td><td>5.0</td><td>39</td><td>Kansas</td><td>3.2</td></tr>
<tr><td>38</td><td>South Carolina</td><td>3.3</td><td>40</td><td>Maine</td><td>3.1</td></tr>
<tr><td>31</td><td>South Dakota</td><td>3.9</td><td>41</td><td>Connecticut</td><td>3.0</td></tr>
<tr><td>21</td><td>Tennessee</td><td>4.3</td><td>42</td><td>New Jersey</td><td>2.8</td></tr>
<tr><td>22</td><td>Texas</td><td>4.2</td><td>43</td><td>Iowa</td><td>2.7</td></tr>
<tr><td>34</td><td>Utah</td><td>3.7</td><td>44</td><td>Wisconsin</td><td>2.3</td></tr>
<tr><td>17</td><td>Vermont</td><td>4.7</td><td>45</td><td>North Dakota</td><td>2.2</td></tr>
<tr><td>36</td><td>Virginia</td><td>3.5</td><td>NA</td><td>California**</td><td>NA</td></tr>
<tr><td>NA</td><td>Washington**</td><td>NA</td><td>NA</td><td>Colorado**</td><td>NA</td></tr>
<tr><td>22</td><td>West Virginia</td><td>4.2</td><td>NA</td><td>Indiana**</td><td>NA</td></tr>
<tr><td>44</td><td>Wisconsin</td><td>2.3</td><td>NA</td><td>Michigan**</td><td>NA</td></tr>
<tr><td>5</td><td>Wyoming</td><td>6.4</td><td>NA</td><td>Washington**</td><td>NA</td></tr>
<tr><td></td><td></td><td></td><td></td><td>District of Columbia**</td><td>NA</td></tr>
</table>

Source: U.S. Department of Education, National Center for Educational Statistics
"Public High School Dropouts and Completers from the Common Core of Data" (NCES 2004-310, November 2003)
**"Event" dropout rates showing the number of 9-12th grade dropouts divided by the number of students enrolled at the beginning of the school year in those grades.*
***Not available.*

ACT Average Composite Score in 2003

National Average = 20.8*

ALPHA ORDER				RANK ORDER		
RANK	STATE	AVERAGE SCORE		RANK	STATE	AVERAGE SCORE
42	Alabama	20.1		1	Oregon	22.6
31	Alaska	21.1		2	Maine	22.5
20	Arizona	21.4		2	Vermont	22.5
38	Arkansas	20.3		2	Washington	22.5
17	California	21.5		5	Massachusetts	22.3
42	Colorado	20.1		5	New York	22.3
9	Connecticut	22.1		7	New Hampshire	22.2
32	Delaware	20.8		7	Wisconsin	22.2
35	Florida	20.5		9	Connecticut	22.1
47	Georgia	19.8		10	Iowa	22.0
12	Hawaii	21.8		10	Minnesota	22.0
29	Idaho	21.2		12	Hawaii	21.8
40	Illinois	20.2		13	Montana	21.7
16	Indiana	21.6		13	Nebraska	21.7
10	Iowa	22.0		13	Rhode Island	21.7
17	Kansas	21.5		16	Indiana	21.6
40	Kentucky	20.2		17	California	21.5
48	Louisiana	19.6		17	Kansas	21.5
2	Maine	22.5		17	Pennsylvania	21.5
33	Maryland	20.7		20	Arizona	21.4
5	Massachusetts	22.3		20	Missouri	21.4
25	Michigan	21.3		20	Ohio	21.4
10	Minnesota	22.0		20	South Dakota	21.4
50	Mississippi	18.7		20	Wyoming	21.4
20	Missouri	21.4		25	Michigan	21.3
13	Montana	21.7		25	Nevada	21.3
13	Nebraska	21.7		25	North Dakota	21.3
25	Nevada	21.3		25	Utah	21.3
7	New Hampshire	22.2		29	Idaho	21.2
29	New Jersey	21.2		29	New Jersey	21.2
45	New Mexico	19.9		31	Alaska	21.1
5	New York	22.3		32	Delaware	20.8
45	North Carolina	19.9		33	Maryland	20.7
25	North Dakota	21.3		34	Virginia	20.6
20	Ohio	21.4		35	Florida	20.5
35	Oklahoma	20.5		35	Oklahoma	20.5
1	Oregon	22.6		37	Tennessee	20.4
17	Pennsylvania	21.5		38	Arkansas	20.3
13	Rhode Island	21.7		38	West Virginia	20.3
49	South Carolina	19.2		40	Illinois	20.2
20	South Dakota	21.4		40	Kentucky	20.2
37	Tennessee	20.4		42	Alabama	20.1
42	Texas	20.1		42	Colorado	20.1
25	Utah	21.3		42	Texas	20.1
2	Vermont	22.5		45	New Mexico	19.9
34	Virginia	20.6		45	North Carolina	19.9
2	Washington	22.5		47	Georgia	19.8
38	West Virginia	20.3		48	Louisiana	19.6
7	Wisconsin	22.2		49	South Carolina	19.2
20	Wyoming	21.4		50	Mississippi	18.7
					District of Columbia	17.5

Source: The American College Testing Program (copyright 2003)
"ACT Average Composite Scores by State" (http://www.act.org/news/data/03/states.html)
**The ACT score range is 1 to 36. More than one million 2003 U.S. high school graduates took the test. Caution should be used in using ACT scores to compare states. The percentage of high school students taking the test varies greatly from one state to another.*

Average Verbal SAT Score in 2003

National Average Score = 507*

ALPHA ORDER				RANK ORDER		
RANK	STATE	AVERAGE SCORE		RANK	STATE	AVERAGE SCORE
17	Alabama	559		1	North Dakota	602
30	Alaska	518		2	South Dakota	588
27	Arizona	524		3	Iowa	586
14	Arkansas	564		4	Wisconsin	585
43	California	499		5	Illinois	583
19	Colorado	551		6	Minnesota	582
34	Connecticut	512		6	Missouri	582
39	Delaware	501		8	Kansas	578
44	Florida	498		9	Nebraska	573
47	Georgia	493		10	Oklahoma	569
50	Hawaii	486		11	Tennessee	568
22	Idaho	540		12	Utah	566
5	Illinois	583		13	Mississippi	565
41	Indiana	500		14	Arkansas	564
3	Iowa	586		14	Michigan	564
8	Kansas	578		16	Louisiana	563
18	Kentucky	554		17	Alabama	559
16	Louisiana	563		18	Kentucky	554
37	Maine	503		19	Colorado	551
36	Maryland	509		20	New Mexico	548
31	Massachusetts	516		20	Wyoming	548
14	Michigan	564		22	Idaho	540
6	Minnesota	582		23	Montana	538
13	Mississippi	565		24	Ohio	536
6	Missouri	582		25	Washington	530
23	Montana	538		26	Oregon	526
9	Nebraska	573		27	Arizona	524
35	Nevada	510		28	New Hampshire	522
28	New Hampshire	522		28	West Virginia	522
39	New Jersey	501		30	Alaska	518
20	New Mexico	548		31	Massachusetts	516
45	New York	496		32	Vermont	515
46	North Carolina	495		33	Virginia	514
1	North Dakota	602		34	Connecticut	512
24	Ohio	536		35	Nevada	510
10	Oklahoma	569		36	Maryland	509
26	Oregon	526		37	Maine	503
41	Pennsylvania	500		38	Rhode Island	502
38	Rhode Island	502		39	Delaware	501
47	South Carolina	493		39	New Jersey	501
2	South Dakota	588		41	Indiana	500
11	Tennessee	568		41	Pennsylvania	500
47	Texas	493		43	California	499
12	Utah	566		44	Florida	498
32	Vermont	515		45	New York	496
33	Virginia	514		46	North Carolina	495
25	Washington	530		47	Georgia	493
28	West Virginia	522		47	South Carolina	493
4	Wisconsin	585		47	Texas	493
20	Wyoming	548		50	Hawaii	486
					District of Columbia	484

Source: The College Board, New York, NY

"College Board News 2003-2004" (www.collegeboard.com/about/news_info/cbsenior/yr2003/html/links.html)
**The College Board strongly cautions against comparing states based on SAT scores alone. The percentage of high school students taking the test varies greatly from one state to another. The SAT was formerly known as the Scholastic Aptitude Test.*

Average Math SAT Score in 2003

National Average Score = 519*

ALPHA ORDER

RANK	STATE	AVERAGE SCORE
17	Alabama	552
31	Alaska	518
27	Arizona	525
15	Arkansas	554
30	California	519
16	Colorado	553
36	Connecticut	514
45	Delaware	501
48	Florida	498
50	Georgia	491
33	Hawaii	516
23	Idaho	540
3	Illinois	596
42	Indiana	504
2	Iowa	597
8	Kansas	582
17	Kentucky	552
13	Louisiana	559
45	Maine	501
34	Maryland	515
28	Massachusetts	522
10	Michigan	576
5	Minnesota	591
19	Mississippi	551
7	Missouri	583
21	Montana	543
9	Nebraska	578
32	Nevada	517
29	New Hampshire	521
34	New Jersey	515
23	New Mexico	540
38	New York	510
41	North Carolina	506
1	North Dakota	613
22	Ohio	541
11	Oklahoma	562
26	Oregon	527
44	Pennsylvania	502
42	Rhode Island	504
49	South Carolina	496
6	South Dakota	588
12	Tennessee	560
47	Texas	500
13	Utah	559
37	Vermont	512
38	Virginia	510
25	Washington	532
38	West Virginia	510
4	Wisconsin	594
20	Wyoming	549

RANK ORDER

RANK	STATE	AVERAGE SCORE
1	North Dakota	613
2	Iowa	597
3	Illinois	596
4	Wisconsin	594
5	Minnesota	591
6	South Dakota	588
7	Missouri	583
8	Kansas	582
9	Nebraska	578
10	Michigan	576
11	Oklahoma	562
12	Tennessee	560
13	Louisiana	559
13	Utah	559
15	Arkansas	554
16	Colorado	553
17	Alabama	552
17	Kentucky	552
19	Mississippi	551
20	Wyoming	549
21	Montana	543
22	Ohio	541
23	Idaho	540
23	New Mexico	540
25	Washington	532
26	Oregon	527
27	Arizona	525
28	Massachusetts	522
29	New Hampshire	521
30	California	519
31	Alaska	518
32	Nevada	517
33	Hawaii	516
34	Maryland	515
34	New Jersey	515
36	Connecticut	514
37	Vermont	512
38	New York	510
38	Virginia	510
38	West Virginia	510
41	North Carolina	506
42	Indiana	504
42	Rhode Island	504
44	Pennsylvania	502
45	Delaware	501
45	Maine	501
47	Texas	500
48	Florida	498
49	South Carolina	496
50	Georgia	491
	District of Columbia	474

Source: The College Board, New York, NY

"College Board News 2003-2004" (www.collegeboard.com/about/news_info/cbsenior/yr2003/html/links.html)

The College Board strongly cautions against comparing states based on SAT scores alone. The percentage of high school students taking the test varies greatly from one state to another. The SAT was formerly known as the Scholastic Aptitude Test.

Education Expenditures by State and Local Governments in 2000

National Total = $521,612,107,000*

ALPHA ORDER

RANK	STATE	EXPENDITURES	% of USA
23	Alabama	$7,768,307,000	1.5%
44	Alaska	1,760,904,000	0.3%
22	Arizona	7,870,687,000	1.5%
34	Arkansas	4,197,707,000	0.8%
1	California	63,559,018,000	12.2%
21	Colorado	7,903,563,000	1.5%
26	Connecticut	6,722,251,000	1.3%
45	Delaware	1,715,010,000	0.3%
5	Florida	22,826,044,000	4.4%
10	Georgia	14,767,624,000	2.8%
43	Hawaii	1,853,891,000	0.4%
40	Idaho	2,132,007,000	0.4%
6	Illinois	22,728,087,000	4.4%
14	Indiana	11,449,565,000	2.2%
29	Iowa	5,964,320,000	1.1%
31	Kansas	4,884,359,000	0.9%
28	Kentucky	6,374,348,000	1.2%
24	Louisiana	7,185,411,000	1.4%
39	Maine	2,227,990,000	0.4%
18	Maryland	10,055,102,000	1.9%
15	Massachusetts	11,444,917,000	2.2%
7	Michigan	22,483,732,000	4.3%
17	Minnesota	10,283,052,000	2.0%
32	Mississippi	4,818,178,000	0.9%
19	Missouri	9,224,225,000	1.8%
46	Montana	1,640,564,000	0.3%
36	Nebraska	3,266,696,000	0.6%
38	Nevada	3,020,130,000	0.6%
41	New Hampshire	2,059,365,000	0.4%
9	New Jersey	18,787,558,000	3.6%
35	New Mexico	3,695,920,000	0.7%
2	New York	40,630,366,000	7.8%
11	North Carolina	14,163,565,000	2.7%
48	North Dakota	1,254,617,000	0.2%
8	Ohio	20,612,205,000	4.0%
30	Oklahoma	5,836,280,000	1.1%
27	Oregon	6,448,195,000	1.2%
4	Pennsylvania	23,255,694,000	4.5%
42	Rhode Island	1,856,613,000	0.4%
25	South Carolina	7,126,017,000	1.4%
49	South Dakota	1,218,178,000	0.2%
20	Tennessee	8,369,231,000	1.6%
3	Texas	39,217,371,000	7.5%
33	Utah	4,233,385,000	0.8%
47	Vermont	1,330,436,000	0.3%
12	Virginia	13,132,025,000	2.5%
13	Washington	11,564,543,000	2.2%
37	West Virginia	3,171,481,000	0.6%
16	Wisconsin	11,427,139,000	2.2%
50	Wyoming	1,124,881,000	0.2%

RANK ORDER

RANK	STATE	EXPENDITURES	% of USA
1	California	$63,559,018,000	12.2%
2	New York	40,630,366,000	7.8%
3	Texas	39,217,371,000	7.5%
4	Pennsylvania	23,255,694,000	4.5%
5	Florida	22,826,044,000	4.4%
6	Illinois	22,728,087,000	4.4%
7	Michigan	22,483,732,000	4.3%
8	Ohio	20,612,205,000	4.0%
9	New Jersey	18,787,558,000	3.6%
10	Georgia	14,767,624,000	2.8%
11	North Carolina	14,163,565,000	2.7%
12	Virginia	13,132,025,000	2.5%
13	Washington	11,564,543,000	2.2%
14	Indiana	11,449,565,000	2.2%
15	Massachusetts	11,444,917,000	2.2%
16	Wisconsin	11,427,139,000	2.2%
17	Minnesota	10,283,052,000	2.0%
18	Maryland	10,055,102,000	1.9%
19	Missouri	9,224,225,000	1.8%
20	Tennessee	8,369,231,000	1.6%
21	Colorado	7,903,563,000	1.5%
22	Arizona	7,870,687,000	1.5%
23	Alabama	7,768,307,000	1.5%
24	Louisiana	7,185,411,000	1.4%
25	South Carolina	7,126,017,000	1.4%
26	Connecticut	6,722,251,000	1.3%
27	Oregon	6,448,195,000	1.2%
28	Kentucky	6,374,348,000	1.2%
29	Iowa	5,964,320,000	1.1%
30	Oklahoma	5,836,280,000	1.1%
31	Kansas	4,884,359,000	0.9%
32	Mississippi	4,818,178,000	0.9%
33	Utah	4,233,385,000	0.8%
34	Arkansas	4,197,707,000	0.8%
35	New Mexico	3,695,920,000	0.7%
36	Nebraska	3,266,696,000	0.6%
37	West Virginia	3,171,481,000	0.6%
38	Nevada	3,020,130,000	0.6%
39	Maine	2,227,990,000	0.4%
40	Idaho	2,132,007,000	0.4%
41	New Hampshire	2,059,365,000	0.4%
42	Rhode Island	1,856,613,000	0.4%
43	Hawaii	1,853,891,000	0.4%
44	Alaska	1,760,904,000	0.3%
45	Delaware	1,715,010,000	0.3%
46	Montana	1,640,564,000	0.3%
47	Vermont	1,330,436,000	0.3%
48	North Dakota	1,254,617,000	0.2%
49	South Dakota	1,218,178,000	0.2%
50	Wyoming	1,124,881,000	0.2%
	District of Columbia	969,353,000	0.2%

Source: U.S. Bureau of the Census, Governments Division
"State and Local Government Finances: 1999-00" (http://www.census.gov/govs/www/estimate00.html)
**Direct general expenditures for higher, secondary, elementary and "other" education. Includes capital outlays.*

Per Capita State and Local Government Expenditures for Education in 2000

National Per Capita = $1,848*

<u>ALPHA ORDER</u>

RANK	STATE	PER CAPITA
35	Alabama	$1,745
1	Alaska	2,805
47	Arizona	1,523
45	Arkansas	1,567
22	California	1,869
24	Colorado	1,827
12	Connecticut	1,970
5	Delaware	2,181
50	Florida	1,422
30	Georgia	1,793
46	Hawaii	1,529
41	Idaho	1,640
24	Illinois	1,827
19	Indiana	1,879
10	Iowa	2,036
27	Kansas	1,814
44	Kentucky	1,574
43	Louisiana	1,608
36	Maine	1,744
16	Maryland	1,893
29	Massachusetts	1,799
3	Michigan	2,258
9	Minnesota	2,084
37	Mississippi	1,691
40	Missouri	1,646
26	Montana	1,816
15	Nebraska	1,907
48	Nevada	1,496
39	New Hampshire	1,660
4	New Jersey	2,228
11	New Mexico	2,029
7	New York	2,138
34	North Carolina	1,752
13	North Dakota	1,957
27	Ohio	1,814
38	Oklahoma	1,690
19	Oregon	1,879
16	Pennsylvania	1,893
32	Rhode Island	1,767
31	South Carolina	1,771
42	South Dakota	1,612
49	Tennessee	1,467
21	Texas	1,871
18	Utah	1,887
5	Vermont	2,181
23	Virginia	1,848
14	Washington	1,956
33	West Virginia	1,755
8	Wisconsin	2,126
2	Wyoming	2,277

<u>RANK ORDER</u>

RANK	STATE	PER CAPITA
1	Alaska	$2,805
2	Wyoming	2,277
3	Michigan	2,258
4	New Jersey	2,228
5	Delaware	2,181
5	Vermont	2,181
7	New York	2,138
8	Wisconsin	2,126
9	Minnesota	2,084
10	Iowa	2,036
11	New Mexico	2,029
12	Connecticut	1,970
13	North Dakota	1,957
14	Washington	1,956
15	Nebraska	1,907
16	Maryland	1,893
16	Pennsylvania	1,893
18	Utah	1,887
19	Indiana	1,879
19	Oregon	1,879
21	Texas	1,871
22	California	1,869
23	Virginia	1,848
24	Colorado	1,827
24	Illinois	1,827
26	Montana	1,816
27	Kansas	1,814
27	Ohio	1,814
29	Massachusetts	1,799
30	Georgia	1,793
31	South Carolina	1,771
32	Rhode Island	1,767
33	West Virginia	1,755
34	North Carolina	1,752
35	Alabama	1,745
36	Maine	1,744
37	Mississippi	1,691
38	Oklahoma	1,690
39	New Hampshire	1,660
40	Missouri	1,646
41	Idaho	1,640
42	South Dakota	1,612
43	Louisiana	1,608
44	Kentucky	1,574
45	Arkansas	1,567
46	Hawaii	1,529
47	Arizona	1,523
48	Nevada	1,496
49	Tennessee	1,467
50	Florida	1,422
	District of Columbia	1,696

Source: Morgan Quitno Press using data from U.S. Bureau of the Census, Governments Division
"State and Local Government Finances: 1999-00" (http://www.census.gov/govs/www/estimate00.html)
*Direct general expenditures for higher, secondary, elementary and "other" education. Includes capital outlays.

Expenditures for Education as a Percent of
All State and Local Government Expenditures in 2000
National Percent = 34.7%*

ALPHA ORDER

ALPHA ORDER

RANK	STATE	PERCENT
27	Alabama	35.2
50	Alaska	23.2
34	Arizona	33.8
11	Arkansas	38.0
40	California	32.5
29	Colorado	35.1
44	Connecticut	31.4
16	Delaware	36.6
46	Florida	30.3
7	Georgia	38.8
49	Hawaii	25.4
16	Idaho	36.6
25	Illinois	35.3
4	Indiana	39.8
10	Iowa	38.3
12	Kansas	37.9
36	Kentucky	33.5
41	Louisiana	32.3
42	Maine	32.0
16	Maryland	36.6
46	Massachusetts	30.3
2	Michigan	41.1
39	Minnesota	33.0
31	Mississippi	34.6
14	Missouri	37.2
22	Montana	36.3
6	Nebraska	38.9
45	Nevada	31.0
20	New Hampshire	36.4
4	New Jersey	39.8
16	New Mexico	36.6
48	New York	29.0
30	North Carolina	35.0
33	North Dakota	34.2
23	Ohio	35.8
1	Oklahoma	42.4
42	Oregon	32.0
25	Pennsylvania	35.3
37	Rhode Island	33.4
27	South Carolina	35.2
24	South Dakota	35.4
38	Tennessee	33.1
3	Texas	41.0
9	Utah	38.4
8	Vermont	38.6
13	Virginia	37.8
32	Washington	34.5
20	West Virginia	36.4
15	Wisconsin	37.1
34	Wyoming	33.8

RANK ORDER

RANK	STATE	PERCENT
1	Oklahoma	42.4
2	Michigan	41.1
3	Texas	41.0
4	Indiana	39.8
4	New Jersey	39.8
6	Nebraska	38.9
7	Georgia	38.8
8	Vermont	38.6
9	Utah	38.4
10	Iowa	38.3
11	Arkansas	38.0
12	Kansas	37.9
13	Virginia	37.8
14	Missouri	37.2
15	Wisconsin	37.1
16	Delaware	36.6
16	Idaho	36.6
16	Maryland	36.6
16	New Mexico	36.6
20	New Hampshire	36.4
20	West Virginia	36.4
22	Montana	36.3
23	Ohio	35.8
24	South Dakota	35.4
25	Illinois	35.3
25	Pennsylvania	35.3
27	Alabama	35.2
27	South Carolina	35.2
29	Colorado	35.1
30	North Carolina	35.0
31	Mississippi	34.6
32	Washington	34.5
33	North Dakota	34.2
34	Arizona	33.8
34	Wyoming	33.8
36	Kentucky	33.5
37	Rhode Island	33.4
38	Tennessee	33.1
39	Minnesota	33.0
40	California	32.5
41	Louisiana	32.3
42	Maine	32.0
42	Oregon	32.0
44	Connecticut	31.4
45	Nevada	31.0
46	Florida	30.3
46	Massachusetts	30.3
48	New York	29.0
49	Hawaii	25.4
50	Alaska	23.2

District of Columbia — 18.8

*Source: Morgan Quitno Press using data from U.S. Bureau of the Census, Governments Division
"State and Local Government Finances: 1999-00" (http://www.census.gov/govs/www/estimate00.html)
*Direct general expenditures for higher, secondary, elementary and "other" education as a percent of all direct
general expenditures. Includes capital outlays.*

Elementary and Secondary Education Expenditures by State and Local Governments in 2000
National Total = $365,180,872,000*

ALPHA ORDER

RANK	STATE	EXPENDITURES	% of USA
24	Alabama	$4,960,858,000	1.4%
43	Alaska	1,334,885,000	0.4%
23	Arizona	5,113,945,000	1.4%
33	Arkansas	2,605,399,000	0.7%
1	California	43,135,742,000	11.8%
22	Colorado	5,183,401,000	1.4%
21	Connecticut	5,218,085,000	1.4%
46	Delaware	1,005,097,000	0.3%
4	Florida	16,808,361,000	4.6%
10	Georgia	10,594,876,000	2.9%
44	Hawaii	1,144,959,000	0.3%
41	Idaho	1,405,863,000	0.4%
5	Illinois	16,465,749,000	4.5%
16	Indiana	7,351,414,000	2.0%
30	Iowa	3,621,038,000	1.0%
31	Kansas	3,081,647,000	0.8%
28	Kentucky	3,948,267,000	1.1%
26	Louisiana	4,723,642,000	1.3%
39	Maine	1,670,848,000	0.5%
18	Maryland	6,719,105,000	1.8%
13	Massachusetts	8,710,178,000	2.4%
7	Michigan	15,094,920,000	4.1%
17	Minnesota	7,163,686,000	2.0%
32	Mississippi	2,939,690,000	0.8%
19	Missouri	6,474,946,000	1.8%
45	Montana	1,036,922,000	0.3%
38	Nebraska	2,068,284,000	0.6%
35	Nevada	2,308,689,000	0.6%
40	New Hampshire	1,528,031,000	0.4%
8	New Jersey	14,861,725,000	4.1%
37	New Mexico	2,133,425,000	0.6%
2	New York	33,237,694,000	9.1%
12	North Carolina	9,099,218,000	2.5%
50	North Dakota	742,408,000	0.2%
9	Ohio	14,494,833,000	4.0%
29	Oklahoma	3,811,679,000	1.0%
27	Oregon	4,223,664,000	1.2%
6	Pennsylvania	16,353,408,000	4.5%
42	Rhode Island	1,346,401,000	0.4%
25	South Carolina	4,830,207,000	1.3%
48	South Dakota	862,172,000	0.2%
20	Tennessee	5,699,080,000	1.6%
3	Texas	28,404,620,000	7.8%
34	Utah	2,414,295,000	0.7%
47	Vermont	881,539,000	0.2%
11	Virginia	9,113,644,000	2.5%
15	Washington	7,667,136,000	2.1%
36	West Virginia	2,147,891,000	0.6%
14	Wisconsin	7,792,624,000	2.1%
49	Wyoming	755,735,000	0.2%

RANK ORDER

RANK	STATE	EXPENDITURES	% of USA
1	California	$43,135,742,000	11.8%
2	New York	33,237,694,000	9.1%
3	Texas	28,404,620,000	7.8%
4	Florida	16,808,361,000	4.6%
5	Illinois	16,465,749,000	4.5%
6	Pennsylvania	16,353,408,000	4.5%
7	Michigan	15,094,920,000	4.1%
8	New Jersey	14,861,725,000	4.1%
9	Ohio	14,494,833,000	4.0%
10	Georgia	10,594,876,000	2.9%
11	Virginia	9,113,644,000	2.5%
12	North Carolina	9,099,218,000	2.5%
13	Massachusetts	8,710,178,000	2.4%
14	Wisconsin	7,792,624,000	2.1%
15	Washington	7,667,136,000	2.1%
16	Indiana	7,351,414,000	2.0%
17	Minnesota	7,163,686,000	2.0%
18	Maryland	6,719,105,000	1.8%
19	Missouri	6,474,946,000	1.8%
20	Tennessee	5,699,080,000	1.6%
21	Connecticut	5,218,085,000	1.4%
22	Colorado	5,183,401,000	1.4%
23	Arizona	5,113,945,000	1.4%
24	Alabama	4,960,858,000	1.4%
25	South Carolina	4,830,207,000	1.3%
26	Louisiana	4,723,642,000	1.3%
27	Oregon	4,223,664,000	1.2%
28	Kentucky	3,948,267,000	1.1%
29	Oklahoma	3,811,679,000	1.0%
30	Iowa	3,621,038,000	1.0%
31	Kansas	3,081,647,000	0.8%
32	Mississippi	2,939,690,000	0.8%
33	Arkansas	2,605,399,000	0.7%
34	Utah	2,414,295,000	0.7%
35	Nevada	2,308,689,000	0.6%
36	West Virginia	2,147,891,000	0.6%
37	New Mexico	2,133,425,000	0.6%
38	Nebraska	2,068,284,000	0.6%
39	Maine	1,670,848,000	0.5%
40	New Hampshire	1,528,031,000	0.4%
41	Idaho	1,405,863,000	0.4%
42	Rhode Island	1,346,401,000	0.4%
43	Alaska	1,334,885,000	0.4%
44	Hawaii	1,144,959,000	0.3%
45	Montana	1,036,922,000	0.3%
46	Delaware	1,005,097,000	0.3%
47	Vermont	881,539,000	0.2%
48	South Dakota	862,172,000	0.2%
49	Wyoming	755,735,000	0.2%
50	North Dakota	742,408,000	0.2%
	District of Columbia	888,947,000	0.2%

Source: U.S. Bureau of the Census, Governments Division
  "State and Local Government Finances: 1999-00" (http://www.census.gov/govs/www/estimate00.html)
*Direct general expenditures. Includes capital outlays.

Per Capita State and Local Government Expenditures for Elementary and Secondary Education in 2000
National Per Capita = $1,294*

RANK	STATE	PER CAPITA
39	Alabama	$1,114
1	Alaska	2,127
47	Arizona	990
49	Arkansas	973
21	California	1,268
29	Colorado	1,198
5	Connecticut	1,529
19	Delaware	1,278
44	Florida	1,047
16	Georgia	1,287
50	Hawaii	944
41	Idaho	1,082
13	Illinois	1,324
26	Indiana	1,207
23	Iowa	1,236
35	Kansas	1,145
48	Kentucky	975
43	Louisiana	1,057
14	Maine	1,308
22	Maryland	1,265
10	Massachusetts	1,369
6	Michigan	1,516
7	Minnesota	1,452
45	Mississippi	1,032
33	Missouri	1,155
34	Montana	1,148
26	Nebraska	1,207
36	Nevada	1,144
24	New Hampshire	1,232
2	New Jersey	1,762
31	New Mexico	1,171
3	New York	1,749
38	North Carolina	1,126
32	North Dakota	1,158
20	Ohio	1,276
40	Oklahoma	1,103
25	Oregon	1,231
12	Pennsylvania	1,331
18	Rhode Island	1,281
28	South Carolina	1,200
37	South Dakota	1,141
46	Tennessee	999
11	Texas	1,355
42	Utah	1,076
9	Vermont	1,445
17	Virginia	1,283
15	Washington	1,297
30	West Virginia	1,188
8	Wisconsin	1,450
4	Wyoming	1,530

RANK	STATE	PER CAPITA
1	Alaska	$2,127
2	New Jersey	1,762
3	New York	1,749
4	Wyoming	1,530
5	Connecticut	1,529
6	Michigan	1,516
7	Minnesota	1,452
8	Wisconsin	1,450
9	Vermont	1,445
10	Massachusetts	1,369
11	Texas	1,355
12	Pennsylvania	1,331
13	Illinois	1,324
14	Maine	1,308
15	Washington	1,297
16	Georgia	1,287
17	Virginia	1,283
18	Rhode Island	1,281
19	Delaware	1,278
20	Ohio	1,276
21	California	1,268
22	Maryland	1,265
23	Iowa	1,236
24	New Hampshire	1,232
25	Oregon	1,231
26	Indiana	1,207
26	Nebraska	1,207
28	South Carolina	1,200
29	Colorado	1,198
30	West Virginia	1,188
31	New Mexico	1,171
32	North Dakota	1,158
33	Missouri	1,155
34	Montana	1,148
35	Kansas	1,145
36	Nevada	1,144
37	South Dakota	1,141
38	North Carolina	1,126
39	Alabama	1,114
40	Oklahoma	1,103
41	Idaho	1,082
42	Utah	1,076
43	Louisiana	1,057
44	Florida	1,047
45	Mississippi	1,032
46	Tennessee	999
47	Arizona	990
48	Kentucky	975
49	Arkansas	973
50	Hawaii	944
	District of Columbia	1,555

Source: Morgan Quitno Press using data from U.S. Bureau of the Census, Governments Division
"State and Local Government Finances: 1999-00" (http://www.census.gov/govs/www/estimate00.html)
*Direct general expenditures. Includes capital outlays.

Expenditures for Elementary and Secondary Education
As a Percent of All State and Local Government Expenditures in 2000
National Percent = 24.3%*

ALPHA ORDER

RANK	STATE	PERCENT
36	Alabama	22.5
49	Alaska	17.6
39	Arizona	22.0
27	Arkansas	23.6
39	California	22.0
30	Colorado	23.0
19	Connecticut	24.4
42	Delaware	21.4
38	Florida	22.3
3	Georgia	27.8
50	Hawaii	15.7
21	Idaho	24.1
9	Illinois	25.6
9	Indiana	25.6
28	Iowa	23.3
23	Kansas	23.9
47	Kentucky	20.8
43	Louisiana	21.2
22	Maine	24.0
18	Maryland	24.5
29	Massachusetts	23.1
5	Michigan	27.6
30	Minnesota	23.0
44	Mississippi	21.1
8	Missouri	26.1
32	Montana	22.9
17	Nebraska	24.6
25	Nevada	23.7
6	New Hampshire	27.0
1	New Jersey	31.5
44	New Mexico	21.1
25	New York	23.7
36	North Carolina	22.5
48	North Dakota	20.2
13	Ohio	25.1
4	Oklahoma	27.7
46	Oregon	20.9
15	Pennsylvania	24.8
20	Rhode Island	24.2
24	South Carolina	23.8
14	South Dakota	25.0
35	Tennessee	22.6
2	Texas	29.7
41	Utah	21.9
9	Vermont	25.6
7	Virginia	26.2
32	Washington	22.9
16	West Virginia	24.7
12	Wisconsin	25.3
34	Wyoming	22.7

RANK ORDER

RANK	STATE	PERCENT
1	New Jersey	31.5
2	Texas	29.7
3	Georgia	27.8
4	Oklahoma	27.7
5	Michigan	27.6
6	New Hampshire	27.0
7	Virginia	26.2
8	Missouri	26.1
9	Illinois	25.6
9	Indiana	25.6
9	Vermont	25.6
12	Wisconsin	25.3
13	Ohio	25.1
14	South Dakota	25.0
15	Pennsylvania	24.8
16	West Virginia	24.7
17	Nebraska	24.6
18	Maryland	24.5
19	Connecticut	24.4
20	Rhode Island	24.2
21	Idaho	24.1
22	Maine	24.0
23	Kansas	23.9
24	South Carolina	23.8
25	Nevada	23.7
25	New York	23.7
27	Arkansas	23.6
28	Iowa	23.3
29	Massachusetts	23.1
30	Colorado	23.0
30	Minnesota	23.0
32	Montana	22.9
32	Washington	22.9
34	Wyoming	22.7
35	Tennessee	22.6
36	Alabama	22.5
36	North Carolina	22.5
38	Florida	22.3
39	Arizona	22.0
39	California	22.0
41	Utah	21.9
42	Delaware	21.4
43	Louisiana	21.2
44	Mississippi	21.1
44	New Mexico	21.1
46	Oregon	20.9
47	Kentucky	20.8
48	North Dakota	20.2
49	Alaska	17.6
50	Hawaii	15.7
	District of Columbia	17.3

Source: Morgan Quitno Press using data from U.S. Bureau of the Census, Governments Division
"State and Local Government Finances: 1999-00" (http://www.census.gov/govs/www/estimate00.html)
*Direct general expenditures for elementary and secondary education as a percent of all direct general
expenditures. Includes capital outlays.

Estimated Per Pupil Public Elementary and Secondary School Current Expenditures in 2003
National Per Pupil = $7,833*

<u>ALPHA ORDER</u>

RANK	STATE	PER PUPIL
47	Alabama	$5,418
8	Alaska	9,594
48	Arizona	5,197
46	Arkansas	5,789
28	California	7,237
31	Colorado	7,200
2	Connecticut	11,263
5	Delaware	10,270
40	Florida	6,411
17	Georgia	8,238
23	Hawaii	7,455
41	Idaho	6,378
9	Illinois	9,376
16	Indiana	8,307
34	Iowa	6,974
22	Kansas	7,606
27	Kentucky	7,322
38	Louisiana	6,698
10	Maine	9,318
19	Maryland	8,124
4	Massachusetts	10,691
14	Michigan	8,642
20	Minnesota	7,782
45	Mississippi	5,822
33	Missouri	7,078
26	Montana	7,388
30	Nebraska	7,203
43	Nevada	6,062
18	New Hampshire	8,151
3	New Jersey	11,119
36	New Mexico	6,834
1	New York	11,507
39	North Carolina	6,547
50	North Dakota	4,773
21	Ohio	7,611
37	Oklahoma	6,829
29	Oregon	7,229
15	Pennsylvania	8,329
7	Rhode Island	9,889
24	South Carolina	7,447
35	South Dakota	6,913
44	Tennessee	6,048
32	Texas	7,152
49	Utah	4,847
6	Vermont	9,957
42	Virginia	6,316
25	Washington	7,420
11	West Virginia	9,119
13	Wisconsin	9,015
12	Wyoming	9,030

<u>RANK ORDER</u>

RANK	STATE	PER PUPIL
1	New York	$11,507
2	Connecticut	11,263
3	New Jersey	11,119
4	Massachusetts	10,691
5	Delaware	10,270
6	Vermont	9,957
7	Rhode Island	9,889
8	Alaska	9,594
9	Illinois	9,376
10	Maine	9,318
11	West Virginia	9,119
12	Wyoming	9,030
13	Wisconsin	9,015
14	Michigan	8,642
15	Pennsylvania	8,329
16	Indiana	8,307
17	Georgia	8,238
18	New Hampshire	8,151
19	Maryland	8,124
20	Minnesota	7,782
21	Ohio	7,611
22	Kansas	7,606
23	Hawaii	7,455
24	South Carolina	7,447
25	Washington	7,420
26	Montana	7,388
27	Kentucky	7,322
28	California	7,237
29	Oregon	7,229
30	Nebraska	7,203
31	Colorado	7,200
32	Texas	7,152
33	Missouri	7,078
34	Iowa	6,974
35	South Dakota	6,913
36	New Mexico	6,834
37	Oklahoma	6,829
38	Louisiana	6,698
39	North Carolina	6,547
40	Florida	6,411
41	Idaho	6,378
42	Virginia	6,316
43	Nevada	6,062
44	Tennessee	6,048
45	Mississippi	5,822
46	Arkansas	5,789
47	Alabama	5,418
48	Arizona	5,197
49	Utah	4,847
50	North Dakota	4,773
	District of Columbia	13,355

Source: National Education Association, Washington, D.C.

"Rankings & Estimates, May 2003" (Copyright © 2003, NEA, used with permission)

*Estimates for school year 2002-2003. Based on student membership.

Higher Education Expenditures by State and Local Governments in 2000

National Total = $134,351,694,000*

ALPHA ORDER

RANK	STATE	EXPENDITURES	% of USA
21	Alabama	$2,373,695,000	1.8%
47	Alaska	374,847,000	0.3%
19	Arizona	2,468,740,000	1.8%
34	Arkansas	1,240,896,000	0.9%
1	California	18,009,807,000	13.4%
18	Colorado	2,513,568,000	1.9%
35	Connecticut	1,195,717,000	0.9%
41	Delaware	554,220,000	0.4%
7	Florida	5,067,239,000	3.8%
13	Georgia	3,363,326,000	2.5%
38	Hawaii	689,072,000	0.5%
40	Idaho	629,656,000	0.5%
8	Illinois	5,050,208,000	3.8%
10	Indiana	3,617,732,000	2.7%
26	Iowa	2,031,922,000	1.5%
30	Kansas	1,666,538,000	1.2%
25	Kentucky	2,033,092,000	1.5%
27	Louisiana	1,960,437,000	1.5%
44	Maine	462,766,000	0.3%
16	Maryland	2,891,786,000	2.2%
23	Massachusetts	2,104,013,000	1.6%
3	Michigan	6,849,901,000	5.1%
17	Minnesota	2,613,362,000	1.9%
32	Mississippi	1,561,995,000	1.2%
22	Missouri	2,281,940,000	1.7%
42	Montana	479,211,000	0.4%
36	Nebraska	1,081,544,000	0.8%
39	Nevada	656,557,000	0.5%
43	New Hampshire	464,297,000	0.3%
12	New Jersey	3,484,316,000	2.6%
33	New Mexico	1,408,786,000	1.0%
4	New York	6,095,308,000	4.5%
9	North Carolina	4,491,586,000	3.3%
45	North Dakota	461,052,000	0.3%
6	Ohio	5,076,566,000	3.8%
29	Oklahoma	1,782,356,000	1.3%
24	Oregon	2,038,504,000	1.5%
5	Pennsylvania	5,106,609,000	3.8%
46	Rhode Island	400,866,000	0.3%
28	South Carolina	1,943,782,000	1.4%
50	South Dakota	305,034,000	0.2%
20	Tennessee	2,379,444,000	1.8%
2	Texas	9,795,418,000	7.3%
31	Utah	1,631,363,000	1.2%
48	Vermont	371,226,000	0.3%
11	Virginia	3,502,053,000	2.6%
14	Washington	3,333,965,000	2.5%
37	West Virginia	836,971,000	0.6%
15	Wisconsin	3,227,670,000	2.4%
49	Wyoming	310,329,000	0.2%

RANK ORDER

RANK	STATE	EXPENDITURES	% of USA
1	California	$18,009,807,000	13.4%
2	Texas	9,795,418,000	7.3%
3	Michigan	6,849,901,000	5.1%
4	New York	6,095,308,000	4.5%
5	Pennsylvania	5,106,609,000	3.8%
6	Ohio	5,076,566,000	3.8%
7	Florida	5,067,239,000	3.8%
8	Illinois	5,050,208,000	3.8%
9	North Carolina	4,491,586,000	3.3%
10	Indiana	3,617,732,000	2.7%
11	Virginia	3,502,053,000	2.6%
12	New Jersey	3,484,316,000	2.6%
13	Georgia	3,363,326,000	2.5%
14	Washington	3,333,965,000	2.5%
15	Wisconsin	3,227,670,000	2.4%
16	Maryland	2,891,786,000	2.2%
17	Minnesota	2,613,362,000	1.9%
18	Colorado	2,513,568,000	1.9%
19	Arizona	2,468,740,000	1.8%
20	Tennessee	2,379,444,000	1.8%
21	Alabama	2,373,695,000	1.8%
22	Missouri	2,281,940,000	1.7%
23	Massachusetts	2,104,013,000	1.6%
24	Oregon	2,038,504,000	1.5%
25	Kentucky	2,033,092,000	1.5%
26	Iowa	2,031,922,000	1.5%
27	Louisiana	1,960,437,000	1.5%
28	South Carolina	1,943,782,000	1.4%
29	Oklahoma	1,782,356,000	1.3%
30	Kansas	1,666,538,000	1.2%
31	Utah	1,631,363,000	1.2%
32	Mississippi	1,561,995,000	1.2%
33	New Mexico	1,408,786,000	1.0%
34	Arkansas	1,240,896,000	0.9%
35	Connecticut	1,195,717,000	0.9%
36	Nebraska	1,081,544,000	0.8%
37	West Virginia	836,971,000	0.6%
38	Hawaii	689,072,000	0.5%
39	Nevada	656,557,000	0.5%
40	Idaho	629,656,000	0.5%
41	Delaware	554,220,000	0.4%
42	Montana	479,211,000	0.4%
43	New Hampshire	464,297,000	0.3%
44	Maine	462,766,000	0.3%
45	North Dakota	461,052,000	0.3%
46	Rhode Island	400,866,000	0.3%
47	Alaska	374,847,000	0.3%
48	Vermont	371,226,000	0.3%
49	Wyoming	310,329,000	0.2%
50	South Dakota	305,034,000	0.2%
	District of Columbia	80,406,000	0.1%

Source: U.S. Bureau of the Census, Governments Division
"State and Local Government Finances: 1999-00" (http://www.census.gov/govs/www/estimate00.html)
**Direct general expenditures. Includes capital outlays.*

Per Capita State and Local Government Expenditures for
Higher Education in 2000
National Per Capita = $476*

<u>ALPHA ORDER</u>

RANK	STATE	PER CAPITA
21	Alabama	$533
12	Alaska	597
30	Arizona	478
32	Arkansas	463
22	California	530
15	Colorado	581
46	Connecticut	350
4	Delaware	705
50	Florida	316
39	Georgia	408
16	Hawaii	568
28	Idaho	484
41	Illinois	406
13	Indiana	594
5	Iowa	694
9	Kansas	619
26	Kentucky	502
35	Louisiana	439
45	Maine	362
20	Maryland	544
47	Massachusetts	331
6	Michigan	688
22	Minnesota	530
19	Mississippi	548
40	Missouri	407
22	Montana	530
7	Nebraska	631
48	Nevada	325
44	New Hampshire	374
38	New Jersey	413
1	New Mexico	773
49	New York	321
18	North Carolina	556
3	North Dakota	719
34	Ohio	447
25	Oklahoma	516
13	Oregon	594
37	Pennsylvania	416
43	Rhode Island	382
29	South Carolina	483
42	South Dakota	404
36	Tennessee	417
31	Texas	467
2	Utah	727
10	Vermont	609
27	Virginia	493
17	Washington	564
32	West Virginia	463
11	Wisconsin	601
8	Wyoming	628

<u>RANK ORDER</u>

RANK	STATE	PER CAPITA
1	New Mexico	$773
2	Utah	727
3	North Dakota	719
4	Delaware	705
5	Iowa	694
6	Michigan	688
7	Nebraska	631
8	Wyoming	628
9	Kansas	619
10	Vermont	609
11	Wisconsin	601
12	Alaska	597
13	Indiana	594
13	Oregon	594
15	Colorado	581
16	Hawaii	568
17	Washington	564
18	North Carolina	556
19	Mississippi	548
20	Maryland	544
21	Alabama	533
22	California	530
22	Minnesota	530
22	Montana	530
25	Oklahoma	516
26	Kentucky	502
27	Virginia	493
28	Idaho	484
29	South Carolina	483
30	Arizona	478
31	Texas	467
32	Arkansas	463
32	West Virginia	463
34	Ohio	447
35	Louisiana	439
36	Tennessee	417
37	Pennsylvania	416
38	New Jersey	413
39	Georgia	408
40	Missouri	407
41	Illinois	406
42	South Dakota	404
43	Rhode Island	382
44	New Hampshire	374
45	Maine	362
46	Connecticut	350
47	Massachusetts	331
48	Nevada	325
49	New York	321
50	Florida	316
	District of Columbia	141

Source: Morgan Quitno Press using data from U.S. Bureau of the Census, Governments Division
"State and Local Government Finances: 1999-00" (http://www.census.gov/govs/www/estimate00.html)
**Direct general expenditures. Includes capital outlays.*

Expenditures for Higher Education as a Percent
Of All State and Local Government Expenditures in 2000
National Percent = 8.9%*

<u>ALPHA ORDER</u>

RANK	STATE	PERCENT
15	Alabama	10.8
49	Alaska	4.9
19	Arizona	10.6
11	Arkansas	11.2
32	California	9.2
11	Colorado	11.2
47	Connecticut	5.6
10	Delaware	11.8
44	Florida	6.7
35	Georgia	8.8
29	Hawaii	9.5
15	Idaho	10.8
40	Illinois	7.8
7	Indiana	12.6
3	Iowa	13.1
4	Kansas	12.9
18	Kentucky	10.7
35	Louisiana	8.8
44	Maine	6.7
21	Maryland	10.5
47	Massachusetts	5.6
9	Michigan	12.5
38	Minnesota	8.4
11	Mississippi	11.2
32	Missouri	9.2
19	Montana	10.6
4	Nebraska	12.9
44	Nevada	6.7
39	New Hampshire	8.2
42	New Jersey	7.4
2	New Mexico	14.0
50	New York	4.4
14	North Carolina	11.1
7	North Dakota	12.6
35	Ohio	8.8
4	Oklahoma	12.9
24	Oregon	10.1
40	Pennsylvania	7.8
43	Rhode Island	7.2
27	South Carolina	9.6
34	South Dakota	8.9
30	Tennessee	9.4
23	Texas	10.2
1	Utah	14.8
15	Vermont	10.8
24	Virginia	10.1
26	Washington	10.0
27	West Virginia	9.6
21	Wisconsin	10.5
31	Wyoming	9.3

<u>RANK ORDER</u>

RANK	STATE	PERCENT
1	Utah	14.8
2	New Mexico	14.0
3	Iowa	13.1
4	Kansas	12.9
4	Nebraska	12.9
4	Oklahoma	12.9
7	Indiana	12.6
7	North Dakota	12.6
9	Michigan	12.5
10	Delaware	11.8
11	Arkansas	11.2
11	Colorado	11.2
11	Mississippi	11.2
14	North Carolina	11.1
15	Alabama	10.8
15	Idaho	10.8
15	Vermont	10.8
18	Kentucky	10.7
19	Arizona	10.6
19	Montana	10.6
21	Maryland	10.5
21	Wisconsin	10.5
23	Texas	10.2
24	Oregon	10.1
24	Virginia	10.1
26	Washington	10.0
27	South Carolina	9.6
27	West Virginia	9.6
29	Hawaii	9.5
30	Tennessee	9.4
31	Wyoming	9.3
32	California	9.2
32	Missouri	9.2
34	South Dakota	8.9
35	Georgia	8.8
35	Louisiana	8.8
35	Ohio	8.8
38	Minnesota	8.4
39	New Hampshire	8.2
40	Illinois	7.8
40	Pennsylvania	7.8
42	New Jersey	7.4
43	Rhode Island	7.2
44	Florida	6.7
44	Maine	6.7
44	Nevada	6.7
47	Connecticut	5.6
47	Massachusetts	5.6
49	Alaska	4.9
50	New York	4.4
	District of Columbia	1.6

Average Faculty Salary at Institutions of Higher Education in 2000

National Average = $55,888*

<u>ALPHA ORDER</u>

RANK	STATE	AVERAGE SALARY
37	Alabama	$47,349
26	Alaska	51,825
11	Arizona	58,430
47	Arkansas	43,523
3	California	65,824
20	Colorado	53,462
2	Connecticut	66,458
5	Delaware	62,647
27	Florida	51,567
19	Georgia	53,666
14	Hawaii	55,776
38	Idaho	47,115
10	Illinois	58,447
21	Indiana	53,388
24	Iowa	51,973
43	Kansas	46,347
36	Kentucky	47,784
39	Louisiana	47,017
31	Maine	49,379
13	Maryland	55,807
4	Massachusetts	65,572
9	Michigan	59,084
23	Minnesota	52,694
44	Mississippi	45,508
28	Missouri	51,247
45	Montana	45,486
35	Nebraska	48,265
12	Nevada	56,656
18	New Hampshire	54,322
1	New Jersey	66,505
42	New Mexico	46,684
6	New York	62,350
22	North Carolina	53,227
50	North Dakota	40,068
15	Ohio	55,098
41	Oklahoma	46,939
32	Oregon	48,812
8	Pennsylvania	59,915
7	Rhode Island	60,482
40	South Carolina	46,991
49	South Dakota	41,728
34	Tennessee	48,513
29	Texas	51,192
25	Utah	51,949
33	Vermont	48,723
16	Virginia	54,864
30	Washington	50,256
46	West Virginia	45,239
17	Wisconsin	54,618
48	Wyoming	42,507

<u>RANK ORDER</u>

RANK	STATE	AVERAGE SALARY
1	New Jersey	$66,505
2	Connecticut	66,458
3	California	65,824
4	Massachusetts	65,572
5	Delaware	62,647
6	New York	62,350
7	Rhode Island	60,482
8	Pennsylvania	59,915
9	Michigan	59,084
10	Illinois	58,447
11	Arizona	58,430
12	Nevada	56,656
13	Maryland	55,807
14	Hawaii	55,776
15	Ohio	55,098
16	Virginia	54,864
17	Wisconsin	54,618
18	New Hampshire	54,322
19	Georgia	53,666
20	Colorado	53,462
21	Indiana	53,388
22	North Carolina	53,227
23	Minnesota	52,694
24	Iowa	51,973
25	Utah	51,949
26	Alaska	51,825
27	Florida	51,567
28	Missouri	51,247
29	Texas	51,192
30	Washington	50,256
31	Maine	49,379
32	Oregon	48,812
33	Vermont	48,723
34	Tennessee	48,513
35	Nebraska	48,265
36	Kentucky	47,784
37	Alabama	47,349
38	Idaho	47,115
39	Louisiana	47,017
40	South Carolina	46,991
41	Oklahoma	46,939
42	New Mexico	46,684
43	Kansas	46,347
44	Mississippi	45,508
45	Montana	45,486
46	West Virginia	45,239
47	Arkansas	43,523
48	Wyoming	42,507
49	South Dakota	41,728
50	North Dakota	40,068
	District of Columbia	66,937

Source: U.S. Department of Education, National Center for Education Statistics
"Digest of Education Statistics 2002" (NCES 2003060, June 2003)
*For 1999-2000 school year. For full-time instructional faculty on 9-month contracts at four-year and two-year public and private degree-granting institutions.

Average Student Costs at Public Institutions of Higher Education in 2002

National Average = $9,199*

ALPHA ORDER

RANK	STATE	AVERAGE COSTS
37	Alabama	$7,654
20	Alaska	9,258
29	Arizona	8,222
45	Arkansas	7,302
12	California	10,320
23	Colorado	8,808
8	Connecticut	11,058
9	Delaware	10,889
26	Florida	8,361
32	Georgia	7,915
31	Hawaii	7,987
46	Idaho	7,163
14	Illinois	10,194
18	Indiana	9,783
28	Iowa	8,253
47	Kansas	6,987
44	Kentucky	7,370
49	Louisiana	6,689
13	Maine	10,259
6	Maryland	11,385
19	Massachusetts	9,370
11	Michigan	10,565
21	Minnesota	9,080
39	Mississippi	7,599
24	Missouri	8,672
27	Montana	8,309
35	Nebraska	7,731
25	Nevada	8,570
3	New Hampshire	12,348
2	New Jersey	12,854
40	New Mexico	7,587
10	New York	10,777
36	North Carolina	7,667
48	North Dakota	6,843
7	Ohio	11,179
50	Oklahoma	6,296
16	Oregon	10,063
4	Pennsylvania	11,861
5	Rhode Island	11,610
15	South Carolina	10,077
41	South Dakota	7,469
34	Tennessee	7,781
30	Texas	8,062
43	Utah	7,393
1	Vermont	13,450
22	Virginia	8,988
17	Washington	9,986
38	West Virginia	7,625
33	Wisconsin	7,786
42	Wyoming	7,421

RANK ORDER

RANK	STATE	AVERAGE COSTS
1	Vermont	$13,450
2	New Jersey	12,854
3	New Hampshire	12,348
4	Pennsylvania	11,861
5	Rhode Island	11,610
6	Maryland	11,385
7	Ohio	11,179
8	Connecticut	11,058
9	Delaware	10,889
10	New York	10,777
11	Michigan	10,565
12	California	10,320
13	Maine	10,259
14	Illinois	10,194
15	South Carolina	10,077
16	Oregon	10,063
17	Washington	9,986
18	Indiana	9,783
19	Massachusetts	9,370
20	Alaska	9,258
21	Minnesota	9,080
22	Virginia	8,988
23	Colorado	8,808
24	Missouri	8,672
25	Nevada	8,570
26	Florida	8,361
27	Montana	8,309
28	Iowa	8,253
29	Arizona	8,222
30	Texas	8,062
31	Hawaii	7,987
32	Georgia	7,915
33	Wisconsin	7,786
34	Tennessee	7,781
35	Nebraska	7,731
36	North Carolina	7,667
37	Alabama	7,654
38	West Virginia	7,625
39	Mississippi	7,599
40	New Mexico	7,587
41	South Dakota	7,469
42	Wyoming	7,421
43	Utah	7,393
44	Kentucky	7,370
45	Arkansas	7,302
46	Idaho	7,163
47	Kansas	6,987
48	North Dakota	6,843
49	Louisiana	6,689
50	Oklahoma	6,296
	District of Columbia**	NA

Source: U.S. Department of Education, National Center for Education Statistics
"Digest of Education Statistics 2002" (NCES 2003060, June 2003)
Data for 2001-2002 school year. Based on average in-state tuition, room and board and fees for full-time students in public four-year institutions for an entire academic year.

**Not available.*

Average Student Costs at Private Institutions of Higher Education in 2002

National Average = $22,968*

ALPHA ORDER

RANK	STATE	AVERAGE COSTS
42	Alabama	$15,269
41	Alaska	15,675
44	Arizona	14,510
45	Arkansas	14,414
7	California	26,203
11	Colorado	24,351
2	Connecticut	29,065
43	Delaware	14,698
23	Florida	20,978
21	Georgia	21,124
36	Hawaii	16,627
48	Idaho	10,163
15	Illinois	22,844
17	Indiana	22,545
25	Iowa	20,341
35	Kansas	16,653
40	Kentucky	15,710
14	Louisiana	23,050
12	Maine	24,132
4	Maryland	27,108
1	Massachusetts	29,970
34	Michigan	17,046
18	Minnesota	22,420
46	Mississippi	14,203
30	Missouri	18,787
39	Montana	15,929
29	Nebraska	18,837
26	Nevada	19,719
6	New Hampshire	26,482
9	New Jersey	25,203
24	New Mexico	20,508
5	New York	26,509
22	North Carolina	21,024
47	North Dakota	11,840
19	Ohio	22,134
37	Oklahoma	16,492
10	Oregon	24,428
8	Pennsylvania	26,002
3	Rhode Island	27,192
31	South Carolina	18,435
38	South Dakota	15,935
28	Tennessee	19,143
33	Texas	18,185
49	Utah	8,992
13	Vermont	23,205
27	Virginia	19,541
16	Washington	22,612
32	West Virginia	18,329
20	Wisconsin	21,330
NA	Wyoming**	NA

RANK ORDER

RANK	STATE	AVERAGE COSTS
1	Massachusetts	$29,970
2	Connecticut	29,065
3	Rhode Island	27,192
4	Maryland	27,108
5	New York	26,509
6	New Hampshire	26,482
7	California	26,203
8	Pennsylvania	26,002
9	New Jersey	25,203
10	Oregon	24,428
11	Colorado	24,351
12	Maine	24,132
13	Vermont	23,205
14	Louisiana	23,050
15	Illinois	22,844
16	Washington	22,612
17	Indiana	22,545
18	Minnesota	22,420
19	Ohio	22,134
20	Wisconsin	21,330
21	Georgia	21,124
22	North Carolina	21,024
23	Florida	20,978
24	New Mexico	20,508
25	Iowa	20,341
26	Nevada	19,719
27	Virginia	19,541
28	Tennessee	19,143
29	Nebraska	18,837
30	Missouri	18,787
31	South Carolina	18,435
32	West Virginia	18,329
33	Texas	18,185
34	Michigan	17,046
35	Kansas	16,653
36	Hawaii	16,627
37	Oklahoma	16,492
38	South Dakota	15,935
39	Montana	15,929
40	Kentucky	15,710
41	Alaska	15,675
42	Alabama	15,269
43	Delaware	14,698
44	Arizona	14,510
45	Arkansas	14,414
46	Mississippi	14,203
47	North Dakota	11,840
48	Idaho	10,163
49	Utah	8,992
NA	Wyoming**	NA
	District of Columbia	28,310

Source: U.S. Department of Education, National Center for Education Statistics
    "Digest of Education Statistics 2002" (NCES 2003060, June 2003)
*Data for 2001-2002 school year. Based on average in-state tuition, room and board and fees for full-time students in private four-year institutions for an entire academic year.
**Not available or not applicable.

Institutions of Higher Education in 2002

National Total = 4,197 Institutions*

<u>ALPHA ORDER</u>

RANK	STATE	INSTITUTIONS	% of USA
20	Alabama	75	1.8%
50	Alaska	8	0.2%
22	Arizona	74	1.8%
31	Arkansas	46	1.1%
1	California	413	9.8%
20	Colorado	75	1.8%
32	Connecticut	45	1.1%
48	Delaware	10	0.2%
7	Florida	166	4.0%
8	Georgia	128	3.0%
43	Hawaii	21	0.5%
46	Idaho	14	0.3%
5	Illinois	184	4.4%
15	Indiana	98	2.3%
24	Iowa	63	1.5%
25	Kansas	62	1.5%
19	Kentucky	79	1.9%
17	Louisiana	85	2.0%
37	Maine	33	0.8%
25	Maryland	62	1.5%
10	Massachusetts	119	2.8%
13	Michigan	107	2.5%
12	Minnesota	114	2.7%
34	Mississippi	41	1.0%
10	Missouri	119	2.8%
41	Montana	24	0.6%
35	Nebraska	38	0.9%
45	Nevada	15	0.4%
40	New Hampshire	25	0.6%
28	New Jersey	57	1.4%
33	New Mexico	44	1.0%
2	New York	309	7.4%
9	North Carolina	121	2.9%
43	North Dakota	21	0.5%
6	Ohio	178	4.2%
30	Oklahoma	52	1.2%
28	Oregon	57	1.4%
3	Pennsylvania	260	6.2%
46	Rhode Island	14	0.3%
25	South Carolina	62	1.5%
39	South Dakota	26	0.6%
16	Tennessee	87	2.1%
4	Texas	198	4.7%
41	Utah	24	0.6%
38	Vermont	27	0.6%
14	Virginia	100	2.4%
18	Washington	80	1.9%
36	West Virginia	37	0.9%
23	Wisconsin	69	1.6%
49	Wyoming	9	0.2%

<u>RANK ORDER</u>

RANK	STATE	INSTITUTIONS	% of USA
1	California	413	9.8%
2	New York	309	7.4%
3	Pennsylvania	260	6.2%
4	Texas	198	4.7%
5	Illinois	184	4.4%
6	Ohio	178	4.2%
7	Florida	166	4.0%
8	Georgia	128	3.0%
9	North Carolina	121	2.9%
10	Massachusetts	119	2.8%
10	Missouri	119	2.8%
12	Minnesota	114	2.7%
13	Michigan	107	2.5%
14	Virginia	100	2.4%
15	Indiana	98	2.3%
16	Tennessee	87	2.1%
17	Louisiana	85	2.0%
18	Washington	80	1.9%
19	Kentucky	79	1.9%
20	Alabama	75	1.8%
20	Colorado	75	1.8%
22	Arizona	74	1.8%
23	Wisconsin	69	1.6%
24	Iowa	63	1.5%
25	Kansas	62	1.5%
25	Maryland	62	1.5%
25	South Carolina	62	1.5%
28	New Jersey	57	1.4%
28	Oregon	57	1.4%
30	Oklahoma	52	1.2%
31	Arkansas	46	1.1%
32	Connecticut	45	1.1%
33	New Mexico	44	1.0%
34	Mississippi	41	1.0%
35	Nebraska	38	0.9%
36	West Virginia	37	0.9%
37	Maine	33	0.8%
38	Vermont	27	0.6%
39	South Dakota	26	0.6%
40	New Hampshire	25	0.6%
41	Montana	24	0.6%
41	Utah	24	0.6%
43	Hawaii	21	0.5%
43	North Dakota	21	0.5%
45	Nevada	15	0.4%
46	Idaho	14	0.3%
46	Rhode Island	14	0.3%
48	Delaware	10	0.2%
49	Wyoming	9	0.2%
50	Alaska	8	0.2%
	District of Columbia	17	0.4%

Source: U.S. Department of Education, National Center for Education Statistics
"Digest of Education Statistics 2002" (NCES 2003060, June 2003)

*For 2001-02 school year. Consists of 2,364 four-year and 1,833 two-year public and private degree-granting institutions. Includes five U.S. Service Schools not shown by state.

Enrollment in Institutions of Higher Education in 2000

National Total = 15,312,289 Students*

ALPHA ORDER

RANK	STATE	STUDENTS	% of USA
23	Alabama	233,962	1.5%
50	Alaska	27,953	0.2%
13	Arizona	342,490	2.2%
34	Arkansas	115,172	0.8%
1	California	2,256,708	14.7%
22	Colorado	263,872	1.7%
32	Connecticut	161,243	1.1%
44	Delaware	43,897	0.3%
5	Florida	707,684	4.6%
12	Georgia	346,204	2.3%
42	Hawaii	60,182	0.4%
40	Idaho	65,594	0.4%
4	Illinois	743,918	4.9%
17	Indiana	314,334	2.1%
25	Iowa	188,974	1.2%
29	Kansas	179,968	1.2%
26	Kentucky	188,341	1.2%
24	Louisiana	223,800	1.5%
43	Maine	58,473	0.4%
20	Maryland	273,745	1.8%
9	Massachusetts	421,142	2.8%
7	Michigan	567,631	3.7%
19	Minnesota	293,445	1.9%
33	Mississippi	137,389	0.9%
15	Missouri	321,348	2.1%
46	Montana	42,240	0.3%
35	Nebraska	112,117	0.7%
37	Nevada	87,893	0.6%
41	New Hampshire	61,718	0.4%
14	New Jersey	335,945	2.2%
36	New Mexico	110,739	0.7%
2	New York	1,043,395	6.8%
10	North Carolina	404,652	2.6%
47	North Dakota	40,248	0.3%
8	Ohio	549,553	3.6%
30	Oklahoma	178,016	1.2%
28	Oregon	183,065	1.2%
6	Pennsylvania	609,521	4.0%
39	Rhode Island	75,450	0.5%
27	South Carolina	185,931	1.2%
45	South Dakota	43,221	0.3%
21	Tennessee	263,910	1.7%
3	Texas	1,033,973	6.8%
31	Utah	163,776	1.1%
48	Vermont	35,489	0.2%
11	Virginia	381,893	2.5%
16	Washington	320,840	2.1%
38	West Virginia	87,888	0.6%
18	Wisconsin	307,179	2.0%
49	Wyoming	30,004	0.2%

RANK ORDER

RANK	STATE	STUDENTS	% of USA
1	California	2,256,708	14.7%
2	New York	1,043,395	6.8%
3	Texas	1,033,973	6.8%
4	Illinois	743,918	4.9%
5	Florida	707,684	4.6%
6	Pennsylvania	609,521	4.0%
7	Michigan	567,631	3.7%
8	Ohio	549,553	3.6%
9	Massachusetts	421,142	2.8%
10	North Carolina	404,652	2.6%
11	Virginia	381,893	2.5%
12	Georgia	346,204	2.3%
13	Arizona	342,490	2.2%
14	New Jersey	335,945	2.2%
15	Missouri	321,348	2.1%
16	Washington	320,840	2.1%
17	Indiana	314,334	2.1%
18	Wisconsin	307,179	2.0%
19	Minnesota	293,445	1.9%
20	Maryland	273,745	1.8%
21	Tennessee	263,910	1.7%
22	Colorado	263,872	1.7%
23	Alabama	233,962	1.5%
24	Louisiana	223,800	1.5%
25	Iowa	188,974	1.2%
26	Kentucky	188,341	1.2%
27	South Carolina	185,931	1.2%
28	Oregon	183,065	1.2%
29	Kansas	179,968	1.2%
30	Oklahoma	178,016	1.2%
31	Utah	163,776	1.1%
32	Connecticut	161,243	1.1%
33	Mississippi	137,389	0.9%
34	Arkansas	115,172	0.8%
35	Nebraska	112,117	0.7%
36	New Mexico	110,739	0.7%
37	Nevada	87,893	0.6%
38	West Virginia	87,888	0.6%
39	Rhode Island	75,450	0.5%
40	Idaho	65,594	0.4%
41	New Hampshire	61,718	0.4%
42	Hawaii	60,182	0.4%
43	Maine	58,473	0.4%
44	Delaware	43,897	0.3%
45	South Dakota	43,221	0.3%
46	Montana	42,240	0.3%
47	North Dakota	40,248	0.3%
48	Vermont	35,489	0.2%
49	Wyoming	30,004	0.2%
50	Alaska	27,953	0.2%
	District of Columbia	72,689	0.5%

Source: U.S. Department of Education, National Center for Education Statistics
"Digest of Education Statistics 2002" (NCES 2003060, June 2003)
**Fall 2000 enrollment. Includes full-time and part-time students at Title IV eligible, degree-granting four-year and two-year institutions. National total includes 13,475 students at U.S. Service Schools.*

Enrollment Rate in Institutions of Higher Education in 2000

National Rate = 564 Students per 1,000 Population 18 to 24 Years Old*

ALPHA ORDER

RANK	STATE	RATE
29	Alabama	532
41	Alaska	488
4	Arizona	666
49	Arkansas	440
3	California	670
12	Colorado	613
18	Connecticut	594
21	Delaware	583
29	Florida	532
50	Georgia	413
31	Hawaii	524
43	Idaho	472
11	Illinois	614
34	Indiana	511
7	Iowa	634
5	Kansas	653
46	Kentucky	469
43	Louisiana	472
23	Maine	563
14	Maryland	607
1	Massachusetts	727
13	Michigan	609
9	Minnesota	624
48	Mississippi	442
16	Missouri	600
39	Montana	493
6	Nebraska	643
40	Nevada	489
17	New Hampshire	597
38	New Jersey	496
9	New Mexico	624
19	New York	591
36	North Carolina	502
28	North Dakota	550
32	Ohio	520
37	Oklahoma	499
25	Oregon	558
26	Pennsylvania	557
2	Rhode Island	708
47	South Carolina	456
26	South Dakota	557
42	Tennessee	481
45	Texas	470
33	Utah	516
8	Vermont	627
24	Virginia	562
22	Washington	574
35	West Virginia	510
20	Wisconsin	590
15	Wyoming	601

RANK ORDER

RANK	STATE	RATE
1	Massachusetts	727
2	Rhode Island	708
3	California	670
4	Arizona	666
5	Kansas	653
6	Nebraska	643
7	Iowa	634
8	Vermont	627
9	Minnesota	624
9	New Mexico	624
11	Illinois	614
12	Colorado	613
13	Michigan	609
14	Maryland	607
15	Wyoming	601
16	Missouri	600
17	New Hampshire	597
18	Connecticut	594
19	New York	591
20	Wisconsin	590
21	Delaware	583
22	Washington	574
23	Maine	563
24	Virginia	562
25	Oregon	558
26	Pennsylvania	557
26	South Dakota	557
28	North Dakota	550
29	Alabama	532
29	Florida	532
31	Hawaii	524
32	Ohio	520
33	Utah	516
34	Indiana	511
35	West Virginia	510
36	North Carolina	502
37	Oklahoma	499
38	New Jersey	496
39	Montana	493
40	Nevada	489
41	Alaska	488
42	Tennessee	481
43	Idaho	472
43	Louisiana	472
45	Texas	470
46	Kentucky	469
47	South Carolina	456
48	Mississippi	442
49	Arkansas	440
50	Georgia	413

District of Columbia	1,001

Source: Morgan Quitno Press using data from U.S. Department of Education, National Center for Education Statistics "Digest of Education Statistics 2002" (NCES 2003060, June 2003)

*Based on fall 2000 enrollment. National rate includes U.S. Service Schools. Includes students at four-year and two-year public and private degree-granting institutions.

Enrollment in Public Institutions of Higher Education in 2000

National Total = 11,752,786 Students*

ALPHA ORDER

RANK	STATE	STUDENTS	% of USA
20	Alabama	207,435	1.8%
49	Alaska	26,559	0.2%
11	Arizona	284,522	2.4%
33	Arkansas	101,775	0.9%
1	California	1,927,771	16.4%
19	Colorado	217,897	1.9%
35	Connecticut	101,027	0.9%
47	Delaware	34,194	0.3%
4	Florida	556,912	4.7%
13	Georgia	271,755	2.3%
40	Hawaii	44,579	0.4%
39	Idaho	53,751	0.5%
5	Illinois	534,155	4.5%
16	Indiana	240,023	2.0%
30	Iowa	135,008	1.1%
25	Kansas	159,976	1.4%
29	Kentucky	151,973	1.3%
23	Louisiana	189,213	1.6%
41	Maine	40,662	0.3%
17	Maryland	223,797	1.9%
24	Massachusetts	183,248	1.6%
6	Michigan	467,861	4.0%
18	Minnesota	218,617	1.9%
31	Mississippi	125,355	1.1%
22	Missouri	201,509	1.7%
43	Montana	37,387	0.3%
36	Nebraska	88,531	0.8%
37	Nevada	83,120	0.7%
45	New Hampshire	35,870	0.3%
14	New Jersey	266,921	2.3%
34	New Mexico	101,450	0.9%
3	New York	583,417	5.0%
9	North Carolina	329,422	2.8%
44	North Dakota	36,014	0.3%
7	Ohio	411,161	3.5%
28	Oklahoma	153,699	1.3%
27	Oregon	154,756	1.3%
8	Pennsylvania	339,229	2.9%
42	Rhode Island	38,458	0.3%
26	South Carolina	155,519	1.3%
46	South Dakota	34,857	0.3%
21	Tennessee	202,530	1.7%
2	Texas	896,534	7.6%
32	Utah	123,046	1.0%
50	Vermont	20,021	0.2%
10	Virginia	313,780	2.7%
12	Washington	273,928	2.3%
38	West Virginia	76,136	0.6%
15	Wisconsin	249,737	2.1%
48	Wyoming	28,715	0.2%

RANK ORDER

RANK	STATE	STUDENTS	% of USA
1	California	1,927,771	16.4%
2	Texas	896,534	7.6%
3	New York	583,417	5.0%
4	Florida	556,912	4.7%
5	Illinois	534,155	4.5%
6	Michigan	467,861	4.0%
7	Ohio	411,161	3.5%
8	Pennsylvania	339,229	2.9%
9	North Carolina	329,422	2.8%
10	Virginia	313,780	2.7%
11	Arizona	284,522	2.4%
12	Washington	273,928	2.3%
13	Georgia	271,755	2.3%
14	New Jersey	266,921	2.3%
15	Wisconsin	249,737	2.1%
16	Indiana	240,023	2.0%
17	Maryland	223,797	1.9%
18	Minnesota	218,617	1.9%
19	Colorado	217,897	1.9%
20	Alabama	207,435	1.8%
21	Tennessee	202,530	1.7%
22	Missouri	201,509	1.7%
23	Louisiana	189,213	1.6%
24	Massachusetts	183,248	1.6%
25	Kansas	159,976	1.4%
26	South Carolina	155,519	1.3%
27	Oregon	154,756	1.3%
28	Oklahoma	153,699	1.3%
29	Kentucky	151,973	1.3%
30	Iowa	135,008	1.1%
31	Mississippi	125,355	1.1%
32	Utah	123,046	1.0%
33	Arkansas	101,775	0.9%
34	New Mexico	101,450	0.9%
35	Connecticut	101,027	0.9%
36	Nebraska	88,531	0.8%
37	Nevada	83,120	0.7%
38	West Virginia	76,136	0.6%
39	Idaho	53,751	0.5%
40	Hawaii	44,579	0.4%
41	Maine	40,662	0.3%
42	Rhode Island	38,458	0.3%
43	Montana	37,387	0.3%
44	North Dakota	36,014	0.3%
45	New Hampshire	35,870	0.3%
46	South Dakota	34,857	0.3%
47	Delaware	34,194	0.3%
48	Wyoming	28,715	0.2%
49	Alaska	26,559	0.2%
50	Vermont	20,021	0.2%
	District of Columbia	5,499	0.0%

Source: U.S. Department of Education, National Center for Education Statistics
"Digest of Education Statistics 2002" (NCES 2003060, June 2003)
*Fall 2000 enrollment. Includes full-time and part-time students at Title IV eligible, degree-granting four-year and two-year institutions. National total includes 13,475 students at U.S. Service Schools.

Enrollment in Private Institutions of Higher Education in 2000

National Total = 3,559,503 Students*

ALPHA ORDER

RANK	STATE	STUDENTS	% of USA
31	Alabama	26,527	0.7%
49	Alaska	1,394	0.0%
19	Arizona	57,968	1.6%
39	Arkansas	13,397	0.4%
2	California	328,937	9.2%
24	Colorado	45,975	1.3%
18	Connecticut	60,216	1.7%
43	Delaware	9,703	0.3%
6	Florida	150,772	4.2%
13	Georgia	74,449	2.1%
37	Hawaii	15,603	0.4%
41	Idaho	11,843	0.3%
5	Illinois	209,763	5.9%
14	Indiana	74,311	2.1%
21	Iowa	53,966	1.5%
35	Kansas	19,992	0.6%
27	Kentucky	36,368	1.0%
28	Louisiana	34,587	1.0%
36	Maine	17,811	0.5%
22	Maryland	49,948	1.4%
4	Massachusetts	237,894	6.7%
10	Michigan	99,770	2.8%
12	Minnesota	74,828	2.1%
40	Mississippi	12,034	0.3%
9	Missouri	119,839	3.4%
46	Montana	4,853	0.1%
34	Nebraska	23,586	0.7%
47	Nevada	4,773	0.1%
32	New Hampshire	25,848	0.7%
15	New Jersey	69,024	1.9%
44	New Mexico	9,289	0.3%
1	New York	459,978	12.9%
11	North Carolina	75,230	2.1%
48	North Dakota	4,234	0.1%
7	Ohio	138,392	3.9%
33	Oklahoma	24,317	0.7%
30	Oregon	28,309	0.8%
3	Pennsylvania	270,292	7.6%
26	Rhode Island	36,992	1.0%
29	South Carolina	30,412	0.9%
45	South Dakota	8,364	0.2%
17	Tennessee	61,380	1.7%
8	Texas	137,439	3.9%
25	Utah	40,730	1.1%
38	Vermont	15,468	0.4%
16	Virginia	68,113	1.9%
23	Washington	46,912	1.3%
42	West Virginia	11,752	0.3%
20	Wisconsin	57,442	1.6%
50	Wyoming	1,289	0.0%

RANK ORDER

RANK	STATE	STUDENTS	% of USA
1	New York	459,978	12.9%
2	California	328,937	9.2%
3	Pennsylvania	270,292	7.6%
4	Massachusetts	237,894	6.7%
5	Illinois	209,763	5.9%
6	Florida	150,772	4.2%
7	Ohio	138,392	3.9%
8	Texas	137,439	3.9%
9	Missouri	119,839	3.4%
10	Michigan	99,770	2.8%
11	North Carolina	75,230	2.1%
12	Minnesota	74,828	2.1%
13	Georgia	74,449	2.1%
14	Indiana	74,311	2.1%
15	New Jersey	69,024	1.9%
16	Virginia	68,113	1.9%
17	Tennessee	61,380	1.7%
18	Connecticut	60,216	1.7%
19	Arizona	57,968	1.6%
20	Wisconsin	57,442	1.6%
21	Iowa	53,966	1.5%
22	Maryland	49,948	1.4%
23	Washington	46,912	1.3%
24	Colorado	45,975	1.3%
25	Utah	40,730	1.1%
26	Rhode Island	36,992	1.0%
27	Kentucky	36,368	1.0%
28	Louisiana	34,587	1.0%
29	South Carolina	30,412	0.9%
30	Oregon	28,309	0.8%
31	Alabama	26,527	0.7%
32	New Hampshire	25,848	0.7%
33	Oklahoma	24,317	0.7%
34	Nebraska	23,586	0.7%
35	Kansas	19,992	0.6%
36	Maine	17,811	0.5%
37	Hawaii	15,603	0.4%
38	Vermont	15,468	0.4%
39	Arkansas	13,397	0.4%
40	Mississippi	12,034	0.3%
41	Idaho	11,843	0.3%
42	West Virginia	11,752	0.3%
43	Delaware	9,703	0.3%
44	New Mexico	9,289	0.3%
45	South Dakota	8,364	0.2%
46	Montana	4,853	0.1%
47	Nevada	4,773	0.1%
48	North Dakota	4,234	0.1%
49	Alaska	1,394	0.0%
50	Wyoming	1,289	0.0%
	District of Columbia	67,190	1.9%

Source: U.S. Department of Education, National Center for Education Statistics
"Digest of Education Statistics 2002" (NCES 2003060, June 2003)
**Fall 2000 enrollment. Includes full-time and part-time students at Title IV eligible, degree-granting four-year and two-year institutions.*

Percent of Population With a Bachelor's Degree or More in 2002

National Percent = 26.7%*

ALPHA ORDER

RANK	STATE	PERCENT
38	Alabama	22.7
26	Alaska	25.6
22	Arizona	26.3
49	Arkansas	18.3
15	California	27.9
2	Colorado	35.7
5	Connecticut	32.6
11	Delaware	29.5
25	Florida	25.7
29	Georgia	25.0
19	Hawaii	26.8
45	Idaho	20.9
16	Illinois	27.3
33	Indiana	23.7
37	Iowa	23.1
12	Kansas	29.1
43	Kentucky	21.6
41	Louisiana	22.1
32	Maine	23.8
1	Maryland	37.6
4	Massachusetts	34.3
39	Michigan	22.5
8	Minnesota	30.5
45	Mississippi	20.9
21	Missouri	26.7
34	Montana	23.6
17	Nebraska	27.1
41	Nevada	22.1
9	New Hampshire	30.1
6	New Jersey	31.4
27	New Mexico	25.4
13	New York	28.8
40	North Carolina	22.4
28	North Dakota	25.3
31	Ohio	24.5
47	Oklahoma	20.4
17	Oregon	27.1
24	Pennsylvania	26.1
9	Rhode Island	30.1
36	South Carolina	23.3
34	South Dakota	23.6
44	Tennessee	21.5
23	Texas	26.2
19	Utah	26.8
7	Vermont	30.8
3	Virginia	34.6
14	Washington	28.3
50	West Virginia	15.9
30	Wisconsin	24.7
48	Wyoming	19.6

RANK ORDER

RANK	STATE	PERCENT
1	Maryland	37.6
2	Colorado	35.7
3	Virginia	34.6
4	Massachusetts	34.3
5	Connecticut	32.6
6	New Jersey	31.4
7	Vermont	30.8
8	Minnesota	30.5
9	New Hampshire	30.1
9	Rhode Island	30.1
11	Delaware	29.5
12	Kansas	29.1
13	New York	28.8
14	Washington	28.3
15	California	27.9
16	Illinois	27.3
17	Nebraska	27.1
17	Oregon	27.1
19	Hawaii	26.8
19	Utah	26.8
21	Missouri	26.7
22	Arizona	26.3
23	Texas	26.2
24	Pennsylvania	26.1
25	Florida	25.7
26	Alaska	25.6
27	New Mexico	25.4
28	North Dakota	25.3
29	Georgia	25.0
30	Wisconsin	24.7
31	Ohio	24.5
32	Maine	23.8
33	Indiana	23.7
34	Montana	23.6
34	South Dakota	23.6
36	South Carolina	23.3
37	Iowa	23.1
38	Alabama	22.7
39	Michigan	22.5
40	North Carolina	22.4
41	Louisiana	22.1
41	Nevada	22.1
43	Kentucky	21.6
44	Tennessee	21.5
45	Idaho	20.9
45	Mississippi	20.9
47	Oklahoma	20.4
48	Wyoming	19.6
49	Arkansas	18.3
50	West Virginia	15.9
	District of Columbia	44.4

Source: U.S. Bureau of the Census
"Educational Attainment of the Population 25 Years and Over, By State"
(http://www.census.gov/population/www/socdemo/education/ppl-169.html)
*Persons age 25 and older.

Public Libraries and Branches in 2001

National Total = 16,421 Libraries and Branches*

ALPHA ORDER

RANK	STATE	LIBRARIES	% of USA
24	Alabama	283	1.7%
43	Alaska	103	0.6%
37	Arizona	176	1.1%
32	Arkansas	209	1.3%
2	California	1,063	6.5%
26	Colorado	243	1.5%
27	Connecticut	242	1.5%
50	Delaware	37	0.2%
10	Florida	473	2.9%
16	Georgia	366	2.2%
49	Hawaii	50	0.3%
40	Idaho	143	0.9%
4	Illinois	786	4.8%
13	Indiana	430	2.6%
8	Iowa	561	3.4%
15	Kansas	373	2.3%
34	Kentucky	189	1.2%
20	Louisiana	329	2.0%
25	Maine	280	1.7%
38	Maryland	175	1.1%
9	Massachusetts	490	3.0%
6	Michigan	654	4.0%
18	Minnesota	359	2.2%
29	Mississippi	237	1.4%
17	Missouri	363	2.2%
41	Montana	107	0.7%
22	Nebraska	289	1.8%
46	Nevada	87	0.5%
28	New Hampshire	238	1.4%
11	New Jersey	458	2.8%
44	New Mexico	101	0.6%
1	New York	1,089	6.6%
14	North Carolina	379	2.3%
45	North Dakota	89	0.5%
5	Ohio	716	4.4%
30	Oklahoma	210	1.3%
30	Oregon	210	1.3%
7	Pennsylvania	636	3.9%
48	Rhode Island	72	0.4%
35	South Carolina	183	1.1%
39	South Dakota	145	0.9%
23	Tennessee	285	1.7%
3	Texas	825	5.0%
41	Utah	107	0.7%
33	Vermont	190	1.2%
19	Virginia	338	2.1%
21	Washington	320	1.9%
36	West Virginia	177	1.1%
12	Wisconsin	455	2.8%
47	Wyoming	74	0.5%

RANK ORDER

RANK	STATE	LIBRARIES	% of USA
1	New York	1,089	6.6%
2	California	1,063	6.5%
3	Texas	825	5.0%
4	Illinois	786	4.8%
5	Ohio	716	4.4%
6	Michigan	654	4.0%
7	Pennsylvania	636	3.9%
8	Iowa	561	3.4%
9	Massachusetts	490	3.0%
10	Florida	473	2.9%
11	New Jersey	458	2.8%
12	Wisconsin	455	2.8%
13	Indiana	430	2.6%
14	North Carolina	379	2.3%
15	Kansas	373	2.3%
16	Georgia	366	2.2%
17	Missouri	363	2.2%
18	Minnesota	359	2.2%
19	Virginia	338	2.1%
20	Louisiana	329	2.0%
21	Washington	320	1.9%
22	Nebraska	289	1.8%
23	Tennessee	285	1.7%
24	Alabama	283	1.7%
25	Maine	280	1.7%
26	Colorado	243	1.5%
27	Connecticut	242	1.5%
28	New Hampshire	238	1.4%
29	Mississippi	237	1.4%
30	Oklahoma	210	1.3%
30	Oregon	210	1.3%
32	Arkansas	209	1.3%
33	Vermont	190	1.2%
34	Kentucky	189	1.2%
35	South Carolina	183	1.1%
36	West Virginia	177	1.1%
37	Arizona	176	1.1%
38	Maryland	175	1.1%
39	South Dakota	145	0.9%
40	Idaho	143	0.9%
41	Montana	107	0.7%
41	Utah	107	0.7%
43	Alaska	103	0.6%
44	New Mexico	101	0.6%
45	North Dakota	89	0.5%
46	Nevada	87	0.5%
47	Wyoming	74	0.5%
48	Rhode Island	72	0.4%
49	Hawaii	50	0.3%
50	Delaware	37	0.2%
	District of Columbia	27	0.2%

Source: U.S. Dept. of Education, Office of Educational Research & Improvement
   "Public Libraries in the United States: FY 2001" (NCES 2003399, June 2003)
*For fiscal year 2001. Total of central and branch outlets. Does not include 879 bookmobiles. There are 9,129 public libraries.

Rate of Public Libraries and Branches in 2001

National Average = 17,362 Population per Library*

ALPHA ORDER

RANK	STATE	RATE
26	Alabama	15,782
44	Alaska	6,142
4	Arizona	30,100
35	Arkansas	12,881
2	California	32,486
19	Colorado	18,225
31	Connecticut	14,184
12	Delaware	21,502
1	Florida	34,578
8	Georgia	22,937
6	Hawaii	24,501
39	Idaho	9,240
24	Illinois	15,925
30	Indiana	14,248
48	Iowa	5,227
41	Kansas	7,240
11	Kentucky	21,520
33	Louisiana	13,574
49	Maine	4,588
3	Maryland	30,762
34	Massachusetts	13,061
28	Michigan	15,298
32	Minnesota	13,886
36	Mississippi	12,058
27	Missouri	15,527
40	Montana	8,467
45	Nebraska	5,948
7	Nevada	24,076
46	New Hampshire	5,290
18	New Jersey	18,568
20	New Mexico	18,110
21	New York	17,516
10	North Carolina	21,623
42	North Dakota	7,149
25	Ohio	15,902
23	Oklahoma	16,510
22	Oregon	16,536
16	Pennsylvania	19,337
29	Rhode Island	14,708
9	South Carolina	22,185
47	South Dakota	5,229
15	Tennessee	20,161
5	Texas	25,867
13	Utah	21,305
50	Vermont	3,226
14	Virginia	21,280
17	Washington	18,727
38	West Virginia	10,179
37	Wisconsin	11,879
43	Wyoming	6,672

RANK ORDER

RANK	STATE	RATE
1	Florida	34,578
2	California	32,486
3	Maryland	30,762
4	Arizona	30,100
5	Texas	25,867
6	Hawaii	24,501
7	Nevada	24,076
8	Georgia	22,937
9	South Carolina	22,185
10	North Carolina	21,623
11	Kentucky	21,520
12	Delaware	21,502
13	Utah	21,305
14	Virginia	21,280
15	Tennessee	20,161
16	Pennsylvania	19,337
17	Washington	18,727
18	New Jersey	18,568
19	Colorado	18,225
20	New Mexico	18,110
21	New York	17,516
22	Oregon	16,536
23	Oklahoma	16,510
24	Illinois	15,925
25	Ohio	15,902
26	Alabama	15,782
27	Missouri	15,527
28	Michigan	15,298
29	Rhode Island	14,708
30	Indiana	14,248
31	Connecticut	14,184
32	Minnesota	13,886
33	Louisiana	13,574
34	Massachusetts	13,061
35	Arkansas	12,881
36	Mississippi	12,058
37	Wisconsin	11,879
38	West Virginia	10,179
39	Idaho	9,240
40	Montana	8,467
41	Kansas	7,240
42	North Dakota	7,149
43	Wyoming	6,672
44	Alaska	6,142
45	Nebraska	5,948
46	New Hampshire	5,290
47	South Dakota	5,229
48	Iowa	5,227
49	Maine	4,588
50	Vermont	3,226
	District of Columbia	21,212

Source: Morgan Quitno Press using data from U.S. Dept. of Education, Office of Educational Research & Improvement "Public Libraries in the United States: FY 2001" (NCES 2003399, June 2003)

*For fiscal year 2001. Total of central and branch outlets. Does not include 879 bookmobiles. There are 9,129 public libraries.

Books in Public Libraries Per Capita in 2001

National Per Capita = 2.8 Books*

<u>ALPHA ORDER</u>

RANK	STATE	BOOKS PER CAPITA
40	Alabama	2.0
19	Alaska	3.6
50	Arizona	1.7
38	Arkansas	2.1
44	California	1.9
30	Colorado	2.6
10	Connecticut	4.1
44	Delaware	1.9
47	Florida	1.8
44	Georgia	1.9
30	Hawaii	2.6
21	Idaho	3.1
16	Illinois	3.7
12	Indiana	3.9
12	Iowa	3.9
5	Kansas	4.7
40	Kentucky	2.0
34	Louisiana	2.4
1	Maine	5.0
22	Maryland	3.0
3	Massachusetts	4.8
26	Michigan	2.7
23	Minnesota	2.9
40	Mississippi	2.0
16	Missouri	3.7
23	Montana	2.9
7	Nebraska	4.6
36	Nevada	2.2
7	New Hampshire	4.6
16	New Jersey	3.7
30	New Mexico	2.6
9	New York	4.4
40	North Carolina	2.0
12	North Dakota	3.9
10	Ohio	4.1
36	Oklahoma	2.2
26	Oregon	2.7
35	Pennsylvania	2.3
15	Rhode Island	3.8
38	South Carolina	2.1
3	South Dakota	4.8
47	Tennessee	1.8
47	Texas	1.8
26	Utah	2.7
5	Vermont	4.7
30	Virginia	2.6
23	Washington	2.9
26	West Virginia	2.7
20	Wisconsin	3.5
2	Wyoming	4.9

<u>RANK ORDER</u>

RANK	STATE	BOOKS PER CAPITA
1	Maine	5.0
2	Wyoming	4.9
3	Massachusetts	4.8
3	South Dakota	4.8
5	Kansas	4.7
5	Vermont	4.7
7	Nebraska	4.6
7	New Hampshire	4.6
9	New York	4.4
10	Connecticut	4.1
10	Ohio	4.1
12	Indiana	3.9
12	Iowa	3.9
12	North Dakota	3.9
15	Rhode Island	3.8
16	Illinois	3.7
16	Missouri	3.7
16	New Jersey	3.7
19	Alaska	3.6
20	Wisconsin	3.5
21	Idaho	3.1
22	Maryland	3.0
23	Minnesota	2.9
23	Montana	2.9
23	Washington	2.9
26	Michigan	2.7
26	Oregon	2.7
26	Utah	2.7
26	West Virginia	2.7
30	Colorado	2.6
30	Hawaii	2.6
30	New Mexico	2.6
30	Virginia	2.6
34	Louisiana	2.4
35	Pennsylvania	2.3
36	Nevada	2.2
36	Oklahoma	2.2
38	Arkansas	2.1
38	South Carolina	2.1
40	Alabama	2.0
40	Kentucky	2.0
40	Mississippi	2.0
40	North Carolina	2.0
44	California	1.9
44	Delaware	1.9
44	Georgia	1.9
47	Florida	1.8
47	Tennessee	1.8
47	Texas	1.8
50	Arizona	1.7
	District of Columbia	4.3

Source: U.S. Dept. of Education, Office of Educational Research & Improvement
"Public Libraries in the United States: FY 2001" (NCES 2003399, June 2003)
For fiscal year 2001. Includes serial volumes but not serial subscriptions.

Per Capita State Art Agencies' Legislative Appropriations in 2004

National Per Capita = $0.78*

<u>ALPHA ORDER</u>

RANK	STATE	PER CAPITA
23	Alabama	$0.73
24	Alaska	0.71
28	Arizona	0.63
35	Arkansas	0.54
48	California	0.05
49	Colorado	0.04
16	Connecticut	1.03
3	Delaware	1.99
40	Florida	0.39
38	Georgia	0.47
1	Hawaii	4.68
31	Idaho	0.60
17	Illinois	0.90
33	Indiana	0.58
38	Iowa	0.47
34	Kansas	0.55
17	Kentucky	0.90
13	Louisiana	1.08
26	Maine	0.67
4	Maryland	1.93
9	Massachusetts	1.13
8	Michigan	1.17
6	Minnesota	1.70
29	Mississippi	0.61
50	Missouri	0.00
44	Montana	0.31
31	Nebraska	0.60
27	Nevada	0.66
36	New Hampshire	0.52
5	New Jersey	1.91
21	New Mexico	0.77
2	New York	2.21
29	North Carolina	0.61
19	North Dakota	0.79
11	Ohio	1.10
11	Oklahoma	1.10
47	Oregon	0.17
9	Pennsylvania	1.13
7	Rhode Island	1.38
21	South Carolina	0.77
25	South Dakota	0.70
45	Tennessee	0.30
46	Texas	0.21
15	Utah	1.04
19	Vermont	0.79
42	Virginia	0.38
43	Washington	0.37
36	West Virginia	0.52
40	Wisconsin	0.39
14	Wyoming	1.05

<u>RANK ORDER</u>

RANK	STATE	PER CAPITA
1	Hawaii	$4.68
2	New York	2.21
3	Delaware	1.99
4	Maryland	1.93
5	New Jersey	1.91
6	Minnesota	1.70
7	Rhode Island	1.38
8	Michigan	1.17
9	Massachusetts	1.13
9	Pennsylvania	1.13
11	Ohio	1.10
11	Oklahoma	1.10
13	Louisiana	1.08
14	Wyoming	1.05
15	Utah	1.04
16	Connecticut	1.03
17	Illinois	0.90
17	Kentucky	0.90
19	North Dakota	0.79
19	Vermont	0.79
21	New Mexico	0.77
21	South Carolina	0.77
23	Alabama	0.73
24	Alaska	0.71
25	South Dakota	0.70
26	Maine	0.67
27	Nevada	0.66
28	Arizona	0.63
29	Mississippi	0.61
29	North Carolina	0.61
31	Idaho	0.60
31	Nebraska	0.60
33	Indiana	0.58
34	Kansas	0.55
35	Arkansas	0.54
36	New Hampshire	0.52
36	West Virginia	0.52
38	Georgia	0.47
38	Iowa	0.47
40	Florida	0.39
40	Wisconsin	0.39
42	Virginia	0.38
43	Washington	0.37
44	Montana	0.31
45	Tennessee	0.30
46	Texas	0.21
47	Oregon	0.17
48	California	0.05
49	Colorado	0.04
50	Missouri	0.00

	District of Columbia	2.84

*Source: Morgan Quitno Press using data from National Assembly of State Arts Agencies
"Legislative Appropriations Annual Survey" (October 2003)*

Fiscal year 2004. Does not include line item appropriations. Line items are legislative appropriations that are not controlled by the state art agencies but are passed through their budgets directly to another entity. Calculated using 2003 census population estimates. National per capita does not include appropriations or population in U.S. territories.

Federal Allocations for Head Start Program in 2002

National Total = $6,327,358,000*

ALPHA ORDER

RANK	STATE	ALLOCATIONS	% of USA
18	Alabama	$100,947,000	1.6%
49	Alaska	12,283,000	0.2%
21	Arizona	94,450,000	1.5%
29	Arkansas	60,467,000	1.0%
1	California	799,391,000	12.6%
28	Colorado	65,129,000	1.0%
31	Connecticut	50,509,000	0.8%
48	Delaware	12,467,000	0.2%
5	Florida	248,753,000	3.9%
9	Georgia	159,480,000	2.5%
39	Hawaii	22,304,000	0.4%
41	Idaho	21,242,000	0.3%
4	Illinois	262,239,000	4.1%
22	Indiana	89,825,000	1.4%
32	Iowa	49,930,000	0.8%
35	Kansas	47,368,000	0.7%
17	Kentucky	104,381,000	1.6%
11	Louisiana	135,394,000	2.1%
38	Maine	26,102,000	0.4%
26	Maryland	75,570,000	1.2%
16	Massachusetts	105,035,000	1.7%
7	Michigan	227,484,000	3.6%
27	Minnesota	69,047,000	1.1%
10	Mississippi	157,653,000	2.5%
14	Missouri	114,130,000	1.8%
42	Montana	19,963,000	0.3%
37	Nebraska	33,870,000	0.5%
43	Nevada	19,355,000	0.3%
47	New Hampshire	13,054,000	0.2%
13	New Jersey	126,712,000	2.0%
34	New Mexico	48,388,000	0.8%
3	New York	419,957,000	6.6%
12	North Carolina	131,280,000	2.1%
45	North Dakota	16,597,000	0.3%
6	Ohio	239,148,000	3.8%
25	Oklahoma	76,072,000	1.2%
30	Oregon	57,731,000	0.9%
8	Pennsylvania	220,606,000	3.5%
40	Rhode Island	21,510,000	0.3%
24	South Carolina	78,995,000	1.2%
44	South Dakota	18,455,000	0.3%
15	Tennessee	112,909,000	1.8%
2	Texas	452,153,000	7.1%
36	Utah	37,787,000	0.6%
46	Vermont	13,228,000	0.2%
20	Virginia	94,724,000	1.5%
19	Washington	97,219,000	1.5%
33	West Virginia	49,225,000	0.8%
23	Wisconsin	87,819,000	1.4%
50	Wyoming	11,339,000	0.2%

RANK ORDER

RANK	STATE	ALLOCATIONS	% of USA
1	California	$799,391,000	12.6%
2	Texas	452,153,000	7.1%
3	New York	419,957,000	6.6%
4	Illinois	262,239,000	4.1%
5	Florida	248,753,000	3.9%
6	Ohio	239,148,000	3.8%
7	Michigan	227,484,000	3.6%
8	Pennsylvania	220,606,000	3.5%
9	Georgia	159,480,000	2.5%
10	Mississippi	157,653,000	2.5%
11	Louisiana	135,394,000	2.1%
12	North Carolina	131,280,000	2.1%
13	New Jersey	126,712,000	2.0%
14	Missouri	114,130,000	1.8%
15	Tennessee	112,909,000	1.8%
16	Massachusetts	105,035,000	1.7%
17	Kentucky	104,381,000	1.6%
18	Alabama	100,947,000	1.6%
19	Washington	97,219,000	1.5%
20	Virginia	94,724,000	1.5%
21	Arizona	94,450,000	1.5%
22	Indiana	89,825,000	1.4%
23	Wisconsin	87,819,000	1.4%
24	South Carolina	78,995,000	1.2%
25	Oklahoma	76,072,000	1.2%
26	Maryland	75,570,000	1.2%
27	Minnesota	69,047,000	1.1%
28	Colorado	65,129,000	1.0%
29	Arkansas	60,467,000	1.0%
30	Oregon	57,731,000	0.9%
31	Connecticut	50,509,000	0.8%
32	Iowa	49,930,000	0.8%
33	West Virginia	49,225,000	0.8%
34	New Mexico	48,388,000	0.8%
35	Kansas	47,368,000	0.7%
36	Utah	37,787,000	0.6%
37	Nebraska	33,870,000	0.5%
38	Maine	26,102,000	0.4%
39	Hawaii	22,304,000	0.4%
40	Rhode Island	21,510,000	0.3%
41	Idaho	21,242,000	0.3%
42	Montana	19,963,000	0.3%
43	Nevada	19,355,000	0.3%
44	South Dakota	18,455,000	0.3%
45	North Dakota	16,597,000	0.3%
46	Vermont	13,228,000	0.2%
47	New Hampshire	13,054,000	0.2%
48	Delaware	12,467,000	0.2%
49	Alaska	12,283,000	0.2%
50	Wyoming	11,339,000	0.2%
	District of Columbia	24,451,000	0.4%

*Source: U.S. Department of Health and Human Services, Administration for Children and Families
"2003 Head Start Fact Sheet" (http://www.acf.dhhs.gov/programs/hsb/research/factsheets/02_hsfs.htm)*

For fiscal year 2002. National total includes $439,926,000 to Migrant and Native American programs and $253,305,000 to U.S. territories.

Enrollment in Head Start in 2001

National Total = 905,235 Enrollees*

ALPHA ORDER

RANK	STATE	ENROLLEES	% of USA
14	Alabama	16,498	1.8%
49	Alaska	1,586	0.2%
23	Arizona	12,865	1.4%
26	Arkansas	10,818	1.2%
1	California	97,667	10.8%
29	Colorado	9,826	1.1%
35	Connecticut	7,207	0.8%
46	Delaware	2,243	0.2%
7	Florida	34,657	3.8%
10	Georgia	23,140	2.6%
40	Hawaii	3,073	0.3%
43	Idaho	2,890	0.3%
4	Illinois	39,805	4.4%
18	Indiana	14,256	1.6%
32	Iowa	7,689	0.8%
31	Kansas	7,897	0.9%
15	Kentucky	16,419	1.8%
11	Louisiana	21,969	2.4%
38	Maine	3,958	0.4%
27	Maryland	10,487	1.2%
22	Massachusetts	13,004	1.4%
6	Michigan	35,112	3.9%
28	Minnesota	10,164	1.1%
9	Mississippi	26,624	2.9%
13	Missouri	17,718	2.0%
41	Montana	2,971	0.3%
37	Nebraska	4,982	0.6%
44	Nevada	2,694	0.3%
48	New Hampshire	1,632	0.2%
17	New Jersey	15,329	1.7%
33	New Mexico	7,618	0.8%
3	New York	48,952	5.4%
12	North Carolina	18,991	2.1%
45	North Dakota	2,287	0.3%
5	Ohio	38,072	4.2%
21	Oklahoma	13,228	1.5%
30	Oregon	9,129	1.0%
8	Pennsylvania	31,104	3.4%
39	Rhode Island	3,150	0.3%
24	South Carolina	12,184	1.3%
42	South Dakota	2,925	0.3%
16	Tennessee	16,344	1.8%
2	Texas	67,572	7.5%
36	Utah	5,403	0.6%
50	Vermont	1,573	0.2%
19	Virginia	13,612	1.5%
25	Washington	11,106	1.2%
34	West Virginia	7,590	0.8%
20	Wisconsin	13,478	1.5%
47	Wyoming	1,757	0.2%

RANK ORDER

RANK	STATE	ENROLLEES	% of USA
1	California	97,667	10.8%
2	Texas	67,572	7.5%
3	New York	48,952	5.4%
4	Illinois	39,805	4.4%
5	Ohio	38,072	4.2%
6	Michigan	35,112	3.9%
7	Florida	34,657	3.8%
8	Pennsylvania	31,104	3.4%
9	Mississippi	26,624	2.9%
10	Georgia	23,140	2.6%
11	Louisiana	21,969	2.4%
12	North Carolina	18,991	2.1%
13	Missouri	17,718	2.0%
14	Alabama	16,498	1.8%
15	Kentucky	16,419	1.8%
16	Tennessee	16,344	1.8%
17	New Jersey	15,329	1.7%
18	Indiana	14,256	1.6%
19	Virginia	13,612	1.5%
20	Wisconsin	13,478	1.5%
21	Oklahoma	13,228	1.5%
22	Massachusetts	13,004	1.4%
23	Arizona	12,865	1.4%
24	South Carolina	12,184	1.3%
25	Washington	11,106	1.2%
26	Arkansas	10,818	1.2%
27	Maryland	10,487	1.2%
28	Minnesota	10,164	1.1%
29	Colorado	9,826	1.1%
30	Oregon	9,129	1.0%
31	Kansas	7,897	0.9%
32	Iowa	7,689	0.8%
33	New Mexico	7,618	0.8%
34	West Virginia	7,590	0.8%
35	Connecticut	7,207	0.8%
36	Utah	5,403	0.6%
37	Nebraska	4,982	0.6%
38	Maine	3,958	0.4%
39	Rhode Island	3,150	0.3%
40	Hawaii	3,073	0.3%
41	Montana	2,971	0.3%
42	South Dakota	2,925	0.3%
43	Idaho	2,890	0.3%
44	Nevada	2,694	0.3%
45	North Dakota	2,287	0.3%
46	Delaware	2,243	0.2%
47	Wyoming	1,757	0.2%
48	New Hampshire	1,632	0.2%
49	Alaska	1,586	0.2%
50	Vermont	1,573	0.2%
	District of Columbia	3,343	0.4%

Source: U.S. Department of Health and Human Services, Administration for Children and Families
"2002 Head Start Fact Sheet" (http://www.acf.dhhs.gov/programs/hsb/research/factsheets/02_hsfs.htm)
For fiscal year 2001. National total includes 56,987 enrollees in Migrant and Native American programs and 43,650 enrollees in U.S. territories.

VI. EMPLOYMENT AND LABOR

Average Annual Wages in 2002

National Average = $36,764*

<table>
<tr><td colspan="3"><u>ALPHA ORDER</u></td><td colspan="3"><u>RANK ORDER</u></td></tr>
<tr><td>RANK</td><td>STATE</td><td>ANNUAL WAGES</td><td>RANK</td><td>STATE</td><td>ANNUAL WAGES</td></tr>
<tr><td>31</td><td>Alabama</td><td>$31,163</td><td>1</td><td>Connecticut</td><td>$46,852</td></tr>
<tr><td>14</td><td>Alaska</td><td>37,134</td><td>2</td><td>New York</td><td>46,328</td></tr>
<tr><td>21</td><td>Arizona</td><td>34,036</td><td>3</td><td>New Jersey</td><td>45,182</td></tr>
<tr><td>46</td><td>Arkansas</td><td>28,074</td><td>4</td><td>Massachusetts</td><td>44,954</td></tr>
<tr><td>5</td><td>California</td><td>41,419</td><td>5</td><td>California</td><td>41,419</td></tr>
<tr><td>11</td><td>Colorado</td><td>38,005</td><td>6</td><td>Illinois</td><td>39,688</td></tr>
<tr><td>1</td><td>Connecticut</td><td>46,852</td><td>7</td><td>Delaware</td><td>39,684</td></tr>
<tr><td>7</td><td>Delaware</td><td>39,684</td><td>8</td><td>Maryland</td><td>39,382</td></tr>
<tr><td>30</td><td>Florida</td><td>32,426</td><td>9</td><td>Washington</td><td>38,242</td></tr>
<tr><td>18</td><td>Georgia</td><td>35,734</td><td>10</td><td>Michigan</td><td>38,135</td></tr>
<tr><td>26</td><td>Hawaii</td><td>32,671</td><td>11</td><td>Colorado</td><td>38,005</td></tr>
<tr><td>45</td><td>Idaho</td><td>28,163</td><td>12</td><td>Minnesota</td><td>37,458</td></tr>
<tr><td>6</td><td>Illinois</td><td>39,688</td><td>13</td><td>Virginia</td><td>37,222</td></tr>
<tr><td>27</td><td>Indiana</td><td>32,603</td><td>14</td><td>Alaska</td><td>37,134</td></tr>
<tr><td>39</td><td>Iowa</td><td>29,668</td><td>15</td><td>Texas</td><td>36,248</td></tr>
<tr><td>34</td><td>Kansas</td><td>30,825</td><td>16</td><td>New Hampshire</td><td>36,176</td></tr>
<tr><td>33</td><td>Kentucky</td><td>30,904</td><td>17</td><td>Pennsylvania</td><td>35,808</td></tr>
<tr><td>36</td><td>Louisiana</td><td>30,115</td><td>18</td><td>Georgia</td><td>35,734</td></tr>
<tr><td>38</td><td>Maine</td><td>29,736</td><td>19</td><td>Rhode Island</td><td>34,810</td></tr>
<tr><td>8</td><td>Maryland</td><td>39,382</td><td>20</td><td>Ohio</td><td>34,214</td></tr>
<tr><td>4</td><td>Massachusetts</td><td>44,954</td><td>21</td><td>Arizona</td><td>34,036</td></tr>
<tr><td>10</td><td>Michigan</td><td>38,135</td><td>22</td><td>Nevada</td><td>33,993</td></tr>
<tr><td>12</td><td>Minnesota</td><td>37,458</td><td>23</td><td>Oregon</td><td>33,684</td></tr>
<tr><td>47</td><td>Mississippi</td><td>26,665</td><td>24</td><td>Missouri</td><td>33,118</td></tr>
<tr><td>24</td><td>Missouri</td><td>33,118</td><td>25</td><td>North Carolina</td><td>32,689</td></tr>
<tr><td>50</td><td>Montana</td><td>26,001</td><td>26</td><td>Hawaii</td><td>32,671</td></tr>
<tr><td>40</td><td>Nebraska</td><td>29,448</td><td>27</td><td>Indiana</td><td>32,603</td></tr>
<tr><td>22</td><td>Nevada</td><td>33,993</td><td>28</td><td>Tennessee</td><td>32,531</td></tr>
<tr><td>16</td><td>New Hampshire</td><td>36,176</td><td>29</td><td>Wisconsin</td><td>32,464</td></tr>
<tr><td>3</td><td>New Jersey</td><td>45,182</td><td>30</td><td>Florida</td><td>32,426</td></tr>
<tr><td>41</td><td>New Mexico</td><td>29,431</td><td>31</td><td>Alabama</td><td>31,163</td></tr>
<tr><td>2</td><td>New York</td><td>46,328</td><td>32</td><td>Vermont</td><td>31,041</td></tr>
<tr><td>25</td><td>North Carolina</td><td>32,689</td><td>33</td><td>Kentucky</td><td>30,904</td></tr>
<tr><td>48</td><td>North Dakota</td><td>26,550</td><td>34</td><td>Kansas</td><td>30,825</td></tr>
<tr><td>20</td><td>Ohio</td><td>34,214</td><td>35</td><td>Utah</td><td>30,585</td></tr>
<tr><td>43</td><td>Oklahoma</td><td>28,654</td><td>36</td><td>Louisiana</td><td>30,115</td></tr>
<tr><td>23</td><td>Oregon</td><td>33,684</td><td>37</td><td>South Carolina</td><td>30,003</td></tr>
<tr><td>17</td><td>Pennsylvania</td><td>35,808</td><td>38</td><td>Maine</td><td>29,736</td></tr>
<tr><td>19</td><td>Rhode Island</td><td>34,810</td><td>39</td><td>Iowa</td><td>29,668</td></tr>
<tr><td>37</td><td>South Carolina</td><td>30,003</td><td>40</td><td>Nebraska</td><td>29,448</td></tr>
<tr><td>49</td><td>South Dakota</td><td>26,360</td><td>41</td><td>New Mexico</td><td>29,431</td></tr>
<tr><td>28</td><td>Tennessee</td><td>32,531</td><td>42</td><td>Wyoming</td><td>28,975</td></tr>
<tr><td>15</td><td>Texas</td><td>36,248</td><td>43</td><td>Oklahoma</td><td>28,654</td></tr>
<tr><td>35</td><td>Utah</td><td>30,585</td><td>44</td><td>West Virginia</td><td>28,612</td></tr>
<tr><td>32</td><td>Vermont</td><td>31,041</td><td>45</td><td>Idaho</td><td>28,163</td></tr>
<tr><td>13</td><td>Virginia</td><td>37,222</td><td>46</td><td>Arkansas</td><td>28,074</td></tr>
<tr><td>9</td><td>Washington</td><td>38,242</td><td>47</td><td>Mississippi</td><td>26,665</td></tr>
<tr><td>44</td><td>West Virginia</td><td>28,612</td><td>48</td><td>North Dakota</td><td>26,550</td></tr>
<tr><td>29</td><td>Wisconsin</td><td>32,464</td><td>49</td><td>South Dakota</td><td>26,360</td></tr>
<tr><td>42</td><td>Wyoming</td><td>28,975</td><td>50</td><td>Montana</td><td>26,001</td></tr>
<tr><td></td><td></td><td></td><td></td><td>District of Columbia</td><td>57,914</td></tr>
</table>

Source: U.S. Department of Labor, Bureau of Labor Statistics
"Quarterly Census of Employment and Wages: Annual Data Tables" (http://www.bls.gov/cew/state2002.pdf)
**Computed by dividing total annual wages of employees covered by unemployment insurance programs by the average monthly number of these employees. Includes bonuses, cash value of meals and lodging, tips and, in many states, employer contributions to certain deferred compensation plans such as 401(k) plans.*

Percent Change in Average Annual Wages: 2001 to 2002

National Percent Change = 1.5% Increase*

ALPHA ORDER

RANK	STATE	PERCENT CHANGE
4	Alabama	3.5
21	Alaska	2.7
37	Arizona	1.9
12	Arkansas	3.0
46	California	0.2
47	Colorado	0.1
49	Connecticut	(0.3)
6	Delaware	3.3
19	Florida	2.8
39	Georgia	1.7
1	Hawaii	4.5
42	Idaho	1.4
41	Illinois	1.5
23	Indiana	2.6
15	Iowa	2.9
31	Kansas	2.2
15	Kentucky	2.9
5	Louisiana	3.4
9	Maine	3.2
12	Maryland	3.0
48	Massachusetts	0.0
35	Michigan	2.0
27	Minnesota	2.4
15	Mississippi	2.9
32	Missouri	2.1
9	Montana	3.2
2	Nebraska	3.8
23	Nevada	2.6
35	New Hampshire	2.0
37	New Jersey	1.9
26	New Mexico	2.5
50	New York	(0.9)
32	North Carolina	2.1
6	North Dakota	3.3
19	Ohio	2.8
29	Oklahoma	2.3
42	Oregon	1.4
27	Pennsylvania	2.4
3	Rhode Island	3.6
23	South Carolina	2.6
12	South Dakota	3.0
9	Tennessee	3.2
45	Texas	0.6
39	Utah	1.7
21	Vermont	2.7
44	Virginia	1.3
32	Washington	2.1
29	West Virginia	2.3
15	Wisconsin	2.9
6	Wyoming	3.3

RANK ORDER

RANK	STATE	PERCENT CHANGE
1	Hawaii	4.5
2	Nebraska	3.8
3	Rhode Island	3.6
4	Alabama	3.5
5	Louisiana	3.4
6	Delaware	3.3
6	North Dakota	3.3
6	Wyoming	3.3
9	Maine	3.2
9	Montana	3.2
9	Tennessee	3.2
12	Arkansas	3.0
12	Maryland	3.0
12	South Dakota	3.0
15	Iowa	2.9
15	Kentucky	2.9
15	Mississippi	2.9
15	Wisconsin	2.9
19	Florida	2.8
19	Ohio	2.8
21	Alaska	2.7
21	Vermont	2.7
23	Indiana	2.6
23	Nevada	2.6
23	South Carolina	2.6
26	New Mexico	2.5
27	Minnesota	2.4
27	Pennsylvania	2.4
29	Oklahoma	2.3
29	West Virginia	2.3
31	Kansas	2.2
32	Missouri	2.1
32	North Carolina	2.1
32	Washington	2.1
35	Michigan	2.0
35	New Hampshire	2.0
37	Arizona	1.9
37	New Jersey	1.9
39	Georgia	1.7
39	Utah	1.7
41	Illinois	1.5
42	Idaho	1.4
42	Oregon	1.4
44	Virginia	1.3
45	Texas	0.6
46	California	0.2
47	Colorado	0.1
48	Massachusetts	0.0
49	Connecticut	(0.3)
50	New York	(0.9)
	District of Columbia	3.6

Source: U.S. Department of Labor, Bureau of Labor Statistics
"Quarterly Census of Employment and Wages: Annual Data Tables" (http://www.bls.gov/cew/state2002.pdf)
**Computed by dividing total annual wages of employees covered by unemployment insurance programs by the average monthly number of these employees. Includes bonuses, cash value of meals and lodging, tips and, in many states, employer contributions to certain deferred compensation plans such as 401(k) plans.*

State Minimum Wage Rates in 2004

National Rate = $5.15 per Hour*

<u>ALPHA ORDER</u>

RANK	STATE	MINIMUM WAGE
NA	Alabama**	NA
2	Alaska	7.15
NA	Arizona**	NA
13	Arkansas	5.15
5	California	6.75
13	Colorado	5.15
3	Connecticut	7.10
11	Delaware	6.15
NA	Florida**	NA
13	Georgia	5.15
9	Hawaii	6.25
13	Idaho	5.15
12	Illinois	5.50
13	Indiana	5.15
13	Iowa	5.15
43	Kansas	2.65
13	Kentucky	5.15
NA	Louisiana**	NA
9	Maine	6.25
13	Maryland	5.15
5	Massachusetts	6.75
13	Michigan	5.15
13	Minnesota	5.15
NA	Mississippi**	NA
13	Missouri	5.15
13	Montana	5.15
13	Nebraska	5.15
13	Nevada	5.15
13	New Hampshire	5.15
13	New Jersey	5.15
13	New Mexico	5.15
13	New York	5.15
13	North Carolina	5.15
13	North Dakota	5.15
42	Ohio	4.25
13	Oklahoma	5.15
4	Oregon	7.05
13	Pennsylvania	5.15
5	Rhode Island	6.75
NA	South Carolina**	NA
13	South Dakota	5.15
NA	Tennessee**	NA
13	Texas	5.15
13	Utah	5.15
5	Vermont	6.75
13	Virginia	5.15
1	Washington	7.16
13	West Virginia	5.15
13	Wisconsin	5.15
13	Wyoming	5.15

<u>RANK ORDER</u>

RANK	STATE	MINIMUM WAGE
1	Washington	$7.16
2	Alaska	7.15
3	Connecticut	7.10
4	Oregon	7.05
5	California	6.75
5	Massachusetts	6.75
5	Rhode Island	6.75
5	Vermont	6.75
9	Hawaii	6.25
9	Maine	6.25
11	Delaware	6.15
12	Illinois	5.50
13	Arkansas	5.15
13	Colorado	5.15
13	Georgia	5.15
13	Idaho	5.15
13	Indiana	5.15
13	Iowa	5.15
13	Kentucky	5.15
13	Maryland	5.15
13	Michigan	5.15
13	Minnesota	5.15
13	Missouri	5.15
13	Montana	5.15
13	Nebraska	5.15
13	Nevada	5.15
13	New Hampshire	5.15
13	New Jersey	5.15
13	New Mexico	5.15
13	New York	5.15
13	North Carolina	5.15
13	North Dakota	5.15
13	Oklahoma	5.15
13	Pennsylvania	5.15
13	South Dakota	5.15
13	Texas	5.15
13	Utah	5.15
13	Virginia	5.15
13	West Virginia	5.15
13	Wisconsin	5.15
13	Wyoming	5.15
42	Ohio	4.25
43	Kansas	2.65
NA	Alabama**	NA
NA	Arizona**	NA
NA	Florida**	NA
NA	Louisiana**	NA
NA	Mississippi**	NA
NA	South Carolina**	NA
NA	Tennessee**	NA

District of Columbia — 6.15

Source: U.S. Department of Labor, Employment Standards Administration
"Minimum Wage Laws in the States" (http://www.dol.gov/esa/minwage/america.htm)
As of January 1, 2004. State minimum wage rates are for those employers and jobs not covered by the federal program.
***No separate state program.*

Average Hourly Earnings of Production Workers
On Manufacturing Payrolls in 2003
National Average = $16.02*

<u>ALPHA ORDER</u>

RANK	STATE	HOURLY EARNINGS
45	Alabama	$13.61
46	Alaska	13.50
30	Arizona	14.60
41	Arkansas	13.90
26	California	15.29
6	Colorado	17.37
3	Connecticut	18.02
8	Delaware	17.31
33	Florida	14.48
35	Georgia	14.38
47	Hawaii	13.39
39	Idaho	14.09
22	Illinois	15.57
6	Indiana	17.37
14	Iowa	16.32
17	Kansas	16.14
19	Kentucky	15.84
11	Louisiana	16.50
13	Maine	16.38
23	Maryland	15.52
10	Massachusetts	16.53
1	Michigan	21.64
20	Minnesota	15.83
48	Mississippi	13.15
2	Missouri	18.06
35	Montana	14.38
25	Nebraska	15.30
34	Nevada	14.41
28	New Hampshire	15.23
18	New Jersey	15.86
48	New Mexico	13.15
9	New York	17.15
42	North Carolina	13.89
37	North Dakota	14.30
5	Ohio	17.96
38	Oklahoma	14.26
24	Oregon	15.50
29	Pennsylvania	15.20
50	Rhode Island	12.93
32	South Carolina	14.52
44	South Dakota	13.73
43	Tennessee	13.79
40	Texas	14.00
27	Utah	15.27
30	Vermont	14.60
15	Virginia	16.24
4	Washington	17.99
15	West Virginia	16.24
12	Wisconsin	16.40
21	Wyoming	15.80

<u>RANK ORDER</u>

RANK	STATE	HOURLY EARNINGS
1	Michigan	$21.64
2	Missouri	18.06
3	Connecticut	18.02
4	Washington	17.99
5	Ohio	17.96
6	Colorado	17.37
6	Indiana	17.37
8	Delaware	17.31
9	New York	17.15
10	Massachusetts	16.53
11	Louisiana	16.50
12	Wisconsin	16.40
13	Maine	16.38
14	Iowa	16.32
15	Virginia	16.24
15	West Virginia	16.24
17	Kansas	16.14
18	New Jersey	15.86
19	Kentucky	15.84
20	Minnesota	15.83
21	Wyoming	15.80
22	Illinois	15.57
23	Maryland	15.52
24	Oregon	15.50
25	Nebraska	15.30
26	California	15.29
27	Utah	15.27
28	New Hampshire	15.23
29	Pennsylvania	15.20
30	Arizona	14.60
30	Vermont	14.60
32	South Carolina	14.52
33	Florida	14.48
34	Nevada	14.41
35	Georgia	14.38
35	Montana	14.38
37	North Dakota	14.30
38	Oklahoma	14.26
39	Idaho	14.09
40	Texas	14.00
41	Arkansas	13.90
42	North Carolina	13.89
43	Tennessee	13.79
44	South Dakota	13.73
45	Alabama	13.61
46	Alaska	13.50
47	Hawaii	13.39
48	Mississippi	13.15
48	New Mexico	13.15
50	Rhode Island	12.93
	District of Columbia**	NA

Source: U.S. Department of Labor, Bureau of Labor Statistics
unpublished data for December 2003 (http://www.bls.gov/sae/home.htm)
Preliminary. Not seasonally adjusted.
**Not available*

Average Weekly Earnings of Production Workers
On Manufacturing Payrolls in 2003
National Average = $664.83*

ALPHA ORDER

RANK	STATE	WEEKLY EARNINGS
44	Alabama	$560.73
49	Alaska	521.10
31	Arizona	600.06
43	Arkansas	562.95
28	California	614.66
8	Colorado	698.27
2	Connecticut	767.65
9	Delaware	697.59
33	Florida	593.68
41	Georgia	570.89
50	Hawaii	484.72
22	Idaho	645.32
19	Illinois	658.61
5	Indiana	727.80
10	Iowa	696.86
16	Kansas	666.58
17	Kentucky	665.28
11	Louisiana	693.00
18	Maine	660.11
26	Maryland	625.46
13	Massachusetts	677.73
1	Michigan	958.65
23	Minnesota	642.70
46	Mississippi	541.78
4	Missouri	733.24
45	Montana	559.38
24	Nebraska	631.89
40	Nevada	574.96
29	New Hampshire	612.25
15	New Jersey	667.71
48	New Mexico	532.58
7	New York	701.44
42	North Carolina	563.93
38	North Dakota	583.44
3	Ohio	748.93
30	Oklahoma	600.35
25	Oregon	627.75
27	Pennsylvania	615.60
47	Rhode Island	532.72
34	South Carolina	589.51
32	South Dakota	595.88
39	Tennessee	581.94
35	Texas	588.00
37	Utah	584.84
36	Vermont	585.46
20	Virginia	656.10
6	Washington	723.20
14	West Virginia	677.21
12	Wisconsin	678.96
21	Wyoming	647.80

RANK ORDER

RANK	STATE	WEEKLY EARNINGS
1	Michigan	$958.65
2	Connecticut	767.65
3	Ohio	748.93
4	Missouri	733.24
5	Indiana	727.80
6	Washington	723.20
7	New York	701.44
8	Colorado	698.27
9	Delaware	697.59
10	Iowa	696.86
11	Louisiana	693.00
12	Wisconsin	678.96
13	Massachusetts	677.73
14	West Virginia	677.21
15	New Jersey	667.71
16	Kansas	666.58
17	Kentucky	665.28
18	Maine	660.11
19	Illinois	658.61
20	Virginia	656.10
21	Wyoming	647.80
22	Idaho	645.32
23	Minnesota	642.70
24	Nebraska	631.89
25	Oregon	627.75
26	Maryland	625.46
27	Pennsylvania	615.60
28	California	614.66
29	New Hampshire	612.25
30	Oklahoma	600.35
31	Arizona	600.06
32	South Dakota	595.88
33	Florida	593.68
34	South Carolina	589.51
35	Texas	588.00
36	Vermont	585.46
37	Utah	584.84
38	North Dakota	583.44
39	Tennessee	581.94
40	Nevada	574.96
41	Georgia	570.89
42	North Carolina	563.93
43	Arkansas	562.95
44	Alabama	560.73
45	Montana	559.38
46	Mississippi	541.78
47	Rhode Island	532.72
48	New Mexico	532.58
49	Alaska	521.10
50	Hawaii	484.72

District of Columbia**   NA

Source: U.S. Department of Labor, Bureau of Labor Statistics
unpublished data for December 2003 (http://www.bls.gov/sae/home.htm)
*Preliminary. Not seasonally adjusted.
**Not available

Average Work Week of Production Workers
On Manufacturing Payrolls in 2003
National Average = 41.5 Hours per Week

ALPHA ORDER

RANK	STATE	WEEKLY HOURS
19	Alabama	41.2
48	Alaska	38.6
22	Arizona	41.1
32	Arkansas	40.5
40	California	40.2
40	Colorado	40.2
5	Connecticut	42.6
37	Delaware	40.3
23	Florida	41.0
46	Georgia	39.7
50	Hawaii	36.2
1	Idaho	45.8
6	Illinois	42.3
13	Indiana	41.9
4	Iowa	42.7
17	Kansas	41.3
10	Kentucky	42.0
10	Louisiana	42.0
37	Maine	40.3
37	Maryland	40.3
23	Massachusetts	41.0
2	Michigan	44.3
28	Minnesota	40.6
19	Mississippi	41.2
28	Missouri	40.6
47	Montana	38.9
17	Nebraska	41.3
45	Nevada	39.9
40	New Hampshire	40.2
8	New Jersey	42.1
32	New Mexico	40.5
26	New York	40.9
28	North Carolina	40.6
27	North Dakota	40.8
14	Ohio	41.7
8	Oklahoma	42.1
32	Oregon	40.5
32	Pennsylvania	40.5
19	Rhode Island	41.2
28	South Carolina	40.6
3	South Dakota	43.4
7	Tennessee	42.2
10	Texas	42.0
49	Utah	38.3
44	Vermont	40.1
36	Virginia	40.4
40	Washington	40.2
14	West Virginia	41.7
16	Wisconsin	41.4
23	Wyoming	41.0

RANK ORDER

RANK	STATE	WEEKLY HOURS
1	Idaho	45.8
2	Michigan	44.3
3	South Dakota	43.4
4	Iowa	42.7
5	Connecticut	42.6
6	Illinois	42.3
7	Tennessee	42.2
8	New Jersey	42.1
8	Oklahoma	42.1
10	Kentucky	42.0
10	Louisiana	42.0
10	Texas	42.0
13	Indiana	41.9
14	Ohio	41.7
14	West Virginia	41.7
16	Wisconsin	41.4
17	Kansas	41.3
17	Nebraska	41.3
19	Alabama	41.2
19	Mississippi	41.2
19	Rhode Island	41.2
22	Arizona	41.1
23	Florida	41.0
23	Massachusetts	41.0
23	Wyoming	41.0
26	New York	40.9
27	North Dakota	40.8
28	Minnesota	40.6
28	Missouri	40.6
28	North Carolina	40.6
28	South Carolina	40.6
32	Arkansas	40.5
32	New Mexico	40.5
32	Oregon	40.5
32	Pennsylvania	40.5
36	Virginia	40.4
37	Delaware	40.3
37	Maine	40.3
37	Maryland	40.3
40	California	40.2
40	Colorado	40.2
40	New Hampshire	40.2
40	Washington	40.2
44	Vermont	40.1
45	Nevada	39.9
46	Georgia	39.7
47	Montana	38.9
48	Alaska	38.6
49	Utah	38.3
50	Hawaii	36.2
	District of Columbia**	NA

Source: U.S. Department of Labor, Bureau of Labor Statistics
    unpublished data for December 2003 (http://www.bls.gov/sae/home.htm)
*Preliminary. Not seasonally adjusted.
**Not available

Average Weekly Unemployment Benefit in 2003

National Average = $261.61 a Week

ALPHA ORDER

RANK	STATE	BENEFIT
48	Alabama	$175.75
47	Alaska	193.04
50	Arizona	173.26
35	Arkansas	228.90
27	California	246.37
7	Colorado	307.68
10	Connecticut	286.19
33	Delaware	230.28
36	Florida	225.02
28	Georgia	243.43
5	Hawaii	312.21
31	Idaho	231.77
11	Illinois	280.94
16	Indiana	263.44
18	Iowa	260.12
13	Kansas	275.99
26	Kentucky	249.62
46	Louisiana	194.93
32	Maine	231.13
23	Maryland	252.14
1	Massachusetts	356.58
9	Michigan	290.52
4	Minnesota	322.15
49	Mississippi	173.43
43	Missouri	205.62
45	Montana	201.41
39	Nebraska	216.16
30	Nevada	236.29
19	New Hampshire	258.60
2	New Jersey	333.67
40	New Mexico	210.63
14	New York	271.55
21	North Carolina	258.33
37	North Dakota	222.30
24	Ohio	251.89
34	Oklahoma	229.45
20	Oregon	258.45
8	Pennsylvania	291.84
6	Rhode Island	308.78
42	South Carolina	210.05
44	South Dakota	201.96
41	Tennessee	210.24
17	Texas	260.80
15	Utah	269.38
22	Vermont	255.08
12	Virginia	276.09
3	Washington	324.40
38	West Virginia	219.87
25	Wisconsin	251.69
29	Wyoming	238.07

RANK ORDER

RANK	STATE	BENEFIT
1	Massachusetts	$356.58
2	New Jersey	333.67
3	Washington	324.40
4	Minnesota	322.15
5	Hawaii	312.21
6	Rhode Island	308.78
7	Colorado	307.68
8	Pennsylvania	291.84
9	Michigan	290.52
10	Connecticut	286.19
11	Illinois	280.94
12	Virginia	276.09
13	Kansas	275.99
14	New York	271.55
15	Utah	269.38
16	Indiana	263.44
17	Texas	260.80
18	Iowa	260.12
19	New Hampshire	258.60
20	Oregon	258.45
21	North Carolina	258.33
22	Vermont	255.08
23	Maryland	252.14
24	Ohio	251.89
25	Wisconsin	251.69
26	Kentucky	249.62
27	California	246.37
28	Georgia	243.43
29	Wyoming	238.07
30	Nevada	236.29
31	Idaho	231.77
32	Maine	231.13
33	Delaware	230.28
34	Oklahoma	229.45
35	Arkansas	228.90
36	Florida	225.02
37	North Dakota	222.30
38	West Virginia	219.87
39	Nebraska	216.16
40	New Mexico	210.63
41	Tennessee	210.24
42	South Carolina	210.05
43	Missouri	205.62
44	South Dakota	201.96
45	Montana	201.41
46	Louisiana	194.93
47	Alaska	193.04
48	Alabama	175.75
49	Mississippi	173.43
50	Arizona	173.26
	District of Columbia	258.43

Source: U.S. Department of Labor, Bureau of Labor Statistics
unpublished data

Workers' Compensation Benefit Payments in 2001

National Total = $49,354,496,000*

ALPHA ORDER

RANK	STATE	PAYMENTS	% of USA
23	Alabama	$562,773,000	1.1%
43	Alaska	171,248,000	0.3%
31	Arizona	392,861,000	0.8%
40	Arkansas	201,136,000	0.4%
1	California	9,604,446,000	19.5%
22	Colorado	581,266,000	1.2%
21	Connecticut	661,471,000	1.3%
45	Delaware	144,588,000	0.3%
3	Florida	2,639,132,000	5.3%
12	Georgia	1,067,327,000	2.2%
36	Hawaii	252,041,000	0.5%
41	Idaho	197,151,000	0.4%
6	Illinois	2,115,569,000	4.3%
25	Indiana	528,005,000	1.1%
30	Iowa	395,981,000	0.8%
33	Kansas	340,343,000	0.7%
26	Kentucky	524,566,000	1.1%
27	Louisiana	501,662,000	1.0%
35	Maine	263,852,000	0.5%
16	Maryland	787,442,000	1.6%
17	Massachusetts	763,795,000	1.5%
9	Michigan	1,477,986,000	3.0%
14	Minnesota	908,100,000	1.8%
34	Mississippi	271,163,000	0.5%
11	Missouri	1,108,464,000	2.2%
42	Montana	172,725,000	0.3%
37	Nebraska	237,045,000	0.5%
32	Nevada	380,756,000	0.8%
38	New Hampshire	214,755,000	0.4%
10	New Jersey	1,198,095,000	2.4%
44	New Mexico	162,022,000	0.3%
2	New York	2,978,224,000	6.0%
15	North Carolina	867,965,000	1.8%
49	North Dakota	79,633,000	0.2%
5	Ohio	2,249,200,000	4.6%
28	Oklahoma	497,008,000	1.0%
29	Oregon	455,625,000	0.9%
4	Pennsylvania	2,440,407,000	4.9%
46	Rhode Island	114,599,000	0.2%
24	South Carolina	532,374,000	1.1%
50	South Dakota	74,950,000	0.2%
19	Tennessee	682,927,000	1.4%
7	Texas	2,043,451,000	4.1%
39	Utah	209,192,000	0.4%
47	Vermont	105,017,000	0.2%
20	Virginia	664,632,000	1.3%
8	Washington	1,637,714,000	3.3%
18	West Virginia	712,495,000	1.4%
13	Wisconsin	921,857,000	1.9%
48	Wyoming	97,706,000	0.2%

RANK ORDER

RANK	STATE	PAYMENTS	% of USA
1	California	$9,604,446,000	19.5%
2	New York	2,978,224,000	6.0%
3	Florida	2,639,132,000	5.3%
4	Pennsylvania	2,440,407,000	4.9%
5	Ohio	2,249,200,000	4.6%
6	Illinois	2,115,569,000	4.3%
7	Texas	2,043,451,000	4.1%
8	Washington	1,637,714,000	3.3%
9	Michigan	1,477,986,000	3.0%
10	New Jersey	1,198,095,000	2.4%
11	Missouri	1,108,464,000	2.2%
12	Georgia	1,067,327,000	2.2%
13	Wisconsin	921,857,000	1.9%
14	Minnesota	908,100,000	1.8%
15	North Carolina	867,965,000	1.8%
16	Maryland	787,442,000	1.6%
17	Massachusetts	763,795,000	1.5%
18	West Virginia	712,495,000	1.4%
19	Tennessee	682,927,000	1.4%
20	Virginia	664,632,000	1.3%
21	Connecticut	661,471,000	1.3%
22	Colorado	581,266,000	1.2%
23	Alabama	562,773,000	1.1%
24	South Carolina	532,374,000	1.1%
25	Indiana	528,005,000	1.1%
26	Kentucky	524,566,000	1.1%
27	Louisiana	501,662,000	1.0%
28	Oklahoma	497,008,000	1.0%
29	Oregon	455,625,000	0.9%
30	Iowa	395,981,000	0.8%
31	Arizona	392,861,000	0.8%
32	Nevada	380,756,000	0.8%
33	Kansas	340,343,000	0.7%
34	Mississippi	271,163,000	0.5%
35	Maine	263,852,000	0.5%
36	Hawaii	252,041,000	0.5%
37	Nebraska	237,045,000	0.5%
38	New Hampshire	214,755,000	0.4%
39	Utah	209,192,000	0.4%
40	Arkansas	201,136,000	0.4%
41	Idaho	197,151,000	0.4%
42	Montana	172,725,000	0.3%
43	Alaska	171,248,000	0.3%
44	New Mexico	162,022,000	0.3%
45	Delaware	144,588,000	0.3%
46	Rhode Island	114,599,000	0.2%
47	Vermont	105,017,000	0.2%
48	Wyoming	97,706,000	0.2%
49	North Dakota	79,633,000	0.2%
50	South Dakota	74,950,000	0.2%
	District of Columbia	92,463,000	0.2%

Source: National Academy of Social Insurance (Washington, DC)
  "Workers' Compensation: Benefits, Coverage and Costs" (http://www.nasi.org)
*Estimated payments from private insurance, state and federal funds and self insurance. National total includes payments for federal civilian employee program, Black Lung Program and other federal programs.

Workers' Compensation Benefit Payment per Covered Worker in 2001

National Average = $389*

ALPHA ORDER

RANK	STATE	AVERAGE
26	Alabama	$326
3	Alaska	644
50	Arizona	179
48	Arkansas	188
2	California	652
35	Colorado	271
13	Connecticut	402
16	Delaware	361
14	Florida	391
31	Georgia	290
5	Hawaii	478
20	Idaho	353
15	Illinois	365
49	Indiana	187
32	Iowa	281
36	Kansas	265
29	Kentucky	309
34	Louisiana	273
7	Maine	456
24	Maryland	343
42	Massachusetts	237
25	Michigan	342
20	Minnesota	353
39	Mississippi	263
9	Missouri	447
6	Montana	466
44	Nebraska	232
10	Nevada	440
19	New Hampshire	357
27	New Jersey	315
41	New Mexico	241
18	New York	359
42	North Carolina	237
36	North Dakota	265
12	Ohio	420
22	Oklahoma	351
30	Oregon	291
8	Pennsylvania	448
40	Rhode Island	261
28	South Carolina	314
45	South Dakota	212
33	Tennessee	275
36	Texas	265
47	Utah	206
17	Vermont	360
46	Virginia	207
4	Washington	625
1	West Virginia	1,073
22	Wisconsin	351
11	Wyoming	429

RANK ORDER

RANK	STATE	AVERAGE
1	West Virginia	$1,073
2	California	652
3	Alaska	644
4	Washington	625
5	Hawaii	478
6	Montana	466
7	Maine	456
8	Pennsylvania	448
9	Missouri	447
10	Nevada	440
11	Wyoming	429
12	Ohio	420
13	Connecticut	402
14	Florida	391
15	Illinois	365
16	Delaware	361
17	Vermont	360
18	New York	359
19	New Hampshire	357
20	Idaho	353
20	Minnesota	353
22	Oklahoma	351
22	Wisconsin	351
24	Maryland	343
25	Michigan	342
26	Alabama	326
27	New Jersey	315
28	South Carolina	314
29	Kentucky	309
30	Oregon	291
31	Georgia	290
32	Iowa	281
33	Tennessee	275
34	Louisiana	273
35	Colorado	271
36	Kansas	265
36	North Dakota	265
36	Texas	265
39	Mississippi	263
40	Rhode Island	261
41	New Mexico	241
42	Massachusetts	237
42	North Carolina	237
44	Nebraska	232
45	South Dakota	212
46	Virginia	207
47	Utah	206
48	Arkansas	188
49	Indiana	187
50	Arizona	179
	District of Columbia	205

Source: Morgan Quitno Press using data from National Academy of Social Insurance (Washington, DC)
"Workers' Compensation: Benefits, Coverage and Costs" (http://www.nasi.org)
*Estimated payments from private insurance, state and federal funds and self insurance. National rate includes payments for federal civilian employee program, Black Lung Program and other federal programs. Total divided by number of workers covered by workers' compensation.

Percent Change in Workers' Compensation Benefit Payments: 2000 to 2001

National Percent Change = 3.5% Increase*

<u>ALPHA ORDER</u>

RANK	STATE	PERCENT CHANGE
21	Alabama	6.3
4	Alaska	17.4
49	Arizona	(23.8)
26	Arkansas	3.4
19	California	7.1
50	Colorado	(30.4)
41	Connecticut	(0.8)
42	Delaware	(1.0)
25	Florida	3.7
16	Georgia	7.2
14	Hawaii	8.9
12	Idaho	9.9
27	Illinois	3.2
45	Indiana	(3.3)
6	Iowa	12.4
40	Kansas	(0.4)
13	Kentucky	9.4
35	Louisiana	1.6
43	Maine	(1.2)
15	Maryland	7.9
47	Massachusetts	(7.8)
38	Michigan	0.3
5	Minnesota	13.8
37	Mississippi	0.7
31	Missouri	2.2
33	Montana	1.7
7	Nebraska	12.2
23	Nevada	5.5
2	New Hampshire	18.1
39	New Jersey	0.0
10	New Mexico	10.7
30	New York	2.4
33	North Carolina	1.7
20	North Dakota	7.0
16	Ohio	7.2
29	Oklahoma	2.5
11	Oregon	10.5
35	Pennsylvania	1.6
24	Rhode Island	4.7
48	South Carolina	(10.8)
8	South Dakota	11.9
21	Tennessee	6.3
32	Texas	1.9
9	Utah	11.4
46	Vermont	(6.5)
44	Virginia	(2.4)
16	Washington	7.2
27	West Virginia	3.2
1	Wisconsin	20.0
3	Wyoming	17.9

<u>RANK ORDER</u>

RANK	STATE	PERCENT CHANGE
1	Wisconsin	20.0
2	New Hampshire	18.1
3	Wyoming	17.9
4	Alaska	17.4
5	Minnesota	13.8
6	Iowa	12.4
7	Nebraska	12.2
8	South Dakota	11.9
9	Utah	11.4
10	New Mexico	10.7
11	Oregon	10.5
12	Idaho	9.9
13	Kentucky	9.4
14	Hawaii	8.9
15	Maryland	7.9
16	Georgia	7.2
16	Ohio	7.2
16	Washington	7.2
19	California	7.1
20	North Dakota	7.0
21	Alabama	6.3
21	Tennessee	6.3
23	Nevada	5.5
24	Rhode Island	4.7
25	Florida	3.7
26	Arkansas	3.4
27	Illinois	3.2
27	West Virginia	3.2
29	Oklahoma	2.5
30	New York	2.4
31	Missouri	2.2
32	Texas	1.9
33	Montana	1.7
33	North Carolina	1.7
35	Louisiana	1.6
35	Pennsylvania	1.6
37	Mississippi	0.7
38	Michigan	0.3
39	New Jersey	0.0
40	Kansas	(0.4)
41	Connecticut	(0.8)
42	Delaware	(1.0)
43	Maine	(1.2)
44	Virginia	(2.4)
45	Indiana	(3.3)
46	Vermont	(6.5)
47	Massachusetts	(7.8)
48	South Carolina	(10.8)
49	Arizona	(23.8)
50	Colorado	(30.4)

District of Columbia	4.3

Source: National Academy of Social Insurance (Washington, DC)
"Workers' Compensation: Benefits, Coverage and Costs" (http://www.nasi.org)
**Estimated payments from private insurance, state and federal funds and self insurance. National rate includes payments for federal civilian employee program, Black Lung Program and other federal programs.*

Civilian Labor Force in 2003

National Total = 146,878,000 Workers*

ALPHA ORDER

RANK	STATE	WORKERS	% of USA
23	Alabama	2,151,900	1.5%
49	Alaska	347,400	0.2%
21	Arizona	2,653,100	1.8%
33	Arkansas	1,310,400	0.9%
1	California	17,681,600	12.0%
22	Colorado	2,485,900	1.7%
28	Connecticut	1,783,400	1.2%
46	Delaware	419,700	0.3%
4	Florida	8,075,500	5.5%
10	Georgia	4,357,500	3.0%
42	Hawaii	609,500	0.4%
41	Idaho	685,800	0.5%
5	Illinois	6,478,400	4.4%
14	Indiana	3,205,000	2.2%
30	Iowa	1,633,200	1.1%
31	Kansas	1,481,900	1.0%
26	Kentucky	1,995,300	1.4%
24	Louisiana	2,064,400	1.4%
40	Maine	697,700	0.5%
19	Maryland	2,930,400	2.0%
13	Massachusetts	3,460,200	2.4%
8	Michigan	5,084,800	3.5%
18	Minnesota	2,934,000	2.0%
32	Mississippi	1,316,700	0.9%
17	Missouri	2,985,500	2.0%
44	Montana	476,200	0.3%
36	Nebraska	989,000	0.7%
35	Nevada	1,104,100	0.8%
39	New Hampshire	716,000	0.5%
9	New Jersey	4,450,700	3.0%
37	New Mexico	898,400	0.6%
3	New York	9,388,600	6.4%
11	North Carolina	4,187,500	2.9%
47	North Dakota	355,400	0.2%
7	Ohio	5,857,800	4.0%
29	Oklahoma	1,688,600	1.1%
27	Oregon	1,820,700	1.2%
6	Pennsylvania	6,205,700	4.2%
43	Rhode Island	562,800	0.4%
25	South Carolina	2,019,600	1.4%
45	South Dakota	425,900	0.3%
20	Tennessee	2,908,700	2.0%
2	Texas	11,033,000	7.5%
34	Utah	1,222,500	0.8%
48	Vermont	352,600	0.2%
12	Virginia	3,796,900	2.6%
15	Washington	3,132,800	2.1%
38	West Virginia	794,100	0.5%
16	Wisconsin	3,093,700	2.1%
50	Wyoming	277,400	0.2%

RANK ORDER

RANK	STATE	WORKERS	% of USA
1	California	17,681,600	12.0%
2	Texas	11,033,000	7.5%
3	New York	9,388,600	6.4%
4	Florida	8,075,500	5.5%
5	Illinois	6,478,400	4.4%
6	Pennsylvania	6,205,700	4.2%
7	Ohio	5,857,800	4.0%
8	Michigan	5,084,800	3.5%
9	New Jersey	4,450,700	3.0%
10	Georgia	4,357,500	3.0%
11	North Carolina	4,187,500	2.9%
12	Virginia	3,796,900	2.6%
13	Massachusetts	3,460,200	2.4%
14	Indiana	3,205,000	2.2%
15	Washington	3,132,800	2.1%
16	Wisconsin	3,093,700	2.1%
17	Missouri	2,985,500	2.0%
18	Minnesota	2,934,000	2.0%
19	Maryland	2,930,400	2.0%
20	Tennessee	2,908,700	2.0%
21	Arizona	2,653,100	1.8%
22	Colorado	2,485,900	1.7%
23	Alabama	2,151,900	1.5%
24	Louisiana	2,064,400	1.4%
25	South Carolina	2,019,600	1.4%
26	Kentucky	1,995,300	1.4%
27	Oregon	1,820,700	1.2%
28	Connecticut	1,783,400	1.2%
29	Oklahoma	1,688,600	1.1%
30	Iowa	1,633,200	1.1%
31	Kansas	1,481,900	1.0%
32	Mississippi	1,316,700	0.9%
33	Arkansas	1,310,400	0.9%
34	Utah	1,222,500	0.8%
35	Nevada	1,104,100	0.8%
36	Nebraska	989,000	0.7%
37	New Mexico	898,400	0.6%
38	West Virginia	794,100	0.5%
39	New Hampshire	716,000	0.5%
40	Maine	697,700	0.5%
41	Idaho	685,800	0.5%
42	Hawaii	609,500	0.4%
43	Rhode Island	562,800	0.4%
44	Montana	476,200	0.3%
45	South Dakota	425,900	0.3%
46	Delaware	419,700	0.3%
47	North Dakota	355,400	0.2%
48	Vermont	352,600	0.2%
49	Alaska	347,400	0.2%
50	Wyoming	277,400	0.2%
	District of Columbia	307,200	0.2%

Source: U.S. Department of Labor, Bureau of Labor Statistics
   "Regional and State Employment and Unemployment" (press release, January 27, 2004)
*Seasonally adjusted preliminary data as of December 2003. National total calculated through a different formula.

Employed Civilian Labor Force in 2003

National Total = 138,479,000 Employed Workers*

ALPHA ORDER

RANK	STATE	EMPLOYED	% of USA
23	Alabama	2,026,900	1.5%
49	Alaska	320,500	0.2%
21	Arizona	2,524,900	1.8%
33	Arkansas	1,238,100	0.9%
1	California	16,555,700	12.0%
22	Colorado	2,342,900	1.7%
27	Connecticut	1,694,200	1.2%
46	Delaware	402,500	0.3%
4	Florida	7,698,200	5.6%
10	Georgia	4,177,700	3.0%
42	Hawaii	584,500	0.4%
41	Idaho	653,000	0.5%
5	Illinois	6,060,700	4.4%
14	Indiana	3,045,700	2.2%
30	Iowa	1,562,000	1.1%
31	Kansas	1,411,000	1.0%
26	Kentucky	1,886,700	1.4%
24	Louisiana	1,944,200	1.4%
40	Maine	662,900	0.5%
18	Maryland	2,801,400	2.0%
13	Massachusetts	3,264,500	2.4%
8	Michigan	4,719,300	3.4%
19	Minnesota	2,795,700	2.0%
32	Mississippi	1,250,300	0.9%
17	Missouri	2,837,500	2.0%
44	Montana	454,700	0.3%
36	Nebraska	951,900	0.7%
35	Nevada	1,055,000	0.8%
39	New Hampshire	686,600	0.5%
9	New Jersey	4,214,800	3.0%
37	New Mexico	847,000	0.6%
3	New York	8,802,600	6.4%
11	North Carolina	3,931,200	2.8%
47	North Dakota	344,100	0.2%
7	Ohio	5,507,100	4.0%
29	Oklahoma	1,601,900	1.2%
28	Oregon	1,688,900	1.2%
6	Pennsylvania	5,889,500	4.3%
43	Rhode Island	534,700	0.4%
25	South Carolina	1,895,600	1.4%
45	South Dakota	411,400	0.3%
20	Tennessee	2,743,800	2.0%
2	Texas	10,330,100	7.5%
34	Utah	1,165,200	0.8%
48	Vermont	338,400	0.2%
12	Virginia	3,658,300	2.6%
16	Washington	2,919,000	2.1%
38	West Virginia	751,900	0.5%
15	Wisconsin	2,934,400	2.1%
50	Wyoming	266,300	0.2%

RANK ORDER

RANK	STATE	EMPLOYED	% of USA
1	California	16,555,700	12.0%
2	Texas	10,330,100	7.5%
3	New York	8,802,600	6.4%
4	Florida	7,698,200	5.6%
5	Illinois	6,060,700	4.4%
6	Pennsylvania	5,889,500	4.3%
7	Ohio	5,507,100	4.0%
8	Michigan	4,719,300	3.4%
9	New Jersey	4,214,800	3.0%
10	Georgia	4,177,700	3.0%
11	North Carolina	3,931,200	2.8%
12	Virginia	3,658,300	2.6%
13	Massachusetts	3,264,500	2.4%
14	Indiana	3,045,700	2.2%
15	Wisconsin	2,934,400	2.1%
16	Washington	2,919,000	2.1%
17	Missouri	2,837,500	2.0%
18	Maryland	2,801,400	2.0%
19	Minnesota	2,795,700	2.0%
20	Tennessee	2,743,800	2.0%
21	Arizona	2,524,900	1.8%
22	Colorado	2,342,900	1.7%
23	Alabama	2,026,900	1.5%
24	Louisiana	1,944,200	1.4%
25	South Carolina	1,895,600	1.4%
26	Kentucky	1,886,700	1.4%
27	Connecticut	1,694,200	1.2%
28	Oregon	1,688,900	1.2%
29	Oklahoma	1,601,900	1.2%
30	Iowa	1,562,000	1.1%
31	Kansas	1,411,000	1.0%
32	Mississippi	1,250,300	0.9%
33	Arkansas	1,238,100	0.9%
34	Utah	1,165,200	0.8%
35	Nevada	1,055,000	0.8%
36	Nebraska	951,900	0.7%
37	New Mexico	847,000	0.6%
38	West Virginia	751,900	0.5%
39	New Hampshire	686,600	0.5%
40	Maine	662,900	0.5%
41	Idaho	653,000	0.5%
42	Hawaii	584,500	0.4%
43	Rhode Island	534,700	0.4%
44	Montana	454,700	0.3%
45	South Dakota	411,400	0.3%
46	Delaware	402,500	0.3%
47	North Dakota	344,100	0.2%
48	Vermont	338,400	0.2%
49	Alaska	320,500	0.2%
50	Wyoming	266,300	0.2%
	District of Columbia	287,000	0.2%

Source: Morgan Quitno Press using data from U.S. Department of Labor, Bureau of Labor Statistics
   "Regional and State Employment and Unemployment" (press release, January 27, 2004)
*Seasonally adjusted preliminary data as of December 2003. National total calculated through a different formula.

Employment to Population Ratio in 2003

National Percent = 61.9% of Population 16 Years and Older Employed*

<u>ALPHA ORDER</u>

RANK	STATE	PERCENT
46	Alabama	57.8
10	Alaska	67.5
33	Arizona	61.1
42	Arkansas	58.7
30	California	62.1
11	Colorado	67.3
22	Connecticut	63.2
24	Delaware	63.0
45	Florida	58.0
18	Georgia	63.9
40	Hawaii	59.5
15	Idaho	64.4
28	Illinois	62.5
16	Indiana	64.2
12	Iowa	67.2
13	Kansas	67.1
47	Kentucky	57.7
49	Louisiana	56.6
24	Maine	63.0
14	Maryland	66.2
20	Massachusetts	63.6
36	Michigan	60.7
1	Minnesota	71.3
48	Mississippi	56.9
18	Missouri	63.9
24	Montana	63.0
2	Nebraska	70.9
20	Nevada	63.6
6	New Hampshire	68.4
24	New Jersey	63.0
39	New Mexico	59.9
43	New York	58.5
35	North Carolina	60.8
8	North Dakota	67.9
30	Ohio	62.1
41	Oklahoma	58.8
33	Oregon	61.1
38	Pennsylvania	60.0
29	Rhode Island	62.3
43	South Carolina	58.5
3	South Dakota	69.7
37	Tennessee	60.3
22	Texas	63.2
4	Utah	69.3
7	Vermont	68.3
17	Virginia	64.1
32	Washington	61.7
50	West Virginia	51.5
5	Wisconsin	68.8
9	Wyoming	67.8

<u>RANK ORDER</u>

RANK	STATE	PERCENT
1	Minnesota	71.3
2	Nebraska	70.9
3	South Dakota	69.7
4	Utah	69.3
5	Wisconsin	68.8
6	New Hampshire	68.4
7	Vermont	68.3
8	North Dakota	67.9
9	Wyoming	67.8
10	Alaska	67.5
11	Colorado	67.3
12	Iowa	67.2
13	Kansas	67.1
14	Maryland	66.2
15	Idaho	64.4
16	Indiana	64.2
17	Virginia	64.1
18	Georgia	63.9
18	Missouri	63.9
20	Massachusetts	63.6
20	Nevada	63.6
22	Connecticut	63.2
22	Texas	63.2
24	Delaware	63.0
24	Maine	63.0
24	Montana	63.0
24	New Jersey	63.0
28	Illinois	62.5
29	Rhode Island	62.3
30	California	62.1
30	Ohio	62.1
32	Washington	61.7
33	Arizona	61.1
33	Oregon	61.1
35	North Carolina	60.8
36	Michigan	60.7
37	Tennessee	60.3
38	Pennsylvania	60.0
39	New Mexico	59.9
40	Hawaii	59.5
41	Oklahoma	58.8
42	Arkansas	58.7
43	New York	58.5
43	South Carolina	58.5
45	Florida	58.0
46	Alabama	57.8
47	Kentucky	57.7
48	Mississippi	56.9
49	Louisiana	56.6
50	West Virginia	51.5

	District of Columbia	61.2

Source: Morgan Quitno Press using data from U.S. Department of Labor, Bureau of Labor Statistics "Regional and State Employment and Unemployment" (press release, January 27, 2004)
**Seasonally adjusted preliminary data as of December 2003.*

Unemployed Civilian Labor Force in 2003

National Total = 8,398,000 Unemployed Workers*

<u>ALPHA ORDER</u>

RANK	STATE	UNEMPLOYED	% of USA
24	Alabama	125,000	1.5%
43	Alaska	26,900	0.3%
23	Arizona	128,200	1.5%
30	Arkansas	72,300	0.9%
1	California	1,125,900	13.4%
18	Colorado	143,000	1.7%
28	Connecticut	89,200	1.1%
46	Delaware	17,200	0.2%
5	Florida	377,300	4.5%
13	Georgia	179,800	2.1%
44	Hawaii	25,000	0.3%
40	Idaho	32,800	0.4%
4	Illinois	417,700	5.0%
15	Indiana	159,300	1.9%
31	Iowa	71,200	0.8%
32	Kansas	70,900	0.8%
27	Kentucky	108,600	1.3%
26	Louisiana	120,200	1.4%
39	Maine	34,800	0.4%
22	Maryland	129,000	1.5%
12	Massachusetts	195,700	2.3%
6	Michigan	365,500	4.4%
20	Minnesota	138,300	1.6%
33	Mississippi	66,400	0.8%
17	Missouri	148,000	1.8%
45	Montana	21,500	0.3%
38	Nebraska	37,100	0.4%
36	Nevada	49,100	0.6%
41	New Hampshire	29,400	0.4%
10	New Jersey	235,900	2.8%
35	New Mexico	51,400	0.6%
3	New York	586,000	7.0%
9	North Carolina	256,300	3.1%
49	North Dakota	11,300	0.1%
7	Ohio	350,700	4.2%
29	Oklahoma	86,700	1.0%
21	Oregon	131,800	1.6%
8	Pennsylvania	316,200	3.8%
42	Rhode Island	28,100	0.3%
25	South Carolina	124,000	1.5%
47	South Dakota	14,500	0.2%
14	Tennessee	164,900	2.0%
2	Texas	702,900	8.4%
34	Utah	57,300	0.7%
48	Vermont	14,200	0.2%
19	Virginia	138,600	1.7%
11	Washington	213,800	2.5%
37	West Virginia	42,200	0.5%
15	Wisconsin	159,300	1.9%
50	Wyoming	11,100	0.1%

<u>RANK ORDER</u>

RANK	STATE	UNEMPLOYED	% of USA
1	California	1,125,900	13.4%
2	Texas	702,900	8.4%
3	New York	586,000	7.0%
4	Illinois	417,700	5.0%
5	Florida	377,300	4.5%
6	Michigan	365,500	4.4%
7	Ohio	350,700	4.2%
8	Pennsylvania	316,200	3.8%
9	North Carolina	256,300	3.1%
10	New Jersey	235,900	2.8%
11	Washington	213,800	2.5%
12	Massachusetts	195,700	2.3%
13	Georgia	179,800	2.1%
14	Tennessee	164,900	2.0%
15	Indiana	159,300	1.9%
15	Wisconsin	159,300	1.9%
17	Missouri	148,000	1.8%
18	Colorado	143,000	1.7%
19	Virginia	138,600	1.7%
20	Minnesota	138,300	1.6%
21	Oregon	131,800	1.6%
22	Maryland	129,000	1.5%
23	Arizona	128,200	1.5%
24	Alabama	125,000	1.5%
25	South Carolina	124,000	1.5%
26	Louisiana	120,200	1.4%
27	Kentucky	108,600	1.3%
28	Connecticut	89,200	1.1%
29	Oklahoma	86,700	1.0%
30	Arkansas	72,300	0.9%
31	Iowa	71,200	0.8%
32	Kansas	70,900	0.8%
33	Mississippi	66,400	0.8%
34	Utah	57,300	0.7%
35	New Mexico	51,400	0.6%
36	Nevada	49,100	0.6%
37	West Virginia	42,200	0.5%
38	Nebraska	37,100	0.4%
39	Maine	34,800	0.4%
40	Idaho	32,800	0.4%
41	New Hampshire	29,400	0.4%
42	Rhode Island	28,100	0.3%
43	Alaska	26,900	0.3%
44	Hawaii	25,000	0.3%
45	Montana	21,500	0.3%
46	Delaware	17,200	0.2%
47	South Dakota	14,500	0.2%
48	Vermont	14,200	0.2%
49	North Dakota	11,300	0.1%
50	Wyoming	11,100	0.1%
	District of Columbia	20,200	0.2%

Source: U.S. Department of Labor, Bureau of Labor Statistics
   "Regional and State Employment and Unemployment" (press release, January 27, 2004)
*Seasonally adjusted preliminary data as of December 2003. National total calculated through a different formula.

Unemployment Rate in 2003

National Rate = 5.7% of Labor Force Unemployed*

ALPHA ORDER

RANK	STATE	PERCENT
12	Alabama	5.8
1	Alaska	7.7
31	Arizona	4.8
18	Arkansas	5.5
5	California	6.4
12	Colorado	5.8
25	Connecticut	5.0
41	Delaware	4.1
34	Florida	4.7
41	Georgia	4.1
41	Hawaii	4.1
31	Idaho	4.8
5	Illinois	6.4
25	Indiana	5.0
38	Iowa	4.4
31	Kansas	4.8
19	Kentucky	5.4
12	Louisiana	5.8
25	Maine	5.0
38	Maryland	4.4
15	Massachusetts	5.7
2	Michigan	7.2
34	Minnesota	4.7
25	Mississippi	5.0
25	Missouri	5.0
37	Montana	4.5
47	Nebraska	3.7
38	Nevada	4.4
41	New Hampshire	4.1
20	New Jersey	5.3
15	New Mexico	5.7
8	New York	6.2
9	North Carolina	6.1
50	North Dakota	3.2
11	Ohio	6.0
23	Oklahoma	5.1
2	Oregon	7.2
23	Pennsylvania	5.1
25	Rhode Island	5.0
9	South Carolina	6.1
49	South Dakota	3.4
15	Tennessee	5.7
5	Texas	6.4
34	Utah	4.7
45	Vermont	4.0
48	Virginia	3.6
4	Washington	6.8
20	West Virginia	5.3
22	Wisconsin	5.2
45	Wyoming	4.0

RANK ORDER

RANK	STATE	PERCENT
1	Alaska	7.7
2	Michigan	7.2
2	Oregon	7.2
4	Washington	6.8
5	California	6.4
5	Illinois	6.4
5	Texas	6.4
8	New York	6.2
9	North Carolina	6.1
9	South Carolina	6.1
11	Ohio	6.0
12	Alabama	5.8
12	Colorado	5.8
12	Louisiana	5.8
15	Massachusetts	5.7
15	New Mexico	5.7
15	Tennessee	5.7
18	Arkansas	5.5
19	Kentucky	5.4
20	New Jersey	5.3
20	West Virginia	5.3
22	Wisconsin	5.2
23	Oklahoma	5.1
23	Pennsylvania	5.1
25	Connecticut	5.0
25	Indiana	5.0
25	Maine	5.0
25	Mississippi	5.0
25	Missouri	5.0
25	Rhode Island	5.0
31	Arizona	4.8
31	Idaho	4.8
31	Kansas	4.8
34	Florida	4.7
34	Minnesota	4.7
34	Utah	4.7
37	Montana	4.5
38	Iowa	4.4
38	Maryland	4.4
38	Nevada	4.4
41	Delaware	4.1
41	Georgia	4.1
41	Hawaii	4.1
41	New Hampshire	4.1
45	Vermont	4.0
45	Wyoming	4.0
47	Nebraska	3.7
48	Virginia	3.6
49	South Dakota	3.4
50	North Dakota	3.2
	District of Columbia	6.6

Source: U.S. Department of Labor, Bureau of Labor Statistics
"Regional and State Employment and Unemployment" (press release, January 27, 2004)
**Seasonally adjusted preliminary data as of December 2003. National rate calculated through a different formula.*

Women in Civilian Labor Force in 2002

National Total = 67,579,000 Women*

<u>ALPHA ORDER</u>

RANK	STATE	WOMEN	% of USA
23	Alabama	999,000	1.5%
49	Alaska	148,000	0.2%
21	Arizona	1,150,000	1.7%
33	Arkansas	604,000	0.9%
1	California	7,832,000	11.6%
22	Colorado	1,079,000	1.6%
27	Connecticut	852,000	1.3%
45	Delaware	206,000	0.3%
4	Florida	3,726,000	5.5%
10	Georgia	1,990,000	2.9%
42	Hawaii	283,000	0.4%
41	Idaho	317,000	0.5%
5	Illinois	3,001,000	4.4%
14	Indiana	1,491,000	2.2%
29	Iowa	792,000	1.2%
31	Kansas	672,000	1.0%
25	Kentucky	936,000	1.4%
26	Louisiana	921,000	1.4%
39	Maine	332,000	0.5%
18	Maryland	1,409,000	2.1%
13	Massachusetts	1,652,000	2.4%
8	Michigan	2,335,000	3.5%
19	Minnesota	1,392,000	2.1%
32	Mississippi	621,000	0.9%
15	Missouri	1,458,000	2.2%
44	Montana	217,000	0.3%
36	Nebraska	457,000	0.7%
35	Nevada	485,000	0.7%
40	New Hampshire	330,000	0.5%
9	New Jersey	2,048,000	3.0%
37	New Mexico	410,000	0.6%
3	New York	4,420,000	6.5%
11	North Carolina	1,959,000	2.9%
48	North Dakota	166,000	0.2%
7	Ohio	2,772,000	4.1%
30	Oklahoma	782,000	1.2%
28	Oregon	841,000	1.2%
6	Pennsylvania	2,951,000	4.4%
43	Rhode Island	267,000	0.4%
24	South Carolina	944,000	1.4%
46	South Dakota	201,000	0.3%
20	Tennessee	1,367,000	2.0%
2	Texas	4,802,000	7.1%
34	Utah	523,000	0.8%
47	Vermont	170,000	0.3%
12	Virginia	1,774,000	2.6%
16	Washington	1,431,000	2.1%
38	West Virginia	367,000	0.5%
17	Wisconsin	1,418,000	2.1%
50	Wyoming	127,000	0.2%

<u>RANK ORDER</u>

RANK	STATE	WOMEN	% of USA
1	California	7,832,000	11.6%
2	Texas	4,802,000	7.1%
3	New York	4,420,000	6.5%
4	Florida	3,726,000	5.5%
5	Illinois	3,001,000	4.4%
6	Pennsylvania	2,951,000	4.4%
7	Ohio	2,772,000	4.1%
8	Michigan	2,335,000	3.5%
9	New Jersey	2,048,000	3.0%
10	Georgia	1,990,000	2.9%
11	North Carolina	1,959,000	2.9%
12	Virginia	1,774,000	2.6%
13	Massachusetts	1,652,000	2.4%
14	Indiana	1,491,000	2.2%
15	Missouri	1,458,000	2.2%
16	Washington	1,431,000	2.1%
17	Wisconsin	1,418,000	2.1%
18	Maryland	1,409,000	2.1%
19	Minnesota	1,392,000	2.1%
20	Tennessee	1,367,000	2.0%
21	Arizona	1,150,000	1.7%
22	Colorado	1,079,000	1.6%
23	Alabama	999,000	1.5%
24	South Carolina	944,000	1.4%
25	Kentucky	936,000	1.4%
26	Louisiana	921,000	1.4%
27	Connecticut	852,000	1.3%
28	Oregon	841,000	1.2%
29	Iowa	792,000	1.2%
30	Oklahoma	782,000	1.2%
31	Kansas	672,000	1.0%
32	Mississippi	621,000	0.9%
33	Arkansas	604,000	0.9%
34	Utah	523,000	0.8%
35	Nevada	485,000	0.7%
36	Nebraska	457,000	0.7%
37	New Mexico	410,000	0.6%
38	West Virginia	367,000	0.5%
39	Maine	332,000	0.5%
40	New Hampshire	330,000	0.5%
41	Idaho	317,000	0.5%
42	Hawaii	283,000	0.4%
43	Rhode Island	267,000	0.4%
44	Montana	217,000	0.3%
45	Delaware	206,000	0.3%
46	South Dakota	201,000	0.3%
47	Vermont	170,000	0.3%
48	North Dakota	166,000	0.2%
49	Alaska	148,000	0.2%
50	Wyoming	127,000	0.2%
	District of Columbia	152,000	0.2%

Source: U.S. Department of Labor, Bureau of Labor Statistics
"Geographic Profiles of Employment and Unemployment, 2002"
*Annual averages.

Percent of Women in the Civilian Labor Force in 2002

National Percent = 59.6% of Women*

<u>ALPHA ORDER</u>

RANK	STATE	PERCENT
47	Alabama	54.7
7	Alaska	66.3
41	Arizona	57.0
46	Arkansas	55.4
36	California	58.8
10	Colorado	64.4
19	Connecticut	62.0
15	Delaware	62.5
44	Florida	55.7
31	Georgia	59.8
24	Hawaii	60.8
19	Idaho	62.0
29	Illinois	60.2
22	Indiana	61.4
3	Iowa	67.1
14	Kansas	62.9
45	Kentucky	55.6
49	Louisiana	52.1
21	Maine	61.6
11	Maryland	64.3
17	Massachusetts	62.3
34	Michigan	58.9
1	Minnesota	71.2
48	Mississippi	54.0
13	Missouri	63.8
25	Montana	60.7
3	Nebraska	67.1
23	Nevada	60.9
9	New Hampshire	65.2
33	New Jersey	59.5
40	New Mexico	57.4
43	New York	56.6
30	North Carolina	59.9
8	North Dakota	65.5
25	Ohio	60.7
39	Oklahoma	57.6
28	Oregon	60.6
34	Pennsylvania	58.9
32	Rhode Island	59.6
42	South Carolina	56.9
2	South Dakota	68.1
38	Tennessee	58.3
36	Texas	58.8
15	Utah	62.5
6	Vermont	66.5
17	Virginia	62.3
25	Washington	60.7
50	West Virginia	48.8
5	Wisconsin	66.7
12	Wyoming	64.2

<u>RANK ORDER</u>

RANK	STATE	PERCENT
1	Minnesota	71.2
2	South Dakota	68.1
3	Iowa	67.1
3	Nebraska	67.1
5	Wisconsin	66.7
6	Vermont	66.5
7	Alaska	66.3
8	North Dakota	65.5
9	New Hampshire	65.2
10	Colorado	64.4
11	Maryland	64.3
12	Wyoming	64.2
13	Missouri	63.8
14	Kansas	62.9
15	Delaware	62.5
15	Utah	62.5
17	Massachusetts	62.3
17	Virginia	62.3
19	Connecticut	62.0
19	Idaho	62.0
21	Maine	61.6
22	Indiana	61.4
23	Nevada	60.9
24	Hawaii	60.8
25	Montana	60.7
25	Ohio	60.7
25	Washington	60.7
28	Oregon	60.6
29	Illinois	60.2
30	North Carolina	59.9
31	Georgia	59.8
32	Rhode Island	59.6
33	New Jersey	59.5
34	Michigan	58.9
34	Pennsylvania	58.9
36	California	58.8
36	Texas	58.8
38	Tennessee	58.3
39	Oklahoma	57.6
40	New Mexico	57.4
41	Arizona	57.0
42	South Carolina	56.9
43	New York	56.6
44	Florida	55.7
45	Kentucky	55.6
46	Arkansas	55.4
47	Alabama	54.7
48	Mississippi	54.0
49	Louisiana	52.1
50	West Virginia	48.8

| | District of Columbia | 61.1 |

Source: U.S. Department of Labor, Bureau of Labor Statistics
   "Geographic Profiles of Employment and Unemployment, 2002"
*Annual averages.

Percent of Civilian Labor Force Comprised of Women in 2002

National Percent = 46.7% of Civilian Labor Force*

ALPHA ORDER

RANK	STATE	PERCENT
17	Alabama	47.5
43	Alaska	45.8
50	Arizona	43.0
24	Arkansas	47.0
45	California	45.0
47	Colorado	44.3
7	Connecticut	48.1
2	Delaware	48.7
40	Florida	46.1
36	Georgia	46.4
4	Hawaii	48.6
37	Idaho	46.3
23	Illinois	47.1
24	Indiana	47.0
17	Iowa	47.5
17	Kansas	47.5
15	Kentucky	47.6
41	Louisiana	45.9
6	Maine	48.4
4	Maryland	48.6
21	Massachusetts	47.4
32	Michigan	46.7
12	Minnesota	47.7
11	Mississippi	47.8
1	Missouri	48.8
30	Montana	46.8
12	Nebraska	47.7
49	Nevada	43.2
32	New Hampshire	46.7
28	New Jersey	46.9
32	New Mexico	46.7
22	New York	47.2
24	North Carolina	47.0
8	North Dakota	48.0
15	Ohio	47.6
38	Oklahoma	46.2
41	Oregon	45.9
28	Pennsylvania	46.9
8	Rhode Island	48.0
8	South Carolina	48.0
12	South Dakota	47.7
32	Tennessee	46.7
46	Texas	44.7
47	Utah	44.3
2	Vermont	48.7
17	Virginia	47.5
38	Washington	46.2
44	West Virginia	45.6
30	Wisconsin	46.8
24	Wyoming	47.0

RANK ORDER

RANK	STATE	PERCENT
1	Missouri	48.8
2	Delaware	48.7
2	Vermont	48.7
4	Hawaii	48.6
4	Maryland	48.6
6	Maine	48.4
7	Connecticut	48.1
8	North Dakota	48.0
8	Rhode Island	48.0
8	South Carolina	48.0
11	Mississippi	47.8
12	Minnesota	47.7
12	Nebraska	47.7
12	South Dakota	47.7
15	Kentucky	47.6
15	Ohio	47.6
17	Alabama	47.5
17	Iowa	47.5
17	Kansas	47.5
17	Virginia	47.5
21	Massachusetts	47.4
22	New York	47.2
23	Illinois	47.1
24	Arkansas	47.0
24	Indiana	47.0
24	North Carolina	47.0
24	Wyoming	47.0
28	New Jersey	46.9
28	Pennsylvania	46.9
30	Montana	46.8
30	Wisconsin	46.8
32	Michigan	46.7
32	New Hampshire	46.7
32	New Mexico	46.7
32	Tennessee	46.7
36	Georgia	46.4
37	Idaho	46.3
38	Oklahoma	46.2
38	Washington	46.2
40	Florida	46.1
41	Louisiana	45.9
41	Oregon	45.9
43	Alaska	45.8
44	West Virginia	45.6
45	California	45.0
46	Texas	44.7
47	Colorado	44.3
47	Utah	44.3
49	Nevada	43.2
50	Arizona	43.0

District of Columbia   50.0

Source: Morgan Quitno Press using data from U.S. Department of Labor, Bureau of Labor Statistics
"Geographic Profiles of Employment and Unemployment, 2002"
*Annual averages.

Percent of Children Under 6 Years Old With All Parents Working: 2002

National Percent = 60.3%

<u>ALPHA ORDER</u>

RANK	STATE	PERCENT
29	Alabama	60.7
28	Alaska	60.8
49	Arizona	51.4
9	Arkansas	66.8
44	California	55.6
45	Colorado	55.5
30	Connecticut	60.2
6	Delaware	68.1
20	Florida	63.1
10	Georgia	66.7
19	Hawaii	63.3
45	Idaho	55.5
36	Illinois	59.5
38	Indiana	58.7
2	Iowa	71.3
22	Kansas	62.8
33	Kentucky	59.9
13	Louisiana	65.9
31	Maine	60.0
8	Maryland	67.8
27	Massachusetts	61.1
37	Michigan	59.4
3	Minnesota	70.9
4	Mississippi	69.0
24	Missouri	62.4
31	Montana	60.0
12	Nebraska	66.3
47	Nevada	54.7
15	New Hampshire	65.1
39	New Jersey	58.2
34	New Mexico	59.7
41	New York	57.1
25	North Carolina	61.9
7	North Dakota	67.9
16	Ohio	64.6
42	Oklahoma	56.5
34	Oregon	59.7
23	Pennsylvania	62.7
13	Rhode Island	65.9
17	South Carolina	64.3
1	South Dakota	71.6
21	Tennessee	62.9
43	Texas	55.8
50	Utah	49.9
10	Vermont	66.7
17	Virginia	64.3
40	Washington	58.0
48	West Virginia	53.7
5	Wisconsin	68.8
26	Wyoming	61.6

<u>RANK ORDER</u>

RANK	STATE	PERCENT
1	South Dakota	71.6
2	Iowa	71.3
3	Minnesota	70.9
4	Mississippi	69.0
5	Wisconsin	68.8
6	Delaware	68.1
7	North Dakota	67.9
8	Maryland	67.8
9	Arkansas	66.8
10	Georgia	66.7
10	Vermont	66.7
12	Nebraska	66.3
13	Louisiana	65.9
13	Rhode Island	65.9
15	New Hampshire	65.1
16	Ohio	64.6
17	South Carolina	64.3
17	Virginia	64.3
19	Hawaii	63.3
20	Florida	63.1
21	Tennessee	62.9
22	Kansas	62.8
23	Pennsylvania	62.7
24	Missouri	62.4
25	North Carolina	61.9
26	Wyoming	61.6
27	Massachusetts	61.1
28	Alaska	60.8
29	Alabama	60.7
30	Connecticut	60.2
31	Maine	60.0
31	Montana	60.0
33	Kentucky	59.9
34	New Mexico	59.7
34	Oregon	59.7
36	Illinois	59.5
37	Michigan	59.4
38	Indiana	58.7
39	New Jersey	58.2
40	Washington	58.0
41	New York	57.1
42	Oklahoma	56.5
43	Texas	55.8
44	California	55.6
45	Colorado	55.5
45	Idaho	55.5
47	Nevada	54.7
48	West Virginia	53.7
49	Arizona	51.4
50	Utah	49.9
	District of Columbia	65.5

Source: U.S. Bureau of the Census
"2002 American Community Survey"

Job Growth: 2002 to 2003

National Percent Change = 0.4% Decrease*

<u>ALPHA ORDER</u>

RANK	STATE	PERCENT CHANGE
33	Alabama	(1.0)
1	Alaska	3.2
4	Arizona	2.7
26	Arkansas	(0.3)
41	California	(1.4)
31	Colorado	(0.9)
35	Connecticut	(1.1)
15	Delaware	0.7
10	Florida	1.7
3	Georgia	3.1
1	Hawaii	3.2
5	Idaho	2.4
25	Illinois	(0.2)
33	Indiana	(1.0)
37	Iowa	(1.2)
37	Kansas	(1.2)
50	Kentucky	(3.6)
43	Louisiana	(2.0)
31	Maine	(0.9)
29	Maryland	(0.8)
44	Massachusetts	(2.5)
48	Michigan	(3.2)
17	Minnesota	0.4
22	Mississippi	(0.1)
18	Missouri	0.3
22	Montana	(0.1)
29	Nebraska	(0.8)
7	Nevada	2.2
26	New Hampshire	(0.3)
18	New Jersey	0.3
6	New Mexico	2.3
41	New York	(1.4)
37	North Carolina	(1.2)
20	North Dakota	0.0
46	Ohio	(2.8)
49	Oklahoma	(3.5)
37	Oregon	(1.2)
20	Pennsylvania	0.0
22	Rhode Island	(0.1)
46	South Carolina	(2.8)
7	South Dakota	2.2
35	Tennessee	(1.1)
16	Texas	0.6
11	Utah	1.3
12	Vermont	1.2
14	Virginia	0.8
13	Washington	1.0
28	West Virginia	(0.4)
45	Wisconsin	(2.6)
9	Wyoming	1.8

<u>RANK ORDER</u>

RANK	STATE	PERCENT CHANGE
1	Alaska	3.2
1	Hawaii	3.2
3	Georgia	3.1
4	Arizona	2.7
5	Idaho	2.4
6	New Mexico	2.3
7	Nevada	2.2
7	South Dakota	2.2
9	Wyoming	1.8
10	Florida	1.7
11	Utah	1.3
12	Vermont	1.2
13	Washington	1.0
14	Virginia	0.8
15	Delaware	0.7
16	Texas	0.6
17	Minnesota	0.4
18	Missouri	0.3
18	New Jersey	0.3
20	North Dakota	0.0
20	Pennsylvania	0.0
22	Mississippi	(0.1)
22	Montana	(0.1)
22	Rhode Island	(0.1)
25	Illinois	(0.2)
26	Arkansas	(0.3)
26	New Hampshire	(0.3)
28	West Virginia	(0.4)
29	Maryland	(0.8)
29	Nebraska	(0.8)
31	Colorado	(0.9)
31	Maine	(0.9)
33	Alabama	(1.0)
33	Indiana	(1.0)
35	Connecticut	(1.1)
35	Tennessee	(1.1)
37	Iowa	(1.2)
37	Kansas	(1.2)
37	North Carolina	(1.2)
37	Oregon	(1.2)
41	California	(1.4)
41	New York	(1.4)
43	Louisiana	(2.0)
44	Massachusetts	(2.5)
45	Wisconsin	(2.6)
46	Ohio	(2.8)
46	South Carolina	(2.8)
48	Michigan	(3.2)
49	Oklahoma	(3.5)
50	Kentucky	(3.6)

District of Columbia   3.1

Source: Morgan Quitno Press using data from U.S. Department of Labor, Bureau of Labor Statistics
"Regional and State Employment and Unemployment" (press release, January 27, 2004)
*Nonfarm jobs. December 2002 to December 2003, seasonally adjusted. National figure based on nonfarm employment from a different survey.

Employees in Nonfarm Payrolls in 2003

National Total = 130,124,000 Employees*

ALPHA ORDER

RANK	STATE	EMPLOYEES	% of USA
24	Alabama	1,873,800	1.4%
48	Alaska	305,000	0.2%
21	Arizona	2,310,800	1.8%
32	Arkansas	1,146,200	0.9%
1	California	14,432,400	11.1%
22	Colorado	2,154,000	1.7%
27	Connecticut	1,644,000	1.3%
44	Delaware	411,600	0.3%
4	Florida	7,353,400	5.7%
10	Georgia	3,967,100	3.0%
42	Hawaii	572,400	0.4%
41	Idaho	575,900	0.4%
5	Illinois	5,881,300	4.5%
14	Indiana	2,872,200	2.2%
30	Iowa	1,442,800	1.1%
31	Kansas	1,346,900	1.0%
26	Kentucky	1,774,400	1.4%
23	Louisiana	1,892,100	1.5%
40	Maine	604,800	0.5%
20	Maryland	2,459,100	1.9%
13	Massachusetts	3,178,300	2.4%
8	Michigan	4,372,300	3.4%
19	Minnesota	2,647,100	2.0%
33	Mississippi	1,130,700	0.9%
18	Missouri	2,663,600	2.0%
45	Montana	397,500	0.3%
36	Nebraska	905,400	0.7%
34	Nevada	1,098,800	0.8%
39	New Hampshire	619,700	0.5%
9	New Jersey	4,021,700	3.1%
37	New Mexico	781,600	0.6%
3	New York	8,405,000	6.5%
11	North Carolina	3,830,500	2.9%
47	North Dakota	331,100	0.3%
7	Ohio	5,341,500	4.1%
29	Oklahoma	1,467,700	1.1%
28	Oregon	1,567,700	1.2%
6	Pennsylvania	5,631,700	4.3%
43	Rhode Island	481,300	0.4%
25	South Carolina	1,776,400	1.4%
46	South Dakota	383,400	0.3%
17	Tennessee	2,667,900	2.1%
2	Texas	9,464,100	7.3%
35	Utah	1,075,900	0.8%
49	Vermont	302,000	0.2%
12	Virginia	3,518,400	2.7%
16	Washington	2,670,200	2.1%
38	West Virginia	723,900	0.6%
15	Wisconsin	2,763,600	2.1%
50	Wyoming	251,600	0.2%

RANK ORDER

RANK	STATE	EMPLOYEES	% of USA
1	California	14,432,400	11.1%
2	Texas	9,464,100	7.3%
3	New York	8,405,000	6.5%
4	Florida	7,353,400	5.7%
5	Illinois	5,881,300	4.5%
6	Pennsylvania	5,631,700	4.3%
7	Ohio	5,341,500	4.1%
8	Michigan	4,372,300	3.4%
9	New Jersey	4,021,700	3.1%
10	Georgia	3,967,100	3.0%
11	North Carolina	3,830,500	2.9%
12	Virginia	3,518,400	2.7%
13	Massachusetts	3,178,300	2.4%
14	Indiana	2,872,200	2.2%
15	Wisconsin	2,763,600	2.1%
16	Washington	2,670,200	2.1%
17	Tennessee	2,667,900	2.1%
18	Missouri	2,663,600	2.0%
19	Minnesota	2,647,100	2.0%
20	Maryland	2,459,100	1.9%
21	Arizona	2,310,800	1.8%
22	Colorado	2,154,000	1.7%
23	Louisiana	1,892,100	1.5%
24	Alabama	1,873,800	1.4%
25	South Carolina	1,776,400	1.4%
26	Kentucky	1,774,400	1.4%
27	Connecticut	1,644,000	1.3%
28	Oregon	1,567,700	1.2%
29	Oklahoma	1,467,700	1.1%
30	Iowa	1,442,800	1.1%
31	Kansas	1,346,900	1.0%
32	Arkansas	1,146,200	0.9%
33	Mississippi	1,130,700	0.9%
34	Nevada	1,098,800	0.8%
35	Utah	1,075,900	0.8%
36	Nebraska	905,400	0.7%
37	New Mexico	781,600	0.6%
38	West Virginia	723,900	0.6%
39	New Hampshire	619,700	0.5%
40	Maine	604,800	0.5%
41	Idaho	575,900	0.4%
42	Hawaii	572,400	0.4%
43	Rhode Island	481,300	0.4%
44	Delaware	411,600	0.3%
45	Montana	397,500	0.3%
46	South Dakota	383,400	0.3%
47	North Dakota	331,100	0.3%
48	Alaska	305,000	0.2%
49	Vermont	302,000	0.2%
50	Wyoming	251,600	0.2%
	District of Columbia	668,700	0.5%

Source: U.S. Department of Labor, Bureau of Labor Statistics
   "Regional and State Employment and Unemployment" (press release, January 27, 2004)
*Seasonally adjusted preliminary data as of December 2003. National total calculated through a different formula.

Employees in Construction in 2003

National Total = 6,873,000 Employees*

ALPHA ORDER

RANK	STATE	EMPLOYEES	% of USA
25	Alabama	102,500	1.5%
47	Alaska	16,500	0.2%
12	Arizona	182,600	2.7%
35	Arkansas	54,300	0.8%
1	California	799,900	11.6%
17	Colorado	148,500	2.2%
33	Connecticut	59,800	0.9%
42	Delaware	24,500	0.4%
3	Florida	459,100	6.7%
10	Georgia	215,400	3.1%
NA	Hawaii***	NA	NA
38	Idaho	37,700	0.5%
5	Illinois	278,000	4.0%
16	Indiana	149,400	2.2%
31	Iowa	64,600	0.9%
30	Kansas	66,600	1.0%
27	Kentucky	81,600	1.2%
21	Louisiana	125,400	1.8%
40	Maine	28,900	0.4%
13	Maryland	164,800	2.4%
19	Massachusetts	133,700	1.9%
11	Michigan	199,400	2.9%
20	Minnesota	125,600	1.8%
34	Mississippi	55,600	0.8%
18	Missouri	135,700	2.0%
43	Montana	23,100	0.3%
37	Nebraska	44,700	0.7%
26	Nevada	100,100	1.5%
41	New Hampshire	26,000	0.4%
14	New Jersey	163,300	2.4%
36	New Mexico	47,700	0.7%
4	New York	329,800	4.8%
8	North Carolina	217,900	3.2%
48	North Dakota	15,600	0.2%
7	Ohio	235,200	3.4%
32	Oklahoma	62,000	0.9%
28	Oregon	79,600	1.2%
6	Pennsylvania	249,100	3.6%
46	Rhode Island	19,900	0.3%
24	South Carolina	108,200	1.6%
45	South Dakota	20,200	0.3%
23	Tennessee	109,100	1.6%
2	Texas	585,500	8.5%
29	Utah	67,900	1.0%
49	Vermont	15,400	0.2%
9	Virginia	215,700	3.1%
15	Washington	162,500	2.4%
39	West Virginia	33,000	0.5%
22	Wisconsin	114,600	1.7%
44	Wyoming	20,400	0.3%

RANK ORDER

RANK	STATE	EMPLOYEES	% of USA
1	California	799,900	11.6%
2	Texas	585,500	8.5%
3	Florida	459,100	6.7%
4	New York	329,800	4.8%
5	Illinois	278,000	4.0%
6	Pennsylvania	249,100	3.6%
7	Ohio	235,200	3.4%
8	North Carolina	217,900	3.2%
9	Virginia	215,700	3.1%
10	Georgia	215,400	3.1%
11	Michigan	199,400	2.9%
12	Arizona	182,600	2.7%
13	Maryland	164,800	2.4%
14	New Jersey	163,300	2.4%
15	Washington	162,500	2.4%
16	Indiana	149,400	2.2%
17	Colorado	148,500	2.2%
18	Missouri	135,700	2.0%
19	Massachusetts	133,700	1.9%
20	Minnesota	125,600	1.8%
21	Louisiana	125,400	1.8%
22	Wisconsin	114,600	1.7%
23	Tennessee	109,100	1.6%
24	South Carolina	108,200	1.6%
25	Alabama	102,500	1.5%
26	Nevada	100,100	1.5%
27	Kentucky	81,600	1.2%
28	Oregon	79,600	1.2%
29	Utah	67,900	1.0%
30	Kansas	66,600	1.0%
31	Iowa	64,600	0.9%
32	Oklahoma	62,000	0.9%
33	Connecticut	59,800	0.9%
34	Mississippi	55,600	0.8%
35	Arkansas	54,300	0.8%
36	New Mexico	47,700	0.7%
37	Nebraska	44,700	0.7%
38	Idaho	37,700	0.5%
39	West Virginia	33,000	0.5%
40	Maine	28,900	0.4%
41	New Hampshire	26,000	0.4%
42	Delaware	24,500	0.4%
43	Montana	23,100	0.3%
44	Wyoming	20,400	0.3%
45	South Dakota	20,200	0.3%
46	Rhode Island	19,900	0.3%
47	Alaska	16,500	0.2%
48	North Dakota	15,600	0.2%
49	Vermont	15,400	0.2%
NA	Hawaii***	NA	NA
	District of Columbia	12,900	0.2%

Source: U.S. Department of Labor, Bureau of Labor Statistics
"Regional and State Employment and Unemployment" (press release, January 27, 2004)
*Seasonally adjusted preliminary data as of December 2003. National total calculated through a different formula.
**Figures for Delaware, DC, Florida and Maryland include employees in mining.
***The Bureau of Labor Statistics no longer publishes seasonally adjusted figures in this category for Hawaii.

Percent of Nonfarm Employees in Construction in 2003

National Percent = 5.3% of Employees*

ALPHA ORDER		
RANK	STATE	PERCENT
18	Alabama	5.5
20	Alaska	5.4
3	Arizona	7.9
31	Arkansas	4.7
18	California	5.5
4	Colorado	6.9
49	Connecticut	3.6
15	Delaware	6.0
9	Florida	6.2
20	Georgia	5.4
NA	Hawaii**	NA
7	Idaho	6.5
31	Illinois	4.7
23	Indiana	5.2
38	Iowa	4.5
27	Kansas	4.9
35	Kentucky	4.6
6	Louisiana	6.6
30	Maine	4.8
5	Maryland	6.7
41	Massachusetts	4.2
35	Michigan	4.6
31	Minnesota	4.7
27	Mississippi	4.9
24	Missouri	5.1
16	Montana	5.8
27	Nebraska	4.9
1	Nevada	9.1
41	New Hampshire	4.2
44	New Jersey	4.1
11	New Mexico	6.1
48	New York	3.9
17	North Carolina	5.7
31	North Dakota	4.7
39	Ohio	4.4
41	Oklahoma	4.2
24	Oregon	5.1
39	Pennsylvania	4.4
44	Rhode Island	4.1
11	South Carolina	6.1
22	South Dakota	5.3
44	Tennessee	4.1
9	Texas	6.2
8	Utah	6.3
24	Vermont	5.1
11	Virginia	6.1
11	Washington	6.1
35	West Virginia	4.6
44	Wisconsin	4.1
2	Wyoming	8.1

RANK ORDER		
RANK	STATE	PERCENT
1	Nevada	9.1
2	Wyoming	8.1
3	Arizona	7.9
4	Colorado	6.9
5	Maryland	6.7
6	Louisiana	6.6
7	Idaho	6.5
8	Utah	6.3
9	Florida	6.2
9	Texas	6.2
11	New Mexico	6.1
11	South Carolina	6.1
11	Virginia	6.1
11	Washington	6.1
15	Delaware	6.0
16	Montana	5.8
17	North Carolina	5.7
18	Alabama	5.5
18	California	5.5
20	Alaska	5.4
20	Georgia	5.4
22	South Dakota	5.3
23	Indiana	5.2
24	Missouri	5.1
24	Oregon	5.1
24	Vermont	5.1
27	Kansas	4.9
27	Mississippi	4.9
27	Nebraska	4.9
30	Maine	4.8
31	Arkansas	4.7
31	Illinois	4.7
31	Minnesota	4.7
31	North Dakota	4.7
35	Kentucky	4.6
35	Michigan	4.6
35	West Virginia	4.6
38	Iowa	4.5
39	Ohio	4.4
39	Pennsylvania	4.4
41	Massachusetts	4.2
41	New Hampshire	4.2
41	Oklahoma	4.2
44	New Jersey	4.1
44	Rhode Island	4.1
44	Tennessee	4.1
44	Wisconsin	4.1
48	New York	3.9
49	Connecticut	3.6
NA	Hawaii**	NA
	District of Columbia	1.9

Source: Morgan Quitno Press using data from U.S. Department of Labor, Bureau of Labor Statistics
"Regional and State Employment and Unemployment" (press release, January 27, 2004)
**Seasonally adjusted preliminary data as of December 2003. National total calculated through a different formula.*
***Figures for Delaware, DC, Florida and Maryland include employees in mining.*
****The Bureau of Labor Statistics no longer publishes seasonally adjusted figures in this category for Hawaii.*

Employees in Education and Health Services in 2003

National Total = 16,674,000 Employees*

<u>ALPHA ORDER</u>

RANK	STATE	EMPLOYEES	% of USA
NA	Alabama**	NA	NA
42	Alaska	33,100	0.2%
21	Arizona	252,300	1.5%
29	Arkansas	140,100	0.8%
1	California	1,540,400	9.2%
24	Colorado	216,500	1.3%
20	Connecticut	267,000	1.6%
40	Delaware	49,800	0.3%
5	Florida	882,600	5.3%
NA	Georgia**	NA	NA
36	Hawaii	66,000	0.4%
NA	Idaho**	NA	NA
7	Illinois	719,000	4.3%
16	Indiana	349,300	2.1%
25	Iowa	193,600	1.2%
NA	Kansas**	NA	NA
23	Kentucky	228,000	1.4%
22	Louisiana	239,500	1.4%
33	Maine	107,900	0.6%
17	Maryland	341,900	2.1%
8	Massachusetts	574,000	3.4%
10	Michigan	542,300	3.3%
14	Minnesota	365,900	2.2%
32	Mississippi	113,700	0.7%
15	Missouri	358,300	2.1%
38	Montana	52,900	0.3%
31	Nebraska	115,800	0.7%
NA	Nevada**	NA	NA
NA	New Hampshire**	NA	NA
9	New Jersey	546,700	3.3%
35	New Mexico	99,800	0.6%
2	New York	1,493,400	9.0%
11	North Carolina	432,500	2.6%
41	North Dakota	47,200	0.3%
6	Ohio	728,800	4.4%
28	Oklahoma	170,700	1.0%
26	Oregon	188,700	1.1%
4	Pennsylvania	993,500	6.0%
NA	Rhode Island**	NA	NA
27	South Carolina	180,000	1.1%
37	South Dakota	56,700	0.3%
19	Tennessee	313,400	1.9%
3	Texas	1,141,800	6.8%
30	Utah	121,400	0.7%
39	Vermont	51,500	0.3%
13	Virginia	367,900	2.2%
18	Washington	316,500	1.9%
34	West Virginia	107,200	0.6%
12	Wisconsin	369,300	2.2%
NA	Wyoming**	NA	NA

<u>RANK ORDER</u>

RANK	STATE	EMPLOYEES	% of USA
1	California	1,540,400	9.2%
2	New York	1,493,400	9.0%
3	Texas	1,141,800	6.8%
4	Pennsylvania	993,500	6.0%
5	Florida	882,600	5.3%
6	Ohio	728,800	4.4%
7	Illinois	719,000	4.3%
8	Massachusetts	574,000	3.4%
9	New Jersey	546,700	3.3%
10	Michigan	542,300	3.3%
11	North Carolina	432,500	2.6%
12	Wisconsin	369,300	2.2%
13	Virginia	367,900	2.2%
14	Minnesota	365,900	2.2%
15	Missouri	358,300	2.1%
16	Indiana	349,300	2.1%
17	Maryland	341,900	2.1%
18	Washington	316,500	1.9%
19	Tennessee	313,400	1.9%
20	Connecticut	267,000	1.6%
21	Arizona	252,300	1.5%
22	Louisiana	239,500	1.4%
23	Kentucky	228,000	1.4%
24	Colorado	216,500	1.3%
25	Iowa	193,600	1.2%
26	Oregon	188,700	1.1%
27	South Carolina	180,000	1.1%
28	Oklahoma	170,700	1.0%
29	Arkansas	140,100	0.8%
30	Utah	121,400	0.7%
31	Nebraska	115,800	0.7%
32	Mississippi	113,700	0.7%
33	Maine	107,900	0.6%
34	West Virginia	107,200	0.6%
35	New Mexico	99,800	0.6%
36	Hawaii	66,000	0.4%
37	South Dakota	56,700	0.3%
38	Montana	52,900	0.3%
39	Vermont	51,500	0.3%
40	Delaware	49,800	0.3%
41	North Dakota	47,200	0.3%
42	Alaska	33,100	0.2%
NA	Alabama**	NA	NA
NA	Georgia**	NA	NA
NA	Idaho**	NA	NA
NA	Kansas**	NA	NA
NA	Nevada**	NA	NA
NA	New Hampshire**	NA	NA
NA	Rhode Island**	NA	NA
NA	Wyoming**	NA	NA
	District of Columbia**	NA	NA

Source: U.S. Department of Labor, Bureau of Labor Statistics
   "Regional and State Employment and Unemployment" (press release, January 27, 2004)
*Seasonally adjusted preliminary data as of December 2003. National total calculated through a different formula.
**The Bureau of Labor Statistics does not publish seasonally adjusted figures in this category for these states.

Percent of Nonfarm Employees in Education and Health Services in 2003

National Percent = 12.8% of Employees*

<u>ALPHA ORDER</u>

RANK	STATE	PERCENT
NA	Alabama**	NA
36	Alaska	10.9
36	Arizona	10.9
23	Arkansas	12.2
38	California	10.7
40	Colorado	10.1
6	Connecticut	16.2
26	Delaware	12.1
28	Florida	12.0
NA	Georgia**	NA
33	Hawaii	11.5
NA	Idaho**	NA
23	Illinois	12.2
23	Indiana	12.2
15	Iowa	13.4
NA	Kansas**	NA
18	Kentucky	12.8
21	Louisiana	12.7
2	Maine	17.8
10	Maryland	13.9
1	Massachusetts	18.1
22	Michigan	12.4
11	Minnesota	13.8
40	Mississippi	10.1
14	Missouri	13.5
17	Montana	13.3
18	Nebraska	12.8
NA	Nevada**	NA
NA	New Hampshire**	NA
12	New Jersey	13.6
18	New Mexico	12.8
2	New York	17.8
34	North Carolina	11.3
9	North Dakota	14.3
12	Ohio	13.6
32	Oklahoma	11.6
28	Oregon	12.0
4	Pennsylvania	17.6
NA	Rhode Island**	NA
40	South Carolina	10.1
7	South Dakota	14.8
31	Tennessee	11.7
26	Texas	12.1
34	Utah	11.3
5	Vermont	17.1
39	Virginia	10.5
30	Washington	11.9
7	West Virginia	14.8
15	Wisconsin	13.4
NA	Wyoming**	NA

<u>RANK ORDER</u>

RANK	STATE	PERCENT
1	Massachusetts	18.1
2	Maine	17.8
2	New York	17.8
4	Pennsylvania	17.6
5	Vermont	17.1
6	Connecticut	16.2
7	South Dakota	14.8
7	West Virginia	14.8
9	North Dakota	14.3
10	Maryland	13.9
11	Minnesota	13.8
12	New Jersey	13.6
12	Ohio	13.6
14	Missouri	13.5
15	Iowa	13.4
15	Wisconsin	13.4
17	Montana	13.3
18	Kentucky	12.8
18	Nebraska	12.8
18	New Mexico	12.8
21	Louisiana	12.7
22	Michigan	12.4
23	Arkansas	12.2
23	Illinois	12.2
23	Indiana	12.2
26	Delaware	12.1
26	Texas	12.1
28	Florida	12.0
28	Oregon	12.0
30	Washington	11.9
31	Tennessee	11.7
32	Oklahoma	11.6
33	Hawaii	11.5
34	North Carolina	11.3
34	Utah	11.3
36	Alaska	10.9
36	Arizona	10.9
38	California	10.7
39	Virginia	10.5
40	Colorado	10.1
40	Mississippi	10.1
40	South Carolina	10.1
NA	Alabama**	NA
NA	Georgia**	NA
NA	Idaho**	NA
NA	Kansas**	NA
NA	Nevada**	NA
NA	New Hampshire**	NA
NA	Rhode Island**	NA
NA	Wyoming**	NA

	District of Columbia**	NA

Source: Morgan Quitno Press using data from U.S. Department of Labor, Bureau of Labor Statistics
"Regional and State Employment and Unemployment" (press release, January 27, 2004)

*Seasonally adjusted preliminary data as of December 2003. National total calculated through a different formula.

**The Bureau of Labor Statistics does not publish seasonally adjusted figures in this category for these states.

Employees in Financial Activities in 2003

National Total = 7,952,000 Employees*

<u>ALPHA ORDER</u>

RANK	STATE	EMPLOYEES	% of USA
23	Alabama	98,000	1.2%
NA	Alaska**	NA	NA
15	Arizona	154,200	1.9%
31	Arkansas	50,800	0.6%
NA	California**	NA	NA
16	Colorado	153,500	1.9%
19	Connecticut	142,800	1.8%
32	Delaware	38,700	0.5%
3	Florida	482,000	6.1%
10	Georgia	211,400	2.7%
NA	Hawaii**	NA	NA
NA	Idaho**	NA	NA
4	Illinois	403,100	5.1%
20	Indiana	138,500	1.7%
24	Iowa	95,400	1.2%
NA	Kansas**	NA	NA
28	Kentucky	84,200	1.1%
22	Louisiana	98,600	1.2%
NA	Maine**	NA	NA
17	Maryland	150,600	1.9%
8	Massachusetts	229,900	2.9%
9	Michigan	218,700	2.8%
12	Minnesota	168,700	2.1%
NA	Mississippi**	NA	NA
14	Missouri	158,600	2.0%
35	Montana	20,200	0.3%
29	Nebraska	63,800	0.8%
30	Nevada	59,100	0.7%
NA	New Hampshire**	NA	NA
7	New Jersey	281,300	3.5%
33	New Mexico	34,400	0.4%
1	New York	703,400	8.8%
NA	North Carolina**	NA	NA
36	North Dakota	18,000	0.2%
6	Ohio	308,200	3.9%
27	Oklahoma	86,100	1.1%
25	Oregon	92,600	1.2%
5	Pennsylvania	339,400	4.3%
NA	Rhode Island**	NA	NA
26	South Carolina	87,500	1.1%
34	South Dakota	28,100	0.4%
21	Tennessee	138,200	1.7%
2	Texas	587,800	7.4%
NA	Utah**	NA	NA
NA	Vermont**	NA	NA
11	Virginia	184,800	2.3%
18	Washington	149,900	1.9%
NA	West Virginia**	NA	NA
13	Wisconsin	159,200	2.0%
NA	Wyoming**	NA	NA

<u>RANK ORDER</u>

RANK	STATE	EMPLOYEES	% of USA
1	New York	703,400	8.8%
2	Texas	587,800	7.4%
3	Florida	482,000	6.1%
4	Illinois	403,100	5.1%
5	Pennsylvania	339,400	4.3%
6	Ohio	308,200	3.9%
7	New Jersey	281,300	3.5%
8	Massachusetts	229,900	2.9%
9	Michigan	218,700	2.8%
10	Georgia	211,400	2.7%
11	Virginia	184,800	2.3%
12	Minnesota	168,700	2.1%
13	Wisconsin	159,200	2.0%
14	Missouri	158,600	2.0%
15	Arizona	154,200	1.9%
16	Colorado	153,500	1.9%
17	Maryland	150,600	1.9%
18	Washington	149,900	1.9%
19	Connecticut	142,800	1.8%
20	Indiana	138,500	1.7%
21	Tennessee	138,200	1.7%
22	Louisiana	98,600	1.2%
23	Alabama	98,000	1.2%
24	Iowa	95,400	1.2%
25	Oregon	92,600	1.2%
26	South Carolina	87,500	1.1%
27	Oklahoma	86,100	1.1%
28	Kentucky	84,200	1.1%
29	Nebraska	63,800	0.8%
30	Nevada	59,100	0.7%
31	Arkansas	50,800	0.6%
32	Delaware	38,700	0.5%
33	New Mexico	34,400	0.4%
34	South Dakota	28,100	0.4%
35	Montana	20,200	0.3%
36	North Dakota	18,000	0.2%
NA	Alaska**	NA	NA
NA	California**	NA	NA
NA	Hawaii**	NA	NA
NA	Idaho**	NA	NA
NA	Kansas**	NA	NA
NA	Maine**	NA	NA
NA	Mississippi**	NA	NA
NA	New Hampshire**	NA	NA
NA	North Carolina**	NA	NA
NA	Rhode Island**	NA	NA
NA	Utah**	NA	NA
NA	Vermont**	NA	NA
NA	West Virginia**	NA	NA
NA	Wyoming**	NA	NA
	District of Columbia**	NA	NA

Source: U.S. Department of Labor, Bureau of Labor Statistics
"Regional and State Employment and Unemployment" (press release, January 27, 2004)
**Seasonally adjusted preliminary data as of December 2003. National total calculated through a different formula.*
Financial activities include insurance and real estate.
***The Bureau of Labor Statistics does not publish seasonally adjusted figures in this category for these states.*

Percent of Nonfarm Employees in Financial Activities in 2003

National Percent = 6.1% of Employees*

ALPHA ORDER

RANK	STATE	PERCENT
27	Alabama	5.2
NA	Alaska**	NA
10	Arizona	6.7
35	Arkansas	4.4
NA	California**	NA
6	Colorado	7.1
2	Connecticut	8.7
1	Delaware	9.4
11	Florida	6.6
25	Georgia	5.3
NA	Hawaii**	NA
NA	Idaho**	NA
9	Illinois	6.9
33	Indiana	4.8
11	Iowa	6.6
NA	Kansas**	NA
34	Kentucky	4.7
27	Louisiana	5.2
NA	Maine**	NA
15	Maryland	6.1
5	Massachusetts	7.2
31	Michigan	5.0
13	Minnesota	6.4
NA	Mississippi**	NA
16	Missouri	6.0
30	Montana	5.1
7	Nebraska	7.0
23	Nevada	5.4
NA	New Hampshire**	NA
7	New Jersey	7.0
35	New Mexico	4.4
3	New York	8.4
NA	North Carolina**	NA
23	North Dakota	5.4
20	Ohio	5.8
18	Oklahoma	5.9
18	Oregon	5.9
16	Pennsylvania	6.0
NA	Rhode Island**	NA
32	South Carolina	4.9
4	South Dakota	7.3
27	Tennessee	5.2
14	Texas	6.2
NA	Utah**	NA
NA	Vermont**	NA
25	Virginia	5.3
22	Washington	5.6
NA	West Virginia**	NA
20	Wisconsin	5.8
NA	Wyoming**	NA

RANK ORDER

RANK	STATE	PERCENT
1	Delaware	9.4
2	Connecticut	8.7
3	New York	8.4
4	South Dakota	7.3
5	Massachusetts	7.2
6	Colorado	7.1
7	Nebraska	7.0
7	New Jersey	7.0
9	Illinois	6.9
10	Arizona	6.7
11	Florida	6.6
11	Iowa	6.6
13	Minnesota	6.4
14	Texas	6.2
15	Maryland	6.1
16	Missouri	6.0
16	Pennsylvania	6.0
18	Oklahoma	5.9
18	Oregon	5.9
20	Ohio	5.8
20	Wisconsin	5.8
22	Washington	5.6
23	Nevada	5.4
23	North Dakota	5.4
25	Georgia	5.3
25	Virginia	5.3
27	Alabama	5.2
27	Louisiana	5.2
27	Tennessee	5.2
30	Montana	5.1
31	Michigan	5.0
32	South Carolina	4.9
33	Indiana	4.8
34	Kentucky	4.7
35	Arkansas	4.4
35	New Mexico	4.4
NA	Alaska**	NA
NA	California**	NA
NA	Hawaii**	NA
NA	Idaho**	NA
NA	Kansas**	NA
NA	Maine**	NA
NA	Mississippi**	NA
NA	New Hampshire**	NA
NA	North Carolina**	NA
NA	Rhode Island**	NA
NA	Utah**	NA
NA	Vermont**	NA
NA	West Virginia**	NA
NA	Wyoming**	NA
	District of Columbia**	NA

Source: Morgan Quitno Press using data from U.S. Department of Labor, Bureau of Labor Statistics
    "Regional and State Employment and Unemployment" (press release, January 27, 2004)
*Seasonally adjusted preliminary data as of December 2003. National total calculated through a different formula.
Financial activities include insurance and real estate.
**The Bureau of Labor Statistics does not publish seasonally adjusted figures in this category for these states.

Employees in Government in 2003

National Total = 21,468,000 Employees*

ALPHA ORDER

RANK	STATE	EMPLOYEES	% of USA
24	Alabama	353,300	1.6%
44	Alaska	82,600	0.4%
21	Arizona	392,300	1.8%
34	Arkansas	197,200	0.9%
1	California	2,410,600	11.2%
23	Colorado	358,100	1.7%
32	Connecticut	241,200	1.1%
49	Delaware	54,800	0.3%
4	Florida	1,084,700	5.1%
11	Georgia	636,700	3.0%
39	Hawaii	118,600	0.6%
40	Idaho	111,000	0.5%
5	Illinois	854,000	4.0%
16	Indiana	420,400	2.0%
31	Iowa	243,800	1.1%
29	Kansas	255,400	1.2%
26	Kentucky	309,600	1.4%
22	Louisiana	377,500	1.8%
41	Maine	103,600	0.5%
14	Maryland	464,000	2.2%
17	Massachusetts	420,000	2.0%
8	Michigan	671,100	3.1%
20	Minnesota	394,700	1.8%
30	Mississippi	246,800	1.1%
15	Missouri	426,000	2.0%
43	Montana	83,800	0.4%
36	Nebraska	159,900	0.7%
38	Nevada	136,200	0.6%
42	New Hampshire	91,200	0.4%
12	New Jersey	625,900	2.9%
35	New Mexico	195,900	0.9%
3	New York	1,478,200	6.9%
9	North Carolina	658,700	3.1%
45	North Dakota	75,800	0.4%
6	Ohio	789,200	3.7%
27	Oklahoma	293,500	1.4%
28	Oregon	271,900	1.3%
7	Pennsylvania	752,900	3.5%
47	Rhode Island	65,600	0.3%
25	South Carolina	331,100	1.5%
46	South Dakota	75,300	0.4%
18	Tennessee	413,200	1.9%
2	Texas	1,671,400	7.8%
33	Utah	197,300	0.9%
50	Vermont	51,600	0.2%
10	Virginia	644,000	3.0%
13	Washington	524,400	2.4%
37	West Virginia	141,100	0.7%
19	Wisconsin	410,400	1.9%
48	Wyoming	63,400	0.3%

RANK ORDER

RANK	STATE	EMPLOYEES	% of USA
1	California	2,410,600	11.2%
2	Texas	1,671,400	7.8%
3	New York	1,478,200	6.9%
4	Florida	1,084,700	5.1%
5	Illinois	854,000	4.0%
6	Ohio	789,200	3.7%
7	Pennsylvania	752,900	3.5%
8	Michigan	671,100	3.1%
9	North Carolina	658,700	3.1%
10	Virginia	644,000	3.0%
11	Georgia	636,700	3.0%
12	New Jersey	625,900	2.9%
13	Washington	524,400	2.4%
14	Maryland	464,000	2.2%
15	Missouri	426,000	2.0%
16	Indiana	420,400	2.0%
17	Massachusetts	420,000	2.0%
18	Tennessee	413,200	1.9%
19	Wisconsin	410,400	1.9%
20	Minnesota	394,700	1.8%
21	Arizona	392,300	1.8%
22	Louisiana	377,500	1.8%
23	Colorado	358,100	1.7%
24	Alabama	353,300	1.6%
25	South Carolina	331,100	1.5%
26	Kentucky	309,600	1.4%
27	Oklahoma	293,500	1.4%
28	Oregon	271,900	1.3%
29	Kansas	255,400	1.2%
30	Mississippi	246,800	1.1%
31	Iowa	243,800	1.1%
32	Connecticut	241,200	1.1%
33	Utah	197,300	0.9%
34	Arkansas	197,200	0.9%
35	New Mexico	195,900	0.9%
36	Nebraska	159,900	0.7%
37	West Virginia	141,100	0.7%
38	Nevada	136,200	0.6%
39	Hawaii	118,600	0.6%
40	Idaho	111,000	0.5%
41	Maine	103,600	0.5%
42	New Hampshire	91,200	0.4%
43	Montana	83,800	0.4%
44	Alaska	82,600	0.4%
45	North Dakota	75,800	0.4%
46	South Dakota	75,300	0.4%
47	Rhode Island	65,600	0.3%
48	Wyoming	63,400	0.3%
49	Delaware	54,800	0.3%
50	Vermont	51,600	0.2%
	District of Columbia	231,000	1.1%

Source: U.S. Department of Labor, Bureau of Labor Statistics
"Regional and State Employment and Unemployment" (press release, January 27, 2004)
**Seasonally adjusted preliminary data as of December 2003. National total calculated through a different formula.*

Percent of Nonfarm Employees in Government in 2003

National Percent = 16.5% of Employees*

<u>ALPHA ORDER</u>

RANK	STATE	PERCENT
15	Alabama	18.9
1	Alaska	27.1
29	Arizona	17.0
25	Arkansas	17.2
31	California	16.7
32	Colorado	16.6
42	Connecticut	14.7
48	Delaware	13.3
40	Florida	14.8
33	Georgia	16.0
7	Hawaii	20.7
13	Idaho	19.3
45	Illinois	14.5
44	Indiana	14.6
30	Iowa	16.9
14	Kansas	19.0
23	Kentucky	17.4
8	Louisiana	20.0
27	Maine	17.1
15	Maryland	18.9
49	Massachusetts	13.2
37	Michigan	15.3
38	Minnesota	14.9
5	Mississippi	21.8
33	Missouri	16.0
6	Montana	21.1
20	Nebraska	17.7
50	Nevada	12.4
42	New Hampshire	14.7
35	New Jersey	15.6
3	New Mexico	25.1
22	New York	17.6
25	North Carolina	17.2
4	North Dakota	22.9
40	Ohio	14.8
8	Oklahoma	20.0
24	Oregon	17.3
47	Pennsylvania	13.4
46	Rhode Island	13.6
17	South Carolina	18.6
10	South Dakota	19.6
36	Tennessee	15.5
20	Texas	17.7
18	Utah	18.3
27	Vermont	17.1
18	Virginia	18.3
10	Washington	19.6
12	West Virginia	19.5
38	Wisconsin	14.9
2	Wyoming	25.2

<u>RANK ORDER</u>

RANK	STATE	PERCENT
1	Alaska	27.1
2	Wyoming	25.2
3	New Mexico	25.1
4	North Dakota	22.9
5	Mississippi	21.8
6	Montana	21.1
7	Hawaii	20.7
8	Louisiana	20.0
8	Oklahoma	20.0
10	South Dakota	19.6
10	Washington	19.6
12	West Virginia	19.5
13	Idaho	19.3
14	Kansas	19.0
15	Alabama	18.9
15	Maryland	18.9
17	South Carolina	18.6
18	Utah	18.3
18	Virginia	18.3
20	Nebraska	17.7
20	Texas	17.7
22	New York	17.6
23	Kentucky	17.4
24	Oregon	17.3
25	Arkansas	17.2
25	North Carolina	17.2
27	Maine	17.1
27	Vermont	17.1
29	Arizona	17.0
30	Iowa	16.9
31	California	16.7
32	Colorado	16.6
33	Georgia	16.0
33	Missouri	16.0
35	New Jersey	15.6
36	Tennessee	15.5
37	Michigan	15.3
38	Minnesota	14.9
38	Wisconsin	14.9
40	Florida	14.8
40	Ohio	14.8
42	Connecticut	14.7
42	New Hampshire	14.7
44	Indiana	14.6
45	Illinois	14.5
46	Rhode Island	13.6
47	Pennsylvania	13.4
48	Delaware	13.3
49	Massachusetts	13.2
50	Nevada	12.4
	District of Columbia	34.5

Source: Morgan Quitno Press using data from U.S. Department of Labor, Bureau of Labor Statistics
"Regional and State Employment and Unemployment" (press release, January 27, 2004)
*Seasonally adjusted preliminary data as of December 2003. National total calculated through a different formula.

Employees in Leisure and Hospitality in 2003

National Total = 12,087,000 Employees*

<u>ALPHA ORDER</u>

RANK	STATE	EMPLOYEES	% of USA
26	Alabama	157,500	1.3%
47	Alaska	29,400	0.2%
22	Arizona	234,600	1.9%
34	Arkansas	88,600	0.7%
1	California	1,405,700	11.6%
17	Colorado	248,900	2.1%
NA	Connecticut**	NA	NA
44	Delaware	38,300	0.3%
3	Florida	831,600	6.9%
9	Georgia	343,300	2.8%
32	Hawaii	101,300	0.8%
40	Idaho	53,400	0.4%
5	Illinois	498,400	4.1%
15	Indiana	267,300	2.2%
NA	Iowa**	NA	NA
31	Kansas	108,600	0.9%
27	Kentucky	154,300	1.3%
24	Louisiana	193,000	1.6%
39	Maine	56,100	0.5%
23	Maryland	208,800	1.7%
14	Massachusetts	282,200	2.3%
8	Michigan	381,700	3.2%
21	Minnesota	237,200	2.0%
30	Mississippi	120,500	1.0%
16	Missouri	258,500	2.1%
41	Montana	51,900	0.4%
36	Nebraska	71,400	0.6%
13	Nevada	301,900	2.5%
38	New Hampshire	64,000	0.5%
11	New Jersey	315,200	2.6%
35	New Mexico	81,500	0.7%
4	New York	652,400	5.4%
10	North Carolina	329,800	2.7%
46	North Dakota	30,400	0.3%
6	Ohio	474,200	3.9%
29	Oklahoma	127,300	1.1%
28	Oregon	153,700	1.3%
7	Pennsylvania	470,400	3.9%
42	Rhode Island	47,500	0.4%
25	South Carolina	190,400	1.6%
43	South Dakota	39,700	0.3%
19	Tennessee	239,500	2.0%
2	Texas	858,000	7.1%
32	Utah	101,300	0.8%
NA	Vermont**	NA	NA
12	Virginia	315,100	2.6%
18	Washington	245,500	2.0%
37	West Virginia	64,700	0.5%
20	Wisconsin	238,400	2.0%
45	Wyoming	31,000	0.3%

<u>RANK ORDER</u>

RANK	STATE	EMPLOYEES	% of USA
1	California	1,405,700	11.6%
2	Texas	858,000	7.1%
3	Florida	831,600	6.9%
4	New York	652,400	5.4%
5	Illinois	498,400	4.1%
6	Ohio	474,200	3.9%
7	Pennsylvania	470,400	3.9%
8	Michigan	381,700	3.2%
9	Georgia	343,300	2.8%
10	North Carolina	329,800	2.7%
11	New Jersey	315,200	2.6%
12	Virginia	315,100	2.6%
13	Nevada	301,900	2.5%
14	Massachusetts	282,200	2.3%
15	Indiana	267,300	2.2%
16	Missouri	258,500	2.1%
17	Colorado	248,900	2.1%
18	Washington	245,500	2.0%
19	Tennessee	239,500	2.0%
20	Wisconsin	238,400	2.0%
21	Minnesota	237,200	2.0%
22	Arizona	234,600	1.9%
23	Maryland	208,800	1.7%
24	Louisiana	193,000	1.6%
25	South Carolina	190,400	1.6%
26	Alabama	157,500	1.3%
27	Kentucky	154,300	1.3%
28	Oregon	153,700	1.3%
29	Oklahoma	127,300	1.1%
30	Mississippi	120,500	1.0%
31	Kansas	108,600	0.9%
32	Hawaii	101,300	0.8%
32	Utah	101,300	0.8%
34	Arkansas	88,600	0.7%
35	New Mexico	81,500	0.7%
36	Nebraska	71,400	0.6%
37	West Virginia	64,700	0.5%
38	New Hampshire	64,000	0.5%
39	Maine	56,100	0.5%
40	Idaho	53,400	0.4%
41	Montana	51,900	0.4%
42	Rhode Island	47,500	0.4%
43	South Dakota	39,700	0.3%
44	Delaware	38,300	0.3%
45	Wyoming	31,000	0.3%
46	North Dakota	30,400	0.3%
47	Alaska	29,400	0.2%
NA	Connecticut**	NA	NA
NA	Iowa**	NA	NA
NA	Vermont**	NA	NA
	District of Columbia	49,400	0.4%

Source: U.S. Department of Labor, Bureau of Labor Statistics
"Regional and State Employment and Unemployment" (press release, January 27, 2004)
**Seasonally adjusted preliminary data as of December 2003. National total calculated through a different formula.*
***The Bureau of Labor Statistics does not publish seasonally adjusted figures in this category for these states.*

Percent of Nonfarm Employees in Leisure and Hospitality in 2003

National Percent = 9.3% of Employees*

ALPHA ORDER

RANK	STATE	PERCENT
41	Alabama	8.4
18	Alaska	9.6
12	Arizona	10.2
47	Arkansas	7.7
16	California	9.7
5	Colorado	11.6
NA	Connecticut**	NA
20	Delaware	9.3
6	Florida	11.3
33	Georgia	8.7
2	Hawaii	17.7
20	Idaho	9.3
39	Illinois	8.5
20	Indiana	9.3
NA	Iowa**	NA
43	Kansas	8.1
33	Kentucky	8.7
12	Louisiana	10.2
20	Maine	9.3
39	Maryland	8.5
30	Massachusetts	8.9
33	Michigan	8.7
27	Minnesota	9.0
7	Mississippi	10.7
16	Missouri	9.7
3	Montana	13.1
44	Nebraska	7.9
1	Nevada	27.5
11	New Hampshire	10.3
45	New Jersey	7.8
9	New Mexico	10.4
45	New York	7.8
37	North Carolina	8.6
24	North Dakota	9.2
30	Ohio	8.9
33	Oklahoma	8.7
15	Oregon	9.8
41	Pennsylvania	8.4
14	Rhode Island	9.9
7	South Carolina	10.7
9	South Dakota	10.4
27	Tennessee	9.0
26	Texas	9.1
19	Utah	9.4
NA	Vermont**	NA
27	Virginia	9.0
24	Washington	9.2
30	West Virginia	8.9
37	Wisconsin	8.6
4	Wyoming	12.3

RANK ORDER

RANK	STATE	PERCENT
1	Nevada	27.5
2	Hawaii	17.7
3	Montana	13.1
4	Wyoming	12.3
5	Colorado	11.6
6	Florida	11.3
7	Mississippi	10.7
7	South Carolina	10.7
9	New Mexico	10.4
9	South Dakota	10.4
11	New Hampshire	10.3
12	Arizona	10.2
12	Louisiana	10.2
14	Rhode Island	9.9
15	Oregon	9.8
16	California	9.7
16	Missouri	9.7
18	Alaska	9.6
19	Utah	9.4
20	Delaware	9.3
20	Idaho	9.3
20	Indiana	9.3
20	Maine	9.3
24	North Dakota	9.2
24	Washington	9.2
26	Texas	9.1
27	Minnesota	9.0
27	Tennessee	9.0
27	Virginia	9.0
30	Massachusetts	8.9
30	Ohio	8.9
30	West Virginia	8.9
33	Georgia	8.7
33	Kentucky	8.7
33	Michigan	8.7
33	Oklahoma	8.7
37	North Carolina	8.6
37	Wisconsin	8.6
39	Illinois	8.5
39	Maryland	8.5
41	Alabama	8.4
41	Pennsylvania	8.4
43	Kansas	8.1
44	Nebraska	7.9
45	New Jersey	7.8
45	New York	7.8
47	Arkansas	7.7
NA	Connecticut**	NA
NA	Iowa**	NA
NA	Vermont**	NA

District of Columbia   7.4

Source: Morgan Quitno Press using data from U.S. Department of Labor, Bureau of Labor Statistics
   "Regional and State Employment and Unemployment" (press release, January 27, 2004)
*Seasonally adjusted preliminary data as of December 2003. National total calculated through a different formula.
**The Bureau of Labor Statistics does not publish seasonally adjusted figures in this category for these states.

Employees in Manufacturing in 2003

National Total = 14,504,000 Employees*

ALPHA ORDER

RANK	STATE	EMPLOYEES	% of USA
NA	Alabama**	NA	NA
NA	Alaska**	NA	NA
25	Arizona	174,200	1.2%
20	Arkansas	205,600	1.4%
1	California	1,573,300	10.8%
28	Colorado	149,900	1.0%
21	Connecticut	200,200	1.4%
NA	Delaware**	NA	NA
11	Florida	392,000	2.7%
NA	Georgia**	NA	NA
NA	Hawaii**	NA	NA
34	Idaho	61,000	0.4%
4	Illinois	725,900	5.0%
9	Indiana	574,800	4.0%
19	Iowa	221,100	1.5%
24	Kansas	177,800	1.2%
17	Kentucky	268,300	1.8%
26	Louisiana	156,600	1.1%
33	Maine	63,800	0.4%
27	Maryland	151,400	1.0%
14	Massachusetts	331,100	2.3%
5	Michigan	722,300	5.0%
13	Minnesota	346,500	2.4%
23	Mississippi	179,200	1.2%
15	Missouri	312,700	2.2%
40	Montana	18,100	0.1%
30	Nebraska	103,900	0.7%
NA	Nevada**	NA	NA
31	New Hampshire	81,100	0.6%
12	New Jersey	355,100	2.4%
37	New Mexico	36,500	0.3%
7	New York	606,200	4.2%
8	North Carolina	596,500	4.1%
39	North Dakota	22,700	0.2%
3	Ohio	838,400	5.8%
NA	Oklahoma**	NA	NA
22	Oregon	198,700	1.4%
6	Pennsylvania	716,000	4.9%
35	Rhode Island	59,400	0.4%
NA	South Carolina**	NA	NA
38	South Dakota	36,200	0.2%
NA	Tennessee**	NA	NA
2	Texas	903,400	6.2%
29	Utah	111,000	0.8%
36	Vermont	38,000	0.3%
16	Virginia	302,800	2.1%
18	Washington	260,700	1.8%
32	West Virginia	64,400	0.4%
10	Wisconsin	508,800	3.5%
NA	Wyoming**	NA	NA

RANK ORDER

RANK	STATE	EMPLOYEES	% of USA
1	California	1,573,300	10.8%
2	Texas	903,400	6.2%
3	Ohio	838,400	5.8%
4	Illinois	725,900	5.0%
5	Michigan	722,300	5.0%
6	Pennsylvania	716,000	4.9%
7	New York	606,200	4.2%
8	North Carolina	596,500	4.1%
9	Indiana	574,800	4.0%
10	Wisconsin	508,800	3.5%
11	Florida	392,000	2.7%
12	New Jersey	355,100	2.4%
13	Minnesota	346,500	2.4%
14	Massachusetts	331,100	2.3%
15	Missouri	312,700	2.2%
16	Virginia	302,800	2.1%
17	Kentucky	268,300	1.8%
18	Washington	260,700	1.8%
19	Iowa	221,100	1.5%
20	Arkansas	205,600	1.4%
21	Connecticut	200,200	1.4%
22	Oregon	198,700	1.4%
23	Mississippi	179,200	1.2%
24	Kansas	177,800	1.2%
25	Arizona	174,200	1.2%
26	Louisiana	156,600	1.1%
27	Maryland	151,400	1.0%
28	Colorado	149,900	1.0%
29	Utah	111,000	0.8%
30	Nebraska	103,900	0.7%
31	New Hampshire	81,100	0.6%
32	West Virginia	64,400	0.4%
33	Maine	63,800	0.4%
34	Idaho	61,000	0.4%
35	Rhode Island	59,400	0.4%
36	Vermont	38,000	0.3%
37	New Mexico	36,500	0.3%
38	South Dakota	36,200	0.2%
39	North Dakota	22,700	0.2%
40	Montana	18,100	0.1%
NA	Alabama**	NA	NA
NA	Alaska**	NA	NA
NA	Delaware**	NA	NA
NA	Georgia**	NA	NA
NA	Hawaii**	NA	NA
NA	Nevada**	NA	NA
NA	Oklahoma**	NA	NA
NA	South Carolina**	NA	NA
NA	Tennessee**	NA	NA
NA	Wyoming**	NA	NA
	District of Columbia**	NA	NA

Source: U.S. Department of Labor, Bureau of Labor Statistics
   "Regional and State Employment and Unemployment" (press release, January 27, 2004)
Seasonally adjusted preliminary data as of December 2003. National total calculated through a different formula.
***The Bureau of Labor Statistics does not publish seasonally adjusted figures in this category for these states.*

Percent of Nonfarm Employees in Manufacturing in 2003

National Percent = 11.1% of Employees*

<u>ALPHA ORDER</u>

RANK	STATE	PERCENT
NA	Alabama**	NA
NA	Alaska**	NA
33	Arizona	7.5
3	Arkansas	17.9
21	California	10.9
35	Colorado	7.0
18	Connecticut	12.2
NA	Delaware**	NA
38	Florida	5.3
NA	Georgia**	NA
NA	Hawaii**	NA
22	Idaho	10.6
16	Illinois	12.3
1	Indiana	20.0
8	Iowa	15.3
10	Kansas	13.2
9	Kentucky	15.1
32	Louisiana	8.3
23	Maine	10.5
37	Maryland	6.2
24	Massachusetts	10.4
4	Michigan	16.5
11	Minnesota	13.1
5	Mississippi	15.8
19	Missouri	11.7
40	Montana	4.6
20	Nebraska	11.5
NA	Nevada**	NA
11	New Hampshire	13.1
30	New Jersey	8.8
39	New Mexico	4.7
34	New York	7.2
7	North Carolina	15.6
36	North Dakota	6.9
6	Ohio	15.7
NA	Oklahoma**	NA
13	Oregon	12.7
13	Pennsylvania	12.7
16	Rhode Island	12.3
NA	South Carolina**	NA
28	South Dakota	9.4
NA	Tennessee**	NA
27	Texas	9.5
25	Utah	10.3
15	Vermont	12.6
31	Virginia	8.6
26	Washington	9.8
29	West Virginia	8.9
2	Wisconsin	18.4
NA	Wyoming**	NA

<u>RANK ORDER</u>

RANK	STATE	PERCENT
1	Indiana	20.0
2	Wisconsin	18.4
3	Arkansas	17.9
4	Michigan	16.5
5	Mississippi	15.8
6	Ohio	15.7
7	North Carolina	15.6
8	Iowa	15.3
9	Kentucky	15.1
10	Kansas	13.2
11	Minnesota	13.1
11	New Hampshire	13.1
13	Oregon	12.7
13	Pennsylvania	12.7
15	Vermont	12.6
16	Illinois	12.3
16	Rhode Island	12.3
18	Connecticut	12.2
19	Missouri	11.7
20	Nebraska	11.5
21	California	10.9
22	Idaho	10.6
23	Maine	10.5
24	Massachusetts	10.4
25	Utah	10.3
26	Washington	9.8
27	Texas	9.5
28	South Dakota	9.4
29	West Virginia	8.9
30	New Jersey	8.8
31	Virginia	8.6
32	Louisiana	8.3
33	Arizona	7.5
34	New York	7.2
35	Colorado	7.0
36	North Dakota	6.9
37	Maryland	6.2
38	Florida	5.3
39	New Mexico	4.7
40	Montana	4.6
NA	Alabama**	NA
NA	Alaska**	NA
NA	Delaware**	NA
NA	Georgia**	NA
NA	Hawaii**	NA
NA	Nevada**	NA
NA	Oklahoma**	NA
NA	South Carolina**	NA
NA	Tennessee**	NA
NA	Wyoming**	NA
	District of Columbia**	NA

Source: Morgan Quitno Press using data from U.S. Department of Labor, Bureau of Labor Statistics
"Regional and State Employment and Unemployment" (press release, January 27, 2004)
**Seasonally adjusted preliminary data as of December 2003. National total calculated through a different formula.*
***The Bureau of Labor Statistics does not publish seasonally adjusted figures in this category for these states.*

Employees in Mining in 2003

National Total = 500,700 Employees*

ALPHA ORDER

RANK	STATE	EMPLOYEES	% of USA
NA	Alabama**	NA	NA
9	Alaska	9,200	1.8%
NA	Arizona**	NA	NA
16	Arkansas	3,600	0.7%
4	California	20,500	4.0%
NA	Colorado**	NA	NA
NA	Connecticut**	NA	NA
NA	Delaware**	NA	NA
NA	Florida**	NA	NA
NA	Georgia**	NA	NA
NA	Hawaii**	NA	NA
17	Idaho	1,600	0.3%
NA	Illinois**	NA	NA
10	Indiana	6,700	1.3%
NA	Iowa**	NA	NA
10	Kansas	6,700	1.3%
NA	Kentucky**	NA	NA
2	Louisiana	45,200	8.9%
NA	Maine**	NA	NA
NA	Maryland**	NA	NA
NA	Massachusetts**	NA	NA
12	Michigan	5,800	1.1%
13	Minnesota	5,400	1.1%
NA	Mississippi**	NA	NA
NA	Missouri**	NA	NA
13	Montana	5,400	1.1%
18	Nebraska	1,300	0.3%
NA	Nevada**	NA	NA
NA	New Hampshire**	NA	NA
NA	New Jersey**	NA	NA
7	New Mexico	13,900	2.7%
NA	New York**	NA	NA
15	North Carolina	4,200	0.8%
NA	North Dakota**	NA	NA
8	Ohio	11,500	2.3%
NA	Oklahoma**	NA	NA
NA	Oregon**	NA	NA
6	Pennsylvania	16,900	3.3%
NA	Rhode Island**	NA	NA
NA	South Carolina**	NA	NA
NA	South Dakota**	NA	NA
NA	Tennessee**	NA	NA
1	Texas	140,200	27.7%
NA	Utah**	NA	NA
NA	Vermont**	NA	NA
NA	Virginia**	NA	NA
NA	Washington**	NA	NA
3	West Virginia	21,200	4.2%
NA	Wisconsin**	NA	NA
5	Wyoming	18,100	3.6%

RANK ORDER

RANK	STATE	EMPLOYEES	% of USA
1	Texas	140,200	27.7%
2	Louisiana	45,200	8.9%
3	West Virginia	21,200	4.2%
4	California	20,500	4.0%
5	Wyoming	18,100	3.6%
6	Pennsylvania	16,900	3.3%
7	New Mexico	13,900	2.7%
8	Ohio	11,500	2.3%
9	Alaska	9,200	1.8%
10	Indiana	6,700	1.3%
10	Kansas	6,700	1.3%
12	Michigan	5,800	1.1%
13	Minnesota	5,400	1.1%
13	Montana	5,400	1.1%
15	North Carolina	4,200	0.8%
16	Arkansas	3,600	0.7%
17	Idaho	1,600	0.3%
18	Nebraska	1,300	0.3%
NA	Alabama**	NA	NA
NA	Arizona**	NA	NA
NA	Colorado**	NA	NA
NA	Connecticut**	NA	NA
NA	Delaware**	NA	NA
NA	Florida**	NA	NA
NA	Georgia**	NA	NA
NA	Hawaii**	NA	NA
NA	Illinois**	NA	NA
NA	Iowa**	NA	NA
NA	Kentucky**	NA	NA
NA	Maine**	NA	NA
NA	Maryland**	NA	NA
NA	Massachusetts**	NA	NA
NA	Mississippi**	NA	NA
NA	Missouri**	NA	NA
NA	Nevada**	NA	NA
NA	New Hampshire**	NA	NA
NA	New Jersey**	NA	NA
NA	New York**	NA	NA
NA	North Dakota**	NA	NA
NA	Oklahoma**	NA	NA
NA	Oregon**	NA	NA
NA	Rhode Island**	NA	NA
NA	South Carolina**	NA	NA
NA	South Dakota**	NA	NA
NA	Tennessee**	NA	NA
NA	Utah**	NA	NA
NA	Vermont**	NA	NA
NA	Virginia**	NA	NA
NA	Washington**	NA	NA
NA	Wisconsin**	NA	NA
	District of Columbia**	NA	NA

Source: U.S. Department of Labor, Bureau of Labor Statistics
"Regional and State Employment and Unemployment" (press release, January 27, 2004)
Not seasonally adjusted preliminary data as of December 2003. National total calculated through a different formula.
**Not available.*

Percent of Nonfarm Employees in Mining in 2003

National Percent = 0.4% of Employees*

<u>ALPHA ORDER</u>

RANK	STATE	PERCENT
NA	Alabama**	NA
2	Alaska	3.0
NA	Arizona**	NA
9	Arkansas	0.3
15	California	0.1
NA	Colorado**	NA
NA	Connecticut**	NA
NA	Delaware**	NA
NA	Florida**	NA
NA	Georgia**	NA
NA	Hawaii**	NA
9	Idaho	0.3
NA	Illinois**	NA
12	Indiana	0.2
NA	Iowa**	NA
8	Kansas	0.5
NA	Kentucky**	NA
4	Louisiana	2.4
NA	Maine**	NA
NA	Maryland**	NA
NA	Massachusetts**	NA
15	Michigan	0.1
12	Minnesota	0.2
NA	Mississippi**	NA
NA	Missouri**	NA
7	Montana	1.4
15	Nebraska	0.1
NA	Nevada**	NA
NA	New Hampshire**	NA
NA	New Jersey**	NA
5	New Mexico	1.8
NA	New York**	NA
15	North Carolina	0.1
NA	North Dakota**	NA
12	Ohio	0.2
NA	Oklahoma**	NA
NA	Oregon**	NA
9	Pennsylvania	0.3
NA	Rhode Island**	NA
NA	South Carolina**	NA
NA	South Dakota**	NA
NA	Tennessee**	NA
6	Texas	1.5
NA	Utah**	NA
NA	Vermont**	NA
NA	Virginia**	NA
NA	Washington**	NA
3	West Virginia	2.9
NA	Wisconsin**	NA
1	Wyoming	7.2

<u>RANK ORDER</u>

RANK	STATE	PERCENT
1	Wyoming	7.2
2	Alaska	3.0
3	West Virginia	2.9
4	Louisiana	2.4
5	New Mexico	1.8
6	Texas	1.5
7	Montana	1.4
8	Kansas	0.5
9	Arkansas	0.3
9	Idaho	0.3
9	Pennsylvania	0.3
12	Indiana	0.2
12	Minnesota	0.2
12	Ohio	0.2
15	California	0.1
15	Michigan	0.1
15	Nebraska	0.1
15	North Carolina	0.1
NA	Alabama**	NA
NA	Arizona**	NA
NA	Colorado**	NA
NA	Connecticut**	NA
NA	Delaware**	NA
NA	Florida**	NA
NA	Georgia**	NA
NA	Hawaii**	NA
NA	Illinois**	NA
NA	Iowa**	NA
NA	Kentucky**	NA
NA	Maine**	NA
NA	Maryland**	NA
NA	Massachusetts**	NA
NA	Mississippi**	NA
NA	Missouri**	NA
NA	Nevada**	NA
NA	New Hampshire**	NA
NA	New Jersey**	NA
NA	New York**	NA
NA	North Dakota**	NA
NA	Oklahoma**	NA
NA	Oregon**	NA
NA	Rhode Island**	NA
NA	South Carolina**	NA
NA	South Dakota**	NA
NA	Tennessee**	NA
NA	Utah**	NA
NA	Vermont**	NA
NA	Virginia**	NA
NA	Washington**	NA
NA	Wisconsin**	NA

| | District of Columbia** | NA |

Source: Morgan Quitno Press using data from U.S. Department of Labor, Bureau of Labor Statistics "Regional and State Employment and Unemployment" (press release, January 27, 2004)
Not seasonally adjusted preliminary data as of December 2003. National total calculated through a different formula.
**Not available.*

Employees in Professional and Business Services in 2003

National Total = 16,224,000 Employees*

<u>ALPHA ORDER</u>

RANK	STATE	EMPLOYEES	% of USA
NA	Alabama**	NA	NA
39	Alaska	24,000	0.1%
15	Arizona	321,700	2.0%
30	Arkansas	99,600	0.6%
1	California	2,116,100	13.0%
19	Colorado	287,600	1.8%
22	Connecticut	196,100	1.2%
34	Delaware	68,400	0.4%
2	Florida	1,271,400	7.8%
10	Georgia	552,300	3.4%
NA	Hawaii**	NA	NA
33	Idaho	73,000	0.4%
5	Illinois	791,200	4.9%
20	Indiana	238,700	1.5%
29	Iowa	109,500	0.7%
NA	Kansas**	NA	NA
26	Kentucky	154,800	1.0%
23	Louisiana	174,200	1.1%
36	Maine	51,300	0.3%
14	Maryland	357,700	2.2%
12	Massachusetts	430,400	2.7%
9	Michigan	563,300	3.5%
17	Minnesota	295,100	1.8%
NA	Mississippi**	NA	NA
NA	Missouri**	NA	NA
38	Montana	32,000	0.2%
31	Nebraska	90,500	0.6%
28	Nevada	120,400	0.7%
NA	New Hampshire**	NA	NA
8	New Jersey	587,100	3.6%
32	New Mexico	89,400	0.6%
4	New York	1,035,400	6.4%
13	North Carolina	423,300	2.6%
40	North Dakota	23,800	0.1%
6	Ohio	600,900	3.7%
25	Oklahoma	158,400	1.0%
24	Oregon	173,900	1.1%
7	Pennsylvania	600,300	3.7%
37	Rhode Island	48,500	0.3%
NA	South Carolina**	NA	NA
NA	South Dakota**	NA	NA
16	Tennessee	316,400	2.0%
3	Texas	1,045,000	6.4%
27	Utah	134,300	0.8%
41	Vermont	20,600	0.1%
11	Virginia	543,000	3.3%
18	Washington	294,200	1.8%
35	West Virginia	58,400	0.4%
21	Wisconsin	238,500	1.5%
42	Wyoming	15,400	0.1%

<u>RANK ORDER</u>

RANK	STATE	EMPLOYEES	% of USA
1	California	2,116,100	13.0%
2	Florida	1,271,400	7.8%
3	Texas	1,045,000	6.4%
4	New York	1,035,400	6.4%
5	Illinois	791,200	4.9%
6	Ohio	600,900	3.7%
7	Pennsylvania	600,300	3.7%
8	New Jersey	587,100	3.6%
9	Michigan	563,300	3.5%
10	Georgia	552,300	3.4%
11	Virginia	543,000	3.3%
12	Massachusetts	430,400	2.7%
13	North Carolina	423,300	2.6%
14	Maryland	357,700	2.2%
15	Arizona	321,700	2.0%
16	Tennessee	316,400	2.0%
17	Minnesota	295,100	1.8%
18	Washington	294,200	1.8%
19	Colorado	287,600	1.8%
20	Indiana	238,700	1.5%
21	Wisconsin	238,500	1.5%
22	Connecticut	196,100	1.2%
23	Louisiana	174,200	1.1%
24	Oregon	173,900	1.1%
25	Oklahoma	158,400	1.0%
26	Kentucky	154,800	1.0%
27	Utah	134,300	0.8%
28	Nevada	120,400	0.7%
29	Iowa	109,500	0.7%
30	Arkansas	99,600	0.6%
31	Nebraska	90,500	0.6%
32	New Mexico	89,400	0.6%
33	Idaho	73,000	0.4%
34	Delaware	68,400	0.4%
35	West Virginia	58,400	0.4%
36	Maine	51,300	0.3%
37	Rhode Island	48,500	0.3%
38	Montana	32,000	0.2%
39	Alaska	24,000	0.1%
40	North Dakota	23,800	0.1%
41	Vermont	20,600	0.1%
42	Wyoming	15,400	0.1%
NA	Alabama**	NA	NA
NA	Hawaii**	NA	NA
NA	Kansas**	NA	NA
NA	Mississippi**	NA	NA
NA	Missouri**	NA	NA
NA	New Hampshire**	NA	NA
NA	South Carolina**	NA	NA
NA	South Dakota**	NA	NA
	District of Columbia	142,300	0.9%

Source: U.S. Department of Labor, Bureau of Labor Statistics
"Regional and State Employment and Unemployment" (press release, January 27, 2004)
**Seasonally adjusted preliminary data as of December 2003. National total calculated through a different formula.*
***The Bureau of Labor Statistics does not publish seasonally adjusted figures in this category for these states.*

Percent of Nonfarm Employees in Professional and Business Services in 2003

National Percent = 12.5% of Employees*

ALPHA ORDER				RANK ORDER		
RANK	**STATE**	**PERCENT**		**RANK**	**STATE**	**PERCENT**
NA	Alabama**	NA		1	Florida	17.3
38	Alaska	7.9		2	Delaware	16.6
7	Arizona	13.9		3	Virginia	15.4
31	Arkansas	8.7		4	California	14.7
4	California	14.7		5	New Jersey	14.6
11	Colorado	13.4		6	Maryland	14.5
16	Connecticut	11.9		7	Arizona	13.9
2	Delaware	16.6		7	Georgia	13.9
1	Florida	17.3		9	Illinois	13.5
7	Georgia	13.9		9	Massachusetts	13.5
NA	Hawaii**	NA		11	Colorado	13.4
13	Idaho	12.7		12	Michigan	12.9
9	Illinois	13.5		13	Idaho	12.7
35	Indiana	8.3		14	Utah	12.5
39	Iowa	7.6		15	New York	12.3
NA	Kansas**	NA		16	Connecticut	11.9
31	Kentucky	8.7		16	Tennessee	11.9
30	Louisiana	9.2		18	New Mexico	11.4
34	Maine	8.5		19	Ohio	11.2
6	Maryland	14.5		20	Minnesota	11.1
9	Massachusetts	13.5		20	North Carolina	11.1
12	Michigan	12.9		20	Oregon	11.1
20	Minnesota	11.1		23	Nevada	11.0
NA	Mississippi**	NA		23	Texas	11.0
NA	Missouri**	NA		23	Washington	11.0
36	Montana	8.1		26	Oklahoma	10.8
29	Nebraska	10.0		27	Pennsylvania	10.7
23	Nevada	11.0		28	Rhode Island	10.1
NA	New Hampshire**	NA		29	Nebraska	10.0
5	New Jersey	14.6		30	Louisiana	9.2
18	New Mexico	11.4		31	Arkansas	8.7
15	New York	12.3		31	Kentucky	8.7
20	North Carolina	11.1		33	Wisconsin	8.6
40	North Dakota	7.2		34	Maine	8.5
19	Ohio	11.2		35	Indiana	8.3
26	Oklahoma	10.8		36	Montana	8.1
20	Oregon	11.1		36	West Virginia	8.1
27	Pennsylvania	10.7		38	Alaska	7.9
28	Rhode Island	10.1		39	Iowa	7.6
NA	South Carolina**	NA		40	North Dakota	7.2
NA	South Dakota**	NA		41	Vermont	6.8
16	Tennessee	11.9		42	Wyoming	6.1
23	Texas	11.0		NA	Alabama**	NA
14	Utah	12.5		NA	Hawaii**	NA
41	Vermont	6.8		NA	Kansas**	NA
3	Virginia	15.4		NA	Mississippi**	NA
23	Washington	11.0		NA	Missouri**	NA
36	West Virginia	8.1		NA	New Hampshire**	NA
33	Wisconsin	8.6		NA	South Carolina**	NA
42	Wyoming	6.1		NA	South Dakota**	NA
					District of Columbia	21.3

Source: Morgan Quitno Press using data from U.S. Department of Labor, Bureau of Labor Statistics "Regional and State Employment and Unemployment" (press release, January 27, 2004)

Seasonally adjusted preliminary data as of December 2003. National total calculated through a different formula.

**The Bureau of Labor Statistics does not publish seasonally adjusted figures in this category for these states.*

Employees in Trade, Transportation and Public Utilities in 2003

National Total = 25,201,000 Employees*

ALPHA ORDER

RANK	STATE	EMPLOYEES	% of USA
24	Alabama	345,600	1.4%
47	Alaska	62,300	0.2%
NA	Arizona**	NA	NA
31	Arkansas	243,300	1.0%
1	California	2,725,400	10.8%
21	Colorado	407,400	1.6%
28	Connecticut	291,300	1.2%
44	Delaware	80,300	0.3%
4	Florida	1,463,600	5.8%
10	Georgia	804,100	3.2%
41	Hawaii	106,100	0.4%
40	Idaho	118,600	0.5%
5	Illinois	1,191,500	4.7%
13	Indiana	574,200	2.3%
27	Iowa	301,100	1.2%
30	Kansas	268,400	1.1%
23	Kentucky	366,600	1.5%
22	Louisiana	380,200	1.5%
39	Maine	125,700	0.5%
20	Maryland	453,300	1.8%
14	Massachusetts	568,400	2.3%
9	Michigan	823,900	3.3%
18	Minnesota	523,500	2.1%
32	Mississippi	219,300	0.9%
16	Missouri	533,500	2.1%
42	Montana	85,400	0.3%
35	Nebraska	197,000	0.8%
34	Nevada	204,200	0.8%
36	New Hampshire	139,200	0.6%
8	New Jersey	884,600	3.5%
37	New Mexico	136,800	0.5%
3	New York	1,475,600	5.9%
11	North Carolina	717,900	2.8%
46	North Dakota	71,600	0.3%
7	Ohio	1,037,300	4.1%
29	Oklahoma	280,900	1.1%
26	Oregon	307,900	1.2%
6	Pennsylvania	1,096,700	4.4%
43	Rhode Island	80,700	0.3%
25	South Carolina	344,500	1.4%
45	South Dakota	79,800	0.3%
15	Tennessee	564,700	2.2%
2	Texas	1,939,800	7.7%
33	Utah	213,800	0.8%
NA	Vermont**	NA	NA
12	Virginia	646,800	2.6%
19	Washington	515,400	2.0%
38	West Virginia	133,400	0.5%
17	Wisconsin	533,100	2.1%
48	Wyoming	48,800	0.2%

RANK ORDER

RANK	STATE	EMPLOYEES	% of USA
1	California	2,725,400	10.8%
2	Texas	1,939,800	7.7%
3	New York	1,475,600	5.9%
4	Florida	1,463,600	5.8%
5	Illinois	1,191,500	4.7%
6	Pennsylvania	1,096,700	4.4%
7	Ohio	1,037,300	4.1%
8	New Jersey	884,600	3.5%
9	Michigan	823,900	3.3%
10	Georgia	804,100	3.2%
11	North Carolina	717,900	2.8%
12	Virginia	646,800	2.6%
13	Indiana	574,200	2.3%
14	Massachusetts	568,400	2.3%
15	Tennessee	564,700	2.2%
16	Missouri	533,500	2.1%
17	Wisconsin	533,100	2.1%
18	Minnesota	523,500	2.1%
19	Washington	515,400	2.0%
20	Maryland	453,300	1.8%
21	Colorado	407,400	1.6%
22	Louisiana	380,200	1.5%
23	Kentucky	366,600	1.5%
24	Alabama	345,600	1.4%
25	South Carolina	344,500	1.4%
26	Oregon	307,900	1.2%
27	Iowa	301,100	1.2%
28	Connecticut	291,300	1.2%
29	Oklahoma	280,900	1.1%
30	Kansas	268,400	1.1%
31	Arkansas	243,300	1.0%
32	Mississippi	219,300	0.9%
33	Utah	213,800	0.8%
34	Nevada	204,200	0.8%
35	Nebraska	197,000	0.8%
36	New Hampshire	139,200	0.6%
37	New Mexico	136,800	0.5%
38	West Virginia	133,400	0.5%
39	Maine	125,700	0.5%
40	Idaho	118,600	0.5%
41	Hawaii	106,100	0.4%
42	Montana	85,400	0.3%
43	Rhode Island	80,700	0.3%
44	Delaware	80,300	0.3%
45	South Dakota	79,800	0.3%
46	North Dakota	71,600	0.3%
47	Alaska	62,300	0.2%
48	Wyoming	48,800	0.2%
NA	Arizona**	NA	NA
NA	Vermont**	NA	NA
	District of Columbia**	NA	NA

Source: U.S. Department of Labor, Bureau of Labor Statistics
   "Regional and State Employment and Unemployment" (press release, January 27, 2004)
*Seasonally adjusted preliminary data as of December 2003. National total calculated through a different formula.
**The Bureau of Labor Statistics does not publish seasonally adjusted figures in this category for these states.

Percent of Nonfarm Employees in
Trade, Transportation and Public Utilities in 2003
National Percent = 19.4% of Employees*

<u>ALPHA ORDER</u>

RANK	STATE	PERCENT
40	Alabama	18.4
14	Alaska	20.4
NA	Arizona**	NA
6	Arkansas	21.2
34	California	18.9
34	Colorado	18.9
45	Connecticut	17.7
25	Delaware	19.5
20	Florida	19.9
15	Georgia	20.3
39	Hawaii	18.5
12	Idaho	20.6
15	Illinois	20.3
18	Indiana	20.0
8	Iowa	20.9
20	Kansas	19.9
11	Kentucky	20.7
17	Louisiana	20.1
9	Maine	20.8
40	Maryland	18.4
44	Massachusetts	17.9
36	Michigan	18.8
23	Minnesota	19.8
27	Mississippi	19.4
18	Missouri	20.0
5	Montana	21.5
3	Nebraska	21.8
38	Nevada	18.6
1	New Hampshire	22.5
2	New Jersey	22.0
47	New Mexico	17.5
46	New York	17.6
37	North Carolina	18.7
4	North Dakota	21.6
27	Ohio	19.4
33	Oklahoma	19.1
24	Oregon	19.6
25	Pennsylvania	19.5
48	Rhode Island	16.8
27	South Carolina	19.4
9	South Dakota	20.8
6	Tennessee	21.2
13	Texas	20.5
20	Utah	19.9
NA	Vermont**	NA
40	Virginia	18.4
31	Washington	19.3
40	West Virginia	18.4
31	Wisconsin	19.3
27	Wyoming	19.4

<u>RANK ORDER</u>

RANK	STATE	PERCENT
1	New Hampshire	22.5
2	New Jersey	22.0
3	Nebraska	21.8
4	North Dakota	21.6
5	Montana	21.5
6	Arkansas	21.2
6	Tennessee	21.2
8	Iowa	20.9
9	Maine	20.8
9	South Dakota	20.8
11	Kentucky	20.7
12	Idaho	20.6
13	Texas	20.5
14	Alaska	20.4
15	Georgia	20.3
15	Illinois	20.3
17	Louisiana	20.1
18	Indiana	20.0
18	Missouri	20.0
20	Florida	19.9
20	Kansas	19.9
20	Utah	19.9
23	Minnesota	19.8
24	Oregon	19.6
25	Delaware	19.5
25	Pennsylvania	19.5
27	Mississippi	19.4
27	Ohio	19.4
27	South Carolina	19.4
27	Wyoming	19.4
31	Washington	19.3
31	Wisconsin	19.3
33	Oklahoma	19.1
34	California	18.9
34	Colorado	18.9
36	Michigan	18.8
37	North Carolina	18.7
38	Nevada	18.6
39	Hawaii	18.5
40	Alabama	18.4
40	Maryland	18.4
40	Virginia	18.4
40	West Virginia	18.4
44	Massachusetts	17.9
45	Connecticut	17.7
46	New York	17.6
47	New Mexico	17.5
48	Rhode Island	16.8
NA	Arizona**	NA
NA	Vermont**	NA
	District of Columbia**	NA

*Source: Morgan Quitno Press using data from U.S. Department of Labor, Bureau of Labor Statistics
   "Regional and State Employment and Unemployment" (press release, January 27, 2004)
*Seasonally adjusted preliminary data as of December 2003. National total calculated through a different formula.
**The Bureau of Labor Statistics does not publish seasonally adjusted figures in this category for these states.*

VII. ENERGY AND ENVIRONMENT

Energy Consumption in 2000

National Total = 98,216,200,000,000,000 Btu's*

ALPHA ORDER

RANK	STATE	BTU'S	% of USA
17	Alabama	1,972,400,000,000,000	2.0%
37	Alaska	632,200,000,000,000	0.6%
26	Arizona	1,215,800,000,000,000	1.2%
30	Arkansas	1,083,700,000,000,000	1.1%
2	California	8,518,700,000,000,000	8.7%
27	Colorado	1,199,900,000,000,000	1.2%
33	Connecticut	863,000,000,000,000	0.9%
46	Delaware	302,600,000,000,000	0.3%
8	Florida	3,943,800,000,000,000	4.0%
11	Georgia	2,769,900,000,000,000	2.8%
47	Hawaii	264,800,000,000,000	0.3%
42	Idaho	511,100,000,000,000	0.5%
5	Illinois	4,417,900,000,000,000	4.5%
10	Indiana	2,777,600,000,000,000	2.8%
29	Iowa	1,099,300,000,000,000	1.1%
32	Kansas	1,035,700,000,000,000	1.1%
18	Kentucky	1,868,200,000,000,000	1.9%
7	Louisiana	3,965,200,000,000,000	4.0%
41	Maine	561,200,000,000,000	0.6%
23	Maryland	1,520,100,000,000,000	1.5%
20	Massachusetts	1,722,800,000,000,000	1.8%
9	Michigan	3,121,900,000,000,000	3.2%
21	Minnesota	1,688,000,000,000,000	1.7%
28	Mississippi	1,143,800,000,000,000	1.2%
22	Missouri	1,659,200,000,000,000	1.7%
39	Montana	594,500,000,000,000	0.6%
40	Nebraska	583,500,000,000,000	0.6%
36	Nevada	632,800,000,000,000	0.6%
45	New Hampshire	329,100,000,000,000	0.3%
12	New Jersey	2,706,600,000,000,000	2.8%
38	New Mexico	620,700,000,000,000	0.6%
4	New York	4,620,000,000,000,000	4.7%
13	North Carolina	2,501,900,000,000,000	2.5%
44	North Dakota	365,400,000,000,000	0.4%
6	Ohio	4,001,800,000,000,000	4.1%
25	Oklahoma	1,400,500,000,000,000	1.4%
31	Oregon	1,079,700,000,000,000	1.1%
3	Pennsylvania	4,779,900,000,000,000	4.9%
48	Rhode Island	250,400,000,000,000	0.3%
24	South Carolina	1,477,100,000,000,000	1.5%
49	South Dakota	246,000,000,000,000	0.3%
16	Tennessee	2,025,900,000,000,000	2.1%
1	Texas	11,588,600,000,000,000	11.8%
35	Utah	718,200,000,000,000	0.7%
50	Vermont	164,600,000,000,000	0.2%
14	Virginia	2,303,600,000,000,000	2.3%
15	Washington	2,173,800,000,000,000	2.2%
34	West Virginia	744,000,000,000,000	0.8%
19	Wisconsin	1,799,700,000,000,000	1.8%
43	Wyoming	417,100,000,000,000	0.4%

RANK ORDER

RANK	STATE	BTU'S	% of USA
1	Texas	11,588,600,000,000,000	11.8%
2	California	8,518,700,000,000,000	8.7%
3	Pennsylvania	4,779,900,000,000,000	4.9%
4	New York	4,620,000,000,000,000	4.7%
5	Illinois	4,417,900,000,000,000	4.5%
6	Ohio	4,001,800,000,000,000	4.1%
7	Louisiana	3,965,200,000,000,000	4.0%
8	Florida	3,943,800,000,000,000	4.0%
9	Michigan	3,121,900,000,000,000	3.2%
10	Indiana	2,777,600,000,000,000	2.8%
11	Georgia	2,769,900,000,000,000	2.8%
12	New Jersey	2,706,600,000,000,000	2.8%
13	North Carolina	2,501,900,000,000,000	2.5%
14	Virginia	2,303,600,000,000,000	2.3%
15	Washington	2,173,800,000,000,000	2.2%
16	Tennessee	2,025,900,000,000,000	2.1%
17	Alabama	1,972,400,000,000,000	2.0%
18	Kentucky	1,868,200,000,000,000	1.9%
19	Wisconsin	1,799,700,000,000,000	1.8%
20	Massachusetts	1,722,800,000,000,000	1.8%
21	Minnesota	1,688,000,000,000,000	1.7%
22	Missouri	1,659,200,000,000,000	1.7%
23	Maryland	1,520,100,000,000,000	1.5%
24	South Carolina	1,477,100,000,000,000	1.5%
25	Oklahoma	1,400,500,000,000,000	1.4%
26	Arizona	1,215,800,000,000,000	1.2%
27	Colorado	1,199,900,000,000,000	1.2%
28	Mississippi	1,143,800,000,000,000	1.2%
29	Iowa	1,099,300,000,000,000	1.1%
30	Arkansas	1,083,700,000,000,000	1.1%
31	Oregon	1,079,700,000,000,000	1.1%
32	Kansas	1,035,700,000,000,000	1.1%
33	Connecticut	863,000,000,000,000	0.9%
34	West Virginia	744,000,000,000,000	0.8%
35	Utah	718,200,000,000,000	0.7%
36	Nevada	632,800,000,000,000	0.6%
37	Alaska	632,200,000,000,000	0.6%
38	New Mexico	620,700,000,000,000	0.6%
39	Montana	594,500,000,000,000	0.6%
40	Nebraska	583,500,000,000,000	0.6%
41	Maine	561,200,000,000,000	0.6%
42	Idaho	511,100,000,000,000	0.5%
43	Wyoming	417,100,000,000,000	0.4%
44	North Dakota	365,400,000,000,000	0.4%
45	New Hampshire	329,100,000,000,000	0.3%
46	Delaware	302,600,000,000,000	0.3%
47	Hawaii	264,800,000,000,000	0.3%
48	Rhode Island	250,400,000,000,000	0.3%
49	South Dakota	246,000,000,000,000	0.3%
50	Vermont	164,600,000,000,000	0.2%
	District of Columbia	166,200,000,000,000	0.2%

Source: U.S. Department of Energy, Energy Information Administration
"Multi-State Data" (http://www.eia.doe.gov/emeu/states/_multi_states.html)
**British Thermal Units: The amount of heat required to raise the temperature of one pound of water one degree.*

Per Capita Energy Consumption in 2000

National Per Capita = 348,007,536 Btu's*

ALPHA ORDER

RANK	STATE	BTU'S
9	Alabama	443,039,325
1	Alaska	1,007,173,843
49	Arizona	235,294,482
13	Arkansas	404,566,747
45	California	250,473,569
40	Colorado	277,320,802
44	Connecticut	252,934,094
17	Delaware	384,736,660
46	Florida	245,698,271
28	Georgia	336,382,624
50	Hawaii	218,361,137
15	Idaho	393,238,241
23	Illinois	355,112,506
8	Indiana	455,945,961
19	Iowa	375,348,870
18	Kansas	384,652,953
7	Kentucky	461,417,021
2	Louisiana	887,115,394
10	Maine	439,369,788
39	Maryland	286,138,571
41	Massachusetts	270,807,266
35	Michigan	313,566,085
25	Minnesota	342,098,735
14	Mississippi	401,498,300
38	Missouri	296,017,871
4	Montana	658,057,860
27	Nebraska	340,555,920
36	Nevada	313,449,189
43	New Hampshire	265,302,240
32	New Jersey	320,942,893
26	New Mexico	340,713,165
47	New York	243,160,966
37	North Carolina	309,554,467
5	North Dakota	569,930,326
24	Ohio	352,160,519
12	Oklahoma	405,424,026
34	Oregon	314,677,030
16	Pennsylvania	389,049,192
48	Rhode Island	238,317,766
21	South Carolina	367,097,652
30	South Dakota	325,490,253
22	Tennessee	355,218,765
6	Texas	553,016,600
33	Utah	320,138,218
42	Vermont	269,857,300
31	Virginia	324,181,314
20	Washington	367,705,081
11	West Virginia	411,657,886
29	Wisconsin	334,867,343
3	Wyoming	844,185,020

RANK ORDER

RANK	STATE	BTU'S
1	Alaska	1,007,173,843
2	Louisiana	887,115,394
3	Wyoming	844,185,020
4	Montana	658,057,860
5	North Dakota	569,930,326
6	Texas	553,016,600
7	Kentucky	461,417,021
8	Indiana	455,945,961
9	Alabama	443,039,325
10	Maine	439,369,788
11	West Virginia	411,657,886
12	Oklahoma	405,424,026
13	Arkansas	404,566,747
14	Mississippi	401,498,300
15	Idaho	393,238,241
16	Pennsylvania	389,049,192
17	Delaware	384,736,660
18	Kansas	384,652,953
19	Iowa	375,348,870
20	Washington	367,705,081
21	South Carolina	367,097,652
22	Tennessee	355,218,765
23	Illinois	355,112,506
24	Ohio	352,160,519
25	Minnesota	342,098,735
26	New Mexico	340,713,165
27	Nebraska	340,555,920
28	Georgia	336,382,624
29	Wisconsin	334,867,343
30	South Dakota	325,490,253
31	Virginia	324,181,314
32	New Jersey	320,942,893
33	Utah	320,138,218
34	Oregon	314,677,030
35	Michigan	313,566,085
36	Nevada	313,449,189
37	North Carolina	309,554,467
38	Missouri	296,017,871
39	Maryland	286,138,571
40	Colorado	277,320,802
41	Massachusetts	270,807,266
42	Vermont	269,857,300
43	New Hampshire	265,302,240
44	Connecticut	252,934,094
45	California	250,473,569
46	Florida	245,698,271
47	New York	243,160,966
48	Rhode Island	238,317,766
49	Arizona	235,294,482
50	Hawaii	218,361,137
	District of Columbia	290,741,917

*Source: Morgan Quitno Press using data from U.S. Department of Energy, Energy Information Administration
"Multi-State Data" (http://www.eia.doe.gov/emeu/states/_multi_states.html)*
British Thermal Units: The amount of heat required to raise the temperature of one pound of water one degree.

Energy Prices in 2000

National Rate = $9.85 per Million Btu's*

<u>ALPHA ORDER</u>

RANK	STATE	RATE
36	Alabama	$9.21
44	Alaska	8.16
4	Arizona	12.81
34	Arkansas	9.61
9	California	11.29
25	Colorado	9.94
5	Connecticut	12.66
30	Delaware	9.88
7	Florida	11.72
22	Georgia	10.16
2	Hawaii	13.39
37	Idaho	9.09
40	Illinois	8.68
46	Indiana	8.06
31	Iowa	9.87
16	Kansas	10.38
43	Kentucky	8.53
48	Louisiana	7.62
23	Maine	10.04
17	Maryland	10.37
10	Massachusetts	11.23
35	Michigan	9.56
28	Minnesota	9.92
32	Mississippi	9.85
13	Missouri	10.91
50	Montana	6.50
25	Nebraska	9.94
10	Nevada	11.23
3	New Hampshire	13.32
27	New Jersey	9.93
14	New Mexico	10.79
6	New York	11.75
12	North Carolina	11.21
49	North Dakota	7.42
19	Ohio	10.28
33	Oklahoma	9.75
20	Oregon	10.27
45	Pennsylvania	8.07
8	Rhode Island	11.60
15	South Carolina	10.43
18	South Dakota	10.35
24	Tennessee	9.95
39	Texas	8.82
41	Utah	8.64
1	Vermont	13.68
21	Virginia	10.19
38	Washington	8.92
42	West Virginia	8.57
29	Wisconsin	9.90
47	Wyoming	7.96

<u>RANK ORDER</u>

RANK	STATE	RATE
1	Vermont	$13.68
2	Hawaii	13.39
3	New Hampshire	13.32
4	Arizona	12.81
5	Connecticut	12.66
6	New York	11.75
7	Florida	11.72
8	Rhode Island	11.60
9	California	11.29
10	Massachusetts	11.23
10	Nevada	11.23
12	North Carolina	11.21
13	Missouri	10.91
14	New Mexico	10.79
15	South Carolina	10.43
16	Kansas	10.38
17	Maryland	10.37
18	South Dakota	10.35
19	Ohio	10.28
20	Oregon	10.27
21	Virginia	10.19
22	Georgia	10.16
23	Maine	10.04
24	Tennessee	9.95
25	Colorado	9.94
25	Nebraska	9.94
27	New Jersey	9.93
28	Minnesota	9.92
29	Wisconsin	9.90
30	Delaware	9.88
31	Iowa	9.87
32	Mississippi	9.85
33	Oklahoma	9.75
34	Arkansas	9.61
35	Michigan	9.56
36	Alabama	9.21
37	Idaho	9.09
38	Washington	8.92
39	Texas	8.82
40	Illinois	8.68
41	Utah	8.64
42	West Virginia	8.57
43	Kentucky	8.53
44	Alaska	8.16
45	Pennsylvania	8.07
46	Indiana	8.06
47	Wyoming	7.96
48	Louisiana	7.62
49	North Dakota	7.42
50	Montana	6.50
	District of Columbia	14.85

Source: U.S. Department of Energy, Energy Information Administration
"Multi-State Data" (http://www.eia.doe.gov/emeu/states/_multi_states.html)
British Thermal Units: The amount of heat required to raise the temperature of one pound of water one degree.

Energy Expenditures in 2000

National Total = $703,194,500,000

ALPHA ORDER

RANK	STATE	EXPENDITURES	% of USA
21	Alabama	$12,038,000,000	1.7%
43	Alaska	2,783,600,000	0.4%
24	Arizona	10,561,900,000	1.5%
33	Arkansas	7,326,000,000	1.0%
2	California	71,058,400,000	10.1%
27	Colorado	8,689,900,000	1.2%
29	Connecticut	8,275,100,000	1.2%
48	Delaware	2,071,600,000	0.3%
4	Florida	31,178,300,000	4.4%
11	Georgia	19,781,800,000	2.8%
44	Hawaii	2,634,100,000	0.4%
41	Idaho	3,158,300,000	0.4%
6	Illinois	30,122,200,000	4.3%
13	Indiana	17,032,800,000	2.4%
28	Iowa	8,314,000,000	1.2%
32	Kansas	7,391,600,000	1.1%
23	Kentucky	11,356,400,000	1.6%
10	Louisiana	20,725,700,000	2.9%
39	Maine	3,772,300,000	0.5%
22	Maryland	11,796,400,000	1.7%
15	Massachusetts	15,458,600,000	2.2%
8	Michigan	22,704,200,000	3.2%
20	Minnesota	12,223,600,000	1.7%
31	Mississippi	7,462,000,000	1.1%
17	Missouri	13,276,600,000	1.9%
42	Montana	2,852,400,000	0.4%
37	Nebraska	4,323,000,000	0.6%
34	Nevada	4,833,700,000	0.7%
40	New Hampshire	3,226,500,000	0.5%
9	New Jersey	21,638,900,000	3.1%
38	New Mexico	4,109,000,000	0.6%
3	New York	42,563,200,000	6.1%
12	North Carolina	19,351,300,000	2.8%
47	North Dakota	2,076,500,000	0.3%
7	Ohio	29,644,900,000	4.2%
26	Oklahoma	9,336,700,000	1.3%
30	Oregon	7,643,800,000	1.1%
5	Pennsylvania	30,483,800,000	4.3%
45	Rhode Island	2,381,000,000	0.3%
25	South Carolina	10,176,200,000	1.4%
49	South Dakota	1,951,600,000	0.3%
16	Tennessee	13,792,000,000	2.0%
1	Texas	74,044,600,000	10.5%
35	Utah	4,561,200,000	0.6%
50	Vermont	1,628,700,000	0.2%
14	Virginia	16,790,900,000	2.4%
18	Washington	13,179,600,000	1.9%
36	West Virginia	4,434,200,000	0.6%
19	Wisconsin	13,058,600,000	1.9%
46	Wyoming	2,242,300,000	0.3%

RANK ORDER

RANK	STATE	EXPENDITURES	% of USA
1	Texas	$74,044,600,000	10.5%
2	California	71,058,400,000	10.1%
3	New York	42,563,200,000	6.1%
4	Florida	31,178,300,000	4.4%
5	Pennsylvania	30,483,800,000	4.3%
6	Illinois	30,122,200,000	4.3%
7	Ohio	29,644,900,000	4.2%
8	Michigan	22,704,200,000	3.2%
9	New Jersey	21,638,900,000	3.1%
10	Louisiana	20,725,700,000	2.9%
11	Georgia	19,781,800,000	2.8%
12	North Carolina	19,351,300,000	2.8%
13	Indiana	17,032,800,000	2.4%
14	Virginia	16,790,900,000	2.4%
15	Massachusetts	15,458,600,000	2.2%
16	Tennessee	13,792,000,000	2.0%
17	Missouri	13,276,600,000	1.9%
18	Washington	13,179,600,000	1.9%
19	Wisconsin	13,058,600,000	1.9%
20	Minnesota	12,223,600,000	1.7%
21	Alabama	12,038,000,000	1.7%
22	Maryland	11,796,400,000	1.7%
23	Kentucky	11,356,400,000	1.6%
24	Arizona	10,561,900,000	1.5%
25	South Carolina	10,176,200,000	1.4%
26	Oklahoma	9,336,700,000	1.3%
27	Colorado	8,689,900,000	1.2%
28	Iowa	8,314,000,000	1.2%
29	Connecticut	8,275,100,000	1.2%
30	Oregon	7,643,800,000	1.1%
31	Mississippi	7,462,000,000	1.1%
32	Kansas	7,391,600,000	1.1%
33	Arkansas	7,326,000,000	1.0%
34	Nevada	4,833,700,000	0.7%
35	Utah	4,561,200,000	0.6%
36	West Virginia	4,434,200,000	0.6%
37	Nebraska	4,323,000,000	0.6%
38	New Mexico	4,109,000,000	0.6%
39	Maine	3,772,300,000	0.5%
40	New Hampshire	3,226,500,000	0.5%
41	Idaho	3,158,300,000	0.4%
42	Montana	2,852,400,000	0.4%
43	Alaska	2,783,600,000	0.4%
44	Hawaii	2,634,100,000	0.4%
45	Rhode Island	2,381,000,000	0.3%
46	Wyoming	2,242,300,000	0.3%
47	North Dakota	2,076,500,000	0.3%
48	Delaware	2,071,600,000	0.3%
49	South Dakota	1,951,600,000	0.3%
50	Vermont	1,628,700,000	0.2%
	District of Columbia	1,530,400,000	0.2%

Source: U.S. Department of Energy, Energy Information Administration
"Multi-State Data" (http://www.eia.doe.gov/emeu/states/_multi_states.html)

Per Capita Energy Expenditures in 2000

National Per Capita = $2,492

<u>ALPHA ORDER</u>

RANK	STATE	PER CAPITA
13	Alabama	$2,704
3	Alaska	4,435
47	Arizona	2,044
12	Arkansas	2,735
46	California	2,089
49	Colorado	2,008
30	Connecticut	2,425
16	Delaware	2,634
50	Florida	1,942
33	Georgia	2,402
45	Hawaii	2,172
27	Idaho	2,430
31	Illinois	2,421
10	Indiana	2,796
8	Iowa	2,839
11	Kansas	2,745
9	Kentucky	2,805
1	Louisiana	4,637
7	Maine	2,953
44	Maryland	2,221
27	Massachusetts	2,430
38	Michigan	2,280
25	Minnesota	2,477
17	Mississippi	2,619
36	Missouri	2,369
6	Montana	3,157
23	Nebraska	2,523
34	Nevada	2,394
19	New Hampshire	2,601
21	New Jersey	2,566
40	New Mexico	2,256
41	New York	2,240
34	North Carolina	2,394
5	North Dakota	3,239
18	Ohio	2,609
14	Oklahoma	2,703
43	Oregon	2,228
24	Pennsylvania	2,481
39	Rhode Island	2,266
22	South Carolina	2,529
20	South Dakota	2,582
32	Tennessee	2,418
4	Texas	3,533
48	Utah	2,033
15	Vermont	2,670
37	Virginia	2,363
42	Washington	2,229
26	West Virginia	2,453
27	Wisconsin	2,430
2	Wyoming	4,538

<u>RANK ORDER</u>

RANK	STATE	PER CAPITA
1	Louisiana	$4,637
2	Wyoming	4,538
3	Alaska	4,435
4	Texas	3,533
5	North Dakota	3,239
6	Montana	3,157
7	Maine	2,953
8	Iowa	2,839
9	Kentucky	2,805
10	Indiana	2,796
11	Kansas	2,745
12	Arkansas	2,735
13	Alabama	2,704
14	Oklahoma	2,703
15	Vermont	2,670
16	Delaware	2,634
17	Mississippi	2,619
18	Ohio	2,609
19	New Hampshire	2,601
20	South Dakota	2,582
21	New Jersey	2,566
22	South Carolina	2,529
23	Nebraska	2,523
24	Pennsylvania	2,481
25	Minnesota	2,477
26	West Virginia	2,453
27	Idaho	2,430
27	Massachusetts	2,430
27	Wisconsin	2,430
30	Connecticut	2,425
31	Illinois	2,421
32	Tennessee	2,418
33	Georgia	2,402
34	Nevada	2,394
34	North Carolina	2,394
36	Missouri	2,369
37	Virginia	2,363
38	Michigan	2,280
39	Rhode Island	2,266
40	New Mexico	2,256
41	New York	2,240
42	Washington	2,229
43	Oregon	2,228
44	Maryland	2,221
45	Hawaii	2,172
46	California	2,089
47	Arizona	2,044
48	Utah	2,033
49	Colorado	2,008
50	Florida	1,942

District of Columbia	2,677

Source: Morgan Quitno Press using data from U.S. Department of Energy, Energy Information Administration
"Multi-State Data" (http://www.eia.doe.gov/emeu/states/_multi_states.html)

Expenditures on Coal in 2000

National Total = $28,728,100,000*

ALPHA ORDER

RANK	STATE	EXPENDITURES	% of USA
5	Alabama	$1,290,600,000	4.5%
44	Alaska	47,200,000	0.2%
17	Arizona	546,100,000	1.9%
28	Arkansas	383,000,000	1.3%
39	California	115,400,000	0.4%
29	Colorado	361,400,000	1.3%
40	Connecticut	83,200,000	0.3%
41	Delaware	73,800,000	0.3%
8	Florida	1,239,900,000	4.3%
6	Georgia	1,269,200,000	4.4%
46	Hawaii	31,200,000	0.1%
48	Idaho	16,300,000	0.1%
9	Illinois	1,225,600,000	4.3%
4	Indiana	1,888,700,000	6.6%
25	Iowa	408,200,000	1.4%
30	Kansas	359,300,000	1.3%
7	Kentucky	1,241,800,000	4.3%
31	Louisiana	326,500,000	1.1%
47	Maine	21,800,000	0.1%
26	Maryland	404,900,000	1.4%
34	Massachusetts	243,600,000	0.8%
12	Michigan	1,048,500,000	3.6%
20	Minnesota	434,300,000	1.5%
36	Mississippi	225,000,000	0.8%
15	Missouri	643,900,000	2.2%
32	Montana	278,600,000	1.0%
38	Nebraska	123,300,000	0.4%
33	Nevada	253,400,000	0.9%
42	New Hampshire	65,500,000	0.2%
37	New Jersey	160,700,000	0.6%
23	New Mexico	420,500,000	1.5%
19	New York	486,800,000	1.7%
11	North Carolina	1,141,800,000	4.0%
21	North Dakota	429,800,000	1.5%
1	Ohio	2,110,000,000	7.3%
27	Oklahoma	383,800,000	1.3%
45	Oregon	41,300,000	0.1%
2	Pennsylvania	2,000,800,000	7.0%
49	Rhode Island	100,000	0.0%
16	South Carolina	613,300,000	2.1%
43	South Dakota	53,800,000	0.2%
13	Tennessee	797,500,000	2.8%
3	Texas	1,902,300,000	6.6%
22	Utah	429,300,000	1.5%
49	Vermont	100,000	0.0%
14	Virginia	714,500,000	2.5%
35	Washington	234,500,000	0.8%
10	West Virginia	1,207,000,000	4.2%
18	Wisconsin	537,300,000	1.9%
24	Wyoming	412,900,000	1.4%

RANK ORDER

RANK	STATE	EXPENDITURES	% of USA
1	Ohio	$2,110,000,000	7.3%
2	Pennsylvania	2,000,800,000	7.0%
3	Texas	1,902,300,000	6.6%
4	Indiana	1,888,700,000	6.6%
5	Alabama	1,290,600,000	4.5%
6	Georgia	1,269,200,000	4.4%
7	Kentucky	1,241,800,000	4.3%
8	Florida	1,239,900,000	4.3%
9	Illinois	1,225,600,000	4.3%
10	West Virginia	1,207,000,000	4.2%
11	North Carolina	1,141,800,000	4.0%
12	Michigan	1,048,500,000	3.6%
13	Tennessee	797,500,000	2.8%
14	Virginia	714,500,000	2.5%
15	Missouri	643,900,000	2.2%
16	South Carolina	613,300,000	2.1%
17	Arizona	546,100,000	1.9%
18	Wisconsin	537,300,000	1.9%
19	New York	486,800,000	1.7%
20	Minnesota	434,300,000	1.5%
21	North Dakota	429,800,000	1.5%
22	Utah	429,300,000	1.5%
23	New Mexico	420,500,000	1.5%
24	Wyoming	412,900,000	1.4%
25	Iowa	408,200,000	1.4%
26	Maryland	404,900,000	1.4%
27	Oklahoma	383,800,000	1.3%
28	Arkansas	383,000,000	1.3%
29	Colorado	361,400,000	1.3%
30	Kansas	359,300,000	1.3%
31	Louisiana	326,500,000	1.1%
32	Montana	278,600,000	1.0%
33	Nevada	253,400,000	0.9%
34	Massachusetts	243,600,000	0.8%
35	Washington	234,500,000	0.8%
36	Mississippi	225,000,000	0.8%
37	New Jersey	160,700,000	0.6%
38	Nebraska	123,300,000	0.4%
39	California	115,400,000	0.4%
40	Connecticut	83,200,000	0.3%
41	Delaware	73,800,000	0.3%
42	New Hampshire	65,500,000	0.2%
43	South Dakota	53,800,000	0.2%
44	Alaska	47,200,000	0.2%
45	Oregon	41,300,000	0.1%
46	Hawaii	31,200,000	0.1%
47	Maine	21,800,000	0.1%
48	Idaho	16,300,000	0.1%
49	Rhode Island	100,000	0.0%
49	Vermont	100,000	0.0%
	District of Columbia	200,000	0.0%

Source: U.S. Department of Energy, Energy Information Administration
"Multi-State Data" (http://www.eia.doe.gov/emeu/states/_multi_states.html)
**For residential, commercial, industrial and electric utility sectors.*

Coal Prices in 2000

National Rate = $1.27 per Million Btu's*

<u>ALPHA ORDER</u>

RANK	STATE	RATE
19	Alabama	$1.43
6	Alaska	2.17
30	Arizona	1.26
19	Arkansas	1.43
9	California	1.65
46	Colorado	0.93
2	Connecticut	2.29
15	Delaware	1.47
10	Florida	1.63
12	Georgia	1.55
8	Hawaii	1.77
34	Idaho	1.19
34	Illinois	1.19
36	Indiana	1.18
48	Iowa	0.92
45	Kansas	0.99
31	Kentucky	1.24
28	Louisiana	1.29
5	Maine	2.19
27	Maryland	1.30
7	Massachusetts	2.12
25	Michigan	1.35
37	Minnesota	1.16
13	Mississippi	1.53
46	Missouri	0.93
11	Montana	1.58
50	Nebraska	0.60
29	Nevada	1.27
14	New Hampshire	1.49
23	New Jersey	1.40
24	New Mexico	1.38
15	New York	1.47
18	North Carolina	1.45
43	North Dakota	1.01
15	Ohio	1.47
43	Oklahoma	1.01
40	Oregon	1.07
26	Pennsylvania	1.33
3	Rhode Island	2.27
21	South Carolina	1.42
42	South Dakota	1.06
38	Tennessee	1.13
32	Texas	1.23
40	Utah	1.07
1	Vermont	2.33
21	Virginia	1.42
4	Washington	2.21
32	West Virginia	1.23
39	Wisconsin	1.08
49	Wyoming	0.82

<u>RANK ORDER</u>

RANK	STATE	RATE
1	Vermont	$2.33
2	Connecticut	2.29
3	Rhode Island	2.27
4	Washington	2.21
5	Maine	2.19
6	Alaska	2.17
7	Massachusetts	2.12
8	Hawaii	1.77
9	California	1.65
10	Florida	1.63
11	Montana	1.58
12	Georgia	1.55
13	Mississippi	1.53
14	New Hampshire	1.49
15	Delaware	1.47
15	New York	1.47
15	Ohio	1.47
18	North Carolina	1.45
19	Alabama	1.43
19	Arkansas	1.43
21	South Carolina	1.42
21	Virginia	1.42
23	New Jersey	1.40
24	New Mexico	1.38
25	Michigan	1.35
26	Pennsylvania	1.33
27	Maryland	1.30
28	Louisiana	1.29
29	Nevada	1.27
30	Arizona	1.26
31	Kentucky	1.24
32	Texas	1.23
32	West Virginia	1.23
34	Idaho	1.19
34	Illinois	1.19
36	Indiana	1.18
37	Minnesota	1.16
38	Tennessee	1.13
39	Wisconsin	1.08
40	Oregon	1.07
40	Utah	1.07
42	South Dakota	1.06
43	North Dakota	1.01
43	Oklahoma	1.01
45	Kansas	0.99
46	Colorado	0.93
46	Missouri	0.93
48	Iowa	0.92
49	Wyoming	0.82
50	Nebraska	0.60
	District of Columbia	1.45

Source: U.S. Department of Energy, Energy Information Administration
   "Multi-State Data" (http://www.eia.doe.gov/emeu/states/_multi_states.html)
**British Thermal Units: The amount of heat required to raise the temperature of one pound of water one degree.*
Prices are for residential, commercial, industrial and electric utility sectors.

Expenditures on Electricity in 2001

National Total = $244,814,200,000*

<u>ALPHA ORDER</u>

RANK	STATE	EXPENDITURES	% of USA
19	Alabama	$4,345,300,000	1.8%
47	Alaska	567,100,000	0.2%
17	Arizona	4,525,600,000	1.8%
31	Arkansas	2,463,500,000	1.0%
1	California	27,482,600,000	11.2%
29	Colorado	2,638,400,000	1.1%
27	Connecticut	2,936,900,000	1.2%
44	Delaware	743,500,000	0.3%
4	Florida	15,376,400,000	6.3%
9	Georgia	7,484,000,000	3.1%
36	Hawaii	1,348,700,000	0.6%
42	Idaho	1,037,300,000	0.4%
7	Illinois	9,310,600,000	3.8%
15	Indiana	5,130,300,000	2.1%
32	Iowa	2,408,000,000	1.0%
33	Kansas	2,223,100,000	0.9%
25	Kentucky	3,361,200,000	1.4%
16	Louisiana	5,069,500,000	2.1%
39	Maine	1,270,300,000	0.5%
22	Maryland	3,983,300,000	1.6%
12	Massachusetts	6,061,800,000	2.5%
10	Michigan	7,068,300,000	2.9%
24	Minnesota	3,618,200,000	1.5%
28	Mississippi	2,719,400,000	1.1%
18	Missouri	4,414,400,000	1.8%
45	Montana	719,800,000	0.3%
37	Nebraska	1,333,200,000	0.5%
34	Nevada	2,171,800,000	0.9%
41	New Hampshire	1,129,200,000	0.5%
11	New Jersey	6,785,200,000	2.8%
38	New Mexico	1,316,400,000	0.5%
3	New York	16,448,900,000	6.7%
8	North Carolina	7,804,200,000	3.2%
50	North Dakota	534,900,000	0.2%
6	Ohio	10,199,500,000	4.2%
26	Oklahoma	3,016,100,000	1.2%
30	Oregon	2,494,300,000	1.0%
5	Pennsylvania	10,757,100,000	4.4%
43	Rhode Island	846,600,000	0.3%
20	South Carolina	4,317,200,000	1.8%
49	South Dakota	548,000,000	0.2%
14	Tennessee	5,324,700,000	2.2%
2	Texas	22,979,100,000	9.4%
40	Utah	1,197,800,000	0.5%
46	Vermont	606,700,000	0.2%
13	Virginia	5,928,400,000	2.4%
21	Washington	4,141,100,000	1.7%
35	West Virginia	1,391,700,000	0.6%
23	Wisconsin	3,930,800,000	1.6%
48	Wyoming	564,000,000	0.2%

<u>RANK ORDER</u>

RANK	STATE	EXPENDITURES	% of USA
1	California	$27,482,600,000	11.2%
2	Texas	22,979,100,000	9.4%
3	New York	16,448,900,000	6.7%
4	Florida	15,376,400,000	6.3%
5	Pennsylvania	10,757,100,000	4.4%
6	Ohio	10,199,500,000	4.2%
7	Illinois	9,310,600,000	3.8%
8	North Carolina	7,804,200,000	3.2%
9	Georgia	7,484,000,000	3.1%
10	Michigan	7,068,300,000	2.9%
11	New Jersey	6,785,200,000	2.8%
12	Massachusetts	6,061,800,000	2.5%
13	Virginia	5,928,400,000	2.4%
14	Tennessee	5,324,700,000	2.2%
15	Indiana	5,130,300,000	2.1%
16	Louisiana	5,069,500,000	2.1%
17	Arizona	4,525,600,000	1.8%
18	Missouri	4,414,400,000	1.8%
19	Alabama	4,345,300,000	1.8%
20	South Carolina	4,317,200,000	1.8%
21	Washington	4,141,100,000	1.7%
22	Maryland	3,983,300,000	1.6%
23	Wisconsin	3,930,800,000	1.6%
24	Minnesota	3,618,200,000	1.5%
25	Kentucky	3,361,200,000	1.4%
26	Oklahoma	3,016,100,000	1.2%
27	Connecticut	2,936,900,000	1.2%
28	Mississippi	2,719,400,000	1.1%
29	Colorado	2,638,400,000	1.1%
30	Oregon	2,494,300,000	1.0%
31	Arkansas	2,463,500,000	1.0%
32	Iowa	2,408,000,000	1.0%
33	Kansas	2,223,100,000	0.9%
34	Nevada	2,171,800,000	0.9%
35	West Virginia	1,391,700,000	0.6%
36	Hawaii	1,348,700,000	0.6%
37	Nebraska	1,333,200,000	0.5%
38	New Mexico	1,316,400,000	0.5%
39	Maine	1,270,300,000	0.5%
40	Utah	1,197,800,000	0.5%
41	New Hampshire	1,129,200,000	0.5%
42	Idaho	1,037,300,000	0.4%
43	Rhode Island	846,600,000	0.3%
44	Delaware	743,500,000	0.3%
45	Montana	719,800,000	0.3%
46	Vermont	606,700,000	0.2%
47	Alaska	567,100,000	0.2%
48	Wyoming	564,000,000	0.2%
49	South Dakota	548,000,000	0.2%
50	North Dakota	534,900,000	0.2%
	District of Columbia	740,100,000	0.3%

Source: U.S. Department of Energy, Energy Information Administration
"Multi-State Data" (http://www.eia.doe.gov/emeu/states/_multi_states.html)
**For residential, commercial, industrial and transportation sectors.*

Electricity Prices in 2001

National Rate = $21.51 per Million Btu's*

<u>ALPHA ORDER</u>

RANK	STATE	RATE
39	Alabama	$16.62
9	Alaska	30.97
16	Arizona	21.30
33	Arkansas	17.89
2	California	34.60
36	Colorado	17.70
10	Connecticut	28.19
18	Delaware	20.60
14	Florida	22.57
26	Georgia	18.77
1	Hawaii	41.34
48	Idaho	14.41
21	Illinois	20.27
44	Indiana	15.57
31	Iowa	18.00
29	Kansas	18.32
50	Kentucky	12.48
19	Louisiana	20.54
8	Maine	31.46
23	Maryland	19.52
4	Massachusetts	33.74
20	Michigan	20.50
35	Minnesota	17.75
28	Mississippi	18.52
37	Missouri	17.67
25	Montana	19.17
43	Nebraska	15.80
12	Nevada	23.12
5	New Hampshire	32.08
11	New Jersey	27.62
17	New Mexico	21.09
3	New York	34.09
24	North Carolina	19.45
41	North Dakota	16.10
22	Ohio	19.57
32	Oklahoma	17.93
42	Oregon	15.93
13	Pennsylvania	23.08
7	Rhode Island	31.62
38	South Carolina	16.91
27	South Dakota	18.62
40	Tennessee	16.52
15	Texas	21.85
46	Utah	15.36
6	Vermont	31.65
30	Virginia	18.18
45	Washington	15.46
47	West Virginia	14.90
34	Wisconsin	17.86
49	Wyoming	13.15

<u>RANK ORDER</u>

RANK	STATE	RATE
1	Hawaii	$41.34
2	California	34.60
3	New York	34.09
4	Massachusetts	33.74
5	New Hampshire	32.08
6	Vermont	31.65
7	Rhode Island	31.62
8	Maine	31.46
9	Alaska	30.97
10	Connecticut	28.19
11	New Jersey	27.62
12	Nevada	23.12
13	Pennsylvania	23.08
14	Florida	22.57
15	Texas	21.85
16	Arizona	21.30
17	New Mexico	21.09
18	Delaware	20.60
19	Louisiana	20.54
20	Michigan	20.50
21	Illinois	20.27
22	Ohio	19.57
23	Maryland	19.52
24	North Carolina	19.45
25	Montana	19.17
26	Georgia	18.77
27	South Dakota	18.62
28	Mississippi	18.52
29	Kansas	18.32
30	Virginia	18.18
31	Iowa	18.00
32	Oklahoma	17.93
33	Arkansas	17.89
34	Wisconsin	17.86
35	Minnesota	17.75
36	Colorado	17.70
37	Missouri	17.67
38	South Carolina	16.91
39	Alabama	16.62
40	Tennessee	16.52
41	North Dakota	16.10
42	Oregon	15.93
43	Nebraska	15.80
44	Indiana	15.57
45	Washington	15.46
46	Utah	15.36
47	West Virginia	14.90
48	Idaho	14.41
49	Wyoming	13.15
50	Kentucky	12.48
	District of Columbia	23.05

Source: U.S. Department of Energy, Energy Information Administration
"Multi-State Data" (http://www.eia.doe.gov/emeu/states/_multi_states.html)
British Thermal Units: The amount of heat required to raise the temperature of one pound of water one degree.
Prices are for residential, commercial, industrial and transportation sectors.

Electricity Prices for Industrial Users in 2001

National Rate = $14.75 per Million Btu's*

<u>ALPHA ORDER</u>

RANK	STATE	RATE
44	Alabama	$11.13
10	Alaska	22.31
19	Arizona	15.37
29	Arkansas	12.98
3	California	28.75
27	Colorado	13.12
9	Connecticut	22.34
21	Delaware	14.89
17	Florida	15.62
36	Georgia	12.55
1	Hawaii	34.22
47	Idaho	10.87
22	Illinois	14.42
41	Indiana	12.03
38	Iowa	12.26
24	Kansas	13.33
50	Kentucky	8.91
14	Louisiana	16.37
6	Maine	25.27
30	Maryland	12.92
2	Massachusetts	29.68
20	Michigan	14.91
25	Minnesota	13.24
31	Mississippi	12.90
32	Missouri	12.88
12	Montana	19.17
45	Nebraska	11.03
11	Nevada	19.24
5	New Hampshire	26.71
7	New Jersey	24.24
16	New Mexico	15.98
15	New York	16.16
23	North Carolina	13.83
42	North Dakota	11.67
34	Ohio	12.61
35	Oklahoma	12.57
37	Oregon	12.34
13	Pennsylvania	17.27
4	Rhode Island	28.70
43	South Carolina	11.32
28	South Dakota	13.06
40	Tennessee	12.08
18	Texas	15.57
48	Utah	10.35
8	Vermont	23.12
39	Virginia	12.21
26	Washington	13.13
46	West Virginia	10.96
33	Wisconsin	12.80
49	Wyoming	10.07

<u>RANK ORDER</u>

RANK	STATE	RATE
1	Hawaii	$34.22
2	Massachusetts	29.68
3	California	28.75
4	Rhode Island	28.70
5	New Hampshire	26.71
6	Maine	25.27
7	New Jersey	24.24
8	Vermont	23.12
9	Connecticut	22.34
10	Alaska	22.31
11	Nevada	19.24
12	Montana	19.17
13	Pennsylvania	17.27
14	Louisiana	16.37
15	New York	16.16
16	New Mexico	15.98
17	Florida	15.62
18	Texas	15.57
19	Arizona	15.37
20	Michigan	14.91
21	Delaware	14.89
22	Illinois	14.42
23	North Carolina	13.83
24	Kansas	13.33
25	Minnesota	13.24
26	Washington	13.13
27	Colorado	13.12
28	South Dakota	13.06
29	Arkansas	12.98
30	Maryland	12.92
31	Mississippi	12.90
32	Missouri	12.88
33	Wisconsin	12.80
34	Ohio	12.61
35	Oklahoma	12.57
36	Georgia	12.55
37	Oregon	12.34
38	Iowa	12.26
39	Virginia	12.21
40	Tennessee	12.08
41	Indiana	12.03
42	North Dakota	11.67
43	South Carolina	11.32
44	Alabama	11.13
45	Nebraska	11.03
46	West Virginia	10.96
47	Idaho	10.87
48	Utah	10.35
49	Wyoming	10.07
50	Kentucky	8.91
	District of Columbia	14.10

Source: U.S. Department of Energy, Energy Information Administration
"Multi-State Data" (http://www.eia.doe.gov/emeu/states/_multi_states.html)
**British Thermal Units: The amount of heat required to raise the temperature of one pound of water one degree.*
Industrial users include manufacturing, mining, construction, agriculture, fisheries and forestry.

Average Monthly Electric Bill for Industrial Customers in 2002

National Average = $6,647 a Month

<u>ALPHA ORDER</u>

RANK	STATE	MONTHLY BILL
11	Alabama	$16,834
40	Alaska	3,765
25	Arizona	7,495
50	Arkansas	2,258
36	California	4,403
35	Colorado	4,944
29	Connecticut	5,922
6	Delaware	26,460
43	Florida	3,553
18	Georgia	11,471
2	Hawaii	53,840
42	Idaho	3,569
5	Illinois	28,826
22	Indiana	8,707
14	Iowa	13,989
46	Kansas	2,987
10	Kentucky	18,046
26	Louisiana	7,074
3	Maine	38,957
27	Maryland	6,624
34	Massachusetts	4,968
21	Michigan	9,502
13	Minnesota	14,929
16	Mississippi	12,361
30	Missouri	5,865
8	Montana	20,470
49	Nebraska	2,302
4	Nevada	37,148
33	New Hampshire	5,163
32	New Jersey	5,363
15	New Mexico	13,963
20	New York	9,928
19	North Carolina	10,545
31	North Dakota	5,446
23	Ohio	8,439
48	Oklahoma	2,575
37	Oregon	4,224
24	Pennsylvania	7,870
41	Rhode Island	3,689
9	South Carolina	19,941
39	South Dakota	4,065
1	Tennessee	58,105
38	Texas	4,219
47	Utah	2,602
7	Vermont	23,492
17	Virginia	12,318
44	Washington	3,230
45	West Virginia	3,035
12	Wisconsin	16,541
28	Wyoming	6,235

<u>RANK ORDER</u>

RANK	STATE	MONTHLY BILL
1	Tennessee	$58,105
2	Hawaii	53,840
3	Maine	38,957
4	Nevada	37,148
5	Illinois	28,826
6	Delaware	26,460
7	Vermont	23,492
8	Montana	20,470
9	South Carolina	19,941
10	Kentucky	18,046
11	Alabama	16,834
12	Wisconsin	16,541
13	Minnesota	14,929
14	Iowa	13,989
15	New Mexico	13,963
16	Mississippi	12,361
17	Virginia	12,318
18	Georgia	11,471
19	North Carolina	10,545
20	New York	9,928
21	Michigan	9,502
22	Indiana	8,707
23	Ohio	8,439
24	Pennsylvania	7,870
25	Arizona	7,495
26	Louisiana	7,074
27	Maryland	6,624
28	Wyoming	6,235
29	Connecticut	5,922
30	Missouri	5,865
31	North Dakota	5,446
32	New Jersey	5,363
33	New Hampshire	5,163
34	Massachusetts	4,968
35	Colorado	4,944
36	California	4,403
37	Oregon	4,224
38	Texas	4,219
39	South Dakota	4,065
40	Alaska	3,765
41	Rhode Island	3,689
42	Idaho	3,569
43	Florida	3,553
44	Washington	3,230
45	West Virginia	3,035
46	Kansas	2,987
47	Utah	2,602
48	Oklahoma	2,575
49	Nebraska	2,302
50	Arkansas	2,258
	District of Columbia*	NA

Average Monthly Electric Bill for Commercial Customers in 2002

National Average = $478 a Month

ALPHA ORDER

RANK	STATE	MONTHLY BILL
41	Alabama	$333
12	Alaska	502
6	Arizona	603
44	Arkansas	290
1	California	767
40	Colorado	340
2	Connecticut	691
8	Delaware	558
19	Florida	462
16	Georgia	475
3	Hawaii	683
38	Idaho	344
9	Illinois	549
32	Indiana	361
47	Iowa	270
33	Kansas	360
48	Kentucky	263
20	Louisiana	458
11	Maine	526
10	Maryland	534
7	Massachusetts	596
13	Michigan	478
25	Minnesota	409
36	Mississippi	347
26	Missouri	397
50	Montana	251
46	Nebraska	276
15	Nevada	477
31	New Hampshire	373
5	New Jersey	615
30	New Mexico	374
4	New York	640
27	North Carolina	393
37	North Dakota	345
13	Ohio	478
42	Oklahoma	305
29	Oregon	378
18	Pennsylvania	471
16	Rhode Island	475
39	South Carolina	342
43	South Dakota	301
35	Tennessee	355
28	Texas	383
22	Utah	429
24	Vermont	416
21	Virginia	455
23	Washington	425
49	West Virginia	259
33	Wisconsin	360
45	Wyoming	281

RANK ORDER

RANK	STATE	MONTHLY BILL
1	California	$767
2	Connecticut	691
3	Hawaii	683
4	New York	640
5	New Jersey	615
6	Arizona	603
7	Massachusetts	596
8	Delaware	558
9	Illinois	549
10	Maryland	534
11	Maine	526
12	Alaska	502
13	Michigan	478
13	Ohio	478
15	Nevada	477
16	Georgia	475
16	Rhode Island	475
18	Pennsylvania	471
19	Florida	462
20	Louisiana	458
21	Virginia	455
22	Utah	429
23	Washington	425
24	Vermont	416
25	Minnesota	409
26	Missouri	397
27	North Carolina	393
28	Texas	383
29	Oregon	378
30	New Mexico	374
31	New Hampshire	373
32	Indiana	361
33	Kansas	360
33	Wisconsin	360
35	Tennessee	355
36	Mississippi	347
37	North Dakota	345
38	Idaho	344
39	South Carolina	342
40	Colorado	340
41	Alabama	333
42	Oklahoma	305
43	South Dakota	301
44	Arkansas	290
45	Wyoming	281
46	Nebraska	276
47	Iowa	270
48	Kentucky	263
49	West Virginia	259
50	Montana	251
	District of Columbia	1,967

Source: U.S. Department of Energy, Energy Information Administration
"Electric Sales and Revenue" (http://www.eia.doe.gov/cneaf/electricity/esr/esr_tabs.html)

Average Monthly Electric Bill for Residential Customers in 2002

National Average = $76.74 a Month

ALPHA ORDER

RANK	STATE	MONTHLY BILL
7	Alabama	$90.43
17	Alaska	80.88
11	Arizona	86.87
19	Arkansas	78.09
27	California	70.88
48	Colorado	50.59
16	Connecticut	81.15
13	Delaware	83.50
2	Florida	97.95
12	Georgia	86.05
1	Hawaii	100.52
33	Idaho	68.99
40	Illinois	64.82
31	Indiana	69.80
26	Iowa	71.38
30	Kansas	70.32
38	Kentucky	65.71
9	Louisiana	90.17
41	Maine	62.52
15	Maryland	81.23
36	Massachusetts	67.14
47	Michigan	56.60
43	Minnesota	60.26
8	Mississippi	90.34
21	Missouri	73.78
44	Montana	58.77
34	Nebraska	67.76
10	Nevada	88.87
28	New Hampshire	70.85
25	New Jersey	72.31
49	New Mexico	49.51
23	New York	72.63
5	North Carolina	90.98
37	North Dakota	66.28
22	Ohio	72.91
24	Oklahoma	72.44
29	Oregon	70.60
18	Pennsylvania	78.91
45	Rhode Island	57.49
4	South Carolina	93.88
32	South Dakota	69.52
13	Tennessee	83.50
3	Texas	94.06
50	Utah	49.14
20	Vermont	75.35
6	Virginia	90.78
35	Washington	67.16
39	West Virginia	65.25
42	Wisconsin	61.18
46	Wyoming	56.85

RANK ORDER

RANK	STATE	MONTHLY BILL
1	Hawaii	$100.52
2	Florida	97.95
3	Texas	94.06
4	South Carolina	93.88
5	North Carolina	90.98
6	Virginia	90.78
7	Alabama	90.43
8	Mississippi	90.34
9	Louisiana	90.17
10	Nevada	88.87
11	Arizona	86.87
12	Georgia	86.05
13	Delaware	83.50
13	Tennessee	83.50
15	Maryland	81.23
16	Connecticut	81.15
17	Alaska	80.88
18	Pennsylvania	78.91
19	Arkansas	78.09
20	Vermont	75.35
21	Missouri	73.78
22	Ohio	72.91
23	New York	72.63
24	Oklahoma	72.44
25	New Jersey	72.31
26	Iowa	71.38
27	California	70.88
28	New Hampshire	70.85
29	Oregon	70.60
30	Kansas	70.32
31	Indiana	69.80
32	South Dakota	69.52
33	Idaho	68.99
34	Nebraska	67.76
35	Washington	67.16
36	Massachusetts	67.14
37	North Dakota	66.28
38	Kentucky	65.71
39	West Virginia	65.25
40	Illinois	64.82
41	Maine	62.52
42	Wisconsin	61.18
43	Minnesota	60.26
44	Montana	58.77
45	Rhode Island	57.49
46	Wyoming	56.85
47	Michigan	56.60
48	Colorado	50.59
49	New Mexico	49.51
50	Utah	49.14
	District of Columbia	60.33

Source: U.S. Department of Energy, Energy Information Administration
"Electric Sales and Revenue" (http://www.eia.doe.gov/cneaf/electricity/esr/esr_tabs.html)

Expenditures on Natural Gas in 2000

National Total = $115,909,700,000*

ALPHA ORDER

RANK	STATE	EXPENDITURES	% of USA
20	Alabama	$1,550,400,000	1.3%
44	Alaska	247,400,000	0.2%
31	Arizona	1,100,100,000	0.9%
27	Arkansas	1,253,700,000	1.1%
2	California	13,512,300,000	11.7%
24	Colorado	1,457,600,000	1.3%
32	Connecticut	996,700,000	0.9%
42	Delaware	293,500,000	0.3%
12	Florida	2,803,000,000	2.4%
13	Georgia	2,479,300,000	2.1%
49	Hawaii	47,400,000	0.0%
41	Idaho	324,300,000	0.3%
4	Illinois	6,681,800,000	5.8%
10	Indiana	3,067,000,000	2.6%
25	Iowa	1,454,200,000	1.3%
26	Kansas	1,358,700,000	1.2%
28	Kentucky	1,219,800,000	1.1%
6	Louisiana	4,985,800,000	4.3%
50	Maine	43,000,000	0.0%
19	Maryland	1,731,300,000	1.5%
11	Massachusetts	2,828,700,000	2.4%
8	Michigan	3,975,300,000	3.4%
16	Minnesota	1,954,100,000	1.7%
29	Mississippi	1,147,600,000	1.0%
17	Missouri	1,870,300,000	1.6%
40	Montana	365,600,000	0.3%
36	Nebraska	668,200,000	0.6%
33	Nevada	950,600,000	0.8%
47	New Hampshire	174,300,000	0.2%
9	New Jersey	3,565,100,000	3.1%
38	New Mexico	570,600,000	0.5%
3	New York	9,694,800,000	8.4%
21	North Carolina	1,539,200,000	1.3%
46	North Dakota	189,400,000	0.2%
5	Ohio	5,543,900,000	4.8%
15	Oklahoma	2,344,100,000	2.0%
30	Oregon	1,135,100,000	1.0%
7	Pennsylvania	4,545,200,000	3.9%
39	Rhode Island	544,000,000	0.5%
34	South Carolina	934,200,000	0.8%
45	South Dakota	197,700,000	0.2%
22	Tennessee	1,504,600,000	1.3%
1	Texas	15,373,300,000	13.3%
35	Utah	679,100,000	0.6%
48	Vermont	56,800,000	0.0%
18	Virginia	1,866,900,000	1.6%
23	Washington	1,475,800,000	1.3%
37	West Virginia	595,100,000	0.5%
14	Wisconsin	2,414,900,000	2.1%
43	Wyoming	260,300,000	0.2%

RANK ORDER

RANK	STATE	EXPENDITURES	% of USA
1	Texas	$15,373,300,000	13.3%
2	California	13,512,300,000	11.7%
3	New York	9,694,800,000	8.4%
4	Illinois	6,681,800,000	5.8%
5	Ohio	5,543,900,000	4.8%
6	Louisiana	4,985,800,000	4.3%
7	Pennsylvania	4,545,200,000	3.9%
8	Michigan	3,975,300,000	3.4%
9	New Jersey	3,565,100,000	3.1%
10	Indiana	3,067,000,000	2.6%
11	Massachusetts	2,828,700,000	2.4%
12	Florida	2,803,000,000	2.4%
13	Georgia	2,479,300,000	2.1%
14	Wisconsin	2,414,900,000	2.1%
15	Oklahoma	2,344,100,000	2.0%
16	Minnesota	1,954,100,000	1.7%
17	Missouri	1,870,300,000	1.6%
18	Virginia	1,866,900,000	1.6%
19	Maryland	1,731,300,000	1.5%
20	Alabama	1,550,400,000	1.3%
21	North Carolina	1,539,200,000	1.3%
22	Tennessee	1,504,600,000	1.3%
23	Washington	1,475,800,000	1.3%
24	Colorado	1,457,600,000	1.3%
25	Iowa	1,454,200,000	1.3%
26	Kansas	1,358,700,000	1.2%
27	Arkansas	1,253,700,000	1.1%
28	Kentucky	1,219,800,000	1.1%
29	Mississippi	1,147,600,000	1.0%
30	Oregon	1,135,100,000	1.0%
31	Arizona	1,100,100,000	0.9%
32	Connecticut	996,700,000	0.9%
33	Nevada	950,600,000	0.8%
34	South Carolina	934,200,000	0.8%
35	Utah	679,100,000	0.6%
36	Nebraska	668,200,000	0.6%
37	West Virginia	595,100,000	0.5%
38	New Mexico	570,600,000	0.5%
39	Rhode Island	544,000,000	0.5%
40	Montana	365,600,000	0.3%
41	Idaho	324,300,000	0.3%
42	Delaware	293,500,000	0.3%
43	Wyoming	260,300,000	0.2%
44	Alaska	247,400,000	0.2%
45	South Dakota	197,700,000	0.2%
46	North Dakota	189,400,000	0.2%
47	New Hampshire	174,300,000	0.2%
48	Vermont	56,800,000	0.0%
49	Hawaii	47,400,000	0.0%
50	Maine	43,000,000	0.0%
	District of Columbia	337,700,000	0.3%

Source: U.S. Department of Energy, Energy Information Administration
"Multi-State Data" (http://www.eia.doe.gov/emeu/states/_multi_states.html)
For residential, commercial, industrial, transportation and electric utility sectors.

Natural Gas Prices in 2000

National Rate = $5.68 per Million Btu's*

<u>ALPHA ORDER</u>

RANK	STATE	RATE
29	Alabama	$5.47
50	Alaska	2.36
22	Arizona	5.90
31	Arkansas	5.45
14	California	6.42
42	Colorado	4.97
5	Connecticut	7.86
26	Delaware	5.63
40	Florida	5.10
16	Georgia	6.32
1	Hawaii**	16.14
44	Idaho	4.86
12	Illinois	6.60
32	Indiana	5.39
13	Iowa	6.44
28	Kansas	5.48
25	Kentucky	5.77
49	Louisiana	4.19
37	Maine	5.18
3	Maryland	8.10
2	Massachusetts	8.15
47	Michigan	4.43
24	Minnesota	5.86
45	Mississippi	4.72
11	Missouri	6.63
15	Montana	6.40
29	Nebraska	5.47
37	Nevada	5.18
4	New Hampshire	7.91
21	New Jersey	5.94
41	New Mexico	4.98
6	New York	7.55
9	North Carolina	6.73
39	North Dakota	5.17
17	Ohio	6.30
34	Oklahoma	5.34
36	Oregon	5.19
8	Pennsylvania	6.80
10	Rhode Island	6.72
20	South Carolina	5.99
19	South Dakota	6.01
23	Tennessee	5.89
48	Texas	4.30
43	Utah	4.88
32	Vermont	5.39
7	Virginia	7.03
35	Washington	5.23
27	West Virginia	5.59
18	Wisconsin	6.29
46	Wyoming	4.52

<u>RANK ORDER</u>

RANK	STATE	RATE
1	Hawaii**	$16.14
2	Massachusetts	8.15
3	Maryland	8.10
4	New Hampshire	7.91
5	Connecticut	7.86
6	New York	7.55
7	Virginia	7.03
8	Pennsylvania	6.80
9	North Carolina	6.73
10	Rhode Island	6.72
11	Missouri	6.63
12	Illinois	6.60
13	Iowa	6.44
14	California	6.42
15	Montana	6.40
16	Georgia	6.32
17	Ohio	6.30
18	Wisconsin	6.29
19	South Dakota	6.01
20	South Carolina	5.99
21	New Jersey	5.94
22	Arizona	5.90
23	Tennessee	5.89
24	Minnesota	5.86
25	Kentucky	5.77
26	Delaware	5.63
27	West Virginia	5.59
28	Kansas	5.48
29	Alabama	5.47
29	Nebraska	5.47
31	Arkansas	5.45
32	Indiana	5.39
32	Vermont	5.39
34	Oklahoma	5.34
35	Washington	5.23
36	Oregon	5.19
37	Maine	5.18
37	Nevada	5.18
39	North Dakota	5.17
40	Florida	5.10
41	New Mexico	4.98
42	Colorado	4.97
43	Utah	4.88
44	Idaho	4.86
45	Mississippi	4.72
46	Wyoming	4.52
47	Michigan	4.43
48	Texas	4.30
49	Louisiana	4.19
50	Alaska	2.36
	District of Columbia	9.91

Source: U.S. Department of Energy, Energy Information Administration
   "Multi-State Data" (http://www.eia.doe.gov/emeu/states/_multi_states.html)
*British Thermal Units: The amount of heat required to raise the temperature of one pound of water one degree.
Prices are for residential, commercial, industrial, transportation and electric utility sectors.
**Hawaii's rate is based on small quantities of liquefied natural gas.

Natural Gas Prices for Industrial Users in 2000

National Rate = $4.71 per Million Btu's*

<u>ALPHA ORDER</u>

RANK	STATE	RATE
32	Alabama	$4.48
50	Alaska	1.98
36	Arizona	4.35
17	Arkansas	5.13
11	California	5.42
48	Colorado	3.47
7	Connecticut	5.81
25	Delaware	4.84
13	Florida	5.33
28	Georgia	4.75
1	Hawaii	9.71
41	Idaho	3.92
8	Illinois	5.69
23	Indiana	4.88
10	Iowa	5.46
39	Kansas	3.98
30	Kentucky	4.63
45	Louisiana	3.78
44	Maine	3.82
2	Maryland	7.61
4	Massachusetts	7.17
47	Michigan	3.73
34	Minnesota	4.38
33	Mississippi	4.47
9	Missouri	5.62
3	Montana	7.26
29	Nebraska	4.72
19	Nevada	4.97
6	New Hampshire	5.84
19	New Jersey	4.97
31	New Mexico	4.56
5	New York	5.96
16	North Carolina	5.15
38	North Dakota	4.04
21	Ohio	4.91
14	Oklahoma	5.26
26	Oregon	4.79
24	Pennsylvania	4.86
15	Rhode Island	5.18
26	South Carolina	4.79
35	South Dakota	4.36
22	Tennessee	4.90
40	Texas	3.97
46	Utah	3.74
49	Vermont	2.95
18	Virginia	5.05
42	Washington	3.90
37	West Virginia	4.18
12	Wisconsin	5.40
43	Wyoming	3.89

<u>RANK ORDER</u>

RANK	STATE	RATE
1	Hawaii	$9.71
2	Maryland	7.61
3	Montana	7.26
4	Massachusetts	7.17
5	New York	5.96
6	New Hampshire	5.84
7	Connecticut	5.81
8	Illinois	5.69
9	Missouri	5.62
10	Iowa	5.46
11	California	5.42
12	Wisconsin	5.40
13	Florida	5.33
14	Oklahoma	5.26
15	Rhode Island	5.18
16	North Carolina	5.15
17	Arkansas	5.13
18	Virginia	5.05
19	Nevada	4.97
19	New Jersey	4.97
21	Ohio	4.91
22	Tennessee	4.90
23	Indiana	4.88
24	Pennsylvania	4.86
25	Delaware	4.84
26	Oregon	4.79
26	South Carolina	4.79
28	Georgia	4.75
29	Nebraska	4.72
30	Kentucky	4.63
31	New Mexico	4.56
32	Alabama	4.48
33	Mississippi	4.47
34	Minnesota	4.38
35	South Dakota	4.36
36	Arizona	4.35
37	West Virginia	4.18
38	North Dakota	4.04
39	Kansas	3.98
40	Texas	3.97
41	Idaho	3.92
42	Washington	3.90
43	Wyoming	3.89
44	Maine	3.82
45	Louisiana	3.78
46	Utah	3.74
47	Michigan	3.73
48	Colorado	3.47
49	Vermont	2.95
50	Alaska	1.98
	District of Columbia**	NA

Source: U.S. Department of Energy, Energy Information Administration
 "Multi-State Data" (http://www.eia.doe.gov/emeu/states/_multi_states.html)
**British Thermal Units: The amount of heat required to raise the temperature of one pound of water one degree.*
Industrial users include manufacturing, mining, construction, agriculture, fisheries and forestry.
***Not available.*

Average Price of Natural Gas Delivered to Residential Customers in 2002

National Average = $7.88 per Thousand Cubic Feet

ALPHA ORDER

RANK	STATE	RATE
8	Alabama	$10.57
44	Alaska	4.26
3	Arizona	12.36
21	Arkansas	8.95
33	California	7.09
42	Colorado	5.40
6	Connecticut	11.11
7	Delaware	11.05
2	Florida	13.91
12	Georgia	9.92
1	Hawaii	23.10
22	Idaho	8.42
37	Illinois	6.32
27	Indiana	7.64
34	Iowa	7.05
24	Kansas	8.06
28	Kentucky	7.56
NA	Louisiana*	NA
4	Maine	11.88
16	Maryland	9.71
NA	Massachusetts*	NA
37	Michigan	6.32
NA	Minnesota*	NA
NA	Mississippi*	NA
25	Missouri	7.94
43	Montana	5.27
39	Nebraska	6.12
17	Nevada	9.69
13	New Hampshire	9.90
32	New Jersey	7.26
40	New Mexico	6.04
14	New York	9.86
19	North Carolina	9.36
NA	North Dakota*	NA
29	Ohio	7.52
NA	Oklahoma*	NA
9	Oregon	10.55
18	Pennsylvania	9.43
5	Rhode Island	11.76
11	South Carolina	10.02
35	South Dakota	6.77
26	Tennessee	7.87
31	Texas	7.27
36	Utah	6.38
10	Vermont	10.39
14	Virginia	9.86
20	Washington	9.35
23	West Virginia	8.37
30	Wisconsin	7.37
41	Wyoming	5.49

RANK ORDER

RANK	STATE	RATE
1	Hawaii	$23.10
2	Florida	13.91
3	Arizona	12.36
4	Maine	11.88
5	Rhode Island	11.76
6	Connecticut	11.11
7	Delaware	11.05
8	Alabama	10.57
9	Oregon	10.55
10	Vermont	10.39
11	South Carolina	10.02
12	Georgia	9.92
13	New Hampshire	9.90
14	New York	9.86
14	Virginia	9.86
16	Maryland	9.71
17	Nevada	9.69
18	Pennsylvania	9.43
19	North Carolina	9.36
20	Washington	9.35
21	Arkansas	8.95
22	Idaho	8.42
23	West Virginia	8.37
24	Kansas	8.06
25	Missouri	7.94
26	Tennessee	7.87
27	Indiana	7.64
28	Kentucky	7.56
29	Ohio	7.52
30	Wisconsin	7.37
31	Texas	7.27
32	New Jersey	7.26
33	California	7.09
34	Iowa	7.05
35	South Dakota	6.77
36	Utah	6.38
37	Illinois	6.32
37	Michigan	6.32
39	Nebraska	6.12
40	New Mexico	6.04
41	Wyoming	5.49
42	Colorado	5.40
43	Montana	5.27
44	Alaska	4.26
NA	Louisiana*	NA
NA	Massachusetts*	NA
NA	Minnesota*	NA
NA	Mississippi*	NA
NA	North Dakota*	NA
NA	Oklahoma*	NA

District of Columbia   11.19

Source: U.S. Department of Energy, Energy Information Administration
"U.S. Natural Gas State Data" (http://www.eia.doe.gov/emeu/states/_states_ng.html, 1/30/04)
*Not available.

Expenditures on Motor Gasoline in 2001

National Total = $185,892,300,000*

<table>
<tr><td colspan="4"><u>ALPHA ORDER</u></td><td colspan="4"><u>RANK ORDER</u></td></tr>
<tr><th>RANK</th><th>STATE</th><th>EXPENDITURES</th><th>% of USA</th><th>RANK</th><th>STATE</th><th>EXPENDITURES</th><th>% of USA</th></tr>
<tr><td>22</td><td>Alabama</td><td>$3,185,300,000</td><td>1.7%</td><td>1</td><td>California</td><td>$22,426,100,000</td><td>12.1%</td></tr>
<tr><td>50</td><td>Alaska</td><td>435,400,000</td><td>0.2%</td><td>2</td><td>Texas</td><td>14,244,800,000</td><td>7.7%</td></tr>
<tr><td>21</td><td>Arizona</td><td>3,516,300,000</td><td>1.9%</td><td>3</td><td>Florida</td><td>9,779,600,000</td><td>5.3%</td></tr>
<tr><td>32</td><td>Arkansas</td><td>1,836,600,000</td><td>1.0%</td><td>4</td><td>New York</td><td>8,031,500,000</td><td>4.3%</td></tr>
<tr><td>1</td><td>California</td><td>22,426,100,000</td><td>12.1%</td><td>5</td><td>Illinois</td><td>7,732,700,000</td><td>4.2%</td></tr>
<tr><td>23</td><td>Colorado</td><td>3,147,900,000</td><td>1.7%</td><td>6</td><td>Ohio</td><td>7,324,900,000</td><td>3.9%</td></tr>
<tr><td>29</td><td>Connecticut</td><td>2,298,000,000</td><td>1.2%</td><td>7</td><td>Pennsylvania</td><td>7,148,700,000</td><td>3.8%</td></tr>
<tr><td>46</td><td>Delaware</td><td>565,900,000</td><td>0.3%</td><td>8</td><td>Michigan</td><td>6,984,800,000</td><td>3.8%</td></tr>
<tr><td>3</td><td>Florida</td><td>9,779,600,000</td><td>5.3%</td><td>9</td><td>Georgia</td><td>5,699,100,000</td><td>3.1%</td></tr>
<tr><td>9</td><td>Georgia</td><td>5,699,100,000</td><td>3.1%</td><td>10</td><td>North Carolina</td><td>5,553,700,000</td><td>3.0%</td></tr>
<tr><td>42</td><td>Hawaii</td><td>754,400,000</td><td>0.4%</td><td>11</td><td>New Jersey</td><td>5,484,300,000</td><td>3.0%</td></tr>
<tr><td>40</td><td>Idaho</td><td>908,700,000</td><td>0.5%</td><td>12</td><td>Virginia</td><td>5,323,400,000</td><td>2.9%</td></tr>
<tr><td>5</td><td>Illinois</td><td>7,732,700,000</td><td>4.2%</td><td>13</td><td>Indiana</td><td>4,311,200,000</td><td>2.3%</td></tr>
<tr><td>13</td><td>Indiana</td><td>4,311,200,000</td><td>2.3%</td><td>14</td><td>Missouri</td><td>4,154,000,000</td><td>2.2%</td></tr>
<tr><td>30</td><td>Iowa</td><td>2,129,500,000</td><td>1.1%</td><td>15</td><td>Massachusetts</td><td>4,134,000,000</td><td>2.2%</td></tr>
<tr><td>33</td><td>Kansas</td><td>1,763,600,000</td><td>0.9%</td><td>16</td><td>Washington</td><td>4,029,300,000</td><td>2.2%</td></tr>
<tr><td>24</td><td>Kentucky</td><td>3,014,500,000</td><td>1.6%</td><td>17</td><td>Minnesota</td><td>3,944,400,000</td><td>2.1%</td></tr>
<tr><td>25</td><td>Louisiana</td><td>2,974,000,000</td><td>1.6%</td><td>18</td><td>Maryland</td><td>3,798,800,000</td><td>2.0%</td></tr>
<tr><td>41</td><td>Maine</td><td>908,600,000</td><td>0.5%</td><td>19</td><td>Tennessee</td><td>3,794,500,000</td><td>2.0%</td></tr>
<tr><td>18</td><td>Maryland</td><td>3,798,800,000</td><td>2.0%</td><td>20</td><td>Wisconsin</td><td>3,689,600,000</td><td>2.0%</td></tr>
<tr><td>15</td><td>Massachusetts</td><td>4,134,000,000</td><td>2.2%</td><td>21</td><td>Arizona</td><td>3,516,300,000</td><td>1.9%</td></tr>
<tr><td>8</td><td>Michigan</td><td>6,984,800,000</td><td>3.8%</td><td>22</td><td>Alabama</td><td>3,185,300,000</td><td>1.7%</td></tr>
<tr><td>17</td><td>Minnesota</td><td>3,944,400,000</td><td>2.1%</td><td>23</td><td>Colorado</td><td>3,147,900,000</td><td>1.7%</td></tr>
<tr><td>31</td><td>Mississippi</td><td>1,993,400,000</td><td>1.1%</td><td>24</td><td>Kentucky</td><td>3,014,500,000</td><td>1.6%</td></tr>
<tr><td>14</td><td>Missouri</td><td>4,154,000,000</td><td>2.2%</td><td>25</td><td>Louisiana</td><td>2,974,000,000</td><td>1.6%</td></tr>
<tr><td>43</td><td>Montana</td><td>751,900,000</td><td>0.4%</td><td>26</td><td>South Carolina</td><td>2,904,800,000</td><td>1.6%</td></tr>
<tr><td>37</td><td>Nebraska</td><td>1,214,900,000</td><td>0.7%</td><td>27</td><td>Oregon</td><td>2,376,600,000</td><td>1.3%</td></tr>
<tr><td>34</td><td>Nevada</td><td>1,448,500,000</td><td>0.8%</td><td>28</td><td>Oklahoma</td><td>2,340,200,000</td><td>1.3%</td></tr>
<tr><td>39</td><td>New Hampshire</td><td>991,400,000</td><td>0.5%</td><td>29</td><td>Connecticut</td><td>2,298,000,000</td><td>1.2%</td></tr>
<tr><td>11</td><td>New Jersey</td><td>5,484,300,000</td><td>3.0%</td><td>30</td><td>Iowa</td><td>2,129,500,000</td><td>1.1%</td></tr>
<tr><td>36</td><td>New Mexico</td><td>1,265,100,000</td><td>0.7%</td><td>31</td><td>Mississippi</td><td>1,993,400,000</td><td>1.1%</td></tr>
<tr><td>4</td><td>New York</td><td>8,031,500,000</td><td>4.3%</td><td>32</td><td>Arkansas</td><td>1,836,600,000</td><td>1.0%</td></tr>
<tr><td>10</td><td>North Carolina</td><td>5,553,700,000</td><td>3.0%</td><td>33</td><td>Kansas</td><td>1,763,600,000</td><td>0.9%</td></tr>
<tr><td>47</td><td>North Dakota</td><td>510,600,000</td><td>0.3%</td><td>34</td><td>Nevada</td><td>1,448,500,000</td><td>0.8%</td></tr>
<tr><td>6</td><td>Ohio</td><td>7,324,900,000</td><td>3.9%</td><td>35</td><td>Utah</td><td>1,393,500,000</td><td>0.7%</td></tr>
<tr><td>28</td><td>Oklahoma</td><td>2,340,200,000</td><td>1.3%</td><td>36</td><td>New Mexico</td><td>1,265,100,000</td><td>0.7%</td></tr>
<tr><td>27</td><td>Oregon</td><td>2,376,600,000</td><td>1.3%</td><td>37</td><td>Nebraska</td><td>1,214,900,000</td><td>0.7%</td></tr>
<tr><td>7</td><td>Pennsylvania</td><td>7,148,700,000</td><td>3.8%</td><td>38</td><td>West Virginia</td><td>1,178,800,000</td><td>0.6%</td></tr>
<tr><td>45</td><td>Rhode Island</td><td>617,600,000</td><td>0.3%</td><td>39</td><td>New Hampshire</td><td>991,400,000</td><td>0.5%</td></tr>
<tr><td>26</td><td>South Carolina</td><td>2,904,800,000</td><td>1.6%</td><td>40</td><td>Idaho</td><td>908,700,000</td><td>0.5%</td></tr>
<tr><td>44</td><td>South Dakota</td><td>618,800,000</td><td>0.3%</td><td>41</td><td>Maine</td><td>908,600,000</td><td>0.5%</td></tr>
<tr><td>19</td><td>Tennessee</td><td>3,794,500,000</td><td>2.0%</td><td>42</td><td>Hawaii</td><td>754,400,000</td><td>0.4%</td></tr>
<tr><td>2</td><td>Texas</td><td>14,244,800,000</td><td>7.7%</td><td>43</td><td>Montana</td><td>751,900,000</td><td>0.4%</td></tr>
<tr><td>35</td><td>Utah</td><td>1,393,500,000</td><td>0.7%</td><td>44</td><td>South Dakota</td><td>618,800,000</td><td>0.3%</td></tr>
<tr><td>48</td><td>Vermont</td><td>503,300,000</td><td>0.3%</td><td>45</td><td>Rhode Island</td><td>617,600,000</td><td>0.3%</td></tr>
<tr><td>12</td><td>Virginia</td><td>5,323,400,000</td><td>2.9%</td><td>46</td><td>Delaware</td><td>565,900,000</td><td>0.3%</td></tr>
<tr><td>16</td><td>Washington</td><td>4,029,300,000</td><td>2.2%</td><td>47</td><td>North Dakota</td><td>510,600,000</td><td>0.3%</td></tr>
<tr><td>38</td><td>West Virginia</td><td>1,178,800,000</td><td>0.6%</td><td>48</td><td>Vermont</td><td>503,300,000</td><td>0.3%</td></tr>
<tr><td>20</td><td>Wisconsin</td><td>3,689,600,000</td><td>2.0%</td><td>49</td><td>Wyoming</td><td>479,400,000</td><td>0.3%</td></tr>
<tr><td>49</td><td>Wyoming</td><td>479,400,000</td><td>0.3%</td><td>50</td><td>Alaska</td><td>435,400,000</td><td>0.2%</td></tr>
<tr><td></td><td></td><td></td><td></td><td></td><td>District of Columbia</td><td>275,100,000</td><td>0.1%</td></tr>
</table>

Source: U.S. Department of Energy, Energy Information Administration
   "Multi-State Data" (http://www.eia.doe.gov/emeu/states/_multi_states.html)
For commercial, industrial and transportation sectors.

Gasoline Used in 2002

National Total = 137,664,309,000 Gallons*

<u>ALPHA ORDER</u>

RANK	STATE	GALLONS	% of USA
19	Alabama	2,624,222,000	1.9%
50	Alaska	260,277,000	0.2%
20	Arizona	2,605,332,000	1.9%
32	Arkansas	1,466,654,000	1.1%
1	California	15,698,946,000	11.4%
26	Colorado	2,105,567,000	1.5%
30	Connecticut	1,589,580,000	1.2%
45	Delaware	426,289,000	0.3%
3	Florida	7,999,217,000	5.8%
9	Georgia	4,960,956,000	3.6%
44	Hawaii	445,623,000	0.3%
41	Idaho	667,739,000	0.5%
7	Illinois	5,212,397,000	3.8%
13	Indiana	3,188,030,000	2.3%
29	Iowa	1,616,809,000	1.2%
33	Kansas	1,230,218,000	0.9%
25	Kentucky	2,158,486,000	1.6%
23	Louisiana	2,349,011,000	1.7%
39	Maine	719,698,000	0.5%
22	Maryland	2,568,457,000	1.9%
16	Massachusetts	2,851,292,000	2.1%
8	Michigan	5,170,129,000	3.8%
18	Minnesota	2,726,586,000	2.0%
28	Mississippi	1,631,883,000	1.2%
14	Missouri	3,164,210,000	2.3%
42	Montana	509,178,000	0.4%
37	Nebraska	888,558,000	0.6%
35	Nevada	1,004,110,000	0.7%
40	New Hampshire	715,392,000	0.5%
11	New Jersey	4,095,002,000	3.0%
36	New Mexico	951,611,000	0.7%
4	New York	5,808,184,000	4.2%
10	North Carolina	4,314,774,000	3.1%
47	North Dakota	366,491,000	0.3%
5	Ohio	5,294,695,000	3.8%
27	Oklahoma	1,796,336,000	1.3%
31	Oregon	1,572,294,000	1.1%
6	Pennsylvania	5,240,740,000	3.8%
46	Rhode Island	403,831,000	0.3%
24	South Carolina	2,345,676,000	1.7%
43	South Dakota	455,689,000	0.3%
15	Tennessee	3,089,576,000	2.2%
2	Texas	11,410,393,000	8.3%
34	Utah	1,038,233,000	0.8%
49	Vermont	346,129,000	0.3%
12	Virginia	3,888,170,000	2.8%
17	Washington	2,759,840,000	2.0%
38	West Virginia	820,458,000	0.6%
21	Wisconsin	2,590,958,000	1.9%
48	Wyoming	353,757,000	0.3%

<u>RANK ORDER</u>

RANK	STATE	GALLONS	% of USA
1	California	15,698,946,000	11.4%
2	Texas	11,410,393,000	8.3%
3	Florida	7,999,217,000	5.8%
4	New York	5,808,184,000	4.2%
5	Ohio	5,294,695,000	3.8%
6	Pennsylvania	5,240,740,000	3.8%
7	Illinois	5,212,397,000	3.8%
8	Michigan	5,170,129,000	3.8%
9	Georgia	4,960,956,000	3.6%
10	North Carolina	4,314,774,000	3.1%
11	New Jersey	4,095,002,000	3.0%
12	Virginia	3,888,170,000	2.8%
13	Indiana	3,188,030,000	2.3%
14	Missouri	3,164,210,000	2.3%
15	Tennessee	3,089,576,000	2.2%
16	Massachusetts	2,851,292,000	2.1%
17	Washington	2,759,840,000	2.0%
18	Minnesota	2,726,586,000	2.0%
19	Alabama	2,624,222,000	1.9%
20	Arizona	2,605,332,000	1.9%
21	Wisconsin	2,590,958,000	1.9%
22	Maryland	2,568,457,000	1.9%
23	Louisiana	2,349,011,000	1.7%
24	South Carolina	2,345,676,000	1.7%
25	Kentucky	2,158,486,000	1.6%
26	Colorado	2,105,567,000	1.5%
27	Oklahoma	1,796,336,000	1.3%
28	Mississippi	1,631,883,000	1.2%
29	Iowa	1,616,809,000	1.2%
30	Connecticut	1,589,580,000	1.2%
31	Oregon	1,572,294,000	1.1%
32	Arkansas	1,466,654,000	1.1%
33	Kansas	1,230,218,000	0.9%
34	Utah	1,038,233,000	0.8%
35	Nevada	1,004,110,000	0.7%
36	New Mexico	951,611,000	0.7%
37	Nebraska	888,558,000	0.6%
38	West Virginia	820,458,000	0.6%
39	Maine	719,698,000	0.5%
40	New Hampshire	715,392,000	0.5%
41	Idaho	667,739,000	0.5%
42	Montana	509,178,000	0.4%
43	South Dakota	455,689,000	0.3%
44	Hawaii	445,623,000	0.3%
45	Delaware	426,289,000	0.3%
46	Rhode Island	403,831,000	0.3%
47	North Dakota	366,491,000	0.3%
48	Wyoming	353,757,000	0.3%
49	Vermont	346,129,000	0.3%
50	Alaska	260,277,000	0.2%
	District of Columbia	166,626,000	0.1%

*Source: U.S. Department of Transportation, Federal Highway Administration
"Highway Statistics 2002" (Table MF-21)*
**Includes gasoline for highway and nonhighway uses. "Gasoline" includes gasohol but excludes "special fuels" such as diesel.*

Per Capita Gasoline Used in 2002

National Per Capita = 478 Gallons*

ALPHA ORDER				RANK ORDER		
RANK	STATE	GALLONS		RANK	STATE	GALLONS
3	Alabama	586		1	Wyoming	709
47	Alaska	406		2	South Dakota	599
29	Arizona	479		3	Alabama	586
15	Arkansas	542		4	Georgia	581
41	California	449		5	North Dakota	578
34	Colorado	468		6	South Carolina	572
37	Connecticut	460		7	Mississippi	569
18	Delaware	529		8	Vermont	562
29	Florida	479		9	New Hampshire	561
4	Georgia	581		10	Montana	559
49	Hawaii	359		11	Missouri	558
28	Idaho	497		12	Maine	556
46	Illinois	414		13	Iowa	551
23	Indiana	518		14	Minnesota	543
13	Iowa	551		15	Arkansas	542
40	Kansas	454		16	Tennessee	534
19	Kentucky	528		16	Virginia	534
20	Louisiana	525		18	Delaware	529
12	Maine	556		19	Kentucky	528
33	Maryland	471		20	Louisiana	525
44	Massachusetts	444		20	Texas	525
24	Michigan	515		22	North Carolina	519
14	Minnesota	543		23	Indiana	518
7	Mississippi	569		24	Michigan	515
11	Missouri	558		24	Oklahoma	515
10	Montana	559		26	Nebraska	514
26	Nebraska	514		26	New Mexico	514
36	Nevada	463		28	Idaho	497
9	New Hampshire	561		29	Arizona	479
31	New Jersey	478		29	Florida	479
26	New Mexico	514		31	New Jersey	478
50	New York	304		32	Wisconsin	476
22	North Carolina	519		33	Maryland	471
5	North Dakota	578		34	Colorado	468
35	Ohio	464		35	Ohio	464
24	Oklahoma	515		36	Nevada	463
43	Oregon	447		37	Connecticut	460
45	Pennsylvania	425		38	Washington	455
48	Rhode Island	378		38	West Virginia	455
6	South Carolina	572		40	Kansas	454
2	South Dakota	599		41	California	449
16	Tennessee	534		42	Utah	448
20	Texas	525		43	Oregon	447
42	Utah	448		44	Massachusetts	444
8	Vermont	562		45	Pennsylvania	425
16	Virginia	534		46	Illinois	414
38	Washington	455		47	Alaska	406
38	West Virginia	455		48	Rhode Island	378
32	Wisconsin	476		49	Hawaii	359
1	Wyoming	709		50	New York	304
					District of Columbia	293

Source: Morgan Quitno Press using data from U.S. Department of Transportation, Federal Highway Administration "Highway Statistics 2002" (Table MF-21)
**Includes gasoline for highway and nonhighway uses. "Gasoline" includes gasohol but excludes "special fuels" such as diesel.*

Daily Production of Crude Oil in 2002

National Total = 5,746,000 Barrels a Day*

ALPHA ORDER

RANK	STATE	BARRELS	% of USA
15	Alabama	24,000	0.4%
2	Alaska	984,000	17.1%
NA	Arizona**	NA	NA
16	Arkansas	20,000	0.3%
3	California	707,000	12.3%
10	Colorado	49,000	0.9%
NA	Connecticut**	NA	NA
NA	Delaware**	NA	NA
19	Florida	10,000	0.2%
NA	Georgia**	NA	NA
NA	Hawaii**	NA	NA
NA	Idaho**	NA	NA
14	Illinois	33,000	0.6%
23	Indiana	5,000	0.1%
NA	Iowa**	NA	NA
8	Kansas	90,000	1.6%
21	Kentucky	7,000	0.1%
4	Louisiana	256,000	4.5%
NA	Maine**	NA	NA
NA	Maryland**	NA	NA
NA	Massachusetts**	NA	NA
16	Michigan	20,000	0.3%
NA	Minnesota**	NA	NA
10	Mississippi	49,000	0.9%
NA	Missouri**	NA	NA
12	Montana	46,000	0.8%
20	Nebraska	8,000	0.1%
26	Nevada	2,000	0.0%
NA	New Hampshire**	NA	NA
NA	New Jersey**	NA	NA
5	New Mexico	184,000	3.2%
NA	New York**	NA	NA
NA	North Carolina**	NA	NA
9	North Dakota	85,000	1.5%
18	Ohio	16,000	0.3%
6	Oklahoma	183,000	3.2%
NA	Oregon**	NA	NA
22	Pennsylvania	6,000	0.1%
NA	Rhode Island**	NA	NA
NA	South Carolina**	NA	NA
25	South Dakota	3,000	0.1%
27	Tennessee	1,000	0.0%
1	Texas	1,129,000	19.6%
13	Utah	37,000	0.6%
NA	Vermont**	NA	NA
NA	Virginia**	NA	NA
NA	Washington**	NA	NA
24	West Virginia	4,000	0.1%
NA	Wisconsin**	NA	NA
7	Wyoming	150,000	2.6%

RANK ORDER

RANK	STATE	BARRELS	% of USA
1	Texas	1,129,000	19.6%
2	Alaska	984,000	17.1%
3	California	707,000	12.3%
4	Louisiana	256,000	4.5%
5	New Mexico	184,000	3.2%
6	Oklahoma	183,000	3.2%
7	Wyoming	150,000	2.6%
8	Kansas	90,000	1.6%
9	North Dakota	85,000	1.5%
10	Colorado	49,000	0.9%
10	Mississippi	49,000	0.9%
12	Montana	46,000	0.8%
13	Utah	37,000	0.6%
14	Illinois	33,000	0.6%
15	Alabama	24,000	0.4%
16	Arkansas	20,000	0.3%
16	Michigan	20,000	0.3%
18	Ohio	16,000	0.3%
19	Florida	10,000	0.2%
20	Nebraska	8,000	0.1%
21	Kentucky	7,000	0.1%
22	Pennsylvania	6,000	0.1%
23	Indiana	5,000	0.1%
24	West Virginia	4,000	0.1%
25	South Dakota	3,000	0.1%
26	Nevada	2,000	0.0%
27	Tennessee	1,000	0.0%
NA	Arizona**	NA	NA
NA	Connecticut**	NA	NA
NA	Delaware**	NA	NA
NA	Georgia**	NA	NA
NA	Hawaii**	NA	NA
NA	Idaho**	NA	NA
NA	Iowa**	NA	NA
NA	Maine**	NA	NA
NA	Maryland**	NA	NA
NA	Massachusetts**	NA	NA
NA	Minnesota**	NA	NA
NA	Missouri**	NA	NA
NA	New Hampshire**	NA	NA
NA	New Jersey**	NA	NA
NA	New York**	NA	NA
NA	North Carolina**	NA	NA
NA	Oregon**	NA	NA
NA	Rhode Island**	NA	NA
NA	South Carolina**	NA	NA
NA	Vermont**	NA	NA
NA	Virginia**	NA	NA
NA	Washington**	NA	NA
NA	Wisconsin**	NA	NA
	District of Columbia**	NA	NA

Source: U.S. Department of Energy, Energy Information Administration
"Production of Crude Oil by PAD District and State, 2002"
*National total includes 1,638,000 barrels in federal offshore production. Figures for Alaska, California, Louisiana and Texas include state offshore production.
**No reported production except for Arizona, Missouri, New York and Virginia which have less than 500 barrels a day of production.

Hazardous Waste Sites on the National Priority List in 2004

National Total = 1,299 Sites*

ALPHA ORDER

RANK	STATE	SITES	% of USA
24	Alabama	15	1.2%
44	Alaska	6	0.5%
40	Arizona	9	0.7%
37	Arkansas	11	0.8%
2	California	98	7.5%
22	Colorado	18	1.4%
23	Connecticut	16	1.2%
24	Delaware	15	1.2%
6	Florida	52	4.0%
24	Georgia	15	1.2%
46	Hawaii	3	0.2%
40	Idaho	9	0.7%
8	Illinois	45	3.5%
14	Indiana	29	2.2%
29	Iowa	14	1.1%
32	Kansas	12	0.9%
29	Kentucky	14	1.1%
24	Louisiana	15	1.2%
32	Maine	12	0.9%
20	Maryland	19	1.5%
12	Massachusetts	32	2.5%
5	Michigan	69	5.3%
18	Minnesota	24	1.8%
45	Mississippi	4	0.3%
16	Missouri	25	1.9%
24	Montana	15	1.2%
37	Nebraska	11	0.8%
49	Nevada	1	0.1%
19	New Hampshire	20	1.5%
1	New Jersey	116	8.9%
32	New Mexico	12	0.9%
4	New York	91	7.0%
14	North Carolina	29	2.2%
50	North Dakota	0	0.0%
11	Ohio	35	2.7%
37	Oklahoma	11	0.8%
32	Oregon	12	0.9%
3	Pennsylvania	95	7.3%
32	Rhode Island	12	0.9%
16	South Carolina	25	1.9%
47	South Dakota	2	0.2%
31	Tennessee	13	1.0%
8	Texas	45	3.5%
20	Utah	19	1.5%
40	Vermont	9	0.7%
13	Virginia	30	2.3%
7	Washington	47	3.6%
43	West Virginia	8	0.6%
10	Wisconsin	40	3.1%
47	Wyoming	2	0.2%

RANK ORDER

RANK	STATE	SITES	% of USA
1	New Jersey	116	8.9%
2	California	98	7.5%
3	Pennsylvania	95	7.3%
4	New York	91	7.0%
5	Michigan	69	5.3%
6	Florida	52	4.0%
7	Washington	47	3.6%
8	Illinois	45	3.5%
8	Texas	45	3.5%
10	Wisconsin	40	3.1%
11	Ohio	35	2.7%
12	Massachusetts	32	2.5%
13	Virginia	30	2.3%
14	Indiana	29	2.2%
14	North Carolina	29	2.2%
16	Missouri	25	1.9%
16	South Carolina	25	1.9%
18	Minnesota	24	1.8%
19	New Hampshire	20	1.5%
20	Maryland	19	1.5%
20	Utah	19	1.5%
22	Colorado	18	1.4%
23	Connecticut	16	1.2%
24	Alabama	15	1.2%
24	Delaware	15	1.2%
24	Georgia	15	1.2%
24	Louisiana	15	1.2%
24	Montana	15	1.2%
29	Iowa	14	1.1%
29	Kentucky	14	1.1%
31	Tennessee	13	1.0%
32	Kansas	12	0.9%
32	Maine	12	0.9%
32	New Mexico	12	0.9%
32	Oregon	12	0.9%
32	Rhode Island	12	0.9%
37	Arkansas	11	0.8%
37	Nebraska	11	0.8%
37	Oklahoma	11	0.8%
40	Arizona	9	0.7%
40	Idaho	9	0.7%
40	Vermont	9	0.7%
43	West Virginia	8	0.6%
44	Alaska	6	0.5%
45	Mississippi	4	0.3%
46	Hawaii	3	0.2%
47	South Dakota	2	0.2%
47	Wyoming	2	0.2%
49	Nevada	1	0.1%
50	North Dakota	0	0.0%
	District of Columbia	1	0.1%

Source: U.S. Environmental Protection Agency
    "National Priorities List (NPL) Sites in the United States"
As of January 2004. Includes final and proposed General Superfund and Federal Facilities Sites. National total includes nine sites in Puerto Rico, two in Guam and two in the Virgin Islands.

Hazardous Waste Sites on the National Priority List
Per 10,000 Square Miles in 2004
National Rate = 3.4 Sites per 10,000 Square Miles*

ALPHA ORDER

RANK	STATE	RATE
29	Alabama	2.9
48	Alaska	0.1
44	Arizona	0.8
34	Arkansas	2.1
19	California	6.2
35	Colorado	1.7
5	Connecticut	28.9
3	Delaware	62.6
11	Florida	8.7
31	Georgia	2.5
22	Hawaii	4.6
41	Idaho	1.1
14	Illinois	7.8
12	Indiana	8.0
31	Iowa	2.5
38	Kansas	1.5
25	Kentucky	3.5
28	Louisiana	3.0
23	Maine	3.6
9	Maryland	15.5
4	Massachusetts	34.6
16	Michigan	7.1
30	Minnesota	2.8
44	Mississippi	0.8
23	Missouri	3.6
42	Montana	1.0
39	Nebraska	1.4
48	Nevada	0.1
6	New Hampshire	21.5
1	New Jersey	141.2
42	New Mexico	1.0
8	New York	16.8
21	North Carolina	5.5
50	North Dakota	0.0
14	Ohio	7.8
37	Oklahoma	1.6
40	Oregon	1.2
7	Pennsylvania	20.6
2	Rhode Island	97.5
12	South Carolina	8.0
46	South Dakota	0.3
27	Tennessee	3.1
35	Texas	1.7
33	Utah	2.2
10	Vermont	9.4
16	Virginia	7.1
18	Washington	6.7
26	West Virginia	3.3
20	Wisconsin	6.1
47	Wyoming	0.2

RANK ORDER

RANK	STATE	RATE
1	New Jersey	141.2
2	Rhode Island	97.5
3	Delaware	62.6
4	Massachusetts	34.6
5	Connecticut	28.9
6	New Hampshire	21.5
7	Pennsylvania	20.6
8	New York	16.8
9	Maryland	15.5
10	Vermont	9.4
11	Florida	8.7
12	Indiana	8.0
12	South Carolina	8.0
14	Illinois	7.8
14	Ohio	7.8
16	Michigan	7.1
16	Virginia	7.1
18	Washington	6.7
19	California	6.2
20	Wisconsin	6.1
21	North Carolina	5.5
22	Hawaii	4.6
23	Maine	3.6
23	Missouri	3.6
25	Kentucky	3.5
26	West Virginia	3.3
27	Tennessee	3.1
28	Louisiana	3.0
29	Alabama	2.9
30	Minnesota	2.8
31	Georgia	2.5
31	Iowa	2.5
33	Utah	2.2
34	Arkansas	2.1
35	Colorado	1.7
35	Texas	1.7
37	Oklahoma	1.6
38	Kansas	1.5
39	Nebraska	1.4
40	Oregon	1.2
41	Idaho	1.1
42	Montana	1.0
42	New Mexico	1.0
44	Arizona	0.8
44	Mississippi	0.8
46	South Dakota	0.3
47	Wyoming	0.2
48	Alaska	0.1
48	Nevada	0.1
50	North Dakota	0.0
	District of Columbia**	NA

Source: Morgan Quitno Press using data from U.S. Environmental Protection Agency
  "National Priorities List (NPL) Sites in the United States"
*As of January 2004. Includes final and proposed General Superfund and Federal Facilities Sites. National rate excludes sites and square miles in Puerto Rico, Guam and the Virgin Islands. Based on land and water area of states.

**The District of Columbia has one site in its 68 square miles.

Toxic Releases: Total Pollution Released in 2001

National Total = 6,141,138,505 Pounds of Toxins*

<u>ALPHA ORDER</u>

RANK	STATE	POUNDS	% of USA
13	Alabama	134,445,577	2.2%
4	Alaska	522,072,731	8.5%
3	Arizona	606,814,321	9.9%
31	Arkansas	44,042,566	0.7%
27	California	58,549,443	1.0%
34	Colorado	37,046,413	0.6%
46	Connecticut	9,755,293	0.2%
43	Delaware	12,074,363	0.2%
15	Florida	123,201,939	2.0%
17	Georgia	116,519,643	1.9%
48	Hawaii	3,066,537	0.0%
23	Idaho	75,181,868	1.2%
12	Illinois	137,749,010	2.2%
8	Indiana	205,557,782	3.3%
32	Iowa	37,873,480	0.6%
36	Kansas	31,666,590	0.5%
19	Kentucky	93,695,654	1.5%
11	Louisiana	145,820,901	2.4%
45	Maine	10,712,685	0.2%
29	Maryland	45,424,212	0.7%
44	Massachusetts	11,085,729	0.2%
14	Michigan	131,916,793	2.1%
35	Minnesota	33,395,310	0.5%
24	Mississippi	71,086,301	1.2%
16	Missouri	119,889,698	2.0%
25	Montana	65,388,178	1.1%
38	Nebraska	26,669,417	0.4%
1	Nevada	783,494,630	12.8%
47	New Hampshire	4,758,653	0.1%
26	New Jersey	58,841,777	1.0%
18	New Mexico	105,833,149	1.7%
30	New York	44,831,050	0.7%
10	North Carolina	147,668,098	2.4%
39	North Dakota	25,277,053	0.4%
6	Ohio	254,563,632	4.1%
37	Oklahoma	28,887,021	0.5%
33	Oregon	37,576,517	0.6%
7	Pennsylvania	207,484,044	3.4%
49	Rhode Island	1,098,100	0.0%
20	South Carolina	81,260,912	1.3%
42	South Dakota	13,527,252	0.2%
9	Tennessee	148,961,221	2.4%
5	Texas	270,535,075	4.4%
2	Utah	767,197,725	12.5%
50	Vermont	363,002	0.0%
22	Virginia	79,783,853	1.3%
40	Washington	23,892,274	0.4%
21	West Virginia	80,140,007	1.3%
28	Wisconsin	46,808,527	0.8%
41	Wyoming	17,591,926	0.3%

<u>RANK ORDER</u>

RANK	STATE	POUNDS	% of USA
1	Nevada	783,494,630	12.8%
2	Utah	767,197,725	12.5%
3	Arizona	606,814,321	9.9%
4	Alaska	522,072,731	8.5%
5	Texas	270,535,075	4.4%
6	Ohio	254,563,632	4.1%
7	Pennsylvania	207,484,044	3.4%
8	Indiana	205,557,782	3.3%
9	Tennessee	148,961,221	2.4%
10	North Carolina	147,668,098	2.4%
11	Louisiana	145,820,901	2.4%
12	Illinois	137,749,010	2.2%
13	Alabama	134,445,577	2.2%
14	Michigan	131,916,793	2.1%
15	Florida	123,201,939	2.0%
16	Missouri	119,889,698	2.0%
17	Georgia	116,519,643	1.9%
18	New Mexico	105,833,149	1.7%
19	Kentucky	93,695,654	1.5%
20	South Carolina	81,260,912	1.3%
21	West Virginia	80,140,007	1.3%
22	Virginia	79,783,853	1.3%
23	Idaho	75,181,868	1.2%
24	Mississippi	71,086,301	1.2%
25	Montana	65,388,178	1.1%
26	New Jersey	58,841,777	1.0%
27	California	58,549,443	1.0%
28	Wisconsin	46,808,527	0.8%
29	Maryland	45,424,212	0.7%
30	New York	44,831,050	0.7%
31	Arkansas	44,042,566	0.7%
32	Iowa	37,873,480	0.6%
33	Oregon	37,576,517	0.6%
34	Colorado	37,046,413	0.6%
35	Minnesota	33,395,310	0.5%
36	Kansas	31,666,590	0.5%
37	Oklahoma	28,887,021	0.5%
38	Nebraska	26,669,417	0.4%
39	North Dakota	25,277,053	0.4%
40	Washington	23,892,274	0.4%
41	Wyoming	17,591,926	0.3%
42	South Dakota	13,527,252	0.2%
43	Delaware	12,074,363	0.2%
44	Massachusetts	11,085,729	0.2%
45	Maine	10,712,685	0.2%
46	Connecticut	9,755,293	0.2%
47	New Hampshire	4,758,653	0.1%
48	Hawaii	3,066,537	0.0%
49	Rhode Island	1,098,100	0.0%
50	Vermont	363,002	0.0%
	District of Columbia	60,573	0.0%

Source: U.S. Environmental Protection Agency, Office of Pollution Prevention and Toxics Information Management "2001 Toxics Release Inventory" (http://www.epa.gov/tri/tridata/tri01/)

**National total does not include 16,858,575 pounds of toxins in U.S. territories. Includes discharges to air, surface water, underground injection and surface land. Includes both original (or manufacturing) industries and those added by EPA since it began tracking releases. Because industries have been added it is not possible to show trends except for the original industries. Those figures are shown in tables 222 and 223.*

Toxic Releases: Total Air Emissions in 2001

National Total = 1,663,716,351 Pounds*

ALPHA ORDER

RANK	STATE	POUNDS	% of USA
10	Alabama	75,567,809	4.5%
43	Alaska	3,201,013	0.2%
38	Arizona	4,600,105	0.3%
23	Arkansas	20,036,562	1.2%
24	California	20,020,008	1.2%
42	Colorado	3,629,554	0.2%
36	Connecticut	4,821,957	0.3%
34	Delaware	6,651,525	0.4%
6	Florida	83,429,911	5.0%
4	Georgia	91,834,154	5.5%
45	Hawaii	2,379,957	0.1%
35	Idaho	5,000,464	0.3%
12	Illinois	59,411,352	3.6%
8	Indiana	77,828,675	4.7%
22	Iowa	24,332,303	1.5%
27	Kansas	14,768,804	0.9%
13	Kentucky	58,703,794	3.5%
9	Louisiana	75,960,815	4.6%
37	Maine	4,657,404	0.3%
18	Maryland	36,076,213	2.2%
33	Massachusetts	7,447,906	0.4%
15	Michigan	56,656,492	3.4%
29	Minnesota	14,252,131	0.9%
17	Mississippi	37,063,726	2.2%
19	Missouri	34,177,643	2.1%
41	Montana	4,292,997	0.3%
32	Nebraska	7,875,435	0.5%
44	Nevada	2,728,933	0.2%
39	New Hampshire	4,496,284	0.3%
30	New Jersey	13,809,784	0.8%
48	New Mexico	1,072,357	0.1%
20	New York	29,629,649	1.8%
2	North Carolina	115,130,332	6.9%
40	North Dakota	4,328,230	0.3%
1	Ohio	121,295,468	7.3%
26	Oklahoma	17,377,943	1.0%
31	Oregon	12,914,088	0.8%
5	Pennsylvania	89,034,059	5.4%
49	Rhode Island	824,582	0.0%
16	South Carolina	54,977,393	3.3%
47	South Dakota	1,799,135	0.1%
7	Tennessee	79,573,558	4.8%
3	Texas	102,748,862	6.2%
25	Utah	19,220,667	1.2%
50	Vermont	136,536	0.0%
14	Virginia	57,216,768	3.4%
28	Washington	14,295,076	0.9%
11	West Virginia	59,430,131	3.6%
21	Wisconsin	25,139,472	1.5%
46	Wyoming	1,817,602	0.1%

RANK ORDER

RANK	STATE	POUNDS	% of USA
1	Ohio	121,295,468	7.3%
2	North Carolina	115,130,332	6.9%
3	Texas	102,748,862	6.2%
4	Georgia	91,834,154	5.5%
5	Pennsylvania	89,034,059	5.4%
6	Florida	83,429,911	5.0%
7	Tennessee	79,573,558	4.8%
8	Indiana	77,828,675	4.7%
9	Louisiana	75,960,815	4.6%
10	Alabama	75,567,809	4.5%
11	West Virginia	59,430,131	3.6%
12	Illinois	59,411,352	3.6%
13	Kentucky	58,703,794	3.5%
14	Virginia	57,216,768	3.4%
15	Michigan	56,656,492	3.4%
16	South Carolina	54,977,393	3.3%
17	Mississippi	37,063,726	2.2%
18	Maryland	36,076,213	2.2%
19	Missouri	34,177,643	2.1%
20	New York	29,629,649	1.8%
21	Wisconsin	25,139,472	1.5%
22	Iowa	24,332,303	1.5%
23	Arkansas	20,036,562	1.2%
24	California	20,020,008	1.2%
25	Utah	19,220,667	1.2%
26	Oklahoma	17,377,943	1.0%
27	Kansas	14,768,804	0.9%
28	Washington	14,295,076	0.9%
29	Minnesota	14,252,131	0.9%
30	New Jersey	13,809,784	0.8%
31	Oregon	12,914,088	0.8%
32	Nebraska	7,875,435	0.5%
33	Massachusetts	7,447,906	0.4%
34	Delaware	6,651,525	0.4%
35	Idaho	5,000,464	0.3%
36	Connecticut	4,821,957	0.3%
37	Maine	4,657,404	0.3%
38	Arizona	4,600,105	0.3%
39	New Hampshire	4,496,284	0.3%
40	North Dakota	4,328,230	0.3%
41	Montana	4,292,997	0.3%
42	Colorado	3,629,554	0.2%
43	Alaska	3,201,013	0.2%
44	Nevada	2,728,933	0.2%
45	Hawaii	2,379,957	0.1%
46	Wyoming	1,817,602	0.1%
47	South Dakota	1,799,135	0.1%
48	New Mexico	1,072,357	0.1%
49	Rhode Island	824,582	0.0%
50	Vermont	136,536	0.0%
	District of Columbia	40,733	0.0%

*Source: U.S. Environmental Protection Agency, Office of Pollution Prevention and Toxics Information Management
"2001 Toxics Release Inventory" (http://www.epa.gov/tri/tridata/tri01/)*
*National total does not include 15,656,707 pounds of emissions in U.S. territories. Includes both original (or
manufacturing) industries and those added by EPA since it began tracking releases.

Toxic Releases: Total Surface Water Discharges in 2001

National Total = 220,628,219 Pounds*

ALPHA ORDER

RANK	STATE	POUNDS	% of USA
15	Alabama	4,713,394	2.1%
41	Alaska	76,438	0.0%
50	Arizona	6,376	0.0%
22	Arkansas	3,190,528	1.4%
14	California	4,924,819	2.2%
20	Colorado	3,752,564	1.7%
37	Connecticut	785,064	0.4%
38	Delaware	573,937	0.3%
32	Florida	1,590,342	0.7%
8	Georgia	8,391,937	3.8%
46	Hawaii	29,770	0.0%
13	Idaho	5,821,110	2.6%
10	Illinois	8,087,041	3.7%
2	Indiana	20,104,003	9.1%
23	Iowa	3,145,360	1.4%
35	Kansas	1,149,296	0.5%
30	Kentucky	2,118,567	1.0%
5	Louisiana	11,908,380	5.4%
17	Maine	3,975,970	1.8%
18	Maryland	3,839,690	1.7%
43	Massachusetts	73,437	0.0%
36	Michigan	1,043,401	0.5%
33	Minnesota	1,571,683	0.7%
4	Mississippi	12,964,677	5.9%
31	Missouri	1,660,217	0.8%
44	Montana	48,785	0.0%
7	Nebraska	9,601,101	4.4%
40	Nevada	82,849	0.0%
48	New Hampshire	10,675	0.0%
21	New Jersey	3,729,623	1.7%
45	New Mexico	40,023	0.0%
12	New York	6,733,053	3.1%
6	North Carolina	9,887,436	4.5%
39	North Dakota	110,470	0.1%
9	Ohio	8,339,219	3.8%
28	Oklahoma	2,391,127	1.1%
25	Oregon	2,912,278	1.3%
3	Pennsylvania	18,741,435	8.5%
49	Rhode Island	10,171	0.0%
26	South Carolina	2,778,925	1.3%
27	South Dakota	2,413,621	1.1%
24	Tennessee	3,067,358	1.4%
1	Texas	26,007,896	11.8%
34	Utah	1,215,070	0.6%
42	Vermont	75,573	0.0%
11	Virginia	6,963,083	3.2%
29	Washington	2,123,223	1.0%
19	West Virginia	3,788,537	1.7%
16	Wisconsin	4,033,349	1.8%
47	Wyoming	11,395	0.0%

RANK ORDER

RANK	STATE	POUNDS	% of USA
1	Texas	26,007,896	11.8%
2	Indiana	20,104,003	9.1%
3	Pennsylvania	18,741,435	8.5%
4	Mississippi	12,964,677	5.9%
5	Louisiana	11,908,380	5.4%
6	North Carolina	9,887,436	4.5%
7	Nebraska	9,601,101	4.4%
8	Georgia	8,391,937	3.8%
9	Ohio	8,339,219	3.8%
10	Illinois	8,087,041	3.7%
11	Virginia	6,963,083	3.2%
12	New York	6,733,053	3.1%
13	Idaho	5,821,110	2.6%
14	California	4,924,819	2.2%
15	Alabama	4,713,394	2.1%
16	Wisconsin	4,033,349	1.8%
17	Maine	3,975,970	1.8%
18	Maryland	3,839,690	1.7%
19	West Virginia	3,788,537	1.7%
20	Colorado	3,752,564	1.7%
21	New Jersey	3,729,623	1.7%
22	Arkansas	3,190,528	1.4%
23	Iowa	3,145,360	1.4%
24	Tennessee	3,067,358	1.4%
25	Oregon	2,912,278	1.3%
26	South Carolina	2,778,925	1.3%
27	South Dakota	2,413,621	1.1%
28	Oklahoma	2,391,127	1.1%
29	Washington	2,123,223	1.0%
30	Kentucky	2,118,567	1.0%
31	Missouri	1,660,217	0.8%
32	Florida	1,590,342	0.7%
33	Minnesota	1,571,683	0.7%
34	Utah	1,215,070	0.6%
35	Kansas	1,149,296	0.5%
36	Michigan	1,043,401	0.5%
37	Connecticut	785,064	0.4%
38	Delaware	573,937	0.3%
39	North Dakota	110,470	0.1%
40	Nevada	82,849	0.0%
41	Alaska	76,438	0.0%
42	Vermont	75,573	0.0%
43	Massachusetts	73,437	0.0%
44	Montana	48,785	0.0%
45	New Mexico	40,023	0.0%
46	Hawaii	29,770	0.0%
47	Wyoming	11,395	0.0%
48	New Hampshire	10,675	0.0%
49	Rhode Island	10,171	0.0%
50	Arizona	6,376	0.0%
	District of Columbia	13,943	0.0%

Source: U.S. Environmental Protection Agency, Office of Pollution Prevention and Toxics Information Management "2001 Toxics Release Inventory" (http://www.epa.gov/tri/tridata/tri01/)
**National total does not include 167,897 pounds of discharges in U.S. territories. Includes both original (or manufacturing) industries and those added by EPA since it began tracking releases.*

Pollution Released by Manufacturing Plants in 2001

National Total = 2,048,246,279 Pounds of Toxins*

ALPHA ORDER

RANK	STATE	POUNDS	% of USA
8	Alabama	76,855,436	3.8%
45	Alaska	2,405,010	0.1%
17	Arizona	55,224,619	2.7%
21	Arkansas	40,479,267	2.0%
23	California	31,707,988	1.5%
39	Colorado	6,578,206	0.3%
40	Connecticut	5,273,469	0.3%
37	Delaware	7,529,187	0.4%
10	Florida	60,639,611	3.0%
15	Georgia	56,461,567	2.8%
48	Hawaii	937,055	0.0%
29	Idaho	20,559,076	1.0%
6	Illinois	85,223,505	4.2%
2	Indiana	135,847,983	6.6%
24	Iowa	27,512,833	1.3%
27	Kansas	22,732,168	1.1%
20	Kentucky	42,207,589	2.1%
5	Louisiana	114,781,224	5.6%
36	Maine	10,541,185	0.5%
35	Maryland	13,735,310	0.7%
41	Massachusetts	4,993,331	0.2%
9	Michigan	67,351,365	3.3%
30	Minnesota	20,002,902	1.0%
12	Mississippi	59,822,014	2.9%
13	Missouri	59,097,407	2.9%
25	Montana	25,502,692	1.2%
33	Nebraska	16,657,768	0.8%
43	Nevada	3,446,680	0.2%
46	New Hampshire	1,354,983	0.1%
19	New Jersey	49,780,644	2.4%
49	New Mexico	923,593	0.0%
26	New York	25,419,840	1.2%
14	North Carolina	58,479,609	2.9%
44	North Dakota	3,224,726	0.2%
4	Ohio	117,112,225	5.7%
28	Oklahoma	22,091,786	1.1%
31	Oregon	19,287,399	0.9%
3	Pennsylvania	127,730,424	6.2%
47	Rhode Island	996,684	0.0%
11	South Carolina	60,138,656	2.9%
42	South Dakota	3,953,500	0.2%
7	Tennessee	81,938,614	4.0%
1	Texas	221,547,637	10.8%
18	Utah	50,720,924	2.5%
50	Vermont	363,002	0.0%
16	Virginia	55,478,204	2.7%
32	Washington	17,773,637	0.9%
34	West Virginia	14,550,450	0.7%
22	Wisconsin	33,973,078	1.7%
38	Wyoming	7,280,378	0.4%

RANK ORDER

RANK	STATE	POUNDS	% of USA
1	Texas	221,547,637	10.8%
2	Indiana	135,847,983	6.6%
3	Pennsylvania	127,730,424	6.2%
4	Ohio	117,112,225	5.7%
5	Louisiana	114,781,224	5.6%
6	Illinois	85,223,505	4.2%
7	Tennessee	81,938,614	4.0%
8	Alabama	76,855,436	3.8%
9	Michigan	67,351,365	3.3%
10	Florida	60,639,611	3.0%
11	South Carolina	60,138,656	2.9%
12	Mississippi	59,822,014	2.9%
13	Missouri	59,097,407	2.9%
14	North Carolina	58,479,609	2.9%
15	Georgia	56,461,567	2.8%
16	Virginia	55,478,204	2.7%
17	Arizona	55,224,619	2.7%
18	Utah	50,720,924	2.5%
19	New Jersey	49,780,644	2.4%
20	Kentucky	42,207,589	2.1%
21	Arkansas	40,479,267	2.0%
22	Wisconsin	33,973,078	1.7%
23	California	31,707,988	1.5%
24	Iowa	27,512,833	1.3%
25	Montana	25,502,692	1.2%
26	New York	25,419,840	1.2%
27	Kansas	22,732,168	1.1%
28	Oklahoma	22,091,786	1.1%
29	Idaho	20,559,076	1.0%
30	Minnesota	20,002,902	1.0%
31	Oregon	19,287,399	0.9%
32	Washington	17,773,637	0.9%
33	Nebraska	16,657,768	0.8%
34	West Virginia	14,550,450	0.7%
35	Maryland	13,735,310	0.7%
36	Maine	10,541,185	0.5%
37	Delaware	7,529,187	0.4%
38	Wyoming	7,280,378	0.4%
39	Colorado	6,578,206	0.3%
40	Connecticut	5,273,469	0.3%
41	Massachusetts	4,993,331	0.2%
42	South Dakota	3,953,500	0.2%
43	Nevada	3,446,680	0.2%
44	North Dakota	3,224,726	0.2%
45	Alaska	2,405,010	0.1%
46	New Hampshire	1,354,983	0.1%
47	Rhode Island	996,684	0.0%
48	Hawaii	937,055	0.0%
49	New Mexico	923,593	0.0%
50	Vermont	363,002	0.0%
	District of Columbia	19,839	0.0%

Source: U.S. Environmental Protection Agency, Office of Pollution Prevention and Toxics Information Management "2001 Toxics Release Inventory" (http://www.epa.gov/tri/tridata/tri01/)

**National total does not include 6,150,618 pounds of toxins in U.S. territories. Includes discharges to air, surface water, underground injection and surface land by what are labeled by the EPA as "original industries" for which data have been collected since 1988. An additional 4,092,892,226 pounds (excluding territories) of toxins were released by industries that have been added by EPA (see table 219).*

Percent Change in Pollution Released by Manufacturing Plants: 1998 to 2001

National Percent Change = 23.3% Decrease*

ALPHA ORDER

RANK	STATE	PERCENT CHANGE
21	Alabama	(19.6)
2	Alaska	65.5
6	Arizona	3.5
14	Arkansas	(13.4)
36	California	(30.4)
20	Colorado	(19.4)
41	Connecticut	(40.3)
11	Delaware	(10.5)
16	Florida	(13.6)
31	Georgia	(25.7)
3	Hawaii	25.1
38	Idaho	(32.5)
18	Illinois	(17.7)
44	Indiana	(44.2)
25	Iowa	(21.1)
33	Kansas	(26.8)
10	Kentucky	(8.2)
26	Louisiana	(23.3)
27	Maine	(24.1)
13	Maryland	(11.6)
37	Massachusetts	(31.0)
19	Michigan	(18.0)
9	Minnesota	(7.4)
17	Mississippi	(14.9)
8	Missouri	(2.8)
49	Montana	(58.8)
4	Nebraska	23.6
14	Nevada	(13.4)
47	New Hampshire	(48.3)
1	New Jersey	136.6
50	New Mexico	(97.5)
40	New York	(37.4)
34	North Carolina	(27.2)
24	North Dakota	(21.0)
35	Ohio	(28.1)
12	Oklahoma	(11.5)
22	Oregon	(19.8)
5	Pennsylvania	18.1
43	Rhode Island	(43.6)
6	South Carolina	3.5
30	South Dakota	(25.1)
32	Tennessee	(25.9)
29	Texas	(24.7)
46	Utah	(48.1)
42	Vermont	(43.1)
23	Virginia	(20.2)
48	Washington	(51.6)
45	West Virginia	(44.7)
28	Wisconsin	(24.6)
39	Wyoming	(33.3)

RANK ORDER

RANK	STATE	PERCENT CHANGE
1	New Jersey	136.6
2	Alaska	65.5
3	Hawaii	25.1
4	Nebraska	23.6
5	Pennsylvania	18.1
6	Arizona	3.5
6	South Carolina	3.5
8	Missouri	(2.8)
9	Minnesota	(7.4)
10	Kentucky	(8.2)
11	Delaware	(10.5)
12	Oklahoma	(11.5)
13	Maryland	(11.6)
14	Arkansas	(13.4)
14	Nevada	(13.4)
16	Florida	(13.6)
17	Mississippi	(14.9)
18	Illinois	(17.7)
19	Michigan	(18.0)
20	Colorado	(19.4)
21	Alabama	(19.6)
22	Oregon	(19.8)
23	Virginia	(20.2)
24	North Dakota	(21.0)
25	Iowa	(21.1)
26	Louisiana	(23.3)
27	Maine	(24.1)
28	Wisconsin	(24.6)
29	Texas	(24.7)
30	South Dakota	(25.1)
31	Georgia	(25.7)
32	Tennessee	(25.9)
33	Kansas	(26.8)
34	North Carolina	(27.2)
35	Ohio	(28.1)
36	California	(30.4)
37	Massachusetts	(31.0)
38	Idaho	(32.5)
39	Wyoming	(33.3)
40	New York	(37.4)
41	Connecticut	(40.3)
42	Vermont	(43.1)
43	Rhode Island	(43.6)
44	Indiana	(44.2)
45	West Virginia	(44.7)
46	Utah	(48.1)
47	New Hampshire	(48.3)
48	Washington	(51.6)
49	Montana	(58.8)
50	New Mexico	(97.5)
	District of Columbia	51.3

Source: Morgan Quitno Press using data from U.S. Environmental Protection Agency
   "2001 Toxics Release Inventory" (http://www.epa.gov/tri/tridata/tri01/)
*National rate does not include toxins in U.S. territories. Includes discharges to air, surface water, underground injection and surface land by what are labeled by the EPA as "original industries" for which data have been collected since 1988. Additional toxins were released by industries that have been added by EPA (see table 217).

VIII. GEOGRAPHY

Total Area of States in Square Miles in 2003

National Total = 3,718,694 Square Miles*

<u>ALPHA ORDER</u>

RANK	STATE	MILES	% of USA
30	Alabama	52,218	1.4%
1	Alaska	616,240	16.6%
6	Arizona	113,998	3.1%
28	Arkansas	53,178	1.4%
3	California	158,854	4.3%
8	Colorado	104,093	2.8%
48	Connecticut	5,543	0.1%
49	Delaware	2,396	0.1%
23	Florida	59,909	1.6%
24	Georgia	58,970	1.6%
47	Hawaii	6,461	0.2%
14	Idaho	83,570	2.2%
25	Illinois	57,914	1.6%
38	Indiana	36,418	1.0%
26	Iowa	56,271	1.5%
15	Kansas	82,276	2.2%
37	Kentucky	40,409	1.1%
31	Louisiana	49,650	1.3%
39	Maine	33,738	0.9%
42	Maryland	12,297	0.3%
45	Massachusetts	9,240	0.2%
11	Michigan	96,716	2.6%
12	Minnesota	86,938	2.3%
32	Mississippi	48,282	1.3%
21	Missouri	69,704	1.9%
4	Montana	147,042	4.0%
16	Nebraska	77,353	2.1%
7	Nevada	110,560	3.0%
44	New Hampshire	9,282	0.2%
46	New Jersey	8,214	0.2%
5	New Mexico	121,589	3.3%
27	New York	54,077	1.5%
29	North Carolina	52,670	1.4%
18	North Dakota	70,699	1.9%
34	Ohio	44,825	1.2%
20	Oklahoma	69,898	1.9%
10	Oregon	97,126	2.6%
33	Pennsylvania	46,055	1.2%
50	Rhode Island	1,231	0.0%
40	South Carolina	31,190	0.8%
17	South Dakota	77,116	2.1%
36	Tennessee	42,143	1.1%
2	Texas	267,256	7.2%
13	Utah	84,898	2.3%
43	Vermont	9,614	0.3%
35	Virginia	42,328	1.1%
19	Washington	70,634	1.9%
41	West Virginia	24,230	0.7%
22	Wisconsin	65,498	1.8%
9	Wyoming	97,813	2.6%

<u>RANK ORDER</u>

RANK	STATE	MILES	% of USA
1	Alaska	616,240	16.6%
2	Texas	267,256	7.2%
3	California	158,854	4.3%
4	Montana	147,042	4.0%
5	New Mexico	121,589	3.3%
6	Arizona	113,998	3.1%
7	Nevada	110,560	3.0%
8	Colorado	104,093	2.8%
9	Wyoming	97,813	2.6%
10	Oregon	97,126	2.6%
11	Michigan	96,716	2.6%
12	Minnesota	86,938	2.3%
13	Utah	84,898	2.3%
14	Idaho	83,570	2.2%
15	Kansas	82,276	2.2%
16	Nebraska	77,353	2.1%
17	South Dakota	77,116	2.1%
18	North Dakota	70,699	1.9%
19	Washington	70,634	1.9%
20	Oklahoma	69,898	1.9%
21	Missouri	69,704	1.9%
22	Wisconsin	65,498	1.8%
23	Florida	59,909	1.6%
24	Georgia	58,970	1.6%
25	Illinois	57,914	1.6%
26	Iowa	56,271	1.5%
27	New York	54,077	1.5%
28	Arkansas	53,178	1.4%
29	North Carolina	52,670	1.4%
30	Alabama	52,218	1.4%
31	Louisiana	49,650	1.3%
32	Mississippi	48,282	1.3%
33	Pennsylvania	46,055	1.2%
34	Ohio	44,825	1.2%
35	Virginia	42,328	1.1%
36	Tennessee	42,143	1.1%
37	Kentucky	40,409	1.1%
38	Indiana	36,418	1.0%
39	Maine	33,738	0.9%
40	South Carolina	31,190	0.8%
41	West Virginia	24,230	0.7%
42	Maryland	12,297	0.3%
43	Vermont	9,614	0.3%
44	New Hampshire	9,282	0.2%
45	Massachusetts	9,240	0.2%
46	New Jersey	8,214	0.2%
47	Hawaii	6,461	0.2%
48	Connecticut	5,543	0.1%
49	Delaware	2,396	0.1%
50	Rhode Island	1,231	0.0%
	District of Columbia	68	0.0%

Source: U.S. Bureau of the Census
"2000 Census of Population and Housing" (Series PHC-1)
*Total of land and water area.

Land Area of States in Square Miles in 2003

National Total = 3,537,422 Square Miles of Land Area*

<u>ALPHA ORDER</u> / <u>RANK ORDER</u>

RANK	STATE	MILES	% of USA		RANK	STATE	MILES	% of USA
28	Alabama	50,744	1.4%		1	Alaska	571,949	16.2%
1	Alaska	571,949	16.2%		2	Texas	261,796	7.4%
6	Arizona	113,634	3.2%		3	California	155,959	4.4%
27	Arkansas	52,068	1.5%		4	Montana	145,552	4.1%
3	California	155,959	4.4%		5	New Mexico	121,355	3.4%
8	Colorado	103,717	2.9%		6	Arizona	113,634	3.2%
48	Connecticut	4,845	0.1%		7	Nevada	109,825	3.1%
49	Delaware	1,954	0.1%		8	Colorado	103,717	2.9%
26	Florida	53,927	1.5%		9	Wyoming	97,100	2.7%
21	Georgia	57,906	1.6%		10	Oregon	95,996	2.7%
47	Hawaii	6,423	0.2%		11	Idaho	82,747	2.3%
11	Idaho	82,747	2.3%		12	Utah	82,143	2.3%
24	Illinois	55,583	1.6%		13	Kansas	81,815	2.3%
38	Indiana	35,867	1.0%		14	Minnesota	79,610	2.3%
23	Iowa	55,869	1.6%		15	Nebraska	76,872	2.2%
13	Kansas	81,815	2.3%		16	South Dakota	75,884	2.1%
36	Kentucky	39,728	1.1%		17	North Dakota	68,976	1.9%
33	Louisiana	43,562	1.2%		18	Missouri	68,886	1.9%
39	Maine	30,861	0.9%		19	Oklahoma	68,667	1.9%
42	Maryland	9,774	0.3%		20	Washington	66,544	1.9%
45	Massachusetts	7,840	0.2%		21	Georgia	57,906	1.6%
22	Michigan	56,804	1.6%		22	Michigan	56,804	1.6%
14	Minnesota	79,610	2.3%		23	Iowa	55,869	1.6%
31	Mississippi	46,907	1.3%		24	Illinois	55,583	1.6%
18	Missouri	68,886	1.9%		25	Wisconsin	54,310	1.5%
4	Montana	145,552	4.1%		26	Florida	53,927	1.5%
15	Nebraska	76,872	2.2%		27	Arkansas	52,068	1.5%
7	Nevada	109,825	3.1%		28	Alabama	50,744	1.4%
44	New Hampshire	8,968	0.3%		29	North Carolina	48,711	1.4%
46	New Jersey	7,417	0.2%		30	New York	47,214	1.3%
5	New Mexico	121,355	3.4%		31	Mississippi	46,907	1.3%
30	New York	47,214	1.3%		32	Pennsylvania	44,816	1.3%
29	North Carolina	48,711	1.4%		33	Louisiana	43,562	1.2%
17	North Dakota	68,976	1.9%		34	Tennessee	41,217	1.2%
35	Ohio	40,948	1.2%		35	Ohio	40,948	1.2%
19	Oklahoma	68,667	1.9%		36	Kentucky	39,728	1.1%
10	Oregon	95,996	2.7%		37	Virginia	39,594	1.1%
32	Pennsylvania	44,816	1.3%		38	Indiana	35,867	1.0%
50	Rhode Island	1,045	0.0%		39	Maine	30,861	0.9%
40	South Carolina	30,109	0.9%		40	South Carolina	30,109	0.9%
16	South Dakota	75,884	2.1%		41	West Virginia	24,078	0.7%
34	Tennessee	41,217	1.2%		42	Maryland	9,774	0.3%
2	Texas	261,796	7.4%		43	Vermont	9,250	0.3%
12	Utah	82,143	2.3%		44	New Hampshire	8,968	0.3%
43	Vermont	9,250	0.3%		45	Massachusetts	7,840	0.2%
37	Virginia	39,594	1.1%		46	New Jersey	7,417	0.2%
20	Washington	66,544	1.9%		47	Hawaii	6,423	0.2%
41	West Virginia	24,078	0.7%		48	Connecticut	4,845	0.1%
25	Wisconsin	54,310	1.5%		49	Delaware	1,954	0.1%
9	Wyoming	97,100	2.7%		50	Rhode Island	1,045	0.0%
						District of Columbia	61	0.0%

Source: U.S. Bureau of the Census
   "2000 Census of Population and Housing" (Series PHC-1)
*Includes dry land temporarily or partially covered by water, such as marshland, swamps, etc.; streams and canals
under one-eighth mile wide; and lakes, reservoirs and ponds under 40 acres.

Water Area of States in Square Miles in 2003

National Total = 181,272 Square Miles of Water*

ALPHA ORDER

RANK	STATE	MILES	% of USA
20	Alabama	1,475	0.8%
1	Alaska	44,292	24.4%
45	Arizona	364	0.2%
27	Arkansas	1,110	0.6%
12	California	2,896	1.6%
43	Colorado	376	0.2%
36	Connecticut	699	0.4%
41	Delaware	442	0.2%
7	Florida	5,983	3.3%
29	Georgia	1,064	0.6%
50	Hawaii	38	0.0%
31	Idaho	823	0.5%
17	Illinois	2,331	1.3%
38	Indiana	551	0.3%
42	Iowa	402	0.2%
40	Kansas	462	0.3%
37	Kentucky	681	0.4%
6	Louisiana	6,089	3.4%
13	Maine	2,877	1.6%
16	Maryland	2,523	1.4%
21	Massachusetts	1,400	0.8%
2	Michigan	39,912	22.0%
4	Minnesota	7,329	4.0%
22	Mississippi	1,375	0.8%
32	Missouri	818	0.5%
19	Montana	1,490	0.8%
39	Nebraska	481	0.3%
34	Nevada	735	0.4%
46	New Hampshire	314	0.2%
33	New Jersey	797	0.4%
47	New Mexico	234	0.1%
5	New York	6,863	3.8%
10	North Carolina	3,960	2.2%
18	North Dakota	1,724	1.0%
11	Ohio	3,877	2.1%
25	Oklahoma	1,231	0.7%
26	Oregon	1,130	0.6%
23	Pennsylvania	1,239	0.7%
48	Rhode Island	187	0.1%
28	South Carolina	1,080	0.6%
24	South Dakota	1,232	0.7%
30	Tennessee	926	0.5%
8	Texas	5,460	3.0%
14	Utah	2,755	1.5%
44	Vermont	365	0.2%
15	Virginia	2,734	1.5%
9	Washington	4,090	2.3%
49	West Virginia	152	0.1%
3	Wisconsin	11,188	6.2%
35	Wyoming	713	0.4%

RANK ORDER

RANK	STATE	MILES	% of USA
1	Alaska	44,292	24.4%
2	Michigan	39,912	22.0%
3	Wisconsin	11,188	6.2%
4	Minnesota	7,329	4.0%
5	New York	6,863	3.8%
6	Louisiana	6,089	3.4%
7	Florida	5,983	3.3%
8	Texas	5,460	3.0%
9	Washington	4,090	2.3%
10	North Carolina	3,960	2.2%
11	Ohio	3,877	2.1%
12	California	2,896	1.6%
13	Maine	2,877	1.6%
14	Utah	2,755	1.5%
15	Virginia	2,734	1.5%
16	Maryland	2,523	1.4%
17	Illinois	2,331	1.3%
18	North Dakota	1,724	1.0%
19	Montana	1,490	0.8%
20	Alabama	1,475	0.8%
21	Massachusetts	1,400	0.8%
22	Mississippi	1,375	0.8%
23	Pennsylvania	1,239	0.7%
24	South Dakota	1,232	0.7%
25	Oklahoma	1,231	0.7%
26	Oregon	1,130	0.6%
27	Arkansas	1,110	0.6%
28	South Carolina	1,080	0.6%
29	Georgia	1,064	0.6%
30	Tennessee	926	0.5%
31	Idaho	823	0.5%
32	Missouri	818	0.5%
33	New Jersey	797	0.4%
34	Nevada	735	0.4%
35	Wyoming	713	0.4%
36	Connecticut	699	0.4%
37	Kentucky	681	0.4%
38	Indiana	551	0.3%
39	Nebraska	481	0.3%
40	Kansas	462	0.3%
41	Delaware	442	0.2%
42	Iowa	402	0.2%
43	Colorado	376	0.2%
44	Vermont	365	0.2%
45	Arizona	364	0.2%
46	New Hampshire	314	0.2%
47	New Mexico	234	0.1%
48	Rhode Island	187	0.1%
49	West Virginia	152	0.1%
50	Hawaii	38	0.0%
	District of Columbia	7	0.0%

Source: U.S. Bureau of the Census
   "2000 Census of Population and Housing" (Series PHC-1)

*Includes permanent inland water surface, such as lakes, reservoirs, and ponds having an area of 40 acres or more,
canals one-eighth mile or more in width; coastal waters behind or sheltered by headlands or islands separated by
less than 1 nautical mile of water, and islands under 40 acres in area. Excludes areas of oceans, bays, etc., lying
within U.S. jurisdiction but not defined as inland water.*

Highest Point of Elevation in Feet

National High Point = 20,320 Feet Above Sea Level (Mt. McKinley, Alaska)

ALPHA ORDER

RANK	STATE	HIGHEST POINT
35	Alabama	2,405
1	Alaska	20,320
12	Arizona	12,633
34	Arkansas	2,753
2	California	14,494
3	Colorado	14,433
36	Connecticut	2,380
49	Delaware	448
50	Florida	345
25	Georgia	4,784
6	Hawaii	13,796
11	Idaho	12,662
45	Illinois	1,235
44	Indiana	1,257
42	Iowa	1,670
28	Kansas	4,039
27	Kentucky	4,139
48	Louisiana	535
22	Maine	5,267
32	Maryland	3,360
31	Massachusetts	3,487
38	Michigan	1,979
37	Minnesota	2,301
47	Mississippi	806
41	Missouri	1,772
10	Montana	12,799
20	Nebraska	5,424
9	Nevada	13,140
18	New Hampshire	6,288
40	New Jersey	1,803
8	New Mexico	13,161
21	New York	5,344
16	North Carolina	6,684
30	North Dakota	3,506
43	Ohio	1,549
23	Oklahoma	4,973
13	Oregon	11,239
33	Pennsylvania	3,213
46	Rhode Island	812
29	South Carolina	3,560
15	South Dakota	7,242
17	Tennessee	6,643
14	Texas	8,749
7	Utah	13,528
26	Vermont	4,393
19	Virginia	5,729
4	Washington	14,410
24	West Virginia	4,861
39	Wisconsin	1,951
5	Wyoming	13,804

RANK ORDER

RANK	STATE	HIGHEST POINT
1	Alaska	20,320
2	California	14,494
3	Colorado	14,433
4	Washington	14,410
5	Wyoming	13,804
6	Hawaii	13,796
7	Utah	13,528
8	New Mexico	13,161
9	Nevada	13,140
10	Montana	12,799
11	Idaho	12,662
12	Arizona	12,633
13	Oregon	11,239
14	Texas	8,749
15	South Dakota	7,242
16	North Carolina	6,684
17	Tennessee	6,643
18	New Hampshire	6,288
19	Virginia	5,729
20	Nebraska	5,424
21	New York	5,344
22	Maine	5,267
23	Oklahoma	4,973
24	West Virginia	4,861
25	Georgia	4,784
26	Vermont	4,393
27	Kentucky	4,139
28	Kansas	4,039
29	South Carolina	3,560
30	North Dakota	3,506
31	Massachusetts	3,487
32	Maryland	3,360
33	Pennsylvania	3,213
34	Arkansas	2,753
35	Alabama	2,405
36	Connecticut	2,380
37	Minnesota	2,301
38	Michigan	1,979
39	Wisconsin	1,951
40	New Jersey	1,803
41	Missouri	1,772
42	Iowa	1,670
43	Ohio	1,549
44	Indiana	1,257
45	Illinois	1,235
46	Rhode Island	812
47	Mississippi	806
48	Louisiana	535
49	Delaware	448
50	Florida	345

District of Columbia   410

Source: U.S. Department of Interior, U.S. Geological Survey
"Elevations and Distances in the United States, 1990"

Lowest Point of Elevation in Feet

National Low Point = 282 Feet Below Sea Level (Death Valley, California)*

ALPHA ORDER

RANK	STATE	LOWEST POINT
3	Alabama	0
3	Alaska	0
26	Arizona	70
25	Arkansas	55
1	California	(282)
50	Colorado	3,350
3	Connecticut	0
3	Delaware	0
3	Florida	0
3	Georgia	0
3	Hawaii	0
42	Idaho	710
32	Illinois	279
34	Indiana	320
37	Iowa	480
41	Kansas	679
31	Kentucky	257
2	Louisiana	(8)
3	Maine	0
3	Maryland	0
3	Massachusetts	0
38	Michigan	571
40	Minnesota	601
3	Mississippi	0
29	Missouri	230
46	Montana	1,800
44	Nebraska	840
36	Nevada	479
3	New Hampshire	0
3	New Jersey	0
48	New Mexico	2,842
3	New York	0
3	North Carolina	0
43	North Dakota	750
35	Ohio	455
33	Oklahoma	289
3	Oregon	0
3	Pennsylvania	0
3	Rhode Island	0
3	South Carolina	0
45	South Dakota	966
28	Tennessee	178
3	Texas	0
47	Utah	2,000
27	Vermont	95
3	Virginia	0
3	Washington	0
30	West Virginia	240
39	Wisconsin	579
49	Wyoming	3,099

RANK ORDER

RANK	STATE	LOWEST POINT
1	California	(282)
2	Louisiana	(8)
3	Alabama*	0
3	Alaska	0
3	Connecticut	0
3	Delaware	0
3	Florida	0
3	Georgia	0
3	Hawaii	0
3	Maine	0
3	Maryland	0
3	Massachusetts	0
3	Mississippi	0
3	New Hampshire	0
3	New Jersey	0
3	New York	0
3	North Carolina	0
3	Oregon	0
3	Pennsylvania	0
3	Rhode Island	0
3	South Carolina	0
3	Texas	0
3	Virginia	0
3	Washington	0
25	Arkansas	55
26	Arizona	70
27	Vermont	95
28	Tennessee	178
29	Missouri	230
30	West Virginia	240
31	Kentucky	257
32	Illinois	279
33	Oklahoma	289
34	Indiana	320
35	Ohio	455
36	Nevada	479
37	Iowa	480
38	Michigan	571
39	Wisconsin	579
40	Minnesota	601
41	Kansas	679
42	Idaho	710
43	North Dakota	750
44	Nebraska	840
45	South Dakota	966
46	Montana	1,800
47	Utah	2,000
48	New Mexico	2,842
49	Wyoming	3,099
50	Colorado	3,350

District of Columbia   1

Source: U.S. Department of Interior, U.S. Geological Survey
  "Elevations and Distances in the United States, 1990"
*States with "0" have sea level as lowest point.

Approximate Mean Elevation in Feet

Approximate National Mean Elevation = 2,500 Feet Above Sea Level

<table>
<tr><td colspan="3"><u>ALPHA ORDER</u></td><td colspan="3"><u>RANK ORDER</u></td></tr>
<tr><td>RANK</td><td>STATE</td><td>MEAN ELEVATION</td><td>RANK</td><td>STATE</td><td>MEAN ELEVATION</td></tr>
<tr><td>40</td><td>Alabama</td><td>500</td><td>1</td><td>Colorado</td><td>6,800</td></tr>
<tr><td>15</td><td>Alaska</td><td>1,900</td><td>2</td><td>Wyoming</td><td>6,700</td></tr>
<tr><td>7</td><td>Arizona</td><td>4,100</td><td>3</td><td>Utah</td><td>6,100</td></tr>
<tr><td>36</td><td>Arkansas</td><td>650</td><td>4</td><td>New Mexico</td><td>5,700</td></tr>
<tr><td>11</td><td>California</td><td>2,900</td><td>5</td><td>Nevada</td><td>5,500</td></tr>
<tr><td>1</td><td>Colorado</td><td>6,800</td><td>6</td><td>Idaho</td><td>5,000</td></tr>
<tr><td>40</td><td>Connecticut</td><td>500</td><td>7</td><td>Arizona</td><td>4,100</td></tr>
<tr><td>50</td><td>Delaware</td><td>60</td><td>8</td><td>Montana</td><td>3,400</td></tr>
<tr><td>48</td><td>Florida</td><td>100</td><td>9</td><td>Oregon</td><td>3,300</td></tr>
<tr><td>37</td><td>Georgia</td><td>600</td><td>10</td><td>Hawaii</td><td>3,030</td></tr>
<tr><td>10</td><td>Hawaii</td><td>3,030</td><td>11</td><td>California</td><td>2,900</td></tr>
<tr><td>6</td><td>Idaho</td><td>5,000</td><td>12</td><td>Nebraska</td><td>2,600</td></tr>
<tr><td>37</td><td>Illinois</td><td>600</td><td>13</td><td>South Dakota</td><td>2,200</td></tr>
<tr><td>34</td><td>Indiana</td><td>700</td><td>14</td><td>Kansas</td><td>2,000</td></tr>
<tr><td>22</td><td>Iowa</td><td>1,100</td><td>15</td><td>Alaska</td><td>1,900</td></tr>
<tr><td>14</td><td>Kansas</td><td>2,000</td><td>15</td><td>North Dakota</td><td>1,900</td></tr>
<tr><td>33</td><td>Kentucky</td><td>750</td><td>17</td><td>Texas</td><td>1,700</td></tr>
<tr><td>48</td><td>Louisiana</td><td>100</td><td>17</td><td>Washington</td><td>1,700</td></tr>
<tr><td>37</td><td>Maine</td><td>600</td><td>19</td><td>West Virginia</td><td>1,500</td></tr>
<tr><td>43</td><td>Maryland</td><td>350</td><td>20</td><td>Oklahoma</td><td>1,300</td></tr>
<tr><td>40</td><td>Massachusetts</td><td>500</td><td>21</td><td>Minnesota</td><td>1,200</td></tr>
<tr><td>29</td><td>Michigan</td><td>900</td><td>22</td><td>Iowa</td><td>1,100</td></tr>
<tr><td>21</td><td>Minnesota</td><td>1,200</td><td>22</td><td>Pennsylvania</td><td>1,100</td></tr>
<tr><td>45</td><td>Mississippi</td><td>300</td><td>24</td><td>Wisconsin</td><td>1,050</td></tr>
<tr><td>32</td><td>Missouri</td><td>800</td><td>25</td><td>New Hampshire</td><td>1,000</td></tr>
<tr><td>8</td><td>Montana</td><td>3,400</td><td>25</td><td>New York</td><td>1,000</td></tr>
<tr><td>12</td><td>Nebraska</td><td>2,600</td><td>25</td><td>Vermont</td><td>1,000</td></tr>
<tr><td>5</td><td>Nevada</td><td>5,500</td><td>28</td><td>Virginia</td><td>950</td></tr>
<tr><td>25</td><td>New Hampshire</td><td>1,000</td><td>29</td><td>Michigan</td><td>900</td></tr>
<tr><td>46</td><td>New Jersey</td><td>250</td><td>29</td><td>Tennessee</td><td>900</td></tr>
<tr><td>4</td><td>New Mexico</td><td>5,700</td><td>31</td><td>Ohio</td><td>850</td></tr>
<tr><td>25</td><td>New York</td><td>1,000</td><td>32</td><td>Missouri</td><td>800</td></tr>
<tr><td>34</td><td>North Carolina</td><td>700</td><td>33</td><td>Kentucky</td><td>750</td></tr>
<tr><td>15</td><td>North Dakota</td><td>1,900</td><td>34</td><td>Indiana</td><td>700</td></tr>
<tr><td>31</td><td>Ohio</td><td>850</td><td>34</td><td>North Carolina</td><td>700</td></tr>
<tr><td>20</td><td>Oklahoma</td><td>1,300</td><td>36</td><td>Arkansas</td><td>650</td></tr>
<tr><td>9</td><td>Oregon</td><td>3,300</td><td>37</td><td>Georgia</td><td>600</td></tr>
<tr><td>22</td><td>Pennsylvania</td><td>1,100</td><td>37</td><td>Illinois</td><td>600</td></tr>
<tr><td>47</td><td>Rhode Island</td><td>200</td><td>37</td><td>Maine</td><td>600</td></tr>
<tr><td>43</td><td>South Carolina</td><td>350</td><td>40</td><td>Alabama</td><td>500</td></tr>
<tr><td>13</td><td>South Dakota</td><td>2,200</td><td>40</td><td>Connecticut</td><td>500</td></tr>
<tr><td>29</td><td>Tennessee</td><td>900</td><td>40</td><td>Massachusetts</td><td>500</td></tr>
<tr><td>17</td><td>Texas</td><td>1,700</td><td>43</td><td>Maryland</td><td>350</td></tr>
<tr><td>3</td><td>Utah</td><td>6,100</td><td>43</td><td>South Carolina</td><td>350</td></tr>
<tr><td>25</td><td>Vermont</td><td>1,000</td><td>45</td><td>Mississippi</td><td>300</td></tr>
<tr><td>28</td><td>Virginia</td><td>950</td><td>46</td><td>New Jersey</td><td>250</td></tr>
<tr><td>17</td><td>Washington</td><td>1,700</td><td>47</td><td>Rhode Island</td><td>200</td></tr>
<tr><td>19</td><td>West Virginia</td><td>1,500</td><td>48</td><td>Florida</td><td>100</td></tr>
<tr><td>24</td><td>Wisconsin</td><td>1,050</td><td>48</td><td>Louisiana</td><td>100</td></tr>
<tr><td>2</td><td>Wyoming</td><td>6,700</td><td>50</td><td>Delaware</td><td>60</td></tr>
<tr><td></td><td></td><td></td><td></td><td>District of Columbia</td><td>150</td></tr>
</table>

Source: U.S. Department of Interior, U.S. Geological Survey
"Elevations and Distances in the United States, 1983"

Percent of Land in Metropolitan Areas in 2000

National Percent = 20.0% of Land*

<u>ALPHA ORDER</u>

RANK	STATE	PERCENT
18	Alabama	33.1
50	Alaska	0.3
8	Arizona	53.9
31	Arkansas	16.6
6	California	59.3
28	Colorado	18.3
3	Connecticut	79.2
9	Delaware	52.0
7	Florida	58.0
25	Georgia	22.2
40	Hawaii	9.3
48	Idaho	3.6
19	Illinois	30.4
14	Indiana	38.2
37	Iowa	11.7
43	Kansas	6.9
32	Kentucky	16.4
17	Louisiana	35.0
47	Maine	4.8
5	Maryland	63.0
4	Massachusetts	70.0
23	Michigan	28.1
26	Minnesota	21.3
36	Mississippi	11.9
29	Missouri	17.6
45	Montana	5.5
49	Nebraska	3.4
21	Nevada	29.5
34	New Hampshire	15.6
1	New Jersey	100.0
39	New Mexico	9.7
11	New York	47.2
16	North Carolina	36.5
38	North Dakota	9.8
12	Ohio	44.7
29	Oklahoma	17.6
35	Oregon	14.9
10	Pennsylvania	47.9
2	Rhode Island	94.8
13	South Carolina	40.2
45	South Dakota	5.5
20	Tennessee	29.9
27	Texas	20.1
40	Utah	9.3
44	Vermont	6.1
15	Virginia	36.8
22	Washington	28.5
33	West Virginia	16.0
24	Wisconsin	23.4
42	Wyoming	8.3

<u>RANK ORDER</u>

RANK	STATE	PERCENT
1	New Jersey	100.0
2	Rhode Island	94.8
3	Connecticut	79.2
4	Massachusetts	70.0
5	Maryland	63.0
6	California	59.3
7	Florida	58.0
8	Arizona	53.9
9	Delaware	52.0
10	Pennsylvania	47.9
11	New York	47.2
12	Ohio	44.7
13	South Carolina	40.2
14	Indiana	38.2
15	Virginia	36.8
16	North Carolina	36.5
17	Louisiana	35.0
18	Alabama	33.1
19	Illinois	30.4
20	Tennessee	29.9
21	Nevada	29.5
22	Washington	28.5
23	Michigan	28.1
24	Wisconsin	23.4
25	Georgia	22.2
26	Minnesota	21.3
27	Texas	20.1
28	Colorado	18.3
29	Missouri	17.6
29	Oklahoma	17.6
31	Arkansas	16.6
32	Kentucky	16.4
33	West Virginia	16.0
34	New Hampshire	15.6
35	Oregon	14.9
36	Mississippi	11.9
37	Iowa	11.7
38	North Dakota	9.8
39	New Mexico	9.7
40	Hawaii	9.3
40	Utah	9.3
42	Wyoming	8.3
43	Kansas	6.9
44	Vermont	6.1
45	Montana	5.5
45	South Dakota	5.5
47	Maine	4.8
48	Idaho	3.6
49	Nebraska	3.4
50	Alaska	0.3
	District of Columbia	100.0

Source: Morgan Quitno Press using data from U.S. Bureau of the Census
unpublished data

*"Metropolitan" refers to metropolitan statistical areas and consolidated metropolitan statistical areas as defined by the U.S. Office of Management and Budget, July 1, 1999. Metropolitan areas currently are being redefined based on the 2000 Census. The new definitions will be completed in 2003.

Percent of Land in Nonmetropolitan Areas in 2000

National Percent = 80.0% of Land*

ALPHA ORDER				RANK ORDER		
RANK	STATE	PERCENT		RANK	STATE	PERCENT
33	Alabama	66.9		1	Alaska	99.7
1	Alaska	99.7		2	Nebraska	96.6
43	Arizona	46.1		3	Idaho	96.4
20	Arkansas	83.4		4	Maine	95.2
45	California	40.7		5	Montana	94.5
23	Colorado	81.7		5	South Dakota	94.5
48	Connecticut	20.8		7	Vermont	93.9
42	Delaware	48.0		8	Kansas	93.1
44	Florida	42.0		9	Wyoming	91.7
26	Georgia	77.8		10	Hawaii	90.7
10	Hawaii	90.7		10	Utah	90.7
3	Idaho	96.4		12	New Mexico	90.3
32	Illinois	69.6		13	North Dakota	90.2
37	Indiana	61.8		14	Iowa	88.3
14	Iowa	88.3		15	Mississippi	88.1
8	Kansas	93.1		16	Oregon	85.1
19	Kentucky	83.6		17	New Hampshire	84.4
34	Louisiana	65.0		18	West Virginia	84.0
4	Maine	95.2		19	Kentucky	83.6
46	Maryland	37.0		20	Arkansas	83.4
47	Massachusetts	30.0		21	Missouri	82.4
28	Michigan	71.9		21	Oklahoma	82.4
25	Minnesota	78.7		23	Colorado	81.7
15	Mississippi	88.1		24	Texas	79.9
21	Missouri	82.4		25	Minnesota	78.7
5	Montana	94.5		26	Georgia	77.8
2	Nebraska	96.6		27	Wisconsin	76.6
30	Nevada	70.5		28	Michigan	71.9
17	New Hampshire	84.4		29	Washington	71.5
50	New Jersey	0.0		30	Nevada	70.5
12	New Mexico	90.3		31	Tennessee	70.1
40	New York	52.8		32	Illinois	69.6
35	North Carolina	63.5		33	Alabama	66.9
13	North Dakota	90.2		34	Louisiana	65.0
39	Ohio	55.3		35	North Carolina	63.5
21	Oklahoma	82.4		36	Virginia	63.2
16	Oregon	85.1		37	Indiana	61.8
41	Pennsylvania	52.1		38	South Carolina	59.8
49	Rhode Island	5.2		39	Ohio	55.3
38	South Carolina	59.8		40	New York	52.8
5	South Dakota	94.5		41	Pennsylvania	52.1
31	Tennessee	70.1		42	Delaware	48.0
24	Texas	79.9		43	Arizona	46.1
10	Utah	90.7		44	Florida	42.0
7	Vermont	93.9		45	California	40.7
36	Virginia	63.2		46	Maryland	37.0
29	Washington	71.5		47	Massachusetts	30.0
18	West Virginia	84.0		48	Connecticut	20.8
27	Wisconsin	76.6		49	Rhode Island	5.2
9	Wyoming	91.7		50	New Jersey	0.0
					District of Columbia	0.0

*Source: Morgan Quitno Press using data from U.S. Bureau of the Census
    unpublished data*

**"Nonmetropolitan" refers to areas outside of metropolitan statistical areas and consolidated metropolitan statistical areas as defined by the U.S. Office of Management and Budget, July 1, 1999. Metropolitan areas currently are being redefined based on the 2000 Census. The new definitions will be completed in 2003.*

Normal Daily Mean Temperature*

<u>ALPHA ORDER</u>

RANK	STATE	MEAN TEMPERATURE
5	Alabama	66.8
50	Alaska	41.5
2	Arizona	72.9
10	Arkansas	62.1
11	California**	61.5
35	Colorado	50.1
34	Connecticut	50.2
22	Delaware	54.4
3	Florida**	72.4
9	Georgia	62.2
1	Hawaii	77.5
28	Idaho	52.0
37	Illinois**	50.0
26	Indiana	52.5
37	Iowa	50.0
18	Kansas	56.4
16	Kentucky	57.0
4	Louisiana	68.8
42	Maine	45.8
20	Maryland	54.6
30	Massachusetts	51.6
45	Michigan**	45.0
48	Minnesota**	42.3
7	Mississippi	64.1
19	Missouri**	55.3
47	Montana	43.8
33	Nebraska	50.7
31	Nevada	51.3
41	New Hampshire	45.9
23	New Jersey	53.5
17	New Mexico	56.8
35	New York**	50.1
13	North Carolina**	60.5
48	North Dakota	42.3
27	Ohio**	52.3
14	Oklahoma	60.1
23	Oregon	53.5
25	Pennsylvania**	53.2
32	Rhode Island	51.1
8	South Carolina	63.6
44	South Dakota	45.1
12	Tennessee**	60.7
6	Texas**	66.3
28	Utah	52.0
43	Vermont	45.2
15	Virginia**	58.6
39	Washington**	49.8
21	West Virginia	54.5
40	Wisconsin	47.5
45	Wyoming	45.0

<u>RANK ORDER</u>

RANK	STATE	MEAN TEMPERATURE
1	Hawaii	77.5
2	Arizona	72.9
3	Florida**	72.4
4	Louisiana	68.8
5	Alabama	66.8
6	Texas**	66.3
7	Mississippi	64.1
8	South Carolina	63.6
9	Georgia	62.2
10	Arkansas	62.1
11	California**	61.5
12	Tennessee**	60.7
13	North Carolina**	60.5
14	Oklahoma	60.1
15	Virginia**	58.6
16	Kentucky	57.0
17	New Mexico	56.8
18	Kansas	56.4
19	Missouri**	55.3
20	Maryland	54.6
21	West Virginia	54.5
22	Delaware	54.4
23	New Jersey	53.5
23	Oregon	53.5
25	Pennsylvania**	53.2
26	Indiana	52.5
27	Ohio**	52.3
28	Idaho	52.0
28	Utah	52.0
30	Massachusetts	51.6
31	Nevada	51.3
32	Rhode Island	51.1
33	Nebraska	50.7
34	Connecticut	50.2
35	Colorado	50.1
35	New York**	50.1
37	Illinois**	50.0
37	Iowa	50.0
39	Washington**	49.8
40	Wisconsin	47.5
41	New Hampshire	45.9
42	Maine	45.8
43	Vermont	45.2
44	South Dakota	45.1
45	Michigan**	45.0
45	Wyoming	45.0
47	Montana	43.8
48	Minnesota**	42.3
48	North Dakota	42.3
50	Alaska	41.5
	District of Columbia	57.5

*Source: U.S. Department of Commerce, National Oceanic and Atmospheric Administration
"Climatography of the United States" (No. 81)*
**Based on standard 30 year period, 1971-2000.*
***Temperatures from multiple reporting cities within one state were averaged to determine a state's mean temperature.*

Percent of Days That Are Sunny*

<u>ALPHA ORDER</u>

RANK	STATE	PERCENT OF DAYS SUNNY
13	Alabama	60
50	Alaska	23
1	Arizona	81
13	Arkansas	60
4	California**	72
6	Colorado	67
37	Connecticut	52
28	Delaware	55
8	Florida**	65
17	Georgia	59
3	Hawaii	74
21	Idaho	58
35	Illinois**	53
41	Indiana	51
28	Iowa	55
11	Kansas	62
35	Kentucky	53
13	Louisiana	60
28	Maine	55
21	Maryland	58
28	Massachusetts	55
46	Michigan**	46
37	Minnesota**	52
17	Mississippi	59
24	Missouri**	57
41	Montana	51
17	Nebraska	59
5	Nevada	69
28	New Hampshire	55
27	New Jersey	56
2	New Mexico	76
37	New York**	52
17	North Carolina**	59
28	North Dakota	55
45	Ohio**	47
9	Oklahoma	64
49	Oregon	39
43	Pennsylvania**	50
28	Rhode Island	55
13	South Carolina	60
24	South Dakota	57
21	Tennessee**	58
6	Texas**	67
11	Utah	62
47	Vermont	44
24	Virginia**	57
48	Washington**	43
44	West Virginia	48
37	Wisconsin	52
9	Wyoming	64

<u>RANK ORDER</u>

RANK	STATE	PERCENT OF DAYS SUNNY
1	Arizona	81
2	New Mexico	76
3	Hawaii	74
4	California**	72
5	Nevada	69
6	Colorado	67
6	Texas**	67
8	Florida**	65
9	Oklahoma	64
9	Wyoming	64
11	Kansas	62
11	Utah	62
13	Alabama	60
13	Arkansas	60
13	Louisiana	60
13	South Carolina	60
17	Georgia	59
17	Mississippi	59
17	Nebraska	59
17	North Carolina**	59
21	Idaho	58
21	Maryland	58
21	Tennessee**	58
24	Missouri**	57
24	South Dakota	57
24	Virginia**	57
27	New Jersey	56
28	Delaware	55
28	Iowa	55
28	Maine	55
28	Massachusetts	55
28	New Hampshire	55
28	North Dakota	55
28	Rhode Island	55
35	Illinois**	53
35	Kentucky	53
37	Connecticut	52
37	Minnesota**	52
37	New York**	52
37	Wisconsin	52
41	Indiana	51
41	Montana	51
43	Pennsylvania**	50
44	West Virginia	48
45	Ohio**	47
46	Michigan**	46
47	Vermont	44
48	Washington**	43
49	Oregon	39
50	Alaska	23
	District of Columbia	55

*Source: U.S. Department of Commerce, National Oceanic and Atmospheric Administration
"Comparative Climatic Data" (annual)*

Averages over various years.
**Percentages from multiple reporting cities within one state were averaged to determine a state's average
percentage of sunny days.*

Average Wind Speed (M.P.H.)*

<table>
<tr><td colspan="3"><u>ALPHA ORDER</u></td><td colspan="3"><u>RANK ORDER</u></td></tr>
<tr><td>RANK</td><td>STATE</td><td>MILES PER HOUR</td><td>RANK</td><td>STATE</td><td>MILES PER HOUR</td></tr>
<tr><td>30</td><td>Alabama</td><td>8.8</td><td>1</td><td>Wyoming</td><td>12.9</td></tr>
<tr><td>39</td><td>Alaska</td><td>8.2</td><td>2</td><td>Montana</td><td>12.6</td></tr>
<tr><td>49</td><td>Arizona</td><td>6.2</td><td>3</td><td>Massachusetts</td><td>12.4</td></tr>
<tr><td>43</td><td>Arkansas</td><td>7.8</td><td>4</td><td>Oklahoma</td><td>12.3</td></tr>
<tr><td>39</td><td>California**</td><td>8.2</td><td>5</td><td>Kansas</td><td>12.2</td></tr>
<tr><td>34</td><td>Colorado</td><td>8.6</td><td>6</td><td>Wisconsin</td><td>11.5</td></tr>
<tr><td>36</td><td>Connecticut</td><td>8.4</td><td>7</td><td>Hawaii</td><td>11.3</td></tr>
<tr><td>25</td><td>Delaware</td><td>9.0</td><td>8</td><td>South Dakota</td><td>11.0</td></tr>
<tr><td>34</td><td>Florida**</td><td>8.6</td><td>9</td><td>Minnesota**</td><td>10.8</td></tr>
<tr><td>22</td><td>Georgia</td><td>9.1</td><td>10</td><td>Iowa</td><td>10.7</td></tr>
<tr><td>7</td><td>Hawaii</td><td>11.3</td><td>11</td><td>Nebraska</td><td>10.5</td></tr>
<tr><td>32</td><td>Idaho</td><td>8.7</td><td>12</td><td>Rhode Island</td><td>10.4</td></tr>
<tr><td>13</td><td>Illinois**</td><td>10.2</td><td>13</td><td>Illinois**</td><td>10.2</td></tr>
<tr><td>19</td><td>Indiana</td><td>9.6</td><td>13</td><td>Missouri**</td><td>10.2</td></tr>
<tr><td>10</td><td>Iowa</td><td>10.7</td><td>13</td><td>North Dakota</td><td>10.2</td></tr>
<tr><td>5</td><td>Kansas</td><td>12.2</td><td>16</td><td>New York**</td><td>10.0</td></tr>
<tr><td>38</td><td>Kentucky</td><td>8.3</td><td>17</td><td>Michigan**</td><td>9.8</td></tr>
<tr><td>39</td><td>Louisiana</td><td>8.2</td><td>17</td><td>New Jersey</td><td>9.8</td></tr>
<tr><td>32</td><td>Maine</td><td>8.7</td><td>19</td><td>Indiana</td><td>9.6</td></tr>
<tr><td>27</td><td>Maryland</td><td>8.9</td><td>20</td><td>Ohio**</td><td>9.3</td></tr>
<tr><td>3</td><td>Massachusetts</td><td>12.4</td><td>20</td><td>Pennsylvania**</td><td>9.3</td></tr>
<tr><td>17</td><td>Michigan**</td><td>9.8</td><td>22</td><td>Georgia</td><td>9.1</td></tr>
<tr><td>9</td><td>Minnesota**</td><td>10.8</td><td>22</td><td>Texas**</td><td>9.1</td></tr>
<tr><td>45</td><td>Mississippi</td><td>7.0</td><td>22</td><td>Virginia**</td><td>9.1</td></tr>
<tr><td>13</td><td>Missouri**</td><td>10.2</td><td>25</td><td>Delaware</td><td>9.0</td></tr>
<tr><td>2</td><td>Montana</td><td>12.6</td><td>25</td><td>Vermont</td><td>9.0</td></tr>
<tr><td>11</td><td>Nebraska</td><td>10.5</td><td>27</td><td>Maryland</td><td>8.9</td></tr>
<tr><td>48</td><td>Nevada</td><td>6.6</td><td>27</td><td>New Mexico</td><td>8.9</td></tr>
<tr><td>47</td><td>New Hampshire</td><td>6.7</td><td>27</td><td>Washington**</td><td>8.9</td></tr>
<tr><td>17</td><td>New Jersey</td><td>9.8</td><td>30</td><td>Alabama</td><td>8.8</td></tr>
<tr><td>27</td><td>New Mexico</td><td>8.9</td><td>30</td><td>Utah</td><td>8.8</td></tr>
<tr><td>16</td><td>New York**</td><td>10.0</td><td>32</td><td>Idaho</td><td>8.7</td></tr>
<tr><td>44</td><td>North Carolina**</td><td>7.5</td><td>32</td><td>Maine</td><td>8.7</td></tr>
<tr><td>13</td><td>North Dakota</td><td>10.2</td><td>34</td><td>Colorado</td><td>8.6</td></tr>
<tr><td>20</td><td>Ohio**</td><td>9.3</td><td>34</td><td>Florida**</td><td>8.6</td></tr>
<tr><td>4</td><td>Oklahoma</td><td>12.3</td><td>36</td><td>Connecticut</td><td>8.4</td></tr>
<tr><td>42</td><td>Oregon</td><td>7.9</td><td>36</td><td>Tennessee**</td><td>8.4</td></tr>
<tr><td>20</td><td>Pennsylvania**</td><td>9.3</td><td>38</td><td>Kentucky</td><td>8.3</td></tr>
<tr><td>12</td><td>Rhode Island</td><td>10.4</td><td>39</td><td>Alaska</td><td>8.2</td></tr>
<tr><td>46</td><td>South Carolina</td><td>6.8</td><td>39</td><td>California**</td><td>8.2</td></tr>
<tr><td>8</td><td>South Dakota</td><td>11.0</td><td>39</td><td>Louisiana</td><td>8.2</td></tr>
<tr><td>36</td><td>Tennessee**</td><td>8.4</td><td>42</td><td>Oregon</td><td>7.9</td></tr>
<tr><td>22</td><td>Texas**</td><td>9.1</td><td>43</td><td>Arkansas</td><td>7.8</td></tr>
<tr><td>30</td><td>Utah</td><td>8.8</td><td>44</td><td>North Carolina**</td><td>7.5</td></tr>
<tr><td>25</td><td>Vermont</td><td>9.0</td><td>45</td><td>Mississippi</td><td>7.0</td></tr>
<tr><td>22</td><td>Virginia**</td><td>9.1</td><td>46</td><td>South Carolina</td><td>6.8</td></tr>
<tr><td>27</td><td>Washington**</td><td>8.9</td><td>47</td><td>New Hampshire</td><td>6.7</td></tr>
<tr><td>50</td><td>West Virginia</td><td>5.9</td><td>48</td><td>Nevada</td><td>6.6</td></tr>
<tr><td>6</td><td>Wisconsin</td><td>11.5</td><td>49</td><td>Arizona</td><td>6.2</td></tr>
<tr><td>1</td><td>Wyoming</td><td>12.9</td><td>50</td><td>West Virginia</td><td>5.9</td></tr>
<tr><td></td><td></td><td></td><td></td><td>District of Columbia</td><td>9.4</td></tr>
</table>

Source: U.S. Department of Commerce, National Oceanic and Atmospheric Administration "Comparative Climatic Data" (annual)

**Averages over various years.*

***Wind speeds from multiple reporting cities within one state were averaged to determine a state's average wind speed.*

Tornadoes in 2002

National Total = 941 Tornadoes*

<u>ALPHA ORDER</u>

RANK	STATE	TORNADOES	% of USA
5	Alabama	35	3.7%
42	Alaska	0	0.0%
42	Arizona	0	0.0%
9	Arkansas	33	3.5%
32	California	6	0.6%
16	Colorado	25	2.7%
33	Connecticut	4	0.4%
42	Delaware	0	0.0%
3	Florida	43	4.6%
17	Georgia	23	2.4%
38	Hawaii	1	0.1%
42	Idaho	0	0.0%
4	Illinois	37	3.9%
20	Indiana	16	1.7%
6	Iowa	34	3.6%
2	Kansas	96	10.2%
22	Kentucky	14	1.5%
6	Louisiana	34	3.6%
35	Maine	3	0.3%
22	Maryland	14	1.5%
38	Massachusetts	1	0.1%
27	Michigan	11	1.2%
6	Minnesota	34	3.6%
11	Mississippi	30	3.2%
12	Missouri	28	3.0%
27	Montana	11	1.2%
13	Nebraska	27	2.9%
38	Nevada	1	0.1%
42	New Hampshire	0	0.0%
42	New Jersey	0	0.0%
42	New Mexico	0	0.0%
22	New York	14	1.5%
27	North Carolina	11	1.2%
18	North Dakota	17	1.8%
15	Ohio	26	2.8%
18	Oklahoma	17	1.8%
36	Oregon	2	0.2%
21	Pennsylvania	15	1.6%
42	Rhode Island	0	0.0%
25	South Carolina	12	1.3%
25	South Dakota	12	1.3%
10	Tennessee	31	3.3%
1	Texas	174	18.5%
33	Utah	4	0.4%
36	Vermont	2	0.2%
31	Virginia	7	0.7%
42	Washington	0	0.0%
38	West Virginia	1	0.1%
13	Wisconsin	27	2.9%
30	Wyoming	8	0.9%

<u>RANK ORDER</u>

RANK	STATE	TORNADOES	% of USA
1	Texas	174	18.5%
2	Kansas	96	10.2%
3	Florida	43	4.6%
4	Illinois	37	3.9%
5	Alabama	35	3.7%
6	Iowa	34	3.6%
6	Louisiana	34	3.6%
6	Minnesota	34	3.6%
9	Arkansas	33	3.5%
10	Tennessee	31	3.3%
11	Mississippi	30	3.2%
12	Missouri	28	3.0%
13	Nebraska	27	2.9%
13	Wisconsin	27	2.9%
15	Ohio	26	2.8%
16	Colorado	25	2.7%
17	Georgia	23	2.4%
18	North Dakota	17	1.8%
18	Oklahoma	17	1.8%
20	Indiana	16	1.7%
21	Pennsylvania	15	1.6%
22	Kentucky	14	1.5%
22	Maryland	14	1.5%
22	New York	14	1.5%
25	South Carolina	12	1.3%
25	South Dakota	12	1.3%
27	Michigan	11	1.2%
27	Montana	11	1.2%
27	North Carolina	11	1.2%
30	Wyoming	8	0.9%
31	Virginia	7	0.7%
32	California	6	0.6%
33	Connecticut	4	0.4%
33	Utah	4	0.4%
35	Maine	3	0.3%
36	Oregon	2	0.2%
36	Vermont	2	0.2%
38	Hawaii	1	0.1%
38	Massachusetts	1	0.1%
38	Nevada	1	0.1%
38	West Virginia	1	0.1%
42	Alaska	0	0.0%
42	Arizona	0	0.0%
42	Delaware	0	0.0%
42	Idaho	0	0.0%
42	New Hampshire	0	0.0%
42	New Jersey	0	0.0%
42	New Mexico	0	0.0%
42	Rhode Island	0	0.0%
42	Washington	0	0.0%
	District of Columbia	0	0.0%

Source: National Weather Service, Storm Prediction Center
 unpublished data

*Preliminary data.

Hazardous Weather Fatalities in 2002

National Total = 481 Fatalities*

ALPHA ORDER

RANK	STATE	FATALITIES	% of USA
9	Alabama	21	4.4%
17	Alaska	7	1.5%
38	Arizona	1	0.2%
22	Arkansas	6	1.2%
6	California	25	5.2%
17	Colorado	7	1.5%
23	Connecticut	5	1.0%
38	Delaware	1	0.2%
5	Florida	30	6.2%
28	Georgia	3	0.6%
30	Hawaii	2	0.4%
14	Idaho	8	1.7%
2	Illinois	52	10.8%
44	Indiana	0	0.0%
44	Iowa	0	0.0%
30	Kansas	2	0.4%
30	Kentucky	2	0.4%
14	Louisiana	8	1.7%
30	Maine	2	0.4%
1	Maryland	54	11.2%
44	Massachusetts	0	0.0%
17	Michigan	7	1.5%
38	Minnesota	1	0.2%
17	Mississippi	7	1.5%
4	Missouri	31	6.4%
30	Montana	2	0.4%
26	Nebraska	4	0.8%
17	Nevada	7	1.5%
44	New Hampshire	0	0.0%
13	New Jersey	9	1.9%
44	New Mexico	0	0.0%
11	New York	14	2.9%
14	North Carolina	8	1.7%
44	North Dakota	0	0.0%
12	Ohio	11	2.3%
38	Oklahoma	1	0.2%
30	Oregon	2	0.4%
3	Pennsylvania	49	10.2%
44	Rhode Island	0	0.0%
23	South Carolina	5	1.0%
30	South Dakota	2	0.4%
6	Tennessee	25	5.2%
8	Texas	24	5.0%
30	Utah	2	0.4%
38	Vermont	1	0.2%
26	Virginia	4	0.8%
23	Washington	5	1.0%
28	West Virginia	3	0.6%
10	Wisconsin	16	3.3%
38	Wyoming	1	0.2%

RANK ORDER

RANK	STATE	FATALITIES	% of USA
1	Maryland	54	11.2%
2	Illinois	52	10.8%
3	Pennsylvania	49	10.2%
4	Missouri	31	6.4%
5	Florida	30	6.2%
6	California	25	5.2%
6	Tennessee	25	5.2%
8	Texas	24	5.0%
9	Alabama	21	4.4%
10	Wisconsin	16	3.3%
11	New York	14	2.9%
12	Ohio	11	2.3%
13	New Jersey	9	1.9%
14	Idaho	8	1.7%
14	Louisiana	8	1.7%
14	North Carolina	8	1.7%
17	Alaska	7	1.5%
17	Colorado	7	1.5%
17	Michigan	7	1.5%
17	Mississippi	7	1.5%
17	Nevada	7	1.5%
22	Arkansas	6	1.2%
23	Connecticut	5	1.0%
23	South Carolina	5	1.0%
23	Washington	5	1.0%
26	Nebraska	4	0.8%
26	Virginia	4	0.8%
28	Georgia	3	0.6%
28	West Virginia	3	0.6%
30	Hawaii	2	0.4%
30	Kansas	2	0.4%
30	Kentucky	2	0.4%
30	Maine	2	0.4%
30	Montana	2	0.4%
30	Oregon	2	0.4%
30	South Dakota	2	0.4%
30	Utah	2	0.4%
38	Arizona	1	0.2%
38	Delaware	1	0.2%
38	Minnesota	1	0.2%
38	Oklahoma	1	0.2%
38	Vermont	1	0.2%
38	Wyoming	1	0.2%
44	Indiana	0	0.0%
44	Iowa	0	0.0%
44	Massachusetts	0	0.0%
44	New Hampshire	0	0.0%
44	New Mexico	0	0.0%
44	North Dakota	0	0.0%
44	Rhode Island	0	0.0%
	District of Columbia	4	0.8%

Source: National Weather Service, Water and Weather Services
"2002 Summary of Hazardous Weather Fatalities" (http://www.nws.noaa.gov/om/severe_weather/state02.pdf)
*Includes lightning, tornado, thunderstorm, extreme temperature, flood, coastal storm, rip current, hurricane, winter storm, fog, avalanche and other weather events.

Cost of Damage from Hazardous Weather in 2002

National Total = $5,181,600,000*

<u>ALPHA ORDER</u>

RANK	STATE	DAMAGE	% of USA
26	Alabama	$36,800,000	0.7%
30	Alaska	32,500,000	0.6%
22	Arizona	73,700,000	1.4%
33	Arkansas	20,400,000	0.4%
10	California	188,800,000	3.6%
21	Colorado	92,800,000	1.8%
44	Connecticut	2,900,000	0.1%
49	Delaware	500,000	0.0%
25	Florida	43,000,000	0.8%
23	Georgia	59,100,000	1.1%
43	Hawaii	3,000,000	0.1%
41	Idaho	4,700,000	0.1%
19	Illinois	96,000,000	1.9%
9	Indiana	194,700,000	3.8%
14	Iowa	117,400,000	2.3%
7	Kansas	200,100,000	3.9%
11	Kentucky	177,300,000	3.4%
1	Louisiana	832,000,000	16.1%
48	Maine	800,000	0.0%
12	Maryland	129,600,000	2.5%
42	Massachusetts	4,100,000	0.1%
31	Michigan	32,400,000	0.6%
5	Minnesota	278,300,000	5.4%
13	Mississippi	118,300,000	2.3%
15	Missouri	115,400,000	2.2%
40	Montana	7,100,000	0.1%
2	Nebraska	633,400,000	12.2%
37	Nevada	9,000,000	0.2%
47	New Hampshire	900,000	0.0%
36	New Jersey	11,600,000	0.2%
39	New Mexico	7,900,000	0.2%
27	New York	36,700,000	0.7%
6	North Carolina	211,700,000	4.1%
45	North Dakota	2,200,000	0.0%
8	Ohio	199,200,000	3.8%
4	Oklahoma	308,500,000	6.0%
35	Oregon	13,300,000	0.3%
28	Pennsylvania	34,700,000	0.7%
50	Rhode Island	200,000	0.0%
17	South Carolina	102,700,000	2.0%
34	South Dakota	14,200,000	0.3%
29	Tennessee	34,500,000	0.7%
3	Texas	310,200,000	6.0%
37	Utah	9,000,000	0.2%
46	Vermont	2,000,000	0.0%
24	Virginia	45,900,000	0.9%
16	Washington	104,800,000	2.0%
20	West Virginia	94,400,000	1.8%
18	Wisconsin	100,900,000	1.9%
32	Wyoming	31,400,000	0.6%

<u>RANK ORDER</u>

RANK	STATE	DAMAGE	% of USA
1	Louisiana	$832,000,000	16.1%
2	Nebraska	633,400,000	12.2%
3	Texas	310,200,000	6.0%
4	Oklahoma	308,500,000	6.0%
5	Minnesota	278,300,000	5.4%
6	North Carolina	211,700,000	4.1%
7	Kansas	200,100,000	3.9%
8	Ohio	199,200,000	3.8%
9	Indiana	194,700,000	3.8%
10	California	188,800,000	3.6%
11	Kentucky	177,300,000	3.4%
12	Maryland	129,600,000	2.5%
13	Mississippi	118,300,000	2.3%
14	Iowa	117,400,000	2.3%
15	Missouri	115,400,000	2.2%
16	Washington	104,800,000	2.0%
17	South Carolina	102,700,000	2.0%
18	Wisconsin	100,900,000	1.9%
19	Illinois	96,000,000	1.9%
20	West Virginia	94,400,000	1.8%
21	Colorado	92,800,000	1.8%
22	Arizona	73,700,000	1.4%
23	Georgia	59,100,000	1.1%
24	Virginia	45,900,000	0.9%
25	Florida	43,000,000	0.8%
26	Alabama	36,800,000	0.7%
27	New York	36,700,000	0.7%
28	Pennsylvania	34,700,000	0.7%
29	Tennessee	34,500,000	0.7%
30	Alaska	32,500,000	0.6%
31	Michigan	32,400,000	0.6%
32	Wyoming	31,400,000	0.6%
33	Arkansas	20,400,000	0.4%
34	South Dakota	14,200,000	0.3%
35	Oregon	13,300,000	0.3%
36	New Jersey	11,600,000	0.2%
37	Nevada	9,000,000	0.2%
37	Utah	9,000,000	0.2%
39	New Mexico	7,900,000	0.2%
40	Montana	7,100,000	0.1%
41	Idaho	4,700,000	0.1%
42	Massachusetts	4,100,000	0.1%
43	Hawaii	3,000,000	0.1%
44	Connecticut	2,900,000	0.1%
45	North Dakota	2,200,000	0.0%
46	Vermont	2,000,000	0.0%
47	New Hampshire	900,000	0.0%
48	Maine	800,000	0.0%
49	Delaware	500,000	0.0%
50	Rhode Island	200,000	0.0%
	District of Columbia	600,000	0.0%

Source: National Weather Service, Water and Weather Services
"2002 Summary of Hazardous Weather Fatalities" (http://www.nws.noaa.gov/om/severe_weather/state02.pdf)
**Includes lightning, tornado, thunderstorm, extreme temperature, flood, coastal storm, rip current, hurricane, winter storm, fog, avalanche and other weather events.*

Acres Owned by the Federal Government in 2002

National Total = 674,099,756 Acres*

ALPHA ORDER

RANK	STATE	ACRES	% of USA
33	Alabama	1,206,419	0.2%
1	Alaska	247,306,686	36.7%
4	Arizona	36,408,100	5.4%
14	Arkansas	4,019,496	0.6%
3	California	47,075,073	7.0%
11	Colorado	23,172,406	3.4%
49	Connecticut	15,374	0.0%
48	Delaware	29,494	0.0%
13	Florida	4,614,638	0.7%
21	Georgia	2,308,447	0.3%
36	Hawaii	672,806	0.1%
6	Idaho	34,383,354	5.1%
37	Illinois	648,540	0.1%
39	Indiana	534,183	0.1%
43	Iowa	303,806	0.0%
38	Kansas	641,130	0.1%
26	Kentucky	1,671,353	0.2%
27	Louisiana	1,494,315	0.2%
46	Maine	163,106	0.0%
44	Maryland	205,686	0.0%
47	Massachusetts	104,832	0.0%
15	Michigan	3,639,440	0.5%
16	Minnesota	3,545,687	0.5%
24	Mississippi	1,981,420	0.3%
22	Missouri	2,240,326	0.3%
9	Montana	29,238,455	4.3%
28	Nebraska	1,459,511	0.2%
2	Nevada	64,455,657	9.6%
34	New Hampshire	830,900	0.1%
45	New Jersey	181,685	0.0%
10	New Mexico	26,518,226	3.9%
42	New York	319,933	0.0%
17	North Carolina	3,497,642	0.5%
29	North Dakota	1,342,704	0.2%
40	Ohio	458,446	0.1%
30	Oklahoma	1,331,302	0.2%
8	Oregon	30,640,290	4.5%
35	Pennsylvania	719,801	0.1%
50	Rhode Island	5,232	0.0%
31	South Carolina	1,234,523	0.2%
20	South Dakota	2,366,754	0.4%
25	Tennessee	1,954,236	0.3%
18	Texas	3,215,460	0.5%
5	Utah	35,025,328	5.2%
41	Vermont	450,170	0.1%
19	Virginia	2,549,105	0.4%
12	Washington	13,156,215	2.0%
32	West Virginia	1,233,549	0.2%
23	Wisconsin	1,986,457	0.3%
7	Wyoming	31,530,863	4.7%

RANK ORDER

RANK	STATE	ACRES	% of USA
1	Alaska	247,306,686	36.7%
2	Nevada	64,455,657	9.6%
3	California	47,075,073	7.0%
4	Arizona	36,408,100	5.4%
5	Utah	35,025,328	5.2%
6	Idaho	34,383,354	5.1%
7	Wyoming	31,530,863	4.7%
8	Oregon	30,640,290	4.5%
9	Montana	29,238,455	4.3%
10	New Mexico	26,518,226	3.9%
11	Colorado	23,172,406	3.4%
12	Washington	13,156,215	2.0%
13	Florida	4,614,638	0.7%
14	Arkansas	4,019,496	0.6%
15	Michigan	3,639,440	0.5%
16	Minnesota	3,545,687	0.5%
17	North Carolina	3,497,642	0.5%
18	Texas	3,215,460	0.5%
19	Virginia	2,549,105	0.4%
20	South Dakota	2,366,754	0.4%
21	Georgia	2,308,447	0.3%
22	Missouri	2,240,326	0.3%
23	Wisconsin	1,986,457	0.3%
24	Mississippi	1,981,420	0.3%
25	Tennessee	1,954,236	0.3%
26	Kentucky	1,671,353	0.2%
27	Louisiana	1,494,315	0.2%
28	Nebraska	1,459,511	0.2%
29	North Dakota	1,342,704	0.2%
30	Oklahoma	1,331,302	0.2%
31	South Carolina	1,234,523	0.2%
32	West Virginia	1,233,549	0.2%
33	Alabama	1,206,419	0.2%
34	New Hampshire	830,900	0.1%
35	Pennsylvania	719,801	0.1%
36	Hawaii	672,806	0.1%
37	Illinois	648,540	0.1%
38	Kansas	641,130	0.1%
39	Indiana	534,183	0.1%
40	Ohio	458,446	0.1%
41	Vermont	450,170	0.1%
42	New York	319,933	0.0%
43	Iowa	303,806	0.0%
44	Maryland	205,686	0.0%
45	New Jersey	181,685	0.0%
46	Maine	163,106	0.0%
47	Massachusetts	104,832	0.0%
48	Delaware	29,494	0.0%
49	Connecticut	15,374	0.0%
50	Rhode Island	5,232	0.0%
	District of Columbia	11,200	0.0%

Source: Government Services Administration, Office of Governmentwide Real Property Policy
"Federal Real Property Profile"

*As of September 30, 2002. Does not include land owned by the federal government in U.S. territories or in foreign countries.

Percent of Land Owned by the Federal Government in 2002

National Percent = 29.7%*

ALPHA ORDER

RANK	STATE	PERCENT
33	Alabama	3.7
2	Alaska	67.7
6	Arizona	50.1
16	Arkansas	12.0
8	California	47.0
9	Colorado	34.9
50	Connecticut	0.5
39	Delaware	2.3
15	Florida	13.3
27	Georgia	6.2
13	Hawaii	16.4
4	Idaho	65.0
43	Illinois	1.8
39	Indiana	2.3
47	Iowa	0.8
45	Kansas	1.2
24	Kentucky	6.6
29	Louisiana	5.2
47	Maine	0.8
34	Maryland	3.3
41	Massachusetts	2.1
18	Michigan	10.0
23	Minnesota	6.9
24	Mississippi	6.6
30	Missouri	5.1
11	Montana	31.3
35	Nebraska	3.0
1	Nevada	91.7
14	New Hampshire	14.4
32	New Jersey	3.8
10	New Mexico	34.1
46	New York	1.0
17	North Carolina	11.1
35	North Dakota	3.0
44	Ohio	1.7
35	Oklahoma	3.0
7	Oregon	49.7
38	Pennsylvania	2.5
47	Rhode Island	0.8
26	South Carolina	6.4
31	South Dakota	4.8
22	Tennessee	7.3
42	Texas	1.9
3	Utah	66.5
21	Vermont	7.6
18	Virginia	10.0
12	Washington	30.8
20	West Virginia	8.0
28	Wisconsin	5.7
5	Wyoming	50.6

RANK ORDER

RANK	STATE	PERCENT
1	Nevada	91.7
2	Alaska	67.7
3	Utah	66.5
4	Idaho	65.0
5	Wyoming	50.6
6	Arizona	50.1
7	Oregon	49.7
8	California	47.0
9	Colorado	34.9
10	New Mexico	34.1
11	Montana	31.3
12	Washington	30.8
13	Hawaii	16.4
14	New Hampshire	14.4
15	Florida	13.3
16	Arkansas	12.0
17	North Carolina	11.1
18	Michigan	10.0
18	Virginia	10.0
20	West Virginia	8.0
21	Vermont	7.6
22	Tennessee	7.3
23	Minnesota	6.9
24	Kentucky	6.6
24	Mississippi	6.6
26	South Carolina	6.4
27	Georgia	6.2
28	Wisconsin	5.7
29	Louisiana	5.2
30	Missouri	5.1
31	South Dakota	4.8
32	New Jersey	3.8
33	Alabama	3.7
34	Maryland	3.3
35	Nebraska	3.0
35	North Dakota	3.0
35	Oklahoma	3.0
38	Pennsylvania	2.5
39	Delaware	2.3
39	Indiana	2.3
41	Massachusetts	2.1
42	Texas	1.9
43	Illinois	1.8
44	Ohio	1.7
45	Kansas	1.2
46	New York	1.0
47	Iowa	0.8
47	Maine	0.8
47	Rhode Island	0.8
50	Connecticut	0.5
	District of Columbia	28.7

Source: Government Services Administration, Office of Governmentwide Real Property Policy
    "Federal Real Property Profile"
*As of September 30, 2002. Does not include land owned by the federal government in U.S. territories or in foreign countries.

National Park Service Land in 2002

National Total = 84,467,821 Acres*

<u>ALPHA ORDER</u>

RANK	STATE	ACRES	% of USA
40	Alabama	21,081	0.0%
1	Alaska	54,640,316	64.7%
3	Arizona	2,834,475	3.4%
25	Arkansas	104,966	0.1%
2	California	8,284,221	9.8%
13	Colorado	670,548	0.8%
46	Connecticut	7,782	0.0%
50	Delaware	0	0.0%
4	Florida	2,637,692	3.1%
34	Georgia	62,861	0.1%
20	Hawaii	251,744	0.3%
11	Idaho	766,856	0.9%
48	Illinois	115	0.0%
42	Indiana	15,288	0.0%
47	Iowa	2,713	0.0%
44	Kansas	11,825	0.0%
27	Kentucky	94,997	0.1%
39	Louisiana	21,155	0.0%
29	Maine	89,867	0.1%
33	Maryland	70,968	0.1%
35	Massachusetts	57,841	0.1%
12	Michigan	718,071	0.9%
19	Minnesota	301,333	0.4%
24	Mississippi	117,051	0.1%
30	Missouri	82,852	0.1%
8	Montana	1,273,088	1.5%
43	Nebraska	12,247	0.0%
10	Nevada	778,532	0.9%
41	New Hampshire	15,566	0.0%
26	New Jersey	98,797	0.1%
15	New Mexico	391,029	0.5%
32	New York	72,464	0.1%
14	North Carolina	403,519	0.5%
31	North Dakota	72,581	0.1%
36	Ohio	34,153	0.0%
45	Oklahoma	10,237	0.0%
21	Oregon	197,907	0.2%
23	Pennsylvania	133,427	0.2%
49	Rhode Island	5	0.0%
37	South Carolina	27,895	0.0%
18	South Dakota	318,968	0.4%
16	Tennessee	379,381	0.4%
9	Texas	1,235,953	1.5%
6	Utah	2,117,068	2.5%
38	Vermont	22,166	0.0%
17	Virginia	355,180	0.4%
7	Washington	1,964,362	2.3%
28	West Virginia	89,930	0.1%
22	Wisconsin	133,763	0.2%
5	Wyoming	2,396,341	2.8%

<u>RANK ORDER</u>

RANK	STATE	ACRES	% of USA
1	Alaska	54,640,316	64.7%
2	California	8,284,221	9.8%
3	Arizona	2,834,475	3.4%
4	Florida	2,637,692	3.1%
5	Wyoming	2,396,341	2.8%
6	Utah	2,117,068	2.5%
7	Washington	1,964,362	2.3%
8	Montana	1,273,088	1.5%
9	Texas	1,235,953	1.5%
10	Nevada	778,532	0.9%
11	Idaho	766,856	0.9%
12	Michigan	718,071	0.9%
13	Colorado	670,548	0.8%
14	North Carolina	403,519	0.5%
15	New Mexico	391,029	0.5%
16	Tennessee	379,381	0.4%
17	Virginia	355,180	0.4%
18	South Dakota	318,968	0.4%
19	Minnesota	301,333	0.4%
20	Hawaii	251,744	0.3%
21	Oregon	197,907	0.2%
22	Wisconsin	133,763	0.2%
23	Pennsylvania	133,427	0.2%
24	Mississippi	117,051	0.1%
25	Arkansas	104,966	0.1%
26	New Jersey	98,797	0.1%
27	Kentucky	94,997	0.1%
28	West Virginia	89,930	0.1%
29	Maine	89,867	0.1%
30	Missouri	82,852	0.1%
31	North Dakota	72,581	0.1%
32	New York	72,464	0.1%
33	Maryland	70,968	0.1%
34	Georgia	62,861	0.1%
35	Massachusetts	57,841	0.1%
36	Ohio	34,153	0.0%
37	South Carolina	27,895	0.0%
38	Vermont	22,166	0.0%
39	Louisiana	21,155	0.0%
40	Alabama	21,081	0.0%
41	New Hampshire	15,566	0.0%
42	Indiana	15,288	0.0%
43	Nebraska	12,247	0.0%
44	Kansas	11,825	0.0%
45	Oklahoma	10,237	0.0%
46	Connecticut	7,782	0.0%
47	Iowa	2,713	0.0%
48	Illinois	115	0.0%
49	Rhode Island	5	0.0%
50	Delaware	0	0.0%
	District of Columbia	6,960	0.0%

Source: National Park Service
"Master Deed Listing - State and County Report by State"
As of September 4, 2002. Includes federal and nonfederal land in national parks, monuments, historic sites, recreation areas, preserves, battlefields, grasslands, seashores, parkways, trails and rivers. Does not include land in national forest or wildlife areas. Includes 59,684 acres in U.S. territories.

Recreation Visits to National Park Service Areas in 2002

National Total = 277,299,880 Visits*

ALPHA ORDER

RANK	STATE	VISITS	% of USA
37	Alabama	576,081	0.2%
29	Alaska	2,150,215	0.8%
5	Arizona	10,227,286	3.7%
27	Arkansas	2,433,642	0.9%
1	California	33,769,299	12.2%
18	Colorado	5,157,377	1.9%
49	Connecticut	16,113	0.0%
50	Delaware	0	0.0%
7	Florida	8,925,852	3.2%
13	Georgia	6,271,091	2.3%
20	Hawaii	4,700,740	1.7%
40	Idaho	481,163	0.2%
41	Illinois	390,076	0.1%
28	Indiana	2,245,373	0.8%
43	Iowa	266,873	0.1%
45	Kansas	126,408	0.0%
24	Kentucky	3,407,104	1.2%
36	Louisiana	757,148	0.3%
26	Maine	2,558,572	0.9%
25	Maryland	3,271,583	1.2%
6	Massachusetts	9,847,828	3.6%
33	Michigan	1,619,565	0.6%
38	Minnesota	531,542	0.2%
12	Mississippi	6,950,837	2.5%
17	Missouri	5,256,509	1.9%
21	Montana	4,020,282	1.4%
44	Nebraska	180,752	0.1%
16	Nevada	5,748,490	2.1%
47	New Hampshire	34,239	0.0%
14	New Jersey	5,861,776	2.1%
32	New Mexico	1,818,551	0.7%
4	New York	15,719,928	5.7%
3	North Carolina	22,594,035	8.1%
39	North Dakota	524,469	0.2%
23	Ohio	3,523,384	1.3%
30	Oklahoma	1,954,370	0.7%
35	Oregon	887,439	0.3%
8	Pennsylvania	8,298,179	3.0%
46	Rhode Island	58,243	0.0%
34	South Carolina	1,562,178	0.6%
22	South Dakota	4,012,981	1.4%
10	Tennessee	7,987,931	2.9%
19	Texas	5,007,121	1.8%
9	Utah	8,189,745	3.0%
48	Vermont	31,940	0.0%
2	Virginia	25,006,802	9.0%
11	Washington	7,665,032	2.8%
31	West Virginia	1,938,035	0.7%
42	Wisconsin	309,204	0.1%
15	Wyoming	5,765,463	2.1%

RANK ORDER

RANK	STATE	VISITS	% of USA
1	California	33,769,299	12.2%
2	Virginia	25,006,802	9.0%
3	North Carolina	22,594,035	8.1%
4	New York	15,719,928	5.7%
5	Arizona	10,227,286	3.7%
6	Massachusetts	9,847,828	3.6%
7	Florida	8,925,852	3.2%
8	Pennsylvania	8,298,179	3.0%
9	Utah	8,189,745	3.0%
10	Tennessee	7,987,931	2.9%
11	Washington	7,665,032	2.8%
12	Mississippi	6,950,837	2.5%
13	Georgia	6,271,091	2.3%
14	New Jersey	5,861,776	2.1%
15	Wyoming	5,765,463	2.1%
16	Nevada	5,748,490	2.1%
17	Missouri	5,256,509	1.9%
18	Colorado	5,157,377	1.9%
19	Texas	5,007,121	1.8%
20	Hawaii	4,700,740	1.7%
21	Montana	4,020,282	1.4%
22	South Dakota	4,012,981	1.4%
23	Ohio	3,523,384	1.3%
24	Kentucky	3,407,104	1.2%
25	Maryland	3,271,583	1.2%
26	Maine	2,558,572	0.9%
27	Arkansas	2,433,642	0.9%
28	Indiana	2,245,373	0.8%
29	Alaska	2,150,215	0.8%
30	Oklahoma	1,954,370	0.7%
31	West Virginia	1,938,035	0.7%
32	New Mexico	1,818,551	0.7%
33	Michigan	1,619,565	0.6%
34	South Carolina	1,562,178	0.6%
35	Oregon	887,439	0.3%
36	Louisiana	757,148	0.3%
37	Alabama	576,081	0.2%
38	Minnesota	531,542	0.2%
39	North Dakota	524,469	0.2%
40	Idaho	481,163	0.2%
41	Illinois	390,076	0.1%
42	Wisconsin	309,204	0.1%
43	Iowa	266,873	0.1%
44	Nebraska	180,752	0.1%
45	Kansas	126,408	0.0%
46	Rhode Island	58,243	0.0%
47	New Hampshire	34,239	0.0%
48	Vermont	31,940	0.0%
49	Connecticut	16,113	0.0%
50	Delaware	0	0.0%
	District of Columbia	24,373,893	8.8%

Source: National Park Service, Public Use Statistics Office
"National Park Service Statistical Abstract 2002" (http://www2.nature.nps.gov/stats/abst2002.pdf)
National total includes 2,287,142 visits in U.S. territories.

State Parks, Recreation Areas and Natural Areas in 2002

National Total = 5,616 Areas*

ALPHA ORDER

RANK	STATE	AREAS	% of USA
48	Alabama	24	0.4%
10	Alaska	139	2.5%
44	Arizona	30	0.5%
33	Arkansas	50	0.9%
4	California	266	4.7%
18	Colorado	115	2.0%
12	Connecticut	130	2.3%
46	Delaware	29	0.5%
9	Florida	150	2.7%
27	Georgia	68	1.2%
26	Hawaii	69	1.2%
42	Idaho	31	0.6%
3	Illinois	313	5.6%
41	Indiana	33	0.6%
8	Iowa	174	3.1%
48	Kansas	24	0.4%
36	Kentucky	49	0.9%
30	Louisiana	57	1.0%
13	Maine	126	2.2%
33	Maryland	50	0.9%
6	Massachusetts	236	4.2%
19	Michigan	99	1.8%
11	Minnesota	133	2.4%
47	Mississippi	28	0.5%
22	Missouri	82	1.5%
2	Montana	374	6.7%
21	Nebraska	85	1.5%
48	Nevada	24	0.4%
22	New Hampshire	82	1.5%
16	New Jersey	116	2.1%
42	New Mexico	31	0.6%
1	New York	824	14.7%
29	North Carolina	59	1.1%
44	North Dakota	30	0.5%
25	Ohio	73	1.3%
33	Oklahoma	50	0.9%
7	Oregon	230	4.1%
15	Pennsylvania	118	2.1%
24	Rhode Island	74	1.3%
31	South Carolina	55	1.0%
16	South Dakota	116	2.1%
32	Tennessee	54	1.0%
14	Texas	123	2.2%
37	Utah	48	0.9%
20	Vermont	98	1.7%
39	Virginia	37	0.7%
5	Washington	260	4.6%
38	West Virginia	47	0.8%
28	Wisconsin	67	1.2%
40	Wyoming	36	0.6%

RANK ORDER

RANK	STATE	AREAS	% of USA
1	New York	824	14.7%
2	Montana	374	6.7%
3	Illinois	313	5.6%
4	California	266	4.7%
5	Washington	260	4.6%
6	Massachusetts	236	4.2%
7	Oregon	230	4.1%
8	Iowa	174	3.1%
9	Florida	150	2.7%
10	Alaska	139	2.5%
11	Minnesota	133	2.4%
12	Connecticut	130	2.3%
13	Maine	126	2.2%
14	Texas	123	2.2%
15	Pennsylvania	118	2.1%
16	New Jersey	116	2.1%
16	South Dakota	116	2.1%
18	Colorado	115	2.0%
19	Michigan	99	1.8%
20	Vermont	98	1.7%
21	Nebraska	85	1.5%
22	Missouri	82	1.5%
22	New Hampshire	82	1.5%
24	Rhode Island	74	1.3%
25	Ohio	73	1.3%
26	Hawaii	69	1.2%
27	Georgia	68	1.2%
28	Wisconsin	67	1.2%
29	North Carolina	59	1.1%
30	Louisiana	57	1.0%
31	South Carolina	55	1.0%
32	Tennessee	54	1.0%
33	Arkansas	50	0.9%
33	Maryland	50	0.9%
33	Oklahoma	50	0.9%
36	Kentucky	49	0.9%
37	Utah	48	0.9%
38	West Virginia	47	0.8%
39	Virginia	37	0.7%
40	Wyoming	36	0.6%
41	Indiana	33	0.6%
42	Idaho	31	0.6%
42	New Mexico	31	0.6%
44	Arizona	30	0.5%
44	North Dakota	30	0.5%
46	Delaware	29	0.5%
47	Mississippi	28	0.5%
48	Alabama	24	0.4%
48	Kansas	24	0.4%
48	Nevada	24	0.4%
	District of Columbia**	NA	NA

Source: The National Association of State Parks Directors "State Park Statistics" (http://www.naspd.org/)

*Includes state parks, recreation areas, natural areas and other areas.
**Not available.

Visitors to State Parks and Recreation Areas in 2002

National Total = 766,021,272 Visitors*

ALPHA ORDER

RANK	STATE	VISITORS	% of USA
37	Alabama	5,456,060	0.7%
40	Alaska	3,661,831	0.5%
43	Arizona	2,515,651	0.3%
29	Arkansas	7,746,050	1.0%
1	California	80,305,625	10.5%
22	Colorado	10,528,250	1.4%
32	Connecticut	7,453,271	1.0%
42	Delaware	3,188,598	0.4%
11	Florida	18,133,491	2.4%
16	Georgia	15,347,739	2.0%
10	Hawaii	18,665,000	2.4%
44	Idaho	2,430,421	0.3%
5	Illinois	44,063,867	5.8%
13	Indiana	17,594,591	2.3%
17	Iowa	15,202,782	2.0%
31	Kansas	7,485,290	1.0%
28	Kentucky	7,831,129	1.0%
47	Louisiana	1,970,404	0.3%
46	Maine	2,280,885	0.3%
24	Maryland	9,838,073	1.3%
20	Massachusetts	12,282,378	1.6%
9	Michigan	25,499,496	3.3%
26	Minnesota	8,342,902	1.1%
38	Mississippi	4,236,392	0.6%
12	Missouri	17,891,769	2.3%
48	Montana	1,339,692	0.2%
23	Nebraska	9,898,403	1.3%
41	Nevada	3,424,684	0.4%
33	New Hampshire	6,689,193	0.9%
19	New Jersey	15,063,934	2.0%
39	New Mexico	4,002,939	0.5%
3	New York	55,528,753	7.2%
21	North Carolina	11,994,637	1.6%
49	North Dakota	1,104,203	0.1%
2	Ohio	59,369,211	7.8%
18	Oklahoma	15,124,642	2.0%
6	Oregon	39,758,298	5.2%
7	Pennsylvania	36,435,843	4.8%
34	Rhode Island	6,350,546	0.8%
25	South Carolina	8,763,101	1.1%
30	South Dakota	7,567,859	1.0%
8	Tennessee	28,821,110	3.8%
14	Texas	17,539,656	2.3%
35	Utah	6,295,779	0.8%
50	Vermont	819,963	0.1%
36	Virginia	6,011,233	0.8%
4	Washington	47,774,327	6.2%
27	West Virginia	8,025,967	1.0%
15	Wisconsin	15,993,799	2.1%
45	Wyoming	2,371,555	0.3%

RANK ORDER

RANK	STATE	VISITORS	% of USA
1	California	80,305,625	10.5%
2	Ohio	59,369,211	7.8%
3	New York	55,528,753	7.2%
4	Washington	47,774,327	6.2%
5	Illinois	44,063,867	5.8%
6	Oregon	39,758,298	5.2%
7	Pennsylvania	36,435,843	4.8%
8	Tennessee	28,821,110	3.8%
9	Michigan	25,499,496	3.3%
10	Hawaii	18,665,000	2.4%
11	Florida	18,133,491	2.4%
12	Missouri	17,891,769	2.3%
13	Indiana	17,594,591	2.3%
14	Texas	17,539,656	2.3%
15	Wisconsin	15,993,799	2.1%
16	Georgia	15,347,739	2.0%
17	Iowa	15,202,782	2.0%
18	Oklahoma	15,124,642	2.0%
19	New Jersey	15,063,934	2.0%
20	Massachusetts	12,282,378	1.6%
21	North Carolina	11,994,637	1.6%
22	Colorado	10,528,250	1.4%
23	Nebraska	9,898,403	1.3%
24	Maryland	9,838,073	1.3%
25	South Carolina	8,763,101	1.1%
26	Minnesota	8,342,902	1.1%
27	West Virginia	8,025,967	1.0%
28	Kentucky	7,831,129	1.0%
29	Arkansas	7,746,050	1.0%
30	South Dakota	7,567,859	1.0%
31	Kansas	7,485,290	1.0%
32	Connecticut	7,453,271	1.0%
33	New Hampshire	6,689,193	0.9%
34	Rhode Island	6,350,546	0.8%
35	Utah	6,295,779	0.8%
36	Virginia	6,011,233	0.8%
37	Alabama	5,456,060	0.7%
38	Mississippi	4,236,392	0.6%
39	New Mexico	4,002,939	0.5%
40	Alaska	3,661,831	0.5%
41	Nevada	3,424,684	0.4%
42	Delaware	3,188,598	0.4%
43	Arizona	2,515,651	0.3%
44	Idaho	2,430,421	0.3%
45	Wyoming	2,371,555	0.3%
46	Maine	2,280,885	0.3%
47	Louisiana	1,970,404	0.3%
48	Montana	1,339,692	0.2%
49	North Dakota	1,104,203	0.1%
50	Vermont	819,963	0.1%
	District of Columbia**	NA	NA

Source: The National Association of State Parks Directors
"State Park Statistics" (http://www.naspd.org/)
*Includes state parks, recreation areas and natural areas. Includes day and overnight visitors.
**Not available.

IX. GOVERNMENT FINANCE: FEDERAL

Federal Tax Burden in 2003

National Total = $1,826,604,000,000*

ALPHA ORDER

RANK	STATE	TAX BURDEN	% of USA
24	Alabama	$20,480,000,000	1.1%
47	Alaska	3,870,000,000	0.2%
23	Arizona	28,473,000,000	1.6%
33	Arkansas	11,705,000,000	0.6%
1	California	258,053,000,000	14.1%
19	Colorado	32,305,000,000	1.8%
16	Connecticut	36,126,000,000	2.0%
44	Delaware	5,419,000,000	0.3%
4	Florida	103,526,000,000	5.7%
11	Georgia	49,084,000,000	2.7%
42	Hawaii	6,536,000,000	0.4%
43	Idaho	6,302,000,000	0.3%
5	Illinois	88,378,000,000	4.8%
18	Indiana	33,183,000,000	1.8%
31	Iowa	15,113,000,000	0.8%
30	Kansas	15,127,000,000	0.8%
28	Kentucky	18,998,000,000	1.0%
26	Louisiana	19,764,000,000	1.1%
40	Maine	6,782,000,000	0.4%
15	Maryland	39,554,000,000	2.2%
10	Massachusetts	60,191,000,000	3.3%
9	Michigan	60,967,000,000	3.3%
17	Minnesota	34,372,000,000	1.9%
34	Mississippi	11,147,000,000	0.6%
21	Missouri	31,079,000,000	1.7%
45	Montana	4,160,000,000	0.2%
37	Nebraska	9,635,000,000	0.5%
32	Nevada	14,118,000,000	0.8%
36	New Hampshire	9,972,000,000	0.5%
7	New Jersey	76,020,000,000	4.2%
38	New Mexico	7,229,000,000	0.4%
2	New York	144,645,000,000	7.9%
14	North Carolina	44,065,000,000	2.4%
50	North Dakota	3,061,000,000	0.2%
8	Ohio	62,295,000,000	3.4%
29	Oklahoma	15,744,000,000	0.9%
25	Oregon	19,970,000,000	1.1%
6	Pennsylvania	76,683,000,000	4.2%
41	Rhode Island	6,762,000,000	0.4%
27	South Carolina	19,133,000,000	1.0%
46	South Dakota	3,918,000,000	0.2%
22	Tennessee	30,264,000,000	1.7%
3	Texas	127,200,000,000	7.0%
35	Utah	10,564,000,000	0.6%
48	Vermont	3,565,000,000	0.2%
12	Virginia	48,705,000,000	2.7%
13	Washington	44,674,000,000	2.4%
39	West Virginia	7,218,000,000	0.4%
20	Wisconsin	31,877,000,000	1.7%
49	Wyoming	3,438,000,000	0.2%

RANK ORDER

RANK	STATE	TAX BURDEN	% of USA
1	California	$258,053,000,000	14.1%
2	New York	144,645,000,000	7.9%
3	Texas	127,200,000,000	7.0%
4	Florida	103,526,000,000	5.7%
5	Illinois	88,378,000,000	4.8%
6	Pennsylvania	76,683,000,000	4.2%
7	New Jersey	76,020,000,000	4.2%
8	Ohio	62,295,000,000	3.4%
9	Michigan	60,967,000,000	3.3%
10	Massachusetts	60,191,000,000	3.3%
11	Georgia	49,084,000,000	2.7%
12	Virginia	48,705,000,000	2.7%
13	Washington	44,674,000,000	2.4%
14	North Carolina	44,065,000,000	2.4%
15	Maryland	39,554,000,000	2.2%
16	Connecticut	36,126,000,000	2.0%
17	Minnesota	34,372,000,000	1.9%
18	Indiana	33,183,000,000	1.8%
19	Colorado	32,305,000,000	1.8%
20	Wisconsin	31,877,000,000	1.7%
21	Missouri	31,079,000,000	1.7%
22	Tennessee	30,264,000,000	1.7%
23	Arizona	28,473,000,000	1.6%
24	Alabama	20,480,000,000	1.1%
25	Oregon	19,970,000,000	1.1%
26	Louisiana	19,764,000,000	1.1%
27	South Carolina	19,133,000,000	1.0%
28	Kentucky	18,998,000,000	1.0%
29	Oklahoma	15,744,000,000	0.9%
30	Kansas	15,127,000,000	0.8%
31	Iowa	15,113,000,000	0.8%
32	Nevada	14,118,000,000	0.8%
33	Arkansas	11,705,000,000	0.6%
34	Mississippi	11,147,000,000	0.6%
35	Utah	10,564,000,000	0.6%
36	New Hampshire	9,972,000,000	0.5%
37	Nebraska	9,635,000,000	0.5%
38	New Mexico	7,229,000,000	0.4%
39	West Virginia	7,218,000,000	0.4%
40	Maine	6,782,000,000	0.4%
41	Rhode Island	6,762,000,000	0.4%
42	Hawaii	6,536,000,000	0.4%
43	Idaho	6,302,000,000	0.3%
44	Delaware	5,419,000,000	0.3%
45	Montana	4,160,000,000	0.2%
46	South Dakota	3,918,000,000	0.2%
47	Alaska	3,870,000,000	0.2%
48	Vermont	3,565,000,000	0.2%
49	Wyoming	3,438,000,000	0.2%
50	North Dakota	3,061,000,000	0.2%
	District of Columbia	5,162,000,000	0.3%

Per Capita Federal Tax Burden in 2003

National Per Capita = $6,282*

ALPHA ORDER

RANK	STATE	PER CAPITA
43	Alabama	$4,542
20	Alaska	5,978
37	Arizona	5,111
47	Arkansas	4,285
7	California	7,280
9	Colorado	7,051
1	Connecticut	10,401
13	Delaware	6,642
18	Florida	6,110
24	Georgia	5,646
31	Hawaii	5,231
39	Idaho	4,633
10	Illinois	6,978
30	Indiana	5,357
35	Iowa	5,131
27	Kansas	5,543
40	Kentucky	4,615
46	Louisiana	4,396
33	Maine	5,221
8	Maryland	7,195
2	Massachusetts	9,318
19	Michigan	6,041
12	Minnesota	6,794
50	Mississippi	3,857
28	Missouri	5,447
42	Montana	4,550
26	Nebraska	5,544
15	Nevada	6,309
4	New Hampshire	7,746
3	New Jersey	8,795
49	New Mexico	3,862
5	New York	7,524
32	North Carolina	5,228
38	North Dakota	4,833
29	Ohio	5,442
45	Oklahoma	4,480
25	Oregon	5,610
17	Pennsylvania	6,209
16	Rhode Island	6,293
40	South Carolina	4,615
36	South Dakota	5,128
34	Tennessee	5,171
22	Texas	5,761
44	Utah	4,494
23	Vermont	5,752
14	Virginia	6,619
6	Washington	7,282
48	West Virginia	4,010
21	Wisconsin	5,827
11	Wyoming	6,871

RANK ORDER

RANK	STATE	PER CAPITA
1	Connecticut	$10,401
2	Massachusetts	9,318
3	New Jersey	8,795
4	New Hampshire	7,746
5	New York	7,524
6	Washington	7,282
7	California	7,280
8	Maryland	7,195
9	Colorado	7,051
10	Illinois	6,978
11	Wyoming	6,871
12	Minnesota	6,794
13	Delaware	6,642
14	Virginia	6,619
15	Nevada	6,309
16	Rhode Island	6,293
17	Pennsylvania	6,209
18	Florida	6,110
19	Michigan	6,041
20	Alaska	5,978
21	Wisconsin	5,827
22	Texas	5,761
23	Vermont	5,752
24	Georgia	5,646
25	Oregon	5,610
26	Nebraska	5,544
27	Kansas	5,543
28	Missouri	5,447
29	Ohio	5,442
30	Indiana	5,357
31	Hawaii	5,231
32	North Carolina	5,228
33	Maine	5,221
34	Tennessee	5,171
35	Iowa	5,131
36	South Dakota	5,128
37	Arizona	5,111
38	North Dakota	4,833
39	Idaho	4,633
40	Kentucky	4,615
40	South Carolina	4,615
42	Montana	4,550
43	Alabama	4,542
44	Utah	4,494
45	Oklahoma	4,480
46	Louisiana	4,396
47	Arkansas	4,285
48	West Virginia	4,010
49	New Mexico	3,862
50	Mississippi	3,857
	District of Columbia	9,069

Source: The Tax Foundation
"Federal Tax Burdens and Expenditures by State" (http://www.taxfoundation.org/sr124.pdf)
*This table attempts to allocate federal tax revenue among the states based on who ultimately bears the burden of taxes as opposed to simply the states where taxes are collected.

Percent Change in Per Capita Federal Tax Burden: 2000 to 2003

National Percent Change = 10.8% Decrease*

ALPHA ORDER

RANK	STATE	PERCENT CHANGE
24	Alabama	(10.6)
47	Alaska	(12.3)
48	Arizona	(12.6)
16	Arkansas	(9.7)
26	California	(10.7)
45	Colorado	(12.1)
24	Connecticut	(10.6)
38	Delaware	(11.5)
48	Florida	(12.6)
43	Georgia	(12.0)
45	Hawaii	(12.1)
35	Idaho	(11.2)
35	Illinois	(11.2)
37	Indiana	(11.3)
16	Iowa	(9.7)
18	Kansas	(9.8)
13	Kentucky	(9.5)
7	Louisiana	(8.7)
4	Maine	(8.2)
19	Maryland	(9.9)
2	Massachusetts	(7.8)
38	Michigan	(11.5)
13	Minnesota	(9.5)
10	Mississippi	(9.2)
29	Missouri	(10.8)
40	Montana	(11.6)
10	Nebraska	(9.2)
50	Nevada	(16.1)
19	New Hampshire	(9.9)
22	New Jersey	(10.4)
22	New Mexico	(10.4)
29	New York	(10.8)
42	North Carolina	(11.8)
1	North Dakota	(7.1)
32	Ohio	(11.0)
10	Oklahoma	(9.2)
33	Oregon	(11.1)
9	Pennsylvania	(9.0)
8	Rhode Island	(8.9)
26	South Carolina	(10.7)
13	South Dakota	(9.5)
26	Tennessee	(10.7)
43	Texas	(12.0)
33	Utah	(11.1)
6	Vermont	(8.6)
29	Virginia	(10.8)
40	Washington	(11.6)
4	West Virginia	(8.2)
21	Wisconsin	(10.2)
3	Wyoming	(7.9)

RANK ORDER

RANK	STATE	PERCENT CHANGE
1	North Dakota	(7.1)
2	Massachusetts	(7.8)
3	Wyoming	(7.9)
4	Maine	(8.2)
4	West Virginia	(8.2)
6	Vermont	(8.6)
7	Louisiana	(8.7)
8	Rhode Island	(8.9)
9	Pennsylvania	(9.0)
10	Mississippi	(9.2)
10	Nebraska	(9.2)
10	Oklahoma	(9.2)
13	Kentucky	(9.5)
13	Minnesota	(9.5)
13	South Dakota	(9.5)
16	Arkansas	(9.7)
16	Iowa	(9.7)
18	Kansas	(9.8)
19	Maryland	(9.9)
19	New Hampshire	(9.9)
21	Wisconsin	(10.2)
22	New Jersey	(10.4)
22	New Mexico	(10.4)
24	Alabama	(10.6)
24	Connecticut	(10.6)
26	California	(10.7)
26	South Carolina	(10.7)
26	Tennessee	(10.7)
29	Missouri	(10.8)
29	New York	(10.8)
29	Virginia	(10.8)
32	Ohio	(11.0)
33	Oregon	(11.1)
33	Utah	(11.1)
35	Idaho	(11.2)
35	Illinois	(11.2)
37	Indiana	(11.3)
38	Delaware	(11.5)
38	Michigan	(11.5)
40	Montana	(11.6)
40	Washington	(11.6)
42	North Carolina	(11.8)
43	Georgia	(12.0)
43	Texas	(12.0)
45	Colorado	(12.1)
45	Hawaii	(12.1)
47	Alaska	(12.3)
48	Arizona	(12.6)
48	Florida	(12.6)
50	Nevada	(16.1)

	District of Columbia	(9.0)

Source: Morgan Quitno Press using data from The Tax Foundation
   "Federal Tax Burdens and Expenditures by State" (http://www.taxfoundation.org/sr124.pdf)
*Percent change calculations based on current dollars not adjusted for inflation.

Federal Expenditures per Dollar of Federal Taxes: 2002

National Median = $1.13 Received for Each Dollar Sent*

<u>ALPHA ORDER</u>

RANK	STATE	PER DOLLAR
7	Alabama	$1.64
3	Alaska	1.91
22	Arizona	1.21
10	Arkansas	1.55
45	California	0.76
42	Colorado	0.78
49	Connecticut	0.65
40	Delaware	0.85
32	Florida	1.01
32	Georgia	1.01
9	Hawaii	1.57
18	Idaho	1.31
43	Illinois	0.77
34	Indiana	1.00
20	Iowa	1.23
25	Kansas	1.13
12	Kentucky	1.50
14	Louisiana	1.48
15	Maine	1.34
21	Maryland	1.22
46	Massachusetts	0.75
37	Michigan	0.88
43	Minnesota	0.77
4	Mississippi	1.89
15	Missouri	1.34
6	Montana	1.67
23	Nebraska	1.19
47	Nevada	0.74
48	New Hampshire	0.66
50	New Jersey	0.62
1	New Mexico	2.37
40	New York	0.85
29	North Carolina	1.07
2	North Dakota	2.07
31	Ohio	1.03
11	Oklahoma	1.52
35	Oregon	0.98
27	Pennsylvania	1.09
28	Rhode Island	1.08
15	South Carolina	1.34
8	South Dakota	1.61
19	Tennessee	1.26
36	Texas	0.92
24	Utah	1.14
25	Vermont	1.13
12	Virginia	1.50
39	Washington	0.87
5	West Virginia	1.82
37	Wisconsin	0.88
30	Wyoming	1.06

<u>RANK ORDER</u>

RANK	STATE	PER DOLLAR
1	New Mexico	$2.37
2	North Dakota	2.07
3	Alaska	1.91
4	Mississippi	1.89
5	West Virginia	1.82
6	Montana	1.67
7	Alabama	1.64
8	South Dakota	1.61
9	Hawaii	1.57
10	Arkansas	1.55
11	Oklahoma	1.52
12	Kentucky	1.50
12	Virginia	1.50
14	Louisiana	1.48
15	Maine	1.34
15	Missouri	1.34
15	South Carolina	1.34
18	Idaho	1.31
19	Tennessee	1.26
20	Iowa	1.23
21	Maryland	1.22
22	Arizona	1.21
23	Nebraska	1.19
24	Utah	1.14
25	Kansas	1.13
25	Vermont	1.13
27	Pennsylvania	1.09
28	Rhode Island	1.08
29	North Carolina	1.07
30	Wyoming	1.06
31	Ohio	1.03
32	Florida	1.01
32	Georgia	1.01
34	Indiana	1.00
35	Oregon	0.98
36	Texas	0.92
37	Michigan	0.88
37	Wisconsin	0.88
39	Washington	0.87
40	Delaware	0.85
40	New York	0.85
42	Colorado	0.78
43	Illinois	0.77
43	Minnesota	0.77
45	California	0.76
46	Massachusetts	0.75
47	Nevada	0.74
48	New Hampshire	0.66
49	Connecticut	0.65
50	New Jersey	0.62
	District of Columbia	6.44

Source: The Tax Foundation
"Federal Tax Burdens and Expenditures by State" (http://www.taxfoundation.org/sr124.pdf)
This table shows how much the federal government spent in each state compared to how much the federal government receives from each state.

Internal Revenue Service Gross Collections in 2002

National Total = $2,016,627,269,000*

<u>ALPHA ORDER</u>

RANK	STATE	COLLECTIONS	% of USA
26	Alabama	$18,650,989,371	0.9%
46	Alaska	3,211,048,300	0.2%
23	Arizona	24,901,726,338	1.2%
25	Arkansas	19,701,605,478	1.0%
1	California	232,301,672,370	11.5%
19	Colorado	36,425,728,559	1.8%
18	Connecticut	39,704,703,727	2.0%
35	Delaware	11,789,203,399	0.6%
5	Florida	94,507,293,792	4.7%
11	Georgia	60,330,806,075	3.0%
42	Hawaii	5,559,959,703	0.3%
41	Idaho	6,894,987,400	0.3%
4	Illinois	111,520,474,945	5.5%
22	Indiana	33,999,215,328	1.7%
32	Iowa	14,570,904,462	0.7%
30	Kansas	16,293,150,929	0.8%
29	Kentucky	17,333,322,804	0.9%
24	Louisiana	22,664,647,541	1.1%
43	Maine	5,302,924,590	0.3%
16	Maryland	41,637,531,279	2.1%
10	Massachusetts	60,389,579,467	3.0%
9	Michigan	66,310,783,861	3.3%
12	Minnesota	58,143,876,558	2.9%
37	Mississippi	9,011,608,013	0.4%
17	Missouri	41,145,978,975	2.0%
47	Montana	3,119,113,776	0.2%
33	Nebraska	12,508,653,750	0.6%
34	Nevada	12,141,753,711	0.6%
39	New Hampshire	7,358,146,111	0.4%
6	New Jersey	91,275,842,895	4.5%
40	New Mexico	7,146,535,897	0.4%
2	New York	182,023,812,811	9.0%
14	North Carolina	47,807,483,920	2.4%
50	North Dakota	2,717,953,098	0.1%
7	Ohio	86,810,682,042	4.3%
28	Oklahoma	18,213,113,718	0.9%
27	Oregon	18,392,990,126	0.9%
8	Pennsylvania	85,488,178,241	4.2%
38	Rhode Island	7,942,125,100	0.4%
31	South Carolina	15,166,634,184	0.8%
45	South Dakota	3,573,354,035	0.2%
20	Tennessee	35,824,876,977	1.8%
3	Texas	146,440,182,371	7.3%
36	Utah	9,117,924,200	0.5%
48	Vermont	3,007,155,502	0.1%
13	Virginia	49,658,845,398	2.5%
15	Washington	42,324,665,394	2.1%
44	West Virginia	4,927,855,354	0.2%
21	Wisconsin	34,648,055,594	1.7%
49	Wyoming	2,735,388,094	0.1%

<u>RANK ORDER</u>

RANK	STATE	COLLECTIONS	% of USA
1	California	$232,301,672,370	11.5%
2	New York	182,023,812,811	9.0%
3	Texas	146,440,182,371	7.3%
4	Illinois	111,520,474,945	5.5%
5	Florida	94,507,293,792	4.7%
6	New Jersey	91,275,842,895	4.5%
7	Ohio	86,810,682,042	4.3%
8	Pennsylvania	85,488,178,241	4.2%
9	Michigan	66,310,783,861	3.3%
10	Massachusetts	60,389,579,467	3.0%
11	Georgia	60,330,806,075	3.0%
12	Minnesota	58,143,876,558	2.9%
13	Virginia	49,658,845,398	2.5%
14	North Carolina	47,807,483,920	2.4%
15	Washington	42,324,665,394	2.1%
16	Maryland	41,637,531,279	2.1%
17	Missouri	41,145,978,975	2.0%
18	Connecticut	39,704,703,727	2.0%
19	Colorado	36,425,728,559	1.8%
20	Tennessee	35,824,876,977	1.8%
21	Wisconsin	34,648,055,594	1.7%
22	Indiana	33,999,215,328	1.7%
23	Arizona	24,901,726,338	1.2%
24	Louisiana	22,664,647,541	1.1%
25	Arkansas	19,701,605,478	1.0%
26	Alabama	18,650,989,371	0.9%
27	Oregon	18,392,990,126	0.9%
28	Oklahoma	18,213,113,718	0.9%
29	Kentucky	17,333,322,804	0.9%
30	Kansas	16,293,150,929	0.8%
31	South Carolina	15,166,634,184	0.8%
32	Iowa	14,570,904,462	0.7%
33	Nebraska	12,508,653,750	0.6%
34	Nevada	12,141,753,711	0.6%
35	Delaware	11,789,203,399	0.6%
36	Utah	9,117,924,200	0.5%
37	Mississippi	9,011,608,013	0.4%
38	Rhode Island	7,942,125,100	0.4%
39	New Hampshire	7,358,146,111	0.4%
40	New Mexico	7,146,535,897	0.4%
41	Idaho	6,894,987,400	0.3%
42	Hawaii	5,559,959,703	0.3%
43	Maine	5,302,924,590	0.3%
44	West Virginia	4,927,855,354	0.2%
45	South Dakota	3,573,354,035	0.2%
46	Alaska	3,211,048,300	0.2%
47	Montana	3,119,113,776	0.2%
48	Vermont	3,007,155,502	0.1%
49	Wyoming	2,735,388,094	0.1%
50	North Dakota	2,717,953,098	0.1%
	District of Columbia	14,750,257,992	0.7%

Source: U.S. Department of the Treasury, Internal Revenue Service
    "Tax Collections" (http://www.irs.gov/)
*Total includes $31,428,303,000 from U.S. citizens abroad and other miscellaneous returns not shown separately.

Per Capita Internal Revenue Service Gross Collections in 2002

National Per Capita = $6,936*

<u>ALPHA ORDER</u>

RANK	STATE	PER CAPITA
43	Alabama	$4,164
35	Alaska	5,006
39	Arizona	4,577
12	Arkansas	7,280
20	California	6,637
8	Colorado	8,093
3	Connecticut	11,480
1	Delaware	14,628
27	Florida	5,662
15	Georgia	7,061
40	Hawaii	4,481
33	Idaho	5,134
7	Illinois	8,860
29	Indiana	5,522
36	Iowa	4,963
24	Kansas	6,008
42	Kentucky	4,238
34	Louisiana	5,063
44	Maine	4,095
9	Maryland	7,639
6	Massachusetts	9,404
21	Michigan	6,603
2	Minnesota	11,571
49	Mississippi	3,144
13	Missouri	7,257
48	Montana	3,426
14	Nebraska	7,241
28	Nevada	5,602
25	New Hampshire	5,774
4	New Jersey	10,644
46	New Mexico	3,859
5	New York	9,513
26	North Carolina	5,756
41	North Dakota	4,288
10	Ohio	7,609
32	Oklahoma	5,219
31	Oregon	5,225
17	Pennsylvania	6,934
11	Rhode Island	7,434
47	South Carolina	3,696
38	South Dakota	4,699
23	Tennessee	6,188
19	Texas	6,737
45	Utah	3,932
37	Vermont	4,879
18	Virginia	6,814
16	Washington	6,976
50	West Virginia	2,730
22	Wisconsin	6,369
30	Wyoming	5,484

<u>RANK ORDER</u>

RANK	STATE	PER CAPITA
1	Delaware	$14,628
2	Minnesota	11,571
3	Connecticut	11,480
4	New Jersey	10,644
5	New York	9,513
6	Massachusetts	9,404
7	Illinois	8,860
8	Colorado	8,093
9	Maryland	7,639
10	Ohio	7,609
11	Rhode Island	7,434
12	Arkansas	7,280
13	Missouri	7,257
14	Nebraska	7,241
15	Georgia	7,061
16	Washington	6,976
17	Pennsylvania	6,934
18	Virginia	6,814
19	Texas	6,737
20	California	6,637
21	Michigan	6,603
22	Wisconsin	6,369
23	Tennessee	6,188
24	Kansas	6,008
25	New Hampshire	5,774
26	North Carolina	5,756
27	Florida	5,662
28	Nevada	5,602
29	Indiana	5,522
30	Wyoming	5,484
31	Oregon	5,225
32	Oklahoma	5,219
33	Idaho	5,134
34	Louisiana	5,063
35	Alaska	5,006
36	Iowa	4,963
37	Vermont	4,879
38	South Dakota	4,699
39	Arizona	4,577
40	Hawaii	4,481
41	North Dakota	4,288
42	Kentucky	4,238
43	Alabama	4,164
44	Maine	4,095
45	Utah	3,932
46	New Mexico	3,859
47	South Carolina	3,696
48	Montana	3,426
49	Mississippi	3,144
50	West Virginia	2,730
	District of Columbia	25,916

Source: Morgan Quitno Press using data from U.S. Department of the Treasury, Internal Revenue Service
   "Tax Collections" (http://www.irs.gov/)
*National per capita does not include collections from U.S. citizens abroad and other miscellaneous returns not shown separately.

Federal Individual Income Tax Collections in 2002

National Total = $1,725,811,146,000*

<u>ALPHA ORDER</u>

RANK	STATE	COLLECTIONS	% of USA
26	Alabama	$16,357,183,189	0.9%
46	Alaska	3,016,939,799	0.2%
24	Arizona	20,916,223,504	1.2%
28	Arkansas	14,487,462,737	0.8%
1	California	202,770,828,300	11.7%
18	Colorado	34,040,705,293	2.0%
19	Connecticut	32,256,165,029	1.9%
37	Delaware	7,779,318,620	0.5%
5	Florida	85,364,367,840	4.9%
12	Georgia	47,323,415,849	2.7%
42	Hawaii	4,779,461,519	0.3%
40	Idaho	6,328,494,431	0.4%
4	Illinois	94,185,655,629	5.5%
21	Indiana	30,643,556,168	1.8%
31	Iowa	12,927,803,725	0.7%
30	Kansas	13,924,986,447	0.8%
27	Kentucky	15,565,771,036	0.9%
23	Louisiana	21,328,977,544	1.2%
43	Maine	4,740,744,012	0.3%
15	Maryland	37,374,228,250	2.2%
10	Massachusetts	54,674,464,156	3.2%
9	Michigan	61,458,413,035	3.6%
11	Minnesota	48,263,155,789	2.8%
36	Mississippi	8,120,055,057	0.5%
17	Missouri	34,242,740,494	2.0%
47	Montana	2,885,949,199	0.2%
33	Nebraska	10,024,823,112	0.6%
34	Nevada	10,020,549,952	0.6%
38	New Hampshire	6,884,266,880	0.4%
6	New Jersey	78,795,054,736	4.6%
39	New Mexico	6,499,143,497	0.4%
2	New York	156,596,002,801	9.1%
14	North Carolina	39,703,323,236	2.3%
49	North Dakota	2,465,135,872	0.1%
8	Ohio	73,026,136,674	4.2%
32	Oklahoma	12,912,374,397	0.7%
25	Oregon	16,863,604,257	1.0%
7	Pennsylvania	73,731,441,789	4.3%
41	Rhode Island	6,170,461,016	0.4%
29	South Carolina	13,929,975,398	0.8%
45	South Dakota	3,452,007,598	0.2%
20	Tennessee	31,669,381,658	1.8%
3	Texas	117,685,965,457	6.8%
35	Utah	8,233,065,054	0.5%
48	Vermont	2,742,096,999	0.2%
13	Virginia	40,766,109,992	2.4%
16	Washington	35,649,249,462	2.1%
44	West Virginia	4,542,538,009	0.3%
22	Wisconsin	29,860,923,335	1.7%
50	Wyoming	2,310,602,524	0.1%

<u>RANK ORDER</u>

RANK	STATE	COLLECTIONS	% of USA
1	California	$202,770,828,300	11.7%
2	New York	156,596,002,801	9.1%
3	Texas	117,685,965,457	6.8%
4	Illinois	94,185,655,629	5.5%
5	Florida	85,364,367,840	4.9%
6	New Jersey	78,795,054,736	4.6%
7	Pennsylvania	73,731,441,789	4.3%
8	Ohio	73,026,136,674	4.2%
9	Michigan	61,458,413,035	3.6%
10	Massachusetts	54,674,464,156	3.2%
11	Minnesota	48,263,155,789	2.8%
12	Georgia	47,323,415,849	2.7%
13	Virginia	40,766,109,992	2.4%
14	North Carolina	39,703,323,236	2.3%
15	Maryland	37,374,228,250	2.2%
16	Washington	35,649,249,462	2.1%
17	Missouri	34,242,740,494	2.0%
18	Colorado	34,040,705,293	2.0%
19	Connecticut	32,256,165,029	1.9%
20	Tennessee	31,669,381,658	1.8%
21	Indiana	30,643,556,168	1.8%
22	Wisconsin	29,860,923,335	1.7%
23	Louisiana	21,328,977,544	1.2%
24	Arizona	20,916,223,504	1.2%
25	Oregon	16,863,604,257	1.0%
26	Alabama	16,357,183,189	0.9%
27	Kentucky	15,565,771,036	0.9%
28	Arkansas	14,487,462,737	0.8%
29	South Carolina	13,929,975,398	0.8%
30	Kansas	13,924,986,447	0.8%
31	Iowa	12,927,803,725	0.7%
32	Oklahoma	12,912,374,397	0.7%
33	Nebraska	10,024,823,112	0.6%
34	Nevada	10,020,549,952	0.6%
35	Utah	8,233,065,054	0.5%
36	Mississippi	8,120,055,057	0.5%
37	Delaware	7,779,318,620	0.5%
38	New Hampshire	6,884,266,880	0.4%
39	New Mexico	6,499,143,497	0.4%
40	Idaho	6,328,494,431	0.4%
41	Rhode Island	6,170,461,016	0.4%
42	Hawaii	4,779,461,519	0.3%
43	Maine	4,740,744,012	0.3%
44	West Virginia	4,542,538,009	0.3%
45	South Dakota	3,452,007,598	0.2%
46	Alaska	3,016,939,799	0.2%
47	Montana	2,885,949,199	0.2%
48	Vermont	2,742,096,999	0.2%
49	North Dakota	2,465,135,872	0.1%
50	Wyoming	2,310,602,524	0.1%
	District of Columbia	11,935,392,181	0.7%

Average Revenue Collection per Federal Individual Income Tax Return in 2002

National Average = $13,184 per Return*

ALPHA ORDER

RANK	STATE	AVERAGE
41	Alabama	$8,652
38	Alaska	9,057
36	Arizona	9,512
14	Arkansas	12,943
10	California	13,481
9	Colorado	16,157
4	Connecticut	19,181
1	Delaware	20,431
27	Florida	11,184
15	Georgia	12,941
43	Hawaii	8,279
26	Idaho	11,235
8	Illinois	16,301
29	Indiana	10,850
35	Iowa	9,656
24	Kansas	11,356
39	Kentucky	8,869
25	Louisiana	11,338
46	Maine	7,738
7	Maryland**	17,188
6	Massachusetts	17,506
11	Michigan	13,404
2	Minnesota	20,237
48	Mississippi	6,978
12	Missouri	13,341
49	Montana	6,762
19	Nebraska	12,439
32	Nevada	10,232
30	New Hampshire	10,826
3	New Jersey	19,287
47	New Mexico	7,648
5	New York	18,110
28	North Carolina	10,879
44	North Dakota	8,186
13	Ohio	13,172
40	Oklahoma	8,781
31	Oregon	10,725
18	Pennsylvania	12,736
21	Rhode Island	12,396
45	South Carolina	7,743
33	South Dakota	9,734
20	Tennessee	12,400
16	Texas	12,806
42	Utah	8,637
37	Vermont	9,066
22	Virginia	12,115
17	Washington	12,801
50	West Virginia	6,051
23	Wisconsin	11,528
34	Wyoming	9,691

RANK ORDER

RANK	STATE	AVERAGE
1	Delaware	$20,431
2	Minnesota	20,237
3	New Jersey	19,287
4	Connecticut	19,181
5	New York	18,110
6	Massachusetts	17,506
7	Maryland**	17,188
8	Illinois	16,301
9	Colorado	16,157
10	California	13,481
11	Michigan	13,404
12	Missouri	13,341
13	Ohio	13,172
14	Arkansas	12,943
15	Georgia	12,941
16	Texas	12,806
17	Washington	12,801
18	Pennsylvania	12,736
19	Nebraska	12,439
20	Tennessee	12,400
21	Rhode Island	12,396
22	Virginia	12,115
23	Wisconsin	11,528
24	Kansas	11,356
25	Louisiana	11,338
26	Idaho	11,235
27	Florida	11,184
28	North Carolina	10,879
29	Indiana	10,850
30	New Hampshire	10,826
31	Oregon	10,725
32	Nevada	10,232
33	South Dakota	9,734
34	Wyoming	9,691
35	Iowa	9,656
36	Arizona	9,512
37	Vermont	9,066
38	Alaska	9,057
39	Kentucky	8,869
40	Oklahoma	8,781
41	Alabama	8,652
42	Utah	8,637
43	Hawaii	8,279
44	North Dakota	8,186
45	South Carolina	7,743
46	Maine	7,738
47	New Mexico	7,648
48	Mississippi	6,978
49	Montana	6,762
50	West Virginia	6,051

District of Columbia**   NA

Source: Morgan Quitno Press using data from U.S. Department of the Treasury, Internal Revenue Service "Tax Collections" and "Number of Returns" (http://www.irs.gov/)

**Total includes collections and returns from U.S. citizens abroad and other miscellaneous returns not shown separately.*

***Maryland's figure includes the District of Columbia.*

Adjusted Gross Income in 2001

National Total = $6,144,619,443,000*

ALPHA ORDER

RANK	STATE	A.G.I.	% of USA
24	Alabama	$72,103,862,000	1.2%
46	Alaska	14,164,363,000	0.2%
23	Arizona	97,892,228,000	1.6%
34	Arkansas	39,556,047,000	0.6%
1	California	797,785,488,000	13.0%
20	Colorado	108,578,215,000	1.8%
18	Connecticut	114,472,787,000	1.9%
44	Delaware	18,484,828,000	0.3%
4	Florida	339,033,617,000	5.5%
12	Georgia	166,756,155,000	2.7%
40	Hawaii	23,882,640,000	0.4%
43	Idaho	21,447,540,000	0.3%
5	Illinois	290,608,112,000	4.7%
16	Indiana	117,976,731,000	1.9%
30	Iowa	52,695,642,000	0.9%
31	Kansas	52,117,375,000*	0.8%
28	Kentucky	67,345,098,000	1.1%
25	Louisiana	70,033,555,000	1.1%
41	Maine	23,877,690,000	0.4%
14	Maryland	138,921,475,000	2.3%
10	Massachusetts	185,543,146,000	3.0%
9	Michigan	208,988,138,000	3.4%
17	Minnesota	116,938,872,000	1.9%
35	Mississippi	39,227,073,000	0.6%
21	Missouri	107,031,790,000	1.7%
45	Montana	14,496,553,000	0.2%
37	Nebraska	32,537,889,000	0.5%
32	Nevada	47,726,925,000	0.8%
38	New Hampshire	32,413,845,000	0.5%
7	New Jersey	247,502,074,000	4.0%
36	New Mexico	33,299,736,000	0.5%
2	New York	484,813,868,000	7.9%
13	North Carolina	154,110,655,000	2.5%
50	North Dakota	10,680,419,000	0.2%
8	Ohio	226,733,944,000	3.7%
29	Oklahoma	55,605,617,000	0.9%
27	Oregon	67,352,647,000	1.1%
6	Pennsylvania	255,829,616,000	4.2%
42	Rhode Island	22,808,544,000	0.4%
26	South Carolina	68,916,663,000	1.1%
47	South Dakota	12,983,789,000	0.2%
22	Tennessee	102,171,197,000	1.7%
3	Texas	413,497,441,000	6.7%
33	Utah	39,764,870,000	0.6%
48	Vermont	12,390,156,000	0.2%
11	Virginia	170,858,125,000	2.8%
15	Washington	138,877,860,000	2.3%
39	West Virginia	26,177,768,000	0.4%
19	Wisconsin	114,224,632,000	1.9%
49	Wyoming	10,727,343,000	0.2%

RANK ORDER

RANK	STATE	A.G.I.	% of USA
1	California	$797,785,488,000	13.0%
2	New York	484,813,868,000	7.9%
3	Texas	413,497,441,000	6.7%
4	Florida	339,033,617,000	5.5%
5	Illinois	290,608,112,000	4.7%
6	Pennsylvania	255,829,616,000	4.2%
7	New Jersey	247,502,074,000	4.0%
8	Ohio	226,733,944,000	3.7%
9	Michigan	208,988,138,000	3.4%
10	Massachusetts	185,543,146,000	3.0%
11	Virginia	170,858,125,000	2.8%
12	Georgia	166,756,155,000	2.7%
13	North Carolina	154,110,655,000	2.5%
14	Maryland	138,921,475,000	2.3%
15	Washington	138,877,860,000	2.3%
16	Indiana	117,976,731,000	1.9%
17	Minnesota	116,938,872,000	1.9%
18	Connecticut	114,472,787,000	1.9%
19	Wisconsin	114,224,632,000	1.9%
20	Colorado	108,578,215,000	1.8%
21	Missouri	107,031,790,000	1.7%
22	Tennessee	102,171,197,000	1.7%
23	Arizona	97,892,228,000	1.6%
24	Alabama	72,103,862,000	1.2%
25	Louisiana	70,033,555,000	1.1%
26	South Carolina	68,916,663,000	1.1%
27	Oregon	67,352,647,000	1.1%
28	Kentucky	67,345,098,000	1.1%
29	Oklahoma	55,605,617,000	0.9%
30	Iowa	52,695,642,000	0.9%
31	Kansas	52,117,375,000	0.8%
32	Nevada	47,726,925,000	0.8%
33	Utah	39,764,870,000	0.6%
34	Arkansas	39,556,047,000	0.6%
35	Mississippi	39,227,073,000	0.6%
36	New Mexico	33,299,736,000	0.5%
37	Nebraska	32,537,889,000	0.5%
38	New Hampshire	32,413,845,000	0.5%
39	West Virginia	26,177,768,000	0.4%
40	Hawaii	23,882,640,000	0.4%
41	Maine	23,877,690,000	0.4%
42	Rhode Island	22,808,544,000	0.4%
43	Idaho	21,447,540,000	0.3%
44	Delaware	18,484,828,000	0.3%
45	Montana	14,496,553,000	0.2%
46	Alaska	14,164,363,000	0.2%
47	South Dakota	12,983,789,000	0.2%
48	Vermont	12,390,156,000	0.2%
49	Wyoming	10,727,343,000	0.2%
50	North Dakota	10,680,419,000	0.2%
	District of Columbia	15,913,850,000	0.3%

Source: U.S. Department of the Treasury, Internal Revenue Service
  "Individual Tax Statistics, State Income" (http://www.irs.gov/)
Total includes $46,740,951,000 from U.S. citizens abroad and other miscellaneous returns not shown separately.

Per Capita Adjusted Gross Income in 2001

National Per Capita = $21,389*

<u>ALPHA ORDER</u>

RANK	STATE	PER CAPITA
44	Alabama	$16,143
15	Alaska	22,388
34	Arizona	18,478
48	Arkansas	14,694
13	California	23,102
7	Colorado	24,516
1	Connecticut	33,349
10	Delaware	23,235
21	Florida	20,729
24	Georgia	19,864
25	Hawaii	19,495
43	Idaho	16,232
11	Illinois	23,217
29	Indiana	19,257
36	Iowa	17,971
28	Kansas	19,299
42	Kentucky	16,558
47	Louisiana	15,681
33	Maine	18,586
4	Maryland	25,806
3	Massachusetts	28,992
19	Michigan	20,888
9	Minnesota	23,457
50	Mississippi	13,727
30	Missouri	18,990
46	Montana	16,001
31	Nebraska	18,928
14	Nevada	22,785
5	New Hampshire	25,746
2	New Jersey	29,104
35	New Mexico	18,205
6	New York	25,416
32	North Carolina	18,805
41	North Dakota	16,786
23	Ohio	19,914
45	Oklahoma	16,038
26	Oregon	19,395
20	Pennsylvania	20,802
17	Rhode Island	21,538
40	South Carolina	16,975
39	South Dakota	17,125
37	Tennessee	17,782
27	Texas	19,376
38	Utah	17,444
22	Vermont	20,215
8	Virginia	23,754
12	Washington	23,174
49	West Virginia	14,530
18	Wisconsin	21,133
16	Wyoming	21,728

<u>RANK ORDER</u>

RANK	STATE	PER CAPITA
1	Connecticut	$33,349
2	New Jersey	29,104
3	Massachusetts	28,992
4	Maryland	25,806
5	New Hampshire	25,746
6	New York	25,416
7	Colorado	24,516
8	Virginia	23,754
9	Minnesota	23,457
10	Delaware	23,235
11	Illinois	23,217
12	Washington	23,174
13	California	23,102
14	Nevada	22,785
15	Alaska	22,388
16	Wyoming	21,728
17	Rhode Island	21,538
18	Wisconsin	21,133
19	Michigan	20,888
20	Pennsylvania	20,802
21	Florida	20,729
22	Vermont	20,215
23	Ohio	19,914
24	Georgia	19,864
25	Hawaii	19,495
26	Oregon	19,395
27	Texas	19,376
28	Kansas	19,299
29	Indiana	19,257
30	Missouri	18,990
31	Nebraska	18,928
32	North Carolina	18,805
33	Maine	18,586
34	Arizona	18,478
35	New Mexico	18,205
36	Iowa	17,971
37	Tennessee	17,782
38	Utah	17,444
39	South Dakota	17,125
40	South Carolina	16,975
41	North Dakota	16,786
42	Kentucky	16,558
43	Idaho	16,232
44	Alabama	16,143
45	Oklahoma	16,038
46	Montana	16,001
47	Louisiana	15,681
48	Arkansas	14,694
49	West Virginia	14,530
50	Mississippi	13,727
	District of Columbia	27,787

Source: Morgan Quitno Press using data from U.S. Department of the Treasury, Internal Revenue Service
"Individual Tax Statistics, State Income" (http://www.irs.gov/)
*National per capita does not include income from U.S. citizens abroad and other miscellaneous returns not shown separately.

Federal Corporate Income Tax Collections in 2002

National Total = $211,437,773,000*

ALPHA ORDER

RANK	STATE	COLLECTIONS	% of USA
27	Alabama	$1,867,638,730	0.9%
48	Alaska	117,146,297	0.1%
25	Arizona	1,896,444,808	0.9%
15	Arkansas	4,721,184,806	2.2%
1	California	21,655,748,195	10.2%
31	Colorado	1,198,433,176	0.6%
12	Connecticut	6,660,592,404	3.2%
20	Delaware	3,823,378,655	1.8%
13	Florida	5,905,368,278	2.8%
7	Georgia	9,761,759,788	4.6%
37	Hawaii	606,173,364	0.3%
40	Idaho	506,781,987	0.2%
4	Illinois	11,992,066,320	5.7%
23	Indiana	2,623,845,551	1.2%
29	Iowa	1,409,806,945	0.7%
35	Kansas	926,707,154	0.4%
30	Kentucky	1,334,004,790	0.6%
34	Louisiana	1,012,378,928	0.5%
42	Maine	340,475,703	0.2%
21	Maryland	3,256,253,267	1.5%
17	Massachusetts	4,304,363,602	2.0%
19	Michigan	4,082,856,396	1.9%
9	Minnesota	8,202,248,323	3.9%
39	Mississippi	554,282,532	0.3%
16	Missouri	4,480,300,460	2.1%
47	Montana	150,459,205	0.1%
24	Nebraska	2,290,868,791	1.1%
26	Nevada	1,886,139,764	0.9%
43	New Hampshire	282,205,346	0.1%
6	New Jersey	9,902,251,930	4.7%
41	New Mexico	431,888,669	0.2%
2	New York	20,979,542,213	9.9%
10	North Carolina	7,365,526,759	3.5%
45	North Dakota	208,395,047	0.1%
5	Ohio	10,015,920,661	4.7%
33	Oklahoma	1,042,779,454	0.5%
32	Oregon	1,046,518,768	0.5%
8	Pennsylvania	8,877,627,779	4.2%
28	Rhode Island	1,681,667,851	0.8%
36	South Carolina	889,444,541	0.4%
49	South Dakota	82,467,110	0.0%
22	Tennessee	2,960,200,580	1.4%
3	Texas	13,702,495,156	6.5%
38	Utah	573,944,368	0.3%
46	Vermont	168,556,701	0.1%
11	Virginia	6,899,626,771	3.3%
14	Washington	5,334,602,577	2.5%
44	West Virginia	233,721,206	0.1%
18	Wisconsin	4,086,680,773	1.9%
50	Wyoming	71,196,465	0.0%

RANK ORDER

RANK	STATE	COLLECTIONS	% of USA
1	California	$21,655,748,195	10.2%
2	New York	20,979,542,213	9.9%
3	Texas	13,702,495,156	6.5%
4	Illinois	11,992,066,320	5.7%
5	Ohio	10,015,920,661	4.7%
6	New Jersey	9,902,251,930	4.7%
7	Georgia	9,761,759,788	4.6%
8	Pennsylvania	8,877,627,779	4.2%
9	Minnesota	8,202,248,323	3.9%
10	North Carolina	7,365,526,759	3.5%
11	Virginia	6,899,626,771	3.3%
12	Connecticut	6,660,592,404	3.2%
13	Florida	5,905,368,278	2.8%
14	Washington	5,334,602,577	2.5%
15	Arkansas	4,721,184,806	2.2%
16	Missouri	4,480,300,460	2.1%
17	Massachusetts	4,304,363,602	2.0%
18	Wisconsin	4,086,680,773	1.9%
19	Michigan	4,082,856,396	1.9%
20	Delaware	3,823,378,655	1.8%
21	Maryland	3,256,253,267	1.5%
22	Tennessee	2,960,200,580	1.4%
23	Indiana	2,623,845,551	1.2%
24	Nebraska	2,290,868,791	1.1%
25	Arizona	1,896,444,808	0.9%
26	Nevada	1,886,139,764	0.9%
27	Alabama	1,867,638,730	0.9%
28	Rhode Island	1,681,667,851	0.8%
29	Iowa	1,409,806,945	0.7%
30	Kentucky	1,334,004,790	0.6%
31	Colorado	1,198,433,176	0.6%
32	Oregon	1,046,518,768	0.5%
33	Oklahoma	1,042,779,454	0.5%
34	Louisiana	1,012,378,928	0.5%
35	Kansas	926,707,154	0.4%
36	South Carolina	889,444,541	0.4%
37	Hawaii	606,173,364	0.3%
38	Utah	573,944,368	0.3%
39	Mississippi	554,282,532	0.3%
40	Idaho	506,781,987	0.2%
41	New Mexico	431,888,669	0.2%
42	Maine	340,475,703	0.2%
43	New Hampshire	282,205,346	0.1%
44	West Virginia	233,721,206	0.1%
45	North Dakota	208,395,047	0.1%
46	Vermont	168,556,701	0.1%
47	Montana	150,459,205	0.1%
48	Alaska	117,146,297	0.1%
49	South Dakota	82,467,110	0.0%
50	Wyoming	71,196,465	0.0%
	District of Columbia	2,490,490,525	1.2%

Source: U.S. Department of the Treasury, Internal Revenue Service
"Tax Collections" (http://www.irs.gov/)

Total includes collections and returns from international sources and others not distributed by state.

Average Revenue Collection per Federal Corporate Income Tax Return in 2002

National Average = $37,024 per Return*

<u>ALPHA ORDER</u>

RANK	STATE	AVERAGE
24	Alabama	$29,130
43	Alaska	11,241
29	Arizona	20,314
3	Arkansas	96,950
17	California	43,656
47	Colorado	9,783
2	Connecticut	110,330
1	Delaware	169,973
46	Florida	10,544
7	Georgia	55,116
27	Hawaii	23,189
32	Idaho	19,209
18	Illinois	42,742
26	Indiana	24,694
25	Iowa	25,675
31	Kansas	19,541
30	Kentucky	20,199
42	Louisiana	11,369
38	Maine	12,291
14	Maryland**	45,045
23	Massachusetts	31,996
28	Michigan	21,041
4	Minnesota	73,238
37	Mississippi	13,955
12	Missouri	45,786
48	Montana	5,992
6	Nebraska	60,464
22	Nevada	32,584
41	New Hampshire	11,468
19	New Jersey	40,001
35	New Mexico	15,614
21	New York	39,319
10	North Carolina	48,678
33	North Dakota	17,880
8	Ohio	53,317
34	Oklahoma	16,586
36	Oregon	15,091
13	Pennsylvania	45,369
5	Rhode Island	68,724
39	South Carolina	12,195
49	South Dakota	5,612
16	Tennessee	44,965
20	Texas	39,948
40	Utah	11,927
45	Vermont	10,549
9	Virginia	51,184
11	Washington	47,346
44	West Virginia	10,787
15	Wisconsin	44,968
50	Wyoming	5,094

<u>RANK ORDER</u>

RANK	STATE	AVERAGE
1	Delaware	$169,973
2	Connecticut	110,330
3	Arkansas	96,950
4	Minnesota	73,238
5	Rhode Island	68,724
6	Nebraska	60,464
7	Georgia	55,116
8	Ohio	53,317
9	Virginia	51,184
10	North Carolina	48,678
11	Washington	47,346
12	Missouri	45,786
13	Pennsylvania	45,369
14	Maryland**	45,045
15	Wisconsin	44,968
16	Tennessee	44,965
17	California	43,656
18	Illinois	42,742
19	New Jersey	40,001
20	Texas	39,948
21	New York	39,319
22	Nevada	32,584
23	Massachusetts	31,996
24	Alabama	29,130
25	Iowa	25,675
26	Indiana	24,694
27	Hawaii	23,189
28	Michigan	21,041
29	Arizona	20,314
30	Kentucky	20,199
31	Kansas	19,541
32	Idaho	19,209
33	North Dakota	17,880
34	Oklahoma	16,586
35	New Mexico	15,614
36	Oregon	15,091
37	Mississippi	13,955
38	Maine	12,291
39	South Carolina	12,195
40	Utah	11,927
41	New Hampshire	11,468
42	Louisiana	11,369
43	Alaska	11,241
44	West Virginia	10,787
45	Vermont	10,549
46	Florida	10,544
47	Colorado	9,783
48	Montana	5,992
49	South Dakota	5,612
50	Wyoming	5,094

District of Columbia**   NA

Source: Morgan Quitno Press using data from U.S. Department of the Treasury, Internal Revenue Service
"Tax Collections" and "Number of Returns" (http://www.irs.gov/)
**Total includes collections and returns from U.S. citizens abroad and other miscellaneous returns not shown separately.*
***Maryland's figure includes the District of Columbia.*

Federal Tax Returns Filed in 2002

National Total = 226,609,232 Returns*

<u>ALPHA ORDER</u>

RANK	STATE	RETURNS	% of USA
25	Alabama	3,058,030	1.3%
48	Alaska	557,048	0.2%
22	Arizona	3,829,758	1.7%
32	Arkansas	1,921,602	0.8%
1	California	25,698,947	11.3%
21	Colorado	3,955,359	1.7%
24	Connecticut	3,109,055	1.4%
45	Delaware	693,751	0.3%
4	Florida	14,282,350	6.3%
10	Georgia	6,122,436	2.7%
42	Hawaii	984,593	0.4%
41	Idaho	1,016,476	0.4%
5	Illinois	10,028,448	4.4%
15	Indiana	4,668,220	2.1%
30	Iowa	2,419,671	1.1%
31	Kansas	2,213,197	1.0%
28	Kentucky	2,867,321	1.3%
23	Louisiana	3,125,022	1.4%
40	Maine	1,124,001	0.5%
14	Maryland**	5,351,860	2.4%
12	Massachusetts	5,747,007	2.5%
8	Michigan	7,543,291	3.3%
19	Minnesota	4,230,403	1.9%
33	Mississippi	1,845,857	0.8%
18	Missouri	4,423,455	2.0%
44	Montana	854,333	0.4%
37	Nebraska	1,306,447	0.6%
34	Nevada	1,672,911	0.7%
39	New Hampshire	1,139,556	0.5%
9	New Jersey	7,470,091	3.3%
36	New Mexico	1,397,856	0.6%
3	New York	15,410,613	6.8%
11	North Carolina	6,111,648	2.7%
49	North Dakota	509,822	0.2%
7	Ohio	9,121,038	4.0%
29	Oklahoma	2,644,045	1.2%
26	Oregon	2,956,346	1.3%
6	Pennsylvania	9,821,996	4.3%
43	Rhode Island	914,244	0.4%
27	South Carolina	2,928,145	1.3%
46	South Dakota	602,964	0.3%
20	Tennessee	4,115,043	1.8%
2	Texas	15,688,260	6.9%
35	Utah	1,638,534	0.7%
47	Vermont	598,172	0.3%
13	Virginia	5,690,382	2.5%
16	Washington	4,583,620	2.0%
38	West Virginia	1,221,872	0.5%
17	Wisconsin	4,480,991	2.0%
50	Wyoming	471,540	0.2%

<u>RANK ORDER</u>

RANK	STATE	RETURNS	% of USA
1	California	25,698,947	11.3%
2	Texas	15,688,260	6.9%
3	New York	15,410,613	6.8%
4	Florida	14,282,350	6.3%
5	Illinois	10,028,448	4.4%
6	Pennsylvania	9,821,996	4.3%
7	Ohio	9,121,038	4.0%
8	Michigan	7,543,291	3.3%
9	New Jersey	7,470,091	3.3%
10	Georgia	6,122,436	2.7%
11	North Carolina	6,111,648	2.7%
12	Massachusetts	5,747,007	2.5%
13	Virginia	5,690,382	2.5%
14	Maryland**	5,351,860	2.4%
15	Indiana	4,668,220	2.1%
16	Washington	4,583,620	2.0%
17	Wisconsin	4,480,991	2.0%
18	Missouri	4,423,455	2.0%
19	Minnesota	4,230,403	1.9%
20	Tennessee	4,115,043	1.8%
21	Colorado	3,955,359	1.7%
22	Arizona	3,829,758	1.7%
23	Louisiana	3,125,022	1.4%
24	Connecticut	3,109,055	1.4%
25	Alabama	3,058,030	1.3%
26	Oregon	2,956,346	1.3%
27	South Carolina	2,928,145	1.3%
28	Kentucky	2,867,321	1.3%
29	Oklahoma	2,644,045	1.2%
30	Iowa	2,419,671	1.1%
31	Kansas	2,213,197	1.0%
32	Arkansas	1,921,602	0.8%
33	Mississippi	1,845,857	0.8%
34	Nevada	1,672,911	0.7%
35	Utah	1,638,534	0.7%
36	New Mexico	1,397,856	0.6%
37	Nebraska	1,306,447	0.6%
38	West Virginia	1,221,872	0.5%
39	New Hampshire	1,139,556	0.5%
40	Maine	1,124,001	0.5%
41	Idaho	1,016,476	0.4%
42	Hawaii	984,593	0.4%
43	Rhode Island	914,244	0.4%
44	Montana	854,333	0.4%
45	Delaware	693,751	0.3%
46	South Dakota	602,964	0.3%
47	Vermont	598,172	0.3%
48	Alaska	557,048	0.2%
49	North Dakota	509,822	0.2%
50	Wyoming	471,540	0.2%
	District of Columbia**	NA	NA

Source: U.S. Department of the Treasury, Internal Revenue Service
"Number of Returns" (http://www.irs.gov/)
**Total includes returns from international sources and other miscellaneous returns not shown separately.*
***Maryland's figure includes the District of Columbia.*

Federal Individual Income Tax Returns Filed in 2002

National Total = 130,904,889 Returns*

ALPHA ORDER

RANK	STATE	RETURNS	% of USA
23	Alabama	1,890,640	1.4%
47	Alaska	333,118	0.3%
21	Arizona	2,198,924	1.7%
33	Arkansas	1,119,332	0.9%
1	California	15,041,642	11.5%
22	Colorado	2,106,853	1.6%
27	Connecticut	1,681,716	1.3%
45	Delaware	380,753	0.3%
4	Florida	7,632,543	5.8%
10	Georgia	3,656,835	2.8%
41	Hawaii	577,321	0.4%
42	Idaho	563,299	0.4%
6	Illinois	5,777,829	4.4%
15	Indiana	2,824,170	2.2%
30	Iowa	1,338,787	1.0%
31	Kansas	1,226,275	0.9%
26	Kentucky	1,755,045	1.3%
24	Louisiana	1,881,184	1.4%
40	Maine	612,648	0.5%
14	Maryland**	2,868,760	2.2%
13	Massachusetts	3,123,187	2.4%
8	Michigan	4,585,063	3.5%
20	Minnesota	2,384,847	1.8%
32	Mississippi	1,163,744	0.9%
18	Missouri	2,566,710	2.0%
44	Montana	426,767	0.3%
37	Nebraska	805,919	0.6%
34	Nevada	979,340	0.7%
39	New Hampshire	635,916	0.5%
9	New Jersey	4,085,427	3.1%
36	New Mexico	849,761	0.6%
3	New York	8,647,067	6.6%
11	North Carolina	3,649,566	2.8%
49	North Dakota	301,150	0.2%
7	Ohio	5,543,846	4.2%
29	Oklahoma	1,470,450	1.1%
28	Oregon	1,572,397	1.2%
5	Pennsylvania	5,789,069	4.4%
43	Rhode Island	497,777	0.4%
25	South Carolina	1,798,975	1.4%
46	South Dakota	354,640	0.3%
19	Tennessee	2,553,908	2.0%
2	Texas	9,189,960	7.0%
35	Utah	953,276	0.7%
48	Vermont	302,456	0.2%
12	Virginia	3,365,046	2.6%
16	Washington	2,784,824	2.1%
38	West Virginia	750,705	0.6%
17	Wisconsin	2,590,240	2.0%
50	Wyoming	238,426	0.2%

RANK ORDER

RANK	STATE	RETURNS	% of USA
1	California	15,041,642	11.5%
2	Texas	9,189,960	7.0%
3	New York	8,647,067	6.6%
4	Florida	7,632,543	5.8%
5	Pennsylvania	5,789,069	4.4%
6	Illinois	5,777,829	4.4%
7	Ohio	5,543,846	4.2%
8	Michigan	4,585,063	3.5%
9	New Jersey	4,085,427	3.1%
10	Georgia	3,656,835	2.8%
11	North Carolina	3,649,566	2.8%
12	Virginia	3,365,046	2.6%
13	Massachusetts	3,123,187	2.4%
14	Maryland**	2,868,760	2.2%
15	Indiana	2,824,170	2.2%
16	Washington	2,784,824	2.1%
17	Wisconsin	2,590,240	2.0%
18	Missouri	2,566,710	2.0%
19	Tennessee	2,553,908	2.0%
20	Minnesota	2,384,847	1.8%
21	Arizona	2,198,924	1.7%
22	Colorado	2,106,853	1.6%
23	Alabama	1,890,640	1.4%
24	Louisiana	1,881,184	1.4%
25	South Carolina	1,798,975	1.4%
26	Kentucky	1,755,045	1.3%
27	Connecticut	1,681,716	1.3%
28	Oregon	1,572,397	1.2%
29	Oklahoma	1,470,450	1.1%
30	Iowa	1,338,787	1.0%
31	Kansas	1,226,275	0.9%
32	Mississippi	1,163,744	0.9%
33	Arkansas	1,119,332	0.9%
34	Nevada	979,340	0.7%
35	Utah	953,276	0.7%
36	New Mexico	849,761	0.6%
37	Nebraska	805,919	0.6%
38	West Virginia	750,705	0.6%
39	New Hampshire	635,916	0.5%
40	Maine	612,648	0.5%
41	Hawaii	577,321	0.4%
42	Idaho	563,299	0.4%
43	Rhode Island	497,777	0.4%
44	Montana	426,767	0.3%
45	Delaware	380,753	0.3%
46	South Dakota	354,640	0.3%
47	Alaska	333,118	0.3%
48	Vermont	302,456	0.2%
49	North Dakota	301,150	0.2%
50	Wyoming	238,426	0.2%
	District of Columbia**	NA	NA

Source: U.S. Department of the Treasury, Internal Revenue Service
"Number of Returns" (http://www.irs.gov/)
*Total includes returns from international sources and other miscellaneous returns not shown separately.
**Maryland's figure includes the District of Columbia.

Federal Corporate Income Tax Returns Filed in 2002

National Total = 5,710,759 Returns*

<u>ALPHA ORDER</u>

RANK	STATE	RETURNS	% of USA
27	Alabama	64,115	1.1%
50	Alaska	10,421	0.2%
20	Arizona	93,357	1.6%
32	Arkansas	48,697	0.9%
3	California	496,060	8.7%
15	Colorado	122,498	2.1%
29	Connecticut	60,370	1.1%
44	Delaware	22,494	0.4%
1	Florida	560,085	9.8%
10	Georgia	177,114	3.1%
40	Hawaii	26,141	0.5%
39	Idaho	26,382	0.5%
5	Illinois	280,570	4.9%
18	Indiana	106,256	1.9%
31	Iowa	54,909	1.0%
34	Kansas	47,424	0.8%
25	Kentucky	66,044	1.2%
22	Louisiana	89,044	1.6%
37	Maine	27,701	0.5%
14	Maryland**	127,577	2.2%
13	Massachusetts	134,528	2.4%
8	Michigan	194,045	3.4%
17	Minnesota	111,995	2.0%
35	Mississippi	39,718	0.7%
19	Missouri	97,852	1.7%
41	Montana	25,109	0.4%
36	Nebraska	37,888	0.7%
30	Nevada	57,885	1.0%
42	New Hampshire	24,607	0.4%
6	New Jersey	247,550	4.3%
38	New Mexico	27,661	0.5%
2	New York	533,568	9.3%
11	North Carolina	151,310	2.6%
49	North Dakota	11,655	0.2%
9	Ohio	187,856	3.3%
28	Oklahoma	62,872	1.1%
24	Oregon	69,345	1.2%
7	Pennsylvania	195,675	3.4%
43	Rhode Island	24,470	0.4%
23	South Carolina	72,938	1.3%
47	South Dakota	14,696	0.3%
26	Tennessee	65,833	1.2%
4	Texas	343,010	6.0%
33	Utah	48,123	0.8%
46	Vermont	15,978	0.3%
12	Virginia	134,800	2.4%
16	Washington	112,672	2.0%
45	West Virginia	21,666	0.4%
21	Wisconsin	90,880	1.6%
48	Wyoming	13,976	0.2%

<u>RANK ORDER</u>

RANK	STATE	RETURNS	% of USA
1	Florida	560,085	9.8%
2	New York	533,568	9.3%
3	California	496,060	8.7%
4	Texas	343,010	6.0%
5	Illinois	280,570	4.9%
6	New Jersey	247,550	4.3%
7	Pennsylvania	195,675	3.4%
8	Michigan	194,045	3.4%
9	Ohio	187,856	3.3%
10	Georgia	177,114	3.1%
11	North Carolina	151,310	2.6%
12	Virginia	134,800	2.4%
13	Massachusetts	134,528	2.4%
14	Maryland**	127,577	2.2%
15	Colorado	122,498	2.1%
16	Washington	112,672	2.0%
17	Minnesota	111,995	2.0%
18	Indiana	106,256	1.9%
19	Missouri	97,852	1.7%
20	Arizona	93,357	1.6%
21	Wisconsin	90,880	1.6%
22	Louisiana	89,044	1.6%
23	South Carolina	72,938	1.3%
24	Oregon	69,345	1.2%
25	Kentucky	66,044	1.2%
26	Tennessee	65,833	1.2%
27	Alabama	64,115	1.1%
28	Oklahoma	62,872	1.1%
29	Connecticut	60,370	1.1%
30	Nevada	57,885	1.0%
31	Iowa	54,909	1.0%
32	Arkansas	48,697	0.9%
33	Utah	48,123	0.8%
34	Kansas	47,424	0.8%
35	Mississippi	39,718	0.7%
36	Nebraska	37,888	0.7%
37	Maine	27,701	0.5%
38	New Mexico	27,661	0.5%
39	Idaho	26,382	0.5%
40	Hawaii	26,141	0.5%
41	Montana	25,109	0.4%
42	New Hampshire	24,607	0.4%
43	Rhode Island	24,470	0.4%
44	Delaware	22,494	0.4%
45	West Virginia	21,666	0.4%
46	Vermont	15,978	0.3%
47	South Dakota	14,696	0.3%
48	Wyoming	13,976	0.2%
49	North Dakota	11,655	0.2%
50	Alaska	10,421	0.2%
	District of Columbia**	NA	NA

Source: U.S. Department of the Treasury, Internal Revenue Service
"Number of Returns" (http://www.irs.gov/)

*Total includes returns from international sources and other miscellaneous returns not shown separately.
**Maryland's figure includes the District of Columbia.

Federal Tax Refunds in 2002

National Total = 109,785,695 Refunds*

<u>ALPHA ORDER</u>

RANK	STATE	REFUNDS	% of USA
24	Alabama	1,735,029	1.6%
48	Alaska	244,855	0.2%
22	Arizona	1,793,182	1.6%
33	Arkansas	1,018,952	0.9%
1	California	12,313,408	11.2%
25	Colorado	1,701,307	1.5%
28	Connecticut	1,380,829	1.3%
45	Delaware	324,368	0.3%
4	Florida	6,428,853	5.9%
11	Georgia	3,160,299	2.9%
42	Hawaii	478,401	0.4%
43	Idaho	459,266	0.4%
7	Illinois	4,706,299	4.3%
15	Indiana	2,434,403	2.2%
32	Iowa	1,046,154	1.0%
34	Kansas	985,523	0.9%
26	Kentucky	1,586,721	1.4%
23	Louisiana	1,744,603	1.6%
41	Maine	515,729	0.5%
18	Maryland	2,189,621	2.0%
14	Massachusetts	2,572,773	2.3%
8	Michigan	3,925,279	3.6%
21	Minnesota	1,892,434	1.7%
31	Mississippi	1,062,246	1.0%
20	Missouri	2,071,490	1.9%
44	Montana	339,822	0.3%
37	Nebraska	697,922	0.6%
36	Nevada	809,253	0.7%
40	New Hampshire	534,462	0.5%
9	New Jersey	3,379,245	3.1%
38	New Mexico	670,426	0.6%
3	New York	7,236,446	6.6%
10	North Carolina	3,345,909	3.0%
49	North Dakota	237,887	0.2%
6	Ohio	4,819,693	4.4%
30	Oklahoma	1,184,438	1.1%
29	Oregon	1,250,726	1.1%
5	Pennsylvania	4,890,930	4.5%
13	Rhode Island	2,704,887	2.5%
27	South Carolina	1,540,782	1.4%
46	South Dakota	285,153	0.3%
16	Tennessee	2,370,098	2.2%
2	Texas	7,493,407	6.8%
35	Utah	814,513	0.7%
47	Vermont	252,602	0.2%
12	Virginia	2,832,006	2.6%
17	Washington	2,320,893	2.1%
39	West Virginia	663,001	0.6%
19	Wisconsin	2,102,069	1.9%
50	Wyoming	199,060	0.2%

<u>RANK ORDER</u>

RANK	STATE	REFUNDS	% of USA
1	California	12,313,408	11.2%
2	Texas	7,493,407	6.8%
3	New York	7,236,446	6.6%
4	Florida	6,428,853	5.9%
5	Pennsylvania	4,890,930	4.5%
6	Ohio	4,819,693	4.4%
7	Illinois	4,706,299	4.3%
8	Michigan	3,925,279	3.6%
9	New Jersey	3,379,245	3.1%
10	North Carolina	3,345,909	3.0%
11	Georgia	3,160,299	2.9%
12	Virginia	2,832,006	2.6%
13	Rhode Island	2,704,887	2.5%
14	Massachusetts	2,572,773	2.3%
15	Indiana	2,434,403	2.2%
16	Tennessee	2,370,098	2.2%
17	Washington	2,320,893	2.1%
18	Maryland	2,189,621	2.0%
19	Wisconsin	2,102,069	1.9%
20	Missouri	2,071,490	1.9%
21	Minnesota	1,892,434	1.7%
22	Arizona	1,793,182	1.6%
23	Louisiana	1,744,603	1.6%
24	Alabama	1,735,029	1.6%
25	Colorado	1,701,307	1.5%
26	Kentucky	1,586,721	1.4%
27	South Carolina	1,540,782	1.4%
28	Connecticut	1,380,829	1.3%
29	Oregon	1,250,726	1.1%
30	Oklahoma	1,184,438	1.1%
31	Mississippi	1,062,246	1.0%
32	Iowa	1,046,154	1.0%
33	Arkansas	1,018,952	0.9%
34	Kansas	985,523	0.9%
35	Utah	814,513	0.7%
36	Nevada	809,253	0.7%
37	Nebraska	697,922	0.6%
38	New Mexico	670,426	0.6%
39	West Virginia	663,001	0.6%
40	New Hampshire	534,462	0.5%
41	Maine	515,729	0.5%
42	Hawaii	478,401	0.4%
43	Idaho	459,266	0.4%
44	Montana	339,822	0.3%
45	Delaware	324,368	0.3%
46	South Dakota	285,153	0.3%
47	Vermont	252,602	0.2%
48	Alaska	244,855	0.2%
49	North Dakota	237,887	0.2%
50	Wyoming	199,060	0.2%
	District of Columbia	226,495	0.2%

Source: U.S. Department of the Treasury, Internal Revenue Service
"Tax Refunds" (http://www.irs.gov/)
**Total includes refunds to international sources and other miscellaneous refunds not shown separately.*

Value of Federal Tax Refunds in 2002

National Total = $283,911,940,000*

ALPHA ORDER

RANK	STATE	REFUNDS	% of USA
25	Alabama	$3,317,553,000	1.2%
48	Alaska	412,871,000	0.1%
23	Arizona	4,086,326,000	1.4%
34	Arkansas	1,793,787,000	0.6%
1	California	33,402,477,000	11.8%
20	Colorado	4,424,011,000	1.6%
17	Connecticut	6,085,732,000	2.1%
41	Delaware	925,701,000	0.3%
6	Florida	14,233,087,000	5.0%
10	Georgia	8,625,383,000	3.0%
43	Hawaii	861,101,000	0.3%
42	Idaho	904,350,000	0.3%
7	Illinois	13,840,685,000	4.9%
18	Indiana	5,192,624,000	1.8%
30	Iowa	2,156,796,000	0.8%
32	Kansas	1,922,186,000	0.7%
27	Kentucky	2,868,770,000	1.0%
24	Louisiana	3,614,030,000	1.3%
44	Maine	832,549,000	0.3%
12	Maryland	7,219,647,000	2.5%
13	Massachusetts	7,027,858,000	2.5%
4	Michigan	14,987,897,000	5.3%
21	Minnesota	4,252,014,000	1.5%
31	Mississippi	1,955,959,000	0.7%
19	Missouri	4,929,013,000	1.7%
45	Montana	569,431,000	0.2%
37	Nebraska	1,204,396,000	0.4%
33	Nevada	1,836,357,000	0.6%
36	New Hampshire	1,240,574,000	0.4%
9	New Jersey	9,679,062,000	3.4%
38	New Mexico	1,155,940,000	0.4%
2	New York	20,170,138,000	7.1%
16	North Carolina	6,369,017,000	2.2%
49	North Dakota	395,728,000	0.1%
5	Ohio	14,396,354,000	5.1%
28	Oklahoma	2,770,356,000	1.0%
29	Oregon	2,353,073,000	0.8%
8	Pennsylvania	10,595,447,000	3.7%
40	Rhode Island	1,050,920,000	0.4%
26	South Carolina	2,876,141,000	1.0%
46	South Dakota	474,726,000	0.2%
14	Tennessee	6,656,657,000	2.3%
3	Texas	18,588,539,000	6.5%
35	Utah	1,484,986,000	0.5%
47	Vermont	436,700,000	0.2%
15	Virginia	6,407,250,000	2.3%
11	Washington	8,606,261,000	3.0%
39	West Virginia	1,108,499,000	0.4%
22	Wisconsin	4,175,321,000	1.5%
50	Wyoming	376,703,000	0.1%

RANK ORDER

RANK	STATE	REFUNDS	% of USA
1	California	$33,402,477,000	11.8%
2	New York	20,170,138,000	7.1%
3	Texas	18,588,539,000	6.5%
4	Michigan	14,987,897,000	5.3%
5	Ohio	14,396,354,000	5.1%
6	Florida	14,233,087,000	5.0%
7	Illinois	13,840,685,000	4.9%
8	Pennsylvania	10,595,447,000	3.7%
9	New Jersey	9,679,062,000	3.4%
10	Georgia	8,625,383,000	3.0%
11	Washington	8,606,261,000	3.0%
12	Maryland	7,219,647,000	2.5%
13	Massachusetts	7,027,858,000	2.5%
14	Tennessee	6,656,657,000	2.3%
15	Virginia	6,407,250,000	2.3%
16	North Carolina	6,369,017,000	2.2%
17	Connecticut	6,085,732,000	2.1%
18	Indiana	5,192,624,000	1.8%
19	Missouri	4,929,013,000	1.7%
20	Colorado	4,424,011,000	1.6%
21	Minnesota	4,252,014,000	1.5%
22	Wisconsin	4,175,321,000	1.5%
23	Arizona	4,086,326,000	1.4%
24	Louisiana	3,614,030,000	1.3%
25	Alabama	3,317,553,000	1.2%
26	South Carolina	2,876,141,000	1.0%
27	Kentucky	2,868,770,000	1.0%
28	Oklahoma	2,770,356,000	1.0%
29	Oregon	2,353,073,000	0.8%
30	Iowa	2,156,796,000	0.8%
31	Mississippi	1,955,959,000	0.7%
32	Kansas	1,922,186,000	0.7%
33	Nevada	1,836,357,000	0.6%
34	Arkansas	1,793,787,000	0.6%
35	Utah	1,484,986,000	0.5%
36	New Hampshire	1,240,574,000	0.4%
37	Nebraska	1,204,396,000	0.4%
38	New Mexico	1,155,940,000	0.4%
39	West Virginia	1,108,499,000	0.4%
40	Rhode Island	1,050,920,000	0.4%
41	Delaware	925,701,000	0.3%
42	Idaho	904,350,000	0.3%
43	Hawaii	861,101,000	0.3%
44	Maine	832,549,000	0.3%
45	Montana	569,431,000	0.2%
46	South Dakota	474,726,000	0.2%
47	Vermont	436,700,000	0.2%
48	Alaska	412,871,000	0.1%
49	North Dakota	395,728,000	0.1%
50	Wyoming	376,703,000	0.1%
	District of Columbia	512,910,000	0.2%

Source: U.S. Department of the Treasury, Internal Revenue Service
"Tax Refunds" (http://www.irs.gov)
Total includes refunds to international sources and other miscellaneous refunds not shown separately.

Average Value of Federal Tax Refunds in 2002

National Average = $2,586*

<u>ALPHA ORDER</u>

RANK	STATE	REFUNDS
31	Alabama	$1,912
44	Alaska	1,686
19	Arizona	2,279
40	Arkansas	1,760
13	California	2,713
14	Colorado	2,600
1	Connecticut	4,407
8	Delaware	2,854
23	Florida	2,214
12	Georgia	2,729
39	Hawaii	1,800
29	Idaho	1,969
6	Illinois	2,941
25	Indiana	2,133
27	Iowa	2,062
30	Kansas	1,950
38	Kentucky	1,808
26	Louisiana	2,072
49	Maine	1,614
4	Maryland	3,297
11	Massachusetts	2,732
2	Michigan	3,818
22	Minnesota	2,247
36	Mississippi	1,841
16	Missouri	2,379
45	Montana	1,676
42	Nebraska	1,726
20	Nevada	2,269
18	New Hampshire	2,321
7	New Jersey	2,864
43	New Mexico	1,724
10	New York	2,787
32	North Carolina	1,904
48	North Dakota	1,664
5	Ohio	2,987
17	Oklahoma	2,339
34	Oregon	1,881
24	Pennsylvania	2,166
50	Rhode Island	389
35	South Carolina	1,867
47	South Dakota	1,665
9	Tennessee	2,809
15	Texas	2,481
37	Utah	1,823
41	Vermont	1,729
21	Virginia	2,262
3	Washington	3,708
46	West Virginia	1,672
28	Wisconsin	1,986
33	Wyoming	1,892

<u>RANK ORDER</u>

RANK	STATE	REFUNDS
1	Connecticut	$4,407
2	Michigan	3,818
3	Washington	3,708
4	Maryland	3,297
5	Ohio	2,987
6	Illinois	2,941
7	New Jersey	2,864
8	Delaware	2,854
9	Tennessee	2,809
10	New York	2,787
11	Massachusetts	2,732
12	Georgia	2,729
13	California	2,713
14	Colorado	2,600
15	Texas	2,481
16	Missouri	2,379
17	Oklahoma	2,339
18	New Hampshire	2,321
19	Arizona	2,279
20	Nevada	2,269
21	Virginia	2,262
22	Minnesota	2,247
23	Florida	2,214
24	Pennsylvania	2,166
25	Indiana	2,133
26	Louisiana	2,072
27	Iowa	2,062
28	Wisconsin	1,986
29	Idaho	1,969
30	Kansas	1,950
31	Alabama	1,912
32	North Carolina	1,904
33	Wyoming	1,892
34	Oregon	1,881
35	South Carolina	1,867
36	Mississippi	1,841
37	Utah	1,823
38	Kentucky	1,808
39	Hawaii	1,800
40	Arkansas	1,760
41	Vermont	1,729
42	Nebraska	1,726
43	New Mexico	1,724
44	Alaska	1,686
45	Montana	1,676
46	West Virginia	1,672
47	South Dakota	1,665
48	North Dakota	1,664
49	Maine	1,614
50	Rhode Island	389
	District of Columbia	2,265

Source: Morgan Quitno Press using data from U.S. Department of the Treasury, Internal Revenue Service
"Tax Refunds" (http://www.irs.gov/)
*Total includes refunds to international sources and other miscellaneous refunds not shown separately.

Value of Federal Individual Income Tax Refunds in 2002

National Total = $210,159,025,000*

ALPHA ORDER

RANK	STATE	REFUNDS	% of USA
24	Alabama	$3,056,145,000	1.5%
48	Alaska	388,161,000	0.2%
20	Arizona	3,383,856,000	1.6%
31	Arkansas	1,659,977,000	0.8%
1	California	25,779,141,000	12.3%
22	Colorado	3,184,033,000	1.5%
25	Connecticut	2,988,692,000	1.4%
44	Delaware	620,909,000	0.3%
4	Florida	12,308,649,000	5.9%
10	Georgia	5,982,909,000	2.8%
42	Hawaii	766,918,000	0.4%
43	Idaho	729,350,000	0.3%
5	Illinois	9,770,131,000	4.6%
15	Indiana	4,453,077,000	2.1%
33	Iowa	1,647,068,000	0.8%
32	Kansas	1,647,183,000	0.8%
27	Kentucky	2,670,275,000	1.3%
23	Louisiana	3,106,337,000	1.5%
41	Maine	791,746,000	0.4%
14	Maryland	4,491,194,000	2.1%
12	Massachusetts	5,318,502,000	2.5%
8	Michigan	7,612,170,000	3.6%
21	Minnesota	3,199,579,000	1.5%
30	Mississippi	1,849,259,000	0.9%
18	Missouri	3,562,135,000	1.7%
45	Montana	489,267,000	0.2%
37	Nebraska	1,070,780,000	0.5%
34	Nevada	1,545,395,000	0.7%
39	New Hampshire	987,148,000	0.5%
9	New Jersey	7,451,374,000	3.5%
36	New Mexico	1,076,678,000	0.5%
2	New York	15,364,274,000	7.3%
11	North Carolina	5,707,006,000	2.7%
50	North Dakota	340,042,000	0.2%
7	Ohio	8,469,711,000	4.0%
29	Oklahoma	1,916,242,000	0.9%
28	Oregon	2,093,635,000	1.0%
6	Pennsylvania	8,747,373,000	4.2%
40	Rhode Island	792,669,000	0.4%
26	South Carolina	2,703,440,000	1.3%
46	South Dakota	440,882,000	0.2%
17	Tennessee	4,050,166,000	1.9%
3	Texas	14,020,851,000	6.7%
35	Utah	1,380,415,000	0.7%
47	Vermont	393,734,000	0.2%
13	Virginia	5,268,562,000	2.5%
16	Washington	4,407,898,000	2.1%
38	West Virginia	1,046,873,000	0.5%
19	Wisconsin	3,442,601,000	1.6%
49	Wyoming	340,703,000	0.2%

RANK ORDER

RANK	STATE	REFUNDS	% of USA
1	California	$25,779,141,000	12.3%
2	New York	15,364,274,000	7.3%
3	Texas	14,020,851,000	6.7%
4	Florida	12,308,649,000	5.9%
5	Illinois	9,770,131,000	4.6%
6	Pennsylvania	8,747,373,000	4.2%
7	Ohio	8,469,711,000	4.0%
8	Michigan	7,612,170,000	3.6%
9	New Jersey	7,451,374,000	3.5%
10	Georgia	5,982,909,000	2.8%
11	North Carolina	5,707,006,000	2.7%
12	Massachusetts	5,318,502,000	2.5%
13	Virginia	5,268,562,000	2.5%
14	Maryland	4,491,194,000	2.1%
15	Indiana	4,453,077,000	2.1%
16	Washington	4,407,898,000	2.1%
17	Tennessee	4,050,166,000	1.9%
18	Missouri	3,562,135,000	1.7%
19	Wisconsin	3,442,601,000	1.6%
20	Arizona	3,383,856,000	1.6%
21	Minnesota	3,199,579,000	1.5%
22	Colorado	3,184,033,000	1.5%
23	Louisiana	3,106,337,000	1.5%
24	Alabama	3,056,145,000	1.5%
25	Connecticut	2,988,692,000	1.4%
26	South Carolina	2,703,440,000	1.3%
27	Kentucky	2,670,275,000	1.3%
28	Oregon	2,093,635,000	1.0%
29	Oklahoma	1,916,242,000	0.9%
30	Mississippi	1,849,259,000	0.9%
31	Arkansas	1,659,977,000	0.8%
32	Kansas	1,647,183,000	0.8%
33	Iowa	1,647,068,000	0.8%
34	Nevada	1,545,395,000	0.7%
35	Utah	1,380,415,000	0.7%
36	New Mexico	1,076,678,000	0.5%
37	Nebraska	1,070,780,000	0.5%
38	West Virginia	1,046,873,000	0.5%
39	New Hampshire	987,148,000	0.5%
40	Rhode Island	792,669,000	0.4%
41	Maine	791,746,000	0.4%
42	Hawaii	766,918,000	0.4%
43	Idaho	729,350,000	0.3%
44	Delaware	620,909,000	0.3%
45	Montana	489,267,000	0.2%
46	South Dakota	440,882,000	0.2%
47	Vermont	393,734,000	0.2%
48	Alaska	388,161,000	0.2%
49	Wyoming	340,703,000	0.2%
50	North Dakota	340,042,000	0.2%
	District of Columbia	472,102,000	0.2%

Source: U.S. Department of the Treasury, Internal Revenue Service
"Tax Refunds" (http://www.irs.gov/)
**Total includes refunds to international sources and other miscellaneous refunds not shown separately.*

Average Value of Federal Individual Income Tax Refunds in 2002

National Average = $1,959*

ALPHA ORDER

RANK	STATE	REFUNDS
24	Alabama	$1,796
42	Alaska	1,635
14	Arizona	1,927
37	Arkansas	1,666
4	California	2,142
15	Colorado	1,924
2	Connecticut	2,215
10	Delaware	1,958
9	Florida	1,965
13	Georgia	1,936
40	Hawaii	1,637
41	Idaho	1,636
5	Illinois	2,121
19	Indiana	1,861
43	Iowa	1,616
34	Kansas	1,715
35	Kentucky	1,712
21	Louisiana	1,823
48	Maine	1,569
7	Maryland	2,092
6	Massachusetts	2,109
8	Michigan	1,981
32	Minnesota	1,731
26	Mississippi	1,777
28	Missouri	1,759
49	Montana	1,494
47	Nebraska	1,575
11	Nevada	1,954
18	New Hampshire	1,893
1	New Jersey	2,255
39	New Mexico	1,641
3	New York	2,168
30	North Carolina	1,741
50	North Dakota	1,475
23	Ohio	1,814
38	Oklahoma	1,657
33	Oregon	1,716
22	Pennsylvania	1,820
20	Rhode Island	1,840
25	South Carolina	1,790
46	South Dakota	1,595
29	Tennessee	1,745
16	Texas	1,922
31	Utah	1,736
45	Vermont	1,607
17	Virginia	1,899
11	Washington	1,954
44	West Virginia	1,611
36	Wisconsin	1,676
26	Wyoming	1,777

RANK ORDER

RANK	STATE	REFUNDS
1	New Jersey	$2,255
2	Connecticut	2,215
3	New York	2,168
4	California	2,142
5	Illinois	2,121
6	Massachusetts	2,109
7	Maryland	2,092
8	Michigan	1,981
9	Florida	1,965
10	Delaware	1,958
11	Nevada	1,954
11	Washington	1,954
13	Georgia	1,936
14	Arizona	1,927
15	Colorado	1,924
16	Texas	1,922
17	Virginia	1,899
18	New Hampshire	1,893
19	Indiana	1,861
20	Rhode Island	1,840
21	Louisiana	1,823
22	Pennsylvania	1,820
23	Ohio	1,814
24	Alabama	1,796
25	South Carolina	1,790
26	Mississippi	1,777
26	Wyoming	1,777
28	Missouri	1,759
29	Tennessee	1,745
30	North Carolina	1,741
31	Utah	1,736
32	Minnesota	1,731
33	Oregon	1,716
34	Kansas	1,715
35	Kentucky	1,712
36	Wisconsin	1,676
37	Arkansas	1,666
38	Oklahoma	1,657
39	New Mexico	1,641
40	Hawaii	1,637
41	Idaho	1,636
42	Alaska	1,635
43	Iowa	1,616
44	West Virginia	1,611
45	Vermont	1,607
46	South Dakota	1,595
47	Nebraska	1,575
48	Maine	1,569
49	Montana	1,494
50	North Dakota	1,475

District of Columbia   2,126

Source: Morgan Quitno Press using data from U.S. Department of the Treasury, Internal Revenue Service
"Tax Refunds" (http://www.irs.gov/)
**Total includes refunds to international sources and other miscellaneous refunds not shown separately.*

Value of Federal Corporate Income Tax Refunds in 2002

National Total = $66,757,609,000*

ALPHA ORDER

RANK	STATE	REFUNDS	% of USA
33	Alabama	$225,022,000	0.3%
49	Alaska	14,813,000	0.0%
23	Arizona	638,532,000	1.0%
38	Arkansas	114,414,000	0.2%
2	California	7,028,410,000	10.5%
17	Colorado	1,172,458,000	1.8%
8	Connecticut	3,026,513,000	4.5%
27	Delaware	293,177,000	0.4%
13	Florida	1,714,077,000	2.6%
11	Georgia	2,514,424,000	3.8%
41	Hawaii	80,379,000	0.1%
34	Idaho	163,893,000	0.2%
7	Illinois	3,879,669,000	5.8%
21	Indiana	689,695,000	1.0%
25	Iowa	495,654,000	0.7%
29	Kansas	251,157,000	0.4%
35	Kentucky	158,414,000	0.2%
26	Louisiana	473,487,000	0.7%
46	Maine	33,029,000	0.0%
9	Maryland	2,617,535,000	3.9%
15	Massachusetts	1,595,747,000	2.4%
1	Michigan	7,244,836,000	10.9%
19	Minnesota	974,945,000	1.5%
39	Mississippi	90,701,000	0.1%
16	Missouri	1,300,092,000	1.9%
42	Montana	73,264,000	0.1%
37	Nebraska	119,155,000	0.2%
28	Nevada	257,583,000	0.4%
32	New Hampshire	225,689,000	0.3%
12	New Jersey	2,048,862,000	3.1%
43	New Mexico	64,443,000	0.1%
4	New York	4,440,610,000	6.7%
24	North Carolina	610,242,000	0.9%
44	North Dakota	50,814,000	0.1%
3	Ohio	5,490,714,000	8.2%
20	Oklahoma	819,537,000	1.2%
31	Oregon	229,967,000	0.3%
14	Pennsylvania	1,685,048,000	2.5%
30	Rhode Island	245,852,000	0.4%
36	South Carolina	147,857,000	0.2%
47	South Dakota	26,330,000	0.0%
10	Tennessee	2,530,221,000	3.8%
5	Texas	4,246,153,000	6.4%
40	Utah	87,123,000	0.1%
45	Vermont	37,813,000	0.1%
18	Virginia	1,034,509,000	1.5%
6	Washington	4,072,126,000	6.1%
48	West Virginia	24,327,000	0.0%
22	Wisconsin	684,890,000	1.0%
50	Wyoming	14,340,000	0.0%

RANK ORDER

RANK	STATE	REFUNDS	% of USA
1	Michigan	$7,244,836,000	10.9%
2	California	7,028,410,000	10.5%
3	Ohio	5,490,714,000	8.2%
4	New York	4,440,610,000	6.7%
5	Texas	4,246,153,000	6.4%
6	Washington	4,072,126,000	6.1%
7	Illinois	3,879,669,000	5.8%
8	Connecticut	3,026,513,000	4.5%
9	Maryland	2,617,535,000	3.9%
10	Tennessee	2,530,221,000	3.8%
11	Georgia	2,514,424,000	3.8%
12	New Jersey	2,048,862,000	3.1%
13	Florida	1,714,077,000	2.6%
14	Pennsylvania	1,685,048,000	2.5%
15	Massachusetts	1,595,747,000	2.4%
16	Missouri	1,300,092,000	1.9%
17	Colorado	1,172,458,000	1.8%
18	Virginia	1,034,509,000	1.5%
19	Minnesota	974,945,000	1.5%
20	Oklahoma	819,537,000	1.2%
21	Indiana	689,695,000	1.0%
22	Wisconsin	684,890,000	1.0%
23	Arizona	638,532,000	1.0%
24	North Carolina	610,242,000	0.9%
25	Iowa	495,654,000	0.7%
26	Louisiana	473,487,000	0.7%
27	Delaware	293,177,000	0.4%
28	Nevada	257,583,000	0.4%
29	Kansas	251,157,000	0.4%
30	Rhode Island	245,852,000	0.4%
31	Oregon	229,967,000	0.3%
32	New Hampshire	225,689,000	0.3%
33	Alabama	225,022,000	0.3%
34	Idaho	163,893,000	0.2%
35	Kentucky	158,414,000	0.2%
36	South Carolina	147,857,000	0.2%
37	Nebraska	119,155,000	0.2%
38	Arkansas	114,414,000	0.2%
39	Mississippi	90,701,000	0.1%
40	Utah	87,123,000	0.1%
41	Hawaii	80,379,000	0.1%
42	Montana	73,264,000	0.1%
43	New Mexico	64,443,000	0.1%
44	North Dakota	50,814,000	0.1%
45	Vermont	37,813,000	0.1%
46	Maine	33,029,000	0.0%
47	South Dakota	26,330,000	0.0%
48	West Virginia	24,327,000	0.0%
49	Alaska	14,813,000	0.0%
50	Wyoming	14,340,000	0.0%
	District of Columbia	22,825,000	0.0%

Source: U.S. Department of the Treasury, Internal Revenue Service
"Tax Refunds" (http://www.irs.gov/)
**Total includes refunds to international sources and other miscellaneous refunds not shown separately.*

Average Value of Federal Corporate Income Tax Refunds in 2002

National Average = $122,090*

ALPHA ORDER

RANK	STATE	REFUNDS
32	Alabama	$44,950
46	Alaska	15,511
19	Arizona	94,794
36	Arkansas	30,543
15	California	128,457
14	Colorado	134,241
1	Connecticut	479,030
9	Delaware	178,440
24	Florida	75,493
6	Georgia	202,368
38	Hawaii	29,870
25	Idaho	67,335
7	Illinois	185,364
20	Indiana	94,105
29	Iowa	55,048
33	Kansas	38,438
34	Kentucky	35,227
26	Louisiana	67,295
47	Maine	13,383
4	Maryland	300,142
13	Massachusetts	137,210
3	Michigan	304,418
21	Minnesota	91,373
44	Mississippi	22,557
17	Missouri	121,983
45	Montana	20,837
43	Nebraska	23,159
27	Nevada	64,331
23	New Hampshire	82,278
12	New Jersey	156,032
42	New Mexico	26,196
10	New York	166,608
31	North Carolina	46,587
41	North Dakota	27,086
28	Ohio	62,195
11	Oklahoma	163,973
35	Oregon	30,794
16	Pennsylvania	126,155
8	Rhode Island	181,040
40	South Carolina	28,358
48	South Dakota	13,054
2	Tennessee	318,187
18	Texas	119,681
39	Utah	28,734
37	Vermont	29,915
22	Virginia	89,320
5	Washington	287,884
49	West Virginia	11,803
30	Wisconsin	55,020
50	Wyoming	9,228

RANK ORDER

RANK	STATE	REFUNDS
1	Connecticut	$479,030
2	Tennessee	318,187
3	Michigan	304,418
4	Maryland	300,142
5	Washington	287,884
6	Georgia	202,368
7	Illinois	185,364
8	Rhode Island	181,040
9	Delaware	178,440
10	New York	166,608
11	Oklahoma	163,973
12	New Jersey	156,032
13	Massachusetts	137,210
14	Colorado	134,241
15	California	128,457
16	Pennsylvania	126,155
17	Missouri	121,983
18	Texas	119,681
19	Arizona	94,794
20	Indiana	94,105
21	Minnesota	91,373
22	Virginia	89,320
23	New Hampshire	82,278
24	Florida	75,493
25	Idaho	67,335
26	Louisiana	67,295
27	Nevada	64,331
28	Ohio	62,195
29	Iowa	55,048
30	Wisconsin	55,020
31	North Carolina	46,587
32	Alabama	44,950
33	Kansas	38,438
34	Kentucky	35,227
35	Oregon	30,794
36	Arkansas	30,543
37	Vermont	29,915
38	Hawaii	29,870
39	Utah	28,734
40	South Carolina	28,358
41	North Dakota	27,086
42	New Mexico	26,196
43	Nebraska	23,159
44	Mississippi	22,557
45	Montana	20,837
46	Alaska	15,511
47	Maine	13,383
48	South Dakota	13,054
49	West Virginia	11,803
50	Wyoming	9,228

District of Columbia   31,483

*Source: Morgan Quitno Press using data from U.S. Department of the Treasury, Internal Revenue Service
"Tax Refunds" (http://www.irs.gov/)*

Total includes refunds to international sources and other miscellaneous refunds not shown separately.

Federal Government Expenditures in 2002

National Total = $1,917,637,000,000*

ALPHA ORDER

RANK	STATE	EXPENDITURES	% of USA
19	Alabama	$34,291,000,000	1.8%
42	Alaska	7,562,000,000	0.4%
18	Arizona	34,761,000,000	1.8%
32	Arkansas	18,372,000,000	1.0%
1	California	206,401,000,000	10.8%
25	Colorado	26,229,000,000	1.4%
27	Connecticut	25,387,000,000	1.3%
48	Delaware	4,766,000,000	0.2%
4	Florida	104,814,000,000	5.5%
10	Georgia	51,336,000,000	2.7%
39	Hawaii	10,474,000,000	0.5%
41	Idaho	8,378,000,000	0.4%
7	Illinois	70,275,000,000	3.7%
20	Indiana	34,200,000,000	1.8%
31	Iowa	18,839,000,000	1.0%
33	Kansas	17,496,000,000	0.9%
22	Kentucky	28,880,000,000	1.5%
21	Louisiana	29,988,000,000	1.6%
40	Maine	9,205,000,000	0.5%
12	Maryland	49,537,000,000	2.6%
14	Massachusetts	47,480,000,000	2.5%
9	Michigan	55,909,000,000	2.9%
24	Minnesota	27,056,000,000	1.4%
29	Mississippi	21,308,000,000	1.1%
15	Missouri	42,347,000,000	2.2%
44	Montana	6,974,000,000	0.4%
37	Nebraska	11,583,000,000	0.6%
38	Nevada	10,737,000,000	0.6%
45	New Hampshire	6,937,000,000	0.4%
11	New Jersey	50,673,000,000	2.6%
34	New Mexico	17,478,000,000	0.9%
2	New York	128,994,000,000	6.7%
13	North Carolina	48,180,000,000	2.5%
46	North Dakota	6,437,000,000	0.3%
8	Ohio	65,976,000,000	3.4%
28	Oklahoma	24,355,000,000	1.3%
30	Oregon	19,839,000,000	1.0%
5	Pennsylvania	85,601,000,000	4.5%
43	Rhode Island	7,503,000,000	0.4%
26	South Carolina	26,103,000,000	1.4%
47	South Dakota	6,315,000,000	0.3%
17	Tennessee	39,276,000,000	2.0%
3	Texas	123,431,000,000	6.4%
36	Utah	12,302,000,000	0.6%
49	Vermont	4,111,000,000	0.2%
6	Virginia	74,537,000,000	3.9%
16	Washington	40,218,000,000	2.1%
35	West Virginia	13,361,000,000	0.7%
23	Wisconsin	28,844,000,000	1.5%
50	Wyoming	3,666,000,000	0.2%

RANK ORDER

RANK	STATE	EXPENDITURES	% of USA
1	California	$206,401,000,000	10.8%
2	New York	128,994,000,000	6.7%
3	Texas	123,431,000,000	6.4%
4	Florida	104,814,000,000	5.5%
5	Pennsylvania	85,601,000,000	4.5%
6	Virginia	74,537,000,000	3.9%
7	Illinois	70,275,000,000	3.7%
8	Ohio	65,976,000,000	3.4%
9	Michigan	55,909,000,000	2.9%
10	Georgia	51,336,000,000	2.7%
11	New Jersey	50,673,000,000	2.6%
12	Maryland	49,537,000,000	2.6%
13	North Carolina	48,180,000,000	2.5%
14	Massachusetts	47,480,000,000	2.5%
15	Missouri	42,347,000,000	2.2%
16	Washington	40,218,000,000	2.1%
17	Tennessee	39,276,000,000	2.0%
18	Arizona	34,761,000,000	1.8%
19	Alabama	34,291,000,000	1.8%
20	Indiana	34,200,000,000	1.8%
21	Louisiana	29,988,000,000	1.6%
22	Kentucky	28,880,000,000	1.5%
23	Wisconsin	28,844,000,000	1.5%
24	Minnesota	27,056,000,000	1.4%
25	Colorado	26,229,000,000	1.4%
26	South Carolina	26,103,000,000	1.4%
27	Connecticut	25,387,000,000	1.3%
28	Oklahoma	24,355,000,000	1.3%
29	Mississippi	21,308,000,000	1.1%
30	Oregon	19,839,000,000	1.0%
31	Iowa	18,839,000,000	1.0%
32	Arkansas	18,372,000,000	1.0%
33	Kansas	17,496,000,000	0.9%
34	New Mexico	17,478,000,000	0.9%
35	West Virginia	13,361,000,000	0.7%
36	Utah	12,302,000,000	0.6%
37	Nebraska	11,583,000,000	0.6%
38	Nevada	10,737,000,000	0.6%
39	Hawaii	10,474,000,000	0.5%
40	Maine	9,205,000,000	0.5%
41	Idaho	8,378,000,000	0.4%
42	Alaska	7,562,000,000	0.4%
43	Rhode Island	7,503,000,000	0.4%
44	Montana	6,974,000,000	0.4%
45	New Hampshire	6,937,000,000	0.4%
46	North Dakota	6,437,000,000	0.3%
47	South Dakota	6,315,000,000	0.3%
48	Delaware	4,766,000,000	0.2%
49	Vermont	4,111,000,000	0.2%
50	Wyoming	3,666,000,000	0.2%
	District of Columbia	33,533,000,000	1.7%

Source: U.S. Bureau of the Census

"Consolidated Federal Funds Report: 2002" (CFFR/02, May 2003, http://www.census.gov/govs/www/cffr02.html)
**Total includes $16,390,000,000 in U.S. territories ($14,062,000,000 in Puerto Rico) and $18,996,000,000 in expenditures not distributed by state.*

Per Capita Federal Government Expenditures in 2002

National Per Capita = $6,536*

<u>ALPHA ORDER</u>

RANK	STATE	PER CAPITA
9	Alabama	$7,656
1	Alaska	11,788
30	Arizona	6,389
21	Arkansas	6,789
37	California	5,897
38	Colorado	5,827
15	Connecticut	7,340
35	Delaware	5,914
32	Florida	6,279
34	Georgia	6,008
6	Hawaii	8,442
33	Idaho	6,238
43	Illinois	5,583
45	Indiana	5,555
29	Iowa	6,417
28	Kansas	6,452
17	Kentucky	7,061
25	Louisiana	6,699
16	Maine	7,109
5	Maryland	9,088
13	Massachusetts	7,394
44	Michigan	5,567
47	Minnesota	5,385
11	Mississippi	7,433
10	Missouri	7,469
8	Montana	7,661
24	Nebraska	6,705
50	Nevada	4,954
46	New Hampshire	5,443
36	New Jersey	5,909
4	New Mexico	9,437
23	New York	6,742
39	North Carolina	5,801
3	North Dakota	10,154
40	Ohio	5,783
19	Oklahoma	6,979
42	Oregon	5,636
20	Pennsylvania	6,943
18	Rhode Island	7,023
31	South Carolina	6,361
7	South Dakota	8,304
22	Tennessee	6,784
41	Texas	5,678
48	Utah	5,305
26	Vermont	6,669
2	Virginia	10,228
27	Washington	6,629
12	West Virginia	7,403
49	Wisconsin	5,303
14	Wyoming	7,349

<u>RANK ORDER</u>

RANK	STATE	PER CAPITA
1	Alaska	$11,788
2	Virginia	10,228
3	North Dakota	10,154
4	New Mexico	9,437
5	Maryland	9,088
6	Hawaii	8,442
7	South Dakota	8,304
8	Montana	7,661
9	Alabama	7,656
10	Missouri	7,469
11	Mississippi	7,433
12	West Virginia	7,403
13	Massachusetts	7,394
14	Wyoming	7,349
15	Connecticut	7,340
16	Maine	7,109
17	Kentucky	7,061
18	Rhode Island	7,023
19	Oklahoma	6,979
20	Pennsylvania	6,943
21	Arkansas	6,789
22	Tennessee	6,784
23	New York	6,742
24	Nebraska	6,705
25	Louisiana	6,699
26	Vermont	6,669
27	Washington	6,629
28	Kansas	6,452
29	Iowa	6,417
30	Arizona	6,389
31	South Carolina	6,361
32	Florida	6,279
33	Idaho	6,238
34	Georgia	6,008
35	Delaware	5,914
36	New Jersey	5,909
37	California	5,897
38	Colorado	5,827
39	North Carolina	5,801
40	Ohio	5,783
41	Texas	5,678
42	Oregon	5,636
43	Illinois	5,583
44	Michigan	5,567
45	Indiana	5,555
46	New Hampshire	5,443
47	Minnesota	5,385
48	Utah	5,305
49	Wisconsin	5,303
50	Nevada	4,954
	District of Columbia	58,917

Source: Morgan Quitno Press using data from U.S. Bureau of the Census
"Consolidated Federal Funds Report: 2002" (CFFR/02, May 2003, http://www.census.gov/govs/www/cffr02.html)
National per capita excludes expenditures and population for territories and undistributed amounts.

Federal Government Grants in 2002

National Total = $412,371,000,000*

ALPHA ORDER

RANK	STATE	GRANTS	% of USA
23	Alabama	$6,344,000,000	1.5%
36	Alaska	3,127,000,000	0.8%
20	Arizona	6,664,000,000	1.6%
32	Arkansas	4,047,000,000	1.0%
1	California	48,084,000,000	11.7%
30	Colorado	4,740,000,000	1.1%
26	Connecticut	5,279,000,000	1.3%
50	Delaware	1,121,000,000	0.3%
5	Florida	16,350,000,000	4.0%
12	Georgia	10,500,000,000	2.5%
44	Hawaii	1,835,000,000	0.4%
43	Idaho	1,837,000,000	0.4%
6	Illinois	14,975,000,000	3.6%
19	Indiana	6,969,000,000	1.7%
31	Iowa	4,060,000,000	1.0%
35	Kansas	3,272,000,000	0.8%
22	Kentucky	6,346,000,000	1.5%
17	Louisiana	7,437,000,000	1.8%
39	Maine	2,270,000,000	0.6%
24	Maryland	6,312,000,000	1.5%
9	Massachusetts	12,339,000,000	3.0%
8	Michigan	13,279,000,000	3.2%
21	Minnesota	6,492,000,000	1.6%
28	Mississippi	5,046,000,000	1.2%
14	Missouri	8,429,000,000	2.0%
41	Montana	1,912,000,000	0.5%
38	Nebraska	2,342,000,000	0.6%
42	Nevada	1,840,000,000	0.4%
45	New Hampshire	1,632,000,000	0.4%
11	New Jersey	10,822,000,000	2.6%
33	New Mexico	3,954,000,000	1.0%
2	New York	42,461,000,000	10.3%
10	North Carolina	10,939,000,000	2.7%
47	North Dakota	1,425,000,000	0.3%
7	Ohio	14,844,000,000	3.6%
27	Oklahoma	5,108,000,000	1.2%
29	Oregon	4,814,000,000	1.2%
4	Pennsylvania	18,017,000,000	4.4%
40	Rhode Island	2,094,000,000	0.5%
25	South Carolina	5,592,000,000	1.4%
46	South Dakota	1,506,000,000	0.4%
13	Tennessee	8,658,000,000	2.1%
3	Texas	24,858,000,000	6.0%
37	Utah	2,697,000,000	0.7%
48	Vermont	1,281,000,000	0.3%
16	Virginia	7,714,000,000	1.9%
15	Washington	8,296,000,000	2.0%
34	West Virginia	3,298,000,000	0.8%
18	Wisconsin	7,255,000,000	1.8%
49	Wyoming	1,234,000,000	0.3%

RANK ORDER

RANK	STATE	GRANTS	% of USA
1	California	$48,084,000,000	11.7%
2	New York	42,461,000,000	10.3%
3	Texas	24,858,000,000	6.0%
4	Pennsylvania	18,017,000,000	4.4%
5	Florida	16,350,000,000	4.0%
6	Illinois	14,975,000,000	3.6%
7	Ohio	14,844,000,000	3.6%
8	Michigan	13,279,000,000	3.2%
9	Massachusetts	12,339,000,000	3.0%
10	North Carolina	10,939,000,000	2.7%
11	New Jersey	10,822,000,000	2.6%
12	Georgia	10,500,000,000	2.5%
13	Tennessee	8,658,000,000	2.1%
14	Missouri	8,429,000,000	2.0%
15	Washington	8,296,000,000	2.0%
16	Virginia	7,714,000,000	1.9%
17	Louisiana	7,437,000,000	1.8%
18	Wisconsin	7,255,000,000	1.8%
19	Indiana	6,969,000,000	1.7%
20	Arizona	6,664,000,000	1.6%
21	Minnesota	6,492,000,000	1.6%
22	Kentucky	6,346,000,000	1.5%
23	Alabama	6,344,000,000	1.5%
24	Maryland	6,312,000,000	1.5%
25	South Carolina	5,592,000,000	1.4%
26	Connecticut	5,279,000,000	1.3%
27	Oklahoma	5,108,000,000	1.2%
28	Mississippi	5,046,000,000	1.2%
29	Oregon	4,814,000,000	1.2%
30	Colorado	4,740,000,000	1.1%
31	Iowa	4,060,000,000	1.0%
32	Arkansas	4,047,000,000	1.0%
33	New Mexico	3,954,000,000	1.0%
34	West Virginia	3,298,000,000	0.8%
35	Kansas	3,272,000,000	0.8%
36	Alaska	3,127,000,000	0.8%
37	Utah	2,697,000,000	0.7%
38	Nebraska	2,342,000,000	0.6%
39	Maine	2,270,000,000	0.6%
40	Rhode Island	2,094,000,000	0.5%
41	Montana	1,912,000,000	0.5%
42	Nevada	1,840,000,000	0.4%
43	Idaho	1,837,000,000	0.4%
44	Hawaii	1,835,000,000	0.4%
45	New Hampshire	1,632,000,000	0.4%
46	South Dakota	1,506,000,000	0.4%
47	North Dakota	1,425,000,000	0.3%
48	Vermont	1,281,000,000	0.3%
49	Wyoming	1,234,000,000	0.3%
50	Delaware	1,121,000,000	0.3%
	District of Columbia	4,832,000,000	1.2%

Source: U.S. Bureau of the Census

"Consolidated Federal Funds Report: 2002" (CFFR/02, May 2003, http://www.census.gov/govs/www/cffr02.html)
*Total includes $5,729,000,000 in U.S. territories ($4,828,000,000 in Puerto Rico) and $65,000,000 in expenditures not distributed by state.

Per Capita Expenditures for Federal Government Grants in 2002

National Per Capita = $1,412*

ALPHA ORDER

RANK	STATE	PER CAPITA
23	Alabama	$1,416
1	Alaska	4,875
40	Arizona	1,225
17	Arkansas	1,495
26	California	1,374
48	Colorado	1,053
16	Connecticut	1,526
24	Delaware	1,391
49	Florida	980
39	Georgia	1,229
20	Hawaii	1,479
27	Idaho	1,368
42	Illinois	1,190
46	Indiana	1,132
25	Iowa	1,383
41	Kansas	1,207
15	Kentucky	1,552
14	Louisiana	1,661
13	Maine	1,753
44	Maryland	1,158
10	Massachusetts	1,921
33	Michigan	1,322
36	Minnesota	1,292
12	Mississippi	1,760
19	Missouri	1,487
6	Montana	2,100
31	Nebraska	1,356
50	Nevada	849
37	New Hampshire	1,281
38	New Jersey	1,262
5	New Mexico	2,135
4	New York	2,219
34	North Carolina	1,317
3	North Dakota	2,248
35	Ohio	1,301
21	Oklahoma	1,464
28	Oregon	1,367
22	Pennsylvania	1,461
9	Rhode Island	1,960
30	South Carolina	1,363
8	South Dakota	1,980
17	Tennessee	1,495
45	Texas	1,144
43	Utah	1,163
7	Vermont	2,078
47	Virginia	1,058
28	Washington	1,367
11	West Virginia	1,827
32	Wisconsin	1,334
2	Wyoming	2,474

RANK ORDER

RANK	STATE	PER CAPITA
1	Alaska	$4,875
2	Wyoming	2,474
3	North Dakota	2,248
4	New York	2,219
5	New Mexico	2,135
6	Montana	2,100
7	Vermont	2,078
8	South Dakota	1,980
9	Rhode Island	1,960
10	Massachusetts	1,921
11	West Virginia	1,827
12	Mississippi	1,760
13	Maine	1,753
14	Louisiana	1,661
15	Kentucky	1,552
16	Connecticut	1,526
17	Arkansas	1,495
17	Tennessee	1,495
19	Missouri	1,487
20	Hawaii	1,479
21	Oklahoma	1,464
22	Pennsylvania	1,461
23	Alabama	1,416
24	Delaware	1,391
25	Iowa	1,383
26	California	1,374
27	Idaho	1,368
28	Oregon	1,367
28	Washington	1,367
30	South Carolina	1,363
31	Nebraska	1,356
32	Wisconsin	1,334
33	Michigan	1,322
34	North Carolina	1,317
35	Ohio	1,301
36	Minnesota	1,292
37	New Hampshire	1,281
38	New Jersey	1,262
39	Georgia	1,229
40	Arizona	1,225
41	Kansas	1,207
42	Illinois	1,190
43	Utah	1,163
44	Maryland	1,158
45	Texas	1,144
46	Indiana	1,132
47	Virginia	1,058
48	Colorado	1,053
49	Florida	980
50	Nevada	849
	District of Columbia	8,490

Source: Morgan Quitno Press using data from U.S. Bureau of the Census
   "Consolidated Federal Funds Report: 2002" (CFFR/02, May 2003, http://www.census.gov/govs/www/cffr02.html)
*National per capita excludes expenditures and population for territories and undistributed amounts.

Federal Government Procurement Contract Awards in 2002

National Total = $270,965,000,000*

ALPHA ORDER

RANK	STATE	CONTRACTS	% of USA
13	Alabama	$6,035,000,000	2.2%
34	Alaska	1,396,000,000	0.5%
10	Arizona	7,291,000,000	2.7%
38	Arkansas	1,095,000,000	0.4%
1	California	34,753,000,000	12.8%
20	Colorado	4,526,000,000	1.7%
12	Connecticut	6,216,000,000	2.3%
50	Delaware	207,000,000	0.1%
5	Florida	9,757,000,000	3.6%
8	Georgia	7,364,000,000	2.7%
33	Hawaii	1,621,000,000	0.6%
35	Idaho	1,357,000,000	0.5%
19	Illinois	4,664,000,000	1.7%
25	Indiana	2,802,000,000	1.0%
40	Iowa	955,000,000	0.4%
32	Kansas	1,653,000,000	0.6%
21	Kentucky	3,978,000,000	1.5%
26	Louisiana	2,773,000,000	1.0%
37	Maine	1,240,000,000	0.5%
4	Maryland	13,488,000,000	5.0%
11	Massachusetts	6,793,000,000	2.5%
22	Michigan	3,539,000,000	1.3%
29	Minnesota	2,228,000,000	0.8%
27	Mississippi	2,734,000,000	1.0%
9	Missouri	7,313,000,000	2.7%
47	Montana	350,000,000	0.1%
43	Nebraska	591,000,000	0.2%
36	Nevada	1,250,000,000	0.5%
41	New Hampshire	788,000,000	0.3%
18	New Jersey	4,840,000,000	1.8%
16	New Mexico	5,393,000,000	2.0%
6	New York	7,417,000,000	2.7%
24	North Carolina	2,923,000,000	1.1%
48	North Dakota	329,000,000	0.1%
17	Ohio	5,243,000,000	1.9%
28	Oklahoma	2,515,000,000	0.9%
39	Oregon	994,000,000	0.4%
7	Pennsylvania	7,415,000,000	2.7%
44	Rhode Island	495,000,000	0.2%
23	South Carolina	3,105,000,000	1.1%
46	South Dakota	378,000,000	0.1%
14	Tennessee	5,912,000,000	2.2%
3	Texas	20,581,000,000	7.6%
30	Utah	2,084,000,000	0.8%
45	Vermont	431,000,000	0.2%
2	Virginia	26,170,000,000	9.7%
15	Washington	5,586,000,000	2.1%
42	West Virginia	602,000,000	0.2%
31	Wisconsin	1,888,000,000	0.7%
49	Wyoming	319,000,000	0.1%

RANK ORDER

RANK	STATE	CONTRACTS	% of USA
1	California	$34,753,000,000	12.8%
2	Virginia	26,170,000,000	9.7%
3	Texas	20,581,000,000	7.6%
4	Maryland	13,488,000,000	5.0%
5	Florida	9,757,000,000	3.6%
6	New York	7,417,000,000	2.7%
7	Pennsylvania	7,415,000,000	2.7%
8	Georgia	7,364,000,000	2.7%
9	Missouri	7,313,000,000	2.7%
10	Arizona	7,291,000,000	2.7%
11	Massachusetts	6,793,000,000	2.5%
12	Connecticut	6,216,000,000	2.3%
13	Alabama	6,035,000,000	2.2%
14	Tennessee	5,912,000,000	2.2%
15	Washington	5,586,000,000	2.1%
16	New Mexico	5,393,000,000	2.0%
17	Ohio	5,243,000,000	1.9%
18	New Jersey	4,840,000,000	1.8%
19	Illinois	4,664,000,000	1.7%
20	Colorado	4,526,000,000	1.7%
21	Kentucky	3,978,000,000	1.5%
22	Michigan	3,539,000,000	1.3%
23	South Carolina	3,105,000,000	1.1%
24	North Carolina	2,923,000,000	1.1%
25	Indiana	2,802,000,000	1.0%
26	Louisiana	2,773,000,000	1.0%
27	Mississippi	2,734,000,000	1.0%
28	Oklahoma	2,515,000,000	0.9%
29	Minnesota	2,228,000,000	0.8%
30	Utah	2,084,000,000	0.8%
31	Wisconsin	1,888,000,000	0.7%
32	Kansas	1,653,000,000	0.6%
33	Hawaii	1,621,000,000	0.6%
34	Alaska	1,396,000,000	0.5%
35	Idaho	1,357,000,000	0.5%
36	Nevada	1,250,000,000	0.5%
37	Maine	1,240,000,000	0.5%
38	Arkansas	1,095,000,000	0.4%
39	Oregon	994,000,000	0.4%
40	Iowa	955,000,000	0.4%
41	New Hampshire	788,000,000	0.3%
42	West Virginia	602,000,000	0.2%
43	Nebraska	591,000,000	0.2%
44	Rhode Island	495,000,000	0.2%
45	Vermont	431,000,000	0.2%
46	South Dakota	378,000,000	0.1%
47	Montana	350,000,000	0.1%
48	North Dakota	329,000,000	0.1%
49	Wyoming	319,000,000	0.1%
50	Delaware	207,000,000	0.1%
	District of Columbia	10,875,000,000	4.0%

Source: U.S. Bureau of the Census

"Consolidated Federal Funds Report: 2002" (CFFR/02, May 2003, http://www.census.gov/govs/www/cffr02.html)
**Total includes $870,000,000 in U.S. territories ($365,000,000 in Puerto Rico) and $15,844,000,000 in expenditures not distributed by state.*

Per Capita Expenditures for Federal Government Procurement Contract Awards in 2002
National Per Capita = $883*

ALPHA ORDER

RANK	STATE	PER CAPITA
6	Alabama	$1,347
4	Alaska	2,176
7	Arizona	1,340
39	Arkansas	405
14	California	993
13	Colorado	1,006
5	Connecticut	1,797
50	Delaware	257
30	Florida	585
21	Georgia	862
8	Hawaii	1,307
12	Idaho	1,010
42	Illinois	371
37	Indiana	455
48	Iowa	325
28	Kansas	610
15	Kentucky	973
26	Louisiana	619
16	Maine	958
3	Maryland	2,475
10	Massachusetts	1,058
43	Michigan	352
38	Minnesota	443
17	Mississippi	954
9	Missouri	1,290
41	Montana	384
46	Nebraska	342
31	Nevada	577
27	New Hampshire	618
32	New Jersey	564
2	New Mexico	2,912
40	New York	388
43	North Carolina	352
33	North Dakota	519
36	Ohio	460
23	Oklahoma	721
49	Oregon	282
29	Pennsylvania	601
35	Rhode Island	463
22	South Carolina	757
34	South Dakota	497
11	Tennessee	1,021
18	Texas	947
20	Utah	899
24	Vermont	699
1	Virginia	3,591
19	Washington	921
47	West Virginia	334
45	Wisconsin	347
25	Wyoming	639

RANK ORDER

RANK	STATE	PER CAPITA
1	Virginia	$3,591
2	New Mexico	2,912
3	Maryland	2,475
4	Alaska	2,176
5	Connecticut	1,797
6	Alabama	1,347
7	Arizona	1,340
8	Hawaii	1,307
9	Missouri	1,290
10	Massachusetts	1,058
11	Tennessee	1,021
12	Idaho	1,010
13	Colorado	1,006
14	California	993
15	Kentucky	973
16	Maine	958
17	Mississippi	954
18	Texas	947
19	Washington	921
20	Utah	899
21	Georgia	862
22	South Carolina	757
23	Oklahoma	721
24	Vermont	699
25	Wyoming	639
26	Louisiana	619
27	New Hampshire	618
28	Kansas	610
29	Pennsylvania	601
30	Florida	585
31	Nevada	577
32	New Jersey	564
33	North Dakota	519
34	South Dakota	497
35	Rhode Island	463
36	Ohio	460
37	Indiana	455
38	Minnesota	443
39	Arkansas	405
40	New York	388
41	Montana	384
42	Illinois	371
43	Michigan	352
43	North Carolina	352
45	Wisconsin	347
46	Nebraska	342
47	West Virginia	334
48	Iowa	325
49	Oregon	282
50	Delaware	257

District of Columbia — 19,107

Source: Morgan Quitno Press using data from U.S. Bureau of the Census
"Consolidated Federal Funds Report: 2002" (CFFR/02, May 2003, http://www.census.gov/govs/www/cffr02.html)
National per capita excludes expenditures and population for territories and undistributed amounts.

Federal Government Direct Payments for Retirement and Disability in 2002
National Total = $612,996,000,000*

ALPHA ORDER

RANK	STATE	PAYMENTS	% of USA
19	Alabama	$11,717,000,000	1.9%
50	Alaska	981,000,000	0.2%
20	Arizona	11,471,000,000	1.9%
30	Arkansas	6,777,000,000	1.1%
1	California	59,256,000,000	9.7%
27	Colorado	8,073,000,000	1.3%
29	Connecticut	7,348,000,000	1.2%
45	Delaware	1,851,000,000	0.3%
2	Florida	43,709,000,000	7.1%
12	Georgia	15,945,000,000	2.6%
40	Hawaii	2,899,000,000	0.5%
42	Idaho	2,713,000,000	0.4%
7	Illinois	24,068,000,000	3.9%
17	Indiana	12,877,000,000	2.1%
32	Iowa	6,570,000,000	1.1%
33	Kansas	5,973,000,000	1.0%
22	Kentucky	9,795,000,000	1.6%
24	Louisiana	9,225,000,000	1.5%
39	Maine	3,267,000,000	0.5%
18	Maryland	12,789,000,000	2.1%
13	Massachusetts	13,436,000,000	2.2%
8	Michigan	21,241,000,000	3.5%
24	Minnesota	9,225,000,000	1.5%
31	Mississippi	6,688,000,000	1.1%
16	Missouri	13,051,000,000	2.1%
44	Montana	2,199,000,000	0.4%
37	Nebraska	3,774,000,000	0.6%
35	Nevada	4,425,000,000	0.7%
41	New Hampshire	2,726,000,000	0.4%
11	New Jersey	17,906,000,000	2.9%
36	New Mexico	4,174,000,000	0.7%
3	New York	39,201,000,000	6.4%
10	North Carolina	17,971,000,000	2.9%
47	North Dakota	1,384,000,000	0.2%
6	Ohio	24,599,000,000	4.0%
26	Oklahoma	8,393,000,000	1.4%
28	Oregon	7,687,000,000	1.3%
5	Pennsylvania	31,194,000,000	5.1%
43	Rhode Island	2,479,000,000	0.4%
23	South Carolina	9,708,000,000	1.6%
46	South Dakota	1,702,000,000	0.3%
14	Tennessee	13,196,000,000	2.2%
4	Texas	37,324,000,000	6.1%
38	Utah	3,723,000,000	0.6%
48	Vermont	1,304,000,000	0.2%
9	Virginia	18,634,000,000	3.0%
15	Washington	13,063,000,000	2.1%
34	West Virginia	5,460,000,000	0.9%
21	Wisconsin	11,158,000,000	1.8%
49	Wyoming	1,095,000,000	0.2%

RANK ORDER

RANK	STATE	PAYMENTS	% of USA
1	California	$59,256,000,000	9.7%
2	Florida	43,709,000,000	7.1%
3	New York	39,201,000,000	6.4%
4	Texas	37,324,000,000	6.1%
5	Pennsylvania	31,194,000,000	5.1%
6	Ohio	24,599,000,000	4.0%
7	Illinois	24,068,000,000	3.9%
8	Michigan	21,241,000,000	3.5%
9	Virginia	18,634,000,000	3.0%
10	North Carolina	17,971,000,000	2.9%
11	New Jersey	17,906,000,000	2.9%
12	Georgia	15,945,000,000	2.6%
13	Massachusetts	13,436,000,000	2.2%
14	Tennessee	13,196,000,000	2.2%
15	Washington	13,063,000,000	2.1%
16	Missouri	13,051,000,000	2.1%
17	Indiana	12,877,000,000	2.1%
18	Maryland	12,789,000,000	2.1%
19	Alabama	11,717,000,000	1.9%
20	Arizona	11,471,000,000	1.9%
21	Wisconsin	11,158,000,000	1.8%
22	Kentucky	9,795,000,000	1.6%
23	South Carolina	9,708,000,000	1.6%
24	Louisiana	9,225,000,000	1.5%
24	Minnesota	9,225,000,000	1.5%
26	Oklahoma	8,393,000,000	1.4%
27	Colorado	8,073,000,000	1.3%
28	Oregon	7,687,000,000	1.3%
29	Connecticut	7,348,000,000	1.2%
30	Arkansas	6,777,000,000	1.1%
31	Mississippi	6,688,000,000	1.1%
32	Iowa	6,570,000,000	1.1%
33	Kansas	5,973,000,000	1.0%
34	West Virginia	5,460,000,000	0.9%
35	Nevada	4,425,000,000	0.7%
36	New Mexico	4,174,000,000	0.7%
37	Nebraska	3,774,000,000	0.6%
38	Utah	3,723,000,000	0.6%
39	Maine	3,267,000,000	0.5%
40	Hawaii	2,899,000,000	0.5%
41	New Hampshire	2,726,000,000	0.4%
42	Idaho	2,713,000,000	0.4%
43	Rhode Island	2,479,000,000	0.4%
44	Montana	2,199,000,000	0.4%
45	Delaware	1,851,000,000	0.3%
46	South Dakota	1,702,000,000	0.3%
47	North Dakota	1,384,000,000	0.2%
48	Vermont	1,304,000,000	0.2%
49	Wyoming	1,095,000,000	0.2%
50	Alaska	981,000,000	0.2%
	District of Columbia	1,876,000,000	0.3%

Source: U.S. Bureau of the Census

"Consolidated Federal Funds Report: 2001" (CFFR/01, April 2002, http://www.census.gov/govs/www/cffr01.html)
Total includes $5,679,000,000 in U.S. territories ($5,282,000,000 in Puerto Rico) and $17,000,000 in expenditures not distributed by state. "Direct Payments for Retirement and Disability" include Social Security, federal retirement and disability payments and veterans benefits.

Per Capita Federal Government Direct Payments for Retirement and Disability in 2002
National Per Capita = $2,109*

ALPHA ORDER

RANK	STATE	PER CAPITA
3	Alabama	$2,616
50	Alaska	1,529
34	Arizona	2,108
7	Arkansas	2,504
48	California	1,693
46	Colorado	1,794
31	Connecticut	2,125
17	Delaware	2,297
2	Florida	2,619
44	Georgia	1,866
13	Hawaii	2,337
42	Idaho	2,020
43	Illinois	1,912
36	Indiana	2,091
20	Iowa	2,238
22	Kansas	2,203
10	Kentucky	2,395
38	Louisiana	2,061
6	Maine	2,523
12	Maryland	2,346
35	Massachusetts	2,092
32	Michigan	2,115
45	Minnesota	1,836
14	Mississippi	2,333
16	Missouri	2,302
8	Montana	2,415
24	Nebraska	2,185
41	Nevada	2,042
30	New Hampshire	2,139
37	New Jersey	2,088
19	New Mexico	2,254
40	New York	2,049
27	North Carolina	2,164
26	North Dakota	2,183
28	Ohio	2,156
9	Oklahoma	2,405
25	Oregon	2,184
5	Pennsylvania	2,530
15	Rhode Island	2,320
11	South Carolina	2,366
20	South Dakota	2,238
18	Tennessee	2,279
47	Texas	1,717
49	Utah	1,606
32	Vermont	2,115
4	Virginia	2,557
29	Washington	2,153
1	West Virginia	3,025
39	Wisconsin	2,051
23	Wyoming	2,195

RANK ORDER

RANK	STATE	PER CAPITA
1	West Virginia	$3,025
2	Florida	2,619
3	Alabama	2,616
4	Virginia	2,557
5	Pennsylvania	2,530
6	Maine	2,523
7	Arkansas	2,504
8	Montana	2,415
9	Oklahoma	2,405
10	Kentucky	2,395
11	South Carolina	2,366
12	Maryland	2,346
13	Hawaii	2,337
14	Mississippi	2,333
15	Rhode Island	2,320
16	Missouri	2,302
17	Delaware	2,297
18	Tennessee	2,279
19	New Mexico	2,254
20	Iowa	2,238
20	South Dakota	2,238
22	Kansas	2,203
23	Wyoming	2,195
24	Nebraska	2,185
25	Oregon	2,184
26	North Dakota	2,183
27	North Carolina	2,164
28	Ohio	2,156
29	Washington	2,153
30	New Hampshire	2,139
31	Connecticut	2,125
32	Michigan	2,115
32	Vermont	2,115
34	Arizona	2,108
35	Massachusetts	2,092
36	Indiana	2,091
37	New Jersey	2,088
38	Louisiana	2,061
39	Wisconsin	2,051
40	New York	2,049
41	Nevada	2,042
42	Idaho	2,020
43	Illinois	1,912
44	Georgia	1,866
45	Minnesota	1,836
46	Colorado	1,794
47	Texas	1,717
48	California	1,693
49	Utah	1,606
50	Alaska	1,529

| | District of Columbia | 3,296 |

Source: Morgan Quitno Press using data from U.S. Bureau of the Census
   "Consolidated Federal Funds Report: 2002" (CFFR/02, May 2003, http://www.census.gov/govs/www/cffr02.html)
*National per capita excludes expenditures and population for territories and undistributed amounts.

Federal Government "Other" Direct Payments in 2002

National Total = $422,239,000,000*

<u>ALPHA ORDER</u>

RANK	STATE	PAYMENTS	% of USA
21	Alabama	$7,086,000,000	1.7%
49	Alaska	560,000,000	0.1%
23	Arizona	6,193,000,000	1.5%
26	Arkansas	5,202,000,000	1.2%
1	California	45,166,000,000	10.7%
31	Colorado	4,753,000,000	1.1%
28	Connecticut	5,088,000,000	1.2%
47	Delaware	1,121,000,000	0.3%
4	Florida	25,961,000,000	6.1%
12	Georgia	10,160,000,000	2.4%
45	Hawaii	1,435,000,000	0.3%
42	Idaho	1,690,000,000	0.4%
6	Illinois	20,223,000,000	4.8%
14	Indiana	9,345,000,000	2.2%
24	Iowa	6,169,000,000	1.5%
33	Kansas	4,614,000,000	1.1%
25	Kentucky	5,906,000,000	1.4%
17	Louisiana	8,092,000,000	1.9%
44	Maine	1,580,000,000	0.4%
19	Maryland	7,285,000,000	1.7%
10	Massachusetts	11,537,000,000	2.7%
8	Michigan	14,564,000,000	3.4%
20	Minnesota	7,089,000,000	1.7%
30	Mississippi	5,000,000,000	1.2%
13	Missouri	9,916,000,000	2.3%
41	Montana	1,752,000,000	0.4%
34	Nebraska	3,767,000,000	0.9%
38	Nevada	2,126,000,000	0.5%
46	New Hampshire	1,216,000,000	0.3%
9	New Jersey	13,131,000,000	3.1%
37	New Mexico	2,154,000,000	0.5%
2	New York	31,389,000,000	7.4%
11	North Carolina	10,369,000,000	2.5%
36	North Dakota	2,643,000,000	0.6%
7	Ohio	16,181,000,000	3.8%
27	Oklahoma	5,187,000,000	1.2%
32	Oregon	4,652,000,000	1.1%
5	Pennsylvania	22,917,000,000	5.4%
43	Rhode Island	1,650,000,000	0.4%
29	South Carolina	5,063,000,000	1.2%
39	South Dakota	2,099,000,000	0.5%
16	Tennessee	8,309,000,000	2.0%
3	Texas	27,648,000,000	6.5%
40	Utah	1,869,000,000	0.4%
48	Vermont	736,000,000	0.2%
15	Virginia	8,515,000,000	2.0%
18	Washington	7,994,000,000	1.9%
35	West Virginia	2,780,000,000	0.7%
22	Wisconsin	6,830,000,000	1.6%
50	Wyoming	553,000,000	0.1%

<u>RANK ORDER</u>

RANK	STATE	PAYMENTS	% of USA
1	California	$45,166,000,000	10.7%
2	New York	31,389,000,000	7.4%
3	Texas	27,648,000,000	6.5%
4	Florida	25,961,000,000	6.1%
5	Pennsylvania	22,917,000,000	5.4%
6	Illinois	20,223,000,000	4.8%
7	Ohio	16,181,000,000	3.8%
8	Michigan	14,564,000,000	3.4%
9	New Jersey	13,131,000,000	3.1%
10	Massachusetts	11,537,000,000	2.7%
11	North Carolina	10,369,000,000	2.5%
12	Georgia	10,160,000,000	2.4%
13	Missouri	9,916,000,000	2.3%
14	Indiana	9,345,000,000	2.2%
15	Virginia	8,515,000,000	2.0%
16	Tennessee	8,309,000,000	2.0%
17	Louisiana	8,092,000,000	1.9%
18	Washington	7,994,000,000	1.9%
19	Maryland	7,285,000,000	1.7%
20	Minnesota	7,089,000,000	1.7%
21	Alabama	7,086,000,000	1.7%
22	Wisconsin	6,830,000,000	1.6%
23	Arizona	6,193,000,000	1.5%
24	Iowa	6,169,000,000	1.5%
25	Kentucky	5,906,000,000	1.4%
26	Arkansas	5,202,000,000	1.2%
27	Oklahoma	5,187,000,000	1.2%
28	Connecticut	5,088,000,000	1.2%
29	South Carolina	5,063,000,000	1.2%
30	Mississippi	5,000,000,000	1.2%
31	Colorado	4,753,000,000	1.1%
32	Oregon	4,652,000,000	1.1%
33	Kansas	4,614,000,000	1.1%
34	Nebraska	3,767,000,000	0.9%
35	West Virginia	2,780,000,000	0.7%
36	North Dakota	2,643,000,000	0.6%
37	New Mexico	2,154,000,000	0.5%
38	Nevada	2,126,000,000	0.5%
39	South Dakota	2,099,000,000	0.5%
40	Utah	1,869,000,000	0.4%
41	Montana	1,752,000,000	0.4%
42	Idaho	1,690,000,000	0.4%
43	Rhode Island	1,650,000,000	0.4%
44	Maine	1,580,000,000	0.4%
45	Hawaii	1,435,000,000	0.3%
46	New Hampshire	1,216,000,000	0.3%
47	Delaware	1,121,000,000	0.3%
48	Vermont	736,000,000	0.2%
49	Alaska	560,000,000	0.1%
50	Wyoming	553,000,000	0.1%
	District of Columbia	2,130,000,000	0.5%

Source: U.S. Bureau of the Census
"Consolidated Federal Funds Report: 2002" (CFFR/02, May 2003, http://www.census.gov/govs/www/cffr02.html)
**Total includes $2,844,000,000 in U.S. territories ($2,658,000,000 in Puerto Rico). "Other Direct Payments" include direct payments for programs other than retirement and disability. These include Medicare, excess earned income tax credits, unemployment compensation, food stamps, housing assistance and agricultural assistance.*

Per Capita Expenditures for Federal Government
"Other" Direct Payments in 2002
National Per Capita = $1,456*

ALPHA ORDER

RANK	STATE	PER CAPITA
15	Alabama	$1,582
49	Alaska	873
44	Arizona	1,138
6	Arkansas	1,922
32	California	1,290
46	Colorado	1,056
22	Connecticut	1,471
28	Delaware	1,391
16	Florida	1,555
40	Georgia	1,189
43	Hawaii	1,157
34	Idaho	1,258
14	Illinois	1,607
20	Indiana	1,518
4	Iowa	2,101
12	Kansas	1,701
24	Kentucky	1,444
8	Louisiana	1,808
38	Maine	1,220
29	Maryland	1,337
9	Massachusetts	1,797
23	Michigan	1,450
27	Minnesota	1,411
11	Mississippi	1,744
10	Missouri	1,749
5	Montana	1,924
3	Nebraska	2,181
47	Nevada	981
48	New Hampshire	954
19	New Jersey	1,531
42	New Mexico	1,163
13	New York	1,640
36	North Carolina	1,248
1	North Dakota	4,169
26	Ohio	1,418
21	Oklahoma	1,486
30	Oregon	1,321
7	Pennsylvania	1,859
17	Rhode Island	1,544
37	South Carolina	1,234
2	South Dakota	2,760
25	Tennessee	1,435
33	Texas	1,272
50	Utah	806
39	Vermont	1,194
41	Virginia	1,168
31	Washington	1,318
18	West Virginia	1,540
35	Wisconsin	1,256
45	Wyoming	1,109

RANK ORDER

RANK	STATE	PER CAPITA
1	North Dakota	$4,169
2	South Dakota	2,760
3	Nebraska	2,181
4	Iowa	2,101
5	Montana	1,924
6	Arkansas	1,922
7	Pennsylvania	1,859
8	Louisiana	1,808
9	Massachusetts	1,797
10	Missouri	1,749
11	Mississippi	1,744
12	Kansas	1,701
13	New York	1,640
14	Illinois	1,607
15	Alabama	1,582
16	Florida	1,555
17	Rhode Island	1,544
18	West Virginia	1,540
19	New Jersey	1,531
20	Indiana	1,518
21	Oklahoma	1,486
22	Connecticut	1,471
23	Michigan	1,450
24	Kentucky	1,444
25	Tennessee	1,435
26	Ohio	1,418
27	Minnesota	1,411
28	Delaware	1,391
29	Maryland	1,337
30	Oregon	1,321
31	Washington	1,318
32	California	1,290
33	Texas	1,272
34	Idaho	1,258
35	Wisconsin	1,256
36	North Carolina	1,248
37	South Carolina	1,234
38	Maine	1,220
39	Vermont	1,194
40	Georgia	1,189
41	Virginia	1,168
42	New Mexico	1,163
43	Hawaii	1,157
44	Arizona	1,138
45	Wyoming	1,109
46	Colorado	1,056
47	Nevada	981
48	New Hampshire	954
49	Alaska	873
50	Utah	806
	District of Columbia	3,742

Source: Morgan Quitno Press using data from U.S. Bureau of the Census
"Consolidated Federal Funds Report: 2002" (CFFR/02, May 2003, http://www.census.gov/govs/www/cffr02.html)
*National per capita excludes expenditures and population for territories and undistributed amounts.

Federal Government Expenditures for Salaries and Wages in 2002

National Total = $199,066,000,000*

ALPHA ORDER

RANK	STATE	SALARIES	% of USA
21	Alabama	$3,109,000,000	1.6%
34	Alaska	1,499,000,000	0.8%
20	Arizona	3,142,000,000	1.6%
36	Arkansas	1,251,000,000	0.6%
1	California	19,143,000,000	9.6%
13	Colorado	4,138,000,000	2.1%
35	Connecticut	1,456,000,000	0.7%
48	Delaware	465,000,000	0.2%
5	Florida	9,038,000,000	4.5%
7	Georgia	7,366,000,000	3.7%
23	Hawaii	2,684,000,000	1.3%
43	Idaho	781,000,000	0.4%
8	Illinois	6,344,000,000	3.2%
26	Indiana	2,208,000,000	1.1%
40	Iowa	1,084,000,000	0.5%
28	Kansas	1,984,000,000	1.0%
22	Kentucky	2,854,000,000	1.4%
25	Louisiana	2,461,000,000	1.2%
41	Maine	848,000,000	0.4%
4	Maryland	9,664,000,000	4.9%
16	Massachusetts	3,376,000,000	1.7%
17	Michigan	3,286,000,000	1.7%
27	Minnesota	2,022,000,000	1.0%
30	Mississippi	1,840,000,000	0.9%
15	Missouri	3,637,000,000	1.8%
44	Montana	760,000,000	0.4%
38	Nebraska	1,109,000,000	0.6%
39	Nevada	1,096,000,000	0.6%
47	New Hampshire	574,000,000	0.3%
14	New Jersey	3,974,000,000	2.0%
31	New Mexico	1,802,000,000	0.9%
6	New York	8,526,000,000	4.3%
10	North Carolina	5,978,000,000	3.0%
45	North Dakota	655,000,000	0.3%
12	Ohio	5,109,000,000	2.6%
19	Oklahoma	3,152,000,000	1.6%
33	Oregon	1,692,000,000	0.8%
9	Pennsylvania	6,058,000,000	3.0%
42	Rhode Island	786,000,000	0.4%
24	South Carolina	2,636,000,000	1.3%
46	South Dakota	631,000,000	0.3%
18	Tennessee	3,200,000,000	1.6%
3	Texas	13,019,000,000	6.5%
29	Utah	1,929,000,000	1.0%
50	Vermont	359,000,000	0.2%
2	Virginia	13,504,000,000	6.8%
11	Washington	5,278,000,000	2.7%
37	West Virginia	1,221,000,000	0.6%
32	Wisconsin	1,713,000,000	0.9%
48	Wyoming	465,000,000	0.2%

RANK ORDER

RANK	STATE	SALARIES	% of USA
1	California	$19,143,000,000	9.6%
2	Virginia	13,504,000,000	6.8%
3	Texas	13,019,000,000	6.5%
4	Maryland	9,664,000,000	4.9%
5	Florida	9,038,000,000	4.5%
6	New York	8,526,000,000	4.3%
7	Georgia	7,366,000,000	3.7%
8	Illinois	6,344,000,000	3.2%
9	Pennsylvania	6,058,000,000	3.0%
10	North Carolina	5,978,000,000	3.0%
11	Washington	5,278,000,000	2.7%
12	Ohio	5,109,000,000	2.6%
13	Colorado	4,138,000,000	2.1%
14	New Jersey	3,974,000,000	2.0%
15	Missouri	3,637,000,000	1.8%
16	Massachusetts	3,376,000,000	1.7%
17	Michigan	3,286,000,000	1.7%
18	Tennessee	3,200,000,000	1.6%
19	Oklahoma	3,152,000,000	1.6%
20	Arizona	3,142,000,000	1.6%
21	Alabama	3,109,000,000	1.6%
22	Kentucky	2,854,000,000	1.4%
23	Hawaii	2,684,000,000	1.3%
24	South Carolina	2,636,000,000	1.3%
25	Louisiana	2,461,000,000	1.2%
26	Indiana	2,208,000,000	1.1%
27	Minnesota	2,022,000,000	1.0%
28	Kansas	1,984,000,000	1.0%
29	Utah	1,929,000,000	1.0%
30	Mississippi	1,840,000,000	0.9%
31	New Mexico	1,802,000,000	0.9%
32	Wisconsin	1,713,000,000	0.9%
33	Oregon	1,692,000,000	0.8%
34	Alaska	1,499,000,000	0.8%
35	Connecticut	1,456,000,000	0.7%
36	Arkansas	1,251,000,000	0.6%
37	West Virginia	1,221,000,000	0.6%
38	Nebraska	1,109,000,000	0.6%
39	Nevada	1,096,000,000	0.6%
40	Iowa	1,084,000,000	0.5%
41	Maine	848,000,000	0.4%
42	Rhode Island	786,000,000	0.4%
43	Idaho	781,000,000	0.4%
44	Montana	760,000,000	0.4%
45	North Dakota	655,000,000	0.3%
46	South Dakota	631,000,000	0.3%
47	New Hampshire	574,000,000	0.3%
48	Delaware	465,000,000	0.2%
48	Wyoming	465,000,000	0.2%
50	Vermont	359,000,000	0.2%
	District of Columbia	13,821,000,000	6.9%

Source: U.S. Bureau of the Census

"Consolidated Federal Funds Report: 2002" (CFFR/02, May 2003, http://www.census.gov/govs/www/cffr02.html)
*Total includes $1,268,000,000 in U.S. territories ($930,000,000 in Puerto Rico) and $3,071,000,000 in expenditures not distributed by state.

Per Capita Expenditures for Federal Government Salaries and Wages in 2002

National Per Capita = $676*

ALPHA ORDER

RANK	STATE	PER CAPITA
19	Alabama	$694
1	Alaska	2,337
29	Arizona	577
41	Arkansas	462
33	California	547
8	Colorado	919
45	Connecticut	421
29	Delaware	577
34	Florida	541
11	Georgia	862
2	Hawaii	2,163
28	Idaho	581
37	Illinois	504
48	Indiana	359
47	Iowa	369
16	Kansas	732
18	Kentucky	698
32	Louisiana	550
21	Maine	655
4	Maryland	1,773
35	Massachusetts	526
49	Michigan	327
46	Minnesota	402
22	Mississippi	642
25	Missouri	641
12	Montana	835
22	Nebraska	642
36	Nevada	506
42	New Hampshire	450
40	New Jersey	463
6	New Mexico	973
44	New York	446
17	North Carolina	720
5	North Dakota	1,033
43	Ohio	448
9	Oklahoma	903
39	Oregon	481
38	Pennsylvania	491
15	Rhode Island	736
22	South Carolina	642
14	South Dakota	830
31	Tennessee	553
26	Texas	599
13	Utah	832
27	Vermont	582
3	Virginia	1,853
10	Washington	870
20	West Virginia	676
50	Wisconsin	315
7	Wyoming	932

RANK ORDER

RANK	STATE	PER CAPITA
1	Alaska	$2,337
2	Hawaii	2,163
3	Virginia	1,853
4	Maryland	1,773
5	North Dakota	1,033
6	New Mexico	973
7	Wyoming	932
8	Colorado	919
9	Oklahoma	903
10	Washington	870
11	Georgia	862
12	Montana	835
13	Utah	832
14	South Dakota	830
15	Rhode Island	736
16	Kansas	732
17	North Carolina	720
18	Kentucky	698
19	Alabama	694
20	West Virginia	676
21	Maine	655
22	Mississippi	642
22	Nebraska	642
22	South Carolina	642
25	Missouri	641
26	Texas	599
27	Vermont	582
28	Idaho	581
29	Arizona	577
29	Delaware	577
31	Tennessee	553
32	Louisiana	550
33	California	547
34	Florida	541
35	Massachusetts	526
36	Nevada	506
37	Illinois	504
38	Pennsylvania	491
39	Oregon	481
40	New Jersey	463
41	Arkansas	462
42	New Hampshire	450
43	Ohio	448
44	New York	446
45	Connecticut	421
46	Minnesota	402
47	Iowa	369
48	Indiana	359
49	Michigan	327
50	Wisconsin	315
	District of Columbia	24,283

Source: Morgan Quitno Press using data from U.S. Bureau of the Census
   "Consolidated Federal Funds Report: 2002" (CFFR/02, May 2003, http://www.census.gov/govs/www/cffr02.html)
*National per capita excludes expenditures and population for territories and undistributed amounts.

Average Salary of Federal Civilian Employees in 2001

National Average = $53,115*

ALPHA ORDER

RANK	STATE	SALARY
13	Alabama	$52,692
20	Alaska	49,365
44	Arizona	45,886
46	Arkansas	44,751
11	California	53,457
8	Colorado	54,185
12	Connecticut	53,146
35	Delaware	47,011
18	Florida	50,650
21	Georgia	49,157
33	Hawaii	47,077
28	Idaho	47,785
6	Illinois	55,284
29	Indiana	47,765
41	Iowa	46,500
30	Kansas	47,655
50	Kentucky	43,102
38	Louisiana	46,732
31	Maine	47,323
1	Maryland	62,321
10	Massachusetts	53,644
9	Michigan	54,163
14	Minnesota	52,284
42	Mississippi	46,386
37	Missouri	46,763
39	Montana	46,596
27	Nebraska	47,871
16	Nevada	51,529
2	New Hampshire	59,476
3	New Jersey	58,237
25	New Mexico	48,028
15	New York	51,972
43	North Carolina	46,340
47	North Dakota	44,724
7	Ohio	54,383
40	Oklahoma	46,510
19	Oregon	50,282
24	Pennsylvania	48,072
5	Rhode Island	57,922
36	South Carolina	46,912
49	South Dakota	43,774
22	Tennessee	49,084
23	Texas	49,049
48	Utah	44,616
34	Vermont	47,071
4	Virginia	58,129
17	Washington	51,442
26	West Virginia	47,969
32	Wisconsin	47,297
45	Wyoming	45,316

RANK ORDER

RANK	STATE	SALARY
1	Maryland	$62,321
2	New Hampshire	59,476
3	New Jersey	58,237
4	Virginia	58,129
5	Rhode Island	57,922
6	Illinois	55,284
7	Ohio	54,383
8	Colorado	54,185
9	Michigan	54,163
10	Massachusetts	53,644
11	California	53,457
12	Connecticut	53,146
13	Alabama	52,692
14	Minnesota	52,284
15	New York	51,972
16	Nevada	51,529
17	Washington	51,442
18	Florida	50,650
19	Oregon	50,282
20	Alaska	49,365
21	Georgia	49,157
22	Tennessee	49,084
23	Texas	49,049
24	Pennsylvania	48,072
25	New Mexico	48,028
26	West Virginia	47,969
27	Nebraska	47,871
28	Idaho	47,785
29	Indiana	47,765
30	Kansas	47,655
31	Maine	47,323
32	Wisconsin	47,297
33	Hawaii	47,077
34	Vermont	47,071
35	Delaware	47,011
36	South Carolina	46,912
37	Missouri	46,763
38	Louisiana	46,732
39	Montana	46,596
40	Oklahoma	46,510
41	Iowa	46,500
42	Mississippi	46,386
43	North Carolina	46,340
44	Arizona	45,886
45	Wyoming	45,316
46	Arkansas	44,751
47	North Dakota	44,724
48	Utah	44,616
49	South Dakota	43,774
50	Kentucky	43,102
	District of Columbia	67,941

Source: Office of Personnel Management
    "The Fact Book 2002 Edition" (http://www.opm.gov/feddata/02factbk.pdf)
*Full-time employees. National average includes employees not shown by state.

Federal Civilian Employees in 2001

National Total = 1,607,722 Full-Time Employees*

<u>ALPHA ORDER</u>

RANK	STATE	EMPLOYEES	% of USA
12	Alabama	35,510	2.2%
34	Alaska	11,223	0.7%
18	Arizona	29,088	1.8%
35	Arkansas	11,052	0.7%
1	California	137,376	8.5%
15	Colorado	32,336	2.0%
44	Connecticut	6,756	0.4%
50	Delaware	2,508	0.2%
6	Florida	61,372	3.8%
5	Georgia	62,938	3.9%
26	Hawaii	19,557	1.2%
40	Idaho	7,490	0.5%
11	Illinois	39,996	2.5%
27	Indiana	19,495	1.2%
42	Iowa	6,992	0.4%
31	Kansas	14,761	0.9%
25	Kentucky	19,624	1.2%
24	Louisiana	19,843	1.2%
37	Maine	8,197	0.5%
3	Maryland	101,461	6.3%
21	Massachusetts	24,369	1.5%
22	Michigan	21,006	1.3%
32	Minnesota	12,975	0.8%
29	Mississippi	16,725	1.0%
16	Missouri	31,767	2.0%
38	Montana	8,009	0.5%
39	Nebraska	7,595	0.5%
41	Nevada	7,294	0.5%
48	New Hampshire	3,083	0.2%
19	New Jersey	25,411	1.6%
23	New Mexico	20,962	1.3%
8	New York	56,478	3.5%
17	North Carolina	30,488	1.9%
46	North Dakota	5,015	0.3%
10	Ohio	42,000	2.6%
14	Oklahoma	32,673	2.0%
28	Oregon	17,270	1.1%
7	Pennsylvania	61,134	3.8%
45	Rhode Island	5,728	0.4%
30	South Carolina	15,707	1.0%
43	South Dakota	6,789	0.4%
13	Tennessee	33,215	2.1%
4	Texas	100,006	6.2%
20	Utah	25,395	1.6%
49	Vermont	2,936	0.2%
2	Virginia	113,781	7.1%
9	Washington	42,105	2.6%
33	West Virginia	12,119	0.8%
36	Wisconsin	11,029	0.7%
47	Wyoming	4,421	0.3%

<u>RANK ORDER</u>

RANK	STATE	EMPLOYEES	% of USA
1	California	137,376	8.5%
2	Virginia	113,781	7.1%
3	Maryland	101,461	6.3%
4	Texas	100,006	6.2%
5	Georgia	62,938	3.9%
6	Florida	61,372	3.8%
7	Pennsylvania	61,134	3.8%
8	New York	56,478	3.5%
9	Washington	42,105	2.6%
10	Ohio	42,000	2.6%
11	Illinois	39,996	2.5%
12	Alabama	35,510	2.2%
13	Tennessee	33,215	2.1%
14	Oklahoma	32,673	2.0%
15	Colorado	32,336	2.0%
16	Missouri	31,767	2.0%
17	North Carolina	30,488	1.9%
18	Arizona	29,088	1.8%
19	New Jersey	25,411	1.6%
20	Utah	25,395	1.6%
21	Massachusetts	24,369	1.5%
22	Michigan	21,006	1.3%
23	New Mexico	20,962	1.3%
24	Louisiana	19,843	1.2%
25	Kentucky	19,624	1.2%
26	Hawaii	19,557	1.2%
27	Indiana	19,495	1.2%
28	Oregon	17,270	1.1%
29	Mississippi	16,725	1.0%
30	South Carolina	15,707	1.0%
31	Kansas	14,761	0.9%
32	Minnesota	12,975	0.8%
33	West Virginia	12,119	0.8%
34	Alaska	11,223	0.7%
35	Arkansas	11,052	0.7%
36	Wisconsin	11,029	0.7%
37	Maine	8,197	0.5%
38	Montana	8,009	0.5%
39	Nebraska	7,595	0.5%
40	Idaho	7,490	0.5%
41	Nevada	7,294	0.5%
42	Iowa	6,992	0.4%
43	South Dakota	6,789	0.4%
44	Connecticut	6,756	0.4%
45	Rhode Island	5,728	0.4%
46	North Dakota	5,015	0.3%
47	Wyoming	4,421	0.3%
48	New Hampshire	3,083	0.2%
49	Vermont	2,936	0.2%
50	Delaware	2,508	0.2%
	District of Columbia	143,768	8.9%

Source: Office of Personnel Management
   "The Fact Book 2002 Edition" (http://www.opm.gov/feddata/02factbk.pdf)
**Full-time employees. National total includes 18,894 employees not shown by state.*

Rate of Federal Civilian Employees in 2001

National Rate = 56 Full-Time Employees per 10,000 Population*

<u>ALPHA ORDER</u>

RANK	STATE	RATE
11	Alabama	79
2	Alaska	177
22	Arizona	55
32	Arkansas	41
33	California	40
14	Colorado	73
49	Connecticut	20
42	Delaware	31
36	Florida	37
13	Georgia	75
3	Hawaii	159
20	Idaho	57
40	Illinois	32
40	Indiana	32
46	Iowa	24
22	Kansas	55
27	Kentucky	48
30	Louisiana	44
17	Maine	64
1	Maryland	188
35	Massachusetts	38
48	Michigan	21
45	Minnesota	26
18	Mississippi	58
21	Missouri	56
10	Montana	88
30	Nebraska	44
39	Nevada	35
46	New Hampshire	24
43	New Jersey	30
5	New Mexico	114
43	New York	30
36	North Carolina	37
11	North Dakota	79
36	Ohio	37
7	Oklahoma	94
25	Oregon	50
25	Pennsylvania	50
24	Rhode Island	54
34	South Carolina	39
8	South Dakota	90
18	Tennessee	58
29	Texas	47
6	Utah	111
27	Vermont	48
4	Virginia	158
15	Washington	70
16	West Virginia	67
49	Wisconsin	20
8	Wyoming	90

<u>RANK ORDER</u>

RANK	STATE	RATE
1	Maryland	188
2	Alaska	177
3	Hawaii	159
4	Virginia	158
5	New Mexico	114
6	Utah	111
7	Oklahoma	94
8	South Dakota	90
8	Wyoming	90
10	Montana	88
11	Alabama	79
11	North Dakota	79
13	Georgia	75
14	Colorado	73
15	Washington	70
16	West Virginia	67
17	Maine	64
18	Mississippi	58
18	Tennessee	58
20	Idaho	57
21	Missouri	56
22	Arizona	55
22	Kansas	55
24	Rhode Island	54
25	Oregon	50
25	Pennsylvania	50
27	Kentucky	48
27	Vermont	48
29	Texas	47
30	Louisiana	44
30	Nebraska	44
32	Arkansas	41
33	California	40
34	South Carolina	39
35	Massachusetts	38
36	Florida	37
36	North Carolina	37
36	Ohio	37
39	Nevada	35
40	Illinois	32
40	Indiana	32
42	Delaware	31
43	New Jersey	30
43	New York	30
45	Minnesota	26
46	Iowa	24
46	New Hampshire	24
48	Michigan	21
49	Connecticut	20
49	Wisconsin	20
	District of Columbia	2,505

Source: Morgan Quitno Press using data from Office of Personnel Management
"The Fact Book 2002 Edition" (http://www.opm.gov/feddata/02factbk.pdf)
**Full-time employees. National rate includes employees not shown by state.*

X. GOVERNMENT FINANCE: STATE AND LOCAL

X. GOVERNMENT FINANCE: STATE AND LOCAL

A Note About Fiscal Years:

<u>State and Local</u>:
Data in these tables relate to the state and local governments' 12-month fiscal years. The data reflect individual government fiscal years that ended between July 1 and the following June 30.

<u>State</u>:
The statistics show state government data for fiscal years that end on June 30, 2001, except for four states with other ending dates: Alabama and Michigan (September 30, 2001), New York (March 31, 2001) and Texas (August 31, 2001).

Note Regarding Government Finance Data

Please note that the U.S. Census Bureau does not have 2001 state-specific state and local government finance data available. Finance data from the 2002 Census of Governments are expected to become available in August of 2004.

State and Local Government Total Revenue in 2000

National Total = $1,942,328,438,000*

<u>ALPHA ORDER</u>

RANK	STATE	REVENUE	% of USA
26	Alabama	$25,726,452,000	1.3%
39	Alaska	10,525,400,000	0.5%
23	Arizona	27,777,897,000	1.4%
34	Arkansas	13,832,882,000	0.7%
1	California	270,380,221,000	13.9%
21	Colorado	29,603,248,000	1.5%
25	Connecticut	25,828,327,000	1.3%
46	Delaware	6,223,665,000	0.3%
4	Florida	92,402,130,000	4.8%
11	Georgia	49,309,807,000	2.5%
41	Hawaii	8,488,284,000	0.4%
42	Idaho	7,590,426,000	0.4%
5	Illinois	80,695,041,000	4.2%
19	Indiana	32,715,990,000	1.7%
30	Iowa	17,220,008,000	0.9%
32	Kansas	16,234,734,000	0.8%
27	Kentucky	25,199,960,000	1.3%
24	Louisiana	27,109,000,000	1.4%
40	Maine	8,554,420,000	0.4%
17	Maryland	33,949,282,000	1.7%
13	Massachusetts	46,102,672,000	2.4%
8	Michigan	70,111,672,000	3.6%
16	Minnesota	38,785,158,000	2.0%
31	Mississippi	16,672,469,000	0.9%
20	Missouri	31,635,209,000	1.6%
47	Montana	5,642,920,000	0.3%
37	Nebraska	11,650,469,000	0.6%
36	Nevada	11,885,072,000	0.6%
45	New Hampshire	6,948,035,000	0.4%
9	New Jersey	62,331,238,000	3.2%
35	New Mexico	13,072,685,000	0.7%
2	New York	188,906,822,000	9.7%
10	North Carolina	50,541,785,000	2.6%
48	North Dakota	4,495,196,000	0.2%
7	Ohio	80,074,128,000	4.1%
29	Oklahoma	18,760,042,000	1.0%
22	Oregon	28,644,114,000	1.5%
6	Pennsylvania	80,545,510,000	4.1%
43	Rhode Island	7,427,400,000	0.4%
28	South Carolina	23,466,665,000	1.2%
49	South Dakota	4,277,467,000	0.2%
18	Tennessee	33,624,769,000	1.7%
3	Texas	120,665,917,000	6.2%
33	Utah	14,953,608,000	0.8%
50	Vermont	4,018,646,000	0.2%
14	Virginia	44,174,553,000	2.3%
12	Washington	46,371,508,000	2.4%
38	West Virginia	10,759,754,000	0.6%
15	Wisconsin	43,002,778,000	2.2%
44	Wyoming	7,029,949,000	0.4%

<u>RANK ORDER</u>

RANK	STATE	REVENUE	% of USA
1	California	$270,380,221,000	13.9%
2	New York	188,906,822,000	9.7%
3	Texas	120,665,917,000	6.2%
4	Florida	92,402,130,000	4.8%
5	Illinois	80,695,041,000	4.2%
6	Pennsylvania	80,545,510,000	4.1%
7	Ohio	80,074,128,000	4.1%
8	Michigan	70,111,672,000	3.6%
9	New Jersey	62,331,238,000	3.2%
10	North Carolina	50,541,785,000	2.6%
11	Georgia	49,309,807,000	2.5%
12	Washington	46,371,508,000	2.4%
13	Massachusetts	46,102,672,000	2.4%
14	Virginia	44,174,553,000	2.3%
15	Wisconsin	43,002,778,000	2.2%
16	Minnesota	38,785,158,000	2.0%
17	Maryland	33,949,282,000	1.7%
18	Tennessee	33,624,769,000	1.7%
19	Indiana	32,715,990,000	1.7%
20	Missouri	31,635,209,000	1.6%
21	Colorado	29,603,248,000	1.5%
22	Oregon	28,644,114,000	1.5%
23	Arizona	27,777,897,000	1.4%
24	Louisiana	27,109,000,000	1.4%
25	Connecticut	25,828,327,000	1.3%
26	Alabama	25,726,452,000	1.3%
27	Kentucky	25,199,960,000	1.3%
28	South Carolina	23,466,665,000	1.2%
29	Oklahoma	18,760,042,000	1.0%
30	Iowa	17,220,008,000	0.9%
31	Mississippi	16,672,469,000	0.9%
32	Kansas	16,234,734,000	0.8%
33	Utah	14,953,608,000	0.8%
34	Arkansas	13,832,882,000	0.7%
35	New Mexico	13,072,685,000	0.7%
36	Nevada	11,885,072,000	0.6%
37	Nebraska	11,650,469,000	0.6%
38	West Virginia	10,759,754,000	0.6%
39	Alaska	10,525,400,000	0.5%
40	Maine	8,554,420,000	0.4%
41	Hawaii	8,488,284,000	0.4%
42	Idaho	7,590,426,000	0.4%
43	Rhode Island	7,427,400,000	0.4%
44	Wyoming	7,029,949,000	0.4%
45	New Hampshire	6,948,035,000	0.4%
46	Delaware	6,223,665,000	0.3%
47	Montana	5,642,920,000	0.3%
48	North Dakota	4,495,196,000	0.2%
49	South Dakota	4,277,467,000	0.2%
50	Vermont	4,018,646,000	0.2%
	District of Columbia	6,383,054,000	0.3%

Source: U.S. Bureau of the Census, Governments Division
"State and Local Government Finances: 1999-2000" (http://www.census.gov/govs/www/estimate00.html)
**Total revenue includes all money received from external sources. This includes taxes, intergovernmental transfers and insurance trust revenue and revenue from government owned utilities and other commercial or auxiliary enterprise.*

Per Capita State and Local Government Revenue in 2000

National Per Capita = $6,882*

<u>ALPHA ORDER</u>

RANK	STATE	PER CAPITA
41	Alabama	$5,779
1	Alaska	16,768
48	Arizona	5,376
50	Arkansas	5,164
6	California	7,950
19	Colorado	6,842
10	Connecticut	7,570
7	Delaware	7,913
43	Florida	5,757
33	Georgia	5,988
18	Hawaii	7,000
39	Idaho	5,840
25	Illinois	6,486
49	Indiana	5,370
37	Iowa	5,880
32	Kansas	6,029
29	Kentucky	6,224
31	Louisiana	6,065
21	Maine	6,697
26	Maryland	6,390
12	Massachusetts	7,247
16	Michigan	7,042
8	Minnesota	7,860
38	Mississippi	5,852
45	Missouri	5,644
28	Montana	6,246
20	Nebraska	6,800
36	Nevada	5,887
46	New Hampshire	5,601
11	New Jersey	7,391
13	New Mexico	7,176
3	New York	9,943
27	North Carolina	6,253
17	North Dakota	7,011
15	Ohio	7,047
47	Oklahoma	5,431
4	Oregon	8,348
24	Pennsylvania	6,556
14	Rhode Island	7,069
40	South Carolina	5,832
44	South Dakota	5,660
35	Tennessee	5,896
42	Texas	5,758
22	Utah	6,666
23	Vermont	6,588
30	Virginia	6,217
9	Washington	7,844
34	West Virginia	5,953
5	Wisconsin	8,001
2	Wyoming	14,228

<u>RANK ORDER</u>

RANK	STATE	PER CAPITA
1	Alaska	$16,768
2	Wyoming	14,228
3	New York	9,943
4	Oregon	8,348
5	Wisconsin	8,001
6	California	7,950
7	Delaware	7,913
8	Minnesota	7,860
9	Washington	7,844
10	Connecticut	7,570
11	New Jersey	7,391
12	Massachusetts	7,247
13	New Mexico	7,176
14	Rhode Island	7,069
15	Ohio	7,047
16	Michigan	7,042
17	North Dakota	7,011
18	Hawaii	7,000
19	Colorado	6,842
20	Nebraska	6,800
21	Maine	6,697
22	Utah	6,666
23	Vermont	6,588
24	Pennsylvania	6,556
25	Illinois	6,486
26	Maryland	6,390
27	North Carolina	6,253
28	Montana	6,246
29	Kentucky	6,224
30	Virginia	6,217
31	Louisiana	6,065
32	Kansas	6,029
33	Georgia	5,988
34	West Virginia	5,953
35	Tennessee	5,896
36	Nevada	5,887
37	Iowa	5,880
38	Mississippi	5,852
39	Idaho	5,840
40	South Carolina	5,832
41	Alabama	5,779
42	Texas	5,758
43	Florida	5,757
44	South Dakota	5,660
45	Missouri	5,644
46	New Hampshire	5,601
47	Oklahoma	5,431
48	Arizona	5,376
49	Indiana	5,370
50	Arkansas	5,164

	District of Columbia	11,166

Source: Morgan Quitno Press using data from U.S. Bureau of the Census, Governments Division
   "State and Local Government Finances: 1999-2000" (http://www.census.gov/govs/www/estimate00.html)
Total revenue includes all money received from external sources. This includes taxes, intergovernmental transfers and insurance trust revenue and revenue from government owned utilities and other commercial or auxiliary enterprise.

State and Local Government Revenue from the Federal Government in 2000

National Total = $291,949,750,000

<u>ALPHA ORDER</u>

RANK	STATE	REVENUE	% of USA
18	Alabama	$5,087,243,000	1.7%
39	Alaska	1,410,843,000	0.5%
25	Arizona	4,475,143,000	1.5%
32	Arkansas	2,822,901,000	1.0%
1	California	38,475,975,000	13.2%
27	Colorado	3,711,484,000	1.3%
28	Connecticut	3,673,657,000	1.3%
50	Delaware	830,479,000	0.3%
5	Florida	11,718,426,000	4.0%
11	Georgia	7,069,968,000	2.4%
41	Hawaii	1,294,197,000	0.4%
44	Idaho	1,150,443,000	0.4%
7	Illinois	10,790,758,000	3.7%
17	Indiana	5,168,994,000	1.8%
31	Iowa	2,885,433,000	1.0%
34	Kansas	2,482,266,000	0.9%
24	Kentucky	4,595,492,000	1.6%
19	Louisiana	5,069,968,000	1.7%
38	Maine	1,630,484,000	0.6%
23	Maryland	4,609,122,000	1.6%
12	Massachusetts	6,439,007,000	2.2%
8	Michigan	10,330,841,000	3.5%
22	Minnesota	4,769,396,000	1.6%
29	Mississippi	3,528,162,000	1.2%
15	Missouri	5,627,998,000	1.9%
40	Montana	1,305,891,000	0.4%
37	Nebraska	1,710,215,000	0.6%
42	Nevada	1,232,620,000	0.4%
46	New Hampshire	1,062,320,000	0.4%
10	New Jersey	7,882,616,000	2.7%
35	New Mexico	2,398,471,000	0.8%
2	New York	29,248,826,000	10.0%
9	North Carolina	9,051,344,000	3.1%
45	North Dakota	1,125,502,000	0.4%
6	Ohio	10,933,057,000	3.7%
30	Oklahoma	3,181,180,000	1.1%
16	Oregon	5,233,082,000	1.8%
4	Pennsylvania	12,497,911,000	4.3%
43	Rhode Island	1,196,383,000	0.4%
26	South Carolina	4,376,690,000	1.5%
49	South Dakota	869,214,000	0.3%
13	Tennessee	6,320,651,000	2.2%
3	Texas	18,575,645,000	6.4%
36	Utah	2,171,908,000	0.7%
47	Vermont	903,249,000	0.3%
21	Virginia	5,009,533,000	1.7%
14	Washington	5,827,523,000	2.0%
33	West Virginia	2,489,321,000	0.9%
20	Wisconsin	5,059,028,000	1.7%
48	Wyoming	890,954,000	0.3%

<u>RANK ORDER</u>

RANK	STATE	REVENUE	% of USA
1	California	$38,475,975,000	13.2%
2	New York	29,248,826,000	10.0%
3	Texas	18,575,645,000	6.4%
4	Pennsylvania	12,497,911,000	4.3%
5	Florida	11,718,426,000	4.0%
6	Ohio	10,933,057,000	3.7%
7	Illinois	10,790,758,000	3.7%
8	Michigan	10,330,841,000	3.5%
9	North Carolina	9,051,344,000	3.1%
10	New Jersey	7,882,616,000	2.7%
11	Georgia	7,069,968,000	2.4%
12	Massachusetts	6,439,007,000	2.2%
13	Tennessee	6,320,651,000	2.2%
14	Washington	5,827,523,000	2.0%
15	Missouri	5,627,998,000	1.9%
16	Oregon	5,233,082,000	1.8%
17	Indiana	5,168,994,000	1.8%
18	Alabama	5,087,243,000	1.7%
19	Louisiana	5,069,968,000	1.7%
20	Wisconsin	5,059,028,000	1.7%
21	Virginia	5,009,533,000	1.7%
22	Minnesota	4,769,396,000	1.6%
23	Maryland	4,609,122,000	1.6%
24	Kentucky	4,595,492,000	1.6%
25	Arizona	4,475,143,000	1.5%
26	South Carolina	4,376,690,000	1.5%
27	Colorado	3,711,484,000	1.3%
28	Connecticut	3,673,657,000	1.3%
29	Mississippi	3,528,162,000	1.2%
30	Oklahoma	3,181,180,000	1.1%
31	Iowa	2,885,433,000	1.0%
32	Arkansas	2,822,901,000	1.0%
33	West Virginia	2,489,321,000	0.9%
34	Kansas	2,482,266,000	0.9%
35	New Mexico	2,398,471,000	0.8%
36	Utah	2,171,908,000	0.7%
37	Nebraska	1,710,215,000	0.6%
38	Maine	1,630,484,000	0.6%
39	Alaska	1,410,843,000	0.5%
40	Montana	1,305,891,000	0.4%
41	Hawaii	1,294,197,000	0.4%
42	Nevada	1,232,620,000	0.4%
43	Rhode Island	1,196,383,000	0.4%
44	Idaho	1,150,443,000	0.4%
45	North Dakota	1,125,502,000	0.4%
46	New Hampshire	1,062,320,000	0.4%
47	Vermont	903,249,000	0.3%
48	Wyoming	890,954,000	0.3%
49	South Dakota	869,214,000	0.3%
50	Delaware	830,479,000	0.3%
	District of Columbia	1,747,936,000	0.6%

Source: U.S. Bureau of the Census, Governments Division
"State and Local Government Finances: 1999-2000" (http://www.census.gov/govs/www/estimate00.html)

Per Capita State and Local Government Revenue
From the Federal Government in 2000
National Per Capita = $1,034

RANK	STATE	PER CAPITA
13	Alabama	$1,143
1	Alaska	2,248
43	Arizona	866
24	Arkansas	1,054
17	California	1,131
45	Colorado	858
21	Connecticut	1,077
23	Delaware	1,056
48	Florida	730
44	Georgia	859
22	Hawaii	1,067
40	Idaho	885
42	Illinois	867
47	Indiana	848
31	Iowa	985
37	Kansas	922
15	Kentucky	1,135
16	Louisiana	1,134
10	Maine	1,277
41	Maryland	868
27	Massachusetts	1,012
25	Michigan	1,038
33	Minnesota	967
11	Mississippi	1,238
28	Missouri	1,004
7	Montana	1,446
29	Nebraska	998
50	Nevada	611
46	New Hampshire	856
36	New Jersey	935
9	New Mexico	1,317
4	New York	1,539
18	North Carolina	1,120
3	North Dakota	1,755
34	Ohio	962
38	Oklahoma	921
5	Oregon	1,525
26	Pennsylvania	1,017
14	Rhode Island	1,139
20	South Carolina	1,088
12	South Dakota	1,150
19	Tennessee	1,108
39	Texas	886
32	Utah	968
6	Vermont	1,481
49	Virginia	705
30	Washington	986
8	West Virginia	1,377
35	Wisconsin	941
2	Wyoming	1,803

RANK	STATE	PER CAPITA
1	Alaska	$2,248
2	Wyoming	1,803
3	North Dakota	1,755
4	New York	1,539
5	Oregon	1,525
6	Vermont	1,481
7	Montana	1,446
8	West Virginia	1,377
9	New Mexico	1,317
10	Maine	1,277
11	Mississippi	1,238
12	South Dakota	1,150
13	Alabama	1,143
14	Rhode Island	1,139
15	Kentucky	1,135
16	Louisiana	1,134
17	California	1,131
18	North Carolina	1,120
19	Tennessee	1,108
20	South Carolina	1,088
21	Connecticut	1,077
22	Hawaii	1,067
23	Delaware	1,056
24	Arkansas	1,054
25	Michigan	1,038
26	Pennsylvania	1,017
27	Massachusetts	1,012
28	Missouri	1,004
29	Nebraska	998
30	Washington	986
31	Iowa	985
32	Utah	968
33	Minnesota	967
34	Ohio	962
35	Wisconsin	941
36	New Jersey	935
37	Kansas	922
38	Oklahoma	921
39	Texas	886
40	Idaho	885
41	Maryland	868
42	Illinois	867
43	Arizona	866
44	Georgia	859
45	Colorado	858
46	New Hampshire	856
47	Indiana	848
48	Florida	730
49	Virginia	705
50	Nevada	611

District of Columbia   3,058

Source: Morgan Quitno Press using data from U.S. Bureau of the Census, Governments Division
"State and Local Government Finances: 1999-2000" (http://www.census.gov/govs/www/estimate00.html)

Percent of State and Local Government Revenue
From the Federal Government in 2000
National Percent = 15.0%*

<u>ALPHA ORDER</u>

RANK	STATE	PERCENT
8	Alabama	19.8
39	Alaska	13.4
20	Arizona	16.1
6	Arkansas	20.4
34	California	14.2
46	Colorado	12.5
34	Connecticut	14.2
41	Delaware	13.3
42	Florida	12.7
33	Georgia	14.3
28	Hawaii	15.2
28	Idaho	15.2
39	Illinois	13.4
22	Indiana	15.8
19	Iowa	16.8
26	Kansas	15.3
15	Kentucky	18.2
11	Louisiana	18.7
9	Maine	19.1
38	Maryland	13.6
36	Massachusetts	14.0
30	Michigan	14.7
47	Minnesota	12.3
5	Mississippi	21.2
17	Missouri	17.8
2	Montana	23.1
30	Nebraska	14.7
50	Nevada	10.4
26	New Hampshire	15.3
44	New Jersey	12.6
13	New Mexico	18.3
23	New York	15.5
16	North Carolina	17.9
1	North Dakota	25.0
37	Ohio	13.7
18	Oklahoma	17.0
13	Oregon	18.3
23	Pennsylvania	15.5
20	Rhode Island	16.1
11	South Carolina	18.7
7	South Dakota	20.3
10	Tennessee	18.8
25	Texas	15.4
32	Utah	14.5
4	Vermont	22.5
49	Virginia	11.3
44	Washington	12.6
2	West Virginia	23.1
48	Wisconsin	11.8
42	Wyoming	12.7

<u>RANK ORDER</u>

RANK	STATE	PERCENT
1	North Dakota	25.0
2	Montana	23.1
2	West Virginia	23.1
4	Vermont	22.5
5	Mississippi	21.2
6	Arkansas	20.4
7	South Dakota	20.3
8	Alabama	19.8
9	Maine	19.1
10	Tennessee	18.8
11	Louisiana	18.7
11	South Carolina	18.7
13	New Mexico	18.3
13	Oregon	18.3
15	Kentucky	18.2
16	North Carolina	17.9
17	Missouri	17.8
18	Oklahoma	17.0
19	Iowa	16.8
20	Arizona	16.1
20	Rhode Island	16.1
22	Indiana	15.8
23	New York	15.5
23	Pennsylvania	15.5
25	Texas	15.4
26	Kansas	15.3
26	New Hampshire	15.3
28	Hawaii	15.2
28	Idaho	15.2
30	Michigan	14.7
30	Nebraska	14.7
32	Utah	14.5
33	Georgia	14.3
34	California	14.2
34	Connecticut	14.2
36	Massachusetts	14.0
37	Ohio	13.7
38	Maryland	13.6
39	Alaska	13.4
39	Illinois	13.4
41	Delaware	13.3
42	Florida	12.7
42	Wyoming	12.7
44	New Jersey	12.6
44	Washington	12.6
46	Colorado	12.5
47	Minnesota	12.3
48	Wisconsin	11.8
49	Virginia	11.3
50	Nevada	10.4
	District of Columbia	27.4

Source: Morgan Quitno Press using data from U.S. Bureau of the Census, Governments Division
  "State and Local Government Finances: 1999-2000" (http://www.census.gov/govs/www/estimate00.html)
*As a percent of total revenue.

State and Local Government Own Source Revenue in 2000

National Total = $1,249,372,731,000*

ALPHA ORDER

RANK	STATE	REVENUE	% of USA
25	Alabama	$15,924,994,000	1.3%
37	Alaska	7,631,362,000	0.6%
23	Arizona	18,388,044,000	1.5%
34	Arkansas	8,758,898,000	0.7%
1	California	169,897,404,000	13.6%
20	Colorado	19,724,146,000	1.6%
21	Connecticut	19,434,795,000	1.6%
45	Delaware	4,372,728,000	0.3%
4	Florida	64,146,076,000	5.1%
10	Georgia	32,620,426,000	2.6%
41	Hawaii	5,797,617,000	0.5%
42	Idaho	4,926,511,000	0.4%
5	Illinois	53,629,207,000	4.3%
17	Indiana	24,580,443,000	2.0%
30	Iowa	12,248,727,000	1.0%
31	Kansas	10,908,616,000	0.9%
28	Kentucky	14,827,525,000	1.2%
24	Louisiana	17,272,187,000	1.4%
40	Maine	5,809,529,000	0.5%
18	Maryland	24,466,408,000	2.0%
12	Massachusetts	31,855,849,000	2.5%
8	Michigan	46,084,318,000	3.7%
15	Minnesota	26,187,820,000	2.1%
32	Mississippi	10,061,883,000	0.8%
19	Missouri	20,276,622,000	1.6%
46	Montana	3,550,564,000	0.3%
38	Nebraska	7,310,291,000	0.6%
35	Nevada	8,359,152,000	0.7%
43	New Hampshire	4,692,436,000	0.4%
9	New Jersey	43,621,774,000	3.5%
36	New Mexico	7,663,508,000	0.6%
2	New York	114,652,517,000	9.2%
11	North Carolina	32,080,095,000	2.6%
47	North Dakota	2,788,303,000	0.2%
7	Ohio	48,084,298,000	3.8%
29	Oklahoma	12,517,011,000	1.0%
26	Oregon	15,736,012,000	1.3%
6	Pennsylvania	52,116,968,000	4.2%
44	Rhode Island	4,551,255,000	0.4%
27	South Carolina	15,350,526,000	1.2%
49	South Dakota	2,621,314,000	0.2%
22	Tennessee	18,502,862,000	1.5%
3	Texas	76,963,568,000	6.2%
33	Utah	9,035,781,000	0.7%
50	Vermont	2,593,701,000	0.2%
13	Virginia	30,424,073,000	2.4%
14	Washington	27,598,554,000	2.2%
39	West Virginia	6,565,317,000	0.5%
16	Wisconsin	25,512,675,000	2.0%
48	Wyoming	2,663,541,000	0.2%

RANK ORDER

RANK	STATE	REVENUE	% of USA
1	California	$169,897,404,000	13.6%
2	New York	114,652,517,000	9.2%
3	Texas	76,963,568,000	6.2%
4	Florida	64,146,076,000	5.1%
5	Illinois	53,629,207,000	4.3%
6	Pennsylvania	52,116,968,000	4.2%
7	Ohio	48,084,298,000	3.8%
8	Michigan	46,084,318,000	3.7%
9	New Jersey	43,621,774,000	3.5%
10	Georgia	32,620,426,000	2.6%
11	North Carolina	32,080,095,000	2.6%
12	Massachusetts	31,855,849,000	2.5%
13	Virginia	30,424,073,000	2.4%
14	Washington	27,598,554,000	2.2%
15	Minnesota	26,187,820,000	2.1%
16	Wisconsin	25,512,675,000	2.0%
17	Indiana	24,580,443,000	2.0%
18	Maryland	24,466,408,000	2.0%
19	Missouri	20,276,622,000	1.6%
20	Colorado	19,724,146,000	1.6%
21	Connecticut	19,434,795,000	1.6%
22	Tennessee	18,502,862,000	1.5%
23	Arizona	18,388,044,000	1.5%
24	Louisiana	17,272,187,000	1.4%
25	Alabama	15,924,994,000	1.3%
26	Oregon	15,736,012,000	1.3%
27	South Carolina	15,350,526,000	1.2%
28	Kentucky	14,827,525,000	1.2%
29	Oklahoma	12,517,011,000	1.0%
30	Iowa	12,248,727,000	1.0%
31	Kansas	10,908,616,000	0.9%
32	Mississippi	10,061,883,000	0.8%
33	Utah	9,035,781,000	0.7%
34	Arkansas	8,758,898,000	0.7%
35	Nevada	8,359,152,000	0.7%
36	New Mexico	7,663,508,000	0.6%
37	Alaska	7,631,362,000	0.6%
38	Nebraska	7,310,291,000	0.6%
39	West Virginia	6,565,317,000	0.5%
40	Maine	5,809,529,000	0.5%
41	Hawaii	5,797,617,000	0.5%
42	Idaho	4,926,511,000	0.4%
43	New Hampshire	4,692,436,000	0.4%
44	Rhode Island	4,551,255,000	0.4%
45	Delaware	4,372,728,000	0.3%
46	Montana	3,550,564,000	0.3%
47	North Dakota	2,788,303,000	0.2%
48	Wyoming	2,663,541,000	0.2%
49	South Dakota	2,621,314,000	0.2%
50	Vermont	2,593,701,000	0.2%
	District of Columbia	3,984,500,000	0.3%

Source: U.S. Bureau of the Census, Governments Division
"State and Local Government Finances: 1999-2000" (http://www.census.gov/govs/www/estimate00.html)
*Own source revenue includes taxes, current charges and miscellaneous general revenue. Excluded are intergovernmental transfers, insurance trust revenue and revenue from government owned utilities and other commercial or auxiliary enterprise.

Per Capita State and Local Government Own Source Revenue in 2000

National Per Capita = $4,427*

ALPHA ORDER

RANK	STATE	PER CAPITA
45	Alabama	$3,577
1	Alaska	12,158
46	Arizona	3,559
49	Arkansas	3,270
9	California	4,995
16	Colorado	4,559
3	Connecticut	5,696
4	Delaware	5,560
32	Florida	3,996
34	Georgia	3,961
10	Hawaii	4,781
38	Idaho	3,790
20	Illinois	4,311
30	Indiana	4,035
27	Iowa	4,182
29	Kansas	4,051
41	Kentucky	3,662
36	Louisiana	3,864
17	Maine	4,548
14	Maryland	4,605
8	Massachusetts	5,007
13	Michigan	4,629
6	Minnesota	5,307
47	Mississippi	3,532
44	Missouri	3,618
35	Montana	3,930
22	Nebraska	4,267
28	Nevada	4,141
39	New Hampshire	3,783
7	New Jersey	5,173
26	New Mexico	4,207
2	New York	6,034
33	North Carolina	3,969
18	North Dakota	4,349
25	Ohio	4,231
43	Oklahoma	3,623
15	Oregon	4,586
24	Pennsylvania	4,242
19	Rhode Island	4,332
37	South Carolina	3,815
48	South Dakota	3,468
50	Tennessee	3,244
40	Texas	3,673
31	Utah	4,028
23	Vermont	4,252
21	Virginia	4,282
12	Washington	4,668
42	West Virginia	3,633
11	Wisconsin	4,747
5	Wyoming	5,391

RANK ORDER

RANK	STATE	PER CAPITA
1	Alaska	$12,158
2	New York	6,034
3	Connecticut	5,696
4	Delaware	5,560
5	Wyoming	5,391
6	Minnesota	5,307
7	New Jersey	5,173
8	Massachusetts	5,007
9	California	4,995
10	Hawaii	4,781
11	Wisconsin	4,747
12	Washington	4,668
13	Michigan	4,629
14	Maryland	4,605
15	Oregon	4,586
16	Colorado	4,559
17	Maine	4,548
18	North Dakota	4,349
19	Rhode Island	4,332
20	Illinois	4,311
21	Virginia	4,282
22	Nebraska	4,267
23	Vermont	4,252
24	Pennsylvania	4,242
25	Ohio	4,231
26	New Mexico	4,207
27	Iowa	4,182
28	Nevada	4,141
29	Kansas	4,051
30	Indiana	4,035
31	Utah	4,028
32	Florida	3,996
33	North Carolina	3,969
34	Georgia	3,961
35	Montana	3,930
36	Louisiana	3,864
37	South Carolina	3,815
38	Idaho	3,790
39	New Hampshire	3,783
40	Texas	3,673
41	Kentucky	3,662
42	West Virginia	3,633
43	Oklahoma	3,623
44	Missouri	3,618
45	Alabama	3,577
46	Arizona	3,559
47	Mississippi	3,532
48	South Dakota	3,468
49	Arkansas	3,270
50	Tennessee	3,244
	District of Columbia	6,970

Source: Morgan Quitno Press using data from U.S. Bureau of the Census, Governments Division "State and Local Government Finances: 1999-2000" (http://www.census.gov/govs/www/estimate00.html)
**Own source revenue includes taxes, current charges and miscellaneous general revenue. Excluded are intergovernmental transfers, insurance trust revenue and revenue from government owned utilities and other commercial or auxiliary enterprise.*

State and Local Government Tax Revenue in 2000

National Total = $872,351,114,000

ALPHA ORDER

RANK	STATE	TAX REVENUE	% of USA
27	Alabama	$9,415,089,000	1.1%
45	Alaska	2,311,801,000	0.3%
21	Arizona	13,333,612,000	1.5%
33	Arkansas	5,961,335,000	0.7%
1	California	120,067,581,000	13.8%
22	Colorado	13,216,188,000	1.5%
19	Connecticut	15,651,070,000	1.8%
44	Delaware	2,618,628,000	0.3%
4	Florida	41,936,682,000	4.8%
11	Georgia	23,253,547,000	2.7%
40	Hawaii	4,101,617,000	0.5%
42	Idaho	3,294,239,000	0.4%
5	Illinois	40,256,016,000	4.6%
18	Indiana	16,363,430,000	1.9%
30	Iowa	8,090,525,000	0.9%
31	Kansas	7,616,353,000	0.9%
25	Kentucky	10,172,414,000	1.2%
24	Louisiana	10,887,408,000	1.2%
39	Maine	4,262,142,000	0.5%
16	Maryland	18,289,881,000	2.1%
10	Massachusetts	24,042,067,000	2.8%
9	Michigan	31,474,162,000	3.6%
17	Minnesota	18,172,885,000	2.1%
32	Mississippi	6,299,396,000	0.7%
20	Missouri	14,313,873,000	1.6%
46	Montana	2,131,839,000	0.2%
36	Nebraska	4,972,968,000	0.6%
35	Nevada	5,824,824,000	0.7%
43	New Hampshire	3,278,375,000	0.4%
8	New Jersey	32,837,939,000	3.8%
37	New Mexico	4,800,578,000	0.6%
2	New York	86,868,188,000	10.0%
12	North Carolina	21,440,029,000	2.5%
48	North Dakota	1,768,115,000	0.2%
7	Ohio	34,238,674,000	3.9%
29	Oklahoma	8,251,421,000	0.9%
28	Oregon	9,411,783,000	1.1%
6	Pennsylvania	36,581,020,000	4.2%
41	Rhode Island	3,412,355,000	0.4%
26	South Carolina	9,542,914,000	1.1%
49	South Dakota	1,735,628,000	0.2%
23	Tennessee	12,431,196,000	1.4%
3	Texas	52,226,535,000	6.0%
34	Utah	5,873,126,000	0.7%
47	Vermont	1,875,546,000	0.2%
13	Virginia	21,082,951,000	2.4%
14	Washington	18,733,865,000	2.1%
38	West Virginia	4,362,304,000	0.5%
15	Wisconsin	18,546,574,000	2.1%
50	Wyoming	1,504,660,000	0.2%

RANK ORDER

RANK	STATE	TAX REVENUE	% of USA
1	California	$120,067,581,000	13.8%
2	New York	86,868,188,000	10.0%
3	Texas	52,226,535,000	6.0%
4	Florida	41,936,682,000	4.8%
5	Illinois	40,256,016,000	4.6%
6	Pennsylvania	36,581,020,000	4.2%
7	Ohio	34,238,674,000	3.9%
8	New Jersey	32,837,939,000	3.8%
9	Michigan	31,474,162,000	3.6%
10	Massachusetts	24,042,067,000	2.8%
11	Georgia	23,253,547,000	2.7%
12	North Carolina	21,440,029,000	2.5%
13	Virginia	21,082,951,000	2.4%
14	Washington	18,733,865,000	2.1%
15	Wisconsin	18,546,574,000	2.1%
16	Maryland	18,289,881,000	2.1%
17	Minnesota	18,172,885,000	2.1%
18	Indiana	16,363,430,000	1.9%
19	Connecticut	15,651,070,000	1.8%
20	Missouri	14,313,873,000	1.6%
21	Arizona	13,333,612,000	1.5%
22	Colorado	13,216,188,000	1.5%
23	Tennessee	12,431,196,000	1.4%
24	Louisiana	10,887,408,000	1.2%
25	Kentucky	10,172,414,000	1.2%
26	South Carolina	9,542,914,000	1.1%
27	Alabama	9,415,089,000	1.1%
28	Oregon	9,411,783,000	1.1%
29	Oklahoma	8,251,421,000	0.9%
30	Iowa	8,090,525,000	0.9%
31	Kansas	7,616,353,000	0.9%
32	Mississippi	6,299,396,000	0.7%
33	Arkansas	5,961,335,000	0.7%
34	Utah	5,873,126,000	0.7%
35	Nevada	5,824,824,000	0.7%
36	Nebraska	4,972,968,000	0.6%
37	New Mexico	4,800,578,000	0.6%
38	West Virginia	4,362,304,000	0.5%
39	Maine	4,262,142,000	0.5%
40	Hawaii	4,101,617,000	0.5%
41	Rhode Island	3,412,355,000	0.4%
42	Idaho	3,294,239,000	0.4%
43	New Hampshire	3,278,375,000	0.4%
44	Delaware	2,618,628,000	0.3%
45	Alaska	2,311,801,000	0.3%
46	Montana	2,131,839,000	0.2%
47	Vermont	1,875,546,000	0.2%
48	North Dakota	1,768,115,000	0.2%
49	South Dakota	1,735,628,000	0.2%
50	Wyoming	1,504,660,000	0.2%
	District of Columbia	3,215,766,000	0.4%

Source: U.S. Bureau of the Census, Governments Division
"State and Local Government Finances: 1999-2000" (http://www.census.gov/govs/www/estimate00.html)

Per Capita State and Local Government Tax Revenue in 2000

National Per Capita = $3,091

<u>ALPHA ORDER</u>

RANK	STATE	PER CAPITA
50	Alabama	$2,115
5	Alaska	3,683
36	Arizona	2,580
47	Arkansas	2,225
7	California	3,530
18	Colorado	3,055
1	Connecticut	4,587
12	Delaware	3,329
35	Florida	2,613
26	Georgia	2,824
10	Hawaii	3,382
38	Idaho	2,535
14	Illinois	3,236
30	Indiana	2,686
27	Iowa	2,762
25	Kansas	2,829
39	Kentucky	2,512
41	Louisiana	2,436
11	Maine	3,337
9	Maryland	3,443
4	Massachusetts	3,779
16	Michigan	3,161
5	Minnesota	3,683
48	Mississippi	2,211
37	Missouri	2,554
45	Montana	2,360
23	Nebraska	2,902
24	Nevada	2,885
32	New Hampshire	2,643
3	New Jersey	3,894
33	New Mexico	2,635
2	New York	4,572
31	North Carolina	2,653
28	North Dakota	2,758
20	Ohio	3,013
43	Oklahoma	2,389
29	Oregon	2,743
21	Pennsylvania	2,977
13	Rhode Island	3,248
44	South Carolina	2,372
46	South Dakota	2,296
49	Tennessee	2,180
40	Texas	2,492
34	Utah	2,618
17	Vermont	3,075
22	Virginia	2,967
15	Washington	3,169
42	West Virginia	2,414
8	Wisconsin	3,451
19	Wyoming	3,045

<u>RANK ORDER</u>

RANK	STATE	PER CAPITA
1	Connecticut	$4,587
2	New York	4,572
3	New Jersey	3,894
4	Massachusetts	3,779
5	Alaska	3,683
5	Minnesota	3,683
7	California	3,530
8	Wisconsin	3,451
9	Maryland	3,443
10	Hawaii	3,382
11	Maine	3,337
12	Delaware	3,329
13	Rhode Island	3,248
14	Illinois	3,236
15	Washington	3,169
16	Michigan	3,161
17	Vermont	3,075
18	Colorado	3,055
19	Wyoming	3,045
20	Ohio	3,013
21	Pennsylvania	2,977
22	Virginia	2,967
23	Nebraska	2,902
24	Nevada	2,885
25	Kansas	2,829
26	Georgia	2,824
27	Iowa	2,762
28	North Dakota	2,758
29	Oregon	2,743
30	Indiana	2,686
31	North Carolina	2,653
32	New Hampshire	2,643
33	New Mexico	2,635
34	Utah	2,618
35	Florida	2,613
36	Arizona	2,580
37	Missouri	2,554
38	Idaho	2,535
39	Kentucky	2,512
40	Texas	2,492
41	Louisiana	2,436
42	West Virginia	2,414
43	Oklahoma	2,389
44	South Carolina	2,372
45	Montana	2,360
46	South Dakota	2,296
47	Arkansas	2,225
48	Mississippi	2,211
49	Tennessee	2,180
50	Alabama	2,115

District of Columbia   5,625

Source: Morgan Quitno Press using data from U.S. Bureau of the Census, Governments Division
"State and Local Government Finances: 1999-2000" (http://www.census.gov/govs/www/estimate00.html)

Percent of State and Local Government Revenue from Taxes in 2000

National Percent = 69.8%

<u>ALPHA ORDER</u>

RANK	STATE	PERCENT
48	Alabama	59.1
50	Alaska	30.3
10	Arizona	72.5
25	Arkansas	68.1
14	California	70.7
30	Colorado	67.0
1	Connecticut	80.5
46	Delaware	59.9
38	Florida	65.4
12	Georgia	71.3
14	Hawaii	70.7
31	Idaho	66.9
5	Illinois	75.1
33	Indiana	66.6
36	Iowa	66.1
19	Kansas	69.8
23	Kentucky	68.6
41	Louisiana	63.0
8	Maine	73.4
7	Maryland	74.8
3	Massachusetts	75.5
24	Michigan	68.3
21	Minnesota	69.4
42	Mississippi	62.6
16	Missouri	70.6
45	Montana	60.0
26	Nebraska	68.0
20	Nevada	69.7
18	New Hampshire	69.9
4	New Jersey	75.3
42	New Mexico	62.6
2	New York	75.8
32	North Carolina	66.8
40	North Dakota	63.4
13	Ohio	71.2
37	Oklahoma	65.9
47	Oregon	59.8
17	Pennsylvania	70.2
6	Rhode Island	75.0
44	South Carolina	62.2
35	South Dakota	66.2
29	Tennessee	67.2
27	Texas	67.9
39	Utah	65.0
11	Vermont	72.3
22	Virginia	69.3
27	Washington	67.9
34	West Virginia	66.4
9	Wisconsin	72.7
49	Wyoming	56.5

<u>RANK ORDER</u>

RANK	STATE	PERCENT
1	Connecticut	80.5
2	New York	75.8
3	Massachusetts	75.5
4	New Jersey	75.3
5	Illinois	75.1
6	Rhode Island	75.0
7	Maryland	74.8
8	Maine	73.4
9	Wisconsin	72.7
10	Arizona	72.5
11	Vermont	72.3
12	Georgia	71.3
13	Ohio	71.2
14	California	70.7
14	Hawaii	70.7
16	Missouri	70.6
17	Pennsylvania	70.2
18	New Hampshire	69.9
19	Kansas	69.8
20	Nevada	69.7
21	Minnesota	69.4
22	Virginia	69.3
23	Kentucky	68.6
24	Michigan	68.3
25	Arkansas	68.1
26	Nebraska	68.0
27	Texas	67.9
27	Washington	67.9
29	Tennessee	67.2
30	Colorado	67.0
31	Idaho	66.9
32	North Carolina	66.8
33	Indiana	66.6
34	West Virginia	66.4
35	South Dakota	66.2
36	Iowa	66.1
37	Oklahoma	65.9
38	Florida	65.4
39	Utah	65.0
40	North Dakota	63.4
41	Louisiana	63.0
42	Mississippi	62.6
42	New Mexico	62.6
44	South Carolina	62.2
45	Montana	60.0
46	Delaware	59.9
47	Oregon	59.8
48	Alabama	59.1
49	Wyoming	56.5
50	Alaska	30.3

District of Columbia — 80.7

Source: Morgan Quitno Press using data from U.S. Bureau of the Census, Governments Division
"State and Local Government Finances: 1999-2000" (http://www.census.gov/govs/www/estimate00.html)

State and Local Government Tax Revenue
As a Percent of Personal Income in 2000
National Percent = 10.4% of Personal Income*

<u>ALPHA ORDER</u>

RANK	STATE	PERCENT
46	Alabama	8.9
3	Alaska	12.3
28	Arizona	10.2
29	Arkansas	10.1
15	California	10.9
43	Colorado	9.3
10	Connecticut	11.1
18	Delaware	10.6
45	Florida	9.2
31	Georgia	10.0
6	Hawaii	12.0
19	Idaho	10.5
31	Illinois	10.0
36	Indiana	9.9
23	Iowa	10.4
25	Kansas	10.3
23	Kentucky	10.4
19	Louisiana	10.5
2	Maine	13.0
29	Maryland	10.1
31	Massachusetts	10.0
16	Michigan	10.7
7	Minnesota	11.4
19	Mississippi	10.5
43	Missouri	9.3
25	Montana	10.3
19	Nebraska	10.5
41	Nevada	9.7
50	New Hampshire	7.9
25	New Jersey	10.3
4	New Mexico	12.1
1	New York	13.1
39	North Carolina	9.8
12	North Dakota	11.0
16	Ohio	10.7
36	Oklahoma	9.9
36	Oregon	9.9
31	Pennsylvania	10.0
10	Rhode Island	11.1
39	South Carolina	9.8
46	South Dakota	8.9
49	Tennessee	8.3
46	Texas	8.9
8	Utah	11.2
8	Vermont	11.2
42	Virginia	9.5
31	Washington	10.0
12	West Virginia	11.0
4	Wisconsin	12.1
12	Wyoming	11.0

<u>RANK ORDER</u>

RANK	STATE	PERCENT
1	New York	13.1
2	Maine	13.0
3	Alaska	12.3
4	New Mexico	12.1
4	Wisconsin	12.1
6	Hawaii	12.0
7	Minnesota	11.4
8	Utah	11.2
8	Vermont	11.2
10	Connecticut	11.1
10	Rhode Island	11.1
12	North Dakota	11.0
12	West Virginia	11.0
12	Wyoming	11.0
15	California	10.9
16	Michigan	10.7
16	Ohio	10.7
18	Delaware	10.6
19	Idaho	10.5
19	Louisiana	10.5
19	Mississippi	10.5
19	Nebraska	10.5
23	Iowa	10.4
23	Kentucky	10.4
25	Kansas	10.3
25	Montana	10.3
25	New Jersey	10.3
28	Arizona	10.2
29	Arkansas	10.1
29	Maryland	10.1
31	Georgia	10.0
31	Illinois	10.0
31	Massachusetts	10.0
31	Pennsylvania	10.0
31	Washington	10.0
36	Indiana	9.9
36	Oklahoma	9.9
36	Oregon	9.9
39	North Carolina	9.8
39	South Carolina	9.8
41	Nevada	9.7
42	Virginia	9.5
43	Colorado	9.3
43	Missouri	9.3
45	Florida	9.2
46	Alabama	8.9
46	South Dakota	8.9
46	Texas	8.9
49	Tennessee	8.3
50	New Hampshire	7.9
	District of Columbia	14.5

*Source: Morgan Quitno Press using data from Bureau of Economic Analysis and U.S. Census Bureau
"State Personal Income" and "State and Local Government Finances: 1999-2000"
*The personal income total used for this table is the sum of state estimates. This total differs from the national
income and product accounts (NIPA) estimate of personal income because it omits the earnings of federal civilian
and military personnel stationed abroad and of U.S. residents employed abroad temporarily by private U.S. firms.*

State and Local Government General Sales Tax Revenue in 2000

National Total = $215,112,414,000*

ALPHA ORDER

RANK	STATE	REVENUE	% of USA
24	Alabama	$2,868,357,000	1.3%
46	Alaska	106,864,000	0.0%
13	Arizona	4,853,286,000	2.3%
30	Arkansas	2,199,195,000	1.0%
1	California	30,439,691,000	14.2%
17	Colorado	3,775,214,000	1.8%
22	Connecticut	3,419,939,000	1.6%
47	Delaware	0	0.0%
4	Florida	15,556,791,000	7.2%
7	Georgia	7,531,299,000	3.5%
36	Hawaii	1,536,276,000	0.7%
40	Idaho	747,134,000	0.3%
9	Illinois	7,275,592,000	3.4%
20	Indiana	3,579,416,000	1.7%
33	Iowa	1,893,062,000	0.9%
29	Kansas	2,211,216,000	1.0%
31	Kentucky	2,171,723,000	1.0%
15	Louisiana	4,324,388,000	2.0%
39	Maine	847,358,000	0.4%
26	Maryland	2,498,184,000	1.2%
21	Massachusetts	3,565,267,000	1.7%
6	Michigan	7,666,399,000	3.6%
18	Minnesota	3,757,366,000	1.7%
28	Mississippi	2,333,384,000	1.1%
16	Missouri	4,107,718,000	1.9%
47	Montana	0	0.0%
37	Nebraska	1,216,962,000	0.6%
32	Nevada	2,061,496,000	1.0%
47	New Hampshire	0	0.0%
12	New Jersey	5,508,046,000	2.6%
34	New Mexico	1,867,700,000	0.9%
3	New York	16,473,484,000	7.7%
14	North Carolina	4,519,995,000	2.1%
44	North Dakota	381,401,000	0.2%
8	Ohio	7,431,610,000	3.5%
27	Oklahoma	2,403,829,000	1.1%
47	Oregon	0	0.0%
10	Pennsylvania	7,220,639,000	3.4%
42	Rhode Island	621,066,000	0.3%
25	South Carolina	2,557,733,000	1.2%
41	South Dakota	627,225,000	0.3%
11	Tennessee	5,701,043,000	2.7%
2	Texas	17,348,954,000	8.1%
35	Utah	1,841,327,000	0.9%
45	Vermont	215,423,000	0.1%
23	Virginia	3,214,162,000	1.5%
5	Washington	8,918,781,000	4.1%
38	West Virginia	917,050,000	0.4%
19	Wisconsin	3,695,182,000	1.7%
43	Wyoming	463,975,000	0.2%

RANK ORDER

RANK	STATE	REVENUE	% of USA
1	California	$30,439,691,000	14.2%
2	Texas	17,348,954,000	8.1%
3	New York	16,473,484,000	7.7%
4	Florida	15,556,791,000	7.2%
5	Washington	8,918,781,000	4.1%
6	Michigan	7,666,399,000	3.6%
7	Georgia	7,531,299,000	3.5%
8	Ohio	7,431,610,000	3.5%
9	Illinois	7,275,592,000	3.4%
10	Pennsylvania	7,220,639,000	3.4%
11	Tennessee	5,701,043,000	2.7%
12	New Jersey	5,508,046,000	2.6%
13	Arizona	4,853,286,000	2.3%
14	North Carolina	4,519,995,000	2.1%
15	Louisiana	4,324,388,000	2.0%
16	Missouri	4,107,718,000	1.9%
17	Colorado	3,775,214,000	1.8%
18	Minnesota	3,757,366,000	1.7%
19	Wisconsin	3,695,182,000	1.7%
20	Indiana	3,579,416,000	1.7%
21	Massachusetts	3,565,267,000	1.7%
22	Connecticut	3,419,939,000	1.6%
23	Virginia	3,214,162,000	1.5%
24	Alabama	2,868,357,000	1.3%
25	South Carolina	2,557,733,000	1.2%
26	Maryland	2,498,184,000	1.2%
27	Oklahoma	2,403,829,000	1.1%
28	Mississippi	2,333,384,000	1.1%
29	Kansas	2,211,216,000	1.0%
30	Arkansas	2,199,195,000	1.0%
31	Kentucky	2,171,723,000	1.0%
32	Nevada	2,061,496,000	1.0%
33	Iowa	1,893,062,000	0.9%
34	New Mexico	1,867,700,000	0.9%
35	Utah	1,841,327,000	0.9%
36	Hawaii	1,536,276,000	0.7%
37	Nebraska	1,216,962,000	0.6%
38	West Virginia	917,050,000	0.4%
39	Maine	847,358,000	0.4%
40	Idaho	747,134,000	0.3%
41	South Dakota	627,225,000	0.3%
42	Rhode Island	621,066,000	0.3%
43	Wyoming	463,975,000	0.2%
44	North Dakota	381,401,000	0.2%
45	Vermont	215,423,000	0.1%
46	Alaska	106,864,000	0.0%
47	Delaware	0	0.0%
47	Montana	0	0.0%
47	New Hampshire	0	0.0%
47	Oregon	0	0.0%
	District of Columbia	640,212,000	0.3%

Source: U.S. Bureau of the Census, Governments Division

"State and Local Government Finances: 1999-2000" (http://www.census.gov/govs/www/estimate00.html)

*Does not include special sales taxes such as those on sale of alcohol, gasoline or tobacco.

Per Capita State and Local Government General Sales Tax Revenue in 2000

National Per Capita = $762*

<u>ALPHA ORDER</u>

RANK	STATE	PER CAPITA
31	Alabama	$644
46	Alaska	170
9	Arizona	939
17	Arkansas	821
12	California	895
13	Colorado	873
5	Connecticut	1,002
47	Delaware	0
7	Florida	969
11	Georgia	915
2	Hawaii	1,267
38	Idaho	575
37	Illinois	585
35	Indiana	588
30	Iowa	646
17	Kansas	821
41	Kentucky	536
8	Louisiana	967
27	Maine	663
43	Maryland	470
39	Massachusetts	560
21	Michigan	770
22	Minnesota	761
20	Mississippi	819
23	Missouri	733
47	Montana	0
24	Nebraska	710
4	Nevada	1,021
47	New Hampshire	0
29	New Jersey	653
3	New Mexico	1,025
14	New York	867
40	North Carolina	559
33	North Dakota	595
28	Ohio	654
25	Oklahoma	696
47	Oregon	0
35	Pennsylvania	588
34	Rhode Island	591
32	South Carolina	636
15	South Dakota	830
6	Tennessee	1,000
16	Texas	828
17	Utah	821
45	Vermont	353
44	Virginia	452
1	Washington	1,509
42	West Virginia	507
26	Wisconsin	688
9	Wyoming	939

<u>RANK ORDER</u>

RANK	STATE	PER CAPITA
1	Washington	$1,509
2	Hawaii	1,267
3	New Mexico	1,025
4	Nevada	1,021
5	Connecticut	1,002
6	Tennessee	1,000
7	Florida	969
8	Louisiana	967
9	Arizona	939
9	Wyoming	939
11	Georgia	915
12	California	895
13	Colorado	873
14	New York	867
15	South Dakota	830
16	Texas	828
17	Arkansas	821
17	Kansas	821
17	Utah	821
20	Mississippi	819
21	Michigan	770
22	Minnesota	761
23	Missouri	733
24	Nebraska	710
25	Oklahoma	696
26	Wisconsin	688
27	Maine	663
28	Ohio	654
29	New Jersey	653
30	Iowa	646
31	Alabama	644
32	South Carolina	636
33	North Dakota	595
34	Rhode Island	591
35	Indiana	588
35	Pennsylvania	588
37	Illinois	585
38	Idaho	575
39	Massachusetts	560
40	North Carolina	559
41	Kentucky	536
42	West Virginia	507
43	Maryland	470
44	Virginia	452
45	Vermont	353
46	Alaska	170
47	Delaware	0
47	Montana	0
47	New Hampshire	0
47	Oregon	0

District of Columbia	1,120

*Source: Morgan Quitno Press using data from U.S. Bureau of the Census, Governments Division
"State and Local Government Finances: 1999-2000" (http://www.census.gov/govs/www/estimate00.html)*
Does not include special sales taxes such as those on sale of alcohol, gasoline or tobacco.

State and Local Government Property Tax Revenue in 2000

National Total = $249,177,604,000

ALPHA ORDER

RANK	STATE	REVENUE	% of USA
36	Alabama	$1,340,152,000	0.5%
44	Alaska	761,244,000	0.3%
20	Arizona	3,905,594,000	1.6%
39	Arkansas	965,665,000	0.4%
1	California	26,235,331,000	10.5%
21	Colorado	3,679,814,000	1.5%
16	Connecticut	5,407,465,000	2.2%
50	Delaware	382,491,000	0.2%
6	Florida	14,098,490,000	5.7%
12	Georgia	5,931,692,000	2.4%
47	Hawaii	602,626,000	0.2%
41	Idaho	867,068,000	0.3%
4	Illinois	14,511,114,000	5.8%
14	Indiana	5,551,586,000	2.2%
26	Iowa	2,599,313,000	1.0%
27	Kansas	2,173,302,000	0.9%
30	Kentucky	1,721,607,000	0.7%
29	Louisiana	1,742,297,000	0.7%
31	Maine	1,598,490,000	0.6%
17	Maryland	4,809,286,000	1.9%
10	Massachusetts	7,642,521,000	3.1%
9	Michigan	9,498,688,000	3.8%
19	Minnesota	4,565,073,000	1.8%
33	Mississippi	1,462,014,000	0.6%
22	Missouri	3,404,879,000	1.4%
40	Montana	907,995,000	0.4%
32	Nebraska	1,548,923,000	0.6%
34	Nevada	1,437,281,000	0.6%
28	New Hampshire	2,027,817,000	0.8%
5	New Jersey	14,448,857,000	5.8%
46	New Mexico	620,463,000	0.2%
2	New York	25,201,914,000	10.1%
18	North Carolina	4,607,461,000	1.8%
48	North Dakota	527,062,000	0.2%
8	Ohio	9,544,118,000	3.8%
38	Oklahoma	1,302,616,000	0.5%
24	Oregon	2,788,611,000	1.1%
7	Pennsylvania	10,066,526,000	4.0%
35	Rhode Island	1,359,523,000	0.5%
25	South Carolina	2,680,143,000	1.1%
45	South Dakota	632,374,000	0.3%
23	Tennessee	2,887,113,000	1.2%
3	Texas	19,817,072,000	8.0%
37	Utah	1,303,192,000	0.5%
43	Vermont	782,200,000	0.3%
11	Virginia	5,985,891,000	2.4%
15	Washington	5,492,563,000	2.2%
42	West Virginia	855,120,000	0.3%
13	Wisconsin	5,689,395,000	2.3%
49	Wyoming	512,791,000	0.2%

RANK ORDER

RANK	STATE	REVENUE	% of USA
1	California	$26,235,331,000	10.5%
2	New York	25,201,914,000	10.1%
3	Texas	19,817,072,000	8.0%
4	Illinois	14,511,114,000	5.8%
5	New Jersey	14,448,857,000	5.8%
6	Florida	14,098,490,000	5.7%
7	Pennsylvania	10,066,526,000	4.0%
8	Ohio	9,544,118,000	3.8%
9	Michigan	9,498,688,000	3.8%
10	Massachusetts	7,642,521,000	3.1%
11	Virginia	5,985,891,000	2.4%
12	Georgia	5,931,692,000	2.4%
13	Wisconsin	5,689,395,000	2.3%
14	Indiana	5,551,586,000	2.2%
15	Washington	5,492,563,000	2.2%
16	Connecticut	5,407,465,000	2.2%
17	Maryland	4,809,286,000	1.9%
18	North Carolina	4,607,461,000	1.8%
19	Minnesota	4,565,073,000	1.8%
20	Arizona	3,905,594,000	1.6%
21	Colorado	3,679,814,000	1.5%
22	Missouri	3,404,879,000	1.4%
23	Tennessee	2,887,113,000	1.2%
24	Oregon	2,788,611,000	1.1%
25	South Carolina	2,680,143,000	1.1%
26	Iowa	2,599,313,000	1.0%
27	Kansas	2,173,302,000	0.9%
28	New Hampshire	2,027,817,000	0.8%
29	Louisiana	1,742,297,000	0.7%
30	Kentucky	1,721,607,000	0.7%
31	Maine	1,598,490,000	0.6%
32	Nebraska	1,548,923,000	0.6%
33	Mississippi	1,462,014,000	0.6%
34	Nevada	1,437,281,000	0.6%
35	Rhode Island	1,359,523,000	0.5%
36	Alabama	1,340,152,000	0.5%
37	Utah	1,303,192,000	0.5%
38	Oklahoma	1,302,616,000	0.5%
39	Arkansas	965,665,000	0.4%
40	Montana	907,995,000	0.4%
41	Idaho	867,068,000	0.3%
42	West Virginia	855,120,000	0.3%
43	Vermont	782,200,000	0.3%
44	Alaska	761,244,000	0.3%
45	South Dakota	632,374,000	0.3%
46	New Mexico	620,463,000	0.2%
47	Hawaii	602,626,000	0.2%
48	North Dakota	527,062,000	0.2%
49	Wyoming	512,791,000	0.2%
50	Delaware	382,491,000	0.2%
	District of Columbia	692,781,000	0.3%

Source: U.S. Bureau of the Census, Governments Division
"State and Local Government Finances: 1999-2000" (http://www.census.gov/govs/www/estimate00.html)

Per Capita State and Local Government Property Tax Revenue in 2000

National Per Capita = $883

<u>ALPHA ORDER</u>

RANK	STATE	PER CAPITA
50	Alabama	$301
8	Alaska	1,213
32	Arizona	756
48	Arkansas	361
31	California	771
23	Colorado	850
3	Connecticut	1,585
43	Delaware	486
22	Florida	878
33	Georgia	720
42	Hawaii	497
35	Idaho	667
10	Illinois	1,166
18	Indiana	911
21	Iowa	888
30	Kansas	807
45	Kentucky	425
46	Louisiana	390
7	Maine	1,251
19	Maryland	905
9	Massachusetts	1,201
14	Michigan	954
17	Minnesota	925
40	Mississippi	513
37	Missouri	607
13	Montana	1,005
20	Nebraska	904
34	Nevada	712
2	New Hampshire	1,635
1	New Jersey	1,713
49	New Mexico	341
4	New York	1,326
39	North Carolina	570
27	North Dakota	822
25	Ohio	840
47	Oklahoma	377
29	Oregon	813
28	Pennsylvania	819
5	Rhode Island	1,294
36	South Carolina	666
26	South Dakota	837
41	Tennessee	506
15	Texas	946
38	Utah	581
6	Vermont	1,282
24	Virginia	842
16	Washington	929
44	West Virginia	473
11	Wisconsin	1,059
12	Wyoming	1,038

<u>RANK ORDER</u>

RANK	STATE	PER CAPITA
1	New Jersey	$1,713
2	New Hampshire	1,635
3	Connecticut	1,585
4	New York	1,326
5	Rhode Island	1,294
6	Vermont	1,282
7	Maine	1,251
8	Alaska	1,213
9	Massachusetts	1,201
10	Illinois	1,166
11	Wisconsin	1,059
12	Wyoming	1,038
13	Montana	1,005
14	Michigan	954
15	Texas	946
16	Washington	929
17	Minnesota	925
18	Indiana	911
19	Maryland	905
20	Nebraska	904
21	Iowa	888
22	Florida	878
23	Colorado	850
24	Virginia	842
25	Ohio	840
26	South Dakota	837
27	North Dakota	822
28	Pennsylvania	819
29	Oregon	813
30	Kansas	807
31	California	771
32	Arizona	756
33	Georgia	720
34	Nevada	712
35	Idaho	667
36	South Carolina	666
37	Missouri	607
38	Utah	581
39	North Carolina	570
40	Mississippi	513
41	Tennessee	506
42	Hawaii	497
43	Delaware	486
44	West Virginia	473
45	Kentucky	425
46	Louisiana	390
47	Oklahoma	377
48	Arkansas	361
49	New Mexico	341
50	Alabama	301

District of Columbia — 1,212

Source: Morgan Quitno Press using data from U.S. Bureau of the Census, Governments Division
"State and Local Government Finances: 1999-2000" (http://www.census.gov/govs/www/estimate00.html)

State and Local Government Property Tax as a Percent Of State and Local Government Total Revenue in 2000
National Percent = 12.8%

<u>ALPHA ORDER</u>

RANK	STATE	PERCENT
49	Alabama	5.2
42	Alaska	7.2
16	Arizona	14.1
44	Arkansas	7.0
34	California	9.7
24	Colorado	12.4
3	Connecticut	20.9
48	Delaware	6.1
12	Florida	15.3
26	Georgia	12.0
43	Hawaii	7.1
31	Idaho	11.4
7	Illinois	18.0
8	Indiana	17.0
13	Iowa	15.1
19	Kansas	13.4
46	Kentucky	6.8
47	Louisiana	6.4
5	Maine	18.7
15	Maryland	14.2
9	Massachusetts	16.6
18	Michigan	13.5
28	Minnesota	11.8
37	Mississippi	8.8
33	Missouri	10.8
11	Montana	16.1
20	Nebraska	13.3
25	Nevada	12.1
1	New Hampshire	29.2
2	New Jersey	23.2
50	New Mexico	4.7
20	New York	13.3
36	North Carolina	9.1
30	North Dakota	11.7
27	Ohio	11.9
45	Oklahoma	6.9
34	Oregon	9.7
23	Pennsylvania	12.5
6	Rhode Island	18.3
31	South Carolina	11.4
14	South Dakota	14.8
39	Tennessee	8.6
10	Texas	16.4
38	Utah	8.7
4	Vermont	19.5
17	Virginia	13.6
28	Washington	11.8
40	West Virginia	7.9
22	Wisconsin	13.2
41	Wyoming	7.3

<u>RANK ORDER</u>

RANK	STATE	PERCENT
1	New Hampshire	29.2
2	New Jersey	23.2
3	Connecticut	20.9
4	Vermont	19.5
5	Maine	18.7
6	Rhode Island	18.3
7	Illinois	18.0
8	Indiana	17.0
9	Massachusetts	16.6
10	Texas	16.4
11	Montana	16.1
12	Florida	15.3
13	Iowa	15.1
14	South Dakota	14.8
15	Maryland	14.2
16	Arizona	14.1
17	Virginia	13.6
18	Michigan	13.5
19	Kansas	13.4
20	Nebraska	13.3
20	New York	13.3
22	Wisconsin	13.2
23	Pennsylvania	12.5
24	Colorado	12.4
25	Nevada	12.1
26	Georgia	12.0
27	Ohio	11.9
28	Minnesota	11.8
28	Washington	11.8
30	North Dakota	11.7
31	Idaho	11.4
31	South Carolina	11.4
33	Missouri	10.8
34	California	9.7
34	Oregon	9.7
36	North Carolina	9.1
37	Mississippi	8.8
38	Utah	8.7
39	Tennessee	8.6
40	West Virginia	7.9
41	Wyoming	7.3
42	Alaska	7.2
43	Hawaii	7.1
44	Arkansas	7.0
45	Oklahoma	6.9
46	Kentucky	6.8
47	Louisiana	6.4
48	Delaware	6.1
49	Alabama	5.2
50	New Mexico	4.7

District of Columbia   10.9

State and Local Government Property Tax Revenue as a Percent Of State and Local Government Own Source Revenue in 2000
National Percent = 19.9%*

<u>ALPHA ORDER</u>

RANK	STATE	PERCENT
49	Alabama	8.4
47	Alaska	10.0
16	Arizona	21.2
43	Arkansas	11.0
37	California	15.4
28	Colorado	18.7
5	Connecticut	27.8
48	Delaware	8.7
14	Florida	22.0
29	Georgia	18.2
44	Hawaii	10.4
31	Idaho	17.6
7	Illinois	27.1
12	Indiana	22.6
16	Iowa	21.2
20	Kansas	19.9
42	Kentucky	11.6
46	Louisiana	10.1
6	Maine	27.5
23	Maryland	19.7
11	Massachusetts	24.0
19	Michigan	20.6
33	Minnesota	17.4
38	Mississippi	14.5
35	Missouri	16.8
9	Montana	25.6
16	Nebraska	21.2
34	Nevada	17.2
1	New Hampshire	43.2
2	New Jersey	33.1
50	New Mexico	8.1
14	New York	22.0
39	North Carolina	14.4
27	North Dakota	18.9
22	Ohio	19.8
44	Oklahoma	10.4
30	Oregon	17.7
25	Pennsylvania	19.3
4	Rhode Island	29.9
32	South Carolina	17.5
10	South Dakota	24.1
36	Tennessee	15.6
8	Texas	25.7
39	Utah	14.4
3	Vermont	30.2
23	Virginia	19.7
20	Washington	19.9
41	West Virginia	13.0
13	Wisconsin	22.3
25	Wyoming	19.3

<u>RANK ORDER</u>

RANK	STATE	PERCENT
1	New Hampshire	43.2
2	New Jersey	33.1
3	Vermont	30.2
4	Rhode Island	29.9
5	Connecticut	27.8
6	Maine	27.5
7	Illinois	27.1
8	Texas	25.7
9	Montana	25.6
10	South Dakota	24.1
11	Massachusetts	24.0
12	Indiana	22.6
13	Wisconsin	22.3
14	Florida	22.0
14	New York	22.0
16	Arizona	21.2
16	Iowa	21.2
16	Nebraska	21.2
19	Michigan	20.6
20	Kansas	19.9
20	Washington	19.9
22	Ohio	19.8
23	Maryland	19.7
23	Virginia	19.7
25	Pennsylvania	19.3
25	Wyoming	19.3
27	North Dakota	18.9
28	Colorado	18.7
29	Georgia	18.2
30	Oregon	17.7
31	Idaho	17.6
32	South Carolina	17.5
33	Minnesota	17.4
34	Nevada	17.2
35	Missouri	16.8
36	Tennessee	15.6
37	California	15.4
38	Mississippi	14.5
39	North Carolina	14.4
39	Utah	14.4
41	West Virginia	13.0
42	Kentucky	11.6
43	Arkansas	11.0
44	Hawaii	10.4
44	Oklahoma	10.4
46	Louisiana	10.1
47	Alaska	10.0
48	Delaware	8.7
49	Alabama	8.4
50	New Mexico	8.1
	District of Columbia	17.4

Source: Morgan Quitno Press using data from U.S. Bureau of the Census, Governments Division
"State and Local Government Finances: 1999-2000" (http://www.census.gov/govs/www/estimate00.html)
**Own source revenue includes taxes, current charges and miscellaneous general revenue. Excluded are intergovernmental transfers, insurance trust revenue and revenue from government owned utilities and other commercial or auxiliary enterprise.*

State and Local Government Total Expenditures in 2000

National Total = $1,746,942,699,000*

ALPHA ORDER

RANK	STATE	EXPENDITURES	% of USA
23	Alabama	$25,319,135,000	1.4%
39	Alaska	8,627,637,000	0.5%
21	Arizona	27,293,135,000	1.6%
34	Arkansas	12,245,158,000	0.7%
1	California	236,644,591,000	13.5%
22	Colorado	26,173,055,000	1.5%
26	Connecticut	24,011,246,000	1.4%
45	Delaware	5,153,049,000	0.3%
4	Florida	84,300,913,000	4.8%
12	Georgia	43,516,518,000	2.5%
40	Hawaii	8,253,845,000	0.5%
43	Idaho	6,404,069,000	0.4%
6	Illinois	74,727,137,000	4.3%
18	Indiana	31,249,891,000	1.8%
29	Iowa	17,274,861,000	1.0%
32	Kansas	14,419,195,000	0.8%
28	Kentucky	21,473,123,000	1.2%
24	Louisiana	25,018,335,000	1.4%
41	Maine	7,652,232,000	0.4%
19	Maryland	30,598,125,000	1.8%
11	Massachusetts	44,361,795,000	2.5%
8	Michigan	61,505,543,000	3.5%
15	Minnesota	35,423,651,000	2.0%
31	Mississippi	15,378,511,000	0.9%
20	Missouri	27,953,327,000	1.6%
46	Montana	4,983,156,000	0.3%
37	Nebraska	10,831,429,000	0.6%
35	Nevada	11,229,943,000	0.6%
44	New Hampshire	6,222,433,000	0.4%
9	New Jersey	54,590,246,000	3.1%
36	New Mexico	11,194,843,000	0.6%
2	New York	171,858,216,000	9.8%
10	North Carolina	46,134,556,000	2.6%
47	North Dakota	4,040,996,000	0.2%
7	Ohio	68,418,276,000	3.9%
30	Oklahoma	15,961,566,000	0.9%
25	Oregon	24,086,300,000	1.4%
5	Pennsylvania	75,623,831,000	4.3%
42	Rhode Island	6,432,385,000	0.4%
27	South Carolina	23,436,064,000	1.3%
49	South Dakota	3,760,194,000	0.2%
17	Tennessee	32,009,918,000	1.8%
3	Texas	109,634,090,000	6.3%
33	Utah	13,044,481,000	0.7%
48	Vermont	3,765,713,000	0.2%
14	Virginia	38,092,479,000	2.2%
13	Washington	41,794,000,000	2.4%
38	West Virginia	9,990,456,000	0.6%
16	Wisconsin	34,558,971,000	2.0%
50	Wyoming	3,743,108,000	0.2%

RANK ORDER

RANK	STATE	EXPENDITURES	% of USA
1	California	$236,644,591,000	13.5%
2	New York	171,858,216,000	9.8%
3	Texas	109,634,090,000	6.3%
4	Florida	84,300,913,000	4.8%
5	Pennsylvania	75,623,831,000	4.3%
6	Illinois	74,727,137,000	4.3%
7	Ohio	68,418,276,000	3.9%
8	Michigan	61,505,543,000	3.5%
9	New Jersey	54,590,246,000	3.1%
10	North Carolina	46,134,556,000	2.6%
11	Massachusetts	44,361,795,000	2.5%
12	Georgia	43,516,518,000	2.5%
13	Washington	41,794,000,000	2.4%
14	Virginia	38,092,479,000	2.2%
15	Minnesota	35,423,651,000	2.0%
16	Wisconsin	34,558,971,000	2.0%
17	Tennessee	32,009,918,000	1.8%
18	Indiana	31,249,891,000	1.8%
19	Maryland	30,598,125,000	1.8%
20	Missouri	27,953,327,000	1.6%
21	Arizona	27,293,135,000	1.6%
22	Colorado	26,173,055,000	1.5%
23	Alabama	25,319,135,000	1.4%
24	Louisiana	25,018,335,000	1.4%
25	Oregon	24,086,300,000	1.4%
26	Connecticut	24,011,246,000	1.4%
27	South Carolina	23,436,064,000	1.3%
28	Kentucky	21,473,123,000	1.2%
29	Iowa	17,274,861,000	1.0%
30	Oklahoma	15,961,566,000	0.9%
31	Mississippi	15,378,511,000	0.9%
32	Kansas	14,419,195,000	0.8%
33	Utah	13,044,481,000	0.7%
34	Arkansas	12,245,158,000	0.7%
35	Nevada	11,229,943,000	0.6%
36	New Mexico	11,194,843,000	0.6%
37	Nebraska	10,831,429,000	0.6%
38	West Virginia	9,990,456,000	0.6%
39	Alaska	8,627,637,000	0.5%
40	Hawaii	8,253,845,000	0.5%
41	Maine	7,652,232,000	0.4%
42	Rhode Island	6,432,385,000	0.4%
43	Idaho	6,404,069,000	0.4%
44	New Hampshire	6,222,433,000	0.4%
45	Delaware	5,153,049,000	0.3%
46	Montana	4,983,156,000	0.3%
47	North Dakota	4,040,996,000	0.2%
48	Vermont	3,765,713,000	0.2%
49	South Dakota	3,760,194,000	0.2%
50	Wyoming	3,743,108,000	0.2%
	District of Columbia	6,526,972,000	0.4%

Source: U.S. Bureau of the Census, Governments Division
"State and Local Government Finances: 1999-2000" (http://www.census.gov/govs/www/estimate00.html)
**Total expenditures includes all money paid other than for retirement of debt and extension of loans. Includes payments from all sources of funds including current revenues and proceeds from borrowing and prior year fund balances. Includes intergovernmental transfers and expenditures for government owned utilities and other commercial or auxiliary enterprise and insurance trust expenditures.*

Per Capita State and Local Government Total Expenditures in 2000

National Per Capita = $6,190*

ALPHA ORDER

RANK	STATE	PER CAPITA
30	Alabama	$5,687
1	Alaska	13,745
41	Arizona	5,282
50	Arkansas	4,571
9	California	6,958
21	Colorado	6,049
6	Connecticut	7,037
11	Delaware	6,552
42	Florida	5,252
40	Georgia	5,285
10	Hawaii	6,806
48	Idaho	4,927
23	Illinois	6,007
44	Indiana	5,130
25	Iowa	5,898
38	Kansas	5,355
39	Kentucky	5,304
32	Louisiana	5,597
24	Maine	5,991
28	Maryland	5,760
8	Massachusetts	6,973
16	Michigan	6,178
4	Minnesota	7,179
36	Mississippi	5,398
46	Missouri	4,987
35	Montana	5,516
14	Nebraska	6,322
33	Nevada	5,563
45	New Hampshire	5,016
12	New Jersey	6,473
19	New Mexico	6,145
2	New York	9,045
29	North Carolina	5,708
15	North Dakota	6,303
22	Ohio	6,021
49	Oklahoma	4,621
7	Oregon	7,020
18	Pennsylvania	6,155
20	Rhode Island	6,122
26	South Carolina	5,824
47	South Dakota	4,975
31	Tennessee	5,613
43	Texas	5,232
27	Utah	5,815
17	Vermont	6,174
37	Virginia	5,361
5	Washington	7,070
34	West Virginia	5,528
13	Wisconsin	6,430
3	Wyoming	7,576

RANK ORDER

RANK	STATE	PER CAPITA
1	Alaska	$13,745
2	New York	9,045
3	Wyoming	7,576
4	Minnesota	7,179
5	Washington	7,070
6	Connecticut	7,037
7	Oregon	7,020
8	Massachusetts	6,973
9	California	6,958
10	Hawaii	6,806
11	Delaware	6,552
12	New Jersey	6,473
13	Wisconsin	6,430
14	Nebraska	6,322
15	North Dakota	6,303
16	Michigan	6,178
17	Vermont	6,174
18	Pennsylvania	6,155
19	New Mexico	6,145
20	Rhode Island	6,122
21	Colorado	6,049
22	Ohio	6,021
23	Illinois	6,007
24	Maine	5,991
25	Iowa	5,898
26	South Carolina	5,824
27	Utah	5,815
28	Maryland	5,760
29	North Carolina	5,708
30	Alabama	5,687
31	Tennessee	5,613
32	Louisiana	5,597
33	Nevada	5,563
34	West Virginia	5,528
35	Montana	5,516
36	Mississippi	5,398
37	Virginia	5,361
38	Kansas	5,355
39	Kentucky	5,304
40	Georgia	5,285
41	Arizona	5,282
42	Florida	5,252
43	Texas	5,232
44	Indiana	5,130
45	New Hampshire	5,016
46	Missouri	4,987
47	South Dakota	4,975
48	Idaho	4,927
49	Oklahoma	4,621
50	Arkansas	4,571
	District of Columbia	11,418

*Source: Morgan Quitno Press using data from U.S. Bureau of the Census, Governments Division
"State and Local Government Finances: 1999-2000" (http://www.census.gov/govs/www/estimate00.html)*
**Total expenditures includes all money paid other than for retirement of debt and extension of loans. Includes payments from all sources of funds including current revenues and proceeds from borrowing and prior year fund balances. Includes intergovernmental transfers and expenditures for government owned utilities and other commercial or auxiliary enterprise and insurance trust expenditures.*

State and Local Government Direct General Expenditures in 2000

National Total = $1,502,767,621,000*

<u>ALPHA ORDER</u>

RANK	STATE	EXPENDITURES	% of USA
24	Alabama	$22,062,478,000	1.5%
39	Alaska	7,600,155,000	0.5%
21	Arizona	23,262,124,000	1.5%
33	Arkansas	11,057,163,000	0.7%
1	California	195,767,410,000	13.0%
22	Colorado	22,527,256,000	1.5%
25	Connecticut	21,419,546,000	1.4%
45	Delaware	4,690,651,000	0.3%
4	Florida	75,290,415,000	5.0%
11	Georgia	38,077,731,000	2.5%
40	Hawaii	7,291,259,000	0.5%
42	Idaho	5,827,839,000	0.4%
6	Illinois	64,403,166,000	4.3%
17	Indiana	28,739,813,000	1.9%
29	Iowa	15,562,762,000	1.0%
32	Kansas	12,884,223,000	0.9%
28	Kentucky	19,020,312,000	1.3%
23	Louisiana	22,277,007,000	1.5%
41	Maine	6,954,682,000	0.5%
18	Maryland	27,446,473,000	1.8%
12	Massachusetts	37,769,841,000	2.5%
8	Michigan	54,750,229,000	3.6%
15	Minnesota	31,166,332,000	2.1%
30	Mississippi	13,932,362,000	0.9%
20	Missouri	24,818,186,000	1.7%
46	Montana	4,522,971,000	0.3%
38	Nebraska	8,405,929,000	0.6%
36	Nevada	9,755,367,000	0.6%
43	New Hampshire	5,663,818,000	0.4%
9	New Jersey	47,230,502,000	3.1%
35	New Mexico	10,098,749,000	0.7%
2	New York	140,020,445,000	9.3%
10	North Carolina	40,434,442,000	2.7%
47	North Dakota	3,673,683,000	0.2%
7	Ohio	57,648,739,000	3.8%
31	Oklahoma	13,767,304,000	0.9%
27	Oregon	20,161,135,000	1.3%
5	Pennsylvania	65,871,207,000	4.4%
44	Rhode Island	5,560,094,000	0.4%
26	South Carolina	20,259,774,000	1.3%
49	South Dakota	3,443,532,000	0.2%
19	Tennessee	25,272,358,000	1.7%
3	Texas	95,761,974,000	6.4%
34	Utah	11,012,530,000	0.7%
48	Vermont	3,446,299,000	0.2%
13	Virginia	34,727,094,000	2.3%
14	Washington	33,475,161,000	2.2%
37	West Virginia	8,711,374,000	0.6%
16	Wisconsin	30,762,068,000	2.0%
50	Wyoming	3,329,687,000	0.2%

<u>RANK ORDER</u>

RANK	STATE	EXPENDITURES	% of USA
1	California	$195,767,410,000	13.0%
2	New York	140,020,445,000	9.3%
3	Texas	95,761,974,000	6.4%
4	Florida	75,290,415,000	5.0%
5	Pennsylvania	65,871,207,000	4.4%
6	Illinois	64,403,166,000	4.3%
7	Ohio	57,648,739,000	3.8%
8	Michigan	54,750,229,000	3.6%
9	New Jersey	47,230,502,000	3.1%
10	North Carolina	40,434,442,000	2.7%
11	Georgia	38,077,731,000	2.5%
12	Massachusetts	37,769,841,000	2.5%
13	Virginia	34,727,094,000	2.3%
14	Washington	33,475,161,000	2.2%
15	Minnesota	31,166,332,000	2.1%
16	Wisconsin	30,762,068,000	2.0%
17	Indiana	28,739,813,000	1.9%
18	Maryland	27,446,473,000	1.8%
19	Tennessee	25,272,358,000	1.7%
20	Missouri	24,818,186,000	1.7%
21	Arizona	23,262,124,000	1.5%
22	Colorado	22,527,256,000	1.5%
23	Louisiana	22,277,007,000	1.5%
24	Alabama	22,062,478,000	1.5%
25	Connecticut	21,419,546,000	1.4%
26	South Carolina	20,259,774,000	1.3%
27	Oregon	20,161,135,000	1.3%
28	Kentucky	19,020,312,000	1.3%
29	Iowa	15,562,762,000	1.0%
30	Mississippi	13,932,362,000	0.9%
31	Oklahoma	13,767,304,000	0.9%
32	Kansas	12,884,223,000	0.9%
33	Arkansas	11,057,163,000	0.7%
34	Utah	11,012,530,000	0.7%
35	New Mexico	10,098,749,000	0.7%
36	Nevada	9,755,367,000	0.6%
37	West Virginia	8,711,374,000	0.6%
38	Nebraska	8,405,929,000	0.6%
39	Alaska	7,600,155,000	0.5%
40	Hawaii	7,291,259,000	0.5%
41	Maine	6,954,682,000	0.5%
42	Idaho	5,827,839,000	0.4%
43	New Hampshire	5,663,818,000	0.4%
44	Rhode Island	5,560,094,000	0.4%
45	Delaware	4,690,651,000	0.3%
46	Montana	4,522,971,000	0.3%
47	North Dakota	3,673,683,000	0.2%
48	Vermont	3,446,299,000	0.2%
49	South Dakota	3,443,532,000	0.2%
50	Wyoming	3,329,687,000	0.2%
	District of Columbia	5,151,970,000	0.3%

Source: U.S. Bureau of the Census, Governments Division
"State and Local Government Finances: 1999-2000" (http://www.census.gov/govs/www/estimate00.html)
**Direct general expenditures include expenditures for current operations, assistance and subsidies, interest on debt and capital outlay. Excludes intergovernmental transfers, expenditures for government owned utilities and other commercial or auxiliary enterprise and insurance trust expenditures.*

Per Capita State and Local Government Direct General Expenditures in 2000

National Per Capita = $5,325*

ALPHA ORDER

RANK	STATE	PER CAPITA
30	Alabama	$4,956
1	Alaska	12,108
45	Arizona	4,502
49	Arkansas	4,128
10	California	5,756
22	Colorado	5,206
5	Connecticut	6,278
7	Delaware	5,964
40	Florida	4,691
41	Georgia	4,624
6	Hawaii	6,013
46	Idaho	4,484
23	Illinois	5,177
38	Indiana	4,718
20	Iowa	5,314
37	Kansas	4,785
39	Kentucky	4,698
29	Louisiana	4,984
18	Maine	5,445
24	Maryland	5,166
8	Massachusetts	5,937
17	Michigan	5,499
4	Minnesota	6,316
33	Mississippi	4,891
48	Missouri	4,428
27	Montana	5,007
32	Nebraska	4,906
35	Nevada	4,832
43	New Hampshire	4,566
15	New Jersey	5,600
16	New Mexico	5,543
2	New York	7,370
28	North Carolina	5,003
11	North Dakota	5,730
25	Ohio	5,073
50	Oklahoma	3,985
9	Oregon	5,876
19	Pennsylvania	5,361
21	Rhode Island	5,292
26	South Carolina	5,035
44	South Dakota	4,556
47	Tennessee	4,431
42	Texas	4,570
31	Utah	4,909
14	Vermont	5,650
34	Virginia	4,887
13	Washington	5,662
36	West Virginia	4,820
12	Wisconsin	5,724
3	Wyoming	6,739

RANK ORDER

RANK	STATE	PER CAPITA
1	Alaska	$12,108
2	New York	7,370
3	Wyoming	6,739
4	Minnesota	6,316
5	Connecticut	6,278
6	Hawaii	6,013
7	Delaware	5,964
8	Massachusetts	5,937
9	Oregon	5,876
10	California	5,756
11	North Dakota	5,730
12	Wisconsin	5,724
13	Washington	5,662
14	Vermont	5,650
15	New Jersey	5,600
16	New Mexico	5,543
17	Michigan	5,499
18	Maine	5,445
19	Pennsylvania	5,361
20	Iowa	5,314
21	Rhode Island	5,292
22	Colorado	5,206
23	Illinois	5,177
24	Maryland	5,166
25	Ohio	5,073
26	South Carolina	5,035
27	Montana	5,007
28	North Carolina	5,003
29	Louisiana	4,984
30	Alabama	4,956
31	Utah	4,909
32	Nebraska	4,906
33	Mississippi	4,891
34	Virginia	4,887
35	Nevada	4,832
36	West Virginia	4,820
37	Kansas	4,785
38	Indiana	4,718
39	Kentucky	4,698
40	Florida	4,691
41	Georgia	4,624
42	Texas	4,570
43	New Hampshire	4,566
44	South Dakota	4,556
45	Arizona	4,502
46	Idaho	4,484
47	Tennessee	4,431
48	Missouri	4,428
49	Arkansas	4,128
50	Oklahoma	3,985
	District of Columbia	9,013

Source: Morgan Quitno Press using data from U.S. Bureau of the Census, Governments Division
"State and Local Government Finances: 1999-2000" (http://www.census.gov/govs/www/estimate00.html)
*Direct general expenditures include expenditures for current operations, assistance and subsidies, interest on debt and capital outlay. Excludes intergovernmental transfers, expenditures for government owned utilities and other commercial or auxiliary enterprise and insurance trust expenditures.

State and Local Government Debt Outstanding in 2000

National Total = $1,451,815,216,000*

ALPHA ORDER

RANK	STATE	DEBT	% of USA
27	Alabama	$16,798,576,000	1.2%
38	Alaska	7,256,519,000	0.5%
18	Arizona	23,598,965,000	1.6%
35	Arkansas	7,828,512,000	0.5%
1	California	177,919,620,000	12.3%
21	Colorado	23,199,133,000	1.6%
19	Connecticut	23,495,016,000	1.6%
44	Delaware	4,584,915,000	0.3%
4	Florida	78,495,159,000	5.4%
13	Georgia	29,948,135,000	2.1%
34	Hawaii	7,909,045,000	0.5%
46	Idaho	3,429,698,000	0.2%
6	Illinois	67,573,181,000	4.7%
22	Indiana	19,868,773,000	1.4%
37	Iowa	7,309,590,000	0.5%
32	Kansas	10,439,970,000	0.7%
20	Kentucky	23,420,480,000	1.6%
26	Louisiana	17,979,760,000	1.2%
43	Maine	5,845,296,000	0.4%
17	Maryland	23,829,590,000	1.6%
7	Massachusetts	55,163,476,000	3.8%
9	Michigan	47,195,342,000	3.3%
15	Minnesota	27,408,508,000	1.9%
33	Mississippi	8,518,722,000	0.6%
23	Missouri	19,285,862,000	1.3%
45	Montana	3,797,793,000	0.3%
42	Nebraska	6,647,814,000	0.5%
29	Nevada	13,235,447,000	0.9%
40	New Hampshire	7,040,746,000	0.5%
8	New Jersey	50,314,502,000	3.5%
36	New Mexico	7,652,261,000	0.5%
2	New York	177,549,900,000	12.2%
14	North Carolina	29,114,420,000	2.0%
49	North Dakota	2,780,540,000	0.2%
10	Ohio	42,086,957,000	2.9%
31	Oklahoma	11,408,557,000	0.8%
28	Oregon	15,606,989,000	1.1%
5	Pennsylvania	73,325,038,000	5.1%
41	Rhode Island	6,877,850,000	0.5%
24	South Carolina	18,670,657,000	1.3%
47	South Dakota	3,288,892,000	0.2%
25	Tennessee	18,376,838,000	1.3%
3	Texas	100,174,846,000	6.9%
30	Utah	12,394,278,000	0.9%
48	Vermont	2,838,976,000	0.2%
12	Virginia	31,546,081,000	2.2%
11	Washington	38,697,244,000	2.7%
39	West Virginia	7,094,022,000	0.5%
16	Wisconsin	25,562,783,000	1.8%
50	Wyoming	2,367,727,000	0.2%

RANK ORDER

RANK	STATE	DEBT	% of USA
1	California	$177,919,620,000	12.3%
2	New York	177,549,900,000	12.2%
3	Texas	100,174,846,000	6.9%
4	Florida	78,495,159,000	5.4%
5	Pennsylvania	73,325,038,000	5.1%
6	Illinois	67,573,181,000	4.7%
7	Massachusetts	55,163,476,000	3.8%
8	New Jersey	50,314,502,000	3.5%
9	Michigan	47,195,342,000	3.3%
10	Ohio	42,086,957,000	2.9%
11	Washington	38,697,244,000	2.7%
12	Virginia	31,546,081,000	2.2%
13	Georgia	29,948,135,000	2.1%
14	North Carolina	29,114,420,000	2.0%
15	Minnesota	27,408,508,000	1.9%
16	Wisconsin	25,562,783,000	1.8%
17	Maryland	23,829,590,000	1.6%
18	Arizona	23,598,965,000	1.6%
19	Connecticut	23,495,016,000	1.6%
20	Kentucky	23,420,480,000	1.6%
21	Colorado	23,199,133,000	1.6%
22	Indiana	19,868,773,000	1.4%
23	Missouri	19,285,862,000	1.3%
24	South Carolina	18,670,657,000	1.3%
25	Tennessee	18,376,838,000	1.3%
26	Louisiana	17,979,760,000	1.2%
27	Alabama	16,798,576,000	1.2%
28	Oregon	15,606,989,000	1.1%
29	Nevada	13,235,447,000	0.9%
30	Utah	12,394,278,000	0.9%
31	Oklahoma	11,408,557,000	0.8%
32	Kansas	10,439,970,000	0.7%
33	Mississippi	8,518,722,000	0.6%
34	Hawaii	7,909,045,000	0.5%
35	Arkansas	7,828,512,000	0.5%
36	New Mexico	7,652,261,000	0.5%
37	Iowa	7,309,590,000	0.5%
38	Alaska	7,256,519,000	0.5%
39	West Virginia	7,094,022,000	0.5%
40	New Hampshire	7,040,746,000	0.5%
41	Rhode Island	6,877,850,000	0.5%
42	Nebraska	6,647,814,000	0.5%
43	Maine	5,845,296,000	0.4%
44	Delaware	4,584,915,000	0.3%
45	Montana	3,797,793,000	0.3%
46	Idaho	3,429,698,000	0.2%
47	South Dakota	3,288,892,000	0.2%
48	Vermont	2,838,976,000	0.2%
49	North Dakota	2,780,540,000	0.2%
50	Wyoming	2,367,727,000	0.2%
	District of Columbia	5,062,215,000	0.3%

Source: U.S. Bureau of the Census, Governments Division
"State and Local Government Finances: 1999-2000" (http://www.census.gov/govs/www/estimate00.html)
Includes short-term, long-term, full faith and credit, nonguaranteed and public debt for private purposes.

Per Capita State and Local Government Debt Outstanding in 2000

National Per Capita = $5,144*

<u>ALPHA ORDER</u>

RANK	STATE	PER CAPITA
39	Alabama	$3,773
1	Alaska	11,561
27	Arizona	4,567
48	Arkansas	2,923
18	California	5,231
17	Colorado	5,362
4	Connecticut	6,886
11	Delaware	5,829
19	Florida	4,890
41	Georgia	3,637
8	Hawaii	6,522
49	Idaho	2,639
16	Illinois	5,432
45	Indiana	3,261
50	Iowa	2,496
38	Kansas	3,877
12	Kentucky	5,785
35	Louisiana	4,023
26	Maine	4,576
29	Maryland	4,486
3	Massachusetts	8,671
23	Michigan	4,740
14	Minnesota	5,555
47	Mississippi	2,990
43	Missouri	3,441
33	Montana	4,204
37	Nebraska	3,880
5	Nevada	6,556
13	New Hampshire	5,676
10	New Jersey	5,966
34	New Mexico	4,200
2	New York	9,345
42	North Carolina	3,602
32	North Dakota	4,337
40	Ohio	3,704
44	Oklahoma	3,303
28	Oregon	4,549
9	Pennsylvania	5,968
6	Rhode Island	6,546
25	South Carolina	4,640
31	South Dakota	4,352
46	Tennessee	3,222
21	Texas	4,780
15	Utah	5,525
24	Vermont	4,654
30	Virginia	4,439
6	Washington	6,546
36	West Virginia	3,925
22	Wisconsin	4,756
20	Wyoming	4,792

<u>RANK ORDER</u>

RANK	STATE	PER CAPITA
1	Alaska	$11,561
2	New York	9,345
3	Massachusetts	8,671
4	Connecticut	6,886
5	Nevada	6,556
6	Rhode Island	6,546
6	Washington	6,546
8	Hawaii	6,522
9	Pennsylvania	5,968
10	New Jersey	5,966
11	Delaware	5,829
12	Kentucky	5,785
13	New Hampshire	5,676
14	Minnesota	5,555
15	Utah	5,525
16	Illinois	5,432
17	Colorado	5,362
18	California	5,231
19	Florida	4,890
20	Wyoming	4,792
21	Texas	4,780
22	Wisconsin	4,756
23	Michigan	4,740
24	Vermont	4,654
25	South Carolina	4,640
26	Maine	4,576
27	Arizona	4,567
28	Oregon	4,549
29	Maryland	4,486
30	Virginia	4,439
31	South Dakota	4,352
32	North Dakota	4,337
33	Montana	4,204
34	New Mexico	4,200
35	Louisiana	4,023
36	West Virginia	3,925
37	Nebraska	3,880
38	Kansas	3,877
39	Alabama	3,773
40	Ohio	3,704
41	Georgia	3,637
42	North Carolina	3,602
43	Missouri	3,441
44	Oklahoma	3,303
45	Indiana	3,261
46	Tennessee	3,222
47	Mississippi	2,990
48	Arkansas	2,923
49	Idaho	2,639
50	Iowa	2,496
	District of Columbia	8,856

Source: Morgan Quitno Press using data from U.S. Bureau of the Census, Governments Division
"State and Local Government Finances: 1999-2000" (http://www.census.gov/govs/www/estimate00.html)
Includes short-term, long-term, full faith and credit, nonguaranteed and public debt for private purposes.

State and Local Government Full-Time Equivalent Employees in 2002

National Total = 15,602,141 FTE Employees*

<u>ALPHA ORDER</u>

RANK	STATE	EMPLOYEES	% of USA
22	Alabama	267,453	1.7%
45	Alaska	50,693	0.3%
23	Arizona	260,028	1.7%
33	Arkansas	150,079	1.0%
1	California	1,775,292	11.4%
25	Colorado	239,808	1.5%
30	Connecticut	180,637	1.2%
46	Delaware	46,598	0.3%
4	Florida	788,804	5.1%
10	Georgia	474,420	3.0%
41	Hawaii	70,461	0.5%
39	Idaho	77,401	0.5%
5	Illinois	642,896	4.1%
14	Indiana	325,170	2.1%
31	Iowa	174,080	1.1%
32	Kansas	173,845	1.1%
26	Kentucky	230,053	1.5%
20	Louisiana	279,380	1.8%
40	Maine	73,701	0.5%
19	Maryland	285,484	1.8%
13	Massachusetts	327,526	2.1%
8	Michigan	506,845	3.2%
21	Minnesota	279,095	1.8%
28	Mississippi	183,434	1.2%
16	Missouri	312,539	2.0%
44	Montana	52,299	0.3%
36	Nebraska	113,929	0.7%
38	Nevada	92,634	0.6%
42	New Hampshire	65,930	0.4%
9	New Jersey	484,903	3.1%
35	New Mexico	118,239	0.8%
3	New York	1,189,388	7.6%
11	North Carolina	473,553	3.0%
49	North Dakota	38,751	0.2%
6	Ohio	608,892	3.9%
27	Oklahoma	204,348	1.3%
29	Oregon	183,390	1.2%
7	Pennsylvania	553,307	3.5%
43	Rhode Island	52,445	0.3%
24	South Carolina	240,582	1.5%
47	South Dakota	42,211	0.3%
17	Tennessee	306,367	2.0%
2	Texas	1,248,838	8.0%
34	Utah	123,340	0.8%
50	Vermont	36,744	0.2%
12	Virginia	411,066	2.6%
15	Washington	318,396	2.0%
37	West Virginia	93,150	0.6%
18	Wisconsin	288,543	1.8%
48	Wyoming	41,144	0.3%

<u>RANK ORDER</u>

RANK	STATE	EMPLOYEES	% of USA
1	California	1,775,292	11.4%
2	Texas	1,248,838	8.0%
3	New York	1,189,388	7.6%
4	Florida	788,804	5.1%
5	Illinois	642,896	4.1%
6	Ohio	608,892	3.9%
7	Pennsylvania	553,307	3.5%
8	Michigan	506,845	3.2%
9	New Jersey	484,903	3.1%
10	Georgia	474,420	3.0%
11	North Carolina	473,553	3.0%
12	Virginia	411,066	2.6%
13	Massachusetts	327,526	2.1%
14	Indiana	325,170	2.1%
15	Washington	318,396	2.0%
16	Missouri	312,539	2.0%
17	Tennessee	306,367	2.0%
18	Wisconsin	288,543	1.8%
19	Maryland	285,484	1.8%
20	Louisiana	279,380	1.8%
21	Minnesota	279,095	1.8%
22	Alabama	267,453	1.7%
23	Arizona	260,028	1.7%
24	South Carolina	240,582	1.5%
25	Colorado	239,808	1.5%
26	Kentucky	230,053	1.5%
27	Oklahoma	204,348	1.3%
28	Mississippi	183,434	1.2%
29	Oregon	183,390	1.2%
30	Connecticut	180,637	1.2%
31	Iowa	174,080	1.1%
32	Kansas	173,845	1.1%
33	Arkansas	150,079	1.0%
34	Utah	123,340	0.8%
35	New Mexico	118,239	0.8%
36	Nebraska	113,929	0.7%
37	West Virginia	93,150	0.6%
38	Nevada	92,634	0.6%
39	Idaho	77,401	0.5%
40	Maine	73,701	0.5%
41	Hawaii	70,461	0.5%
42	New Hampshire	65,930	0.4%
43	Rhode Island	52,445	0.3%
44	Montana	52,299	0.3%
45	Alaska	50,693	0.3%
46	Delaware	46,598	0.3%
47	South Dakota	42,211	0.3%
48	Wyoming	41,144	0.3%
49	North Dakota	38,751	0.2%
50	Vermont	36,744	0.2%
	District of Columbia	44,030	0.3%

Source: U.S. Bureau of the Census, Governments Division
"State and Local Employment and Payroll - March 2002" (http://www.census.gov/govs/www/apesstl02.html)
*As of March 2002.

Rate of State and Local Government FTE Employees in 2002

National Rate = 542 State/Local Government Employees per 10,000 Population*

<u>ALPHA ORDER</u>

RANK	STATE	RATE
10	Alabama	597
2	Alaska	790
47	Arizona	478
25	Arkansas	555
44	California	507
31	Colorado	533
38	Connecticut	522
15	Delaware	578
48	Florida	473
25	Georgia	555
21	Hawaii	568
16	Idaho	576
42	Illinois	511
35	Indiana	528
12	Iowa	593
4	Kansas	641
24	Kentucky	563
7	Louisiana	624
20	Maine	569
37	Maryland	524
43	Massachusetts	510
45	Michigan	505
25	Minnesota	555
5	Mississippi	640
29	Missouri	551
18	Montana	574
3	Nebraska	659
50	Nevada	427
40	New Hampshire	517
22	New Jersey	565
6	New Mexico	638
8	New York	622
19	North Carolina	570
9	North Dakota	611
30	Ohio	534
13	Oklahoma	586
39	Oregon	521
49	Pennsylvania	449
46	Rhode Island	491
13	South Carolina	586
25	South Dakota	555
34	Tennessee	529
17	Texas	575
32	Utah	532
11	Vermont	596
23	Virginia	564
36	Washington	525
41	West Virginia	516
33	Wisconsin	530
1	Wyoming	825

<u>RANK ORDER</u>

RANK	STATE	RATE
1	Wyoming	825
2	Alaska	790
3	Nebraska	659
4	Kansas	641
5	Mississippi	640
6	New Mexico	638
7	Louisiana	624
8	New York	622
9	North Dakota	611
10	Alabama	597
11	Vermont	596
12	Iowa	593
13	Oklahoma	586
13	South Carolina	586
15	Delaware	578
16	Idaho	576
17	Texas	575
18	Montana	574
19	North Carolina	570
20	Maine	569
21	Hawaii	568
22	New Jersey	565
23	Virginia	564
24	Kentucky	563
25	Arkansas	555
25	Georgia	555
25	Minnesota	555
25	South Dakota	555
29	Missouri	551
30	Ohio	534
31	Colorado	533
32	Utah	532
33	Wisconsin	530
34	Tennessee	529
35	Indiana	528
36	Washington	525
37	Maryland	524
38	Connecticut	522
39	Oregon	521
40	New Hampshire	517
41	West Virginia	516
42	Illinois	511
43	Massachusetts	510
44	California	507
45	Michigan	505
46	Rhode Island	491
47	Arizona	478
48	Florida	473
49	Pennsylvania	449
50	Nevada	427
	District of Columbia	774

Source: Morgan Quitno Press using data from U.S. Bureau of the Census, Governments Division
"State and Local Employment and Payroll - March 2002" (http://www.census.gov/govs/www/apesstl02.html)
*Full-time equivalent as of March 2002.

Average Annual Earnings of Full-Time State and Local Government Employees in 2002
National Average = $40,243*

ALPHA ORDER

RANK	STATE	EARNINGS
38	Alabama	$33,027
6	Alaska	45,622
21	Arizona	37,554
49	Arkansas	29,901
2	California	50,840
15	Colorado	40,776
4	Connecticut	46,863
17	Delaware	40,469
22	Florida	37,029
31	Georgia	34,108
20	Hawaii	37,920
43	Idaho	32,674
12	Illinois	41,805
29	Indiana	34,884
24	Iowa	36,228
32	Kansas	33,891
45	Kentucky	31,780
47	Louisiana	31,317
35	Maine	33,362
10	Maryland	44,417
9	Massachusetts	44,513
11	Michigan	42,298
13	Minnesota	41,766
50	Mississippi	28,432
41	Missouri	32,749
44	Montana	32,585
33	Nebraska	33,764
8	Nevada	45,030
26	New Hampshire	35,750
3	New Jersey	49,677
37	New Mexico	33,028
1	New York	50,862
27	North Carolina	35,462
34	North Dakota	33,611
19	Ohio	38,435
46	Oklahoma	31,519
18	Oregon	39,688
14	Pennsylvania	41,209
5	Rhode Island	45,948
40	South Carolina	32,861
48	South Dakota	30,938
39	Tennessee	32,908
30	Texas	34,271
25	Utah	35,924
28	Vermont	35,403
23	Virginia	36,749
7	Washington	45,428
42	West Virginia	32,730
16	Wisconsin	40,649
36	Wyoming	33,153

RANK ORDER

RANK	STATE	EARNINGS
1	New York	$50,862
2	California	50,840
3	New Jersey	49,677
4	Connecticut	46,863
5	Rhode Island	45,948
6	Alaska	45,622
7	Washington	45,428
8	Nevada	45,030
9	Massachusetts	44,513
10	Maryland	44,417
11	Michigan	42,298
12	Illinois	41,805
13	Minnesota	41,766
14	Pennsylvania	41,209
15	Colorado	40,776
16	Wisconsin	40,649
17	Delaware	40,469
18	Oregon	39,688
19	Ohio	38,435
20	Hawaii	37,920
21	Arizona	37,554
22	Florida	37,029
23	Virginia	36,749
24	Iowa	36,228
25	Utah	35,924
26	New Hampshire	35,750
27	North Carolina	35,462
28	Vermont	35,403
29	Indiana	34,884
30	Texas	34,271
31	Georgia	34,108
32	Kansas	33,891
33	Nebraska	33,764
34	North Dakota	33,611
35	Maine	33,362
36	Wyoming	33,153
37	New Mexico	33,028
38	Alabama	33,027
39	Tennessee	32,908
40	South Carolina	32,861
41	Missouri	32,749
42	West Virginia	32,730
43	Idaho	32,674
44	Montana	32,585
45	Kentucky	31,780
46	Oklahoma	31,519
47	Louisiana	31,317
48	South Dakota	30,938
49	Arkansas	29,901
50	Mississippi	28,432
	District of Columbia	50,677

Source: Morgan Quitno Press using data from U.S. Bureau of the Census, Governments Division
"State and Local Employment and Payroll - March 2002" (http://www.census.gov/govs/www/apesstl02.html)
*March 2002 total payroll (multiplied by 12) divided by full-time equivalent employees.

State Government Total Revenue in 2001

National Total = $1,180,303,656,000*

ALPHA ORDER

RANK	STATE	REVENUE	% of USA
23	Alabama	$17,859,899,000	1.5%
39	Alaska	6,185,917,000	0.5%
28	Arizona	15,488,897,000	1.3%
31	Arkansas	10,330,394,000	0.9%
1	California	176,080,892,000	14.9%
19	Colorado	19,774,425,000	1.7%
25	Connecticut	17,750,445,000	1.5%
44	Delaware	5,114,008,000	0.4%
6	Florida	46,370,565,000	3.9%
13	Georgia	25,250,019,000	2.1%
38	Hawaii	6,591,146,000	0.6%
42	Idaho	5,286,097,000	0.4%
5	Illinois	47,348,197,000	4.0%
17	Indiana	20,766,968,000	1.8%
32	Iowa	10,255,453,000	0.9%
35	Kansas	8,713,237,000	0.7%
21	Kentucky	18,550,297,000	1.6%
24	Louisiana	17,811,457,000	1.5%
43	Maine	5,207,414,000	0.4%
16	Maryland	20,938,683,000	1.8%
11	Massachusetts	29,303,913,000	2.5%
8	Michigan	43,346,782,000	3.7%
12	Minnesota	26,135,477,000	2.2%
30	Mississippi	11,692,949,000	1.0%
18	Missouri	20,133,937,000	1.7%
46	Montana	4,224,359,000	0.4%
40	Nebraska	5,943,922,000	0.5%
37	Nevada	6,643,897,000	0.6%
45	New Hampshire	4,574,828,000	0.4%
9	New Jersey	42,788,178,000	3.6%
34	New Mexico	9,099,224,000	0.8%
2	New York	112,438,570,000	9.5%
10	North Carolina	32,202,748,000	2.7%
47	North Dakota	3,373,244,000	0.3%
4	Ohio	52,802,649,000	4.5%
29	Oklahoma	12,745,926,000	1.1%
22	Oregon	18,218,617,000	1.5%
7	Pennsylvania	45,887,490,000	3.9%
41	Rhode Island	5,483,128,000	0.5%
27	South Carolina	16,865,229,000	1.4%
48	South Dakota	3,170,959,000	0.3%
26	Tennessee	17,344,232,000	1.5%
3	Texas	65,525,245,000	5.6%
33	Utah	9,131,656,000	0.8%
49	Vermont	3,143,100,000	0.3%
15	Virginia	22,760,130,000	1.9%
14	Washington	23,646,114,000	2.0%
36	West Virginia	8,296,556,000	0.7%
20	Wisconsin	18,826,011,000	1.6%
50	Wyoming	2,880,176,000	0.2%

RANK ORDER

RANK	STATE	REVENUE	% of USA
1	California	$176,080,892,000	14.9%
2	New York	112,438,570,000	9.5%
3	Texas	65,525,245,000	5.6%
4	Ohio	52,802,649,000	4.5%
5	Illinois	47,348,197,000	4.0%
6	Florida	46,370,565,000	3.9%
7	Pennsylvania	45,887,490,000	3.9%
8	Michigan	43,346,782,000	3.7%
9	New Jersey	42,788,178,000	3.6%
10	North Carolina	32,202,748,000	2.7%
11	Massachusetts	29,303,913,000	2.5%
12	Minnesota	26,135,477,000	2.2%
13	Georgia	25,250,019,000	2.1%
14	Washington	23,646,114,000	2.0%
15	Virginia	22,760,130,000	1.9%
16	Maryland	20,938,683,000	1.8%
17	Indiana	20,766,968,000	1.8%
18	Missouri	20,133,937,000	1.7%
19	Colorado	19,774,425,000	1.7%
20	Wisconsin	18,826,011,000	1.6%
21	Kentucky	18,550,297,000	1.6%
22	Oregon	18,218,617,000	1.5%
23	Alabama	17,859,899,000	1.5%
24	Louisiana	17,811,457,000	1.5%
25	Connecticut	17,750,445,000	1.5%
26	Tennessee	17,344,232,000	1.5%
27	South Carolina	16,865,229,000	1.4%
28	Arizona	15,488,897,000	1.3%
29	Oklahoma	12,745,926,000	1.1%
30	Mississippi	11,692,949,000	1.0%
31	Arkansas	10,330,394,000	0.9%
32	Iowa	10,255,453,000	0.9%
33	Utah	9,131,656,000	0.8%
34	New Mexico	9,099,224,000	0.8%
35	Kansas	8,713,237,000	0.7%
36	West Virginia	8,296,556,000	0.7%
37	Nevada	6,643,897,000	0.6%
38	Hawaii	6,591,146,000	0.6%
39	Alaska	6,185,917,000	0.5%
40	Nebraska	5,943,922,000	0.5%
41	Rhode Island	5,483,128,000	0.5%
42	Idaho	5,286,097,000	0.4%
43	Maine	5,207,414,000	0.4%
44	Delaware	5,114,008,000	0.4%
45	New Hampshire	4,574,828,000	0.4%
46	Montana	4,224,359,000	0.4%
47	North Dakota	3,373,244,000	0.3%
48	South Dakota	3,170,959,000	0.3%
49	Vermont	3,143,100,000	0.3%
50	Wyoming	2,880,176,000	0.2%
	District of Columbia**	NA	NA

Source: U.S. Bureau of the Census, Governments Division
    "2001 State Government Finances" (http://www.census.gov/govs/www/state01.html)
*Total revenue includes all money received from external sources. This includes taxes, intergovernmental transfers and insurance trust revenue and revenue from government owned utilities and other commercial or auxiliary enterprise.
**Not applicable.

Per Capita State Government Total Revenue in 2001

National Per Capita = $4,148*

<u>ALPHA ORDER</u>

RANK	STATE	PER CAPITA
28	Alabama	$3,999
1	Alaska	9,777
49	Arizona	2,924
33	Arkansas	3,837
12	California	5,099
20	Colorado	4,465
10	Connecticut	5,171
2	Delaware	6,428
50	Florida	2,835
48	Georgia	3,008
5	Hawaii	5,380
27	Idaho	4,001
34	Illinois	3,783
42	Indiana	3,390
39	Iowa	3,497
43	Kansas	3,227
19	Kentucky	4,561
29	Louisiana	3,988
25	Maine	4,053
32	Maryland	3,890
18	Massachusetts	4,579
21	Michigan	4,332
8	Minnesota	5,243
24	Mississippi	4,092
38	Missouri	3,572
15	Montana	4,663
41	Nebraska	3,458
44	Nevada	3,172
37	New Hampshire	3,634
13	New Jersey	5,031
14	New Mexico	4,975
3	New York	5,895
31	North Carolina	3,929
6	North Dakota	5,301
16	Ohio	4,638
36	Oklahoma	3,676
7	Oregon	5,246
35	Pennsylvania	3,731
9	Rhode Island	5,178
23	South Carolina	4,154
22	South Dakota	4,182
47	Tennessee	3,019
46	Texas	3,070
26	Utah	4,006
11	Vermont	5,128
45	Virginia	3,164
30	Washington	3,946
17	West Virginia	4,605
40	Wisconsin	3,483
4	Wyoming	5,834

<u>RANK ORDER</u>

RANK	STATE	PER CAPITA
1	Alaska	$9,777
2	Delaware	6,428
3	New York	5,895
4	Wyoming	5,834
5	Hawaii	5,380
6	North Dakota	5,301
7	Oregon	5,246
8	Minnesota	5,243
9	Rhode Island	5,178
10	Connecticut	5,171
11	Vermont	5,128
12	California	5,099
13	New Jersey	5,031
14	New Mexico	4,975
15	Montana	4,663
16	Ohio	4,638
17	West Virginia	4,605
18	Massachusetts	4,579
19	Kentucky	4,561
20	Colorado	4,465
21	Michigan	4,332
22	South Dakota	4,182
23	South Carolina	4,154
24	Mississippi	4,092
25	Maine	4,053
26	Utah	4,006
27	Idaho	4,001
28	Alabama	3,999
29	Louisiana	3,988
30	Washington	3,946
31	North Carolina	3,929
32	Maryland	3,890
33	Arkansas	3,837
34	Illinois	3,783
35	Pennsylvania	3,731
36	Oklahoma	3,676
37	New Hampshire	3,634
38	Missouri	3,572
39	Iowa	3,497
40	Wisconsin	3,483
41	Nebraska	3,458
42	Indiana	3,390
43	Kansas	3,227
44	Nevada	3,172
45	Virginia	3,164
46	Texas	3,070
47	Tennessee	3,019
48	Georgia	3,008
49	Arizona	2,924
50	Florida	2,835

District of Columbia** NA

Source: Morgan Quitno Press using data from U.S. Bureau of the Census, Governments Division
   "2001 State Government Finances" (http://www.census.gov/govs/www/state01.html)
*Total revenue includes all money received from external sources. This includes taxes, intergovernmental transfers and insurance trust revenue and revenue from government owned utilities and other commercial or auxiliary enterprise.
**Not applicable.

State Government Intergovernmental Revenue in 2001

National Total = $305,618,536,000*

ALPHA ORDER

RANK	STATE	REVENUE	% of USA
16	Alabama	$5,715,592,000	1.9%
41	Alaska	1,289,816,000	0.4%
26	Arizona	4,449,959,000	1.5%
31	Arkansas	3,057,182,000	1.0%
1	California	40,145,150,000	13.1%
30	Colorado	3,471,257,000	1.1%
28	Connecticut	3,729,883,000	1.2%
50	Delaware	901,160,000	0.3%
5	Florida	11,838,853,000	3.9%
11	Georgia	7,392,034,000	2.4%
44	Hawaii	1,213,905,000	0.4%
43	Idaho	1,232,331,000	0.4%
7	Illinois	11,027,128,000	3.6%
18	Indiana	5,595,841,000	1.8%
32	Iowa	2,892,204,000	0.9%
33	Kansas	2,659,435,000	0.9%
25	Kentucky	4,562,924,000	1.5%
19	Louisiana	5,280,258,000	1.7%
38	Maine	1,625,685,000	0.5%
24	Maryland	4,763,735,000	1.6%
14	Massachusetts	6,096,675,000	2.0%
8	Michigan	10,693,583,000	3.5%
21	Minnesota	4,981,133,000	1.6%
27	Mississippi	3,856,416,000	1.3%
17	Missouri	5,612,433,000	1.8%
40	Montana	1,318,446,000	0.4%
37	Nebraska	1,626,621,000	0.5%
45	Nevada	1,161,832,000	0.4%
42	New Hampshire	1,258,365,000	0.4%
10	New Jersey	8,595,009,000	2.8%
34	New Mexico	2,452,808,000	0.8%
2	New York	35,575,036,000	11.6%
9	North Carolina	9,546,520,000	3.1%
48	North Dakota	998,857,000	0.3%
6	Ohio	11,770,390,000	3.9%
29	Oklahoma	3,539,625,000	1.2%
20	Oregon	5,043,882,000	1.7%
4	Pennsylvania	12,597,237,000	4.1%
39	Rhode Island	1,546,611,000	0.5%
23	South Carolina	4,792,650,000	1.6%
46	South Dakota	1,033,882,000	0.3%
12	Tennessee	6,806,855,000	2.2%
3	Texas	18,733,876,000	6.1%
36	Utah	2,064,525,000	0.7%
49	Vermont	976,421,000	0.3%
22	Virginia	4,857,443,000	1.6%
15	Washington	5,908,876,000	1.9%
35	West Virginia	2,200,549,000	0.7%
13	Wisconsin	6,118,475,000	2.0%
47	Wyoming	1,009,173,000	0.3%

RANK ORDER

RANK	STATE	REVENUE	% of USA
1	California	$40,145,150,000	13.1%
2	New York	35,575,036,000	11.6%
3	Texas	18,733,876,000	6.1%
4	Pennsylvania	12,597,237,000	4.1%
5	Florida	11,838,853,000	3.9%
6	Ohio	11,770,390,000	3.9%
7	Illinois	11,027,128,000	3.6%
8	Michigan	10,693,583,000	3.5%
9	North Carolina	9,546,520,000	3.1%
10	New Jersey	8,595,009,000	2.8%
11	Georgia	7,392,034,000	2.4%
12	Tennessee	6,806,855,000	2.2%
13	Wisconsin	6,118,475,000	2.0%
14	Massachusetts	6,096,675,000	2.0%
15	Washington	5,908,876,000	1.9%
16	Alabama	5,715,592,000	1.9%
17	Missouri	5,612,433,000	1.8%
18	Indiana	5,595,841,000	1.8%
19	Louisiana	5,280,258,000	1.7%
20	Oregon	5,043,882,000	1.7%
21	Minnesota	4,981,133,000	1.6%
22	Virginia	4,857,443,000	1.6%
23	South Carolina	4,792,650,000	1.6%
24	Maryland	4,763,735,000	1.6%
25	Kentucky	4,562,924,000	1.5%
26	Arizona	4,449,959,000	1.5%
27	Mississippi	3,856,416,000	1.3%
28	Connecticut	3,729,883,000	1.2%
29	Oklahoma	3,539,625,000	1.2%
30	Colorado	3,471,257,000	1.1%
31	Arkansas	3,057,182,000	1.0%
32	Iowa	2,892,204,000	0.9%
33	Kansas	2,659,435,000	0.9%
34	New Mexico	2,452,808,000	0.8%
35	West Virginia	2,200,549,000	0.7%
36	Utah	2,064,525,000	0.7%
37	Nebraska	1,626,621,000	0.5%
38	Maine	1,625,685,000	0.5%
39	Rhode Island	1,546,611,000	0.5%
40	Montana	1,318,446,000	0.4%
41	Alaska	1,289,816,000	0.4%
42	New Hampshire	1,258,365,000	0.4%
43	Idaho	1,232,331,000	0.4%
44	Hawaii	1,213,905,000	0.4%
45	Nevada	1,161,832,000	0.4%
46	South Dakota	1,033,882,000	0.3%
47	Wyoming	1,009,173,000	0.3%
48	North Dakota	998,857,000	0.3%
49	Vermont	976,421,000	0.3%
50	Delaware	901,160,000	0.3%
	District of Columbia**	NA	NA

Source: U.S. Bureau of the Census, Governments Division
   "2001 State Government Finances" (http://www.census.gov/govs/www/state01.html)
*Includes revenue from federal and local government sources.
**Not applicable.

Per Capita State Government Intergovernmental Revenue in 2001

National Per Capita = $1,074*

ALPHA ORDER

RANK	STATE	PER CAPITA
12	Alabama	$1,280
2	Alaska	2,039
46	Arizona	840
20	Arkansas	1,136
19	California	1,163
47	Colorado	784
24	Connecticut	1,087
21	Delaware	1,133
48	Florida	724
43	Georgia	881
33	Hawaii	991
39	Idaho	933
43	Illinois	881
40	Indiana	913
34	Iowa	986
36	Kansas	985
23	Kentucky	1,122
16	Louisiana	1,182
13	Maine	1,265
42	Maryland	885
37	Massachusetts	953
25	Michigan	1,069
31	Minnesota	999
10	Mississippi	1,349
32	Missouri	996
7	Montana	1,455
38	Nebraska	946
50	Nevada	555
30	New Hampshire	1,000
29	New Jersey	1,011
11	New Mexico	1,341
3	New York	1,865
18	North Carolina	1,165
5	North Dakota	1,570
26	Ohio	1,034
28	Oklahoma	1,021
8	Oregon	1,452
27	Pennsylvania	1,024
6	Rhode Island	1,460
17	South Carolina	1,181
9	South Dakota	1,364
15	Tennessee	1,185
45	Texas	878
41	Utah	906
4	Vermont	1,593
49	Virginia	675
34	Washington	986
14	West Virginia	1,221
22	Wisconsin	1,132
1	Wyoming	2,044

RANK ORDER

RANK	STATE	PER CAPITA
1	Wyoming	$2,044
2	Alaska	2,039
3	New York	1,865
4	Vermont	1,593
5	North Dakota	1,570
6	Rhode Island	1,460
7	Montana	1,455
8	Oregon	1,452
9	South Dakota	1,364
10	Mississippi	1,349
11	New Mexico	1,341
12	Alabama	1,280
13	Maine	1,265
14	West Virginia	1,221
15	Tennessee	1,185
16	Louisiana	1,182
17	South Carolina	1,181
18	North Carolina	1,165
19	California	1,163
20	Arkansas	1,136
21	Delaware	1,133
22	Wisconsin	1,132
23	Kentucky	1,122
24	Connecticut	1,087
25	Michigan	1,069
26	Ohio	1,034
27	Pennsylvania	1,024
28	Oklahoma	1,021
29	New Jersey	1,011
30	New Hampshire	1,000
31	Minnesota	999
32	Missouri	996
33	Hawaii	991
34	Iowa	986
34	Washington	986
36	Kansas	985
37	Massachusetts	953
38	Nebraska	946
39	Idaho	933
40	Indiana	913
41	Utah	906
42	Maryland	885
43	Georgia	881
43	Illinois	881
45	Texas	878
46	Arizona	840
47	Colorado	784
48	Florida	724
49	Virginia	675
50	Nevada	555
	District of Columbia**	NA

Source: Morgan Quitno Press using data from U.S. Bureau of the Census, Governments Division
 "2001 State Government Finances" (http://www.census.gov/govs/www/state01.html)
*Includes revenue from federal and local government sources.
**Not applicable.

State Government Own Source Revenue in 2001

National Total = $743,677,801,000*

ALPHA ORDER

RANK	STATE	REVENUE	% of USA
26	Alabama	$10,016,054,000	1.3%
38	Alaska	4,753,491,000	0.6%
22	Arizona	10,715,678,000	1.4%
31	Arkansas	6,746,954,000	0.9%
1	California	108,831,636,000	14.6%
24	Colorado	10,396,747,000	1.4%
19	Connecticut	12,553,639,000	1.7%
42	Delaware	3,557,869,000	0.5%
4	Florida	32,358,906,000	4.4%
13	Georgia	18,019,383,000	2.4%
36	Hawaii	4,831,283,000	0.6%
43	Idaho	3,326,415,000	0.4%
7	Illinois	29,199,495,000	3.9%
18	Indiana	14,142,122,000	1.9%
30	Iowa	7,437,221,000	1.0%
33	Kansas	6,367,225,000	0.9%
23	Kentucky	10,612,693,000	1.4%
21	Louisiana	11,530,174,000	1.6%
41	Maine	3,774,127,000	0.5%
17	Maryland	14,278,238,000	1.9%
10	Massachusetts	23,191,023,000	3.1%
6	Michigan	29,925,828,000	4.0%
14	Minnesota	16,769,149,000	2.3%
32	Mississippi	6,463,658,000	0.9%
20	Missouri	11,915,377,000	1.6%
46	Montana	2,283,908,000	0.3%
40	Nebraska	4,247,903,000	0.6%
39	Nevada	4,614,499,000	0.6%
45	New Hampshire	2,741,178,000	0.4%
9	New Jersey	25,777,976,000	3.5%
34	New Mexico	6,300,243,000	0.8%
2	New York	56,226,741,000	7.6%
11	North Carolina	19,845,324,000	2.7%
48	North Dakota	1,841,523,000	0.2%
8	Ohio	26,425,310,000	3.6%
29	Oklahoma	8,653,832,000	1.2%
27	Oregon	9,152,504,000	1.2%
5	Pennsylvania	31,583,379,000	4.2%
44	Rhode Island	3,218,356,000	0.4%
28	South Carolina	9,079,889,000	1.2%
50	South Dakota	1,550,277,000	0.2%
25	Tennessee	10,234,623,000	1.4%
3	Texas	41,862,519,000	5.6%
35	Utah	6,106,704,000	0.8%
47	Vermont	2,130,247,000	0.3%
12	Virginia	19,336,164,000	2.6%
15	Washington	16,509,430,000	2.2%
37	West Virginia	4,758,001,000	0.6%
16	Wisconsin	15,765,390,000	2.1%
49	Wyoming	1,717,496,000	0.2%

RANK ORDER

RANK	STATE	REVENUE	% of USA
1	California	$108,831,636,000	14.6%
2	New York	56,226,741,000	7.6%
3	Texas	41,862,519,000	5.6%
4	Florida	32,358,906,000	4.4%
5	Pennsylvania	31,583,379,000	4.2%
6	Michigan	29,925,828,000	4.0%
7	Illinois	29,199,495,000	3.9%
8	Ohio	26,425,310,000	3.6%
9	New Jersey	25,777,976,000	3.5%
10	Massachusetts	23,191,023,000	3.1%
11	North Carolina	19,845,324,000	2.7%
12	Virginia	19,336,164,000	2.6%
13	Georgia	18,019,383,000	2.4%
14	Minnesota	16,769,149,000	2.3%
15	Washington	16,509,430,000	2.2%
16	Wisconsin	15,765,390,000	2.1%
17	Maryland	14,278,238,000	1.9%
18	Indiana	14,142,122,000	1.9%
19	Connecticut	12,553,639,000	1.7%
20	Missouri	11,915,377,000	1.6%
21	Louisiana	11,530,174,000	1.6%
22	Arizona	10,715,678,000	1.4%
23	Kentucky	10,612,693,000	1.4%
24	Colorado	10,396,747,000	1.4%
25	Tennessee	10,234,623,000	1.4%
26	Alabama	10,016,054,000	1.3%
27	Oregon	9,152,504,000	1.2%
28	South Carolina	9,079,889,000	1.2%
29	Oklahoma	8,653,832,000	1.2%
30	Iowa	7,437,221,000	1.0%
31	Arkansas	6,746,954,000	0.9%
32	Mississippi	6,463,658,000	0.9%
33	Kansas	6,367,225,000	0.9%
34	New Mexico	6,300,243,000	0.8%
35	Utah	6,106,704,000	0.8%
36	Hawaii	4,831,283,000	0.6%
37	West Virginia	4,758,001,000	0.6%
38	Alaska	4,753,491,000	0.6%
39	Nevada	4,614,499,000	0.6%
40	Nebraska	4,247,903,000	0.6%
41	Maine	3,774,127,000	0.5%
42	Delaware	3,557,869,000	0.5%
43	Idaho	3,326,415,000	0.4%
44	Rhode Island	3,218,356,000	0.4%
45	New Hampshire	2,741,178,000	0.4%
46	Montana	2,283,908,000	0.3%
47	Vermont	2,130,247,000	0.3%
48	North Dakota	1,841,523,000	0.2%
49	Wyoming	1,717,496,000	0.2%
50	South Dakota	1,550,277,000	0.2%
	District of Columbia**	NA	NA

Source: U.S. Bureau of the Census, Governments Division

"2001 State Government Finances" (http://www.census.gov/govs/www/state01.html)

*Own source revenue includes taxes, current charges and miscellaneous general revenue. Excluded are intergovernmental transfers, insurance trust revenue and revenue from government owned utilities and other commercial or auxiliary enterprise.

**Not applicable.

Per Capita State Government Own Source Revenue in 2001

National Per Capita = $2,614*

<u>ALPHA ORDER</u>

RANK	STATE	PER CAPITA
40	Alabama	$2,243
1	Alaska	7,513
47	Arizona	2,023
30	Arkansas	2,506
10	California	3,152
35	Colorado	2,348
4	Connecticut	3,657
2	Delaware	4,472
48	Florida	1,979
44	Georgia	2,146
3	Hawaii	3,944
29	Idaho	2,518
36	Illinois	2,333
38	Indiana	2,308
27	Iowa	2,536
34	Kansas	2,358
24	Kentucky	2,609
25	Louisiana	2,582
15	Maine	2,938
21	Maryland	2,652
5	Massachusetts	3,624
13	Michigan	2,991
9	Minnesota	3,364
39	Mississippi	2,262
45	Missouri	2,114
28	Montana	2,521
32	Nebraska	2,471
42	Nevada	2,203
43	New Hampshire	2,177
12	New Jersey	3,031
8	New Mexico	3,444
14	New York	2,948
33	North Carolina	2,422
17	North Dakota	2,894
37	Ohio	2,321
31	Oklahoma	2,496
23	Oregon	2,636
26	Pennsylvania	2,568
11	Rhode Island	3,039
41	South Carolina	2,237
46	South Dakota	2,045
50	Tennessee	1,781
49	Texas	1,962
20	Utah	2,679
7	Vermont	3,476
19	Virginia	2,688
18	Washington	2,755
22	West Virginia	2,641
16	Wisconsin	2,917
6	Wyoming	3,479

<u>RANK ORDER</u>

RANK	STATE	PER CAPITA
1	Alaska	$7,513
2	Delaware	4,472
3	Hawaii	3,944
4	Connecticut	3,657
5	Massachusetts	3,624
6	Wyoming	3,479
7	Vermont	3,476
8	New Mexico	3,444
9	Minnesota	3,364
10	California	3,152
11	Rhode Island	3,039
12	New Jersey	3,031
13	Michigan	2,991
14	New York	2,948
15	Maine	2,938
16	Wisconsin	2,917
17	North Dakota	2,894
18	Washington	2,755
19	Virginia	2,688
20	Utah	2,679
21	Maryland	2,652
22	West Virginia	2,641
23	Oregon	2,636
24	Kentucky	2,609
25	Louisiana	2,582
26	Pennsylvania	2,568
27	Iowa	2,536
28	Montana	2,521
29	Idaho	2,518
30	Arkansas	2,506
31	Oklahoma	2,496
32	Nebraska	2,471
33	North Carolina	2,422
34	Kansas	2,358
35	Colorado	2,348
36	Illinois	2,333
37	Ohio	2,321
38	Indiana	2,308
39	Mississippi	2,262
40	Alabama	2,243
41	South Carolina	2,237
42	Nevada	2,203
43	New Hampshire	2,177
44	Georgia	2,146
45	Missouri	2,114
46	South Dakota	2,045
47	Arizona	2,023
48	Florida	1,979
49	Texas	1,962
50	Tennessee	1,781

District of Columbia**   NA

Source: Morgan Quitno Press using data from U.S. Bureau of the Census, Governments Division "2001 State Government Finances" (http://www.census.gov/govs/www/state01.html)
Own source revenue includes taxes, current charges and miscellaneous general revenue. Excluded are intergovernmental transfers, insurance trust revenue and revenue from government owned utilities and other commercial or auxiliary enterprise.
**Not applicable.*

State Government Tax Revenue in 2002

National Total = $533,432,378,000

ALPHA ORDER

RANK	STATE	STATE TAXES	% of USA
26	Alabama	$6,878,923,000	1.3%
49	Alaska	1,089,504,000	0.2%
21	Arizona	8,477,001,000	1.6%
30	Arkansas	5,034,109,000	0.9%
1	California	77,755,376,000	14.6%
25	Colorado	6,923,171,000	1.3%
19	Connecticut	9,032,787,000	1.7%
42	Delaware	2,173,600,000	0.4%
4	Florida	24,815,964,000	4.7%
12	Georgia	13,772,147,000	2.6%
38	Hawaii	3,420,671,000	0.6%
41	Idaho	2,271,075,000	0.4%
5	Illinois	22,460,190,000	4.2%
18	Indiana	9,994,595,000	1.9%
31	Iowa	5,006,251,000	0.9%
32	Kansas	4,808,361,000	0.9%
22	Kentucky	7,974,690,000	1.5%
24	Louisiana	7,345,994,000	1.4%
40	Maine	2,626,830,000	0.5%
17	Maryland	10,821,276,000	2.0%
11	Massachusetts	14,819,794,000	2.8%
7	Michigan	21,864,052,000	4.1%
13	Minnesota	12,936,369,000	2.4%
33	Mississippi	4,728,905,000	0.9%
20	Missouri	8,678,611,000	1.6%
46	Montana	1,442,731,000	0.3%
39	Nebraska	2,992,522,000	0.6%
34	Nevada	3,945,329,000	0.7%
44	New Hampshire	1,883,924,000	0.4%
9	New Jersey	18,328,814,000	3.4%
36	New Mexico	3,628,055,000	0.7%
2	New York	43,262,137,000	8.1%
10	North Carolina	15,535,277,000	2.9%
47	North Dakota	1,117,299,000	0.2%
8	Ohio	19,616,569,000	3.7%
27	Oklahoma	6,052,680,000	1.1%
29	Oregon	5,139,322,000	1.0%
6	Pennsylvania	22,135,537,000	4.1%
43	Rhode Island	2,127,609,000	0.4%
28	South Carolina	5,748,585,000	1.1%
50	South Dakota	976,596,000	0.2%
23	Tennessee	7,797,681,000	1.5%
3	Texas	28,662,395,000	5.4%
35	Utah	3,925,382,000	0.7%
45	Vermont	1,533,982,000	0.3%
14	Virginia	12,781,149,000	2.4%
15	Washington	12,628,567,000	2.4%
37	West Virginia	3,551,756,000	0.7%
16	Wisconsin	11,813,832,000	2.2%
48	Wyoming	1,094,402,000	0.2%

RANK ORDER

RANK	STATE	STATE TAXES	% of USA
1	California	$77,755,376,000	14.6%
2	New York	43,262,137,000	8.1%
3	Texas	28,662,395,000	5.4%
4	Florida	24,815,964,000	4.7%
5	Illinois	22,460,190,000	4.2%
6	Pennsylvania	22,135,537,000	4.1%
7	Michigan	21,864,052,000	4.1%
8	Ohio	19,616,569,000	3.7%
9	New Jersey	18,328,814,000	3.4%
10	North Carolina	15,535,277,000	2.9%
11	Massachusetts	14,819,794,000	2.8%
12	Georgia	13,772,147,000	2.6%
13	Minnesota	12,936,369,000	2.4%
14	Virginia	12,781,149,000	2.4%
15	Washington	12,628,567,000	2.4%
16	Wisconsin	11,813,832,000	2.2%
17	Maryland	10,821,276,000	2.0%
18	Indiana	9,994,595,000	1.9%
19	Connecticut	9,032,787,000	1.7%
20	Missouri	8,678,611,000	1.6%
21	Arizona	8,477,001,000	1.6%
22	Kentucky	7,974,690,000	1.5%
23	Tennessee	7,797,681,000	1.5%
24	Louisiana	7,345,994,000	1.4%
25	Colorado	6,923,171,000	1.3%
26	Alabama	6,878,923,000	1.3%
27	Oklahoma	6,052,680,000	1.1%
28	South Carolina	5,748,585,000	1.1%
29	Oregon	5,139,322,000	1.0%
30	Arkansas	5,034,109,000	0.9%
31	Iowa	5,006,251,000	0.9%
32	Kansas	4,808,361,000	0.9%
33	Mississippi	4,728,905,000	0.9%
34	Nevada	3,945,329,000	0.7%
35	Utah	3,925,382,000	0.7%
36	New Mexico	3,628,055,000	0.7%
37	West Virginia	3,551,756,000	0.7%
38	Hawaii	3,420,671,000	0.6%
39	Nebraska	2,992,522,000	0.6%
40	Maine	2,626,830,000	0.5%
41	Idaho	2,271,075,000	0.4%
42	Delaware	2,173,600,000	0.4%
43	Rhode Island	2,127,609,000	0.4%
44	New Hampshire	1,883,924,000	0.4%
45	Vermont	1,533,982,000	0.3%
46	Montana	1,442,731,000	0.3%
47	North Dakota	1,117,299,000	0.2%
48	Wyoming	1,094,402,000	0.2%
49	Alaska	1,089,504,000	0.2%
50	South Dakota	976,596,000	0.2%
	District of Columbia*	NA	NA

Source: U.S. Bureau of the Census, Governments Division
"2002 State Government Tax Collections" (http://www.census.gov/govs/www/statetax02.html)
**Not applicable.*

Per Capita State Government Tax Revenue in 2002

National Per Capita = $1,856

<u>ALPHA ORDER</u>

RANK	STATE	PER CAPITA
42	Alabama	$1,536
32	Alaska	1,698
40	Arizona	1,558
21	Arkansas	1,860
8	California	2,221
41	Colorado	1,538
3	Connecticut	2,612
2	Delaware	2,697
44	Florida	1,487
38	Georgia	1,612
1	Hawaii	2,757
34	Idaho	1,691
24	Illinois	1,784
37	Indiana	1,623
31	Iowa	1,705
25	Kansas	1,773
19	Kentucky	1,950
36	Louisiana	1,641
14	Maine	2,029
16	Maryland	1,985
6	Massachusetts	2,308
10	Michigan	2,177
4	Minnesota	2,575
35	Mississippi	1,650
43	Missouri	1,531
39	Montana	1,585
29	Nebraska	1,732
22	Nevada	1,820
45	New Hampshire	1,478
12	New Jersey	2,137
18	New Mexico	1,959
7	New York	2,261
20	North Carolina	1,870
26	North Dakota	1,763
30	Ohio	1,719
28	Oklahoma	1,734
46	Oregon	1,460
23	Pennsylvania	1,795
15	Rhode Island	1,992
47	South Carolina	1,401
50	South Dakota	1,284
48	Tennessee	1,347
49	Texas	1,319
33	Utah	1,693
5	Vermont	2,489
27	Virginia	1,754
13	Washington	2,081
17	West Virginia	1,968
11	Wisconsin	2,172
9	Wyoming	2,194

<u>RANK ORDER</u>

RANK	STATE	PER CAPITA
1	Hawaii	$2,757
2	Delaware	2,697
3	Connecticut	2,612
4	Minnesota	2,575
5	Vermont	2,489
6	Massachusetts	2,308
7	New York	2,261
8	California	2,221
9	Wyoming	2,194
10	Michigan	2,177
11	Wisconsin	2,172
12	New Jersey	2,137
13	Washington	2,081
14	Maine	2,029
15	Rhode Island	1,992
16	Maryland	1,985
17	West Virginia	1,968
18	New Mexico	1,959
19	Kentucky	1,950
20	North Carolina	1,870
21	Arkansas	1,860
22	Nevada	1,820
23	Pennsylvania	1,795
24	Illinois	1,784
25	Kansas	1,773
26	North Dakota	1,763
27	Virginia	1,754
28	Oklahoma	1,734
29	Nebraska	1,732
30	Ohio	1,719
31	Iowa	1,705
32	Alaska	1,698
33	Utah	1,693
34	Idaho	1,691
35	Mississippi	1,650
36	Louisiana	1,641
37	Indiana	1,623
38	Georgia	1,612
39	Montana	1,585
40	Arizona	1,558
41	Colorado	1,538
42	Alabama	1,536
43	Missouri	1,531
44	Florida	1,487
45	New Hampshire	1,478
46	Oregon	1,460
47	South Carolina	1,401
48	Tennessee	1,347
49	Texas	1,319
50	South Dakota	1,284
	District of Columbia*	NA

Source: Morgan Quitno Press using data from U.S. Bureau of the Census, Governments Division
   "2002 State Government Tax Collections" (http://www.census.gov/govs/www/statetax02.html)
*Not applicable.

State Government Tax Revenue as a Percent of Personal Income in 2002

National Percent = 6.0% of Personal Income*

<u>ALPHA ORDER</u>

RANK	STATE	PERCENT
25	Alabama	6.1
41	Alaska	5.3
30	Arizona	5.9
6	Arkansas	7.9
18	California	6.7
48	Colorado	4.6
25	Connecticut	6.1
3	Delaware	8.3
45	Florida	5.0
36	Georgia	5.6
1	Hawaii	9.1
16	Idaho	6.8
41	Illinois	5.3
34	Indiana	5.7
25	Iowa	6.1
25	Kansas	6.1
7	Kentucky	7.6
20	Louisiana	6.5
10	Maine	7.3
37	Maryland	5.5
30	Massachusetts	5.9
11	Michigan	7.2
7	Minnesota	7.6
9	Mississippi	7.4
41	Missouri	5.3
21	Montana	6.4
30	Nebraska	5.9
29	Nevada	6.0
50	New Hampshire	4.3
39	New Jersey	5.4
5	New Mexico	8.2
24	New York	6.3
16	North Carolina	6.8
19	North Dakota	6.6
30	Ohio	5.9
15	Oklahoma	6.9
44	Oregon	5.1
34	Pennsylvania	5.7
21	Rhode Island	6.4
37	South Carolina	5.5
47	South Dakota	4.8
46	Tennessee	4.9
48	Texas	4.6
14	Utah	7.0
2	Vermont	8.4
39	Virginia	5.4
21	Washington	6.4
3	West Virginia	8.3
11	Wisconsin	7.2
11	Wyoming	7.2

<u>RANK ORDER</u>

RANK	STATE	PERCENT
1	Hawaii	9.1
2	Vermont	8.4
3	Delaware	8.3
3	West Virginia	8.3
5	New Mexico	8.2
6	Arkansas	7.9
7	Kentucky	7.6
7	Minnesota	7.6
9	Mississippi	7.4
10	Maine	7.3
11	Michigan	7.2
11	Wisconsin	7.2
11	Wyoming	7.2
14	Utah	7.0
15	Oklahoma	6.9
16	Idaho	6.8
16	North Carolina	6.8
18	California	6.7
19	North Dakota	6.6
20	Louisiana	6.5
21	Montana	6.4
21	Rhode Island	6.4
21	Washington	6.4
24	New York	6.3
25	Alabama	6.1
25	Connecticut	6.1
25	Iowa	6.1
25	Kansas	6.1
29	Nevada	6.0
30	Arizona	5.9
30	Massachusetts	5.9
30	Nebraska	5.9
30	Ohio	5.9
34	Indiana	5.7
34	Pennsylvania	5.7
36	Georgia	5.6
37	Maryland	5.5
37	South Carolina	5.5
39	New Jersey	5.4
39	Virginia	5.4
41	Alaska	5.3
41	Illinois	5.3
41	Missouri	5.3
44	Oregon	5.1
45	Florida	5.0
46	Tennessee	4.9
47	South Dakota	4.8
48	Colorado	4.6
48	Texas	4.6
50	New Hampshire	4.3

	District of Columbia**	NA

Source: Morgan Quitno Press using data from U.S. Bureau of the Census, Governments Division
"2002 State Government Tax Collections" (http://www.census.gov/govs/www/statetax02.html)
U.S. Department of Commerce, Bureau of Economic Analysis
"Annual State Personal Income" (http://www.bea.doc.gov/bea/regional/spil)
*National figure does not include personal income or taxes from the District of Columbia.
**Not applicable.

State Government Individual Income Tax Revenue in 2002

National Total = $185,032,712,000

ALPHA ORDER

RANK	STATE	INCOME TAX	% of USA
21	Alabama	$2,399,852,000	1.3%
44	Alaska	0	0.0%
23	Arizona	2,090,645,000	1.1%
29	Arkansas	1,488,250,000	0.8%
1	California	33,046,665,000	17.9%
19	Colorado	3,475,760,000	1.9%
15	Connecticut	3,685,244,000	2.0%
38	Delaware	716,647,000	0.4%
44	Florida	0	0.0%
10	Georgia	6,487,638,000	3.5%
31	Hawaii	1,111,590,000	0.6%
36	Idaho	842,375,000	0.5%
6	Illinois	6,951,265,000	3.8%
18	Indiana	3,540,819,000	1.9%
27	Iowa	1,769,347,000	1.0%
25	Kansas	1,854,848,000	1.0%
20	Kentucky	2,678,330,000	1.4%
26	Louisiana	1,779,506,000	1.0%
32	Maine	1,072,810,000	0.6%
14	Maryland	4,704,368,000	2.5%
4	Massachusetts	7,912,934,000	4.3%
11	Michigan	6,125,270,000	3.3%
12	Minnesota	5,444,715,000	2.9%
34	Mississippi	985,117,000	0.5%
17	Missouri	3,615,417,000	2.0%
39	Montana	517,568,000	0.3%
30	Nebraska	1,153,444,000	0.6%
44	Nevada	0	0.0%
43	New Hampshire	71,433,000	0.0%
7	New Jersey	6,836,992,000	3.7%
35	New Mexico	982,891,000	0.5%
2	New York	25,573,667,000	13.8%
5	North Carolina	7,265,242,000	3.9%
41	North Dakota	199,590,000	0.1%
3	Ohio	8,335,554,000	4.5%
22	Oklahoma	2,286,110,000	1.2%
16	Oregon	3,674,962,000	2.0%
8	Pennsylvania	6,734,729,000	3.6%
37	Rhode Island	823,521,000	0.4%
24	South Carolina	1,952,498,000	1.1%
44	South Dakota	0	0.0%
42	Tennessee	146,293,000	0.1%
44	Texas	0	0.0%
28	Utah	1,605,310,000	0.9%
40	Vermont	374,445,000	0.2%
9	Virginia	6,710,771,000	3.6%
44	Washington	0	0.0%
33	West Virginia	1,034,665,000	0.6%
13	Wisconsin	4,973,615,000	2.7%
44	Wyoming	0	0.0%

RANK ORDER

RANK	STATE	INCOME TAX	% of USA
1	California	$33,046,665,000	17.9%
2	New York	25,573,667,000	13.8%
3	Ohio	8,335,554,000	4.5%
4	Massachusetts	7,912,934,000	4.3%
5	North Carolina	7,265,242,000	3.9%
6	Illinois	6,951,265,000	3.8%
7	New Jersey	6,836,992,000	3.7%
8	Pennsylvania	6,734,729,000	3.6%
9	Virginia	6,710,771,000	3.6%
10	Georgia	6,487,638,000	3.5%
11	Michigan	6,125,270,000	3.3%
12	Minnesota	5,444,715,000	2.9%
13	Wisconsin	4,973,615,000	2.7%
14	Maryland	4,704,368,000	2.5%
15	Connecticut	3,685,244,000	2.0%
16	Oregon	3,674,962,000	2.0%
17	Missouri	3,615,417,000	2.0%
18	Indiana	3,540,819,000	1.9%
19	Colorado	3,475,760,000	1.9%
20	Kentucky	2,678,330,000	1.4%
21	Alabama	2,399,852,000	1.3%
22	Oklahoma	2,286,110,000	1.2%
23	Arizona	2,090,645,000	1.1%
24	South Carolina	1,952,498,000	1.1%
25	Kansas	1,854,848,000	1.0%
26	Louisiana	1,779,506,000	1.0%
27	Iowa	1,769,347,000	1.0%
28	Utah	1,605,310,000	0.9%
29	Arkansas	1,488,250,000	0.8%
30	Nebraska	1,153,444,000	0.6%
31	Hawaii	1,111,590,000	0.6%
32	Maine	1,072,810,000	0.6%
33	West Virginia	1,034,665,000	0.6%
34	Mississippi	985,117,000	0.5%
35	New Mexico	982,891,000	0.5%
36	Idaho	842,375,000	0.5%
37	Rhode Island	823,521,000	0.4%
38	Delaware	716,647,000	0.4%
39	Montana	517,568,000	0.3%
40	Vermont	374,445,000	0.2%
41	North Dakota	199,590,000	0.1%
42	Tennessee	146,293,000	0.1%
43	New Hampshire	71,433,000	0.0%
44	Alaska	0	0.0%
44	Florida	0	0.0%
44	Nevada	0	0.0%
44	South Dakota	0	0.0%
44	Texas	0	0.0%
44	Washington	0	0.0%
44	Wyoming	0	0.0%
	District of Columbia*	NA	NA

Source: U.S. Bureau of the Census, Governments Division
"2002 State Government Tax Collections" (http://www.census.gov/govs/www/statetax02.html)
*Not applicable.

Per Capita State Government Individual Income Tax Revenue in 2002

National Per Capita = $644

<table>
<tr><td colspan="3"><u>ALPHA ORDER</u></td><td colspan="3"><u>RANK ORDER</u></td></tr>
<tr><td>RANK</td><td>STATE</td><td>PER CAPITA</td><td>RANK</td><td>STATE</td><td>PER CAPITA</td></tr>
<tr><td>35</td><td>Alabama</td><td>$536</td><td>1</td><td>New York</td><td>$1,337</td></tr>
<tr><td>44</td><td>Alaska</td><td>0</td><td>2</td><td>Massachusetts</td><td>1,232</td></tr>
<tr><td>39</td><td>Arizona</td><td>384</td><td>3</td><td>Minnesota</td><td>1,084</td></tr>
<tr><td>33</td><td>Arkansas</td><td>550</td><td>4</td><td>Connecticut</td><td>1,066</td></tr>
<tr><td>6</td><td>California</td><td>944</td><td>5</td><td>Oregon</td><td>1,044</td></tr>
<tr><td>15</td><td>Colorado</td><td>772</td><td>6</td><td>California</td><td>944</td></tr>
<tr><td>4</td><td>Connecticut</td><td>1,066</td><td>7</td><td>Virginia</td><td>921</td></tr>
<tr><td>10</td><td>Delaware</td><td>889</td><td>8</td><td>Wisconsin</td><td>914</td></tr>
<tr><td>44</td><td>Florida</td><td>0</td><td>9</td><td>Hawaii</td><td>896</td></tr>
<tr><td>17</td><td>Georgia</td><td>759</td><td>10</td><td>Delaware</td><td>889</td></tr>
<tr><td>9</td><td>Hawaii</td><td>896</td><td>11</td><td>North Carolina</td><td>875</td></tr>
<tr><td>25</td><td>Idaho</td><td>627</td><td>12</td><td>Maryland</td><td>863</td></tr>
<tr><td>32</td><td>Illinois</td><td>552</td><td>13</td><td>Maine</td><td>828</td></tr>
<tr><td>29</td><td>Indiana</td><td>575</td><td>14</td><td>New Jersey</td><td>797</td></tr>
<tr><td>28</td><td>Iowa</td><td>603</td><td>15</td><td>Colorado</td><td>772</td></tr>
<tr><td>20</td><td>Kansas</td><td>684</td><td>16</td><td>Rhode Island</td><td>771</td></tr>
<tr><td>22</td><td>Kentucky</td><td>655</td><td>17</td><td>Georgia</td><td>759</td></tr>
<tr><td>38</td><td>Louisiana</td><td>398</td><td>18</td><td>Ohio</td><td>731</td></tr>
<tr><td>13</td><td>Maine</td><td>828</td><td>19</td><td>Utah</td><td>692</td></tr>
<tr><td>12</td><td>Maryland</td><td>863</td><td>20</td><td>Kansas</td><td>684</td></tr>
<tr><td>2</td><td>Massachusetts</td><td>1,232</td><td>21</td><td>Nebraska</td><td>668</td></tr>
<tr><td>26</td><td>Michigan</td><td>610</td><td>22</td><td>Kentucky</td><td>655</td></tr>
<tr><td>3</td><td>Minnesota</td><td>1,084</td><td>22</td><td>Oklahoma</td><td>655</td></tr>
<tr><td>40</td><td>Mississippi</td><td>344</td><td>24</td><td>Missouri</td><td>638</td></tr>
<tr><td>24</td><td>Missouri</td><td>638</td><td>25</td><td>Idaho</td><td>627</td></tr>
<tr><td>31</td><td>Montana</td><td>569</td><td>26</td><td>Michigan</td><td>610</td></tr>
<tr><td>21</td><td>Nebraska</td><td>668</td><td>27</td><td>Vermont</td><td>607</td></tr>
<tr><td>44</td><td>Nevada</td><td>0</td><td>28</td><td>Iowa</td><td>603</td></tr>
<tr><td>42</td><td>New Hampshire</td><td>56</td><td>29</td><td>Indiana</td><td>575</td></tr>
<tr><td>14</td><td>New Jersey</td><td>797</td><td>30</td><td>West Virginia</td><td>573</td></tr>
<tr><td>36</td><td>New Mexico</td><td>531</td><td>31</td><td>Montana</td><td>569</td></tr>
<tr><td>1</td><td>New York</td><td>1,337</td><td>32</td><td>Illinois</td><td>552</td></tr>
<tr><td>11</td><td>North Carolina</td><td>875</td><td>33</td><td>Arkansas</td><td>550</td></tr>
<tr><td>41</td><td>North Dakota</td><td>315</td><td>34</td><td>Pennsylvania</td><td>546</td></tr>
<tr><td>18</td><td>Ohio</td><td>731</td><td>35</td><td>Alabama</td><td>536</td></tr>
<tr><td>22</td><td>Oklahoma</td><td>655</td><td>36</td><td>New Mexico</td><td>531</td></tr>
<tr><td>5</td><td>Oregon</td><td>1,044</td><td>37</td><td>South Carolina</td><td>476</td></tr>
<tr><td>34</td><td>Pennsylvania</td><td>546</td><td>38</td><td>Louisiana</td><td>398</td></tr>
<tr><td>16</td><td>Rhode Island</td><td>771</td><td>39</td><td>Arizona</td><td>384</td></tr>
<tr><td>37</td><td>South Carolina</td><td>476</td><td>40</td><td>Mississippi</td><td>344</td></tr>
<tr><td>44</td><td>South Dakota</td><td>0</td><td>41</td><td>North Dakota</td><td>315</td></tr>
<tr><td>43</td><td>Tennessee</td><td>25</td><td>42</td><td>New Hampshire</td><td>56</td></tr>
<tr><td>44</td><td>Texas</td><td>0</td><td>43</td><td>Tennessee</td><td>25</td></tr>
<tr><td>19</td><td>Utah</td><td>692</td><td>44</td><td>Alaska</td><td>0</td></tr>
<tr><td>27</td><td>Vermont</td><td>607</td><td>44</td><td>Florida</td><td>0</td></tr>
<tr><td>7</td><td>Virginia</td><td>921</td><td>44</td><td>Nevada</td><td>0</td></tr>
<tr><td>44</td><td>Washington</td><td>0</td><td>44</td><td>South Dakota</td><td>0</td></tr>
<tr><td>30</td><td>West Virginia</td><td>573</td><td>44</td><td>Texas</td><td>0</td></tr>
<tr><td>8</td><td>Wisconsin</td><td>914</td><td>44</td><td>Washington</td><td>0</td></tr>
<tr><td>44</td><td>Wyoming</td><td>0</td><td>44</td><td>Wyoming</td><td>0</td></tr>
<tr><td></td><td></td><td></td><td></td><td>District of Columbia*</td><td>NA</td></tr>
</table>

*Source: Morgan Quitno Press using data from U.S. Bureau of the Census, Governments Division
"2002 State Government Tax Collections" (http://www.census.gov/govs/www/statetax02.html)*
Not applicable.

State Government Corporation Net Income Tax Revenue in 2002

National Total = $25,887,521,000

ALPHA ORDER

RANK	STATE	REVENUE	% of USA
19	Alabama	$322,636,000	1.2%
23	Alaska	269,273,000	1.0%
18	Arizona	346,280,000	1.3%
32	Arkansas	161,021,000	0.6%
1	California	5,333,036,000	20.6%
28	Colorado	205,217,000	0.8%
33	Connecticut	149,454,000	0.6%
25	Delaware	251,643,000	1.0%
5	Florida	1,218,864,000	4.7%
12	Georgia	568,080,000	2.2%
42	Hawaii	52,640,000	0.2%
40	Idaho	76,769,000	0.3%
4	Illinois	2,061,540,000	8.0%
11	Indiana	667,162,000	2.6%
38	Iowa	88,310,000	0.3%
35	Kansas	121,931,000	0.5%
22	Kentucky	302,129,000	1.2%
24	Louisiana	264,419,000	1.0%
39	Maine	77,366,000	0.3%
17	Maryland	359,420,000	1.4%
8	Massachusetts	812,257,000	3.1%
3	Michigan	2,065,241,000	8.0%
13	Minnesota	542,771,000	2.1%
30	Mississippi	195,814,000	0.8%
21	Missouri	302,301,000	1.2%
41	Montana	68,173,000	0.3%
37	Nebraska	107,628,000	0.4%
47	Nevada	0	0.0%
16	New Hampshire	377,313,000	1.5%
7	New Jersey	1,101,296,000	4.3%
34	New Mexico	124,327,000	0.5%
2	New York	2,257,935,000	8.7%
10	North Carolina	668,124,000	2.6%
43	North Dakota	49,990,000	0.2%
9	Ohio	761,050,000	2.9%
31	Oklahoma	173,701,000	0.7%
29	Oregon	196,257,000	0.8%
6	Pennsylvania	1,198,438,000	4.6%
46	Rhode Island	28,273,000	0.1%
27	South Carolina	217,327,000	0.8%
44	South Dakota	40,547,000	0.2%
15	Tennessee	502,977,000	1.9%
47	Texas	0	0.0%
36	Utah	110,989,000	0.4%
45	Vermont	37,306,000	0.1%
20	Virginia	308,554,000	1.2%
47	Washington	0	0.0%
26	West Virginia	220,158,000	0.9%
14	Wisconsin	521,584,000	2.0%
47	Wyoming	0	0.0%

RANK ORDER

RANK	STATE	REVENUE	% of USA
1	California	$5,333,036,000	20.6%
2	New York	2,257,935,000	8.7%
3	Michigan	2,065,241,000	8.0%
4	Illinois	2,061,540,000	8.0%
5	Florida	1,218,864,000	4.7%
6	Pennsylvania	1,198,438,000	4.6%
7	New Jersey	1,101,296,000	4.3%
8	Massachusetts	812,257,000	3.1%
9	Ohio	761,050,000	2.9%
10	North Carolina	668,124,000	2.6%
11	Indiana	667,162,000	2.6%
12	Georgia	568,080,000	2.2%
13	Minnesota	542,771,000	2.1%
14	Wisconsin	521,584,000	2.0%
15	Tennessee	502,977,000	1.9%
16	New Hampshire	377,313,000	1.5%
17	Maryland	359,420,000	1.4%
18	Arizona	346,280,000	1.3%
19	Alabama	322,636,000	1.2%
20	Virginia	308,554,000	1.2%
21	Missouri	302,301,000	1.2%
22	Kentucky	302,129,000	1.2%
23	Alaska	269,273,000	1.0%
24	Louisiana	264,419,000	1.0%
25	Delaware	251,643,000	1.0%
26	West Virginia	220,158,000	0.9%
27	South Carolina	217,327,000	0.8%
28	Colorado	205,217,000	0.8%
29	Oregon	196,257,000	0.8%
30	Mississippi	195,814,000	0.8%
31	Oklahoma	173,701,000	0.7%
32	Arkansas	161,021,000	0.6%
33	Connecticut	149,454,000	0.6%
34	New Mexico	124,327,000	0.5%
35	Kansas	121,931,000	0.5%
36	Utah	110,989,000	0.4%
37	Nebraska	107,628,000	0.4%
38	Iowa	88,310,000	0.3%
39	Maine	77,366,000	0.3%
40	Idaho	76,769,000	0.3%
41	Montana	68,173,000	0.3%
42	Hawaii	52,640,000	0.2%
43	North Dakota	49,990,000	0.2%
44	South Dakota	40,547,000	0.2%
45	Vermont	37,306,000	0.1%
46	Rhode Island	28,273,000	0.1%
47	Nevada	0	0.0%
47	Texas	0	0.0%
47	Washington	0	0.0%
47	Wyoming	0	0.0%
	District of Columbia*	NA	NA

Source: U.S. Bureau of the Census, Governments Division
"2002 State Government Tax Collections" (http://www.census.gov/govs/www/statetax02.html)
*Not applicable.

Per Capita State Government Corporation Net Income Tax Revenue in 2002

National Per Capita = $90

<u>ALPHA ORDER</u>

RANK	STATE	PER CAPITA
21	Alabama	$72
1	Alaska	420
27	Arizona	64
31	Arkansas	59
6	California	152
40	Colorado	46
42	Connecticut	43
2	Delaware	312
20	Florida	73
25	Georgia	66
43	Hawaii	42
33	Idaho	57
5	Illinois	164
11	Indiana	108
45	Iowa	30
41	Kansas	45
19	Kentucky	74
31	Louisiana	59
30	Maine	60
25	Maryland	66
8	Massachusetts	126
4	Michigan	206
11	Minnesota	108
22	Mississippi	68
35	Missouri	53
18	Montana	75
28	Nebraska	62
47	Nevada	0
3	New Hampshire	296
7	New Jersey	128
23	New Mexico	67
10	New York	118
16	North Carolina	80
17	North Dakota	79
23	Ohio	67
38	Oklahoma	50
34	Oregon	56
13	Pennsylvania	97
46	Rhode Island	26
35	South Carolina	53
35	South Dakota	53
15	Tennessee	87
47	Texas	0
39	Utah	48
29	Vermont	61
43	Virginia	42
47	Washington	0
9	West Virginia	122
14	Wisconsin	96
47	Wyoming	0

<u>RANK ORDER</u>

RANK	STATE	PER CAPITA
1	Alaska	$420
2	Delaware	312
3	New Hampshire	296
4	Michigan	206
5	Illinois	164
6	California	152
7	New Jersey	128
8	Massachusetts	126
9	West Virginia	122
10	New York	118
11	Indiana	108
11	Minnesota	108
13	Pennsylvania	97
14	Wisconsin	96
15	Tennessee	87
16	North Carolina	80
17	North Dakota	79
18	Montana	75
19	Kentucky	74
20	Florida	73
21	Alabama	72
22	Mississippi	68
23	New Mexico	67
23	Ohio	67
25	Georgia	66
25	Maryland	66
27	Arizona	64
28	Nebraska	62
29	Vermont	61
30	Maine	60
31	Arkansas	59
31	Louisiana	59
33	Idaho	57
34	Oregon	56
35	Missouri	53
35	South Carolina	53
35	South Dakota	53
38	Oklahoma	50
39	Utah	48
40	Colorado	46
41	Kansas	45
42	Connecticut	43
43	Hawaii	42
43	Virginia	42
45	Iowa	30
46	Rhode Island	26
47	Nevada	0
47	Texas	0
47	Washington	0
47	Wyoming	0
	District of Columbia*	NA

Source: Morgan Quitno Press using data from U.S. Bureau of the Census, Governments Division
   "2002 State Government Tax Collections" (http://www.census.gov/govs/www/statetax02.html)
*Not applicable.

State Government General Sales Tax Revenue in 2002

National Total = $178,941,291,000*

ALPHA ORDER

RANK	STATE	SALES TAX	% of USA
31	Alabama	$1,748,235,000	1.0%
46	Alaska	0	0.0%
13	Arizona	4,289,778,000	2.4%
28	Arkansas	1,918,140,000	1.1%
1	California	23,816,406,000	13.3%
29	Colorado	1,901,972,000	1.1%
19	Connecticut	3,043,971,000	1.7%
46	Delaware	0	0.0%
3	Florida	14,408,709,000	8.1%
11	Georgia	4,833,521,000	2.7%
33	Hawaii	1,612,333,000	0.9%
40	Idaho	795,384,000	0.4%
8	Illinois	6,419,156,000	3.6%
14	Indiana	3,798,490,000	2.1%
32	Iowa	1,747,016,000	1.0%
30	Kansas	1,799,485,000	1.0%
26	Kentucky	2,312,224,000	1.3%
25	Louisiana	2,326,873,000	1.3%
39	Maine	836,134,000	0.5%
22	Maryland	2,690,434,000	1.5%
16	Massachusetts	3,695,874,000	2.1%
6	Michigan	7,784,308,000	4.4%
15	Minnesota	3,740,660,000	2.1%
23	Mississippi	2,340,474,000	1.3%
20	Missouri	2,854,718,000	1.6%
46	Montana	0	0.0%
37	Nebraska	1,069,185,000	0.6%
27	Nevada	2,070,013,000	1.2%
46	New Hampshire	0	0.0%
10	New Jersey	5,996,839,000	3.4%
36	New Mexico	1,337,321,000	0.7%
4	New York	8,607,718,000	4.8%
18	North Carolina	3,212,098,000	1.8%
44	North Dakota	335,613,000	0.2%
9	Ohio	6,391,475,000	3.6%
34	Oklahoma	1,529,465,000	0.9%
46	Oregon	0	0.0%
7	Pennsylvania	7,330,422,000	4.1%
41	Rhode Island	731,597,000	0.4%
24	South Carolina	2,335,170,000	1.3%
42	South Dakota	523,001,000	0.3%
12	Tennessee	4,674,896,000	2.6%
2	Texas	14,559,504,000	8.1%
35	Utah	1,500,278,000	0.8%
45	Vermont	214,841,000	0.1%
21	Virginia	2,799,526,000	1.6%
5	Washington	7,904,003,000	4.4%
38	West Virginia	962,756,000	0.5%
17	Wisconsin	3,695,796,000	2.1%
43	Wyoming	445,479,000	0.2%

RANK ORDER

RANK	STATE	SALES TAX	% of USA
1	California	$23,816,406,000	13.3%
2	Texas	14,559,504,000	8.1%
3	Florida	14,408,709,000	8.1%
4	New York	8,607,718,000	4.8%
5	Washington	7,904,003,000	4.4%
6	Michigan	7,784,308,000	4.4%
7	Pennsylvania	7,330,422,000	4.1%
8	Illinois	6,419,156,000	3.6%
9	Ohio	6,391,475,000	3.6%
10	New Jersey	5,996,839,000	3.4%
11	Georgia	4,833,521,000	2.7%
12	Tennessee	4,674,896,000	2.6%
13	Arizona	4,289,778,000	2.4%
14	Indiana	3,798,490,000	2.1%
15	Minnesota	3,740,660,000	2.1%
16	Massachusetts	3,695,874,000	2.1%
17	Wisconsin	3,695,796,000	2.1%
18	North Carolina	3,212,098,000	1.8%
19	Connecticut	3,043,971,000	1.7%
20	Missouri	2,854,718,000	1.6%
21	Virginia	2,799,526,000	1.6%
22	Maryland	2,690,434,000	1.5%
23	Mississippi	2,340,474,000	1.3%
24	South Carolina	2,335,170,000	1.3%
25	Louisiana	2,326,873,000	1.3%
26	Kentucky	2,312,224,000	1.3%
27	Nevada	2,070,013,000	1.2%
28	Arkansas	1,918,140,000	1.1%
29	Colorado	1,901,972,000	1.1%
30	Kansas	1,799,485,000	1.0%
31	Alabama	1,748,235,000	1.0%
32	Iowa	1,747,016,000	1.0%
33	Hawaii	1,612,333,000	0.9%
34	Oklahoma	1,529,465,000	0.9%
35	Utah	1,500,278,000	0.8%
36	New Mexico	1,337,321,000	0.7%
37	Nebraska	1,069,185,000	0.6%
38	West Virginia	962,756,000	0.5%
39	Maine	836,134,000	0.5%
40	Idaho	795,384,000	0.4%
41	Rhode Island	731,597,000	0.4%
42	South Dakota	523,001,000	0.3%
43	Wyoming	445,479,000	0.2%
44	North Dakota	335,613,000	0.2%
45	Vermont	214,841,000	0.1%
46	Alaska	0	0.0%
46	Delaware	0	0.0%
46	Montana	0	0.0%
46	New Hampshire	0	0.0%
46	Oregon	0	0.0%
	District of Columbia**	NA	NA

Per Capita State Government General Sales Tax Revenue in 2002

National Per Capita = $623*

<u>ALPHA ORDER</u>

RANK	STATE	PER CAPITA
42	Alabama	$390
46	Alaska	0
9	Arizona	788
13	Arkansas	709
17	California	680
41	Colorado	423
5	Connecticut	880
46	Delaware	0
6	Florida	863
30	Georgia	566
2	Hawaii	1,300
27	Idaho	592
36	Illinois	510
24	Indiana	617
25	Iowa	595
20	Kansas	664
31	Kentucky	565
35	Louisiana	520
22	Maine	646
38	Maryland	494
28	Massachusetts	576
10	Michigan	775
11	Minnesota	744
7	Mississippi	816
37	Missouri	504
46	Montana	0
23	Nebraska	619
3	Nevada	955
46	New Hampshire	0
14	New Jersey	699
12	New Mexico	722
39	New York	450
43	North Carolina	387
34	North Dakota	529
32	Ohio	560
40	Oklahoma	438
46	Oregon	0
25	Pennsylvania	595
16	Rhode Island	685
29	South Carolina	569
15	South Dakota	688
8	Tennessee	807
19	Texas	670
21	Utah	647
45	Vermont	349
44	Virginia	384
1	Washington	1,303
33	West Virginia	533
18	Wisconsin	679
4	Wyoming	893

<u>RANK ORDER</u>

RANK	STATE	PER CAPITA
1	Washington	$1,303
2	Hawaii	1,300
3	Nevada	955
4	Wyoming	893
5	Connecticut	880
6	Florida	863
7	Mississippi	816
8	Tennessee	807
9	Arizona	788
10	Michigan	775
11	Minnesota	744
12	New Mexico	722
13	Arkansas	709
14	New Jersey	699
15	South Dakota	688
16	Rhode Island	685
17	California	680
18	Wisconsin	679
19	Texas	670
20	Kansas	664
21	Utah	647
22	Maine	646
23	Nebraska	619
24	Indiana	617
25	Iowa	595
25	Pennsylvania	595
27	Idaho	592
28	Massachusetts	576
29	South Carolina	569
30	Georgia	566
31	Kentucky	565
32	Ohio	560
33	West Virginia	533
34	North Dakota	529
35	Louisiana	520
36	Illinois	510
37	Missouri	504
38	Maryland	494
39	New York	450
40	Oklahoma	438
41	Colorado	423
42	Alabama	390
43	North Carolina	387
44	Virginia	384
45	Vermont	349
46	Alaska	0
46	Delaware	0
46	Montana	0
46	New Hampshire	0
46	Oregon	0
	District of Columbia**	NA

Source: Morgan Quitno Press using data from U.S. Bureau of the Census, Governments Division
"2002 State Government Tax Collections" (http://www.census.gov/govs/www/statetax02.html)
*Does not include special sales taxes such as those on sale of alcohol, gasoline or tobacco.
**Not applicable.

State Government Motor Fuels Sales Tax Revenue in 2002

National Total = $31,907,961,000

<u>ALPHA ORDER</u>

RANK	STATE	FUEL TAX	% of USA
23	Alabama	$511,927,000	1.6%
50	Alaska	40,352,000	0.1%
18	Arizona	624,655,000	2.0%
27	Arkansas	415,050,000	1.3%
1	California	3,295,903,000	10.3%
20	Colorado	569,079,000	1.8%
26	Connecticut	424,669,000	1.3%
46	Delaware	107,713,000	0.3%
3	Florida	1,808,863,000	5.7%
17	Georgia	649,746,000	2.0%
48	Hawaii	78,088,000	0.2%
38	Idaho	213,778,000	0.7%
5	Illinois	1,373,522,000	4.3%
16	Indiana	665,619,000	2.1%
33	Iowa	343,147,000	1.1%
32	Kansas	376,241,000	1.2%
25	Kentucky	461,333,000	1.4%
21	Louisiana	558,892,000	1.8%
40	Maine	191,694,000	0.6%
13	Maryland	703,390,000	2.2%
15	Massachusetts	666,751,000	2.1%
8	Michigan	1,089,813,000	3.4%
19	Minnesota	620,241,000	1.9%
30	Mississippi	410,258,000	1.3%
14	Missouri	692,448,000	2.2%
41	Montana	191,440,000	0.6%
35	Nebraska	308,147,000	1.0%
37	Nevada	266,101,000	0.8%
44	New Hampshire	120,006,000	0.4%
22	New Jersey	523,819,000	1.6%
39	New Mexico	199,515,000	0.6%
24	New York	492,185,000	1.5%
7	North Carolina	1,209,386,000	3.8%
45	North Dakota	110,848,000	0.3%
6	Ohio	1,372,423,000	4.3%
29	Oklahoma	410,353,000	1.3%
31	Oregon	398,309,000	1.2%
4	Pennsylvania	1,753,338,000	5.5%
42	Rhode Island	130,134,000	0.4%
28	South Carolina	411,074,000	1.3%
43	South Dakota	123,427,000	0.4%
11	Tennessee	814,468,000	2.6%
2	Texas	2,835,232,000	8.9%
34	Utah	336,411,000	1.1%
47	Vermont	86,440,000	0.3%
10	Virginia	848,528,000	2.7%
12	Washington	742,699,000	2.3%
36	West Virginia	300,049,000	0.9%
9	Wisconsin	955,404,000	3.0%
49	Wyoming	75,053,000	0.2%

<u>RANK ORDER</u>

RANK	STATE	FUEL TAX	% of USA
1	California	$3,295,903,000	10.3%
2	Texas	2,835,232,000	8.9%
3	Florida	1,808,863,000	5.7%
4	Pennsylvania	1,753,338,000	5.5%
5	Illinois	1,373,522,000	4.3%
6	Ohio	1,372,423,000	4.3%
7	North Carolina	1,209,386,000	3.8%
8	Michigan	1,089,813,000	3.4%
9	Wisconsin	955,404,000	3.0%
10	Virginia	848,528,000	2.7%
11	Tennessee	814,468,000	2.6%
12	Washington	742,699,000	2.3%
13	Maryland	703,390,000	2.2%
14	Missouri	692,448,000	2.2%
15	Massachusetts	666,751,000	2.1%
16	Indiana	665,619,000	2.1%
17	Georgia	649,746,000	2.0%
18	Arizona	624,655,000	2.0%
19	Minnesota	620,241,000	1.9%
20	Colorado	569,079,000	1.8%
21	Louisiana	558,892,000	1.8%
22	New Jersey	523,819,000	1.6%
23	Alabama	511,927,000	1.6%
24	New York	492,185,000	1.5%
25	Kentucky	461,333,000	1.4%
26	Connecticut	424,669,000	1.3%
27	Arkansas	415,050,000	1.3%
28	South Carolina	411,074,000	1.3%
29	Oklahoma	410,353,000	1.3%
30	Mississippi	410,258,000	1.3%
31	Oregon	398,309,000	1.2%
32	Kansas	376,241,000	1.2%
33	Iowa	343,147,000	1.1%
34	Utah	336,411,000	1.1%
35	Nebraska	308,147,000	1.0%
36	West Virginia	300,049,000	0.9%
37	Nevada	266,101,000	0.8%
38	Idaho	213,778,000	0.7%
39	New Mexico	199,515,000	0.6%
40	Maine	191,694,000	0.6%
41	Montana	191,440,000	0.6%
42	Rhode Island	130,134,000	0.4%
43	South Dakota	123,427,000	0.4%
44	New Hampshire	120,006,000	0.4%
45	North Dakota	110,848,000	0.3%
46	Delaware	107,713,000	0.3%
47	Vermont	86,440,000	0.3%
48	Hawaii	78,088,000	0.2%
49	Wyoming	75,053,000	0.2%
50	Alaska	40,352,000	0.1%
	District of Columbia*	NA	NA

Source: U.S. Bureau of the Census, Governments Division
"2002 State Government Tax Collections" (http://www.census.gov/govs/www/statetax02.html)
*Not applicable.

Per Capita State Government Motor Fuel Sales Tax Revenue in 2002

National Per Capita = $111

ALPHA ORDER

RANK	STATE	PER CAPITA
34	Alabama	$114
47	Alaska	63
33	Arizona	115
8	Arkansas	153
44	California	94
21	Colorado	126
23	Connecticut	123
18	Delaware	134
39	Florida	108
46	Georgia	76
47	Hawaii	63
7	Idaho	159
37	Illinois	109
39	Indiana	108
31	Iowa	117
17	Kansas	139
35	Kentucky	113
22	Louisiana	125
10	Maine	148
20	Maryland	129
42	Massachusetts	104
37	Michigan	109
23	Minnesota	123
13	Mississippi	143
26	Missouri	122
1	Montana	210
2	Nebraska	178
23	Nevada	123
44	New Hampshire	94
49	New Jersey	61
39	New Mexico	108
50	New York	26
11	North Carolina	146
4	North Dakota	175
29	Ohio	120
30	Oklahoma	118
35	Oregon	113
14	Pennsylvania	142
26	Rhode Island	122
43	South Carolina	100
6	South Dakota	162
15	Tennessee	141
19	Texas	130
12	Utah	145
16	Vermont	140
32	Virginia	116
26	Washington	122
5	West Virginia	166
3	Wisconsin	176
9	Wyoming	150

RANK ORDER

RANK	STATE	PER CAPITA
1	Montana	$210
2	Nebraska	178
3	Wisconsin	176
4	North Dakota	175
5	West Virginia	166
6	South Dakota	162
7	Idaho	159
8	Arkansas	153
9	Wyoming	150
10	Maine	148
11	North Carolina	146
12	Utah	145
13	Mississippi	143
14	Pennsylvania	142
15	Tennessee	141
16	Vermont	140
17	Kansas	139
18	Delaware	134
19	Texas	130
20	Maryland	129
21	Colorado	126
22	Louisiana	125
23	Connecticut	123
23	Minnesota	123
23	Nevada	123
26	Missouri	122
26	Rhode Island	122
26	Washington	122
29	Ohio	120
30	Oklahoma	118
31	Iowa	117
32	Virginia	116
33	Arizona	115
34	Alabama	114
35	Kentucky	113
35	Oregon	113
37	Illinois	109
37	Michigan	109
39	Florida	108
39	Indiana	108
39	New Mexico	108
42	Massachusetts	104
43	South Carolina	100
44	California	94
44	New Hampshire	94
46	Georgia	76
47	Alaska	63
47	Hawaii	63
49	New Jersey	61
50	New York	26
	District of Columbia*	NA

Source: Morgan Quitno Press using data from U.S. Bureau of the Census, Governments Division
   "2002 State Government Tax Collections" (http://www.census.gov/govs/www/statetax02.html)
*Not applicable.

State Tax Rates on Gasoline in 2003

National Median = 20.10 Cents per Gallon*

<u>ALPHA ORDER</u>

RANK	STATE	CENTS PER GALLON
36	Alabama	18.00
49	Alaska	8.00
36	Arizona	18.00
22	Arkansas	21.50
36	California	18.00
18	Colorado	22.00
8	Connecticut	25.00
14	Delaware	23.00
47	Florida	14.10
50	Georgia	7.50
43	Hawaii	16.00
4	Idaho	26.00
31	Illinois	19.80
45	Indiana	15.00
26	Iowa	20.10
14	Kansas	23.00
42	Kentucky	16.40
27	Louisiana	20.00
18	Maine	22.00
13	Maryland	23.50
24	Massachusetts	21.00
33	Michigan	19.00
27	Minnesota	20.00
35	Mississippi	18.40
40	Missouri	17.03
3	Montana	27.00
6	Nebraska	25.50
10	Nevada	24.00
32	New Hampshire	19.50
46	New Jersey	14.50
34	New Mexico	18.90
17	New York	22.60
12	North Carolina	23.65
24	North Dakota	21.00
18	Ohio	22.00
41	Oklahoma	17.00
10	Oregon	24.00
5	Pennsylvania	25.90
1	Rhode Island	31.00
43	South Carolina	16.00
18	South Dakota	22.00
23	Tennessee	21.40
27	Texas	20.00
9	Utah	24.50
27	Vermont	20.00
39	Virginia	17.50
14	Washington	23.00
7	West Virginia	25.35
2	Wisconsin	28.10
48	Wyoming	14.00

<u>RANK ORDER</u>

RANK	STATE	CENTS PER GALLON
1	Rhode Island	31.00
2	Wisconsin	28.10
3	Montana	27.00
4	Idaho	26.00
5	Pennsylvania	25.90
6	Nebraska	25.50
7	West Virginia	25.35
8	Connecticut	25.00
9	Utah	24.50
10	Nevada	24.00
10	Oregon	24.00
12	North Carolina	23.65
13	Maryland	23.50
14	Delaware	23.00
14	Kansas	23.00
14	Washington	23.00
17	New York	22.60
18	Colorado	22.00
18	Maine	22.00
18	Ohio	22.00
18	South Dakota	22.00
22	Arkansas	21.50
23	Tennessee	21.40
24	Massachusetts	21.00
24	North Dakota	21.00
26	Iowa	20.10
27	Louisiana	20.00
27	Minnesota	20.00
27	Texas	20.00
27	Vermont	20.00
31	Illinois	19.80
32	New Hampshire	19.50
33	Michigan	19.00
34	New Mexico	18.90
35	Mississippi	18.40
36	Alabama	18.00
36	Arizona	18.00
36	California	18.00
39	Virginia	17.50
40	Missouri	17.03
41	Oklahoma	17.00
42	Kentucky	16.40
43	Hawaii	16.00
43	South Carolina	16.00
45	Indiana	15.00
46	New Jersey	14.50
47	Florida	14.10
48	Wyoming	14.00
49	Alaska	8.00
50	Georgia	7.50

	District of Columbia	20.00

Source: Federation of Tax Administrators
"Motor Fuel Excise Tax Rates" (http://www.taxadmin.org/fta/rate/mf.pdf)
As of January 1, 2003. Federal gasoline tax rate is an additional 18.4 cents per gallon. Many states also allow additional local option taxes on gasoline.

State Government Motor Vehicle and Operators' License Tax Revenue in 2002

National Total = $16,941,994,000

<u>ALPHA ORDER</u>

RANK	STATE	REVENUE	% of USA
26	Alabama	$196,187,000	1.2%
49	Alaska	37,304,000	0.2%
28	Arizona	167,154,000	1.0%
37	Arkansas	110,658,000	0.7%
1	California	1,891,776,000	11.2%
27	Colorado	168,083,000	1.0%
21	Connecticut	274,407,000	1.6%
50	Delaware	32,050,000	0.2%
4	Florida	1,061,703,000	6.3%
19	Georgia	292,912,000	1.7%
43	Hawaii	79,775,000	0.5%
35	Idaho	116,768,000	0.7%
2	Illinois	1,414,163,000	8.3%
25	Indiana	197,937,000	1.2%
13	Iowa	371,739,000	2.2%
29	Kansas	153,672,000	0.9%
24	Kentucky	202,233,000	1.2%
33	Louisiana	125,213,000	0.7%
42	Maine	89,127,000	0.5%
23	Maryland	219,790,000	1.3%
17	Massachusetts	328,136,000	1.9%
5	Michigan	934,087,000	5.5%
10	Minnesota	524,564,000	3.1%
31	Mississippi	135,303,000	0.8%
22	Missouri	258,226,000	1.5%
32	Montana	131,507,000	0.8%
39	Nebraska	93,425,000	0.6%
30	Nevada	142,721,000	0.8%
41	New Hampshire	90,388,000	0.5%
12	New Jersey	404,163,000	2.4%
34	New Mexico	123,394,000	0.7%
7	New York	767,228,000	4.5%
11	North Carolina	480,185,000	2.8%
44	North Dakota	55,873,000	0.3%
8	Ohio	660,769,000	3.9%
9	Oklahoma	581,092,000	3.4%
18	Oregon	293,495,000	1.7%
6	Pennsylvania	825,285,000	4.9%
46	Rhode Island	53,777,000	0.3%
36	South Carolina	111,977,000	0.7%
48	South Dakota	43,512,000	0.3%
20	Tennessee	276,616,000	1.6%
3	Texas	1,100,546,000	6.5%
38	Utah	94,866,000	0.6%
47	Vermont	43,685,000	0.3%
16	Virginia	343,154,000	2.0%
14	Washington	349,542,000	2.1%
40	West Virginia	91,260,000	0.5%
15	Wisconsin	346,381,000	2.0%
45	Wyoming	54,186,000	0.3%

<u>RANK ORDER</u>

RANK	STATE	REVENUE	% of USA
1	California	$1,891,776,000	11.2%
2	Illinois	1,414,163,000	8.3%
3	Texas	1,100,546,000	6.5%
4	Florida	1,061,703,000	6.3%
5	Michigan	934,087,000	5.5%
6	Pennsylvania	825,285,000	4.9%
7	New York	767,228,000	4.5%
8	Ohio	660,769,000	3.9%
9	Oklahoma	581,092,000	3.4%
10	Minnesota	524,564,000	3.1%
11	North Carolina	480,185,000	2.8%
12	New Jersey	404,163,000	2.4%
13	Iowa	371,739,000	2.2%
14	Washington	349,542,000	2.1%
15	Wisconsin	346,381,000	2.0%
16	Virginia	343,154,000	2.0%
17	Massachusetts	328,136,000	1.9%
18	Oregon	293,495,000	1.7%
19	Georgia	292,912,000	1.7%
20	Tennessee	276,616,000	1.6%
21	Connecticut	274,407,000	1.6%
22	Missouri	258,226,000	1.5%
23	Maryland	219,790,000	1.3%
24	Kentucky	202,233,000	1.2%
25	Indiana	197,937,000	1.2%
26	Alabama	196,187,000	1.2%
27	Colorado	168,083,000	1.0%
28	Arizona	167,154,000	1.0%
29	Kansas	153,672,000	0.9%
30	Nevada	142,721,000	0.8%
31	Mississippi	135,303,000	0.8%
32	Montana	131,507,000	0.8%
33	Louisiana	125,213,000	0.7%
34	New Mexico	123,394,000	0.7%
35	Idaho	116,768,000	0.7%
36	South Carolina	111,977,000	0.7%
37	Arkansas	110,658,000	0.7%
38	Utah	94,866,000	0.6%
39	Nebraska	93,425,000	0.6%
40	West Virginia	91,260,000	0.5%
41	New Hampshire	90,388,000	0.5%
42	Maine	89,127,000	0.5%
43	Hawaii	79,775,000	0.5%
44	North Dakota	55,873,000	0.3%
45	Wyoming	54,186,000	0.3%
46	Rhode Island	53,777,000	0.3%
47	Vermont	43,685,000	0.3%
48	South Dakota	43,512,000	0.3%
49	Alaska	37,304,000	0.2%
50	Delaware	32,050,000	0.2%
	District of Columbia*	NA	NA

Source: U.S. Bureau of the Census, Governments Division
"2002 State Government Tax Collections" (http://www.census.gov/govs/www/statetax02.html)
**Not applicable.*

Per Capita State Government Motor Vehicle and Operators' License Tax Revenue in 2002
National Per Capita = $59.95

<u>ALPHA ORDER</u>

RANK	STATE	PER CAPITA
39	Alabama	$43.80
21	Alaska	58.15
48	Arizona	30.72
41	Arkansas	40.89
28	California	54.05
45	Colorado	37.34
11	Connecticut	79.34
44	Delaware	39.77
20	Florida	63.61
46	Georgia	34.28
18	Hawaii	64.30
9	Idaho	86.94
4	Illinois	112.36
47	Indiana	32.15
3	Iowa	126.62
26	Kansas	56.67
33	Kentucky	49.45
49	Louisiana	27.97
14	Maine	68.83
42	Maryland	40.32
29	Massachusetts	51.10
7	Michigan	93.01
6	Minnesota	104.40
35	Mississippi	47.20
38	Missouri	45.55
2	Montana	144.45
27	Nebraska	54.08
17	Nevada	65.85
12	New Hampshire	70.93
36	New Jersey	47.13
16	New Mexico	66.63
43	New York	40.10
23	North Carolina	57.81
8	North Dakota	88.14
22	Ohio	57.92
1	Oklahoma	166.52
10	Oregon	83.37
15	Pennsylvania	66.94
32	Rhode Island	50.34
50	South Carolina	27.29
25	South Dakota	57.22
34	Tennessee	47.78
30	Texas	50.63
40	Utah	40.91
13	Vermont	70.87
37	Virginia	47.09
24	Washington	57.61
31	West Virginia	50.56
19	Wisconsin	63.68
5	Wyoming	108.63

<u>RANK ORDER</u>

RANK	STATE	PER CAPITA
1	Oklahoma	$166.52
2	Montana	144.45
3	Iowa	126.62
4	Illinois	112.36
5	Wyoming	108.63
6	Minnesota	104.40
7	Michigan	93.01
8	North Dakota	88.14
9	Idaho	86.94
10	Oregon	83.37
11	Connecticut	79.34
12	New Hampshire	70.93
13	Vermont	70.87
14	Maine	68.83
15	Pennsylvania	66.94
16	New Mexico	66.63
17	Nevada	65.85
18	Hawaii	64.30
19	Wisconsin	63.68
20	Florida	63.61
21	Alaska	58.15
22	Ohio	57.92
23	North Carolina	57.81
24	Washington	57.61
25	South Dakota	57.22
26	Kansas	56.67
27	Nebraska	54.08
28	California	54.05
29	Massachusetts	51.10
30	Texas	50.63
31	West Virginia	50.56
32	Rhode Island	50.34
33	Kentucky	49.45
34	Tennessee	47.78
35	Mississippi	47.20
36	New Jersey	47.13
37	Virginia	47.09
38	Missouri	45.55
39	Alabama	43.80
40	Utah	40.91
41	Arkansas	40.89
42	Maryland	40.32
43	New York	40.10
44	Delaware	39.77
45	Colorado	37.34
46	Georgia	34.28
47	Indiana	32.15
48	Arizona	30.72
49	Louisiana	27.97
50	South Carolina	27.29

District of Columbia*   NA

State Government Tobacco Product Sales Tax Revenue in 2002

National Total = $8,902,017,000

ALPHA ORDER

RANK	STATE	TOBACCO TAX	% of USA
31	Alabama	$63,782,000	0.7%
36	Alaska	45,810,000	0.5%
16	Arizona	161,754,000	1.8%
24	Arkansas	93,073,000	1.0%
1	California	1,102,807,000	12.4%
29	Colorado	66,244,000	0.7%
17	Connecticut	158,348,000	1.8%
41	Delaware	27,652,000	0.3%
5	Florida	466,464,000	5.2%
22	Georgia	94,099,000	1.1%
30	Hawaii	65,546,000	0.7%
40	Idaho	28,392,000	0.3%
6	Illinois	464,447,000	5.2%
19	Indiana	123,215,000	1.4%
21	Iowa	94,480,000	1.1%
34	Kansas	52,342,000	0.6%
47	Kentucky	16,828,000	0.2%
18	Louisiana	128,521,000	1.4%
23	Maine	94,082,000	1.1%
13	Maryland	209,881,000	2.4%
12	Massachusetts	274,997,000	3.1%
3	Michigan	670,022,000	7.5%
15	Minnesota	173,544,000	1.9%
33	Mississippi	55,612,000	0.6%
20	Missouri	106,817,000	1.2%
49	Montana	13,281,000	0.1%
37	Nebraska	44,164,000	0.5%
32	Nevada	63,739,000	0.7%
27	New Hampshire	82,625,000	0.9%
7	New Jersey	406,856,000	4.6%
46	New Mexico	17,780,000	0.2%
2	New York	1,010,949,000	11.4%
38	North Carolina	41,531,000	0.5%
44	North Dakota	21,573,000	0.2%
11	Ohio	281,291,000	3.2%
28	Oklahoma	71,501,000	0.8%
14	Oregon	175,034,000	2.0%
9	Pennsylvania	317,442,000	3.6%
26	Rhode Island	83,099,000	0.9%
42	South Carolina	26,627,000	0.3%
45	South Dakota	18,724,000	0.2%
25	Tennessee	83,573,000	0.9%
4	Texas	540,034,000	6.1%
35	Utah	50,994,000	0.6%
43	Vermont	26,599,000	0.3%
48	Virginia	15,125,000	0.2%
8	Washington	330,730,000	3.7%
39	West Virginia	32,219,000	0.4%
10	Wisconsin	302,701,000	3.4%
50	Wyoming	5,067,000	0.1%

RANK ORDER

RANK	STATE	TOBACCO TAX	% of USA
1	California	$1,102,807,000	12.4%
2	New York	1,010,949,000	11.4%
3	Michigan	670,022,000	7.5%
4	Texas	540,034,000	6.1%
5	Florida	466,464,000	5.2%
6	Illinois	464,447,000	5.2%
7	New Jersey	406,856,000	4.6%
8	Washington	330,730,000	3.7%
9	Pennsylvania	317,442,000	3.6%
10	Wisconsin	302,701,000	3.4%
11	Ohio	281,291,000	3.2%
12	Massachusetts	274,997,000	3.1%
13	Maryland	209,881,000	2.4%
14	Oregon	175,034,000	2.0%
15	Minnesota	173,544,000	1.9%
16	Arizona	161,754,000	1.8%
17	Connecticut	158,348,000	1.8%
18	Louisiana	128,521,000	1.4%
19	Indiana	123,215,000	1.4%
20	Missouri	106,817,000	1.2%
21	Iowa	94,480,000	1.1%
22	Georgia	94,099,000	1.1%
23	Maine	94,082,000	1.1%
24	Arkansas	93,073,000	1.0%
25	Tennessee	83,573,000	0.9%
26	Rhode Island	83,099,000	0.9%
27	New Hampshire	82,625,000	0.9%
28	Oklahoma	71,501,000	0.8%
29	Colorado	66,244,000	0.7%
30	Hawaii	65,546,000	0.7%
31	Alabama	63,782,000	0.7%
32	Nevada	63,739,000	0.7%
33	Mississippi	55,612,000	0.6%
34	Kansas	52,342,000	0.6%
35	Utah	50,994,000	0.6%
36	Alaska	45,810,000	0.5%
37	Nebraska	44,164,000	0.5%
38	North Carolina	41,531,000	0.5%
39	West Virginia	32,219,000	0.4%
40	Idaho	28,392,000	0.3%
41	Delaware	27,652,000	0.3%
42	South Carolina	26,627,000	0.3%
43	Vermont	26,599,000	0.3%
44	North Dakota	21,573,000	0.2%
45	South Dakota	18,724,000	0.2%
46	New Mexico	17,780,000	0.2%
47	Kentucky	16,828,000	0.2%
48	Virginia	15,125,000	0.2%
49	Montana	13,281,000	0.1%
50	Wyoming	5,067,000	0.1%
	District of Columbia*	NA	NA

Source: U.S. Bureau of the Census, Governments Division
"2002 State Government Tax Collections" (http://www.census.gov/govs/www/statetax02.html)
*Not applicable.

Per Capita State Government Tobacco Sales Tax Revenue in 2002

National Per Capita = $30.97

ALPHA ORDER

RANK	STATE	PER CAPITA
43	Alabama	$14.24
3	Alaska	71.41
23	Arizona	29.73
18	Arkansas	34.39
22	California	31.51
40	Colorado	14.72
12	Connecticut	45.78
19	Delaware	34.31
26	Florida	27.95
44	Georgia	11.01
8	Hawaii	52.83
33	Idaho	21.14
16	Illinois	36.90
35	Indiana	20.01
21	Iowa	32.18
37	Kansas	19.30
49	Kentucky	4.11
25	Louisiana	28.71
2	Maine	72.66
15	Maryland	38.51
14	Massachusetts	42.82
4	Michigan	66.71
17	Minnesota	34.54
36	Mississippi	19.40
38	Missouri	18.84
41	Montana	14.59
28	Nebraska	25.56
24	Nevada	29.41
5	New Hampshire	64.83
11	New Jersey	47.45
46	New Mexico	9.60
8	New York	52.83
48	North Carolina	5.00
20	North Dakota	34.03
30	Ohio	24.66
34	Oklahoma	20.49
10	Oregon	49.72
27	Pennsylvania	25.75
1	Rhode Island	77.78
47	South Carolina	6.49
31	South Dakota	24.62
42	Tennessee	14.43
29	Texas	24.84
32	Utah	21.99
13	Vermont	43.15
50	Virginia	2.08
7	Washington	54.51
39	West Virginia	17.85
6	Wisconsin	55.65
45	Wyoming	10.16

RANK ORDER

RANK	STATE	PER CAPITA
1	Rhode Island	$77.78
2	Maine	72.66
3	Alaska	71.41
4	Michigan	66.71
5	New Hampshire	64.83
6	Wisconsin	55.65
7	Washington	54.51
8	Hawaii	52.83
8	New York	52.83
10	Oregon	49.72
11	New Jersey	47.45
12	Connecticut	45.78
13	Vermont	43.15
14	Massachusetts	42.82
15	Maryland	38.51
16	Illinois	36.90
17	Minnesota	34.54
18	Arkansas	34.39
19	Delaware	34.31
20	North Dakota	34.03
21	Iowa	32.18
22	California	31.51
23	Arizona	29.73
24	Nevada	29.41
25	Louisiana	28.71
26	Florida	27.95
27	Pennsylvania	25.75
28	Nebraska	25.56
29	Texas	24.84
30	Ohio	24.66
31	South Dakota	24.62
32	Utah	21.99
33	Idaho	21.14
34	Oklahoma	20.49
35	Indiana	20.01
36	Mississippi	19.40
37	Kansas	19.30
38	Missouri	18.84
39	West Virginia	17.85
40	Colorado	14.72
41	Montana	14.59
42	Tennessee	14.43
43	Alabama	14.24
44	Georgia	11.01
45	Wyoming	10.16
46	New Mexico	9.60
47	South Carolina	6.49
48	North Carolina	5.00
49	Kentucky	4.11
50	Virginia	2.08

District of Columbia*　　　　NA

*Source: Morgan Quitno Press using data from U.S. Bureau of the Census, Governments Division
"2002 State Government Tax Collections" (http://www.census.gov/govs/www/statetax02.html)
Not applicable.

State Tax on a Pack of Cigarettes in 2004

National Median = 60.0 Cents per Pack*

ALPHA ORDER

RANK	STATE	CENTS PER PACK
46	Alabama	16.5
12	Alaska	100.0
11	Arizona	118.0
26	Arkansas	59.0
18	California	87.0
42	Colorado	20.0
3	Connecticut	151.0
29	Delaware	55.0
40	Florida	33.9
37	Georgia	37.0
7	Hawaii**	130.0
27	Idaho	57.0
16	Illinois	98.0
28	Indiana	55.5
38	Iowa	36.0
20	Kansas	79.0
49	Kentucky	3.0
38	Louisiana	36.0
12	Maine	100.0
12	Maryland	100.0
3	Massachusetts	151.0
9	Michigan	125.0
34	Minnesota	48.0
44	Mississippi	18.0
45	Missouri	17.0
22	Montana	70.0
24	Nebraska	64.0
19	Nevada	80.0
33	New Hampshire	52.0
1	New Jersey	205.0
17	New Mexico	91.0
5	New York	150.0
48	North Carolina	5.0
35	North Dakota	44.0
29	Ohio	55.0
41	Oklahoma	23.0
8	Oregon	128.0
12	Pennsylvania**	100.0
2	Rhode Island	171.0
47	South Carolina	7.0
32	South Dakota	53.0
42	Tennessee	20.0
36	Texas	41.0
23	Utah	69.5
10	Vermont	119.0
50	Virginia	2.5
6	Washington	142.5
29	West Virginia	55.0
21	Wisconsin	77.0
25	Wyoming	60.0

RANK ORDER

RANK	STATE	CENTS PER PACK
1	New Jersey	205.0
2	Rhode Island	171.0
3	Connecticut	151.0
3	Massachusetts	151.0
5	New York	150.0
6	Washington	142.5
7	Hawaii**	130.0
8	Oregon	128.0
9	Michigan	125.0
10	Vermont	119.0
11	Arizona	118.0
12	Alaska	100.0
12	Maine	100.0
12	Maryland	100.0
12	Pennsylvania**	100.0
16	Illinois	98.0
17	New Mexico	91.0
18	California	87.0
19	Nevada	80.0
20	Kansas	79.0
21	Wisconsin	77.0
22	Montana	70.0
23	Utah	69.5
24	Nebraska	64.0
25	Wyoming	60.0
26	Arkansas	59.0
27	Idaho	57.0
28	Indiana	55.5
29	Delaware	55.0
29	Ohio	55.0
29	West Virginia	55.0
32	South Dakota	53.0
33	New Hampshire	52.0
34	Minnesota	48.0
35	North Dakota	44.0
36	Texas	41.0
37	Georgia	37.0
38	Iowa	36.0
38	Louisiana	36.0
40	Florida	33.9
41	Oklahoma	23.0
42	Colorado	20.0
42	Tennessee	20.0
44	Mississippi	18.0
45	Missouri	17.0
46	Alabama	16.5
47	South Carolina	7.0
48	North Carolina	5.0
49	Kentucky	3.0
50	Virginia	2.5
	District of Columbia	100.0

Source: Federation of Tax Administrators
"State Cigarette Excise Tax Rates" (http://www.taxadmin.org/fta/rate/tobacco.pdf)
*As of January 1, 2004. Many states also allow additional local option taxes on cigarettes.
**On January 7, 2004, the rate per pack will rise in Pennsylvania to $1.35. On July 1, 2004, the rate per pack will rise in Hawaii to $1.40.*

State Government Alcoholic Beverage Sales Tax Revenue in 2002

National Total = $4,258,016,000

ALPHA ORDER

RANK	STATE	LIQUOR TAX	% of USA
12	Alabama	$129,876,000	3.1%
40	Alaska	12,889,000	0.3%
22	Arizona	52,641,000	1.2%
31	Arkansas	30,739,000	0.7%
3	California	292,627,000	6.9%
32	Colorado	30,028,000	0.7%
26	Connecticut	41,619,000	1.0%
44	Delaware	11,739,000	0.3%
2	Florida	547,682,000	12.9%
8	Georgia	144,022,000	3.4%
28	Hawaii	39,090,000	0.9%
48	Idaho	6,212,000	0.1%
9	Illinois	140,854,000	3.3%
30	Indiana	34,473,000	0.8%
42	Iowa	12,508,000	0.3%
15	Kansas	81,834,000	1.9%
18	Kentucky	72,545,000	1.7%
23	Louisiana	51,360,000	1.2%
25	Maine	42,891,000	1.0%
35	Maryland	25,754,000	0.6%
19	Massachusetts	65,927,000	1.5%
10	Michigan	138,310,000	3.2%
21	Minnesota	57,495,000	1.4%
27	Mississippi	39,690,000	0.9%
34	Missouri	25,907,000	0.6%
36	Montana	18,388,000	0.4%
37	Nebraska	17,534,000	0.4%
38	Nevada	16,717,000	0.4%
43	New Hampshire	11,882,000	0.3%
16	New Jersey	81,280,000	1.9%
29	New Mexico	35,471,000	0.8%
6	New York	177,991,000	4.2%
4	North Carolina	213,986,000	5.0%
49	North Dakota	5,494,000	0.1%
14	Ohio	85,837,000	2.0%
20	Oklahoma	64,729,000	1.5%
41	Oregon	12,684,000	0.3%
5	Pennsylvania	197,426,000	4.6%
46	Rhode Island	10,271,000	0.2%
13	South Carolina	124,110,000	2.9%
45	South Dakota	11,143,000	0.3%
17	Tennessee	80,107,000	1.9%
1	Texas	560,197,000	13.2%
33	Utah	26,080,000	0.6%
39	Vermont	15,578,000	0.4%
11	Virginia	132,878,000	3.1%
7	Washington	174,170,000	4.1%
47	West Virginia	8,621,000	0.2%
24	Wisconsin	45,581,000	1.1%
50	Wyoming	1,149,000	0.0%

RANK ORDER

RANK	STATE	LIQUOR TAX	% of USA
1	Texas	$560,197,000	13.2%
2	Florida	547,682,000	12.9%
3	California	292,627,000	6.9%
4	North Carolina	213,986,000	5.0%
5	Pennsylvania	197,426,000	4.6%
6	New York	177,991,000	4.2%
7	Washington	174,170,000	4.1%
8	Georgia	144,022,000	3.4%
9	Illinois	140,854,000	3.3%
10	Michigan	138,310,000	3.2%
11	Virginia	132,878,000	3.1%
12	Alabama	129,876,000	3.1%
13	South Carolina	124,110,000	2.9%
14	Ohio	85,837,000	2.0%
15	Kansas	81,834,000	1.9%
16	New Jersey	81,280,000	1.9%
17	Tennessee	80,107,000	1.9%
18	Kentucky	72,545,000	1.7%
19	Massachusetts	65,927,000	1.5%
20	Oklahoma	64,729,000	1.5%
21	Minnesota	57,495,000	1.4%
22	Arizona	52,641,000	1.2%
23	Louisiana	51,360,000	1.2%
24	Wisconsin	45,581,000	1.1%
25	Maine	42,891,000	1.0%
26	Connecticut	41,619,000	1.0%
27	Mississippi	39,690,000	0.9%
28	Hawaii	39,090,000	0.9%
29	New Mexico	35,471,000	0.8%
30	Indiana	34,473,000	0.8%
31	Arkansas	30,739,000	0.7%
32	Colorado	30,028,000	0.7%
33	Utah	26,080,000	0.6%
34	Missouri	25,907,000	0.6%
35	Maryland	25,754,000	0.6%
36	Montana	18,388,000	0.4%
37	Nebraska	17,534,000	0.4%
38	Nevada	16,717,000	0.4%
39	Vermont	15,578,000	0.4%
40	Alaska	12,889,000	0.3%
41	Oregon	12,684,000	0.3%
42	Iowa	12,508,000	0.3%
43	New Hampshire	11,882,000	0.3%
44	Delaware	11,739,000	0.3%
45	South Dakota	11,143,000	0.3%
46	Rhode Island	10,271,000	0.2%
47	West Virginia	8,621,000	0.2%
48	Idaho	6,212,000	0.1%
49	North Dakota	5,494,000	0.1%
50	Wyoming	1,149,000	0.0%
	District of Columbia*	NA	NA

Source: U.S. Bureau of the Census, Governments Division
"2002 State Government Tax Collections" (http://www.census.gov/govs/www/statetax02.html)
*Not applicable.

Per Capita State Government Alcoholic Beverage Sales Tax Revenue in 2002

National Per Capita = $14.82

<u>ALPHA ORDER</u>

RANK	STATE	PER CAPITA
6	Alabama	$29.00
12	Alaska	20.09
32	Arizona	9.67
27	Arkansas	11.36
39	California	8.36
42	Colorado	6.67
24	Connecticut	12.03
20	Delaware	14.57
2	Florida	32.81
17	Georgia	16.86
3	Hawaii	31.51
46	Idaho	4.63
29	Illinois	11.19
43	Indiana	5.60
48	Iowa	4.26
5	Kansas	30.18
16	Kentucky	17.74
25	Louisiana	11.47
1	Maine	33.12
45	Maryland	4.73
30	Massachusetts	10.27
23	Michigan	13.77
26	Minnesota	11.44
21	Mississippi	13.85
47	Missouri	4.57
11	Montana	20.20
31	Nebraska	10.15
40	Nevada	7.71
35	New Hampshire	9.32
34	New Jersey	9.48
13	New Mexico	19.15
36	New York	9.30
9	North Carolina	25.76
37	North Dakota	8.67
41	Ohio	7.52
14	Oklahoma	18.55
49	Oregon	3.60
18	Pennsylvania	16.01
33	Rhode Island	9.61
4	South Carolina	30.24
19	South Dakota	14.65
22	Tennessee	13.84
8	Texas	25.77
28	Utah	11.25
10	Vermont	25.27
15	Virginia	18.23
7	Washington	28.71
44	West Virginia	4.78
38	Wisconsin	8.38
50	Wyoming	2.30

<u>RANK ORDER</u>

RANK	STATE	PER CAPITA
1	Maine	$33.12
2	Florida	32.81
3	Hawaii	31.51
4	South Carolina	30.24
5	Kansas	30.18
6	Alabama	29.00
7	Washington	28.71
8	Texas	25.77
9	North Carolina	25.76
10	Vermont	25.27
11	Montana	20.20
12	Alaska	20.09
13	New Mexico	19.15
14	Oklahoma	18.55
15	Virginia	18.23
16	Kentucky	17.74
17	Georgia	16.86
18	Pennsylvania	16.01
19	South Dakota	14.65
20	Delaware	14.57
21	Mississippi	13.85
22	Tennessee	13.84
23	Michigan	13.77
24	Connecticut	12.03
25	Louisiana	11.47
26	Minnesota	11.44
27	Arkansas	11.36
28	Utah	11.25
29	Illinois	11.19
30	Massachusetts	10.27
31	Nebraska	10.15
32	Arizona	9.67
33	Rhode Island	9.61
34	New Jersey	9.48
35	New Hampshire	9.32
36	New York	9.30
37	North Dakota	8.67
38	Wisconsin	8.38
39	California	8.36
40	Nevada	7.71
41	Ohio	7.52
42	Colorado	6.67
43	Indiana	5.60
44	West Virginia	4.78
45	Maryland	4.73
46	Idaho	4.63
47	Missouri	4.57
48	Iowa	4.26
49	Oregon	3.60
50	Wyoming	2.30
	District of Columbia*	NA

Source: Morgan Quitno Press using data from U.S. Bureau of the Census, Governments Division
"2002 State Government Tax Collections" (http://www.census.gov/govs/www/statetax02.html)
*Not applicable.

State Government Total Expenditures in 2001

National Total = $1,184,146,099,000*

ALPHA ORDER

RANK	STATE	EXPENDITURES	% of USA
25	Alabama	$16,718,151,000	1.4%
36	Alaska	9,047,480,000	0.8%
24	Arizona	17,143,148,000	1.4%
32	Arkansas	10,597,097,000	0.9%
1	California	170,470,259,000	14.4%
28	Colorado	15,685,926,000	1.3%
21	Connecticut	18,189,210,000	1.5%
45	Delaware	4,311,551,000	0.4%
5	Florida	50,264,767,000	4.2%
12	Georgia	27,860,155,000	2.4%
38	Hawaii	6,792,058,000	0.6%
43	Idaho	4,951,659,000	0.4%
8	Illinois	45,170,257,000	3.8%
17	Indiana	21,583,665,000	1.8%
29	Iowa	12,271,461,000	1.0%
33	Kansas	10,196,910,000	0.9%
23	Kentucky	17,330,724,000	1.5%
26	Louisiana	16,410,263,000	1.4%
41	Maine	5,737,911,000	0.5%
18	Maryland	21,484,098,000	1.8%
10	Massachusetts	32,435,081,000	2.7%
7	Michigan	46,657,684,000	3.9%
16	Minnesota	24,612,196,000	2.1%
30	Mississippi	11,727,422,000	1.0%
19	Missouri	18,888,113,000	1.6%
46	Montana	4,048,049,000	0.3%
40	Nebraska	6,111,217,000	0.5%
39	Nevada	6,747,035,000	0.6%
44	New Hampshire	4,411,243,000	0.4%
9	New Jersey	37,659,554,000	3.2%
35	New Mexico	9,173,756,000	0.8%
2	New York	106,598,603,000	9.0%
11	North Carolina	31,626,851,000	2.7%
48	North Dakota	2,897,950,000	0.2%
6	Ohio	47,880,092,000	4.0%
31	Oklahoma	11,416,492,000	1.0%
27	Oregon	16,321,295,000	1.4%
4	Pennsylvania	51,488,402,000	4.3%
42	Rhode Island	5,350,551,000	0.5%
22	South Carolina	18,078,717,000	1.5%
49	South Dakota	2,690,165,000	0.2%
20	Tennessee	18,385,079,000	1.6%
3	Texas	64,685,858,000	5.5%
34	Utah	9,253,469,000	0.8%
47	Vermont	3,370,929,000	0.3%
14	Virginia	26,786,593,000	2.3%
13	Washington	27,824,006,000	2.3%
37	West Virginia	7,300,483,000	0.6%
15	Wisconsin	24,857,238,000	2.1%
50	Wyoming	2,645,226,000	0.2%

RANK ORDER

RANK	STATE	EXPENDITURES	% of USA
1	California	$170,470,259,000	14.4%
2	New York	106,598,603,000	9.0%
3	Texas	64,685,858,000	5.5%
4	Pennsylvania	51,488,402,000	4.3%
5	Florida	50,264,767,000	4.2%
6	Ohio	47,880,092,000	4.0%
7	Michigan	46,657,684,000	3.9%
8	Illinois	45,170,257,000	3.8%
9	New Jersey	37,659,554,000	3.2%
10	Massachusetts	32,435,081,000	2.7%
11	North Carolina	31,626,851,000	2.7%
12	Georgia	27,860,155,000	2.4%
13	Washington	27,824,006,000	2.3%
14	Virginia	26,786,593,000	2.3%
15	Wisconsin	24,857,238,000	2.1%
16	Minnesota	24,612,196,000	2.1%
17	Indiana	21,583,665,000	1.8%
18	Maryland	21,484,098,000	1.8%
19	Missouri	18,888,113,000	1.6%
20	Tennessee	18,385,079,000	1.6%
21	Connecticut	18,189,210,000	1.5%
22	South Carolina	18,078,717,000	1.5%
23	Kentucky	17,330,724,000	1.5%
24	Arizona	17,143,148,000	1.4%
25	Alabama	16,718,151,000	1.4%
26	Louisiana	16,410,263,000	1.4%
27	Oregon	16,321,295,000	1.4%
28	Colorado	15,685,926,000	1.3%
29	Iowa	12,271,461,000	1.0%
30	Mississippi	11,727,422,000	1.0%
31	Oklahoma	11,416,492,000	1.0%
32	Arkansas	10,597,097,000	0.9%
33	Kansas	10,196,910,000	0.9%
34	Utah	9,253,469,000	0.8%
35	New Mexico	9,173,756,000	0.8%
36	Alaska	9,047,480,000	0.8%
37	West Virginia	7,300,483,000	0.6%
38	Hawaii	6,792,058,000	0.6%
39	Nevada	6,747,035,000	0.6%
40	Nebraska	6,111,217,000	0.5%
41	Maine	5,737,911,000	0.5%
42	Rhode Island	5,350,551,000	0.5%
43	Idaho	4,951,659,000	0.4%
44	New Hampshire	4,411,243,000	0.4%
45	Delaware	4,311,551,000	0.4%
46	Montana	4,048,049,000	0.3%
47	Vermont	3,370,929,000	0.3%
48	North Dakota	2,897,950,000	0.2%
49	South Dakota	2,690,165,000	0.2%
50	Wyoming	2,645,226,000	0.2%
	District of Columbia**	NA	NA

Source: U.S. Bureau of the Census, Governments Division
"2001 State Government Finances" (http://www.census.gov/govs/www/state01.html)

*Total expenditures includes all money paid other than for retirement of debt and extension of loans. Includes payments from all sources of funds including current revenues and proceeds from borrowing and prior year fund balances. Includes intergovernmental transfers and expenditures for government owned utilities and other commercial or auxiliary enterprise and insurance trust expenditures. **Not applicable.

Per Capita State Government Total Expenditures in 2001

National Per Capita = $4,162*

ALPHA ORDER

RANK	STATE	PER CAPITA
34	Alabama	$3,743
1	Alaska	14,300
46	Arizona	3,236
30	Arkansas	3,936
12	California	4,936
40	Colorado	3,542
7	Connecticut	5,299
5	Delaware	5,419
49	Florida	3,073
44	Georgia	3,319
3	Hawaii	5,544
33	Idaho	3,748
37	Illinois	3,609
41	Indiana	3,523
25	Iowa	4,185
32	Kansas	3,776
22	Kentucky	4,261
36	Louisiana	3,674
19	Maine	4,466
29	Maryland	3,991
8	Massachusetts	5,068
14	Michigan	4,663
11	Minnesota	4,937
26	Mississippi	4,104
43	Missouri	3,351
18	Montana	4,468
38	Nebraska	3,555
47	Nevada	3,221
42	New Hampshire	3,504
21	New Jersey	4,428
10	New Mexico	5,015
2	New York	5,588
31	North Carolina	3,859
17	North Dakota	4,554
23	Ohio	4,205
45	Oklahoma	3,293
13	Oregon	4,700
24	Pennsylvania	4,187
9	Rhode Island	5,052
20	South Carolina	4,453
39	South Dakota	3,548
48	Tennessee	3,200
50	Texas	3,031
27	Utah	4,059
4	Vermont	5,500
35	Virginia	3,724
15	Washington	4,643
28	West Virginia	4,052
16	Wisconsin	4,599
6	Wyoming	5,358

RANK ORDER

RANK	STATE	PER CAPITA
1	Alaska	$14,300
2	New York	5,588
3	Hawaii	5,544
4	Vermont	5,500
5	Delaware	5,419
6	Wyoming	5,358
7	Connecticut	5,299
8	Massachusetts	5,068
9	Rhode Island	5,052
10	New Mexico	5,015
11	Minnesota	4,937
12	California	4,936
13	Oregon	4,700
14	Michigan	4,663
15	Washington	4,643
16	Wisconsin	4,599
17	North Dakota	4,554
18	Montana	4,468
19	Maine	4,466
20	South Carolina	4,453
21	New Jersey	4,428
22	Kentucky	4,261
23	Ohio	4,205
24	Pennsylvania	4,187
25	Iowa	4,185
26	Mississippi	4,104
27	Utah	4,059
28	West Virginia	4,052
29	Maryland	3,991
30	Arkansas	3,936
31	North Carolina	3,859
32	Kansas	3,776
33	Idaho	3,748
34	Alabama	3,743
35	Virginia	3,724
36	Louisiana	3,674
37	Illinois	3,609
38	Nebraska	3,555
39	South Dakota	3,548
40	Colorado	3,542
41	Indiana	3,523
42	New Hampshire	3,504
43	Missouri	3,351
44	Georgia	3,319
45	Oklahoma	3,293
46	Arizona	3,236
47	Nevada	3,221
48	Tennessee	3,200
49	Florida	3,073
50	Texas	3,031

District of Columbia**   NA

Source: Morgan Quitno Press using data from U.S. Bureau of the Census, Governments Division
   "2001 State Government Finances" (http://www.census.gov/govs/www/state01.html)
*Total expenditures includes all money paid other than for retirement of debt and extension of loans. Includes payments from all sources of funds including current revenues and proceeds from borrowing and prior year fund balances. Includes intergovernmental transfers and expenditures for government owned utilities and other commercial or auxiliary enterprise and insurance trust expenditures. **Not applicable.

State Government Direct General Expenditures in 2001

National Total = $693,010,511,000*

ALPHA ORDER

RANK	STATE	EXPENDITURES	% of USA
24	Alabama	$11,163,261,000	1.6%
30	Alaska	7,402,157,000	1.1%
28	Arizona	9,089,057,000	1.3%
32	Arkansas	6,906,308,000	1.0%
1	California	75,834,873,000	10.9%
26	Colorado	9,793,044,000	1.4%
18	Connecticut	12,845,134,000	1.9%
43	Delaware	3,164,166,000	0.5%
5	Florida	31,584,767,000	4.6%
12	Georgia	17,279,162,000	2.5%
36	Hawaii	6,020,302,000	0.9%
44	Idaho	3,063,026,000	0.4%
6	Illinois	27,474,902,000	4.0%
17	Indiana	13,202,816,000	1.9%
29	Iowa	7,914,449,000	1.1%
33	Kansas	6,452,441,000	0.9%
22	Kentucky	12,015,655,000	1.7%
25	Louisiana	10,669,394,000	1.5%
39	Maine	4,236,015,000	0.6%
15	Maryland	14,239,944,000	2.1%
9	Massachusetts	22,601,784,000	3.3%
8	Michigan	24,107,153,000	3.5%
16	Minnesota	13,762,013,000	2.0%
31	Mississippi	7,255,892,000	1.0%
21	Missouri	12,320,707,000	1.8%
46	Montana	2,755,864,000	0.4%
40	Nebraska	4,158,449,000	0.6%
42	Nevada	3,599,541,000	0.5%
45	New Hampshire	2,849,891,000	0.4%
10	New Jersey	21,395,015,000	3.1%
37	New Mexico	5,837,259,000	0.8%
2	New York	54,523,983,000	7.9%
11	North Carolina	19,550,727,000	2.8%
48	North Dakota	2,104,159,000	0.3%
7	Ohio	24,440,667,000	3.5%
35	Oklahoma	6,311,419,000	0.9%
27	Oregon	9,518,882,000	1.4%
4	Pennsylvania	32,396,418,000	4.7%
41	Rhode Island	3,944,731,000	0.6%
23	South Carolina	11,506,436,000	1.7%
49	South Dakota	2,010,620,000	0.3%
20	Tennessee	12,552,746,000	1.8%
3	Texas	40,978,796,000	5.9%
34	Utah	6,387,904,000	0.9%
47	Vermont	2,280,543,000	0.3%
14	Virginia	17,000,319,000	2.5%
13	Washington	17,020,682,000	2.5%
38	West Virginia	5,176,922,000	0.7%
19	Wisconsin	12,798,037,000	1.8%
50	Wyoming	1,512,079,000	0.2%

RANK ORDER

RANK	STATE	EXPENDITURES	% of USA
1	California	$75,834,873,000	10.9%
2	New York	54,523,983,000	7.9%
3	Texas	40,978,796,000	5.9%
4	Pennsylvania	32,396,418,000	4.7%
5	Florida	31,584,767,000	4.6%
6	Illinois	27,474,902,000	4.0%
7	Ohio	24,440,667,000	3.5%
8	Michigan	24,107,153,000	3.5%
9	Massachusetts	22,601,784,000	3.3%
10	New Jersey	21,395,015,000	3.1%
11	North Carolina	19,550,727,000	2.8%
12	Georgia	17,279,162,000	2.5%
13	Washington	17,020,682,000	2.5%
14	Virginia	17,000,319,000	2.5%
15	Maryland	14,239,944,000	2.1%
16	Minnesota	13,762,013,000	2.0%
17	Indiana	13,202,816,000	1.9%
18	Connecticut	12,845,134,000	1.9%
19	Wisconsin	12,798,037,000	1.8%
20	Tennessee	12,552,746,000	1.8%
21	Missouri	12,320,707,000	1.8%
22	Kentucky	12,015,655,000	1.7%
23	South Carolina	11,506,436,000	1.7%
24	Alabama	11,163,261,000	1.6%
25	Louisiana	10,669,394,000	1.5%
26	Colorado	9,793,044,000	1.4%
27	Oregon	9,518,882,000	1.4%
28	Arizona	9,089,057,000	1.3%
29	Iowa	7,914,449,000	1.1%
30	Alaska	7,402,157,000	1.1%
31	Mississippi	7,255,892,000	1.0%
32	Arkansas	6,906,308,000	1.0%
33	Kansas	6,452,441,000	0.9%
34	Utah	6,387,904,000	0.9%
35	Oklahoma	6,311,419,000	0.9%
36	Hawaii	6,020,302,000	0.9%
37	New Mexico	5,837,259,000	0.8%
38	West Virginia	5,176,922,000	0.7%
39	Maine	4,236,015,000	0.6%
40	Nebraska	4,158,449,000	0.6%
41	Rhode Island	3,944,731,000	0.6%
42	Nevada	3,599,541,000	0.5%
43	Delaware	3,164,166,000	0.5%
44	Idaho	3,063,026,000	0.4%
45	New Hampshire	2,849,891,000	0.4%
46	Montana	2,755,864,000	0.4%
47	Vermont	2,280,543,000	0.3%
48	North Dakota	2,104,159,000	0.3%
49	South Dakota	2,010,620,000	0.3%
50	Wyoming	1,512,079,000	0.2%
	District of Columbia**	NA	NA

Source: U.S. Bureau of the Census, Governments Division
   "2001 State Government Finances" (http://www.census.gov/govs/www/state01.html)
*Direct general expenditures include expenditures for current operations, assistance and subsidies, interest on debt and capital outlay. Excludes intergovernmental transfers, expenditures for government owned utilities and other commercial or auxiliary enterprise and insurance trust expenditures.
**Not applicable.

Per Capita State Government Direct General Expenditures in 2001

National Per Capita = $2,436*

ALPHA ORDER

RANK	STATE	PER CAPITA
28	Alabama	$2,499
1	Alaska	11,700
50	Arizona	1,716
25	Arkansas	2,565
39	California	2,196
38	Colorado	2,211
4	Connecticut	3,742
3	Delaware	3,977
46	Florida	1,931
45	Georgia	2,058
2	Hawaii	4,914
36	Idaho	2,318
40	Illinois	2,195
43	Indiana	2,155
21	Iowa	2,699
31	Kansas	2,389
13	Kentucky	2,954
31	Louisiana	2,389
9	Maine	3,297
23	Maryland	2,645
7	Massachusetts	3,532
30	Michigan	2,409
19	Minnesota	2,761
26	Mississippi	2,539
41	Missouri	2,186
12	Montana	3,042
29	Nebraska	2,419
49	Nevada	1,718
37	New Hampshire	2,264
27	New Jersey	2,516
10	New Mexico	3,191
15	New York	2,858
33	North Carolina	2,386
8	North Dakota	3,307
44	Ohio	2,147
48	Oklahoma	1,820
20	Oregon	2,741
24	Pennsylvania	2,634
5	Rhode Island	3,725
17	South Carolina	2,834
22	South Dakota	2,652
42	Tennessee	2,185
47	Texas	1,920
18	Utah	2,802
6	Vermont	3,721
35	Virginia	2,364
16	Washington	2,840
14	West Virginia	2,873
34	Wisconsin	2,368
11	Wyoming	3,063

RANK ORDER

RANK	STATE	PER CAPITA
1	Alaska	$11,700
2	Hawaii	4,914
3	Delaware	3,977
4	Connecticut	3,742
5	Rhode Island	3,725
6	Vermont	3,721
7	Massachusetts	3,532
8	North Dakota	3,307
9	Maine	3,297
10	New Mexico	3,191
11	Wyoming	3,063
12	Montana	3,042
13	Kentucky	2,954
14	West Virginia	2,873
15	New York	2,858
16	Washington	2,840
17	South Carolina	2,834
18	Utah	2,802
19	Minnesota	2,761
20	Oregon	2,741
21	Iowa	2,699
22	South Dakota	2,652
23	Maryland	2,645
24	Pennsylvania	2,634
25	Arkansas	2,565
26	Mississippi	2,539
27	New Jersey	2,516
28	Alabama	2,499
29	Nebraska	2,419
30	Michigan	2,409
31	Kansas	2,389
31	Louisiana	2,389
33	North Carolina	2,386
34	Wisconsin	2,368
35	Virginia	2,364
36	Idaho	2,318
37	New Hampshire	2,264
38	Colorado	2,211
39	California	2,196
40	Illinois	2,195
41	Missouri	2,186
42	Tennessee	2,185
43	Indiana	2,155
44	Ohio	2,147
45	Georgia	2,058
46	Florida	1,931
47	Texas	1,920
48	Oklahoma	1,820
49	Nevada	1,718
50	Arizona	1,716

District of Columbia** NA

Source: Morgan Quitno Press using data from U.S. Bureau of the Census, Governments Division
   "2001 State Government Finances" (http://www.census.gov/govs/www/state01.html)
*Direct general expenditures include expenditures for current operations, assistance and subsidies, interest on debt and capital outlay. Excludes intergovernmental transfers, expenditures for government owned utilities and other commercial or auxiliary enterprise and insurance trust expenditures.
**Not applicable.

State Government Debt Outstanding in 2001

National Total = $576,599,213,000*

ALPHA ORDER

RANK	STATE	DEBT	% of USA
28	Alabama	$5,577,158,000	1.0%
31	Alaska	4,507,108,000	0.8%
38	Arizona	3,710,911,000	0.6%
41	Arkansas	2,841,828,000	0.5%
2	California	62,343,083,000	10.8%
30	Colorado	4,917,187,000	0.9%
8	Connecticut	19,027,060,000	3.3%
36	Delaware	3,888,567,000	0.7%
10	Florida	18,613,380,000	3.2%
22	Georgia	7,520,051,000	1.3%
29	Hawaii	5,300,649,000	0.9%
44	Idaho	2,341,978,000	0.4%
4	Illinois	30,247,654,000	5.2%
19	Indiana	8,517,915,000	1.5%
43	Iowa	2,542,400,000	0.4%
47	Kansas	2,183,859,000	0.4%
20	Kentucky	8,347,565,000	1.4%
21	Louisiana	7,977,398,000	1.4%
33	Maine	4,210,901,000	0.7%
15	Maryland	11,661,413,000	2.0%
3	Massachusetts	42,149,219,000	7.3%
6	Michigan	20,114,054,000	3.5%
26	Minnesota	5,623,878,000	1.0%
37	Mississippi	3,819,476,000	0.7%
16	Missouri	11,373,216,000	2.0%
42	Montana	2,739,648,000	0.5%
48	Nebraska	1,799,628,000	0.3%
40	Nevada	3,387,247,000	0.6%
27	New Hampshire	5,607,884,000	1.0%
5	New Jersey	29,727,858,000	5.2%
32	New Mexico	4,304,803,000	0.7%
1	New York	80,384,892,000	13.9%
17	North Carolina	9,998,034,000	1.7%
49	North Dakota	1,549,350,000	0.3%
9	Ohio	18,748,257,000	3.3%
24	Oklahoma	5,985,516,000	1.0%
23	Oregon	6,417,534,000	1.1%
7	Pennsylvania	19,249,044,000	3.3%
25	Rhode Island	5,832,702,000	1.0%
18	South Carolina	9,560,312,000	1.7%
46	South Dakota	2,215,512,000	0.4%
39	Tennessee	3,387,622,000	0.6%
11	Texas	16,815,848,000	2.9%
35	Utah	4,022,974,000	0.7%
45	Vermont	2,325,609,000	0.4%
12	Virginia	12,963,092,000	2.2%
13	Washington	12,607,489,000	2.2%
34	West Virginia	4,091,919,000	0.7%
14	Wisconsin	12,172,209,000	2.1%
50	Wyoming	1,346,322,000	0.2%

RANK ORDER

RANK	STATE	DEBT	% of USA
1	New York	$80,384,892,000	13.9%
2	California	62,343,083,000	10.8%
3	Massachusetts	42,149,219,000	7.3%
4	Illinois	30,247,654,000	5.2%
5	New Jersey	29,727,858,000	5.2%
6	Michigan	20,114,054,000	3.5%
7	Pennsylvania	19,249,044,000	3.3%
8	Connecticut	19,027,060,000	3.3%
9	Ohio	18,748,257,000	3.3%
10	Florida	18,613,380,000	3.2%
11	Texas	16,815,848,000	2.9%
12	Virginia	12,963,092,000	2.2%
13	Washington	12,607,489,000	2.2%
14	Wisconsin	12,172,209,000	2.1%
15	Maryland	11,661,413,000	2.0%
16	Missouri	11,373,216,000	2.0%
17	North Carolina	9,998,034,000	1.7%
18	South Carolina	9,560,312,000	1.7%
19	Indiana	8,517,915,000	1.5%
20	Kentucky	8,347,565,000	1.4%
21	Louisiana	7,977,398,000	1.4%
22	Georgia	7,520,051,000	1.3%
23	Oregon	6,417,534,000	1.1%
24	Oklahoma	5,985,516,000	1.0%
25	Rhode Island	5,832,702,000	1.0%
26	Minnesota	5,623,878,000	1.0%
27	New Hampshire	5,607,884,000	1.0%
28	Alabama	5,577,158,000	1.0%
29	Hawaii	5,300,649,000	0.9%
30	Colorado	4,917,187,000	0.9%
31	Alaska	4,507,108,000	0.8%
32	New Mexico	4,304,803,000	0.7%
33	Maine	4,210,901,000	0.7%
34	West Virginia	4,091,919,000	0.7%
35	Utah	4,022,974,000	0.7%
36	Delaware	3,888,567,000	0.7%
37	Mississippi	3,819,476,000	0.7%
38	Arizona	3,710,911,000	0.6%
39	Tennessee	3,387,622,000	0.6%
40	Nevada	3,387,247,000	0.6%
41	Arkansas	2,841,828,000	0.5%
42	Montana	2,739,648,000	0.5%
43	Iowa	2,542,400,000	0.4%
44	Idaho	2,341,978,000	0.4%
45	Vermont	2,325,609,000	0.4%
46	South Dakota	2,215,512,000	0.4%
47	Kansas	2,183,859,000	0.4%
48	Nebraska	1,799,628,000	0.3%
49	North Dakota	1,549,350,000	0.3%
50	Wyoming	1,346,322,000	0.2%
	District of Columbia**	NA	NA

Source: U.S. Bureau of the Census, Governments Division
"2001 State Government Finances" (http://www.census.gov/govs/www/state01.html)
*Includes short-term, long-term, full faith and credit, nonguaranteed and public debt for private purposes.
**Not applicable.

Per Capita State Government Debt Outstanding in 2001

National Per Capita = $2,027*

<u>ALPHA ORDER</u>

RANK	STATE	PER CAPITA
38	Alabama	$1,249
1	Alaska	7,124
49	Arizona	700
43	Arkansas	1,056
27	California	1,805
42	Colorado	1,110
3	Connecticut	5,543
5	Delaware	4,888
40	Florida	1,138
45	Georgia	896
7	Hawaii	4,327
30	Idaho	1,772
16	Illinois	2,416
36	Indiana	1,390
46	Iowa	867
47	Kansas	809
23	Kentucky	2,052
29	Louisiana	1,786
11	Maine	3,278
21	Maryland	2,166
2	Massachusetts	6,586
25	Michigan	2,010
41	Minnesota	1,128
37	Mississippi	1,337
24	Missouri	2,018
12	Montana	3,024
44	Nebraska	1,047
34	Nevada	1,617
6	New Hampshire	4,454
10	New Jersey	3,496
18	New Mexico	2,353
8	New York	4,214
39	North Carolina	1,220
15	North Dakota	2,435
33	Ohio	1,647
32	Oklahoma	1,726
26	Oregon	1,848
35	Pennsylvania	1,565
4	Rhode Island	5,508
17	South Carolina	2,355
13	South Dakota	2,922
50	Tennessee	590
48	Texas	788
31	Utah	1,765
9	Vermont	3,794
28	Virginia	1,802
22	Washington	2,104
19	West Virginia	2,271
20	Wisconsin	2,252
14	Wyoming	2,727

<u>RANK ORDER</u>

RANK	STATE	PER CAPITA
1	Alaska	$7,124
2	Massachusetts	6,586
3	Connecticut	5,543
4	Rhode Island	5,508
5	Delaware	4,888
6	New Hampshire	4,454
7	Hawaii	4,327
8	New York	4,214
9	Vermont	3,794
10	New Jersey	3,496
11	Maine	3,278
12	Montana	3,024
13	South Dakota	2,922
14	Wyoming	2,727
15	North Dakota	2,435
16	Illinois	2,416
17	South Carolina	2,355
18	New Mexico	2,353
19	West Virginia	2,271
20	Wisconsin	2,252
21	Maryland	2,166
22	Washington	2,104
23	Kentucky	2,052
24	Missouri	2,018
25	Michigan	2,010
26	Oregon	1,848
27	California	1,805
28	Virginia	1,802
29	Louisiana	1,786
30	Idaho	1,772
31	Utah	1,765
32	Oklahoma	1,726
33	Ohio	1,647
34	Nevada	1,617
35	Pennsylvania	1,565
36	Indiana	1,390
37	Mississippi	1,337
38	Alabama	1,249
39	North Carolina	1,220
40	Florida	1,138
41	Minnesota	1,128
42	Colorado	1,110
43	Arkansas	1,056
44	Nebraska	1,047
45	Georgia	896
46	Iowa	867
47	Kansas	809
48	Texas	788
49	Arizona	700
50	Tennessee	590
	District of Columbia**	NA

*Source: Morgan Quitno Press using data from U.S. Bureau of the Census, Governments Division
"2001 State Government Finances" (http://www.census.gov/govs/www/state01.html)*
Includes short-term, long-term, full faith and credit, nonguaranteed and public debt for private purposes.
***Not applicable.*

State Government Full-Time Equivalent Employees in 2002

National Total = 4,222,751 FTE Employees*

<u>ALPHA ORDER</u>

RANK	STATE	EMPLOYEES	% of USA
19	Alabama	85,665	2.0%
40	Alaska	24,811	0.6%
26	Arizona	66,387	1.6%
32	Arkansas	53,231	1.3%
1	California	378,362	9.0%
28	Colorado	65,932	1.6%
25	Connecticut	66,869	1.6%
39	Delaware	24,826	0.6%
4	Florida	184,793	4.4%
11	Georgia	122,825	2.9%
30	Hawaii	55,972	1.3%
42	Idaho	23,845	0.6%
7	Illinois	146,669	3.5%
18	Indiana	90,254	2.1%
33	Iowa	52,261	1.2%
36	Kansas	44,372	1.1%
22	Kentucky	78,126	1.9%
16	Louisiana	91,752	2.2%
43	Maine	21,904	0.5%
15	Maryland	92,244	2.2%
14	Massachusetts	95,435	2.3%
8	Michigan	142,860	3.4%
23	Minnesota	75,725	1.8%
29	Mississippi	56,952	1.3%
17	Missouri	91,713	2.2%
46	Montana	17,776	0.4%
38	Nebraska	33,155	0.8%
41	Nevada	24,454	0.6%
45	New Hampshire	19,995	0.5%
6	New Jersey	147,813	3.5%
35	New Mexico	45,490	1.1%
3	New York	252,512	6.0%
10	North Carolina	134,898	3.2%
47	North Dakota	16,625	0.4%
9	Ohio	138,086	3.3%
27	Oklahoma	66,341	1.6%
31	Oregon	55,292	1.3%
5	Pennsylvania	157,088	3.7%
44	Rhode Island	20,085	0.5%
21	South Carolina	78,362	1.9%
49	South Dakota	13,136	0.3%
20	Tennessee	83,862	2.0%
2	Texas	269,674	6.4%
34	Utah	49,092	1.2%
48	Vermont	13,721	0.3%
12	Virginia	120,793	2.9%
13	Washington	114,329	2.7%
37	West Virginia	34,279	0.8%
24	Wisconsin	70,873	1.7%
50	Wyoming	11,235	0.3%

<u>RANK ORDER</u>

RANK	STATE	EMPLOYEES	% of USA
1	California	378,362	9.0%
2	Texas	269,674	6.4%
3	New York	252,512	6.0%
4	Florida	184,793	4.4%
5	Pennsylvania	157,088	3.7%
6	New Jersey	147,813	3.5%
7	Illinois	146,669	3.5%
8	Michigan	142,860	3.4%
9	Ohio	138,086	3.3%
10	North Carolina	134,898	3.2%
11	Georgia	122,825	2.9%
12	Virginia	120,793	2.9%
13	Washington	114,329	2.7%
14	Massachusetts	95,435	2.3%
15	Maryland	92,244	2.2%
16	Louisiana	91,752	2.2%
17	Missouri	91,713	2.2%
18	Indiana	90,254	2.1%
19	Alabama	85,665	2.0%
20	Tennessee	83,862	2.0%
21	South Carolina	78,362	1.9%
22	Kentucky	78,126	1.9%
23	Minnesota	75,725	1.8%
24	Wisconsin	70,873	1.7%
25	Connecticut	66,869	1.6%
26	Arizona	66,387	1.6%
27	Oklahoma	66,341	1.6%
28	Colorado	65,932	1.6%
29	Mississippi	56,952	1.3%
30	Hawaii	55,972	1.3%
31	Oregon	55,292	1.3%
32	Arkansas	53,231	1.3%
33	Iowa	52,261	1.2%
34	Utah	49,092	1.2%
35	New Mexico	45,490	1.1%
36	Kansas	44,372	1.1%
37	West Virginia	34,279	0.8%
38	Nebraska	33,155	0.8%
39	Delaware	24,826	0.6%
40	Alaska	24,811	0.6%
41	Nevada	24,454	0.6%
42	Idaho	23,845	0.6%
43	Maine	21,904	0.5%
44	Rhode Island	20,085	0.5%
45	New Hampshire	19,995	0.5%
46	Montana	17,776	0.4%
47	North Dakota	16,625	0.4%
48	Vermont	13,721	0.3%
49	South Dakota	13,136	0.3%
50	Wyoming	11,235	0.3%
	District of Columbia**	NA	NA

Source: U.S. Bureau of the Census, Governments Division
 "2002 State Government Employment and Payroll" (http://www.census.gov/govs/www/apesst02.html)
**As of March 2002.*
***Not applicable.*

Rate of State Government FTE Employees in 2002

National Rate = 147 State Government Employees per 10,000 Population*

ALPHA ORDER

RANK	STATE	RATE
15	Alabama	191
2	Alaska	387
45	Arizona	122
11	Arkansas	197
50	California	108
37	Colorado	146
13	Connecticut	193
3	Delaware	308
49	Florida	111
39	Georgia	144
1	Hawaii	451
22	Idaho	178
47	Illinois	117
36	Indiana	147
22	Iowa	178
29	Kansas	164
15	Kentucky	191
9	Louisiana	205
26	Maine	169
26	Maryland	169
35	Massachusetts	149
40	Michigan	142
34	Minnesota	151
10	Mississippi	199
30	Missouri	162
12	Montana	195
14	Nebraska	192
48	Nevada	113
32	New Hampshire	157
25	New Jersey	172
5	New Mexico	246
41	New York	132
30	North Carolina	162
4	North Dakota	262
46	Ohio	121
18	Oklahoma	190
32	Oregon	157
43	Pennsylvania	127
20	Rhode Island	188
15	South Carolina	191
24	South Dakota	173
38	Tennessee	145
44	Texas	124
8	Utah	212
7	Vermont	223
28	Virginia	166
20	Washington	188
18	West Virginia	190
42	Wisconsin	130
6	Wyoming	225

RANK ORDER

RANK	STATE	RATE
1	Hawaii	451
2	Alaska	387
3	Delaware	308
4	North Dakota	262
5	New Mexico	246
6	Wyoming	225
7	Vermont	223
8	Utah	212
9	Louisiana	205
10	Mississippi	199
11	Arkansas	197
12	Montana	195
13	Connecticut	193
14	Nebraska	192
15	Alabama	191
15	Kentucky	191
15	South Carolina	191
18	Oklahoma	190
18	West Virginia	190
20	Rhode Island	188
20	Washington	188
22	Idaho	178
22	Iowa	178
24	South Dakota	173
25	New Jersey	172
26	Maine	169
26	Maryland	169
28	Virginia	166
29	Kansas	164
30	Missouri	162
30	North Carolina	162
32	New Hampshire	157
32	Oregon	157
34	Minnesota	151
35	Massachusetts	149
36	Indiana	147
37	Colorado	146
38	Tennessee	145
39	Georgia	144
40	Michigan	142
41	New York	132
42	Wisconsin	130
43	Pennsylvania	127
44	Texas	124
45	Arizona	122
46	Ohio	121
47	Illinois	117
48	Nevada	113
49	Florida	111
50	California	108
	District of Columbia**	NA

Source: Morgan Quitno Press using data from U.S. Bureau of the Census, Governments Division
"2002 State Government Employment and Payroll" (http://www.census.gov/govs/www/apesst02.html)
*Full-time equivalent as of March 2002.
**Not applicable.

Average Annual Earnings of FTE State Government Employees in 2002

National Average = $42,165*

ALPHA ORDER

RANK	STATE	EARNINGS
28	Alabama	$38,010
8	Alaska	46,527
33	Arizona	37,336
44	Arkansas	34,466
1	California	54,597
9	Colorado	46,453
4	Connecticut	49,094
18	Delaware	41,043
30	Florida	37,846
35	Georgia	36,471
34	Hawaii	37,108
39	Idaho	35,401
16	Illinois	43,001
36	Indiana	36,025
12	Iowa	44,601
25	Kansas	38,846
32	Kentucky	37,385
40	Louisiana	35,372
24	Maine	38,912
10	Maryland	45,466
6	Massachusetts	47,269
11	Michigan	44,942
5	Minnesota	48,025
50	Mississippi	32,505
49	Missouri	32,874
31	Montana	37,511
48	Nebraska	33,179
17	Nevada	42,479
23	New Hampshire	39,034
2	New Jersey	51,451
41	New Mexico	34,731
3	New York	50,875
27	North Carolina	38,378
47	North Dakota	33,556
19	Ohio	41,025
37	Oklahoma	35,886
21	Oregon	39,905
14	Pennsylvania	43,385
7	Rhode Island	46,682
42	South Carolina	34,654
43	South Dakota	34,571
45	Tennessee	34,378
26	Texas	38,684
29	Utah	37,900
20	Vermont	40,843
22	Virginia	39,434
15	Washington	43,096
46	West Virginia	34,094
13	Wisconsin	44,208
38	Wyoming	35,433

RANK ORDER

RANK	STATE	EARNINGS
1	California	$54,597
2	New Jersey	51,451
3	New York	50,875
4	Connecticut	49,094
5	Minnesota	48,025
6	Massachusetts	47,269
7	Rhode Island	46,682
8	Alaska	46,527
9	Colorado	46,453
10	Maryland	45,466
11	Michigan	44,942
12	Iowa	44,601
13	Wisconsin	44,208
14	Pennsylvania	43,385
15	Washington	43,096
16	Illinois	43,001
17	Nevada	42,479
18	Delaware	41,043
19	Ohio	41,025
20	Vermont	40,843
21	Oregon	39,905
22	Virginia	39,434
23	New Hampshire	39,034
24	Maine	38,912
25	Kansas	38,846
26	Texas	38,684
27	North Carolina	38,378
28	Alabama	38,010
29	Utah	37,900
30	Florida	37,846
31	Montana	37,511
32	Kentucky	37,385
33	Arizona	37,336
34	Hawaii	37,108
35	Georgia	36,471
36	Indiana	36,025
37	Oklahoma	35,886
38	Wyoming	35,433
39	Idaho	35,401
40	Louisiana	35,372
41	New Mexico	34,731
42	South Carolina	34,654
43	South Dakota	34,571
44	Arkansas	34,466
45	Tennessee	34,378
46	West Virginia	34,094
47	North Dakota	33,556
48	Nebraska	33,179
49	Missouri	32,874
50	Mississippi	32,505

District of Columbia**   NA

Source: Morgan Quitno Press using data from U.S. Bureau of the Census, Governments Division
   "2002 State Government Employment and Payroll" (http://www.census.gov/govs/www/apesst02.html)
*March 2002 total payroll (multiplied by 12) divided by full-time equivalent employees.

Local Government Total Revenue in 2000

National Total = $1,013,824,631,000*

ALPHA ORDER

RANK	STATE	REVENUE	% of USA
23	Alabama	$13,045,686,000	1.3%
42	Alaska	2,834,723,000	0.3%
19	Arizona	17,364,747,000	1.7%
36	Arkansas	5,718,268,000	0.6%
1	California	160,439,009,000	15.8%
21	Colorado	15,788,669,000	1.6%
26	Connecticut	11,190,025,000	1.1%
46	Delaware	1,920,650,000	0.2%
4	Florida	55,504,603,000	5.5%
10	Georgia	27,036,116,000	2.7%
49	Hawaii	1,703,365,000	0.2%
39	Idaho	3,294,439,000	0.3%
5	Illinois	45,243,179,000	4.5%
18	Indiana	18,045,743,000	1.8%
28	Iowa	9,052,574,000	0.9%
30	Kansas	8,704,929,000	0.9%
29	Kentucky	8,723,401,000	0.9%
24	Louisiana	12,152,540,000	1.2%
41	Maine	3,196,963,000	0.3%
20	Maryland	16,865,660,000	1.7%
13	Massachusetts	21,421,771,000	2.1%
8	Michigan	36,411,119,000	3.6%
15	Minnesota	19,251,253,000	1.9%
32	Mississippi	7,401,304,000	0.7%
22	Missouri	15,641,048,000	1.5%
44	Montana	2,132,257,000	0.2%
34	Nebraska	6,877,068,000	0.7%
33	Nevada	7,112,700,000	0.7%
40	New Hampshire	3,204,850,000	0.3%
9	New Jersey	29,133,282,000	2.9%
37	New Mexico	5,011,174,000	0.5%
2	New York	115,278,236,000	11.4%
11	North Carolina	26,160,067,000	2.6%
48	North Dakota	1,790,748,000	0.2%
7	Ohio	37,393,555,000	3.7%
31	Oklahoma	8,523,708,000	0.8%
25	Oregon	11,786,233,000	1.2%
6	Pennsylvania	38,472,303,000	3.8%
43	Rhode Island	2,485,994,000	0.2%
27	South Carolina	10,947,521,000	1.1%
47	South Dakota	1,820,562,000	0.2%
17	Tennessee	18,777,884,000	1.9%
3	Texas	65,509,832,000	6.5%
35	Utah	6,633,146,000	0.7%
50	Vermont	1,579,681,000	0.2%
14	Virginia	21,171,860,000	2.1%
12	Washington	22,702,634,000	2.2%
38	West Virginia	3,776,882,000	0.4%
16	Wisconsin	19,137,241,000	1.9%
45	Wyoming	2,070,375,000	0.2%

RANK ORDER

RANK	STATE	REVENUE	% of USA
1	California	$160,439,009,000	15.8%
2	New York	115,278,236,000	11.4%
3	Texas	65,509,832,000	6.5%
4	Florida	55,504,603,000	5.5%
5	Illinois	45,243,179,000	4.5%
6	Pennsylvania	38,472,303,000	3.8%
7	Ohio	37,393,555,000	3.7%
8	Michigan	36,411,119,000	3.6%
9	New Jersey	29,133,282,000	2.9%
10	Georgia	27,036,116,000	2.7%
11	North Carolina	26,160,067,000	2.6%
12	Washington	22,702,634,000	2.2%
13	Massachusetts	21,421,771,000	2.1%
14	Virginia	21,171,860,000	2.1%
15	Minnesota	19,251,253,000	1.9%
16	Wisconsin	19,137,241,000	1.9%
17	Tennessee	18,777,884,000	1.9%
18	Indiana	18,045,743,000	1.8%
19	Arizona	17,364,747,000	1.7%
20	Maryland	16,865,660,000	1.7%
21	Colorado	15,788,669,000	1.6%
22	Missouri	15,641,048,000	1.5%
23	Alabama	13,045,686,000	1.3%
24	Louisiana	12,152,540,000	1.2%
25	Oregon	11,786,233,000	1.2%
26	Connecticut	11,190,025,000	1.1%
27	South Carolina	10,947,521,000	1.1%
28	Iowa	9,052,574,000	0.9%
29	Kentucky	8,723,401,000	0.9%
30	Kansas	8,704,929,000	0.9%
31	Oklahoma	8,523,708,000	0.8%
32	Mississippi	7,401,304,000	0.7%
33	Nevada	7,112,700,000	0.7%
34	Nebraska	6,877,068,000	0.7%
35	Utah	6,633,146,000	0.7%
36	Arkansas	5,718,268,000	0.6%
37	New Mexico	5,011,174,000	0.5%
38	West Virginia	3,776,882,000	0.4%
39	Idaho	3,294,439,000	0.3%
40	New Hampshire	3,204,850,000	0.3%
41	Maine	3,196,963,000	0.3%
42	Alaska	2,834,723,000	0.3%
43	Rhode Island	2,485,994,000	0.2%
44	Montana	2,132,257,000	0.2%
45	Wyoming	2,070,375,000	0.2%
46	Delaware	1,920,650,000	0.2%
47	South Dakota	1,820,562,000	0.2%
48	North Dakota	1,790,748,000	0.2%
49	Hawaii	1,703,365,000	0.2%
50	Vermont	1,579,681,000	0.2%
	District of Columbia	6,383,054,000	0.6%

Source: U.S. Bureau of the Census, Governments Division
"State and Local Government Finances: 1999-2000" (http://www.census.gov/govs/www/estimate00.html)
Total revenue includes all money received from external sources. This includes taxes, intergovernmental transfers and insurance trust revenue and revenue from government owned utilities and other commercial or auxiliary enterprise.

Per Capita Local Government Total Revenue in 2000

National Per Capita = $3,592*

<u>ALPHA ORDER</u>

RANK	STATE	PER CAPITA
31	Alabama	$2,930
3	Alaska	4,516
17	Arizona	3,361
48	Arkansas	2,135
2	California	4,717
9	Colorado	3,649
21	Connecticut	3,280
43	Delaware	2,442
13	Florida	3,458
20	Georgia	3,283
50	Hawaii	1,405
40	Idaho	2,535
10	Illinois	3,637
29	Indiana	2,962
27	Iowa	3,091
23	Kansas	3,233
47	Kentucky	2,155
36	Louisiana	2,719
41	Maine	2,503
24	Maryland	3,175
16	Massachusetts	3,367
8	Michigan	3,657
6	Minnesota	3,902
37	Mississippi	2,598
33	Missouri	2,791
46	Montana	2,360
5	Nebraska	4,014
12	Nevada	3,523
39	New Hampshire	2,584
14	New Jersey	3,455
34	New Mexico	2,751
1	New York	6,067
22	North Carolina	3,237
32	North Dakota	2,793
19	Ohio	3,291
42	Oklahoma	2,467
15	Oregon	3,435
25	Pennsylvania	3,131
45	Rhode Island	2,366
35	South Carolina	2,721
44	South Dakota	2,409
18	Tennessee	3,292
26	Texas	3,126
30	Utah	2,957
38	Vermont	2,590
28	Virginia	2,979
7	Washington	3,840
49	West Virginia	2,090
11	Wisconsin	3,561
4	Wyoming	4,190

<u>RANK ORDER</u>

RANK	STATE	PER CAPITA
1	New York	$6,067
2	California	4,717
3	Alaska	4,516
4	Wyoming	4,190
5	Nebraska	4,014
6	Minnesota	3,902
7	Washington	3,840
8	Michigan	3,657
9	Colorado	3,649
10	Illinois	3,637
11	Wisconsin	3,561
12	Nevada	3,523
13	Florida	3,458
14	New Jersey	3,455
15	Oregon	3,435
16	Massachusetts	3,367
17	Arizona	3,361
18	Tennessee	3,292
19	Ohio	3,291
20	Georgia	3,283
21	Connecticut	3,280
22	North Carolina	3,237
23	Kansas	3,233
24	Maryland	3,175
25	Pennsylvania	3,131
26	Texas	3,126
27	Iowa	3,091
28	Virginia	2,979
29	Indiana	2,962
30	Utah	2,957
31	Alabama	2,930
32	North Dakota	2,793
33	Missouri	2,791
34	New Mexico	2,751
35	South Carolina	2,721
36	Louisiana	2,719
37	Mississippi	2,598
38	Vermont	2,590
39	New Hampshire	2,584
40	Idaho	2,535
41	Maine	2,503
42	Oklahoma	2,467
43	Delaware	2,442
44	South Dakota	2,409
45	Rhode Island	2,366
46	Montana	2,360
47	Kentucky	2,155
48	Arkansas	2,135
49	West Virginia	2,090
50	Hawaii	1,405

District of Columbia	11,166

*Source: Morgan Quitno Press using data from U.S. Bureau of the Census, Governments Division
"State and Local Government Finances: 1999-2000" (http://www.census.gov/govs/www/estimate00.html)
Total revenue includes all money received from external sources. This includes taxes, intergovernmental transfers and insurance trust revenue and revenue from government owned utilities and other commercial or auxiliary enterprise.

Local Government Revenue from the Federal Government in 2000

National Total = $32,835,984,000

ALPHA ORDER

RANK	STATE	REVENUE	% of USA
24	Alabama	$342,610,000	1.0%
34	Alaska	213,427,000	0.6%
14	Arizona	635,092,000	1.9%
42	Arkansas	116,445,000	0.4%
1	California	4,820,620,000	14.7%
18	Colorado	431,155,000	1.3%
28	Connecticut	286,411,000	0.9%
49	Delaware	41,786,000	0.1%
5	Florida	1,813,217,000	5.5%
13	Georgia	659,329,000	2.0%
36	Hawaii	170,244,000	0.5%
46	Idaho	80,393,000	0.2%
6	Illinois	1,515,606,000	4.6%
22	Indiana	376,643,000	1.1%
31	Iowa	253,548,000	0.8%
41	Kansas	117,311,000	0.4%
29	Kentucky	276,236,000	0.8%
25	Louisiana	340,092,000	1.0%
45	Maine	83,465,000	0.3%
16	Maryland	586,765,000	1.8%
9	Massachusetts	1,011,368,000	3.1%
7	Michigan	1,163,001,000	3.5%
21	Minnesota	388,585,000	1.2%
35	Mississippi	178,944,000	0.5%
20	Missouri	423,383,000	1.3%
40	Montana	119,289,000	0.4%
37	Nebraska	169,434,000	0.5%
32	Nevada	234,178,000	0.7%
47	New Hampshire	68,047,000	0.2%
17	New Jersey	572,256,000	1.7%
30	New Mexico	266,433,000	0.8%
2	New York	3,042,897,000	9.3%
10	North Carolina	996,205,000	3.0%
38	North Dakota	151,905,000	0.5%
8	Ohio	1,090,786,000	3.3%
33	Oklahoma	218,787,000	0.7%
15	Oregon	607,793,000	1.9%
4	Pennsylvania	1,993,414,000	6.1%
43	Rhode Island	105,860,000	0.3%
26	South Carolina	321,936,000	1.0%
44	South Dakota	88,239,000	0.3%
23	Tennessee	354,516,000	1.1%
3	Texas	2,013,660,000	6.1%
27	Utah	294,359,000	0.9%
50	Vermont	26,292,000	0.1%
12	Virginia	695,518,000	2.1%
11	Washington	732,693,000	2.2%
39	West Virginia	124,064,000	0.4%
19	Wisconsin	426,335,000	1.3%
48	Wyoming	47,476,000	0.1%

RANK ORDER

RANK	STATE	REVENUE	% of USA
1	California	$4,820,620,000	14.7%
2	New York	3,042,897,000	9.3%
3	Texas	2,013,660,000	6.1%
4	Pennsylvania	1,993,414,000	6.1%
5	Florida	1,813,217,000	5.5%
6	Illinois	1,515,606,000	4.6%
7	Michigan	1,163,001,000	3.5%
8	Ohio	1,090,786,000	3.3%
9	Massachusetts	1,011,368,000	3.1%
10	North Carolina	996,205,000	3.0%
11	Washington	732,693,000	2.2%
12	Virginia	695,518,000	2.1%
13	Georgia	659,329,000	2.0%
14	Arizona	635,092,000	1.9%
15	Oregon	607,793,000	1.9%
16	Maryland	586,765,000	1.8%
17	New Jersey	572,256,000	1.7%
18	Colorado	431,155,000	1.3%
19	Wisconsin	426,335,000	1.3%
20	Missouri	423,383,000	1.3%
21	Minnesota	388,585,000	1.2%
22	Indiana	376,643,000	1.1%
23	Tennessee	354,516,000	1.1%
24	Alabama	342,610,000	1.0%
25	Louisiana	340,092,000	1.0%
26	South Carolina	321,936,000	1.0%
27	Utah	294,359,000	0.9%
28	Connecticut	286,411,000	0.9%
29	Kentucky	276,236,000	0.8%
30	New Mexico	266,433,000	0.8%
31	Iowa	253,548,000	0.8%
32	Nevada	234,178,000	0.7%
33	Oklahoma	218,787,000	0.7%
34	Alaska	213,427,000	0.6%
35	Mississippi	178,944,000	0.5%
36	Hawaii	170,244,000	0.5%
37	Nebraska	169,434,000	0.5%
38	North Dakota	151,905,000	0.5%
39	West Virginia	124,064,000	0.4%
40	Montana	119,289,000	0.4%
41	Kansas	117,311,000	0.4%
42	Arkansas	116,445,000	0.4%
43	Rhode Island	105,860,000	0.3%
44	South Dakota	88,239,000	0.3%
45	Maine	83,465,000	0.3%
46	Idaho	80,393,000	0.2%
47	New Hampshire	68,047,000	0.2%
48	Wyoming	47,476,000	0.1%
49	Delaware	41,786,000	0.1%
50	Vermont	26,292,000	0.1%
	District of Columbia	1,747,936,000	5.3%

Source: U.S. Bureau of the Census, Governments Division
"State and Local Government Finances: 1999-2000" (http://www.census.gov/govs/www/estimate00.html)

Per Capita Local Government Revenue from the Federal Government in 2000

National Per Capita = $116

<u>ALPHA ORDER</u>

RANK	STATE	PER CAPITA
34	Alabama	$77
1	Alaska	340
13	Arizona	123
49	Arkansas	43
8	California	142
22	Colorado	100
29	Connecticut	84
47	Delaware	53
19	Florida	113
30	Georgia	80
9	Hawaii	140
43	Idaho	62
15	Illinois	122
43	Indiana	62
28	Iowa	87
48	Kansas	44
38	Kentucky	68
35	Louisiana	76
40	Maine	65
20	Maryland	110
6	Massachusetts	159
16	Michigan	117
32	Minnesota	79
41	Mississippi	63
35	Missouri	76
10	Montana	132
23	Nebraska	99
18	Nevada	116
46	New Hampshire	55
38	New Jersey	68
7	New Mexico	146
5	New York	160
13	North Carolina	123
2	North Dakota	237
25	Ohio	96
41	Oklahoma	63
3	Oregon	177
4	Pennsylvania	162
21	Rhode Island	101
30	South Carolina	80
16	South Dakota	117
43	Tennessee	62
25	Texas	96
11	Utah	131
49	Vermont	43
24	Virginia	98
12	Washington	124
37	West Virginia	69
32	Wisconsin	79
25	Wyoming	96

<u>RANK ORDER</u>

RANK	STATE	PER CAPITA
1	Alaska	$340
2	North Dakota	237
3	Oregon	177
4	Pennsylvania	162
5	New York	160
6	Massachusetts	159
7	New Mexico	146
8	California	142
9	Hawaii	140
10	Montana	132
11	Utah	131
12	Washington	124
13	Arizona	123
13	North Carolina	123
15	Illinois	122
16	Michigan	117
16	South Dakota	117
18	Nevada	116
19	Florida	113
20	Maryland	110
21	Rhode Island	101
22	Colorado	100
23	Nebraska	99
24	Virginia	98
25	Ohio	96
25	Texas	96
25	Wyoming	96
28	Iowa	87
29	Connecticut	84
30	Georgia	80
30	South Carolina	80
32	Minnesota	79
32	Wisconsin	79
34	Alabama	77
35	Louisiana	76
35	Missouri	76
37	West Virginia	69
38	Kentucky	68
38	New Jersey	68
40	Maine	65
41	Mississippi	63
41	Oklahoma	63
43	Idaho	62
43	Indiana	62
43	Tennessee	62
46	New Hampshire	55
47	Delaware	53
48	Kansas	44
49	Arkansas	43
49	Vermont	43

District of Columbia 3,058

Source: Morgan Quitno Press using data from U.S. Bureau of the Census, Governments Division
"State and Local Government Finances: 1999-2000" (http://www.census.gov/govs/www/estimate00.html)

Local Government Own Source Revenue in 2000

National Total = $538,970,886,000*

ALPHA ORDER

RANK	STATE	REVENUE	% of USA
25	Alabama	$6,589,272,000	1.2%
43	Alaska	1,502,559,000	0.3%
22	Arizona	8,249,538,000	1.5%
36	Arkansas	2,375,114,000	0.4%
1	California	70,240,489,000	13.0%
17	Colorado	10,100,139,000	1.9%
24	Connecticut	6,597,013,000	1.2%
49	Delaware	866,874,000	0.2%
4	Florida	32,751,912,000	6.1%
10	Georgia	15,684,362,000	2.9%
45	Hawaii	1,196,743,000	0.2%
41	Idaho	1,798,055,000	0.3%
5	Illinois	25,084,245,000	4.7%
14	Indiana	10,675,512,000	2.0%
28	Iowa	5,087,739,000	0.9%
30	Kansas	4,748,694,000	0.9%
31	Kentucky	4,519,684,000	0.8%
23	Louisiana	7,184,919,000	1.3%
37	Maine	2,091,256,000	0.4%
15	Maryland	10,674,691,000	2.0%
16	Massachusetts	10,224,221,000	1.9%
9	Michigan	15,963,852,000	3.0%
18	Minnesota	9,667,142,000	1.8%
33	Mississippi	3,895,709,000	0.7%
20	Missouri	9,047,196,000	1.7%
44	Montana	1,260,277,000	0.2%
35	Nebraska	3,172,969,000	0.6%
32	Nevada	3,942,857,000	0.7%
38	New Hampshire	1,973,650,000	0.4%
8	New Jersey	19,127,778,000	3.5%
39	New Mexico	1,963,315,000	0.4%
2	New York	62,407,726,000	11.6%
11	North Carolina	12,908,472,000	2.4%
48	North Dakota	992,790,000	0.2%
6	Ohio	21,992,119,000	4.1%
29	Oklahoma	4,780,855,000	0.9%
27	Oregon	6,322,103,000	1.2%
7	Pennsylvania	21,001,531,000	3.9%
42	Rhode Island	1,608,399,000	0.3%
26	South Carolina	6,412,361,000	1.2%
47	South Dakota	1,132,517,000	0.2%
21	Tennessee	8,695,096,000	1.6%
3	Texas	38,802,134,000	7.2%
34	Utah	3,227,994,000	0.6%
50	Vermont	568,425,000	0.1%
12	Virginia	12,175,398,000	2.3%
13	Washington	11,534,702,000	2.1%
40	West Virginia	1,939,712,000	0.4%
19	Wisconsin	9,064,107,000	1.7%
46	Wyoming	1,162,169,000	0.2%

RANK ORDER

RANK	STATE	REVENUE	% of USA
1	California	$70,240,489,000	13.0%
2	New York	62,407,726,000	11.6%
3	Texas	38,802,134,000	7.2%
4	Florida	32,751,912,000	6.1%
5	Illinois	25,084,245,000	4.7%
6	Ohio	21,992,119,000	4.1%
7	Pennsylvania	21,001,531,000	3.9%
8	New Jersey	19,127,778,000	3.5%
9	Michigan	15,963,852,000	3.0%
10	Georgia	15,684,362,000	2.9%
11	North Carolina	12,908,472,000	2.4%
12	Virginia	12,175,398,000	2.3%
13	Washington	11,534,702,000	2.1%
14	Indiana	10,675,512,000	2.0%
15	Maryland	10,674,691,000	2.0%
16	Massachusetts	10,224,221,000	1.9%
17	Colorado	10,100,139,000	1.9%
18	Minnesota	9,667,142,000	1.8%
19	Wisconsin	9,064,107,000	1.7%
20	Missouri	9,047,196,000	1.7%
21	Tennessee	8,695,096,000	1.6%
22	Arizona	8,249,538,000	1.5%
23	Louisiana	7,184,919,000	1.3%
24	Connecticut	6,597,013,000	1.2%
25	Alabama	6,589,272,000	1.2%
26	South Carolina	6,412,361,000	1.2%
27	Oregon	6,322,103,000	1.2%
28	Iowa	5,087,739,000	0.9%
29	Oklahoma	4,780,855,000	0.9%
30	Kansas	4,748,694,000	0.9%
31	Kentucky	4,519,684,000	0.8%
32	Nevada	3,942,857,000	0.7%
33	Mississippi	3,895,709,000	0.7%
34	Utah	3,227,994,000	0.6%
35	Nebraska	3,172,969,000	0.6%
36	Arkansas	2,375,114,000	0.4%
37	Maine	2,091,256,000	0.4%
38	New Hampshire	1,973,650,000	0.4%
39	New Mexico	1,963,315,000	0.4%
40	West Virginia	1,939,712,000	0.4%
41	Idaho	1,798,055,000	0.3%
42	Rhode Island	1,608,399,000	0.3%
43	Alaska	1,502,559,000	0.3%
44	Montana	1,260,277,000	0.2%
45	Hawaii	1,196,743,000	0.2%
46	Wyoming	1,162,169,000	0.2%
47	South Dakota	1,132,517,000	0.2%
48	North Dakota	992,790,000	0.2%
49	Delaware	866,874,000	0.2%
50	Vermont	568,425,000	0.1%
	District of Columbia	3,984,500,000	0.7%

Source: U.S. Bureau of the Census, Governments Division
"State and Local Government Finances: 1999-2000" (http://www.census.gov/govs/www/estimate00.html)
**Own source revenue includes taxes, current charges and miscellaneous general revenue. Excluded are intergovernmental transfers, insurance trust revenue and revenue from government owned utilities and other commercial or auxiliary enterprise.*

Per Capita Local Government Own Source Revenue in 2000

National Per Capita = $1,910*

<u>ALPHA ORDER</u>

RANK	STATE	PER CAPITA
38	Alabama	$1,480
2	Alaska	2,394
30	Arizona	1,597
50	Arkansas	887
6	California	2,065
4	Colorado	2,334
14	Connecticut	1,933
45	Delaware	1,102
7	Florida	2,040
15	Georgia	1,905
48	Hawaii	987
42	Idaho	1,383
8	Illinois	2,016
20	Indiana	1,752
21	Iowa	1,737
19	Kansas	1,764
44	Kentucky	1,116
27	Louisiana	1,607
25	Maine	1,637
9	Maryland	2,009
27	Massachusetts	1,607
29	Michigan	1,603
10	Minnesota	1,959
43	Mississippi	1,367
26	Missouri	1,614
40	Montana	1,395
16	Nebraska	1,852
11	Nevada	1,953
33	New Hampshire	1,591
5	New Jersey	2,268
46	New Mexico	1,078
1	New York	3,285
30	North Carolina	1,597
34	North Dakota	1,548
13	Ohio	1,935
41	Oklahoma	1,384
18	Oregon	1,843
23	Pennsylvania	1,709
35	Rhode Island	1,531
32	South Carolina	1,594
37	South Dakota	1,498
36	Tennessee	1,525
16	Texas	1,852
39	Utah	1,439
49	Vermont	932
22	Virginia	1,713
12	Washington	1,951
47	West Virginia	1,073
24	Wisconsin	1,687
3	Wyoming	2,352

<u>RANK ORDER</u>

RANK	STATE	PER CAPITA
1	New York	$3,285
2	Alaska	2,394
3	Wyoming	2,352
4	Colorado	2,334
5	New Jersey	2,268
6	California	2,065
7	Florida	2,040
8	Illinois	2,016
9	Maryland	2,009
10	Minnesota	1,959
11	Nevada	1,953
12	Washington	1,951
13	Ohio	1,935
14	Connecticut	1,933
15	Georgia	1,905
16	Nebraska	1,852
16	Texas	1,852
18	Oregon	1,843
19	Kansas	1,764
20	Indiana	1,752
21	Iowa	1,737
22	Virginia	1,713
23	Pennsylvania	1,709
24	Wisconsin	1,687
25	Maine	1,637
26	Missouri	1,614
27	Louisiana	1,607
27	Massachusetts	1,607
29	Michigan	1,603
30	Arizona	1,597
30	North Carolina	1,597
32	South Carolina	1,594
33	New Hampshire	1,591
34	North Dakota	1,548
35	Rhode Island	1,531
36	Tennessee	1,525
37	South Dakota	1,498
38	Alabama	1,480
39	Utah	1,439
40	Montana	1,395
41	Oklahoma	1,384
42	Idaho	1,383
43	Mississippi	1,367
44	Kentucky	1,116
45	Delaware	1,102
46	New Mexico	1,078
47	West Virginia	1,073
48	Hawaii	987
49	Vermont	932
50	Arkansas	887

District of Columbia   6,970

Source: Morgan Quitno Press using data from U.S. Bureau of the Census, Governments Division
"State and Local Government Finances: 1999-2000" (http://www.census.gov/govs/www/estimate00.html)
*Own source revenue includes taxes, current charges and miscellaneous general revenue. Excluded are intergovernmental transfers, insurance trust revenue and revenue from government owned utilities and other commercial or auxiliary enterprise.

Local Government Tax Revenue in 2000

National Total = $332,695,777,000

ALPHA ORDER

RANK	STATE	TAX REVENUE	% of USA
27	Alabama	$2,976,651,000	0.9%
43	Alaska	888,514,000	0.3%
21	Arizona	5,232,875,000	1.6%
39	Arkansas	1,090,774,000	0.3%
2	California	36,259,622,000	10.9%
16	Colorado	6,141,141,000	1.8%
20	Connecticut	5,479,828,000	1.6%
49	Delaware	486,497,000	0.1%
5	Florida	17,119,419,000	5.1%
9	Georgia	9,742,272,000	2.9%
45	Hawaii	766,874,000	0.2%
42	Idaho	916,988,000	0.3%
4	Illinois	17,467,217,000	5.3%
14	Indiana	6,259,077,000	1.9%
28	Iowa	2,905,131,000	0.9%
29	Kansas	2,768,118,000	0.8%
30	Kentucky	2,477,804,000	0.7%
24	Louisiana	4,375,026,000	1.3%
35	Maine	1,601,062,000	0.5%
12	Maryland	7,935,434,000	2.4%
13	Massachusetts	7,889,193,000	2.4%
10	Michigan	8,717,759,000	2.6%
22	Minnesota	4,834,353,000	1.5%
36	Mississippi	1,587,802,000	0.5%
19	Missouri	5,742,325,000	1.7%
46	Montana	721,079,000	0.2%
33	Nebraska	1,991,921,000	0.6%
32	Nevada	2,107,569,000	0.6%
37	New Hampshire	1,582,290,000	0.5%
6	New Jersey	14,690,335,000	4.4%
40	New Mexico	1,057,400,000	0.3%
1	New York	45,132,347,000	13.6%
17	North Carolina	6,124,643,000	1.8%
47	North Dakota	595,742,000	0.2%
7	Ohio	14,562,309,000	4.4%
31	Oklahoma	2,411,399,000	0.7%
25	Oregon	3,466,108,000	1.0%
8	Pennsylvania	14,114,114,000	4.2%
38	Rhode Island	1,377,446,000	0.4%
26	South Carolina	3,161,523,000	1.0%
44	South Dakota	808,383,000	0.2%
23	Tennessee	4,691,606,000	1.4%
3	Texas	24,802,393,000	7.5%
34	Utah	1,894,429,000	0.6%
50	Vermont	392,391,000	0.1%
11	Virginia	8,434,916,000	2.5%
15	Washington	6,166,482,000	1.9%
41	West Virginia	1,019,038,000	0.3%
18	Wisconsin	5,971,382,000	1.8%
48	Wyoming	541,010,000	0.2%

RANK ORDER

RANK	STATE	TAX REVENUE	% of USA
1	New York	$45,132,347,000	13.6%
2	California	36,259,622,000	10.9%
3	Texas	24,802,393,000	7.5%
4	Illinois	17,467,217,000	5.3%
5	Florida	17,119,419,000	5.1%
6	New Jersey	14,690,335,000	4.4%
7	Ohio	14,562,309,000	4.4%
8	Pennsylvania	14,114,114,000	4.2%
9	Georgia	9,742,272,000	2.9%
10	Michigan	8,717,759,000	2.6%
11	Virginia	8,434,916,000	2.5%
12	Maryland	7,935,434,000	2.4%
13	Massachusetts	7,889,193,000	2.4%
14	Indiana	6,259,077,000	1.9%
15	Washington	6,166,482,000	1.9%
16	Colorado	6,141,141,000	1.8%
17	North Carolina	6,124,643,000	1.8%
18	Wisconsin	5,971,382,000	1.8%
19	Missouri	5,742,325,000	1.7%
20	Connecticut	5,479,828,000	1.6%
21	Arizona	5,232,875,000	1.6%
22	Minnesota	4,834,353,000	1.5%
23	Tennessee	4,691,606,000	1.4%
24	Louisiana	4,375,026,000	1.3%
25	Oregon	3,466,108,000	1.0%
26	South Carolina	3,161,523,000	1.0%
27	Alabama	2,976,651,000	0.9%
28	Iowa	2,905,131,000	0.9%
29	Kansas	2,768,118,000	0.8%
30	Kentucky	2,477,804,000	0.7%
31	Oklahoma	2,411,399,000	0.7%
32	Nevada	2,107,569,000	0.6%
33	Nebraska	1,991,921,000	0.6%
34	Utah	1,894,429,000	0.6%
35	Maine	1,601,062,000	0.5%
36	Mississippi	1,587,802,000	0.5%
37	New Hampshire	1,582,290,000	0.5%
38	Rhode Island	1,377,446,000	0.4%
39	Arkansas	1,090,774,000	0.3%
40	New Mexico	1,057,400,000	0.3%
41	West Virginia	1,019,038,000	0.3%
42	Idaho	916,988,000	0.3%
43	Alaska	888,514,000	0.3%
44	South Dakota	808,383,000	0.2%
45	Hawaii	766,874,000	0.2%
46	Montana	721,079,000	0.2%
47	North Dakota	595,742,000	0.2%
48	Wyoming	541,010,000	0.2%
49	Delaware	486,497,000	0.1%
50	Vermont	392,391,000	0.1%
	District of Columbia	3,215,766,000	1.0%

Source: U.S. Bureau of the Census, Governments Division
"State and Local Government Finances: 1999-2000" (http://www.census.gov/govs/www/estimate00.html)

Per Capita Local Government Tax Revenue in 2000

National Per Capita = $1,179

<u>ALPHA ORDER</u>

RANK	STATE	PER CAPITA
42	Alabama	$669
6	Alaska	1,416
28	Arizona	1,013
50	Arkansas	407
22	California	1,066
5	Colorado	1,419
3	Connecticut	1,606
45	Delaware	619
21	Florida	1,067
15	Georgia	1,183
44	Hawaii	632
40	Idaho	706
7	Illinois	1,404
26	Indiana	1,027
30	Iowa	992
25	Kansas	1,028
46	Kentucky	612
32	Louisiana	979
11	Maine	1,253
4	Maryland	1,494
12	Massachusetts	1,240
34	Michigan	876
31	Minnesota	980
49	Mississippi	557
27	Missouri	1,024
37	Montana	798
16	Nebraska	1,163
23	Nevada	1,044
10	New Hampshire	1,276
2	New Jersey	1,742
47	New Mexico	580
1	New York	2,375
39	North Carolina	758
33	North Dakota	929
9	Ohio	1,281
41	Oklahoma	698
29	Oregon	1,010
17	Pennsylvania	1,149
8	Rhode Island	1,311
38	South Carolina	786
20	South Dakota	1,070
36	Tennessee	823
14	Texas	1,184
35	Utah	844
43	Vermont	643
13	Virginia	1,187
24	Washington	1,043
48	West Virginia	564
18	Wisconsin	1,111
19	Wyoming	1,095

<u>RANK ORDER</u>

RANK	STATE	PER CAPITA
1	New York	$2,375
2	New Jersey	1,742
3	Connecticut	1,606
4	Maryland	1,494
5	Colorado	1,419
6	Alaska	1,416
7	Illinois	1,404
8	Rhode Island	1,311
9	Ohio	1,281
10	New Hampshire	1,276
11	Maine	1,253
12	Massachusetts	1,240
13	Virginia	1,187
14	Texas	1,184
15	Georgia	1,183
16	Nebraska	1,163
17	Pennsylvania	1,149
18	Wisconsin	1,111
19	Wyoming	1,095
20	South Dakota	1,070
21	Florida	1,067
22	California	1,066
23	Nevada	1,044
24	Washington	1,043
25	Kansas	1,028
26	Indiana	1,027
27	Missouri	1,024
28	Arizona	1,013
29	Oregon	1,010
30	Iowa	992
31	Minnesota	980
32	Louisiana	979
33	North Dakota	929
34	Michigan	876
35	Utah	844
36	Tennessee	823
37	Montana	798
38	South Carolina	786
39	North Carolina	758
40	Idaho	706
41	Oklahoma	698
42	Alabama	669
43	Vermont	643
44	Hawaii	632
45	Delaware	619
46	Kentucky	612
47	New Mexico	580
48	West Virginia	564
49	Mississippi	557
50	Arkansas	407

District of Columbia	5,625

Source: Morgan Quitno Press using data from U.S. Bureau of the Census, Governments Division
"State and Local Government Finances: 1999-2000" (http://www.census.gov/govs/www/estimate00.html)

Local Government Total Expenditures in 2000

National Total = $996,266,752,000*

ALPHA ORDER

RANK	STATE	EXPENDITURES	% of USA
23	Alabama	$13,357,344,000	1.3%
42	Alaska	2,931,164,000	0.3%
19	Arizona	17,091,688,000	1.7%
36	Arkansas	5,381,089,000	0.5%
1	California	150,812,757,000	15.1%
20	Colorado	15,943,066,000	1.6%
27	Connecticut	10,659,647,000	1.1%
47	Delaware	1,800,220,000	0.2%
4	Florida	53,358,062,000	5.4%
11	Georgia	25,931,363,000	2.6%
48	Hawaii	1,792,295,000	0.2%
39	Idaho	3,192,379,000	0.3%
5	Illinois	45,623,807,000	4.6%
18	Indiana	17,753,153,000	1.8%
28	Iowa	9,081,657,000	0.9%
31	Kansas	8,157,696,000	0.8%
29	Kentucky	9,073,523,000	0.9%
25	Louisiana	12,186,914,000	1.2%
40	Maine	3,107,955,000	0.3%
21	Maryland	15,742,961,000	1.6%
13	Massachusetts	21,571,660,000	2.2%
8	Michigan	36,046,030,000	3.6%
16	Minnesota	19,799,163,000	2.0%
32	Mississippi	7,655,694,000	0.8%
22	Missouri	15,187,767,000	1.5%
45	Montana	2,028,823,000	0.2%
34	Nebraska	6,639,596,000	0.7%
33	Nevada	7,430,453,000	0.7%
41	New Hampshire	2,966,550,000	0.3%
9	New Jersey	28,659,632,000	2.9%
37	New Mexico	4,963,389,000	0.5%
2	New York	111,561,910,000	11.2%
10	North Carolina	26,145,002,000	2.6%
49	North Dakota	1,785,895,000	0.2%
7	Ohio	36,945,677,000	3.7%
30	Oklahoma	8,380,572,000	0.8%
24	Oregon	12,233,130,000	1.2%
6	Pennsylvania	39,166,454,000	3.9%
43	Rhode Island	2,437,526,000	0.2%
26	South Carolina	11,023,557,000	1.1%
46	South Dakota	1,806,134,000	0.2%
17	Tennessee	19,561,393,000	2.0%
3	Texas	65,969,872,000	6.6%
35	Utah	6,438,200,000	0.6%
50	Vermont	1,469,563,000	0.1%
14	Virginia	20,932,317,000	2.1%
12	Washington	22,292,633,000	2.2%
38	West Virginia	3,804,143,000	0.4%
15	Wisconsin	19,829,441,000	2.0%
44	Wyoming	2,028,864,000	0.2%

RANK ORDER

RANK	STATE	EXPENDITURES	% of USA
1	California	$150,812,757,000	15.1%
2	New York	111,561,910,000	11.2%
3	Texas	65,969,872,000	6.6%
4	Florida	53,358,062,000	5.4%
5	Illinois	45,623,807,000	4.6%
6	Pennsylvania	39,166,454,000	3.9%
7	Ohio	36,945,677,000	3.7%
8	Michigan	36,046,030,000	3.6%
9	New Jersey	28,659,632,000	2.9%
10	North Carolina	26,145,002,000	2.6%
11	Georgia	25,931,363,000	2.6%
12	Washington	22,292,633,000	2.2%
13	Massachusetts	21,571,660,000	2.2%
14	Virginia	20,932,317,000	2.1%
15	Wisconsin	19,829,441,000	2.0%
16	Minnesota	19,799,163,000	2.0%
17	Tennessee	19,561,393,000	2.0%
18	Indiana	17,753,153,000	1.8%
19	Arizona	17,091,688,000	1.7%
20	Colorado	15,943,066,000	1.6%
21	Maryland	15,742,961,000	1.6%
22	Missouri	15,187,767,000	1.5%
23	Alabama	13,357,344,000	1.3%
24	Oregon	12,233,130,000	1.2%
25	Louisiana	12,186,914,000	1.2%
26	South Carolina	11,023,557,000	1.1%
27	Connecticut	10,659,647,000	1.1%
28	Iowa	9,081,657,000	0.9%
29	Kentucky	9,073,523,000	0.9%
30	Oklahoma	8,380,572,000	0.8%
31	Kansas	8,157,696,000	0.8%
32	Mississippi	7,655,694,000	0.8%
33	Nevada	7,430,453,000	0.7%
34	Nebraska	6,639,596,000	0.7%
35	Utah	6,438,200,000	0.6%
36	Arkansas	5,381,089,000	0.5%
37	New Mexico	4,963,389,000	0.5%
38	West Virginia	3,804,143,000	0.4%
39	Idaho	3,192,379,000	0.3%
40	Maine	3,107,955,000	0.3%
41	New Hampshire	2,966,550,000	0.3%
42	Alaska	2,931,164,000	0.3%
43	Rhode Island	2,437,526,000	0.2%
44	Wyoming	2,028,864,000	0.2%
45	Montana	2,028,823,000	0.2%
46	South Dakota	1,806,134,000	0.2%
47	Delaware	1,800,220,000	0.2%
48	Hawaii	1,792,295,000	0.2%
49	North Dakota	1,785,895,000	0.2%
50	Vermont	1,469,563,000	0.1%
	District of Columbia	6,526,972,000	0.7%

Source: U.S. Bureau of the Census, Governments Division
"State and Local Government Finances: 1999-2000" (http://www.census.gov/govs/www/estimate00.html)
**Total expenditures includes all money paid other than for retirement of debt and extension of loans. Includes payments from all sources of funds including current revenues and proceeds from borrowing and prior year fund balances. Includes intergovernmental transfers and expenditures for government owned utilities and other commercial or auxiliary enterprise and insurance trust expenditures.*

Per Capita Local Government Total Expenditures in 2000

National Per Capita = $3,530*

<u>ALPHA ORDER</u>

RANK	STATE	PER CAPITA
27	Alabama	$3,000
2	Alaska	4,670
18	Arizona	3,308
49	Arkansas	2,009
3	California	4,434
9	Colorado	3,685
24	Connecticut	3,124
45	Delaware	2,289
17	Florida	3,324
22	Georgia	3,149
50	Hawaii	1,478
38	Idaho	2,456
11	Illinois	3,667
30	Indiana	2,914
25	Iowa	3,101
26	Kansas	3,030
47	Kentucky	2,241
34	Louisiana	2,727
39	Maine	2,433
28	Maryland	2,963
16	Massachusetts	3,391
12	Michigan	3,620
5	Minnesota	4,013
37	Mississippi	2,687
36	Missouri	2,710
46	Montana	2,246
6	Nebraska	3,875
10	Nevada	3,681
42	New Hampshire	2,391
15	New Jersey	3,398
35	New Mexico	2,724
1	New York	5,872
20	North Carolina	3,235
32	North Dakota	2,786
19	Ohio	3,251
40	Oklahoma	2,426
13	Oregon	3,565
21	Pennsylvania	3,188
44	Rhode Island	2,320
33	South Carolina	2,740
43	South Dakota	2,390
14	Tennessee	3,430
23	Texas	3,148
31	Utah	2,870
41	Vermont	2,409
29	Virginia	2,946
7	Washington	3,771
48	West Virginia	2,105
8	Wisconsin	3,690
4	Wyoming	4,106

<u>RANK ORDER</u>

RANK	STATE	PER CAPITA
1	New York	$5,872
2	Alaska	4,670
3	California	4,434
4	Wyoming	4,106
5	Minnesota	4,013
6	Nebraska	3,875
7	Washington	3,771
8	Wisconsin	3,690
9	Colorado	3,685
10	Nevada	3,681
11	Illinois	3,667
12	Michigan	3,620
13	Oregon	3,565
14	Tennessee	3,430
15	New Jersey	3,398
16	Massachusetts	3,391
17	Florida	3,324
18	Arizona	3,308
19	Ohio	3,251
20	North Carolina	3,235
21	Pennsylvania	3,188
22	Georgia	3,149
23	Texas	3,148
24	Connecticut	3,124
25	Iowa	3,101
26	Kansas	3,030
27	Alabama	3,000
28	Maryland	2,963
29	Virginia	2,946
30	Indiana	2,914
31	Utah	2,870
32	North Dakota	2,786
33	South Carolina	2,740
34	Louisiana	2,727
35	New Mexico	2,724
36	Missouri	2,710
37	Mississippi	2,687
38	Idaho	2,456
39	Maine	2,433
40	Oklahoma	2,426
41	Vermont	2,409
42	New Hampshire	2,391
43	South Dakota	2,390
44	Rhode Island	2,320
45	Delaware	2,289
46	Montana	2,246
47	Kentucky	2,241
48	West Virginia	2,105
49	Arkansas	2,009
50	Hawaii	1,478

District of Columbia — 11,418

Source: Morgan Quitno Press using data from U.S. Bureau of the Census, Governments Division
"State and Local Government Finances: 1999-2000" (http://www.census.gov/govs/www/estimate00.html)
*Total expenditures includes all money paid other than for retirement of debt and extension of loans. Includes payments from all sources of funds including current revenues and proceeds from borrowing and prior year fund balances. Includes intergovernmental transfers and expenditures for government owned utilities and other commercial or auxiliary enterprise and insurance trust expenditures.

Local Government Direct General Expenditures in 2000

National Total = $865,114,373,000*

<u>ALPHA ORDER</u>

RANK	STATE	EXPENDITURES	% of USA
23	Alabama	$11,571,224,000	1.3%
42	Alaska	2,654,932,000	0.3%
19	Arizona	14,177,354,000	1.6%
35	Arkansas	4,815,865,000	0.6%
1	California	126,952,673,000	14.7%
21	Colorado	13,744,781,000	1.6%
26	Connecticut	9,926,121,000	1.1%
48	Delaware	1,633,972,000	0.2%
4	Florida	46,878,162,000	5.4%
11	Georgia	22,165,718,000	2.6%
49	Hawaii	1,473,668,000	0.2%
39	Idaho	3,066,844,000	0.4%
5	Illinois	39,557,933,000	4.6%
17	Indiana	16,287,706,000	1.9%
28	Iowa	8,254,253,000	1.0%
31	Kansas	7,361,387,000	0.9%
29	Kentucky	8,103,668,000	0.9%
24	Louisiana	11,215,844,000	1.3%
40	Maine	3,016,979,000	0.3%
18	Maryland	14,521,232,000	1.7%
16	Massachusetts	17,189,111,000	2.0%
8	Michigan	32,947,508,000	3.8%
15	Minnesota	17,801,862,000	2.1%
32	Mississippi	7,131,336,000	0.8%
22	Missouri	13,509,676,000	1.6%
44	Montana	1,958,595,000	0.2%
37	Nebraska	4,455,154,000	0.5%
33	Nevada	6,636,685,000	0.8%
41	New Hampshire	2,832,622,000	0.3%
9	New Jersey	27,709,799,000	3.2%
36	New Mexico	4,560,696,000	0.5%
2	New York	90,676,069,000	10.5%
10	North Carolina	22,493,779,000	2.6%
46	North Dakota	1,694,822,000	0.2%
7	Ohio	34,437,126,000	4.0%
30	Oklahoma	7,710,171,000	0.9%
25	Oregon	10,926,080,000	1.3%
6	Pennsylvania	35,304,305,000	4.1%
43	Rhode Island	2,250,264,000	0.3%
27	South Carolina	9,871,251,000	1.1%
47	South Dakota	1,663,919,000	0.2%
20	Tennessee	13,814,845,000	1.6%
3	Texas	57,541,189,000	6.7%
34	Utah	5,033,913,000	0.6%
50	Vermont	1,310,297,000	0.2%
12	Virginia	19,250,900,000	2.2%
14	Washington	17,895,234,000	2.1%
38	West Virginia	3,580,801,000	0.4%
13	Wisconsin	18,480,141,000	2.1%
45	Wyoming	1,913,937,000	0.2%

<u>RANK ORDER</u>

RANK	STATE	EXPENDITURES	% of USA
1	California	$126,952,673,000	14.7%
2	New York	90,676,069,000	10.5%
3	Texas	57,541,189,000	6.7%
4	Florida	46,878,162,000	5.4%
5	Illinois	39,557,933,000	4.6%
6	Pennsylvania	35,304,305,000	4.1%
7	Ohio	34,437,126,000	4.0%
8	Michigan	32,947,508,000	3.8%
9	New Jersey	27,709,799,000	3.2%
10	North Carolina	22,493,779,000	2.6%
11	Georgia	22,165,718,000	2.6%
12	Virginia	19,250,900,000	2.2%
13	Wisconsin	18,480,141,000	2.1%
14	Washington	17,895,234,000	2.1%
15	Minnesota	17,801,862,000	2.1%
16	Massachusetts	17,189,111,000	2.0%
17	Indiana	16,287,706,000	1.9%
18	Maryland	14,521,232,000	1.7%
19	Arizona	14,177,354,000	1.6%
20	Tennessee	13,814,845,000	1.6%
21	Colorado	13,744,781,000	1.6%
22	Missouri	13,509,676,000	1.6%
23	Alabama	11,571,224,000	1.3%
24	Louisiana	11,215,844,000	1.3%
25	Oregon	10,926,080,000	1.3%
26	Connecticut	9,926,121,000	1.1%
27	South Carolina	9,871,251,000	1.1%
28	Iowa	8,254,253,000	1.0%
29	Kentucky	8,103,668,000	0.9%
30	Oklahoma	7,710,171,000	0.9%
31	Kansas	7,361,387,000	0.9%
32	Mississippi	7,131,336,000	0.8%
33	Nevada	6,636,685,000	0.8%
34	Utah	5,033,913,000	0.6%
35	Arkansas	4,815,865,000	0.6%
36	New Mexico	4,560,696,000	0.5%
37	Nebraska	4,455,154,000	0.5%
38	West Virginia	3,580,801,000	0.4%
39	Idaho	3,066,844,000	0.4%
40	Maine	3,016,979,000	0.3%
41	New Hampshire	2,832,622,000	0.3%
42	Alaska	2,654,932,000	0.3%
43	Rhode Island	2,250,264,000	0.3%
44	Montana	1,958,595,000	0.2%
45	Wyoming	1,913,937,000	0.2%
46	North Dakota	1,694,822,000	0.2%
47	South Dakota	1,663,919,000	0.2%
48	Delaware	1,633,972,000	0.2%
49	Hawaii	1,473,668,000	0.2%
50	Vermont	1,310,297,000	0.2%
	District of Columbia	5,151,970,000	0.6%

Source: U.S. Bureau of the Census, Governments Division
"State and Local Government Finances: 1999-2000" (http://www.census.gov/govs/www/estimate00.html)
*Direct general expenditures include expenditures for current operations, assistance and subsidies, interest on debt and capital outlay. Excludes intergovernmental transfers, expenditures for government owned utilities and other commercial or auxiliary enterprise and insurance trust expenditures.

Per Capita Local Government Direct General Expenditures in 2000

National Per Capita = $3,065*

<u>ALPHA ORDER</u>

RANK	STATE	PER CAPITA
30	Alabama	$2,599
2	Alaska	4,230
21	Arizona	2,744
49	Arkansas	1,798
4	California	3,733
12	Colorado	3,177
16	Connecticut	2,909
46	Delaware	2,077
15	Florida	2,921
26	Georgia	2,692
50	Hawaii	1,215
38	Idaho	2,360
11	Illinois	3,180
27	Indiana	2,674
18	Iowa	2,818
22	Kansas	2,734
47	Kentucky	2,001
31	Louisiana	2,509
37	Maine	2,362
23	Maryland	2,733
25	Massachusetts	2,702
7	Michigan	3,309
5	Minnesota	3,608
32	Mississippi	2,503
36	Missouri	2,410
43	Montana	2,168
29	Nebraska	2,600
8	Nevada	3,287
39	New Hampshire	2,284
9	New Jersey	3,286
32	New Mexico	2,503
1	New York	4,772
19	North Carolina	2,783
28	North Dakota	2,643
13	Ohio	3,030
41	Oklahoma	2,232
10	Oregon	3,184
17	Pennsylvania	2,874
45	Rhode Island	2,142
34	South Carolina	2,453
42	South Dakota	2,202
35	Tennessee	2,422
20	Texas	2,746
40	Utah	2,244
44	Vermont	2,148
24	Virginia	2,709
14	Washington	3,027
48	West Virginia	1,981
6	Wisconsin	3,439
3	Wyoming	3,874

<u>RANK ORDER</u>

RANK	STATE	PER CAPITA
1	New York	$4,772
2	Alaska	4,230
3	Wyoming	3,874
4	California	3,733
5	Minnesota	3,608
6	Wisconsin	3,439
7	Michigan	3,309
8	Nevada	3,287
9	New Jersey	3,286
10	Oregon	3,184
11	Illinois	3,180
12	Colorado	3,177
13	Ohio	3,030
14	Washington	3,027
15	Florida	2,921
16	Connecticut	2,909
17	Pennsylvania	2,874
18	Iowa	2,818
19	North Carolina	2,783
20	Texas	2,746
21	Arizona	2,744
22	Kansas	2,734
23	Maryland	2,733
24	Virginia	2,709
25	Massachusetts	2,702
26	Georgia	2,692
27	Indiana	2,674
28	North Dakota	2,643
29	Nebraska	2,600
30	Alabama	2,599
31	Louisiana	2,509
32	Mississippi	2,503
32	New Mexico	2,503
34	South Carolina	2,453
35	Tennessee	2,422
36	Missouri	2,410
37	Maine	2,362
38	Idaho	2,360
39	New Hampshire	2,284
40	Utah	2,244
41	Oklahoma	2,232
42	South Dakota	2,202
43	Montana	2,168
44	Vermont	2,148
45	Rhode Island	2,142
46	Delaware	2,077
47	Kentucky	2,001
48	West Virginia	1,981
49	Arkansas	1,798
50	Hawaii	1,215

District of Columbia   9,013

Source: Morgan Quitno Press using data from U.S. Bureau of the Census, Governments Division
"State and Local Government L?nent Finances: 1999-2000" (http://www.census.gov/govs/www/estimate00.html)
**Direct general expenditures include expenditures for current operations, assistance and subsidies, interest on debt and capital outlay. Excludes intergovernmental transfers, expenditures for government owned utilities and other commercial or auxiliary enterprise and insurance trust expenditures.*

Local Government Debt Outstanding in 2000

National Total = $903,939,398,000*

ALPHA ORDER

RANK	STATE	DEBT	% of USA
24	Alabama	$11,506,782,000	1.3%
39	Alaska	3,106,021,000	0.3%
13	Arizona	20,497,732,000	2.3%
33	Arkansas	5,082,953,000	0.6%
1	California	120,749,554,000	13.4%
16	Colorado	18,768,343,000	2.1%
34	Connecticut	5,038,742,000	0.6%
43	Delaware	1,323,872,000	0.1%
4	Florida	60,313,703,000	6.7%
10	Georgia	22,862,245,000	2.5%
40	Hawaii	2,316,838,000	0.3%
47	Idaho	1,150,426,000	0.1%
6	Illinois	38,745,191,000	4.3%
22	Indiana	11,974,310,000	1.3%
36	Iowa	4,947,663,000	0.5%
29	Kansas	8,528,146,000	0.9%
18	Kentucky	15,667,958,000	1.7%
26	Louisiana	10,209,564,000	1.1%
41	Maine	1,784,833,000	0.2%
21	Maryland	12,464,426,000	1.4%
17	Massachusetts	16,202,409,000	1.8%
7	Michigan	27,750,462,000	3.1%
11	Minnesota	21,806,456,000	2.4%
32	Mississippi	5,296,594,000	0.6%
27	Missouri	9,466,147,000	1.0%
45	Montana	1,240,451,000	0.1%
35	Nebraska	4,967,490,000	0.5%
25	Nevada	10,245,296,000	1.1%
42	New Hampshire	1,542,179,000	0.2%
12	New Jersey	21,376,219,000	2.4%
37	New Mexico	4,027,029,000	0.4%
2	New York	98,933,910,000	10.9%
14	North Carolina	19,778,045,000	2.2%
44	North Dakota	1,260,812,000	0.1%
9	Ohio	23,999,571,000	2.7%
31	Oklahoma	5,745,375,000	0.6%
28	Oregon	9,372,129,000	1.0%
5	Pennsylvania	54,730,056,000	6.1%
46	Rhode Island	1,196,759,000	0.1%
23	South Carolina	11,613,346,000	1.3%
49	South Dakota	983,997,000	0.1%
19	Tennessee	15,084,523,000	1.7%
3	Texas	80,946,696,000	9.0%
30	Utah	8,508,860,000	0.9%
50	Vermont	673,817,000	0.1%
15	Virginia	19,535,459,000	2.2%
8	Washington	26,962,945,000	3.0%
38	West Virginia	3,363,696,000	0.4%
20	Wisconsin	14,108,940,000	1.6%
48	Wyoming	1,118,213,000	0.1%

RANK ORDER

RANK	STATE	DEBT	% of USA
1	California	$120,749,554,000	13.4%
2	New York	98,933,910,000	10.9%
3	Texas	80,946,696,000	9.0%
4	Florida	60,313,703,000	6.7%
5	Pennsylvania	54,730,056,000	6.1%
6	Illinois	38,745,191,000	4.3%
7	Michigan	27,750,462,000	3.1%
8	Washington	26,962,945,000	3.0%
9	Ohio	23,999,571,000	2.7%
10	Georgia	22,862,245,000	2.5%
11	Minnesota	21,806,456,000	2.4%
12	New Jersey	21,376,219,000	2.4%
13	Arizona	20,497,732,000	2.3%
14	North Carolina	19,778,045,000	2.2%
15	Virginia	19,535,459,000	2.2%
16	Colorado	18,768,343,000	2.1%
17	Massachusetts	16,202,409,000	1.8%
18	Kentucky	15,667,958,000	1.7%
19	Tennessee	15,084,523,000	1.7%
20	Wisconsin	14,108,940,000	1.6%
21	Maryland	12,464,426,000	1.4%
22	Indiana	11,974,310,000	1.3%
23	South Carolina	11,613,346,000	1.3%
24	Alabama	11,506,782,000	1.3%
25	Nevada	10,245,296,000	1.1%
26	Louisiana	10,209,564,000	1.1%
27	Missouri	9,466,147,000	1.0%
28	Oregon	9,372,129,000	1.0%
29	Kansas	8,528,146,000	0.9%
30	Utah	8,508,860,000	0.9%
31	Oklahoma	5,745,375,000	0.6%
32	Mississippi	5,296,594,000	0.6%
33	Arkansas	5,082,953,000	0.6%
34	Connecticut	5,038,742,000	0.6%
35	Nebraska	4,967,490,000	0.5%
36	Iowa	4,947,663,000	0.5%
37	New Mexico	4,027,029,000	0.4%
38	West Virginia	3,363,696,000	0.4%
39	Alaska	3,106,021,000	0.3%
40	Hawaii	2,316,838,000	0.3%
41	Maine	1,784,833,000	0.2%
42	New Hampshire	1,542,179,000	0.2%
43	Delaware	1,323,872,000	0.1%
44	North Dakota	1,260,812,000	0.1%
45	Montana	1,240,451,000	0.1%
46	Rhode Island	1,196,759,000	0.1%
47	Idaho	1,150,426,000	0.1%
48	Wyoming	1,118,213,000	0.1%
49	South Dakota	983,997,000	0.1%
50	Vermont	673,817,000	0.1%
	District of Columbia	5,062,215,000	0.6%

Source: U.S. Bureau of the Census, Governments Division
"State and Local Government Finances: 1999-2000" (http://www.census.gov/govs/www/estimate00.html)
**Includes short-term, long-term, full faith and credit, nonguaranteed and public debt for private purposes.*

Per Capita Local Government Debt Outstanding in 2000

National Per Capita = $3,203*

ALPHA ORDER

RANK	STATE	PER CAPITA
24	Alabama	$2,585
3	Alaska	4,948
8	Arizona	3,967
36	Arkansas	1,898
13	California	3,550
7	Colorado	4,338
43	Connecticut	1,477
41	Delaware	1,683
12	Florida	3,758
19	Georgia	2,776
35	Hawaii	1,911
50	Idaho	885
15	Illinois	3,114
34	Indiana	1,966
39	Iowa	1,689
14	Kansas	3,167
9	Kentucky	3,870
29	Louisiana	2,284
44	Maine	1,397
28	Maryland	2,346
25	Massachusetts	2,547
18	Michigan	2,787
6	Minnesota	4,419
38	Mississippi	1,859
39	Missouri	1,689
45	Montana	1,373
16	Nebraska	2,899
2	Nevada	5,075
47	New Hampshire	1,243
26	New Jersey	2,535
31	New Mexico	2,211
1	New York	5,207
27	North Carolina	2,447
33	North Dakota	1,967
32	Ohio	2,112
42	Oklahoma	1,663
21	Oregon	2,731
5	Pennsylvania	4,455
48	Rhode Island	1,139
17	South Carolina	2,886
46	South Dakota	1,302
22	Tennessee	2,645
10	Texas	3,863
11	Utah	3,793
49	Vermont	1,105
20	Virginia	2,749
4	Washington	4,561
37	West Virginia	1,861
23	Wisconsin	2,625
30	Wyoming	2,263

RANK ORDER

RANK	STATE	PER CAPITA
1	New York	$5,207
2	Nevada	5,075
3	Alaska	4,948
4	Washington	4,561
5	Pennsylvania	4,455
6	Minnesota	4,419
7	Colorado	4,338
8	Arizona	3,967
9	Kentucky	3,870
10	Texas	3,863
11	Utah	3,793
12	Florida	3,758
13	California	3,550
14	Kansas	3,167
15	Illinois	3,114
16	Nebraska	2,899
17	South Carolina	2,886
18	Michigan	2,787
19	Georgia	2,776
20	Virginia	2,749
21	Oregon	2,731
22	Tennessee	2,645
23	Wisconsin	2,625
24	Alabama	2,585
25	Massachusetts	2,547
26	New Jersey	2,535
27	North Carolina	2,447
28	Maryland	2,346
29	Louisiana	2,284
30	Wyoming	2,263
31	New Mexico	2,211
32	Ohio	2,112
33	North Dakota	1,967
34	Indiana	1,966
35	Hawaii	1,911
36	Arkansas	1,898
37	West Virginia	1,861
38	Mississippi	1,859
39	Iowa	1,689
39	Missouri	1,689
41	Delaware	1,683
42	Oklahoma	1,663
43	Connecticut	1,477
44	Maine	1,397
45	Montana	1,373
46	South Dakota	1,302
47	New Hampshire	1,243
48	Rhode Island	1,139
49	Vermont	1,105
50	Idaho	885

District of Columbia	8,856

Source: Morgan Quitno Press using data from U.S. Bureau of the Census, Governments Division
"State and Local Government Finances: 1999-2000" (http://www.census.gov/govs/www/estimate00.html)
*Includes short-term, long-term, full faith and credit, nonguaranteed and public debt for private purposes.

Local Government Full-Time Equivalent Employees in 2002

National Total = 11,379,390 FTE Employees*

<u>ALPHA ORDER</u>

RANK	STATE	EMPLOYEES	% of USA
23	Alabama	181,788	1.6%
46	Alaska	25,882	0.2%
20	Arizona	193,641	1.7%
33	Arkansas	96,848	0.9%
1	California	1,396,930	12.3%
24	Colorado	173,876	1.5%
32	Connecticut	113,768	1.0%
49	Delaware	21,772	0.2%
4	Florida	604,011	5.3%
9	Georgia	351,595	3.1%
50	Hawaii	14,489	0.1%
39	Idaho	53,556	0.5%
5	Illinois	496,227	4.4%
13	Indiana	234,916	2.1%
31	Iowa	121,819	1.1%
28	Kansas	129,473	1.1%
26	Kentucky	151,927	1.3%
22	Louisiana	187,628	1.6%
40	Maine	51,797	0.5%
21	Maryland	193,240	1.7%
14	Massachusetts	232,091	2.0%
8	Michigan	363,985	3.2%
19	Minnesota	203,370	1.8%
30	Mississippi	126,482	1.1%
16	Missouri	220,826	1.9%
42	Montana	34,523	0.3%
34	Nebraska	80,774	0.7%
37	Nevada	68,180	0.6%
41	New Hampshire	45,935	0.4%
11	New Jersey	337,090	3.0%
36	New Mexico	72,749	0.6%
3	New York	936,876	8.2%
10	North Carolina	338,655	3.0%
48	North Dakota	22,126	0.2%
6	Ohio	470,806	4.1%
27	Oklahoma	138,007	1.2%
29	Oregon	128,098	1.1%
7	Pennsylvania	396,219	3.5%
43	Rhode Island	32,360	0.3%
25	South Carolina	162,220	1.4%
45	South Dakota	29,075	0.3%
15	Tennessee	222,505	2.0%
2	Texas	979,164	8.6%
35	Utah	74,248	0.7%
47	Vermont	23,023	0.2%
12	Virginia	290,273	2.6%
18	Washington	204,067	1.8%
38	West Virginia	58,871	0.5%
17	Wisconsin	217,670	1.9%
44	Wyoming	29,909	0.3%

<u>RANK ORDER</u>

RANK	STATE	EMPLOYEES	% of USA
1	California	1,396,930	12.3%
2	Texas	979,164	8.6%
3	New York	936,876	8.2%
4	Florida	604,011	5.3%
5	Illinois	496,227	4.4%
6	Ohio	470,806	4.1%
7	Pennsylvania	396,219	3.5%
8	Michigan	363,985	3.2%
9	Georgia	351,595	3.1%
10	North Carolina	338,655	3.0%
11	New Jersey	337,090	3.0%
12	Virginia	290,273	2.6%
13	Indiana	234,916	2.1%
14	Massachusetts	232,091	2.0%
15	Tennessee	222,505	2.0%
16	Missouri	220,826	1.9%
17	Wisconsin	217,670	1.9%
18	Washington	204,067	1.8%
19	Minnesota	203,370	1.8%
20	Arizona	193,641	1.7%
21	Maryland	193,240	1.7%
22	Louisiana	187,628	1.6%
23	Alabama	181,788	1.6%
24	Colorado	173,876	1.5%
25	South Carolina	162,220	1.4%
26	Kentucky	151,927	1.3%
27	Oklahoma	138,007	1.2%
28	Kansas	129,473	1.1%
29	Oregon	128,098	1.1%
30	Mississippi	126,482	1.1%
31	Iowa	121,819	1.1%
32	Connecticut	113,768	1.0%
33	Arkansas	96,848	0.9%
34	Nebraska	80,774	0.7%
35	Utah	74,248	0.7%
36	New Mexico	72,749	0.6%
37	Nevada	68,180	0.6%
38	West Virginia	58,871	0.5%
39	Idaho	53,556	0.5%
40	Maine	51,797	0.5%
41	New Hampshire	45,935	0.4%
42	Montana	34,523	0.3%
43	Rhode Island	32,360	0.3%
44	Wyoming	29,909	0.3%
45	South Dakota	29,075	0.3%
46	Alaska	25,882	0.2%
47	Vermont	23,023	0.2%
48	North Dakota	22,126	0.2%
49	Delaware	21,772	0.2%
50	Hawaii	14,489	0.1%
	District of Columbia	44,030	0.4%

Source: U.S. Bureau of the Census, Governments Division
"Local Government Employment and Payroll - March 2002" (http://www.census.gov/govs/www/apesloc02.html)
*As of March 2002.

Rate of Local Government FTE Employees in 2002

National Rate = 395 Local Government Employees per 10,000 Population*

ALPHA ORDER

RANK	STATE	RATE
12	Alabama	406
14	Alaska	403
39	Arizona	356
38	Arkansas	358
17	California	399
26	Colorado	386
43	Connecticut	329
49	Delaware	270
34	Florida	362
10	Georgia	412
50	Hawaii	117
17	Idaho	399
22	Illinois	394
28	Indiana	382
8	Iowa	415
3	Kansas	477
32	Kentucky	371
7	Louisiana	419
15	Maine	400
40	Maryland	355
36	Massachusetts	361
34	Michigan	362
13	Minnesota	405
6	Mississippi	441
25	Missouri	389
30	Montana	379
4	Nebraska	468
47	Nevada	315
37	New Hampshire	360
23	New Jersey	393
23	New Mexico	393
2	New York	490
11	North Carolina	408
41	North Dakota	349
9	Ohio	413
20	Oklahoma	395
33	Oregon	364
45	Pennsylvania	321
48	Rhode Island	303
20	South Carolina	395
28	South Dakota	382
27	Tennessee	384
5	Texas	450
46	Utah	320
31	Vermont	374
19	Virginia	398
42	Washington	336
44	West Virginia	326
15	Wisconsin	400
1	Wyoming	600

RANK ORDER

RANK	STATE	RATE
1	Wyoming	600
2	New York	490
3	Kansas	477
4	Nebraska	468
5	Texas	450
6	Mississippi	441
7	Louisiana	419
8	Iowa	415
9	Ohio	413
10	Georgia	412
11	North Carolina	408
12	Alabama	406
13	Minnesota	405
14	Alaska	403
15	Maine	400
15	Wisconsin	400
17	California	399
17	Idaho	399
19	Virginia	398
20	Oklahoma	395
20	South Carolina	395
22	Illinois	394
23	New Jersey	393
23	New Mexico	393
25	Missouri	389
26	Colorado	386
27	Tennessee	384
28	Indiana	382
28	South Dakota	382
30	Montana	379
31	Vermont	374
32	Kentucky	371
33	Oregon	364
34	Florida	362
34	Michigan	362
36	Massachusetts	361
37	New Hampshire	360
38	Arkansas	358
39	Arizona	356
40	Maryland	355
41	North Dakota	349
42	Washington	336
43	Connecticut	329
44	West Virginia	326
45	Pennsylvania	321
46	Utah	320
47	Nevada	315
48	Rhode Island	303
49	Delaware	270
50	Hawaii	117
	District of Columbia	774

Source: Morgan Quitno Press using data from U.S. Bureau of the Census, Governments Division
"Local Government Employment and Payroll - March 2002" (http://www.census.gov/govs/www/apesloc02.html)
*Full-time equivalent as of March 2002.

Average Annual Earnings of FTE Local Government Employees in 2002

National Average = $39,530*

<u>ALPHA ORDER</u>

RANK	STATE	EARNINGS
43	Alabama	$30,680
8	Alaska	44,754
21	Arizona	37,629
49	Arkansas	27,392
2	California	49,823
19	Colorado	38,624
6	Connecticut	45,552
15	Delaware	39,815
22	Florida	36,778
30	Georgia	33,282
13	Hawaii	41,059
41	Idaho	31,460
11	Illinois	41,452
25	Indiana	34,445
33	Iowa	32,636
36	Kansas	32,193
48	Kentucky	28,897
46	Louisiana	29,335
42	Maine	31,014
9	Maryland	43,916
10	Massachusetts	43,379
12	Michigan	41,260
18	Minnesota	39,436
50	Mississippi	26,599
32	Missouri	32,697
44	Montana	30,049
28	Nebraska	34,005
5	Nevada	45,946
26	New Hampshire	34,321
3	New Jersey	48,900
39	New Mexico	31,963
1	New York	50,859
27	North Carolina	34,300
29	North Dakota	33,652
20	Ohio	37,675
45	Oklahoma	29,419
16	Oregon	39,595
14	Pennsylvania	40,347
7	Rhode Island	45,492
38	South Carolina	31,995
47	South Dakota	29,297
34	Tennessee	32,354
31	Texas	33,056
24	Utah	34,618
37	Vermont	32,161
23	Virginia	35,632
4	Washington	46,735
40	West Virginia	31,936
17	Wisconsin	39,490
35	Wyoming	32,296

<u>RANK ORDER</u>

RANK	STATE	EARNINGS
1	New York	$50,859
2	California	49,823
3	New Jersey	48,900
4	Washington	46,735
5	Nevada	45,946
6	Connecticut	45,552
7	Rhode Island	45,492
8	Alaska	44,754
9	Maryland	43,916
10	Massachusetts	43,379
11	Illinois	41,452
12	Michigan	41,260
13	Hawaii	41,059
14	Pennsylvania	40,347
15	Delaware	39,815
16	Oregon	39,595
17	Wisconsin	39,490
18	Minnesota	39,436
19	Colorado	38,624
20	Ohio	37,675
21	Arizona	37,629
22	Florida	36,778
23	Virginia	35,632
24	Utah	34,618
25	Indiana	34,445
26	New Hampshire	34,321
27	North Carolina	34,300
28	Nebraska	34,005
29	North Dakota	33,652
30	Georgia	33,282
31	Texas	33,056
32	Missouri	32,697
33	Iowa	32,636
34	Tennessee	32,354
35	Wyoming	32,296
36	Kansas	32,193
37	Vermont	32,161
38	South Carolina	31,995
39	New Mexico	31,963
40	West Virginia	31,936
41	Idaho	31,460
42	Maine	31,014
43	Alabama	30,680
44	Montana	30,049
45	Oklahoma	29,419
46	Louisiana	29,335
47	South Dakota	29,297
48	Kentucky	28,897
49	Arkansas	27,392
50	Mississippi	26,599
	District of Columbia	50,677

XI. HEALTH

Persons Not Covered by Health Insurance in 2002

National Total = 43,574,000 Uninsured

<u>ALPHA ORDER</u>

RANK	STATE	UNINSURED	% of USA
23	Alabama	564,000	1.3%
44	Alaska	119,000	0.3%
13	Arizona	916,000	2.1%
29	Arkansas	440,000	1.0%
1	California	6,398,000	14.7%
18	Colorado	720,000	1.7%
33	Connecticut	356,000	0.8%
48	Delaware	79,000	0.2%
4	Florida	2,843,000	6.5%
8	Georgia	1,354,000	3.1%
43	Hawaii	123,000	0.3%
38	Idaho	233,000	0.5%
5	Illinois	1,767,000	4.1%
16	Indiana	797,000	1.8%
36	Iowa	277,000	0.6%
35	Kansas	280,000	0.6%
24	Kentucky	548,000	1.3%
15	Louisiana	820,000	1.9%
40	Maine	144,000	0.3%
17	Maryland	730,000	1.7%
20	Massachusetts	644,000	1.5%
11	Michigan	1,158,000	2.7%
31	Minnesota	397,000	0.9%
28	Mississippi	465,000	1.1%
19	Missouri	646,000	1.5%
41	Montana	139,000	0.3%
39	Nebraska	174,000	0.4%
30	Nevada	418,000	1.0%
42	New Hampshire	125,000	0.3%
10	New Jersey	1,197,000	2.7%
32	New Mexico	388,000	0.9%
3	New York	3,042,000	7.0%
7	North Carolina	1,368,000	3.1%
49	North Dakota	69,000	0.2%
9	Ohio	1,344,000	3.1%
22	Oklahoma	601,000	1.4%
26	Oregon	511,000	1.2%
6	Pennsylvania	1,380,000	3.2%
45	Rhode Island	104,000	0.2%
27	South Carolina	500,000	1.1%
47	South Dakota	85,000	0.2%
21	Tennessee	614,000	1.4%
2	Texas	5,556,000	12.8%
34	Utah	310,000	0.7%
50	Vermont	66,000	0.2%
12	Virginia	962,000	2.2%
14	Washington	850,000	2.0%
37	West Virginia	255,000	0.6%
25	Wisconsin	538,000	1.2%
46	Wyoming	86,000	0.2%

<u>RANK ORDER</u>

RANK	STATE	UNINSURED	% of USA
1	California	6,398,000	14.7%
2	Texas	5,556,000	12.8%
3	New York	3,042,000	7.0%
4	Florida	2,843,000	6.5%
5	Illinois	1,767,000	4.1%
6	Pennsylvania	1,380,000	3.2%
7	North Carolina	1,368,000	3.1%
8	Georgia	1,354,000	3.1%
9	Ohio	1,344,000	3.1%
10	New Jersey	1,197,000	2.7%
11	Michigan	1,158,000	2.7%
12	Virginia	962,000	2.2%
13	Arizona	916,000	2.1%
14	Washington	850,000	2.0%
15	Louisiana	820,000	1.9%
16	Indiana	797,000	1.8%
17	Maryland	730,000	1.7%
18	Colorado	720,000	1.7%
19	Missouri	646,000	1.5%
20	Massachusetts	644,000	1.5%
21	Tennessee	614,000	1.4%
22	Oklahoma	601,000	1.4%
23	Alabama	564,000	1.3%
24	Kentucky	548,000	1.3%
25	Wisconsin	538,000	1.2%
26	Oregon	511,000	1.2%
27	South Carolina	500,000	1.1%
28	Mississippi	465,000	1.1%
29	Arkansas	440,000	1.0%
30	Nevada	418,000	1.0%
31	Minnesota	397,000	0.9%
32	New Mexico	388,000	0.9%
33	Connecticut	356,000	0.8%
34	Utah	310,000	0.7%
35	Kansas	280,000	0.6%
36	Iowa	277,000	0.6%
37	West Virginia	255,000	0.6%
38	Idaho	233,000	0.5%
39	Nebraska	174,000	0.4%
40	Maine	144,000	0.3%
41	Montana	139,000	0.3%
42	New Hampshire	125,000	0.3%
43	Hawaii	123,000	0.3%
44	Alaska	119,000	0.3%
45	Rhode Island	104,000	0.2%
46	Wyoming	86,000	0.2%
47	South Dakota	85,000	0.2%
48	Delaware	79,000	0.2%
49	North Dakota	69,000	0.2%
50	Vermont	66,000	0.2%
	District of Columbia	74,000	0.2%

Source: U.S. Bureau of the Census
"Health Insurance Coverage Status by State for All People: 2002"
(http://ferret.bls.census.gov/macro/032003/health/h06_000.htm)

Percent of Population Not Covered by Health Insurance in 2002

National Percent = 14.7% of Population*

ALPHA ORDER

RANK	STATE	PERCENT
26	Alabama	13.0
6	Alaska	17.8
9	Arizona	17.1
14	Arkansas	15.6
3	California	18.7
16	Colorado	15.3
39	Connecticut	10.2
44	Delaware	9.5
7	Florida	17.5
13	Georgia	15.7
40	Hawaii	9.7
10	Idaho	16.4
20	Illinois	13.9
28	Indiana	12.0
47	Iowa	8.6
33	Kansas	10.9
24	Kentucky	13.2
4	Louisiana	18.6
34	Maine	10.8
28	Maryland	12.0
46	Massachusetts	9.0
37	Michigan	10.4
50	Minnesota	8.0
14	Mississippi	15.6
37	Missouri	10.4
17	Montana	15.2
42	Nebraska	9.6
7	Nevada	17.5
45	New Hampshire	9.2
25	New Jersey	13.1
2	New Mexico	22.0
12	New York	15.8
18	North Carolina	14.9
35	North Dakota	10.7
31	Ohio	11.4
5	Oklahoma	18.2
23	Oregon	13.3
40	Pennsylvania	9.7
49	Rhode Island	8.3
27	South Carolina	12.3
36	South Dakota	10.6
32	Tennessee	11.0
1	Texas	24.1
21	Utah	13.6
42	Vermont	9.6
28	Virginia	12.0
21	Washington	13.6
19	West Virginia	14.0
48	Wisconsin	8.4
10	Wyoming	16.4

RANK ORDER

RANK	STATE	PERCENT
1	Texas	24.1
2	New Mexico	22.0
3	California	18.7
4	Louisiana	18.6
5	Oklahoma	18.2
6	Alaska	17.8
7	Florida	17.5
7	Nevada	17.5
9	Arizona	17.1
10	Idaho	16.4
10	Wyoming	16.4
12	New York	15.8
13	Georgia	15.7
14	Arkansas	15.6
14	Mississippi	15.6
16	Colorado	15.3
17	Montana	15.2
18	North Carolina	14.9
19	West Virginia	14.0
20	Illinois	13.9
21	Utah	13.6
21	Washington	13.6
23	Oregon	13.3
24	Kentucky	13.2
25	New Jersey	13.1
26	Alabama	13.0
27	South Carolina	12.3
28	Indiana	12.0
28	Maryland	12.0
28	Virginia	12.0
31	Ohio	11.4
32	Tennessee	11.0
33	Kansas	10.9
34	Maine	10.8
35	North Dakota	10.7
36	South Dakota	10.6
37	Michigan	10.4
37	Missouri	10.4
39	Connecticut	10.2
40	Hawaii	9.7
40	Pennsylvania	9.7
42	Nebraska	9.6
42	Vermont	9.6
44	Delaware	9.5
45	New Hampshire	9.2
46	Massachusetts	9.0
47	Iowa	8.6
48	Wisconsin	8.4
49	Rhode Island	8.3
50	Minnesota	8.0
	District of Columbia	13.2

Source: U.S. Bureau of the Census
"Percent of People Without Health Insurance Coverage for the Entire Year by State"
(http://www.census.gov/hhes/hlthins/hlthin02/hi02t4.pdf)
*Three-year average for 2000 through 2002.

Percent of Population Lacking Access to Primary Care in 2003

National Percent = 11.5% of Population*

<u>ALPHA ORDER</u>

RANK	STATE	PERCENT
2	Alabama	26.4
19	Alaska	13.4
18	Arizona	13.6
29	Arkansas	9.9
31	California	9.3
30	Colorado	9.7
43	Connecticut	6.5
35	Delaware	8.2
13	Florida	15.6
12	Georgia	16.4
48	Hawaii	4.4
7	Idaho	19.0
22	Illinois	12.7
35	Indiana	8.2
34	Iowa	8.8
14	Kansas	15.5
16	Kentucky	14.7
8	Louisiana	18.5
35	Maine	8.2
40	Maryland	7.6
47	Massachusetts	5.4
26	Michigan	10.9
25	Minnesota	11.5
1	Mississippi	28.2
3	Missouri	24.7
9	Montana	17.6
46	Nebraska	5.5
21	Nevada	12.8
45	New Hampshire	5.9
50	New Jersey	2.9
4	New Mexico	23.0
28	New York	10.1
35	North Carolina	8.2
6	North Dakota	19.4
42	Ohio	7.2
32	Oklahoma	9.2
39	Oregon	7.7
44	Pennsylvania	6.3
32	Rhode Island	9.2
11	South Carolina	17.0
5	South Dakota	19.5
23	Tennessee	11.8
17	Texas	14.4
15	Utah	15.4
49	Vermont	3.3
40	Virginia	7.6
23	Washington	11.8
20	West Virginia	13.2
27	Wisconsin	10.3
10	Wyoming	17.1

<u>RANK ORDER</u>

RANK	STATE	PERCENT
1	Mississippi	28.2
2	Alabama	26.4
3	Missouri	24.7
4	New Mexico	23.0
5	South Dakota	19.5
6	North Dakota	19.4
7	Idaho	19.0
8	Louisiana	18.5
9	Montana	17.6
10	Wyoming	17.1
11	South Carolina	17.0
12	Georgia	16.4
13	Florida	15.6
14	Kansas	15.5
15	Utah	15.4
16	Kentucky	14.7
17	Texas	14.4
18	Arizona	13.6
19	Alaska	13.4
20	West Virginia	13.2
21	Nevada	12.8
22	Illinois	12.7
23	Tennessee	11.8
23	Washington	11.8
25	Minnesota	11.5
26	Michigan	10.9
27	Wisconsin	10.3
28	New York	10.1
29	Arkansas	9.9
30	Colorado	9.7
31	California	9.3
32	Oklahoma	9.2
32	Rhode Island	9.2
34	Iowa	8.8
35	Delaware	8.2
35	Indiana	8.2
35	Maine	8.2
35	North Carolina	8.2
39	Oregon	7.7
40	Maryland	7.6
40	Virginia	7.6
42	Ohio	7.2
43	Connecticut	6.5
44	Pennsylvania	6.3
45	New Hampshire	5.9
46	Nebraska	5.5
47	Massachusetts	5.4
48	Hawaii	4.4
49	Vermont	3.3
50	New Jersey	2.9

District of Columbia	26.5

Source: Morgan Quitno Press using data from U.S. Dept. of Health and Human Services, Div. of Shortage Designation "Selected Statistics on Health Professional Shortage Areas"

*Percent of population considered under-served by primary medical practitioners (Family & General Practice doctors, Internists, Ob/Gyns and Pediatricians). An under-served population does not have primary medical care within reasonable economic and geographic bounds.

Personal Health Care Expenditures in 1998

National Total = $1,016,129,000,000*

ALPHA ORDER

RANK	STATE	EXPENDITURES	% of USA
22	Alabama	$15,611,000,000	1.5%
48	Alaska	2,085,000,000	0.2%
24	Arizona	15,010,000,000	1.5%
33	Arkansas	8,532,000,000	0.8%
1	California	112,848,000,000	11.1%
26	Colorado	13,552,000,000	1.3%
23	Connecticut	15,336,000,000	1.5%
44	Delaware	3,070,000,000	0.3%
4	Florida	60,306,000,000	5.9%
11	Georgia	27,213,000,000	2.7%
41	Hawaii	4,579,000,000	0.5%
43	Idaho	3,419,000,000	0.3%
6	Illinois	44,170,000,000	4.3%
15	Indiana	21,221,000,000	2.1%
30	Iowa	10,192,000,000	1.0%
31	Kansas	9,309,000,000	0.9%
25	Kentucky	14,471,000,000	1.4%
21	Louisiana	16,434,000,000	1.6%
39	Maine	4,895,000,000	0.5%
19	Maryland	19,507,000,000	1.9%
10	Massachusetts	30,198,000,000	3.0%
8	Michigan	35,256,000,000	3.5%
17	Minnesota	19,989,000,000	2.0%
32	Mississippi	9,034,000,000	0.9%
16	Missouri	21,150,000,000	2.1%
45	Montana	2,855,000,000	0.3%
35	Nebraska	6,109,000,000	0.6%
37	Nevada	5,581,000,000	0.5%
40	New Hampshire	4,610,000,000	0.5%
9	New Jersey	32,772,000,000	3.2%
38	New Mexico	5,364,000,000	0.5%
2	New York	85,156,000,000	8.4%
12	North Carolina	26,853,000,000	2.6%
47	North Dakota	2,669,000,000	0.3%
7	Ohio	41,798,000,000	4.1%
29	Oklahoma	10,897,000,000	1.1%
28	Oregon	10,950,000,000	1.1%
5	Pennsylvania	50,760,000,000	5.0%
42	Rhode Island	4,400,000,000	0.4%
27	South Carolina	13,006,000,000	1.3%
46	South Dakota	2,774,000,000	0.3%
14	Tennessee	21,798,000,000	2.1%
3	Texas	68,385,000,000	6.7%
36	Utah	5,933,000,000	0.6%
49	Vermont	2,052,000,000	0.2%
13	Virginia	22,158,000,000	2.2%
20	Washington	19,331,000,000	1.9%
34	West Virginia	7,015,000,000	0.7%
18	Wisconsin	19,806,000,000	1.9%
50	Wyoming	1,398,000,000	0.1%

RANK ORDER

RANK	STATE	EXPENDITURES	% of USA
1	California	$112,848,000,000	11.1%
2	New York	85,156,000,000	8.4%
3	Texas	68,385,000,000	6.7%
4	Florida	60,306,000,000	5.9%
5	Pennsylvania	50,760,000,000	5.0%
6	Illinois	44,170,000,000	4.3%
7	Ohio	41,798,000,000	4.1%
8	Michigan	35,256,000,000	3.5%
9	New Jersey	32,772,000,000	3.2%
10	Massachusetts	30,198,000,000	3.0%
11	Georgia	27,213,000,000	2.7%
12	North Carolina	26,853,000,000	2.6%
13	Virginia	22,158,000,000	2.2%
14	Tennessee	21,798,000,000	2.1%
15	Indiana	21,221,000,000	2.1%
16	Missouri	21,150,000,000	2.1%
17	Minnesota	19,989,000,000	2.0%
18	Wisconsin	19,806,000,000	1.9%
19	Maryland	19,507,000,000	1.9%
20	Washington	19,331,000,000	1.9%
21	Louisiana	16,434,000,000	1.6%
22	Alabama	15,611,000,000	1.5%
23	Connecticut	15,336,000,000	1.5%
24	Arizona	15,010,000,000	1.5%
25	Kentucky	14,471,000,000	1.4%
26	Colorado	13,552,000,000	1.3%
27	South Carolina	13,006,000,000	1.3%
28	Oregon	10,950,000,000	1.1%
29	Oklahoma	10,897,000,000	1.1%
30	Iowa	10,192,000,000	1.0%
31	Kansas	9,309,000,000	0.9%
32	Mississippi	9,034,000,000	0.9%
33	Arkansas	8,532,000,000	0.8%
34	West Virginia	7,015,000,000	0.7%
35	Nebraska	6,109,000,000	0.6%
36	Utah	5,933,000,000	0.6%
37	Nevada	5,581,000,000	0.5%
38	New Mexico	5,364,000,000	0.5%
39	Maine	4,895,000,000	0.5%
40	New Hampshire	4,610,000,000	0.5%
41	Hawaii	4,579,000,000	0.5%
42	Rhode Island	4,400,000,000	0.4%
43	Idaho	3,419,000,000	0.3%
44	Delaware	3,070,000,000	0.3%
45	Montana	2,855,000,000	0.3%
46	South Dakota	2,774,000,000	0.3%
47	North Dakota	2,669,000,000	0.3%
48	Alaska	2,085,000,000	0.2%
49	Vermont	2,052,000,000	0.2%
50	Wyoming	1,398,000,000	0.1%
	District of Columbia	4,312,000,000	0.4%

Source: U.S. Department of Health and Human Services, Centers for Medicare and Medicaid Services
"State Health Care Expenditures" (http://www.cms.hhs.gov/statistics/nhe/)
*By state of provider. Includes hospital care, physician services, dental services, home health care, drugs, vision products, nursing home care and other personal health care services and products. Revised figures.

Per Capita Personal Health Care Expenditures in 1998

National Per Capita = $3,760*

ALPHA ORDER

RANK	STATE	PER CAPITA
27	Alabama	$3,588
37	Alaska	3,389
45	Arizona	3,216
39	Arkansas	3,361
34	California	3,453
35	Colorado	3,414
3	Connecticut	4,686
8	Delaware	4,126
10	Florida	4,045
28	Georgia	3,564
16	Hawaii	3,846
50	Idaho	2,778
24	Illinois	3,660
25	Indiana	3,592
29	Iowa	3,562
31	Kansas	3,528
22	Kentucky	3,678
20	Louisiana	3,767
12	Maine	3,924
17	Maryland	3,802
1	Massachusetts	4,915
26	Michigan	3,590
5	Minnesota	4,229
41	Mississippi	3,283
13	Missouri	3,890
44	Montana	3,246
22	Nebraska	3,678
46	Nevada	3,201
14	New Hampshire	3,888
9	New Jersey	4,048
47	New Mexico	3,094
2	New York	4,689
30	North Carolina	3,559
7	North Dakota	4,185
21	Ohio	3,719
43	Oklahoma	3,263
40	Oregon	3,336
5	Pennsylvania	4,229
4	Rhode Island	4,455
38	South Carolina	3,387
18	South Dakota	3,796
11	Tennessee	4,012
33	Texas	3,469
49	Utah	2,824
32	Vermont	3,475
42	Virginia	3,264
36	Washington	3,399
15	West Virginia	3,872
19	Wisconsin	3,793
48	Wyoming	2,912

RANK ORDER

RANK	STATE	PER CAPITA
1	Massachusetts	$4,915
2	New York	4,689
3	Connecticut	4,686
4	Rhode Island	4,455
5	Minnesota	4,229
5	Pennsylvania	4,229
7	North Dakota	4,185
8	Delaware	4,126
9	New Jersey	4,048
10	Florida	4,045
11	Tennessee	4,012
12	Maine	3,924
13	Missouri	3,890
14	New Hampshire	3,888
15	West Virginia	3,872
16	Hawaii	3,846
17	Maryland	3,802
18	South Dakota	3,796
19	Wisconsin	3,793
20	Louisiana	3,767
21	Ohio	3,719
22	Kentucky	3,678
22	Nebraska	3,678
24	Illinois	3,660
25	Indiana	3,592
26	Michigan	3,590
27	Alabama	3,588
28	Georgia	3,564
29	Iowa	3,562
30	North Carolina	3,559
31	Kansas	3,528
32	Vermont	3,475
33	Texas	3,469
34	California	3,453
35	Colorado	3,414
36	Washington	3,399
37	Alaska	3,389
38	South Carolina	3,387
39	Arkansas	3,361
40	Oregon	3,336
41	Mississippi	3,283
42	Virginia	3,264
43	Oklahoma	3,263
44	Montana	3,246
45	Arizona	3,216
46	Nevada	3,201
47	New Mexico	3,094
48	Wyoming	2,912
49	Utah	2,824
50	Idaho	2,778

| | District of Columbia | 8,270 |

Source: MQ Press using data from U.S. Dept of Health & Human Services, Centers for Medicare and Medicaid Services "State Health Care Expenditures" (http://www.cms.hhs.gov/statistics/nhe/)

*By state of provider. Per capita calculated using resident population. These figures may be skewed due to residents crossing state borders for care. Includes hospital care, physician services, dental services, home health care, drugs, vision products, nursing home care and other personal health care services and products. Revised figures

Nonfederal Physicians in 2002

National Total = 819,643 Physicians*

<u>ALPHA ORDER</u>

RANK	STATE	PHYSICIANS	% of USA
26	Alabama	9,905	1.2%
49	Alaska	1,346	0.2%
22	Arizona	12,543	1.5%
32	Arkansas	5,841	0.7%
1	California	99,720	12.2%
24	Colorado	12,027	1.5%
21	Connecticut	13,717	1.7%
46	Delaware	2,158	0.3%
4	Florida	47,403	5.8%
14	Georgia	19,585	2.4%
40	Hawaii	3,929	0.5%
43	Idaho	2,464	0.3%
6	Illinois	36,439	4.4%
20	Indiana	14,103	1.7%
31	Iowa	5,991	0.7%
29	Kansas	6,491	0.8%
28	Kentucky	9,799	1.2%
23	Louisiana	12,515	1.5%
41	Maine	3,748	0.5%
11	Maryland	22,513	2.7%
8	Massachusetts	29,474	3.6%
10	Michigan	25,475	3.1%
17	Minnesota	14,709	1.8%
33	Mississippi	5,433	0.7%
19	Missouri	14,277	1.7%
45	Montana	2,288	0.3%
37	Nebraska	4,402	0.5%
38	Nevada	4,285	0.5%
42	New Hampshire	3,661	0.4%
9	New Jersey	28,435	3.5%
35	New Mexico	4,562	0.6%
2	New York	79,889	9.7%
12	North Carolina	22,204	2.7%
48	North Dakota	1,603	0.2%
7	Ohio	31,232	3.8%
30	Oklahoma	6,474	0.8%
27	Oregon	9,892	1.2%
5	Pennsylvania	39,886	4.9%
39	Rhode Island	3,953	0.5%
25	South Carolina	9,912	1.2%
47	South Dakota	1,714	0.2%
16	Tennessee	15,795	1.9%
3	Texas	48,156	5.9%
34	Utah	5,156	0.6%
44	Vermont	2,451	0.3%
13	Virginia	20,499	2.5%
15	Washington	17,371	2.1%
36	West Virginia	4,415	0.5%
18	Wisconsin	14,636	1.8%
50	Wyoming	1,008	0.1%

<u>RANK ORDER</u>

RANK	STATE	PHYSICIANS	% of USA
1	California	99,720	12.2%
2	New York	79,889	9.7%
3	Texas	48,156	5.9%
4	Florida	47,403	5.8%
5	Pennsylvania	39,886	4.9%
6	Illinois	36,439	4.4%
7	Ohio	31,232	3.8%
8	Massachusetts	29,474	3.6%
9	New Jersey	28,435	3.5%
10	Michigan	25,475	3.1%
11	Maryland	22,513	2.7%
12	North Carolina	22,204	2.7%
13	Virginia	20,499	2.5%
14	Georgia	19,585	2.4%
15	Washington	17,371	2.1%
16	Tennessee	15,795	1.9%
17	Minnesota	14,709	1.8%
18	Wisconsin	14,636	1.8%
19	Missouri	14,277	1.7%
20	Indiana	14,103	1.7%
21	Connecticut	13,717	1.7%
22	Arizona	12,543	1.5%
23	Louisiana	12,515	1.5%
24	Colorado	12,027	1.5%
25	South Carolina	9,912	1.2%
26	Alabama	9,905	1.2%
27	Oregon	9,892	1.2%
28	Kentucky	9,799	1.2%
29	Kansas	6,491	0.8%
30	Oklahoma	6,474	0.8%
31	Iowa	5,991	0.7%
32	Arkansas	5,841	0.7%
33	Mississippi	5,433	0.7%
34	Utah	5,156	0.6%
35	New Mexico	4,562	0.6%
36	West Virginia	4,415	0.5%
37	Nebraska	4,402	0.5%
38	Nevada	4,285	0.5%
39	Rhode Island	3,953	0.5%
40	Hawaii	3,929	0.5%
41	Maine	3,748	0.5%
42	New Hampshire	3,661	0.4%
43	Idaho	2,464	0.3%
44	Vermont	2,451	0.3%
45	Montana	2,288	0.3%
46	Delaware	2,158	0.3%
47	South Dakota	1,714	0.2%
48	North Dakota	1,603	0.2%
49	Alaska	1,346	0.2%
50	Wyoming	1,008	0.1%
	District of Columbia	4,159	0.5%

Source: American Medical Association (Chicago, Illinois)
"Physician Characteristics and Distribution in the U.S." (2004 Edition)
As of December 31, 2002. Total does not include 12,002 physicians in U.S. territories and possessions, at APO's and FPO's and whose addresses are unknown.

Rate of Nonfederal Physicians in 2002

National Rate = 285 Physicians per 100,000 Population*

ALPHA ORDER

RANK	STATE	RATE
42	Alabama	221
44	Alaska	210
36	Arizona	231
43	Arkansas	216
15	California	285
24	Colorado	267
5	Connecticut	397
23	Delaware	268
16	Florida	284
37	Georgia	229
9	Hawaii	317
50	Idaho	183
11	Illinois	290
37	Indiana	229
45	Iowa	204
35	Kansas	239
34	Kentucky	240
19	Louisiana	280
12	Maine	289
3	Maryland	413
1	Massachusetts	459
27	Michigan	254
10	Minnesota	293
48	Mississippi	190
29	Missouri	252
30	Montana	251
26	Nebraska	255
47	Nevada	198
13	New Hampshire	287
7	New Jersey	332
31	New Mexico	246
2	New York	418
24	North Carolina	267
28	North Dakota	253
20	Ohio	274
49	Oklahoma	186
17	Oregon	281
8	Pennsylvania	324
6	Rhode Island	370
33	South Carolina	242
39	South Dakota	225
21	Tennessee	273
40	Texas	222
40	Utah	222
4	Vermont	398
17	Virginia	281
14	Washington	286
32	West Virginia	245
22	Wisconsin	269
46	Wyoming	202

RANK ORDER

RANK	STATE	RATE
1	Massachusetts	459
2	New York	418
3	Maryland	413
4	Vermont	398
5	Connecticut	397
6	Rhode Island	370
7	New Jersey	332
8	Pennsylvania	324
9	Hawaii	317
10	Minnesota	293
11	Illinois	290
12	Maine	289
13	New Hampshire	287
14	Washington	286
15	California	285
16	Florida	284
17	Oregon	281
17	Virginia	281
19	Louisiana	280
20	Ohio	274
21	Tennessee	273
22	Wisconsin	269
23	Delaware	268
24	Colorado	267
24	North Carolina	267
26	Nebraska	255
27	Michigan	254
28	North Dakota	253
29	Missouri	252
30	Montana	251
31	New Mexico	246
32	West Virginia	245
33	South Carolina	242
34	Kentucky	240
35	Kansas	239
36	Arizona	231
37	Georgia	229
37	Indiana	229
39	South Dakota	225
40	Texas	222
40	Utah	222
42	Alabama	221
43	Arkansas	216
44	Alaska	210
45	Iowa	204
46	Wyoming	202
47	Nevada	198
48	Mississippi	190
49	Oklahoma	186
50	Idaho	183

	District of Columbia	731

Source: Morgan Quitno Press using data from American Medical Association (Chicago, Illinois) "Physician Characteristics and Distribution in the U.S." (2004 Edition)

*As of December 31, 2002. National rate does not include physicians in U.S. territories and possessions, at APO's and FPO's and whose addresses are unknown.

Rate of Registered Nurses in 2002

National Rate = 778 Nurses per 100,000 Population*

ALPHA ORDER				RANK ORDER		
RANK	STATE	RATE		RANK	STATE	RATE
30	Alabama	781		1	Massachusetts	1,117
25	Alaska	809		2	South Dakota	1,106
47	Arizona	596		3	Rhode Island	1,050
40	Arkansas	690		4	Minnesota	1,021
49	California	589		5	North Dakota	975
41	Colorado	649		6	Pennsylvania	953
14	Connecticut	906		7	Nebraska	945
28	Delaware	803		8	Iowa	943
32	Florida	779		9	Maine	934
42	Georgia	647		10	New Hampshire	931
45	Hawaii	619		11	Ohio	919
35	Idaho	748		12	Kansas	918
30	Illinois	781		13	Tennessee	916
25	Indiana	809		14	Connecticut	906
8	Iowa	943		15	Missouri	896
12	Kansas	918		16	Vermont	883
19	Kentucky	861		17	West Virginia	871
24	Louisiana	816		18	Maryland	863
9	Maine	934		19	Kentucky	861
18	Maryland	863		20	New Jersey	857
1	Massachusetts	1,117		21	Wisconsin	856
33	Michigan	773		22	New York	855
4	Minnesota	1,021		23	Montana	840
25	Mississippi	809		24	Louisiana	816
15	Missouri	896		25	Alaska	809
23	Montana	840		25	Indiana	809
7	Nebraska	945		25	Mississippi	809
50	Nevada	588		28	Delaware	803
10	New Hampshire	931		29	North Carolina	798
20	New Jersey	857		30	Alabama	781
43	New Mexico	630		30	Illinois	781
22	New York	855		32	Florida	779
29	North Carolina	798		33	Michigan	773
5	North Dakota	975		34	Oregon	749
11	Ohio	919		35	Idaho	748
45	Oklahoma	619		36	Washington	728
34	Oregon	749		37	Wyoming	708
6	Pennsylvania	953		38	South Carolina	697
3	Rhode Island	1,050		38	Virginia	697
38	South Carolina	697		40	Arkansas	690
2	South Dakota	1,106		41	Colorado	649
13	Tennessee	916		42	Georgia	647
44	Texas	628		43	New Mexico	630
47	Utah	596		44	Texas	628
16	Vermont	883		45	Hawaii	619
38	Virginia	697		45	Oklahoma	619
36	Washington	728		47	Arizona	596
17	West Virginia	871		47	Utah	596
21	Wisconsin	856		49	California	589
37	Wyoming	708		50	Nevada	588
					District of Columbia	1,418

Source: Morgan Quitno Press using data from U.S. Department of Labor, Bureau of Labor Statistics "Occupational Employment and Wages, 2002" (http://www.bls.gov/oes/)

**Does not include self-employed.*

Rate of Dentists in 2001

National Rate = 59 Dentists per 100,000 Population*

<table>
<tr><td colspan="3"><u>ALPHA ORDER</u></td><td colspan="3"><u>RANK ORDER</u></td></tr>
<tr><td>RANK</td><td>STATE</td><td>RATE</td><td>RANK</td><td>STATE</td><td>RATE</td></tr>
<tr><td>45</td><td>Alabama</td><td>43</td><td>1</td><td>Hawaii</td><td>81</td></tr>
<tr><td>7</td><td>Alaska</td><td>72</td><td>1</td><td>Massachusetts</td><td>81</td></tr>
<tr><td>41</td><td>Arizona</td><td>46</td><td>3</td><td>New York</td><td>80</td></tr>
<tr><td>48</td><td>Arkansas</td><td>40</td><td>4</td><td>Connecticut</td><td>78</td></tr>
<tr><td>8</td><td>California</td><td>68</td><td>4</td><td>New Jersey</td><td>78</td></tr>
<tr><td>13</td><td>Colorado</td><td>64</td><td>6</td><td>Maryland</td><td>75</td></tr>
<tr><td>4</td><td>Connecticut</td><td>78</td><td>7</td><td>Alaska</td><td>72</td></tr>
<tr><td>45</td><td>Delaware</td><td>43</td><td>8</td><td>California</td><td>68</td></tr>
<tr><td>29</td><td>Florida</td><td>52</td><td>9</td><td>Oregon</td><td>67</td></tr>
<tr><td>43</td><td>Georgia</td><td>44</td><td>10</td><td>Washington</td><td>66</td></tr>
<tr><td>1</td><td>Hawaii</td><td>81</td><td>11</td><td>Illinois</td><td>65</td></tr>
<tr><td>25</td><td>Idaho</td><td>53</td><td>11</td><td>Pennsylvania</td><td>65</td></tr>
<tr><td>11</td><td>Illinois</td><td>65</td><td>13</td><td>Colorado</td><td>64</td></tr>
<tr><td>34</td><td>Indiana</td><td>48</td><td>13</td><td>Nebraska</td><td>64</td></tr>
<tr><td>25</td><td>Iowa</td><td>53</td><td>15</td><td>Utah</td><td>63</td></tr>
<tr><td>31</td><td>Kansas</td><td>51</td><td>16</td><td>Minnesota</td><td>60</td></tr>
<tr><td>22</td><td>Kentucky</td><td>56</td><td>17</td><td>Michigan</td><td>59</td></tr>
<tr><td>37</td><td>Louisiana</td><td>47</td><td>17</td><td>Wisconsin</td><td>59</td></tr>
<tr><td>37</td><td>Maine</td><td>47</td><td>19</td><td>New Hampshire</td><td>58</td></tr>
<tr><td>6</td><td>Maryland</td><td>75</td><td>19</td><td>Vermont</td><td>58</td></tr>
<tr><td>1</td><td>Massachusetts</td><td>81</td><td>21</td><td>Virginia</td><td>57</td></tr>
<tr><td>17</td><td>Michigan</td><td>59</td><td>22</td><td>Kentucky</td><td>56</td></tr>
<tr><td>16</td><td>Minnesota</td><td>60</td><td>22</td><td>Montana</td><td>56</td></tr>
<tr><td>49</td><td>Mississippi</td><td>39</td><td>22</td><td>Rhode Island</td><td>56</td></tr>
<tr><td>32</td><td>Missouri</td><td>49</td><td>25</td><td>Idaho</td><td>53</td></tr>
<tr><td>22</td><td>Montana</td><td>56</td><td>25</td><td>Iowa</td><td>53</td></tr>
<tr><td>13</td><td>Nebraska</td><td>64</td><td>25</td><td>Ohio</td><td>53</td></tr>
<tr><td>50</td><td>Nevada</td><td>37</td><td>25</td><td>Wyoming</td><td>53</td></tr>
<tr><td>19</td><td>New Hampshire</td><td>58</td><td>29</td><td>Florida</td><td>52</td></tr>
<tr><td>4</td><td>New Jersey</td><td>78</td><td>29</td><td>Tennessee</td><td>52</td></tr>
<tr><td>43</td><td>New Mexico</td><td>44</td><td>31</td><td>Kansas</td><td>51</td></tr>
<tr><td>3</td><td>New York</td><td>80</td><td>32</td><td>Missouri</td><td>49</td></tr>
<tr><td>47</td><td>North Carolina</td><td>42</td><td>32</td><td>Oklahoma</td><td>49</td></tr>
<tr><td>34</td><td>North Dakota</td><td>48</td><td>34</td><td>Indiana</td><td>48</td></tr>
<tr><td>25</td><td>Ohio</td><td>53</td><td>34</td><td>North Dakota</td><td>48</td></tr>
<tr><td>32</td><td>Oklahoma</td><td>49</td><td>34</td><td>South Dakota</td><td>48</td></tr>
<tr><td>9</td><td>Oregon</td><td>67</td><td>37</td><td>Louisiana</td><td>47</td></tr>
<tr><td>11</td><td>Pennsylvania</td><td>65</td><td>37</td><td>Maine</td><td>47</td></tr>
<tr><td>22</td><td>Rhode Island</td><td>56</td><td>37</td><td>Texas</td><td>47</td></tr>
<tr><td>42</td><td>South Carolina</td><td>45</td><td>37</td><td>West Virginia</td><td>47</td></tr>
<tr><td>34</td><td>South Dakota</td><td>48</td><td>41</td><td>Arizona</td><td>46</td></tr>
<tr><td>29</td><td>Tennessee</td><td>52</td><td>42</td><td>South Carolina</td><td>45</td></tr>
<tr><td>37</td><td>Texas</td><td>47</td><td>43</td><td>Georgia</td><td>44</td></tr>
<tr><td>15</td><td>Utah</td><td>63</td><td>43</td><td>New Mexico</td><td>44</td></tr>
<tr><td>19</td><td>Vermont</td><td>58</td><td>45</td><td>Alabama</td><td>43</td></tr>
<tr><td>21</td><td>Virginia</td><td>57</td><td>45</td><td>Delaware</td><td>43</td></tr>
<tr><td>10</td><td>Washington</td><td>66</td><td>47</td><td>North Carolina</td><td>42</td></tr>
<tr><td>37</td><td>West Virginia</td><td>47</td><td>48</td><td>Arkansas</td><td>40</td></tr>
<tr><td>17</td><td>Wisconsin</td><td>59</td><td>49</td><td>Mississippi</td><td>39</td></tr>
<tr><td>25</td><td>Wyoming</td><td>53</td><td>50</td><td>Nevada</td><td>37</td></tr>
<tr><td></td><td></td><td></td><td></td><td>District of Columbia</td><td>126</td></tr>
</table>

Source: Morgan Quitno Press using data from American Dental Association
    "Distribution of Dentists, by Region and State, 2001"
*Professionally active dentists. National rate includes dentists for whom state is not known. National rate does not include dentists in territories nor dentists in the Armed Forces stationed overseas.

Community Hospitals in 2002

National Total = 4,927 Hospitals*

<u>ALPHA ORDER</u>

RANK	STATE	HOSPITALS	% of USA
19	Alabama	106	2.2%
47	Alaska	19	0.4%
31	Arizona	61	1.2%
23	Arkansas	87	1.8%
2	California	383	7.8%
29	Colorado	68	1.4%
42	Connecticut	35	0.7%
50	Delaware	6	0.1%
4	Florida	202	4.1%
8	Georgia	146	3.0%
45	Hawaii	25	0.5%
39	Idaho	39	0.8%
6	Illinois	192	3.9%
18	Indiana	112	2.3%
16	Iowa	116	2.4%
11	Kansas	132	2.7%
21	Kentucky	104	2.1%
12	Louisiana	128	2.6%
40	Maine	37	0.8%
36	Maryland	49	1.0%
28	Massachusetts	78	1.6%
9	Michigan	145	2.9%
10	Minnesota	133	2.7%
22	Mississippi	91	1.8%
15	Missouri	119	2.4%
34	Montana	53	1.1%
24	Nebraska	86	1.7%
44	Nevada	26	0.5%
43	New Hampshire	28	0.6%
27	New Jersey	81	1.6%
41	New Mexico	36	0.7%
3	New York	211	4.3%
17	North Carolina	113	2.3%
37	North Dakota	42	0.9%
7	Ohio	168	3.4%
20	Oklahoma	105	2.1%
32	Oregon	60	1.2%
5	Pennsylvania	201	4.1%
49	Rhode Island	11	0.2%
30	South Carolina	62	1.3%
35	South Dakota	51	1.0%
13	Tennessee	125	2.5%
1	Texas	416	8.4%
37	Utah	42	0.9%
48	Vermont	14	0.3%
24	Virginia	86	1.7%
24	Washington	86	1.7%
33	West Virginia	57	1.2%
14	Wisconsin	120	2.4%
46	Wyoming	24	0.5%

<u>RANK ORDER</u>

RANK	STATE	HOSPITALS	% of USA
1	Texas	416	8.4%
2	California	383	7.8%
3	New York	211	4.3%
4	Florida	202	4.1%
5	Pennsylvania	201	4.1%
6	Illinois	192	3.9%
7	Ohio	168	3.4%
8	Georgia	146	3.0%
9	Michigan	145	2.9%
10	Minnesota	133	2.7%
11	Kansas	132	2.7%
12	Louisiana	128	2.6%
13	Tennessee	125	2.5%
14	Wisconsin	120	2.4%
15	Missouri	119	2.4%
16	Iowa	116	2.4%
17	North Carolina	113	2.3%
18	Indiana	112	2.3%
19	Alabama	106	2.2%
20	Oklahoma	105	2.1%
21	Kentucky	104	2.1%
22	Mississippi	91	1.8%
23	Arkansas	87	1.8%
24	Nebraska	86	1.7%
24	Virginia	86	1.7%
24	Washington	86	1.7%
27	New Jersey	81	1.6%
28	Massachusetts	78	1.6%
29	Colorado	68	1.4%
30	South Carolina	62	1.3%
31	Arizona	61	1.2%
32	Oregon	60	1.2%
33	West Virginia	57	1.2%
34	Montana	53	1.1%
35	South Dakota	51	1.0%
36	Maryland	49	1.0%
37	North Dakota	42	0.9%
37	Utah	42	0.9%
39	Idaho	39	0.8%
40	Maine	37	0.8%
41	New Mexico	36	0.7%
42	Connecticut	35	0.7%
43	New Hampshire	28	0.6%
44	Nevada	26	0.5%
45	Hawaii	25	0.5%
46	Wyoming	24	0.5%
47	Alaska	19	0.4%
48	Vermont	14	0.3%
49	Rhode Island	11	0.2%
50	Delaware	6	0.1%
	District of Columbia	10	0.2%

Source: American Hospital Association (Chicago, IL)
   "Hospital Statistics" (2004 edition)
*Community hospitals are all nonfederal, short-term, general and special hospitals whose facilities and services are available to the public.

Rate of Community Hospitals in 2002

National Rate = 1.7 Community Hospitals per 100,000 Population*

ALPHA ORDER

RANK	STATE	RATE
18	Alabama	2.4
11	Alaska	3.0
43	Arizona	1.1
8	Arkansas	3.2
43	California	1.1
32	Colorado	1.5
46	Connecticut	1.0
50	Delaware	0.7
39	Florida	1.2
29	Georgia	1.7
24	Hawaii	2.0
13	Idaho	2.9
32	Illinois	1.5
27	Indiana	1.8
7	Iowa	4.0
5	Kansas	4.9
17	Kentucky	2.5
13	Louisiana	2.9
13	Maine	2.9
48	Maryland	0.9
39	Massachusetts	1.2
36	Michigan	1.4
16	Minnesota	2.6
8	Mississippi	3.2
23	Missouri	2.1
3	Montana	5.8
4	Nebraska	5.0
39	Nevada	1.2
20	New Hampshire	2.2
48	New Jersey	0.9
25	New Mexico	1.9
43	New York	1.1
36	North Carolina	1.4
2	North Dakota	6.6
32	Ohio	1.5
11	Oklahoma	3.0
29	Oregon	1.7
31	Pennsylvania	1.6
46	Rhode Island	1.0
32	South Carolina	1.5
1	South Dakota	6.7
20	Tennessee	2.2
25	Texas	1.9
27	Utah	1.8
19	Vermont	2.3
39	Virginia	1.2
36	Washington	1.4
8	West Virginia	3.2
20	Wisconsin	2.2
6	Wyoming	4.8

RANK ORDER

RANK	STATE	RATE
1	South Dakota	6.7
2	North Dakota	6.6
3	Montana	5.8
4	Nebraska	5.0
5	Kansas	4.9
6	Wyoming	4.8
7	Iowa	4.0
8	Arkansas	3.2
8	Mississippi	3.2
8	West Virginia	3.2
11	Alaska	3.0
11	Oklahoma	3.0
13	Idaho	2.9
13	Louisiana	2.9
13	Maine	2.9
16	Minnesota	2.6
17	Kentucky	2.5
18	Alabama	2.4
19	Vermont	2.3
20	New Hampshire	2.2
20	Tennessee	2.2
20	Wisconsin	2.2
23	Missouri	2.1
24	Hawaii	2.0
25	New Mexico	1.9
25	Texas	1.9
27	Indiana	1.8
27	Utah	1.8
29	Georgia	1.7
29	Oregon	1.7
31	Pennsylvania	1.6
32	Colorado	1.5
32	Illinois	1.5
32	Ohio	1.5
32	South Carolina	1.5
36	Michigan	1.4
36	North Carolina	1.4
36	Washington	1.4
39	Florida	1.2
39	Massachusetts	1.2
39	Nevada	1.2
39	Virginia	1.2
43	Arizona	1.1
43	California	1.1
43	New York	1.1
46	Connecticut	1.0
46	Rhode Island	1.0
48	Maryland	0.9
48	New Jersey	0.9
50	Delaware	0.7
	District of Columbia	1.8

*Community hospitals are all nonfederal, short-term, general and special hospitals whose facilities and services are available to the public.

Births in 2002

National Total = 4,021,726 Live Births*

ALPHA ORDER

RANK	STATE	BIRTHS	% of USA
24	Alabama	58,967	1.5%
47	Alaska	9,938	0.2%
13	Arizona	87,837	2.2%
34	Arkansas	37,437	0.9%
1	California	529,357	13.2%
21	Colorado	68,418	1.7%
30	Connecticut	42,001	1.0%
44	Delaware	11,090	0.3%
4	Florida	205,579	5.1%
8	Georgia	133,300	3.3%
40	Hawaii	17,477	0.4%
38	Idaho	20,970	0.5%
5	Illinois	180,622	4.5%
14	Indiana	85,081	2.1%
33	Iowa	37,559	0.9%
32	Kansas	39,412	1.0%
26	Kentucky	54,233	1.3%
23	Louisiana	64,872	1.6%
42	Maine	13,559	0.3%
19	Maryland	73,323	1.8%
15	Massachusetts	80,645	2.0%
9	Michigan	129,967	3.2%
22	Minnesota	68,025	1.7%
31	Mississippi	41,518	1.0%
18	Missouri	75,251	1.9%
45	Montana	11,049	0.3%
37	Nebraska	25,383	0.6%
35	Nevada	32,571	0.8%
41	New Hampshire	14,442	0.4%
11	New Jersey	114,751	2.9%
36	New Mexico	27,753	0.7%
3	New York	251,415	6.3%
10	North Carolina	117,335	2.9%
48	North Dakota	7,757	0.2%
6	Ohio	148,720	3.7%
27	Oklahoma	50,387	1.3%
29	Oregon	45,192	1.1%
7	Pennsylvania	142,850	3.6%
43	Rhode Island	12,894	0.3%
25	South Carolina	54,570	1.4%
46	South Dakota	10,698	0.3%
17	Tennessee	77,482	1.9%
2	Texas	372,450	9.3%
28	Utah	49,182	1.2%
50	Vermont	6,387	0.2%
12	Virginia	99,672	2.5%
16	Washington	79,028	2.0%
39	West Virginia	20,712	0.5%
20	Wisconsin	68,560	1.7%
49	Wyoming	6,550	0.2%

RANK ORDER

RANK	STATE	BIRTHS	% of USA
1	California	529,357	13.2%
2	Texas	372,450	9.3%
3	New York	251,415	6.3%
4	Florida	205,579	5.1%
5	Illinois	180,622	4.5%
6	Ohio	148,720	3.7%
7	Pennsylvania	142,850	3.6%
8	Georgia	133,300	3.3%
9	Michigan	129,967	3.2%
10	North Carolina	117,335	2.9%
11	New Jersey	114,751	2.9%
12	Virginia	99,672	2.5%
13	Arizona	87,837	2.2%
14	Indiana	85,081	2.1%
15	Massachusetts	80,645	2.0%
16	Washington	79,028	2.0%
17	Tennessee	77,482	1.9%
18	Missouri	75,251	1.9%
19	Maryland	73,323	1.8%
20	Wisconsin	68,560	1.7%
21	Colorado	68,418	1.7%
22	Minnesota	68,025	1.7%
23	Louisiana	64,872	1.6%
24	Alabama	58,967	1.5%
25	South Carolina	54,570	1.4%
26	Kentucky	54,233	1.3%
27	Oklahoma	50,387	1.3%
28	Utah	49,182	1.2%
29	Oregon	45,192	1.1%
30	Connecticut	42,001	1.0%
31	Mississippi	41,518	1.0%
32	Kansas	39,412	1.0%
33	Iowa	37,559	0.9%
34	Arkansas	37,437	0.9%
35	Nevada	32,571	0.8%
36	New Mexico	27,753	0.7%
37	Nebraska	25,383	0.6%
38	Idaho	20,970	0.5%
39	West Virginia	20,712	0.5%
40	Hawaii	17,477	0.4%
41	New Hampshire	14,442	0.4%
42	Maine	13,559	0.3%
43	Rhode Island	12,894	0.3%
44	Delaware	11,090	0.3%
45	Montana	11,049	0.3%
46	South Dakota	10,698	0.3%
47	Alaska	9,938	0.2%
48	North Dakota	7,757	0.2%
49	Wyoming	6,550	0.2%
50	Vermont	6,387	0.2%
	District of Columbia	7,498	0.2%

Source: U.S. Department of Health and Human Services, National Center for Health Statistics
   "National Vital Statistics Reports" (Vol. 52, No. 10, December 17, 2003)
*Final data by state of residence.

Birth Rate in 2002

National Rate = 13.9 Live Births per 1,000 Population*

ALPHA ORDER

RANK	STATE	RATE
31	Alabama	13.1
6	Alaska	15.4
3	Arizona	16.1
20	Arkansas	13.8
8	California	15.1
7	Colorado	15.2
43	Connecticut	12.1
22	Delaware	13.7
41	Florida	12.3
4	Georgia	15.6
19	Hawaii	14.0
4	Idaho	15.6
16	Illinois	14.3
20	Indiana	13.8
37	Iowa	12.8
12	Kansas	14.5
28	Kentucky	13.3
12	Louisiana	14.5
49	Maine	10.5
25	Maryland	13.4
40	Massachusetts	12.5
36	Michigan	12.9
24	Minnesota	13.6
12	Mississippi	14.5
28	Missouri	13.3
43	Montana	12.1
11	Nebraska	14.7
9	Nevada	15.0
48	New Hampshire	11.3
25	New Jersey	13.4
9	New Mexico	15.0
31	New York	13.1
17	North Carolina	14.1
42	North Dakota	12.2
34	Ohio	13.0
15	Oklahoma	14.4
37	Oregon	12.8
46	Pennsylvania	11.6
43	Rhode Island	12.1
28	South Carolina	13.3
17	South Dakota	14.1
25	Tennessee	13.4
2	Texas	17.1
1	Utah	21.2
50	Vermont	10.4
22	Virginia	13.7
34	Washington	13.0
47	West Virginia	11.5
39	Wisconsin	12.6
31	Wyoming	13.1

RANK ORDER

RANK	STATE	RATE
1	Utah	21.2
2	Texas	17.1
3	Arizona	16.1
4	Georgia	15.6
4	Idaho	15.6
6	Alaska	15.4
7	Colorado	15.2
8	California	15.1
9	Nevada	15.0
9	New Mexico	15.0
11	Nebraska	14.7
12	Kansas	14.5
12	Louisiana	14.5
12	Mississippi	14.5
15	Oklahoma	14.4
16	Illinois	14.3
17	North Carolina	14.1
17	South Dakota	14.1
19	Hawaii	14.0
20	Arkansas	13.8
20	Indiana	13.8
22	Delaware	13.7
22	Virginia	13.7
24	Minnesota	13.6
25	Maryland	13.4
25	New Jersey	13.4
25	Tennessee	13.4
28	Kentucky	13.3
28	Missouri	13.3
28	South Carolina	13.3
31	Alabama	13.1
31	New York	13.1
31	Wyoming	13.1
34	Ohio	13.0
34	Washington	13.0
36	Michigan	12.9
37	Iowa	12.8
37	Oregon	12.8
39	Wisconsin	12.6
40	Massachusetts	12.5
41	Florida	12.3
42	North Dakota	12.2
43	Connecticut	12.1
43	Montana	12.1
43	Rhode Island	12.1
46	Pennsylvania	11.6
47	West Virginia	11.5
48	New Hampshire	11.3
49	Maine	10.5
50	Vermont	10.4

	District of Columbia	13.1

Source: U.S. Department of Health and Human Services, National Center for Health Statistics
  "National Vital Statistics Reports" (Vol. 52, No. 10, December 17, 2003)
*Final data by state of residence.

Births to White Women in 2002

National Total = 3,174,760 Live Births to White Women*

<u>ALPHA ORDER</u>

RANK	STATE	BIRTHS	% of USA
26	Alabama	39,978	1.3%
47	Alaska	6,377	0.2%
12	Arizona	77,043	2.4%
33	Arkansas	29,209	0.9%
1	California	428,549	13.5%
17	Colorado	62,425	2.0%
32	Connecticut	34,654	1.1%
45	Delaware	7,925	0.2%
4	Florida	152,855	4.8%
9	Georgia	85,809	2.7%
50	Hawaii	3,953	0.1%
38	Idaho	20,151	0.6%
5	Illinois	140,163	4.4%
13	Indiana	74,309	2.3%
30	Iowa	35,112	1.1%
31	Kansas	34,904	1.1%
22	Kentucky	48,399	1.5%
28	Louisiana	36,757	1.2%
41	Maine	13,049	0.4%
24	Maryland	45,198	1.4%
15	Massachusetts	66,689	2.1%
8	Michigan	102,590	3.2%
21	Minnesota	58,023	1.8%
37	Mississippi	22,618	0.7%
18	Missouri	62,374	2.0%
43	Montana	9,512	0.3%
36	Nebraska	22,980	0.7%
34	Nevada	26,979	0.8%
40	New Hampshire	13,691	0.4%
11	New Jersey	84,493	2.7%
35	New Mexico	23,281	0.7%
3	New York	181,212	5.7%
10	North Carolina	85,210	2.7%
46	North Dakota	6,762	0.2%
6	Ohio	122,887	3.9%
27	Oklahoma	39,508	1.2%
25	Oregon	41,047	1.3%
7	Pennsylvania	117,817	3.7%
42	Rhode Island	11,036	0.3%
29	South Carolina	35,373	1.1%
44	South Dakota	8,657	0.3%
19	Tennessee	59,627	1.9%
2	Texas	317,150	10.0%
23	Utah	46,572	1.5%
48	Vermont	6,239	0.2%
14	Virginia	71,415	2.2%
16	Washington	66,519	2.1%
39	West Virginia	19,877	0.6%
20	Wisconsin	58,979	1.9%
49	Wyoming	6,147	0.2%

<u>RANK ORDER</u>

RANK	STATE	BIRTHS	% of USA
1	California	428,549	13.5%
2	Texas	317,150	10.0%
3	New York	181,212	5.7%
4	Florida	152,855	4.8%
5	Illinois	140,163	4.4%
6	Ohio	122,887	3.9%
7	Pennsylvania	117,817	3.7%
8	Michigan	102,590	3.2%
9	Georgia	85,809	2.7%
10	North Carolina	85,210	2.7%
11	New Jersey	84,493	2.7%
12	Arizona	77,043	2.4%
13	Indiana	74,309	2.3%
14	Virginia	71,415	2.2%
15	Massachusetts	66,689	2.1%
16	Washington	66,519	2.1%
17	Colorado	62,425	2.0%
18	Missouri	62,374	2.0%
19	Tennessee	59,627	1.9%
20	Wisconsin	58,979	1.9%
21	Minnesota	58,023	1.8%
22	Kentucky	48,399	1.5%
23	Utah	46,572	1.5%
24	Maryland	45,198	1.4%
25	Oregon	41,047	1.3%
26	Alabama	39,978	1.3%
27	Oklahoma	39,508	1.2%
28	Louisiana	36,757	1.2%
29	South Carolina	35,373	1.1%
30	Iowa	35,112	1.1%
31	Kansas	34,904	1.1%
32	Connecticut	34,654	1.1%
33	Arkansas	29,209	0.9%
34	Nevada	26,979	0.8%
35	New Mexico	23,281	0.7%
36	Nebraska	22,980	0.7%
37	Mississippi	22,618	0.7%
38	Idaho	20,151	0.6%
39	West Virginia	19,877	0.6%
40	New Hampshire	13,691	0.4%
41	Maine	13,049	0.4%
42	Rhode Island	11,036	0.3%
43	Montana	9,512	0.3%
44	South Dakota	8,657	0.3%
45	Delaware	7,925	0.2%
46	North Dakota	6,762	0.2%
47	Alaska	6,377	0.2%
48	Vermont	6,239	0.2%
49	Wyoming	6,147	0.2%
50	Hawaii	3,953	0.1%
	District of Columbia	2,677	0.1%

Source: U.S. Department of Health and Human Services, National Center for Health Statistics
"National Vital Statistics Reports" (Vol. 52, No. 10, December 17, 2003)
**Final data by state of residence. By race of mother.*

Births to Black Women in 2002

National Total = 593,691 Live Births to Black Women*

<u>ALPHA ORDER</u>

RANK	STATE	BIRTHS	% of USA
15	Alabama	18,292	3.1%
41	Alaska	432	0.1%
31	Arizona	2,779	0.5%
22	Arkansas	7,427	1.3%
5	California	32,653	5.5%
29	Colorado	2,934	0.5%
24	Connecticut	5,195	0.9%
32	Delaware	2,708	0.5%
2	Florida	46,238	7.8%
3	Georgia	42,777	7.2%
40	Hawaii	475	0.1%
45	Idaho	103	0.0%
6	Illinois	31,833	5.4%
20	Indiana	9,332	1.6%
35	Iowa	1,263	0.2%
30	Kansas	2,890	0.5%
25	Kentucky	4,943	0.8%
8	Louisiana	26,659	4.5%
44	Maine	174	0.0%
9	Maryland	24,214	4.1%
21	Massachusetts	8,344	1.4%
11	Michigan	22,440	3.8%
26	Minnesota	4,862	0.8%
16	Mississippi	18,202	3.1%
19	Missouri	11,028	1.9%
50	Montana	37	0.0%
34	Nebraska	1,442	0.2%
33	Nevada	2,611	0.4%
43	New Hampshire	225	0.0%
14	New Jersey	19,952	3.4%
39	New Mexico	511	0.1%
1	New York	49,590	8.4%
7	North Carolina	27,571	4.6%
47	North Dakota	90	0.0%
10	Ohio	22,547	3.8%
27	Oklahoma	4,704	0.8%
37	Oregon	941	0.2%
13	Pennsylvania	20,265	3.4%
36	Rhode Island	1,145	0.2%
17	South Carolina	18,183	3.1%
45	South Dakota	103	0.0%
18	Tennessee	16,304	2.7%
4	Texas	41,642	7.0%
42	Utah	339	0.1%
49	Vermont	44	0.0%
12	Virginia	22,084	3.7%
28	Washington	3,393	0.6%
38	West Virginia	679	0.1%
23	Wisconsin	6,418	1.1%
48	Wyoming	54	0.0%

<u>RANK ORDER</u>

RANK	STATE	BIRTHS	% of USA
1	New York	49,590	8.4%
2	Florida	46,238	7.8%
3	Georgia	42,777	7.2%
4	Texas	41,642	7.0%
5	California	32,653	5.5%
6	Illinois	31,833	5.4%
7	North Carolina	27,571	4.6%
8	Louisiana	26,659	4.5%
9	Maryland	24,214	4.1%
10	Ohio	22,547	3.8%
11	Michigan	22,440	3.8%
12	Virginia	22,084	3.7%
13	Pennsylvania	20,265	3.4%
14	New Jersey	19,952	3.4%
15	Alabama	18,292	3.1%
16	Mississippi	18,202	3.1%
17	South Carolina	18,183	3.1%
18	Tennessee	16,304	2.7%
19	Missouri	11,028	1.9%
20	Indiana	9,332	1.6%
21	Massachusetts	8,344	1.4%
22	Arkansas	7,427	1.3%
23	Wisconsin	6,418	1.1%
24	Connecticut	5,195	0.9%
25	Kentucky	4,943	0.8%
26	Minnesota	4,862	0.8%
27	Oklahoma	4,704	0.8%
28	Washington	3,393	0.6%
29	Colorado	2,934	0.5%
30	Kansas	2,890	0.5%
31	Arizona	2,779	0.5%
32	Delaware	2,708	0.5%
33	Nevada	2,611	0.4%
34	Nebraska	1,442	0.2%
35	Iowa	1,263	0.2%
36	Rhode Island	1,145	0.2%
37	Oregon	941	0.2%
38	West Virginia	679	0.1%
39	New Mexico	511	0.1%
40	Hawaii	475	0.1%
41	Alaska	432	0.1%
42	Utah	339	0.1%
43	New Hampshire	225	0.0%
44	Maine	174	0.0%
45	Idaho	103	0.0%
45	South Dakota	103	0.0%
47	North Dakota	90	0.0%
48	Wyoming	54	0.0%
49	Vermont	44	0.0%
50	Montana	37	0.0%
	District of Columbia	4,620	0.8%

Source: U.S. Department of Health and Human Services, National Center for Health Statistics
"National Vital Statistics Reports" (Vol. 52, No. 10, December 17, 2003)
Final data by state of residence. By race of mother.

Births to Hispanic Women in 2002

National Total = 876,642 Live Births to Hispanic Women*

ALPHA ORDER

RANK	STATE	BIRTHS	% of USA
34	Alabama	2,569	0.3%
42	Alaska	799	0.1%
6	Arizona	37,938	4.3%
32	Arkansas	3,050	0.3%
1	California	263,061	30.0%
8	Colorado	21,029	2.4%
19	Connecticut	6,982	0.8%
40	Delaware	1,316	0.2%
4	Florida	51,619	5.9%
9	Georgia	16,819	1.9%
35	Hawaii	2,422	0.3%
33	Idaho	2,788	0.3%
5	Illinois	41,022	4.7%
21	Indiana	6,169	0.7%
36	Iowa	2,390	0.3%
25	Kansas	5,023	0.6%
38	Kentucky	1,630	0.2%
39	Louisiana	1,383	0.2%
47	Maine	167	0.0%
22	Maryland	6,062	0.7%
15	Massachusetts	9,592	1.1%
18	Michigan	7,265	0.8%
27	Minnesota	4,646	0.5%
41	Mississippi	823	0.1%
30	Missouri	3,267	0.4%
45	Montana	382	0.0%
29	Nebraska	3,313	0.4%
13	Nevada	11,386	1.3%
44	New Hampshire	503	0.1%
7	New Jersey	24,664	2.8%
11	New Mexico	14,623	1.7%
3	New York	54,700	6.2%
10	North Carolina	15,064	1.7%
48	North Dakota	149	0.0%
26	Ohio	4,817	0.5%
24	Oklahoma	5,259	0.6%
17	Oregon	8,040	0.9%
16	Pennsylvania	8,696	1.0%
37	Rhode Island	2,328	0.3%
31	South Carolina	3,175	0.4%
46	South Dakota	318	0.0%
28	Tennessee	4,348	0.5%
2	Texas	178,968	20.4%
20	Utah	6,952	0.8%
50	Vermont	32	0.0%
14	Virginia	9,790	1.1%
12	Washington	12,349	1.4%
49	West Virginia	84	0.0%
23	Wisconsin	5,295	0.6%
43	Wyoming	622	0.1%

RANK ORDER

RANK	STATE	BIRTHS	% of USA
1	California	263,061	30.0%
2	Texas	178,968	20.4%
3	New York	54,700	6.2%
4	Florida	51,619	5.9%
5	Illinois	41,022	4.7%
6	Arizona	37,938	4.3%
7	New Jersey	24,664	2.8%
8	Colorado	21,029	2.4%
9	Georgia	16,819	1.9%
10	North Carolina	15,064	1.7%
11	New Mexico	14,623	1.7%
12	Washington	12,349	1.4%
13	Nevada	11,386	1.3%
14	Virginia	9,790	1.1%
15	Massachusetts	9,592	1.1%
16	Pennsylvania	8,696	1.0%
17	Oregon	8,040	0.9%
18	Michigan	7,265	0.8%
19	Connecticut	6,982	0.8%
20	Utah	6,952	0.8%
21	Indiana	6,169	0.7%
22	Maryland	6,062	0.7%
23	Wisconsin	5,295	0.6%
24	Oklahoma	5,259	0.6%
25	Kansas	5,023	0.6%
26	Ohio	4,817	0.5%
27	Minnesota	4,646	0.5%
28	Tennessee	4,348	0.5%
29	Nebraska	3,313	0.4%
30	Missouri	3,267	0.4%
31	South Carolina	3,175	0.4%
32	Arkansas	3,050	0.3%
33	Idaho	2,788	0.3%
34	Alabama	2,569	0.3%
35	Hawaii	2,422	0.3%
36	Iowa	2,390	0.3%
37	Rhode Island	2,328	0.3%
38	Kentucky	1,630	0.2%
39	Louisiana	1,383	0.2%
40	Delaware	1,316	0.2%
41	Mississippi	823	0.1%
42	Alaska	799	0.1%
43	Wyoming	622	0.1%
44	New Hampshire	503	0.1%
45	Montana	382	0.0%
46	South Dakota	318	0.0%
47	Maine	167	0.0%
48	North Dakota	149	0.0%
49	West Virginia	84	0.0%
50	Vermont	32	0.0%
	District of Columbia	954	0.1%

Source: U.S. Department of Health and Human Services, National Center for Health Statistics
"National Vital Statistics Reports" (Vol. 52, No. 10, December 17, 2003)
**Final data by state of residence. By race of mother. Persons of Hispanic origin may be of any race.*

Births of Low Birthweight in 2002

National Total = 314,077 Live Births*

<u>ALPHA ORDER</u>

RANK	STATE	BIRTHS	% of USA
21	Alabama	5,825	1.9%
47	Alaska	579	0.2%
20	Arizona	5,938	1.9%
30	Arkansas	3,204	1.0%
1	California	33,824	10.8%
17	Colorado	6,067	1.9%
29	Connecticut	3,258	1.0%
41	Delaware	1,102	0.4%
4	Florida	17,320	5.5%
7	Georgia	11,915	3.8%
39	Hawaii	1,450	0.5%
40	Idaho	1,284	0.4%
5	Illinois	14,725	4.7%
16	Indiana	6,463	2.1%
34	Iowa	2,489	0.8%
32	Kansas	2,757	0.9%
23	Kentucky	4,657	1.5%
14	Louisiana	6,774	2.2%
44	Maine	853	0.3%
15	Maryland	6,607	2.1%
18	Massachusetts	6,046	1.9%
10	Michigan	10,363	3.3%
27	Minnesota	4,251	1.4%
24	Mississippi	4,635	1.5%
19	Missouri	6,034	1.9%
46	Montana	755	0.2%
38	Nebraska	1,817	0.6%
35	Nevada	2,445	0.8%
43	New Hampshire	914	0.3%
11	New Jersey	9,185	2.9%
36	New Mexico	2,225	0.7%
3	New York	19,802	6.3%
9	North Carolina	10,514	3.3%
49	North Dakota	486	0.2%
6	Ohio	12,334	3.9%
28	Oklahoma	4,019	1.3%
33	Oregon	2,608	0.8%
8	Pennsylvania	11,685	3.7%
42	Rhode Island	1,019	0.3%
22	South Carolina	5,455	1.7%
45	South Dakota	765	0.2%
13	Tennessee	7,106	2.3%
2	Texas	28,646	9.1%
31	Utah	3,164	1.0%
50	Vermont	409	0.1%
12	Virginia	7,888	2.5%
25	Washington	4,604	1.5%
37	West Virginia	1,855	0.6%
26	Wisconsin	4,538	1.4%
48	Wyoming	553	0.2%

<u>RANK ORDER</u>

RANK	STATE	BIRTHS	% of USA
1	California	33,824	10.8%
2	Texas	28,646	9.1%
3	New York	19,802	6.3%
4	Florida	17,320	5.5%
5	Illinois	14,725	4.7%
6	Ohio	12,334	3.9%
7	Georgia	11,915	3.8%
8	Pennsylvania	11,685	3.7%
9	North Carolina	10,514	3.3%
10	Michigan	10,363	3.3%
11	New Jersey	9,185	2.9%
12	Virginia	7,888	2.5%
13	Tennessee	7,106	2.3%
14	Louisiana	6,774	2.2%
15	Maryland	6,607	2.1%
16	Indiana	6,463	2.1%
17	Colorado	6,067	1.9%
18	Massachusetts	6,046	1.9%
19	Missouri	6,034	1.9%
20	Arizona	5,938	1.9%
21	Alabama	5,825	1.9%
22	South Carolina	5,455	1.7%
23	Kentucky	4,657	1.5%
24	Mississippi	4,635	1.5%
25	Washington	4,604	1.5%
26	Wisconsin	4,538	1.4%
27	Minnesota	4,251	1.4%
28	Oklahoma	4,019	1.3%
29	Connecticut	3,258	1.0%
30	Arkansas	3,204	1.0%
31	Utah	3,164	1.0%
32	Kansas	2,757	0.9%
33	Oregon	2,608	0.8%
34	Iowa	2,489	0.8%
35	Nevada	2,445	0.8%
36	New Mexico	2,225	0.7%
37	West Virginia	1,855	0.6%
38	Nebraska	1,817	0.6%
39	Hawaii	1,450	0.5%
40	Idaho	1,284	0.4%
41	Delaware	1,102	0.4%
42	Rhode Island	1,019	0.3%
43	New Hampshire	914	0.3%
44	Maine	853	0.3%
45	South Dakota	765	0.2%
46	Montana	755	0.2%
47	Alaska	579	0.2%
48	Wyoming	553	0.2%
49	North Dakota	486	0.2%
50	Vermont	409	0.1%
	District of Columbia	866	0.3%

Source: U.S. Department of Health and Human Services, National Center for Health Statistics
   "National Vital Statistics Reports" (Vol. 52, No. 10, December 17, 2003)
*Final data by state of residence. Births of less than 2,500 grams (5 pounds 8 ounces).

Births of Low Birthweight as a Percent of All Births in 2002

National Percent = 7.8% of Live Births*

<u>ALPHA ORDER</u>

RANK	STATE	PERCENT
4	Alabama	9.9
49	Alaska	5.8
36	Arizona	6.8
12	Arkansas	8.6
40	California	6.4
10	Colorado	8.9
28	Connecticut	7.8
4	Delaware	9.9
14	Florida	8.4
10	Georgia	8.9
16	Hawaii	8.3
47	Idaho	6.1
18	Illinois	8.2
30	Indiana	7.6
38	Iowa	6.6
35	Kansas	7.0
12	Kentucky	8.6
2	Louisiana	10.4
43	Maine	6.3
7	Maryland	9.0
31	Massachusetts	7.5
20	Michigan	8.0
43	Minnesota	6.3
1	Mississippi	11.2
20	Missouri	8.0
36	Montana	6.8
33	Nebraska	7.2
31	Nevada	7.5
43	New Hampshire	6.3
20	New Jersey	8.0
20	New Mexico	8.0
25	New York	7.9
7	North Carolina	9.0
43	North Dakota	6.3
16	Ohio	8.3
20	Oklahoma	8.0
49	Oregon	5.8
18	Pennsylvania	8.2
25	Rhode Island	7.9
3	South Carolina	10.0
33	South Dakota	7.2
6	Tennessee	9.2
29	Texas	7.7
40	Utah	6.4
40	Vermont	6.4
25	Virginia	7.9
48	Washington	5.9
7	West Virginia	9.0
38	Wisconsin	6.6
14	Wyoming	8.4

<u>RANK ORDER</u>

RANK	STATE	PERCENT
1	Mississippi	11.2
2	Louisiana	10.4
3	South Carolina	10.0
4	Alabama	9.9
4	Delaware	9.9
6	Tennessee	9.2
7	Maryland	9.0
7	North Carolina	9.0
7	West Virginia	9.0
10	Colorado	8.9
10	Georgia	8.9
12	Arkansas	8.6
12	Kentucky	8.6
14	Florida	8.4
14	Wyoming	8.4
16	Hawaii	8.3
16	Ohio	8.3
18	Illinois	8.2
18	Pennsylvania	8.2
20	Michigan	8.0
20	Missouri	8.0
20	New Jersey	8.0
20	New Mexico	8.0
20	Oklahoma	8.0
25	New York	7.9
25	Rhode Island	7.9
25	Virginia	7.9
28	Connecticut	7.8
29	Texas	7.7
30	Indiana	7.6
31	Massachusetts	7.5
31	Nevada	7.5
33	Nebraska	7.2
33	South Dakota	7.2
35	Kansas	7.0
36	Arizona	6.8
36	Montana	6.8
38	Iowa	6.6
38	Wisconsin	6.6
40	California	6.4
40	Utah	6.4
40	Vermont	6.4
43	Maine	6.3
43	Minnesota	6.3
43	New Hampshire	6.3
43	North Dakota	6.3
47	Idaho	6.1
48	Washington	5.9
49	Alaska	5.8
49	Oregon	5.8
	District of Columbia	11.6

Source: U.S. Department of Health and Human Services, National Center for Health Statistics
    "National Vital Statistics Reports" (Vol. 52, No. 10, December 17, 2003)
*Final data by state of residence. Births of less than 2,500 grams (5 pounds 8 ounces).

Teenage Birth Rate in 2002

National Rate = 43.0 Live Births per 1,000 Women 15 to 19 Years Old*

ALPHA ORDER

RANK	STATE	RATE
9	Alabama	54.5
25	Alaska	39.5
4	Arizona	61.2
5	Arkansas	59.9
23	California	41.1
15	Colorado	47.0
46	Connecticut	25.8
16	Delaware	46.3
19	Florida	44.5
8	Georgia	55.7
28	Hawaii	38.2
27	Idaho	39.1
22	Illinois	42.2
18	Indiana	44.6
39	Iowa	32.5
21	Kansas	43.0
14	Kentucky	51.0
6	Louisiana	58.1
47	Maine	25.4
36	Maryland	35.4
49	Massachusetts	23.3
37	Michigan	34.8
43	Minnesota	27.5
1	Mississippi	64.7
20	Missouri	44.1
34	Montana	36.4
31	Nebraska	37.0
11	Nevada	53.9
50	New Hampshire	20.0
45	New Jersey	26.8
3	New Mexico	62.4
42	New York	29.5
13	North Carolina	52.2
44	North Dakota	27.2
25	Ohio	39.5
7	Oklahoma	58.0
32	Oregon	36.8
41	Pennsylvania	31.6
35	Rhode Island	35.6
12	South Carolina	53.0
29	South Dakota	38.0
10	Tennessee	54.3
2	Texas	64.4
32	Utah	36.8
48	Vermont	24.2
30	Virginia	37.6
38	Washington	33.0
17	West Virginia	45.5
40	Wisconsin	32.3
24	Wyoming	39.9

RANK ORDER

RANK	STATE	RATE
1	Mississippi	64.7
2	Texas	64.4
3	New Mexico	62.4
4	Arizona	61.2
5	Arkansas	59.9
6	Louisiana	58.1
7	Oklahoma	58.0
8	Georgia	55.7
9	Alabama	54.5
10	Tennessee	54.3
11	Nevada	53.9
12	South Carolina	53.0
13	North Carolina	52.2
14	Kentucky	51.0
15	Colorado	47.0
16	Delaware	46.3
17	West Virginia	45.5
18	Indiana	44.6
19	Florida	44.5
20	Missouri	44.1
21	Kansas	43.0
22	Illinois	42.2
23	California	41.1
24	Wyoming	39.9
25	Alaska	39.5
25	Ohio	39.5
27	Idaho	39.1
28	Hawaii	38.2
29	South Dakota	38.0
30	Virginia	37.6
31	Nebraska	37.0
32	Oregon	36.8
32	Utah	36.8
34	Montana	36.4
35	Rhode Island	35.6
36	Maryland	35.4
37	Michigan	34.8
38	Washington	33.0
39	Iowa	32.5
40	Wisconsin	32.3
41	Pennsylvania	31.6
42	New York	29.5
43	Minnesota	27.5
44	North Dakota	27.2
45	New Jersey	26.8
46	Connecticut	25.8
47	Maine	25.4
48	Vermont	24.2
49	Massachusetts	23.3
50	New Hampshire	20.0

District of Columbia	69.1

Source: U.S. Department of Health and Human Services, National Center for Health Statistics
"National Vital Statistics Reports" (Vol. 52, No. 10, December 17, 2003)
Final data by state of residence.

Births to Unmarried Women as a Percent of All Births in 2002

National Percent = 34.0% of Live Births*

<u>ALPHA ORDER</u>

RANK	STATE	PERCENT
19	Alabama	34.8
24	Alaska	34.0
5	Arizona	40.4
10	Arkansas	37.1
28	California	33.0
46	Colorado	26.8
41	Connecticut	29.1
4	Delaware	40.6
7	Florida	39.3
8	Georgia	37.8
25	Hawaii	33.6
49	Idaho	21.9
19	Illinois	34.8
11	Indiana	36.4
39	Iowa	29.3
34	Kansas	31.1
27	Kentucky	33.2
2	Louisiana	47.0
31	Maine	32.6
19	Maryland	34.8
46	Massachusetts	26.8
23	Michigan	34.1
45	Minnesota	27.4
1	Mississippi	47.1
17	Missouri	35.2
30	Montana	32.8
44	Nebraska	28.6
9	Nevada	37.4
48	New Hampshire	24.6
39	New Jersey	29.3
3	New Mexico	46.9
14	New York	35.7
22	North Carolina	34.7
42	North Dakota	29.0
16	Ohio	35.4
11	Oklahoma	36.4
35	Oregon	30.9
26	Pennsylvania	33.4
14	Rhode Island	35.7
5	South Carolina	40.4
18	South Dakota	35.0
13	Tennessee	36.2
32	Texas	32.4
50	Utah	17.2
33	Vermont	31.9
36	Virginia	30.3
43	Washington	28.8
29	West Virginia	32.9
38	Wisconsin	30.0
36	Wyoming	30.3

<u>RANK ORDER</u>

RANK	STATE	PERCENT
1	Mississippi	47.1
2	Louisiana	47.0
3	New Mexico	46.9
4	Delaware	40.6
5	Arizona	40.4
5	South Carolina	40.4
7	Florida	39.3
8	Georgia	37.8
9	Nevada	37.4
10	Arkansas	37.1
11	Indiana	36.4
11	Oklahoma	36.4
13	Tennessee	36.2
14	New York	35.7
14	Rhode Island	35.7
16	Ohio	35.4
17	Missouri	35.2
18	South Dakota	35.0
19	Alabama	34.8
19	Illinois	34.8
19	Maryland	34.8
22	North Carolina	34.7
23	Michigan	34.1
24	Alaska	34.0
25	Hawaii	33.6
26	Pennsylvania	33.4
27	Kentucky	33.2
28	California	33.0
29	West Virginia	32.9
30	Montana	32.8
31	Maine	32.6
32	Texas	32.4
33	Vermont	31.9
34	Kansas	31.1
35	Oregon	30.9
36	Virginia	30.3
36	Wyoming	30.3
38	Wisconsin	30.0
39	Iowa	29.3
39	New Jersey	29.3
41	Connecticut	29.1
42	North Dakota	29.0
43	Washington	28.8
44	Nebraska	28.6
45	Minnesota	27.4
46	Colorado	26.8
46	Massachusetts	26.8
48	New Hampshire	24.6
49	Idaho	21.9
50	Utah	17.2
	District of Columbia	56.5

*Source: U.S. Department of Health and Human Services, National Center for Health Statistics
"National Vital Statistics Reports" (Vol. 52, No. 10, December 17, 2003)*
*Final data by state of residence.

Percent of Mothers Receiving Late or No Prenatal Care in 2002

National Percent = 3.6% of Mothers*

<u>ALPHA ORDER</u>

RANK	STATE	PERCENT
15	Alabama	3.8
11	Alaska	4.6
3	Arizona	6.6
6	Arkansas	4.9
40	California	2.6
12	Colorado	4.5
45	Connecticut	2.0
19	Delaware	3.5
31	Florida	2.9
25	Georgia	3.4
19	Hawaii	3.5
25	Idaho	3.4
31	Illinois	2.9
19	Indiana	3.5
43	Iowa	2.2
36	Kansas	2.8
41	Kentucky	2.5
17	Louisiana	3.6
48	Maine	1.6
17	Maryland	3.6
45	Massachusetts	2.0
19	Michigan	3.5
42	Minnesota	2.3
28	Mississippi	3.1
38	Missouri	2.7
36	Montana	2.8
28	Nebraska	3.1
2	Nevada	7.1
50	New Hampshire	1.4
6	New Jersey	4.9
1	New Mexico	7.9
9	New York	4.7
31	North Carolina	2.9
38	North Dakota	2.7
31	Ohio	2.9
4	Oklahoma	5.4
15	Oregon	3.8
19	Pennsylvania	3.5
49	Rhode Island	1.5
9	South Carolina	4.7
13	South Dakota	4.4
14	Tennessee	3.9
5	Texas	5.0
6	Utah	4.9
47	Vermont	1.7
19	Virginia	3.5
28	Washington	3.1
43	West Virginia	2.2
27	Wisconsin	3.2
31	Wyoming	2.9

<u>RANK ORDER</u>

RANK	STATE	PERCENT
1	New Mexico	7.9
2	Nevada	7.1
3	Arizona	6.6
4	Oklahoma	5.4
5	Texas	5.0
6	Arkansas	4.9
6	New Jersey	4.9
6	Utah	4.9
9	New York	4.7
9	South Carolina	4.7
11	Alaska	4.6
12	Colorado	4.5
13	South Dakota	4.4
14	Tennessee	3.9
15	Alabama	3.8
15	Oregon	3.8
17	Louisiana	3.6
17	Maryland	3.6
19	Delaware	3.5
19	Hawaii	3.5
19	Indiana	3.5
19	Michigan	3.5
19	Pennsylvania	3.5
19	Virginia	3.5
25	Georgia	3.4
25	Idaho	3.4
27	Wisconsin	3.2
28	Mississippi	3.1
28	Nebraska	3.1
28	Washington	3.1
31	Florida	2.9
31	Illinois	2.9
31	North Carolina	2.9
31	Ohio	2.9
31	Wyoming	2.9
36	Kansas	2.8
36	Montana	2.8
38	Missouri	2.7
38	North Dakota	2.7
40	California	2.6
41	Kentucky	2.5
42	Minnesota	2.3
43	Iowa	2.2
43	West Virginia	2.2
45	Connecticut	2.0
45	Massachusetts	2.0
47	Vermont	1.7
48	Maine	1.6
49	Rhode Island	1.5
50	New Hampshire	1.4
	District of Columbia	7.4

Source: U.S. Department of Health and Human Services, National Center for Health Statistics "National Vital Statistics Reports" (Vol. 52, No. 10, December 17, 2003)
**Final data by state of residence. "Late" means care begun in third trimester.*

Reported Legal Abortions in 2000

Reporting States' Total = 857,475 Abortions*

<u>ALPHA ORDER</u>

RANK	STATE	ABORTIONS	% of USA
17	Alabama	13,553	1.6%
NA	Alaska**	NA	NA
24	Arizona	10,064	1.2%
30	Arkansas	5,501	0.6%
NA	California**	NA	NA
35	Colorado	4,215	0.5%
18	Connecticut	12,908	1.5%
33	Delaware	5,082	0.6%
2	Florida	88,563	10.3%
8	Georgia	31,678	3.7%
37	Hawaii	3,941	0.5%
46	Idaho	801	0.1%
4	Illinois	45,884	5.4%
20	Indiana	12,272	1.4%
29	Iowa	5,747	0.7%
21	Kansas	12,225	1.4%
34	Kentucky	4,630	0.5%
22	Louisiana	11,384	1.3%
41	Maine	2,536	0.3%
19	Maryland	12,337	1.4%
11	Massachusetts	27,180	3.2%
12	Michigan	26,807	3.1%
15	Minnesota	14,468	1.7%
38	Mississippi	3,758	0.4%
25	Missouri	7,884	0.9%
42	Montana	2,441	0.3%
36	Nebraska	4,178	0.5%
28	Nevada	5,972	0.7%
NA	New Hampshire**	NA	NA
7	New Jersey	33,026	3.9%
31	New Mexico	5,465	0.6%
1	New York	129,678	15.1%
9	North Carolina	30,157	3.5%
44	North Dakota	1,341	0.2%
5	Ohio	38,140	4.4%
27	Oklahoma	7,182	0.8%
16	Oregon	14,194	1.7%
6	Pennsylvania	35,630	4.2%
32	Rhode Island	5,413	0.6%
26	South Carolina	7,527	0.9%
45	South Dakota	878	0.1%
14	Tennessee	17,479	2.0%
3	Texas	76,121	8.9%
39	Utah	3,509	0.4%
43	Vermont	1,781	0.2%
10	Virginia	27,999	3.3%
13	Washington	25,692	3.0%
40	West Virginia	2,549	0.3%
23	Wisconsin	11,040	1.3%
47	Wyoming	6	0.0%

<u>RANK ORDER</u>

RANK	STATE	ABORTIONS	% of USA
1	New York	129,678	15.1%
2	Florida	88,563	10.3%
3	Texas	76,121	8.9%
4	Illinois	45,884	5.4%
5	Ohio	38,140	4.4%
6	Pennsylvania	35,630	4.2%
7	New Jersey	33,026	3.9%
8	Georgia	31,678	3.7%
9	North Carolina	30,157	3.5%
10	Virginia	27,999	3.3%
11	Massachusetts	27,180	3.2%
12	Michigan	26,807	3.1%
13	Washington	25,692	3.0%
14	Tennessee	17,479	2.0%
15	Minnesota	14,468	1.7%
16	Oregon	14,194	1.7%
17	Alabama	13,553	1.6%
18	Connecticut	12,908	1.5%
19	Maryland	12,337	1.4%
20	Indiana	12,272	1.4%
21	Kansas	12,225	1.4%
22	Louisiana	11,384	1.3%
23	Wisconsin	11,040	1.3%
24	Arizona	10,064	1.2%
25	Missouri	7,884	0.9%
26	South Carolina	7,527	0.9%
27	Oklahoma	7,182	0.8%
28	Nevada	5,972	0.7%
29	Iowa	5,747	0.7%
30	Arkansas	5,501	0.6%
31	New Mexico	5,465	0.6%
32	Rhode Island	5,413	0.6%
33	Delaware	5,082	0.6%
34	Kentucky	4,630	0.5%
35	Colorado	4,215	0.5%
36	Nebraska	4,178	0.5%
37	Hawaii	3,941	0.5%
38	Mississippi	3,758	0.4%
39	Utah	3,509	0.4%
40	West Virginia	2,549	0.3%
41	Maine	2,536	0.3%
42	Montana	2,441	0.3%
43	Vermont	1,781	0.2%
44	North Dakota	1,341	0.2%
45	South Dakota	878	0.1%
46	Idaho	801	0.1%
47	Wyoming	6	0.0%
NA	Alaska**	NA	NA
NA	California**	NA	NA
NA	New Hampshire**	NA	NA
	District of Columbia	6,659	0.8%

Source: U.S. Department of Health and Human Services, Centers for Disease Control and Prevention
"Abortion Surveillance-United States, 2000" (Morbidity Mortality Weekly Report, Vol. 52, No. SS-12, 11/28/03)
**By state of occurrence. Total is for reporting states only.*
***Not reported.*

Reported Legal Abortions per 1,000 Live Births in 2000

Reporting States' Ratio = 245 Abortions per 1,000 Live Births*

ALPHA ORDER

RANK	STATE	RATIO
21	Alabama	214
NA	Alaska**	NA
39	Arizona	118
34	Arkansas	146
NA	California**	NA
45	Colorado	64
9	Connecticut	300
2	Delaware	460
3	Florida	434
17	Georgia	239
18	Hawaii	225
46	Idaho	39
14	Illinois	248
36	Indiana	140
33	Iowa	150
8	Kansas	308
43	Kentucky	83
30	Louisiana	168
27	Maine	186
31	Maryland	166
5	Massachusetts	333
25	Michigan	197
21	Minnesota	214
41	Mississippi	85
40	Missouri	103
19	Montana	223
29	Nebraska	170
26	Nevada	194
NA	New Hampshire**	NA
10	New Jersey	286
24	New Mexico	201
1	New York	501
13	North Carolina	251
28	North Dakota	175
15	Ohio	245
35	Oklahoma	144
7	Oregon	310
16	Pennsylvania	244
4	Rhode Island	433
37	South Carolina	134
41	South Dakota	85
20	Tennessee	220
23	Texas	209
44	Utah	74
12	Vermont	274
11	Virginia	283
6	Washington	317
38	West Virginia	122
32	Wisconsin	159
NA	Wyoming**	NA

RANK ORDER

RANK	STATE	RATIO
1	New York	501
2	Delaware	460
3	Florida	434
4	Rhode Island	433
5	Massachusetts	333
6	Washington	317
7	Oregon	310
8	Kansas	308
9	Connecticut	300
10	New Jersey	286
11	Virginia	283
12	Vermont	274
13	North Carolina	251
14	Illinois	248
15	Ohio	245
16	Pennsylvania	244
17	Georgia	239
18	Hawaii	225
19	Montana	223
20	Tennessee	220
21	Alabama	214
21	Minnesota	214
23	Texas	209
24	New Mexico	201
25	Michigan	197
26	Nevada	194
27	Maine	186
28	North Dakota	175
29	Nebraska	170
30	Louisiana	168
31	Maryland	166
32	Wisconsin	159
33	Iowa	150
34	Arkansas	146
35	Oklahoma	144
36	Indiana	140
37	South Carolina	134
38	West Virginia	122
39	Arizona	118
40	Missouri	103
41	Mississippi	85
41	South Dakota	85
43	Kentucky	83
44	Utah	74
45	Colorado	64
46	Idaho	39
NA	Alaska**	NA
NA	California**	NA
NA	New Hampshire**	NA
NA	Wyoming**	NA

District of Columbia — 869

Source: U.S. Department of Health and Human Services, Centers for Disease Control and Prevention
"Abortion Surveillance-United States, 2000" (Morbidity Mortality Weekly Report, Vol. 52, No. SS-12, 11/28/03)
*By state of occurrence. National figure is for reporting states only.
**Not reported.

Infant Deaths in 2001

National Total = 27,568 Infant Deaths*

<u>ALPHA ORDER</u>

RANK	STATE	DEATHS	% of USA
18	Alabama	567	2.1%
44	Alaska	81	0.3%
17	Arizona	592	2.1%
29	Arkansas	309	1.1%
1	California	2,830	10.3%
25	Colorado	388	1.4%
31	Connecticut	260	0.9%
40	Delaware	115	0.4%
3	Florida	1,495	5.4%
7	Georgia	1,146	4.2%
41	Hawaii	106	0.4%
39	Idaho	129	0.5%
5	Illinois	1,413	5.1%
14	Indiana	650	2.4%
34	Iowa	212	0.8%
30	Kansas	287	1.0%
28	Kentucky	325	1.2%
15	Louisiana	643	2.3%
43	Maine	84	0.3%
16	Maryland	594	2.2%
24	Massachusetts	405	1.5%
8	Michigan	1,069	3.9%
27	Minnesota	361	1.3%
23	Mississippi	445	1.6%
19	Missouri	558	2.0%
46	Montana	74	0.3%
37	Nebraska	168	0.6%
35	Nevada	180	0.7%
48	New Hampshire	56	0.2%
11	New Jersey	747	2.7%
36	New Mexico	174	0.6%
4	New York	1,482	5.4%
10	North Carolina	1,009	3.7%
47	North Dakota	67	0.2%
6	Ohio	1,161	4.2%
26	Oklahoma	366	1.3%
32	Oregon	246	0.9%
9	Pennsylvania	1,033	3.7%
42	Rhode Island	86	0.3%
20	South Carolina	496	1.8%
45	South Dakota	78	0.3%
13	Tennessee	681	2.5%
2	Texas	2,171	7.9%
33	Utah	232	0.8%
50	Vermont	35	0.1%
11	Virginia	747	2.7%
22	Washington	459	1.7%
38	West Virginia	148	0.5%
21	Wisconsin	491	1.8%
49	Wyoming	36	0.1%

<u>RANK ORDER</u>

RANK	STATE	DEATHS	% of USA
1	California	2,830	10.3%
2	Texas	2,171	7.9%
3	Florida	1,495	5.4%
4	New York	1,482	5.4%
5	Illinois	1,413	5.1%
6	Ohio	1,161	4.2%
7	Georgia	1,146	4.2%
8	Michigan	1,069	3.9%
9	Pennsylvania	1,033	3.7%
10	North Carolina	1,009	3.7%
11	New Jersey	747	2.7%
11	Virginia	747	2.7%
13	Tennessee	681	2.5%
14	Indiana	650	2.4%
15	Louisiana	643	2.3%
16	Maryland	594	2.2%
17	Arizona	592	2.1%
18	Alabama	567	2.1%
19	Missouri	558	2.0%
20	South Carolina	496	1.8%
21	Wisconsin	491	1.8%
22	Washington	459	1.7%
23	Mississippi	445	1.6%
24	Massachusetts	405	1.5%
25	Colorado	388	1.4%
26	Oklahoma	366	1.3%
27	Minnesota	361	1.3%
28	Kentucky	325	1.2%
29	Arkansas	309	1.1%
30	Kansas	287	1.0%
31	Connecticut	260	0.9%
32	Oregon	246	0.9%
33	Utah	232	0.8%
34	Iowa	212	0.8%
35	Nevada	180	0.7%
36	New Mexico	174	0.6%
37	Nebraska	168	0.6%
38	West Virginia	148	0.5%
39	Idaho	129	0.5%
40	Delaware	115	0.4%
41	Hawaii	106	0.4%
42	Rhode Island	86	0.3%
43	Maine	84	0.3%
44	Alaska	81	0.3%
45	South Dakota	78	0.3%
46	Montana	74	0.3%
47	North Dakota	67	0.2%
48	New Hampshire	56	0.2%
49	Wyoming	36	0.1%
50	Vermont	35	0.1%
	District of Columbia	81	0.3%

Source: U.S. Department of Health and Human Services, National Center for Health Statistics
 "National Vital Statistics Reports" (Vol. 52, No. 3, September 18, 2003)
*Final data. Deaths under 1 year old by state of residence.

Infant Mortality Rate in 2001

National Rate = 6.8 Infant Deaths per 1,000 Live Births*

ALPHA ORDER

RANK	STATE	RATE
4	Alabama	9.4
11	Alaska	8.1
26	Arizona	6.9
10	Arkansas	8.3
45	California	5.4
39	Colorado	5.8
34	Connecticut	6.1
1	Delaware	10.7
21	Florida	7.3
8	Georgia	8.6
32	Hawaii	6.2
32	Idaho	6.2
14	Illinois	7.7
17	Indiana	7.5
43	Iowa	5.6
18	Kansas	7.4
36	Kentucky	5.9
3	Louisiana	9.8
34	Maine	6.1
11	Maryland	8.1
48	Massachusetts	5.0
13	Michigan	8.0
47	Minnesota	5.3
2	Mississippi	10.5
18	Missouri	7.4
29	Montana	6.7
27	Nebraska	6.8
42	Nevada	5.7
50	New Hampshire	3.8
30	New Jersey	6.5
31	New Mexico	6.4
39	New York	5.8
9	North Carolina	8.5
6	North Dakota	8.8
14	Ohio	7.7
21	Oklahoma	7.3
45	Oregon	5.4
23	Pennsylvania	7.2
27	Rhode Island	6.8
5	South Carolina	8.9
18	South Dakota	7.4
7	Tennessee	8.7
36	Texas	5.9
49	Utah	4.8
44	Vermont	5.5
16	Virginia	7.6
39	Washington	5.8
23	West Virginia	7.2
25	Wisconsin	7.1
36	Wyoming	5.9

RANK ORDER

RANK	STATE	RATE
1	Delaware	10.7
2	Mississippi	10.5
3	Louisiana	9.8
4	Alabama	9.4
5	South Carolina	8.9
6	North Dakota	8.8
7	Tennessee	8.7
8	Georgia	8.6
9	North Carolina	8.5
10	Arkansas	8.3
11	Alaska	8.1
11	Maryland	8.1
13	Michigan	8.0
14	Illinois	7.7
14	Ohio	7.7
16	Virginia	7.6
17	Indiana	7.5
18	Kansas	7.4
18	Missouri	7.4
18	South Dakota	7.4
21	Florida	7.3
21	Oklahoma	7.3
23	Pennsylvania	7.2
23	West Virginia	7.2
25	Wisconsin	7.1
26	Arizona	6.9
27	Nebraska	6.8
27	Rhode Island	6.8
29	Montana	6.7
30	New Jersey	6.5
31	New Mexico	6.4
32	Hawaii	6.2
32	Idaho	6.2
34	Connecticut	6.1
34	Maine	6.1
36	Kentucky	5.9
36	Texas	5.9
36	Wyoming	5.9
39	Colorado	5.8
39	New York	5.8
39	Washington	5.8
42	Nevada	5.7
43	Iowa	5.6
44	Vermont	5.5
45	California	5.4
45	Oregon	5.4
47	Minnesota	5.3
48	Massachusetts	5.0
49	Utah	4.8
50	New Hampshire	3.8
	District of Columbia	10.6

Source: U.S. Department of Health and Human Services, National Center for Health Statistics "National Vital Statistics Reports" (Vol. 52, No. 3, September 18, 2003)
Final data. Deaths under 1 year old by state of residence.

Deaths in 2001

National Total = 2,416,425 Deaths*

ALPHA ORDER

RANK	STATE	DEATHS	% of USA
18	Alabama	45,316	1.9%
50	Alaska	2,974	0.1%
22	Arizona	41,058	1.7%
32	Arkansas	27,759	1.1%
1	California	234,044	9.7%
29	Colorado	28,294	1.2%
28	Connecticut	29,827	1.2%
45	Delaware	7,112	0.3%
2	Florida	167,269	6.9%
11	Georgia	64,485	2.7%
43	Hawaii	8,394	0.3%
42	Idaho	9,753	0.4%
7	Illinois	105,430	4.4%
14	Indiana	55,198	2.3%
31	Iowa	27,791	1.2%
33	Kansas	24,647	1.0%
23	Kentucky	39,861	1.6%
21	Louisiana	41,757	1.7%
39	Maine	12,421	0.5%
20	Maryland	43,839	1.8%
12	Massachusetts	56,754	2.3%
8	Michigan	86,424	3.6%
24	Minnesota	37,735	1.6%
30	Mississippi	28,259	1.2%
16	Missouri	54,982	2.3%
44	Montana	8,265	0.3%
36	Nebraska	15,174	0.6%
35	Nevada	16,285	0.7%
41	New Hampshire	9,815	0.4%
9	New Jersey	74,710	3.1%
37	New Mexico	14,129	0.6%
3	New York	159,240	6.6%
10	North Carolina	70,934	2.9%
47	North Dakota	6,048	0.3%
6	Ohio	108,027	4.5%
26	Oklahoma	34,682	1.4%
27	Oregon	30,158	1.2%
5	Pennsylvania	129,729	5.4%
40	Rhode Island	10,021	0.4%
25	South Carolina	36,612	1.5%
46	South Dakota	6,923	0.3%
15	Tennessee	55,151	2.3%
4	Texas	152,779	6.3%
38	Utah	12,662	0.5%
48	Vermont	5,201	0.2%
13	Virginia	56,280	2.3%
19	Washington	44,642	1.8%
34	West Virginia	20,967	0.9%
17	Wisconsin	46,628	1.9%
49	Wyoming	4,029	0.2%

RANK ORDER

RANK	STATE	DEATHS	% of USA
1	California	234,044	9.7%
2	Florida	167,269	6.9%
3	New York	159,240	6.6%
4	Texas	152,779	6.3%
5	Pennsylvania	129,729	5.4%
6	Ohio	108,027	4.5%
7	Illinois	105,430	4.4%
8	Michigan	86,424	3.6%
9	New Jersey	74,710	3.1%
10	North Carolina	70,934	2.9%
11	Georgia	64,485	2.7%
12	Massachusetts	56,754	2.3%
13	Virginia	56,280	2.3%
14	Indiana	55,198	2.3%
15	Tennessee	55,151	2.3%
16	Missouri	54,982	2.3%
17	Wisconsin	46,628	1.9%
18	Alabama	45,316	1.9%
19	Washington	44,642	1.8%
20	Maryland	43,839	1.8%
21	Louisiana	41,757	1.7%
22	Arizona	41,058	1.7%
23	Kentucky	39,861	1.6%
24	Minnesota	37,735	1.6%
25	South Carolina	36,612	1.5%
26	Oklahoma	34,682	1.4%
27	Oregon	30,158	1.2%
28	Connecticut	29,827	1.2%
29	Colorado	28,294	1.2%
30	Mississippi	28,259	1.2%
31	Iowa	27,791	1.2%
32	Arkansas	27,759	1.1%
33	Kansas	24,647	1.0%
34	West Virginia	20,967	0.9%
35	Nevada	16,285	0.7%
36	Nebraska	15,174	0.6%
37	New Mexico	14,129	0.6%
38	Utah	12,662	0.5%
39	Maine	12,421	0.5%
40	Rhode Island	10,021	0.4%
41	New Hampshire	9,815	0.4%
42	Idaho	9,753	0.4%
43	Hawaii	8,394	0.3%
44	Montana	8,265	0.3%
45	Delaware	7,112	0.3%
46	South Dakota	6,923	0.3%
47	North Dakota	6,048	0.3%
48	Vermont	5,201	0.2%
49	Wyoming	4,029	0.2%
50	Alaska	2,974	0.1%
	District of Columbia	5,951	0.2%

Source: U.S. Department of Health and Human Services, National Center for Health Statistics "National Vital Statistics Reports" (Vol. 52, No. 3, September 18, 2003)

**Final data by state of residence.*

Death Rate in 2001

National Rate = 848.5 Deaths per 100,000 Population*

ALPHA ORDER

RANK	STATE	RATE
5	Alabama	1,014.0
50	Alaska	469.4
39	Arizona	773.7
3	Arkansas	1,030.1
47	California	676.4
48	Colorado	638.5
26	Connecticut	868.4
22	Delaware	892.8
4	Florida	1,021.6
41	Georgia	767.2
46	Hawaii	684.1
44	Idaho	738.5
32	Illinois	842.1
21	Indiana	900.9
14	Iowa	947.9
19	Kansas	912.1
8	Kentucky	979.7
16	Louisiana	934.1
10	Maine	967.0
35	Maryland	813.9
23	Massachusetts	886.6
29	Michigan	863.7
42	Minnesota	757.0
7	Mississippi	988.2
9	Missouri	975.3
17	Montana	912.9
24	Nebraska	882.2
38	Nevada	776.3
37	New Hampshire	779.4
25	New Jersey	877.8
40	New Mexico	771.7
33	New York	834.4
28	North Carolina	864.4
12	North Dakota	950.1
13	Ohio	948.5
6	Oklahoma	999.6
27	Oregon	868.2
2	Pennsylvania	1,054.4
15	Rhode Island	945.7
20	South Carolina	901.3
17	South Dakota	912.9
11	Tennessee	959.2
45	Texas	714.9
49	Utah	555.7
31	Vermont	848.5
36	Virginia	782.0
43	Washington	744.9
1	West Virginia	1,164.2
30	Wisconsin	862.5
34	Wyoming	816.0

RANK ORDER

RANK	STATE	RATE
1	West Virginia	1,164.2
2	Pennsylvania	1,054.4
3	Arkansas	1,030.1
4	Florida	1,021.6
5	Alabama	1,014.0
6	Oklahoma	999.6
7	Mississippi	988.2
8	Kentucky	979.7
9	Missouri	975.3
10	Maine	967.0
11	Tennessee	959.2
12	North Dakota	950.1
13	Ohio	948.5
14	Iowa	947.9
15	Rhode Island	945.7
16	Louisiana	934.1
17	Montana	912.9
17	South Dakota	912.9
19	Kansas	912.1
20	South Carolina	901.3
21	Indiana	900.9
22	Delaware	892.8
23	Massachusetts	886.6
24	Nebraska	882.2
25	New Jersey	877.8
26	Connecticut	868.4
27	Oregon	868.2
28	North Carolina	864.4
29	Michigan	863.7
30	Wisconsin	862.5
31	Vermont	848.5
32	Illinois	842.1
33	New York	834.4
34	Wyoming	816.0
35	Maryland	813.9
36	Virginia	782.0
37	New Hampshire	779.4
38	Nevada	776.3
39	Arizona	773.7
40	New Mexico	771.7
41	Georgia	767.2
42	Minnesota	757.0
43	Washington	744.9
44	Idaho	738.5
45	Texas	714.9
46	Hawaii	684.1
47	California	676.4
48	Colorado	638.5
49	Utah	555.7
50	Alaska	469.4
	District of Columbia	1,037.1

Source: U.S. Department of Health and Human Services, National Center for Health Statistics
     "National Vital Statistics Reports" (Vol. 52, No. 3, September 18, 2003)
*Final data by state of residence. Not age-adjusted.

Age-Adjusted Death Rate in 2001

National Rate = 854.5 Deaths per 100,000 Population*

<u>ALPHA ORDER</u>

RANK	STATE	RATE
4	Alabama	992.9
28	Alaska	825.8
42	Arizona	787.4
9	Arkansas	948.1
47	California	775.1
41	Colorado	787.8
48	Connecticut	767.8
16	Delaware	891.9
36	Florida	799.7
8	Georgia	956.5
50	Hawaii	652.6
38	Idaho	798.0
22	Illinois	857.3
14	Indiana	908.3
44	Iowa	777.4
26	Kansas	839.8
5	Kentucky	987.7
2	Louisiana	1,005.9
24	Maine	843.2
17	Maryland	881.4
34	Massachusetts	801.4
19	Michigan	877.6
49	Minnesota	744.9
1	Mississippi	1,023.2
13	Missouri	909.5
25	Montana	840.3
39	Nebraska	793.5
11	Nevada	922.6
37	New Hampshire	798.5
27	New Jersey	831.9
30	New Mexico	825.4
35	New York	800.9
12	North Carolina	911.0
46	North Dakota	775.9
15	Ohio	905.7
7	Oklahoma	959.7
29	Oregon	825.6
20	Pennsylvania	869.9
33	Rhode Island	806.4
10	South Carolina	939.1
43	South Dakota	784.8
6	Tennessee	972.9
18	Texas	877.8
45	Utah	776.8
31	Vermont	811.2
21	Virginia	862.2
40	Washington	792.9
3	West Virginia	994.9
32	Wisconsin	806.5
23	Wyoming	851.7

<u>RANK ORDER</u>

RANK	STATE	RATE
1	Mississippi	1,023.2
2	Louisiana	1,005.9
3	West Virginia	994.9
4	Alabama	992.9
5	Kentucky	987.7
6	Tennessee	972.9
7	Oklahoma	959.7
8	Georgia	956.5
9	Arkansas	948.1
10	South Carolina	939.1
11	Nevada	922.6
12	North Carolina	911.0
13	Missouri	909.5
14	Indiana	908.3
15	Ohio	905.7
16	Delaware	891.9
17	Maryland	881.4
18	Texas	877.8
19	Michigan	877.6
20	Pennsylvania	869.9
21	Virginia	862.2
22	Illinois	857.3
23	Wyoming	851.7
24	Maine	843.2
25	Montana	840.3
26	Kansas	839.8
27	New Jersey	831.9
28	Alaska	825.8
29	Oregon	825.6
30	New Mexico	825.4
31	Vermont	811.2
32	Wisconsin	806.5
33	Rhode Island	806.4
34	Massachusetts	801.4
35	New York	800.9
36	Florida	799.7
37	New Hampshire	798.5
38	Idaho	798.0
39	Nebraska	793.5
40	Washington	792.9
41	Colorado	787.8
42	Arizona	787.4
43	South Dakota	784.8
44	Iowa	777.4
45	Utah	776.8
46	North Dakota	775.9
47	California	775.1
48	Connecticut	767.8
49	Minnesota	744.9
50	Hawaii	652.6

District of Columbia   1,038.2

Source: U.S. Department of Health and Human Services, National Center for Health Statistics
    "National Vital Statistics Reports" (Vol. 52, No. 3, September 18, 2003)
**Final data by state of residence. Age-adjusted rates eliminate the distorting effects of the aging of the population.*
Rates based on the year 2000 standard population.

Estimated Deaths by Cancer in 2004

National Estimated Total = 563,700 Deaths

<u>ALPHA ORDER</u>

RANK	STATE	DEATHS	% of USA
20	Alabama	10,000	1.8%
50	Alaska	780	0.1%
21	Arizona	9,710	1.7%
32	Arkansas	6,100	1.1%
1	California	55,340	9.8%
30	Colorado	6,390	1.1%
28	Connecticut	7,010	1.2%
45	Delaware	1,810	0.3%
2	Florida	40,090	7.1%
11	Georgia	14,600	2.6%
43	Hawaii	2,090	0.4%
42	Idaho	2,250	0.4%
6	Illinois	24,840	4.4%
13	Indiana	13,250	2.4%
29	Iowa	6,570	1.2%
33	Kansas	5,330	0.9%
23	Kentucky	9,360	1.7%
22	Louisiana	9,700	1.7%
38	Maine	3,100	0.5%
19	Maryland	10,430	1.9%
12	Massachusetts	13,620	2.4%
8	Michigan	19,870	3.5%
23	Minnesota	9,360	1.7%
31	Mississippi	6,230	1.1%
16	Missouri	12,480	2.2%
44	Montana	2,060	0.4%
36	Nebraska	3,410	0.6%
35	Nevada	4,530	0.8%
40	New Hampshire	2,590	0.5%
9	New Jersey	18,060	3.2%
37	New Mexico	3,110	0.6%
3	New York	36,340	6.4%
10	North Carolina	16,580	2.9%
47	North Dakota	1,340	0.2%
7	Ohio	24,480	4.3%
26	Oklahoma	7,640	1.4%
27	Oregon	7,120	1.3%
5	Pennsylvania	29,910	5.3%
41	Rhode Island	2,450	0.4%
25	South Carolina	8,860	1.6%
46	South Dakota	1,650	0.3%
15	Tennessee	12,710	2.3%
4	Texas	34,830	6.2%
39	Utah	2,620	0.5%
48	Vermont	1,300	0.2%
14	Virginia	12,850	2.3%
17	Washington	11,280	2.0%
34	West Virginia	4,710	0.8%
18	Wisconsin	10,780	1.9%
49	Wyoming	1,000	0.2%

<u>RANK ORDER</u>

RANK	STATE	DEATHS	% of USA
1	California	55,340	9.8%
2	Florida	40,090	7.1%
3	New York	36,340	6.4%
4	Texas	34,830	6.2%
5	Pennsylvania	29,910	5.3%
6	Illinois	24,840	4.4%
7	Ohio	24,480	4.3%
8	Michigan	19,870	3.5%
9	New Jersey	18,060	3.2%
10	North Carolina	16,580	2.9%
11	Georgia	14,600	2.6%
12	Massachusetts	13,620	2.4%
13	Indiana	13,250	2.4%
14	Virginia	12,850	2.3%
15	Tennessee	12,710	2.3%
16	Missouri	12,480	2.2%
17	Washington	11,280	2.0%
18	Wisconsin	10,780	1.9%
19	Maryland	10,430	1.9%
20	Alabama	10,000	1.8%
21	Arizona	9,710	1.7%
22	Louisiana	9,700	1.7%
23	Kentucky	9,360	1.7%
23	Minnesota	9,360	1.7%
25	South Carolina	8,860	1.6%
26	Oklahoma	7,640	1.4%
27	Oregon	7,120	1.3%
28	Connecticut	7,010	1.2%
29	Iowa	6,570	1.2%
30	Colorado	6,390	1.1%
31	Mississippi	6,230	1.1%
32	Arkansas	6,100	1.1%
33	Kansas	5,330	0.9%
34	West Virginia	4,710	0.8%
35	Nevada	4,530	0.8%
36	Nebraska	3,410	0.6%
37	New Mexico	3,110	0.6%
38	Maine	3,100	0.5%
39	Utah	2,620	0.5%
40	New Hampshire	2,590	0.5%
41	Rhode Island	2,450	0.4%
42	Idaho	2,250	0.4%
43	Hawaii	2,090	0.4%
44	Montana	2,060	0.4%
45	Delaware	1,810	0.3%
46	South Dakota	1,650	0.3%
47	North Dakota	1,340	0.2%
48	Vermont	1,300	0.2%
49	Wyoming	1,000	0.2%
50	Alaska	780	0.1%
	District of Columbia	1,180	0.2%

Source: American Cancer Society
"Cancer Facts & Figures 2004" (Copyright 2004, Reprinted with permission from the American Cancer Society)

Estimated Death Rate by Cancer in 2004

National Estimated Rate = 193.8 Deaths per 100,000 Population*

ALPHA ORDER

RANK	STATE	RATE
10	Alabama	222.2
49	Alaska	120.2
40	Arizona	174.0
8	Arkansas	223.8
47	California	156.0
48	Colorado	140.4
26	Connecticut	201.2
11	Delaware	221.4
4	Florida	235.6
42	Georgia	168.1
43	Hawaii	166.2
45	Idaho	164.7
33	Illinois	196.3
19	Indiana	213.9
9	Iowa	223.2
35	Kansas	195.7
6	Kentucky	227.3
17	Louisiana	215.7
3	Maine	237.4
37	Maryland	189.3
21	Massachusetts	211.7
31	Michigan	197.1
38	Minnesota	185.0
15	Mississippi	216.2
12	Missouri	218.8
7	Montana	224.5
34	Nebraska	196.1
25	Nevada	202.1
27	New Hampshire	201.1
24	New Jersey	209.1
44	New Mexico	165.9
36	New York	189.4
30	North Carolina	197.2
22	North Dakota	211.4
18	Ohio	214.1
13	Oklahoma	217.6
28	Oregon	200.0
2	Pennsylvania	241.9
5	Rhode Island	227.7
20	South Carolina	213.6
16	South Dakota	215.9
13	Tennessee	217.6
46	Texas	157.5
50	Utah	111.4
23	Vermont	210.0
40	Virginia	174.0
39	Washington	184.0
1	West Virginia	260.2
32	Wisconsin	197.0
29	Wyoming	199.5

RANK ORDER

RANK	STATE	RATE
1	West Virginia	260.2
2	Pennsylvania	241.9
3	Maine	237.4
4	Florida	235.6
5	Rhode Island	227.7
6	Kentucky	227.3
7	Montana	224.5
8	Arkansas	223.8
9	Iowa	223.2
10	Alabama	222.2
11	Delaware	221.4
12	Missouri	218.8
13	Oklahoma	217.6
13	Tennessee	217.6
15	Mississippi	216.2
16	South Dakota	215.9
17	Louisiana	215.7
18	Ohio	214.1
19	Indiana	213.9
20	South Carolina	213.6
21	Massachusetts	211.7
22	North Dakota	211.4
23	Vermont	210.0
24	New Jersey	209.1
25	Nevada	202.1
26	Connecticut	201.2
27	New Hampshire	201.1
28	Oregon	200.0
29	Wyoming	199.5
30	North Carolina	197.2
31	Michigan	197.1
32	Wisconsin	197.0
33	Illinois	196.3
34	Nebraska	196.1
35	Kansas	195.7
36	New York	189.4
37	Maryland	189.3
38	Minnesota	185.0
39	Washington	184.0
40	Arizona	174.0
40	Virginia	174.0
42	Georgia	168.1
43	Hawaii	166.2
44	New Mexico	165.9
45	Idaho	164.7
46	Texas	157.5
47	California	156.0
48	Colorado	140.4
49	Alaska	120.2
50	Utah	111.4
	District of Columbia	209.4

Estimated New Cancer Cases in 2004

National Estimated Total = 1,368,030 New Cases*

ALPHA ORDER

RANK	STATE	CASES	% of USA
20	Alabama	24,270	1.8%
50	Alaska	1,890	0.1%
21	Arizona	23,560	1.7%
32	Arkansas	14,800	1.1%
1	California	134,300	9.8%
30	Colorado	15,510	1.1%
28	Connecticut	17,010	1.2%
45	Delaware	4,390	0.3%
2	Florida	97,290	7.1%
11	Georgia	35,430	2.6%
43	Hawaii	5,070	0.4%
42	Idaho	5,460	0.4%
6	Illinois	60,280	4.4%
13	Indiana	32,160	2.4%
29	Iowa	15,940	1.2%
33	Kansas	12,940	0.9%
23	Kentucky	22,720	1.7%
22	Louisiana	23,540	1.7%
38	Maine	7,520	0.5%
19	Maryland	25,310	1.9%
12	Massachusetts	33,050	2.4%
8	Michigan	48,220	3.5%
23	Minnesota	22,720	1.7%
31	Mississippi	15,120	1.1%
16	Missouri	30,290	2.2%
44	Montana	5,000	0.4%
36	Nebraska	8,280	0.6%
35	Nevada	10,990	0.8%
40	New Hampshire	6,290	0.5%
9	New Jersey	43,830	3.2%
37	New Mexico	7,550	0.6%
3	New York	88,190	6.4%
10	North Carolina	40,240	2.9%
47	North Dakota	3,250	0.2%
7	Ohio	59,410	4.3%
26	Oklahoma	18,540	1.4%
27	Oregon	17,280	1.3%
5	Pennsylvania	72,590	5.3%
41	Rhode Island	5,950	0.4%
25	South Carolina	21,500	1.6%
46	South Dakota	4,000	0.3%
15	Tennessee	30,850	2.3%
4	Texas	84,530	6.2%
39	Utah	6,360	0.5%
48	Vermont	3,150	0.2%
14	Virginia	31,190	2.3%
17	Washington	27,380	2.0%
34	West Virginia	11,430	0.8%
18	Wisconsin	26,160	1.9%
49	Wyoming	2,430	0.2%

RANK ORDER

RANK	STATE	CASES	% of USA
1	California	134,300	9.8%
2	Florida	97,290	7.1%
3	New York	88,190	6.4%
4	Texas	84,530	6.2%
5	Pennsylvania	72,590	5.3%
6	Illinois	60,280	4.4%
7	Ohio	59,410	4.3%
8	Michigan	48,220	3.5%
9	New Jersey	43,830	3.2%
10	North Carolina	40,240	2.9%
11	Georgia	35,430	2.6%
12	Massachusetts	33,050	2.4%
13	Indiana	32,160	2.4%
14	Virginia	31,190	2.3%
15	Tennessee	30,850	2.3%
16	Missouri	30,290	2.2%
17	Washington	27,380	2.0%
18	Wisconsin	26,160	1.9%
19	Maryland	25,310	1.9%
20	Alabama	24,270	1.8%
21	Arizona	23,560	1.7%
22	Louisiana	23,540	1.7%
23	Kentucky	22,720	1.7%
23	Minnesota	22,720	1.7%
25	South Carolina	21,500	1.6%
26	Oklahoma	18,540	1.4%
27	Oregon	17,280	1.3%
28	Connecticut	17,010	1.2%
29	Iowa	15,940	1.2%
30	Colorado	15,510	1.1%
31	Mississippi	15,120	1.1%
32	Arkansas	14,800	1.1%
33	Kansas	12,940	0.9%
34	West Virginia	11,430	0.8%
35	Nevada	10,990	0.8%
36	Nebraska	8,280	0.6%
37	New Mexico	7,550	0.6%
38	Maine	7,520	0.5%
39	Utah	6,360	0.5%
40	New Hampshire	6,290	0.5%
41	Rhode Island	5,950	0.4%
42	Idaho	5,460	0.4%
43	Hawaii	5,070	0.4%
44	Montana	5,000	0.4%
45	Delaware	4,390	0.3%
46	South Dakota	4,000	0.3%
47	North Dakota	3,250	0.2%
48	Vermont	3,150	0.2%
49	Wyoming	2,430	0.2%
50	Alaska	1,890	0.1%
	District of Columbia	2,860	0.2%

Source: American Cancer Society
"Cancer Facts & Figures 2004" (Copyright 2004, Reprinted with permission from the American Cancer Society)
**These estimates are offered as a rough guide and should not be regarded as definitive. They are calculated according to the distribution of estimated 2004 cancer deaths by state. Totals do not include basal and squamous cell skin cancers or in situ carcinomas except urinary bladder.*

Estimated Rate of New Cancer Cases in 2004

National Estimated Rate = 470.4 New Cases per 100,000 Population*

ALPHA ORDER

RANK	STATE	RATE
10	Alabama	539.2
49	Alaska	291.3
41	Arizona	422.2
8	Arkansas	543.0
47	California	378.5
48	Colorado	340.8
27	Connecticut	488.3
11	Delaware	537.0
4	Florida	571.7
42	Georgia	408.0
43	Hawaii	403.1
45	Idaho	399.6
33	Illinois	476.4
19	Indiana	519.1
9	Iowa	541.4
35	Kansas	475.1
6	Kentucky	551.7
16	Louisiana	523.5
3	Maine	575.9
37	Maryland	459.4
21	Massachusetts	513.7
31	Michigan	478.4
38	Minnesota	449.1
15	Mississippi	524.8
12	Missouri	531.0
7	Montana	544.9
34	Nebraska	476.1
25	Nevada	490.4
26	New Hampshire	488.5
24	New Jersey	507.4
44	New Mexico	402.7
36	New York	459.6
30	North Carolina	478.6
22	North Dakota	512.8
18	Ohio	519.5
14	Oklahoma	528.0
28	Oregon	485.4
2	Pennsylvania	587.0
5	Rhode Island	552.9
20	South Carolina	518.4
17	South Dakota	523.3
13	Tennessee	528.1
46	Texas	382.2
50	Utah	270.5
23	Vermont	508.8
40	Virginia	422.3
39	Washington	446.6
1	West Virginia	631.4
32	Wisconsin	478.0
29	Wyoming	484.8

RANK ORDER

RANK	STATE	RATE
1	West Virginia	631.4
2	Pennsylvania	587.0
3	Maine	575.9
4	Florida	571.7
5	Rhode Island	552.9
6	Kentucky	551.7
7	Montana	544.9
8	Arkansas	543.0
9	Iowa	541.4
10	Alabama	539.2
11	Delaware	537.0
12	Missouri	531.0
13	Tennessee	528.1
14	Oklahoma	528.0
15	Mississippi	524.8
16	Louisiana	523.5
17	South Dakota	523.3
18	Ohio	519.5
19	Indiana	519.1
20	South Carolina	518.4
21	Massachusetts	513.7
22	North Dakota	512.8
23	Vermont	508.8
24	New Jersey	507.4
25	Nevada	490.4
26	New Hampshire	488.5
27	Connecticut	488.3
28	Oregon	485.4
29	Wyoming	484.8
30	North Carolina	478.6
31	Michigan	478.4
32	Wisconsin	478.0
33	Illinois	476.4
34	Nebraska	476.1
35	Kansas	475.1
36	New York	459.6
37	Maryland	459.4
38	Minnesota	449.1
39	Washington	446.6
40	Virginia	422.3
41	Arizona	422.2
42	Georgia	408.0
43	Hawaii	403.1
44	New Mexico	402.7
45	Idaho	399.6
46	Texas	382.2
47	California	378.5
48	Colorado	340.8
49	Alaska	291.3
50	Utah	270.5
	District of Columbia	507.6

Source: Morgan Quitno Press using data from American Cancer Society
"Cancer Facts & Figures 2004" (Copyright 2004, Reprinted with permission from the American Cancer Society)
**These estimates are offered as a rough guide and should not be regarded as definitive. They are calculated according to the distribution of estimated 2004 cancer deaths by state. Totals do not include basal and squamous cell skin cancers or in situ carcinomas except urinary bladder.*

Deaths by Accidents in 2001

National Total = 101,537 Deaths*

ALPHA ORDER

RANK	STATE	DEATHS	% of USA
16	Alabama	2,211	2.2%
45	Alaska	345	0.3%
12	Arizona	2,475	2.4%
30	Arkansas	1,277	1.3%
1	California	8,132	8.0%
24	Colorado	1,720	1.7%
32	Connecticut	1,056	1.0%
47	Delaware	290	0.3%
3	Florida	6,969	6.9%
9	Georgia	3,396	3.3%
44	Hawaii	372	0.4%
39	Idaho	568	0.6%
6	Illinois	4,077	4.0%
17	Indiana	2,185	2.2%
33	Iowa	1,051	1.0%
31	Kansas	1,156	1.1%
21	Kentucky	1,990	2.0%
20	Louisiana	2,029	2.0%
40	Maine	490	0.5%
28	Maryland	1,339	1.3%
27	Massachusetts	1,506	1.5%
10	Michigan	3,291	3.2%
23	Minnesota	1,797	1.8%
26	Mississippi	1,571	1.5%
13	Missouri	2,455	2.4%
41	Montana	468	0.5%
38	Nebraska	633	0.6%
36	Nevada	739	0.7%
43	New Hampshire	374	0.4%
15	New Jersey	2,405	2.4%
34	New Mexico	1,020	1.0%
4	New York	4,982	4.9%
8	North Carolina	3,438	3.4%
49	North Dakota	238	0.2%
7	Ohio	3,857	3.8%
25	Oklahoma	1,700	1.7%
29	Oregon	1,313	1.3%
5	Pennsylvania	4,552	4.5%
46	Rhode Island	293	0.3%
22	South Carolina	1,960	1.9%
42	South Dakota	382	0.4%
11	Tennessee	2,709	2.7%
2	Texas	7,920	7.8%
37	Utah	643	0.6%
50	Vermont	230	0.2%
14	Virginia	2,432	2.4%
19	Washington	2,072	2.0%
35	West Virginia	834	0.8%
18	Wisconsin	2,100	2.1%
48	Wyoming	272	0.3%

RANK ORDER

RANK	STATE	DEATHS	% of USA
1	California	8,132	8.0%
2	Texas	7,920	7.8%
3	Florida	6,969	6.9%
4	New York	4,982	4.9%
5	Pennsylvania	4,552	4.5%
6	Illinois	4,077	4.0%
7	Ohio	3,857	3.8%
8	North Carolina	3,438	3.4%
9	Georgia	3,396	3.3%
10	Michigan	3,291	3.2%
11	Tennessee	2,709	2.7%
12	Arizona	2,475	2.4%
13	Missouri	2,455	2.4%
14	Virginia	2,432	2.4%
15	New Jersey	2,405	2.4%
16	Alabama	2,211	2.2%
17	Indiana	2,185	2.2%
18	Wisconsin	2,100	2.1%
19	Washington	2,072	2.0%
20	Louisiana	2,029	2.0%
21	Kentucky	1,990	2.0%
22	South Carolina	1,960	1.9%
23	Minnesota	1,797	1.8%
24	Colorado	1,720	1.7%
25	Oklahoma	1,700	1.7%
26	Mississippi	1,571	1.5%
27	Massachusetts	1,506	1.5%
28	Maryland	1,339	1.3%
29	Oregon	1,313	1.3%
30	Arkansas	1,277	1.3%
31	Kansas	1,156	1.1%
32	Connecticut	1,056	1.0%
33	Iowa	1,051	1.0%
34	New Mexico	1,020	1.0%
35	West Virginia	834	0.8%
36	Nevada	739	0.7%
37	Utah	643	0.6%
38	Nebraska	633	0.6%
39	Idaho	568	0.6%
40	Maine	490	0.5%
41	Montana	468	0.5%
42	South Dakota	382	0.4%
43	New Hampshire	374	0.4%
44	Hawaii	372	0.4%
45	Alaska	345	0.3%
46	Rhode Island	293	0.3%
47	Delaware	290	0.3%
48	Wyoming	272	0.3%
49	North Dakota	238	0.2%
50	Vermont	230	0.2%
	District of Columbia	223	0.2%

Source: U.S. Department of Health and Human Services, National Center for Health Statistics
   "National Vital Statistics Reports" (Vol. 52, No. 3, September 18, 2003)
*Final data by state of residence. Includes motor vehicle deaths, poisoning, falls, drowning and other accidents.

Age-Adjusted Death Rate by Accidents in 2001

National Rate = 35.7 Deaths per 100,000 Population*

<u>ALPHA ORDER</u>

RANK	STATE	RATE
6	Alabama	49.2
1	Alaska	60.4
10	Arizona	47.3
13	Arkansas	46.4
49	California	24.4
20	Colorado	41.5
44	Connecticut	29.5
28	Delaware	36.3
22	Florida	40.5
17	Georgia	43.6
43	Hawaii	29.7
16	Idaho	44.0
39	Illinois	32.7
30	Indiana	35.7
40	Iowa	32.3
21	Kansas	41.3
7	Kentucky	48.7
13	Louisiana	46.4
29	Maine	36.0
46	Maryland	25.7
50	Massachusetts	22.0
38	Michigan	33.1
31	Minnesota	35.2
3	Mississippi	55.6
19	Missouri	42.4
5	Montana	49.9
34	Nebraska	34.7
25	Nevada	37.2
42	New Hampshire	29.9
45	New Jersey	27.7
2	New Mexico	57.6
47	New York	25.6
18	North Carolina	42.6
36	North Dakota	33.8
37	Ohio	33.3
9	Oklahoma	48.3
26	Oregon	36.8
35	Pennsylvania	34.4
48	Rhode Island	25.1
7	South Carolina	48.7
12	South Dakota	47.0
11	Tennessee	47.1
23	Texas	39.5
40	Utah	32.3
27	Vermont	36.4
32	Virginia	35.1
32	Washington	35.1
15	West Virginia	44.6
24	Wisconsin	37.3
4	Wyoming	55.4

<u>RANK ORDER</u>

RANK	STATE	RATE
1	Alaska	60.4
2	New Mexico	57.6
3	Mississippi	55.6
4	Wyoming	55.4
5	Montana	49.9
6	Alabama	49.2
7	Kentucky	48.7
7	South Carolina	48.7
9	Oklahoma	48.3
10	Arizona	47.3
11	Tennessee	47.1
12	South Dakota	47.0
13	Arkansas	46.4
13	Louisiana	46.4
15	West Virginia	44.6
16	Idaho	44.0
17	Georgia	43.6
18	North Carolina	42.6
19	Missouri	42.4
20	Colorado	41.5
21	Kansas	41.3
22	Florida	40.5
23	Texas	39.5
24	Wisconsin	37.3
25	Nevada	37.2
26	Oregon	36.8
27	Vermont	36.4
28	Delaware	36.3
29	Maine	36.0
30	Indiana	35.7
31	Minnesota	35.2
32	Virginia	35.1
32	Washington	35.1
34	Nebraska	34.7
35	Pennsylvania	34.4
36	North Dakota	33.8
37	Ohio	33.3
38	Michigan	33.1
39	Illinois	32.7
40	Iowa	32.3
40	Utah	32.3
42	New Hampshire	29.9
43	Hawaii	29.7
44	Connecticut	29.5
45	New Jersey	27.7
46	Maryland	25.7
47	New York	25.6
48	Rhode Island	25.1
49	California	24.4
50	Massachusetts	22.0
	District of Columbia	38.3

Source: U.S. Department of Health and Human Services, National Center for Health Statistics
"National Vital Statistics Reports" (Vol. 52, No. 3, September 18, 2003)
**Final data by state of residence. Includes motor vehicle deaths, poisoning, falls, drowning and other accidents.*
Age-adjusted rates based on the year 2000 standard population.

Deaths by Cerebrovascular Diseases in 2001

National Total = 163,538 Deaths*

ALPHA ORDER

RANK	STATE	DEATHS	% of USA
19	Alabama	2,998	1.8%
50	Alaska	158	0.1%
26	Arizona	2,480	1.5%
28	Arkansas	2,256	1.4%
1	California	18,088	11.1%
33	Colorado	1,825	1.1%
30	Connecticut	2,003	1.2%
47	Delaware	383	0.2%
3	Florida	10,414	6.4%
10	Georgia	4,312	2.6%
41	Hawaii	766	0.5%
40	Idaho	781	0.5%
6	Illinois	7,230	4.4%
14	Indiana	3,877	2.4%
29	Iowa	2,218	1.4%
32	Kansas	1,848	1.1%
25	Kentucky	2,557	1.6%
23	Louisiana	2,638	1.6%
39	Maine	822	0.5%
20	Maryland	2,882	1.8%
18	Massachusetts	3,535	2.2%
8	Michigan	5,701	3.5%
22	Minnesota	2,727	1.7%
31	Mississippi	1,935	1.2%
15	Missouri	3,796	2.3%
44	Montana	578	0.4%
35	Nebraska	1,130	0.7%
36	Nevada	913	0.6%
42	New Hampshire	633	0.4%
13	New Jersey	4,007	2.5%
38	New Mexico	824	0.5%
5	New York	7,706	4.7%
9	North Carolina	5,401	3.3%
45	North Dakota	507	0.3%
7	Ohio	6,891	4.2%
27	Oklahoma	2,384	1.5%
24	Oregon	2,588	1.6%
4	Pennsylvania	8,619	5.3%
43	Rhode Island	614	0.4%
21	South Carolina	2,832	1.7%
46	South Dakota	490	0.3%
12	Tennessee	4,037	2.5%
2	Texas	10,612	6.5%
37	Utah	870	0.5%
48	Vermont	323	0.2%
11	Virginia	4,129	2.5%
16	Washington	3,765	2.3%
34	West Virginia	1,272	0.8%
17	Wisconsin	3,658	2.2%
49	Wyoming	260	0.2%

RANK ORDER

RANK	STATE	DEATHS	% of USA
1	California	18,088	11.1%
2	Texas	10,612	6.5%
3	Florida	10,414	6.4%
4	Pennsylvania	8,619	5.3%
5	New York	7,706	4.7%
6	Illinois	7,230	4.4%
7	Ohio	6,891	4.2%
8	Michigan	5,701	3.5%
9	North Carolina	5,401	3.3%
10	Georgia	4,312	2.6%
11	Virginia	4,129	2.5%
12	Tennessee	4,037	2.5%
13	New Jersey	4,007	2.5%
14	Indiana	3,877	2.4%
15	Missouri	3,796	2.3%
16	Washington	3,765	2.3%
17	Wisconsin	3,658	2.2%
18	Massachusetts	3,535	2.2%
19	Alabama	2,998	1.8%
20	Maryland	2,882	1.8%
21	South Carolina	2,832	1.7%
22	Minnesota	2,727	1.7%
23	Louisiana	2,638	1.6%
24	Oregon	2,588	1.6%
25	Kentucky	2,557	1.6%
26	Arizona	2,480	1.5%
27	Oklahoma	2,384	1.5%
28	Arkansas	2,256	1.4%
29	Iowa	2,218	1.4%
30	Connecticut	2,003	1.2%
31	Mississippi	1,935	1.2%
32	Kansas	1,848	1.1%
33	Colorado	1,825	1.1%
34	West Virginia	1,272	0.8%
35	Nebraska	1,130	0.7%
36	Nevada	913	0.6%
37	Utah	870	0.5%
38	New Mexico	824	0.5%
39	Maine	822	0.5%
40	Idaho	781	0.5%
41	Hawaii	766	0.5%
42	New Hampshire	633	0.4%
43	Rhode Island	614	0.4%
44	Montana	578	0.4%
45	North Dakota	507	0.3%
46	South Dakota	490	0.3%
47	Delaware	383	0.2%
48	Vermont	323	0.2%
49	Wyoming	260	0.2%
50	Alaska	158	0.1%
	District of Columbia	265	0.2%

Source: U.S. Department of Health and Human Services, National Center for Health Statistics
    "National Vital Statistics Reports" (Vol. 52, No. 3, September 18, 2003)
*Final data by state of residence. Cerebrovascular diseases include stroke and other disorders of the blood vessels of the brain.

Age-Adjusted Death Rate by Cerebrovascular Diseases in 2001

National Rate = 57.9 Deaths per 100,000 Population*

<u>ALPHA ORDER</u>

RANK	STATE	RATE
9	Alabama	66.0
29	Alaska	57.4
46	Arizona	48.2
1	Arkansas	75.9
19	California	61.2
37	Colorado	53.9
42	Connecticut	49.6
44	Delaware	49.2
47	Florida	47.6
7	Georgia	67.3
22	Hawaii	59.8
13	Idaho	64.7
26	Illinois	58.4
16	Indiana	63.7
25	Iowa	58.8
21	Kansas	60.3
14	Kentucky	64.4
12	Louisiana	64.8
36	Maine	54.7
23	Maryland	59.6
45	Massachusetts	48.6
27	Michigan	58.2
38	Minnesota	52.5
5	Mississippi	70.5
18	Missouri	61.6
28	Montana	57.6
31	Nebraska	57.3
35	Nevada	55.1
40	New Hampshire	52.0
49	New Jersey	44.2
42	New Mexico	49.6
50	New York	38.4
4	North Carolina	71.3
20	North Dakota	60.4
29	Ohio	57.4
10	Oklahoma	65.6
6	Oregon	69.5
34	Pennsylvania	55.5
48	Rhode Island	47.4
2	South Carolina	75.0
38	South Dakota	52.5
3	Tennessee	72.3
15	Texas	63.8
32	Utah	56.4
41	Vermont	50.2
11	Virginia	65.4
8	Washington	67.2
24	West Virginia	59.4
17	Wisconsin	61.7
33	Wyoming	56.1

<u>RANK ORDER</u>

RANK	STATE	RATE
1	Arkansas	75.9
2	South Carolina	75.0
3	Tennessee	72.3
4	North Carolina	71.3
5	Mississippi	70.5
6	Oregon	69.5
7	Georgia	67.3
8	Washington	67.2
9	Alabama	66.0
10	Oklahoma	65.6
11	Virginia	65.4
12	Louisiana	64.8
13	Idaho	64.7
14	Kentucky	64.4
15	Texas	63.8
16	Indiana	63.7
17	Wisconsin	61.7
18	Missouri	61.6
19	California	61.2
20	North Dakota	60.4
21	Kansas	60.3
22	Hawaii	59.8
23	Maryland	59.6
24	West Virginia	59.4
25	Iowa	58.8
26	Illinois	58.4
27	Michigan	58.2
28	Montana	57.6
29	Alaska	57.4
29	Ohio	57.4
31	Nebraska	57.3
32	Utah	56.4
33	Wyoming	56.1
34	Pennsylvania	55.5
35	Nevada	55.1
36	Maine	54.7
37	Colorado	53.9
38	Minnesota	52.5
38	South Dakota	52.5
40	New Hampshire	52.0
41	Vermont	50.2
42	Connecticut	49.6
42	New Mexico	49.6
44	Delaware	49.2
45	Massachusetts	48.6
46	Arizona	48.2
47	Florida	47.6
48	Rhode Island	47.4
49	New Jersey	44.2
50	New York	38.4
	District of Columbia	46.4

Source: U.S. Department of Health and Human Services, National Center for Health Statistics
"National Vital Statistics Reports" (Vol. 52, No. 3, September 18, 2003)
Final data by state of residence. Cerebrovascular diseases include stroke and other disorders of the blood vessels of the brain. Age-adjusted rates based on the year 2000 standard population.

Deaths by Chronic Lower Respiratory Diseases in 2001

National Total = 123,013 Deaths*

ALPHA ORDER

RANK	STATE	DEATHS	% of USA
21	Alabama	2,204	1.8%
50	Alaska	147	0.1%
18	Arizona	2,499	2.0%
32	Arkansas	1,368	1.1%
1	California	12,965	10.5%
25	Colorado	1,836	1.5%
30	Connecticut	1,486	1.2%
46	Delaware	306	0.2%
2	Florida	8,954	7.3%
11	Georgia	3,097	2.5%
48	Hawaii	280	0.2%
41	Idaho	581	0.5%
7	Illinois	4,776	3.9%
10	Indiana	3,136	2.5%
29	Iowa	1,552	1.3%
31	Kansas	1,444	1.2%
20	Kentucky	2,265	1.8%
26	Louisiana	1,763	1.4%
37	Maine	800	0.7%
24	Maryland	1,907	1.6%
15	Massachusetts	2,810	2.3%
8	Michigan	4,148	3.4%
23	Minnesota	1,909	1.6%
33	Mississippi	1,333	1.1%
14	Missouri	2,882	2.3%
40	Montana	583	0.5%
36	Nebraska	882	0.7%
35	Nevada	1,136	0.9%
39	New Hampshire	616	0.5%
13	New Jersey	2,911	2.4%
38	New Mexico	775	0.6%
4	New York	6,906	5.6%
9	North Carolina	3,514	2.9%
45	North Dakota	308	0.3%
5	Ohio	5,881	4.8%
22	Oklahoma	1,922	1.6%
28	Oregon	1,726	1.4%
6	Pennsylvania	5,845	4.8%
43	Rhode Island	511	0.4%
27	South Carolina	1,731	1.4%
44	South Dakota	362	0.3%
12	Tennessee	2,941	2.4%
3	Texas	7,739	6.3%
42	Utah	525	0.4%
47	Vermont	305	0.2%
16	Virginia	2,744	2.2%
17	Washington	2,634	2.1%
34	West Virginia	1,273	1.0%
19	Wisconsin	2,375	1.9%
49	Wyoming	270	0.2%

RANK ORDER

RANK	STATE	DEATHS	% of USA
1	California	12,965	10.5%
2	Florida	8,954	7.3%
3	Texas	7,739	6.3%
4	New York	6,906	5.6%
5	Ohio	5,881	4.8%
6	Pennsylvania	5,845	4.8%
7	Illinois	4,776	3.9%
8	Michigan	4,148	3.4%
9	North Carolina	3,514	2.9%
10	Indiana	3,136	2.5%
11	Georgia	3,097	2.5%
12	Tennessee	2,941	2.4%
13	New Jersey	2,911	2.4%
14	Missouri	2,882	2.3%
15	Massachusetts	2,810	2.3%
16	Virginia	2,744	2.2%
17	Washington	2,634	2.1%
18	Arizona	2,499	2.0%
19	Wisconsin	2,375	1.9%
20	Kentucky	2,265	1.8%
21	Alabama	2,204	1.8%
22	Oklahoma	1,922	1.6%
23	Minnesota	1,909	1.6%
24	Maryland	1,907	1.6%
25	Colorado	1,836	1.5%
26	Louisiana	1,763	1.4%
27	South Carolina	1,731	1.4%
28	Oregon	1,726	1.4%
29	Iowa	1,552	1.3%
30	Connecticut	1,486	1.2%
31	Kansas	1,444	1.2%
32	Arkansas	1,368	1.1%
33	Mississippi	1,333	1.1%
34	West Virginia	1,273	1.0%
35	Nevada	1,136	0.9%
36	Nebraska	882	0.7%
37	Maine	800	0.7%
38	New Mexico	775	0.6%
39	New Hampshire	616	0.5%
40	Montana	583	0.5%
41	Idaho	581	0.5%
42	Utah	525	0.4%
43	Rhode Island	511	0.4%
44	South Dakota	362	0.3%
45	North Dakota	308	0.3%
46	Delaware	306	0.2%
47	Vermont	305	0.2%
48	Hawaii	280	0.2%
49	Wyoming	270	0.2%
50	Alaska	147	0.1%
	District of Columbia	150	0.1%

*Source: U.S. Department of Health and Human Services, National Center for Health Statistics
"National Vital Statistics Reports" (Vol. 52, No. 3, September 18, 2003)*
Final data by state of residence. Chronic lower respiratory diseases are diseases of the lungs including bronchitis, emphysema and asthma. Includes allied conditions.

Age-Adjusted Death Rate by Chronic Lower Respiratory Diseases in 2001

National Rate = 43.7 Deaths per 100,000 Population*

ALPHA ORDER

RANK	STATE	RATE
18	Alabama	48.0
13	Alaska	49.6
23	Arizona	47.3
25	Arkansas	46.2
30	California	43.9
7	Colorado	53.5
45	Connecticut	38.0
46	Delaware	37.9
37	Florida	40.9
19	Georgia	47.9
50	Hawaii	21.6
16	Idaho	48.4
41	Illinois	39.3
10	Indiana	51.9
31	Iowa	43.5
12	Kansas	49.9
5	Kentucky	56.2
32	Louisiana	43.0
6	Maine	54.1
42	Maryland	39.2
39	Massachusetts	39.7
34	Michigan	42.3
43	Minnesota	38.7
15	Mississippi	48.7
22	Missouri	47.7
2	Montana	59.1
24	Nebraska	46.5
1	Nevada	65.6
11	New Hampshire	50.8
49	New Jersey	32.4
27	New Mexico	45.6
47	New York	34.8
28	North Carolina	45.4
40	North Dakota	39.5
14	Ohio	49.0
8	Oklahoma	53.0
20	Oregon	47.8
44	Pennsylvania	38.2
38	Rhode Island	40.8
29	South Carolina	44.4
35	South Dakota	41.5
9	Tennessee	52.0
26	Texas	46.1
48	Utah	33.6
17	Vermont	48.1
33	Virginia	42.8
20	Washington	47.8
3	West Virginia	58.9
36	Wisconsin	41.4
4	Wyoming	57.5

RANK ORDER

RANK	STATE	RATE
1	Nevada	65.6
2	Montana	59.1
3	West Virginia	58.9
4	Wyoming	57.5
5	Kentucky	56.2
6	Maine	54.1
7	Colorado	53.5
8	Oklahoma	53.0
9	Tennessee	52.0
10	Indiana	51.9
11	New Hampshire	50.8
12	Kansas	49.9
13	Alaska	49.6
14	Ohio	49.0
15	Mississippi	48.7
16	Idaho	48.4
17	Vermont	48.1
18	Alabama	48.0
19	Georgia	47.9
20	Oregon	47.8
20	Washington	47.8
22	Missouri	47.7
23	Arizona	47.3
24	Nebraska	46.5
25	Arkansas	46.2
26	Texas	46.1
27	New Mexico	45.6
28	North Carolina	45.4
29	South Carolina	44.4
30	California	43.9
31	Iowa	43.5
32	Louisiana	43.0
33	Virginia	42.8
34	Michigan	42.3
35	South Dakota	41.5
36	Wisconsin	41.4
37	Florida	40.9
38	Rhode Island	40.8
39	Massachusetts	39.7
40	North Dakota	39.5
41	Illinois	39.3
42	Maryland	39.2
43	Minnesota	38.7
44	Pennsylvania	38.2
45	Connecticut	38.0
46	Delaware	37.9
47	New York	34.8
48	Utah	33.6
49	New Jersey	32.4
50	Hawaii	21.6
	District of Columbia	26.5

*Source: U.S. Department of Health and Human Services, National Center for Health Statistics
"National Vital Statistics Reports" (Vol. 52, No. 3, September 18, 2003)*
**Final data by state of residence. Chronic lower respiratory diseases are diseases of the lungs including bronchitis, emphysema and asthma. Includes allied conditions. Age-adjusted rates based on the year 2000 standard population.*

Deaths by Diseases of the Heart in 2001

National Total = 700,142 Deaths*

ALPHA ORDER

RANK	STATE	DEATHS	% of USA
17	Alabama	13,207	1.9%
50	Alaska	603	0.1%
24	Arizona	10,588	1.5%
29	Arkansas	8,263	1.2%
1	California	68,234	9.7%
34	Colorado	6,293	0.9%
28	Connecticut	8,582	1.2%
44	Delaware	2,033	0.3%
3	Florida	50,629	7.2%
11	Georgia	17,478	2.5%
43	Hawaii	2,310	0.3%
42	Idaho	2,489	0.4%
7	Illinois	30,990	4.4%
14	Indiana	15,682	2.2%
30	Iowa	8,250	1.2%
32	Kansas	6,716	1.0%
20	Kentucky	11,808	1.7%
21	Louisiana	11,474	1.6%
38	Maine	3,272	0.5%
19	Maryland	12,310	1.8%
15	Massachusetts	15,144	2.2%
8	Michigan	26,896	3.8%
27	Minnesota	8,760	1.3%
26	Mississippi	9,050	1.3%
12	Missouri	16,633	2.4%
46	Montana	1,970	0.3%
36	Nebraska	4,150	0.6%
35	Nevada	4,393	0.6%
41	New Hampshire	2,835	0.4%
9	New Jersey	22,704	3.2%
37	New Mexico	3,423	0.5%
2	New York	56,643	8.1%
10	North Carolina	18,792	2.7%
47	North Dakota	1,700	0.2%
6	Ohio	32,453	4.6%
23	Oklahoma	10,840	1.5%
31	Oregon	7,075	1.0%
5	Pennsylvania	39,438	5.6%
39	Rhode Island	3,076	0.4%
25	South Carolina	9,471	1.4%
45	South Dakota	1,985	0.3%
13	Tennessee	15,688	2.2%
4	Texas	43,199	6.2%
40	Utah	2,896	0.4%
48	Vermont	1,429	0.2%
16	Virginia	14,913	2.1%
22	Washington	11,281	1.6%
33	West Virginia	6,325	0.9%
18	Wisconsin	13,023	1.9%
49	Wyoming	985	0.1%

RANK ORDER

RANK	STATE	DEATHS	% of USA
1	California	68,234	9.7%
2	New York	56,643	8.1%
3	Florida	50,629	7.2%
4	Texas	43,199	6.2%
5	Pennsylvania	39,438	5.6%
6	Ohio	32,453	4.6%
7	Illinois	30,990	4.4%
8	Michigan	26,896	3.8%
9	New Jersey	22,704	3.2%
10	North Carolina	18,792	2.7%
11	Georgia	17,478	2.5%
12	Missouri	16,633	2.4%
13	Tennessee	15,688	2.2%
14	Indiana	15,682	2.2%
15	Massachusetts	15,144	2.2%
16	Virginia	14,913	2.1%
17	Alabama	13,207	1.9%
18	Wisconsin	13,023	1.9%
19	Maryland	12,310	1.8%
20	Kentucky	11,808	1.7%
21	Louisiana	11,474	1.6%
22	Washington	11,281	1.6%
23	Oklahoma	10,840	1.5%
24	Arizona	10,588	1.5%
25	South Carolina	9,471	1.4%
26	Mississippi	9,050	1.3%
27	Minnesota	8,760	1.3%
28	Connecticut	8,582	1.2%
29	Arkansas	8,263	1.2%
30	Iowa	8,250	1.2%
31	Oregon	7,075	1.0%
32	Kansas	6,716	1.0%
33	West Virginia	6,325	0.9%
34	Colorado	6,293	0.9%
35	Nevada	4,393	0.6%
36	Nebraska	4,150	0.6%
37	New Mexico	3,423	0.5%
38	Maine	3,272	0.5%
39	Rhode Island	3,076	0.4%
40	Utah	2,896	0.4%
41	New Hampshire	2,835	0.4%
42	Idaho	2,489	0.4%
43	Hawaii	2,310	0.3%
44	Delaware	2,033	0.3%
45	South Dakota	1,985	0.3%
46	Montana	1,970	0.3%
47	North Dakota	1,700	0.2%
48	Vermont	1,429	0.2%
49	Wyoming	985	0.1%
50	Alaska	603	0.1%
	District of Columbia	1,761	0.3%

Source: U.S. Department of Health and Human Services, National Center for Health Statistics
   "National Vital Statistics Reports" (Vol. 52, No. 3, September 18, 2003)
*Final data by state of residence.

Age-Adjusted Death Rate by Diseases of the Heart in 2001

National Rate = 247.8 Deaths per 100,000 Population*

ALPHA ORDER

RANK ORDER

RANK	STATE	RATE		RANK	STATE	RATE
5	Alabama	289.3		1	Mississippi	329.0
46	Alaska	187.7		2	Oklahoma	298.1
41	Arizona	204.5		3	West Virginia	296.0
8	Arkansas	279.1		4	Kentucky	294.0
28	California	230.4		5	Alabama	289.3
48	Colorado	181.0		6	New York	282.2
35	Connecticut	216.4		7	Louisiana	280.1
16	Delaware	257.2		8	Arkansas	279.1
25	Florida	233.2		9	Tennessee	278.2
13	Georgia	268.0		10	Michigan	273.8
49	Hawaii	179.5		11	Missouri	271.9
40	Idaho	205.1		12	Ohio	271.0
20	Illinois	251.5		13	Georgia	268.0
14	Indiana	258.0		14	Indiana	258.0
29	Iowa	224.0		15	Pennsylvania	257.8
29	Kansas	224.0		16	Delaware	257.2
4	Kentucky	294.0		17	Nevada	257.1
7	Louisiana	280.1		18	Texas	255.1
33	Maine	218.8		19	Maryland	251.6
19	Maryland	251.6		20	Illinois	251.5
38	Massachusetts	210.4		21	New Jersey	250.8
10	Michigan	273.8		22	South Carolina	245.5
50	Minnesota	171.0		23	North Carolina	244.0
1	Mississippi	329.0		24	Rhode Island	240.5
11	Missouri	271.9		25	Florida	233.2
44	Montana	197.9		26	Virginia	231.9
36	Nebraska	210.9		27	New Hampshire	230.9
17	Nevada	257.1		28	California	230.4
27	New Hampshire	230.9		29	Iowa	224.0
21	New Jersey	250.8		29	Kansas	224.0
42	New Mexico	203.4		31	Wisconsin	222.3
6	New York	282.2		32	Vermont	221.4
23	North Carolina	244.0		33	Maine	218.8
36	North Dakota	210.9		34	South Dakota	218.1
12	Ohio	271.0		35	Connecticut	216.4
2	Oklahoma	298.1		36	Nebraska	210.9
45	Oregon	191.6		36	North Dakota	210.9
15	Pennsylvania	257.8		38	Massachusetts	210.4
24	Rhode Island	240.5		39	Wyoming	209.5
22	South Carolina	245.5		40	Idaho	205.1
34	South Dakota	218.1		41	Arizona	204.5
9	Tennessee	278.2		42	New Mexico	203.4
18	Texas	255.1		43	Washington	201.2
47	Utah	185.2		44	Montana	197.9
32	Vermont	221.4		45	Oregon	191.6
26	Virginia	231.9		46	Alaska	187.7
43	Washington	201.2		47	Utah	185.2
3	West Virginia	296.0		48	Colorado	181.0
31	Wisconsin	222.3		49	Hawaii	179.5
39	Wyoming	209.5		50	Minnesota	171.0

District of Columbia   308.5

*Source: U.S. Department of Health and Human Services, National Center for Health Statistics
"National Vital Statistics Reports" (Vol. 52, No. 3, September 18, 2003)*
*Final data by state of residence. Age-adjusted rates based on the year 2000 standard population.

Deaths by Suicide in 2001

National Total = 30,622 Suicides*

ALPHA ORDER

RANK	STATE	SUICIDES	% of USA
21	Alabama	512	1.7%
46	Alaska	102	0.3%
12	Arizona	767	2.5%
30	Arkansas	382	1.2%
1	California	2,831	9.2%
14	Colorado	722	2.4%
37	Connecticut	283	0.9%
44	Delaware	108	0.4%
2	Florida	2,314	7.6%
10	Georgia	935	3.1%
43	Hawaii	136	0.4%
38	Idaho	210	0.7%
7	Illinois	1,139	3.7%
15	Indiana	715	2.3%
34	Iowa	304	1.0%
35	Kansas	293	1.0%
23	Kentucky	495	1.6%
24	Louisiana	493	1.6%
42	Maine	161	0.5%
27	Maryland	454	1.5%
28	Massachusetts	426	1.4%
8	Michigan	1,051	3.4%
25	Minnesota	480	1.6%
32	Mississippi	328	1.1%
13	Missouri	725	2.4%
40	Montana	175	0.6%
39	Nebraska	187	0.6%
29	Nevada	387	1.3%
41	New Hampshire	167	0.5%
19	New Jersey	588	1.9%
31	New Mexico	362	1.2%
5	New York	1,253	4.1%
9	North Carolina	997	3.3%
49	North Dakota	79	0.3%
6	Ohio	1,219	4.0%
20	Oklahoma	515	1.7%
22	Oregon	505	1.6%
4	Pennsylvania	1,276	4.2%
47	Rhode Island	88	0.3%
26	South Carolina	467	1.5%
45	South Dakota	105	0.3%
17	Tennessee	711	2.3%
3	Texas	2,225	7.3%
33	Utah	321	1.0%
50	Vermont	72	0.2%
11	Virginia	797	2.6%
16	Washington	712	2.3%
36	West Virginia	286	0.9%
18	Wisconsin	639	2.1%
48	Wyoming	83	0.3%

RANK ORDER

RANK	STATE	SUICIDES	% of USA
1	California	2,831	9.2%
2	Florida	2,314	7.6%
3	Texas	2,225	7.3%
4	Pennsylvania	1,276	4.2%
5	New York	1,253	4.1%
6	Ohio	1,219	4.0%
7	Illinois	1,139	3.7%
8	Michigan	1,051	3.4%
9	North Carolina	997	3.3%
10	Georgia	935	3.1%
11	Virginia	797	2.6%
12	Arizona	767	2.5%
13	Missouri	725	2.4%
14	Colorado	722	2.4%
15	Indiana	715	2.3%
16	Washington	712	2.3%
17	Tennessee	711	2.3%
18	Wisconsin	639	2.1%
19	New Jersey	588	1.9%
20	Oklahoma	515	1.7%
21	Alabama	512	1.7%
22	Oregon	505	1.6%
23	Kentucky	495	1.6%
24	Louisiana	493	1.6%
25	Minnesota	480	1.6%
26	South Carolina	467	1.5%
27	Maryland	454	1.5%
28	Massachusetts	426	1.4%
29	Nevada	387	1.3%
30	Arkansas	382	1.2%
31	New Mexico	362	1.2%
32	Mississippi	328	1.1%
33	Utah	321	1.0%
34	Iowa	304	1.0%
35	Kansas	293	1.0%
36	West Virginia	286	0.9%
37	Connecticut	283	0.9%
38	Idaho	210	0.7%
39	Nebraska	187	0.6%
40	Montana	175	0.6%
41	New Hampshire	167	0.5%
42	Maine	161	0.5%
43	Hawaii	136	0.4%
44	Delaware	108	0.4%
45	South Dakota	105	0.3%
46	Alaska	102	0.3%
47	Rhode Island	88	0.3%
48	Wyoming	83	0.3%
49	North Dakota	79	0.3%
50	Vermont	72	0.2%
	District of Columbia	40	0.1%

*Source: U.S. Department of Health and Human Services, National Center for Health Statistics
    "National Vital Statistics Reports" (Vol. 52, No. 3, September 18, 2003)*
*Final data by state of residence.

Age-Adjusted Death Rate by Suicide in 2001

National Rate = 10.7 Deaths per 100,000 Population*

ALPHA ORDER

RANK	STATE	RATE
29	Alabama	11.3
7	Alaska	15.9
11	Arizona	14.8
13	Arkansas	14.2
44	California	8.5
4	Colorado	16.5
46	Connecticut	8.2
16	Delaware	13.3
15	Florida	13.5
28	Georgia	11.4
34	Hawaii	10.9
6	Idaho	16.3
43	Illinois	9.1
25	Indiana	11.7
40	Iowa	10.1
34	Kansas	10.9
23	Kentucky	11.9
32	Louisiana	11.2
22	Maine	12.0
45	Maryland	8.4
49	Massachusetts	6.5
39	Michigan	10.5
42	Minnesota	9.6
25	Mississippi	11.7
18	Missouri	12.7
2	Montana	19.1
34	Nebraska	10.9
3	Nevada	18.8
17	New Hampshire	13.1
48	New Jersey	6.8
1	New Mexico	20.2
49	New York	6.5
21	North Carolina	12.1
18	North Dakota	12.7
38	Ohio	10.6
10	Oklahoma	14.9
12	Oregon	14.4
40	Pennsylvania	10.1
47	Rhode Island	8.0
29	South Carolina	11.3
14	South Dakota	13.9
20	Tennessee	12.2
34	Texas	10.9
8	Utah	15.4
29	Vermont	11.3
33	Virginia	11.0
24	Washington	11.8
9	West Virginia	15.0
25	Wisconsin	11.7
5	Wyoming	16.4

RANK ORDER

RANK	STATE	RATE
1	New Mexico	20.2
2	Montana	19.1
3	Nevada	18.8
4	Colorado	16.5
5	Wyoming	16.4
6	Idaho	16.3
7	Alaska	15.9
8	Utah	15.4
9	West Virginia	15.0
10	Oklahoma	14.9
11	Arizona	14.8
12	Oregon	14.4
13	Arkansas	14.2
14	South Dakota	13.9
15	Florida	13.5
16	Delaware	13.3
17	New Hampshire	13.1
18	Missouri	12.7
18	North Dakota	12.7
20	Tennessee	12.2
21	North Carolina	12.1
22	Maine	12.0
23	Kentucky	11.9
24	Washington	11.8
25	Indiana	11.7
25	Mississippi	11.7
25	Wisconsin	11.7
28	Georgia	11.4
29	Alabama	11.3
29	South Carolina	11.3
29	Vermont	11.3
32	Louisiana	11.2
33	Virginia	11.0
34	Hawaii	10.9
34	Kansas	10.9
34	Nebraska	10.9
34	Texas	10.9
38	Ohio	10.6
39	Michigan	10.5
40	Iowa	10.1
40	Pennsylvania	10.1
42	Minnesota	9.6
43	Illinois	9.1
44	California	8.5
45	Maryland	8.4
46	Connecticut	8.2
47	Rhode Island	8.0
48	New Jersey	6.8
49	Massachusetts	6.5
49	New York	6.5
	District of Columbia	6.5

Source: U.S. Department of Health and Human Services, National Center for Health Statistics
"National Vital Statistics Reports" (Vol. 52, No. 3, September 18, 2003)
**Final data by state of residence. Age-adjusted rates based on the year 2000 standard population.*

Deaths by AIDS in 2001

National Total = 14,175 Deaths*

ALPHA ORDER

RANK	STATE	DEATHS	% of USA
17	Alabama	214	1.5%
45	Alaska	7	0.0%
21	Arizona	156	1.1%
31	Arkansas	64	0.5%
3	California	1,505	10.6%
26	Colorado	93	0.7%
20	Connecticut	193	1.4%
30	Delaware	67	0.5%
2	Florida	1,664	11.7%
6	Georgia	722	5.1%
39	Hawaii	26	0.2%
42	Idaho	12	0.1%
8	Illinois	518	3.7%
23	Indiana	119	0.8%
40	Iowa	18	0.1%
34	Kansas	39	0.3%
27	Kentucky	90	0.6%
11	Louisiana	404	2.9%
41	Maine	14	0.1%
7	Maryland	572	4.0%
16	Massachusetts	249	1.8%
15	Michigan	255	1.8%
33	Minnesota	53	0.4%
19	Mississippi	202	1.4%
22	Missouri	147	1.0%
46	Montana	5	0.0%
36	Nebraska	33	0.2%
28	Nevada	76	0.5%
44	New Hampshire	9	0.1%
5	New Jersey	785	5.5%
34	New Mexico	39	0.3%
1	New York	2,085	14.7%
10	North Carolina	464	3.3%
47	North Dakota	4	0.0%
18	Ohio	207	1.5%
25	Oklahoma	99	0.7%
32	Oregon	63	0.4%
9	Pennsylvania	496	3.5%
37	Rhode Island	30	0.2%
12	South Carolina	310	2.2%
47	South Dakota	4	0.0%
13	Tennessee	277	2.0%
4	Texas	1,055	7.4%
42	Utah	12	0.1%
47	Vermont	4	0.0%
14	Virginia	275	1.9%
24	Washington	113	0.8%
38	West Virginia	29	0.2%
29	Wisconsin	73	0.5%
50	Wyoming	2	0.0%

RANK ORDER

RANK	STATE	DEATHS	% of USA
1	New York	2,085	14.7%
2	Florida	1,664	11.7%
3	California	1,505	10.6%
4	Texas	1,055	7.4%
5	New Jersey	785	5.5%
6	Georgia	722	5.1%
7	Maryland	572	4.0%
8	Illinois	518	3.7%
9	Pennsylvania	496	3.5%
10	North Carolina	464	3.3%
11	Louisiana	404	2.9%
12	South Carolina	310	2.2%
13	Tennessee	277	2.0%
14	Virginia	275	1.9%
15	Michigan	255	1.8%
16	Massachusetts	249	1.8%
17	Alabama	214	1.5%
18	Ohio	207	1.5%
19	Mississippi	202	1.4%
20	Connecticut	193	1.4%
21	Arizona	156	1.1%
22	Missouri	147	1.0%
23	Indiana	119	0.8%
24	Washington	113	0.8%
25	Oklahoma	99	0.7%
26	Colorado	93	0.7%
27	Kentucky	90	0.6%
28	Nevada	76	0.5%
29	Wisconsin	73	0.5%
30	Delaware	67	0.5%
31	Arkansas	64	0.5%
32	Oregon	63	0.4%
33	Minnesota	53	0.4%
34	Kansas	39	0.3%
34	New Mexico	39	0.3%
36	Nebraska	33	0.2%
37	Rhode Island	30	0.2%
38	West Virginia	29	0.2%
39	Hawaii	26	0.2%
40	Iowa	18	0.1%
41	Maine	14	0.1%
42	Idaho	12	0.1%
42	Utah	12	0.1%
44	New Hampshire	9	0.1%
45	Alaska	7	0.0%
46	Montana	5	0.0%
47	North Dakota	4	0.0%
47	South Dakota	4	0.0%
47	Vermont	4	0.0%
50	Wyoming	2	0.0%
	District of Columbia	223	1.6%

Source: U.S. Department of Health and Human Services, National Center for Health Statistics
"National Vital Statistics Reports" (Vol. 52, No. 3, September 18, 2003)
*AIDS is Acquired Immunodeficiency Syndrome. It is a specific group of diseases or conditions which are indicative of severe immunosuppression related to infection with the Human Immunodeficiency Virus (HIV).

Age-Adjusted Death Rate by AIDS in 2001

National Rate = 5.0 Deaths per 100,000 Population*

<u>ALPHA ORDER</u>

RANK	STATE	RATE
13	Alabama	4.9
NA	Alaska**	NA
21	Arizona	3.1
25	Arkansas	2.5
15	California	4.4
30	Colorado	2.0
11	Connecticut	5.4
7	Delaware	8.3
2	Florida	10.4
6	Georgia	8.5
29	Hawaii	2.1
NA	Idaho**	NA
16	Illinois	4.2
30	Indiana	2.0
NA	Iowa**	NA
37	Kansas	1.5
27	Kentucky	2.2
4	Louisiana	9.3
NA	Maine**	NA
3	Maryland	10.1
18	Massachusetts	3.7
25	Michigan	2.5
39	Minnesota	1.0
9	Mississippi	7.4
24	Missouri	2.7
NA	Montana**	NA
30	Nebraska	2.0
20	Nevada	3.6
NA	New Hampshire**	NA
5	New Jersey	8.9
27	New Mexico	2.2
1	New York	10.7
10	North Carolina	5.6
NA	North Dakota**	NA
33	Ohio	1.9
22	Oklahoma	2.9
33	Oregon	1.9
17	Pennsylvania	4.0
23	Rhode Island	2.8
8	South Carolina	7.6
NA	South Dakota**	NA
14	Tennessee	4.8
12	Texas	5.1
NA	Utah**	NA
NA	Vermont**	NA
18	Virginia	3.7
35	Washington	1.8
36	West Virginia	1.7
38	Wisconsin	1.3
NA	Wyoming**	NA

<u>RANK ORDER</u>

RANK	STATE	RATE
1	New York	10.7
2	Florida	10.4
3	Maryland	10.1
4	Louisiana	9.3
5	New Jersey	8.9
6	Georgia	8.5
7	Delaware	8.3
8	South Carolina	7.6
9	Mississippi	7.4
10	North Carolina	5.6
11	Connecticut	5.4
12	Texas	5.1
13	Alabama	4.9
14	Tennessee	4.8
15	California	4.4
16	Illinois	4.2
17	Pennsylvania	4.0
18	Massachusetts	3.7
18	Virginia	3.7
20	Nevada	3.6
21	Arizona	3.1
22	Oklahoma	2.9
23	Rhode Island	2.8
24	Missouri	2.7
25	Arkansas	2.5
25	Michigan	2.5
27	Kentucky	2.2
27	New Mexico	2.2
29	Hawaii	2.1
30	Colorado	2.0
30	Indiana	2.0
30	Nebraska	2.0
33	Ohio	1.9
33	Oregon	1.9
35	Washington	1.8
36	West Virginia	1.7
37	Kansas	1.5
38	Wisconsin	1.3
39	Minnesota	1.0
NA	Alaska**	NA
NA	Idaho**	NA
NA	Iowa**	NA
NA	Maine**	NA
NA	Montana**	NA
NA	New Hampshire**	NA
NA	North Dakota**	NA
NA	South Dakota**	NA
NA	Utah**	NA
NA	Vermont**	NA
NA	Wyoming**	NA
	District of Columbia	38.1

*Source: U.S. Department of Health and Human Services, National Center for Health Statistics
"National Vital Statistics Reports" (Vol. 52, No. 3, September 18, 2003)*

AIDS is Acquired Immunodeficiency Syndrome. It is a specific group of diseases or conditions which are indicative of severe immunosuppression related to infection with the Human Immunodeficiency Virus (HIV). Age-adjusted rates based on the year 2000 standard population.

**Insufficient data to determine a reliable rate.*

AIDS Cases Reported in 2003

National Total = 41,832 New AIDS Cases*

ALPHA ORDER

RANK	STATE	CASES	% of USA
22	Alabama	441	1.1%
46	Alaska	15	0.0%
16	Arizona	646	1.5%
31	Arkansas	172	0.4%
2	California	5,802	13.9%
25	Colorado	343	0.8%
17	Connecticut	631	1.5%
28	Delaware	202	0.5%
3	Florida	4,409	10.5%
6	Georgia	1,825	4.4%
36	Hawaii	97	0.2%
44	Idaho	24	0.1%
7	Illinois	1,718	4.1%
20	Indiana	514	1.2%
39	Iowa	82	0.2%
37	Kansas	91	0.2%
30	Kentucky	200	0.5%
18	Louisiana	610	1.5%
41	Maine	52	0.1%
9	Maryland	1,441	3.4%
19	Massachusetts	599	1.4%
15	Michigan	703	1.7%
33	Minnesota	162	0.4%
23	Mississippi	438	1.0%
24	Missouri	365	0.9%
48	Montana	13	0.0%
41	Nebraska	52	0.1%
26	Nevada	254	0.6%
43	New Hampshire	36	0.1%
8	New Jersey	1,448	3.5%
34	New Mexico	102	0.2%
1	New York	6,208	14.8%
10	North Carolina	1,060	2.5%
50	North Dakota	2	0.0%
13	Ohio	757	1.8%
28	Oklahoma	202	0.5%
27	Oregon	242	0.6%
5	Pennsylvania	2,058	4.9%
34	Rhode Island	102	0.2%
14	South Carolina	756	1.8%
47	South Dakota	14	0.0%
12	Tennessee	800	1.9%
4	Texas	3,582	8.6%
40	Utah	72	0.2%
45	Vermont	16	0.0%
11	Virginia	856	2.0%
21	Washington	491	1.2%
38	West Virginia	86	0.2%
32	Wisconsin	171	0.4%
49	Wyoming	7	0.0%

RANK ORDER

RANK	STATE	CASES	% of USA
1	New York	6,208	14.8%
2	California	5,802	13.9%
3	Florida	4,409	10.5%
4	Texas	3,582	8.6%
5	Pennsylvania	2,058	4.9%
6	Georgia	1,825	4.4%
7	Illinois	1,718	4.1%
8	New Jersey	1,448	3.5%
9	Maryland	1,441	3.4%
10	North Carolina	1,060	2.5%
11	Virginia	856	2.0%
12	Tennessee	800	1.9%
13	Ohio	757	1.8%
14	South Carolina	756	1.8%
15	Michigan	703	1.7%
16	Arizona	646	1.5%
17	Connecticut	631	1.5%
18	Louisiana	610	1.5%
19	Massachusetts	599	1.4%
20	Indiana	514	1.2%
21	Washington	491	1.2%
22	Alabama	441	1.1%
23	Mississippi	438	1.0%
24	Missouri	365	0.9%
25	Colorado	343	0.8%
26	Nevada	254	0.6%
27	Oregon	242	0.6%
28	Delaware	202	0.5%
28	Oklahoma	202	0.5%
30	Kentucky	200	0.5%
31	Arkansas	172	0.4%
32	Wisconsin	171	0.4%
33	Minnesota	162	0.4%
34	New Mexico	102	0.2%
34	Rhode Island	102	0.2%
36	Hawaii	97	0.2%
37	Kansas	91	0.2%
38	West Virginia	86	0.2%
39	Iowa	82	0.2%
40	Utah	72	0.2%
41	Maine	52	0.1%
41	Nebraska	52	0.1%
43	New Hampshire	36	0.1%
44	Idaho	24	0.1%
45	Vermont	16	0.0%
46	Alaska	15	0.0%
47	South Dakota	14	0.0%
48	Montana	13	0.0%
49	Wyoming	7	0.0%
50	North Dakota	2	0.0%

| | District of Columbia | 863 | 2.1% |

Source: U.S. Department of Health and Human Services, National Center for Health Statistics
"Morbidity and Mortality Weekly Report" (January 2, 2004, Vol. 52, Nos. 51 & 52)
**Provisional data. AIDS is Acquired Immunodeficiency Syndrome. It is a specific group of diseases or conditions which are indicative of severe immunosuppression related to infection with the Human Immunodeficiency Virus (HIV). National total does not include 1,025 new cases in Puerto Rico.*

AIDS Rate in 2003

National Rate = 14.4 New AIDS Cases Reported per 100,000 Population*

ALPHA ORDER

RANK	STATE	RATE
20	Alabama	9.8
45	Alaska	2.3
17	Arizona	11.6
31	Arkansas	6.3
10	California	16.4
26	Colorado	7.5
7	Connecticut	18.1
4	Delaware	24.7
3	Florida	25.9
5	Georgia	21.0
25	Hawaii	7.7
46	Idaho	1.8
14	Illinois	13.6
23	Indiana	8.3
42	Iowa	2.8
37	Kansas	3.3
34	Kentucky	4.9
14	Louisiana	13.6
36	Maine	4.0
2	Maryland	26.2
22	Massachusetts	9.3
27	Michigan	7.0
38	Minnesota	3.2
12	Mississippi	15.2
30	Missouri	6.4
48	Montana	1.4
41	Nebraska	3.0
19	Nevada	11.3
42	New Hampshire	2.8
8	New Jersey	16.8
33	New Mexico	5.4
1	New York	32.3
16	North Carolina	12.6
50	North Dakota	0.3
29	Ohio	6.6
32	Oklahoma	5.8
28	Oregon	6.8
9	Pennsylvania	16.6
21	Rhode Island	9.5
6	South Carolina	18.2
46	South Dakota	1.8
13	Tennessee	13.7
11	Texas	16.2
39	Utah	3.1
44	Vermont	2.6
17	Virginia	11.6
24	Washington	8.0
35	West Virginia	4.8
39	Wisconsin	3.1
48	Wyoming	1.4

RANK ORDER

RANK	STATE	RATE
1	New York	32.3
2	Maryland	26.2
3	Florida	25.9
4	Delaware	24.7
5	Georgia	21.0
6	South Carolina	18.2
7	Connecticut	18.1
8	New Jersey	16.8
9	Pennsylvania	16.6
10	California	16.4
11	Texas	16.2
12	Mississippi	15.2
13	Tennessee	13.7
14	Illinois	13.6
14	Louisiana	13.6
16	North Carolina	12.6
17	Arizona	11.6
17	Virginia	11.6
19	Nevada	11.3
20	Alabama	9.8
21	Rhode Island	9.5
22	Massachusetts	9.3
23	Indiana	8.3
24	Washington	8.0
25	Hawaii	7.7
26	Colorado	7.5
27	Michigan	7.0
28	Oregon	6.8
29	Ohio	6.6
30	Missouri	6.4
31	Arkansas	6.3
32	Oklahoma	5.8
33	New Mexico	5.4
34	Kentucky	4.9
35	West Virginia	4.8
36	Maine	4.0
37	Kansas	3.3
38	Minnesota	3.2
39	Utah	3.1
39	Wisconsin	3.1
41	Nebraska	3.0
42	Iowa	2.8
42	New Hampshire	2.8
44	Vermont	2.6
45	Alaska	2.3
46	Idaho	1.8
46	South Dakota	1.8
48	Montana	1.4
48	Wyoming	1.4
50	North Dakota	0.3

| | District of Columbia | 153.2 |

Source: Morgan Quitno Press using data from U.S. Dept. of Health & Human Serv's, National Center for Health Statistics "Morbidity and Mortality Weekly Report" (January 2, 2004, Vol. 52, Nos. 51 & 52)

Provisional data. AIDS is Acquired Immunodeficiency Syndrome. It is a specific group of diseases or conditions which are indicative of severe immunosuppression related to infection with the Human Immunodeficiency Virus (HIV). National rate does not include cases or population in U.S. territories.

Adult Per Capita Alcohol Consumption in 2000

National Per Capita = 2.5 Gallons Consumed per Adult 21 Years and Older*

ALPHA ORDER

RANK	STATE	PER CAPITA
39	Alabama	2.2
5	Alaska	3.1
7	Arizona	2.9
46	Arkansas	2.0
28	California	2.5
6	Colorado	3.0
28	Connecticut	2.5
3	Delaware	3.3
7	Florida	2.9
28	Georgia	2.5
20	Hawaii	2.6
15	Idaho	2.7
20	Illinois	2.6
36	Indiana	2.3
36	Iowa	2.3
43	Kansas	2.1
46	Kentucky	2.0
12	Louisiana	2.8
20	Maine	2.6
34	Maryland	2.4
7	Massachusetts	2.9
34	Michigan	2.4
15	Minnesota	2.7
28	Mississippi	2.5
20	Missouri	2.6
7	Montana	2.9
20	Nebraska	2.6
2	Nevada	4.2
1	New Hampshire	4.6
28	New Jersey	2.5
12	New Mexico	2.8
43	New York	2.1
39	North Carolina	2.2
12	North Dakota	2.8
36	Ohio	2.3
46	Oklahoma	2.0
20	Oregon	2.6
39	Pennsylvania	2.2
20	Rhode Island	2.6
15	South Carolina	2.7
15	South Dakota	2.7
43	Tennessee	2.1
20	Texas	2.6
50	Utah	1.6
15	Vermont	2.7
39	Virginia	2.2
28	Washington	2.5
49	West Virginia	1.9
4	Wisconsin	3.2
7	Wyoming	2.9

RANK ORDER

RANK	STATE	PER CAPITA
1	New Hampshire	4.6
2	Nevada	4.2
3	Delaware	3.3
4	Wisconsin	3.2
5	Alaska	3.1
6	Colorado	3.0
7	Arizona	2.9
7	Florida	2.9
7	Massachusetts	2.9
7	Montana	2.9
7	Wyoming	2.9
12	Louisiana	2.8
12	New Mexico	2.8
12	North Dakota	2.8
15	Idaho	2.7
15	Minnesota	2.7
15	South Carolina	2.7
15	South Dakota	2.7
15	Vermont	2.7
20	Hawaii	2.6
20	Illinois	2.6
20	Maine	2.6
20	Missouri	2.6
20	Nebraska	2.6
20	Oregon	2.6
20	Rhode Island	2.6
20	Texas	2.6
28	California	2.5
28	Connecticut	2.5
28	Georgia	2.5
28	Mississippi	2.5
28	New Jersey	2.5
28	Washington	2.5
34	Maryland	2.4
34	Michigan	2.4
36	Indiana	2.3
36	Iowa	2.3
36	Ohio	2.3
39	Alabama	2.2
39	North Carolina	2.2
39	Pennsylvania	2.2
39	Virginia	2.2
43	Kansas	2.1
43	New York	2.1
43	Tennessee	2.1
46	Arkansas	2.0
46	Kentucky	2.0
46	Oklahoma	2.0
49	West Virginia	1.9
50	Utah	1.6

| | District of Columbia | 4.0 |

Source: Morgan Quitno Press using data from U.S. Dept. of HHS, National Institute on Alcohol Abuse and Alcoholism "Volume Beverage and Ethanol Consumption for States" (http://www.niaaa.nih.gov/databases/consum02.txt)
*This is apparent consumption of actual alcohol, not entire volume of an alcoholic beverage (e.g. wine is roughly 11% absolute alcohol content). Apparent consumption is based on several sources which together approximate sales but do not actually measure consumption. Accordingly, figures for some states may be skewed by purchases by nonresidents.

Percent of Adults Who Smoke: 2002

National Median = 23.1% of Adults*

ALPHA ORDER

RANK	STATE	PERCENT
17	Alabama	24.4
2	Alaska	29.4
22	Arizona	23.5
12	Arkansas	26.3
49	California	16.4
45	Colorado	20.4
46	Connecticut	19.5
14	Delaware	24.7
34	Florida	22.1
24	Georgia	23.3
43	Hawaii	21.1
44	Idaho	20.6
27	Illinois	22.9
5	Indiana	27.7
26	Iowa	23.1
34	Kansas	22.1
1	Kentucky	32.6
19	Louisiana	23.9
21	Maine	23.6
36	Maryland	22.0
48	Massachusetts	19.0
18	Michigan	24.2
37	Minnesota	21.7
6	Mississippi	27.4
8	Missouri	26.6
40	Montana	21.3
29	Nebraska	22.8
13	Nevada	26.0
25	New Hampshire	23.2
47	New Jersey	19.1
41	New Mexico	21.2
32	New York	22.4
11	North Carolina	26.4
38	North Dakota	21.5
8	Ohio	26.6
7	Oklahoma	26.7
32	Oregon	22.4
15	Pennsylvania	24.6
31	Rhode Island	22.5
8	South Carolina	26.6
30	South Dakota	22.6
4	Tennessee	27.8
27	Texas	22.9
50	Utah	12.7
41	Vermont	21.2
15	Virginia	24.6
38	Washington	21.5
3	West Virginia	28.4
23	Wisconsin	23.4
20	Wyoming	23.7

RANK ORDER

RANK	STATE	PERCENT
1	Kentucky	32.6
2	Alaska	29.4
3	West Virginia	28.4
4	Tennessee	27.8
5	Indiana	27.7
6	Mississippi	27.4
7	Oklahoma	26.7
8	Missouri	26.6
8	Ohio	26.6
8	South Carolina	26.6
11	North Carolina	26.4
12	Arkansas	26.3
13	Nevada	26.0
14	Delaware	24.7
15	Pennsylvania	24.6
15	Virginia	24.6
17	Alabama	24.4
18	Michigan	24.2
19	Louisiana	23.9
20	Wyoming	23.7
21	Maine	23.6
22	Arizona	23.5
23	Wisconsin	23.4
24	Georgia	23.3
25	New Hampshire	23.2
26	Iowa	23.1
27	Illinois	22.9
27	Texas	22.9
29	Nebraska	22.8
30	South Dakota	22.6
31	Rhode Island	22.5
32	New York	22.4
32	Oregon	22.4
34	Florida	22.1
34	Kansas	22.1
36	Maryland	22.0
37	Minnesota	21.7
38	North Dakota	21.5
38	Washington	21.5
40	Montana	21.3
41	New Mexico	21.2
41	Vermont	21.2
43	Hawaii	21.1
44	Idaho	20.6
45	Colorado	20.4
46	Connecticut	19.5
47	New Jersey	19.1
48	Massachusetts	19.0
49	California	16.4
50	Utah	12.7
	District of Columbia	20.4

Source: U.S. Department of Health and Human Services, Centers for Disease Control and Prevention
"2002 Behavioral Risk Factor Surveillance Summary Prevalence Data" (http://apps.nccd.cdc.gov/brfss/)
**Persons 18 and older who have smoked more than 100 cigarettes during their lifetime and who currently smoke everyday or some days.*

Percent of Adults Overweight: 2002

National Median = 37.0% of Adults*

ALPHA ORDER

RANK	STATE	PERCENT
22	Alabama	37.0
9	Alaska	37.7
32	Arizona	36.6
19	Arkansas	37.2
13	California	37.5
22	Colorado	37.0
22	Connecticut	37.0
38	Delaware	36.2
11	Florida	37.6
49	Georgia	35.4
41	Hawaii	36.0
21	Idaho	37.1
15	Illinois	37.3
19	Indiana	37.2
4	Iowa	38.3
14	Kansas	37.4
6	Kentucky	38.1
44	Louisiana	35.6
7	Maine	38.0
2	Maryland	38.5
35	Massachusetts	36.3
27	Michigan	36.9
33	Minnesota	36.5
35	Mississippi	36.3
22	Missouri	37.0
8	Montana	37.9
22	Nebraska	37.0
15	Nevada	37.3
2	New Hampshire	38.5
15	New Jersey	37.3
30	New Mexico	36.7
30	New York	36.7
48	North Carolina	35.5
5	North Dakota	38.2
42	Ohio	35.8
42	Oklahoma	35.8
27	Oregon	36.9
44	Pennsylvania	35.6
11	Rhode Island	37.6
44	South Carolina	35.6
1	South Dakota	39.4
29	Tennessee	36.8
15	Texas	37.3
39	Utah	36.1
44	Vermont	35.6
50	Virginia	35.1
9	Washington	37.7
39	West Virginia	36.1
35	Wisconsin	36.3
34	Wyoming	36.4

RANK ORDER

RANK	STATE	PERCENT
1	South Dakota	39.4
2	Maryland	38.5
2	New Hampshire	38.5
4	Iowa	38.3
5	North Dakota	38.2
6	Kentucky	38.1
7	Maine	38.0
8	Montana	37.9
9	Alaska	37.7
9	Washington	37.7
11	Florida	37.6
11	Rhode Island	37.6
13	California	37.5
14	Kansas	37.4
15	Illinois	37.3
15	Nevada	37.3
15	New Jersey	37.3
15	Texas	37.3
19	Arkansas	37.2
19	Indiana	37.2
21	Idaho	37.1
22	Alabama	37.0
22	Colorado	37.0
22	Connecticut	37.0
22	Missouri	37.0
22	Nebraska	37.0
27	Michigan	36.9
27	Oregon	36.9
29	Tennessee	36.8
30	New Mexico	36.7
30	New York	36.7
32	Arizona	36.6
33	Minnesota	36.5
34	Wyoming	36.4
35	Massachusetts	36.3
35	Mississippi	36.3
35	Wisconsin	36.3
38	Delaware	36.2
39	Utah	36.1
39	West Virginia	36.1
41	Hawaii	36.0
42	Ohio	35.8
42	Oklahoma	35.8
44	Louisiana	35.6
44	Pennsylvania	35.6
44	South Carolina	35.6
44	Vermont	35.6
48	North Carolina	35.5
49	Georgia	35.4
50	Virginia	35.1
	District of Columbia	32.1

Source: U.S. Department of Health and Human Services, Centers for Disease Control and Prevention
"2002 Behavioral Risk Factor Surveillance Summary Prevalence Data" (http://apps.nccd.cdc.gov/brfss/)
Persons 18 and older. Overweight is defined as a Body Mass Index (BMI) of 25.0 to 29.9 regardless of sex. BMI is a ratio of height to weight. As an example, a person 5' 8" and weighing 171 pounds has a BMI of 26. See http://www.cdc.gov/nccdphp/dnpa/bmi/bmi-adult.htm.

Percent of Children Aged 19 to 35 Months Fully Immunized in 2002

National Percent = 65.5%*

<u>ALPHA ORDER</u>   <u>RANK ORDER</u>

RANK	STATE	PERCENT		RANK	STATE	PERCENT
5	Alabama	73.3		1	Rhode Island	80.7
44	Alaska	56.2		2	Massachusetts	78.0
39	Arizona	59.0		3	Georgia	76.5
12	Arkansas	68.3		4	South Carolina	73.8
17	California	67.1		5	Alabama	73.3
45	Colorado	56.1		6	Connecticut	72.8
6	Connecticut	72.8		7	Michigan	71.7
9	Delaware	69.7		8	Maryland	70.7
18	Florida	66.4		9	Delaware	69.7
3	Georgia	76.5		9	North Carolina	69.7
11	Hawaii	69.1		11	Hawaii	69.1
48	Idaho	52.6		12	Arkansas	68.3
41	Illinois	58.1		13	Pennsylvania	67.6
37	Indiana	59.4		14	Wisconsin	67.5
40	Iowa	58.2		15	New York	67.3
46	Kansas	55.1		15	Tennessee	67.3
27	Kentucky	63.6		17	California	67.1
31	Louisiana	61.9		18	Florida	66.4
29	Maine	62.1		19	New Hampshire	66.2
8	Maryland	70.7		20	West Virginia	65.8
2	Massachusetts	78.0		21	New Jersey	65.5
7	Michigan	71.7		22	Nevada	65.3
32	Minnesota	61.5		23	Texas	65.0
26	Mississippi	63.9		24	Virginia	64.8
36	Missouri	60.1		25	Nebraska	64.3
50	Montana	49.4		26	Mississippi	63.9
25	Nebraska	64.3		27	Kentucky	63.6
22	Nevada	65.3		28	Ohio	63.5
19	New Hampshire	66.2		29	Maine	62.1
21	New Jersey	65.5		30	South Dakota	62.0
38	New Mexico	59.1		31	Louisiana	61.9
15	New York	67.3		32	Minnesota	61.5
9	North Carolina	69.7		33	Utah	61.4
43	North Dakota	56.3		34	Oklahoma	60.3
28	Ohio	63.5		34	Oregon	60.3
34	Oklahoma	60.3		36	Missouri	60.1
34	Oregon	60.3		37	Indiana	59.4
13	Pennsylvania	67.6		38	New Mexico	59.1
1	Rhode Island	80.7		39	Arizona	59.0
4	South Carolina	73.8		40	Iowa	58.2
30	South Dakota	62.0		41	Illinois	58.1
15	Tennessee	67.3		42	Vermont	57.7
23	Texas	65.0		43	North Dakota	56.3
33	Utah	61.4		44	Alaska	56.2
42	Vermont	57.7		45	Colorado	56.1
24	Virginia	64.8		46	Kansas	55.1
49	Washington	51.9		47	Wyoming	54.1
20	West Virginia	65.8		48	Idaho	52.6
14	Wisconsin	67.5		49	Washington	51.9
47	Wyoming	54.1		50	Montana	49.4
					District of Columbia	68.3

*Source: U.S. Department of Health and Human Services, Centers for Disease Control and Prevention
"State Vaccination Coverage Levels" (Morbidity and Mortality Weekly Report, Vol. 52, No. 31, August 8, 2003)*
**Fully immunized (4:3:1:3:3:1 series) children received four doses of DTP/DT/DTaP (Diphtheria, Tetanus, Pertussis
(Whooping Cough), Acellular Pertussis), three doses of OPV (Oral Poliovirus Vaccine), one dose of MCV
(Measles-Containing Vaccine), three doses of Hib (Haemophilus influenzae type b), three doses of Hepatitis B
vaccine and one dose of Varicella (chickenpox) vaccine. This differs from previous "fully" immunized tables.*

XII. HOUSEHOLDS & HOUSING

Households in 2002

National Total = 107,366,878 Households*

<u>ALPHA ORDER</u>

RANK	STATE	HOUSEHOLDS	% of USA
23	Alabama	1,729,893	1.6%
49	Alaska	225,474	0.2%
20	Arizona	2,014,316	1.9%
31	Arkansas	1,062,677	1.0%
1	California	11,705,477	10.9%
22	Colorado	1,804,111	1.7%
29	Connecticut	1,305,518	1.2%
45	Delaware	306,205	0.3%
4	Florida	6,568,733	6.1%
11	Georgia	3,078,258	2.9%
42	Hawaii	415,479	0.4%
40	Idaho	489,032	0.5%
6	Illinois	4,627,667	4.3%
15	Indiana	2,345,780	2.2%
30	Iowa	1,145,564	1.1%
32	Kansas	1,056,896	1.0%
25	Kentucky	1,599,319	1.5%
24	Louisiana	1,664,877	1.6%
39	Maine	536,194	0.5%
19	Maryland	2,019,463	1.9%
13	Massachusetts	2,432,176	2.3%
8	Michigan	3,844,635	3.6%
21	Minnesota	1,992,524	1.9%
33	Mississippi	1,047,324	1.0%
17	Missouri	2,252,604	2.1%
44	Montana	357,296	0.3%
38	Nebraska	677,159	0.6%
34	Nevada	808,077	0.8%
41	New Hampshire	485,903	0.5%
10	New Jersey	3,081,928	2.9%
37	New Mexico	681,931	0.6%
3	New York	7,060,516	6.6%
9	North Carolina	3,207,447	3.0%
47	North Dakota	254,689	0.2%
7	Ohio	4,447,307	4.1%
28	Oklahoma	1,338,651	1.2%
27	Oregon	1,409,433	1.3%
5	Pennsylvania	4,821,279	4.5%
43	Rhode Island	408,272	0.4%
26	South Carolina	1,563,144	1.5%
46	South Dakota	291,851	0.3%
16	Tennessee	2,257,080	2.1%
2	Texas	7,521,712	7.0%
35	Utah	744,627	0.7%
48	Vermont	242,201	0.2%
12	Virginia	2,773,044	2.6%
14	Washington	2,358,892	2.2%
36	West Virginia	719,655	0.7%
18	Wisconsin	2,142,645	2.0%
50	Wyoming	199,848	0.2%

<u>RANK ORDER</u>

RANK	STATE	HOUSEHOLDS	% of USA
1	California	11,705,477	10.9%
2	Texas	7,521,712	7.0%
3	New York	7,060,516	6.6%
4	Florida	6,568,733	6.1%
5	Pennsylvania	4,821,279	4.5%
6	Illinois	4,627,667	4.3%
7	Ohio	4,447,307	4.1%
8	Michigan	3,844,635	3.6%
9	North Carolina	3,207,447	3.0%
10	New Jersey	3,081,928	2.9%
11	Georgia	3,078,258	2.9%
12	Virginia	2,773,044	2.6%
13	Massachusetts	2,432,176	2.3%
14	Washington	2,358,892	2.2%
15	Indiana	2,345,780	2.2%
16	Tennessee	2,257,080	2.1%
17	Missouri	2,252,604	2.1%
18	Wisconsin	2,142,645	2.0%
19	Maryland	2,019,463	1.9%
20	Arizona	2,014,316	1.9%
21	Minnesota	1,992,524	1.9%
22	Colorado	1,804,111	1.7%
23	Alabama	1,729,893	1.6%
24	Louisiana	1,664,877	1.6%
25	Kentucky	1,599,319	1.5%
26	South Carolina	1,563,144	1.5%
27	Oregon	1,409,433	1.3%
28	Oklahoma	1,338,651	1.2%
29	Connecticut	1,305,518	1.2%
30	Iowa	1,145,564	1.1%
31	Arkansas	1,062,677	1.0%
32	Kansas	1,056,896	1.0%
33	Mississippi	1,047,324	1.0%
34	Nevada	808,077	0.8%
35	Utah	744,627	0.7%
36	West Virginia	719,655	0.7%
37	New Mexico	681,931	0.6%
38	Nebraska	677,159	0.6%
39	Maine	536,194	0.5%
40	Idaho	489,032	0.5%
41	New Hampshire	485,903	0.5%
42	Hawaii	415,479	0.4%
43	Rhode Island	408,272	0.4%
44	Montana	357,296	0.3%
45	Delaware	306,205	0.3%
46	South Dakota	291,851	0.3%
47	North Dakota	254,689	0.2%
48	Vermont	242,201	0.2%
49	Alaska	225,474	0.2%
50	Wyoming	199,848	0.2%
	District of Columbia	242,095	0.2%

Source: U.S. Bureau of the Census
"2002 American Community Survey"

*A household includes all persons who occupy a housing unit. A household consists of a single family, one person living alone, two or more families living together, or any other group of related or unrelated persons who share living arrangements.

Persons per Household in 2003

National Rate = 2.61 Persons per Household*

<table>
<tr><th colspan="3">ALPHA ORDER</th><th colspan="3">RANK ORDER</th></tr>
<tr><th>RANK</th><th>STATE</th><th>PERSONS</th><th>RANK</th><th>STATE</th><th>PERSONS</th></tr>
<tr><td>25</td><td>Alabama</td><td>2.53</td><td>1</td><td>Utah</td><td>3.06</td></tr>
<tr><td>5</td><td>Alaska</td><td>2.77</td><td>2</td><td>California</td><td>2.93</td></tr>
<tr><td>10</td><td>Arizona</td><td>2.65</td><td>3</td><td>Hawaii</td><td>2.91</td></tr>
<tr><td>35</td><td>Arkansas</td><td>2.48</td><td>4</td><td>Texas</td><td>2.82</td></tr>
<tr><td>2</td><td>California</td><td>2.93</td><td>5</td><td>Alaska</td><td>2.77</td></tr>
<tr><td>44</td><td>Colorado</td><td>2.44</td><td>6</td><td>New Jersey</td><td>2.72</td></tr>
<tr><td>17</td><td>Connecticut</td><td>2.57</td><td>7</td><td>Georgia</td><td>2.70</td></tr>
<tr><td>18</td><td>Delaware</td><td>2.55</td><td>8</td><td>Idaho</td><td>2.68</td></tr>
<tr><td>35</td><td>Florida</td><td>2.48</td><td>9</td><td>New Mexico</td><td>2.67</td></tr>
<tr><td>7</td><td>Georgia</td><td>2.70</td><td>10</td><td>Arizona</td><td>2.65</td></tr>
<tr><td>3</td><td>Hawaii</td><td>2.91</td><td>10</td><td>Illinois</td><td>2.65</td></tr>
<tr><td>8</td><td>Idaho</td><td>2.68</td><td>10</td><td>Mississippi</td><td>2.65</td></tr>
<tr><td>10</td><td>Illinois</td><td>2.65</td><td>10</td><td>Nevada</td><td>2.65</td></tr>
<tr><td>18</td><td>Indiana</td><td>2.55</td><td>14</td><td>Maryland</td><td>2.64</td></tr>
<tr><td>39</td><td>Iowa</td><td>2.47</td><td>15</td><td>New York</td><td>2.63</td></tr>
<tr><td>33</td><td>Kansas</td><td>2.49</td><td>16</td><td>Louisiana</td><td>2.61</td></tr>
<tr><td>33</td><td>Kentucky</td><td>2.49</td><td>17</td><td>Connecticut</td><td>2.57</td></tr>
<tr><td>16</td><td>Louisiana</td><td>2.61</td><td>18</td><td>Delaware</td><td>2.55</td></tr>
<tr><td>50</td><td>Maine</td><td>2.35</td><td>18</td><td>Indiana</td><td>2.55</td></tr>
<tr><td>14</td><td>Maryland</td><td>2.64</td><td>18</td><td>Massachusetts</td><td>2.55</td></tr>
<tr><td>18</td><td>Massachusetts</td><td>2.55</td><td>18</td><td>Michigan</td><td>2.55</td></tr>
<tr><td>18</td><td>Michigan</td><td>2.55</td><td>18</td><td>New Hampshire</td><td>2.55</td></tr>
<tr><td>43</td><td>Minnesota</td><td>2.45</td><td>18</td><td>Virginia</td><td>2.55</td></tr>
<tr><td>10</td><td>Mississippi</td><td>2.65</td><td>24</td><td>South Carolina</td><td>2.54</td></tr>
<tr><td>44</td><td>Missouri</td><td>2.44</td><td>25</td><td>Alabama</td><td>2.53</td></tr>
<tr><td>35</td><td>Montana</td><td>2.48</td><td>26</td><td>Oklahoma</td><td>2.52</td></tr>
<tr><td>35</td><td>Nebraska</td><td>2.48</td><td>26</td><td>Rhode Island</td><td>2.52</td></tr>
<tr><td>10</td><td>Nevada</td><td>2.65</td><td>28</td><td>North Carolina</td><td>2.51</td></tr>
<tr><td>18</td><td>New Hampshire</td><td>2.55</td><td>28</td><td>South Dakota</td><td>2.51</td></tr>
<tr><td>6</td><td>New Jersey</td><td>2.72</td><td>28</td><td>Washington</td><td>2.51</td></tr>
<tr><td>9</td><td>New Mexico</td><td>2.67</td><td>31</td><td>Ohio</td><td>2.50</td></tr>
<tr><td>15</td><td>New York</td><td>2.63</td><td>31</td><td>Tennessee</td><td>2.50</td></tr>
<tr><td>28</td><td>North Carolina</td><td>2.51</td><td>33</td><td>Kansas</td><td>2.49</td></tr>
<tr><td>49</td><td>North Dakota</td><td>2.40</td><td>33</td><td>Kentucky</td><td>2.49</td></tr>
<tr><td>31</td><td>Ohio</td><td>2.50</td><td>35</td><td>Arkansas</td><td>2.48</td></tr>
<tr><td>26</td><td>Oklahoma</td><td>2.52</td><td>35</td><td>Florida</td><td>2.48</td></tr>
<tr><td>44</td><td>Oregon</td><td>2.44</td><td>35</td><td>Montana</td><td>2.48</td></tr>
<tr><td>39</td><td>Pennsylvania</td><td>2.47</td><td>35</td><td>Nebraska</td><td>2.48</td></tr>
<tr><td>26</td><td>Rhode Island</td><td>2.52</td><td>39</td><td>Iowa</td><td>2.47</td></tr>
<tr><td>24</td><td>South Carolina</td><td>2.54</td><td>39</td><td>Pennsylvania</td><td>2.47</td></tr>
<tr><td>28</td><td>South Dakota</td><td>2.51</td><td>39</td><td>Wisconsin</td><td>2.47</td></tr>
<tr><td>31</td><td>Tennessee</td><td>2.50</td><td>42</td><td>Vermont</td><td>2.46</td></tr>
<tr><td>4</td><td>Texas</td><td>2.82</td><td>43</td><td>Minnesota</td><td>2.45</td></tr>
<tr><td>1</td><td>Utah</td><td>3.06</td><td>44</td><td>Colorado</td><td>2.44</td></tr>
<tr><td>42</td><td>Vermont</td><td>2.46</td><td>44</td><td>Missouri</td><td>2.44</td></tr>
<tr><td>18</td><td>Virginia</td><td>2.55</td><td>44</td><td>Oregon</td><td>2.44</td></tr>
<tr><td>28</td><td>Washington</td><td>2.51</td><td>44</td><td>West Virginia</td><td>2.44</td></tr>
<tr><td>44</td><td>West Virginia</td><td>2.44</td><td>48</td><td>Wyoming</td><td>2.43</td></tr>
<tr><td>39</td><td>Wisconsin</td><td>2.47</td><td>49</td><td>North Dakota</td><td>2.40</td></tr>
<tr><td>48</td><td>Wyoming</td><td>2.43</td><td>50</td><td>Maine</td><td>2.35</td></tr>
<tr><td></td><td></td><td></td><td></td><td>District of Columbia</td><td>2.21</td></tr>
</table>

Source: U.S. Bureau of the Census
"2002 American Community Survey"
**A household includes all persons who occupy a housing unit. A household consists of a single family, one person living alone, two or more families living together, or any other group of related or unrelated persons who share living arrangements.*

Percent of Households with One Person in 2002

National Percent = 26.7% of Households

<table>
<tr><th colspan="3">ALPHA ORDER</th><th colspan="3">RANK ORDER</th></tr>
<tr><th>RANK</th><th>STATE</th><th>PERCENT</th><th>RANK</th><th>STATE</th><th>PERCENT</th></tr>
<tr><td>37</td><td>Alabama</td><td>25.6</td><td>1</td><td>North Dakota</td><td>30.5</td></tr>
<tr><td>49</td><td>Alaska</td><td>22.4</td><td>2</td><td>New York</td><td>29.5</td></tr>
<tr><td>42</td><td>Arizona</td><td>24.4</td><td>3</td><td>Kansas</td><td>28.8</td></tr>
<tr><td>31</td><td>Arkansas</td><td>26.2</td><td>4</td><td>Pennsylvania</td><td>28.5</td></tr>
<tr><td>40</td><td>California</td><td>25.1</td><td>4</td><td>West Virginia</td><td>28.5</td></tr>
<tr><td>25</td><td>Colorado</td><td>26.9</td><td>6</td><td>Ohio</td><td>28.4</td></tr>
<tr><td>29</td><td>Connecticut</td><td>26.4</td><td>7</td><td>Michigan</td><td>28.3</td></tr>
<tr><td>41</td><td>Delaware</td><td>24.8</td><td>7</td><td>Oregon</td><td>28.3</td></tr>
<tr><td>15</td><td>Florida</td><td>27.7</td><td>9</td><td>South Dakota</td><td>28.1</td></tr>
<tr><td>31</td><td>Georgia</td><td>26.2</td><td>9</td><td>Wyoming</td><td>28.1</td></tr>
<tr><td>48</td><td>Hawaii</td><td>22.8</td><td>11</td><td>Illinois</td><td>28.0</td></tr>
<tr><td>47</td><td>Idaho</td><td>23.0</td><td>11</td><td>Montana</td><td>28.0</td></tr>
<tr><td>11</td><td>Illinois</td><td>28.0</td><td>11</td><td>Washington</td><td>28.0</td></tr>
<tr><td>27</td><td>Indiana</td><td>26.7</td><td>14</td><td>Rhode Island</td><td>27.8</td></tr>
<tr><td>18</td><td>Iowa</td><td>27.5</td><td>15</td><td>Florida</td><td>27.7</td></tr>
<tr><td>3</td><td>Kansas</td><td>28.8</td><td>15</td><td>Massachusetts</td><td>27.7</td></tr>
<tr><td>33</td><td>Kentucky</td><td>26.1</td><td>17</td><td>Nebraska</td><td>27.6</td></tr>
<tr><td>26</td><td>Louisiana</td><td>26.8</td><td>18</td><td>Iowa</td><td>27.5</td></tr>
<tr><td>39</td><td>Maine</td><td>25.2</td><td>18</td><td>Minnesota</td><td>27.5</td></tr>
<tr><td>36</td><td>Maryland</td><td>25.8</td><td>18</td><td>Wisconsin</td><td>27.5</td></tr>
<tr><td>15</td><td>Massachusetts</td><td>27.7</td><td>21</td><td>Tennessee</td><td>27.4</td></tr>
<tr><td>7</td><td>Michigan</td><td>28.3</td><td>22</td><td>Oklahoma</td><td>27.1</td></tr>
<tr><td>18</td><td>Minnesota</td><td>27.5</td><td>23</td><td>Missouri</td><td>27.0</td></tr>
<tr><td>46</td><td>Mississippi</td><td>24.1</td><td>23</td><td>New Mexico</td><td>27.0</td></tr>
<tr><td>23</td><td>Missouri</td><td>27.0</td><td>25</td><td>Colorado</td><td>26.9</td></tr>
<tr><td>11</td><td>Montana</td><td>28.0</td><td>26</td><td>Louisiana</td><td>26.8</td></tr>
<tr><td>17</td><td>Nebraska</td><td>27.6</td><td>27</td><td>Indiana</td><td>26.7</td></tr>
<tr><td>30</td><td>Nevada</td><td>26.3</td><td>27</td><td>North Carolina</td><td>26.7</td></tr>
<tr><td>44</td><td>New Hampshire</td><td>24.2</td><td>29</td><td>Connecticut</td><td>26.4</td></tr>
<tr><td>43</td><td>New Jersey</td><td>24.3</td><td>30</td><td>Nevada</td><td>26.3</td></tr>
<tr><td>23</td><td>New Mexico</td><td>27.0</td><td>31</td><td>Arkansas</td><td>26.2</td></tr>
<tr><td>2</td><td>New York</td><td>29.5</td><td>31</td><td>Georgia</td><td>26.2</td></tr>
<tr><td>27</td><td>North Carolina</td><td>26.7</td><td>33</td><td>Kentucky</td><td>26.1</td></tr>
<tr><td>1</td><td>North Dakota</td><td>30.5</td><td>34</td><td>South Carolina</td><td>26.0</td></tr>
<tr><td>6</td><td>Ohio</td><td>28.4</td><td>34</td><td>Virginia</td><td>26.0</td></tr>
<tr><td>22</td><td>Oklahoma</td><td>27.1</td><td>36</td><td>Maryland</td><td>25.8</td></tr>
<tr><td>7</td><td>Oregon</td><td>28.3</td><td>37</td><td>Alabama</td><td>25.6</td></tr>
<tr><td>4</td><td>Pennsylvania</td><td>28.5</td><td>37</td><td>Vermont</td><td>25.6</td></tr>
<tr><td>14</td><td>Rhode Island</td><td>27.8</td><td>39</td><td>Maine</td><td>25.2</td></tr>
<tr><td>34</td><td>South Carolina</td><td>26.0</td><td>40</td><td>California</td><td>25.1</td></tr>
<tr><td>9</td><td>South Dakota</td><td>28.1</td><td>41</td><td>Delaware</td><td>24.8</td></tr>
<tr><td>21</td><td>Tennessee</td><td>27.4</td><td>42</td><td>Arizona</td><td>24.4</td></tr>
<tr><td>44</td><td>Texas</td><td>24.2</td><td>43</td><td>New Jersey</td><td>24.3</td></tr>
<tr><td>50</td><td>Utah</td><td>17.1</td><td>44</td><td>New Hampshire</td><td>24.2</td></tr>
<tr><td>37</td><td>Vermont</td><td>25.6</td><td>44</td><td>Texas</td><td>24.2</td></tr>
<tr><td>34</td><td>Virginia</td><td>26.0</td><td>46</td><td>Mississippi</td><td>24.1</td></tr>
<tr><td>11</td><td>Washington</td><td>28.0</td><td>47</td><td>Idaho</td><td>23.0</td></tr>
<tr><td>4</td><td>West Virginia</td><td>28.5</td><td>48</td><td>Hawaii</td><td>22.8</td></tr>
<tr><td>18</td><td>Wisconsin</td><td>27.5</td><td>49</td><td>Alaska</td><td>22.4</td></tr>
<tr><td>9</td><td>Wyoming</td><td>28.1</td><td>50</td><td>Utah</td><td>17.1</td></tr>
<tr><td></td><td></td><td></td><td></td><td>District of Columbia</td><td>44.5</td></tr>
</table>

Source: Morgan Quitno Press using data from U.S. Bureau of the Census
    "2002 American Community Survey"

Percent of Households Headed by Married Couples in 2002

National Percent = 50.7% of Households

<u>ALPHA ORDER</u>

RANK	STATE	PERCENT
16	Alabama	52.9
3	Alaska	55.1
19	Arizona	52.6
11	Arkansas	53.3
42	California	49.4
23	Colorado	52.0
20	Connecticut	52.5
29	Delaware	51.2
44	Florida	48.9
36	Georgia	50.1
18	Hawaii	52.7
2	Idaho	58.1
39	Illinois	49.9
22	Indiana	52.1
7	Iowa	53.9
28	Kansas	51.8
14	Kentucky	53.1
49	Louisiana	47.0
20	Maine	52.5
35	Maryland	50.2
43	Massachusetts	49.3
34	Michigan	50.6
16	Minnesota	52.9
46	Mississippi	48.8
23	Missouri	52.0
6	Montana	54.1
8	Nebraska	53.6
47	Nevada	48.5
4	New Hampshire	54.8
5	New Jersey	54.2
44	New Mexico	48.9
50	New York	45.3
32	North Carolina	50.9
29	North Dakota	51.2
39	Ohio	49.9
14	Oklahoma	53.1
38	Oregon	50.0
33	Pennsylvania	50.8
47	Rhode Island	48.5
39	South Carolina	49.9
10	South Dakota	53.4
31	Tennessee	51.1
11	Texas	53.3
1	Utah	63.8
9	Vermont	53.5
26	Virginia	51.9
36	Washington	50.1
26	West Virginia	51.9
23	Wisconsin	52.0
13	Wyoming	53.2

<u>RANK ORDER</u>

RANK	STATE	PERCENT
1	Utah	63.8
2	Idaho	58.1
3	Alaska	55.1
4	New Hampshire	54.8
5	New Jersey	54.2
6	Montana	54.1
7	Iowa	53.9
8	Nebraska	53.6
9	Vermont	53.5
10	South Dakota	53.4
11	Arkansas	53.3
11	Texas	53.3
13	Wyoming	53.2
14	Kentucky	53.1
14	Oklahoma	53.1
16	Alabama	52.9
16	Minnesota	52.9
18	Hawaii	52.7
19	Arizona	52.6
20	Connecticut	52.5
20	Maine	52.5
22	Indiana	52.1
23	Colorado	52.0
23	Missouri	52.0
23	Wisconsin	52.0
26	Virginia	51.9
26	West Virginia	51.9
28	Kansas	51.8
29	Delaware	51.2
29	North Dakota	51.2
31	Tennessee	51.1
32	North Carolina	50.9
33	Pennsylvania	50.8
34	Michigan	50.6
35	Maryland	50.2
36	Georgia	50.1
36	Washington	50.1
38	Oregon	50.0
39	Illinois	49.9
39	Ohio	49.9
39	South Carolina	49.9
42	California	49.4
43	Massachusetts	49.3
44	Florida	48.9
44	New Mexico	48.9
46	Mississippi	48.8
47	Nevada	48.5
47	Rhode Island	48.5
49	Louisiana	47.0
50	New York	45.3
	District of Columbia	22.2

Source: Morgan Quitno Press using data from U.S. Bureau of the Census
"2002 American Community Survey"

Percent of Households Headed by Single Mothers in 2002

National Percent = 12.4% of Households*

<u>ALPHA ORDER</u>

RANK	STATE	PERCENT
6	Alabama	14.1
35	Alaska	10.6
30	Arizona	11.3
20	Arkansas	12.2
12	California	12.9
39	Colorado	9.8
24	Connecticut	11.9
9	Delaware	13.3
17	Florida	12.3
4	Georgia	14.7
24	Hawaii	11.9
50	Idaho	7.9
17	Illinois	12.3
28	Indiana	11.4
43	Iowa	9.1
32	Kansas	11.0
20	Kentucky	12.2
2	Louisiana	17.6
31	Maine	11.1
7	Maryland	14.0
17	Massachusetts	12.3
24	Michigan	11.9
45	Minnesota	8.9
1	Mississippi	18.0
28	Missouri	11.4
49	Montana	8.3
47	Nebraska	8.7
20	Nevada	12.2
36	New Hampshire	10.3
16	New Jersey	12.4
9	New Mexico	13.3
4	New York	14.7
9	North Carolina	13.3
48	North Dakota	8.4
15	Ohio	12.7
33	Oklahoma	10.9
36	Oregon	10.3
27	Pennsylvania	11.5
8	Rhode Island	13.4
3	South Carolina	15.1
46	South Dakota	8.8
12	Tennessee	12.9
12	Texas	12.9
42	Utah	9.3
41	Vermont	9.5
23	Virginia	12.1
36	Washington	10.3
34	West Virginia	10.7
40	Wisconsin	9.6
44	Wyoming	9.0

<u>RANK ORDER</u>

RANK	STATE	PERCENT
1	Mississippi	18.0
2	Louisiana	17.6
3	South Carolina	15.1
4	Georgia	14.7
4	New York	14.7
6	Alabama	14.1
7	Maryland	14.0
8	Rhode Island	13.4
9	Delaware	13.3
9	New Mexico	13.3
9	North Carolina	13.3
12	California	12.9
12	Tennessee	12.9
12	Texas	12.9
15	Ohio	12.7
16	New Jersey	12.4
17	Florida	12.3
17	Illinois	12.3
17	Massachusetts	12.3
20	Arkansas	12.2
20	Kentucky	12.2
20	Nevada	12.2
23	Virginia	12.1
24	Connecticut	11.9
24	Hawaii	11.9
24	Michigan	11.9
27	Pennsylvania	11.5
28	Indiana	11.4
28	Missouri	11.4
30	Arizona	11.3
31	Maine	11.1
32	Kansas	11.0
33	Oklahoma	10.9
34	West Virginia	10.7
35	Alaska	10.6
36	New Hampshire	10.3
36	Oregon	10.3
36	Washington	10.3
39	Colorado	9.8
40	Wisconsin	9.6
41	Vermont	9.5
42	Utah	9.3
43	Iowa	9.1
44	Wyoming	9.0
45	Minnesota	8.9
46	South Dakota	8.8
47	Nebraska	8.7
48	North Dakota	8.4
49	Montana	8.3
50	Idaho	7.9
	District of Columbia	19.5

Source: Morgan Quitno Press using data from U.S. Bureau of the Census
"2002 American Community Survey"
*No spouse present in household with children under 18 years old.

Percent of Households Headed by Single Fathers in 2002

National Percent = 3.2% of Households*

<u>ALPHA ORDER</u>

RANK	STATE	PERCENT
49	Alabama	2.1
1	Alaska	4.8
8	Arizona	4.0
43	Arkansas	2.6
5	California	4.1
3	Colorado	4.4
38	Connecticut	2.7
21	Delaware	3.1
18	Florida	3.3
38	Georgia	2.7
9	Hawaii	3.9
29	Idaho	3.0
21	Illinois	3.1
9	Indiana	3.9
17	Iowa	3.4
35	Kansas	2.8
31	Kentucky	2.9
29	Louisiana	3.0
38	Maine	2.7
21	Maryland	3.1
50	Massachusetts	1.9
21	Michigan	3.1
21	Minnesota	3.1
4	Mississippi	4.3
31	Missouri	2.9
16	Montana	3.5
13	Nebraska	3.6
5	Nevada	4.1
35	New Hampshire	2.8
45	New Jersey	2.4
2	New Mexico	4.7
35	New York	2.8
31	North Carolina	2.9
45	North Dakota	2.4
13	Ohio	3.6
21	Oklahoma	3.1
21	Oregon	3.1
38	Pennsylvania	2.7
48	Rhode Island	2.3
45	South Carolina	2.4
11	South Dakota	3.7
31	Tennessee	2.9
18	Texas	3.3
13	Utah	3.6
38	Vermont	2.7
43	Virginia	2.6
20	Washington	3.2
21	West Virginia	3.1
11	Wisconsin	3.7
5	Wyoming	4.1

<u>RANK ORDER</u>

RANK	STATE	PERCENT
1	Alaska	4.8
2	New Mexico	4.7
3	Colorado	4.4
4	Mississippi	4.3
5	California	4.1
5	Nevada	4.1
5	Wyoming	4.1
8	Arizona	4.0
9	Hawaii	3.9
9	Indiana	3.9
11	South Dakota	3.7
11	Wisconsin	3.7
13	Nebraska	3.6
13	Ohio	3.6
13	Utah	3.6
16	Montana	3.5
17	Iowa	3.4
18	Florida	3.3
18	Texas	3.3
20	Washington	3.2
21	Delaware	3.1
21	Illinois	3.1
21	Maryland	3.1
21	Michigan	3.1
21	Minnesota	3.1
21	Oklahoma	3.1
21	Oregon	3.1
21	West Virginia	3.1
29	Idaho	3.0
29	Louisiana	3.0
31	Kentucky	2.9
31	Missouri	2.9
31	North Carolina	2.9
31	Tennessee	2.9
35	Kansas	2.8
35	New Hampshire	2.8
35	New York	2.8
38	Connecticut	2.7
38	Georgia	2.7
38	Maine	2.7
38	Pennsylvania	2.7
38	Vermont	2.7
43	Arkansas	2.6
43	Virginia	2.6
45	New Jersey	2.4
45	North Dakota	2.4
45	South Carolina	2.4
48	Rhode Island	2.3
49	Alabama	2.1
50	Massachusetts	1.9
	District of Columbia	2.2

Source: Morgan Quitno Press using data from U.S. Bureau of the Census
"2002 American Community Survey"
*A household includes all persons who occupy a housing unit. A household consists of a single family, one person living alone, two or more families living together, or any other group of related or unrelated persons who share living arrangements.

Housing Units in 2002

National Total = 119,302,132 Housing Units*

ALPHA ORDER

RANK	STATE	HOUSING UNITS	% of USA
22	Alabama	2,014,536	1.7%
49	Alaska	265,377	0.2%
19	Arizona	2,328,720	2.0%
31	Arkansas	1,202,028	1.0%
1	California	12,507,767	10.5%
23	Colorado	1,929,092	1.6%
29	Connecticut	1,402,643	1.2%
45	Delaware	352,031	0.3%
4	Florida	7,624,378	6.4%
10	Georgia	3,487,088	2.9%
42	Hawaii	470,512	0.4%
41	Idaho	552,117	0.5%
6	Illinois	4,981,258	4.2%
14	Indiana	2,615,750	2.2%
30	Iowa	1,257,184	1.1%
33	Kansas	1,159,276	1.0%
26	Kentucky	1,796,900	1.5%
24	Louisiana	1,880,122	1.6%
39	Maine	664,613	0.6%
20	Maryland	2,197,126	1.8%
13	Massachusetts	2,649,029	2.2%
8	Michigan	4,331,986	3.6%
21	Minnesota	2,132,632	1.8%
32	Mississippi	1,195,133	1.0%
17	Missouri	2,503,187	2.1%
44	Montana	417,106	0.3%
38	Nebraska	738,870	0.6%
34	Nevada	901,597	0.8%
40	New Hampshire	561,178	0.5%
11	New Jersey	3,372,572	2.8%
37	New Mexico	805,293	0.7%
3	New York	7,754,508	6.5%
9	North Carolina	3,707,129	3.1%
48	North Dakota	294,165	0.2%
7	Ohio	4,875,496	4.1%
27	Oklahoma	1,541,518	1.3%
28	Oregon	1,495,582	1.3%
5	Pennsylvania	5,328,251	4.5%
43	Rhode Island	443,761	0.4%
25	South Carolina	1,825,531	1.5%
46	South Dakota	332,360	0.3%
16	Tennessee	2,519,825	2.1%
2	Texas	8,502,060	7.1%
36	Utah	808,593	0.7%
47	Vermont	299,570	0.3%
12	Virginia	3,006,877	2.5%
15	Washington	2,530,215	2.1%
35	West Virginia	852,165	0.7%
18	Wisconsin	2,386,848	2.0%
50	Wyoming	227,941	0.2%

RANK ORDER

RANK	STATE	HOUSING UNITS	% of USA
1	California	12,507,767	10.5%
2	Texas	8,502,060	7.1%
3	New York	7,754,508	6.5%
4	Florida	7,624,378	6.4%
5	Pennsylvania	5,328,251	4.5%
6	Illinois	4,981,258	4.2%
7	Ohio	4,875,496	4.1%
8	Michigan	4,331,986	3.6%
9	North Carolina	3,707,129	3.1%
10	Georgia	3,487,088	2.9%
11	New Jersey	3,372,572	2.8%
12	Virginia	3,006,877	2.5%
13	Massachusetts	2,649,029	2.2%
14	Indiana	2,615,750	2.2%
15	Washington	2,530,215	2.1%
16	Tennessee	2,519,825	2.1%
17	Missouri	2,503,187	2.1%
18	Wisconsin	2,386,848	2.0%
19	Arizona	2,328,720	2.0%
20	Maryland	2,197,126	1.8%
21	Minnesota	2,132,632	1.8%
22	Alabama	2,014,536	1.7%
23	Colorado	1,929,092	1.6%
24	Louisiana	1,880,122	1.6%
25	South Carolina	1,825,531	1.5%
26	Kentucky	1,796,900	1.5%
27	Oklahoma	1,541,518	1.3%
28	Oregon	1,495,582	1.3%
29	Connecticut	1,402,643	1.2%
30	Iowa	1,257,184	1.1%
31	Arkansas	1,202,028	1.0%
32	Mississippi	1,195,133	1.0%
33	Kansas	1,159,276	1.0%
34	Nevada	901,597	0.8%
35	West Virginia	852,165	0.7%
36	Utah	808,593	0.7%
37	New Mexico	805,293	0.7%
38	Nebraska	738,870	0.6%
39	Maine	664,613	0.6%
40	New Hampshire	561,178	0.5%
41	Idaho	552,117	0.5%
42	Hawaii	470,512	0.4%
43	Rhode Island	443,761	0.4%
44	Montana	417,106	0.3%
45	Delaware	352,031	0.3%
46	South Dakota	332,360	0.3%
47	Vermont	299,570	0.3%
48	North Dakota	294,165	0.2%
49	Alaska	265,377	0.2%
50	Wyoming	227,941	0.2%
	District of Columbia	272,636	0.2%

Source: U.S. Bureau of the Census
"Housing Unit Estimates" (http://eire.census.gov/popest/data/household/HU-EST2002-01.php)
*A housing unit is a house, an apartment, a mobile home, a group of rooms, or a single room that is occupied (or if vacant, is intended for occupancy) as separate living quarters. Separate living quarters are those in which the occupants live and eat separately from any other persons in the building and which have direct access from the outside of the building or through a common hall.

Housing Units per Square Mile in 2002

National Average = 33.7 Housing Units*

ALPHA ORDER

RANK	STATE	HOUSING UNITS
25	Alabama	39.7
50	Alaska	0.5
37	Arizona	20.5
33	Arkansas	23.1
12	California	80.2
38	Colorado	18.6
4	Connecticut	289.5
6	Delaware	180.2
8	Florida	141.4
21	Georgia	60.2
16	Hawaii	73.3
44	Idaho	6.7
11	Illinois	89.6
17	Indiana	72.9
34	Iowa	22.5
40	Kansas	14.2
22	Kentucky	45.2
24	Louisiana	43.2
36	Maine	21.5
5	Maryland	224.8
3	Massachusetts	337.9
13	Michigan	76.3
31	Minnesota	26.8
32	Mississippi	25.5
27	Missouri	36.3
48	Montana	2.9
42	Nebraska	9.6
43	Nevada	8.2
18	New Hampshire	62.6
1	New Jersey	454.7
45	New Mexico	6.6
7	New York	164.2
14	North Carolina	76.1
47	North Dakota	4.3
9	Ohio	119.1
35	Oklahoma	22.4
39	Oregon	15.6
10	Pennsylvania	118.9
2	Rhode Island	424.7
20	South Carolina	60.6
46	South Dakota	4.4
19	Tennessee	61.1
29	Texas	32.5
41	Utah	9.8
30	Vermont	32.4
15	Virginia	75.9
26	Washington	38.0
28	West Virginia	35.4
23	Wisconsin	43.9
49	Wyoming	2.3

RANK ORDER

RANK	STATE	HOUSING UNITS
1	New Jersey	454.7
2	Rhode Island	424.7
3	Massachusetts	337.9
4	Connecticut	289.5
5	Maryland	224.8
6	Delaware	180.2
7	New York	164.2
8	Florida	141.4
9	Ohio	119.1
10	Pennsylvania	118.9
11	Illinois	89.6
12	California	80.2
13	Michigan	76.3
14	North Carolina	76.1
15	Virginia	75.9
16	Hawaii	73.3
17	Indiana	72.9
18	New Hampshire	62.6
19	Tennessee	61.1
20	South Carolina	60.6
21	Georgia	60.2
22	Kentucky	45.2
23	Wisconsin	43.9
24	Louisiana	43.2
25	Alabama	39.7
26	Washington	38.0
27	Missouri	36.3
28	West Virginia	35.4
29	Texas	32.5
30	Vermont	32.4
31	Minnesota	26.8
32	Mississippi	25.5
33	Arkansas	23.1
34	Iowa	22.5
35	Oklahoma	22.4
36	Maine	21.5
37	Arizona	20.5
38	Colorado	18.6
39	Oregon	15.6
40	Kansas	14.2
41	Utah	9.8
42	Nebraska	9.6
43	Nevada	8.2
44	Idaho	6.7
45	New Mexico	6.6
46	South Dakota	4.4
47	North Dakota	4.3
48	Montana	2.9
49	Wyoming	2.3
50	Alaska	0.5

District of Columbia   4,469.4

Source: Morgan Quitno Press using data from U.S. Bureau of the Census
"Housing Unit Estimates" (http://eire.census.gov/popest/data/household/HU-EST2002-01.php)
Based on land area. A housing unit is a house, an apartment, a mobile home, a group of rooms, or a single room that is occupied (or if vacant, is intended for occupancy) as separate living quarters. Separate living quarters are those in which the occupants live and eat separately from any other persons in the building and which have direct access from the outside of the building or through a common hall.

New Housing Units Authorized in 2003

National Total = 1,862,365 Units*

ALPHA ORDER

RANK	STATE	UNITS	% of USA
25	Alabama	26,012	1.4%
46	Alaska	3,545	0.2%
6	Arizona	73,070	3.9%
33	Arkansas	14,177	0.8%
2	California	192,273	10.3%
17	Colorado	39,446	2.1%
37	Connecticut	10,758	0.6%
40	Delaware	7,786	0.4%
1	Florida	211,078	11.3%
4	Georgia	94,773	5.1%
42	Hawaii	7,222	0.4%
32	Idaho	14,903	0.8%
7	Illinois	61,411	3.3%
15	Indiana	40,270	2.2%
30	Iowa	16,654	0.9%
34	Kansas	13,748	0.7%
28	Kentucky	20,183	1.1%
27	Louisiana	20,313	1.1%
41	Maine	7,361	0.4%
22	Maryland	30,125	1.6%
29	Massachusetts	19,273	1.0%
10	Michigan	51,486	2.8%
16	Minnesota	40,086	2.2%
36	Mississippi	12,052	0.6%
23	Missouri	27,307	1.5%
45	Montana	3,645	0.2%
38	Nebraska	10,130	0.5%
13	Nevada	43,140	2.3%
39	New Hampshire	7,861	0.4%
21	New Jersey	32,369	1.7%
35	New Mexico	13,400	0.7%
11	New York	49,998	2.7%
5	North Carolina	77,982	4.2%
47	North Dakota	3,535	0.2%
9	Ohio	52,419	2.8%
31	Oklahoma	15,248	0.8%
24	Oregon	26,103	1.4%
14	Pennsylvania	42,315	2.3%
50	Rhode Island	2,349	0.1%
20	South Carolina	36,733	2.0%
43	South Dakota	4,835	0.3%
19	Tennessee	37,427	2.0%
3	Texas	174,170	9.4%
26	Utah	22,226	1.2%
48	Vermont	2,792	0.1%
8	Virginia	56,951	3.1%
12	Washington	43,580	2.3%
44	West Virginia	4,584	0.2%
18	Wisconsin	39,212	2.1%
49	Wyoming	2,622	0.1%

RANK ORDER

RANK	STATE	UNITS	% of USA
1	Florida	211,078	11.3%
2	California	192,273	10.3%
3	Texas	174,170	9.4%
4	Georgia	94,773	5.1%
5	North Carolina	77,982	4.2%
6	Arizona	73,070	3.9%
7	Illinois	61,411	3.3%
8	Virginia	56,951	3.1%
9	Ohio	52,419	2.8%
10	Michigan	51,486	2.8%
11	New York	49,998	2.7%
12	Washington	43,580	2.3%
13	Nevada	43,140	2.3%
14	Pennsylvania	42,315	2.3%
15	Indiana	40,270	2.2%
16	Minnesota	40,086	2.2%
17	Colorado	39,446	2.1%
18	Wisconsin	39,212	2.1%
19	Tennessee	37,427	2.0%
20	South Carolina	36,733	2.0%
21	New Jersey	32,369	1.7%
22	Maryland	30,125	1.6%
23	Missouri	27,307	1.5%
24	Oregon	26,103	1.4%
25	Alabama	26,012	1.4%
26	Utah	22,226	1.2%
27	Louisiana	20,313	1.1%
28	Kentucky	20,183	1.1%
29	Massachusetts	19,273	1.0%
30	Iowa	16,654	0.9%
31	Oklahoma	15,248	0.8%
32	Idaho	14,903	0.8%
33	Arkansas	14,177	0.8%
34	Kansas	13,748	0.7%
35	New Mexico	13,400	0.7%
36	Mississippi	12,052	0.6%
37	Connecticut	10,758	0.6%
38	Nebraska	10,130	0.5%
39	New Hampshire	7,861	0.4%
40	Delaware	7,786	0.4%
41	Maine	7,361	0.4%
42	Hawaii	7,222	0.4%
43	South Dakota	4,835	0.3%
44	West Virginia	4,584	0.2%
45	Montana	3,645	0.2%
46	Alaska	3,545	0.2%
47	North Dakota	3,535	0.2%
48	Vermont	2,792	0.1%
49	Wyoming	2,622	0.1%
50	Rhode Island	2,349	0.1%
	District of Columbia	1,427	0.1%

Source: U.S. Bureau of the Census
    "New Privately Owned Housing Units Authorized" (http://www.census.gov/const/C40/Table2/t2yu200312.txt)
*Preliminary and unadjusted. Includes single and multifamily privately owned units. Based on approximately 19,000 places in the U.S. having building permit systems.

Value of New Housing Units Authorized in 2003

National Total = $246,076,883,000*

ALPHA ORDER

RANK	STATE	VALUE	% of USA
26	Alabama	$2,918,562,000	1.2%
44	Alaska	562,270,000	0.2%
5	Arizona	10,350,824,000	4.2%
36	Arkansas	1,484,807,000	0.6%
1	California	32,187,415,000	13.1%
12	Colorado	6,297,876,000	2.6%
32	Connecticut	1,892,954,000	0.8%
42	Delaware	793,515,000	0.3%
2	Florida	27,694,765,000	11.3%
4	Georgia	10,506,434,000	4.3%
37	Hawaii	1,302,680,000	0.5%
31	Idaho	1,928,530,000	0.8%
7	Illinois	9,043,655,000	3.7%
16	Indiana	5,456,773,000	2.2%
30	Iowa	2,123,650,000	0.9%
34	Kansas	1,749,449,000	0.7%
28	Kentucky	2,226,956,000	0.9%
29	Louisiana	2,195,749,000	0.9%
41	Maine	979,054,000	0.4%
22	Maryland	3,758,778,000	1.5%
25	Massachusetts	3,005,319,000	1.2%
10	Michigan	6,815,614,000	2.8%
14	Minnesota	5,974,467,000	2.4%
38	Mississippi	1,254,535,000	0.5%
24	Missouri	3,369,554,000	1.4%
46	Montana	392,347,000	0.2%
39	Nebraska	1,226,156,000	0.5%
18	Nevada	4,923,935,000	2.0%
40	New Hampshire	1,101,929,000	0.4%
23	New Jersey	3,624,295,000	1.5%
35	New Mexico	1,672,430,000	0.7%
13	New York	6,033,743,000	2.5%
6	North Carolina	10,035,807,000	4.1%
47	North Dakota	388,314,000	0.2%
8	Ohio	7,544,726,000	3.1%
33	Oklahoma	1,837,882,000	0.7%
21	Oregon	3,849,338,000	1.6%
15	Pennsylvania	5,502,784,000	2.2%
50	Rhode Island	339,789,000	0.1%
19	South Carolina	4,466,671,000	1.8%
45	South Dakota	518,055,000	0.2%
20	Tennessee	4,465,006,000	1.8%
3	Texas	19,429,344,000	7.9%
27	Utah	2,886,290,000	1.2%
49	Vermont	371,999,000	0.2%
9	Virginia	6,945,755,000	2.8%
11	Washington	6,303,247,000	2.6%
43	West Virginia	580,185,000	0.2%
17	Wisconsin	5,286,208,000	2.1%
48	Wyoming	379,661,000	0.2%

RANK ORDER

RANK	STATE	VALUE	% of USA
1	California	$32,187,415,000	13.1%
2	Florida	27,694,765,000	11.3%
3	Texas	19,429,344,000	7.9%
4	Georgia	10,506,434,000	4.3%
5	Arizona	10,350,824,000	4.2%
6	North Carolina	10,035,807,000	4.1%
7	Illinois	9,043,655,000	3.7%
8	Ohio	7,544,726,000	3.1%
9	Virginia	6,945,755,000	2.8%
10	Michigan	6,815,614,000	2.8%
11	Washington	6,303,247,000	2.6%
12	Colorado	6,297,876,000	2.6%
13	New York	6,033,743,000	2.5%
14	Minnesota	5,974,467,000	2.4%
15	Pennsylvania	5,502,784,000	2.2%
16	Indiana	5,456,773,000	2.2%
17	Wisconsin	5,286,208,000	2.1%
18	Nevada	4,923,935,000	2.0%
19	South Carolina	4,466,671,000	1.8%
20	Tennessee	4,465,006,000	1.8%
21	Oregon	3,849,338,000	1.6%
22	Maryland	3,758,778,000	1.5%
23	New Jersey	3,624,295,000	1.5%
24	Missouri	3,369,554,000	1.4%
25	Massachusetts	3,005,319,000	1.2%
26	Alabama	2,918,562,000	1.2%
27	Utah	2,886,290,000	1.2%
28	Kentucky	2,226,956,000	0.9%
29	Louisiana	2,195,749,000	0.9%
30	Iowa	2,123,650,000	0.9%
31	Idaho	1,928,530,000	0.8%
32	Connecticut	1,892,954,000	0.8%
33	Oklahoma	1,837,882,000	0.7%
34	Kansas	1,749,449,000	0.7%
35	New Mexico	1,672,430,000	0.7%
36	Arkansas	1,484,807,000	0.6%
37	Hawaii	1,302,680,000	0.5%
38	Mississippi	1,254,535,000	0.5%
39	Nebraska	1,226,156,000	0.5%
40	New Hampshire	1,101,929,000	0.4%
41	Maine	979,054,000	0.4%
42	Delaware	793,515,000	0.3%
43	West Virginia	580,185,000	0.2%
44	Alaska	562,270,000	0.2%
45	South Dakota	518,055,000	0.2%
46	Montana	392,347,000	0.2%
47	North Dakota	388,314,000	0.2%
48	Wyoming	379,661,000	0.2%
49	Vermont	371,999,000	0.2%
50	Rhode Island	339,789,000	0.1%
	District of Columbia	96,797,000	0.0%

Source: U.S. Bureau of the Census
"New Privately Owned Housing Units Authorized" (http://www.census.gov/const/C40/Table2/t2yv200312.txt)
**Preliminary and unadjusted. Includes single and multifamily privately owned units. Based on approximately 19,000 places in the U.S. having building permit systems.*

Average Value of New Housing Units in 2003

National Average = $132,131 per Unit*

<u>ALPHA ORDER</u>

RANK	STATE	VALUE
39	Alabama	$112,201
5	Alaska	158,609
14	Arizona	141,656
48	Arkansas	104,734
3	California	167,405
4	Colorado	159,658
2	Connecticut	175,958
50	Delaware	101,916
21	Florida	131,206
42	Georgia	110,859
1	Hawaii	180,377
24	Idaho	129,405
9	Illinois	147,264
16	Indiana	135,505
26	Iowa	127,516
27	Kansas	127,251
43	Kentucky	110,338
45	Louisiana	108,096
19	Maine	133,006
30	Maryland	124,773
6	Massachusetts	155,934
20	Michigan	132,378
7	Minnesota	149,041
49	Mississippi	104,094
31	Missouri	123,395
46	Montana	107,640
34	Nebraska	121,042
38	Nevada	114,139
15	New Hampshire	140,177
40	New Jersey	111,968
29	New Mexico	124,808
35	New York	120,680
25	North Carolina	128,694
44	North Dakota	109,848
13	Ohio	143,931
36	Oklahoma	120,533
8	Oregon	147,467
22	Pennsylvania	130,043
11	Rhode Island	144,653
33	South Carolina	121,598
47	South Dakota	107,147
37	Tennessee	119,299
41	Texas	111,554
23	Utah	129,861
18	Vermont	133,237
32	Virginia	121,960
12	Washington	144,636
28	West Virginia	126,567
17	Wisconsin	134,811
10	Wyoming	144,798

<u>RANK ORDER</u>

RANK	STATE	VALUE
1	Hawaii	$180,377
2	Connecticut	175,958
3	California	167,405
4	Colorado	159,658
5	Alaska	158,609
6	Massachusetts	155,934
7	Minnesota	149,041
8	Oregon	147,467
9	Illinois	147,264
10	Wyoming	144,798
11	Rhode Island	144,653
12	Washington	144,636
13	Ohio	143,931
14	Arizona	141,656
15	New Hampshire	140,177
16	Indiana	135,505
17	Wisconsin	134,811
18	Vermont	133,237
19	Maine	133,006
20	Michigan	132,378
21	Florida	131,206
22	Pennsylvania	130,043
23	Utah	129,861
24	Idaho	129,405
25	North Carolina	128,694
26	Iowa	127,516
27	Kansas	127,251
28	West Virginia	126,567
29	New Mexico	124,808
30	Maryland	124,773
31	Missouri	123,395
32	Virginia	121,960
33	South Carolina	121,598
34	Nebraska	121,042
35	New York	120,680
36	Oklahoma	120,533
37	Tennessee	119,299
38	Nevada	114,139
39	Alabama	112,201
40	New Jersey	111,968
41	Texas	111,554
42	Georgia	110,859
43	Kentucky	110,338
44	North Dakota	109,848
45	Louisiana	108,096
46	Montana	107,640
47	South Dakota	107,147
48	Arkansas	104,734
49	Mississippi	104,094
50	Delaware	101,916
	District of Columbia	67,833

Source: Morgan Quitno Press using data from U.S. Bureau of the Census
"New Privately Owned Housing Units Authorized" (http://www.census.gov/const/C40/Table2/t2yu200312.txt)
**Preliminary and unadjusted. Includes single and multifamily privately owned units. Based on approximately 19,000 places in the U.S. having building permit systems.*

Median Value of Owner-Occupied Housing in 2002

National Median = $136,929

<table>
<tr><td colspan="3">ALPHA ORDER</td><td colspan="3">RANK ORDER</td></tr>
<tr><td>RANK</td><td>STATE</td><td>MEDIAN</td><td>RANK</td><td>STATE</td><td>MEDIAN</td></tr>
<tr><td>43</td><td>Alabama</td><td>$93,917</td><td>1</td><td>Hawaii</td><td>$291,576</td></tr>
<tr><td>12</td><td>Alaska</td><td>162,526</td><td>2</td><td>California</td><td>275,526</td></tr>
<tr><td>20</td><td>Arizona</td><td>136,434</td><td>3</td><td>Massachusetts</td><td>249,161</td></tr>
<tr><td>50</td><td>Arkansas</td><td>79,043</td><td>4</td><td>New Jersey</td><td>210,483</td></tr>
<tr><td>2</td><td>California</td><td>275,526</td><td>5</td><td>Colorado</td><td>199,039</td></tr>
<tr><td>5</td><td>Colorado</td><td>199,039</td><td>6</td><td>Connecticut</td><td>196,143</td></tr>
<tr><td>6</td><td>Connecticut</td><td>196,143</td><td>7</td><td>Washington</td><td>189,148</td></tr>
<tr><td>19</td><td>Delaware</td><td>145,004</td><td>8</td><td>New York</td><td>176,438</td></tr>
<tr><td>24</td><td>Florida</td><td>128,120</td><td>9</td><td>New Hampshire</td><td>173,699</td></tr>
<tr><td>22</td><td>Georgia</td><td>131,221</td><td>10</td><td>Maryland</td><td>165,784</td></tr>
<tr><td>1</td><td>Hawaii</td><td>291,576</td><td>11</td><td>Rhode Island</td><td>165,458</td></tr>
<tr><td>30</td><td>Idaho</td><td>115,744</td><td>12</td><td>Alaska</td><td>162,526</td></tr>
<tr><td>17</td><td>Illinois</td><td>147,353</td><td>13</td><td>Oregon</td><td>160,185</td></tr>
<tr><td>37</td><td>Indiana</td><td>100,762</td><td>14</td><td>Nevada</td><td>157,407</td></tr>
<tr><td>45</td><td>Iowa</td><td>88,176</td><td>15</td><td>Minnesota</td><td>155,212</td></tr>
<tr><td>42</td><td>Kansas</td><td>94,005</td><td>16</td><td>Utah</td><td>151,775</td></tr>
<tr><td>38</td><td>Kentucky</td><td>98,132</td><td>17</td><td>Illinois</td><td>147,353</td></tr>
<tr><td>39</td><td>Louisiana</td><td>94,786</td><td>18</td><td>Virginia</td><td>145,437</td></tr>
<tr><td>27</td><td>Maine</td><td>121,036</td><td>19</td><td>Delaware</td><td>145,004</td></tr>
<tr><td>10</td><td>Maryland</td><td>165,784</td><td>20</td><td>Arizona</td><td>136,434</td></tr>
<tr><td>3</td><td>Massachusetts</td><td>249,161</td><td>21</td><td>Michigan</td><td>133,270</td></tr>
<tr><td>21</td><td>Michigan</td><td>133,270</td><td>22</td><td>Georgia</td><td>131,221</td></tr>
<tr><td>15</td><td>Minnesota</td><td>155,212</td><td>23</td><td>Vermont</td><td>130,492</td></tr>
<tr><td>49</td><td>Mississippi</td><td>79,425</td><td>24</td><td>Florida</td><td>128,120</td></tr>
<tr><td>36</td><td>Missouri</td><td>102,252</td><td>25</td><td>Wisconsin</td><td>122,259</td></tr>
<tr><td>33</td><td>Montana</td><td>106,735</td><td>26</td><td>North Carolina</td><td>121,181</td></tr>
<tr><td>41</td><td>Nebraska</td><td>94,191</td><td>27</td><td>Maine</td><td>121,036</td></tr>
<tr><td>14</td><td>Nevada</td><td>157,407</td><td>28</td><td>South Carolina</td><td>116,614</td></tr>
<tr><td>9</td><td>New Hampshire</td><td>173,699</td><td>29</td><td>New Mexico</td><td>116,080</td></tr>
<tr><td>4</td><td>New Jersey</td><td>210,483</td><td>30</td><td>Idaho</td><td>115,744</td></tr>
<tr><td>29</td><td>New Mexico</td><td>116,080</td><td>31</td><td>Ohio</td><td>113,072</td></tr>
<tr><td>8</td><td>New York</td><td>176,438</td><td>32</td><td>Wyoming</td><td>110,586</td></tr>
<tr><td>26</td><td>North Carolina</td><td>121,181</td><td>33</td><td>Montana</td><td>106,735</td></tr>
<tr><td>47</td><td>North Dakota</td><td>80,317</td><td>34</td><td>Tennessee</td><td>106,070</td></tr>
<tr><td>31</td><td>Ohio</td><td>113,072</td><td>35</td><td>Pennsylvania</td><td>102,871</td></tr>
<tr><td>48</td><td>Oklahoma</td><td>79,839</td><td>36</td><td>Missouri</td><td>102,252</td></tr>
<tr><td>13</td><td>Oregon</td><td>160,185</td><td>37</td><td>Indiana</td><td>100,762</td></tr>
<tr><td>35</td><td>Pennsylvania</td><td>102,871</td><td>38</td><td>Kentucky</td><td>98,132</td></tr>
<tr><td>11</td><td>Rhode Island</td><td>165,458</td><td>39</td><td>Louisiana</td><td>94,786</td></tr>
<tr><td>28</td><td>South Carolina</td><td>116,614</td><td>40</td><td>Texas</td><td>94,559</td></tr>
<tr><td>44</td><td>South Dakota</td><td>90,022</td><td>41</td><td>Nebraska</td><td>94,191</td></tr>
<tr><td>34</td><td>Tennessee</td><td>106,070</td><td>42</td><td>Kansas</td><td>94,005</td></tr>
<tr><td>40</td><td>Texas</td><td>94,559</td><td>43</td><td>Alabama</td><td>93,917</td></tr>
<tr><td>16</td><td>Utah</td><td>151,775</td><td>44</td><td>South Dakota</td><td>90,022</td></tr>
<tr><td>23</td><td>Vermont</td><td>130,492</td><td>45</td><td>Iowa</td><td>88,176</td></tr>
<tr><td>18</td><td>Virginia</td><td>145,437</td><td>46</td><td>West Virginia</td><td>81,695</td></tr>
<tr><td>7</td><td>Washington</td><td>189,148</td><td>47</td><td>North Dakota</td><td>80,317</td></tr>
<tr><td>46</td><td>West Virginia</td><td>81,695</td><td>48</td><td>Oklahoma</td><td>79,839</td></tr>
<tr><td>25</td><td>Wisconsin</td><td>122,259</td><td>49</td><td>Mississippi</td><td>79,425</td></tr>
<tr><td>32</td><td>Wyoming</td><td>110,586</td><td>50</td><td>Arkansas</td><td>79,043</td></tr>
<tr><td></td><td></td><td></td><td></td><td>District of Columbia</td><td>212,428</td></tr>
</table>

Source: U.S. Bureau of the Census
*   "2002 American Community Survey"*

Percent Change in House Prices: 1999 to 2003

National Percent Change = 38.2% Increase*

ALPHA ORDER

RANK	STATE	PERCENT CHANGE
40	Alabama	19.8
37	Alaska	21.8
16	Arizona	31.6
43	Arkansas	19.5
4	California	67.7
13	Colorado	42.4
10	Connecticut	46.8
14	Delaware	39.5
9	Florida	48.3
17	Georgia	30.6
21	Hawaii	29.6
48	Idaho	18.0
18	Illinois	30.3
47	Indiana	18.4
34	Iowa	22.6
29	Kansas	25.5
35	Kentucky	22.3
31	Louisiana	23.5
8	Maine	51.4
11	Maryland	43.9
1	Massachusetts	71.6
19	Michigan	30.0
7	Minnesota	53.2
40	Mississippi	19.8
22	Missouri	29.4
24	Montana	28.0
44	Nebraska	19.3
25	Nevada	27.8
3	New Hampshire	68.3
5	New Jersey	55.2
49	New Mexico	16.9
6	New York	54.6
39	North Carolina	20.8
44	North Dakota	19.3
38	Ohio	21.5
31	Oklahoma	23.5
36	Oregon	22.0
19	Pennsylvania	30.0
2	Rhode Island	69.2
29	South Carolina	25.5
31	South Dakota	23.5
46	Tennessee	18.8
28	Texas	26.9
50	Utah	10.5
15	Vermont	39.3
12	Virginia	42.7
27	Washington	27.3
40	West Virginia	19.8
25	Wisconsin	27.8
23	Wyoming	28.6

RANK ORDER

RANK	STATE	PERCENT CHANGE
1	Massachusetts	71.6
2	Rhode Island	69.2
3	New Hampshire	68.3
4	California	67.7
5	New Jersey	55.2
6	New York	54.6
7	Minnesota	53.2
8	Maine	51.4
9	Florida	48.3
10	Connecticut	46.8
11	Maryland	43.9
12	Virginia	42.7
13	Colorado	42.4
14	Delaware	39.5
15	Vermont	39.3
16	Arizona	31.6
17	Georgia	30.6
18	Illinois	30.3
19	Michigan	30.0
19	Pennsylvania	30.0
21	Hawaii	29.6
22	Missouri	29.4
23	Wyoming	28.6
24	Montana	28.0
25	Nevada	27.8
25	Wisconsin	27.8
27	Washington	27.3
28	Texas	26.9
29	Kansas	25.5
29	South Carolina	25.5
31	Louisiana	23.5
31	Oklahoma	23.5
31	South Dakota	23.5
34	Iowa	22.6
35	Kentucky	22.3
36	Oregon	22.0
37	Alaska	21.8
38	Ohio	21.5
39	North Carolina	20.8
40	Alabama	19.8
40	Mississippi	19.8
40	West Virginia	19.8
43	Arkansas	19.5
44	Nebraska	19.3
44	North Dakota	19.3
46	Tennessee	18.8
47	Indiana	18.4
48	Idaho	18.0
49	New Mexico	16.9
50	Utah	10.5

District of Columbia	82.9

*Source: Office of Federal Housing Enterprise Oversight
"House Price Index" (http://www.ofheo.gov/HPI.asp)
Single-family house prices. As of September 30, 2003.

Median Monthly Mortgage Payment in 2002

National Median = $1,168*

ALPHA ORDER

RANK	STATE	MEDIAN
42	Alabama	$892
10	Alaska	1,363
21	Arizona	1,105
49	Arkansas	772
3	California	1,592
11	Colorado	1,333
5	Connecticut	1,477
19	Delaware	1,149
23	Florida	1,091
20	Georgia	1,125
1	Hawaii	1,691
33	Idaho	972
13	Illinois	1,284
38	Indiana	928
43	Iowa	879
31	Kansas	988
45	Kentucky	870
43	Louisiana	879
34	Maine	971
9	Maryland	1,366
4	Massachusetts	1,486
25	Michigan	1,085
17	Minnesota	1,167
48	Mississippi	827
37	Missouri	946
40	Montana	908
32	Nebraska	977
14	Nevada	1,267
8	New Hampshire	1,377
2	New Jersey	1,672
35	New Mexico	963
6	New York	1,411
27	North Carolina	1,071
46	North Dakota	852
29	Ohio	1,028
47	Oklahoma	832
16	Oregon	1,217
28	Pennsylvania	1,062
12	Rhode Island	1,305
30	South Carolina	995
41	South Dakota	895
36	Tennessee	962
22	Texas	1,096
18	Utah	1,155
26	Vermont	1,082
15	Virginia	1,228
7	Washington	1,405
50	West Virginia	762
24	Wisconsin	1,088
39	Wyoming	913

RANK ORDER

RANK	STATE	MEDIAN
1	Hawaii	$1,691
2	New Jersey	1,672
3	California	1,592
4	Massachusetts	1,486
5	Connecticut	1,477
6	New York	1,411
7	Washington	1,405
8	New Hampshire	1,377
9	Maryland	1,366
10	Alaska	1,363
11	Colorado	1,333
12	Rhode Island	1,305
13	Illinois	1,284
14	Nevada	1,267
15	Virginia	1,228
16	Oregon	1,217
17	Minnesota	1,167
18	Utah	1,155
19	Delaware	1,149
20	Georgia	1,125
21	Arizona	1,105
22	Texas	1,096
23	Florida	1,091
24	Wisconsin	1,088
25	Michigan	1,085
26	Vermont	1,082
27	North Carolina	1,071
28	Pennsylvania	1,062
29	Ohio	1,028
30	South Carolina	995
31	Kansas	988
32	Nebraska	977
33	Idaho	972
34	Maine	971
35	New Mexico	963
36	Tennessee	962
37	Missouri	946
38	Indiana	928
39	Wyoming	913
40	Montana	908
41	South Dakota	895
42	Alabama	892
43	Iowa	879
43	Louisiana	879
45	Kentucky	870
46	North Dakota	852
47	Oklahoma	832
48	Mississippi	827
49	Arkansas	772
50	West Virginia	762
	District of Columbia	1,549

Source: U.S. Bureau of the Census
  "2002 American Community Survey"
*For owner-occupied housing.

Existing Home Sales in 2003

National Total = 7,398,000 Homes*

<u>ALPHA ORDER</u>

RANK	STATE	HOMES	% of USA
23	Alabama	127,000	1.7%
43	Alaska	23,100	0.3%
6	Arizona	264,200	3.6%
31	Arkansas	69,500	0.9%
1	California	713,300	9.6%
15	Colorado	166,500	2.3%
35	Connecticut	58,200	0.8%
48	Delaware	12,000	0.2%
2	Florida	703,400	9.5%
9	Georgia	208,700	2.8%
40	Hawaii	35,600	0.5%
39	Idaho	39,100	0.5%
5	Illinois	299,100	4.0%
19	Indiana	151,900	2.1%
32	Iowa	68,600	0.9%
29	Kansas	85,200	1.2%
27	Kentucky	105,500	1.4%
25	Louisiana	113,800	1.5%
37	Maine	42,800	0.6%
21	Maryland	140,700	1.9%
28	Massachusetts	103,900	1.4%
12	Michigan	194,400	2.6%
16	Minnesota	163,100	2.2%
33	Mississippi	65,200	0.9%
17	Missouri	157,500	2.1%
42	Montana	26,900	0.4%
38	Nebraska	42,100	0.6%
26	Nevada	107,500	1.5%
NA	New Hampshire**	NA	NA
20	New Jersey	147,200	2.0%
36	New Mexico	44,800	0.6%
12	New York	194,400	2.6%
4	North Carolina	314,000	4.2%
47	North Dakota	14,400	0.2%
7	Ohio	252,500	3.4%
22	Oklahoma	136,100	1.8%
30	Oregon	83,000	1.1%
11	Pennsylvania	200,800	2.7%
44	Rhode Island	21,400	0.3%
18	South Carolina	155,300	2.1%
44	South Dakota	21,400	0.3%
10	Tennessee	202,000	2.7%
3	Texas	677,200	9.2%
34	Utah	60,700	0.8%
NA	Vermont**	NA	NA
14	Virginia	180,100	2.4%
8	Washington	219,500	3.0%
41	West Virginia	33,600	0.5%
24	Wisconsin	123,400	1.7%
46	Wyoming	15,200	0.2%

<u>RANK ORDER</u>

RANK	STATE	HOMES	% of USA
1	California	713,300	9.6%
2	Florida	703,400	9.5%
3	Texas	677,200	9.2%
4	North Carolina	314,000	4.2%
5	Illinois	299,100	4.0%
6	Arizona	264,200	3.6%
7	Ohio	252,500	3.4%
8	Washington	219,500	3.0%
9	Georgia	208,700	2.8%
10	Tennessee	202,000	2.7%
11	Pennsylvania	200,800	2.7%
12	Michigan	194,400	2.6%
12	New York	194,400	2.6%
14	Virginia	180,100	2.4%
15	Colorado	166,500	2.3%
16	Minnesota	163,100	2.2%
17	Missouri	157,500	2.1%
18	South Carolina	155,300	2.1%
19	Indiana	151,900	2.1%
20	New Jersey	147,200	2.0%
21	Maryland	140,700	1.9%
22	Oklahoma	136,100	1.8%
23	Alabama	127,000	1.7%
24	Wisconsin	123,400	1.7%
25	Louisiana	113,800	1.5%
26	Nevada	107,500	1.5%
27	Kentucky	105,500	1.4%
28	Massachusetts	103,900	1.4%
29	Kansas	85,200	1.2%
30	Oregon	83,000	1.1%
31	Arkansas	69,500	0.9%
32	Iowa	68,600	0.9%
33	Mississippi	65,200	0.9%
34	Utah	60,700	0.8%
35	Connecticut	58,200	0.8%
36	New Mexico	44,800	0.6%
37	Maine	42,800	0.6%
38	Nebraska	42,100	0.6%
39	Idaho	39,100	0.5%
40	Hawaii	35,600	0.5%
41	West Virginia	33,600	0.5%
42	Montana	26,900	0.4%
43	Alaska	23,100	0.3%
44	Rhode Island	21,400	0.3%
44	South Dakota	21,400	0.3%
46	Wyoming	15,200	0.2%
47	North Dakota	14,400	0.2%
48	Delaware	12,000	0.2%
NA	New Hampshire**	NA	NA
NA	Vermont**	NA	NA
	District of Columbia	16,300	0.2%

Source: National Association of Realtors®, Economics and Research Division
    "Existing Home Sales" (http://www.realtor.org/Research.nsf/Pages/EHSdata)
*Preliminary data. Includes existing houses, apartment condos and co-ops. Excludes new construction.
**Not available.

Percent Change in Existing Home Sales: 2002 to 2003

National Percent Change = 18.7% Increase*

ALPHA ORDER

RANK	STATE	PERCENT CHANGE
5	Alabama	26.7
41	Alaska	11.1
3	Arizona	29.4
40	Arkansas	11.4
25	California	16.2
42	Colorado	10.8
33	Connecticut	13.2
10	Delaware	23.7
20	Florida	19.1
39	Georgia	11.7
12	Hawaii	23.6
10	Idaho	23.7
31	Illinois	13.5
46	Indiana	4.8
30	Iowa	14.5
26	Kansas	15.4
17	Kentucky	21.5
13	Louisiana	23.2
33	Maine	13.2
32	Maryland	13.3
24	Massachusetts	16.3
27	Michigan	15.2
44	Minnesota	8.1
18	Mississippi	20.7
15	Missouri	22.2
37	Montana	12.1
8	Nebraska	23.8
1	Nevada	37.6
NA	New Hampshire**	NA
45	New Jersey	6.7
8	New Mexico	23.8
47	New York	3.9
5	North Carolina	26.7
16	North Dakota	22.0
14	Ohio	22.8
19	Oklahoma	19.7
23	Oregon	17.6
36	Pennsylvania	12.3
28	Rhode Island	15.1
4	South Carolina	27.2
22	South Dakota	18.2
7	Tennessee	24.7
38	Texas	11.9
43	Utah	10.4
NA	Vermont**	NA
28	Virginia	15.1
2	Washington	36.7
20	West Virginia	19.1
35	Wisconsin	12.4
48	Wyoming	3.4

RANK ORDER

RANK	STATE	PERCENT CHANGE
1	Nevada	37.6
2	Washington	36.7
3	Arizona	29.4
4	South Carolina	27.2
5	Alabama	26.7
5	North Carolina	26.7
7	Tennessee	24.7
8	Nebraska	23.8
8	New Mexico	23.8
10	Delaware	23.7
10	Idaho	23.7
12	Hawaii	23.6
13	Louisiana	23.2
14	Ohio	22.8
15	Missouri	22.2
16	North Dakota	22.0
17	Kentucky	21.5
18	Mississippi	20.7
19	Oklahoma	19.7
20	Florida	19.1
20	West Virginia	19.1
22	South Dakota	18.2
23	Oregon	17.6
24	Massachusetts	16.3
25	California	16.2
26	Kansas	15.4
27	Michigan	15.2
28	Rhode Island	15.1
28	Virginia	15.1
30	Iowa	14.5
31	Illinois	13.5
32	Maryland	13.3
33	Connecticut	13.2
33	Maine	13.2
35	Wisconsin	12.4
36	Pennsylvania	12.3
37	Montana	12.1
38	Texas	11.9
39	Georgia	11.7
40	Arkansas	11.4
41	Alaska	11.1
42	Colorado	10.8
43	Utah	10.4
44	Minnesota	8.1
45	New Jersey	6.7
46	Indiana	4.8
47	New York	3.9
48	Wyoming	3.4
NA	New Hampshire**	NA
NA	Vermont**	NA
	District of Columbia	19.9

Homeownership Rate in 2002

National Rate = 67.9%*

<u>ALPHA ORDER</u>

RANK	STATE	PERCENT
13	Alabama	73.5
38	Alaska	67.3
43	Arizona	65.9
25	Arkansas	70.2
48	California	58.0
35	Colorado	69.1
22	Connecticut	71.6
5	Delaware	75.6
36	Florida	68.7
21	Georgia	71.7
49	Hawaii	57.4
15	Idaho	73.0
25	Illinois	70.2
6	Indiana	75.0
11	Iowa	73.9
25	Kansas	70.2
13	Kentucky	73.5
40	Louisiana	67.1
11	Maine	73.9
18	Maryland	72.0
46	Massachusetts	62.7
4	Michigan	76.0
1	Minnesota	77.3
7	Mississippi	74.8
8	Missouri	74.6
34	Montana	69.3
37	Nebraska	68.4
44	Nevada	65.5
31	New Hampshire	69.5
39	New Jersey	67.2
24	New Mexico	70.3
50	New York	55.0
30	North Carolina	70.0
31	North Dakota	69.5
18	Ohio	72.0
33	Oklahoma	69.4
42	Oregon	66.2
10	Pennsylvania	74.0
47	Rhode Island	59.6
1	South Carolina	77.3
23	South Dakota	71.5
29	Tennessee	70.1
45	Texas	63.8
17	Utah	72.7
25	Vermont	70.2
9	Virginia	74.3
41	Washington	67.0
3	West Virginia	77.0
18	Wisconsin	72.0
16	Wyoming	72.8

<u>RANK ORDER</u>

RANK	STATE	PERCENT
1	Minnesota	77.3
1	South Carolina	77.3
3	West Virginia	77.0
4	Michigan	76.0
5	Delaware	75.6
6	Indiana	75.0
7	Mississippi	74.8
8	Missouri	74.6
9	Virginia	74.3
10	Pennsylvania	74.0
11	Iowa	73.9
11	Maine	73.9
13	Alabama	73.5
13	Kentucky	73.5
15	Idaho	73.0
16	Wyoming	72.8
17	Utah	72.7
18	Maryland	72.0
18	Ohio	72.0
18	Wisconsin	72.0
21	Georgia	71.7
22	Connecticut	71.6
23	South Dakota	71.5
24	New Mexico	70.3
25	Arkansas	70.2
25	Illinois	70.2
25	Kansas	70.2
25	Vermont	70.2
29	Tennessee	70.1
30	North Carolina	70.0
31	New Hampshire	69.5
31	North Dakota	69.5
33	Oklahoma	69.4
34	Montana	69.3
35	Colorado	69.1
36	Florida	68.7
37	Nebraska	68.4
38	Alaska	67.3
39	New Jersey	67.2
40	Louisiana	67.1
41	Washington	67.0
42	Oregon	66.2
43	Arizona	65.9
44	Nevada	65.5
45	Texas	63.8
46	Massachusetts	62.7
47	Rhode Island	59.6
48	California	58.0
49	Hawaii	57.4
50	New York	55.0

	STATE	PERCENT
	District of Columbia	44.1

Source: U.S. Bureau of the Census
"Housing Vacancies and Homeownership, Annual Statistics: 2002"
(http://www.census.gov/hhes/www/housing/hvs/annual02/ann02t13.html)
*Percent of households occupied by the owner.

Median Monthly Rental Payment in 2002

National Median = $655*

ALPHA ORDER

RANK	STATE	MEDIAN
44	Alabama	$488
6	Alaska	761
20	Arizona	659
42	Arkansas	497
1	California	840
9	Colorado	730
9	Connecticut	730
15	Delaware	679
14	Florida	702
18	Georgia	664
2	Hawaii	832
37	Idaho	529
17	Illinois	665
32	Indiana	545
41	Iowa	498
32	Kansas	545
47	Kentucky	480
43	Louisiana	495
31	Maine	552
7	Maryland	738
4	Massachusetts	799
26	Michigan	585
21	Minnesota	651
39	Mississippi	511
34	Missouri	538
48	Montana	478
36	Nebraska	536
5	Nevada	762
8	New Hampshire	732
3	New Jersey	808
38	New Mexico	528
11	New York	727
25	North Carolina	590
50	North Dakota	433
30	Ohio	557
40	Oklahoma	503
19	Oregon	663
28	Pennsylvania	577
23	Rhode Island	622
29	South Carolina	565
45	South Dakota	481
35	Tennessee	537
22	Texas	629
16	Utah	667
24	Vermont	601
13	Virginia	707
12	Washington	710
49	West Virginia	448
27	Wisconsin	580
45	Wyoming	481

RANK ORDER

RANK	STATE	MEDIAN
1	California	$840
2	Hawaii	832
3	New Jersey	808
4	Massachusetts	799
5	Nevada	762
6	Alaska	761
7	Maryland	738
8	New Hampshire	732
9	Colorado	730
9	Connecticut	730
11	New York	727
12	Washington	710
13	Virginia	707
14	Florida	702
15	Delaware	679
16	Utah	667
17	Illinois	665
18	Georgia	664
19	Oregon	663
20	Arizona	659
21	Minnesota	651
22	Texas	629
23	Rhode Island	622
24	Vermont	601
25	North Carolina	590
26	Michigan	585
27	Wisconsin	580
28	Pennsylvania	577
29	South Carolina	565
30	Ohio	557
31	Maine	552
32	Indiana	545
32	Kansas	545
34	Missouri	538
35	Tennessee	537
36	Nebraska	536
37	Idaho	529
38	New Mexico	528
39	Mississippi	511
40	Oklahoma	503
41	Iowa	498
42	Arkansas	497
43	Louisiana	495
44	Alabama	488
45	South Dakota	481
45	Wyoming	481
47	Kentucky	480
48	Montana	478
49	West Virginia	448
50	North Dakota	433
	District of Columbia	693

Source: U.S. Bureau of the Census
"2002 American Community Survey"
*For renter-occupied housing.

State and Local Government Expenditures
For Housing and Community Development in 2000
National Total = $26,589,639,000*

ALPHA ORDER

RANK	STATE	EXPENDITURES	% of USA
23	Alabama	$304,238,000	1.1%
29	Alaska	185,293,000	0.7%
21	Arizona	353,512,000	1.3%
36	Arkansas	127,699,000	0.5%
1	California	4,546,635,000	17.1%
20	Colorado	377,258,000	1.4%
16	Connecticut	480,577,000	1.8%
46	Delaware	78,764,000	0.3%
8	Florida	934,281,000	3.5%
14	Georgia	601,971,000	2.3%
27	Hawaii	266,278,000	1.0%
49	Idaho	25,266,000	0.1%
4	Illinois	1,482,599,000	5.6%
17	Indiana	477,872,000	1.8%
34	Iowa	132,197,000	0.5%
38	Kansas	113,363,000	0.4%
32	Kentucky	143,046,000	0.5%
24	Louisiana	302,311,000	1.1%
39	Maine	112,635,000	0.4%
11	Maryland	632,444,000	2.4%
6	Massachusetts	1,210,473,000	4.6%
26	Michigan	275,245,000	1.0%
15	Minnesota	591,414,000	2.2%
33	Mississippi	133,980,000	0.5%
25	Missouri	300,692,000	1.1%
47	Montana	62,331,000	0.2%
40	Nebraska	112,051,000	0.4%
31	Nevada	147,363,000	0.6%
43	New Hampshire	91,404,000	0.3%
9	New Jersey	751,574,000	2.8%
44	New Mexico	91,163,000	0.3%
2	New York	2,979,475,000	11.2%
13	North Carolina	603,236,000	2.3%
42	North Dakota	92,315,000	0.3%
7	Ohio	981,297,000	3.7%
30	Oklahoma	147,614,000	0.6%
18	Oregon	469,032,000	1.8%
5	Pennsylvania	1,255,540,000	4.7%
35	Rhode Island	128,262,000	0.5%
28	South Carolina	201,666,000	0.8%
48	South Dakota	31,490,000	0.1%
19	Tennessee	461,003,000	1.7%
3	Texas	1,809,067,000	6.8%
37	Utah	115,042,000	0.4%
45	Vermont	81,410,000	0.3%
12	Virginia	615,328,000	2.3%
10	Washington	647,184,000	2.4%
41	West Virginia	104,353,000	0.4%
22	Wisconsin	350,629,000	1.3%
50	Wyoming	11,539,000	0.0%

RANK ORDER

RANK	STATE	EXPENDITURES	% of USA
1	California	$4,546,635,000	17.1%
2	New York	2,979,475,000	11.2%
3	Texas	1,809,067,000	6.8%
4	Illinois	1,482,599,000	5.6%
5	Pennsylvania	1,255,540,000	4.7%
6	Massachusetts	1,210,473,000	4.6%
7	Ohio	981,297,000	3.7%
8	Florida	934,281,000	3.5%
9	New Jersey	751,574,000	2.8%
10	Washington	647,184,000	2.4%
11	Maryland	632,444,000	2.4%
12	Virginia	615,328,000	2.3%
13	North Carolina	603,236,000	2.3%
14	Georgia	601,971,000	2.3%
15	Minnesota	591,414,000	2.2%
16	Connecticut	480,577,000	1.8%
17	Indiana	477,872,000	1.8%
18	Oregon	469,032,000	1.8%
19	Tennessee	461,003,000	1.7%
20	Colorado	377,258,000	1.4%
21	Arizona	353,512,000	1.3%
22	Wisconsin	350,629,000	1.3%
23	Alabama	304,238,000	1.1%
24	Louisiana	302,311,000	1.1%
25	Missouri	300,692,000	1.1%
26	Michigan	275,245,000	1.0%
27	Hawaii	266,278,000	1.0%
28	South Carolina	201,666,000	0.8%
29	Alaska	185,293,000	0.7%
30	Oklahoma	147,614,000	0.6%
31	Nevada	147,363,000	0.6%
32	Kentucky	143,046,000	0.5%
33	Mississippi	133,980,000	0.5%
34	Iowa	132,197,000	0.5%
35	Rhode Island	128,262,000	0.5%
36	Arkansas	127,699,000	0.5%
37	Utah	115,042,000	0.4%
38	Kansas	113,363,000	0.4%
39	Maine	112,635,000	0.4%
40	Nebraska	112,051,000	0.4%
41	West Virginia	104,353,000	0.4%
42	North Dakota	92,315,000	0.3%
43	New Hampshire	91,404,000	0.3%
44	New Mexico	91,163,000	0.3%
45	Vermont	81,410,000	0.3%
46	Delaware	78,764,000	0.3%
47	Montana	62,331,000	0.2%
48	South Dakota	31,490,000	0.1%
49	Idaho	25,266,000	0.1%
50	Wyoming	11,539,000	0.0%
	District of Columbia	58,228,000	0.2%

Source: U.S. Bureau of the Census, Governments Division
"State and Local Government Finances: 1999-2000" (http://www.census.gov/govs/www/estimate00.html)
**Direct general expenditures.*

Per Capita State and Local Government Expenditures
For Housing and Community Development in 2000
National Per Capita = $94.21*

<u>ALPHA ORDER</u>

RANK	STATE	PER CAPITA
31	Alabama	$68.34
1	Alaska	295.19
30	Arizona	68.42
41	Arkansas	47.67
8	California	133.68
19	Colorado	87.19
6	Connecticut	140.85
16	Delaware	100.14
35	Florida	58.21
27	Georgia	73.10
2	Hawaii	219.58
50	Idaho	19.44
12	Illinois	119.17
24	Indiana	78.44
43	Iowa	45.14
45	Kansas	42.10
47	Kentucky	35.33
32	Louisiana	67.63
18	Maine	88.18
13	Maryland	119.05
3	Massachusetts	190.27
48	Michigan	27.65
11	Minnesota	119.86
42	Mississippi	47.03
37	Missouri	53.65
29	Montana	68.99
33	Nebraska	65.40
28	Nevada	72.99
26	New Hampshire	73.68
17	New Jersey	89.12
40	New Mexico	50.04
4	New York	156.82
25	North Carolina	74.64
5	North Dakota	143.99
21	Ohio	86.35
44	Oklahoma	42.73
7	Oregon	136.70
15	Pennsylvania	102.19
10	Rhode Island	122.07
39	South Carolina	50.12
46	South Dakota	41.67
23	Tennessee	80.83
22	Texas	86.33
38	Utah	51.28
9	Vermont	133.47
20	Virginia	86.59
14	Washington	109.47
36	West Virginia	57.74
34	Wisconsin	65.24
49	Wyoming	23.35

<u>RANK ORDER</u>

RANK	STATE	PER CAPITA
1	Alaska	$295.19
2	Hawaii	219.58
3	Massachusetts	190.27
4	New York	156.82
5	North Dakota	143.99
6	Connecticut	140.85
7	Oregon	136.70
8	California	133.68
9	Vermont	133.47
10	Rhode Island	122.07
11	Minnesota	119.86
12	Illinois	119.17
13	Maryland	119.05
14	Washington	109.47
15	Pennsylvania	102.19
16	Delaware	100.14
17	New Jersey	89.12
18	Maine	88.18
19	Colorado	87.19
20	Virginia	86.59
21	Ohio	86.35
22	Texas	86.33
23	Tennessee	80.83
24	Indiana	78.44
25	North Carolina	74.64
26	New Hampshire	73.68
27	Georgia	73.10
28	Nevada	72.99
29	Montana	68.99
30	Arizona	68.42
31	Alabama	68.34
32	Louisiana	67.63
33	Nebraska	65.40
34	Wisconsin	65.24
35	Florida	58.21
36	West Virginia	57.74
37	Missouri	53.65
38	Utah	51.28
39	South Carolina	50.12
40	New Mexico	50.04
41	Arkansas	47.67
42	Mississippi	47.03
43	Iowa	45.14
44	Oklahoma	42.73
45	Kansas	42.10
46	South Dakota	41.67
47	Kentucky	35.33
48	Michigan	27.65
49	Wyoming	23.35
50	Idaho	19.44

District of Columbia   101.86

*Source: Morgan Quitno Press using data from U.S. Bureau of the Census, Governments Division
"State and Local Government Finances: 1999-2000" (http://www.census.gov/govs/www/estimate00.html)
Direct general expenditures.

XIII. POPULATION

XIII. POPULATION (continued)

Population in 2003

National Total = 290,809,777*

<u>ALPHA ORDER</u>

RANK	STATE	POPULATION	% of USA
23	Alabama	4,500,752	1.5%
47	Alaska	648,818	0.2%
18	Arizona	5,580,811	1.9%
32	Arkansas	2,725,714	0.9%
1	California	35,484,453	12.2%
22	Colorado	4,550,688	1.6%
29	Connecticut	3,483,372	1.2%
45	Delaware	817,491	0.3%
4	Florida	17,019,068	5.9%
9	Georgia	8,684,715	3.0%
42	Hawaii	1,257,608	0.4%
39	Idaho	1,366,332	0.5%
5	Illinois	12,653,544	4.4%
14	Indiana	6,195,643	2.1%
30	Iowa	2,944,062	1.0%
33	Kansas	2,723,507	0.9%
26	Kentucky	4,117,827	1.4%
24	Louisiana	4,496,334	1.5%
40	Maine	1,305,728	0.4%
19	Maryland	5,508,909	1.9%
13	Massachusetts	6,433,422	2.2%
8	Michigan	10,079,985	3.5%
21	Minnesota	5,059,375	1.7%
31	Mississippi	2,881,281	1.0%
17	Missouri	5,704,484	2.0%
44	Montana	917,621	0.3%
38	Nebraska	1,739,291	0.6%
35	Nevada	2,241,154	0.8%
41	New Hampshire	1,287,687	0.4%
10	New Jersey	8,638,396	3.0%
36	New Mexico	1,874,614	0.6%
3	New York	19,190,115	6.6%
11	North Carolina	8,407,248	2.9%
48	North Dakota	633,837	0.2%
7	Ohio	11,435,798	3.9%
28	Oklahoma	3,511,532	1.2%
27	Oregon	3,559,596	1.2%
6	Pennsylvania	12,365,455	4.3%
43	Rhode Island	1,076,164	0.4%
25	South Carolina	4,147,152	1.4%
46	South Dakota	764,309	0.3%
16	Tennessee	5,841,748	2.0%
2	Texas	22,118,509	7.6%
34	Utah	2,351,467	0.8%
49	Vermont	619,107	0.2%
12	Virginia	7,386,330	2.5%
15	Washington	6,131,445	2.1%
37	West Virginia	1,810,354	0.6%
20	Wisconsin	5,472,299	1.9%
50	Wyoming	501,242	0.2%

<u>RANK ORDER</u>

RANK	STATE	POPULATION	% of USA
1	California	35,484,453	12.2%
2	Texas	22,118,509	7.6%
3	New York	19,190,115	6.6%
4	Florida	17,019,068	5.9%
5	Illinois	12,653,544	4.4%
6	Pennsylvania	12,365,455	4.3%
7	Ohio	11,435,798	3.9%
8	Michigan	10,079,985	3.5%
9	Georgia	8,684,715	3.0%
10	New Jersey	8,638,396	3.0%
11	North Carolina	8,407,248	2.9%
12	Virginia	7,386,330	2.5%
13	Massachusetts	6,433,422	2.2%
14	Indiana	6,195,643	2.1%
15	Washington	6,131,445	2.1%
16	Tennessee	5,841,748	2.0%
17	Missouri	5,704,484	2.0%
18	Arizona	5,580,811	1.9%
19	Maryland	5,508,909	1.9%
20	Wisconsin	5,472,299	1.9%
21	Minnesota	5,059,375	1.7%
22	Colorado	4,550,688	1.6%
23	Alabama	4,500,752	1.5%
24	Louisiana	4,496,334	1.5%
25	South Carolina	4,147,152	1.4%
26	Kentucky	4,117,827	1.4%
27	Oregon	3,559,596	1.2%
28	Oklahoma	3,511,532	1.2%
29	Connecticut	3,483,372	1.2%
30	Iowa	2,944,062	1.0%
31	Mississippi	2,881,281	1.0%
32	Arkansas	2,725,714	0.9%
33	Kansas	2,723,507	0.9%
34	Utah	2,351,467	0.8%
35	Nevada	2,241,154	0.8%
36	New Mexico	1,874,614	0.6%
37	West Virginia	1,810,354	0.6%
38	Nebraska	1,739,291	0.6%
39	Idaho	1,366,332	0.5%
40	Maine	1,305,728	0.4%
41	New Hampshire	1,287,687	0.4%
42	Hawaii	1,257,608	0.4%
43	Rhode Island	1,076,164	0.4%
44	Montana	917,621	0.3%
45	Delaware	817,491	0.3%
46	South Dakota	764,309	0.3%
47	Alaska	648,818	0.2%
48	North Dakota	633,837	0.2%
49	Vermont	619,107	0.2%
50	Wyoming	501,242	0.2%
	District of Columbia	563,384	0.2%

Source: U.S. Bureau of the Census
"Population Estimates" (December 18, 2003, http://eire.census.gov/popest/estimates.php)
Resident population.

Population in 2002

National Total = 287,973,924*

<u>ALPHA ORDER</u>

RANK	STATE	POPULATION	% of USA
23	Alabama	4,478,896	1.6%
47	Alaska	641,482	0.2%
19	Arizona	5,441,125	1.9%
33	Arkansas	2,706,268	0.9%
1	California	35,001,986	12.2%
22	Colorado	4,501,051	1.6%
29	Connecticut	3,458,587	1.2%
45	Delaware	805,945	0.3%
4	Florida	16,691,701	5.8%
10	Georgia	8,544,005	3.0%
42	Hawaii	1,240,663	0.4%
39	Idaho	1,343,124	0.5%
5	Illinois	12,586,447	4.4%
14	Indiana	6,156,913	2.1%
30	Iowa	2,935,840	1.0%
32	Kansas	2,711,769	0.9%
26	Kentucky	4,089,822	1.4%
24	Louisiana	4,476,192	1.6%
40	Maine	1,294,894	0.4%
18	Maryland	5,450,525	1.9%
13	Massachusetts	6,421,800	2.2%
8	Michigan	10,043,221	3.5%
21	Minnesota	5,024,791	1.7%
31	Mississippi	2,866,733	1.0%
17	Missouri	5,669,544	2.0%
44	Montana	910,372	0.3%
38	Nebraska	1,727,564	0.6%
35	Nevada	2,167,455	0.8%
41	New Hampshire	1,274,405	0.4%
9	New Jersey	8,575,252	3.0%
36	New Mexico	1,852,044	0.6%
3	New York	19,134,293	6.6%
11	North Carolina	8,305,820	2.9%
48	North Dakota	633,911	0.2%
7	Ohio	11,408,699	4.0%
28	Oklahoma	3,489,700	1.2%
27	Oregon	3,520,355	1.2%
6	Pennsylvania	12,328,827	4.3%
43	Rhode Island	1,068,326	0.4%
25	South Carolina	4,103,770	1.4%
46	South Dakota	760,437	0.3%
16	Tennessee	5,789,796	2.0%
2	Texas	21,736,925	7.5%
34	Utah	2,318,789	0.8%
49	Vermont	616,408	0.2%
12	Virginia	7,287,829	2.5%
15	Washington	6,067,060	2.1%
37	West Virginia	1,804,884	0.6%
20	Wisconsin	5,439,692	1.9%
50	Wyoming	498,830	0.2%

<u>RANK ORDER</u>

RANK	STATE	POPULATION	% of USA
1	California	35,001,986	12.2%
2	Texas	21,736,925	7.5%
3	New York	19,134,293	6.6%
4	Florida	16,691,701	5.8%
5	Illinois	12,586,447	4.4%
6	Pennsylvania	12,328,827	4.3%
7	Ohio	11,408,699	4.0%
8	Michigan	10,043,221	3.5%
9	New Jersey	8,575,252	3.0%
10	Georgia	8,544,005	3.0%
11	North Carolina	8,305,820	2.9%
12	Virginia	7,287,829	2.5%
13	Massachusetts	6,421,800	2.2%
14	Indiana	6,156,913	2.1%
15	Washington	6,067,060	2.1%
16	Tennessee	5,789,796	2.0%
17	Missouri	5,669,544	2.0%
18	Maryland	5,450,525	1.9%
19	Arizona	5,441,125	1.9%
20	Wisconsin	5,439,692	1.9%
21	Minnesota	5,024,791	1.7%
22	Colorado	4,501,051	1.6%
23	Alabama	4,478,896	1.6%
24	Louisiana	4,476,192	1.6%
25	South Carolina	4,103,770	1.4%
26	Kentucky	4,089,822	1.4%
27	Oregon	3,520,355	1.2%
28	Oklahoma	3,489,700	1.2%
29	Connecticut	3,458,587	1.2%
30	Iowa	2,935,840	1.0%
31	Mississippi	2,866,733	1.0%
32	Kansas	2,711,769	0.9%
33	Arkansas	2,706,268	0.9%
34	Utah	2,318,789	0.8%
35	Nevada	2,167,455	0.8%
36	New Mexico	1,852,044	0.6%
37	West Virginia	1,804,884	0.6%
38	Nebraska	1,727,564	0.6%
39	Idaho	1,343,124	0.5%
40	Maine	1,294,894	0.4%
41	New Hampshire	1,274,405	0.4%
42	Hawaii	1,240,663	0.4%
43	Rhode Island	1,068,326	0.4%
44	Montana	910,372	0.3%
45	Delaware	805,945	0.3%
46	South Dakota	760,437	0.3%
47	Alaska	641,482	0.2%
48	North Dakota	633,911	0.2%
49	Vermont	616,408	0.2%
50	Wyoming	498,830	0.2%
	District of Columbia	569,157	0.2%

Source: U.S. Bureau of the Census
   "Population Estimates" (December 18, 2003, http://eire.census.gov/popest/estimates.php)
Resident population. Revised estimates.

Numerical Population Change: 2002 to 2003

National Total = 2,835,853 Increase*

ALPHA ORDER

RANK	STATE	GAIN/LOSS	% of USA
30	Alabama	21,856	0.8%
44	Alaska	7,336	0.3%
5	Arizona	139,686	4.9%
33	Arkansas	19,446	0.7%
1	California	482,467	17.0%
15	Colorado	49,637	1.8%
27	Connecticut	24,785	0.9%
40	Delaware	11,546	0.4%
3	Florida	327,367	11.5%
4	Georgia	140,710	5.0%
34	Hawaii	16,945	0.6%
28	Idaho	23,208	0.8%
9	Illinois	67,097	2.4%
18	Indiana	38,730	1.4%
42	Iowa	8,222	0.3%
37	Kansas	11,738	0.4%
25	Kentucky	28,005	1.0%
32	Louisiana	20,142	0.7%
41	Maine	10,834	0.4%
12	Maryland	58,384	2.1%
39	Massachusetts	11,622	0.4%
19	Michigan	36,764	1.3%
22	Minnesota	34,584	1.2%
35	Mississippi	14,548	0.5%
21	Missouri	34,940	1.2%
45	Montana	7,249	0.3%
38	Nebraska	11,727	0.4%
8	Nevada	73,699	2.6%
36	New Hampshire	13,282	0.5%
11	New Jersey	63,144	2.2%
29	New Mexico	22,570	0.8%
13	New York	55,822	2.0%
6	North Carolina	101,428	3.6%
50	North Dakota	(74)	0.0%
26	Ohio	27,099	1.0%
31	Oklahoma	21,832	0.8%
17	Oregon	39,241	1.4%
20	Pennsylvania	36,628	1.3%
43	Rhode Island	7,838	0.3%
16	South Carolina	43,382	1.5%
47	South Dakota	3,872	0.1%
14	Tennessee	51,952	1.8%
2	Texas	381,584	13.5%
23	Utah	32,678	1.2%
48	Vermont	2,699	0.1%
7	Virginia	98,501	3.5%
10	Washington	64,385	2.3%
46	West Virginia	5,470	0.2%
24	Wisconsin	32,607	1.1%
49	Wyoming	2,412	0.1%

RANK ORDER

RANK	STATE	GAIN/LOSS	% of USA
1	California	482,467	17.0%
2	Texas	381,584	13.5%
3	Florida	327,367	11.5%
4	Georgia	140,710	5.0%
5	Arizona	139,686	4.9%
6	North Carolina	101,428	3.6%
7	Virginia	98,501	3.5%
8	Nevada	73,699	2.6%
9	Illinois	67,097	2.4%
10	Washington	64,385	2.3%
11	New Jersey	63,144	2.2%
12	Maryland	58,384	2.1%
13	New York	55,822	2.0%
14	Tennessee	51,952	1.8%
15	Colorado	49,637	1.8%
16	South Carolina	43,382	1.5%
17	Oregon	39,241	1.4%
18	Indiana	38,730	1.4%
19	Michigan	36,764	1.3%
20	Pennsylvania	36,628	1.3%
21	Missouri	34,940	1.2%
22	Minnesota	34,584	1.2%
23	Utah	32,678	1.2%
24	Wisconsin	32,607	1.1%
25	Kentucky	28,005	1.0%
26	Ohio	27,099	1.0%
27	Connecticut	24,785	0.9%
28	Idaho	23,208	0.8%
29	New Mexico	22,570	0.8%
30	Alabama	21,856	0.8%
31	Oklahoma	21,832	0.8%
32	Louisiana	20,142	0.7%
33	Arkansas	19,446	0.7%
34	Hawaii	16,945	0.6%
35	Mississippi	14,548	0.5%
36	New Hampshire	13,282	0.5%
37	Kansas	11,738	0.4%
38	Nebraska	11,727	0.4%
39	Massachusetts	11,622	0.4%
40	Delaware	11,546	0.4%
41	Maine	10,834	0.4%
42	Iowa	8,222	0.3%
43	Rhode Island	7,838	0.3%
44	Alaska	7,336	0.3%
45	Montana	7,249	0.3%
46	West Virginia	5,470	0.2%
47	South Dakota	3,872	0.1%
48	Vermont	2,699	0.1%
49	Wyoming	2,412	0.1%
50	North Dakota	(74)	0.0%

District of Columbia   (5,773)

Source: U.S. Bureau of the Census, Governments Division
"Annual Estimates of Population Changes" (http://eire.census.gov/popest/data/states/tables/NST-EST2003-03.php)
*Resident population from July 1, 2002 to July 1, 2003.

Percent Change in Population: 2002 to 2003

National Percent Change = 1.0% Increase*

<u>ALPHA ORDER</u>

RANK	STATE	PERCENT CHANGE
35	Alabama	0.5
14	Alaska	1.1
2	Arizona	2.6
24	Arkansas	0.7
7	California	1.4
14	Colorado	1.1
24	Connecticut	0.7
7	Delaware	1.4
3	Florida	2.0
6	Georgia	1.6
7	Hawaii	1.4
5	Idaho	1.7
35	Illinois	0.5
31	Indiana	0.6
44	Iowa	0.3
40	Kansas	0.4
24	Kentucky	0.7
40	Louisiana	0.4
22	Maine	0.8
14	Maryland	1.1
48	Massachusetts	0.2
40	Michigan	0.4
24	Minnesota	0.7
35	Mississippi	0.5
31	Missouri	0.6
22	Montana	0.8
24	Nebraska	0.7
1	Nevada	3.4
20	New Hampshire	1.0
24	New Jersey	0.7
12	New Mexico	1.2
44	New York	0.3
12	North Carolina	1.2
50	North Dakota	0.0
48	Ohio	0.2
31	Oklahoma	0.6
14	Oregon	1.1
44	Pennsylvania	0.3
24	Rhode Island	0.7
14	South Carolina	1.1
35	South Dakota	0.5
21	Tennessee	0.9
4	Texas	1.8
7	Utah	1.4
40	Vermont	0.4
7	Virginia	1.4
14	Washington	1.1
44	West Virginia	0.3
31	Wisconsin	0.6
35	Wyoming	0.5

<u>RANK ORDER</u>

RANK	STATE	PERCENT CHANGE
1	Nevada	3.4
2	Arizona	2.6
3	Florida	2.0
4	Texas	1.8
5	Idaho	1.7
6	Georgia	1.6
7	California	1.4
7	Delaware	1.4
7	Hawaii	1.4
7	Utah	1.4
7	Virginia	1.4
12	New Mexico	1.2
12	North Carolina	1.2
14	Alaska	1.1
14	Colorado	1.1
14	Maryland	1.1
14	Oregon	1.1
14	South Carolina	1.1
14	Washington	1.1
20	New Hampshire	1.0
21	Tennessee	0.9
22	Maine	0.8
22	Montana	0.8
24	Arkansas	0.7
24	Connecticut	0.7
24	Kentucky	0.7
24	Minnesota	0.7
24	Nebraska	0.7
24	New Jersey	0.7
24	Rhode Island	0.7
31	Indiana	0.6
31	Missouri	0.6
31	Oklahoma	0.6
31	Wisconsin	0.6
35	Alabama	0.5
35	Illinois	0.5
35	Mississippi	0.5
35	South Dakota	0.5
35	Wyoming	0.5
40	Kansas	0.4
40	Louisiana	0.4
40	Michigan	0.4
40	Vermont	0.4
44	Iowa	0.3
44	New York	0.3
44	Pennsylvania	0.3
44	West Virginia	0.3
48	Massachusetts	0.2
48	Ohio	0.2
50	North Dakota	0.0
	District of Columbia	(1.0)

Source: U.S. Bureau of the Census, Governments Division
"Annual Estimates of Population Changes" (http://eire.census.gov/popest/data/states/tables/NST-EST2003-03.php)
Resident population from July 1, 2002 to July 1, 2003.

Population in 2000 Census

National Total = 281,421,906*

<u>ALPHA ORDER</u>

RANK	STATE	POPULATION	% of USA
23	Alabama	4,447,100	1.6%
48	Alaska	626,932	0.2%
20	Arizona	5,130,632	1.8%
33	Arkansas	2,673,400	0.9%
1	California	33,871,648	12.0%
24	Colorado	4,301,261	1.5%
29	Connecticut	3,405,565	1.2%
45	Delaware	783,600	0.3%
4	Florida	15,982,378	5.7%
10	Georgia	8,186,453	2.9%
42	Hawaii	1,211,537	0.4%
39	Idaho	1,293,953	0.5%
5	Illinois	12,419,293	4.4%
14	Indiana	6,080,485	2.2%
30	Iowa	2,926,324	1.0%
32	Kansas	2,688,418	1.0%
25	Kentucky	4,041,769	1.4%
22	Louisiana	4,468,976	1.6%
40	Maine	1,274,923	0.5%
19	Maryland	5,296,486	1.9%
13	Massachusetts	6,349,097	2.3%
8	Michigan	9,938,444	3.5%
21	Minnesota	4,919,479	1.7%
31	Mississippi	2,844,658	1.0%
17	Missouri	5,595,211	2.0%
44	Montana	902,195	0.3%
38	Nebraska	1,711,263	0.6%
35	Nevada	1,998,257	0.7%
41	New Hampshire	1,235,786	0.4%
9	New Jersey	8,414,350	3.0%
36	New Mexico	1,819,046	0.6%
3	New York	18,976,457	6.7%
11	North Carolina	8,049,313	2.9%
47	North Dakota	642,200	0.2%
7	Ohio	11,353,140	4.0%
27	Oklahoma	3,450,654	1.2%
28	Oregon	3,421,399	1.2%
6	Pennsylvania	12,281,054	4.4%
43	Rhode Island	1,048,319	0.4%
26	South Carolina	4,012,012	1.4%
46	South Dakota	754,844	0.3%
16	Tennessee	5,689,283	2.0%
2	Texas	20,851,820	7.4%
34	Utah	2,233,169	0.8%
49	Vermont	608,827	0.2%
12	Virginia	7,078,515	2.5%
15	Washington	5,894,121	2.1%
37	West Virginia	1,808,344	0.6%
18	Wisconsin	5,363,675	1.9%
50	Wyoming	493,782	0.2%

<u>RANK ORDER</u>

RANK	STATE	POPULATION	% of USA
1	California	33,871,648	12.0%
2	Texas	20,851,820	7.4%
3	New York	18,976,457	6.7%
4	Florida	15,982,378	5.7%
5	Illinois	12,419,293	4.4%
6	Pennsylvania	12,281,054	4.4%
7	Ohio	11,353,140	4.0%
8	Michigan	9,938,444	3.5%
9	New Jersey	8,414,350	3.0%
10	Georgia	8,186,453	2.9%
11	North Carolina	8,049,313	2.9%
12	Virginia	7,078,515	2.5%
13	Massachusetts	6,349,097	2.3%
14	Indiana	6,080,485	2.2%
15	Washington	5,894,121	2.1%
16	Tennessee	5,689,283	2.0%
17	Missouri	5,595,211	2.0%
18	Wisconsin	5,363,675	1.9%
19	Maryland	5,296,486	1.9%
20	Arizona	5,130,632	1.8%
21	Minnesota	4,919,479	1.7%
22	Louisiana	4,468,976	1.6%
23	Alabama	4,447,100	1.6%
24	Colorado	4,301,261	1.5%
25	Kentucky	4,041,769	1.4%
26	South Carolina	4,012,012	1.4%
27	Oklahoma	3,450,654	1.2%
28	Oregon	3,421,399	1.2%
29	Connecticut	3,405,565	1.2%
30	Iowa	2,926,324	1.0%
31	Mississippi	2,844,658	1.0%
32	Kansas	2,688,418	1.0%
33	Arkansas	2,673,400	0.9%
34	Utah	2,233,169	0.8%
35	Nevada	1,998,257	0.7%
36	New Mexico	1,819,046	0.6%
37	West Virginia	1,808,344	0.6%
38	Nebraska	1,711,263	0.6%
39	Idaho	1,293,953	0.5%
40	Maine	1,274,923	0.5%
41	New Hampshire	1,235,786	0.4%
42	Hawaii	1,211,537	0.4%
43	Rhode Island	1,048,319	0.4%
44	Montana	902,195	0.3%
45	Delaware	783,600	0.3%
46	South Dakota	754,844	0.3%
47	North Dakota	642,200	0.2%
48	Alaska	626,932	0.2%
49	Vermont	608,827	0.2%
50	Wyoming	493,782	0.2%
	District of Columbia	572,059	0.2%

Source: U.S. Bureau of the Census

"First Census 2000 Results" (December 28, 2000, http://www.census.gov/main/www/cen2000.html)
Resident population as of April 2000 Census.

Population (Resident and Overseas) in 2000

National Total = 281,998,273*

ALPHA ORDER

RANK	STATE	POPULATION	% of USA
23	Alabama	4,461,130	1.6%
48	Alaska	628,933	0.2%
20	Arizona	5,140,683	1.8%
33	Arkansas	2,679,733	1.0%
1	California	33,930,798	12.0%
24	Colorado	4,311,882	1.5%
29	Connecticut	3,409,535	1.2%
45	Delaware	785,068	0.3%
4	Florida	16,028,890	5.7%
10	Georgia	8,206,975	2.9%
42	Hawaii	1,216,642	0.4%
39	Idaho	1,297,274	0.5%
5	Illinois	12,439,042	4.4%
14	Indiana	6,090,782	2.2%
30	Iowa	2,931,923	1.0%
32	Kansas	2,693,824	1.0%
25	Kentucky	4,049,431	1.4%
22	Louisiana	4,480,271	1.6%
40	Maine	1,277,731	0.5%
19	Maryland	5,307,886	1.9%
13	Massachusetts	6,355,568	2.3%
8	Michigan	9,955,829	3.5%
21	Minnesota	4,925,670	1.7%
31	Mississippi	2,852,927	1.0%
17	Missouri	5,606,260	2.0%
44	Montana	905,316	0.3%
38	Nebraska	1,715,369	0.6%
35	Nevada	2,002,032	0.7%
41	New Hampshire	1,238,415	0.4%
9	New Jersey	8,424,354	3.0%
36	New Mexico	1,823,821	0.6%
3	New York	19,004,973	6.7%
11	North Carolina	8,067,673	2.9%
47	North Dakota	643,756	0.2%
7	Ohio	11,374,540	4.0%
27	Oklahoma	3,458,819	1.2%
28	Oregon	3,428,543	1.2%
6	Pennsylvania	12,300,670	4.4%
43	Rhode Island	1,049,662	0.4%
26	South Carolina	4,025,061	1.4%
46	South Dakota	756,874	0.3%
16	Tennessee	5,700,037	2.0%
2	Texas	20,903,994	7.4%
34	Utah	2,236,714	0.8%
49	Vermont	609,890	0.2%
12	Virginia	7,100,702	2.5%
15	Washington	5,908,684	2.1%
37	West Virginia	1,813,077	0.6%
18	Wisconsin	5,371,210	1.9%
50	Wyoming	495,304	0.2%

RANK ORDER

RANK	STATE	POPULATION	% of USA
1	California	33,930,798	12.0%
2	Texas	20,903,994	7.4%
3	New York	19,004,973	6.7%
4	Florida	16,028,890	5.7%
5	Illinois	12,439,042	4.4%
6	Pennsylvania	12,300,670	4.4%
7	Ohio	11,374,540	4.0%
8	Michigan	9,955,829	3.5%
9	New Jersey	8,424,354	3.0%
10	Georgia	8,206,975	2.9%
11	North Carolina	8,067,673	2.9%
12	Virginia	7,100,702	2.5%
13	Massachusetts	6,355,568	2.3%
14	Indiana	6,090,782	2.2%
15	Washington	5,908,684	2.1%
16	Tennessee	5,700,037	2.0%
17	Missouri	5,606,260	2.0%
18	Wisconsin	5,371,210	1.9%
19	Maryland	5,307,886	1.9%
20	Arizona	5,140,683	1.8%
21	Minnesota	4,925,670	1.7%
22	Louisiana	4,480,271	1.6%
23	Alabama	4,461,130	1.6%
24	Colorado	4,311,882	1.5%
25	Kentucky	4,049,431	1.4%
26	South Carolina	4,025,061	1.4%
27	Oklahoma	3,458,819	1.2%
28	Oregon	3,428,543	1.2%
29	Connecticut	3,409,535	1.2%
30	Iowa	2,931,923	1.0%
31	Mississippi	2,852,927	1.0%
32	Kansas	2,693,824	1.0%
33	Arkansas	2,679,733	1.0%
34	Utah	2,236,714	0.8%
35	Nevada	2,002,032	0.7%
36	New Mexico	1,823,821	0.6%
37	West Virginia	1,813,077	0.6%
38	Nebraska	1,715,369	0.6%
39	Idaho	1,297,274	0.5%
40	Maine	1,277,731	0.5%
41	New Hampshire	1,238,415	0.4%
42	Hawaii	1,216,642	0.4%
43	Rhode Island	1,049,662	0.4%
44	Montana	905,316	0.3%
45	Delaware	785,068	0.3%
46	South Dakota	756,874	0.3%
47	North Dakota	643,756	0.2%
48	Alaska	628,933	0.2%
49	Vermont	609,890	0.2%
50	Wyoming	495,304	0.2%
	District of Columbia	574,096	0.2%

Source: Morgan Quitno Press using data from U.S. Bureau of the Census
"First Census 2000 Results" (December 28, 2000, http://www.census.gov/main/www/cen2000.html)

**This is the total of resident and overseas population. Overseas population includes U.S. military and federal civilian employees (and their dependents living with them) allocated to their home state or the District of Columbia, as reported by the employing federal agencies. This is the same population as that used for congressional apportionment except that the population for the District of Columbia is removed for that purpose.*

U.S. Population Living Overseas in 2000

National Total = 576,367*

<u>ALPHA ORDER</u>

RANK	STATE	OVERSEAS	% of USA
13	Alabama	14,030	2.4%
45	Alaska	2,001	0.3%
21	Arizona	10,051	1.7%
29	Arkansas	6,333	1.1%
1	California	59,150	10.3%
19	Colorado	10,621	1.8%
37	Connecticut	3,970	0.7%
48	Delaware	1,468	0.3%
3	Florida	46,512	8.1%
7	Georgia	20,522	3.6%
33	Hawaii	5,105	0.9%
40	Idaho	3,321	0.6%
8	Illinois	19,749	3.4%
20	Indiana	10,297	1.8%
31	Iowa	5,599	1.0%
32	Kansas	5,406	0.9%
25	Kentucky	7,662	1.3%
16	Louisiana	11,295	2.0%
42	Maine	2,808	0.5%
15	Maryland	11,400	2.0%
28	Massachusetts	6,471	1.1%
11	Michigan	17,385	3.0%
30	Minnesota	6,191	1.1%
23	Mississippi	8,269	1.4%
17	Missouri	11,049	1.9%
41	Montana	3,121	0.5%
36	Nebraska	4,106	0.7%
38	Nevada	3,775	0.7%
43	New Hampshire	2,629	0.5%
22	New Jersey	10,004	1.7%
34	New Mexico	4,775	0.8%
4	New York	28,516	4.9%
10	North Carolina	18,360	3.2%
46	North Dakota	1,556	0.3%
6	Ohio	21,400	3.7%
24	Oklahoma	8,165	1.4%
27	Oregon	7,144	1.2%
9	Pennsylvania	19,616	3.4%
49	Rhode Island	1,343	0.2%
14	South Carolina	13,049	2.3%
44	South Dakota	2,030	0.4%
18	Tennessee	10,754	1.9%
2	Texas	52,174	9.1%
39	Utah	3,545	0.6%
50	Vermont	1,063	0.2%
5	Virginia	22,187	3.8%
12	Washington	14,563	2.5%
35	West Virginia	4,733	0.8%
26	Wisconsin	7,535	1.3%
47	Wyoming	1,522	0.3%

<u>RANK ORDER</u>

RANK	STATE	OVERSEAS	% of USA
1	California	59,150	10.3%
2	Texas	52,174	9.1%
3	Florida	46,512	8.1%
4	New York	28,516	4.9%
5	Virginia	22,187	3.8%
6	Ohio	21,400	3.7%
7	Georgia	20,522	3.6%
8	Illinois	19,749	3.4%
9	Pennsylvania	19,616	3.4%
10	North Carolina	18,360	3.2%
11	Michigan	17,385	3.0%
12	Washington	14,563	2.5%
13	Alabama	14,030	2.4%
14	South Carolina	13,049	2.3%
15	Maryland	11,400	2.0%
16	Louisiana	11,295	2.0%
17	Missouri	11,049	1.9%
18	Tennessee	10,754	1.9%
19	Colorado	10,621	1.8%
20	Indiana	10,297	1.8%
21	Arizona	10,051	1.7%
22	New Jersey	10,004	1.7%
23	Mississippi	8,269	1.4%
24	Oklahoma	8,165	1.4%
25	Kentucky	7,662	1.3%
26	Wisconsin	7,535	1.3%
27	Oregon	7,144	1.2%
28	Massachusetts	6,471	1.1%
29	Arkansas	6,333	1.1%
30	Minnesota	6,191	1.1%
31	Iowa	5,599	1.0%
32	Kansas	5,406	0.9%
33	Hawaii	5,105	0.9%
34	New Mexico	4,775	0.8%
35	West Virginia	4,733	0.8%
36	Nebraska	4,106	0.7%
37	Connecticut	3,970	0.7%
38	Nevada	3,775	0.7%
39	Utah	3,545	0.6%
40	Idaho	3,321	0.6%
41	Montana	3,121	0.5%
42	Maine	2,808	0.5%
43	New Hampshire	2,629	0.5%
44	South Dakota	2,030	0.4%
45	Alaska	2,001	0.3%
46	North Dakota	1,556	0.3%
47	Wyoming	1,522	0.3%
48	Delaware	1,468	0.3%
49	Rhode Island	1,343	0.2%
50	Vermont	1,063	0.2%
	District of Columbia	2,037	0.4%

Source: U.S. Bureau of the Census
"First Census 2000 Results" (December 28, 2000, http://www.census.gov/main/www/cen2000.html)
Includes overseas U.S. military and federal civilian employees (and their dependents living with them) allocated to their home state or the District of Columbia, as reported by the employing federal agencies.

Resident State Population in 1990

National Total = 248,790,925*

RANK	STATE	POPULATION	% of USA
22	Alabama	4,040,389	1.6%
49	Alaska	550,043	0.2%
24	Arizona	3,665,339	1.5%
33	Arkansas	2,350,624	0.9%
1	California	29,811,427	12.0%
26	Colorado	3,294,473	1.3%
27	Connecticut	3,287,116	1.3%
46	Delaware	666,168	0.3%
4	Florida	12,938,071	5.2%
11	Georgia	6,478,149	2.6%
41	Hawaii	1,108,229	0.4%
42	Idaho	1,006,734	0.4%
6	Illinois	11,430,602	4.6%
14	Indiana	5,544,156	2.2%
30	Iowa	2,776,831	1.1%
32	Kansas	2,477,588	1.0%
23	Kentucky	3,686,892	1.5%
21	Louisiana	4,221,826	1.7%
38	Maine	1,227,928	0.5%
19	Maryland	4,780,753	1.9%
13	Massachusetts	6,016,425	2.4%
8	Michigan	9,295,287	3.7%
20	Minnesota	4,375,665	1.8%
31	Mississippi	2,575,475	1.0%
15	Missouri	5,116,901	2.1%
44	Montana	799,065	0.3%
36	Nebraska	1,578,417	0.6%
39	Nevada	1,201,675	0.5%
40	New Hampshire	1,109,252	0.4%
9	New Jersey	7,747,750	3.1%
37	New Mexico	1,515,069	0.6%
2	New York	17,990,778	7.2%
10	North Carolina	6,632,448	2.7%
47	North Dakota	638,800	0.3%
7	Ohio	10,847,115	4.4%
28	Oklahoma	3,145,576	1.3%
29	Oregon	2,842,337	1.1%
5	Pennsylvania	11,882,842	4.8%
43	Rhode Island	1,003,464	0.4%
25	South Carolina	3,486,310	1.4%
45	South Dakota	696,004	0.3%
17	Tennessee	4,877,203	2.0%
3	Texas	16,986,335	6.8%
35	Utah	1,722,850	0.7%
48	Vermont	562,758	0.2%
12	Virginia	6,189,197	2.5%
18	Washington	4,866,669	2.0%
34	West Virginia	1,793,477	0.7%
16	Wisconsin	4,891,954	2.0%
50	Wyoming	453,589	0.2%

RANK	STATE	POPULATION	% of USA
1	California	29,811,427	12.0%
2	New York	17,990,778	7.2%
3	Texas	16,986,335	6.8%
4	Florida	12,938,071	5.2%
5	Pennsylvania	11,882,842	4.8%
6	Illinois	11,430,602	4.6%
7	Ohio	10,847,115	4.4%
8	Michigan	9,295,287	3.7%
9	New Jersey	7,747,750	3.1%
10	North Carolina	6,632,448	2.7%
11	Georgia	6,478,149	2.6%
12	Virginia	6,189,197	2.5%
13	Massachusetts	6,016,425	2.4%
14	Indiana	5,544,156	2.2%
15	Missouri	5,116,901	2.1%
16	Wisconsin	4,891,954	2.0%
17	Tennessee	4,877,203	2.0%
18	Washington	4,866,669	2.0%
19	Maryland	4,780,753	1.9%
20	Minnesota	4,375,665	1.8%
21	Louisiana	4,221,826	1.7%
22	Alabama	4,040,389	1.6%
23	Kentucky	3,686,892	1.5%
24	Arizona	3,665,339	1.5%
25	South Carolina	3,486,310	1.4%
26	Colorado	3,294,473	1.3%
27	Connecticut	3,287,116	1.3%
28	Oklahoma	3,145,576	1.3%
29	Oregon	2,842,337	1.1%
30	Iowa	2,776,831	1.1%
31	Mississippi	2,575,475	1.0%
32	Kansas	2,477,588	1.0%
33	Arkansas	2,350,624	0.9%
34	West Virginia	1,793,477	0.7%
35	Utah	1,722,850	0.7%
36	Nebraska	1,578,417	0.6%
37	New Mexico	1,515,069	0.6%
38	Maine	1,227,928	0.5%
39	Nevada	1,201,675	0.5%
40	New Hampshire	1,109,252	0.4%
41	Hawaii	1,108,229	0.4%
42	Idaho	1,006,734	0.4%
43	Rhode Island	1,003,464	0.4%
44	Montana	799,065	0.3%
45	South Dakota	696,004	0.3%
46	Delaware	666,168	0.3%
47	North Dakota	638,800	0.3%
48	Vermont	562,758	0.2%
49	Alaska	550,043	0.2%
50	Wyoming	453,589	0.2%
	District of Columbia	606,900	0.2%

Source: U.S. Bureau of the Census
    "State Population Estimates" (December 29, 1999, http://www.census.gov/population/estimates/state/st-99-3.txt)
*This is the decennial census dated April 1, 1990. The counts shown here include corrections processed through December 1998.

Percent Change in Population: 1990 to 2000

National Percent Change = 13.2% Increase*

<u>ALPHA ORDER</u>

RANK	STATE	PERCENT CHANGE
25	Alabama	10.1
17	Alaska	14.0
2	Arizona	40.0
19	Arkansas	13.7
18	California	13.8
3	Colorado	30.6
47	Connecticut	3.6
13	Delaware	17.6
7	Florida	23.5
6	Georgia	26.4
30	Hawaii	9.3
5	Idaho	28.5
34	Illinois	8.6
26	Indiana	9.7
43	Iowa	5.4
35	Kansas	8.5
26	Kentucky	9.7
40	Louisiana	5.9
46	Maine	3.8
23	Maryland	10.8
41	Massachusetts	5.5
39	Michigan	6.9
21	Minnesota	12.4
24	Mississippi	10.5
30	Missouri	9.3
20	Montana	12.9
37	Nebraska	8.4
1	Nevada	66.3
22	New Hampshire	11.4
32	New Jersey	8.9
12	New Mexico	20.1
41	New York	5.5
9	North Carolina	21.4
50	North Dakota	0.5
44	Ohio	4.7
26	Oklahoma	9.7
11	Oregon	20.4
48	Pennsylvania	3.4
45	Rhode Island	4.5
15	South Carolina	15.1
35	South Dakota	8.5
14	Tennessee	16.7
8	Texas	22.8
4	Utah	29.6
38	Vermont	8.2
16	Virginia	14.4
10	Washington	21.1
49	West Virginia	0.8
29	Wisconsin	9.6
32	Wyoming	8.9

<u>RANK ORDER</u>

RANK	STATE	PERCENT CHANGE
1	Nevada	66.3
2	Arizona	40.0
3	Colorado	30.6
4	Utah	29.6
5	Idaho	28.5
6	Georgia	26.4
7	Florida	23.5
8	Texas	22.8
9	North Carolina	21.4
10	Washington	21.1
11	Oregon	20.4
12	New Mexico	20.1
13	Delaware	17.6
14	Tennessee	16.7
15	South Carolina	15.1
16	Virginia	14.4
17	Alaska	14.0
18	California	13.8
19	Arkansas	13.7
20	Montana	12.9
21	Minnesota	12.4
22	New Hampshire	11.4
23	Maryland	10.8
24	Mississippi	10.5
25	Alabama	10.1
26	Indiana	9.7
26	Kentucky	9.7
26	Oklahoma	9.7
29	Wisconsin	9.6
30	Hawaii	9.3
30	Missouri	9.3
32	New Jersey	8.9
32	Wyoming	8.9
34	Illinois	8.6
35	Kansas	8.5
35	South Dakota	8.5
37	Nebraska	8.4
38	Vermont	8.2
39	Michigan	6.9
40	Louisiana	5.9
41	Massachusetts	5.5
41	New York	5.5
43	Iowa	5.4
44	Ohio	4.7
45	Rhode Island	4.5
46	Maine	3.8
47	Connecticut	3.6
48	Pennsylvania	3.4
49	West Virginia	0.8
50	North Dakota	0.5

District of Columbia   (5.7)

Source: U.S. Bureau of the Census

"First Census 2000 Results" (December 28, 2000, http://www.census.gov/main/www/cen2000.html)

**From April 1, 1990 to April 1, 2000.*

Population per Square Mile in 2003

National Rate = 82.2 Persons per Square Mile*

<u>ALPHA ORDER</u>

RANK	STATE	RATE
26	Alabama	88.7
50	Alaska	1.1
36	Arizona	49.1
34	Arkansas	52.3
12	California	227.5
37	Colorado	43.9
4	Connecticut	719.0
6	Delaware	418.4
8	Florida	315.6
18	Georgia	150.0
13	Hawaii	195.8
44	Idaho	16.5
11	Illinois	227.7
16	Indiana	172.7
33	Iowa	52.7
40	Kansas	33.3
22	Kentucky	103.7
23	Louisiana	103.2
38	Maine	42.3
5	Maryland	563.6
3	Massachusetts	820.6
15	Michigan	177.5
31	Minnesota	63.6
32	Mississippi	61.4
28	Missouri	82.8
48	Montana	6.3
42	Nebraska	22.6
43	Nevada	20.4
19	New Hampshire	143.6
1	New Jersey	1,164.7
45	New Mexico	15.4
7	New York	406.4
17	North Carolina	172.6
47	North Dakota	9.2
9	Ohio	279.3
35	Oklahoma	51.1
39	Oregon	37.1
10	Pennsylvania	275.9
2	Rhode Island	1,029.8
21	South Carolina	137.7
46	South Dakota	10.1
20	Tennessee	141.7
27	Texas	84.5
41	Utah	28.6
30	Vermont	66.9
14	Virginia	186.6
25	Washington	92.1
29	West Virginia	75.2
24	Wisconsin	100.8
49	Wyoming	5.2

<u>RANK ORDER</u>

RANK	STATE	RATE
1	New Jersey	1,164.7
2	Rhode Island	1,029.8
3	Massachusetts	820.6
4	Connecticut	719.0
5	Maryland	563.6
6	Delaware	418.4
7	New York	406.4
8	Florida	315.6
9	Ohio	279.3
10	Pennsylvania	275.9
11	Illinois	227.7
12	California	227.5
13	Hawaii	195.8
14	Virginia	186.6
15	Michigan	177.5
16	Indiana	172.7
17	North Carolina	172.6
18	Georgia	150.0
19	New Hampshire	143.6
20	Tennessee	141.7
21	South Carolina	137.7
22	Kentucky	103.7
23	Louisiana	103.2
24	Wisconsin	100.8
25	Washington	92.1
26	Alabama	88.7
27	Texas	84.5
28	Missouri	82.8
29	West Virginia	75.2
30	Vermont	66.9
31	Minnesota	63.6
32	Mississippi	61.4
33	Iowa	52.7
34	Arkansas	52.3
35	Oklahoma	51.1
36	Arizona	49.1
37	Colorado	43.9
38	Maine	42.3
39	Oregon	37.1
40	Kansas	33.3
41	Utah	28.6
42	Nebraska	22.6
43	Nevada	20.4
44	Idaho	16.5
45	New Mexico	15.4
46	South Dakota	10.1
47	North Dakota	9.2
48	Montana	6.3
49	Wyoming	5.2
50	Alaska	1.1
	District of Columbia	9,235.8

*Source: Morgan Quitno Press using data from U.S. Bureau of the Census
"Population Estimates" (December 18, 2003, http://eire.census.gov/popest/estimates.php)*
Resident population. Based on land area of states.

Population per Square Mile in 2000

National Rate = 79.8 Persons per Square Mile*

<u>ALPHA ORDER</u>

RANK	STATE	RATE
26	Alabama	87.7
50	Alaska	1.1
36	Arizona	45.5
34	Arkansas	51.4
12	California	218.1
37	Colorado	41.7
4	Connecticut	704.2
6	Delaware	402.3
8	Florida	297.6
18	Georgia	142.2
13	Hawaii	188.8
44	Idaho	15.7
11	Illinois	223.8
16	Indiana	169.8
33	Iowa	52.4
40	Kansas	32.9
23	Kentucky	101.9
22	Louisiana	102.6
38	Maine	41.4
5	Maryland	543.5
3	Massachusetts	811.7
15	Michigan	175.3
31	Minnesota	62.0
32	Mississippi	60.7
27	Missouri	81.4
48	Montana	6.2
42	Nebraska	22.3
43	Nevada	18.4
20	New Hampshire	138.3
1	New Jersey	1,136.7
45	New Mexico	15.0
6	New York	402.3
17	North Carolina	165.9
47	North Dakota	9.3
9	Ohio	277.5
35	Oklahoma	50.3
39	Oregon	35.7
10	Pennsylvania	274.1
2	Rhode Island	1,005.5
21	South Carolina	133.6
46	South Dakota	10.0
19	Tennessee	138.4
28	Texas	80.0
41	Utah	27.3
30	Vermont	65.9
14	Virginia	179.5
25	Washington	88.8
29	West Virginia	75.0
24	Wisconsin	98.9
49	Wyoming	5.1

<u>RANK ORDER</u>

RANK	STATE	RATE
1	New Jersey	1,136.7
2	Rhode Island	1,005.5
3	Massachusetts	811.7
4	Connecticut	704.2
5	Maryland	543.5
6	Delaware	402.3
6	New York	402.3
8	Florida	297.6
9	Ohio	277.5
10	Pennsylvania	274.1
11	Illinois	223.8
12	California	218.1
13	Hawaii	188.8
14	Virginia	179.5
15	Michigan	175.3
16	Indiana	169.8
17	North Carolina	165.9
18	Georgia	142.2
19	Tennessee	138.4
20	New Hampshire	138.3
21	South Carolina	133.6
22	Louisiana	102.6
23	Kentucky	101.9
24	Wisconsin	98.9
25	Washington	88.8
26	Alabama	87.7
27	Missouri	81.4
28	Texas	80.0
29	West Virginia	75.0
30	Vermont	65.9
31	Minnesota	62.0
32	Mississippi	60.7
33	Iowa	52.4
34	Arkansas	51.4
35	Oklahoma	50.3
36	Arizona	45.5
37	Colorado	41.7
38	Maine	41.4
39	Oregon	35.7
40	Kansas	32.9
41	Utah	27.3
42	Nebraska	22.3
43	Nevada	18.4
44	Idaho	15.7
45	New Mexico	15.0
46	South Dakota	10.0
47	North Dakota	9.3
48	Montana	6.2
49	Wyoming	5.1
50	Alaska	1.1
	District of Columbia	9,371.2

*Source: Morgan Quitno Press using data from U.S. Bureau of the Census
"Population Estimates" (December 20, 2002, http://eire.census.gov/popest/estimates.php)*
**Resident population. Based on land area of states.*

Population per Square Mile in 1990

National Rate = 70.4 Persons per Square Mile*

ALPHA ORDER

RANK	STATE	RATE
25	Alabama	79.6
50	Alaska	1.0
37	Arizona	32.3
35	Arkansas	45.1
12	California	191.1
38	Colorado	31.8
4	Connecticut	678.5
7	Delaware	340.8
10	Florida	239.9
21	Georgia	111.8
13	Hawaii	172.5
44	Idaho	12.2
11	Illinois	205.6
16	Indiana	154.6
33	Iowa	49.7
39	Kansas	30.3
23	Kentucky	92.8
22	Louisiana	96.9
36	Maine	39.8
5	Maryland	489.1
3	Massachusetts	767.6
14	Michigan	163.6
31	Minnesota	55.0
32	Mississippi	54.9
27	Missouri	74.3
48	Montana	5.5
42	Nebraska	20.5
45	Nevada	10.9
18	New Hampshire	123.7
1	New Jersey	1,044.3
43	New Mexico	12.5
6	New York	381.0
17	North Carolina	136.1
46	North Dakota	9.3
9	Ohio	264.9
34	Oklahoma	45.8
40	Oregon	29.6
8	Pennsylvania	265.1
2	Rhode Island	960.3
20	South Carolina	115.8
47	South Dakota	9.2
19	Tennessee	118.3
29	Texas	64.9
41	Utah	21.0
30	Vermont	60.8
15	Virginia	156.3
28	Washington	73.1
26	West Virginia	74.5
24	Wisconsin	90.1
49	Wyoming	4.7

RANK ORDER

RANK	STATE	RATE
1	New Jersey	1,044.3
2	Rhode Island	960.3
3	Massachusetts	767.6
4	Connecticut	678.5
5	Maryland	489.1
6	New York	381.0
7	Delaware	340.8
8	Pennsylvania	265.1
9	Ohio	264.9
10	Florida	239.9
11	Illinois	205.6
12	California	191.1
13	Hawaii	172.5
14	Michigan	163.6
15	Virginia	156.3
16	Indiana	154.6
17	North Carolina	136.1
18	New Hampshire	123.7
19	Tennessee	118.3
20	South Carolina	115.8
21	Georgia	111.8
22	Louisiana	96.9
23	Kentucky	92.8
24	Wisconsin	90.1
25	Alabama	79.6
26	West Virginia	74.5
27	Missouri	74.3
28	Washington	73.1
29	Texas	64.9
30	Vermont	60.8
31	Minnesota	55.0
32	Mississippi	54.9
33	Iowa	49.7
34	Oklahoma	45.8
35	Arkansas	45.1
36	Maine	39.8
37	Arizona	32.3
38	Colorado	31.8
39	Kansas	30.3
40	Oregon	29.6
41	Utah	21.0
42	Nebraska	20.5
43	New Mexico	12.5
44	Idaho	12.2
45	Nevada	10.9
46	North Dakota	9.3
47	South Dakota	9.2
48	Montana	5.5
49	Wyoming	4.7
50	Alaska	1.0
	District of Columbia	9,949.2

Source: Morgan Quitno Press using data from U.S. Bureau of the Census
"State Population Estimates" (December 29, 1999, http://www.census.gov/population/estimates/state/st-99-3.txt)
**The is the decennial census dated April 1, 1990. The counts shown here include corrections processed through December 1998.*

Percent of Population Living in a Metropolitan Area in 2000

National Percent = 80.3% of Population*

<u>ALPHA ORDER</u>

RANK	STATE	PERCENT
27	Alabama	69.9
43	Alaska	41.5
9	Arizona	88.2
38	Arkansas	49.4
2	California	96.7
14	Colorado	83.9
4	Connecticut	95.6
18	Delaware	80.0
6	Florida	92.8
28	Georgia	69.2
23	Hawaii	72.3
44	Idaho	39.3
11	Illinois	84.9
24	Indiana	72.2
40	Iowa	45.3
36	Kansas	56.6
39	Kentucky	48.8
21	Louisiana	75.4
45	Maine	36.6
7	Maryland	92.7
3	Massachusetts	95.9
16	Michigan	82.2
25	Minnesota	70.4
46	Mississippi	36.0
31	Missouri	67.8
48	Montana	33.9
37	Nebraska	52.6
10	Nevada	87.5
34	New Hampshire	59.9
1	New Jersey	100.0
35	New Mexico	56.9
8	New York	92.1
32	North Carolina	67.5
41	North Dakota	44.2
17	Ohio	81.2
33	Oklahoma	60.8
22	Oregon	73.1
13	Pennsylvania	84.6
5	Rhode Island	94.1
26	South Carolina	70.0
47	South Dakota	34.6
29	Tennessee	67.9
12	Texas	84.8
20	Utah	76.5
50	Vermont	27.8
19	Virginia	78.1
15	Washington	83.1
42	West Virginia	42.3
29	Wisconsin	67.9
49	Wyoming	30.0

<u>RANK ORDER</u>

RANK	STATE	PERCENT
1	New Jersey	100.0
2	California	96.7
3	Massachusetts	95.9
4	Connecticut	95.6
5	Rhode Island	94.1
6	Florida	92.8
7	Maryland	92.7
8	New York	92.1
9	Arizona	88.2
10	Nevada	87.5
11	Illinois	84.9
12	Texas	84.8
13	Pennsylvania	84.6
14	Colorado	83.9
15	Washington	83.1
16	Michigan	82.2
17	Ohio	81.2
18	Delaware	80.0
19	Virginia	78.1
20	Utah	76.5
21	Louisiana	75.4
22	Oregon	73.1
23	Hawaii	72.3
24	Indiana	72.2
25	Minnesota	70.4
26	South Carolina	70.0
27	Alabama	69.9
28	Georgia	69.2
29	Tennessee	67.9
29	Wisconsin	67.9
31	Missouri	67.8
32	North Carolina	67.5
33	Oklahoma	60.8
34	New Hampshire	59.9
35	New Mexico	56.9
36	Kansas	56.6
37	Nebraska	52.6
38	Arkansas	49.4
39	Kentucky	48.8
40	Iowa	45.3
41	North Dakota	44.2
42	West Virginia	42.3
43	Alaska	41.5
44	Idaho	39.3
45	Maine	36.6
46	Mississippi	36.0
47	South Dakota	34.6
48	Montana	33.9
49	Wyoming	30.0
50	Vermont	27.8

District of Columbia	100.0

*Source: U.S. Bureau of the Census
    unpublished data*

**"Metropolitan" refers to metropolitan statistical areas and consolidated metropolitan statistical areas as defined by the U.S. Office of Management and Budget, June 30, 1999.*

Percent of Population Living in a Nonmetropolitan Area in 2000

National Percent = 19.7% of Population*

<u>ALPHA ORDER</u>

RANK	STATE	PERCENT
24	Alabama	30.1
8	Alaska	58.5
42	Arizona	11.8
13	Arkansas	50.6
49	California	3.3
37	Colorado	16.1
47	Connecticut	4.4
33	Delaware	20.0
45	Florida	7.2
23	Georgia	30.8
28	Hawaii	27.7
7	Idaho	60.7
40	Illinois	15.1
27	Indiana	27.8
11	Iowa	54.7
15	Kansas	43.4
12	Kentucky	51.2
30	Louisiana	24.6
6	Maine	63.4
44	Maryland	7.3
48	Massachusetts	4.1
35	Michigan	17.8
26	Minnesota	29.6
5	Mississippi	64.0
20	Missouri	32.2
3	Montana	66.1
14	Nebraska	47.4
41	Nevada	12.5
17	New Hampshire	40.1
50	New Jersey	0.0
16	New Mexico	43.1
43	New York	7.9
19	North Carolina	32.5
10	North Dakota	55.8
34	Ohio	18.8
18	Oklahoma	39.2
29	Oregon	26.9
38	Pennsylvania	15.4
46	Rhode Island	5.9
25	South Carolina	30.0
4	South Dakota	65.4
21	Tennessee	32.1
39	Texas	15.2
31	Utah	23.5
1	Vermont	72.2
32	Virginia	21.9
36	Washington	16.9
9	West Virginia	57.7
21	Wisconsin	32.1
2	Wyoming	70.0

<u>RANK ORDER</u>

RANK	STATE	PERCENT
1	Vermont	72.2
2	Wyoming	70.0
3	Montana	66.1
4	South Dakota	65.4
5	Mississippi	64.0
6	Maine	63.4
7	Idaho	60.7
8	Alaska	58.5
9	West Virginia	57.7
10	North Dakota	55.8
11	Iowa	54.7
12	Kentucky	51.2
13	Arkansas	50.6
14	Nebraska	47.4
15	Kansas	43.4
16	New Mexico	43.1
17	New Hampshire	40.1
18	Oklahoma	39.2
19	North Carolina	32.5
20	Missouri	32.2
21	Tennessee	32.1
21	Wisconsin	32.1
23	Georgia	30.8
24	Alabama	30.1
25	South Carolina	30.0
26	Minnesota	29.6
27	Indiana	27.8
28	Hawaii	27.7
29	Oregon	26.9
30	Louisiana	24.6
31	Utah	23.5
32	Virginia	21.9
33	Delaware	20.0
34	Ohio	18.8
35	Michigan	17.8
36	Washington	16.9
37	Colorado	16.1
38	Pennsylvania	15.4
39	Texas	15.2
40	Illinois	15.1
41	Nevada	12.5
42	Arizona	11.8
43	New York	7.9
44	Maryland	7.3
45	Florida	7.2
46	Rhode Island	5.9
47	Connecticut	4.4
48	Massachusetts	4.1
49	California	3.3
50	New Jersey	0.0
	District of Columbia	0.0

Source: U.S. Bureau of the Census
unpublished data

*"Nonmetropolitan" are the areas outside metropolitan areas as defined by the Office of Management and Budget as of June 30, 1999.

Male Population in 2002

National Total = 141,660,978 Males

ALPHA ORDER

RANK	STATE	MALES	% of USA
24	Alabama	2,169,135	1.5%
47	Alaska	333,121	0.2%
18	Arizona	2,725,856	1.9%
33	Arkansas	1,324,566	0.9%
1	California	17,516,452	12.4%
22	Colorado	2,270,151	1.6%
29	Connecticut	1,679,226	1.2%
45	Delaware	392,375	0.3%
4	Florida	8,171,203	5.8%
9	Georgia	4,217,976	3.0%
42	Hawaii	624,098	0.4%
39	Idaho	671,945	0.5%
5	Illinois	6,177,306	4.4%
14	Indiana	3,025,295	2.1%
30	Iowa	1,442,028	1.0%
32	Kansas	1,343,815	0.9%
25	Kentucky	2,001,568	1.4%
23	Louisiana	2,172,234	1.5%
40	Maine	630,137	0.4%
20	Maryland	2,639,040	1.9%
13	Massachusetts	3,102,377	2.2%
8	Michigan	4,934,223	3.5%
21	Minnesota	2,487,372	1.8%
31	Mississippi	1,388,879	1.0%
17	Missouri	2,761,830	1.9%
44	Montana	453,137	0.3%
38	Nebraska	853,495	0.6%
35	Nevada	1,107,082	0.8%
41	New Hampshire	627,621	0.4%
10	New Jersey	4,173,927	2.9%
36	New Mexico	912,159	0.6%
3	New York	9,251,295	6.5%
11	North Carolina	4,081,520	2.9%
48	North Dakota	316,578	0.2%
7	Ohio	5,553,185	3.9%
28	Oklahoma	1,719,873	1.2%
27	Oregon	1,747,855	1.2%
6	Pennsylvania	5,966,139	4.2%
43	Rhode Island	514,729	0.4%
26	South Carolina	1,995,285	1.4%
46	South Dakota	377,961	0.3%
16	Tennessee	2,826,216	2.0%
2	Texas	10,825,924	7.6%
34	Utah	1,161,454	0.8%
49	Vermont	302,244	0.2%
12	Virginia	3,580,749	2.5%
15	Washington	3,023,056	2.1%
37	West Virginia	877,003	0.6%
19	Wisconsin	2,689,757	1.9%
50	Wyoming	250,878	0.2%

RANK ORDER

RANK	STATE	MALES	% of USA
1	California	17,516,452	12.4%
2	Texas	10,825,924	7.6%
3	New York	9,251,295	6.5%
4	Florida	8,171,203	5.8%
5	Illinois	6,177,306	4.4%
6	Pennsylvania	5,966,139	4.2%
7	Ohio	5,553,185	3.9%
8	Michigan	4,934,223	3.5%
9	Georgia	4,217,976	3.0%
10	New Jersey	4,173,927	2.9%
11	North Carolina	4,081,520	2.9%
12	Virginia	3,580,749	2.5%
13	Massachusetts	3,102,377	2.2%
14	Indiana	3,025,295	2.1%
15	Washington	3,023,056	2.1%
16	Tennessee	2,826,216	2.0%
17	Missouri	2,761,830	1.9%
18	Arizona	2,725,856	1.9%
19	Wisconsin	2,689,757	1.9%
20	Maryland	2,639,040	1.9%
21	Minnesota	2,487,372	1.8%
22	Colorado	2,270,151	1.6%
23	Louisiana	2,172,234	1.5%
24	Alabama	2,169,135	1.5%
25	Kentucky	2,001,568	1.4%
26	South Carolina	1,995,285	1.4%
27	Oregon	1,747,855	1.2%
28	Oklahoma	1,719,873	1.2%
29	Connecticut	1,679,226	1.2%
30	Iowa	1,442,028	1.0%
31	Mississippi	1,388,879	1.0%
32	Kansas	1,343,815	0.9%
33	Arkansas	1,324,566	0.9%
34	Utah	1,161,454	0.8%
35	Nevada	1,107,082	0.8%
36	New Mexico	912,159	0.6%
37	West Virginia	877,003	0.6%
38	Nebraska	853,495	0.6%
39	Idaho	671,945	0.5%
40	Maine	630,137	0.4%
41	New Hampshire	627,621	0.4%
42	Hawaii	624,098	0.4%
43	Rhode Island	514,729	0.4%
44	Montana	453,137	0.3%
45	Delaware	392,375	0.3%
46	South Dakota	377,961	0.3%
47	Alaska	333,121	0.2%
48	North Dakota	316,578	0.2%
49	Vermont	302,244	0.2%
50	Wyoming	250,878	0.2%
	District of Columbia	269,648	0.2%

Source: U.S. Bureau of the Census
"Table ST-EST2002-ASRO-01 - State Characteristic Estimates" (September 18, 2003)

Female Population in 2002

National Total = 146,707,720 Females

<table>
<tr><td colspan="4"><u>ALPHA ORDER</u></td><td colspan="4"><u>RANK ORDER</u></td></tr>
<tr><td>RANK</td><td>STATE</td><td>FEMALES</td><td>% of USA</td><td>RANK</td><td>STATE</td><td>FEMALES</td><td>% of USA</td></tr>
<tr><td>22</td><td>Alabama</td><td>2,317,373</td><td>1.6%</td><td>1</td><td>California</td><td>17,599,581</td><td>12.0%</td></tr>
<tr><td>49</td><td>Alaska</td><td>310,665</td><td>0.2%</td><td>2</td><td>Texas</td><td>10,953,969</td><td>7.5%</td></tr>
<tr><td>20</td><td>Arizona</td><td>2,730,597</td><td>1.9%</td><td>3</td><td>New York</td><td>9,906,237</td><td>6.8%</td></tr>
<tr><td>32</td><td>Arkansas</td><td>1,385,513</td><td>0.9%</td><td>4</td><td>Florida</td><td>8,541,946</td><td>5.8%</td></tr>
<tr><td>1</td><td>California</td><td>17,599,581</td><td>12.0%</td><td>5</td><td>Illinois</td><td>6,423,314</td><td>4.4%</td></tr>
<tr><td>24</td><td>Colorado</td><td>2,236,391</td><td>1.5%</td><td>6</td><td>Pennsylvania</td><td>6,368,952</td><td>4.3%</td></tr>
<tr><td>27</td><td>Connecticut</td><td>1,781,277</td><td>1.2%</td><td>7</td><td>Ohio</td><td>5,868,082</td><td>4.0%</td></tr>
<tr><td>45</td><td>Delaware</td><td>415,010</td><td>0.3%</td><td>8</td><td>Michigan</td><td>5,116,223</td><td>3.5%</td></tr>
<tr><td>4</td><td>Florida</td><td>8,541,946</td><td>5.8%</td><td>9</td><td>New Jersey</td><td>4,416,373</td><td>3.0%</td></tr>
<tr><td>10</td><td>Georgia</td><td>4,342,334</td><td>3.0%</td><td>10</td><td>Georgia</td><td>4,342,334</td><td>3.0%</td></tr>
<tr><td>42</td><td>Hawaii</td><td>620,800</td><td>0.4%</td><td>11</td><td>North Carolina</td><td>4,238,626</td><td>2.9%</td></tr>
<tr><td>39</td><td>Idaho</td><td>669,186</td><td>0.5%</td><td>12</td><td>Virginia</td><td>3,712,793</td><td>2.5%</td></tr>
<tr><td>5</td><td>Illinois</td><td>6,423,314</td><td>4.4%</td><td>13</td><td>Massachusetts</td><td>3,325,424</td><td>2.3%</td></tr>
<tr><td>14</td><td>Indiana</td><td>3,133,773</td><td>2.1%</td><td>14</td><td>Indiana</td><td>3,133,773</td><td>2.1%</td></tr>
<tr><td>30</td><td>Iowa</td><td>1,494,732</td><td>1.0%</td><td>15</td><td>Washington</td><td>3,045,940</td><td>2.1%</td></tr>
<tr><td>33</td><td>Kansas</td><td>1,372,069</td><td>0.9%</td><td>16</td><td>Tennessee</td><td>2,971,073</td><td>2.0%</td></tr>
<tr><td>26</td><td>Kentucky</td><td>2,091,323</td><td>1.4%</td><td>17</td><td>Missouri</td><td>2,910,749</td><td>2.0%</td></tr>
<tr><td>23</td><td>Louisiana</td><td>2,310,412</td><td>1.6%</td><td>18</td><td>Maryland</td><td>2,819,097</td><td>1.9%</td></tr>
<tr><td>40</td><td>Maine</td><td>664,327</td><td>0.5%</td><td>19</td><td>Wisconsin</td><td>2,751,439</td><td>1.9%</td></tr>
<tr><td>18</td><td>Maryland</td><td>2,819,097</td><td>1.9%</td><td>20</td><td>Arizona</td><td>2,730,597</td><td>1.9%</td></tr>
<tr><td>13</td><td>Massachusetts</td><td>3,325,424</td><td>2.3%</td><td>21</td><td>Minnesota</td><td>2,532,348</td><td>1.7%</td></tr>
<tr><td>8</td><td>Michigan</td><td>5,116,223</td><td>3.5%</td><td>22</td><td>Alabama</td><td>2,317,373</td><td>1.6%</td></tr>
<tr><td>21</td><td>Minnesota</td><td>2,532,348</td><td>1.7%</td><td>23</td><td>Louisiana</td><td>2,310,412</td><td>1.6%</td></tr>
<tr><td>31</td><td>Mississippi</td><td>1,482,903</td><td>1.0%</td><td>24</td><td>Colorado</td><td>2,236,391</td><td>1.5%</td></tr>
<tr><td>17</td><td>Missouri</td><td>2,910,749</td><td>2.0%</td><td>25</td><td>South Carolina</td><td>2,111,898</td><td>1.4%</td></tr>
<tr><td>44</td><td>Montana</td><td>456,316</td><td>0.3%</td><td>26</td><td>Kentucky</td><td>2,091,323</td><td>1.4%</td></tr>
<tr><td>38</td><td>Nebraska</td><td>875,685</td><td>0.6%</td><td>27</td><td>Connecticut</td><td>1,781,277</td><td>1.2%</td></tr>
<tr><td>35</td><td>Nevada</td><td>1,066,409</td><td>0.7%</td><td>28</td><td>Oklahoma</td><td>1,773,841</td><td>1.2%</td></tr>
<tr><td>41</td><td>New Hampshire</td><td>647,435</td><td>0.4%</td><td>29</td><td>Oregon</td><td>1,773,660</td><td>1.2%</td></tr>
<tr><td>9</td><td>New Jersey</td><td>4,416,373</td><td>3.0%</td><td>30</td><td>Iowa</td><td>1,494,732</td><td>1.0%</td></tr>
<tr><td>36</td><td>New Mexico</td><td>942,900</td><td>0.6%</td><td>31</td><td>Mississippi</td><td>1,482,903</td><td>1.0%</td></tr>
<tr><td>3</td><td>New York</td><td>9,906,237</td><td>6.8%</td><td>32</td><td>Arkansas</td><td>1,385,513</td><td>0.9%</td></tr>
<tr><td>11</td><td>North Carolina</td><td>4,238,626</td><td>2.9%</td><td>33</td><td>Kansas</td><td>1,372,069</td><td>0.9%</td></tr>
<tr><td>47</td><td>North Dakota</td><td>317,532</td><td>0.2%</td><td>34</td><td>Utah</td><td>1,154,802</td><td>0.8%</td></tr>
<tr><td>7</td><td>Ohio</td><td>5,868,082</td><td>4.0%</td><td>35</td><td>Nevada</td><td>1,066,409</td><td>0.7%</td></tr>
<tr><td>28</td><td>Oklahoma</td><td>1,773,841</td><td>1.2%</td><td>36</td><td>New Mexico</td><td>942,900</td><td>0.6%</td></tr>
<tr><td>29</td><td>Oregon</td><td>1,773,660</td><td>1.2%</td><td>37</td><td>West Virginia</td><td>924,870</td><td>0.6%</td></tr>
<tr><td>6</td><td>Pennsylvania</td><td>6,368,952</td><td>4.3%</td><td>38</td><td>Nebraska</td><td>875,685</td><td>0.6%</td></tr>
<tr><td>43</td><td>Rhode Island</td><td>554,996</td><td>0.4%</td><td>39</td><td>Idaho</td><td>669,186</td><td>0.5%</td></tr>
<tr><td>25</td><td>South Carolina</td><td>2,111,898</td><td>1.4%</td><td>40</td><td>Maine</td><td>664,327</td><td>0.5%</td></tr>
<tr><td>46</td><td>South Dakota</td><td>383,102</td><td>0.3%</td><td>41</td><td>New Hampshire</td><td>647,435</td><td>0.4%</td></tr>
<tr><td>16</td><td>Tennessee</td><td>2,971,073</td><td>2.0%</td><td>42</td><td>Hawaii</td><td>620,800</td><td>0.4%</td></tr>
<tr><td>2</td><td>Texas</td><td>10,953,969</td><td>7.5%</td><td>43</td><td>Rhode Island</td><td>554,996</td><td>0.4%</td></tr>
<tr><td>34</td><td>Utah</td><td>1,154,802</td><td>0.8%</td><td>44</td><td>Montana</td><td>456,316</td><td>0.3%</td></tr>
<tr><td>48</td><td>Vermont</td><td>314,348</td><td>0.2%</td><td>45</td><td>Delaware</td><td>415,010</td><td>0.3%</td></tr>
<tr><td>12</td><td>Virginia</td><td>3,712,793</td><td>2.5%</td><td>46</td><td>South Dakota</td><td>383,102</td><td>0.3%</td></tr>
<tr><td>15</td><td>Washington</td><td>3,045,940</td><td>2.1%</td><td>47</td><td>North Dakota</td><td>317,532</td><td>0.2%</td></tr>
<tr><td>37</td><td>West Virginia</td><td>924,870</td><td>0.6%</td><td>48</td><td>Vermont</td><td>314,348</td><td>0.2%</td></tr>
<tr><td>19</td><td>Wisconsin</td><td>2,751,439</td><td>1.9%</td><td>49</td><td>Alaska</td><td>310,665</td><td>0.2%</td></tr>
<tr><td>50</td><td>Wyoming</td><td>247,825</td><td>0.2%</td><td>50</td><td>Wyoming</td><td>247,825</td><td>0.2%</td></tr>
<tr><td></td><td></td><td></td><td></td><td></td><td>District of Columbia</td><td>301,250</td><td>0.2%</td></tr>
</table>

Source: U.S. Bureau of the Census
"Table ST-EST2002-ASRO-01 - State Characteristic Estimates" (September 18, 2003)

Male to Female Ratio in 2002

National Ratio = 96.6 Males per 100 Females

<u>ALPHA ORDER</u>

RANK	STATE	RATIO
46	Alabama	93.6
1	Alaska	107.2
8	Arizona	99.8
33	Arkansas	95.6
10	California	99.5
3	Colorado	101.5
42	Connecticut	94.3
39	Delaware	94.5
31	Florida	95.7
20	Georgia	97.1
6	Hawaii	100.5
7	Idaho	100.4
29	Illinois	96.2
24	Indiana	96.5
24	Iowa	96.5
17	Kansas	97.9
31	Kentucky	95.7
43	Louisiana	94.0
35	Maine	94.9
46	Maryland	93.6
49	Massachusetts	93.3
26	Michigan	96.4
16	Minnesota	98.2
44	Mississippi	93.7
35	Missouri	94.9
11	Montana	99.3
19	Nebraska	97.5
2	Nevada	103.8
22	New Hampshire	96.9
39	New Jersey	94.5
23	New Mexico	96.7
48	New York	93.4
28	North Carolina	96.3
9	North Dakota	99.7
38	Ohio	94.6
21	Oklahoma	97.0
15	Oregon	98.5
44	Pennsylvania	93.7
50	Rhode Island	92.7
39	South Carolina	94.5
14	South Dakota	98.7
34	Tennessee	95.1
13	Texas	98.8
5	Utah	100.6
30	Vermont	96.1
26	Virginia	96.4
12	Washington	99.2
37	West Virginia	94.8
18	Wisconsin	97.8
4	Wyoming	101.2

<u>RANK ORDER</u>

RANK	STATE	RATIO
1	Alaska	107.2
2	Nevada	103.8
3	Colorado	101.5
4	Wyoming	101.2
5	Utah	100.6
6	Hawaii	100.5
7	Idaho	100.4
8	Arizona	99.8
9	North Dakota	99.7
10	California	99.5
11	Montana	99.3
12	Washington	99.2
13	Texas	98.8
14	South Dakota	98.7
15	Oregon	98.5
16	Minnesota	98.2
17	Kansas	97.9
18	Wisconsin	97.8
19	Nebraska	97.5
20	Georgia	97.1
21	Oklahoma	97.0
22	New Hampshire	96.9
23	New Mexico	96.7
24	Indiana	96.5
24	Iowa	96.5
26	Michigan	96.4
26	Virginia	96.4
28	North Carolina	96.3
29	Illinois	96.2
30	Vermont	96.1
31	Florida	95.7
31	Kentucky	95.7
33	Arkansas	95.6
34	Tennessee	95.1
35	Maine	94.9
35	Missouri	94.9
37	West Virginia	94.8
38	Ohio	94.6
39	Delaware	94.5
39	New Jersey	94.5
39	South Carolina	94.5
42	Connecticut	94.3
43	Louisiana	94.0
44	Mississippi	93.7
44	Pennsylvania	93.7
46	Alabama	93.6
46	Maryland	93.6
48	New York	93.4
49	Massachusetts	93.3
50	Rhode Island	92.7
	District of Columbia	89.5

Source: Morgan Quitno Press using data from U.S. Bureau of the Census
"Table ST-EST2002-ASRO-01 - State Characteristic Estimates" (September 18, 2003)

White Population in 2002

National Total = 232,646,166 White Persons*

ALPHA ORDER

RANK	STATE	WHITES	% of USA
24	Alabama	3,206,224	1.4%
49	Alaska	457,047	0.2%
18	Arizona	4,790,117	2.1%
32	Arkansas	2,200,990	0.9%
1	California	27,263,239	11.7%
21	Colorado	4,071,785	1.8%
26	Connecticut	2,959,926	1.3%
45	Delaware	617,680	0.3%
4	Florida	13,502,040	5.8%
11	Georgia	5,782,168	2.5%
50	Hawaii	327,249	0.1%
39	Idaho	1,280,333	0.6%
6	Illinois	10,025,164	4.3%
13	Indiana	5,481,336	2.4%
28	Iowa	2,789,000	1.2%
31	Kansas	2,427,957	1.0%
22	Kentucky	3,703,170	1.6%
27	Louisiana	2,884,468	1.2%
40	Maine	1,256,973	0.5%
23	Maryland	3,587,707	1.5%
12	Massachusetts	5,626,212	2.4%
8	Michigan	8,196,618	3.5%
20	Minnesota	4,539,575	2.0%
35	Mississippi	1,762,785	0.8%
17	Missouri	4,850,303	2.1%
43	Montana	827,903	0.4%
37	Nebraska	1,594,647	0.7%
34	Nevada	1,830,195	0.8%
41	New Hampshire	1,229,961	0.5%
9	New Jersey	6,667,293	2.9%
38	New Mexico	1,577,817	0.7%
3	New York	14,161,142	6.1%
10	North Carolina	6,178,210	2.7%
47	North Dakota	587,085	0.3%
7	Ohio	9,769,002	4.2%
30	Oklahoma	2,744,090	1.2%
25	Oregon	3,204,971	1.4%
5	Pennsylvania	10,678,879	4.6%
42	Rhode Island	957,030	0.4%
29	South Carolina	2,787,151	1.2%
44	South Dakota	676,544	0.3%
19	Tennessee	4,694,327	2.0%
2	Texas	18,216,487	7.8%
33	Utah	2,168,114	0.9%
46	Vermont	597,699	0.3%
14	Virginia	5,403,615	2.3%
15	Washington	5,202,229	2.2%
36	West Virginia	1,713,753	0.7%
16	Wisconsin	4,912,827	2.1%
48	Wyoming	472,890	0.2%

RANK ORDER

RANK	STATE	WHITES	% of USA
1	California	27,263,239	11.7%
2	Texas	18,216,487	7.8%
3	New York	14,161,142	6.1%
4	Florida	13,502,040	5.8%
5	Pennsylvania	10,678,879	4.6%
6	Illinois	10,025,164	4.3%
7	Ohio	9,769,002	4.2%
8	Michigan	8,196,618	3.5%
9	New Jersey	6,667,293	2.9%
10	North Carolina	6,178,210	2.7%
11	Georgia	5,782,168	2.5%
12	Massachusetts	5,626,212	2.4%
13	Indiana	5,481,336	2.4%
14	Virginia	5,403,615	2.3%
15	Washington	5,202,229	2.2%
16	Wisconsin	4,912,827	2.1%
17	Missouri	4,850,303	2.1%
18	Arizona	4,790,117	2.1%
19	Tennessee	4,694,327	2.0%
20	Minnesota	4,539,575	2.0%
21	Colorado	4,071,785	1.8%
22	Kentucky	3,703,170	1.6%
23	Maryland	3,587,707	1.5%
24	Alabama	3,206,224	1.4%
25	Oregon	3,204,971	1.4%
26	Connecticut	2,959,926	1.3%
27	Louisiana	2,884,468	1.2%
28	Iowa	2,789,000	1.2%
29	South Carolina	2,787,151	1.2%
30	Oklahoma	2,744,090	1.2%
31	Kansas	2,427,957	1.0%
32	Arkansas	2,200,990	0.9%
33	Utah	2,168,114	0.9%
34	Nevada	1,830,195	0.8%
35	Mississippi	1,762,785	0.8%
36	West Virginia	1,713,753	0.7%
37	Nebraska	1,594,647	0.7%
38	New Mexico	1,577,817	0.7%
39	Idaho	1,280,333	0.6%
40	Maine	1,256,973	0.5%
41	New Hampshire	1,229,961	0.5%
42	Rhode Island	957,030	0.4%
43	Montana	827,903	0.4%
44	South Dakota	676,544	0.3%
45	Delaware	617,680	0.3%
46	Vermont	597,699	0.3%
47	North Dakota	587,085	0.3%
48	Wyoming	472,890	0.2%
49	Alaska	457,047	0.2%
50	Hawaii	327,249	0.1%
	District of Columbia	202,239	0.1%

Source: U.S. Bureau of the Census
"Population by Race" (http://eire.census.gov/popest/data/states/ST-EST2002-ASRO-03.php)
"White" is defined by Census as a person having origins in any of the original peoples of Europe, North Africa, or the Middle East. There are 196,844,959 non-Hispanic whites. Census states "Race is a self-identification data item in which respondents choose the race or races with which they most closely identify."

Percent of Population White in 2002

National Percent = 80.7% White*

<u>ALPHA ORDER</u>

RANK	STATE	PERCENT
43	Alabama	71.5
44	Alaska	71.0
21	Arizona	87.8
32	Arkansas	81.2
37	California	77.6
14	Colorado	90.4
25	Connecticut	85.5
39	Delaware	76.5
34	Florida	80.8
46	Georgia	67.5
50	Hawaii	26.3
4	Idaho	95.5
35	Illinois	79.6
19	Indiana	89.0
6	Iowa	95.0
18	Kansas	89.4
13	Kentucky	90.5
48	Louisiana	64.3
1	Maine	97.1
47	Maryland	65.7
22	Massachusetts	87.5
31	Michigan	81.6
14	Minnesota	90.4
49	Mississippi	61.4
25	Missouri	85.5
11	Montana	91.0
10	Nebraska	92.2
29	Nevada	84.2
3	New Hampshire	96.5
37	New Jersey	77.6
28	New Mexico	85.1
42	New York	73.9
40	North Carolina	74.3
9	North Dakota	92.6
25	Ohio	85.5
36	Oklahoma	78.5
11	Oregon	91.0
23	Pennsylvania	86.6
17	Rhode Island	89.5
45	South Carolina	67.9
20	South Dakota	88.9
33	Tennessee	81.0
30	Texas	83.6
8	Utah	93.6
2	Vermont	96.9
41	Virginia	74.1
24	Washington	85.7
5	West Virginia	95.1
16	Wisconsin	90.3
7	Wyoming	94.8

<u>RANK ORDER</u>

RANK	STATE	PERCENT
1	Maine	97.1
2	Vermont	96.9
3	New Hampshire	96.5
4	Idaho	95.5
5	West Virginia	95.1
6	Iowa	95.0
7	Wyoming	94.8
8	Utah	93.6
9	North Dakota	92.6
10	Nebraska	92.2
11	Montana	91.0
11	Oregon	91.0
13	Kentucky	90.5
14	Colorado	90.4
14	Minnesota	90.4
16	Wisconsin	90.3
17	Rhode Island	89.5
18	Kansas	89.4
19	Indiana	89.0
20	South Dakota	88.9
21	Arizona	87.8
22	Massachusetts	87.5
23	Pennsylvania	86.6
24	Washington	85.7
25	Connecticut	85.5
25	Missouri	85.5
25	Ohio	85.5
28	New Mexico	85.1
29	Nevada	84.2
30	Texas	83.6
31	Michigan	81.6
32	Arkansas	81.2
33	Tennessee	81.0
34	Florida	80.8
35	Illinois	79.6
36	Oklahoma	78.5
37	California	77.6
37	New Jersey	77.6
39	Delaware	76.5
40	North Carolina	74.3
41	Virginia	74.1
42	New York	73.9
43	Alabama	71.5
44	Alaska	71.0
45	South Carolina	67.9
46	Georgia	67.5
47	Maryland	65.7
48	Louisiana	64.3
49	Mississippi	61.4
50	Hawaii	26.3

	District of Columbia	35.4

Source: Morgan Quitno Press using data from U.S. Bureau of the Census
    "Population by Race" (http://eire.census.gov/popest/data/states/ST-EST2002-ASRO-03.php)
*"White" is defined by Census as a person having origins in any of the original peoples of Europe, North Africa, or the Middle East. Non-Hispanic whites comprise 68.3% of the total population. Census states "Race is a self-identification data item in which respondents choose the race or races with which they most closely identify."

Black Population in 2002

National Total = 36,745,974 Black Persons*

ALPHA ORDER

RANK	STATE	BLACKS	% of USA
16	Alabama	1,181,698	3.2%
41	Alaska	24,105	0.1%
30	Arizona	180,659	0.5%
21	Arkansas	434,579	1.2%
5	California	2,435,921	6.6%
29	Colorado	186,605	0.5%
23	Connecticut	346,397	0.9%
32	Delaware	156,942	0.4%
2	Florida	2,633,683	7.2%
4	Georgia	2,462,419	6.7%
40	Hawaii	27,674	0.1%
45	Idaho	7,093	0.0%
6	Illinois	1,920,014	5.2%
20	Indiana	525,151	1.4%
35	Iowa	65,312	0.2%
31	Kansas	161,052	0.4%
25	Kentucky	306,118	0.8%
9	Louisiana	1,473,150	4.0%
44	Maine	7,812	0.0%
8	Maryland	1,536,785	4.2%
22	Massachusetts	428,263	1.2%
11	Michigan	1,442,625	3.9%
28	Minnesota	190,029	0.5%
17	Mississippi	1,057,123	2.9%
19	Missouri	650,856	1.8%
50	Montana	3,377	0.0%
34	Nebraska	72,079	0.2%
33	Nevada	149,908	0.4%
43	New Hampshire	11,298	0.0%
14	New Jersey	1,249,045	3.4%
39	New Mexico	41,333	0.1%
1	New York	3,408,528	9.3%
7	North Carolina	1,817,634	4.9%
47	North Dakota	4,931	0.0%
12	Ohio	1,331,310	3.6%
26	Oklahoma	271,763	0.7%
37	Oregon	61,836	0.2%
13	Pennsylvania	1,273,637	3.5%
36	Rhode Island	62,506	0.2%
15	South Carolina	1,228,173	3.3%
46	South Dakota	5,892	0.0%
18	Tennessee	964,709	2.6%
3	Texas	2,527,946	6.9%
42	Utah	21,574	0.1%
49	Vermont	3,634	0.0%
10	Virginia	1,458,697	4.0%
27	Washington	209,823	0.6%
38	West Virginia	58,909	0.2%
24	Wisconsin	319,026	0.9%
48	Wyoming	4,489	0.0%

RANK ORDER

RANK	STATE	BLACKS	% of USA
1	New York	3,408,528	9.3%
2	Florida	2,633,683	7.2%
3	Texas	2,527,946	6.9%
4	Georgia	2,462,419	6.7%
5	California	2,435,921	6.6%
6	Illinois	1,920,014	5.2%
7	North Carolina	1,817,634	4.9%
8	Maryland	1,536,785	4.2%
9	Louisiana	1,473,150	4.0%
10	Virginia	1,458,697	4.0%
11	Michigan	1,442,625	3.9%
12	Ohio	1,331,310	3.6%
13	Pennsylvania	1,273,637	3.5%
14	New Jersey	1,249,045	3.4%
15	South Carolina	1,228,173	3.3%
16	Alabama	1,181,698	3.2%
17	Mississippi	1,057,123	2.9%
18	Tennessee	964,709	2.6%
19	Missouri	650,856	1.8%
20	Indiana	525,151	1.4%
21	Arkansas	434,579	1.2%
22	Massachusetts	428,263	1.2%
23	Connecticut	346,397	0.9%
24	Wisconsin	319,026	0.9%
25	Kentucky	306,118	0.8%
26	Oklahoma	271,763	0.7%
27	Washington	209,823	0.6%
28	Minnesota	190,029	0.5%
29	Colorado	186,605	0.5%
30	Arizona	180,659	0.5%
31	Kansas	161,052	0.4%
32	Delaware	156,942	0.4%
33	Nevada	149,908	0.4%
34	Nebraska	72,079	0.2%
35	Iowa	65,312	0.2%
36	Rhode Island	62,506	0.2%
37	Oregon	61,836	0.2%
38	West Virginia	58,909	0.2%
39	New Mexico	41,333	0.1%
40	Hawaii	27,674	0.1%
41	Alaska	24,105	0.1%
42	Utah	21,574	0.1%
43	New Hampshire	11,298	0.0%
44	Maine	7,812	0.0%
45	Idaho	7,093	0.0%
46	South Dakota	5,892	0.0%
47	North Dakota	4,931	0.0%
48	Wyoming	4,489	0.0%
49	Vermont	3,634	0.0%
50	Montana	3,377	0.0%
	District of Columbia	341,852	0.9%

Source: U.S. Bureau of the Census
    "Population by Race" (http://eire.census.gov/popest/data/states/ST-EST2002-ASRO-03.php)
*"Black" is defined by Census as a person having origins in any of the Black racial groups of Africa. Census
states "Race is a self-identification data item in which respondents choose the race or races with which they most
closely identify."

Percent of Population Black in 2002

National Percent = 12.7% Black*

ALPHA ORDER				RANK ORDER		
RANK	STATE	PERCENT		RANK	STATE	PERCENT
6	Alabama	26.3		1	Mississippi	36.8
34	Alaska	3.7		2	Louisiana	32.9
36	Arizona	3.3		3	South Carolina	29.9
12	Arkansas	16.0		4	Georgia	28.8
25	California	6.9		5	Maryland	28.2
32	Colorado	4.1		6	Alabama	26.3
21	Connecticut	10.0		7	North Carolina	21.8
9	Delaware	19.4		8	Virginia	20.0
13	Florida	15.8		9	Delaware	19.4
4	Georgia	28.8		10	New York	17.8
38	Hawaii	2.2		11	Tennessee	16.6
49	Idaho	0.5		12	Arkansas	16.0
14	Illinois	15.2		13	Florida	15.8
22	Indiana	8.5		14	Illinois	15.2
38	Iowa	2.2		15	New Jersey	14.5
28	Kansas	5.9		16	Michigan	14.4
24	Kentucky	7.5		17	Ohio	11.7
2	Louisiana	32.9		18	Texas	11.6
47	Maine	0.6		19	Missouri	11.5
5	Maryland	28.2		20	Pennsylvania	10.3
27	Massachusetts	6.7		21	Connecticut	10.0
16	Michigan	14.4		22	Indiana	8.5
33	Minnesota	3.8		23	Oklahoma	7.8
1	Mississippi	36.8		24	Kentucky	7.5
19	Missouri	11.5		25	California	6.9
50	Montana	0.4		25	Nevada	6.9
31	Nebraska	4.2		27	Massachusetts	6.7
25	Nevada	6.9		28	Kansas	5.9
42	New Hampshire	0.9		28	Wisconsin	5.9
15	New Jersey	14.5		30	Rhode Island	5.8
38	New Mexico	2.2		31	Nebraska	4.2
10	New York	17.8		32	Colorado	4.1
7	North Carolina	21.8		33	Minnesota	3.8
45	North Dakota	0.8		34	Alaska	3.7
17	Ohio	11.7		35	Washington	3.5
23	Oklahoma	7.8		36	Arizona	3.3
41	Oregon	1.8		36	West Virginia	3.3
20	Pennsylvania	10.3		38	Hawaii	2.2
30	Rhode Island	5.8		38	Iowa	2.2
3	South Carolina	29.9		38	New Mexico	2.2
45	South Dakota	0.8		41	Oregon	1.8
11	Tennessee	16.6		42	New Hampshire	0.9
18	Texas	11.6		42	Utah	0.9
42	Utah	0.9		42	Wyoming	0.9
47	Vermont	0.6		45	North Dakota	0.8
8	Virginia	20.0		45	South Dakota	0.8
35	Washington	3.5		47	Maine	0.6
36	West Virginia	3.3		47	Vermont	0.6
28	Wisconsin	5.9		49	Idaho	0.5
42	Wyoming	0.9		50	Montana	0.4

District of Columbia — 59.9

Source: Morgan Quitno Press using data from U.S. Bureau of the Census
"Population by Race" (http://eire.census.gov/popest/data/states/ST-EST2002-ASRO-03.php)
**"Black" is defined by Census as a person having origins in any of the Black racial groups of Africa. Census states "Race is a self-identification data item in which respondents choose the race or races with which they most closely identify."*

Hispanic Population in 2002

National Total = 38,761,301 Hispanics*

ALPHA ORDER

RANK	STATE	HISPANICS	% of USA
38	Alabama	86,322	0.2%
43	Alaska	28,237	0.1%
6	Arizona	1,476,738	3.8%
35	Arkansas	97,073	0.3%
1	California	11,936,707	30.8%
8	Colorado	818,274	2.1%
18	Connecticut	345,424	0.9%
41	Delaware	41,263	0.1%
4	Florida	3,019,305	7.8%
10	Georgia	516,530	1.3%
36	Hawaii	91,092	0.2%
31	Idaho	113,935	0.3%
5	Illinois	1,681,402	4.3%
21	Indiana	236,367	0.6%
37	Iowa	89,627	0.2%
25	Kansas	206,715	0.5%
39	Kentucky	68,838	0.2%
30	Louisiana	114,584	0.3%
48	Maine	10,298	0.0%
20	Maryland	256,510	0.7%
12	Massachusetts	467,276	1.2%
17	Michigan	349,166	0.9%
27	Minnesota	158,752	0.4%
40	Mississippi	42,904	0.1%
29	Missouri	127,322	0.3%
45	Montana	19,092	0.0%
33	Nebraska	103,580	0.3%
13	Nevada	462,690	1.2%
44	New Hampshire	22,479	0.1%
7	New Jersey	1,220,733	3.1%
9	New Mexico	796,171	2.1%
3	New York	3,073,430	7.9%
14	North Carolina	444,463	1.1%
49	North Dakota	8,198	0.0%
22	Ohio	228,959	0.6%
26	Oklahoma	192,769	0.5%
19	Oregon	312,442	0.8%
15	Pennsylvania	415,700	1.1%
34	Rhode Island	98,947	0.3%
32	South Carolina	109,285	0.3%
47	South Dakota	11,486	0.0%
28	Tennessee	139,861	0.4%
2	Texas	7,314,341	18.9%
23	Utah	224,304	0.6%
50	Vermont	5,813	0.0%
16	Virginia	378,060	1.0%
11	Washington	490,448	1.3%
46	West Virginia	12,507	0.0%
24	Wisconsin	209,074	0.5%
42	Wyoming	33,352	0.1%

RANK ORDER

RANK	STATE	HISPANICS	% of USA
1	California	11,936,707	30.8%
2	Texas	7,314,341	18.9%
3	New York	3,073,430	7.9%
4	Florida	3,019,305	7.8%
5	Illinois	1,681,402	4.3%
6	Arizona	1,476,738	3.8%
7	New Jersey	1,220,733	3.1%
8	Colorado	818,274	2.1%
9	New Mexico	796,171	2.1%
10	Georgia	516,530	1.3%
11	Washington	490,448	1.3%
12	Massachusetts	467,276	1.2%
13	Nevada	462,690	1.2%
14	North Carolina	444,463	1.1%
15	Pennsylvania	415,700	1.1%
16	Virginia	378,060	1.0%
17	Michigan	349,166	0.9%
18	Connecticut	345,424	0.9%
19	Oregon	312,442	0.8%
20	Maryland	256,510	0.7%
21	Indiana	236,367	0.6%
22	Ohio	228,959	0.6%
23	Utah	224,304	0.6%
24	Wisconsin	209,074	0.5%
25	Kansas	206,715	0.5%
26	Oklahoma	192,769	0.5%
27	Minnesota	158,752	0.4%
28	Tennessee	139,861	0.4%
29	Missouri	127,322	0.3%
30	Louisiana	114,584	0.3%
31	Idaho	113,935	0.3%
32	South Carolina	109,285	0.3%
33	Nebraska	103,580	0.3%
34	Rhode Island	98,947	0.3%
35	Arkansas	97,073	0.3%
36	Hawaii	91,092	0.2%
37	Iowa	89,627	0.2%
38	Alabama	86,322	0.2%
39	Kentucky	68,838	0.2%
40	Mississippi	42,904	0.1%
41	Delaware	41,263	0.1%
42	Wyoming	33,352	0.1%
43	Alaska	28,237	0.1%
44	New Hampshire	22,479	0.1%
45	Montana	19,092	0.0%
46	West Virginia	12,507	0.0%
47	South Dakota	11,486	0.0%
48	Maine	10,298	0.0%
49	North Dakota	8,198	0.0%
50	Vermont	5,813	0.0%
	District of Columbia	52,456	0.1%

Source: U.S. Bureau of the Census
   "Population by Race" (http://eire.census.gov/popest/data/states/ST-EST2002-ASRO-03.php)
*Persons of Hispanic origin may be of any race. Census states "Race is a self-identification data item in which respondents choose the race or races with which they most closely identify."

Percent of Population Hispanic in 2002

National Percent = 13.4% Hispanic*

ALPHA ORDER

RANK	STATE	PERCENT
42	Alabama	1.9
28	Alaska	4.4
4	Arizona	27.1
31	Arkansas	3.6
2	California	34.0
6	Colorado	18.2
11	Connecticut	10.0
26	Delaware	5.1
7	Florida	18.1
21	Georgia	6.0
18	Hawaii	7.3
15	Idaho	8.5
10	Illinois	13.3
29	Indiana	3.8
35	Iowa	3.1
17	Kansas	7.6
44	Kentucky	1.7
37	Louisiana	2.6
49	Maine	0.8
27	Maryland	4.7
18	Massachusetts	7.3
32	Michigan	3.5
34	Minnesota	3.2
45	Mississippi	1.5
39	Missouri	2.2
40	Montana	2.1
21	Nebraska	6.0
5	Nevada	21.3
43	New Hampshire	1.8
9	New Jersey	14.2
1	New Mexico	42.9
8	New York	16.0
24	North Carolina	5.3
47	North Dakota	1.3
41	Ohio	2.0
23	Oklahoma	5.5
14	Oregon	8.9
33	Pennsylvania	3.4
13	Rhode Island	9.2
36	South Carolina	2.7
45	South Dakota	1.5
38	Tennessee	2.4
3	Texas	33.6
12	Utah	9.7
48	Vermont	0.9
25	Virginia	5.2
16	Washington	8.1
50	West Virginia	0.7
29	Wisconsin	3.8
20	Wyoming	6.7

RANK ORDER

RANK	STATE	PERCENT
1	New Mexico	42.9
2	California	34.0
3	Texas	33.6
4	Arizona	27.1
5	Nevada	21.3
6	Colorado	18.2
7	Florida	18.1
8	New York	16.0
9	New Jersey	14.2
10	Illinois	13.3
11	Connecticut	10.0
12	Utah	9.7
13	Rhode Island	9.2
14	Oregon	8.9
15	Idaho	8.5
16	Washington	8.1
17	Kansas	7.6
18	Hawaii	7.3
18	Massachusetts	7.3
20	Wyoming	6.7
21	Georgia	6.0
21	Nebraska	6.0
23	Oklahoma	5.5
24	North Carolina	5.3
25	Virginia	5.2
26	Delaware	5.1
27	Maryland	4.7
28	Alaska	4.4
29	Indiana	3.8
29	Wisconsin	3.8
31	Arkansas	3.6
32	Michigan	3.5
33	Pennsylvania	3.4
34	Minnesota	3.2
35	Iowa	3.1
36	South Carolina	2.7
37	Louisiana	2.6
38	Tennessee	2.4
39	Missouri	2.2
40	Montana	2.1
41	Ohio	2.0
42	Alabama	1.9
43	New Hampshire	1.8
44	Kentucky	1.7
45	Mississippi	1.5
45	South Dakota	1.5
47	North Dakota	1.3
48	Vermont	0.9
49	Maine	0.8
50	West Virginia	0.7

District of Columbia — 9.2

Source: Morgan Quitno Press using data from U.S. Bureau of the Census
"Population by Race" (http://eire.census.gov/popest/data/states/ST-EST2002-ASRO-03.php)
**Persons of Hispanic origin may be of any race. Census states "Race is a self-identification data item in which respondents choose the race or races with which they most closely identify."*

Asian Population in 2002

National Total = 11,559,022 Asians*

<u>ALPHA ORDER</u>

RANK	STATE	ASIANS	% of USA
33	Alabama	36,486	0.3%
36	Alaska	26,855	0.2%
20	Arizona	110,541	1.0%
38	Arkansas	23,559	0.2%
1	California	4,060,600	35.1%
19	Colorado	111,826	1.0%
23	Connecticut	97,350	0.8%
41	Delaware	19,690	0.2%
8	Florida	315,569	2.7%
14	Georgia	201,226	1.7%
5	Hawaii	538,818	4.7%
43	Idaho	14,044	0.1%
6	Illinois	481,424	4.2%
25	Indiana	69,776	0.6%
30	Iowa	44,486	0.4%
29	Kansas	54,719	0.5%
34	Kentucky	35,182	0.3%
27	Louisiana	62,029	0.5%
45	Maine	10,605	0.1%
12	Maryland	239,830	2.1%
10	Massachusetts	273,019	2.4%
13	Michigan	206,197	1.8%
15	Minnesota	158,940	1.4%
40	Mississippi	21,615	0.2%
24	Missouri	71,883	0.6%
48	Montana	5,383	0.0%
37	Nebraska	26,431	0.2%
21	Nevada	102,534	0.9%
42	New Hampshire	18,864	0.2%
4	New Jersey	544,139	4.7%
39	New Mexico	23,322	0.2%
2	New York	1,206,600	10.4%
17	North Carolina	135,006	1.2%
49	North Dakota	4,401	0.0%
16	Ohio	157,417	1.4%
28	Oklahoma	54,721	0.5%
18	Oregon	115,455	1.0%
11	Pennsylvania	251,874	2.2%
35	Rhode Island	28,096	0.2%
31	South Carolina	42,795	0.4%
47	South Dakota	5,422	0.0%
26	Tennessee	66,729	0.6%
3	Texas	648,519	5.6%
32	Utah	42,144	0.4%
46	Vermont	6,095	0.1%
9	Virginia	297,661	2.6%
7	Washington	356,026	3.1%
44	West Virginia	11,173	0.1%
22	Wisconsin	101,174	0.9%
50	Wyoming	3,288	0.0%

<u>RANK ORDER</u>

RANK	STATE	ASIANS	% of USA
1	California	4,060,600	35.1%
2	New York	1,206,600	10.4%
3	Texas	648,519	5.6%
4	New Jersey	544,139	4.7%
5	Hawaii	538,818	4.7%
6	Illinois	481,424	4.2%
7	Washington	356,026	3.1%
8	Florida	315,569	2.7%
9	Virginia	297,661	2.6%
10	Massachusetts	273,019	2.4%
11	Pennsylvania	251,874	2.2%
12	Maryland	239,830	2.1%
13	Michigan	206,197	1.8%
14	Georgia	201,226	1.7%
15	Minnesota	158,940	1.4%
16	Ohio	157,417	1.4%
17	North Carolina	135,006	1.2%
18	Oregon	115,455	1.0%
19	Colorado	111,826	1.0%
20	Arizona	110,541	1.0%
21	Nevada	102,534	0.9%
22	Wisconsin	101,174	0.9%
23	Connecticut	97,350	0.8%
24	Missouri	71,883	0.6%
25	Indiana	69,776	0.6%
26	Tennessee	66,729	0.6%
27	Louisiana	62,029	0.5%
28	Oklahoma	54,721	0.5%
29	Kansas	54,719	0.5%
30	Iowa	44,486	0.4%
31	South Carolina	42,795	0.4%
32	Utah	42,144	0.4%
33	Alabama	36,486	0.3%
34	Kentucky	35,182	0.3%
35	Rhode Island	28,096	0.2%
36	Alaska	26,855	0.2%
37	Nebraska	26,431	0.2%
38	Arkansas	23,559	0.2%
39	New Mexico	23,322	0.2%
40	Mississippi	21,615	0.2%
41	Delaware	19,690	0.2%
42	New Hampshire	18,864	0.2%
43	Idaho	14,044	0.1%
44	West Virginia	11,173	0.1%
45	Maine	10,605	0.1%
46	Vermont	6,095	0.1%
47	South Dakota	5,422	0.0%
48	Montana	5,383	0.0%
49	North Dakota	4,401	0.0%
50	Wyoming	3,288	0.0%
	District of Columbia	17,484	0.2%

Source: U.S. Bureau of the Census
"Population by Race" (http://eire.census.gov/popest/data/states/ST-EST2002-ASRO-03.php)
**Census states "Race is a self-identification data item in which respondents choose the race or races with which they most closely identify."*

Percent of Population Asian in 2002

National Percent = 4.0% Asian*

<table>
<tr><td colspan="3">ALPHA ORDER</td><td colspan="3">RANK ORDER</td></tr>
<tr><td>RANK</td><td>STATE</td><td>PERCENT</td><td>RANK</td><td>STATE</td><td>PERCENT</td></tr>
<tr><td>43</td><td>Alabama</td><td>0.8</td><td>1</td><td>Hawaii</td><td>43.3</td></tr>
<tr><td>8</td><td>Alaska</td><td>4.2</td><td>2</td><td>California</td><td>11.6</td></tr>
<tr><td>21</td><td>Arizona</td><td>2.0</td><td>3</td><td>New Jersey</td><td>6.3</td></tr>
<tr><td>41</td><td>Arkansas</td><td>0.9</td><td>3</td><td>New York</td><td>6.3</td></tr>
<tr><td>2</td><td>California</td><td>11.6</td><td>5</td><td>Washington</td><td>5.9</td></tr>
<tr><td>17</td><td>Colorado</td><td>2.5</td><td>6</td><td>Nevada</td><td>4.7</td></tr>
<tr><td>15</td><td>Connecticut</td><td>2.8</td><td>7</td><td>Maryland</td><td>4.4</td></tr>
<tr><td>18</td><td>Delaware</td><td>2.4</td><td>8</td><td>Alaska</td><td>4.2</td></tr>
<tr><td>24</td><td>Florida</td><td>1.9</td><td>8</td><td>Massachusetts</td><td>4.2</td></tr>
<tr><td>18</td><td>Georgia</td><td>2.4</td><td>10</td><td>Virginia</td><td>4.1</td></tr>
<tr><td>1</td><td>Hawaii</td><td>43.3</td><td>11</td><td>Illinois</td><td>3.8</td></tr>
<tr><td>38</td><td>Idaho</td><td>1.0</td><td>12</td><td>Oregon</td><td>3.3</td></tr>
<tr><td>11</td><td>Illinois</td><td>3.8</td><td>13</td><td>Minnesota</td><td>3.2</td></tr>
<tr><td>37</td><td>Indiana</td><td>1.1</td><td>14</td><td>Texas</td><td>3.0</td></tr>
<tr><td>29</td><td>Iowa</td><td>1.5</td><td>15</td><td>Connecticut</td><td>2.8</td></tr>
<tr><td>21</td><td>Kansas</td><td>2.0</td><td>16</td><td>Rhode Island</td><td>2.6</td></tr>
<tr><td>41</td><td>Kentucky</td><td>0.9</td><td>17</td><td>Colorado</td><td>2.5</td></tr>
<tr><td>32</td><td>Louisiana</td><td>1.4</td><td>18</td><td>Delaware</td><td>2.4</td></tr>
<tr><td>43</td><td>Maine</td><td>0.8</td><td>18</td><td>Georgia</td><td>2.4</td></tr>
<tr><td>7</td><td>Maryland</td><td>4.4</td><td>20</td><td>Michigan</td><td>2.1</td></tr>
<tr><td>8</td><td>Massachusetts</td><td>4.2</td><td>21</td><td>Arizona</td><td>2.0</td></tr>
<tr><td>20</td><td>Michigan</td><td>2.1</td><td>21</td><td>Kansas</td><td>2.0</td></tr>
<tr><td>13</td><td>Minnesota</td><td>3.2</td><td>21</td><td>Pennsylvania</td><td>2.0</td></tr>
<tr><td>43</td><td>Mississippi</td><td>0.8</td><td>24</td><td>Florida</td><td>1.9</td></tr>
<tr><td>34</td><td>Missouri</td><td>1.3</td><td>24</td><td>Wisconsin</td><td>1.9</td></tr>
<tr><td>49</td><td>Montana</td><td>0.6</td><td>26</td><td>Utah</td><td>1.8</td></tr>
<tr><td>29</td><td>Nebraska</td><td>1.5</td><td>27</td><td>North Carolina</td><td>1.6</td></tr>
<tr><td>6</td><td>Nevada</td><td>4.7</td><td>27</td><td>Oklahoma</td><td>1.6</td></tr>
<tr><td>29</td><td>New Hampshire</td><td>1.5</td><td>29</td><td>Iowa</td><td>1.5</td></tr>
<tr><td>3</td><td>New Jersey</td><td>6.3</td><td>29</td><td>Nebraska</td><td>1.5</td></tr>
<tr><td>34</td><td>New Mexico</td><td>1.3</td><td>29</td><td>New Hampshire</td><td>1.5</td></tr>
<tr><td>3</td><td>New York</td><td>6.3</td><td>32</td><td>Louisiana</td><td>1.4</td></tr>
<tr><td>27</td><td>North Carolina</td><td>1.6</td><td>32</td><td>Ohio</td><td>1.4</td></tr>
<tr><td>46</td><td>North Dakota</td><td>0.7</td><td>34</td><td>Missouri</td><td>1.3</td></tr>
<tr><td>32</td><td>Ohio</td><td>1.4</td><td>34</td><td>New Mexico</td><td>1.3</td></tr>
<tr><td>27</td><td>Oklahoma</td><td>1.6</td><td>36</td><td>Tennessee</td><td>1.2</td></tr>
<tr><td>12</td><td>Oregon</td><td>3.3</td><td>37</td><td>Indiana</td><td>1.1</td></tr>
<tr><td>21</td><td>Pennsylvania</td><td>2.0</td><td>38</td><td>Idaho</td><td>1.0</td></tr>
<tr><td>16</td><td>Rhode Island</td><td>2.6</td><td>38</td><td>South Carolina</td><td>1.0</td></tr>
<tr><td>38</td><td>South Carolina</td><td>1.0</td><td>38</td><td>Vermont</td><td>1.0</td></tr>
<tr><td>46</td><td>South Dakota</td><td>0.7</td><td>41</td><td>Arkansas</td><td>0.9</td></tr>
<tr><td>36</td><td>Tennessee</td><td>1.2</td><td>41</td><td>Kentucky</td><td>0.9</td></tr>
<tr><td>14</td><td>Texas</td><td>3.0</td><td>43</td><td>Alabama</td><td>0.8</td></tr>
<tr><td>26</td><td>Utah</td><td>1.8</td><td>43</td><td>Maine</td><td>0.8</td></tr>
<tr><td>38</td><td>Vermont</td><td>1.0</td><td>43</td><td>Mississippi</td><td>0.8</td></tr>
<tr><td>10</td><td>Virginia</td><td>4.1</td><td>46</td><td>North Dakota</td><td>0.7</td></tr>
<tr><td>5</td><td>Washington</td><td>5.9</td><td>46</td><td>South Dakota</td><td>0.7</td></tr>
<tr><td>49</td><td>West Virginia</td><td>0.6</td><td>46</td><td>Wyoming</td><td>0.7</td></tr>
<tr><td>24</td><td>Wisconsin</td><td>1.9</td><td>49</td><td>Montana</td><td>0.6</td></tr>
<tr><td>46</td><td>Wyoming</td><td>0.7</td><td>49</td><td>West Virginia</td><td>0.6</td></tr>
<tr><td></td><td></td><td></td><td></td><td>District of Columbia</td><td>3.1</td></tr>
</table>

Source: Morgan Quitno Press using data from U.S. Bureau of the Census
"Population by Race" (http://eire.census.gov/popest/data/states/ST-EST2002-ASRO-03.php)
**Census states "Race is a self-identification data item in which respondents choose the race or races with which they most closely identify."*

American Indian Population in 2002

National Total = 2,752,158 American Indians*

ALPHA ORDER

RANK	STATE	INDIANS	% of USA
29	Alabama	22,840	0.8%
8	Alaska	100,494	3.7%
2	Arizona	286,680	10.4%
32	Arkansas	18,477	0.7%
1	California	410,501	14.9%
15	Colorado	51,182	1.9%
41	Connecticut	11,275	0.4%
49	Delaware	3,087	0.1%
10	Florida	66,138	2.4%
24	Georgia	25,991	0.9%
46	Hawaii	3,863	0.1%
31	Idaho	19,268	0.7%
18	Illinois	38,815	1.4%
35	Indiana	17,249	0.6%
42	Iowa	10,058	0.4%
22	Kansas	26,085	0.9%
43	Kentucky	9,437	0.3%
23	Louisiana	26,073	0.9%
44	Maine	7,291	0.3%
34	Maryland	17,379	0.6%
33	Massachusetts	18,354	0.7%
12	Michigan	60,105	2.2%
14	Minnesota	57,340	2.1%
39	Mississippi	12,431	0.5%
25	Missouri	25,953	0.9%
13	Montana	58,048	2.1%
37	Nebraska	16,280	0.6%
20	Nevada	31,281	1.1%
48	New Hampshire	3,213	0.1%
27	New Jersey	25,741	0.9%
4	New Mexico	183,972	6.7%
7	New York	103,337	3.8%
6	North Carolina	106,454	3.9%
21	North Dakota	31,104	1.1%
26	Ohio	25,870	0.9%
3	Oklahoma	278,124	10.1%
17	Oregon	48,341	1.8%
30	Pennsylvania	20,900	0.8%
45	Rhode Island	6,105	0.2%
38	South Carolina	15,069	0.5%
11	South Dakota	63,390	2.3%
36	Tennessee	16,576	0.6%
5	Texas	145,954	5.3%
19	Utah	32,886	1.2%
50	Vermont	2,492	0.1%
28	Virginia	23,778	0.9%
9	Washington	99,446	3.6%
47	West Virginia	3,686	0.1%
16	Wisconsin	50,042	1.8%
40	Wyoming	11,641	0.4%

RANK ORDER

RANK	STATE	INDIANS	% of USA
1	California	410,501	14.9%
2	Arizona	286,680	10.4%
3	Oklahoma	278,124	10.1%
4	New Mexico	183,972	6.7%
5	Texas	145,954	5.3%
6	North Carolina	106,454	3.9%
7	New York	103,337	3.8%
8	Alaska	100,494	3.7%
9	Washington	99,446	3.6%
10	Florida	66,138	2.4%
11	South Dakota	63,390	2.3%
12	Michigan	60,105	2.2%
13	Montana	58,048	2.1%
14	Minnesota	57,340	2.1%
15	Colorado	51,182	1.9%
16	Wisconsin	50,042	1.8%
17	Oregon	48,341	1.8%
18	Illinois	38,815	1.4%
19	Utah	32,886	1.2%
20	Nevada	31,281	1.1%
21	North Dakota	31,104	1.1%
22	Kansas	26,085	0.9%
23	Louisiana	26,073	0.9%
24	Georgia	25,991	0.9%
25	Missouri	25,953	0.9%
26	Ohio	25,870	0.9%
27	New Jersey	25,741	0.9%
28	Virginia	23,778	0.9%
29	Alabama	22,840	0.8%
30	Pennsylvania	20,900	0.8%
31	Idaho	19,268	0.7%
32	Arkansas	18,477	0.7%
33	Massachusetts	18,354	0.7%
34	Maryland	17,379	0.6%
35	Indiana	17,249	0.6%
36	Tennessee	16,576	0.6%
37	Nebraska	16,280	0.6%
38	South Carolina	15,069	0.5%
39	Mississippi	12,431	0.5%
40	Wyoming	11,641	0.4%
41	Connecticut	11,275	0.4%
42	Iowa	10,058	0.4%
43	Kentucky	9,437	0.3%
44	Maine	7,291	0.3%
45	Rhode Island	6,105	0.2%
46	Hawaii	3,863	0.1%
47	West Virginia	3,686	0.1%
48	New Hampshire	3,213	0.1%
49	Delaware	3,087	0.1%
50	Vermont	2,492	0.1%
	District of Columbia	2,062	0.1%

Source: U.S. Bureau of the Census
"Population by Race" (http://eire.census.gov/popest/data/states/ST-EST2002-ASRO-03.php)
**Includes Alaska Native populations. Census states "Race is a self-identification data item in which respondents choose the race or races with which they most closely identify."*

Percent of Population American Indian in 2002

National Percent = 1.0% American Indian*

ALPHA ORDER

RANK	STATE	PERCENT
27	Alabama	0.5
1	Alaska	15.6
6	Arizona	5.3
21	Arkansas	0.7
15	California	1.2
16	Colorado	1.1
35	Connecticut	0.3
30	Delaware	0.4
30	Florida	0.4
35	Georgia	0.3
35	Hawaii	0.3
10	Idaho	1.4
35	Illinois	0.3
35	Indiana	0.3
35	Iowa	0.3
18	Kansas	1.0
47	Kentucky	0.2
23	Louisiana	0.6
23	Maine	0.6
35	Maryland	0.3
35	Massachusetts	0.3
23	Michigan	0.6
16	Minnesota	1.1
30	Mississippi	0.4
27	Missouri	0.5
5	Montana	6.4
19	Nebraska	0.9
10	Nevada	1.4
35	New Hampshire	0.3
35	New Jersey	0.3
2	New Mexico	9.9
27	New York	0.5
14	North Carolina	1.3
7	North Dakota	4.9
47	Ohio	0.2
4	Oklahoma	8.0
10	Oregon	1.4
47	Pennsylvania	0.2
23	Rhode Island	0.6
30	South Carolina	0.4
3	South Dakota	8.3
35	Tennessee	0.3
21	Texas	0.7
10	Utah	1.4
30	Vermont	0.4
35	Virginia	0.3
9	Washington	1.6
47	West Virginia	0.2
19	Wisconsin	0.9
8	Wyoming	2.3

RANK ORDER

RANK	STATE	PERCENT
1	Alaska	15.6
2	New Mexico	9.9
3	South Dakota	8.3
4	Oklahoma	8.0
5	Montana	6.4
6	Arizona	5.3
7	North Dakota	4.9
8	Wyoming	2.3
9	Washington	1.6
10	Idaho	1.4
10	Nevada	1.4
10	Oregon	1.4
10	Utah	1.4
14	North Carolina	1.3
15	California	1.2
16	Colorado	1.1
16	Minnesota	1.1
18	Kansas	1.0
19	Nebraska	0.9
19	Wisconsin	0.9
21	Arkansas	0.7
21	Texas	0.7
23	Louisiana	0.6
23	Maine	0.6
23	Michigan	0.6
23	Rhode Island	0.6
27	Alabama	0.5
27	Missouri	0.5
27	New York	0.5
30	Delaware	0.4
30	Florida	0.4
30	Mississippi	0.4
30	South Carolina	0.4
30	Vermont	0.4
35	Connecticut	0.3
35	Georgia	0.3
35	Hawaii	0.3
35	Illinois	0.3
35	Indiana	0.3
35	Iowa	0.3
35	Maryland	0.3
35	Massachusetts	0.3
35	New Hampshire	0.3
35	New Jersey	0.3
35	Tennessee	0.3
35	Virginia	0.3
47	Kentucky	0.2
47	Ohio	0.2
47	Pennsylvania	0.2
47	West Virginia	0.2

| | District of Columbia | 0.4 |

Mixed Race Population in 2002

National Total = 4,181,064 Mixed Race*

ALPHA ORDER

RANK	STATE	MIXED RACE	% of USA
29	Alabama	37,527	0.9%
34	Alaska	31,672	0.8%
17	Arizona	78,800	1.9%
35	Arkansas	30,283	0.7%
1	California	803,081	19.2%
16	Colorado	78,846	1.9%
28	Connecticut	43,117	1.0%
46	Delaware	9,574	0.2%
5	Florida	183,297	4.4%
14	Georgia	82,389	2.0%
3	Hawaii	237,196	5.7%
38	Idaho	18,705	0.4%
10	Illinois	127,288	3.0%
23	Indiana	62,809	1.5%
36	Iowa	26,514	0.6%
27	Kansas	44,197	1.1%
30	Kentucky	37,110	0.9%
31	Louisiana	35,317	0.8%
44	Maine	11,316	0.3%
20	Maryland	73,351	1.8%
19	Massachusetts	76,857	1.8%
8	Michigan	141,343	3.4%
21	Minnesota	71,283	1.7%
40	Mississippi	16,972	0.4%
22	Missouri	69,776	1.7%
42	Montana	14,183	0.3%
39	Nebraska	18,567	0.4%
26	Nevada	49,725	1.2%
45	New Hampshire	11,240	0.3%
13	New Jersey	97,836	2.3%
37	New Mexico	26,289	0.6%
2	New York	260,268	6.2%
18	North Carolina	77,357	1.9%
49	North Dakota	6,311	0.2%
9	Ohio	134,098	3.2%
7	Oklahoma	141,974	3.4%
15	Oregon	81,368	1.9%
11	Pennsylvania	104,960	2.5%
41	Rhode Island	14,738	0.4%
33	South Carolina	31,824	0.8%
47	South Dakota	9,496	0.2%
25	Tennessee	52,114	1.2%
4	Texas	218,168	5.2%
32	Utah	33,526	0.8%
48	Vermont	6,502	0.2%
12	Virginia	104,695	2.5%
6	Washington	174,535	4.2%
43	West Virginia	13,866	0.3%
24	Wisconsin	55,986	1.3%
50	Wyoming	6,024	0.1%

RANK ORDER

RANK	STATE	MIXED RACE	% of USA
1	California	803,081	19.2%
2	New York	260,268	6.2%
3	Hawaii	237,196	5.7%
4	Texas	218,168	5.2%
5	Florida	183,297	4.4%
6	Washington	174,535	4.2%
7	Oklahoma	141,974	3.4%
8	Michigan	141,343	3.4%
9	Ohio	134,098	3.2%
10	Illinois	127,288	3.0%
11	Pennsylvania	104,960	2.5%
12	Virginia	104,695	2.5%
13	New Jersey	97,836	2.3%
14	Georgia	82,389	2.0%
15	Oregon	81,368	1.9%
16	Colorado	78,846	1.9%
17	Arizona	78,800	1.9%
18	North Carolina	77,357	1.9%
19	Massachusetts	76,857	1.8%
20	Maryland	73,351	1.8%
21	Minnesota	71,283	1.7%
22	Missouri	69,776	1.7%
23	Indiana	62,809	1.5%
24	Wisconsin	55,986	1.3%
25	Tennessee	52,114	1.2%
26	Nevada	49,725	1.2%
27	Kansas	44,197	1.1%
28	Connecticut	43,117	1.0%
29	Alabama	37,527	0.9%
30	Kentucky	37,110	0.9%
31	Louisiana	35,317	0.8%
32	Utah	33,526	0.8%
33	South Carolina	31,824	0.8%
34	Alaska	31,672	0.8%
35	Arkansas	30,283	0.7%
36	Iowa	26,514	0.6%
37	New Mexico	26,289	0.6%
38	Idaho	18,705	0.4%
39	Nebraska	18,567	0.4%
40	Mississippi	16,972	0.4%
41	Rhode Island	14,738	0.4%
42	Montana	14,183	0.3%
43	West Virginia	13,866	0.3%
44	Maine	11,316	0.3%
45	New Hampshire	11,240	0.3%
46	Delaware	9,574	0.2%
47	South Dakota	9,496	0.2%
48	Vermont	6,502	0.2%
49	North Dakota	6,311	0.2%
50	Wyoming	6,024	0.1%
	District of Columbia	6,794	0.2%

Source: U.S. Bureau of the Census
   "Population by Race" (http://eire.census.gov/popest/data/states/ST-EST2002-ASRO-03.php)
Census states "Race is a self-identification data item in which respondents choose the race or races with which they most closely identify." The 2000 Census was the first to allow respondents to identify themselves as one or more races.

Percent of Population of Mixed Race in 2002

National Percent = 1.4% Mixed Race*

<table>
<tr><th colspan="3">ALPHA ORDER</th><th colspan="3">RANK ORDER</th></tr>
<tr><th>RANK</th><th>STATE</th><th>PERCENT</th><th>RANK</th><th>STATE</th><th>PERCENT</th></tr>
<tr><td>46</td><td>Alabama</td><td>0.8</td><td>1</td><td>Hawaii</td><td>19.1</td></tr>
<tr><td>2</td><td>Alaska</td><td>4.9</td><td>2</td><td>Alaska</td><td>4.9</td></tr>
<tr><td>11</td><td>Arizona</td><td>1.4</td><td>3</td><td>Oklahoma</td><td>4.1</td></tr>
<tr><td>28</td><td>Arkansas</td><td>1.1</td><td>4</td><td>Washington</td><td>2.9</td></tr>
<tr><td>5</td><td>California</td><td>2.3</td><td>5</td><td>California</td><td>2.3</td></tr>
<tr><td>8</td><td>Colorado</td><td>1.7</td><td>5</td><td>Nevada</td><td>2.3</td></tr>
<tr><td>21</td><td>Connecticut</td><td>1.2</td><td>5</td><td>Oregon</td><td>2.3</td></tr>
<tr><td>21</td><td>Delaware</td><td>1.2</td><td>8</td><td>Colorado</td><td>1.7</td></tr>
<tr><td>28</td><td>Florida</td><td>1.1</td><td>9</td><td>Kansas</td><td>1.6</td></tr>
<tr><td>33</td><td>Georgia</td><td>1.0</td><td>9</td><td>Montana</td><td>1.6</td></tr>
<tr><td>1</td><td>Hawaii</td><td>19.1</td><td>11</td><td>Arizona</td><td>1.4</td></tr>
<tr><td>11</td><td>Idaho</td><td>1.4</td><td>11</td><td>Idaho</td><td>1.4</td></tr>
<tr><td>33</td><td>Illinois</td><td>1.0</td><td>11</td><td>Michigan</td><td>1.4</td></tr>
<tr><td>33</td><td>Indiana</td><td>1.0</td><td>11</td><td>Minnesota</td><td>1.4</td></tr>
<tr><td>39</td><td>Iowa</td><td>0.9</td><td>11</td><td>New Mexico</td><td>1.4</td></tr>
<tr><td>9</td><td>Kansas</td><td>1.6</td><td>11</td><td>New York</td><td>1.4</td></tr>
<tr><td>39</td><td>Kentucky</td><td>0.9</td><td>11</td><td>Rhode Island</td><td>1.4</td></tr>
<tr><td>46</td><td>Louisiana</td><td>0.8</td><td>11</td><td>Utah</td><td>1.4</td></tr>
<tr><td>39</td><td>Maine</td><td>0.9</td><td>11</td><td>Virginia</td><td>1.4</td></tr>
<tr><td>20</td><td>Maryland</td><td>1.3</td><td>20</td><td>Maryland</td><td>1.3</td></tr>
<tr><td>21</td><td>Massachusetts</td><td>1.2</td><td>21</td><td>Connecticut</td><td>1.2</td></tr>
<tr><td>11</td><td>Michigan</td><td>1.4</td><td>21</td><td>Delaware</td><td>1.2</td></tr>
<tr><td>11</td><td>Minnesota</td><td>1.4</td><td>21</td><td>Massachusetts</td><td>1.2</td></tr>
<tr><td>50</td><td>Mississippi</td><td>0.6</td><td>21</td><td>Missouri</td><td>1.2</td></tr>
<tr><td>21</td><td>Missouri</td><td>1.2</td><td>21</td><td>Ohio</td><td>1.2</td></tr>
<tr><td>9</td><td>Montana</td><td>1.6</td><td>21</td><td>South Dakota</td><td>1.2</td></tr>
<tr><td>28</td><td>Nebraska</td><td>1.1</td><td>21</td><td>Wyoming</td><td>1.2</td></tr>
<tr><td>5</td><td>Nevada</td><td>2.3</td><td>28</td><td>Arkansas</td><td>1.1</td></tr>
<tr><td>39</td><td>New Hampshire</td><td>0.9</td><td>28</td><td>Florida</td><td>1.1</td></tr>
<tr><td>28</td><td>New Jersey</td><td>1.1</td><td>28</td><td>Nebraska</td><td>1.1</td></tr>
<tr><td>11</td><td>New Mexico</td><td>1.4</td><td>28</td><td>New Jersey</td><td>1.1</td></tr>
<tr><td>11</td><td>New York</td><td>1.4</td><td>28</td><td>Vermont</td><td>1.1</td></tr>
<tr><td>39</td><td>North Carolina</td><td>0.9</td><td>33</td><td>Georgia</td><td>1.0</td></tr>
<tr><td>33</td><td>North Dakota</td><td>1.0</td><td>33</td><td>Illinois</td><td>1.0</td></tr>
<tr><td>21</td><td>Ohio</td><td>1.2</td><td>33</td><td>Indiana</td><td>1.0</td></tr>
<tr><td>3</td><td>Oklahoma</td><td>4.1</td><td>33</td><td>North Dakota</td><td>1.0</td></tr>
<tr><td>5</td><td>Oregon</td><td>2.3</td><td>33</td><td>Texas</td><td>1.0</td></tr>
<tr><td>39</td><td>Pennsylvania</td><td>0.9</td><td>33</td><td>Wisconsin</td><td>1.0</td></tr>
<tr><td>11</td><td>Rhode Island</td><td>1.4</td><td>39</td><td>Iowa</td><td>0.9</td></tr>
<tr><td>46</td><td>South Carolina</td><td>0.8</td><td>39</td><td>Kentucky</td><td>0.9</td></tr>
<tr><td>21</td><td>South Dakota</td><td>1.2</td><td>39</td><td>Maine</td><td>0.9</td></tr>
<tr><td>39</td><td>Tennessee</td><td>0.9</td><td>39</td><td>New Hampshire</td><td>0.9</td></tr>
<tr><td>33</td><td>Texas</td><td>1.0</td><td>39</td><td>North Carolina</td><td>0.9</td></tr>
<tr><td>11</td><td>Utah</td><td>1.4</td><td>39</td><td>Pennsylvania</td><td>0.9</td></tr>
<tr><td>28</td><td>Vermont</td><td>1.1</td><td>39</td><td>Tennessee</td><td>0.9</td></tr>
<tr><td>11</td><td>Virginia</td><td>1.4</td><td>46</td><td>Alabama</td><td>0.8</td></tr>
<tr><td>4</td><td>Washington</td><td>2.9</td><td>46</td><td>Louisiana</td><td>0.8</td></tr>
<tr><td>46</td><td>West Virginia</td><td>0.8</td><td>46</td><td>South Carolina</td><td>0.8</td></tr>
<tr><td>33</td><td>Wisconsin</td><td>1.0</td><td>46</td><td>West Virginia</td><td>0.8</td></tr>
<tr><td>21</td><td>Wyoming</td><td>1.2</td><td>50</td><td>Mississippi</td><td>0.6</td></tr>
</table>

District of Columbia   1.2

Source: Morgan Quitno Press using data from U.S. Bureau of the Census
"Population by Race" (http://eire.census.gov/popest/data/states/ST-EST2002-ASRO-03.php)
*Census states "Race is a self-identification data item in which respondents choose the race or races with which they most closely identify." The 2000 Census was the first to allow respondents to identify themselves as one or more races.

Projected State Population in 2025

National Total = 335,050,000

<u>ALPHA ORDER</u>

RANK	STATE	POPULATION	% of USA
22	Alabama	5,224,000	1.6%
45	Alaska	885,000	0.3%
17	Arizona	6,412,000	1.9%
32	Arkansas	3,055,000	0.9%
1	California	49,285,000	14.7%
23	Colorado	5,188,000	1.5%
29	Connecticut	3,739,000	1.1%
47	Delaware	861,000	0.3%
3	Florida	20,710,000	6.2%
9	Georgia	9,869,000	2.9%
39	Hawaii	1,812,000	0.5%
40	Idaho	1,739,000	0.5%
5	Illinois	13,440,000	4.0%
16	Indiana	6,546,000	2.0%
33	Iowa	3,040,000	0.9%
31	Kansas	3,108,000	0.9%
27	Kentucky	4,314,000	1.3%
24	Louisiana	5,133,000	1.5%
42	Maine	1,423,000	0.4%
18	Maryland	6,274,000	1.9%
14	Massachusetts	6,902,000	2.1%
8	Michigan	10,078,000	3.0%
21	Minnesota	5,510,000	1.6%
30	Mississippi	3,142,000	0.9%
19	Missouri	6,250,000	1.9%
44	Montana	1,121,000	0.3%
37	Nebraska	1,930,000	0.6%
36	Nevada	2,312,000	0.7%
41	New Hampshire	1,439,000	0.4%
10	New Jersey	9,558,000	2.9%
35	New Mexico	2,612,000	0.8%
4	New York	19,830,000	5.9%
11	North Carolina	9,349,000	2.8%
48	North Dakota	729,000	0.2%
7	Ohio	11,744,000	3.5%
28	Oklahoma	4,057,000	1.2%
26	Oregon	4,349,000	1.3%
6	Pennsylvania	12,683,000	3.8%
43	Rhode Island	1,141,000	0.3%
25	South Carolina	4,645,000	1.4%
46	South Dakota	866,000	0.3%
15	Tennessee	6,665,000	2.0%
2	Texas	27,183,000	8.1%
34	Utah	2,883,000	0.9%
50	Vermont	678,000	0.2%
12	Virginia	8,466,000	2.5%
13	Washington	7,808,000	2.3%
38	West Virginia	1,845,000	0.6%
20	Wisconsin	5,867,000	1.8%
49	Wyoming	694,000	0.2%

<u>RANK ORDER</u>

RANK	STATE	POPULATION	% of USA
1	California	49,285,000	14.7%
2	Texas	27,183,000	8.1%
3	Florida	20,710,000	6.2%
4	New York	19,830,000	5.9%
5	Illinois	13,440,000	4.0%
6	Pennsylvania	12,683,000	3.8%
7	Ohio	11,744,000	3.5%
8	Michigan	10,078,000	3.0%
9	Georgia	9,869,000	2.9%
10	New Jersey	9,558,000	2.9%
11	North Carolina	9,349,000	2.8%
12	Virginia	8,466,000	2.5%
13	Washington	7,808,000	2.3%
14	Massachusetts	6,902,000	2.1%
15	Tennessee	6,665,000	2.0%
16	Indiana	6,546,000	2.0%
17	Arizona	6,412,000	1.9%
18	Maryland	6,274,000	1.9%
19	Missouri	6,250,000	1.9%
20	Wisconsin	5,867,000	1.8%
21	Minnesota	5,510,000	1.6%
22	Alabama	5,224,000	1.6%
23	Colorado	5,188,000	1.5%
24	Louisiana	5,133,000	1.5%
25	South Carolina	4,645,000	1.4%
26	Oregon	4,349,000	1.3%
27	Kentucky	4,314,000	1.3%
28	Oklahoma	4,057,000	1.2%
29	Connecticut	3,739,000	1.1%
30	Mississippi	3,142,000	0.9%
31	Kansas	3,108,000	0.9%
32	Arkansas	3,055,000	0.9%
33	Iowa	3,040,000	0.9%
34	Utah	2,883,000	0.9%
35	New Mexico	2,612,000	0.8%
36	Nevada	2,312,000	0.7%
37	Nebraska	1,930,000	0.6%
38	West Virginia	1,845,000	0.6%
39	Hawaii	1,812,000	0.5%
40	Idaho	1,739,000	0.5%
41	New Hampshire	1,439,000	0.4%
42	Maine	1,423,000	0.4%
43	Rhode Island	1,141,000	0.3%
44	Montana	1,121,000	0.3%
45	Alaska	885,000	0.3%
46	South Dakota	866,000	0.3%
47	Delaware	861,000	0.3%
48	North Dakota	729,000	0.2%
49	Wyoming	694,000	0.2%
50	Vermont	678,000	0.2%
	District of Columbia	655,000	0.2%

Source: U.S. Bureau of the Census
   "Projections of Total Population of States: 1995-2025 "
   (http://www.census.gov/population/projections/state/stpjpop.txt)

Projected Percent Change in Population: 2000 to 2025

National Projected Percent Change = 19.1% Increase*

<u>ALPHA ORDER</u>

RANK	STATE	PERCENT CHANGE
19	Alabama	17.5
4	Alaska	41.2
12	Arizona	25.0
28	Arkansas	14.3
2	California	45.5
14	Colorado	20.6
38	Connecticut	9.8
37	Delaware	9.9
9	Florida	29.6
14	Georgia	20.6
1	Hawaii	49.6
6	Idaho	34.4
42	Illinois	8.2
43	Indiana	7.7
46	Iowa	3.9
25	Kansas	15.6
44	Kentucky	6.7
26	Louisiana	14.9
34	Maine	11.6
17	Maryland	18.5
41	Massachusetts	8.7
50	Michigan	1.4
32	Minnesota	12.0
36	Mississippi	10.5
33	Missouri	11.7
13	Montana	24.3
31	Nebraska	12.8
24	Nevada	15.7
21	New Hampshire	16.4
29	New Jersey	13.6
3	New Mexico	43.6
45	New York	4.5
22	North Carolina	16.1
30	North Dakota	13.5
47	Ohio	3.4
18	Oklahoma	17.6
11	Oregon	27.1
48	Pennsylvania	3.3
40	Rhode Island	8.8
23	South Carolina	15.8
27	South Dakota	14.7
20	Tennessee	17.2
8	Texas	30.4
10	Utah	29.1
35	Vermont	11.4
16	Virginia	19.6
7	Washington	32.5
49	West Virginia	2.0
39	Wisconsin	9.4
5	Wyoming	40.5

<u>RANK ORDER</u>

RANK	STATE	PERCENT CHANGE
1	Hawaii	49.6
2	California	45.5
3	New Mexico	43.6
4	Alaska	41.2
5	Wyoming	40.5
6	Idaho	34.4
7	Washington	32.5
8	Texas	30.4
9	Florida	29.6
10	Utah	29.1
11	Oregon	27.1
12	Arizona	25.0
13	Montana	24.3
14	Colorado	20.6
14	Georgia	20.6
16	Virginia	19.6
17	Maryland	18.5
18	Oklahoma	17.6
19	Alabama	17.5
20	Tennessee	17.2
21	New Hampshire	16.4
22	North Carolina	16.1
23	South Carolina	15.8
24	Nevada	15.7
25	Kansas	15.6
26	Louisiana	14.9
27	South Dakota	14.7
28	Arkansas	14.3
29	New Jersey	13.6
30	North Dakota	13.5
31	Nebraska	12.8
32	Minnesota	12.0
33	Missouri	11.7
34	Maine	11.6
35	Vermont	11.4
36	Mississippi	10.5
37	Delaware	9.9
38	Connecticut	9.8
39	Wisconsin	9.4
40	Rhode Island	8.8
41	Massachusetts	8.7
42	Illinois	8.2
43	Indiana	7.7
44	Kentucky	6.7
45	New York	4.5
46	Iowa	3.9
47	Ohio	3.4
48	Pennsylvania	3.3
49	West Virginia	2.0
50	Michigan	1.4

District of Columbia 14.5

Source: Morgan Quitno Press using data from U.S. Bureau of the Census
"Projections of Total Population of States: 1995-2025 " (www.census.gov/population/projections/state/stpjpop.txt)
and "First Census 2000 Results" (December 28, 2000, http://www.census.gov/main/www/cen2000.html)

Projected Percent of Population White in 2025

National Projected Percent = 78.3% White*

<u>ALPHA ORDER</u>

RANK	STATE	PERCENT
40	Alabama	72.4
46	Alaska	63.1
19	Arizona	87.3
28	Arkansas	83.0
37	California	73.8
14	Colorado	89.1
30	Connecticut	82.0
38	Delaware	73.5
33	Florida	79.9
45	Georgia	63.7
50	Hawaii	31.2
4	Idaho	95.5
35	Illinois	78.2
15	Indiana	88.8
6	Iowa	94.0
16	Kansas	88.2
11	Kentucky	90.8
48	Louisiana	61.3
1	Maine	97.5
49	Maryland	60.2
29	Massachusetts	82.5
34	Michigan	79.5
17	Minnesota	88.1
47	Mississippi	61.7
23	Missouri	85.1
12	Montana	89.8
10	Nebraska	90.9
26	Nevada	83.6
3	New Hampshire	96.5
41	New Jersey	71.3
25	New Mexico	83.9
43	New York	69.7
39	North Carolina	73.0
13	North Dakota	89.7
27	Ohio	83.5
36	Oklahoma	78.0
9	Oregon	91.1
24	Pennsylvania	84.5
21	Rhode Island	85.6
44	South Carolina	68.3
18	South Dakota	87.6
32	Tennessee	80.0
31	Texas	81.3
8	Utah	92.7
2	Vermont	97.2
42	Virginia	70.3
22	Washington	85.3
5	West Virginia	95.1
20	Wisconsin	86.8
7	Wyoming	93.4

<u>RANK ORDER</u>

RANK	STATE	PERCENT
1	Maine	97.5
2	Vermont	97.2
3	New Hampshire	96.5
4	Idaho	95.5
5	West Virginia	95.1
6	Iowa	94.0
7	Wyoming	93.4
8	Utah	92.7
9	Oregon	91.1
10	Nebraska	90.9
11	Kentucky	90.8
12	Montana	89.8
13	North Dakota	89.7
14	Colorado	89.1
15	Indiana	88.8
16	Kansas	88.2
17	Minnesota	88.1
18	South Dakota	87.6
19	Arizona	87.3
20	Wisconsin	86.8
21	Rhode Island	85.6
22	Washington	85.3
23	Missouri	85.1
24	Pennsylvania	84.5
25	New Mexico	83.9
26	Nevada	83.6
27	Ohio	83.5
28	Arkansas	83.0
29	Massachusetts	82.5
30	Connecticut	82.0
31	Texas	81.3
32	Tennessee	80.0
33	Florida	79.9
34	Michigan	79.5
35	Illinois	78.2
36	Oklahoma	78.0
37	California	73.8
38	Delaware	73.5
39	North Carolina	73.0
40	Alabama	72.4
41	New Jersey	71.3
42	Virginia	70.3
43	New York	69.7
44	South Carolina	68.3
45	Georgia	63.7
46	Alaska	63.1
47	Mississippi	61.7
48	Louisiana	61.3
49	Maryland	60.2
50	Hawaii	31.2
	District of Columbia	36.5

Source: Morgan Quitno Press using data from U.S. Bureau of the Census
"Projected State Populations, by Sex, Race, and Hispanic Origin: 1995-2025 "
(http://www.census.gov/population/projections/state/stpjrace.txt)
**"White" is defined by Census as a person having origins in any of the original peoples of Europe, North Africa, or the Middle East.*

Projected Percent of Population Black in 2025

National Projected Percent = 14.2% Black*

ALPHA ORDER

RANK	STATE	PERCENT
6	Alabama	26.1
34	Alaska	4.4
34	Arizona	4.4
16	Arkansas	15.3
30	California	7.0
31	Colorado	6.0
19	Connecticut	13.1
9	Delaware	23.1
13	Florida	17.2
3	Georgia	33.7
40	Hawaii	2.3
44	Idaho	1.0
15	Illinois	16.2
24	Indiana	9.4
39	Iowa	3.0
27	Kansas	8.0
27	Kentucky	8.0
2	Louisiana	36.0
49	Maine	0.6
4	Maryland	33.0
23	Massachusetts	9.5
14	Michigan	16.9
33	Minnesota	5.1
1	Mississippi	37.0
20	Missouri	12.8
50	Montana	0.5
32	Nebraska	5.6
25	Nevada	8.7
44	New Hampshire	1.0
12	New Jersey	18.0
38	New Mexico	3.4
10	New York	20.4
7	North Carolina	24.0
48	North Dakota	0.7
18	Ohio	14.1
22	Oklahoma	10.7
40	Oregon	2.3
21	Pennsylvania	12.1
27	Rhode Island	8.0
5	South Carolina	30.2
47	South Dakota	0.8
11	Tennessee	18.3
17	Texas	14.2
43	Utah	1.4
46	Vermont	0.9
8	Virginia	23.3
36	Washington	3.6
36	West Virginia	3.6
26	Wisconsin	8.5
42	Wyoming	1.6

RANK ORDER

RANK	STATE	PERCENT
1	Mississippi	37.0
2	Louisiana	36.0
3	Georgia	33.7
4	Maryland	33.0
5	South Carolina	30.2
6	Alabama	26.1
7	North Carolina	24.0
8	Virginia	23.3
9	Delaware	23.1
10	New York	20.4
11	Tennessee	18.3
12	New Jersey	18.0
13	Florida	17.2
14	Michigan	16.9
15	Illinois	16.2
16	Arkansas	15.3
17	Texas	14.2
18	Ohio	14.1
19	Connecticut	13.1
20	Missouri	12.8
21	Pennsylvania	12.1
22	Oklahoma	10.7
23	Massachusetts	9.5
24	Indiana	9.4
25	Nevada	8.7
26	Wisconsin	8.5
27	Kansas	8.0
27	Kentucky	8.0
27	Rhode Island	8.0
30	California	7.0
31	Colorado	6.0
32	Nebraska	5.6
33	Minnesota	5.1
34	Alaska	4.4
34	Arizona	4.4
36	Washington	3.6
36	West Virginia	3.6
38	New Mexico	3.4
39	Iowa	3.0
40	Hawaii	2.3
40	Oregon	2.3
42	Wyoming	1.6
43	Utah	1.4
44	Idaho	1.0
44	New Hampshire	1.0
46	Vermont	0.9
47	South Dakota	0.8
48	North Dakota	0.7
49	Maine	0.6
50	Montana	0.5
	District of Columbia	58.9

Source: Morgan Quitno Press using data from U.S. Bureau of the Census
"Projected State Populations, by Sex, Race, and Hispanic Origin: 1995-2025 "
(http://www.census.gov/population/projections/state/stpjrace.txt)
*"Black" is defined by Census as a person having origins in any of the Black racial groups of Africa.

Projected Percent of Population Hispanic in 2025

National Projected Percent = 17.6% Hispanic*

<u>ALPHA ORDER</u>

RANK	STATE	PERCENT
49	Alabama	1.2
22	Alaska	6.7
4	Arizona	32.2
39	Arkansas	2.2
2	California	43.1
8	Colorado	20.6
11	Connecticut	15.4
26	Delaware	5.6
6	Florida	23.9
32	Georgia	3.5
16	Hawaii	10.3
14	Idaho	11.8
10	Illinois	16.9
31	Indiana	3.7
35	Iowa	3.2
20	Kansas	9.0
47	Kentucky	1.3
28	Louisiana	4.4
46	Maine	1.4
21	Maryland	7.0
13	Massachusetts	13.5
29	Michigan	4.3
32	Minnesota	3.5
49	Mississippi	1.2
36	Missouri	2.8
32	Montana	3.5
25	Nebraska	5.8
5	Nevada	25.2
38	New Hampshire	2.4
9	New Jersey	19.5
1	New Mexico	47.5
7	New York	21.7
39	North Carolina	2.2
41	North Dakota	1.9
37	Ohio	2.7
24	Oklahoma	6.0
18	Oregon	9.9
27	Pennsylvania	5.0
11	Rhode Island	15.4
43	South Carolina	1.7
44	South Dakota	1.6
44	Tennessee	1.6
3	Texas	37.6
19	Utah	9.2
42	Vermont	1.8
23	Virginia	6.4
17	Washington	10.2
47	West Virginia	1.3
30	Wisconsin	4.0
15	Wyoming	10.7

<u>RANK ORDER</u>

RANK	STATE	PERCENT
1	New Mexico	47.5
2	California	43.1
3	Texas	37.6
4	Arizona	32.2
5	Nevada	25.2
6	Florida	23.9
7	New York	21.7
8	Colorado	20.6
9	New Jersey	19.5
10	Illinois	16.9
11	Connecticut	15.4
11	Rhode Island	15.4
13	Massachusetts	13.5
14	Idaho	11.8
15	Wyoming	10.7
16	Hawaii	10.3
17	Washington	10.2
18	Oregon	9.9
19	Utah	9.2
20	Kansas	9.0
21	Maryland	7.0
22	Alaska	6.7
23	Virginia	6.4
24	Oklahoma	6.0
25	Nebraska	5.8
26	Delaware	5.6
27	Pennsylvania	5.0
28	Louisiana	4.4
29	Michigan	4.3
30	Wisconsin	4.0
31	Indiana	3.7
32	Georgia	3.5
32	Minnesota	3.5
32	Montana	3.5
35	Iowa	3.2
36	Missouri	2.8
37	Ohio	2.7
38	New Hampshire	2.4
39	Arkansas	2.2
39	North Carolina	2.2
41	North Dakota	1.9
42	Vermont	1.8
43	South Carolina	1.7
44	South Dakota	1.6
44	Tennessee	1.6
46	Maine	1.4
47	Kentucky	1.3
47	West Virginia	1.3
49	Alabama	1.2
49	Mississippi	1.2
	District of Columbia	12.2

Source: Morgan Quitno Press using data from U.S. Bureau of the Census
   "Projected State Populations, by Sex, Race, and Hispanic Origin: 1995-2025 "
   (http://www.census.gov/population/projections/state/stpjrace.txt)
*Persons of Hispanic origin may be of any race.

Projected Percent of Population Asian in 2025

National Percent = 6.6% Asian*

<u>ALPHA ORDER</u>

RANK	STATE	PERCENT
45	Alabama	1.1
2	Alaska	21.8
22	Arizona	3.0
48	Arkansas	1.0
3	California	18.4
18	Colorado	3.8
15	Connecticut	4.6
21	Delaware	3.1
25	Florida	2.5
25	Georgia	2.5
1	Hawaii	66.1
35	Idaho	1.7
12	Illinois	5.4
39	Indiana	1.5
25	Iowa	2.5
24	Kansas	2.7
45	Kentucky	1.1
28	Louisiana	2.2
42	Maine	1.3
8	Maryland	6.5
7	Massachusetts	7.7
23	Michigan	2.9
13	Minnesota	5.0
48	Mississippi	1.0
37	Missouri	1.6
43	Montana	1.2
28	Nebraska	2.2
9	Nevada	6.1
32	New Hampshire	2.1
4	New Jersey	10.4
28	New Mexico	2.2
5	New York	9.5
34	North Carolina	1.9
40	North Dakota	1.4
32	Ohio	2.1
28	Oklahoma	2.2
14	Oregon	4.9
20	Pennsylvania	3.2
11	Rhode Island	5.5
43	South Carolina	1.2
48	South Dakota	1.0
40	Tennessee	1.4
16	Texas	3.9
16	Utah	3.9
37	Vermont	1.6
9	Virginia	6.1
6	Washington	9.1
45	West Virginia	1.1
19	Wisconsin	3.6
35	Wyoming	1.7

<u>RANK ORDER</u>

RANK	STATE	PERCENT
1	Hawaii	66.1
2	Alaska	21.8
3	California	18.4
4	New Jersey	10.4
5	New York	9.5
6	Washington	9.1
7	Massachusetts	7.7
8	Maryland	6.5
9	Nevada	6.1
9	Virginia	6.1
11	Rhode Island	5.5
12	Illinois	5.4
13	Minnesota	5.0
14	Oregon	4.9
15	Connecticut	4.6
16	Texas	3.9
16	Utah	3.9
18	Colorado	3.8
19	Wisconsin	3.6
20	Pennsylvania	3.2
21	Delaware	3.1
22	Arizona	3.0
23	Michigan	2.9
24	Kansas	2.7
25	Florida	2.5
25	Georgia	2.5
25	Iowa	2.5
28	Louisiana	2.2
28	Nebraska	2.2
28	New Mexico	2.2
28	Oklahoma	2.2
32	New Hampshire	2.1
32	Ohio	2.1
34	North Carolina	1.9
35	Idaho	1.7
35	Wyoming	1.7
37	Missouri	1.6
37	Vermont	1.6
39	Indiana	1.5
40	North Dakota	1.4
40	Tennessee	1.4
42	Maine	1.3
43	Montana	1.2
43	South Carolina	1.2
45	Alabama	1.1
45	Kentucky	1.1
45	West Virginia	1.1
48	Arkansas	1.0
48	Mississippi	1.0
48	South Dakota	1.0

District of Columbia — 4.4

Source: Morgan Quitno Press using data from U.S. Bureau of the Census
"Projected State Populations, by Sex, Race, and Hispanic Origin: 1995-2025 "
(http://www.census.gov/population/projections/state/stpjrace.txt)
*Includes Pacific Islanders.

Projected Percent of Population American Indian in 2025

National Projected Percent = 1.0% American Indian*

<u>ALPHA ORDER</u>

RANK	STATE	PERCENT
30	Alabama	0.4
1	Alaska	10.7
7	Arizona	5.2
22	Arkansas	0.7
21	California	0.8
16	Colorado	1.2
33	Connecticut	0.3
45	Delaware	0.2
30	Florida	0.4
45	Georgia	0.2
30	Hawaii	0.4
12	Idaho	1.8
33	Illinois	0.3
33	Indiana	0.3
25	Iowa	0.5
16	Kansas	1.2
45	Kentucky	0.2
25	Louisiana	0.5
25	Maine	0.5
33	Maryland	0.3
33	Massachusetts	0.3
22	Michigan	0.7
10	Minnesota	1.9
33	Mississippi	0.3
25	Missouri	0.5
5	Montana	8.2
15	Nebraska	1.3
14	Nevada	1.5
33	New Hampshire	0.3
33	New Jersey	0.3
2	New Mexico	10.5
25	New York	0.5
16	North Carolina	1.2
6	North Dakota	8.1
33	Ohio	0.3
4	Oklahoma	9.0
13	Oregon	1.7
45	Pennsylvania	0.2
20	Rhode Island	0.9
45	South Carolina	0.2
3	South Dakota	10.3
33	Tennessee	0.3
24	Texas	0.6
9	Utah	2.0
33	Vermont	0.3
33	Virginia	0.3
10	Washington	1.9
50	West Virginia	0.1
19	Wisconsin	1.1
8	Wyoming	3.9

<u>RANK ORDER</u>

RANK	STATE	PERCENT
1	Alaska	10.7
2	New Mexico	10.5
3	South Dakota	10.3
4	Oklahoma	9.0
5	Montana	8.2
6	North Dakota	8.1
7	Arizona	5.2
8	Wyoming	3.9
9	Utah	2.0
10	Minnesota	1.9
10	Washington	1.9
12	Idaho	1.8
13	Oregon	1.7
14	Nevada	1.5
15	Nebraska	1.3
16	Colorado	1.2
16	Kansas	1.2
16	North Carolina	1.2
19	Wisconsin	1.1
20	Rhode Island	0.9
21	California	0.8
22	Arkansas	0.7
22	Michigan	0.7
24	Texas	0.6
25	Iowa	0.5
25	Louisiana	0.5
25	Maine	0.5
25	Missouri	0.5
25	New York	0.5
30	Alabama	0.4
30	Florida	0.4
30	Hawaii	0.4
33	Connecticut	0.3
33	Illinois	0.3
33	Indiana	0.3
33	Maryland	0.3
33	Massachusetts	0.3
33	Mississippi	0.3
33	New Hampshire	0.3
33	New Jersey	0.3
33	Ohio	0.3
33	Tennessee	0.3
33	Vermont	0.3
33	Virginia	0.3
45	Delaware	0.2
45	Georgia	0.2
45	Kentucky	0.2
45	Pennsylvania	0.2
45	South Carolina	0.2
50	West Virginia	0.1
	District of Columbia	0.0

Source: Morgan Quitno Press using data from U.S. Bureau of the Census
"Projected State Populations, by Sex, Race, and Hispanic Origin: 1995-2025 "
(http://www.census.gov/population/projections/state/stpjrace.txt)
**Includes Eskimo and Aleut populations.*

Median Age in 2002

National Median = 35.9 Years Old

<u>ALPHA ORDER</u>

RANK	STATE	MEDIAN AGE
29	Alabama	36.4
44	Alaska	34.2
44	Arizona	34.2
22	Arkansas	36.7
48	California	33.6
41	Colorado	34.7
8	Connecticut	38.1
18	Delaware	36.9
4	Florida	39.3
47	Georgia	33.7
14	Hawaii	37.4
46	Idaho	33.8
39	Illinois	35.1
38	Indiana	35.6
9	Iowa	37.9
34	Kansas	35.8
16	Kentucky	37.2
42	Louisiana	34.6
1	Maine	40.0
23	Maryland	36.6
13	Massachusetts	37.5
30	Michigan	36.2
30	Minnesota	36.2
43	Mississippi	34.4
19	Missouri	36.8
4	Montana	39.3
34	Nebraska	35.8
40	Nevada	35.0
7	New Hampshire	38.2
12	New Jersey	37.6
37	New Mexico	35.7
25	New York	36.5
34	North Carolina	35.8
14	North Dakota	37.4
25	Ohio	36.5
32	Oklahoma	36.1
19	Oregon	36.8
6	Pennsylvania	38.9
9	Rhode Island	37.9
25	South Carolina	36.5
23	South Dakota	36.6
19	Tennessee	36.8
49	Texas	32.8
50	Utah	28.1
3	Vermont	39.4
25	Virginia	36.5
32	Washington	36.1
1	West Virginia	40.0
17	Wisconsin	37.0
11	Wyoming	37.8

<u>RANK ORDER</u>

RANK	STATE	MEDIAN AGE
1	Maine	40.0
1	West Virginia	40.0
3	Vermont	39.4
4	Florida	39.3
4	Montana	39.3
6	Pennsylvania	38.9
7	New Hampshire	38.2
8	Connecticut	38.1
9	Iowa	37.9
9	Rhode Island	37.9
11	Wyoming	37.8
12	New Jersey	37.6
13	Massachusetts	37.5
14	Hawaii	37.4
14	North Dakota	37.4
16	Kentucky	37.2
17	Wisconsin	37.0
18	Delaware	36.9
19	Missouri	36.8
19	Oregon	36.8
19	Tennessee	36.8
22	Arkansas	36.7
23	Maryland	36.6
23	South Dakota	36.6
25	New York	36.5
25	Ohio	36.5
25	South Carolina	36.5
25	Virginia	36.5
29	Alabama	36.4
30	Michigan	36.2
30	Minnesota	36.2
32	Oklahoma	36.1
32	Washington	36.1
34	Kansas	35.8
34	Nebraska	35.8
34	North Carolina	35.8
37	New Mexico	35.7
38	Indiana	35.6
39	Illinois	35.1
40	Nevada	35.0
41	Colorado	34.7
42	Louisiana	34.6
43	Mississippi	34.4
44	Alaska	34.2
44	Arizona	34.2
46	Idaho	33.8
47	Georgia	33.7
48	California	33.6
49	Texas	32.8
50	Utah	28.1
	District of Columbia	35.9

Source: U.S. Bureau of the Census
"2002 American Community Survey"

Population Under 5 Years Old in 2002

National Total = 19,609,147

<u>ALPHA ORDER</u>

RANK	STATE	POPULATION	% of USA
24	Alabama	298,697	1.5%
47	Alaska	49,477	0.3%
14	Arizona	419,740	2.1%
33	Arkansas	183,668	0.9%
1	California	2,544,993	13.0%
22	Colorado	320,757	1.6%
29	Connecticut	223,611	1.1%
45	Delaware	51,293	0.3%
4	Florida	1,035,177	5.3%
9	Georgia	648,667	3.3%
40	Hawaii	83,507	0.4%
38	Idaho	99,950	0.5%
5	Illinois	889,948	4.5%
13	Indiana	429,345	2.2%
34	Iowa	180,971	0.9%
32	Kansas	187,892	1.0%
26	Kentucky	253,219	1.3%
21	Louisiana	322,952	1.6%
42	Maine	65,113	0.3%
19	Maryland	365,545	1.9%
16	Massachusetts	387,614	2.0%
8	Michigan	663,586	3.4%
23	Minnesota	318,995	1.6%
31	Mississippi	209,456	1.1%
18	Missouri	367,340	1.9%
44	Montana	52,793	0.3%
37	Nebraska	117,787	0.6%
35	Nevada	160,805	0.8%
41	New Hampshire	73,407	0.4%
11	New Jersey	567,489	2.9%
36	New Mexico	132,123	0.7%
3	New York	1,228,144	6.3%
10	North Carolina	585,105	3.0%
48	North Dakota	36,525	0.2%
6	Ohio	764,553	3.9%
27	Oklahoma	238,637	1.2%
28	Oregon	226,208	1.2%
7	Pennsylvania	712,121	3.6%
43	Rhode Island	60,340	0.3%
25	South Carolina	266,500	1.4%
46	South Dakota	50,879	0.3%
17	Tennessee	383,745	2.0%
2	Texas	1,718,456	8.8%
30	Utah	218,989	1.1%
49	Vermont	31,681	0.2%
12	Virginia	485,338	2.5%
15	Washington	396,508	2.0%
39	West Virginia	96,979	0.5%
20	Wisconsin	338,384	1.7%
50	Wyoming	30,231	0.2%

<u>RANK ORDER</u>

RANK	STATE	POPULATION	% of USA
1	California	2,544,993	13.0%
2	Texas	1,718,456	8.8%
3	New York	1,228,144	6.3%
4	Florida	1,035,177	5.3%
5	Illinois	889,948	4.5%
6	Ohio	764,553	3.9%
7	Pennsylvania	712,121	3.6%
8	Michigan	663,586	3.4%
9	Georgia	648,667	3.3%
10	North Carolina	585,105	3.0%
11	New Jersey	567,489	2.9%
12	Virginia	485,338	2.5%
13	Indiana	429,345	2.2%
14	Arizona	419,740	2.1%
15	Washington	396,508	2.0%
16	Massachusetts	387,614	2.0%
17	Tennessee	383,745	2.0%
18	Missouri	367,340	1.9%
19	Maryland	365,545	1.9%
20	Wisconsin	338,384	1.7%
21	Louisiana	322,952	1.6%
22	Colorado	320,757	1.6%
23	Minnesota	318,995	1.6%
24	Alabama	298,697	1.5%
25	South Carolina	266,500	1.4%
26	Kentucky	253,219	1.3%
27	Oklahoma	238,637	1.2%
28	Oregon	226,208	1.2%
29	Connecticut	223,611	1.1%
30	Utah	218,989	1.1%
31	Mississippi	209,456	1.1%
32	Kansas	187,892	1.0%
33	Arkansas	183,668	0.9%
34	Iowa	180,971	0.9%
35	Nevada	160,805	0.8%
36	New Mexico	132,123	0.7%
37	Nebraska	117,787	0.6%
38	Idaho	99,950	0.5%
39	West Virginia	96,979	0.5%
40	Hawaii	83,507	0.4%
41	New Hampshire	73,407	0.4%
42	Maine	65,113	0.3%
43	Rhode Island	60,340	0.3%
44	Montana	52,793	0.3%
45	Delaware	51,293	0.3%
46	South Dakota	50,879	0.3%
47	Alaska	49,477	0.3%
48	North Dakota	36,525	0.2%
49	Vermont	31,681	0.2%
50	Wyoming	30,231	0.2%
	District of Columbia	33,907	0.2%

Source: U.S. Bureau of the Census
"Table ST-EST2002-ASRO-01 - State Characteristic Estimates" (September 18, 2003)

Percent of Population Under 5 Years Old in 2002

National Percent = 6.8% of Population

<table>
<tr><td colspan="3"><u>ALPHA ORDER</u></td><td colspan="3"><u>RANK ORDER</u></td></tr>
<tr><td>RANK</td><td>STATE</td><td>PERCENT</td><td>RANK</td><td>STATE</td><td>PERCENT</td></tr>
<tr><td>20</td><td>Alabama</td><td>6.7</td><td>1</td><td>Utah</td><td>9.5</td></tr>
<tr><td>3</td><td>Alaska</td><td>7.7</td><td>2</td><td>Texas</td><td>7.9</td></tr>
<tr><td>3</td><td>Arizona</td><td>7.7</td><td>3</td><td>Alaska</td><td>7.7</td></tr>
<tr><td>17</td><td>Arkansas</td><td>6.8</td><td>3</td><td>Arizona</td><td>7.7</td></tr>
<tr><td>9</td><td>California</td><td>7.2</td><td>5</td><td>Georgia</td><td>7.6</td></tr>
<tr><td>11</td><td>Colorado</td><td>7.1</td><td>6</td><td>Idaho</td><td>7.5</td></tr>
<tr><td>29</td><td>Connecticut</td><td>6.5</td><td>7</td><td>Nevada</td><td>7.4</td></tr>
<tr><td>33</td><td>Delaware</td><td>6.4</td><td>8</td><td>Mississippi</td><td>7.3</td></tr>
<tr><td>37</td><td>Florida</td><td>6.2</td><td>9</td><td>California</td><td>7.2</td></tr>
<tr><td>5</td><td>Georgia</td><td>7.6</td><td>9</td><td>Louisiana</td><td>7.2</td></tr>
<tr><td>20</td><td>Hawaii</td><td>6.7</td><td>11</td><td>Colorado</td><td>7.1</td></tr>
<tr><td>6</td><td>Idaho</td><td>7.5</td><td>11</td><td>Illinois</td><td>7.1</td></tr>
<tr><td>11</td><td>Illinois</td><td>7.1</td><td>11</td><td>New Mexico</td><td>7.1</td></tr>
<tr><td>14</td><td>Indiana</td><td>7.0</td><td>14</td><td>Indiana</td><td>7.0</td></tr>
<tr><td>37</td><td>Iowa</td><td>6.2</td><td>14</td><td>North Carolina</td><td>7.0</td></tr>
<tr><td>16</td><td>Kansas</td><td>6.9</td><td>16</td><td>Kansas</td><td>6.9</td></tr>
<tr><td>37</td><td>Kentucky</td><td>6.2</td><td>17</td><td>Arkansas</td><td>6.8</td></tr>
<tr><td>9</td><td>Louisiana</td><td>7.2</td><td>17</td><td>Nebraska</td><td>6.8</td></tr>
<tr><td>50</td><td>Maine</td><td>5.0</td><td>17</td><td>Oklahoma</td><td>6.8</td></tr>
<tr><td>20</td><td>Maryland</td><td>6.7</td><td>20</td><td>Alabama</td><td>6.7</td></tr>
<tr><td>42</td><td>Massachusetts</td><td>6.0</td><td>20</td><td>Hawaii</td><td>6.7</td></tr>
<tr><td>26</td><td>Michigan</td><td>6.6</td><td>20</td><td>Maryland</td><td>6.7</td></tr>
<tr><td>33</td><td>Minnesota</td><td>6.4</td><td>20</td><td>Ohio</td><td>6.7</td></tr>
<tr><td>8</td><td>Mississippi</td><td>7.3</td><td>20</td><td>South Dakota</td><td>6.7</td></tr>
<tr><td>29</td><td>Missouri</td><td>6.5</td><td>20</td><td>Virginia</td><td>6.7</td></tr>
<tr><td>43</td><td>Montana</td><td>5.8</td><td>26</td><td>Michigan</td><td>6.6</td></tr>
<tr><td>17</td><td>Nebraska</td><td>6.8</td><td>26</td><td>New Jersey</td><td>6.6</td></tr>
<tr><td>7</td><td>Nevada</td><td>7.4</td><td>26</td><td>Tennessee</td><td>6.6</td></tr>
<tr><td>43</td><td>New Hampshire</td><td>5.8</td><td>29</td><td>Connecticut</td><td>6.5</td></tr>
<tr><td>26</td><td>New Jersey</td><td>6.6</td><td>29</td><td>Missouri</td><td>6.5</td></tr>
<tr><td>11</td><td>New Mexico</td><td>7.1</td><td>29</td><td>South Carolina</td><td>6.5</td></tr>
<tr><td>33</td><td>New York</td><td>6.4</td><td>29</td><td>Washington</td><td>6.5</td></tr>
<tr><td>14</td><td>North Carolina</td><td>7.0</td><td>33</td><td>Delaware</td><td>6.4</td></tr>
<tr><td>43</td><td>North Dakota</td><td>5.8</td><td>33</td><td>Minnesota</td><td>6.4</td></tr>
<tr><td>20</td><td>Ohio</td><td>6.7</td><td>33</td><td>New York</td><td>6.4</td></tr>
<tr><td>17</td><td>Oklahoma</td><td>6.8</td><td>33</td><td>Oregon</td><td>6.4</td></tr>
<tr><td>33</td><td>Oregon</td><td>6.4</td><td>37</td><td>Florida</td><td>6.2</td></tr>
<tr><td>43</td><td>Pennsylvania</td><td>5.8</td><td>37</td><td>Iowa</td><td>6.2</td></tr>
<tr><td>47</td><td>Rhode Island</td><td>5.6</td><td>37</td><td>Kentucky</td><td>6.2</td></tr>
<tr><td>29</td><td>South Carolina</td><td>6.5</td><td>37</td><td>Wisconsin</td><td>6.2</td></tr>
<tr><td>20</td><td>South Dakota</td><td>6.7</td><td>41</td><td>Wyoming</td><td>6.1</td></tr>
<tr><td>26</td><td>Tennessee</td><td>6.6</td><td>42</td><td>Massachusetts</td><td>6.0</td></tr>
<tr><td>2</td><td>Texas</td><td>7.9</td><td>43</td><td>Montana</td><td>5.8</td></tr>
<tr><td>1</td><td>Utah</td><td>9.5</td><td>43</td><td>New Hampshire</td><td>5.8</td></tr>
<tr><td>49</td><td>Vermont</td><td>5.1</td><td>43</td><td>North Dakota</td><td>5.8</td></tr>
<tr><td>20</td><td>Virginia</td><td>6.7</td><td>43</td><td>Pennsylvania</td><td>5.8</td></tr>
<tr><td>29</td><td>Washington</td><td>6.5</td><td>47</td><td>Rhode Island</td><td>5.6</td></tr>
<tr><td>48</td><td>West Virginia</td><td>5.4</td><td>48</td><td>West Virginia</td><td>5.4</td></tr>
<tr><td>37</td><td>Wisconsin</td><td>6.2</td><td>49</td><td>Vermont</td><td>5.1</td></tr>
<tr><td>41</td><td>Wyoming</td><td>6.1</td><td>50</td><td>Maine</td><td>5.0</td></tr>
<tr><td></td><td></td><td></td><td></td><td>District of Columbia</td><td>5.9</td></tr>
</table>

Source: Morgan Quitno Press using data from U.S. Bureau of the Census
"Table ST-EST2002-ASRO-01 - State Characteristic Estimates" (September 18, 2003)

Population 5 to 17 Years Old in 2002

National Total = 53,285,336

<u>ALPHA ORDER</u>

RANK	STATE	POPULATION	% of USA
24	Alabama	808,411	1.5%
46	Alaska	142,951	0.3%
16	Arizona	1,057,116	2.0%
34	Arkansas	493,854	0.9%
1	California	6,907,398	13.0%
23	Colorado	830,361	1.6%
27	Connecticut	649,242	1.2%
47	Delaware	138,405	0.3%
4	Florida	2,847,094	5.3%
9	Georgia	1,619,810	3.0%
42	Hawaii	212,007	0.4%
39	Idaho	270,489	0.5%
5	Illinois	2,364,575	4.4%
13	Indiana	1,165,512	2.2%
31	Iowa	517,074	1.0%
32	Kansas	508,627	1.0%
26	Kentucky	678,369	1.3%
22	Louisiana	862,722	1.6%
41	Maine	213,945	0.4%
19	Maryland	1,014,380	1.9%
15	Massachusetts	1,075,726	2.0%
8	Michigan	1,906,678	3.6%
21	Minnesota	933,130	1.8%
30	Mississippi	551,291	1.0%
17	Missouri	1,030,121	1.9%
44	Montana	163,527	0.3%
37	Nebraska	321,606	0.6%
35	Nevada	411,785	0.8%
40	New Hampshire	234,964	0.4%
10	New Jersey	1,559,902	2.9%
36	New Mexico	368,383	0.7%
3	New York	3,385,107	6.4%
11	North Carolina	1,483,735	2.8%
48	North Dakota	110,287	0.2%
7	Ohio	2,115,374	4.0%
28	Oklahoma	634,923	1.2%
29	Oregon	628,899	1.2%
6	Pennsylvania	2,151,331	4.0%
43	Rhode Island	178,908	0.3%
25	South Carolina	712,663	1.3%
45	South Dakota	144,746	0.3%
18	Tennessee	1,020,916	1.9%
2	Texas	4,383,860	8.2%
33	Utah	494,023	0.9%
49	Vermont	107,981	0.2%
12	Virginia	1,294,070	2.4%
14	Washington	1,116,852	2.1%
38	West Virginia	292,192	0.5%
20	Wisconsin	999,680	1.9%
50	Wyoming	92,113	0.2%

<u>RANK ORDER</u>

RANK	STATE	POPULATION	% of USA
1	California	6,907,398	13.0%
2	Texas	4,383,860	8.2%
3	New York	3,385,107	6.4%
4	Florida	2,847,094	5.3%
5	Illinois	2,364,575	4.4%
6	Pennsylvania	2,151,331	4.0%
7	Ohio	2,115,374	4.0%
8	Michigan	1,906,678	3.6%
9	Georgia	1,619,810	3.0%
10	New Jersey	1,559,902	2.9%
11	North Carolina	1,483,735	2.8%
12	Virginia	1,294,070	2.4%
13	Indiana	1,165,512	2.2%
14	Washington	1,116,852	2.1%
15	Massachusetts	1,075,726	2.0%
16	Arizona	1,057,116	2.0%
17	Missouri	1,030,121	1.9%
18	Tennessee	1,020,916	1.9%
19	Maryland	1,014,380	1.9%
20	Wisconsin	999,680	1.9%
21	Minnesota	933,130	1.8%
22	Louisiana	862,722	1.6%
23	Colorado	830,361	1.6%
24	Alabama	808,411	1.5%
25	South Carolina	712,663	1.3%
26	Kentucky	678,369	1.3%
27	Connecticut	649,242	1.2%
28	Oklahoma	634,923	1.2%
29	Oregon	628,899	1.2%
30	Mississippi	551,291	1.0%
31	Iowa	517,074	1.0%
32	Kansas	508,627	1.0%
33	Utah	494,023	0.9%
34	Arkansas	493,854	0.9%
35	Nevada	411,785	0.8%
36	New Mexico	368,383	0.7%
37	Nebraska	321,606	0.6%
38	West Virginia	292,192	0.5%
39	Idaho	270,489	0.5%
40	New Hampshire	234,964	0.4%
41	Maine	213,945	0.4%
42	Hawaii	212,007	0.4%
43	Rhode Island	178,908	0.3%
44	Montana	163,527	0.3%
45	South Dakota	144,746	0.3%
46	Alaska	142,951	0.3%
47	Delaware	138,405	0.3%
48	North Dakota	110,287	0.2%
49	Vermont	107,981	0.2%
50	Wyoming	92,113	0.2%
	District of Columbia	78,221	0.1%

Source: U.S. Bureau of the Census
"Table ST-EST2002-ASRO-01 - State Characteristic Estimates" (September 18, 2003)

Percent of Population 5 to 17 Years Old in 2002

National Percent = 18.5% of Population

ALPHA ORDER

RANK	STATE	PERCENT
31	Alabama	18.0
1	Alaska	22.2
7	Arizona	19.4
27	Arkansas	18.2
6	California	19.7
23	Colorado	18.4
15	Connecticut	18.8
43	Delaware	17.1
44	Florida	17.0
12	Georgia	18.9
44	Hawaii	17.0
3	Idaho	20.2
15	Illinois	18.8
12	Indiana	18.9
37	Iowa	17.6
17	Kansas	18.7
48	Kentucky	16.6
8	Louisiana	19.2
49	Maine	16.5
18	Maryland	18.6
46	Massachusetts	16.7
10	Michigan	19.0
18	Minnesota	18.6
8	Mississippi	19.2
27	Missouri	18.2
31	Montana	18.0
18	Nebraska	18.6
12	Nevada	18.9
23	New Hampshire	18.4
27	New Jersey	18.2
5	New Mexico	19.9
35	New York	17.7
34	North Carolina	17.8
40	North Dakota	17.4
21	Ohio	18.5
27	Oklahoma	18.2
33	Oregon	17.9
40	Pennsylvania	17.4
46	Rhode Island	16.7
40	South Carolina	17.4
10	South Dakota	19.0
37	Tennessee	17.6
4	Texas	20.1
2	Utah	21.3
39	Vermont	17.5
35	Virginia	17.7
23	Washington	18.4
50	West Virginia	16.2
23	Wisconsin	18.4
21	Wyoming	18.5

RANK ORDER

RANK	STATE	PERCENT
1	Alaska	22.2
2	Utah	21.3
3	Idaho	20.2
4	Texas	20.1
5	New Mexico	19.9
6	California	19.7
7	Arizona	19.4
8	Louisiana	19.2
8	Mississippi	19.2
10	Michigan	19.0
10	South Dakota	19.0
12	Georgia	18.9
12	Indiana	18.9
12	Nevada	18.9
15	Connecticut	18.8
15	Illinois	18.8
17	Kansas	18.7
18	Maryland	18.6
18	Minnesota	18.6
18	Nebraska	18.6
21	Ohio	18.5
21	Wyoming	18.5
23	Colorado	18.4
23	New Hampshire	18.4
23	Washington	18.4
23	Wisconsin	18.4
27	Arkansas	18.2
27	Missouri	18.2
27	New Jersey	18.2
27	Oklahoma	18.2
31	Alabama	18.0
31	Montana	18.0
33	Oregon	17.9
34	North Carolina	17.8
35	New York	17.7
35	Virginia	17.7
37	Iowa	17.6
37	Tennessee	17.6
39	Vermont	17.5
40	North Dakota	17.4
40	Pennsylvania	17.4
40	South Carolina	17.4
43	Delaware	17.1
44	Florida	17.0
44	Hawaii	17.0
46	Massachusetts	16.7
46	Rhode Island	16.7
48	Kentucky	16.6
49	Maine	16.5
50	West Virginia	16.2

District of Columbia 13.7

Source: Morgan Quitno Press using data from U.S. Bureau of the Census
"Table ST-EST2002-ASRO-01 - State Characteristic Estimates" (September 18, 2003)

Population 18 Years Old and Older in 2002

National Total = 215,474,215

<u>ALPHA ORDER</u>

RANK	STATE	POPULATION	% of USA
22	Alabama	3,379,400	1.6%
49	Alaska	451,358	0.2%
20	Arizona	3,979,597	1.8%
32	Arkansas	2,032,557	0.9%
1	California	25,663,642	11.9%
23	Colorado	3,355,424	1.6%
29	Connecticut	2,587,650	1.2%
45	Delaware	617,687	0.3%
4	Florida	12,830,878	6.0%
10	Georgia	6,291,833	2.9%
42	Hawaii	949,384	0.4%
40	Idaho	970,692	0.5%
6	Illinois	9,346,097	4.3%
14	Indiana	4,564,211	2.1%
30	Iowa	2,238,715	1.0%
33	Kansas	2,019,365	0.9%
25	Kentucky	3,161,303	1.5%
24	Louisiana	3,296,972	1.5%
39	Maine	1,015,406	0.5%
19	Maryland	4,078,212	1.9%
13	Massachusetts	4,964,461	2.3%
8	Michigan	7,480,182	3.5%
21	Minnesota	3,767,595	1.7%
31	Mississippi	2,111,035	1.0%
17	Missouri	4,275,118	2.0%
44	Montana	693,133	0.3%
38	Nebraska	1,289,787	0.6%
35	Nevada	1,600,901	0.7%
41	New Hampshire	966,685	0.4%
9	New Jersey	6,462,909	3.0%
37	New Mexico	1,354,553	0.6%
3	New York	14,544,281	6.7%
11	North Carolina	6,251,306	2.9%
47	North Dakota	487,298	0.2%
7	Ohio	8,541,340	4.0%
28	Oklahoma	2,620,154	1.2%
27	Oregon	2,666,408	1.2%
5	Pennsylvania	9,471,639	4.4%
43	Rhode Island	830,477	0.4%
26	South Carolina	3,128,020	1.5%
46	South Dakota	565,438	0.3%
16	Tennessee	4,392,628	2.0%
2	Texas	15,677,577	7.3%
34	Utah	1,603,244	0.7%
48	Vermont	476,930	0.2%
12	Virginia	5,514,134	2.6%
15	Washington	4,555,636	2.1%
36	West Virginia	1,412,702	0.7%
18	Wisconsin	4,103,132	1.9%
50	Wyoming	376,359	0.2%

<u>RANK ORDER</u>

RANK	STATE	POPULATION	% of USA
1	California	25,663,642	11.9%
2	Texas	15,677,577	7.3%
3	New York	14,544,281	6.7%
4	Florida	12,830,878	6.0%
5	Pennsylvania	9,471,639	4.4%
6	Illinois	9,346,097	4.3%
7	Ohio	8,541,340	4.0%
8	Michigan	7,480,182	3.5%
9	New Jersey	6,462,909	3.0%
10	Georgia	6,291,833	2.9%
11	North Carolina	6,251,306	2.9%
12	Virginia	5,514,134	2.6%
13	Massachusetts	4,964,461	2.3%
14	Indiana	4,564,211	2.1%
15	Washington	4,555,636	2.1%
16	Tennessee	4,392,628	2.0%
17	Missouri	4,275,118	2.0%
18	Wisconsin	4,103,132	1.9%
19	Maryland	4,078,212	1.9%
20	Arizona	3,979,597	1.8%
21	Minnesota	3,767,595	1.7%
22	Alabama	3,379,400	1.6%
23	Colorado	3,355,424	1.6%
24	Louisiana	3,296,972	1.5%
25	Kentucky	3,161,303	1.5%
26	South Carolina	3,128,020	1.5%
27	Oregon	2,666,408	1.2%
28	Oklahoma	2,620,154	1.2%
29	Connecticut	2,587,650	1.2%
30	Iowa	2,238,715	1.0%
31	Mississippi	2,111,035	1.0%
32	Arkansas	2,032,557	0.9%
33	Kansas	2,019,365	0.9%
34	Utah	1,603,244	0.7%
35	Nevada	1,600,901	0.7%
36	West Virginia	1,412,702	0.7%
37	New Mexico	1,354,553	0.6%
38	Nebraska	1,289,787	0.6%
39	Maine	1,015,406	0.5%
40	Idaho	970,692	0.5%
41	New Hampshire	966,685	0.4%
42	Hawaii	949,384	0.4%
43	Rhode Island	830,477	0.4%
44	Montana	693,133	0.3%
45	Delaware	617,687	0.3%
46	South Dakota	565,438	0.3%
47	North Dakota	487,298	0.2%
48	Vermont	476,930	0.2%
49	Alaska	451,358	0.2%
50	Wyoming	376,359	0.2%
	District of Columbia	458,770	0.2%

Source: U.S. Bureau of the Census
"Table ST-EST2002-ASRO-01 - State Characteristic Estimates" (September 18, 2003)

Percent of Population 18 Years Old and Older in 2002

National Percent = 74.7% of Population

<u>ALPHA ORDER</u>

RANK	STATE	PERCENT
23	Alabama	75.3
49	Alaska	70.1
46	Arizona	72.9
28	Arkansas	75.0
44	California	73.1
34	Colorado	74.5
30	Connecticut	74.8
10	Delaware	76.5
7	Florida	76.8
41	Georgia	73.5
11	Hawaii	76.3
47	Idaho	72.4
38	Illinois	74.2
39	Indiana	74.1
12	Iowa	76.2
35	Kansas	74.4
5	Kentucky	77.2
41	Louisiana	73.5
1	Maine	78.4
32	Maryland	74.7
5	Massachusetts	77.2
35	Michigan	74.4
25	Minnesota	75.1
41	Mississippi	73.5
21	Missouri	75.4
12	Montana	76.2
33	Nebraska	74.6
40	Nevada	73.7
16	New Hampshire	75.8
24	New Jersey	75.2
45	New Mexico	73.0
15	New York	75.9
25	North Carolina	75.1
7	North Dakota	76.8
30	Ohio	74.8
28	Oklahoma	75.0
18	Oregon	75.7
7	Pennsylvania	76.8
3	Rhode Island	77.6
12	South Carolina	76.2
37	South Dakota	74.3
16	Tennessee	75.8
48	Texas	72.0
50	Utah	69.2
4	Vermont	77.3
19	Virginia	75.6
25	Washington	75.1
1	West Virginia	78.4
21	Wisconsin	75.4
20	Wyoming	75.5

<u>RANK ORDER</u>

RANK	STATE	PERCENT
1	Maine	78.4
1	West Virginia	78.4
3	Rhode Island	77.6
4	Vermont	77.3
5	Kentucky	77.2
5	Massachusetts	77.2
7	Florida	76.8
7	North Dakota	76.8
7	Pennsylvania	76.8
10	Delaware	76.5
11	Hawaii	76.3
12	Iowa	76.2
12	Montana	76.2
12	South Carolina	76.2
15	New York	75.9
16	New Hampshire	75.8
16	Tennessee	75.8
18	Oregon	75.7
19	Virginia	75.6
20	Wyoming	75.5
21	Missouri	75.4
21	Wisconsin	75.4
23	Alabama	75.3
24	New Jersey	75.2
25	Minnesota	75.1
25	North Carolina	75.1
25	Washington	75.1
28	Arkansas	75.0
28	Oklahoma	75.0
30	Connecticut	74.8
30	Ohio	74.8
32	Maryland	74.7
33	Nebraska	74.6
34	Colorado	74.5
35	Kansas	74.4
35	Michigan	74.4
37	South Dakota	74.3
38	Illinois	74.2
39	Indiana	74.1
40	Nevada	73.7
41	Georgia	73.5
41	Louisiana	73.5
41	Mississippi	73.5
44	California	73.1
45	New Mexico	73.0
46	Arizona	72.9
47	Idaho	72.4
48	Texas	72.0
49	Alaska	70.1
50	Utah	69.2
	District of Columbia	80.4

Source: Morgan Quitno Press using data from U.S. Bureau of the Census
"Table ST-EST2002-ASRO-01 - State Characteristic Estimates" (September 18, 2003)

Population 18 to 24 Years Old in 2002

National Total = 28,341,732

ALPHA ORDER

RANK	STATE	POPULATION	% of USA
23	Alabama	452,196	1.6%
49	Alaska	58,738	0.2%
19	Arizona	540,015	1.9%
34	Arkansas	272,391	1.0%
1	California	3,551,492	12.5%
24	Colorado	447,869	1.6%
33	Connecticut	287,412	1.0%
46	Delaware	81,501	0.3%
4	Florida	1,403,624	5.0%
9	Georgia	868,937	3.1%
40	Hawaii	123,045	0.4%
39	Idaho	149,036	0.5%
5	Illinois	1,228,541	4.3%
13	Indiana	628,691	2.2%
31	Iowa	314,972	1.1%
32	Kansas	291,509	1.0%
26	Kentucky	419,536	1.5%
21	Louisiana	495,811	1.7%
41	Maine	118,126	0.4%
22	Maryland	488,911	1.7%
14	Massachusetts	597,865	2.1%
8	Michigan	970,466	3.4%
20	Minnesota	507,071	1.8%
29	Mississippi	322,625	1.1%
16	Missouri	567,574	2.0%
44	Montana	92,915	0.3%
37	Nebraska	184,586	0.7%
36	Nevada	187,297	0.7%
42	New Hampshire	114,725	0.4%
12	New Jersey	693,034	2.4%
35	New Mexico	191,698	0.7%
3	New York	1,815,216	6.4%
10	North Carolina	815,438	2.9%
47	North Dakota	76,034	0.3%
7	Ohio	1,098,431	3.9%
27	Oklahoma	377,256	1.3%
28	Oregon	338,287	1.2%
6	Pennsylvania	1,153,224	4.1%
43	Rhode Island	114,090	0.4%
25	South Carolina	429,425	1.5%
45	South Dakota	82,635	0.3%
18	Tennessee	553,941	2.0%
2	Texas	2,287,194	8.1%
30	Utah	321,169	1.1%
48	Vermont	62,147	0.2%
11	Virginia	720,847	2.5%
15	Washington	593,628	2.1%
38	West Virginia	173,743	0.6%
17	Wisconsin	556,567	2.0%
50	Wyoming	54,248	0.2%

RANK ORDER

RANK	STATE	POPULATION	% of USA
1	California	3,551,492	12.5%
2	Texas	2,287,194	8.1%
3	New York	1,815,216	6.4%
4	Florida	1,403,624	5.0%
5	Illinois	1,228,541	4.3%
6	Pennsylvania	1,153,224	4.1%
7	Ohio	1,098,431	3.9%
8	Michigan	970,466	3.4%
9	Georgia	868,937	3.1%
10	North Carolina	815,438	2.9%
11	Virginia	720,847	2.5%
12	New Jersey	693,034	2.4%
13	Indiana	628,691	2.2%
14	Massachusetts	597,865	2.1%
15	Washington	593,628	2.1%
16	Missouri	567,574	2.0%
17	Wisconsin	556,567	2.0%
18	Tennessee	553,941	2.0%
19	Arizona	540,015	1.9%
20	Minnesota	507,071	1.8%
21	Louisiana	495,811	1.7%
22	Maryland	488,911	1.7%
23	Alabama	452,196	1.6%
24	Colorado	447,869	1.6%
25	South Carolina	429,425	1.5%
26	Kentucky	419,536	1.5%
27	Oklahoma	377,256	1.3%
28	Oregon	338,287	1.2%
29	Mississippi	322,625	1.1%
30	Utah	321,169	1.1%
31	Iowa	314,972	1.1%
32	Kansas	291,509	1.0%
33	Connecticut	287,412	1.0%
34	Arkansas	272,391	1.0%
35	New Mexico	191,698	0.7%
36	Nevada	187,297	0.7%
37	Nebraska	184,586	0.7%
38	West Virginia	173,743	0.6%
39	Idaho	149,036	0.5%
40	Hawaii	123,045	0.4%
41	Maine	118,126	0.4%
42	New Hampshire	114,725	0.4%
43	Rhode Island	114,090	0.4%
44	Montana	92,915	0.3%
45	South Dakota	82,635	0.3%
46	Delaware	81,501	0.3%
47	North Dakota	76,034	0.3%
48	Vermont	62,147	0.2%
49	Alaska	58,738	0.2%
50	Wyoming	54,248	0.2%
	District of Columbia	66,003	0.2%

Source: U.S. Bureau of the Census
"Population Estimates Data Sets" (http://eire.census.gov/popest/estimates_dataset.php)

Percent of Population 18 to 24 Years Old in 2002

National Percent = 9.8% of Population

<table>
<tr><td colspan="3"><u>ALPHA ORDER</u></td><td colspan="3"><u>RANK ORDER</u></td></tr>
<tr><td>RANK</td><td>STATE</td><td>PERCENT</td><td>RANK</td><td>STATE</td><td>PERCENT</td></tr>
<tr><td>21</td><td>Alabama</td><td>10.1</td><td>1</td><td>Utah</td><td>13.9</td></tr>
<tr><td>43</td><td>Alaska</td><td>9.1</td><td>2</td><td>North Dakota</td><td>12.0</td></tr>
<tr><td>28</td><td>Arizona</td><td>9.9</td><td>3</td><td>Mississippi</td><td>11.2</td></tr>
<tr><td>21</td><td>Arkansas</td><td>10.1</td><td>4</td><td>Idaho</td><td>11.1</td></tr>
<tr><td>21</td><td>California</td><td>10.1</td><td>4</td><td>Louisiana</td><td>11.1</td></tr>
<tr><td>28</td><td>Colorado</td><td>9.9</td><td>6</td><td>South Dakota</td><td>10.9</td></tr>
<tr><td>49</td><td>Connecticut</td><td>8.3</td><td>6</td><td>Wyoming</td><td>10.9</td></tr>
<tr><td>21</td><td>Delaware</td><td>10.1</td><td>8</td><td>Oklahoma</td><td>10.8</td></tr>
<tr><td>48</td><td>Florida</td><td>8.4</td><td>9</td><td>Iowa</td><td>10.7</td></tr>
<tr><td>17</td><td>Georgia</td><td>10.2</td><td>9</td><td>Kansas</td><td>10.7</td></tr>
<tr><td>28</td><td>Hawaii</td><td>9.9</td><td>9</td><td>Nebraska</td><td>10.7</td></tr>
<tr><td>4</td><td>Idaho</td><td>11.1</td><td>9</td><td>Rhode Island</td><td>10.7</td></tr>
<tr><td>34</td><td>Illinois</td><td>9.7</td><td>13</td><td>South Carolina</td><td>10.5</td></tr>
<tr><td>17</td><td>Indiana</td><td>10.2</td><td>13</td><td>Texas</td><td>10.5</td></tr>
<tr><td>9</td><td>Iowa</td><td>10.7</td><td>15</td><td>Kentucky</td><td>10.3</td></tr>
<tr><td>9</td><td>Kansas</td><td>10.7</td><td>15</td><td>New Mexico</td><td>10.3</td></tr>
<tr><td>15</td><td>Kentucky</td><td>10.3</td><td>17</td><td>Georgia</td><td>10.2</td></tr>
<tr><td>4</td><td>Louisiana</td><td>11.1</td><td>17</td><td>Indiana</td><td>10.2</td></tr>
<tr><td>43</td><td>Maine</td><td>9.1</td><td>17</td><td>Montana</td><td>10.2</td></tr>
<tr><td>45</td><td>Maryland</td><td>9.0</td><td>17</td><td>Wisconsin</td><td>10.2</td></tr>
<tr><td>41</td><td>Massachusetts</td><td>9.3</td><td>21</td><td>Alabama</td><td>10.1</td></tr>
<tr><td>34</td><td>Michigan</td><td>9.7</td><td>21</td><td>Arkansas</td><td>10.1</td></tr>
<tr><td>21</td><td>Minnesota</td><td>10.1</td><td>21</td><td>California</td><td>10.1</td></tr>
<tr><td>3</td><td>Mississippi</td><td>11.2</td><td>21</td><td>Delaware</td><td>10.1</td></tr>
<tr><td>27</td><td>Missouri</td><td>10.0</td><td>21</td><td>Minnesota</td><td>10.1</td></tr>
<tr><td>17</td><td>Montana</td><td>10.2</td><td>21</td><td>Vermont</td><td>10.1</td></tr>
<tr><td>9</td><td>Nebraska</td><td>10.7</td><td>27</td><td>Missouri</td><td>10.0</td></tr>
<tr><td>47</td><td>Nevada</td><td>8.6</td><td>28</td><td>Arizona</td><td>9.9</td></tr>
<tr><td>45</td><td>New Hampshire</td><td>9.0</td><td>28</td><td>Colorado</td><td>9.9</td></tr>
<tr><td>50</td><td>New Jersey</td><td>8.1</td><td>28</td><td>Hawaii</td><td>9.9</td></tr>
<tr><td>15</td><td>New Mexico</td><td>10.3</td><td>28</td><td>Virginia</td><td>9.9</td></tr>
<tr><td>40</td><td>New York</td><td>9.5</td><td>32</td><td>North Carolina</td><td>9.8</td></tr>
<tr><td>32</td><td>North Carolina</td><td>9.8</td><td>32</td><td>Washington</td><td>9.8</td></tr>
<tr><td>2</td><td>North Dakota</td><td>12.0</td><td>34</td><td>Illinois</td><td>9.7</td></tr>
<tr><td>36</td><td>Ohio</td><td>9.6</td><td>34</td><td>Michigan</td><td>9.7</td></tr>
<tr><td>8</td><td>Oklahoma</td><td>10.8</td><td>36</td><td>Ohio</td><td>9.6</td></tr>
<tr><td>36</td><td>Oregon</td><td>9.6</td><td>36</td><td>Oregon</td><td>9.6</td></tr>
<tr><td>41</td><td>Pennsylvania</td><td>9.3</td><td>36</td><td>Tennessee</td><td>9.6</td></tr>
<tr><td>9</td><td>Rhode Island</td><td>10.7</td><td>36</td><td>West Virginia</td><td>9.6</td></tr>
<tr><td>13</td><td>South Carolina</td><td>10.5</td><td>40</td><td>New York</td><td>9.5</td></tr>
<tr><td>6</td><td>South Dakota</td><td>10.9</td><td>41</td><td>Massachusetts</td><td>9.3</td></tr>
<tr><td>36</td><td>Tennessee</td><td>9.6</td><td>41</td><td>Pennsylvania</td><td>9.3</td></tr>
<tr><td>13</td><td>Texas</td><td>10.5</td><td>43</td><td>Alaska</td><td>9.1</td></tr>
<tr><td>1</td><td>Utah</td><td>13.9</td><td>43</td><td>Maine</td><td>9.1</td></tr>
<tr><td>21</td><td>Vermont</td><td>10.1</td><td>45</td><td>Maryland</td><td>9.0</td></tr>
<tr><td>28</td><td>Virginia</td><td>9.9</td><td>45</td><td>New Hampshire</td><td>9.0</td></tr>
<tr><td>32</td><td>Washington</td><td>9.8</td><td>47</td><td>Nevada</td><td>8.6</td></tr>
<tr><td>36</td><td>West Virginia</td><td>9.6</td><td>48</td><td>Florida</td><td>8.4</td></tr>
<tr><td>17</td><td>Wisconsin</td><td>10.2</td><td>49</td><td>Connecticut</td><td>8.3</td></tr>
<tr><td>6</td><td>Wyoming</td><td>10.9</td><td>50</td><td>New Jersey</td><td>8.1</td></tr>
<tr><td></td><td></td><td></td><td></td><td>District of Columbia</td><td>11.6</td></tr>
</table>

Source: Morgan Quitno Press using data from U.S. Bureau of the Census
"Table ST-EST2002-ASRO-01 - State Characteristic Estimates" (September 18, 2003)

Population 25 to 44 Years Old in 2002

National Total = 85,915,373

ALPHA ORDER

RANK	STATE	POPULATION	% of USA
23	Alabama	1,279,779	1.5%
47	Alaska	196,544	0.2%
19	Arizona	1,583,361	1.8%
33	Arkansas	751,746	0.9%
1	California	11,114,775	12.9%
22	Colorado	1,431,917	1.7%
28	Connecticut	1,003,335	1.2%
44	Delaware	242,522	0.3%
4	Florida	4,647,821	5.4%
9	Georgia	2,745,385	3.2%
39	Hawaii	438,939	0.5%
41	Idaho	370,814	0.4%
5	Illinois	3,798,969	4.4%
15	Indiana	1,769,594	2.1%
31	Iowa	800,251	0.9%
32	Kansas	766,581	0.9%
25	Kentucky	1,229,843	1.4%
24	Louisiana	1,263,486	1.5%
42	Maine	369,757	0.4%
17	Maryland	1,679,618	2.0%
13	Massachusetts	1,994,198	2.3%
8	Michigan	2,926,216	3.4%
21	Minnesota	1,506,335	1.8%
30	Mississippi	802,231	0.9%
18	Missouri	1,630,149	1.9%
45	Montana	239,836	0.3%
38	Nebraska	484,132	0.6%
34	Nevada	677,925	0.8%
40	New Hampshire	381,883	0.4%
10	New Jersey	2,609,928	3.0%
36	New Mexico	513,228	0.6%
3	New York	5,848,430	6.8%
11	North Carolina	2,527,255	2.9%
49	North Dakota	169,632	0.2%
7	Ohio	3,249,727	3.8%
29	Oklahoma	996,950	1.2%
27	Oregon	1,026,700	1.2%
6	Pennsylvania	3,418,780	4.0%
43	Rhode Island	315,167	0.4%
26	South Carolina	1,205,672	1.4%
46	South Dakota	202,667	0.2%
16	Tennessee	1,722,479	2.0%
2	Texas	6,623,524	7.7%
35	Utah	673,752	0.8%
48	Vermont	173,448	0.2%
12	Virginia	2,259,419	2.6%
14	Washington	1,867,436	2.2%
37	West Virginia	486,211	0.6%
20	Wisconsin	1,567,784	1.8%
50	Wyoming	133,170	0.2%

RANK ORDER

RANK	STATE	POPULATION	% of USA
1	California	11,114,775	12.9%
2	Texas	6,623,524	7.7%
3	New York	5,848,430	6.8%
4	Florida	4,647,821	5.4%
5	Illinois	3,798,969	4.4%
6	Pennsylvania	3,418,780	4.0%
7	Ohio	3,249,727	3.8%
8	Michigan	2,926,216	3.4%
9	Georgia	2,745,385	3.2%
10	New Jersey	2,609,928	3.0%
11	North Carolina	2,527,255	2.9%
12	Virginia	2,259,419	2.6%
13	Massachusetts	1,994,198	2.3%
14	Washington	1,867,436	2.2%
15	Indiana	1,769,594	2.1%
16	Tennessee	1,722,479	2.0%
17	Maryland	1,679,618	2.0%
18	Missouri	1,630,149	1.9%
19	Arizona	1,583,361	1.8%
20	Wisconsin	1,567,784	1.8%
21	Minnesota	1,506,335	1.8%
22	Colorado	1,431,917	1.7%
23	Alabama	1,279,779	1.5%
24	Louisiana	1,263,486	1.5%
25	Kentucky	1,229,843	1.4%
26	South Carolina	1,205,672	1.4%
27	Oregon	1,026,700	1.2%
28	Connecticut	1,003,335	1.2%
29	Oklahoma	996,950	1.2%
30	Mississippi	802,231	0.9%
31	Iowa	800,251	0.9%
32	Kansas	766,581	0.9%
33	Arkansas	751,746	0.9%
34	Nevada	677,925	0.8%
35	Utah	673,752	0.8%
36	New Mexico	513,228	0.6%
37	West Virginia	486,211	0.6%
38	Nebraska	484,132	0.6%
39	Hawaii	438,939	0.5%
40	New Hampshire	381,883	0.4%
41	Idaho	370,814	0.4%
42	Maine	369,757	0.4%
43	Rhode Island	315,167	0.4%
44	Delaware	242,522	0.3%
45	Montana	239,836	0.3%
46	South Dakota	202,667	0.2%
47	Alaska	196,544	0.2%
48	Vermont	173,448	0.2%
49	North Dakota	169,632	0.2%
50	Wyoming	133,170	0.2%
	District of Columbia	196,072	0.2%

Source: U.S. Bureau of the Census
"Population Estimates Data Sets" (http://eire.census.gov/popest/estimates_dataset.php)

Percent of Population 25 to 44 Years Old in 2002

National Percent = 29.8% of Population

RANK	STATE	PERCENT		RANK	STATE	PERCENT
32	Alabama	28.5		1	Hawaii	35.3
10	Alaska	30.5		2	Georgia	32.1
26	Arizona	29.0		3	Colorado	31.8
41	Arkansas	27.7		4	California	31.7
4	California	31.7		5	Nevada	31.2
3	Colorado	31.8		6	Massachusetts	31.0
26	Connecticut	29.0		6	Virginia	31.0
16	Delaware	30.0		8	Maryland	30.8
40	Florida	27.8		8	Washington	30.8
2	Georgia	32.1		10	Alaska	30.5
1	Hawaii	35.3		10	New York	30.5
44	Idaho	27.6		12	New Jersey	30.4
15	Illinois	30.1		12	North Carolina	30.4
29	Indiana	28.7		12	Texas	30.4
45	Iowa	27.2		15	Illinois	30.1
35	Kansas	28.2		16	Delaware	30.0
16	Kentucky	30.0		16	Kentucky	30.0
35	Louisiana	28.2		16	Minnesota	30.0
31	Maine	28.6		16	New Hampshire	30.0
8	Maryland	30.8		20	Tennessee	29.7
6	Massachusetts	31.0		21	Rhode Island	29.5
24	Michigan	29.1		22	South Carolina	29.4
16	Minnesota	30.0		23	Oregon	29.2
39	Mississippi	27.9		24	Michigan	29.1
29	Missouri	28.7		24	Utah	29.1
50	Montana	26.4		26	Arizona	29.0
38	Nebraska	28.0		26	Connecticut	29.0
5	Nevada	31.2		28	Wisconsin	28.8
16	New Hampshire	30.0		29	Indiana	28.7
12	New Jersey	30.4		29	Missouri	28.7
41	New Mexico	27.7		31	Maine	28.6
10	New York	30.5		32	Alabama	28.5
12	North Carolina	30.4		32	Ohio	28.5
47	North Dakota	26.8		32	Oklahoma	28.5
32	Ohio	28.5		35	Kansas	28.2
32	Oklahoma	28.5		35	Louisiana	28.2
23	Oregon	29.2		37	Vermont	28.1
41	Pennsylvania	27.7		38	Nebraska	28.0
21	Rhode Island	29.5		39	Mississippi	27.9
22	South Carolina	29.4		40	Florida	27.8
49	South Dakota	26.6		41	Arkansas	27.7
20	Tennessee	29.7		41	New Mexico	27.7
12	Texas	30.4		41	Pennsylvania	27.7
24	Utah	29.1		44	Idaho	27.6
37	Vermont	28.1		45	Iowa	27.2
6	Virginia	31.0		46	West Virginia	27.0
8	Washington	30.8		47	North Dakota	26.8
46	West Virginia	27.0		48	Wyoming	26.7
28	Wisconsin	28.8		49	South Dakota	26.6
48	Wyoming	26.7		50	Montana	26.4
					District of Columbia	34.3

Source: Morgan Quitno Press using data from U.S. Bureau of the Census
  "Table ST-EST2002-ASRO-01 - State Characteristic Estimates" (September 18, 2003)

Population 45 to 64 Years Old in 2002

National Total = 67,314,928

<u>ALPHA ORDER</u>

RANK	STATE	POPULATION	% of USA
22	Alabama	1,075,114	1.6%
47	Alaska	170,623	0.3%
20	Arizona	1,184,494	1.8%
32	Arkansas	644,910	1.0%
1	California	7,617,740	11.3%
23	Colorado	1,073,355	1.6%
29	Connecticut	840,436	1.2%
45	Delaware	191,573	0.3%
4	Florida	3,998,246	5.9%
11	Georgia	1,897,107	2.8%
39	Hawaii	349,989	0.5%
42	Idaho	306,906	0.5%
6	Illinois	2,866,367	4.3%
15	Indiana	1,430,367	2.1%
30	Iowa	699,171	1.0%
33	Kansas	622,696	0.9%
25	Kentucky	1,017,011	1.5%
24	Louisiana	1,031,130	1.5%
40	Maine	345,625	0.5%
18	Maryland	1,321,928	2.0%
13	Massachusetts	1,537,881	2.3%
8	Michigan	2,405,659	3.6%
21	Minnesota	1,176,207	1.7%
31	Mississippi	646,409	1.0%
17	Missouri	1,348,283	2.0%
44	Montana	243,507	0.4%
38	Nebraska	394,998	0.6%
34	Nevada	515,745	0.8%
41	New Hampshire	321,967	0.5%
9	New Jersey	2,077,528	3.1%
36	New Mexico	438,834	0.7%
3	New York	4,515,381	6.7%
10	North Carolina	1,939,973	2.9%
49	North Dakota	149,892	0.2%
7	Ohio	2,727,791	4.1%
28	Oklahoma	849,653	1.3%
27	Oregon	892,116	1.3%
5	Pennsylvania	3,027,917	4.5%
43	Rhode Island	254,144	0.4%
26	South Carolina	1,002,717	1.5%
46	South Dakota	175,226	0.3%
16	Tennessee	1,418,267	2.1%
2	Texas	4,703,299	7.0%
37	Utah	420,087	0.6%
48	Vermont	164,880	0.2%
12	Virginia	1,757,359	2.6%
14	Washington	1,487,466	2.2%
35	West Virginia	482,303	0.7%
19	Wisconsin	1,290,891	1.9%
50	Wyoming	132,114	0.2%

<u>RANK ORDER</u>

RANK	STATE	POPULATION	% of USA
1	California	7,617,740	11.3%
2	Texas	4,703,299	7.0%
3	New York	4,515,381	6.7%
4	Florida	3,998,246	5.9%
5	Pennsylvania	3,027,917	4.5%
6	Illinois	2,866,367	4.3%
7	Ohio	2,727,791	4.1%
8	Michigan	2,405,659	3.6%
9	New Jersey	2,077,528	3.1%
10	North Carolina	1,939,973	2.9%
11	Georgia	1,897,107	2.8%
12	Virginia	1,757,359	2.6%
13	Massachusetts	1,537,881	2.3%
14	Washington	1,487,466	2.2%
15	Indiana	1,430,367	2.1%
16	Tennessee	1,418,267	2.1%
17	Missouri	1,348,283	2.0%
18	Maryland	1,321,928	2.0%
19	Wisconsin	1,290,891	1.9%
20	Arizona	1,184,494	1.8%
21	Minnesota	1,176,207	1.7%
22	Alabama	1,075,114	1.6%
23	Colorado	1,073,355	1.6%
24	Louisiana	1,031,130	1.5%
25	Kentucky	1,017,011	1.5%
26	South Carolina	1,002,717	1.5%
27	Oregon	892,116	1.3%
28	Oklahoma	849,653	1.3%
29	Connecticut	840,436	1.2%
30	Iowa	699,171	1.0%
31	Mississippi	646,409	1.0%
32	Arkansas	644,910	1.0%
33	Kansas	622,696	0.9%
34	Nevada	515,745	0.8%
35	West Virginia	482,303	0.7%
36	New Mexico	438,834	0.7%
37	Utah	420,087	0.6%
38	Nebraska	394,998	0.6%
39	Hawaii	349,989	0.5%
40	Maine	345,625	0.5%
41	New Hampshire	321,967	0.5%
42	Idaho	306,906	0.5%
43	Rhode Island	254,144	0.4%
44	Montana	243,507	0.4%
45	Delaware	191,573	0.3%
46	South Dakota	175,226	0.3%
47	Alaska	170,623	0.3%
48	Vermont	164,880	0.2%
49	North Dakota	149,892	0.2%
50	Wyoming	132,114	0.2%
	District of Columbia	131,646	0.2%

Source: U.S. Bureau of the Census
"Table ST-EST2002-ASRO-01 - State Characteristic Estimates" (September 18, 2003)

Percent of Population 45 to 64 Years Old in 2002

National Percent = 23.3% of Population

ALPHA ORDER

RANK	STATE	PERCENT
20	Alabama	24.0
6	Alaska	26.5
47	Arizona	21.7
25	Arkansas	23.8
47	California	21.7
25	Colorado	23.8
15	Connecticut	24.3
30	Delaware	23.7
21	Florida	23.9
46	Georgia	22.2
1	Hawaii	28.1
41	Idaho	22.9
44	Illinois	22.7
38	Indiana	23.2
25	Iowa	23.8
41	Kansas	22.9
10	Kentucky	24.8
39	Louisiana	23.0
4	Maine	26.7
17	Maryland	24.2
21	Massachusetts	23.9
21	Michigan	23.9
36	Minnesota	23.4
45	Mississippi	22.5
25	Missouri	23.8
2	Montana	26.8
43	Nebraska	22.8
30	Nevada	23.7
8	New Hampshire	25.3
17	New Jersey	24.2
30	New Mexico	23.7
34	New York	23.6
37	North Carolina	23.3
34	North Dakota	23.6
21	Ohio	23.9
15	Oklahoma	24.3
8	Oregon	25.3
11	Pennsylvania	24.5
25	Rhode Island	23.8
14	South Carolina	24.4
39	South Dakota	23.0
11	Tennessee	24.5
49	Texas	21.6
50	Utah	18.1
4	Vermont	26.7
19	Virginia	24.1
11	Washington	24.5
2	West Virginia	26.8
30	Wisconsin	23.7
6	Wyoming	26.5

RANK ORDER

RANK	STATE	PERCENT
1	Hawaii	28.1
2	Montana	26.8
2	West Virginia	26.8
4	Maine	26.7
4	Vermont	26.7
6	Alaska	26.5
6	Wyoming	26.5
8	New Hampshire	25.3
8	Oregon	25.3
10	Kentucky	24.8
11	Pennsylvania	24.5
11	Tennessee	24.5
11	Washington	24.5
14	South Carolina	24.4
15	Connecticut	24.3
15	Oklahoma	24.3
17	Maryland	24.2
17	New Jersey	24.2
19	Virginia	24.1
20	Alabama	24.0
21	Florida	23.9
21	Massachusetts	23.9
21	Michigan	23.9
21	Ohio	23.9
25	Arkansas	23.8
25	Colorado	23.8
25	Iowa	23.8
25	Missouri	23.8
25	Rhode Island	23.8
30	Delaware	23.7
30	Nevada	23.7
30	New Mexico	23.7
30	Wisconsin	23.7
34	New York	23.6
34	North Dakota	23.6
36	Minnesota	23.4
37	North Carolina	23.3
38	Indiana	23.2
39	Louisiana	23.0
39	South Dakota	23.0
41	Idaho	22.9
41	Kansas	22.9
43	Nebraska	22.8
44	Illinois	22.7
45	Mississippi	22.5
46	Georgia	22.2
47	Arizona	21.7
47	California	21.7
49	Texas	21.6
50	Utah	18.1

| | District of Columbia | 23.1 |

Source: Morgan Quitno Press using data from U.S. Bureau of the Census
   "Table ST-EST2002-ASRO-01 - State Characteristic Estimates" (September 18, 2003)

Population 65 Years Old and Older in 2002

National Total = 35,601,911

<u>ALPHA ORDER</u>

RANK	STATE	POPULATION	% of USA
22	Alabama	588,542	1.7%
50	Alaska	39,200	0.1%
18	Arizona	701,243	2.0%
31	Arkansas	376,387	1.1%
1	California	3,716,836	10.4%
29	Colorado	434,472	1.2%
26	Connecticut	472,314	1.3%
46	Delaware	105,488	0.3%
2	Florida	2,854,838	8.0%
13	Georgia	813,652	2.3%
40	Hawaii	166,910	0.5%
43	Idaho	151,141	0.4%
7	Illinois	1,499,249	4.2%
14	Indiana	757,451	2.1%
30	Iowa	432,785	1.2%
32	Kansas	355,094	1.0%
24	Kentucky	509,476	1.4%
23	Louisiana	520,446	1.5%
39	Maine	186,383	0.5%
20	Maryland	616,699	1.7%
11	Massachusetts	863,695	2.4%
8	Michigan	1,231,920	3.5%
21	Minnesota	601,741	1.7%
33	Mississippi	346,251	1.0%
15	Missouri	757,197	2.1%
44	Montana	122,806	0.3%
36	Nebraska	232,134	0.7%
35	Nevada	240,255	0.7%
41	New Hampshire	152,577	0.4%
9	New Jersey	1,121,197	3.1%
37	New Mexico	221,454	0.6%
3	New York	2,473,510	6.9%
10	North Carolina	998,391	2.8%
47	North Dakota	94,076	0.3%
6	Ohio	1,513,372	4.3%
27	Oklahoma	460,459	1.3%
28	Oregon	443,968	1.2%
5	Pennsylvania	1,908,962	5.4%
42	Rhode Island	152,286	0.4%
25	South Carolina	503,256	1.4%
45	South Dakota	108,322	0.3%
16	Tennessee	719,177	2.0%
4	Texas	2,152,896	6.0%
38	Utah	199,041	0.6%
48	Vermont	79,241	0.2%
12	Virginia	817,441	2.3%
19	Washington	677,532	1.9%
34	West Virginia	275,974	0.8%
17	Wisconsin	706,418	2.0%
49	Wyoming	59,222	0.2%

<u>RANK ORDER</u>

RANK	STATE	POPULATION	% of USA
1	California	3,716,836	10.4%
2	Florida	2,854,838	8.0%
3	New York	2,473,510	6.9%
4	Texas	2,152,896	6.0%
5	Pennsylvania	1,908,962	5.4%
6	Ohio	1,513,372	4.3%
7	Illinois	1,499,249	4.2%
8	Michigan	1,231,920	3.5%
9	New Jersey	1,121,197	3.1%
10	North Carolina	998,391	2.8%
11	Massachusetts	863,695	2.4%
12	Virginia	817,441	2.3%
13	Georgia	813,652	2.3%
14	Indiana	757,451	2.1%
15	Missouri	757,197	2.1%
16	Tennessee	719,177	2.0%
17	Wisconsin	706,418	2.0%
18	Arizona	701,243	2.0%
19	Washington	677,532	1.9%
20	Maryland	616,699	1.7%
21	Minnesota	601,741	1.7%
22	Alabama	588,542	1.7%
23	Louisiana	520,446	1.5%
24	Kentucky	509,476	1.4%
25	South Carolina	503,256	1.4%
26	Connecticut	472,314	1.3%
27	Oklahoma	460,459	1.3%
28	Oregon	443,968	1.2%
29	Colorado	434,472	1.2%
30	Iowa	432,785	1.2%
31	Arkansas	376,387	1.1%
32	Kansas	355,094	1.0%
33	Mississippi	346,251	1.0%
34	West Virginia	275,974	0.8%
35	Nevada	240,255	0.7%
36	Nebraska	232,134	0.7%
37	New Mexico	221,454	0.6%
38	Utah	199,041	0.6%
39	Maine	186,383	0.5%
40	Hawaii	166,910	0.5%
41	New Hampshire	152,577	0.4%
42	Rhode Island	152,286	0.4%
43	Idaho	151,141	0.4%
44	Montana	122,806	0.3%
45	South Dakota	108,322	0.3%
46	Delaware	105,488	0.3%
47	North Dakota	94,076	0.3%
48	Vermont	79,241	0.2%
49	Wyoming	59,222	0.2%
50	Alaska	39,200	0.1%
	District of Columbia	68,534	0.2%

Source: U.S. Bureau of the Census
"Table ST-EST2002-ASRO-01 - State Characteristic Estimates" (September 18, 2003)

Percent of Population 65 Years Old and Older in 2002

National Percent = 12.3% of Population

<table>
<tr><td colspan="3"><u>ALPHA ORDER</u></td><td colspan="3"><u>RANK ORDER</u></td></tr>
<tr><td>RANK</td><td>STATE</td><td>PERCENT</td><td>RANK</td><td>STATE</td><td>PERCENT</td></tr>
<tr><td>18</td><td>Alabama</td><td>13.1</td><td>1</td><td>Florida</td><td>17.1</td></tr>
<tr><td>50</td><td>Alaska</td><td>6.1</td><td>2</td><td>Pennsylvania</td><td>15.5</td></tr>
<tr><td>23</td><td>Arizona</td><td>12.9</td><td>3</td><td>West Virginia</td><td>15.3</td></tr>
<tr><td>9</td><td>Arkansas</td><td>13.9</td><td>4</td><td>North Dakota</td><td>14.8</td></tr>
<tr><td>45</td><td>California</td><td>10.6</td><td>5</td><td>Iowa</td><td>14.7</td></tr>
<tr><td>47</td><td>Colorado</td><td>9.6</td><td>6</td><td>Maine</td><td>14.4</td></tr>
<tr><td>10</td><td>Connecticut</td><td>13.6</td><td>7</td><td>Rhode Island</td><td>14.2</td></tr>
<tr><td>18</td><td>Delaware</td><td>13.1</td><td>7</td><td>South Dakota</td><td>14.2</td></tr>
<tr><td>1</td><td>Florida</td><td>17.1</td><td>9</td><td>Arkansas</td><td>13.9</td></tr>
<tr><td>48</td><td>Georgia</td><td>9.5</td><td>10</td><td>Connecticut</td><td>13.6</td></tr>
<tr><td>12</td><td>Hawaii</td><td>13.4</td><td>11</td><td>Montana</td><td>13.5</td></tr>
<tr><td>40</td><td>Idaho</td><td>11.3</td><td>12</td><td>Hawaii</td><td>13.4</td></tr>
<tr><td>36</td><td>Illinois</td><td>11.9</td><td>12</td><td>Massachusetts</td><td>13.4</td></tr>
<tr><td>29</td><td>Indiana</td><td>12.3</td><td>12</td><td>Nebraska</td><td>13.4</td></tr>
<tr><td>5</td><td>Iowa</td><td>14.7</td><td>15</td><td>Missouri</td><td>13.3</td></tr>
<tr><td>18</td><td>Kansas</td><td>13.1</td><td>15</td><td>Ohio</td><td>13.3</td></tr>
<tr><td>27</td><td>Kentucky</td><td>12.4</td><td>17</td><td>Oklahoma</td><td>13.2</td></tr>
<tr><td>39</td><td>Louisiana</td><td>11.6</td><td>18</td><td>Alabama</td><td>13.1</td></tr>
<tr><td>6</td><td>Maine</td><td>14.4</td><td>18</td><td>Delaware</td><td>13.1</td></tr>
<tr><td>40</td><td>Maryland</td><td>11.3</td><td>18</td><td>Kansas</td><td>13.1</td></tr>
<tr><td>12</td><td>Massachusetts</td><td>13.4</td><td>18</td><td>New Jersey</td><td>13.1</td></tr>
<tr><td>29</td><td>Michigan</td><td>12.3</td><td>22</td><td>Wisconsin</td><td>13.0</td></tr>
<tr><td>33</td><td>Minnesota</td><td>12.0</td><td>23</td><td>Arizona</td><td>12.9</td></tr>
<tr><td>32</td><td>Mississippi</td><td>12.1</td><td>23</td><td>New York</td><td>12.9</td></tr>
<tr><td>15</td><td>Missouri</td><td>13.3</td><td>23</td><td>Vermont</td><td>12.9</td></tr>
<tr><td>11</td><td>Montana</td><td>13.5</td><td>26</td><td>Oregon</td><td>12.6</td></tr>
<tr><td>12</td><td>Nebraska</td><td>13.4</td><td>27</td><td>Kentucky</td><td>12.4</td></tr>
<tr><td>44</td><td>Nevada</td><td>11.1</td><td>27</td><td>Tennessee</td><td>12.4</td></tr>
<tr><td>33</td><td>New Hampshire</td><td>12.0</td><td>29</td><td>Indiana</td><td>12.3</td></tr>
<tr><td>18</td><td>New Jersey</td><td>13.1</td><td>29</td><td>Michigan</td><td>12.3</td></tr>
<tr><td>36</td><td>New Mexico</td><td>11.9</td><td>29</td><td>South Carolina</td><td>12.3</td></tr>
<tr><td>23</td><td>New York</td><td>12.9</td><td>32</td><td>Mississippi</td><td>12.1</td></tr>
<tr><td>33</td><td>North Carolina</td><td>12.0</td><td>33</td><td>Minnesota</td><td>12.0</td></tr>
<tr><td>4</td><td>North Dakota</td><td>14.8</td><td>33</td><td>New Hampshire</td><td>12.0</td></tr>
<tr><td>15</td><td>Ohio</td><td>13.3</td><td>33</td><td>North Carolina</td><td>12.0</td></tr>
<tr><td>17</td><td>Oklahoma</td><td>13.2</td><td>36</td><td>Illinois</td><td>11.9</td></tr>
<tr><td>26</td><td>Oregon</td><td>12.6</td><td>36</td><td>New Mexico</td><td>11.9</td></tr>
<tr><td>2</td><td>Pennsylvania</td><td>15.5</td><td>36</td><td>Wyoming</td><td>11.9</td></tr>
<tr><td>7</td><td>Rhode Island</td><td>14.2</td><td>39</td><td>Louisiana</td><td>11.6</td></tr>
<tr><td>29</td><td>South Carolina</td><td>12.3</td><td>40</td><td>Idaho</td><td>11.3</td></tr>
<tr><td>7</td><td>South Dakota</td><td>14.2</td><td>40</td><td>Maryland</td><td>11.3</td></tr>
<tr><td>27</td><td>Tennessee</td><td>12.4</td><td>42</td><td>Virginia</td><td>11.2</td></tr>
<tr><td>46</td><td>Texas</td><td>9.9</td><td>42</td><td>Washington</td><td>11.2</td></tr>
<tr><td>49</td><td>Utah</td><td>8.6</td><td>44</td><td>Nevada</td><td>11.1</td></tr>
<tr><td>23</td><td>Vermont</td><td>12.9</td><td>45</td><td>California</td><td>10.6</td></tr>
<tr><td>42</td><td>Virginia</td><td>11.2</td><td>46</td><td>Texas</td><td>9.9</td></tr>
<tr><td>42</td><td>Washington</td><td>11.2</td><td>47</td><td>Colorado</td><td>9.6</td></tr>
<tr><td>3</td><td>West Virginia</td><td>15.3</td><td>48</td><td>Georgia</td><td>9.5</td></tr>
<tr><td>22</td><td>Wisconsin</td><td>13.0</td><td>49</td><td>Utah</td><td>8.6</td></tr>
<tr><td>36</td><td>Wyoming</td><td>11.9</td><td>50</td><td>Alaska</td><td>6.1</td></tr>
<tr><td></td><td></td><td></td><td></td><td>District of Columbia</td><td>12.0</td></tr>
</table>

Population 85 Years Old and Older in 2002

National Total = 4,593,063

ALPHA ORDER

RANK	STATE	POPULATION	% of USA
22	Alabama	71,436	1.6%
50	Alaska	3,073	0.1%
20	Arizona	77,568	1.7%
32	Arkansas	48,960	1.1%
1	California	470,826	10.3%
31	Colorado	53,101	1.2%
23	Connecticut	70,079	1.5%
47	Delaware	11,821	0.3%
2	Florida	360,332	7.8%
16	Georgia	95,660	2.1%
41	Hawaii	20,353	0.4%
43	Idaho	19,701	0.4%
6	Illinois	206,861	4.5%
14	Indiana	98,317	2.1%
24	Iowa	68,523	1.5%
30	Kansas	53,908	1.2%
27	Kentucky	61,272	1.3%
26	Louisiana	61,368	1.3%
37	Maine	25,025	0.5%
21	Maryland	73,543	1.6%
10	Massachusetts	125,214	2.7%
8	Michigan	155,891	3.4%
18	Minnesota	91,625	2.0%
33	Mississippi	44,530	1.0%
13	Missouri	102,956	2.2%
45	Montana	16,568	0.4%
34	Nebraska	35,528	0.8%
40	Nevada	20,508	0.4%
42	New Hampshire	19,966	0.4%
9	New Jersey	148,920	3.2%
36	New Mexico	25,820	0.6%
3	New York	337,060	7.3%
11	North Carolina	115,539	2.5%
46	North Dakota	15,544	0.3%
7	Ohio	190,926	4.2%
28	Oklahoma	58,325	1.3%
25	Oregon	63,297	1.4%
4	Pennsylvania	258,789	5.6%
39	Rhode Island	22,707	0.5%
29	South Carolina	55,259	1.2%
44	South Dakota	17,021	0.4%
19	Tennessee	86,838	1.9%
5	Texas	255,611	5.6%
38	Utah	24,078	0.5%
48	Vermont	10,768	0.2%
15	Virginia	95,835	2.1%
17	Washington	93,072	2.0%
35	West Virginia	33,292	0.7%
12	Wisconsin	103,150	2.2%
49	Wyoming	7,273	0.2%

RANK ORDER

RANK	STATE	POPULATION	% of USA
1	California	470,826	10.3%
2	Florida	360,332	7.8%
3	New York	337,060	7.3%
4	Pennsylvania	258,789	5.6%
5	Texas	255,611	5.6%
6	Illinois	206,861	4.5%
7	Ohio	190,926	4.2%
8	Michigan	155,891	3.4%
9	New Jersey	148,920	3.2%
10	Massachusetts	125,214	2.7%
11	North Carolina	115,539	2.5%
12	Wisconsin	103,150	2.2%
13	Missouri	102,956	2.2%
14	Indiana	98,317	2.1%
15	Virginia	95,835	2.1%
16	Georgia	95,660	2.1%
17	Washington	93,072	2.0%
18	Minnesota	91,625	2.0%
19	Tennessee	86,838	1.9%
20	Arizona	77,568	1.7%
21	Maryland	73,543	1.6%
22	Alabama	71,436	1.6%
23	Connecticut	70,079	1.5%
24	Iowa	68,523	1.5%
25	Oregon	63,297	1.4%
26	Louisiana	61,368	1.3%
27	Kentucky	61,272	1.3%
28	Oklahoma	58,325	1.3%
29	South Carolina	55,259	1.2%
30	Kansas	53,908	1.2%
31	Colorado	53,101	1.2%
32	Arkansas	48,960	1.1%
33	Mississippi	44,530	1.0%
34	Nebraska	35,528	0.8%
35	West Virginia	33,292	0.7%
36	New Mexico	25,820	0.6%
37	Maine	25,025	0.5%
38	Utah	24,078	0.5%
39	Rhode Island	22,707	0.5%
40	Nevada	20,508	0.4%
41	Hawaii	20,353	0.4%
42	New Hampshire	19,966	0.4%
43	Idaho	19,701	0.4%
44	South Dakota	17,021	0.4%
45	Montana	16,568	0.4%
46	North Dakota	15,544	0.3%
47	Delaware	11,821	0.3%
48	Vermont	10,768	0.2%
49	Wyoming	7,273	0.2%
50	Alaska	3,073	0.1%
	District of Columbia	9,426	0.2%

Source: U.S. Bureau of the Census
"Table ST-EST2002-ASRO-01 - State Characteristic Estimates" (September 18, 2003)

Percent of Population 85 Years Old and Older in 2002

National Percent = 1.6% of Population

ALPHA ORDER

RANK	STATE	PERCENT
24	Alabama	1.6
50	Alaska	0.5
37	Arizona	1.4
13	Arkansas	1.8
41	California	1.3
45	Colorado	1.2
8	Connecticut	2.0
31	Delaware	1.5
3	Florida	2.2
47	Georgia	1.1
24	Hawaii	1.6
31	Idaho	1.5
24	Illinois	1.6
24	Indiana	1.6
2	Iowa	2.3
8	Kansas	2.0
31	Kentucky	1.5
37	Louisiana	1.4
10	Maine	1.9
41	Maryland	1.3
10	Massachusetts	1.9
24	Michigan	1.6
13	Minnesota	1.8
24	Mississippi	1.6
13	Missouri	1.8
13	Montana	1.8
5	Nebraska	2.1
49	Nevada	0.9
24	New Hampshire	1.6
20	New Jersey	1.7
37	New Mexico	1.4
13	New York	1.8
37	North Carolina	1.4
1	North Dakota	2.5
20	Ohio	1.7
20	Oklahoma	1.7
13	Oregon	1.8
5	Pennsylvania	2.1
5	Rhode Island	2.1
41	South Carolina	1.3
3	South Dakota	2.2
31	Tennessee	1.5
45	Texas	1.2
48	Utah	1.0
20	Vermont	1.7
41	Virginia	1.3
31	Washington	1.5
13	West Virginia	1.8
10	Wisconsin	1.9
31	Wyoming	1.5

RANK ORDER

RANK	STATE	PERCENT
1	North Dakota	2.5
2	Iowa	2.3
3	Florida	2.2
3	South Dakota	2.2
5	Nebraska	2.1
5	Pennsylvania	2.1
5	Rhode Island	2.1
8	Connecticut	2.0
8	Kansas	2.0
10	Maine	1.9
10	Massachusetts	1.9
10	Wisconsin	1.9
13	Arkansas	1.8
13	Minnesota	1.8
13	Missouri	1.8
13	Montana	1.8
13	New York	1.8
13	Oregon	1.8
13	West Virginia	1.8
20	New Jersey	1.7
20	Ohio	1.7
20	Oklahoma	1.7
20	Vermont	1.7
24	Alabama	1.6
24	Hawaii	1.6
24	Illinois	1.6
24	Indiana	1.6
24	Michigan	1.6
24	Mississippi	1.6
24	New Hampshire	1.6
31	Delaware	1.5
31	Idaho	1.5
31	Kentucky	1.5
31	Tennessee	1.5
31	Washington	1.5
31	Wyoming	1.5
37	Arizona	1.4
37	Louisiana	1.4
37	New Mexico	1.4
37	North Carolina	1.4
41	California	1.3
41	Maryland	1.3
41	South Carolina	1.3
41	Virginia	1.3
45	Colorado	1.2
45	Texas	1.2
47	Georgia	1.1
48	Utah	1.0
49	Nevada	0.9
50	Alaska	0.5
	District of Columbia	1.7

Source: Morgan Quitno Press using data from U.S. Bureau of the Census
"Table ST-EST2002-ASRO-01 - State Characteristic Estimates" (September 18, 2003)

Domestic Migration of Population: 2002 to 2003

National Net Migration = 0 People*

<u>ALPHA ORDER</u>

RANK	STATE	NET MIGRATION
25	Alabama	4,525
33	Alaska	(320)
2	Arizona	61,200
20	Arkansas	5,255
49	California	(94,861)
42	Colorado	(10,611)
34	Connecticut	(1,234)
18	Delaware	5,762
1	Florida	177,734
4	Georgia	31,785
26	Hawaii	2,129
11	Idaho	10,132
48	Illinois	(73,980)
29	Indiana	1,019
38	Iowa	(5,535)
40	Kansas	(9,568)
13	Kentucky	8,592
41	Louisiana	(10,605)
12	Maine	9,862
14	Maryland	8,266
47	Massachusetts	(45,099)
44	Michigan	(25,583)
39	Minnesota	(7,705)
37	Mississippi	(2,588)
15	Missouri	7,871
23	Montana	5,033
35	Nebraska	(1,319)
3	Nevada	44,718
17	New Hampshire	6,472
46	New Jersey	(33,225)
22	New Mexico	5,074
50	New York	(170,041)
6	North Carolina	25,100
36	North Dakota	(2,049)
45	Ohio	(27,497)
30	Oklahoma	400
10	Oregon	13,300
16	Pennsylvania	7,841
27	Rhode Island	1,843
8	South Carolina	19,735
31	South Dakota	(30)
7	Tennessee	19,942
9	Texas	15,998
43	Utah	(11,263)
28	Vermont	1,272
5	Virginia	28,412
19	Washington	5,687
21	West Virginia	5,140
24	Wisconsin	4,981
32	Wyoming	(130)

<u>RANK ORDER</u>

RANK	STATE	NET MIGRATION
1	Florida	177,734
2	Arizona	61,200
3	Nevada	44,718
4	Georgia	31,785
5	Virginia	28,412
6	North Carolina	25,100
7	Tennessee	19,942
8	South Carolina	19,735
9	Texas	15,998
10	Oregon	13,300
11	Idaho	10,132
12	Maine	9,862
13	Kentucky	8,592
14	Maryland	8,266
15	Missouri	7,871
16	Pennsylvania	7,841
17	New Hampshire	6,472
18	Delaware	5,762
19	Washington	5,687
20	Arkansas	5,255
21	West Virginia	5,140
22	New Mexico	5,074
23	Montana	5,033
24	Wisconsin	4,981
25	Alabama	4,525
26	Hawaii	2,129
27	Rhode Island	1,843
28	Vermont	1,272
29	Indiana	1,019
30	Oklahoma	400
31	South Dakota	(30)
32	Wyoming	(130)
33	Alaska	(320)
34	Connecticut	(1,234)
35	Nebraska	(1,319)
36	North Dakota	(2,049)
37	Mississippi	(2,588)
38	Iowa	(5,535)
39	Minnesota	(7,705)
40	Kansas	(9,568)
41	Louisiana	(10,605)
42	Colorado	(10,611)
43	Utah	(11,263)
44	Michigan	(25,583)
45	Ohio	(27,497)
46	New Jersey	(33,225)
47	Massachusetts	(45,099)
48	Illinois	(73,980)
49	California	(94,861)
50	New York	(170,041)
	District of Columbia	(11,837)

Source: U.S. Bureau of the Census
  "Components of Population Change" (December 18, 2003, http://eire.census.gov/popest/estimates.php)
From July 1, 2002 to July 1, 2003. Includes armed forces residing in each state. Net Domestic Migration is the difference between domestic inmigration to an area and domestic outmigration from it during the period. Domestic inmigration and outmigration consist of moves where both the origins and destinations are within the United States (excluding Puerto Rico).

Net International Migration: 2002 to 2003

National Net = 1,286,118 Immigrants*

ALPHA ORDER

RANK	STATE	IMMIGRANTS	% of USA
34	Alabama	5,064	0.4%
43	Alaska	1,067	0.1%
8	Arizona	34,266	2.7%
36	Arkansas	4,363	0.3%
1	California	288,051	22.4%
14	Colorado	22,766	1.8%
17	Connecticut	15,542	1.2%
41	Delaware	2,263	0.2%
4	Florida	107,303	8.3%
7	Georgia	38,914	3.0%
31	Hawaii	5,835	0.5%
39	Idaho	2,907	0.2%
5	Illinois	66,911	5.2%
22	Indiana	11,147	0.9%
30	Iowa	5,950	0.5%
27	Kansas	7,806	0.6%
33	Kentucky	5,416	0.4%
38	Louisiana	3,833	0.3%
44	Maine	952	0.1%
15	Maryland	22,204	1.7%
9	Massachusetts	33,447	2.6%
13	Michigan	25,279	2.0%
20	Minnesota	14,589	1.1%
42	Mississippi	1,935	0.2%
26	Missouri	8,623	0.7%
50	Montana	405	0.0%
35	Nebraska	4,560	0.4%
21	Nevada	13,501	1.0%
40	New Hampshire	2,292	0.2%
6	New Jersey	59,067	4.6%
32	New Mexico	5,567	0.4%
2	New York	136,185	10.6%
10	North Carolina	31,395	2.4%
47	North Dakota	715	0.1%
18	Ohio	15,478	1.2%
28	Oklahoma	7,424	0.6%
19	Oregon	14,755	1.1%
16	Pennsylvania	21,201	1.6%
37	Rhode Island	3,856	0.3%
29	South Carolina	6,997	0.5%
46	South Dakota	760	0.1%
24	Tennessee	10,057	0.8%
3	Texas	135,010	10.5%
23	Utah	10,225	0.8%
45	Vermont	889	0.1%
11	Virginia	27,462	2.1%
12	Washington	27,216	2.1%
48	West Virginia	643	0.0%
25	Wisconsin	9,427	0.7%
49	Wyoming	418	0.0%

RANK ORDER

RANK	STATE	IMMIGRANTS	% of USA
1	California	288,051	22.4%
2	New York	136,185	10.6%
3	Texas	135,010	10.5%
4	Florida	107,303	8.3%
5	Illinois	66,911	5.2%
6	New Jersey	59,067	4.6%
7	Georgia	38,914	3.0%
8	Arizona	34,266	2.7%
9	Massachusetts	33,447	2.6%
10	North Carolina	31,395	2.4%
11	Virginia	27,462	2.1%
12	Washington	27,216	2.1%
13	Michigan	25,279	2.0%
14	Colorado	22,766	1.8%
15	Maryland	22,204	1.7%
16	Pennsylvania	21,201	1.6%
17	Connecticut	15,542	1.2%
18	Ohio	15,478	1.2%
19	Oregon	14,755	1.1%
20	Minnesota	14,589	1.1%
21	Nevada	13,501	1.0%
22	Indiana	11,147	0.9%
23	Utah	10,225	0.8%
24	Tennessee	10,057	0.8%
25	Wisconsin	9,427	0.7%
26	Missouri	8,623	0.7%
27	Kansas	7,806	0.6%
28	Oklahoma	7,424	0.6%
29	South Carolina	6,997	0.5%
30	Iowa	5,950	0.5%
31	Hawaii	5,835	0.5%
32	New Mexico	5,567	0.4%
33	Kentucky	5,416	0.4%
34	Alabama	5,064	0.4%
35	Nebraska	4,560	0.4%
36	Arkansas	4,363	0.3%
37	Rhode Island	3,856	0.3%
38	Louisiana	3,833	0.3%
39	Idaho	2,907	0.2%
40	New Hampshire	2,292	0.2%
41	Delaware	2,263	0.2%
42	Mississippi	1,935	0.2%
43	Alaska	1,067	0.1%
44	Maine	952	0.1%
45	Vermont	889	0.1%
46	South Dakota	760	0.1%
47	North Dakota	715	0.1%
48	West Virginia	643	0.0%
49	Wyoming	418	0.0%
50	Montana	405	0.0%
	District of Columbia	4,180	0.3%

Source: U.S. Bureau of the Census
   "Components of Population Change" (December 18, 2003, http://eire.census.gov/popest/estimates.php)
From July 1, 2002 to July 1, 2003. Net International Migration is the difference between migration to an area from outside the United States (immigration) and migration from the area to outside the United States (emigration) during the period. Includes legal immigration and estimates of undocumented immigration.

Percent of Population Foreign Born: 2002

National Percent = 11.8% of Population*

ALPHA ORDER

RANK	STATE	PERCENT
42	Alabama	2.6
25	Alaska	5.4
8	Arizona	13.2
41	Arkansas	2.9
1	California	26.9
15	Colorado	9.8
11	Connecticut	12.1
22	Delaware	6.1
4	Florida	17.9
19	Georgia	7.7
4	Hawaii	17.9
25	Idaho	5.4
9	Illinois	13.1
36	Indiana	3.4
34	Iowa	3.5
30	Kansas	4.2
45	Kentucky	2.1
42	Louisiana	2.6
40	Maine	3.0
13	Maryland	10.8
9	Massachusetts	13.1
24	Michigan	5.5
21	Minnesota	6.4
50	Mississippi	1.1
39	Missouri	3.1
48	Montana	1.6
29	Nebraska	4.4
6	Nevada	17.0
28	New Hampshire	4.5
3	New Jersey	18.9
17	New Mexico	8.9
2	New York	20.9
23	North Carolina	6.0
45	North Dakota	2.1
37	Ohio	3.3
30	Oklahoma	4.2
16	Oregon	9.0
27	Pennsylvania	4.6
12	Rhode Island	11.6
34	South Carolina	3.5
47	South Dakota	1.9
37	Tennessee	3.3
7	Texas	15.2
20	Utah	7.1
33	Vermont	3.8
18	Virginia	8.8
14	Washington	10.7
49	West Virginia	1.2
32	Wisconsin	4.0
44	Wyoming	2.4

RANK ORDER

RANK	STATE	PERCENT
1	California	26.9
2	New York	20.9
3	New Jersey	18.9
4	Florida	17.9
4	Hawaii	17.9
6	Nevada	17.0
7	Texas	15.2
8	Arizona	13.2
9	Illinois	13.1
9	Massachusetts	13.1
11	Connecticut	12.1
12	Rhode Island	11.6
13	Maryland	10.8
14	Washington	10.7
15	Colorado	9.8
16	Oregon	9.0
17	New Mexico	8.9
18	Virginia	8.8
19	Georgia	7.7
20	Utah	7.1
21	Minnesota	6.4
22	Delaware	6.1
23	North Carolina	6.0
24	Michigan	5.5
25	Alaska	5.4
25	Idaho	5.4
27	Pennsylvania	4.6
28	New Hampshire	4.5
29	Nebraska	4.4
30	Kansas	4.2
30	Oklahoma	4.2
32	Wisconsin	4.0
33	Vermont	3.8
34	Iowa	3.5
34	South Carolina	3.5
36	Indiana	3.4
37	Ohio	3.3
37	Tennessee	3.3
39	Missouri	3.1
40	Maine	3.0
41	Arkansas	2.9
42	Alabama	2.6
42	Louisiana	2.6
44	Wyoming	2.4
45	Kentucky	2.1
45	North Dakota	2.1
47	South Dakota	1.9
48	Montana	1.6
49	West Virginia	1.2
50	Mississippi	1.1
	District of Columbia	14.6

Source: U.S. Bureau of the Census
   "2002 American Community Survey"
*"Foreign born" are persons not born in the United States, Puerto Rico, a U.S. Island Area or abroad of American parent or parents.

Percent of Population Speaking a Language Other Than English in 2002

National Percent = 18.3%*

ALPHA ORDER

RANK	STATE	PERCENT
48	Alabama	3.7
17	Alaska	12.7
7	Arizona	25.8
45	Arkansas	4.2
1	California	40.6
14	Colorado	15.6
13	Connecticut	18.0
23	Delaware	9.7
8	Florida	24.1
22	Georgia	9.9
6	Hawaii	26.3
24	Idaho	9.6
10	Illinois	19.9
26	Indiana	8.4
38	Iowa	5.8
32	Kansas	7.6
47	Kentucky	3.8
25	Louisiana	8.5
35	Maine	7.2
16	Maryland	13.2
12	Massachusetts	18.7
27	Michigan	8.2
21	Minnesota	10.0
49	Mississippi	2.9
39	Missouri	5.6
46	Montana	4.1
30	Nebraska	7.7
9	Nevada	23.5
33	New Hampshire	7.4
5	New Jersey	26.4
2	New Mexico	34.4
4	New York	27.4
27	North Carolina	8.2
39	North Dakota	5.6
36	Ohio	6.0
33	Oklahoma	7.4
19	Oregon	12.0
27	Pennsylvania	8.2
11	Rhode Island	19.0
42	South Carolina	5.4
39	South Dakota	5.6
44	Tennessee	4.7
3	Texas	31.5
18	Utah	12.3
43	Vermont	4.9
20	Virginia	11.5
15	Washington	14.3
50	West Virginia	2.3
30	Wisconsin	7.7
37	Wyoming	5.9

RANK ORDER

RANK	STATE	PERCENT
1	California	40.6
2	New Mexico	34.4
3	Texas	31.5
4	New York	27.4
5	New Jersey	26.4
6	Hawaii	26.3
7	Arizona	25.8
8	Florida	24.1
9	Nevada	23.5
10	Illinois	19.9
11	Rhode Island	19.0
12	Massachusetts	18.7
13	Connecticut	18.0
14	Colorado	15.6
15	Washington	14.3
16	Maryland	13.2
17	Alaska	12.7
18	Utah	12.3
19	Oregon	12.0
20	Virginia	11.5
21	Minnesota	10.0
22	Georgia	9.9
23	Delaware	9.7
24	Idaho	9.6
25	Louisiana	8.5
26	Indiana	8.4
27	Michigan	8.2
27	North Carolina	8.2
27	Pennsylvania	8.2
30	Nebraska	7.7
30	Wisconsin	7.7
32	Kansas	7.6
33	New Hampshire	7.4
33	Oklahoma	7.4
35	Maine	7.2
36	Ohio	6.0
37	Wyoming	5.9
38	Iowa	5.8
39	Missouri	5.6
39	North Dakota	5.6
39	South Dakota	5.6
42	South Carolina	5.4
43	Vermont	4.9
44	Tennessee	4.7
45	Arkansas	4.2
46	Montana	4.1
47	Kentucky	3.8
48	Alabama	3.7
49	Mississippi	2.9
50	West Virginia	2.3

	District of Columbia	16.7

Source: U.S. Bureau of the Census
   "2002 American Community Survey"
*Population five years old and older.

Percent of Population Speaking Spanish at Home in 2002

National Percent = 11.1%*

<u>ALPHA ORDER</u>

RANK	STATE	PERCENT
39	Alabama	2.1
34	Alaska	2.6
4	Arizona	19.9
31	Arkansas	2.9
3	California	26.8
10	Colorado	11.4
11	Connecticut	8.3
20	Delaware	5.1
5	Florida	17.3
18	Georgia	5.8
40	Hawaii	1.8
13	Idaho	7.5
9	Illinois	11.6
27	Indiana	3.4
33	Iowa	2.8
25	Kansas	4.3
40	Kentucky	1.8
38	Louisiana	2.2
50	Maine	0.7
21	Maryland	5.0
16	Massachusetts	6.5
35	Michigan	2.5
30	Minnesota	3.0
46	Mississippi	1.6
37	Missouri	2.3
45	Montana	1.7
23	Nebraska	4.8
6	Nevada	17.0
40	New Hampshire	1.8
8	New Jersey	12.8
1	New Mexico	28.0
7	New York	14.0
19	North Carolina	5.4
47	North Dakota	1.2
40	Ohio	1.8
24	Oklahoma	4.4
15	Oregon	6.9
31	Pennsylvania	2.9
12	Rhode Island	7.9
29	South Carolina	3.2
40	South Dakota	1.8
36	Tennessee	2.4
2	Texas	27.4
14	Utah	7.3
48	Vermont	0.8
22	Virginia	4.9
17	Washington	5.9
48	West Virginia	0.8
28	Wisconsin	3.3
26	Wyoming	3.6

<u>RANK ORDER</u>

RANK	STATE	PERCENT
1	New Mexico	28.0
2	Texas	27.4
3	California	26.8
4	Arizona	19.9
5	Florida	17.3
6	Nevada	17.0
7	New York	14.0
8	New Jersey	12.8
9	Illinois	11.6
10	Colorado	11.4
11	Connecticut	8.3
12	Rhode Island	7.9
13	Idaho	7.5
14	Utah	7.3
15	Oregon	6.9
16	Massachusetts	6.5
17	Washington	5.9
18	Georgia	5.8
19	North Carolina	5.4
20	Delaware	5.1
21	Maryland	5.0
22	Virginia	4.9
23	Nebraska	4.8
24	Oklahoma	4.4
25	Kansas	4.3
26	Wyoming	3.6
27	Indiana	3.4
28	Wisconsin	3.3
29	South Carolina	3.2
30	Minnesota	3.0
31	Arkansas	2.9
31	Pennsylvania	2.9
33	Iowa	2.8
34	Alaska	2.6
35	Michigan	2.5
36	Tennessee	2.4
37	Missouri	2.3
38	Louisiana	2.2
39	Alabama	2.1
40	Hawaii	1.8
40	Kentucky	1.8
40	New Hampshire	1.8
40	Ohio	1.8
40	South Dakota	1.8
45	Montana	1.7
46	Mississippi	1.6
47	North Dakota	1.2
48	Vermont	0.8
48	West Virginia	0.8
50	Maine	0.7

District of Columbia	9.8

Source: U.S. Bureau of the Census
    "2002 American Community Survey"
*Population five years old and older.

Marriages in 2002

National Total = 2,255,000 Marriages*

ALPHA ORDER

RANK	STATE	MARRIAGES	% of USA
16	Alabama	42,675	1.9%
46	Alaska	5,511	0.2%
24	Arizona	36,199	1.6%
20	Arkansas	37,818	1.7%
1	California	217,880	9.7%
25	Colorado	35,600	1.6%
35	Connecticut	16,188	0.7%
47	Delaware	4,925	0.2%
3	Florida	159,263	7.1%
13	Georgia	58,382	2.6%
29	Hawaii	25,334	1.1%
38	Idaho	14,405	0.6%
6	Illinois	83,208	3.7%
15	Indiana	43,903	1.9%
34	Iowa	18,139	0.8%
32	Kansas	19,809	0.9%
21	Kentucky	36,576	1.6%
26	Louisiana	35,577	1.6%
41	Maine	10,900	0.5%
19	Maryland	37,969	1.7%
22	Massachusetts	36,523	1.6%
10	Michigan	65,164	2.9%
28	Minnesota	31,782	1.4%
33	Mississippi	18,952	0.8%
17	Missouri	41,934	1.9%
44	Montana	6,317	0.3%
39	Nebraska	13,005	0.6%
5	Nevada	123,303	5.5%
40	New Hampshire	10,978	0.5%
14	New Jersey	51,355	2.3%
37	New Mexico	14,662	0.7%
4	New York	134,345	6.0%
12	North Carolina	61,046	2.7%
49	North Dakota	4,555	0.2%
7	Ohio	80,373	3.6%
NA	Oklahoma**	NA	NA
30	Oregon	24,901	1.1%
9	Pennsylvania	69,647	3.1%
42	Rhode Island	8,272	0.4%
23	South Carolina	36,380	1.6%
43	South Dakota	6,789	0.3%
8	Tennessee	76,531	3.4%
2	Texas	192,630	8.5%
31	Utah	22,728	1.0%
45	Vermont	5,963	0.3%
11	Virginia	63,152	2.8%
18	Washington	38,125	1.7%
36	West Virginia	14,887	0.7%
27	Wisconsin	34,295	1.5%
48	Wyoming	4,717	0.2%

RANK ORDER

RANK	STATE	MARRIAGES	% of USA
1	California	217,880	9.7%
2	Texas	192,630	8.5%
3	Florida	159,263	7.1%
4	New York	134,345	6.0%
5	Nevada	123,303	5.5%
6	Illinois	83,208	3.7%
7	Ohio	80,373	3.6%
8	Tennessee	76,531	3.4%
9	Pennsylvania	69,647	3.1%
10	Michigan	65,164	2.9%
11	Virginia	63,152	2.8%
12	North Carolina	61,046	2.7%
13	Georgia	58,382	2.6%
14	New Jersey	51,355	2.3%
15	Indiana	43,903	1.9%
16	Alabama	42,675	1.9%
17	Missouri	41,934	1.9%
18	Washington	38,125	1.7%
19	Maryland	37,969	1.7%
20	Arkansas	37,818	1.7%
21	Kentucky	36,576	1.6%
22	Massachusetts	36,523	1.6%
23	South Carolina	36,380	1.6%
24	Arizona	36,199	1.6%
25	Colorado	35,600	1.6%
26	Louisiana	35,577	1.6%
27	Wisconsin	34,295	1.5%
28	Minnesota	31,782	1.4%
29	Hawaii	25,334	1.1%
30	Oregon	24,901	1.1%
31	Utah	22,728	1.0%
32	Kansas	19,809	0.9%
33	Mississippi	18,952	0.8%
34	Iowa	18,139	0.8%
35	Connecticut	16,188	0.7%
36	West Virginia	14,887	0.7%
37	New Mexico	14,662	0.7%
38	Idaho	14,405	0.6%
39	Nebraska	13,005	0.6%
40	New Hampshire	10,978	0.5%
41	Maine	10,900	0.5%
42	Rhode Island	8,272	0.4%
43	South Dakota	6,789	0.3%
44	Montana	6,317	0.3%
45	Vermont	5,963	0.3%
46	Alaska	5,511	0.2%
47	Delaware	4,925	0.2%
48	Wyoming	4,717	0.2%
49	North Dakota	4,555	0.2%
NA	Oklahoma**	NA	NA
	District of Columbia	3,039	0.1%

*Source: U.S. Department of Health and Human Services, National Center for Health Statistics
    "National Vital Statistics Reports" (Vol. 51, No. 10)*
Provisional data by state of occurrence.
**Not available.*

Marriage Rate in 2002

National Rate = 7.8 Marriages per 1,000 Population*

<u>ALPHA ORDER</u>

RANK	STATE	RATE
8	Alabama	9.5
16	Alaska	8.6
36	Arizona	6.7
3	Arkansas	14.0
43	California	6.2
20	Colorado	7.9
49	Connecticut	4.7
45	Delaware	6.1
8	Florida	9.5
35	Georgia	6.8
2	Hawaii	20.4
5	Idaho	10.7
37	Illinois	6.6
29	Indiana	7.1
43	Iowa	6.2
26	Kansas	7.3
11	Kentucky	8.9
20	Louisiana	7.9
18	Maine	8.4
31	Maryland	7.0
47	Massachusetts	5.7
39	Michigan	6.5
40	Minnesota	6.3
37	Mississippi	6.6
25	Missouri	7.4
34	Montana	6.9
24	Nebraska	7.5
1	Nevada	56.9
16	New Hampshire	8.6
46	New Jersey	6.0
20	New Mexico	7.9
31	New York	7.0
26	North Carolina	7.3
28	North Dakota	7.2
31	Ohio	7.0
NA	Oklahoma**	NA
29	Oregon	7.1
48	Pennsylvania	5.6
23	Rhode Island	7.7
11	South Carolina	8.9
11	South Dakota	8.9
4	Tennessee	13.2
11	Texas	8.9
6	Utah	9.8
7	Vermont	9.7
15	Virginia	8.7
40	Washington	6.3
19	West Virginia	8.2
40	Wisconsin	6.3
8	Wyoming	9.5

<u>RANK ORDER</u>

RANK	STATE	RATE
1	Nevada	56.9
2	Hawaii	20.4
3	Arkansas	14.0
4	Tennessee	13.2
5	Idaho	10.7
6	Utah	9.8
7	Vermont	9.7
8	Alabama	9.5
8	Florida	9.5
8	Wyoming	9.5
11	Kentucky	8.9
11	South Carolina	8.9
11	South Dakota	8.9
11	Texas	8.9
15	Virginia	8.7
16	Alaska	8.6
16	New Hampshire	8.6
18	Maine	8.4
19	West Virginia	8.2
20	Colorado	7.9
20	Louisiana	7.9
20	New Mexico	7.9
23	Rhode Island	7.7
24	Nebraska	7.5
25	Missouri	7.4
26	Kansas	7.3
26	North Carolina	7.3
28	North Dakota	7.2
29	Indiana	7.1
29	Oregon	7.1
31	Maryland	7.0
31	New York	7.0
31	Ohio	7.0
34	Montana	6.9
35	Georgia	6.8
36	Arizona	6.7
37	Illinois	6.6
37	Mississippi	6.6
39	Michigan	6.5
40	Minnesota	6.3
40	Washington	6.3
40	Wisconsin	6.3
43	California	6.2
43	Iowa	6.2
45	Delaware	6.1
46	New Jersey	6.0
47	Massachusetts	5.7
48	Pennsylvania	5.6
49	Connecticut	4.7
NA	Oklahoma**	NA

District of Columbia   5.3

Source: Morgan Quitno Press using data from U.S. Dept. of Health and Human Services, Nat'l Center for Health Statistics "National Vital Statistics Reports" (Vol. 51, No. 10)

*Provisional data by state of occurrence.

**Not available.

Divorces in 2002

Reporting States' Total = 958,978 Divorces*

<u>ALPHA ORDER</u>

RANK	STATE	DIVORCES	% of USA
15	Alabama	24,611	2.6%
41	Alaska	2,631	0.3%
14	Arizona	25,896	2.7%
21	Arkansas	16,931	1.8%
NA	California**	NA	NA
18	Colorado	21,113	2.2%
29	Connecticut	9,942	1.0%
45	Delaware	2,424	0.3%
1	Florida	86,565	9.0%
9	Georgia	31,495	3.3%
38	Hawaii	4,612	0.5%
34	Idaho	7,008	0.7%
8	Illinois	36,854	3.8%
NA	Indiana**	NA	NA
32	Iowa	8,624	0.9%
28	Kansas	10,289	1.1%
17	Kentucky	21,139	2.2%
NA	Louisiana**	NA	NA
37	Maine	5,018	0.5%
23	Maryland	16,426	1.7%
22	Massachusetts	16,661	1.7%
5	Michigan	37,836	3.9%
25	Minnesota	15,594	1.6%
26	Mississippi	14,226	1.5%
16	Missouri	22,913	2.4%
44	Montana	2,516	0.3%
35	Nebraska	6,340	0.7%
19	Nevada	20,926	2.2%
36	New Hampshire	5,900	0.6%
12	New Jersey	29,191	3.0%
33	New Mexico	8,099	0.8%
3	New York	71,616	7.5%
6	North Carolina	37,298	3.9%
46	North Dakota	1,819	0.2%
4	Ohio	45,955	4.8%
NA	Oklahoma**	NA	NA
24	Oregon	16,166	1.7%
7	Pennsylvania	37,105	3.9%
39	Rhode Island	3,336	0.3%
27	South Carolina	13,317	1.4%
43	South Dakota	2,556	0.3%
10	Tennessee	31,456	3.3%
2	Texas	83,996	8.8%
31	Utah	9,552	1.0%
42	Vermont	2,574	0.3%
11	Virginia	30,836	3.2%
13	Washington	27,964	2.9%
30	West Virginia	9,939	1.0%
20	Wisconsin	17,705	1.8%
40	Wyoming	2,654	0.3%

<u>RANK ORDER</u>

RANK	STATE	DIVORCES	% of USA
1	Florida	86,565	9.0%
2	Texas	83,996	8.8%
3	New York	71,616	7.5%
4	Ohio	45,955	4.8%
5	Michigan	37,836	3.9%
6	North Carolina	37,298	3.9%
7	Pennsylvania	37,105	3.9%
8	Illinois	36,854	3.8%
9	Georgia	31,495	3.3%
10	Tennessee	31,456	3.3%
11	Virginia	30,836	3.2%
12	New Jersey	29,191	3.0%
13	Washington	27,964	2.9%
14	Arizona	25,896	2.7%
15	Alabama	24,611	2.6%
16	Missouri	22,913	2.4%
17	Kentucky	21,139	2.2%
18	Colorado	21,113	2.2%
19	Nevada	20,926	2.2%
20	Wisconsin	17,705	1.8%
21	Arkansas	16,931	1.8%
22	Massachusetts	16,661	1.7%
23	Maryland	16,426	1.7%
24	Oregon	16,166	1.7%
25	Minnesota	15,594	1.6%
26	Mississippi	14,226	1.5%
27	South Carolina	13,317	1.4%
28	Kansas	10,289	1.1%
29	Connecticut	9,942	1.0%
30	West Virginia	9,939	1.0%
31	Utah	9,552	1.0%
32	Iowa	8,624	0.9%
33	New Mexico	8,099	0.8%
34	Idaho	7,008	0.7%
35	Nebraska	6,340	0.7%
36	New Hampshire	5,900	0.6%
37	Maine	5,018	0.5%
38	Hawaii	4,612	0.5%
39	Rhode Island	3,336	0.3%
40	Wyoming	2,654	0.3%
41	Alaska	2,631	0.3%
42	Vermont	2,574	0.3%
43	South Dakota	2,556	0.3%
44	Montana	2,516	0.3%
45	Delaware	2,424	0.3%
46	North Dakota	1,819	0.2%
NA	California**	NA	NA
NA	Indiana**	NA	NA
NA	Louisiana**	NA	NA
NA	Oklahoma**	NA	NA
	District of Columbia	1,354	0.1%

Source: U.S. Department of Health and Human Services, National Center for Health Statistics
"National Vital Statistics Reports" (Vol. 51, No. 10)
*Provisional data by state of occurrence. National total is only for reporting states.
**Not available.

Divorce Rate in 2002

Reporting States' Rate = 4.0 Divorces per 1,000 Population*

ALPHA ORDER

RANK	STATE	RATE
3	Alabama	5.5
20	Alaska	4.1
11	Arizona	4.8
2	Arkansas	6.3
NA	California**	NA
12	Colorado	4.7
41	Connecticut	2.9
38	Delaware	3.0
7	Florida	5.2
28	Georgia	3.7
28	Hawaii	3.7
7	Idaho	5.2
41	Illinois	2.9
NA	Indiana**	NA
41	Iowa	2.9
26	Kansas	3.8
7	Kentucky	5.2
NA	Louisiana**	NA
24	Maine	3.9
38	Maryland	3.0
46	Massachusetts	2.6
26	Michigan	3.8
36	Minnesota	3.1
10	Mississippi	5.0
22	Missouri	4.0
45	Montana	2.8
28	Nebraska	3.7
1	Nevada	9.7
13	New Hampshire	4.6
32	New Jersey	3.4
17	New Mexico	4.4
28	New York	3.7
16	North Carolina	4.5
41	North Dakota	2.9
22	Ohio	4.0
NA	Oklahoma**	NA
13	Oregon	4.6
38	Pennsylvania	3.0
36	Rhode Island	3.1
35	South Carolina	3.2
32	South Dakota	3.4
5	Tennessee	5.4
24	Texas	3.9
20	Utah	4.1
18	Vermont	4.2
18	Virginia	4.2
13	Washington	4.6
3	West Virginia	5.5
34	Wisconsin	3.3
6	Wyoming	5.3

RANK ORDER

RANK	STATE	RATE
1	Nevada	9.7
2	Arkansas	6.3
3	Alabama	5.5
3	West Virginia	5.5
5	Tennessee	5.4
6	Wyoming	5.3
7	Florida	5.2
7	Idaho	5.2
7	Kentucky	5.2
10	Mississippi	5.0
11	Arizona	4.8
12	Colorado	4.7
13	New Hampshire	4.6
13	Oregon	4.6
13	Washington	4.6
16	North Carolina	4.5
17	New Mexico	4.4
18	Vermont	4.2
18	Virginia	4.2
20	Alaska	4.1
20	Utah	4.1
22	Missouri	4.0
22	Ohio	4.0
24	Maine	3.9
24	Texas	3.9
26	Kansas	3.8
26	Michigan	3.8
28	Georgia	3.7
28	Hawaii	3.7
28	Nebraska	3.7
28	New York	3.7
32	New Jersey	3.4
32	South Dakota	3.4
34	Wisconsin	3.3
35	South Carolina	3.2
36	Minnesota	3.1
36	Rhode Island	3.1
38	Delaware	3.0
38	Maryland	3.0
38	Pennsylvania	3.0
41	Connecticut	2.9
41	Illinois	2.9
41	Iowa	2.9
41	North Dakota	2.9
45	Montana	2.8
46	Massachusetts	2.6
NA	California**	NA
NA	Indiana**	NA
NA	Louisiana**	NA
NA	Oklahoma**	NA

District of Columbia   2.4

Source: Morgan Quitno Press using data from U.S. Dept. of Health and Human Services, Nat'l Center for Health Statistics
"National Vital Statistics Reports" (Vol. 51, No. 10)
*Provisional data by state of occurrence. National rate is only for reporting states.
**Not available.

Average Family Size in 2002

National Average = 3.19 Persons per Family

<u>ALPHA ORDER</u>

RANK	STATE	PERSONS
35	Alabama	3.03
8	Alaska	3.27
14	Arizona	3.18
43	Arkansas	3.00
1	California	3.56
45	Colorado	2.99
18	Connecticut	3.14
31	Delaware	3.04
31	Florida	3.04
6	Georgia	3.28
2	Hawaii	3.45
15	Idaho	3.16
6	Illinois	3.28
22	Indiana	3.10
38	Iowa	3.02
25	Kansas	3.08
46	Kentucky	2.98
12	Louisiana	3.19
50	Maine	2.80
12	Maryland	3.19
16	Massachusetts	3.15
16	Michigan	3.15
41	Minnesota	3.01
18	Mississippi	3.14
46	Missouri	2.98
35	Montana	3.03
31	Nebraska	3.04
11	Nevada	3.23
35	New Hampshire	3.03
8	New Jersey	3.27
10	New Mexico	3.24
5	New York	3.29
29	North Carolina	3.05
38	North Dakota	3.02
25	Ohio	3.08
27	Oklahoma	3.07
38	Oregon	3.02
31	Pennsylvania	3.04
20	Rhode Island	3.11
28	South Carolina	3.06
23	South Dakota	3.09
29	Tennessee	3.05
4	Texas	3.40
2	Utah	3.45
49	Vermont	2.95
23	Virginia	3.09
20	Washington	3.11
43	West Virginia	3.00
41	Wisconsin	3.01
48	Wyoming	2.96

<u>RANK ORDER</u>

RANK	STATE	PERSONS
1	California	3.56
2	Hawaii	3.45
2	Utah	3.45
4	Texas	3.40
5	New York	3.29
6	Georgia	3.28
6	Illinois	3.28
8	Alaska	3.27
8	New Jersey	3.27
10	New Mexico	3.24
11	Nevada	3.23
12	Louisiana	3.19
12	Maryland	3.19
14	Arizona	3.18
15	Idaho	3.16
16	Massachusetts	3.15
16	Michigan	3.15
18	Connecticut	3.14
18	Mississippi	3.14
20	Rhode Island	3.11
20	Washington	3.11
22	Indiana	3.10
23	South Dakota	3.09
23	Virginia	3.09
25	Kansas	3.08
25	Ohio	3.08
27	Oklahoma	3.07
28	South Carolina	3.06
29	North Carolina	3.05
29	Tennessee	3.05
31	Delaware	3.04
31	Florida	3.04
31	Nebraska	3.04
31	Pennsylvania	3.04
35	Alabama	3.03
35	Montana	3.03
35	New Hampshire	3.03
38	Iowa	3.02
38	North Dakota	3.02
38	Oregon	3.02
41	Minnesota	3.01
41	Wisconsin	3.01
43	Arkansas	3.00
43	West Virginia	3.00
45	Colorado	2.99
46	Kentucky	2.98
46	Missouri	2.98
48	Wyoming	2.96
49	Vermont	2.95
50	Maine	2.80

District of Columbia 3.13

Source: U.S. Bureau of the Census
   "2002 American Community Survey"

Seats in the U.S. House of Representatives in 2004

National Total = 435 Seats*

ALPHA ORDER

RANK	STATE	SEATS	% of USA
22	Alabama	7	1.6%
44	Alaska	1	0.2%
18	Arizona	8	1.8%
31	Arkansas	4	0.9%
1	California	53	12.2%
22	Colorado	7	1.6%
27	Connecticut	5	1.1%
44	Delaware	1	0.2%
4	Florida	25	5.7%
9	Georgia	13	3.0%
39	Hawaii	2	0.5%
39	Idaho	2	0.5%
5	Illinois	19	4.4%
14	Indiana	9	2.1%
27	Iowa	5	1.1%
31	Kansas	4	0.9%
25	Kentucky	6	1.4%
22	Louisiana	7	1.6%
39	Maine	2	0.5%
18	Maryland	8	1.8%
13	Massachusetts	10	2.3%
8	Michigan	15	3.4%
18	Minnesota	8	1.8%
31	Mississippi	4	0.9%
14	Missouri	9	2.1%
44	Montana	1	0.2%
34	Nebraska	3	0.7%
34	Nevada	3	0.7%
39	New Hampshire	2	0.5%
9	New Jersey	13	3.0%
34	New Mexico	3	0.7%
3	New York	29	6.7%
9	North Carolina	13	3.0%
44	North Dakota	1	0.2%
7	Ohio	18	4.1%
27	Oklahoma	5	1.1%
27	Oregon	5	1.1%
5	Pennsylvania	19	4.4%
39	Rhode Island	2	0.5%
25	South Carolina	6	1.4%
44	South Dakota	1	0.2%
14	Tennessee	9	2.1%
2	Texas	32	7.4%
34	Utah	3	0.7%
44	Vermont	1	0.2%
12	Virginia	11	2.5%
14	Washington	9	2.1%
34	West Virginia	3	0.7%
18	Wisconsin	8	1.8%
44	Wyoming	1	0.2%

RANK ORDER

RANK	STATE	SEATS	% of USA
1	California	53	12.2%
2	Texas	32	7.4%
3	New York	29	6.7%
4	Florida	25	5.7%
5	Illinois	19	4.4%
5	Pennsylvania	19	4.4%
7	Ohio	18	4.1%
8	Michigan	15	3.4%
9	Georgia	13	3.0%
9	New Jersey	13	3.0%
9	North Carolina	13	3.0%
12	Virginia	11	2.5%
13	Massachusetts	10	2.3%
14	Indiana	9	2.1%
14	Missouri	9	2.1%
14	Tennessee	9	2.1%
14	Washington	9	2.1%
18	Arizona	8	1.8%
18	Maryland	8	1.8%
18	Minnesota	8	1.8%
18	Wisconsin	8	1.8%
22	Alabama	7	1.6%
22	Colorado	7	1.6%
22	Louisiana	7	1.6%
25	Kentucky	6	1.4%
25	South Carolina	6	1.4%
27	Connecticut	5	1.1%
27	Iowa	5	1.1%
27	Oklahoma	5	1.1%
27	Oregon	5	1.1%
31	Arkansas	4	0.9%
31	Kansas	4	0.9%
31	Mississippi	4	0.9%
34	Nebraska	3	0.7%
34	Nevada	3	0.7%
34	New Mexico	3	0.7%
34	Utah	3	0.7%
34	West Virginia	3	0.7%
39	Hawaii	2	0.5%
39	Idaho	2	0.5%
39	Maine	2	0.5%
39	New Hampshire	2	0.5%
39	Rhode Island	2	0.5%
44	Alaska	1	0.2%
44	Delaware	1	0.2%
44	Montana	1	0.2%
44	North Dakota	1	0.2%
44	South Dakota	1	0.2%
44	Vermont	1	0.2%
44	Wyoming	1	0.2%
	District of Columbia**	0	0.0%

Source: U.S. Bureau of the Census
    "Congressional Apportionment" (http://www.census.gov/population/www/censusdata/apportionment.html)
*This table shows the number of seats after reapportionment of the 2000 Census. This apportionment became effective with the Congress elected in November 2002 and that took office in January 2003.
**The District of Columbia has one non-voting delegate. Each state has two members in the U.S. Senate.

Estimated Population per U.S. House Seat in 2004

National Rate = 667,233 Persons per House Member*

ALPHA ORDER

RANK	STATE	RATE
37	Alabama	642,965
33	Alaska	648,818
9	Arizona	697,601
18	Arkansas	681,429
24	California	669,518
31	Colorado	650,098
10	Connecticut	696,674
2	Delaware	817,491
21	Florida	680,763
25	Georgia	668,055
43	Hawaii	628,804
17	Idaho	683,166
26	Illinois	665,976
14	Indiana	688,405
47	Iowa	588,812
20	Kansas	680,877
15	Kentucky	686,305
38	Louisiana	642,333
29	Maine	652,864
13	Maryland	688,614
36	Massachusetts	643,342
22	Michigan	671,999
42	Minnesota	632,422
6	Mississippi	720,320
41	Missouri	633,832
1	Montana	917,621
48	Nebraska	579,764
5	Nevada	747,051
35	New Hampshire	643,844
27	New Jersey	664,492
44	New Mexico	624,871
28	New York	661,728
34	North Carolina	646,711
40	North Dakota	633,837
39	Ohio	635,322
8	Oklahoma	702,306
7	Oregon	711,919
30	Pennsylvania	650,813
49	Rhode Island	538,082
12	South Carolina	691,192
4	South Dakota	764,309
32	Tennessee	649,083
11	Texas	691,203
3	Utah	783,822
45	Vermont	619,107
23	Virginia	671,485
19	Washington	681,272
46	West Virginia	603,451
16	Wisconsin	684,037
50	Wyoming	501,242

RANK ORDER

RANK	STATE	RATE
1	Montana	917,621
2	Delaware	817,491
3	Utah	783,822
4	South Dakota	764,309
5	Nevada	747,051
6	Mississippi	720,320
7	Oregon	711,919
8	Oklahoma	702,306
9	Arizona	697,601
10	Connecticut	696,674
11	Texas	691,203
12	South Carolina	691,192
13	Maryland	688,614
14	Indiana	688,405
15	Kentucky	686,305
16	Wisconsin	684,037
17	Idaho	683,166
18	Arkansas	681,429
19	Washington	681,272
20	Kansas	680,877
21	Florida	680,763
22	Michigan	671,999
23	Virginia	671,485
24	California	669,518
25	Georgia	668,055
26	Illinois	665,976
27	New Jersey	664,492
28	New York	661,728
29	Maine	652,864
30	Pennsylvania	650,813
31	Colorado	650,098
32	Tennessee	649,083
33	Alaska	648,818
34	North Carolina	646,711
35	New Hampshire	643,844
36	Massachusetts	643,342
37	Alabama	642,965
38	Louisiana	642,333
39	Ohio	635,322
40	North Dakota	633,837
41	Missouri	633,832
42	Minnesota	632,422
43	Hawaii	628,804
44	New Mexico	624,871
45	Vermont	619,107
46	West Virginia	603,451
47	Iowa	588,812
48	Nebraska	579,764
49	Rhode Island	538,082
50	Wyoming	501,242
	District of Columbia**	NA

Source: Morgan Quitno Press using data from U.S. Bureau of the Census
   "Congressional Apportionment" (http://blue.census.gov/population/www/censusdata/apportionment.html)
*National rate does not include population of the District of Columbia. D.C. has one non-voting delegate. Each state has two members in the U.S. Senate. This table is based only on U.S. Representatives and not U.S. Senate members. This table reflects reapportionment resulting from the 2000 census.
**Not applicable.

State Legislators in 2004

National Total = 7,382 Legislators*

ALPHA ORDER

RANK	STATE	LEGISLATORS	% of USA
27	Alabama	140	1.9%
49	Alaska	60	0.8%
43	Arizona	90	1.2%
30	Arkansas	135	1.8%
35	California	120	1.6%
42	Colorado	100	1.4%
9	Connecticut	187	2.5%
48	Delaware	62	0.8%
18	Florida	160	2.2%
3	Georgia	236	3.2%
46	Hawaii	76	1.0%
39	Idaho	105	1.4%
13	Illinois	177	2.4%
19	Indiana	150	2.0%
19	Iowa	150	2.0%
17	Kansas	165	2.2%
29	Kentucky	138	1.9%
25	Louisiana	144	2.0%
10	Maine	186	2.5%
8	Maryland	188	2.5%
6	Massachusetts	200	2.7%
23	Michigan	148	2.0%
5	Minnesota	201	2.7%
14	Mississippi	174	2.4%
7	Missouri	197	2.7%
19	Montana	150	2.0%
50	Nebraska	49	0.7%
47	Nevada	63	0.9%
1	New Hampshire	424	5.7%
35	New Jersey	120	1.6%
38	New Mexico	112	1.5%
4	New York	212	2.9%
15	North Carolina	170	2.3%
26	North Dakota	141	1.9%
32	Ohio	132	1.8%
22	Oklahoma	149	2.0%
43	Oregon	90	1.2%
2	Pennsylvania	253	3.4%
37	Rhode Island	113	1.5%
15	South Carolina	170	2.3%
39	South Dakota	105	1.4%
32	Tennessee	132	1.8%
11	Texas	181	2.5%
41	Utah	104	1.4%
12	Vermont	180	2.4%
27	Virginia	140	1.9%
24	Washington	147	2.0%
31	West Virginia	134	1.8%
32	Wisconsin	132	1.8%
43	Wyoming	90	1.2%

RANK ORDER

RANK	STATE	LEGISLATORS	% of USA
1	New Hampshire	424	5.7%
2	Pennsylvania	253	3.4%
3	Georgia	236	3.2%
4	New York	212	2.9%
5	Minnesota	201	2.7%
6	Massachusetts	200	2.7%
7	Missouri	197	2.7%
8	Maryland	188	2.5%
9	Connecticut	187	2.5%
10	Maine	186	2.5%
11	Texas	181	2.5%
12	Vermont	180	2.4%
13	Illinois	177	2.4%
14	Mississippi	174	2.4%
15	North Carolina	170	2.3%
15	South Carolina	170	2.3%
17	Kansas	165	2.2%
18	Florida	160	2.2%
19	Indiana	150	2.0%
19	Iowa	150	2.0%
19	Montana	150	2.0%
22	Oklahoma	149	2.0%
23	Michigan	148	2.0%
24	Washington	147	2.0%
25	Louisiana	144	2.0%
26	North Dakota	141	1.9%
27	Alabama	140	1.9%
27	Virginia	140	1.9%
29	Kentucky	138	1.9%
30	Arkansas	135	1.8%
31	West Virginia	134	1.8%
32	Ohio	132	1.8%
32	Tennessee	132	1.8%
32	Wisconsin	132	1.8%
35	California	120	1.6%
35	New Jersey	120	1.6%
37	Rhode Island	113	1.5%
38	New Mexico	112	1.5%
39	Idaho	105	1.4%
39	South Dakota	105	1.4%
41	Utah	104	1.4%
42	Colorado	100	1.4%
43	Arizona	90	1.2%
43	Oregon	90	1.2%
43	Wyoming	90	1.2%
46	Hawaii	76	1.0%
47	Nevada	63	0.9%
48	Delaware	62	0.8%
49	Alaska	60	0.8%
50	Nebraska	49	0.7%
	District of Columbia**	NA	NA

Source: National Conference of State Legislatures (Denver, CO)
"2004 Partisan Composition of State Legislatures"
(http://www.ncsl.org/ncsldb/elect98/partcomp.cfm?yearsel=2004)
**There are 1,971 state senators (including Nebraska's 49 unicameral seats) and 5,411 state house members.*
***Not applicable.*

Population per State Legislator in 2004

National Rate = 39,318 Population per Legislator*

ALPHA ORDER

RANK	STATE	RATE
23	Alabama	32,148
42	Alaska	10,814
9	Arizona	62,009
32	Arkansas	20,190
1	California	295,704
13	Colorado	45,507
34	Connecticut	18,628
40	Delaware	13,185
3	Florida	106,369
19	Georgia	36,800
37	Hawaii	16,547
41	Idaho	13,013
7	Illinois	71,489
17	Indiana	41,304
33	Iowa	19,627
38	Kansas	16,506
25	Kentucky	29,839
24	Louisiana	31,225
45	Maine	7,020
26	Maryland	29,303
22	Massachusetts	32,167
8	Michigan	68,108
28	Minnesota	25,171
36	Mississippi	16,559
27	Missouri	28,957
46	Montana	6,117
21	Nebraska	35,496
20	Nevada	35,574
50	New Hampshire	3,037
6	New Jersey	71,987
35	New Mexico	16,738
4	New York	90,519
11	North Carolina	49,454
48	North Dakota	4,495
5	Ohio	86,635
30	Oklahoma	23,567
18	Oregon	39,551
12	Pennsylvania	48,875
43	Rhode Island	9,524
29	South Carolina	24,395
44	South Dakota	7,279
14	Tennessee	44,256
2	Texas	122,202
31	Utah	22,610
49	Vermont	3,439
10	Virginia	52,760
15	Washington	41,711
39	West Virginia	13,510
16	Wisconsin	41,457
47	Wyoming	5,569

RANK ORDER

RANK	STATE	RATE
1	California	295,704
2	Texas	122,202
3	Florida	106,369
4	New York	90,519
5	Ohio	86,635
6	New Jersey	71,987
7	Illinois	71,489
8	Michigan	68,108
9	Arizona	62,009
10	Virginia	52,760
11	North Carolina	49,454
12	Pennsylvania	48,875
13	Colorado	45,507
14	Tennessee	44,256
15	Washington	41,711
16	Wisconsin	41,457
17	Indiana	41,304
18	Oregon	39,551
19	Georgia	36,800
20	Nevada	35,574
21	Nebraska	35,496
22	Massachusetts	32,167
23	Alabama	32,148
24	Louisiana	31,225
25	Kentucky	29,839
26	Maryland	29,303
27	Missouri	28,957
28	Minnesota	25,171
29	South Carolina	24,395
30	Oklahoma	23,567
31	Utah	22,610
32	Arkansas	20,190
33	Iowa	19,627
34	Connecticut	18,628
35	New Mexico	16,738
36	Mississippi	16,559
37	Hawaii	16,547
38	Kansas	16,506
39	West Virginia	13,510
40	Delaware	13,185
41	Idaho	13,013
42	Alaska	10,814
43	Rhode Island	9,524
44	South Dakota	7,279
45	Maine	7,020
46	Montana	6,117
47	Wyoming	5,569
48	North Dakota	4,495
49	Vermont	3,439
50	New Hampshire	3,037

District of Columbia** NA

Source: Morgan Quitno Press using data from National Conference of State Legislatures (Denver, CO)
   "2004 Partisan Composition of State Legislatures"
      (http://www.ncsl.org/ncsldb/elect98/partcomp.cfm?yearsel=2004)
*There are 1,971 state senators (including Nebraska's 49 unicameral seats) and 5,411 state house members.
National rate does not include population for the District of Columbia.
**Not applicable.

Registered Voters in 2000

National Total = 156,421,311*

<u>ALPHA ORDER</u>

RANK	STATE	REGISTERED	% of USA
22	Alabama	2,528,963	1.6%
45	Alaska	473,648	0.3%
25	Arizona	2,173,122	1.4%
32	Arkansas	1,555,809	1.0%
1	California	15,707,307	10.0%
23	Colorado	2,274,152	1.5%
28	Connecticut	1,874,245	1.2%
44	Delaware	505,360	0.3%
4	Florida	8,752,717	5.6%
14	Georgia	3,859,960	2.5%
43	Hawaii	637,349	0.4%
40	Idaho	728,085	0.5%
7	Illinois	7,129,026	4.6%
12	Indiana	4,000,809	2.6%
29	Iowa	1,841,346	1.2%
31	Kansas	1,623,623	1.0%
21	Kentucky	2,556,815	1.6%
19	Louisiana	2,730,380	1.7%
38	Maine	882,337	0.6%
20	Maryland	2,715,366	1.7%
11	Massachusetts	4,008,796	2.6%
8	Michigan	6,861,342	4.4%
17	Minnesota	3,265,324	2.1%
30	Mississippi	1,739,858	1.1%
13	Missouri	3,860,672	2.5%
41	Montana	698,260	0.4%
34	Nebraska	1,085,217	0.7%
37	Nevada	898,347	0.6%
39	New Hampshire	856,519	0.5%
10	New Jersey	4,710,768	3.0%
36	New Mexico	972,895	0.6%
2	New York	11,262,816	7.2%
9	North Carolina	5,122,123	3.3%
NA	North Dakota**	NA	NA
6	Ohio	7,537,822	4.8%
24	Oklahoma	2,233,602	1.4%
27	Oregon	1,943,699	1.2%
5	Pennsylvania	7,781,997	5.0%
42	Rhode Island	655,107	0.4%
26	South Carolina	2,157,006	1.4%
46	South Dakota	471,152	0.3%
18	Tennessee	3,181,108	2.0%
3	Texas	10,267,639	6.6%
33	Utah	1,123,238	0.7%
47	Vermont	427,354	0.3%
15	Virginia	3,770,273	2.4%
16	Washington	3,335,714	2.1%
35	West Virginia	1,067,822	0.7%
NA	Wisconsin**	NA	NA
48	Wyoming	220,012	0.1%

<u>RANK ORDER</u>

RANK	STATE	REGISTERED	% of USA
1	California	15,707,307	10.0%
2	New York	11,262,816	7.2%
3	Texas	10,267,639	6.6%
4	Florida	8,752,717	5.6%
5	Pennsylvania	7,781,997	5.0%
6	Ohio	7,537,822	4.8%
7	Illinois	7,129,026	4.6%
8	Michigan	6,861,342	4.4%
9	North Carolina	5,122,123	3.3%
10	New Jersey	4,710,768	3.0%
11	Massachusetts	4,008,796	2.6%
12	Indiana	4,000,809	2.6%
13	Missouri	3,860,672	2.5%
14	Georgia	3,859,960	2.5%
15	Virginia	3,770,273	2.4%
16	Washington	3,335,714	2.1%
17	Minnesota	3,265,324	2.1%
18	Tennessee	3,181,108	2.0%
19	Louisiana	2,730,380	1.7%
20	Maryland	2,715,366	1.7%
21	Kentucky	2,556,815	1.6%
22	Alabama	2,528,963	1.6%
23	Colorado	2,274,152	1.5%
24	Oklahoma	2,233,602	1.4%
25	Arizona	2,173,122	1.4%
26	South Carolina	2,157,006	1.4%
27	Oregon	1,943,699	1.2%
28	Connecticut	1,874,245	1.2%
29	Iowa	1,841,346	1.2%
30	Mississippi	1,739,858	1.1%
31	Kansas	1,623,623	1.0%
32	Arkansas	1,555,809	1.0%
33	Utah	1,123,238	0.7%
34	Nebraska	1,085,217	0.7%
35	West Virginia	1,067,822	0.7%
36	New Mexico	972,895	0.6%
37	Nevada	898,347	0.6%
38	Maine	882,337	0.6%
39	New Hampshire	856,519	0.5%
40	Idaho	728,085	0.5%
41	Montana	698,260	0.4%
42	Rhode Island	655,107	0.4%
43	Hawaii	637,349	0.4%
44	Delaware	505,360	0.3%
45	Alaska	473,648	0.3%
46	South Dakota	471,152	0.3%
47	Vermont	427,354	0.3%
48	Wyoming	220,012	0.1%
NA	North Dakota**	NA	NA
NA	Wisconsin**	NA	NA
	District of Columbia	354,410	0.2%

Source: Federal Election Commission
    "Voter Registration and Turnout - 2000" (http://www.fec.gov/pages/2000turnout/reg&to00.htm)

*As reported by states.

**North Dakota has no voter registration and Wisconsin has election day registration at the polls.

Percent of Eligible Voters Reported Registered in 2000

National Percent = 76.0%*

ALPHA ORDER

RANK	STATE	PERCENT
32	Alabama	75.9
1	Alaska	110.0
48	Arizona	59.9
25	Arkansas	80.7
46	California	63.2
38	Colorado	74.1
36	Connecticut	75.0
15	Delaware	86.8
37	Florida	74.3
44	Georgia	65.5
41	Hawaii	70.1
27	Idaho	79.1
26	Illinois	79.4
9	Indiana	89.9
18	Iowa	85.1
23	Kansas	81.9
17	Kentucky	85.4
22	Louisiana	83.9
8	Maine	91.2
42	Maryland	69.2
21	Massachusetts	84.4
5	Michigan	93.3
7	Minnesota	92.1
20	Mississippi	84.9
3	Missouri	94.0
2	Montana	104.5
13	Nebraska	87.9
45	Nevada	64.6
3	New Hampshire	94.0
33	New Jersey	75.4
28	New Mexico	77.0
24	New York	81.6
11	North Carolina	88.4
NA	North Dakota**	NA
10	Ohio	89.4
12	Oklahoma	88.2
29	Oregon	76.8
19	Pennsylvania	85.0
14	Rhode Island	87.0
39	South Carolina	72.5
15	South Dakota	86.8
33	Tennessee	75.4
43	Texas	69.1
30	Utah	76.7
6	Vermont	92.9
40	Virginia	71.6
31	Washington	76.4
33	West Virginia	75.4
NA	Wisconsin**	NA
47	Wyoming	61.5

RANK ORDER

RANK	STATE	PERCENT
1	Alaska	110.0
2	Montana	104.5
3	Missouri	94.0
3	New Hampshire	94.0
5	Michigan	93.3
6	Vermont	92.9
7	Minnesota	92.1
8	Maine	91.2
9	Indiana	89.9
10	Ohio	89.4
11	North Carolina	88.4
12	Oklahoma	88.2
13	Nebraska	87.9
14	Rhode Island	87.0
15	Delaware	86.8
15	South Dakota	86.8
17	Kentucky	85.4
18	Iowa	85.1
19	Pennsylvania	85.0
20	Mississippi	84.9
21	Massachusetts	84.4
22	Louisiana	83.9
23	Kansas	81.9
24	New York	81.6
25	Arkansas	80.7
26	Illinois	79.4
27	Idaho	79.1
28	New Mexico	77.0
29	Oregon	76.8
30	Utah	76.7
31	Washington	76.4
32	Alabama	75.9
33	New Jersey	75.4
33	Tennessee	75.4
33	West Virginia	75.4
36	Connecticut	75.0
37	Florida	74.3
38	Colorado	74.1
39	South Carolina	72.5
40	Virginia	71.6
41	Hawaii	70.1
42	Maryland	69.2
43	Texas	69.1
44	Georgia	65.5
45	Nevada	64.6
46	California	63.2
47	Wyoming	61.5
48	Arizona	59.9
NA	North Dakota**	NA
NA	Wisconsin**	NA
	District of Columbia	86.2

Source: Federal Election Commission
    "Voter Registration and Turnout - 2000" (http://www.fec.gov/pages/2000turnout/reg&to00.htm)
*As a percent of voting age population.
**North Dakota has no voter registration and Wisconsin has election day registration at the polls.

Persons Voting in 2000

National Total = 105,586,274*

<table>
<tr><td colspan="4"><u>ALPHA ORDER</u></td><td colspan="4"><u>RANK ORDER</u></td></tr>
<tr><td>RANK</td><td>STATE</td><td>VOTERS</td><td>% of USA</td><td>RANK</td><td>STATE</td><td>VOTERS</td><td>% of USA</td></tr>
<tr><td>23</td><td>Alabama</td><td>1,666,272</td><td>1.6%</td><td>1</td><td>California</td><td>10,965,822</td><td>10.4%</td></tr>
<tr><td>49</td><td>Alaska</td><td>285,560</td><td>0.3%</td><td>2</td><td>New York</td><td>6,960,215</td><td>6.6%</td></tr>
<tr><td>26</td><td>Arizona</td><td>1,532,016</td><td>1.5%</td><td>3</td><td>Texas</td><td>6,407,037</td><td>6.1%</td></tr>
<tr><td>33</td><td>Arkansas</td><td>921,781</td><td>0.9%</td><td>4</td><td>Florida</td><td>5,963,110</td><td>5.6%</td></tr>
<tr><td>1</td><td>California</td><td>10,965,822</td><td>10.4%</td><td>5</td><td>Pennsylvania</td><td>4,912,185</td><td>4.7%</td></tr>
<tr><td>22</td><td>Colorado</td><td>1,741,368</td><td>1.6%</td><td>6</td><td>Illinois</td><td>4,742,115</td><td>4.5%</td></tr>
<tr><td>27</td><td>Connecticut</td><td>1,459,526</td><td>1.4%</td><td>7</td><td>Ohio</td><td>4,701,998</td><td>4.5%</td></tr>
<tr><td>45</td><td>Delaware</td><td>327,529</td><td>0.3%</td><td>8</td><td>Michigan</td><td>4,232,501</td><td>4.0%</td></tr>
<tr><td>4</td><td>Florida</td><td>5,963,110</td><td>5.6%</td><td>9</td><td>New Jersey</td><td>3,187,226</td><td>3.0%</td></tr>
<tr><td>14</td><td>Georgia</td><td>2,583,208</td><td>2.4%</td><td>10</td><td>North Carolina</td><td>2,914,990</td><td>2.8%</td></tr>
<tr><td>44</td><td>Hawaii</td><td>367,951</td><td>0.3%</td><td>11</td><td>Virginia</td><td>2,789,808</td><td>2.6%</td></tr>
<tr><td>41</td><td>Idaho</td><td>501,615</td><td>0.5%</td><td>12</td><td>Massachusetts</td><td>2,734,006</td><td>2.6%</td></tr>
<tr><td>6</td><td>Illinois</td><td>4,742,115</td><td>4.5%</td><td>13</td><td>Wisconsin</td><td>2,598,607</td><td>2.5%</td></tr>
<tr><td>18</td><td>Indiana</td><td>2,180,305</td><td>2.1%</td><td>14</td><td>Georgia</td><td>2,583,208</td><td>2.4%</td></tr>
<tr><td>29</td><td>Iowa</td><td>1,314,395</td><td>1.2%</td><td>15</td><td>Washington</td><td>2,487,433</td><td>2.4%</td></tr>
<tr><td>31</td><td>Kansas</td><td>1,072,216</td><td>1.0%</td><td>16</td><td>Minnesota</td><td>2,438,685</td><td>2.3%</td></tr>
<tr><td>24</td><td>Kentucky</td><td>1,544,026</td><td>1.5%</td><td>17</td><td>Missouri</td><td>2,359,892</td><td>2.2%</td></tr>
<tr><td>21</td><td>Louisiana</td><td>1,765,656</td><td>1.7%</td><td>18</td><td>Indiana</td><td>2,180,305</td><td>2.1%</td></tr>
<tr><td>36</td><td>Maine</td><td>651,817</td><td>0.6%</td><td>19</td><td>Tennessee</td><td>2,076,181</td><td>2.0%</td></tr>
<tr><td>20</td><td>Maryland</td><td>2,023,735</td><td>1.9%</td><td>20</td><td>Maryland</td><td>2,023,735</td><td>1.9%</td></tr>
<tr><td>12</td><td>Massachusetts</td><td>2,734,006</td><td>2.6%</td><td>21</td><td>Louisiana</td><td>1,765,656</td><td>1.7%</td></tr>
<tr><td>8</td><td>Michigan</td><td>4,232,501</td><td>4.0%</td><td>22</td><td>Colorado</td><td>1,741,368</td><td>1.6%</td></tr>
<tr><td>16</td><td>Minnesota</td><td>2,438,685</td><td>2.3%</td><td>23</td><td>Alabama</td><td>1,666,272</td><td>1.6%</td></tr>
<tr><td>32</td><td>Mississippi</td><td>994,184</td><td>0.9%</td><td>24</td><td>Kentucky</td><td>1,544,026</td><td>1.5%</td></tr>
<tr><td>17</td><td>Missouri</td><td>2,359,892</td><td>2.2%</td><td>25</td><td>Oregon</td><td>1,533,968</td><td>1.5%</td></tr>
<tr><td>42</td><td>Montana</td><td>410,986</td><td>0.4%</td><td>26</td><td>Arizona</td><td>1,532,016</td><td>1.5%</td></tr>
<tr><td>35</td><td>Nebraska</td><td>697,019</td><td>0.7%</td><td>27</td><td>Connecticut</td><td>1,459,526</td><td>1.4%</td></tr>
<tr><td>38</td><td>Nevada</td><td>608,970</td><td>0.6%</td><td>28</td><td>South Carolina</td><td>1,386,331</td><td>1.3%</td></tr>
<tr><td>40</td><td>New Hampshire</td><td>569,081</td><td>0.5%</td><td>29</td><td>Iowa</td><td>1,314,395</td><td>1.2%</td></tr>
<tr><td>9</td><td>New Jersey</td><td>3,187,226</td><td>3.0%</td><td>30</td><td>Oklahoma</td><td>1,234,229</td><td>1.2%</td></tr>
<tr><td>39</td><td>New Mexico</td><td>598,605</td><td>0.6%</td><td>31</td><td>Kansas</td><td>1,072,216</td><td>1.0%</td></tr>
<tr><td>2</td><td>New York</td><td>6,960,215</td><td>6.6%</td><td>32</td><td>Mississippi</td><td>994,184</td><td>0.9%</td></tr>
<tr><td>10</td><td>North Carolina</td><td>2,914,990</td><td>2.8%</td><td>33</td><td>Arkansas</td><td>921,781</td><td>0.9%</td></tr>
<tr><td>48</td><td>North Dakota</td><td>288,256</td><td>0.3%</td><td>34</td><td>Utah</td><td>770,754</td><td>0.7%</td></tr>
<tr><td>7</td><td>Ohio</td><td>4,701,998</td><td>4.5%</td><td>35</td><td>Nebraska</td><td>697,019</td><td>0.7%</td></tr>
<tr><td>30</td><td>Oklahoma</td><td>1,234,229</td><td>1.2%</td><td>36</td><td>Maine</td><td>651,817</td><td>0.6%</td></tr>
<tr><td>25</td><td>Oregon</td><td>1,533,968</td><td>1.5%</td><td>37</td><td>West Virginia</td><td>648,124</td><td>0.6%</td></tr>
<tr><td>5</td><td>Pennsylvania</td><td>4,912,185</td><td>4.7%</td><td>38</td><td>Nevada</td><td>608,970</td><td>0.6%</td></tr>
<tr><td>43</td><td>Rhode Island</td><td>408,783</td><td>0.4%</td><td>39</td><td>New Mexico</td><td>598,605</td><td>0.6%</td></tr>
<tr><td>28</td><td>South Carolina</td><td>1,386,331</td><td>1.3%</td><td>40</td><td>New Hampshire</td><td>569,081</td><td>0.5%</td></tr>
<tr><td>46</td><td>South Dakota</td><td>316,269</td><td>0.3%</td><td>41</td><td>Idaho</td><td>501,615</td><td>0.5%</td></tr>
<tr><td>19</td><td>Tennessee</td><td>2,076,181</td><td>2.0%</td><td>42</td><td>Montana</td><td>410,986</td><td>0.4%</td></tr>
<tr><td>3</td><td>Texas</td><td>6,407,037</td><td>6.1%</td><td>43</td><td>Rhode Island</td><td>408,783</td><td>0.4%</td></tr>
<tr><td>34</td><td>Utah</td><td>770,754</td><td>0.7%</td><td>44</td><td>Hawaii</td><td>367,951</td><td>0.3%</td></tr>
<tr><td>47</td><td>Vermont</td><td>294,308</td><td>0.3%</td><td>45</td><td>Delaware</td><td>327,529</td><td>0.3%</td></tr>
<tr><td>11</td><td>Virginia</td><td>2,789,808</td><td>2.6%</td><td>46</td><td>South Dakota</td><td>316,269</td><td>0.3%</td></tr>
<tr><td>15</td><td>Washington</td><td>2,487,433</td><td>2.4%</td><td>47</td><td>Vermont</td><td>294,308</td><td>0.3%</td></tr>
<tr><td>37</td><td>West Virginia</td><td>648,124</td><td>0.6%</td><td>48</td><td>North Dakota</td><td>288,256</td><td>0.3%</td></tr>
<tr><td>13</td><td>Wisconsin</td><td>2,598,607</td><td>2.5%</td><td>49</td><td>Alaska</td><td>285,560</td><td>0.3%</td></tr>
<tr><td>50</td><td>Wyoming</td><td>213,726</td><td>0.2%</td><td>50</td><td>Wyoming</td><td>213,726</td><td>0.2%</td></tr>
<tr><td></td><td></td><td></td><td></td><td></td><td>District of Columbia</td><td>201,894</td><td>0.2%</td></tr>
</table>

Source: Federal Election Commission
  "Voter Registration and Turnout - 2000" (http://www.fec.gov/pages/2000turnout/reg&to00.htm)
**Refers to the total vote cast for the highest office on the ballot in 2000. These figures may be inconsistent with other reported turnout figures since research suggests that approximately 2% of voters fail to vote for the highest office on a fairly consistent basis.*

Percent of Eligible Population Reported Voting in 2000

National Percent = 51.3%*

<u>ALPHA ORDER</u>

RANK	STATE	PERCENT
36	Alabama	50.0
3	Alaska	66.4
49	Arizona	42.3
41	Arkansas	47.8
45	California	44.1
18	Colorado	56.8
12	Connecticut	58.4
20	Delaware	56.3
33	Florida	50.6
46	Georgia	43.8
50	Hawaii	40.5
22	Idaho	54.5
28	Illinois	52.8
38	Indiana	49.0
8	Iowa	60.7
25	Kansas	54.1
30	Kentucky	51.6
24	Louisiana	54.2
2	Maine	67.3
30	Maryland	51.6
14	Massachusetts	57.6
15	Michigan	57.5
1	Minnesota	68.8
40	Mississippi	48.6
15	Missouri	57.5
7	Montana	61.5
19	Nebraska	56.5
46	Nevada	43.8
6	New Hampshire	62.5
32	New Jersey	51.0
42	New Mexico	47.4
34	New York	50.4
35	North Carolina	50.3
10	North Dakota	60.4
21	Ohio	55.8
39	Oklahoma	48.8
9	Oregon	60.6
26	Pennsylvania	53.7
23	Rhode Island	54.3
43	South Carolina	46.6
13	South Dakota	58.2
37	Tennessee	49.2
48	Texas	43.1
29	Utah	52.6
5	Vermont	64.0
27	Virginia	53.0
17	Washington	56.9
44	West Virginia	45.8
4	Wisconsin	66.1
11	Wyoming	59.7

<u>RANK ORDER</u>

RANK	STATE	PERCENT
1	Minnesota	68.8
2	Maine	67.3
3	Alaska	66.4
4	Wisconsin	66.1
5	Vermont	64.0
6	New Hampshire	62.5
7	Montana	61.5
8	Iowa	60.7
9	Oregon	60.6
10	North Dakota	60.4
11	Wyoming	59.7
12	Connecticut	58.4
13	South Dakota	58.2
14	Massachusetts	57.6
15	Michigan	57.5
15	Missouri	57.5
17	Washington	56.9
18	Colorado	56.8
19	Nebraska	56.5
20	Delaware	56.3
21	Ohio	55.8
22	Idaho	54.5
23	Rhode Island	54.3
24	Louisiana	54.2
25	Kansas	54.1
26	Pennsylvania	53.7
27	Virginia	53.0
28	Illinois	52.8
29	Utah	52.6
30	Kentucky	51.6
30	Maryland	51.6
32	New Jersey	51.0
33	Florida	50.6
34	New York	50.4
35	North Carolina	50.3
36	Alabama	50.0
37	Tennessee	49.2
38	Indiana	49.0
39	Oklahoma	48.8
40	Mississippi	48.6
41	Arkansas	47.8
42	New Mexico	47.4
43	South Carolina	46.6
44	West Virginia	45.8
45	California	44.1
46	Georgia	43.8
46	Nevada	43.8
48	Texas	43.1
49	Arizona	42.3
50	Hawaii	40.5

District of Columbia	49.1

Source: Federal Election Commission
   "Voter Registration and Turnout - 2000" (http://www.fec.gov/pages/2000turnout/reg&to00.htm)

*Refers to the total vote cast for the highest office on the ballot in 2000. These figures may be inconsistent with other reported turnout figures since research suggests that approximately 2% of voters fail to vote for the highest office on a fairly consistent basis.

XIV. SOCIAL WELFARE

Poverty Rate in 2002

National Rate = 11.7% of Population in Poverty*

<table>
<tr><td colspan="3">ALPHA ORDER</td><td colspan="3">RANK ORDER</td></tr>
<tr><td>RANK</td><td>STATE</td><td>PERCENT</td><td>RANK</td><td>STATE</td><td>PERCENT</td></tr>
<tr><td>8</td><td>Alabama</td><td>14.6</td><td>1</td><td>Arkansas</td><td>18.0</td></tr>
<tr><td>42</td><td>Alaska</td><td>8.3</td><td>2</td><td>New Mexico</td><td>17.8</td></tr>
<tr><td>13</td><td>Arizona</td><td>13.3</td><td>3</td><td>Mississippi</td><td>17.6</td></tr>
<tr><td>1</td><td>Arkansas</td><td>18.0</td><td>4</td><td>Louisiana</td><td>17.0</td></tr>
<tr><td>16</td><td>California</td><td>12.8</td><td>5</td><td>West Virginia</td><td>16.0</td></tr>
<tr><td>35</td><td>Colorado</td><td>9.4</td><td>6</td><td>Texas</td><td>15.3</td></tr>
<tr><td>46</td><td>Connecticut</td><td>7.8</td><td>7</td><td>Oklahoma</td><td>14.7</td></tr>
<tr><td>45</td><td>Delaware</td><td>8.1</td><td>8</td><td>Alabama</td><td>14.6</td></tr>
<tr><td>17</td><td>Florida</td><td>12.1</td><td>9</td><td>Tennessee</td><td>14.2</td></tr>
<tr><td>17</td><td>Georgia</td><td>12.1</td><td>10</td><td>New York</td><td>14.0</td></tr>
<tr><td>25</td><td>Hawaii</td><td>10.6</td><td>11</td><td>Montana</td><td>13.7</td></tr>
<tr><td>20</td><td>Idaho</td><td>11.8</td><td>12</td><td>South Carolina</td><td>13.5</td></tr>
<tr><td>22</td><td>Illinois</td><td>11.2</td><td>13</td><td>Arizona</td><td>13.3</td></tr>
<tr><td>39</td><td>Indiana</td><td>8.7</td><td>14</td><td>Kentucky</td><td>13.1</td></tr>
<tr><td>42</td><td>Iowa</td><td>8.3</td><td>14</td><td>North Carolina</td><td>13.1</td></tr>
<tr><td>35</td><td>Kansas</td><td>9.4</td><td>16</td><td>California</td><td>12.8</td></tr>
<tr><td>14</td><td>Kentucky</td><td>13.1</td><td>17</td><td>Florida</td><td>12.1</td></tr>
<tr><td>4</td><td>Louisiana</td><td>17.0</td><td>17</td><td>Georgia</td><td>12.1</td></tr>
<tr><td>21</td><td>Maine</td><td>11.3</td><td>19</td><td>North Dakota</td><td>11.9</td></tr>
<tr><td>48</td><td>Maryland</td><td>7.3</td><td>20</td><td>Idaho</td><td>11.8</td></tr>
<tr><td>31</td><td>Massachusetts</td><td>9.6</td><td>21</td><td>Maine</td><td>11.3</td></tr>
<tr><td>26</td><td>Michigan</td><td>10.3</td><td>22</td><td>Illinois</td><td>11.2</td></tr>
<tr><td>49</td><td>Minnesota</td><td>6.5</td><td>22</td><td>Oregon</td><td>11.2</td></tr>
<tr><td>3</td><td>Mississippi</td><td>17.6</td><td>24</td><td>Washington</td><td>10.8</td></tr>
<tr><td>31</td><td>Missouri</td><td>9.6</td><td>25</td><td>Hawaii</td><td>10.6</td></tr>
<tr><td>11</td><td>Montana</td><td>13.7</td><td>26</td><td>Michigan</td><td>10.3</td></tr>
<tr><td>33</td><td>Nebraska</td><td>9.5</td><td>26</td><td>Rhode Island</td><td>10.3</td></tr>
<tr><td>42</td><td>Nevada</td><td>8.3</td><td>28</td><td>South Dakota</td><td>10.2</td></tr>
<tr><td>50</td><td>New Hampshire</td><td>5.6</td><td>29</td><td>Ohio</td><td>10.1</td></tr>
<tr><td>46</td><td>New Jersey</td><td>7.8</td><td>30</td><td>Vermont</td><td>9.9</td></tr>
<tr><td>2</td><td>New Mexico</td><td>17.8</td><td>31</td><td>Massachusetts</td><td>9.6</td></tr>
<tr><td>10</td><td>New York</td><td>14.0</td><td>31</td><td>Missouri</td><td>9.6</td></tr>
<tr><td>14</td><td>North Carolina</td><td>13.1</td><td>33</td><td>Nebraska</td><td>9.5</td></tr>
<tr><td>19</td><td>North Dakota</td><td>11.9</td><td>33</td><td>Wyoming</td><td>9.5</td></tr>
<tr><td>29</td><td>Ohio</td><td>10.1</td><td>35</td><td>Colorado</td><td>9.4</td></tr>
<tr><td>7</td><td>Oklahoma</td><td>14.7</td><td>35</td><td>Kansas</td><td>9.4</td></tr>
<tr><td>22</td><td>Oregon</td><td>11.2</td><td>37</td><td>Utah</td><td>9.3</td></tr>
<tr><td>38</td><td>Pennsylvania</td><td>9.2</td><td>38</td><td>Pennsylvania</td><td>9.2</td></tr>
<tr><td>26</td><td>Rhode Island</td><td>10.3</td><td>39</td><td>Indiana</td><td>8.7</td></tr>
<tr><td>12</td><td>South Carolina</td><td>13.5</td><td>39</td><td>Virginia</td><td>8.7</td></tr>
<tr><td>28</td><td>South Dakota</td><td>10.2</td><td>41</td><td>Wisconsin</td><td>8.6</td></tr>
<tr><td>9</td><td>Tennessee</td><td>14.2</td><td>42</td><td>Alaska</td><td>8.3</td></tr>
<tr><td>6</td><td>Texas</td><td>15.3</td><td>42</td><td>Iowa</td><td>8.3</td></tr>
<tr><td>37</td><td>Utah</td><td>9.3</td><td>42</td><td>Nevada</td><td>8.3</td></tr>
<tr><td>30</td><td>Vermont</td><td>9.9</td><td>45</td><td>Delaware</td><td>8.1</td></tr>
<tr><td>39</td><td>Virginia</td><td>8.7</td><td>46</td><td>Connecticut</td><td>7.8</td></tr>
<tr><td>24</td><td>Washington</td><td>10.8</td><td>46</td><td>New Jersey</td><td>7.8</td></tr>
<tr><td>5</td><td>West Virginia</td><td>16.0</td><td>48</td><td>Maryland</td><td>7.3</td></tr>
<tr><td>41</td><td>Wisconsin</td><td>8.6</td><td>49</td><td>Minnesota</td><td>6.5</td></tr>
<tr><td>33</td><td>Wyoming</td><td>9.5</td><td>50</td><td>New Hampshire</td><td>5.6</td></tr>
<tr><td></td><td></td><td></td><td></td><td>District of Columbia</td><td>16.8</td></tr>
</table>

Source: U.S. Bureau of the Census
"Poverty in the United States: 2002" (http://www.census.gov/hhes/www/poverty02.html)
**Three-year average: 2000-2002. The poverty threshold for a family of four in 2002 was $18,392.*

Percent of Senior Citizens Living in Poverty in 2002

National Percent = 9.6%*

ALPHA ORDER

RANK	STATE	PERCENT
2	Alabama	14.2
50	Alaska	3.2
37	Arizona	8.0
13	Arkansas	10.9
45	California	7.3
23	Colorado	9.3
48	Connecticut	5.9
40	Delaware	7.7
20	Florida	9.9
7	Georgia	13.0
40	Hawaii	7.7
29	Idaho	8.7
29	Illinois	8.7
38	Indiana	7.9
32	Iowa	8.5
28	Kansas	8.8
2	Kentucky	14.2
2	Louisiana	14.2
16	Maine	10.4
35	Maryland	8.1
26	Massachusetts	9.0
42	Michigan	7.5
39	Minnesota	7.8
1	Mississippi	18.4
22	Missouri	9.5
24	Montana	9.1
24	Nebraska	9.1
21	Nevada	9.7
29	New Hampshire	8.7
45	New Jersey	7.3
6	New Mexico	13.7
12	New York	11.2
10	North Carolina	12.4
2	North Dakota	14.2
32	Ohio	8.5
14	Oklahoma	10.8
27	Oregon	8.9
34	Pennsylvania	8.3
19	Rhode Island	10.0
8	South Carolina	12.6
16	South Dakota	10.4
8	Tennessee	12.6
11	Texas	12.0
49	Utah	5.1
42	Vermont	7.5
18	Virginia	10.3
47	Washington	7.0
15	West Virginia	10.5
44	Wisconsin	7.4
35	Wyoming	8.1

RANK ORDER

RANK	STATE	PERCENT
1	Mississippi	18.4
2	Alabama	14.2
2	Kentucky	14.2
2	Louisiana	14.2
2	North Dakota	14.2
6	New Mexico	13.7
7	Georgia	13.0
8	South Carolina	12.6
8	Tennessee	12.6
10	North Carolina	12.4
11	Texas	12.0
12	New York	11.2
13	Arkansas	10.9
14	Oklahoma	10.8
15	West Virginia	10.5
16	Maine	10.4
16	South Dakota	10.4
18	Virginia	10.3
19	Rhode Island	10.0
20	Florida	9.9
21	Nevada	9.7
22	Missouri	9.5
23	Colorado	9.3
24	Montana	9.1
24	Nebraska	9.1
26	Massachusetts	9.0
27	Oregon	8.9
28	Kansas	8.8
29	Idaho	8.7
29	Illinois	8.7
29	New Hampshire	8.7
32	Iowa	8.5
32	Ohio	8.5
34	Pennsylvania	8.3
35	Maryland	8.1
35	Wyoming	8.1
37	Arizona	8.0
38	Indiana	7.9
39	Minnesota	7.8
40	Delaware	7.7
40	Hawaii	7.7
42	Michigan	7.5
42	Vermont	7.5
44	Wisconsin	7.4
45	California	7.3
45	New Jersey	7.3
47	Washington	7.0
48	Connecticut	5.9
49	Utah	5.1
50	Alaska	3.2
	District of Columbia	16.6

Source: U.S. Bureau of the Census
     "2002 American Community Survey"
*People 65 years and over living with incomes below the poverty level.

Percent of Children Living in Poverty in 2002

National Percent = 17.2%*

<u>ALPHA ORDER</u>

RANK	STATE	PERCENT
5	Alabama	23.3
48	Alaska	9.6
11	Arizona	20.1
7	Arkansas	21.4
16	California	18.2
41	Colorado	12.1
47	Connecticut	9.8
43	Delaware	11.2
17	Florida	18.1
18	Georgia	17.3
33	Hawaii	13.7
28	Idaho	14.9
23	Illinois	15.7
31	Indiana	14.3
33	Iowa	13.7
24	Kansas	15.6
9	Kentucky	20.5
2	Louisiana	27.2
25	Maine	15.4
45	Maryland	10.9
42	Massachusetts	11.9
26	Michigan	15.3
44	Minnesota	11.1
1	Mississippi	28.6
22	Missouri	16.0
14	Montana	19.1
37	Nebraska	13.1
20	Nevada	16.6
50	New Hampshire	7.2
46	New Jersey	10.4
3	New Mexico	26.7
15	New York	18.7
10	North Carolina	20.3
37	North Dakota	13.1
21	Ohio	16.5
8	Oklahoma	21.1
19	Oregon	16.8
28	Pennsylvania	14.9
27	Rhode Island	15.0
12	South Carolina	19.8
32	South Dakota	14.0
13	Tennessee	19.4
6	Texas	21.5
37	Utah	13.1
49	Vermont	8.9
37	Virginia	13.1
30	Washington	14.7
4	West Virginia	24.7
35	Wisconsin	13.5
36	Wyoming	13.3

<u>RANK ORDER</u>

RANK	STATE	PERCENT
1	Mississippi	28.6
2	Louisiana	27.2
3	New Mexico	26.7
4	West Virginia	24.7
5	Alabama	23.3
6	Texas	21.5
7	Arkansas	21.4
8	Oklahoma	21.1
9	Kentucky	20.5
10	North Carolina	20.3
11	Arizona	20.1
12	South Carolina	19.8
13	Tennessee	19.4
14	Montana	19.1
15	New York	18.7
16	California	18.2
17	Florida	18.1
18	Georgia	17.3
19	Oregon	16.8
20	Nevada	16.6
21	Ohio	16.5
22	Missouri	16.0
23	Illinois	15.7
24	Kansas	15.6
25	Maine	15.4
26	Michigan	15.3
27	Rhode Island	15.0
28	Idaho	14.9
28	Pennsylvania	14.9
30	Washington	14.7
31	Indiana	14.3
32	South Dakota	14.0
33	Hawaii	13.7
33	Iowa	13.7
35	Wisconsin	13.5
36	Wyoming	13.3
37	Nebraska	13.1
37	North Dakota	13.1
37	Utah	13.1
37	Virginia	13.1
41	Colorado	12.1
42	Massachusetts	11.9
43	Delaware	11.2
44	Minnesota	11.1
45	Maryland	10.9
46	New Jersey	10.4
47	Connecticut	9.8
48	Alaska	9.6
49	Vermont	8.9
50	New Hampshire	7.2
	District of Columbia	27.0

Source: U.S. Bureau of the Census
"2002 American Community Survey"
Children 17 and under living in families with incomes below the poverty level.

Percent of Families Living in Poverty in 2002

National Percent = 9.6%*

ALPHA ORDER

RANK	STATE	PERCENT
4	Alabama	13.3
43	Alaska	6.1
14	Arizona	10.5
9	Arkansas	11.5
17	California	10.0
40	Colorado	6.7
47	Connecticut	5.5
45	Delaware	5.8
19	Florida	9.6
14	Georgia	10.5
33	Hawaii	7.9
19	Idaho	9.6
25	Illinois	8.7
36	Indiana	7.7
36	Iowa	7.7
29	Kansas	8.3
6	Kentucky	12.8
1	Louisiana	16.1
23	Maine	9.1
43	Maryland	6.1
42	Massachusetts	6.6
27	Michigan	8.4
47	Minnesota	5.5
1	Mississippi	16.1
24	Missouri	8.8
16	Montana	10.4
33	Nebraska	7.9
21	Nevada	9.5
50	New Hampshire	4.6
45	New Jersey	5.8
3	New Mexico	15.6
13	New York	10.6
12	North Carolina	11.0
30	North Dakota	8.1
22	Ohio	9.2
10	Oklahoma	11.4
18	Oregon	9.9
30	Pennsylvania	8.1
30	Rhode Island	8.1
11	South Carolina	11.3
25	South Dakota	8.7
8	Tennessee	11.6
6	Texas	12.8
33	Utah	7.9
49	Vermont	5.4
39	Virginia	7.5
27	Washington	8.4
5	West Virginia	13.2
40	Wisconsin	6.7
38	Wyoming	7.6

RANK ORDER

RANK	STATE	PERCENT
1	Louisiana	16.1
1	Mississippi	16.1
3	New Mexico	15.6
4	Alabama	13.3
5	West Virginia	13.2
6	Kentucky	12.8
6	Texas	12.8
8	Tennessee	11.6
9	Arkansas	11.5
10	Oklahoma	11.4
11	South Carolina	11.3
12	North Carolina	11.0
13	New York	10.6
14	Arizona	10.5
14	Georgia	10.5
16	Montana	10.4
17	California	10.0
18	Oregon	9.9
19	Florida	9.6
19	Idaho	9.6
21	Nevada	9.5
22	Ohio	9.2
23	Maine	9.1
24	Missouri	8.8
25	Illinois	8.7
25	South Dakota	8.7
27	Michigan	8.4
27	Washington	8.4
29	Kansas	8.3
30	North Dakota	8.1
30	Pennsylvania	8.1
30	Rhode Island	8.1
33	Hawaii	7.9
33	Nebraska	7.9
33	Utah	7.9
36	Indiana	7.7
36	Iowa	7.7
38	Wyoming	7.6
39	Virginia	7.5
40	Colorado	6.7
40	Wisconsin	6.7
42	Massachusetts	6.6
43	Alaska	6.1
43	Maryland	6.1
45	Delaware	5.8
45	New Jersey	5.8
47	Connecticut	5.5
47	Minnesota	5.5
49	Vermont	5.4
50	New Hampshire	4.6

District of Columbia	15.7

Source: Morgan Quitno Press using data from U.S. Bureau of the Census
   "2002 American Community Survey"
Families living with incomes below the poverty level.

Percent of Female-Headed Families with Children Living in Poverty in 2002

National Percent = 28.3%*

<u>ALPHA ORDER</u>

RANK	STATE	PERCENT
4	Alabama	39.3
48	Alaska	18.6
26	Arizona	27.7
15	Arkansas	31.5
36	California	25.1
44	Colorado	20.1
43	Connecticut	20.5
46	Delaware	19.3
34	Florida	26.0
18	Georgia	30.7
35	Hawaii	25.2
13	Idaho	32.5
29	Illinois	27.3
30	Indiana	26.9
22	Iowa	28.6
39	Kansas	24.4
6	Kentucky	35.5
2	Louisiana	41.9
14	Maine	31.6
49	Maryland	17.5
40	Massachusetts	24.0
32	Michigan	26.7
42	Minnesota	20.6
1	Mississippi	42.6
33	Missouri	26.3
17	Montana	31.2
20	Nebraska	29.0
41	Nevada	23.2
50	New Hampshire	17.2
44	New Jersey	20.1
3	New Mexico	40.0
25	New York	27.8
7	North Carolina	35.1
27	North Dakota	27.6
21	Ohio	28.7
8	Oklahoma	34.4
16	Oregon	31.3
31	Pennsylvania	26.8
23	Rhode Island	28.3
9	South Carolina	34.1
19	South Dakota	29.3
10	Tennessee	32.8
11	Texas	32.6
24	Utah	28.0
46	Vermont	19.3
38	Virginia	24.8
27	Washington	27.6
5	West Virginia	38.1
37	Wisconsin	25.0
11	Wyoming	32.6

<u>RANK ORDER</u>

RANK	STATE	PERCENT
1	Mississippi	42.6
2	Louisiana	41.9
3	New Mexico	40.0
4	Alabama	39.3
5	West Virginia	38.1
6	Kentucky	35.5
7	North Carolina	35.1
8	Oklahoma	34.4
9	South Carolina	34.1
10	Tennessee	32.8
11	Texas	32.6
11	Wyoming	32.6
13	Idaho	32.5
14	Maine	31.6
15	Arkansas	31.5
16	Oregon	31.3
17	Montana	31.2
18	Georgia	30.7
19	South Dakota	29.3
20	Nebraska	29.0
21	Ohio	28.7
22	Iowa	28.6
23	Rhode Island	28.3
24	Utah	28.0
25	New York	27.8
26	Arizona	27.7
27	North Dakota	27.6
27	Washington	27.6
29	Illinois	27.3
30	Indiana	26.9
31	Pennsylvania	26.8
32	Michigan	26.7
33	Missouri	26.3
34	Florida	26.0
35	Hawaii	25.2
36	California	25.1
37	Wisconsin	25.0
38	Virginia	24.8
39	Kansas	24.4
40	Massachusetts	24.0
41	Nevada	23.2
42	Minnesota	20.6
43	Connecticut	20.5
44	Colorado	20.1
44	New Jersey	20.1
46	Delaware	19.3
46	Vermont	19.3
48	Alaska	18.6
49	Maryland	17.5
50	New Hampshire	17.2
	District of Columbia	29.7

State and Local Government Expenditures for Public Welfare Programs in 2000

National Total = $233,350,301,000*

ALPHA ORDER

RANK	STATE	EXPENDITURES	% of USA
22	Alabama	$3,525,348,000	1.5%
43	Alaska	809,983,000	0.3%
27	Arizona	2,945,496,000	1.3%
31	Arkansas	1,999,464,000	0.9%
1	California	29,214,190,000	12.5%
28	Colorado	2,731,258,000	1.2%
24	Connecticut	3,116,019,000	1.3%
48	Delaware	547,945,000	0.2%
6	Florida	9,506,230,000	4.1%
13	Georgia	5,567,703,000	2.4%
40	Hawaii	1,039,848,000	0.4%
44	Idaho	790,122,000	0.3%
7	Illinois	8,852,772,000	3.8%
18	Indiana	4,264,341,000	1.8%
30	Iowa	2,258,615,000	1.0%
37	Kansas	1,353,527,000	0.6%
19	Kentucky	4,096,471,000	1.8%
25	Louisiana	3,071,229,000	1.3%
33	Maine	1,585,593,000	0.7%
21	Maryland	4,009,293,000	1.7%
9	Massachusetts	6,309,121,000	2.7%
8	Michigan	8,241,898,000	3.5%
11	Minnesota	5,970,165,000	2.6%
29	Mississippi	2,320,418,000	1.0%
20	Missouri	4,041,191,000	1.7%
47	Montana	555,235,000	0.2%
36	Nebraska	1,425,248,000	0.6%
41	Nevada	885,963,000	0.4%
39	New Hampshire	1,112,840,000	0.5%
12	New Jersey	5,822,565,000	2.5%
34	New Mexico	1,515,110,000	0.6%
2	New York	29,185,151,000	12.5%
10	North Carolina	6,299,233,000	2.7%
46	North Dakota	579,839,000	0.2%
5	Ohio	9,566,967,000	4.1%
42	Oklahoma	885,377,000	0.4%
26	Oregon	3,070,360,000	1.3%
3	Pennsylvania	13,318,054,000	5.7%
38	Rhode Island	1,143,940,000	0.5%
23	South Carolina	3,457,708,000	1.5%
49	South Dakota	487,763,000	0.2%
15	Tennessee	4,871,818,000	2.1%
4	Texas	11,459,507,000	4.9%
35	Utah	1,472,568,000	0.6%
45	Vermont	701,101,000	0.3%
16	Virginia	4,487,388,000	1.9%
14	Washington	5,099,818,000	2.2%
32	West Virginia	1,762,774,000	0.8%
17	Wisconsin	4,469,954,000	1.9%
50	Wyoming	291,419,000	0.1%

RANK ORDER

RANK	STATE	EXPENDITURES	% of USA
1	California	$29,214,190,000	12.5%
2	New York	29,185,151,000	12.5%
3	Pennsylvania	13,318,054,000	5.7%
4	Texas	11,459,507,000	4.9%
5	Ohio	9,566,967,000	4.1%
6	Florida	9,506,230,000	4.1%
7	Illinois	8,852,772,000	3.8%
8	Michigan	8,241,898,000	3.5%
9	Massachusetts	6,309,121,000	2.7%
10	North Carolina	6,299,233,000	2.7%
11	Minnesota	5,970,165,000	2.6%
12	New Jersey	5,822,565,000	2.5%
13	Georgia	5,567,703,000	2.4%
14	Washington	5,099,818,000	2.2%
15	Tennessee	4,871,818,000	2.1%
16	Virginia	4,487,388,000	1.9%
17	Wisconsin	4,469,954,000	1.9%
18	Indiana	4,264,341,000	1.8%
19	Kentucky	4,096,471,000	1.8%
20	Missouri	4,041,191,000	1.7%
21	Maryland	4,009,293,000	1.7%
22	Alabama	3,525,348,000	1.5%
23	South Carolina	3,457,708,000	1.5%
24	Connecticut	3,116,019,000	1.3%
25	Louisiana	3,071,229,000	1.3%
26	Oregon	3,070,360,000	1.3%
27	Arizona	2,945,496,000	1.3%
28	Colorado	2,731,258,000	1.2%
29	Mississippi	2,320,418,000	1.0%
30	Iowa	2,258,615,000	1.0%
31	Arkansas	1,999,464,000	0.9%
32	West Virginia	1,762,774,000	0.8%
33	Maine	1,585,593,000	0.7%
34	New Mexico	1,515,110,000	0.6%
35	Utah	1,472,568,000	0.6%
36	Nebraska	1,425,248,000	0.6%
37	Kansas	1,353,527,000	0.6%
38	Rhode Island	1,143,940,000	0.5%
39	New Hampshire	1,112,840,000	0.5%
40	Hawaii	1,039,848,000	0.4%
41	Nevada	885,963,000	0.4%
42	Oklahoma	885,377,000	0.4%
43	Alaska	809,983,000	0.3%
44	Idaho	790,122,000	0.3%
45	Vermont	701,101,000	0.3%
46	North Dakota	579,839,000	0.2%
47	Montana	555,235,000	0.2%
48	Delaware	547,945,000	0.2%
49	South Dakota	487,763,000	0.2%
50	Wyoming	291,419,000	0.1%
	District of Columbia	1,254,361,000	0.5%

Source: U.S. Bureau of the Census, Governments Division
"State and Local Government Finances: 1999-2000" (http://www.census.gov/govs/www/estimate00.html)
**Direct general expenditures. Includes funds for cash assistance programs, medical and other vendor payments,*
welfare institutions and other public welfare programs.

Per Capita State and Local Government Expenditures
For Public Welfare Programs in 2000
National Per Capita = $827*

ALPHA ORDER

RANK	STATE	PER CAPITA
26	Alabama	$792
2	Alaska	1,290
46	Arizona	570
30	Arkansas	746
16	California	859
41	Colorado	631
11	Connecticut	913
34	Delaware	697
44	Florida	592
37	Georgia	676
18	Hawaii	857
43	Idaho	608
32	Illinois	712
33	Indiana	700
28	Iowa	771
48	Kansas	503
8	Kentucky	1,012
36	Louisiana	687
3	Maine	1,241
29	Maryland	755
9	Massachusetts	992
24	Michigan	828
4	Minnesota	1,210
25	Mississippi	815
31	Missouri	721
42	Montana	615
21	Nebraska	832
49	Nevada	439
13	New Hampshire	897
35	New Jersey	690
21	New Mexico	832
1	New York	1,536
27	North Carolina	779
12	North Dakota	904
20	Ohio	842
50	Oklahoma	256
14	Oregon	895
7	Pennsylvania	1,084
6	Rhode Island	1,089
16	South Carolina	859
39	South Dakota	645
19	Tennessee	854
47	Texas	547
38	Utah	656
5	Vermont	1,149
40	Virginia	632
15	Washington	863
10	West Virginia	975
21	Wisconsin	832
45	Wyoming	590

RANK ORDER

RANK	STATE	PER CAPITA
1	New York	$1,536
2	Alaska	1,290
3	Maine	1,241
4	Minnesota	1,210
5	Vermont	1,149
6	Rhode Island	1,089
7	Pennsylvania	1,084
8	Kentucky	1,012
9	Massachusetts	992
10	West Virginia	975
11	Connecticut	913
12	North Dakota	904
13	New Hampshire	897
14	Oregon	895
15	Washington	863
16	California	859
16	South Carolina	859
18	Hawaii	857
19	Tennessee	854
20	Ohio	842
21	Nebraska	832
21	New Mexico	832
21	Wisconsin	832
24	Michigan	828
25	Mississippi	815
26	Alabama	792
27	North Carolina	779
28	Iowa	771
29	Maryland	755
30	Arkansas	746
31	Missouri	721
32	Illinois	712
33	Indiana	700
34	Delaware	697
35	New Jersey	690
36	Louisiana	687
37	Georgia	676
38	Utah	656
39	South Dakota	645
40	Virginia	632
41	Colorado	631
42	Montana	615
43	Idaho	608
44	Florida	592
45	Wyoming	590
46	Arizona	570
47	Texas	547
48	Kansas	503
49	Nevada	439
50	Oklahoma	256

District of Columbia	2,194

Source: Morgan Quitno Press using data from U.S. Bureau of the Census, Governments Division
"State and Local Government Finances: 1999-2000" (http://www.census.gov/govs/www/estimate00.html)
*Direct general expenditures. Includes funds for cash assistance programs, medical and other vendor payments, welfare institutions and other public welfare programs.

State and Local Government Spending for Public Welfare Programs
As a Percent of All State and Local Government Expenditures in 2000
National Percent = 15.5%*

ALPHA ORDER

RANK	STATE	PERCENT
18	Alabama	16.0
46	Alaska	10.7
39	Arizona	12.7
11	Arkansas	18.1
25	California	14.9
43	Colorado	12.1
29	Connecticut	14.5
45	Delaware	11.7
40	Florida	12.6
27	Georgia	14.6
32	Hawaii	14.3
36	Idaho	13.6
35	Illinois	13.7
26	Indiana	14.8
29	Iowa	14.5
47	Kansas	10.5
2	Kentucky	21.5
34	Louisiana	13.8
1	Maine	22.8
27	Maryland	14.6
14	Massachusetts	16.7
23	Michigan	15.1
10	Minnesota	19.2
14	Mississippi	16.7
17	Missouri	16.3
41	Montana	12.3
13	Nebraska	17.0
48	Nevada	9.1
8	New Hampshire	19.6
41	New Jersey	12.3
24	New Mexico	15.0
3	New York	20.8
20	North Carolina	15.6
19	North Dakota	15.8
16	Ohio	16.6
50	Oklahoma	6.4
21	Oregon	15.2
6	Pennsylvania	20.2
4	Rhode Island	20.6
12	South Carolina	17.1
33	South Dakota	14.2
9	Tennessee	19.3
44	Texas	12.0
37	Utah	13.4
5	Vermont	20.3
38	Virginia	12.9
21	Washington	15.2
6	West Virginia	20.2
29	Wisconsin	14.5
49	Wyoming	8.8

RANK ORDER

RANK	STATE	PERCENT
1	Maine	22.8
2	Kentucky	21.5
3	New York	20.8
4	Rhode Island	20.6
5	Vermont	20.3
6	Pennsylvania	20.2
6	West Virginia	20.2
8	New Hampshire	19.6
9	Tennessee	19.3
10	Minnesota	19.2
11	Arkansas	18.1
12	South Carolina	17.1
13	Nebraska	17.0
14	Massachusetts	16.7
14	Mississippi	16.7
16	Ohio	16.6
17	Missouri	16.3
18	Alabama	16.0
19	North Dakota	15.8
20	North Carolina	15.6
21	Oregon	15.2
21	Washington	15.2
23	Michigan	15.1
24	New Mexico	15.0
25	California	14.9
26	Indiana	14.8
27	Georgia	14.6
27	Maryland	14.6
29	Connecticut	14.5
29	Iowa	14.5
29	Wisconsin	14.5
32	Hawaii	14.3
33	South Dakota	14.2
34	Louisiana	13.8
35	Illinois	13.7
36	Idaho	13.6
37	Utah	13.4
38	Virginia	12.9
39	Arizona	12.7
40	Florida	12.6
41	Montana	12.3
41	New Jersey	12.3
43	Colorado	12.1
44	Texas	12.0
45	Delaware	11.7
46	Alaska	10.7
47	Kansas	10.5
48	Nevada	9.1
49	Wyoming	8.8
50	Oklahoma	6.4

District of Columbia	24.3

Source: Morgan Quitno Press using data from U.S. Bureau of the Census, Governments Division
"State and Local Government Finances: 1999-2000" (http://www.census.gov/govs/www/estimate00.html)
*As a percent of direct general expenditures. Includes funds for cash assistance programs, medical and other vendor payments, welfare institutions and other public welfare programs.

Social Security (OASDI) Payments in 2001

National Total = $431,737,000,000*

<u>ALPHA ORDER</u>

RANK	STATE	PAYMENTS	% of USA
20	Alabama	$7,428,000,000	1.7%
50	Alaska	506,000,000	0.1%
19	Arizona	7,713,000,000	1.8%
31	Arkansas	4,495,000,000	1.0%
1	California	40,358,000,000	9.3%
30	Colorado	5,004,000,000	1.2%
26	Connecticut	6,015,000,000	1.4%
45	Delaware	1,357,000,000	0.3%
2	Florida	30,455,000,000	7.1%
11	Georgia	10,172,000,000	2.4%
43	Hawaii	1,752,000,000	0.4%
41	Idaho	1,829,000,000	0.4%
7	Illinois	18,397,000,000	4.3%
13	Indiana	9,899,000,000	2.3%
29	Iowa	5,149,000,000	1.2%
33	Kansas	4,273,000,000	1.0%
23	Kentucky	6,578,000,000	1.5%
25	Louisiana	6,248,000,000	1.4%
39	Maine	2,199,000,000	0.5%
21	Maryland	7,057,000,000	1.6%
12	Massachusetts	10,161,000,000	2.4%
8	Michigan	16,827,000,000	3.9%
22	Minnesota	7,048,000,000	1.6%
32	Mississippi	4,374,000,000	1.0%
15	Missouri	9,415,000,000	2.2%
44	Montana	1,451,000,000	0.3%
36	Nebraska	2,663,000,000	0.6%
35	Nevada	2,869,000,000	0.7%
40	New Hampshire	1,970,000,000	0.5%
9	New Jersey	14,221,000,000	3.3%
37	New Mexico	2,451,000,000	0.6%
3	New York	30,142,000,000	7.0%
10	North Carolina	12,458,000,000	2.9%
47	North Dakota	1,020,000,000	0.2%
6	Ohio	18,598,000,000	4.3%
28	Oklahoma	5,429,000,000	1.3%
27	Oregon	5,536,000,000	1.3%
5	Pennsylvania	23,270,000,000	5.4%
42	Rhode Island	1,821,000,000	0.4%
24	South Carolina	6,355,000,000	1.5%
46	South Dakota	1,186,000,000	0.3%
16	Tennessee	9,109,000,000	2.1%
4	Texas	24,367,000,000	5.6%
38	Utah	2,300,000,000	0.5%
48	Vermont	973,000,000	0.2%
14	Virginia	9,707,000,000	2.2%
18	Washington	8,427,000,000	2.0%
34	West Virginia	3,690,000,000	0.9%
17	Wisconsin	8,818,000,000	2.0%
49	Wyoming	737,000,000	0.2%

<u>RANK ORDER</u>

RANK	STATE	PAYMENTS	% of USA
1	California	$40,358,000,000	9.3%
2	Florida	30,455,000,000	7.1%
3	New York	30,142,000,000	7.0%
4	Texas	24,367,000,000	5.6%
5	Pennsylvania	23,270,000,000	5.4%
6	Ohio	18,598,000,000	4.3%
7	Illinois	18,397,000,000	4.3%
8	Michigan	16,827,000,000	3.9%
9	New Jersey	14,221,000,000	3.3%
10	North Carolina	12,458,000,000	2.9%
11	Georgia	10,172,000,000	2.4%
12	Massachusetts	10,161,000,000	2.4%
13	Indiana	9,899,000,000	2.3%
14	Virginia	9,707,000,000	2.2%
15	Missouri	9,415,000,000	2.2%
16	Tennessee	9,109,000,000	2.1%
17	Wisconsin	8,818,000,000	2.0%
18	Washington	8,427,000,000	2.0%
19	Arizona	7,713,000,000	1.8%
20	Alabama	7,428,000,000	1.7%
21	Maryland	7,057,000,000	1.6%
22	Minnesota	7,048,000,000	1.6%
23	Kentucky	6,578,000,000	1.5%
24	South Carolina	6,355,000,000	1.5%
25	Louisiana	6,248,000,000	1.4%
26	Connecticut	6,015,000,000	1.4%
27	Oregon	5,536,000,000	1.3%
28	Oklahoma	5,429,000,000	1.3%
29	Iowa	5,149,000,000	1.2%
30	Colorado	5,004,000,000	1.2%
31	Arkansas	4,495,000,000	1.0%
32	Mississippi	4,374,000,000	1.0%
33	Kansas	4,273,000,000	1.0%
34	West Virginia	3,690,000,000	0.9%
35	Nevada	2,869,000,000	0.7%
36	Nebraska	2,663,000,000	0.6%
37	New Mexico	2,451,000,000	0.6%
38	Utah	2,300,000,000	0.5%
39	Maine	2,199,000,000	0.5%
40	New Hampshire	1,970,000,000	0.5%
41	Idaho	1,829,000,000	0.4%
42	Rhode Island	1,821,000,000	0.4%
43	Hawaii	1,752,000,000	0.4%
44	Montana	1,451,000,000	0.3%
45	Delaware	1,357,000,000	0.3%
46	South Dakota	1,186,000,000	0.3%
47	North Dakota	1,020,000,000	0.2%
48	Vermont	973,000,000	0.2%
49	Wyoming	737,000,000	0.2%
50	Alaska	506,000,000	0.1%
	District of Columbia	603,000,000	0.1%

Source: Social Security Administration
"Social Security Bulletin, Annual Statistical Supplement 2002"
**"OASDI" is Old Age, Survivors and Disability Insurance. National total includes $6,831,000,000 in payments to recipients in U.S. territories and foreign countries.*

Per Capita Social Security (OASDI) Payments in 2001

National Per Capita = $1,490*

<u>ALPHA ORDER</u>

RANK	STATE	PER CAPITA
13	Alabama	$1,663
50	Alaska	800
35	Arizona	1,456
11	Arkansas	1,670
46	California	1,169
48	Colorado	1,130
5	Connecticut	1,752
8	Delaware	1,706
3	Florida	1,862
45	Georgia	1,212
36	Hawaii	1,430
40	Idaho	1,384
34	Illinois	1,470
17	Indiana	1,616
4	Iowa	1,756
24	Kansas	1,582
16	Kentucky	1,617
39	Louisiana	1,399
7	Maine	1,712
44	Maryland	1,311
21	Massachusetts	1,588
9	Michigan	1,682
37	Minnesota	1,414
31	Mississippi	1,531
11	Missouri	1,670
19	Montana	1,602
30	Nebraska	1,549
41	Nevada	1,370
27	New Hampshire	1,565
10	New Jersey	1,672
43	New Mexico	1,340
25	New York	1,580
32	North Carolina	1,520
18	North Dakota	1,603
14	Ohio	1,633
26	Oklahoma	1,566
20	Oregon	1,594
2	Pennsylvania	1,892
6	Rhode Island	1,720
27	South Carolina	1,565
29	South Dakota	1,564
23	Tennessee	1,585
47	Texas	1,142
49	Utah	1,009
22	Vermont	1,587
42	Virginia	1,350
38	Washington	1,406
1	West Virginia	2,048
15	Wisconsin	1,631
33	Wyoming	1,493

<u>RANK ORDER</u>

RANK	STATE	PER CAPITA
1	West Virginia	$2,048
2	Pennsylvania	1,892
3	Florida	1,862
4	Iowa	1,756
5	Connecticut	1,752
6	Rhode Island	1,720
7	Maine	1,712
8	Delaware	1,706
9	Michigan	1,682
10	New Jersey	1,672
11	Arkansas	1,670
11	Missouri	1,670
13	Alabama	1,663
14	Ohio	1,633
15	Wisconsin	1,631
16	Kentucky	1,617
17	Indiana	1,616
18	North Dakota	1,603
19	Montana	1,602
20	Oregon	1,594
21	Massachusetts	1,588
22	Vermont	1,587
23	Tennessee	1,585
24	Kansas	1,582
25	New York	1,580
26	Oklahoma	1,566
27	New Hampshire	1,565
27	South Carolina	1,565
29	South Dakota	1,564
30	Nebraska	1,549
31	Mississippi	1,531
32	North Carolina	1,520
33	Wyoming	1,493
34	Illinois	1,470
35	Arizona	1,456
36	Hawaii	1,430
37	Minnesota	1,414
38	Washington	1,406
39	Louisiana	1,399
40	Idaho	1,384
41	Nevada	1,370
42	Virginia	1,350
43	New Mexico	1,340
44	Maryland	1,311
45	Georgia	1,212
46	California	1,169
47	Texas	1,142
48	Colorado	1,130
49	Utah	1,009
50	Alaska	800
	District of Columbia	1,053

Source: Morgan Quitno Press using data from Social Security Administration
   "Social Security Bulletin, Annual Statistical Supplement 2002"
*"OASDI" is Old Age, Survivors and Disability Insurance. National per capita does not include payments or population in U.S. territories and foreign countries.

Social Security (OASDI) Monthly Payments in 2001

National Total = $36,502,038,000*

ALPHA ORDER

RANK	STATE	PAYMENTS	% of USA
20	Alabama	$620,613,000	1.7%
50	Alaska	42,565,000	0.1%
19	Arizona	661,819,000	1.8%
31	Arkansas	376,725,000	1.0%
1	California	3,426,450,000	9.4%
30	Colorado	423,930,000	1.2%
25	Connecticut	514,766,000	1.4%
45	Delaware	115,438,000	0.3%
2	Florida	2,608,198,000	7.1%
12	Georgia	855,079,000	2.3%
43	Hawaii	151,425,000	0.4%
41	Idaho	156,206,000	0.4%
7	Illinois	1,552,962,000	4.3%
13	Indiana	835,033,000	2.3%
29	Iowa	435,115,000	1.2%
33	Kansas	361,698,000	1.0%
23	Kentucky	545,155,000	1.5%
26	Louisiana	512,450,000	1.4%
39	Maine	185,804,000	0.5%
22	Maryland	597,970,000	1.6%
11	Massachusetts	861,023,000	2.4%
8	Michigan	1,417,417,000	3.9%
21	Minnesota	598,469,000	1.6%
32	Mississippi	364,131,000	1.0%
15	Missouri	794,396,000	2.2%
44	Montana	122,720,000	0.3%
36	Nebraska	225,622,000	0.6%
35	Nevada	247,601,000	0.7%
40	New Hampshire	168,120,000	0.5%
9	New Jersey	1,211,848,000	3.3%
37	New Mexico	207,291,000	0.6%
3	New York	2,558,064,000	7.0%
10	North Carolina	1,057,006,000	2.9%
47	North Dakota	85,354,000	0.2%
6	Ohio	1,557,857,000	4.3%
28	Oklahoma	456,195,000	1.2%
27	Oregon	472,815,000	1.3%
5	Pennsylvania	1,964,668,000	5.4%
42	Rhode Island	155,252,000	0.4%
24	South Carolina	537,308,000	1.5%
46	South Dakota	99,980,000	0.3%
16	Tennessee	764,758,000	2.1%
4	Texas	2,046,477,000	5.6%
38	Utah	196,288,000	0.5%
48	Vermont	82,333,000	0.2%
14	Virginia	819,775,000	2.2%
18	Washington	718,799,000	2.0%
34	West Virginia	303,684,000	0.8%
17	Wisconsin	750,118,000	2.1%
49	Wyoming	62,905,000	0.2%

RANK ORDER

RANK	STATE	PAYMENTS	% of USA
1	California	$3,426,450,000	9.4%
2	Florida	2,608,198,000	7.1%
3	New York	2,558,064,000	7.0%
4	Texas	2,046,477,000	5.6%
5	Pennsylvania	1,964,668,000	5.4%
6	Ohio	1,557,857,000	4.3%
7	Illinois	1,552,962,000	4.3%
8	Michigan	1,417,417,000	3.9%
9	New Jersey	1,211,848,000	3.3%
10	North Carolina	1,057,006,000	2.9%
11	Massachusetts	861,023,000	2.4%
12	Georgia	855,079,000	2.3%
13	Indiana	835,033,000	2.3%
14	Virginia	819,775,000	2.2%
15	Missouri	794,396,000	2.2%
16	Tennessee	764,758,000	2.1%
17	Wisconsin	750,118,000	2.1%
18	Washington	718,799,000	2.0%
19	Arizona	661,819,000	1.8%
20	Alabama	620,613,000	1.7%
21	Minnesota	598,469,000	1.6%
22	Maryland	597,970,000	1.6%
23	Kentucky	545,155,000	1.5%
24	South Carolina	537,308,000	1.5%
25	Connecticut	514,766,000	1.4%
26	Louisiana	512,450,000	1.4%
27	Oregon	472,815,000	1.3%
28	Oklahoma	456,195,000	1.2%
29	Iowa	435,115,000	1.2%
30	Colorado	423,930,000	1.2%
31	Arkansas	376,725,000	1.0%
32	Mississippi	364,131,000	1.0%
33	Kansas	361,698,000	1.0%
34	West Virginia	303,684,000	0.8%
35	Nevada	247,601,000	0.7%
36	Nebraska	225,622,000	0.6%
37	New Mexico	207,291,000	0.6%
38	Utah	196,288,000	0.5%
39	Maine	185,804,000	0.5%
40	New Hampshire	168,120,000	0.5%
41	Idaho	156,206,000	0.4%
42	Rhode Island	155,252,000	0.4%
43	Hawaii	151,425,000	0.4%
44	Montana	122,720,000	0.3%
45	Delaware	115,438,000	0.3%
46	South Dakota	99,980,000	0.3%
47	North Dakota	85,354,000	0.2%
48	Vermont	82,333,000	0.2%
49	Wyoming	62,905,000	0.2%
50	Alaska	42,565,000	0.1%
	District of Columbia	50,880,000	0.1%

Source: Social Security Administration
   "Social Security Bulletin, Annual Statistical Supplement 2002"
*For December 2001. "OASDI" is Old Age, Survivors and Disability Insurance. National total includes
$560,872,000 in payments to recipients in U.S. territories and foreign countries.

Social Security (OASDI) Beneficiaries in 2001

National Total = 45,874,040*

<u>ALPHA ORDER</u>

RANK	STATE	BENEFICIARIES	% of USA
19	Alabama	841,730	1.8%
50	Alaska	56,940	0.1%
20	Arizona	813,180	1.8%
32	Arkansas	520,680	1.1%
1	California	4,247,470	9.3%
29	Colorado	542,210	1.2%
27	Connecticut	580,180	1.3%
45	Delaware	137,170	0.3%
2	Florida	3,235,390	7.1%
11	Georgia	1,125,190	2.5%
43	Hawaii	188,920	0.4%
41	Idaho	199,640	0.4%
7	Illinois	1,845,500	4.0%
16	Indiana	1,000,050	2.2%
30	Iowa	541,280	1.2%
33	Kansas	440,620	1.0%
21	Kentucky	746,330	1.6%
24	Louisiana	716,220	1.6%
38	Maine	253,810	0.6%
23	Maryland	733,940	1.6%
12	Massachusetts	1,061,920	2.3%
8	Michigan	1,658,480	3.6%
22	Minnesota	746,100	1.6%
31	Mississippi	523,460	1.1%
14	Missouri	1,012,790	2.2%
44	Montana	159,180	0.3%
36	Nebraska	285,900	0.6%
35	Nevada	299,910	0.7%
40	New Hampshire	204,140	0.4%
10	New Jersey	1,355,570	3.0%
37	New Mexico	285,250	0.6%
3	New York	3,014,910	6.6%
9	North Carolina	1,373,880	3.0%
47	North Dakota	114,380	0.2%
6	Ohio	1,921,920	4.2%
26	Oklahoma	597,270	1.3%
28	Oregon	577,570	1.3%
5	Pennsylvania	2,365,850	5.2%
42	Rhode Island	191,520	0.4%
25	South Carolina	703,930	1.5%
46	South Dakota	136,560	0.3%
15	Tennessee	1,010,900	2.2%
4	Texas	2,672,950	5.8%
39	Utah	246,330	0.5%
48	Vermont	105,330	0.2%
13	Virginia	1,053,340	2.3%
18	Washington	858,510	1.9%
34	West Virginia	394,510	0.9%
17	Wisconsin	905,450	2.0%
49	Wyoming	78,420	0.2%

<u>RANK ORDER</u>

RANK	STATE	BENEFICIARIES	% of USA
1	California	4,247,470	9.3%
2	Florida	3,235,390	7.1%
3	New York	3,014,910	6.6%
4	Texas	2,672,950	5.8%
5	Pennsylvania	2,365,850	5.2%
6	Ohio	1,921,920	4.2%
7	Illinois	1,845,500	4.0%
8	Michigan	1,658,480	3.6%
9	North Carolina	1,373,880	3.0%
10	New Jersey	1,355,570	3.0%
11	Georgia	1,125,190	2.5%
12	Massachusetts	1,061,920	2.3%
13	Virginia	1,053,340	2.3%
14	Missouri	1,012,790	2.2%
15	Tennessee	1,010,900	2.2%
16	Indiana	1,000,050	2.2%
17	Wisconsin	905,450	2.0%
18	Washington	858,510	1.9%
19	Alabama	841,730	1.8%
20	Arizona	813,180	1.8%
21	Kentucky	746,330	1.6%
22	Minnesota	746,100	1.6%
23	Maryland	733,940	1.6%
24	Louisiana	716,220	1.6%
25	South Carolina	703,930	1.5%
26	Oklahoma	597,270	1.3%
27	Connecticut	580,180	1.3%
28	Oregon	577,570	1.3%
29	Colorado	542,210	1.2%
30	Iowa	541,280	1.2%
31	Mississippi	523,460	1.1%
32	Arkansas	520,680	1.1%
33	Kansas	440,620	1.0%
34	West Virginia	394,510	0.9%
35	Nevada	299,910	0.7%
36	Nebraska	285,900	0.6%
37	New Mexico	285,250	0.6%
38	Maine	253,810	0.6%
39	Utah	246,330	0.5%
40	New Hampshire	204,140	0.4%
41	Idaho	199,640	0.4%
42	Rhode Island	191,520	0.4%
43	Hawaii	188,920	0.4%
44	Montana	159,180	0.3%
45	Delaware	137,170	0.3%
46	South Dakota	136,560	0.3%
47	North Dakota	114,380	0.2%
48	Vermont	105,330	0.2%
49	Wyoming	78,420	0.2%
50	Alaska	56,940	0.1%
	District of Columbia	73,390	0.2%

Source: Social Security Administration
"Social Security Bulletin, Annual Statistical Supplement 2002"
For December 2001. "OASDI" is Old Age, Survivors and Disability Insurance. National total includes 1,114,230 beneficiaries in U.S. territories and foreign countries.

Average Monthly Social Security (OASDI) Payment in 2001

National Average = $772.60 Each Month per Beneficiary*

ALPHA ORDER

RANK	STATE	AVERAGE BENEFIT
43	Alabama	$741.40
21	Alaska	773.80
4	Arizona	814.00
46	Arkansas	725.40
13	California	790.80
20	Colorado	779.40
8	Connecticut	801.00
7	Delaware	805.40
16	Florida	785.00
38	Georgia	752.80
12	Hawaii	791.60
23	Idaho	771.00
10	Illinois	796.80
17	Indiana	783.20
40	Iowa	747.60
34	Kansas	757.80
31	Kentucky	759.80
37	Louisiana	754.00
49	Maine	711.80
6	Maryland	807.80
26	Massachusetts	767.40
3	Michigan	830.40
35	Minnesota	756.60
48	Mississippi	713.80
31	Missouri	759.80
29	Montana	761.80
45	Nebraska	735.80
1	Nevada	847.80
19	New Hampshire	782.00
2	New Jersey	835.40
42	New Mexico	742.60
4	New York	814.00
39	North Carolina	748.00
47	North Dakota	714.00
25	Ohio	767.80
30	Oklahoma	760.20
18	Oregon	782.20
15	Pennsylvania	785.20
28	Rhode Island	764.60
36	South Carolina	756.40
50	South Dakota	702.80
44	Tennessee	740.60
33	Texas	759.40
24	Utah	769.80
41	Vermont	745.80
22	Virginia	772.00
11	Washington	792.80
9	West Virginia	800.20
27	Wisconsin	767.20
14	Wyoming	789.80

RANK ORDER

RANK	STATE	AVERAGE BENEFIT
1	Nevada	$847.80
2	New Jersey	835.40
3	Michigan	830.40
4	Arizona	814.00
4	New York	814.00
6	Maryland	807.80
7	Delaware	805.40
8	Connecticut	801.00
9	West Virginia	800.20
10	Illinois	796.80
11	Washington	792.80
12	Hawaii	791.60
13	California	790.80
14	Wyoming	789.80
15	Pennsylvania	785.20
16	Florida	785.00
17	Indiana	783.20
18	Oregon	782.20
19	New Hampshire	782.00
20	Colorado	779.40
21	Alaska	773.80
22	Virginia	772.00
23	Idaho	771.00
24	Utah	769.80
25	Ohio	767.80
26	Massachusetts	767.40
27	Wisconsin	767.20
28	Rhode Island	764.60
29	Montana	761.80
30	Oklahoma	760.20
31	Kentucky	759.80
31	Missouri	759.80
33	Texas	759.40
34	Kansas	757.80
35	Minnesota	756.60
36	South Carolina	756.40
37	Louisiana	754.00
38	Georgia	752.80
39	North Carolina	748.00
40	Iowa	747.60
41	Vermont	745.80
42	New Mexico	742.60
43	Alabama	741.40
44	Tennessee	740.60
45	Nebraska	735.80
46	Arkansas	725.40
47	North Dakota	714.00
48	Mississippi	713.80
49	Maine	711.80
50	South Dakota	702.80
	District of Columbia	712.60

Source: Social Security Administration
   "Social Security Bulletin, Annual Statistical Supplement 2002"
*As of December 2001. "OASDI" is Old Age, Survivors and Disability Insurance.

Medicare Benefit Payments in 2001

National Total = $236,492,552,000*

ALPHA ORDER

RANK	STATE	BENEFITS	% of USA
18	Alabama	$4,270,957,000	1.8%
50	Alaska	169,288,000	0.1%
23	Arizona	3,322,292,000	1.4%
28	Arkansas	2,420,406,000	1.0%
1	California	24,858,719,000	10.5%
27	Colorado	2,698,488,000	1.1%
26	Connecticut	3,117,052,000	1.3%
47	Delaware	500,000,000	0.2%
2	Florida	21,580,488,000	9.1%
17	Georgia	4,397,178,000	1.9%
42	Hawaii	717,998,000	0.3%
41	Idaho	741,441,000	0.3%
7	Illinois	8,001,947,000	3.4%
13	Indiana	4,999,250,000	2.1%
34	Iowa	1,632,032,000	0.7%
31	Kansas	2,141,312,000	0.9%
21	Kentucky	3,640,057,000	1.5%
14	Louisiana	4,902,926,000	2.1%
40	Maine	875,798,000	0.4%
16	Maryland	4,611,432,000	1.9%
11	Massachusetts	5,963,041,000	2.5%
8	Michigan	7,012,604,000	3.0%
25	Minnesota	3,136,907,000	1.3%
32	Mississippi	2,140,391,000	0.9%
15	Missouri	4,755,402,000	2.0%
44	Montana	663,416,000	0.3%
35	Nebraska	1,366,977,000	0.6%
36	Nevada	1,272,774,000	0.5%
43	New Hampshire	714,188,000	0.3%
9	New Jersey	6,885,642,000	2.9%
39	New Mexico	879,540,000	0.4%
3	New York	20,436,630,000	8.6%
10	North Carolina	6,797,677,000	2.9%
46	North Dakota	562,654,000	0.2%
6	Ohio	10,685,164,000	4.5%
29	Oklahoma	2,343,403,000	1.0%
30	Oregon	2,181,557,000	0.9%
5	Pennsylvania	15,141,847,000	6.4%
37	Rhode Island	1,146,888,000	0.5%
22	South Carolina	3,356,574,000	1.4%
45	South Dakota	622,092,000	0.3%
12	Tennessee	5,545,549,000	2.3%
4	Texas	16,336,061,000	6.9%
38	Utah	1,077,334,000	0.5%
48	Vermont	361,871,000	0.2%
20	Virginia	3,897,031,000	1.6%
24	Washington	3,209,406,000	1.4%
33	West Virginia	1,822,039,000	0.8%
19	Wisconsin	3,961,455,000	1.7%
49	Wyoming	281,639,000	0.1%

RANK ORDER

RANK	STATE	BENEFITS	% of USA
1	California	$24,858,719,000	10.5%
2	Florida	21,580,488,000	9.1%
3	New York	20,436,630,000	8.6%
4	Texas	16,336,061,000	6.9%
5	Pennsylvania	15,141,847,000	6.4%
6	Ohio	10,685,164,000	4.5%
7	Illinois	8,001,947,000	3.4%
8	Michigan	7,012,604,000	3.0%
9	New Jersey	6,885,642,000	2.9%
10	North Carolina	6,797,677,000	2.9%
11	Massachusetts	5,963,041,000	2.5%
12	Tennessee	5,545,549,000	2.3%
13	Indiana	4,999,250,000	2.1%
14	Louisiana	4,902,926,000	2.1%
15	Missouri	4,755,402,000	2.0%
16	Maryland	4,611,432,000	1.9%
17	Georgia	4,397,178,000	1.9%
18	Alabama	4,270,957,000	1.8%
19	Wisconsin	3,961,455,000	1.7%
20	Virginia	3,897,031,000	1.6%
21	Kentucky	3,640,057,000	1.5%
22	South Carolina	3,356,574,000	1.4%
23	Arizona	3,322,292,000	1.4%
24	Washington	3,209,406,000	1.4%
25	Minnesota	3,136,907,000	1.3%
26	Connecticut	3,117,052,000	1.3%
27	Colorado	2,698,488,000	1.1%
28	Arkansas	2,420,406,000	1.0%
29	Oklahoma	2,343,403,000	1.0%
30	Oregon	2,181,557,000	0.9%
31	Kansas	2,141,312,000	0.9%
32	Mississippi	2,140,391,000	0.9%
33	West Virginia	1,822,039,000	0.8%
34	Iowa	1,632,032,000	0.7%
35	Nebraska	1,366,977,000	0.6%
36	Nevada	1,272,774,000	0.5%
37	Rhode Island	1,146,888,000	0.5%
38	Utah	1,077,334,000	0.5%
39	New Mexico	879,540,000	0.4%
40	Maine	875,798,000	0.4%
41	Idaho	741,441,000	0.3%
42	Hawaii	717,998,000	0.3%
43	New Hampshire	714,188,000	0.3%
44	Montana	663,416,000	0.3%
45	South Dakota	622,092,000	0.3%
46	North Dakota	562,654,000	0.2%
47	Delaware	500,000,000	0.2%
48	Vermont	361,871,000	0.2%
49	Wyoming	281,639,000	0.1%
50	Alaska	169,288,000	0.1%
	District of Columbia	792,265,000	0.3%

Source: U.S. Department of Health and Human Services, Centers for Medicare and Medicaid Services
"Medicare Estimated Benefit Payments by State" (www.cms.gov/statistics/feeforservice/BenefitPayments01.pdf)
For fiscal year 2001. Includes payments to aged and disabled enrollees. Total includes $1,454,823,000 in payments to enrollees in Puerto Rico and $88,652,000 to enrollees in "other outlying areas."

Medicare Enrollees in 2002

National Total = 40,488,878 Enrollees*

ALPHA ORDER

RANK	STATE	ENROLLEES	% of USA
20	Alabama	705,555	1.7%
50	Alaska	45,788	0.1%
19	Arizona	708,210	1.7%
31	Arkansas	446,152	1.1%
1	California	4,009,429	9.9%
29	Colorado	483,706	1.2%
26	Connecticut	518,344	1.3%
46	Delaware	116,363	0.3%
2	Florida	2,876,168	7.1%
12	Georgia	951,439	2.3%
43	Hawaii	171,259	0.4%
41	Idaho	172,787	0.4%
7	Illinois	1,645,851	4.1%
15	Indiana	865,366	2.1%
30	Iowa	479,455	1.2%
33	Kansas	391,782	1.0%
23	Kentucky	637,212	1.6%
24	Louisiana	611,863	1.5%
38	Maine	222,917	0.6%
22	Maryland	663,739	1.6%
11	Massachusetts	963,270	2.4%
8	Michigan	1,426,169	3.5%
21	Minnesota	667,407	1.6%
32	Mississippi	429,046	1.1%
14	Missouri	873,816	2.2%
44	Montana	140,156	0.3%
36	Nebraska	255,862	0.6%
35	Nevada	261,371	0.6%
40	New Hampshire	175,828	0.4%
9	New Jersey	1,212,966	3.0%
37	New Mexico	243,922	0.6%
3	New York	2,746,660	6.8%
10	North Carolina	1,178,169	2.9%
47	North Dakota	103,208	0.3%
6	Ohio	1,712,918	4.2%
27	Oklahoma	514,542	1.3%
28	Oregon	503,783	1.2%
5	Pennsylvania	2,100,640	5.2%
42	Rhode Island	172,106	0.4%
25	South Carolina	592,039	1.5%
45	South Dakota	120,720	0.3%
16	Tennessee	855,278	2.1%
4	Texas	2,338,394	5.8%
39	Utah	214,881	0.5%
48	Vermont	91,382	0.2%
13	Virginia	926,579	2.3%
18	Washington	759,088	1.9%
34	West Virginia	343,210	0.8%
17	Wisconsin	794,181	2.0%
49	Wyoming	67,356	0.2%

RANK ORDER

RANK	STATE	ENROLLEES	% of USA
1	California	4,009,429	9.9%
2	Florida	2,876,168	7.1%
3	New York	2,746,660	6.8%
4	Texas	2,338,394	5.8%
5	Pennsylvania	2,100,640	5.2%
6	Ohio	1,712,918	4.2%
7	Illinois	1,645,851	4.1%
8	Michigan	1,426,169	3.5%
9	New Jersey	1,212,966	3.0%
10	North Carolina	1,178,169	2.9%
11	Massachusetts	963,270	2.4%
12	Georgia	951,439	2.3%
13	Virginia	926,579	2.3%
14	Missouri	873,816	2.2%
15	Indiana	865,366	2.1%
16	Tennessee	855,278	2.1%
17	Wisconsin	794,181	2.0%
18	Washington	759,088	1.9%
19	Arizona	708,210	1.7%
20	Alabama	705,555	1.7%
21	Minnesota	667,407	1.6%
22	Maryland	663,739	1.6%
23	Kentucky	637,212	1.6%
24	Louisiana	611,863	1.5%
25	South Carolina	592,039	1.5%
26	Connecticut	518,344	1.3%
27	Oklahoma	514,542	1.3%
28	Oregon	503,783	1.2%
29	Colorado	483,706	1.2%
30	Iowa	479,455	1.2%
31	Arkansas	446,152	1.1%
32	Mississippi	429,046	1.1%
33	Kansas	391,782	1.0%
34	West Virginia	343,210	0.8%
35	Nevada	261,371	0.6%
36	Nebraska	255,862	0.6%
37	New Mexico	243,922	0.6%
38	Maine	222,917	0.6%
39	Utah	214,881	0.5%
40	New Hampshire	175,828	0.4%
41	Idaho	172,787	0.4%
42	Rhode Island	172,106	0.4%
43	Hawaii	171,259	0.4%
44	Montana	140,156	0.3%
45	South Dakota	120,720	0.3%
46	Delaware	116,363	0.3%
47	North Dakota	103,208	0.3%
48	Vermont	91,382	0.2%
49	Wyoming	67,356	0.2%
50	Alaska	45,788	0.1%
	District of Columbia	74,175	0.2%

Source: U.S. Department of Health and Human Services, Centers for Medicare and Medicaid Services "Medicare Enrollment" (http://www.cms.gov/statistics/enrollment/stenrtrend99_02.asp)

*As of July 2002. Includes aged and disabled enrollees. Total includes 561,768 enrollees in Puerto Rico and 344,603 enrollees in other outlying areas, foreign countries or whose address is unknown.

Medicare Payments per Enrollee in 2001

National Rate = $6,003*

<u>ALPHA ORDER</u>

RANK	STATE	PER ENROLLEE
12	Alabama	$6,144
48	Alaska	3,864
33	Arizona	4,811
21	Arkansas	5,478
9	California	6,285
19	Colorado	5,674
13	Connecticut	6,037
40	Delaware	4,387
2	Florida	7,603
36	Georgia	4,713
43	Hawaii	4,266
39	Idaho	4,399
32	Illinois	4,879
15	Indiana	5,826
50	Iowa	3,414
22	Kansas	5,475
17	Kentucky	5,781
1	Louisiana	8,099
47	Maine	3,993
6	Maryland	7,045
11	Massachusetts	6,202
31	Michigan	4,959
35	Minnesota	4,750
29	Mississippi	5,055
20	Missouri	5,486
34	Montana	4,798
24	Nebraska	5,367
28	Nevada	5,080
45	New Hampshire	4,135
18	New Jersey	5,702
49	New Mexico	3,689
3	New York	7,489
14	North Carolina	5,886
23	North Dakota	5,456
10	Ohio	6,266
37	Oklahoma	4,590
38	Oregon	4,401
4	Pennsylvania	7,226
7	Rhode Island	6,675
16	South Carolina	5,791
26	South Dakota	5,183
8	Tennessee	6,584
5	Texas	7,104
27	Utah	5,120
46	Vermont	4,019
42	Virginia	4,285
41	Washington	4,303
25	West Virginia	5,361
30	Wisconsin	5,031
44	Wyoming	4,239

<u>RANK ORDER</u>

RANK	STATE	PER ENROLLEE
1	Louisiana	$8,099
2	Florida	7,603
3	New York	7,489
4	Pennsylvania	7,226
5	Texas	7,104
6	Maryland	7,045
7	Rhode Island	6,675
8	Tennessee	6,584
9	California	6,285
10	Ohio	6,266
11	Massachusetts	6,202
12	Alabama	6,144
13	Connecticut	6,037
14	North Carolina	5,886
15	Indiana	5,826
16	South Carolina	5,791
17	Kentucky	5,781
18	New Jersey	5,702
19	Colorado	5,674
20	Missouri	5,486
21	Arkansas	5,478
22	Kansas	5,475
23	North Dakota	5,456
24	Nebraska	5,367
25	West Virginia	5,361
26	South Dakota	5,183
27	Utah	5,120
28	Nevada	5,080
29	Mississippi	5,055
30	Wisconsin	5,031
31	Michigan	4,959
32	Illinois	4,879
33	Arizona	4,811
34	Montana	4,798
35	Minnesota	4,750
36	Georgia	4,713
37	Oklahoma	4,590
38	Oregon	4,401
39	Idaho	4,399
40	Delaware	4,387
41	Washington	4,303
42	Virginia	4,285
43	Hawaii	4,266
44	Wyoming	4,239
45	New Hampshire	4,135
46	Vermont	4,019
47	Maine	3,993
48	Alaska	3,864
49	New Mexico	3,689
50	Iowa	3,414
	District of Columbia	10,606

*Source: MQ Press using data from U.S. Dept of Health & Human Services, Centers for Medicare and Medicaid Services "Medicare Estimated Benefit Payments by State" (www.cms.gov/statistics/feeforservice/BenefitPayments01.pdf) *For fiscal year 2001. Includes aged and disabled enrollees. National rate does not include payments or enrollees in Puerto Rico and in "other outlying areas." Payments are based on the state of the provider or plan. Thus data showing payments per beneficiary should be viewed as estimates and interpreted with caution.*

Percent of Population Enrolled in Medicare in 2002

National Percent = 13.7% of Population*

ALPHA ORDER

RANK	STATE	PERCENT
10	Alabama	15.8
50	Alaska	7.1
39	Arizona	13.0
5	Arkansas	16.5
45	California	11.5
48	Colorado	10.7
14	Connecticut	15.0
23	Delaware	14.4
2	Florida	17.2
46	Georgia	11.1
32	Hawaii	13.8
40	Idaho	12.9
38	Illinois	13.1
30	Indiana	14.1
6	Iowa	16.3
23	Kansas	14.4
11	Kentucky	15.6
34	Louisiana	13.7
2	Maine	17.2
43	Maryland	12.2
14	Massachusetts	15.0
28	Michigan	14.2
36	Minnesota	13.3
14	Mississippi	15.0
12	Missouri	15.4
12	Montana	15.4
18	Nebraska	14.8
44	Nevada	12.1
32	New Hampshire	13.8
30	New Jersey	14.1
37	New Mexico	13.2
23	New York	14.4
28	North Carolina	14.2
6	North Dakota	16.3
14	Ohio	15.0
21	Oklahoma	14.7
27	Oregon	14.3
4	Pennsylvania	17.0
8	Rhode Island	16.1
23	South Carolina	14.4
9	South Dakota	15.9
18	Tennessee	14.8
47	Texas	10.8
49	Utah	9.3
18	Vermont	14.8
41	Virginia	12.7
42	Washington	12.5
1	West Virginia	19.0
22	Wisconsin	14.6
35	Wyoming	13.5

RANK ORDER

RANK	STATE	PERCENT
1	West Virginia	19.0
2	Florida	17.2
2	Maine	17.2
4	Pennsylvania	17.0
5	Arkansas	16.5
6	Iowa	16.3
6	North Dakota	16.3
8	Rhode Island	16.1
9	South Dakota	15.9
10	Alabama	15.8
11	Kentucky	15.6
12	Missouri	15.4
12	Montana	15.4
14	Connecticut	15.0
14	Massachusetts	15.0
14	Mississippi	15.0
14	Ohio	15.0
18	Nebraska	14.8
18	Tennessee	14.8
18	Vermont	14.8
21	Oklahoma	14.7
22	Wisconsin	14.6
23	Delaware	14.4
23	Kansas	14.4
23	New York	14.4
23	South Carolina	14.4
27	Oregon	14.3
28	Michigan	14.2
28	North Carolina	14.2
30	Indiana	14.1
30	New Jersey	14.1
32	Hawaii	13.8
32	New Hampshire	13.8
34	Louisiana	13.7
35	Wyoming	13.5
36	Minnesota	13.3
37	New Mexico	13.2
38	Illinois	13.1
39	Arizona	13.0
40	Idaho	12.9
41	Virginia	12.7
42	Washington	12.5
43	Maryland	12.2
44	Nevada	12.1
45	California	11.5
46	Georgia	11.1
47	Texas	10.8
48	Colorado	10.7
49	Utah	9.3
50	Alaska	7.1
	District of Columbia	13.0

Source: MQ Press using data from U.S. Dept of Health & Human Services, Centers for Medicare and Medicaid Services
"Medicare Enrollment" (http://www.cms.gov/statistics/enrollment/stenrtrend99_02.asp)
*For fiscal year 2002. Includes aged and disabled enrollees. National rate includes only residents of the 50 states and the District of Columbia.

Medicaid Expenditures in 2002

National Total = $246,283,943,000*

<u>ALPHA ORDER</u>

RANK	STATE	EXPENDITURES	% of USA
26	Alabama	$3,093,271,000	1.3%
44	Alaska	685,773,000	0.3%
23	Arizona	3,541,599,000	1.4%
32	Arkansas	2,237,818,000	0.9%
2	California	26,890,541,000	10.9%
30	Colorado	2,323,069,000	0.9%
24	Connecticut	3,456,339,000	1.4%
46	Delaware	634,046,000	0.3%
5	Florida	9,871,508,000	4.0%
12	Georgia	6,241,211,000	2.5%
43	Hawaii	740,007,000	0.3%
42	Idaho	773,535,000	0.3%
7	Illinois	8,809,060,000	3.6%
17	Indiana	4,448,318,000	1.8%
28	Iowa	2,575,146,000	1.0%
33	Kansas	1,836,717,000	0.7%
21	Kentucky	3,763,204,000	1.5%
16	Louisiana	4,885,972,000	2.0%
36	Maine	1,430,109,000	0.6%
22	Maryland	3,613,476,000	1.5%
8	Massachusetts	8,063,005,000	3.3%
10	Michigan	7,562,053,000	3.1%
18	Minnesota	4,414,511,000	1.8%
27	Mississippi	2,877,014,000	1.2%
14	Missouri	5,360,608,000	2.2%
47	Montana	571,456,000	0.2%
38	Nebraska	1,339,132,000	0.5%
41	Nevada	808,198,000	0.3%
39	New Hampshire	1,016,095,000	0.4%
9	New Jersey	7,745,878,000	3.1%
34	New Mexico	1,776,812,000	0.7%
1	New York	36,295,107,000	14.7%
11	North Carolina	6,723,599,000	2.7%
49	North Dakota	461,402,000	0.2%
6	Ohio	9,658,041,000	3.9%
31	Oklahoma	2,260,404,000	0.9%
29	Oregon	2,571,561,000	1.0%
4	Pennsylvania	12,130,925,000	4.9%
37	Rhode Island	1,358,501,000	0.6%
25	South Carolina	3,292,901,000	1.3%
48	South Dakota	549,884,000	0.2%
13	Tennessee	5,787,079,000	2.3%
3	Texas	13,523,486,000	5.5%
40	Utah	984,161,000	0.4%
45	Vermont	660,732,000	0.3%
20	Virginia	3,812,166,000	1.5%
15	Washington	5,168,512,000	2.1%
35	West Virginia	1,584,166,000	0.6%
19	Wisconsin	4,193,175,000	1.7%
50	Wyoming	274,565,000	0.1%

<u>RANK ORDER</u>

RANK	STATE	EXPENDITURES	% of USA
1	New York	$36,295,107,000	14.7%
2	California	26,890,541,000	10.9%
3	Texas	13,523,486,000	5.5%
4	Pennsylvania	12,130,925,000	4.9%
5	Florida	9,871,508,000	4.0%
6	Ohio	9,658,041,000	3.9%
7	Illinois	8,809,060,000	3.6%
8	Massachusetts	8,063,005,000	3.3%
9	New Jersey	7,745,878,000	3.1%
10	Michigan	7,562,053,000	3.1%
11	North Carolina	6,723,599,000	2.7%
12	Georgia	6,241,211,000	2.5%
13	Tennessee	5,787,079,000	2.3%
14	Missouri	5,360,608,000	2.2%
15	Washington	5,168,512,000	2.1%
16	Louisiana	4,885,972,000	2.0%
17	Indiana	4,448,318,000	1.8%
18	Minnesota	4,414,511,000	1.8%
19	Wisconsin	4,193,175,000	1.7%
20	Virginia	3,812,166,000	1.5%
21	Kentucky	3,763,204,000	1.5%
22	Maryland	3,613,476,000	1.5%
23	Arizona	3,541,599,000	1.4%
24	Connecticut	3,456,339,000	1.4%
25	South Carolina	3,292,901,000	1.3%
26	Alabama	3,093,271,000	1.3%
27	Mississippi	2,877,014,000	1.2%
28	Iowa	2,575,146,000	1.0%
29	Oregon	2,571,561,000	1.0%
30	Colorado	2,323,069,000	0.9%
31	Oklahoma	2,260,404,000	0.9%
32	Arkansas	2,237,818,000	0.9%
33	Kansas	1,836,717,000	0.7%
34	New Mexico	1,776,812,000	0.7%
35	West Virginia	1,584,166,000	0.6%
36	Maine	1,430,109,000	0.6%
37	Rhode Island	1,358,501,000	0.6%
38	Nebraska	1,339,132,000	0.5%
39	New Hampshire	1,016,095,000	0.4%
40	Utah	984,161,000	0.4%
41	Nevada	808,198,000	0.3%
42	Idaho	773,535,000	0.3%
43	Hawaii	740,007,000	0.3%
44	Alaska	685,773,000	0.3%
45	Vermont	660,732,000	0.3%
46	Delaware	634,046,000	0.3%
47	Montana	571,456,000	0.2%
48	South Dakota	549,884,000	0.2%
49	North Dakota	461,402,000	0.2%
50	Wyoming	274,565,000	0.1%
	District of Columbia	1,021,773,000	0.4%

*Source: U.S. Department of Health and Human Services, Centers for Medicare and Medicaid Services
"Medicaid Financial Statistics Tables (HCFA-64 Report)"*
For fiscal year 2002. National total includes $586,322,000 in expenditures in U.S. territories. Includes Medical Assistance Payments and Administrative Costs.

Percent Change in Medicaid Expenditures: 1998 to 2002

National Percent Change = 38.9% Increase*

<u>ALPHA ORDER</u>

RANK	STATE	PERCENT CHANGE
42	Alabama	30.1
3	Alaska	72.5
2	Arizona	77.2
14	Arkansas	49.9
32	California	37.5
29	Colorado	39.2
49	Connecticut	18.1
22	Delaware	43.3
16	Florida	49.3
4	Georgia	67.1
48	Hawaii	20.0
6	Idaho	66.3
46	Illinois	24.8
7	Indiana	66.2
1	Iowa	82.0
9	Kansas	58.8
27	Kentucky	40.5
16	Louisiana	49.3
45	Maine	26.9
43	Maryland	29.8
23	Massachusetts	42.4
47	Michigan	21.6
30	Minnesota	38.3
5	Mississippi	66.9
10	Missouri	57.5
32	Montana	37.5
16	Nebraska	49.3
19	Nevada	49.1
39	New Hampshire	31.4
36	New Jersey	35.5
7	New Mexico	66.2
44	New York	29.7
24	North Carolina	42.1
38	North Dakota	34.0
25	Ohio	41.5
12	Oklahoma	54.4
31	Oregon	38.2
34	Pennsylvania	37.1
35	Rhode Island	36.2
28	South Carolina	40.2
14	South Dakota	49.9
26	Tennessee	41.3
41	Texas	30.6
37	Utah	34.9
13	Vermont	53.6
11	Virginia	54.8
21	Washington	43.9
50	West Virginia	12.3
20	Wisconsin	45.6
40	Wyoming	30.8

<u>RANK ORDER</u>

RANK	STATE	PERCENT CHANGE
1	Iowa	82.0
2	Arizona	77.2
3	Alaska	72.5
4	Georgia	67.1
5	Mississippi	66.9
6	Idaho	66.3
7	Indiana	66.2
7	New Mexico	66.2
9	Kansas	58.8
10	Missouri	57.5
11	Virginia	54.8
12	Oklahoma	54.4
13	Vermont	53.6
14	Arkansas	49.9
14	South Dakota	49.9
16	Florida	49.3
16	Louisiana	49.3
16	Nebraska	49.3
19	Nevada	49.1
20	Wisconsin	45.6
21	Washington	43.9
22	Delaware	43.3
23	Massachusetts	42.4
24	North Carolina	42.1
25	Ohio	41.5
26	Tennessee	41.3
27	Kentucky	40.5
28	South Carolina	40.2
29	Colorado	39.2
30	Minnesota	38.3
31	Oregon	38.2
32	California	37.5
32	Montana	37.5
34	Pennsylvania	37.1
35	Rhode Island	36.2
36	New Jersey	35.5
37	Utah	34.9
38	North Dakota	34.0
39	New Hampshire	31.4
40	Wyoming	30.8
41	Texas	30.6
42	Alabama	30.1
43	Maryland	29.8
44	New York	29.7
45	Maine	26.9
46	Illinois	24.8
47	Michigan	21.6
48	Hawaii	20.0
49	Connecticut	18.1
50	West Virginia	12.3
	District of Columbia	12.7

Source: MQ Press using data from U.S. Dept of Health & Human Services, Centers for Medicare and Medicaid Services "Medicaid Financial Statistics Tables (HCFA-64 Report)"
*For fiscal years 2002 and 1998. National figure includes expenditures in U.S. territories.

Medicaid Enrollment in 2002

National Total = 41,149,422 Enrollees*

ALPHA ORDER

RANK	STATE	ENROLLEES	% of USA
19	Alabama	735,706	1.8%
45	Alaska	91,698	0.2%
16	Arizona	821,748	2.0%
27	Arkansas	526,877	1.3%
1	California	6,190,430	15.0%
32	Colorado	313,183	0.8%
31	Connecticut	385,239	0.9%
44	Delaware	124,828	0.3%
4	Florida	2,109,603	5.1%
9	Georgia	1,323,205	3.2%
38	Hawaii	177,531	0.4%
42	Idaho	151,390	0.4%
5	Illinois	1,695,647	4.1%
20	Indiana	686,712	1.7%
34	Iowa	265,042	0.6%
35	Kansas	235,797	0.6%
24	Kentucky	604,120	1.5%
15	Louisiana	833,918	2.0%
36	Maine	221,230	0.5%
22	Maryland	662,755	1.6%
12	Massachusetts	962,342	2.3%
10	Michigan	1,191,456	2.9%
25	Minnesota	556,386	1.4%
23	Mississippi	650,800	1.6%
14	Missouri	930,232	2.3%
48	Montana	76,482	0.2%
37	Nebraska	211,712	0.5%
41	Nevada	164,388	0.4%
47	New Hampshire	90,028	0.2%
18	New Jersey	759,644	1.8%
30	New Mexico	389,298	0.9%
2	New York	3,388,931	8.2%
11	North Carolina	1,052,041	2.6%
50	North Dakota	52,913	0.1%
6	Ohio	1,545,000	3.8%
28	Oklahoma	462,533	1.1%
29	Oregon	427,547	1.0%
7	Pennsylvania	1,458,694	3.5%
39	Rhode Island	175,500	0.4%
17	South Carolina	771,490	1.9%
46	South Dakota	90,766	0.2%
8	Tennessee	1,324,011	3.2%
3	Texas	2,412,854	5.9%
40	Utah	170,775	0.4%
43	Vermont	132,502	0.3%
26	Virginia	530,423	1.3%
13	Washington	946,329	2.3%
33	West Virginia	288,072	0.7%
21	Wisconsin	676,395	1.6%
49	Wyoming	54,656	0.1%

RANK ORDER

RANK	STATE	ENROLLEES	% of USA
1	California	6,190,430	15.0%
2	New York	3,388,931	8.2%
3	Texas	2,412,854	5.9%
4	Florida	2,109,603	5.1%
5	Illinois	1,695,647	4.1%
6	Ohio	1,545,000	3.8%
7	Pennsylvania	1,458,694	3.5%
8	Tennessee	1,324,011	3.2%
9	Georgia	1,323,205	3.2%
10	Michigan	1,191,456	2.9%
11	North Carolina	1,052,041	2.6%
12	Massachusetts	962,342	2.3%
13	Washington	946,329	2.3%
14	Missouri	930,232	2.3%
15	Louisiana	833,918	2.0%
16	Arizona	821,748	2.0%
17	South Carolina	771,490	1.9%
18	New Jersey	759,644	1.8%
19	Alabama	735,706	1.8%
20	Indiana	686,712	1.7%
21	Wisconsin	676,395	1.6%
22	Maryland	662,755	1.6%
23	Mississippi	650,800	1.6%
24	Kentucky	604,120	1.5%
25	Minnesota	556,386	1.4%
26	Virginia	530,423	1.3%
27	Arkansas	526,877	1.3%
28	Oklahoma	462,533	1.1%
29	Oregon	427,547	1.0%
30	New Mexico	389,298	0.9%
31	Connecticut	385,239	0.9%
32	Colorado	313,183	0.8%
33	West Virginia	288,072	0.7%
34	Iowa	265,042	0.6%
35	Kansas	235,797	0.6%
36	Maine	221,230	0.5%
37	Nebraska	211,712	0.5%
38	Hawaii	177,531	0.4%
39	Rhode Island	175,500	0.4%
40	Utah	170,775	0.4%
41	Nevada	164,388	0.4%
42	Idaho	151,390	0.4%
43	Vermont	132,502	0.3%
44	Delaware	124,828	0.3%
45	Alaska	91,698	0.2%
46	South Dakota	90,766	0.2%
47	New Hampshire	90,028	0.2%
48	Montana	76,482	0.2%
49	Wyoming	54,656	0.1%
50	North Dakota	52,913	0.1%
	District of Columbia	128,837	0.3%

Source: U.S. Department of Health and Human Services, Centers for Medicare and Medicaid Services "Medicaid Managed Care State Enrollment" (http://www.cms.gov/medicaid/managedcare/mmcpr02.pdf)
As of December 31, 2002. National total includes 919,726 Medicaid enrollees in Puerto Rico and the Virgin Islands.

Medicaid Expenditures per Enrollee in 2002

National Rate = $5,985 per Enrollee*

<u>ALPHA ORDER</u>

RANK	STATE	PER ENROLLEE
49	Alabama	$4,204
12	Alaska	7,479
46	Arizona	4,310
48	Arkansas	4,247
45	California	4,344
14	Colorado	7,418
5	Connecticut	8,972
35	Delaware	5,079
41	Florida	4,679
40	Georgia	4,717
50	Hawaii	4,168
34	Idaho	5,110
33	Illinois	5,195
16	Indiana	6,478
4	Iowa	9,716
10	Kansas	7,789
22	Kentucky	6,229
26	Louisiana	5,859
17	Maine	6,464
32	Maryland	5,452
7	Massachusetts	8,379
19	Michigan	6,347
9	Minnesota	7,934
43	Mississippi	4,421
27	Missouri	5,763
13	Montana	7,472
20	Nebraska	6,325
38	Nevada	4,916
1	New Hampshire	11,286
3	New Jersey	10,197
42	New Mexico	4,564
2	New York	10,710
18	North Carolina	6,391
6	North Dakota	8,720
21	Ohio	6,251
39	Oklahoma	4,887
25	Oregon	6,015
8	Pennsylvania	8,316
11	Rhode Island	7,741
47	South Carolina	4,268
24	South Dakota	6,058
44	Tennessee	4,371
29	Texas	5,605
27	Utah	5,763
37	Vermont	4,987
15	Virginia	7,187
31	Washington	5,462
30	West Virginia	5,499
23	Wisconsin	6,199
36	Wyoming	5,024

<u>RANK ORDER</u>

RANK	STATE	PER ENROLLEE
1	New Hampshire	$11,286
2	New York	10,710
3	New Jersey	10,197
4	Iowa	9,716
5	Connecticut	8,972
6	North Dakota	8,720
7	Massachusetts	8,379
8	Pennsylvania	8,316
9	Minnesota	7,934
10	Kansas	7,789
11	Rhode Island	7,741
12	Alaska	7,479
13	Montana	7,472
14	Colorado	7,418
15	Virginia	7,187
16	Indiana	6,478
17	Maine	6,464
18	North Carolina	6,391
19	Michigan	6,347
20	Nebraska	6,325
21	Ohio	6,251
22	Kentucky	6,229
23	Wisconsin	6,199
24	South Dakota	6,058
25	Oregon	6,015
26	Louisiana	5,859
27	Missouri	5,763
27	Utah	5,763
29	Texas	5,605
30	West Virginia	5,499
31	Washington	5,462
32	Maryland	5,452
33	Illinois	5,195
34	Idaho	5,110
35	Delaware	5,079
36	Wyoming	5,024
37	Vermont	4,987
38	Nevada	4,916
39	Oklahoma	4,887
40	Georgia	4,717
41	Florida	4,679
42	New Mexico	4,564
43	Mississippi	4,421
44	Tennessee	4,371
45	California	4,344
46	Arizona	4,310
47	South Carolina	4,268
48	Arkansas	4,247
49	Alabama	4,204
50	Hawaii	4,168

| | District of Columbia | 7,931 |

Source: MQ Press using data from U.S. Dept of Health & Human Services, Centers for Medicare and Medicaid Services "Medicaid Financial Statistics Tables (HCFA-64 Report)"
*For fiscal year 2002. National figure includes expenditures and enrollees in U.S. territories. Includes Medical Assistance Payments and Administrative Costs.

Percent of Population Receiving Public Aid in 2001

National Percent = 4.2% of Population*

<table>
<tr><td colspan="3"><u>ALPHA ORDER</u></td><td colspan="3"><u>RANK ORDER</u></td></tr>
<tr><td>RANK</td><td>STATE</td><td>PERCENT</td><td>RANK</td><td>STATE</td><td>PERCENT</td></tr>
<tr><td>10</td><td>Alabama</td><td>4.6</td><td>1</td><td>California</td><td>6.6</td></tr>
<tr><td>15</td><td>Alaska</td><td>4.2</td><td>2</td><td>Rhode Island</td><td>6.5</td></tr>
<tr><td>27</td><td>Arizona</td><td>3.3</td><td>3</td><td>West Virginia</td><td>6.4</td></tr>
<tr><td>15</td><td>Arkansas</td><td>4.2</td><td>4</td><td>Kentucky</td><td>6.3</td></tr>
<tr><td>1</td><td>California</td><td>6.6</td><td>5</td><td>Mississippi</td><td>5.9</td></tr>
<tr><td>47</td><td>Colorado</td><td>1.9</td><td>6</td><td>Tennessee</td><td>5.7</td></tr>
<tr><td>34</td><td>Connecticut</td><td>3.1</td><td>7</td><td>New York</td><td>5.6</td></tr>
<tr><td>34</td><td>Delaware</td><td>3.1</td><td>8</td><td>New Mexico</td><td>5.3</td></tr>
<tr><td>30</td><td>Florida</td><td>3.2</td><td>9</td><td>Louisiana</td><td>5.2</td></tr>
<tr><td>22</td><td>Georgia</td><td>3.9</td><td>10</td><td>Alabama</td><td>4.6</td></tr>
<tr><td>11</td><td>Hawaii</td><td>4.4</td><td>11</td><td>Hawaii</td><td>4.4</td></tr>
<tr><td>49</td><td>Idaho</td><td>1.6</td><td>12</td><td>Maine</td><td>4.3</td></tr>
<tr><td>30</td><td>Illinois</td><td>3.2</td><td>12</td><td>Massachusetts</td><td>4.3</td></tr>
<tr><td>24</td><td>Indiana</td><td>3.7</td><td>12</td><td>Vermont</td><td>4.3</td></tr>
<tr><td>27</td><td>Iowa</td><td>3.3</td><td>15</td><td>Alaska</td><td>4.2</td></tr>
<tr><td>41</td><td>Kansas</td><td>2.6</td><td>15</td><td>Arkansas</td><td>4.2</td></tr>
<tr><td>4</td><td>Kentucky</td><td>6.3</td><td>15</td><td>Michigan</td><td>4.2</td></tr>
<tr><td>9</td><td>Louisiana</td><td>5.2</td><td>15</td><td>Missouri</td><td>4.2</td></tr>
<tr><td>12</td><td>Maine</td><td>4.3</td><td>15</td><td>Pennsylvania</td><td>4.2</td></tr>
<tr><td>37</td><td>Maryland</td><td>2.9</td><td>20</td><td>Washington</td><td>4.1</td></tr>
<tr><td>12</td><td>Massachusetts</td><td>4.3</td><td>21</td><td>South Carolina</td><td>4.0</td></tr>
<tr><td>15</td><td>Michigan</td><td>4.2</td><td>22</td><td>Georgia</td><td>3.9</td></tr>
<tr><td>30</td><td>Minnesota</td><td>3.2</td><td>23</td><td>Ohio</td><td>3.8</td></tr>
<tr><td>5</td><td>Mississippi</td><td>5.9</td><td>24</td><td>Indiana</td><td>3.7</td></tr>
<tr><td>15</td><td>Missouri</td><td>4.2</td><td>25</td><td>North Carolina</td><td>3.5</td></tr>
<tr><td>27</td><td>Montana</td><td>3.3</td><td>25</td><td>Texas</td><td>3.5</td></tr>
<tr><td>39</td><td>Nebraska</td><td>2.7</td><td>27</td><td>Arizona</td><td>3.3</td></tr>
<tr><td>44</td><td>Nevada</td><td>2.5</td><td>27</td><td>Iowa</td><td>3.3</td></tr>
<tr><td>46</td><td>New Hampshire</td><td>2.1</td><td>27</td><td>Montana</td><td>3.3</td></tr>
<tr><td>36</td><td>New Jersey</td><td>3.0</td><td>30</td><td>Florida</td><td>3.2</td></tr>
<tr><td>8</td><td>New Mexico</td><td>5.3</td><td>30</td><td>Illinois</td><td>3.2</td></tr>
<tr><td>7</td><td>New York</td><td>5.6</td><td>30</td><td>Minnesota</td><td>3.2</td></tr>
<tr><td>25</td><td>North Carolina</td><td>3.5</td><td>30</td><td>Oklahoma</td><td>3.2</td></tr>
<tr><td>41</td><td>North Dakota</td><td>2.6</td><td>34</td><td>Connecticut</td><td>3.1</td></tr>
<tr><td>23</td><td>Ohio</td><td>3.8</td><td>34</td><td>Delaware</td><td>3.1</td></tr>
<tr><td>30</td><td>Oklahoma</td><td>3.2</td><td>36</td><td>New Jersey</td><td>3.0</td></tr>
<tr><td>39</td><td>Oregon</td><td>2.7</td><td>37</td><td>Maryland</td><td>2.9</td></tr>
<tr><td>15</td><td>Pennsylvania</td><td>4.2</td><td>38</td><td>Virginia</td><td>2.8</td></tr>
<tr><td>2</td><td>Rhode Island</td><td>6.5</td><td>39</td><td>Nebraska</td><td>2.7</td></tr>
<tr><td>21</td><td>South Carolina</td><td>4.0</td><td>39</td><td>Oregon</td><td>2.7</td></tr>
<tr><td>41</td><td>South Dakota</td><td>2.6</td><td>41</td><td>Kansas</td><td>2.6</td></tr>
<tr><td>6</td><td>Tennessee</td><td>5.7</td><td>41</td><td>North Dakota</td><td>2.6</td></tr>
<tr><td>25</td><td>Texas</td><td>3.5</td><td>41</td><td>South Dakota</td><td>2.6</td></tr>
<tr><td>48</td><td>Utah</td><td>1.8</td><td>44</td><td>Nevada</td><td>2.5</td></tr>
<tr><td>12</td><td>Vermont</td><td>4.3</td><td>45</td><td>Wisconsin</td><td>2.4</td></tr>
<tr><td>38</td><td>Virginia</td><td>2.8</td><td>46</td><td>New Hampshire</td><td>2.1</td></tr>
<tr><td>20</td><td>Washington</td><td>4.1</td><td>47</td><td>Colorado</td><td>1.9</td></tr>
<tr><td>3</td><td>West Virginia</td><td>6.4</td><td>48</td><td>Utah</td><td>1.8</td></tr>
<tr><td>45</td><td>Wisconsin</td><td>2.4</td><td>49</td><td>Idaho</td><td>1.6</td></tr>
<tr><td>50</td><td>Wyoming</td><td>1.3</td><td>50</td><td>Wyoming</td><td>1.3</td></tr>
<tr><td></td><td></td><td></td><td></td><td>District of Columbia</td><td>11.0</td></tr>
</table>

*Source: Morgan Quitno Press using data from U.S. Social Security Administration and
U.S. Department of Health and Human Services*

*As of December 2001. Includes recipients of Temporary Assistance to Needy Families (TANF) and Supplemental
Security Income payments.*

Social Security Supplemental Security Income Beneficiaries in 2001

National Total = 6,687,811 Beneficiaries*

<u>ALPHA ORDER</u>

RANK	STATE	BENEFICIARIES	% of USA
15	Alabama	161,521	2.4%
48	Alaska	9,123	0.1%
26	Arizona	84,796	1.3%
25	Arkansas	85,088	1.3%
1	California	1,106,294	16.5%
31	Colorado	53,466	0.8%
32	Connecticut	49,586	0.7%
46	Delaware	12,197	0.2%
4	Florida	386,334	5.8%
9	Georgia	198,063	3.0%
40	Hawaii	21,303	0.3%
42	Idaho	18,840	0.3%
6	Illinois	249,004	3.7%
23	Indiana	89,118	1.3%
34	Iowa	40,716	0.6%
35	Kansas	36,600	0.5%
11	Kentucky	175,925	2.6%
13	Louisiana	166,181	2.5%
36	Maine	30,138	0.5%
22	Maryland	89,180	1.3%
12	Massachusetts	166,874	2.5%
8	Michigan	210,492	3.1%
29	Minnesota	65,538	1.0%
18	Mississippi	128,449	1.9%
19	Missouri	113,258	1.7%
43	Montana	14,206	0.2%
39	Nebraska	21,471	0.3%
38	Nevada	27,161	0.4%
47	New Hampshire	11,942	0.2%
16	New Jersey	147,747	2.2%
33	New Mexico	47,579	0.7%
2	New York	622,764	9.3%
10	North Carolina	191,630	2.9%
49	North Dakota	8,129	0.1%
7	Ohio	241,763	3.6%
28	Oklahoma	72,756	1.1%
30	Oregon	54,099	0.8%
5	Pennsylvania	294,467	4.4%
37	Rhode Island	28,623	0.4%
20	South Carolina	106,881	1.6%
44	South Dakota	12,698	0.2%
14	Tennessee	162,920	2.4%
3	Texas	418,235	6.3%
41	Utah	20,545	0.3%
45	Vermont	12,554	0.2%
17	Virginia	132,808	2.0%
21	Washington	104,700	1.6%
27	West Virginia	72,953	1.1%
24	Wisconsin	85,333	1.3%
50	Wyoming	5,790	0.1%

<u>RANK ORDER</u>

RANK	STATE	BENEFICIARIES	% of USA
1	California	1,106,294	16.5%
2	New York	622,764	9.3%
3	Texas	418,235	6.3%
4	Florida	386,334	5.8%
5	Pennsylvania	294,467	4.4%
6	Illinois	249,004	3.7%
7	Ohio	241,763	3.6%
8	Michigan	210,492	3.1%
9	Georgia	198,063	3.0%
10	North Carolina	191,630	2.9%
11	Kentucky	175,925	2.6%
12	Massachusetts	166,874	2.5%
13	Louisiana	166,181	2.5%
14	Tennessee	162,920	2.4%
15	Alabama	161,521	2.4%
16	New Jersey	147,747	2.2%
17	Virginia	132,808	2.0%
18	Mississippi	128,449	1.9%
19	Missouri	113,258	1.7%
20	South Carolina	106,881	1.6%
21	Washington	104,700	1.6%
22	Maryland	89,180	1.3%
23	Indiana	89,118	1.3%
24	Wisconsin	85,333	1.3%
25	Arkansas	85,088	1.3%
26	Arizona	84,796	1.3%
27	West Virginia	72,953	1.1%
28	Oklahoma	72,756	1.1%
29	Minnesota	65,538	1.0%
30	Oregon	54,099	0.8%
31	Colorado	53,466	0.8%
32	Connecticut	49,586	0.7%
33	New Mexico	47,579	0.7%
34	Iowa	40,716	0.6%
35	Kansas	36,600	0.5%
36	Maine	30,138	0.5%
37	Rhode Island	28,623	0.4%
38	Nevada	27,161	0.4%
39	Nebraska	21,471	0.3%
40	Hawaii	21,303	0.3%
41	Utah	20,545	0.3%
42	Idaho	18,840	0.3%
43	Montana	14,206	0.2%
44	South Dakota	12,698	0.2%
45	Vermont	12,554	0.2%
46	Delaware	12,197	0.2%
47	New Hampshire	11,942	0.2%
48	Alaska	9,123	0.1%
49	North Dakota	8,129	0.1%
50	Wyoming	5,790	0.1%
	District of Columbia	19,973	0.3%

Source: Social Security Administration
  "Social Security Bulletin, Annual Statistical Supplement 2002"
*For December 2001. National total includes 677 beneficiaries in U.S. territories or otherwise not distributed by state.

Average Monthly Social Security Supplemental Security Income Payment: 2001

National Average = $393.96 Each Month per Beneficiary*

<u>ALPHA ORDER</u>

RANK	STATE	AVERAGE BENEFIT
38	Alabama	$342.90
25	Alaska	359.31
14	Arizona	374.72
49	Arkansas	324.61
1	California	499.77
28	Colorado	355.70
13	Connecticut	375.96
23	Delaware	362.24
19	Florida	366.75
43	Georgia	338.42
4	Hawaii	411.55
31	Idaho	350.66
8	Illinois	400.65
17	Indiana	367.45
41	Iowa	338.89
30	Kansas	353.45
22	Kentucky	364.25
24	Louisiana	359.52
45	Maine	330.72
12	Maryland	379.02
5	Massachusetts	409.80
9	Michigan	398.60
20	Minnesota	366.42
44	Mississippi	336.49
27	Missouri	357.05
33	Montana	349.97
40	Nebraska	339.03
21	Nevada	364.76
34	New Hampshire	349.52
11	New Jersey	387.95
32	New Mexico	350.29
2	New York	435.05
48	North Carolina	325.51
50	North Dakota	310.10
10	Ohio	392.06
35	Oklahoma	348.99
16	Oregon	369.79
6	Pennsylvania	408.22
7	Rhode Island	401.60
42	South Carolina	338.52
46	South Dakota	327.31
36	Tennessee	346.52
47	Texas	326.80
18	Utah	367.38
29	Vermont	354.53
37	Virginia	344.18
3	Washington	413.66
15	West Virginia	373.25
26	Wisconsin	359.30
39	Wyoming	342.71

<u>RANK ORDER</u>

RANK	STATE	AVERAGE BENEFIT
1	California	$499.77
2	New York	435.05
3	Washington	413.66
4	Hawaii	411.55
5	Massachusetts	409.80
6	Pennsylvania	408.22
7	Rhode Island	401.60
8	Illinois	400.65
9	Michigan	398.60
10	Ohio	392.06
11	New Jersey	387.95
12	Maryland	379.02
13	Connecticut	375.96
14	Arizona	374.72
15	West Virginia	373.25
16	Oregon	369.79
17	Indiana	367.45
18	Utah	367.38
19	Florida	366.75
20	Minnesota	366.42
21	Nevada	364.76
22	Kentucky	364.25
23	Delaware	362.24
24	Louisiana	359.52
25	Alaska	359.31
26	Wisconsin	359.30
27	Missouri	357.05
28	Colorado	355.70
29	Vermont	354.53
30	Kansas	353.45
31	Idaho	350.66
32	New Mexico	350.29
33	Montana	349.97
34	New Hampshire	349.52
35	Oklahoma	348.99
36	Tennessee	346.52
37	Virginia	344.18
38	Alabama	342.90
39	Wyoming	342.71
40	Nebraska	339.03
41	Iowa	338.89
42	South Carolina	338.52
43	Georgia	338.42
44	Mississippi	336.49
45	Maine	330.72
46	South Dakota	327.31
47	Texas	326.80
48	North Carolina	325.51
49	Arkansas	324.61
50	North Dakota	310.10
	District of Columbia	394.61

Source: Morgan Quitno Press using data from Social Security Administration
"Social Security Bulletin, Annual Statistical Supplement 2002"
As of December 2001. National average includes payments to beneficiaries in U.S. territories and foreign countries.

Recipients of Temporary Assistance to Needy Families (TANF) Payments: 2003

National Total = 4,963,771 Monthly Recipients*

ALPHA ORDER

RANK	STATE	RECIPIENTS	% of USA
27	Alabama	44,646	0.9%
43	Alaska	15,927	0.3%
12	Arizona	111,334	2.2%
40	Arkansas	25,382	0.5%
1	California	1,085,627	21.9%
36	Colorado	34,862	0.7%
29	Connecticut	43,292	0.9%
46	Delaware	12,351	0.2%
11	Florida	119,080	2.4%
10	Georgia	132,003	2.7%
39	Hawaii	25,409	0.5%
49	Idaho	3,204	0.1%
16	Illinois	99,952	2.0%
9	Indiana	140,571	2.8%
23	Iowa	51,713	1.0%
32	Kansas	39,093	0.8%
19	Kentucky	76,688	1.5%
22	Louisiana	56,157	1.1%
33	Maine	37,562	0.8%
21	Maryland	62,066	1.3%
14	Massachusetts	108,469	2.2%
5	Michigan	202,469	4.1%
17	Minnesota	93,665	1.9%
26	Mississippi	45,191	0.9%
13	Missouri	108,561	2.2%
42	Montana	18,074	0.4%
37	Nebraska	27,079	0.5%
38	Nevada	25,832	0.5%
44	New Hampshire	15,061	0.3%
15	New Jersey	101,854	2.1%
30	New Mexico	42,999	0.9%
2	New York	341,004	6.9%
18	North Carolina	83,906	1.7%
47	North Dakota	8,602	0.2%
6	Ohio	188,108	3.8%
34	Oklahoma	35,974	0.7%
28	Oregon	43,591	0.9%
4	Pennsylvania	207,429	4.2%
35	Rhode Island	35,714	0.7%
24	South Carolina	48,028	1.0%
48	South Dakota	6,143	0.1%
7	Tennessee	180,466	3.6%
3	Texas	333,435	6.7%
41	Utah	21,800	0.4%
45	Vermont	12,737	0.3%
20	Virginia	70,199	1.4%
8	Washington	140,721	2.8%
31	West Virginia	41,478	0.8%
25	Wisconsin	47,712	1.0%
50	Wyoming	729	0.0%

RANK ORDER

RANK	STATE	RECIPIENTS	% of USA
1	California	1,085,627	21.9%
2	New York	341,004	6.9%
3	Texas	333,435	6.7%
4	Pennsylvania	207,429	4.2%
5	Michigan	202,469	4.1%
6	Ohio	188,108	3.8%
7	Tennessee	180,466	3.6%
8	Washington	140,721	2.8%
9	Indiana	140,571	2.8%
10	Georgia	132,003	2.7%
11	Florida	119,080	2.4%
12	Arizona	111,334	2.2%
13	Missouri	108,561	2.2%
14	Massachusetts	108,469	2.2%
15	New Jersey	101,854	2.1%
16	Illinois	99,952	2.0%
17	Minnesota	93,665	1.9%
18	North Carolina	83,906	1.7%
19	Kentucky	76,688	1.5%
20	Virginia	70,199	1.4%
21	Maryland	62,066	1.3%
22	Louisiana	56,157	1.1%
23	Iowa	51,713	1.0%
24	South Carolina	48,028	1.0%
25	Wisconsin	47,712	1.0%
26	Mississippi	45,191	0.9%
27	Alabama	44,646	0.9%
28	Oregon	43,591	0.9%
29	Connecticut	43,292	0.9%
30	New Mexico	42,999	0.9%
31	West Virginia	41,478	0.8%
32	Kansas	39,093	0.8%
33	Maine	37,562	0.8%
34	Oklahoma	35,974	0.7%
35	Rhode Island	35,714	0.7%
36	Colorado	34,862	0.7%
37	Nebraska	27,079	0.5%
38	Nevada	25,832	0.5%
39	Hawaii	25,409	0.5%
40	Arkansas	25,382	0.5%
41	Utah	21,800	0.4%
42	Montana	18,074	0.4%
43	Alaska	15,927	0.3%
44	New Hampshire	15,061	0.3%
45	Vermont	12,737	0.3%
46	Delaware	12,351	0.2%
47	North Dakota	8,602	0.2%
48	South Dakota	6,143	0.1%
49	Idaho	3,204	0.1%
50	Wyoming	729	0.0%
	District of Columbia	43,136	0.9%

Source: U.S. Department of Health and Human Services, Administration for Children and Families
   "Total Number of Families and Recipients" (http://www.acf.hhs.gov/news/stats/Mar02-Mar03.htm)
*As of March 2003. Welfare reform replaced the Aid to Families with Dependent Children program (AFDC) with Temporary Assistance to Needy Families (TANF) as of July 1, 1997. National total includes 66,686 recipients in U.S. territories (54,544 in Puerto Rico).

Percent Change in TANF Recipients: 2002 to 2003

National Percent Change = 4.3% Decrease*

<u>ALPHA ORDER</u>

RANK	STATE	PERCENT CHANGE
12	Alabama	5.2
47	Alaska	(16.2)
3	Arizona	20.4
42	Arkansas	(10.3)
35	California	(7.6)
7	Colorado	8.6
48	Connecticut	(18.2)
21	Delaware	0.0
31	Florida	(5.0)
15	Georgia	3.5
46	Hawaii	(15.9)
2	Idaho	32.6
50	Illinois	(28.8)
18	Indiana	1.5
30	Iowa	(4.9)
6	Kansas	9.8
23	Kentucky	(1.0)
34	Louisiana	(7.0)
1	Maine	41.8
36	Maryland	(7.7)
19	Massachusetts	1.2
33	Michigan	(6.2)
23	Minnesota	(1.0)
4	Mississippi	13.3
41	Missouri	(10.2)
10	Montana	5.6
11	Nebraska	5.3
44	Nevada	(11.0)
17	New Hampshire	1.6
26	New Jersey	(2.1)
42	New Mexico	(10.3)
45	New York	(12.6)
38	North Carolina	(8.1)
13	North Dakota	4.6
27	Ohio	(2.5)
22	Oklahoma	(0.6)
16	Oregon	3.0
28	Pennsylvania	(3.1)
39	Rhode Island	(9.1)
40	South Carolina	(10.1)
37	South Dakota	(8.0)
5	Tennessee	10.2
20	Texas	1.0
8	Utah	8.0
32	Vermont	(5.6)
14	Virginia	4.1
25	Washington	(1.3)
29	West Virginia	(3.8)
9	Wisconsin	6.8
49	Wyoming	(19.5)

<u>RANK ORDER</u>

RANK	STATE	PERCENT CHANGE
1	Maine	41.8
2	Idaho	32.6
3	Arizona	20.4
4	Mississippi	13.3
5	Tennessee	10.2
6	Kansas	9.8
7	Colorado	8.6
8	Utah	8.0
9	Wisconsin	6.8
10	Montana	5.6
11	Nebraska	5.3
12	Alabama	5.2
13	North Dakota	4.6
14	Virginia	4.1
15	Georgia	3.5
16	Oregon	3.0
17	New Hampshire	1.6
18	Indiana	1.5
19	Massachusetts	1.2
20	Texas	1.0
21	Delaware	0.0
22	Oklahoma	(0.6)
23	Kentucky	(1.0)
23	Minnesota	(1.0)
25	Washington	(1.3)
26	New Jersey	(2.1)
27	Ohio	(2.5)
28	Pennsylvania	(3.1)
29	West Virginia	(3.8)
30	Iowa	(4.9)
31	Florida	(5.0)
32	Vermont	(5.6)
33	Michigan	(6.2)
34	Louisiana	(7.0)
35	California	(7.6)
36	Maryland	(7.7)
37	South Dakota	(8.0)
38	North Carolina	(8.1)
39	Rhode Island	(9.1)
40	South Carolina	(10.1)
41	Missouri	(10.2)
42	Arkansas	(10.3)
42	New Mexico	(10.3)
44	Nevada	(11.0)
45	New York	(12.6)
46	Hawaii	(15.9)
47	Alaska	(16.2)
48	Connecticut	(18.2)
49	Wyoming	(19.5)
50	Illinois	(28.8)

District of Columbia	1.5

*Source: Morgan Quitno Press using data from U.S. Dept. of HHS, Administration for Children and Families
    "Total Number of Families and Recipients" (http://www.acf.hhs.gov/news/stats/Mar02-Mar03.htm)*
**March 2002 to March 2003.   Welfare reform replaced the Aid to Families with Dependent Children program (AFDC)
with Temporary Assistance to Needy Families (TANF) as of July 1, 1997. National percent includes recipients in
U.S. territories.*

Average Monthly TANF Assistance per Recipient in 2002

National Average = $163.94*

<table>
<tr><td colspan="3"><u>ALPHA ORDER</u></td><td colspan="3"><u>RANK ORDER</u></td></tr>
<tr><td>RANK</td><td>STATE</td><td>PER RECIPIENT</td><td>RANK</td><td>STATE</td><td>PER RECIPIENT</td></tr>
<tr><td>44</td><td>Alabama</td><td>$68.45</td><td>1</td><td>Pennsylvania</td><td>$314.21</td></tr>
<tr><td>3</td><td>Alaska</td><td>245.01</td><td>2</td><td>California</td><td>269.90</td></tr>
<tr><td>35</td><td>Arizona</td><td>106.81</td><td>3</td><td>Alaska</td><td>245.01</td></tr>
<tr><td>38</td><td>Arkansas</td><td>101.98</td><td>4</td><td>Oregon</td><td>237.52</td></tr>
<tr><td>2</td><td>California</td><td>269.90</td><td>5</td><td>Massachusetts</td><td>231.76</td></tr>
<tr><td>25</td><td>Colorado</td><td>136.65</td><td>6</td><td>New York</td><td>208.07</td></tr>
<tr><td>9</td><td>Connecticut</td><td>193.93</td><td>7</td><td>New Hampshire</td><td>204.22</td></tr>
<tr><td>33</td><td>Delaware</td><td>108.59</td><td>8</td><td>Vermont</td><td>195.47</td></tr>
<tr><td>30</td><td>Florida</td><td>117.49</td><td>9</td><td>Connecticut</td><td>193.93</td></tr>
<tr><td>NA</td><td>Georgia**</td><td>NA</td><td>10</td><td>Wisconsin</td><td>189.76</td></tr>
<tr><td>11</td><td>Hawaii</td><td>177.10</td><td>11</td><td>Hawaii</td><td>177.10</td></tr>
<tr><td>13</td><td>Idaho</td><td>164.06</td><td>12</td><td>Washington</td><td>172.61</td></tr>
<tr><td>48</td><td>Illinois</td><td>54.97</td><td>13</td><td>Idaho</td><td>164.06</td></tr>
<tr><td>40</td><td>Indiana</td><td>95.33</td><td>14</td><td>North Dakota</td><td>162.04</td></tr>
<tr><td>29</td><td>Iowa</td><td>123.10</td><td>15</td><td>Rhode Island</td><td>160.19</td></tr>
<tr><td>31</td><td>Kansas</td><td>116.70</td><td>16</td><td>Utah</td><td>155.12</td></tr>
<tr><td>36</td><td>Kentucky</td><td>106.37</td><td>17</td><td>Montana</td><td>153.88</td></tr>
<tr><td>42</td><td>Louisiana</td><td>89.06</td><td>18</td><td>Maine</td><td>150.78</td></tr>
<tr><td>18</td><td>Maine</td><td>150.78</td><td>19</td><td>Minnesota</td><td>144.70</td></tr>
<tr><td>21</td><td>Maryland</td><td>141.52</td><td>20</td><td>New Jersey</td><td>143.65</td></tr>
<tr><td>5</td><td>Massachusetts</td><td>231.76</td><td>21</td><td>Maryland</td><td>141.52</td></tr>
<tr><td>27</td><td>Michigan</td><td>132.62</td><td>22</td><td>Ohio</td><td>140.75</td></tr>
<tr><td>19</td><td>Minnesota</td><td>144.70</td><td>23</td><td>Nebraska</td><td>138.13</td></tr>
<tr><td>47</td><td>Mississippi</td><td>63.69</td><td>24</td><td>South Dakota</td><td>136.77</td></tr>
<tr><td>41</td><td>Missouri</td><td>93.37</td><td>25</td><td>Colorado</td><td>136.65</td></tr>
<tr><td>17</td><td>Montana</td><td>153.88</td><td>26</td><td>West Virginia</td><td>136.16</td></tr>
<tr><td>23</td><td>Nebraska</td><td>138.13</td><td>27</td><td>Michigan</td><td>132.62</td></tr>
<tr><td>28</td><td>Nevada</td><td>124.65</td><td>28</td><td>Nevada</td><td>124.65</td></tr>
<tr><td>7</td><td>New Hampshire</td><td>204.22</td><td>29</td><td>Iowa</td><td>123.10</td></tr>
<tr><td>20</td><td>New Jersey</td><td>143.65</td><td>30</td><td>Florida</td><td>117.49</td></tr>
<tr><td>34</td><td>New Mexico</td><td>107.28</td><td>31</td><td>Kansas</td><td>116.70</td></tr>
<tr><td>6</td><td>New York</td><td>208.07</td><td>32</td><td>Virginia</td><td>113.84</td></tr>
<tr><td>39</td><td>North Carolina</td><td>101.60</td><td>33</td><td>Delaware</td><td>108.59</td></tr>
<tr><td>14</td><td>North Dakota</td><td>162.04</td><td>34</td><td>New Mexico</td><td>107.28</td></tr>
<tr><td>22</td><td>Ohio</td><td>140.75</td><td>35</td><td>Arizona</td><td>106.81</td></tr>
<tr><td>NA</td><td>Oklahoma**</td><td>NA</td><td>36</td><td>Kentucky</td><td>106.37</td></tr>
<tr><td>4</td><td>Oregon</td><td>237.52</td><td>37</td><td>Wyoming</td><td>103.00</td></tr>
<tr><td>1</td><td>Pennsylvania</td><td>314.21</td><td>38</td><td>Arkansas</td><td>101.98</td></tr>
<tr><td>15</td><td>Rhode Island</td><td>160.19</td><td>39</td><td>North Carolina</td><td>101.60</td></tr>
<tr><td>46</td><td>South Carolina</td><td>64.01</td><td>40</td><td>Indiana</td><td>95.33</td></tr>
<tr><td>24</td><td>South Dakota</td><td>136.77</td><td>41</td><td>Missouri</td><td>93.37</td></tr>
<tr><td>45</td><td>Tennessee</td><td>65.25</td><td>42</td><td>Louisiana</td><td>89.06</td></tr>
<tr><td>43</td><td>Texas</td><td>71.15</td><td>43</td><td>Texas</td><td>71.15</td></tr>
<tr><td>16</td><td>Utah</td><td>155.12</td><td>44</td><td>Alabama</td><td>68.45</td></tr>
<tr><td>8</td><td>Vermont</td><td>195.47</td><td>45</td><td>Tennessee</td><td>65.25</td></tr>
<tr><td>32</td><td>Virginia</td><td>113.84</td><td>46</td><td>South Carolina</td><td>64.01</td></tr>
<tr><td>12</td><td>Washington</td><td>172.61</td><td>47</td><td>Mississippi</td><td>63.69</td></tr>
<tr><td>26</td><td>West Virginia</td><td>136.16</td><td>48</td><td>Illinois</td><td>54.97</td></tr>
<tr><td>10</td><td>Wisconsin</td><td>189.76</td><td>NA</td><td>Georgia**</td><td>NA</td></tr>
<tr><td>37</td><td>Wyoming</td><td>103.00</td><td>NA</td><td>Oklahoma**</td><td>NA</td></tr>
<tr><td></td><td></td><td></td><td></td><td>District of Columbia</td><td>129.13</td></tr>
</table>

Source: U.S. Department of Health and Human Services, Administration for Children and Families
"Average Monthly Amount of Assistance" (http://www.acf.hhs.gov/programs/ofa/annualreport5/0207c.htm)
**For first half of fiscal year 2002.   Welfare reform replaced the Aid to Families with Dependent Children program (AFDC) with Temporary Assistance to Needy Families (TANF) as of July 1, 1997. National average includes recipients in U.S. territories.*
***Not available.*

Food Stamp Benefits in 2003

National Total = $21,412,045,317*

ALPHA ORDER

RANK	STATE	BENEFITS	% of USA
17	Alabama	$466,123,805	2.2%
44	Alaska	65,728,367	0.3%
14	Arizona	497,638,214	2.3%
25	Arkansas	304,339,830	1.4%
2	California	1,811,713,551	8.5%
31	Colorado	203,312,158	0.9%
33	Connecticut	164,849,374	0.8%
46	Delaware	47,791,321	0.2%
5	Florida	987,926,276	4.6%
9	Georgia	782,410,910	3.7%
34	Hawaii	156,191,451	0.7%
41	Idaho	76,579,605	0.4%
4	Illinois	1,052,739,082	4.9%
16	Indiana	483,696,911	2.3%
35	Iowa	149,243,938	0.7%
36	Kansas	140,386,993	0.7%
15	Kentucky	486,231,294	2.3%
11	Louisiana	685,267,266	3.2%
37	Maine	124,070,012	0.6%
26	Maryland	256,947,694	1.2%
27	Massachusetts	253,770,540	1.2%
8	Michigan	783,076,440	3.7%
29	Minnesota	227,113,189	1.1%
24	Mississippi	335,073,821	1.6%
13	Missouri	567,586,201	2.7%
42	Montana	68,950,529	0.3%
40	Nebraska	89,301,600	0.4%
38	Nevada	112,673,472	0.5%
47	New Hampshire	39,886,906	0.2%
23	New Jersey	338,820,775	1.6%
32	New Mexico	183,505,381	0.9%
3	New York	1,676,508,940	7.8%
12	North Carolina	645,418,451	3.0%
49	North Dakota	36,702,542	0.2%
6	Ohio	880,174,745	4.1%
22	Oklahoma	362,457,507	1.7%
20	Oregon	380,986,642	1.8%
7	Pennsylvania	785,458,544	3.7%
43	Rhode Island	68,800,619	0.3%
18	South Carolina	443,355,574	2.1%
45	South Dakota	50,515,060	0.2%
10	Tennessee	721,795,073	3.4%
1	Texas	1,880,851,630	8.8%
39	Utah	102,204,854	0.5%
48	Vermont	37,629,392	0.2%
21	Virginia	366,234,127	1.7%
19	Washington	394,382,981	1.8%
30	West Virginia	216,064,512	1.0%
28	Wisconsin	233,462,769	1.1%
50	Wyoming	24,054,276	0.1%

RANK ORDER

RANK	STATE	BENEFITS	% of USA
1	Texas	$1,880,851,630	8.8%
2	California	1,811,713,551	8.5%
3	New York	1,676,508,940	7.8%
4	Illinois	1,052,739,082	4.9%
5	Florida	987,926,276	4.6%
6	Ohio	880,174,745	4.1%
7	Pennsylvania	785,458,544	3.7%
8	Michigan	783,076,440	3.7%
9	Georgia	782,410,910	3.7%
10	Tennessee	721,795,073	3.4%
11	Louisiana	685,267,266	3.2%
12	North Carolina	645,418,451	3.0%
13	Missouri	567,586,201	2.7%
14	Arizona	497,638,214	2.3%
15	Kentucky	486,231,294	2.3%
16	Indiana	483,696,911	2.3%
17	Alabama	466,123,805	2.2%
18	South Carolina	443,355,574	2.1%
19	Washington	394,382,981	1.8%
20	Oregon	380,986,642	1.8%
21	Virginia	366,234,127	1.7%
22	Oklahoma	362,457,507	1.7%
23	New Jersey	338,820,775	1.6%
24	Mississippi	335,073,821	1.6%
25	Arkansas	304,339,830	1.4%
26	Maryland	256,947,694	1.2%
27	Massachusetts	253,770,540	1.2%
28	Wisconsin	233,462,769	1.1%
29	Minnesota	227,113,189	1.1%
30	West Virginia	216,064,512	1.0%
31	Colorado	203,312,158	0.9%
32	New Mexico	183,505,381	0.9%
33	Connecticut	164,849,374	0.8%
34	Hawaii	156,191,451	0.7%
35	Iowa	149,243,938	0.7%
36	Kansas	140,386,993	0.7%
37	Maine	124,070,012	0.6%
38	Nevada	112,673,472	0.5%
39	Utah	102,204,854	0.5%
40	Nebraska	89,301,600	0.4%
41	Idaho	76,579,605	0.4%
42	Montana	68,950,529	0.3%
43	Rhode Island	68,800,619	0.3%
44	Alaska	65,728,367	0.3%
45	South Dakota	50,515,060	0.2%
46	Delaware	47,791,321	0.2%
47	New Hampshire	39,886,906	0.2%
48	Vermont	37,629,392	0.2%
49	North Dakota	36,702,542	0.2%
50	Wyoming	24,054,276	0.1%
	District of Columbia	90,113,910	0.4%

Source: U.S. Department of Agriculture, Food, Nutrition and Consumer Services
   "Food Stamp Program: Benefits" (http://www.fns.usda.gov/pd/fsfybft.htm)
*Preliminary for year ending December 19, 2003. National total includes $71,926,263 to U.S. territories. Costs are for benefits only and exclude administrative expenditures.

Monthly Food Stamp Recipients in 2003

National Total = 21,261,633 Recipients*

ALPHA ORDER

RANK	STATE	RECIPIENTS	% of USA
15	Alabama	472,066	2.2%
45	Alaska	50,687	0.2%
17	Arizona	466,153	2.2%
25	Arkansas	310,359	1.5%
2	California	1,708,354	8.0%
31	Colorado	208,053	1.0%
33	Connecticut	180,512	0.8%
46	Delaware	46,027	0.2%
4	Florida	1,041,315	4.9%
9	Georgia	750,208	3.5%
39	Hawaii	100,382	0.5%
41	Idaho	81,524	0.4%
5	Illinois	953,929	4.5%
16	Indiana	470,182	2.2%
35	Iowa	153,816	0.7%
34	Kansas	160,705	0.8%
14	Kentucky	502,677	2.4%
11	Louisiana	655,300	3.1%
36	Maine	132,582	0.6%
28	Maryland	252,220	1.2%
27	Massachusetts	292,200	1.4%
7	Michigan	837,629	3.9%
30	Minnesota	234,631	1.1%
23	Mississippi	355,783	1.7%
13	Missouri	591,532	2.8%
43	Montana	71,320	0.3%
40	Nebraska	99,243	0.5%
37	Nevada	111,352	0.5%
47	New Hampshire	44,783	0.2%
24	New Jersey	339,047	1.6%
32	New Mexico	194,795	0.9%
3	New York	1,434,936	6.7%
12	North Carolina	649,426	3.1%
49	North Dakota	39,663	0.2%
6	Ohio	855,401	4.0%
22	Oklahoma	379,743	1.8%
20	Oregon	398,377	1.9%
8	Pennsylvania	822,696	3.9%
42	Rhode Island	74,068	0.3%
18	South Carolina	450,556	2.1%
44	South Dakota	51,176	0.2%
10	Tennessee	728,305	3.4%
1	Texas	1,875,492	8.8%
38	Utah	105,630	0.5%
48	Vermont	41,333	0.2%
21	Virginia	393,911	1.9%
19	Washington	403,992	1.9%
29	West Virginia	246,890	1.2%
26	Wisconsin	296,719	1.4%
50	Wyoming	25,306	0.1%

RANK ORDER

RANK	STATE	RECIPIENTS	% of USA
1	Texas	1,875,492	8.8%
2	California	1,708,354	8.0%
3	New York	1,434,936	6.7%
4	Florida	1,041,315	4.9%
5	Illinois	953,929	4.5%
6	Ohio	855,401	4.0%
7	Michigan	837,629	3.9%
8	Pennsylvania	822,696	3.9%
9	Georgia	750,208	3.5%
10	Tennessee	728,305	3.4%
11	Louisiana	655,300	3.1%
12	North Carolina	649,426	3.1%
13	Missouri	591,532	2.8%
14	Kentucky	502,677	2.4%
15	Alabama	472,066	2.2%
16	Indiana	470,182	2.2%
17	Arizona	466,153	2.2%
18	South Carolina	450,556	2.1%
19	Washington	403,992	1.9%
20	Oregon	398,377	1.9%
21	Virginia	393,911	1.9%
22	Oklahoma	379,743	1.8%
23	Mississippi	355,783	1.7%
24	New Jersey	339,047	1.6%
25	Arkansas	310,359	1.5%
26	Wisconsin	296,719	1.4%
27	Massachusetts	292,200	1.4%
28	Maryland	252,220	1.2%
29	West Virginia	246,890	1.2%
30	Minnesota	234,631	1.1%
31	Colorado	208,053	1.0%
32	New Mexico	194,795	0.9%
33	Connecticut	180,512	0.8%
34	Kansas	160,705	0.8%
35	Iowa	153,816	0.7%
36	Maine	132,582	0.6%
37	Nevada	111,352	0.5%
38	Utah	105,630	0.5%
39	Hawaii	100,382	0.5%
40	Nebraska	99,243	0.5%
41	Idaho	81,524	0.4%
42	Rhode Island	74,068	0.3%
43	Montana	71,320	0.3%
44	South Dakota	51,176	0.2%
45	Alaska	50,687	0.2%
46	Delaware	46,027	0.2%
47	New Hampshire	44,783	0.2%
48	Vermont	41,333	0.2%
49	North Dakota	39,663	0.2%
50	Wyoming	25,306	0.1%
	District of Columbia	81,777	0.4%

Source: U.S. Department of Agriculture, Food, Nutrition and Consumer Services
"Food Stamp Program: Number of Persons Participating" (http://www.fns.usda.gov/pd/fsfypart.htm)
*Preliminary for fiscal year 2003. National total includes 36,872 recipients in U.S. territories.

Average Monthly Food Stamp Benefit per Recipient in 2003

National Average = $83.92 per Recipient*

ALPHA ORDER

RANK	STATE	PER RECIPIENT
18	Alabama	$82.28
2	Alaska	108.06
5	Arizona	88.96
21	Arkansas	81.72
6	California	88.38
22	Colorado	81.43
43	Connecticut	76.10
9	Delaware	86.53
34	Florida	79.06
8	Georgia	86.91
1	Hawaii	129.66
37	Idaho	78.28
4	Illinois	91.97
11	Indiana	85.73
24	Iowa	80.86
48	Kansas	72.80
27	Kentucky	80.61
7	Louisiana	87.14
38	Maine	77.98
12	Maryland	84.90
49	Massachusetts	72.37
39	Michigan	77.91
25	Minnesota	80.66
36	Mississippi	78.48
29	Missouri	79.96
28	Montana	80.56
45	Nebraska	74.99
13	Nevada	84.32
46	New Hampshire	74.22
15	New Jersey	83.28
35	New Mexico	78.50
3	New York	97.36
16	North Carolina	82.82
42	North Dakota	77.11
10	Ohio	85.75
32	Oklahoma	79.54
30	Oregon	79.70
31	Pennsylvania	79.56
41	Rhode Island	77.41
20	South Carolina	82.00
19	South Dakota	82.26
17	Tennessee	82.59
14	Texas	83.57
26	Utah	80.63
44	Vermont	75.87
40	Virginia	77.48
23	Washington	81.35
47	West Virginia	72.93
50	Wisconsin	65.57
33	Wyoming	79.21

RANK ORDER

RANK	STATE	PER RECIPIENT
1	Hawaii	$129.66
2	Alaska	108.06
3	New York	97.36
4	Illinois	91.97
5	Arizona	88.96
6	California	88.38
7	Louisiana	87.14
8	Georgia	86.91
9	Delaware	86.53
10	Ohio	85.75
11	Indiana	85.73
12	Maryland	84.90
13	Nevada	84.32
14	Texas	83.57
15	New Jersey	83.28
16	North Carolina	82.82
17	Tennessee	82.59
18	Alabama	82.28
19	South Dakota	82.26
20	South Carolina	82.00
21	Arkansas	81.72
22	Colorado	81.43
23	Washington	81.35
24	Iowa	80.86
25	Minnesota	80.66
26	Utah	80.63
27	Kentucky	80.61
28	Montana	80.56
29	Missouri	79.96
30	Oregon	79.70
31	Pennsylvania	79.56
32	Oklahoma	79.54
33	Wyoming	79.21
34	Florida	79.06
35	New Mexico	78.50
36	Mississippi	78.48
37	Idaho	78.28
38	Maine	77.98
39	Michigan	77.91
40	Virginia	77.48
41	Rhode Island	77.41
42	North Dakota	77.11
43	Connecticut	76.10
44	Vermont	75.87
45	Nebraska	74.99
46	New Hampshire	74.22
47	West Virginia	72.93
48	Kansas	72.80
49	Massachusetts	72.37
50	Wisconsin	65.57
	District of Columbia	91.83

Source: U.S. Department of Agriculture, Food, Nutrition and Consumer Services
   "Food Stamp Program: Average Monthly Benefit per Person" (http://www.fns.usda.gov/pd/fsavgben.htm)
*Preliminary for fiscal year 2003. National average includes recipients in U.S. territories.

Percent of Population Receiving Food Stamps in 2003

National Percent = 7.1%*

<u>ALPHA ORDER</u>

RANK	STATE	PERCENT
10	Alabama	10.5
19	Alaska	7.8
16	Arizona	8.4
6	Arkansas	11.4
43	California	4.8
44	Colorado	4.6
39	Connecticut	5.2
36	Delaware	5.6
32	Florida	6.1
14	Georgia	8.6
18	Hawaii	8.0
33	Idaho	6.0
23	Illinois	7.5
22	Indiana	7.6
39	Iowa	5.2
34	Kansas	5.9
5	Kentucky	12.2
1	Louisiana	14.6
13	Maine	10.2
44	Maryland	4.6
47	Massachusetts	4.5
17	Michigan	8.3
44	Minnesota	4.6
4	Mississippi	12.3
11	Missouri	10.4
19	Montana	7.8
35	Nebraska	5.7
41	Nevada	5.0
50	New Hampshire	3.5
49	New Jersey	3.9
11	New Mexico	10.4
23	New York	7.5
21	North Carolina	7.7
31	North Dakota	6.3
23	Ohio	7.5
9	Oklahoma	10.8
7	Oregon	11.2
27	Pennsylvania	6.7
26	Rhode Island	6.9
8	South Carolina	10.9
27	South Dakota	6.7
3	Tennessee	12.5
15	Texas	8.5
47	Utah	4.5
27	Vermont	6.7
38	Virginia	5.3
30	Washington	6.6
2	West Virginia	13.6
37	Wisconsin	5.4
41	Wyoming	5.0

<u>RANK ORDER</u>

RANK	STATE	PERCENT
1	Louisiana	14.6
2	West Virginia	13.6
3	Tennessee	12.5
4	Mississippi	12.3
5	Kentucky	12.2
6	Arkansas	11.4
7	Oregon	11.2
8	South Carolina	10.9
9	Oklahoma	10.8
10	Alabama	10.5
11	Missouri	10.4
11	New Mexico	10.4
13	Maine	10.2
14	Georgia	8.6
15	Texas	8.5
16	Arizona	8.4
17	Michigan	8.3
18	Hawaii	8.0
19	Alaska	7.8
19	Montana	7.8
21	North Carolina	7.7
22	Indiana	7.6
23	Illinois	7.5
23	New York	7.5
23	Ohio	7.5
26	Rhode Island	6.9
27	Pennsylvania	6.7
27	South Dakota	6.7
27	Vermont	6.7
30	Washington	6.6
31	North Dakota	6.3
32	Florida	6.1
33	Idaho	6.0
34	Kansas	5.9
35	Nebraska	5.7
36	Delaware	5.6
37	Wisconsin	5.4
38	Virginia	5.3
39	Connecticut	5.2
39	Iowa	5.2
41	Nevada	5.0
41	Wyoming	5.0
43	California	4.8
44	Colorado	4.6
44	Maryland	4.6
44	Minnesota	4.6
47	Massachusetts	4.5
47	Utah	4.5
49	New Jersey	3.9
50	New Hampshire	3.5
	District of Columbia	14.5

*Source: Morgan Quitno Press using data from U.S. Department of Agriculture, Food, Nutrition and Consumer Services
"Food Stamp Program: Number of Persons Participating" (http://www.fns.usda.gov/pd/fsfypart.htm)*
Preliminary data for fiscal year 2003. National rate does not include recipients in U.S. territories.

Households Receiving Food Stamps in 2003

National Total = 9,155,214 Households*

<u>ALPHA ORDER</u>

RANK	STATE	HOUSEHOLDS	% of USA
18	Alabama	185,028	2.0%
48	Alaska	17,797	0.2%
20	Arizona	181,146	2.0%
26	Arkansas	124,288	1.4%
3	California	661,219	7.2%
32	Colorado	90,096	1.0%
31	Connecticut	94,147	1.0%
47	Delaware	19,141	0.2%
4	Florida	502,669	5.5%
10	Georgia	314,687	3.4%
38	Hawaii	48,766	0.5%
42	Idaho	32,428	0.4%
5	Illinois	422,487	4.6%
16	Indiana	196,688	2.1%
35	Iowa	66,436	0.7%
34	Kansas	70,845	0.8%
14	Kentucky	209,532	2.3%
12	Louisiana	250,388	2.7%
36	Maine	65,760	0.7%
28	Maryland	114,885	1.3%
25	Massachusetts	135,195	1.5%
8	Michigan	364,166	4.0%
29	Minnesota	110,088	1.2%
24	Mississippi	142,641	1.6%
13	Missouri	248,540	2.7%
43	Montana	30,208	0.3%
39	Nebraska	42,507	0.5%
37	Nevada	49,214	0.5%
44	New Hampshire	22,150	0.2%
22	New Jersey	157,874	1.7%
33	New Mexico	74,645	0.8%
1	New York	723,371	7.9%
11	North Carolina	276,321	3.0%
49	North Dakota	17,273	0.2%
6	Ohio	379,354	4.1%
23	Oklahoma	152,628	1.7%
15	Oregon	199,205	2.2%
7	Pennsylvania	373,597	4.1%
41	Rhode Island	34,121	0.4%
19	South Carolina	184,771	2.0%
46	South Dakota	20,018	0.2%
9	Tennessee	314,792	3.4%
2	Texas	719,754	7.9%
40	Utah	41,282	0.5%
45	Vermont	20,519	0.2%
21	Virginia	174,196	1.9%
17	Washington	192,735	2.1%
30	West Virginia	105,365	1.2%
27	Wisconsin	119,455	1.3%
50	Wyoming	10,205	0.1%

<u>RANK ORDER</u>

RANK	STATE	HOUSEHOLDS	% of USA
1	New York	723,371	7.9%
2	Texas	719,754	7.9%
3	California	661,219	7.2%
4	Florida	502,669	5.5%
5	Illinois	422,487	4.6%
6	Ohio	379,354	4.1%
7	Pennsylvania	373,597	4.1%
8	Michigan	364,166	4.0%
9	Tennessee	314,792	3.4%
10	Georgia	314,687	3.4%
11	North Carolina	276,321	3.0%
12	Louisiana	250,388	2.7%
13	Missouri	248,540	2.7%
14	Kentucky	209,532	2.3%
15	Oregon	199,205	2.2%
16	Indiana	196,688	2.1%
17	Washington	192,735	2.1%
18	Alabama	185,028	2.0%
19	South Carolina	184,771	2.0%
20	Arizona	181,146	2.0%
21	Virginia	174,196	1.9%
22	New Jersey	157,874	1.7%
23	Oklahoma	152,628	1.7%
24	Mississippi	142,641	1.6%
25	Massachusetts	135,195	1.5%
26	Arkansas	124,288	1.4%
27	Wisconsin	119,455	1.3%
28	Maryland	114,885	1.3%
29	Minnesota	110,088	1.2%
30	West Virginia	105,365	1.2%
31	Connecticut	94,147	1.0%
32	Colorado	90,096	1.0%
33	New Mexico	74,645	0.8%
34	Kansas	70,845	0.8%
35	Iowa	66,436	0.7%
36	Maine	65,760	0.7%
37	Nevada	49,214	0.5%
38	Hawaii	48,766	0.5%
39	Nebraska	42,507	0.5%
40	Utah	41,282	0.5%
41	Rhode Island	34,121	0.4%
42	Idaho	32,428	0.4%
43	Montana	30,208	0.3%
44	New Hampshire	22,150	0.2%
45	Vermont	20,519	0.2%
46	South Dakota	20,018	0.2%
47	Delaware	19,141	0.2%
48	Alaska	17,797	0.2%
49	North Dakota	17,273	0.2%
50	Wyoming	10,205	0.1%
	District of Columbia	39,104	0.4%

Source: U.S. Department of Agriculture, Food, Nutrition and Consumer Services
"Food Stamp Program: Number of Persons Participating" (http://www.fns.usda.gov/pd/fsfypart.htm)
Preliminary for fiscal year 2003. National total includes 11,492 households in U.S. territories.

Percent of Households Receiving Food Stamps in 2003

National Percent = 8.5% of Households*

ALPHA ORDER

RANK	STATE	PERCENT
14	Alabama	10.7
28	Alaska	7.9
20	Arizona	9.0
9	Arkansas	11.7
42	California	5.6
49	Colorado	5.0
31	Connecticut	7.2
36	Delaware	6.3
29	Florida	7.7
15	Georgia	10.2
9	Hawaii	11.7
35	Idaho	6.6
19	Illinois	9.1
25	Indiana	8.4
40	Iowa	5.8
34	Kansas	6.7
6	Kentucky	13.1
1	Louisiana	15.0
7	Maine	12.3
41	Maryland	5.7
42	Massachusetts	5.6
18	Michigan	9.5
45	Minnesota	5.5
5	Mississippi	13.6
12	Missouri	11.0
22	Montana	8.5
36	Nebraska	6.3
39	Nevada	6.1
50	New Hampshire	4.6
47	New Jersey	5.1
13	New Mexico	10.9
15	New York	10.2
21	North Carolina	8.6
33	North Dakota	6.8
22	Ohio	8.5
11	Oklahoma	11.4
3	Oregon	14.1
29	Pennsylvania	7.7
25	Rhode Island	8.4
8	South Carolina	11.8
32	South Dakota	6.9
4	Tennessee	13.9
17	Texas	9.6
45	Utah	5.5
22	Vermont	8.5
36	Virginia	6.3
27	Washington	8.2
2	West Virginia	14.6
42	Wisconsin	5.6
47	Wyoming	5.1

RANK ORDER

RANK	STATE	PERCENT
1	Louisiana	15.0
2	West Virginia	14.6
3	Oregon	14.1
4	Tennessee	13.9
5	Mississippi	13.6
6	Kentucky	13.1
7	Maine	12.3
8	South Carolina	11.8
9	Arkansas	11.7
9	Hawaii	11.7
11	Oklahoma	11.4
12	Missouri	11.0
13	New Mexico	10.9
14	Alabama	10.7
15	Georgia	10.2
15	New York	10.2
17	Texas	9.6
18	Michigan	9.5
19	Illinois	9.1
20	Arizona	9.0
21	North Carolina	8.6
22	Montana	8.5
22	Ohio	8.5
22	Vermont	8.5
25	Indiana	8.4
25	Rhode Island	8.4
27	Washington	8.2
28	Alaska	7.9
29	Florida	7.7
29	Pennsylvania	7.7
31	Connecticut	7.2
32	South Dakota	6.9
33	North Dakota	6.8
34	Kansas	6.7
35	Idaho	6.6
36	Delaware	6.3
36	Nebraska	6.3
36	Virginia	6.3
39	Nevada	6.1
40	Iowa	5.8
41	Maryland	5.7
42	California	5.6
42	Massachusetts	5.6
42	Wisconsin	5.6
45	Minnesota	5.5
45	Utah	5.5
47	New Jersey	5.1
47	Wyoming	5.1
49	Colorado	5.0
50	New Hampshire	4.6

District of Columbia   16.2

Source: Morgan Quitno Press using data from U.S. Department of Agriculture, Food, Nutrition and Consumer Services
"Food Stamp Program: Number of Persons Participating" (http://www.fns.usda.gov/pd/fsfypart.htm)
*Food stamp program households are for fiscal year 2003. Percent calculated using 2002 estimated total households. National percent excludes households in U.S. territories.

Average Monthly Participants in Women, Infants and Children (WIC) Special Nutrition Program in 2003
National Total = 7,630,815 Participants*

ALPHA ORDER

RANK	STATE	PARTICIPANTS	% of USA
19	Alabama	120,377	1.6%
41	Alaska	25,510	0.3%
11	Arizona	156,319	2.0%
29	Arkansas	85,712	1.1%
1	California	1,274,472	16.7%
30	Colorado	81,196	1.1%
35	Connecticut	51,721	0.7%
46	Delaware	17,785	0.2%
4	Florida	354,572	4.6%
7	Georgia	246,267	3.2%
40	Hawaii	32,788	0.4%
39	Idaho	34,754	0.5%
5	Illinois	266,975	3.5%
18	Indiana	124,683	1.6%
31	Iowa	64,585	0.8%
34	Kansas	61,307	0.8%
21	Kentucky	113,055	1.5%
15	Louisiana	133,403	1.7%
43	Maine	21,743	0.3%
27	Maryland	101,285	1.3%
20	Massachusetts	114,026	1.5%
9	Michigan	216,531	2.8%
23	Minnesota	110,117	1.4%
26	Mississippi	103,244	1.4%
16	Missouri	129,961	1.7%
44	Montana	21,387	0.3%
38	Nebraska	38,328	0.5%
37	Nevada	44,544	0.6%
47	New Hampshire	16,701	0.2%
14	New Jersey	136,272	1.8%
33	New Mexico	62,252	0.8%
3	New York	458,177	6.0%
10	North Carolina	211,577	2.8%
49	North Dakota	13,969	0.2%
6	Ohio	256,062	3.4%
22	Oklahoma	111,688	1.5%
28	Oregon	96,469	1.3%
8	Pennsylvania	229,627	3.0%
42	Rhode Island	22,434	0.3%
25	South Carolina	104,967	1.4%
45	South Dakota	20,631	0.3%
12	Tennessee	152,828	2.0%
2	Texas	824,449	10.8%
32	Utah	64,001	0.8%
48	Vermont	16,201	0.2%
17	Virginia	125,205	1.6%
13	Washington	152,538	2.0%
36	West Virginia	49,837	0.7%
24	Wisconsin	105,717	1.4%
50	Wyoming	12,037	0.2%

RANK ORDER

RANK	STATE	PARTICIPANTS	% of USA
1	California	1,274,472	16.7%
2	Texas	824,449	10.8%
3	New York	458,177	6.0%
4	Florida	354,572	4.6%
5	Illinois	266,975	3.5%
6	Ohio	256,062	3.4%
7	Georgia	246,267	3.2%
8	Pennsylvania	229,627	3.0%
9	Michigan	216,531	2.8%
10	North Carolina	211,577	2.8%
11	Arizona	156,319	2.0%
12	Tennessee	152,828	2.0%
13	Washington	152,538	2.0%
14	New Jersey	136,272	1.8%
15	Louisiana	133,403	1.7%
16	Missouri	129,961	1.7%
17	Virginia	125,205	1.6%
18	Indiana	124,683	1.6%
19	Alabama	120,377	1.6%
20	Massachusetts	114,026	1.5%
21	Kentucky	113,055	1.5%
22	Oklahoma	111,688	1.5%
23	Minnesota	110,117	1.4%
24	Wisconsin	105,717	1.4%
25	South Carolina	104,967	1.4%
26	Mississippi	103,244	1.4%
27	Maryland	101,285	1.3%
28	Oregon	96,469	1.3%
29	Arkansas	85,712	1.1%
30	Colorado	81,196	1.1%
31	Iowa	64,585	0.8%
32	Utah	64,001	0.8%
33	New Mexico	62,252	0.8%
34	Kansas	61,307	0.8%
35	Connecticut	51,721	0.7%
36	West Virginia	49,837	0.7%
37	Nevada	44,544	0.6%
38	Nebraska	38,328	0.5%
39	Idaho	34,754	0.5%
40	Hawaii	32,788	0.4%
41	Alaska	25,510	0.3%
42	Rhode Island	22,434	0.3%
43	Maine	21,743	0.3%
44	Montana	21,387	0.3%
45	South Dakota	20,631	0.3%
46	Delaware	17,785	0.2%
47	New Hampshire	16,701	0.2%
48	Vermont	16,201	0.2%
49	North Dakota	13,969	0.2%
50	Wyoming	12,037	0.2%
	District of Columbia	15,723	0.2%

Source: U.S. Department of Agriculture, Food, Nutrition and Consumer Services
"WIC Program: Total Participation" (http://www.fns.usda.gov/pd/wifypart.htm)
**Preliminary data for fiscal year 2003. National total includes 224,805 participants in outlying areas not shown separately (Puerto Rico has 207,838 participants).*

Average Monthly Benefit per Participant in Women, Infant and Children (WIC) Special Nutrition Program in 2003
National Average = $35.23*

ALPHA ORDER				RANK ORDER		
RANK	STATE	AVERAGE BENEFIT		RANK	STATE	AVERAGE BENEFIT
9	Alabama	$38.10		1	Hawaii	$48.59
2	Alaska	40.30		2	Alaska	40.30
8	Arizona	38.44		3	Washington	39.35
24	Arkansas	33.08		4	New York	39.10
5	California	39.07		5	California	39.07
22	Colorado	33.32		6	Connecticut	39.03
6	Connecticut	39.03		7	North Dakota	38.85
39	Delaware	31.13		8	Arizona	38.44
15	Florida	36.08		9	Alabama	38.10
23	Georgia	33.16		10	Vermont	37.87
1	Hawaii	48.59		11	Illinois	37.67
49	Idaho	28.22		12	Louisiana	37.52
11	Illinois	37.67		13	Tennessee	37.24
45	Indiana	29.33		14	Mississippi	36.73
41	Iowa	30.78		15	Florida	36.08
37	Kansas	31.33		16	Oregon	35.75
17	Kentucky	35.65		17	Kentucky	35.65
12	Louisiana	37.52		18	New Jersey	34.29
50	Maine	25.88		19	Rhode Island	34.17
40	Maryland	30.98		20	West Virginia	33.96
33	Massachusetts	31.97		21	Montana	33.50
34	Michigan	31.90		22	Colorado	33.32
30	Minnesota	32.26		23	Georgia	33.16
14	Mississippi	36.73		24	Arkansas	33.08
38	Missouri	31.17		25	Virginia	32.74
21	Montana	33.50		26	North Carolina	32.58
29	Nebraska	32.29		27	South Dakota	32.57
32	Nevada	31.99		28	Wisconsin	32.34
46	New Hampshire	28.97		29	Nebraska	32.29
18	New Jersey	34.29		30	Minnesota	32.26
31	New Mexico	32.18		31	New Mexico	32.18
4	New York	39.10		32	Nevada	31.99
26	North Carolina	32.58		33	Massachusetts	31.97
7	North Dakota	38.85		34	Michigan	31.90
42	Ohio	30.73		35	Pennsylvania	31.68
43	Oklahoma	29.56		36	South Carolina	31.41
16	Oregon	35.75		37	Kansas	31.33
35	Pennsylvania	31.68		38	Missouri	31.17
19	Rhode Island	34.17		39	Delaware	31.13
36	South Carolina	31.41		40	Maryland	30.98
27	South Dakota	32.57		41	Iowa	30.78
13	Tennessee	37.24		42	Ohio	30.73
44	Texas	29.46		43	Oklahoma	29.56
48	Utah	28.89		44	Texas	29.46
10	Vermont	37.87		45	Indiana	29.33
25	Virginia	32.74		46	New Hampshire	28.97
3	Washington	39.35		46	Wyoming	28.97
20	West Virginia	33.96		48	Utah	28.89
28	Wisconsin	32.34		49	Idaho	28.22
46	Wyoming	28.97		50	Maine	25.88
				District of Columbia		38.70

Source: U.S. Department of Agriculture, Food, Nutrition and Consumer Services
   "WIC Program: Average Benefit per Person per Month" (http://www.fns.usda.gov/pd/wifyavgfd$.htm)
*Preliminary data for fiscal year 2003. National average includes outlying areas and Indian reservations not shown separately.

Percent of Public Elementary and Secondary School Students Eligible for Free or Reduced-Price Meals in 2002
Reporting States' Percent = 36.6%*

ALPHA ORDER

RANK	STATE	PERCENT
6	Alabama	48.7
44	Alaska	25.2
NA	Arizona**	NA
10	Arkansas	47.2
9	California	47.3
38	Colorado	27.5
NA	Connecticut**	NA
21	Delaware	34.6
12	Florida	44.6
13	Georgia	44.2
15	Hawaii	41.9
18	Idaho	35.6
19	Illinois	35.2
28	Indiana	31.1
40	Iowa	26.7
22	Kansas	34.1
5	Kentucky	49.1
2	Louisiana	59.1
32	Maine	29.6
30	Maryland	29.7
43	Massachusetts	25.3
26	Michigan	31.2
41	Minnesota	26.4
1	Mississippi	65.3
20	Missouri	35.1
24	Montana	31.5
26	Nebraska	31.2
30	Nevada	29.7
46	New Hampshire	14.8
37	New Jersey	27.8
3	New Mexico	54.7
14	New York	43.2
16	North Carolina	38.4
36	North Dakota	28.0
39	Ohio	27.4
6	Oklahoma	48.7
17	Oregon	36.1
35	Pennsylvania	28.4
23	Rhode Island	33.6
6	South Carolina	48.7
29	South Dakota	30.1
NA	Tennessee**	NA
11	Texas	45.4
34	Utah	29.2
45	Vermont	23.8
33	Virginia	29.3
25	Washington	31.4
4	West Virginia	50.4
42	Wisconsin	26.0
NA	Wyoming**	NA

RANK ORDER

RANK	STATE	PERCENT
1	Mississippi	65.3
2	Louisiana	59.1
3	New Mexico	54.7
4	West Virginia	50.4
5	Kentucky	49.1
6	Alabama	48.7
6	Oklahoma	48.7
6	South Carolina	48.7
9	California	47.3
10	Arkansas	47.2
11	Texas	45.4
12	Florida	44.6
13	Georgia	44.2
14	New York	43.2
15	Hawaii	41.9
16	North Carolina	38.4
17	Oregon	36.1
18	Idaho	35.6
19	Illinois	35.2
20	Missouri	35.1
21	Delaware	34.6
22	Kansas	34.1
23	Rhode Island	33.6
24	Montana	31.5
25	Washington	31.4
26	Michigan	31.2
26	Nebraska	31.2
28	Indiana	31.1
29	South Dakota	30.1
30	Maryland	29.7
30	Nevada	29.7
32	Maine	29.6
33	Virginia	29.3
34	Utah	29.2
35	Pennsylvania	28.4
36	North Dakota	28.0
37	New Jersey	27.8
38	Colorado	27.5
39	Ohio	27.4
40	Iowa	26.7
41	Minnesota	26.4
42	Wisconsin	26.0
43	Massachusetts	25.3
44	Alaska	25.2
45	Vermont	23.8
46	New Hampshire	14.8
NA	Arizona**	NA
NA	Connecticut**	NA
NA	Tennessee**	NA
NA	Wyoming**	NA

	District of Columbia	55.3

Source: U.S. Department of Education, National Center for Education Statistics
"Overview of Public Elementary and Secondary Schools and Districts: School Year 2001-2002" (NCES 2003-411)
*For school year 2001-2002. National percent is only for reporting states.
**Not available.

Child Support Collections in 2002

National Total = $19,910,176,795*

ALPHA ORDER

RANK	STATE	COLLECTIONS	% of USA
28	Alabama	$210,793,885	1.1%
40	Alaska	81,297,436	0.4%
25	Arizona	229,628,128	1.2%
36	Arkansas	128,845,269	0.6%
1	California	1,761,395,793	8.8%
29	Colorado	202,513,277	1.0%
27	Connecticut	216,686,470	1.1%
43	Delaware	59,507,990	0.3%
7	Florida	803,427,506	4.0%
16	Georgia	415,190,279	2.1%
42	Hawaii	73,490,476	0.4%
38	Idaho	95,669,488	0.5%
13	Illinois	460,100,983	2.3%
15	Indiana	430,195,033	2.2%
24	Iowa	255,489,996	1.3%
33	Kansas	134,192,271	0.7%
21	Kentucky	280,917,646	1.4%
23	Louisiana	260,352,264	1.3%
37	Maine	96,058,639	0.5%
19	Maryland	396,325,538	2.0%
18	Massachusetts	402,684,665	2.0%
3	Michigan	1,443,730,382	7.3%
11	Minnesota	537,089,362	2.7%
30	Mississippi	169,034,476	0.8%
17	Missouri	410,866,655	2.1%
49	Montana	43,450,853	0.2%
32	Nebraska	143,218,162	0.7%
39	Nevada	91,416,297	0.5%
41	New Hampshire	76,021,041	0.4%
8	New Jersey	774,655,477	3.9%
45	New Mexico	51,872,707	0.3%
6	New York	1,289,224,609	6.5%
12	North Carolina	468,742,468	2.4%
46	North Dakota	50,844,528	0.3%
2	Ohio	1,617,586,413	8.1%
35	Oklahoma	131,791,800	0.7%
22	Oregon	275,879,302	1.4%
5	Pennsylvania	1,331,920,478	6.7%
44	Rhode Island	53,269,669	0.3%
26	South Carolina	224,346,732	1.1%
47	South Dakota	50,621,425	0.3%
20	Tennessee	318,253,081	1.6%
4	Texas	1,346,898,110	6.8%
34	Utah	133,052,785	0.7%
50	Vermont	41,502,260	0.2%
14	Virginia	436,704,128	2.2%
9	Washington	590,896,606	3.0%
31	West Virginia	151,193,843	0.8%
10	Wisconsin	574,178,130	2.9%
48	Wyoming	46,608,491	0.2%

RANK ORDER

RANK	STATE	COLLECTIONS	% of USA
1	California	$1,761,395,793	8.8%
2	Ohio	1,617,586,413	8.1%
3	Michigan	1,443,730,382	7.3%
4	Texas	1,346,898,110	6.8%
5	Pennsylvania	1,331,920,478	6.7%
6	New York	1,289,224,609	6.5%
7	Florida	803,427,506	4.0%
8	New Jersey	774,655,477	3.9%
9	Washington	590,896,606	3.0%
10	Wisconsin	574,178,130	2.9%
11	Minnesota	537,089,362	2.7%
12	North Carolina	468,742,468	2.4%
13	Illinois	460,100,983	2.3%
14	Virginia	436,704,128	2.2%
15	Indiana	430,195,033	2.2%
16	Georgia	415,190,279	2.1%
17	Missouri	410,866,655	2.1%
18	Massachusetts	402,684,665	2.0%
19	Maryland	396,325,538	2.0%
20	Tennessee	318,253,081	1.6%
21	Kentucky	280,917,646	1.4%
22	Oregon	275,879,302	1.4%
23	Louisiana	260,352,264	1.3%
24	Iowa	255,489,996	1.3%
25	Arizona	229,628,128	1.2%
26	South Carolina	224,346,732	1.1%
27	Connecticut	216,686,470	1.1%
28	Alabama	210,793,885	1.1%
29	Colorado	202,513,277	1.0%
30	Mississippi	169,034,476	0.8%
31	West Virginia	151,193,843	0.8%
32	Nebraska	143,218,162	0.7%
33	Kansas	134,192,271	0.7%
34	Utah	133,052,785	0.7%
35	Oklahoma	131,791,800	0.7%
36	Arkansas	128,845,269	0.6%
37	Maine	96,058,639	0.5%
38	Idaho	95,669,488	0.5%
39	Nevada	91,416,297	0.5%
40	Alaska	81,297,436	0.4%
41	New Hampshire	76,021,041	0.4%
42	Hawaii	73,490,476	0.4%
43	Delaware	59,507,990	0.3%
44	Rhode Island	53,269,669	0.3%
45	New Mexico	51,872,707	0.3%
46	North Dakota	50,844,528	0.3%
47	South Dakota	50,621,425	0.3%
48	Wyoming	46,608,491	0.2%
49	Montana	43,450,853	0.2%
50	Vermont	41,502,260	0.2%
	District of Columbia	40,543,493	0.2%

Source: U.S. Department of Health and Human Services, Office of Child Support Enforcement
   "Child Support Enforcement" (http://www.acf.hhs.gov/programs/cse/pubs/2003/reports/prelim_datareport/)
Fiscal year 2002. Total does not include $226,690,276 collected in U.S. territories.

Cost Effectiveness of Child Support Collection Efforts in 2002

National Average = $4.13 Collected for Every Dollar of Administrative Expense*

ALPHA ORDER

RANK	STATE	RATIO
42	Alabama	$3.64
26	Alaska	4.49
31	Arizona	4.25
47	Arkansas	2.66
49	California	1.91
40	Colorado	3.66
39	Connecticut	3.76
40	Delaware	3.66
36	Florida	4.03
32	Georgia	4.24
5	Hawaii	6.53
13	Idaho	5.29
45	Illinois	2.80
1	Indiana	7.80
11	Iowa	5.63
48	Kansas	2.61
20	Kentucky	4.71
16	Louisiana	4.87
30	Maine	4.28
33	Maryland	4.19
10	Massachusetts	5.77
23	Michigan	4.59
35	Minnesota	4.05
3	Mississippi	7.12
22	Missouri	4.63
34	Montana	4.10
43	Nebraska	2.87
43	Nevada	2.87
29	New Hampshire	4.37
18	New Jersey	4.83
50	New Mexico	1.46
26	New York	4.49
28	North Carolina	4.43
20	North Dakota	4.71
19	Ohio	4.81
45	Oklahoma	2.80
9	Oregon	5.85
4	Pennsylvania	6.85
24	Rhode Island	4.52
8	South Carolina	5.87
2	South Dakota	7.59
25	Tennessee	4.50
12	Texas	5.41
38	Utah	3.89
37	Vermont	3.93
6	Virginia	6.34
15	Washington	4.95
16	West Virginia	4.87
7	Wisconsin	6.11
14	Wyoming	5.00

RANK ORDER

RANK	STATE	RATIO
1	Indiana	$7.80
2	South Dakota	7.59
3	Mississippi	7.12
4	Pennsylvania	6.85
5	Hawaii	6.53
6	Virginia	6.34
7	Wisconsin	6.11
8	South Carolina	5.87
9	Oregon	5.85
10	Massachusetts	5.77
11	Iowa	5.63
12	Texas	5.41
13	Idaho	5.29
14	Wyoming	5.00
15	Washington	4.95
16	Louisiana	4.87
16	West Virginia	4.87
18	New Jersey	4.83
19	Ohio	4.81
20	Kentucky	4.71
20	North Dakota	4.71
22	Missouri	4.63
23	Michigan	4.59
24	Rhode Island	4.52
25	Tennessee	4.50
26	Alaska	4.49
26	New York	4.49
28	North Carolina	4.43
29	New Hampshire	4.37
30	Maine	4.28
31	Arizona	4.25
32	Georgia	4.24
33	Maryland	4.19
34	Montana	4.10
35	Minnesota	4.05
36	Florida	4.03
37	Vermont	3.93
38	Utah	3.89
39	Connecticut	3.76
40	Colorado	3.66
40	Delaware	3.66
42	Alabama	3.64
43	Nebraska	2.87
43	Nevada	2.87
45	Illinois	2.80
45	Oklahoma	2.80
47	Arkansas	2.66
48	Kansas	2.61
49	California	1.91
50	New Mexico	1.46
	District of Columbia	2.69

Source: U.S. Department of Health and Human Services, Office of Child Support Enforcement
"Child Support Enforcement" (http://www.acf.hhs.gov/programs/cse/pubs/2003/reports/prelim_datareport/)
*This table shows ratios based on the Child Support Performance and Incentive Act of 1998 (CSPIA).

XV. TRANSPORTATION

Federal Highway Funds in 2004

National Total = $27,711,870,953*

ALPHA ORDER

RANK	STATE	FUNDS	% of USA
16	Alabama	$543,109,952	2.0%
33	Alaska	318,576,348	1.1%
21	Arizona	469,800,345	1.7%
29	Arkansas	354,248,023	1.3%
1	California	2,587,736,464	9.3%
28	Colorado	355,828,826	1.3%
26	Connecticut	408,081,032	1.5%
50	Delaware	119,631,816	0.4%
5	Florida	1,322,497,812	4.8%
6	Georgia	971,879,012	3.5%
47	Hawaii	139,448,551	0.5%
40	Idaho	207,687,024	0.7%
8	Illinois	914,397,232	3.3%
14	Indiana	633,715,415	2.3%
32	Iowa	322,957,321	1.2%
34	Kansas	314,831,521	1.1%
20	Kentucky	476,819,989	1.7%
24	Louisiana	436,824,448	1.6%
46	Maine	142,147,805	0.5%
23	Maryland	449,842,879	1.6%
18	Massachusetts	504,009,600	1.8%
9	Michigan	849,446,787	3.1%
27	Minnesota	404,224,722	1.5%
30	Mississippi	333,204,117	1.2%
13	Missouri	634,036,110	2.3%
36	Montana	266,850,264	1.0%
39	Nebraska	209,568,810	0.8%
41	Nevada	196,008,967	0.7%
48	New Hampshire	139,336,963	0.5%
11	New Jersey	731,121,297	2.6%
37	New Mexico	265,757,701	1.0%
3	New York	1,394,407,699	5.0%
10	North Carolina	769,907,419	2.8%
44	North Dakota	177,482,854	0.6%
7	Ohio	938,861,449	3.4%
25	Oklahoma	417,254,466	1.5%
31	Oregon	328,148,519	1.2%
4	Pennsylvania	1,338,851,823	4.8%
45	Rhode Island	160,317,515	0.6%
22	South Carolina	452,450,091	1.6%
42	South Dakota	192,988,037	0.7%
15	Tennessee	608,826,783	2.2%
2	Texas	2,158,988,444	7.8%
38	Utah	211,589,145	0.8%
49	Vermont	123,585,708	0.4%
12	Virginia	692,188,304	2.5%
19	Washington	482,581,113	1.7%
35	West Virginia	303,082,607	1.1%
17	Wisconsin	535,460,215	1.9%
43	Wyoming	188,237,776	0.7%

RANK ORDER

RANK	STATE	FUNDS	% of USA
1	California	$2,587,736,464	9.3%
2	Texas	2,158,988,444	7.8%
3	New York	1,394,407,699	5.0%
4	Pennsylvania	1,338,851,823	4.8%
5	Florida	1,322,497,812	4.8%
6	Georgia	971,879,012	3.5%
7	Ohio	938,861,449	3.4%
8	Illinois	914,397,232	3.3%
9	Michigan	849,446,787	3.1%
10	North Carolina	769,907,419	2.8%
11	New Jersey	731,121,297	2.6%
12	Virginia	692,188,304	2.5%
13	Missouri	634,036,110	2.3%
14	Indiana	633,715,415	2.3%
15	Tennessee	608,826,783	2.2%
16	Alabama	543,109,952	2.0%
17	Wisconsin	535,460,215	1.9%
18	Massachusetts	504,009,600	1.8%
19	Washington	482,581,113	1.7%
20	Kentucky	476,819,989	1.7%
21	Arizona	469,800,345	1.7%
22	South Carolina	452,450,091	1.6%
23	Maryland	449,842,879	1.6%
24	Louisiana	436,824,448	1.6%
25	Oklahoma	417,254,466	1.5%
26	Connecticut	408,081,032	1.5%
27	Minnesota	404,224,722	1.5%
28	Colorado	355,828,826	1.3%
29	Arkansas	354,248,023	1.3%
30	Mississippi	333,204,117	1.2%
31	Oregon	328,148,519	1.2%
32	Iowa	322,957,321	1.2%
33	Alaska	318,576,348	1.1%
34	Kansas	314,831,521	1.1%
35	West Virginia	303,082,607	1.1%
36	Montana	266,850,264	1.0%
37	New Mexico	265,757,701	1.0%
38	Utah	211,589,145	0.8%
39	Nebraska	209,568,810	0.8%
40	Idaho	207,687,024	0.7%
41	Nevada	196,008,967	0.7%
42	South Dakota	192,988,037	0.7%
43	Wyoming	188,237,776	0.7%
44	North Dakota	177,482,854	0.6%
45	Rhode Island	160,317,515	0.6%
46	Maine	142,147,805	0.5%
47	Hawaii	139,448,551	0.5%
48	New Hampshire	139,336,963	0.5%
49	Vermont	123,585,708	0.4%
50	Delaware	119,631,816	0.4%
	District of Columbia	106,961,571	0.4%

Source: U.S. Department of Transportation, Federal Highway Administration
"FHWA Apportionment under SAFETEA" (http://www.fhwa.dot.gov/reauthorization/apportionmentsbyyear.htm)
**Fiscal Year 2004 apportionments. National total includes $106,072,260 apportioned to Puerto Rico.*

Per Capita Federal Highway Funds in 2004

National Per Capita = $95*

<u>ALPHA ORDER</u>

RANK	STATE	PER CAPITA
13	Alabama	$121
1	Alaska	491
39	Arizona	84
12	Arkansas	130
48	California	73
45	Colorado	78
16	Connecticut	117
10	Delaware	146
45	Florida	78
20	Georgia	112
21	Hawaii	111
8	Idaho	152
50	Illinois	72
29	Indiana	102
23	Iowa	110
17	Kansas	116
17	Kentucky	116
32	Louisiana	97
24	Maine	109
41	Maryland	82
45	Massachusetts	78
39	Michigan	84
43	Minnesota	80
17	Mississippi	116
21	Missouri	111
3	Montana	291
14	Nebraska	120
37	Nevada	87
26	New Hampshire	108
38	New Jersey	85
11	New Mexico	142
48	New York	73
34	North Carolina	92
4	North Dakota	280
41	Ohio	82
15	Oklahoma	119
34	Oregon	92
26	Pennsylvania	108
9	Rhode Island	149
24	South Carolina	109
5	South Dakota	253
28	Tennessee	104
30	Texas	98
36	Utah	90
6	Vermont	200
33	Virginia	94
44	Washington	79
7	West Virginia	167
30	Wisconsin	98
2	Wyoming	376

<u>RANK ORDER</u>

RANK	STATE	PER CAPITA
1	Alaska	$491
2	Wyoming	376
3	Montana	291
4	North Dakota	280
5	South Dakota	253
6	Vermont	200
7	West Virginia	167
8	Idaho	152
9	Rhode Island	149
10	Delaware	146
11	New Mexico	142
12	Arkansas	130
13	Alabama	121
14	Nebraska	120
15	Oklahoma	119
16	Connecticut	117
17	Kansas	116
17	Kentucky	116
17	Mississippi	116
20	Georgia	112
21	Hawaii	111
21	Missouri	111
23	Iowa	110
24	Maine	109
24	South Carolina	109
26	New Hampshire	108
26	Pennsylvania	108
28	Tennessee	104
29	Indiana	102
30	Texas	98
30	Wisconsin	98
32	Louisiana	97
33	Virginia	94
34	North Carolina	92
34	Oregon	92
36	Utah	90
37	Nevada	87
38	New Jersey	85
39	Arizona	84
39	Michigan	84
41	Maryland	82
41	Ohio	82
43	Minnesota	80
44	Washington	79
45	Colorado	78
45	Florida	78
45	Massachusetts	78
48	California	73
48	New York	73
50	Illinois	72

	District of Columbia	190

Source: Morgan Quitno Press using data from U.S. Department of Transportation, Federal Highway Administration
"FHWA Apportionment under SAFETEA" (http://www.fhwa.dot.gov/reauthorization/apportionmentsbyyear.htm)
*Fiscal Year 2004 apportionments. Rates calculated with July 2003 population estimates.

Federally-Funded Road and Street Mileage in 2002

National Total = 956,479 Miles*

ALPHA ORDER

RANK	STATE	MILES	% of USA
16	Alabama	23,923	2.5%
45	Alaska	4,241	0.4%
33	Arizona	12,239	1.3%
19	Arkansas	21,019	2.2%
2	California	54,335	5.7%
29	Colorado	16,753	1.8%
44	Connecticut	6,031	0.6%
50	Delaware	1,452	0.2%
15	Florida	24,240	2.5%
9	Georgia	30,370	3.2%
49	Hawaii	1,546	0.2%
35	Idaho	10,383	1.1%
3	Illinois	34,443	3.6%
17	Indiana	22,225	2.3%
14	Iowa	25,643	2.7%
4	Kansas	34,287	3.6%
31	Kentucky	14,443	1.5%
32	Louisiana	12,577	1.3%
43	Maine	6,415	0.7%
41	Maryland	7,463	0.8%
34	Massachusetts	10,740	1.1%
5	Michigan	33,255	3.5%
6	Minnesota	31,504	3.3%
20	Mississippi	20,736	2.2%
8	Missouri	30,444	3.2%
30	Montana	14,575	1.5%
22	Nebraska	20,340	2.1%
42	Nevada	6,425	0.7%
47	New Hampshire	3,288	0.3%
38	New Jersey	9,830	1.0%
37	New Mexico	9,995	1.0%
13	New York	26,165	2.7%
21	North Carolina	20,559	2.1%
25	North Dakota	18,107	1.9%
10	Ohio	27,991	2.9%
7	Oklahoma	31,314	3.3%
26	Oregon	17,894	1.9%
12	Pennsylvania	27,292	2.9%
48	Rhode Island	1,690	0.2%
27	South Carolina	17,389	1.8%
23	South Dakota	19,652	2.1%
28	Tennessee	16,950	1.8%
1	Texas	78,188	8.2%
39	Utah	8,183	0.9%
46	Vermont	3,860	0.4%
18	Virginia	21,162	2.2%
24	Washington	18,811	2.0%
36	West Virginia	10,249	1.1%
11	Wisconsin	27,779	2.9%
40	Wyoming	7,632	0.8%

RANK ORDER

RANK	STATE	MILES	% of USA
1	Texas	78,188	8.2%
2	California	54,335	5.7%
3	Illinois	34,443	3.6%
4	Kansas	34,287	3.6%
5	Michigan	33,255	3.5%
6	Minnesota	31,504	3.3%
7	Oklahoma	31,314	3.3%
8	Missouri	30,444	3.2%
9	Georgia	30,370	3.2%
10	Ohio	27,991	2.9%
11	Wisconsin	27,779	2.9%
12	Pennsylvania	27,292	2.9%
13	New York	26,165	2.7%
14	Iowa	25,643	2.7%
15	Florida	24,240	2.5%
16	Alabama	23,923	2.5%
17	Indiana	22,225	2.3%
18	Virginia	21,162	2.2%
19	Arkansas	21,019	2.2%
20	Mississippi	20,736	2.2%
21	North Carolina	20,559	2.1%
22	Nebraska	20,340	2.1%
23	South Dakota	19,652	2.1%
24	Washington	18,811	2.0%
25	North Dakota	18,107	1.9%
26	Oregon	17,894	1.9%
27	South Carolina	17,389	1.8%
28	Tennessee	16,950	1.8%
29	Colorado	16,753	1.8%
30	Montana	14,575	1.5%
31	Kentucky	14,443	1.5%
32	Louisiana	12,577	1.3%
33	Arizona	12,239	1.3%
34	Massachusetts	10,740	1.1%
35	Idaho	10,383	1.1%
36	West Virginia	10,249	1.1%
37	New Mexico	9,995	1.0%
38	New Jersey	9,830	1.0%
39	Utah	8,183	0.9%
40	Wyoming	7,632	0.8%
41	Maryland	7,463	0.8%
42	Nevada	6,425	0.7%
43	Maine	6,415	0.7%
44	Connecticut	6,031	0.6%
45	Alaska	4,241	0.4%
46	Vermont	3,860	0.4%
47	New Hampshire	3,288	0.3%
48	Rhode Island	1,690	0.2%
49	Hawaii	1,546	0.2%
50	Delaware	1,452	0.2%
	District of Columbia	452	0.0%

Source: U.S. Department of Transportation, Federal Highway Administration
"Highway Statistics 2002" (Table HM-15)
*Does not include 2,854 federally-funded miles of highway in Puerto Rico.

Percent of Public Road and Street Mileage Federally-Funded in 2002

National Percent = 24.1% of Public Road and Street Mileage*

ALPHA ORDER

RANK	STATE	PERCENT
21	Alabama	25.3
4	Alaska	30.0
37	Arizona	21.4
38	Arkansas	21.3
2	California	32.4
45	Colorado	19.4
6	Connecticut	28.7
23	Delaware	24.8
43	Florida	20.2
18	Georgia	26.2
1	Hawaii	36.0
35	Idaho	22.2
22	Illinois	24.9
28	Indiana	23.6
33	Iowa	22.6
20	Kansas	25.4
48	Kentucky	18.4
42	Louisiana	20.6
7	Maine	28.3
26	Maryland	24.2
3	Massachusetts	30.3
13	Michigan	27.3
27	Minnesota	23.8
8	Mississippi	28.1
25	Missouri	24.4
40	Montana	21.0
36	Nebraska	21.8
48	Nevada	18.4
39	New Hampshire	21.2
15	New Jersey	26.9
50	New Mexico	16.3
30	New York	22.9
43	North Carolina	20.2
41	North Dakota	20.9
34	Ohio	22.4
10	Oklahoma	27.8
15	Oregon	26.9
32	Pennsylvania	22.7
9	Rhode Island	27.9
17	South Carolina	26.3
29	South Dakota	23.5
46	Tennessee	19.2
19	Texas	25.9
46	Utah	19.2
14	Vermont	27.0
5	Virginia	29.8
30	Washington	22.9
12	West Virginia	27.7
24	Wisconsin	24.6
10	Wyoming	27.8

RANK ORDER

RANK	STATE	PERCENT
1	Hawaii	36.0
2	California	32.4
3	Massachusetts	30.3
4	Alaska	30.0
5	Virginia	29.8
6	Connecticut	28.7
7	Maine	28.3
8	Mississippi	28.1
9	Rhode Island	27.9
10	Oklahoma	27.8
10	Wyoming	27.8
12	West Virginia	27.7
13	Michigan	27.3
14	Vermont	27.0
15	New Jersey	26.9
15	Oregon	26.9
17	South Carolina	26.3
18	Georgia	26.2
19	Texas	25.9
20	Kansas	25.4
21	Alabama	25.3
22	Illinois	24.9
23	Delaware	24.8
24	Wisconsin	24.6
25	Missouri	24.4
26	Maryland	24.2
27	Minnesota	23.8
28	Indiana	23.6
29	South Dakota	23.5
30	New York	22.9
30	Washington	22.9
32	Pennsylvania	22.7
33	Iowa	22.6
34	Ohio	22.4
35	Idaho	22.2
36	Nebraska	21.8
37	Arizona	21.4
38	Arkansas	21.3
39	New Hampshire	21.2
40	Montana	21.0
41	North Dakota	20.9
42	Louisiana	20.6
43	Florida	20.2
43	North Carolina	20.2
45	Colorado	19.4
46	Tennessee	19.2
46	Utah	19.2
48	Kentucky	18.4
48	Nevada	18.4
50	New Mexico	16.3

District of Columbia   29.4

Source: Morgan Quitno Press using data from U.S. Department of Transportation, Federal Highway Administration "Highway Statistics 2002" (Table HM-15)
*National percent does not include federally-funded highway miles in Puerto Rico.

Public Road and Street Mileage in 2002

National Total = 3,966,494 Miles*

<u>ALPHA ORDER</u>

RANK	STATE	MILES	% of USA
18	Alabama	94,435	2.4%
47	Alaska	14,117	0.4%
34	Arizona	57,165	1.4%
17	Arkansas	98,482	2.5%
2	California	167,898	4.2%
23	Colorado	86,310	2.2%
44	Connecticut	21,042	0.5%
49	Delaware	5,845	0.1%
10	Florida	119,785	3.0%
11	Georgia	115,778	2.9%
50	Hawaii	4,299	0.1%
35	Idaho	46,731	1.2%
3	Illinois	138,337	3.5%
19	Indiana	94,288	2.4%
13	Iowa	113,449	2.9%
4	Kansas	135,038	3.4%
26	Kentucky	78,372	2.0%
33	Louisiana	60,912	1.5%
43	Maine	22,693	0.6%
41	Maryland	30,815	0.8%
39	Massachusetts	35,458	0.9%
8	Michigan	122,029	3.1%
5	Minnesota	132,121	3.3%
27	Mississippi	73,902	1.9%
7	Missouri	124,686	3.1%
29	Montana	69,502	1.8%
20	Nebraska	93,171	2.3%
40	Nevada	34,853	0.9%
45	New Hampshire	15,504	0.4%
38	New Jersey	36,559	0.9%
32	New Mexico	61,384	1.5%
12	New York	114,022	2.9%
16	North Carolina	101,743	2.6%
22	North Dakota	86,588	2.2%
6	Ohio	124,885	3.1%
15	Oklahoma	112,531	2.8%
30	Oregon	66,642	1.7%
9	Pennsylvania	120,298	3.0%
48	Rhode Island	6,051	0.2%
31	South Carolina	66,194	1.7%
24	South Dakota	83,611	2.1%
21	Tennessee	88,287	2.2%
1	Texas	301,777	7.6%
36	Utah	42,611	1.1%
46	Vermont	14,292	0.4%
28	Virginia	70,950	1.8%
25	Washington	82,181	2.1%
37	West Virginia	36,994	0.9%
14	Wisconsin	112,919	2.8%
42	Wyoming	27,423	0.7%

<u>RANK ORDER</u>

RANK	STATE	MILES	% of USA
1	Texas	301,777	7.6%
2	California	167,898	4.2%
3	Illinois	138,337	3.5%
4	Kansas	135,038	3.4%
5	Minnesota	132,121	3.3%
6	Ohio	124,885	3.1%
7	Missouri	124,686	3.1%
8	Michigan	122,029	3.1%
9	Pennsylvania	120,298	3.0%
10	Florida	119,785	3.0%
11	Georgia	115,778	2.9%
12	New York	114,022	2.9%
13	Iowa	113,449	2.9%
14	Wisconsin	112,919	2.8%
15	Oklahoma	112,531	2.8%
16	North Carolina	101,743	2.6%
17	Arkansas	98,482	2.5%
18	Alabama	94,435	2.4%
19	Indiana	94,288	2.4%
20	Nebraska	93,171	2.3%
21	Tennessee	88,287	2.2%
22	North Dakota	86,588	2.2%
23	Colorado	86,310	2.2%
24	South Dakota	83,611	2.1%
25	Washington	82,181	2.1%
26	Kentucky	78,372	2.0%
27	Mississippi	73,902	1.9%
28	Virginia	70,950	1.8%
29	Montana	69,502	1.8%
30	Oregon	66,642	1.7%
31	South Carolina	66,194	1.7%
32	New Mexico	61,384	1.5%
33	Louisiana	60,912	1.5%
34	Arizona	57,165	1.4%
35	Idaho	46,731	1.2%
36	Utah	42,611	1.1%
37	West Virginia	36,994	0.9%
38	New Jersey	36,559	0.9%
39	Massachusetts	35,458	0.9%
40	Nevada	34,853	0.9%
41	Maryland	30,815	0.8%
42	Wyoming	27,423	0.7%
43	Maine	22,693	0.6%
44	Connecticut	21,042	0.5%
45	New Hampshire	15,504	0.4%
46	Vermont	14,292	0.4%
47	Alaska	14,117	0.4%
48	Rhode Island	6,051	0.2%
49	Delaware	5,845	0.1%
50	Hawaii	4,299	0.1%
	District of Columbia	1,535	0.0%

Interstate Highway Mileage in 2002

National Total = 46,483 Miles*

ALPHA ORDER

RANK	STATE	MILES	% of USA
24	Alabama	905	1.9%
15	Alaska	1,083	2.3%
13	Arizona	1,168	2.5%
35	Arkansas	656	1.4%
2	California	2,454	5.3%
19	Colorado	954	2.1%
45	Connecticut	346	0.7%
50	Delaware	41	0.1%
7	Florida	1,471	3.2%
8	Georgia	1,245	2.7%
49	Hawaii	55	0.1%
36	Idaho	611	1.3%
3	Illinois	2,170	4.7%
12	Indiana	1,169	2.5%
28	Iowa	782	1.7%
26	Kansas	874	1.9%
30	Kentucky	762	1.6%
25	Louisiana	904	1.9%
44	Maine	367	0.8%
42	Maryland	481	1.0%
38	Massachusetts	566	1.2%
9	Michigan	1,240	2.7%
22	Minnesota	913	2.0%
33	Mississippi	685	1.5%
11	Missouri	1,181	2.5%
10	Montana	1,191	2.6%
41	Nebraska	482	1.0%
39	Nevada	560	1.2%
47	New Hampshire	224	0.5%
43	New Jersey	431	0.9%
18	New Mexico	1,000	2.2%
5	New York	1,674	3.6%
17	North Carolina	1,020	2.2%
37	North Dakota	572	1.2%
6	Ohio	1,573	3.4%
21	Oklahoma	931	2.0%
32	Oregon	728	1.6%
4	Pennsylvania	1,757	3.8%
48	Rhode Island	70	0.2%
27	South Carolina	842	1.8%
34	South Dakota	678	1.5%
16	Tennessee	1,073	2.3%
1	Texas	3,234	7.0%
20	Utah	940	2.0%
46	Vermont	320	0.7%
14	Virginia	1,117	2.4%
29	Washington	764	1.6%
40	West Virginia	549	1.2%
31	Wisconsin	744	1.6%
22	Wyoming	913	2.0%

RANK ORDER

RANK	STATE	MILES	% of USA
1	Texas	3,234	7.0%
2	California	2,454	5.3%
3	Illinois	2,170	4.7%
4	Pennsylvania	1,757	3.8%
5	New York	1,674	3.6%
6	Ohio	1,573	3.4%
7	Florida	1,471	3.2%
8	Georgia	1,245	2.7%
9	Michigan	1,240	2.7%
10	Montana	1,191	2.6%
11	Missouri	1,181	2.5%
12	Indiana	1,169	2.5%
13	Arizona	1,168	2.5%
14	Virginia	1,117	2.4%
15	Alaska	1,083	2.3%
16	Tennessee	1,073	2.3%
17	North Carolina	1,020	2.2%
18	New Mexico	1,000	2.2%
19	Colorado	954	2.1%
20	Utah	940	2.0%
21	Oklahoma	931	2.0%
22	Minnesota	913	2.0%
22	Wyoming	913	2.0%
24	Alabama	905	1.9%
25	Louisiana	904	1.9%
26	Kansas	874	1.9%
27	South Carolina	842	1.8%
28	Iowa	782	1.7%
29	Washington	764	1.6%
30	Kentucky	762	1.6%
31	Wisconsin	744	1.6%
32	Oregon	728	1.6%
33	Mississippi	685	1.5%
34	South Dakota	678	1.5%
35	Arkansas	656	1.4%
36	Idaho	611	1.3%
37	North Dakota	572	1.2%
38	Massachusetts	566	1.2%
39	Nevada	560	1.2%
40	West Virginia	549	1.2%
41	Nebraska	482	1.0%
42	Maryland	481	1.0%
43	New Jersey	431	0.9%
44	Maine	367	0.8%
45	Connecticut	346	0.7%
46	Vermont	320	0.7%
47	New Hampshire	224	0.5%
48	Rhode Island	70	0.2%
49	Hawaii	55	0.1%
50	Delaware	41	0.1%
	District of Columbia	13	0.0%

Source: U.S. Department of Transportation, Federal Highway Administration
   "Highway Statistics 2002" (Table HM-15)
*Does not include 265 miles of highway in Puerto Rico that are part of the interstate system.

Rural Road and Street Mileage in 2002

National Total = 3,071,768 Rural Miles*

<u>ALPHA ORDER</u>

RANK	STATE	MILES	% of USA
20	Alabama	73,466	2.4%
46	Alaska	12,273	0.4%
35	Arizona	37,575	1.2%
10	Arkansas	87,681	2.9%
16	California	82,816	2.7%
22	Colorado	71,266	2.3%
47	Connecticut	6,109	0.2%
48	Delaware	3,828	0.1%
32	Florida	50,933	1.7%
12	Georgia	87,458	2.8%
49	Hawaii	2,180	0.1%
34	Idaho	42,430	1.4%
6	Illinois	101,504	3.3%
19	Indiana	73,893	2.4%
5	Iowa	103,535	3.4%
2	Kansas	124,528	4.1%
25	Kentucky	66,483	2.2%
33	Louisiana	46,962	1.5%
40	Maine	20,060	0.7%
41	Maryland	16,176	0.5%
45	Massachusetts	12,280	0.4%
9	Michigan	92,091	3.0%
3	Minnesota	116,016	3.8%
26	Mississippi	65,697	2.1%
4	Missouri	107,110	3.5%
24	Montana	66,899	2.2%
11	Nebraska	87,578	2.9%
38	Nevada	29,187	1.0%
43	New Hampshire	12,505	0.4%
44	New Jersey	12,305	0.4%
30	New Mexico	54,543	1.8%
21	New York	72,560	2.4%
18	North Carolina	77,629	2.5%
15	North Dakota	84,753	2.8%
14	Ohio	84,968	2.8%
7	Oklahoma	99,122	3.2%
29	Oregon	55,470	1.8%
13	Pennsylvania	85,585	2.8%
50	Rhode Island	1,333	0.0%
28	South Carolina	55,520	1.8%
17	South Dakota	81,475	2.7%
23	Tennessee	70,203	2.3%
1	Texas	218,572	7.1%
36	Utah	34,637	1.1%
42	Vermont	12,909	0.4%
31	Virginia	51,759	1.7%
27	Washington	63,008	2.1%
37	West Virginia	33,910	1.1%
8	Wisconsin	96,046	3.1%
39	Wyoming	24,942	0.8%

<u>RANK ORDER</u>

RANK	STATE	MILES	% of USA
1	Texas	218,572	7.1%
2	Kansas	124,528	4.1%
3	Minnesota	116,016	3.8%
4	Missouri	107,110	3.5%
5	Iowa	103,535	3.4%
6	Illinois	101,504	3.3%
7	Oklahoma	99,122	3.2%
8	Wisconsin	96,046	3.1%
9	Michigan	92,091	3.0%
10	Arkansas	87,681	2.9%
11	Nebraska	87,578	2.9%
12	Georgia	87,458	2.8%
13	Pennsylvania	85,585	2.8%
14	Ohio	84,968	2.8%
15	North Dakota	84,753	2.8%
16	California	82,816	2.7%
17	South Dakota	81,475	2.7%
18	North Carolina	77,629	2.5%
19	Indiana	73,893	2.4%
20	Alabama	73,466	2.4%
21	New York	72,560	2.4%
22	Colorado	71,266	2.3%
23	Tennessee	70,203	2.3%
24	Montana	66,899	2.2%
25	Kentucky	66,483	2.2%
26	Mississippi	65,697	2.1%
27	Washington	63,008	2.1%
28	South Carolina	55,520	1.8%
29	Oregon	55,470	1.8%
30	New Mexico	54,543	1.8%
31	Virginia	51,759	1.7%
32	Florida	50,933	1.7%
33	Louisiana	46,962	1.5%
34	Idaho	42,430	1.4%
35	Arizona	37,575	1.2%
36	Utah	34,637	1.1%
37	West Virginia	33,910	1.1%
38	Nevada	29,187	1.0%
39	Wyoming	24,942	0.8%
40	Maine	20,060	0.7%
41	Maryland	16,176	0.5%
42	Vermont	12,909	0.4%
43	New Hampshire	12,505	0.4%
44	New Jersey	12,305	0.4%
45	Massachusetts	12,280	0.4%
46	Alaska	12,273	0.4%
47	Connecticut	6,109	0.2%
48	Delaware	3,828	0.1%
49	Hawaii	2,180	0.1%
50	Rhode Island	1,333	0.0%
	District of Columbia	0	0.0%

Source: U.S. Department of Transportation, Federal Highway Administration
  "Highway Statistics 2002" (Table HM-10)
Does not include 7,993 miles of rural roads and streets in Puerto Rico.

Urban Road and Street Mileage in 2002

National Total = 894,726 Urban Miles*

ALPHA ORDER

RANK	STATE	MILES	% of USA
13	Alabama	20,969	2.3%
48	Alaska	1,844	0.2%
15	Arizona	19,590	2.2%
29	Arkansas	10,801	1.2%
1	California	85,082	9.5%
22	Colorado	15,044	1.7%
23	Connecticut	14,933	1.7%
47	Delaware	2,017	0.2%
3	Florida	68,852	7.7%
9	Georgia	28,320	3.2%
46	Hawaii	2,119	0.2%
39	Idaho	4,301	0.5%
6	Illinois	36,833	4.1%
14	Indiana	20,395	2.3%
32	Iowa	9,914	1.1%
31	Kansas	10,510	1.2%
27	Kentucky	11,889	1.3%
25	Louisiana	13,950	1.6%
42	Maine	2,633	0.3%
24	Maryland	14,639	1.6%
12	Massachusetts	23,178	2.6%
8	Michigan	29,938	3.3%
21	Minnesota	16,105	1.8%
33	Mississippi	8,205	0.9%
19	Missouri	17,576	2.0%
43	Montana	2,603	0.3%
37	Nebraska	5,593	0.6%
36	Nevada	5,666	0.6%
41	New Hampshire	2,999	0.3%
10	New Jersey	24,254	2.7%
35	New Mexico	6,841	0.8%
4	New York	41,462	4.6%
11	North Carolina	24,114	2.7%
49	North Dakota	1,835	0.2%
5	Ohio	39,917	4.5%
26	Oklahoma	13,409	1.5%
28	Oregon	11,172	1.2%
7	Pennsylvania	34,713	3.9%
38	Rhode Island	4,718	0.5%
30	South Carolina	10,674	1.2%
45	South Dakota	2,136	0.2%
18	Tennessee	18,084	2.0%
2	Texas	83,205	9.3%
34	Utah	7,974	0.9%
50	Vermont	1,383	0.2%
16	Virginia	19,191	2.1%
17	Washington	19,173	2.1%
40	West Virginia	3,084	0.3%
20	Wisconsin	16,873	1.9%
44	Wyoming	2,481	0.3%

RANK ORDER

RANK	STATE	MILES	% of USA
1	California	85,082	9.5%
2	Texas	83,205	9.3%
3	Florida	68,852	7.7%
4	New York	41,462	4.6%
5	Ohio	39,917	4.5%
6	Illinois	36,833	4.1%
7	Pennsylvania	34,713	3.9%
8	Michigan	29,938	3.3%
9	Georgia	28,320	3.2%
10	New Jersey	24,254	2.7%
11	North Carolina	24,114	2.7%
12	Massachusetts	23,178	2.6%
13	Alabama	20,969	2.3%
14	Indiana	20,395	2.3%
15	Arizona	19,590	2.2%
16	Virginia	19,191	2.1%
17	Washington	19,173	2.1%
18	Tennessee	18,084	2.0%
19	Missouri	17,576	2.0%
20	Wisconsin	16,873	1.9%
21	Minnesota	16,105	1.8%
22	Colorado	15,044	1.7%
23	Connecticut	14,933	1.7%
24	Maryland	14,639	1.6%
25	Louisiana	13,950	1.6%
26	Oklahoma	13,409	1.5%
27	Kentucky	11,889	1.3%
28	Oregon	11,172	1.2%
29	Arkansas	10,801	1.2%
30	South Carolina	10,674	1.2%
31	Kansas	10,510	1.2%
32	Iowa	9,914	1.1%
33	Mississippi	8,205	0.9%
34	Utah	7,974	0.9%
35	New Mexico	6,841	0.8%
36	Nevada	5,666	0.6%
37	Nebraska	5,593	0.6%
38	Rhode Island	4,718	0.5%
39	Idaho	4,301	0.5%
40	West Virginia	3,084	0.3%
41	New Hampshire	2,999	0.3%
42	Maine	2,633	0.3%
43	Montana	2,603	0.3%
44	Wyoming	2,481	0.3%
45	South Dakota	2,136	0.2%
46	Hawaii	2,119	0.2%
47	Delaware	2,017	0.2%
48	Alaska	1,844	0.2%
49	North Dakota	1,835	0.2%
50	Vermont	1,383	0.2%
	District of Columbia	1,535	0.2%

Source: U.S. Department of Transportation, Federal Highway Administration
   "Highway Statistics 2002" (Table HM-10)
*Does not include 7,188 miles of urban roads and streets in Puerto Rico.

Bridges in 2003

National Total = 589,783 Bridges*

<u>ALPHA ORDER</u>

RANK	STATE	BRIDGES	% of USA
15	Alabama	15,714	2.7%
47	Alaska	1,174	0.2%
30	Arizona	6,948	1.2%
23	Arkansas	12,454	2.1%
7	California	23,755	4.0%
27	Colorado	8,098	1.4%
38	Connecticut	4,172	0.7%
49	Delaware	840	0.1%
24	Florida	11,450	1.9%
17	Georgia	14,455	2.5%
48	Hawaii	1,097	0.2%
39	Idaho	4,053	0.7%
3	Illinois	25,661	4.4%
11	Indiana	18,138	3.1%
5	Iowa	24,992	4.2%
4	Kansas	25,627	4.3%
19	Kentucky	13,526	2.3%
20	Louisiana	13,392	2.3%
44	Maine	2,364	0.4%
36	Maryland	4,995	0.8%
35	Massachusetts	5,000	0.8%
25	Michigan	10,654	1.8%
22	Minnesota	12,976	2.2%
14	Mississippi	16,830	2.9%
6	Missouri	23,787	4.0%
34	Montana	5,100	0.9%
16	Nebraska	15,455	2.6%
46	Nevada	1,612	0.3%
45	New Hampshire	2,349	0.4%
32	New Jersey	6,377	1.1%
40	New Mexico	3,835	0.7%
12	New York	17,368	2.9%
13	North Carolina	17,193	2.9%
37	North Dakota	4,518	0.8%
2	Ohio	27,902	4.7%
8	Oklahoma	23,251	3.9%
29	Oregon	7,201	1.2%
9	Pennsylvania	21,889	3.7%
50	Rhode Island	748	0.1%
26	South Carolina	9,149	1.6%
33	South Dakota	5,966	1.0%
10	Tennessee	19,489	3.3%
1	Texas	48,494	8.2%
42	Utah	2,793	0.5%
43	Vermont	2,686	0.5%
21	Virginia	13,056	2.2%
28	Washington	7,436	1.3%
31	West Virginia	6,868	1.2%
18	Wisconsin	13,613	2.3%
41	Wyoming	3,038	0.5%

<u>RANK ORDER</u>

RANK	STATE	BRIDGES	% of USA
1	Texas	48,494	8.2%
2	Ohio	27,902	4.7%
3	Illinois	25,661	4.4%
4	Kansas	25,627	4.3%
5	Iowa	24,992	4.2%
6	Missouri	23,787	4.0%
7	California	23,755	4.0%
8	Oklahoma	23,251	3.9%
9	Pennsylvania	21,889	3.7%
10	Tennessee	19,489	3.3%
11	Indiana	18,138	3.1%
12	New York	17,368	2.9%
13	North Carolina	17,193	2.9%
14	Mississippi	16,830	2.9%
15	Alabama	15,714	2.7%
16	Nebraska	15,455	2.6%
17	Georgia	14,455	2.5%
18	Wisconsin	13,613	2.3%
19	Kentucky	13,526	2.3%
20	Louisiana	13,392	2.3%
21	Virginia	13,056	2.2%
22	Minnesota	12,976	2.2%
23	Arkansas	12,454	2.1%
24	Florida	11,450	1.9%
25	Michigan	10,654	1.8%
26	South Carolina	9,149	1.6%
27	Colorado	8,098	1.4%
28	Washington	7,436	1.3%
29	Oregon	7,201	1.2%
30	Arizona	6,948	1.2%
31	West Virginia	6,868	1.2%
32	New Jersey	6,377	1.1%
33	South Dakota	5,966	1.0%
34	Montana	5,100	0.9%
35	Massachusetts	5,000	0.8%
36	Maryland	4,995	0.8%
37	North Dakota	4,518	0.8%
38	Connecticut	4,172	0.7%
39	Idaho	4,053	0.7%
40	New Mexico	3,835	0.7%
41	Wyoming	3,038	0.5%
42	Utah	2,793	0.5%
43	Vermont	2,686	0.5%
44	Maine	2,364	0.4%
45	New Hampshire	2,349	0.4%
46	Nevada	1,612	0.3%
47	Alaska	1,174	0.2%
48	Hawaii	1,097	0.2%
49	Delaware	840	0.1%
50	Rhode Island	748	0.1%
	District of Columbia	245	0.0%

Source: U.S. Department of Transportation, Federal Highway Administration
"Deficient Bridges by State and Highway System, 2003" (http://www.fhwa.dot.gov/bridge/deficient.htm)
As of December 2003. Includes federal-aid and nonfederal-aid system bridges. National total does not include 2,135 bridges in Puerto Rico.

Deficient Bridges in 2003

National Total = 156,663 Deficient Bridges*

<u>ALPHA ORDER</u>

RANK	STATE	BRIDGES	% of USA
12	Alabama	4,752	3.0%
48	Alaska	345	0.2%
43	Arizona	705	0.5%
20	Arkansas	3,272	2.1%
7	California	6,599	4.2%
34	Colorado	1,325	0.8%
35	Connecticut	1,303	0.8%
50	Delaware	119	0.1%
27	Florida	2,079	1.3%
22	Georgia	2,990	1.9%
45	Hawaii	508	0.3%
42	Idaho	717	0.5%
14	Illinois	4,354	2.8%
16	Indiana	4,085	2.6%
5	Iowa	7,092	4.5%
9	Kansas	5,929	3.8%
18	Kentucky	3,963	2.5%
15	Louisiana	4,309	2.8%
39	Maine	832	0.5%
33	Maryland	1,403	0.9%
25	Massachusetts	2,507	1.6%
21	Michigan	3,070	2.0%
31	Minnesota	1,684	1.1%
10	Mississippi	5,006	3.2%
4	Missouri	8,311	5.3%
37	Montana	1,060	0.7%
17	Nebraska	4,065	2.6%
49	Nevada	202	0.1%
40	New Hampshire	785	0.5%
26	New Jersey	2,262	1.4%
41	New Mexico	720	0.5%
8	New York	6,408	4.1%
11	North Carolina	4,919	3.1%
36	North Dakota	1,083	0.7%
6	Ohio	7,019	4.5%
3	Oklahoma	8,991	5.7%
30	Oregon	1,714	1.1%
2	Pennsylvania	9,082	5.8%
47	Rhode Island	383	0.2%
28	South Carolina	1,983	1.3%
32	South Dakota	1,488	0.9%
13	Tennessee	4,550	2.9%
1	Texas	10,080	6.4%
46	Utah	498	0.3%
38	Vermont	948	0.6%
19	Virginia	3,383	2.2%
29	Washington	1,898	1.2%
24	West Virginia	2,541	1.6%
23	Wisconsin	2,561	1.6%
44	Wyoming	628	0.4%

<u>RANK ORDER</u>

RANK	STATE	BRIDGES	% of USA
1	Texas	10,080	6.4%
2	Pennsylvania	9,082	5.8%
3	Oklahoma	8,991	5.7%
4	Missouri	8,311	5.3%
5	Iowa	7,092	4.5%
6	Ohio	7,019	4.5%
7	California	6,599	4.2%
8	New York	6,408	4.1%
9	Kansas	5,929	3.8%
10	Mississippi	5,006	3.2%
11	North Carolina	4,919	3.1%
12	Alabama	4,752	3.0%
13	Tennessee	4,550	2.9%
14	Illinois	4,354	2.8%
15	Louisiana	4,309	2.8%
16	Indiana	4,085	2.6%
17	Nebraska	4,065	2.6%
18	Kentucky	3,963	2.5%
19	Virginia	3,383	2.2%
20	Arkansas	3,272	2.1%
21	Michigan	3,070	2.0%
22	Georgia	2,990	1.9%
23	Wisconsin	2,561	1.6%
24	West Virginia	2,541	1.6%
25	Massachusetts	2,507	1.6%
26	New Jersey	2,262	1.4%
27	Florida	2,079	1.3%
28	South Carolina	1,983	1.3%
29	Washington	1,898	1.2%
30	Oregon	1,714	1.1%
31	Minnesota	1,684	1.1%
32	South Dakota	1,488	0.9%
33	Maryland	1,403	0.9%
34	Colorado	1,325	0.8%
35	Connecticut	1,303	0.8%
36	North Dakota	1,083	0.7%
37	Montana	1,060	0.7%
38	Vermont	948	0.6%
39	Maine	832	0.5%
40	New Hampshire	785	0.5%
41	New Mexico	720	0.5%
42	Idaho	717	0.5%
43	Arizona	705	0.5%
44	Wyoming	628	0.4%
45	Hawaii	508	0.3%
46	Utah	498	0.3%
47	Rhode Island	383	0.2%
48	Alaska	345	0.2%
49	Nevada	202	0.1%
50	Delaware	119	0.1%
	District of Columbia	153	0.1%

Source: U.S. Department of Transportation, Federal Highway Administration
    "Deficient Bridges by State and Highway System, 2003" (http://www.fhwa.dot.gov/bridge/deficient.htm)
*As of December 2003. Includes federal-aid and nonfederal-aid system bridges. National total does not include 1,060 deficient bridges in Puerto Rico. Bridges classified as deficient are either functionally obsolete or structurally deficient and are not necessarily unsafe.

Deficient Bridges as a Percent of Total Bridges in 2003

National Percent = 26.6% of Bridges are Deficient*

ALPHA ORDER

RANK	STATE	PERCENT
15	Alabama	30.2
17	Alaska	29.4
50	Arizona	10.1
24	Arkansas	26.3
23	California	27.8
46	Colorado	16.4
14	Connecticut	31.2
47	Delaware	14.2
42	Florida	18.2
38	Georgia	20.7
3	Hawaii	46.3
44	Idaho	17.7
45	Illinois	17.0
34	Indiana	22.5
21	Iowa	28.4
33	Kansas	23.1
18	Kentucky	29.3
13	Louisiana	32.2
10	Maine	35.2
22	Maryland	28.1
2	Massachusetts	50.1
19	Michigan	28.8
48	Minnesota	13.0
16	Mississippi	29.7
11	Missouri	34.9
36	Montana	20.8
24	Nebraska	26.3
49	Nevada	12.5
12	New Hampshire	33.4
8	New Jersey	35.5
40	New Mexico	18.8
7	New York	36.9
20	North Carolina	28.6
30	North Dakota	24.0
28	Ohio	25.2
5	Oklahoma	38.7
31	Oregon	23.8
4	Pennsylvania	41.5
1	Rhode Island	51.2
35	South Carolina	21.7
29	South Dakota	24.9
32	Tennessee	23.3
36	Texas	20.8
43	Utah	17.8
9	Vermont	35.3
26	Virginia	25.9
27	Washington	25.5
6	West Virginia	37.0
40	Wisconsin	18.8
38	Wyoming	20.7

RANK ORDER

RANK	STATE	PERCENT
1	Rhode Island	51.2
2	Massachusetts	50.1
3	Hawaii	46.3
4	Pennsylvania	41.5
5	Oklahoma	38.7
6	West Virginia	37.0
7	New York	36.9
8	New Jersey	35.5
9	Vermont	35.3
10	Maine	35.2
11	Missouri	34.9
12	New Hampshire	33.4
13	Louisiana	32.2
14	Connecticut	31.2
15	Alabama	30.2
16	Mississippi	29.7
17	Alaska	29.4
18	Kentucky	29.3
19	Michigan	28.8
20	North Carolina	28.6
21	Iowa	28.4
22	Maryland	28.1
23	California	27.8
24	Arkansas	26.3
24	Nebraska	26.3
26	Virginia	25.9
27	Washington	25.5
28	Ohio	25.2
29	South Dakota	24.9
30	North Dakota	24.0
31	Oregon	23.8
32	Tennessee	23.3
33	Kansas	23.1
34	Indiana	22.5
35	South Carolina	21.7
36	Montana	20.8
36	Texas	20.8
38	Georgia	20.7
38	Wyoming	20.7
40	New Mexico	18.8
40	Wisconsin	18.8
42	Florida	18.2
43	Utah	17.8
44	Idaho	17.7
45	Illinois	17.0
46	Colorado	16.4
47	Delaware	14.2
48	Minnesota	13.0
49	Nevada	12.5
50	Arizona	10.1

District of Columbia — 62.4

Source: Morgan Quitno Press using data from U.S. Department of Transportation, Federal Highway Administration
"Deficient Bridges by State and Highway System, 2003" (http://www.fhwa.dot.gov/bridge/deficient.htm)
*As of December 2003. Includes federal-aid and nonfederal-aid system bridges. National percent does not include bridges in Puerto Rico. Bridges classified as deficient are either functionally obsolete or structurally deficient and are not necessarily unsafe.

Vehicle-Miles of Travel in 2002

National Total = 2,855,756,000,000 Miles

<u>ALPHA ORDER</u>

RANK	STATE	MILES	% of USA
17	Alabama	57,515,000,000	2.0%
50	Alaska	4,896,000,000	0.2%
22	Arizona	51,334,000,000	1.8%
32	Arkansas	30,080,000,000	1.1%
1	California	320,942,000,000	11.2%
26	Colorado	43,545,000,000	1.5%
30	Connecticut	31,205,000,000	1.1%
46	Delaware	8,875,000,000	0.3%
3	Florida	178,367,000,000	6.2%
5	Georgia	108,321,000,000	3.8%
45	Hawaii	8,886,000,000	0.3%
40	Idaho	14,167,000,000	0.5%
7	Illinois	105,401,000,000	3.7%
12	Indiana	72,523,000,000	2.5%
31	Iowa	30,847,000,000	1.1%
33	Kansas	28,443,000,000	1.0%
24	Kentucky	46,841,000,000	1.6%
27	Louisiana	43,295,000,000	1.5%
39	Maine	14,727,000,000	0.5%
20	Maryland	53,702,000,000	1.9%
21	Massachusetts	53,266,000,000	1.9%
9	Michigan	100,144,000,000	3.5%
19	Minnesota	54,562,000,000	1.9%
28	Mississippi	36,429,000,000	1.3%
15	Missouri	68,163,000,000	2.4%
42	Montana	10,395,000,000	0.4%
37	Nebraska	18,719,000,000	0.7%
38	Nevada	17,966,000,000	0.6%
41	New Hampshire	12,578,000,000	0.4%
13	New Jersey	69,942,000,000	2.4%
35	New Mexico	22,789,000,000	0.8%
4	New York	133,057,000,000	4.7%
10	North Carolina	92,894,000,000	3.3%
49	North Dakota	7,336,000,000	0.3%
6	Ohio	107,861,000,000	3.8%
25	Oklahoma	45,731,000,000	1.6%
29	Oregon	34,578,000,000	1.2%
8	Pennsylvania	104,476,000,000	3.7%
48	Rhode Island	8,142,000,000	0.3%
23	South Carolina	47,290,000,000	1.7%
47	South Dakota	8,499,000,000	0.3%
14	Tennessee	68,229,000,000	2.4%
2	Texas	221,026,000,000	7.7%
34	Utah	24,564,000,000	0.9%
43	Vermont	9,677,000,000	0.3%
11	Virginia	77,450,000,000	2.7%
18	Washington	54,776,000,000	1.9%
36	West Virginia	20,005,000,000	0.7%
16	Wisconsin	58,746,000,000	2.1%
44	Wyoming	9,007,000,000	0.3%

<u>RANK ORDER</u>

RANK	STATE	MILES	% of USA
1	California	320,942,000,000	11.2%
2	Texas	221,026,000,000	7.7%
3	Florida	178,367,000,000	6.2%
4	New York	133,057,000,000	4.7%
5	Georgia	108,321,000,000	3.8%
6	Ohio	107,861,000,000	3.8%
7	Illinois	105,401,000,000	3.7%
8	Pennsylvania	104,476,000,000	3.7%
9	Michigan	100,144,000,000	3.5%
10	North Carolina	92,894,000,000	3.3%
11	Virginia	77,450,000,000	2.7%
12	Indiana	72,523,000,000	2.5%
13	New Jersey	69,942,000,000	2.4%
14	Tennessee	68,229,000,000	2.4%
15	Missouri	68,163,000,000	2.4%
16	Wisconsin	58,746,000,000	2.1%
17	Alabama	57,515,000,000	2.0%
18	Washington	54,776,000,000	1.9%
19	Minnesota	54,562,000,000	1.9%
20	Maryland	53,702,000,000	1.9%
21	Massachusetts	53,266,000,000	1.9%
22	Arizona	51,334,000,000	1.8%
23	South Carolina	47,290,000,000	1.7%
24	Kentucky	46,841,000,000	1.6%
25	Oklahoma	45,731,000,000	1.6%
26	Colorado	43,545,000,000	1.5%
27	Louisiana	43,295,000,000	1.5%
28	Mississippi	36,429,000,000	1.3%
29	Oregon	34,578,000,000	1.2%
30	Connecticut	31,205,000,000	1.1%
31	Iowa	30,847,000,000	1.1%
32	Arkansas	30,080,000,000	1.1%
33	Kansas	28,443,000,000	1.0%
34	Utah	24,564,000,000	0.9%
35	New Mexico	22,789,000,000	0.8%
36	West Virginia	20,005,000,000	0.7%
37	Nebraska	18,719,000,000	0.7%
38	Nevada	17,966,000,000	0.6%
39	Maine	14,727,000,000	0.5%
40	Idaho	14,167,000,000	0.5%
41	New Hampshire	12,578,000,000	0.4%
42	Montana	10,395,000,000	0.4%
43	Vermont	9,677,000,000	0.3%
44	Wyoming	9,007,000,000	0.3%
45	Hawaii	8,886,000,000	0.3%
46	Delaware	8,875,000,000	0.3%
47	South Dakota	8,499,000,000	0.3%
48	Rhode Island	8,142,000,000	0.3%
49	North Dakota	7,336,000,000	0.3%
50	Alaska	4,896,000,000	0.2%
	District of Columbia	3,547,000,000	0.1%

Highway Fatalities in 2002

National Total = 42,815 Fatalities

ALPHA ORDER

RANK	STATE	FATALITIES	% of USA
15	Alabama	1,033	2.4%
48	Alaska	87	0.2%
13	Arizona	1,117	2.6%
28	Arkansas	640	1.5%
1	California	4,078	9.5%
23	Colorado	742	1.7%
37	Connecticut	322	0.8%
45	Delaware	124	0.3%
3	Florida	3,132	7.3%
6	Georgia	1,523	3.6%
46	Hawaii	119	0.3%
40	Idaho	264	0.6%
9	Illinois	1,411	3.3%
21	Indiana	792	1.8%
34	Iowa	404	0.9%
29	Kansas	512	1.2%
16	Kentucky	915	2.1%
19	Louisiana	875	2.0%
41	Maine	216	0.5%
25	Maryland	659	1.5%
30	Massachusetts	459	1.1%
10	Michigan	1,277	3.0%
27	Minnesota	657	1.5%
18	Mississippi	885	2.1%
11	Missouri	1,208	2.8%
39	Montana	270	0.6%
38	Nebraska	307	0.7%
35	Nevada	381	0.9%
44	New Hampshire	127	0.3%
22	New Jersey	773	1.8%
31	New Mexico	449	1.0%
7	New York	1,522	3.6%
5	North Carolina	1,575	3.7%
47	North Dakota	97	0.2%
8	Ohio	1,418	3.3%
24	Oklahoma	734	1.7%
33	Oregon	436	1.0%
4	Pennsylvania	1,614	3.8%
49	Rhode Island	84	0.2%
14	South Carolina	1,053	2.5%
42	South Dakota	180	0.4%
12	Tennessee	1,175	2.7%
2	Texas	3,725	8.7%
36	Utah	328	0.8%
50	Vermont	78	0.2%
17	Virginia	914	2.1%
25	Washington	659	1.5%
32	West Virginia	439	1.0%
20	Wisconsin	803	1.9%
43	Wyoming	176	0.4%

RANK ORDER

RANK	STATE	FATALITIES	% of USA
1	California	4,078	9.5%
2	Texas	3,725	8.7%
3	Florida	3,132	7.3%
4	Pennsylvania	1,614	3.8%
5	North Carolina	1,575	3.7%
6	Georgia	1,523	3.6%
7	New York	1,522	3.6%
8	Ohio	1,418	3.3%
9	Illinois	1,411	3.3%
10	Michigan	1,277	3.0%
11	Missouri	1,208	2.8%
12	Tennessee	1,175	2.7%
13	Arizona	1,117	2.6%
14	South Carolina	1,053	2.5%
15	Alabama	1,033	2.4%
16	Kentucky	915	2.1%
17	Virginia	914	2.1%
18	Mississippi	885	2.1%
19	Louisiana	875	2.0%
20	Wisconsin	803	1.9%
21	Indiana	792	1.8%
22	New Jersey	773	1.8%
23	Colorado	742	1.7%
24	Oklahoma	734	1.7%
25	Maryland	659	1.5%
25	Washington	659	1.5%
27	Minnesota	657	1.5%
28	Arkansas	640	1.5%
29	Kansas	512	1.2%
30	Massachusetts	459	1.1%
31	New Mexico	449	1.0%
32	West Virginia	439	1.0%
33	Oregon	436	1.0%
34	Iowa	404	0.9%
35	Nevada	381	0.9%
36	Utah	328	0.8%
37	Connecticut	322	0.8%
38	Nebraska	307	0.7%
39	Montana	270	0.6%
40	Idaho	264	0.6%
41	Maine	216	0.5%
42	South Dakota	180	0.4%
43	Wyoming	176	0.4%
44	New Hampshire	127	0.3%
45	Delaware	124	0.3%
46	Hawaii	119	0.3%
47	North Dakota	97	0.2%
48	Alaska	87	0.2%
49	Rhode Island	84	0.2%
50	Vermont	78	0.2%
	District of Columbia	47	0.1%

Source: U.S. Department of Transportation, National Highway Safety Administration
"Traffic Safety Facts 2002" (http://www-nrd.nhtsa.dot.gov/pdf/nrd-30/NCSA/TSFAnn/TSF2002Final.pdf)

Highway Fatality Rate in 2002

National Rate = 1.5 Fatalities per 100 Million Vehicle-Miles of Travel

ALPHA ORDER

RANK	STATE	RATE
14	Alabama	1.8
14	Alaska	1.8
3	Arizona	2.2
6	Arkansas	2.1
30	California	1.3
19	Colorado	1.7
46	Connecticut	1.0
27	Delaware	1.4
14	Florida	1.8
27	Georgia	1.4
30	Hawaii	1.3
13	Idaho	1.9
30	Illinois	1.3
43	Indiana	1.1
30	Iowa	1.3
14	Kansas	1.8
9	Kentucky	2.0
9	Louisiana	2.0
25	Maine	1.5
39	Maryland	1.2
49	Massachusetts	0.9
30	Michigan	1.3
39	Minnesota	1.2
2	Mississippi	2.4
14	Missouri	1.8
1	Montana	2.6
23	Nebraska	1.6
6	Nevada	2.1
46	New Hampshire	1.0
43	New Jersey	1.1
9	New Mexico	2.0
43	New York	1.1
19	North Carolina	1.7
30	North Dakota	1.3
30	Ohio	1.3
23	Oklahoma	1.6
30	Oregon	1.3
25	Pennsylvania	1.5
46	Rhode Island	1.0
3	South Carolina	2.2
6	South Dakota	2.1
19	Tennessee	1.7
19	Texas	1.7
30	Utah	1.3
50	Vermont	0.8
39	Virginia	1.2
39	Washington	1.2
3	West Virginia	2.2
27	Wisconsin	1.4
9	Wyoming	2.0

RANK ORDER

RANK	STATE	RATE
1	Montana	2.6
2	Mississippi	2.4
3	Arizona	2.2
3	South Carolina	2.2
3	West Virginia	2.2
6	Arkansas	2.1
6	Nevada	2.1
6	South Dakota	2.1
9	Kentucky	2.0
9	Louisiana	2.0
9	New Mexico	2.0
9	Wyoming	2.0
13	Idaho	1.9
14	Alabama	1.8
14	Alaska	1.8
14	Florida	1.8
14	Kansas	1.8
14	Missouri	1.8
19	Colorado	1.7
19	North Carolina	1.7
19	Tennessee	1.7
19	Texas	1.7
23	Nebraska	1.6
23	Oklahoma	1.6
25	Maine	1.5
25	Pennsylvania	1.5
27	Delaware	1.4
27	Georgia	1.4
27	Wisconsin	1.4
30	California	1.3
30	Hawaii	1.3
30	Illinois	1.3
30	Iowa	1.3
30	Michigan	1.3
30	North Dakota	1.3
30	Ohio	1.3
30	Oregon	1.3
30	Utah	1.3
39	Maryland	1.2
39	Minnesota	1.2
39	Virginia	1.2
39	Washington	1.2
43	Indiana	1.1
43	New Jersey	1.1
43	New York	1.1
46	Connecticut	1.0
46	New Hampshire	1.0
46	Rhode Island	1.0
49	Massachusetts	0.9
50	Vermont	0.8
	District of Columbia	1.3

Source: U.S. Department of Transportation, National Highway Safety Administration
"Traffic Safety Facts 2002" (http://www-nrd.nhtsa.dot.gov/pdf/nrd-30/NCSA/TSFAnn/TSF2002Final.pdf)

Percent of Traffic Fatalities Who Were Motorcyclists: 2002

National Percent = 7.6%*

ALPHA ORDER

RANK	STATE	PERCENT
48	Alabama	4.2
3	Alaska	13.8
18	Arizona	8.4
37	Arkansas	5.9
21	California	7.9
11	Colorado	9.8
2	Connecticut	14.6
39	Delaware	5.6
8	Florida	10.2
39	Georgia	5.6
1	Hawaii	20.2
47	Idaho	4.5
26	Illinois	7.1
5	Indiana	11.1
10	Iowa	10.1
33	Kansas	6.3
45	Kentucky	4.9
24	Louisiana	7.5
35	Maine	6.0
23	Maryland	7.6
4	Massachusetts	12.6
28	Michigan	6.8
25	Minnesota	7.2
49	Mississippi	2.9
44	Missouri	5.0
16	Montana	8.9
45	Nebraska	4.9
15	Nevada	9.2
12	New Hampshire	9.4
42	New Jersey	5.3
26	New Mexico	7.1
14	New York	9.3
22	North Carolina	7.8
50	North Dakota	1.0
12	Ohio	9.4
43	Oklahoma	5.2
35	Oregon	6.0
19	Pennsylvania	8.3
6	Rhode Island	10.7
17	South Carolina	8.5
7	South Dakota	10.6
33	Tennessee	6.3
30	Texas	6.6
41	Utah	5.5
32	Vermont	6.4
37	Virginia	5.9
20	Washington	8.2
30	West Virginia	6.6
8	Wisconsin	10.2
28	Wyoming	6.8

RANK ORDER

RANK	STATE	PERCENT
1	Hawaii	20.2
2	Connecticut	14.6
3	Alaska	13.8
4	Massachusetts	12.6
5	Indiana	11.1
6	Rhode Island	10.7
7	South Dakota	10.6
8	Florida	10.2
8	Wisconsin	10.2
10	Iowa	10.1
11	Colorado	9.8
12	New Hampshire	9.4
12	Ohio	9.4
14	New York	9.3
15	Nevada	9.2
16	Montana	8.9
17	South Carolina	8.5
18	Arizona	8.4
19	Pennsylvania	8.3
20	Washington	8.2
21	California	7.9
22	North Carolina	7.8
23	Maryland	7.6
24	Louisiana	7.5
25	Minnesota	7.2
26	Illinois	7.1
26	New Mexico	7.1
28	Michigan	6.8
28	Wyoming	6.8
30	Texas	6.6
30	West Virginia	6.6
32	Vermont	6.4
33	Kansas	6.3
33	Tennessee	6.3
35	Maine	6.0
35	Oregon	6.0
37	Arkansas	5.9
37	Virginia	5.9
39	Delaware	5.6
39	Georgia	5.6
41	Utah	5.5
42	New Jersey	5.3
43	Oklahoma	5.2
44	Missouri	5.0
45	Kentucky	4.9
45	Nebraska	4.9
47	Idaho	4.5
48	Alabama	4.2
49	Mississippi	2.9
50	North Dakota	1.0
	District of Columbia	14.9

Source: U.S. Department of Transportation, National Highway Traffic Safety Administration
    "Traffic Safety Facts 2002, Motorcycles" (http://www-nrd.nhtsa.dot.gov/pdf/nrd-30/NCSA/TSF2002/2002mcyfacts.pdf)
*In 2001 (2002 data not available), motorcycles accounted for two percent of all registered vehicles and 0.3 percent
of all vehicle miles traveled.

Percent of Traffic Fatalities That Were Speeding-Related: 2002

National Percent = 32.0%*

ALPHA ORDER				RANK ORDER		
RANK	STATE	PERCENT		RANK	STATE	PERCENT
13	Alabama	39.8		1	Kansas	58.6
21	Alaska	37.9		2	Rhode Island	54.8
16	Arizona	39.0		3	Connecticut	47.8
44	Arkansas	19.5		4	South Carolina	47.0
24	California	36.0		5	Vermont	46.2
8	Colorado	43.0		6	Pennsylvania	45.2
3	Connecticut	47.8		7	South Dakota	43.3
29	Delaware	32.3		8	Colorado	43.0
45	Florida	17.8		9	Missouri	42.1
42	Georgia	20.6		10	Oklahoma	41.7
25	Hawaii	34.5		11	Texas	41.5
28	Idaho	33.3		12	Wyoming	40.3
23	Illinois	37.6		13	Alabama	39.8
40	Indiana	23.4		14	Washington	39.5
49	Iowa	12.1		15	New Mexico	39.4
1	Kansas	58.6		16	Arizona	39.0
43	Kentucky	19.6		17	Nevada	38.8
48	Louisiana	12.2		18	Maine	38.4
18	Maine	38.4		19	Massachusetts	38.3
29	Maryland	32.3		20	North Carolina	38.2
19	Massachusetts	38.3		21	Alaska	37.9
41	Michigan	22.5		22	Montana	37.8
37	Minnesota	27.2		23	Illinois	37.6
38	Mississippi	26.2		24	California	36.0
9	Missouri	42.1		25	Hawaii	34.5
22	Montana	37.8		26	Wisconsin	34.4
47	Nebraska	14.3		27	North Dakota	34.0
17	Nevada	38.8		28	Idaho	33.3
35	New Hampshire	29.9		29	Delaware	32.3
50	New Jersey	6.3		29	Maryland	32.3
15	New Mexico	39.4		31	New York	31.9
31	New York	31.9		32	Oregon	31.0
20	North Carolina	38.2		32	West Virginia	31.0
27	North Dakota	34.0		34	Utah	30.5
46	Ohio	17.3		35	New Hampshire	29.9
10	Oklahoma	41.7		36	Virginia	27.5
32	Oregon	31.0		37	Minnesota	27.2
6	Pennsylvania	45.2		38	Mississippi	26.2
2	Rhode Island	54.8		39	Tennessee	24.9
4	South Carolina	47.0		40	Indiana	23.4
7	South Dakota	43.3		41	Michigan	22.5
39	Tennessee	24.9		42	Georgia	20.6
11	Texas	41.5		43	Kentucky	19.6
34	Utah	30.5		44	Arkansas	19.5
5	Vermont	46.2		45	Florida	17.8
36	Virginia	27.5		46	Ohio	17.3
14	Washington	39.5		47	Nebraska	14.3
32	West Virginia	31.0		48	Louisiana	12.2
26	Wisconsin	34.4		49	Iowa	12.1
12	Wyoming	40.3		50	New Jersey	6.3
					District of Columbia	36.2

Source: Morgan Quitno Press using data from U.S. Department of Transportation, National Highway Traffic Safety Admin.
"Traffic Safety Facts 2002, Speeding" (http://www-nrd.nhtsa.dot.gov/pdf/nrd-30/NCSA/TSF2002/2002spdfacts.pdf)
*A speeding-related crash is if the driver was charged with a speeding-related offense or if an officer indicated that racing, driving too fast for conditions, or exceeding the posted speed limit was a contributing factor in the crash.

Percent of Vehicles Involved in Fatal Crashes That Were Large Trucks: 2002

National Percent = 7.8%*

ALPHA ORDER				RANK ORDER		
RANK	STATE	PERCENT		RANK	STATE	PERCENT
18	Alabama	9.0		1	North Dakota	14.4
48	Alaska	3.6		2	Nebraska	14.3
43	Arizona	6.0		3	Wyoming	13.3
10	Arkansas	9.6		4	Kansas	11.4
41	California	6.2		5	Iowa	11.2
44	Colorado	5.1		6	Oklahoma	11.0
47	Connecticut	4.1		7	Indiana	10.4
10	Delaware	9.6		8	New Mexico	10.0
28	Florida	7.9		9	West Virginia	9.9
15	Georgia	9.2		10	Arkansas	9.6
50	Hawaii	2.4		10	Delaware	9.6
21	Idaho	8.5		10	Utah	9.6
22	Illinois	8.3		13	Kentucky	9.3
7	Indiana	10.4		13	Ohio	9.3
5	Iowa	11.2		15	Georgia	9.2
4	Kansas	11.4		15	Missouri	9.2
13	Kentucky	9.3		15	Vermont	9.2
19	Louisiana	8.7		18	Alabama	9.0
30	Maine	7.7		19	Louisiana	8.7
39	Maryland	6.3		19	Minnesota	8.7
49	Massachusetts	3.5		21	Idaho	8.5
35	Michigan	6.6		22	Illinois	8.3
19	Minnesota	8.7		22	Tennessee	8.3
37	Mississippi	6.5		24	New Hampshire	8.2
15	Missouri	9.2		24	Wisconsin	8.2
33	Montana	7.1		26	Oregon	8.1
2	Nebraska	14.3		27	Texas	8.0
38	Nevada	6.4		28	Florida	7.9
24	New Hampshire	8.2		28	Pennsylvania	7.9
45	New Jersey	4.7		30	Maine	7.7
8	New Mexico	10.0		30	North Carolina	7.7
39	New York	6.3		32	South Dakota	7.3
30	North Carolina	7.7		33	Montana	7.1
1	North Dakota	14.4		34	Virginia	6.9
13	Ohio	9.3		35	Michigan	6.6
6	Oklahoma	11.0		35	South Carolina	6.6
26	Oregon	8.1		37	Mississippi	6.5
28	Pennsylvania	7.9		38	Nevada	6.4
46	Rhode Island	4.2		39	Maryland	6.3
35	South Carolina	6.6		39	New York	6.3
32	South Dakota	7.3		41	California	6.2
22	Tennessee	8.3		42	Washington	6.1
27	Texas	8.0		43	Arizona	6.0
10	Utah	9.6		44	Colorado	5.1
15	Vermont	9.2		45	New Jersey	4.7
34	Virginia	6.9		46	Rhode Island	4.2
42	Washington	6.1		47	Connecticut	4.1
9	West Virginia	9.9		48	Alaska	3.6
24	Wisconsin	8.2		49	Massachusetts	3.5
3	Wyoming	13.3		50	Hawaii	2.4
					District of Columbia	0.0

Source: U.S. Department of Transportation, National Highway Traffic Safety Administration
"Traffic Safety Facts 2002, Large Trucks" (http://www-nrd.nhtsa.dot.gov/pdf/nrd-30/NCSA/TSF2002/2002trkfacts.pdf)
**Large trucks are those with gross vehicle weight greater than 10,000 pounds. In 2001 (2002 data not available),*
large trucks accounted for four percent of all registered vehicles and seven percent of all vehicle miles traveled.

Safety Belt Usage Rate in 2002

National Rate = 75.0% Use Safety Belts*

ALPHA ORDER

RANK	STATE	PERCENT
16	Alabama	79
38	Alaska	66
23	Arizona	74
41	Arkansas	64
2	California	91
25	Colorado	73
17	Connecticut	78
28	Delaware	71
21	Florida	75
19	Georgia	77
3	Hawaii	90
43	Idaho	63
23	Illinois	74
26	Indiana	72
11	Iowa	82
47	Kansas	61
45	Kentucky	62
34	Louisiana	69
NA	Maine**	NA
6	Maryland	86
48	Massachusetts	51
9	Michigan	83
14	Minnesota	80
45	Mississippi	62
34	Missouri	69
17	Montana	78
30	Nebraska	70
21	Nevada	75
NA	New Hampshire**	NA
12	New Jersey	81
4	New Mexico	88
9	New York	83
8	North Carolina	84
43	North Dakota	63
30	Ohio	70
30	Oklahoma	70
4	Oregon	88
20	Pennsylvania	76
28	Rhode Island	71
38	South Carolina	66
41	South Dakota	64
36	Tennessee	67
12	Texas	81
14	Utah	80
7	Vermont	85
30	Virginia	70
1	Washington	93
26	West Virginia	72
38	Wisconsin	66
36	Wyoming	67

RANK ORDER

RANK	STATE	PERCENT
1	Washington	93
2	California	91
3	Hawaii	90
4	New Mexico	88
4	Oregon	88
6	Maryland	86
7	Vermont	85
8	North Carolina	84
9	Michigan	83
9	New York	83
11	Iowa	82
12	New Jersey	81
12	Texas	81
14	Minnesota	80
14	Utah	80
16	Alabama	79
17	Connecticut	78
17	Montana	78
19	Georgia	77
20	Pennsylvania	76
21	Florida	75
21	Nevada	75
23	Arizona	74
23	Illinois	74
25	Colorado	73
26	Indiana	72
26	West Virginia	72
28	Delaware	71
28	Rhode Island	71
30	Nebraska	70
30	Ohio	70
30	Oklahoma	70
30	Virginia	70
34	Louisiana	69
34	Missouri	69
36	Tennessee	67
36	Wyoming	67
38	Alaska	66
38	South Carolina	66
38	Wisconsin	66
41	Arkansas	64
41	South Dakota	64
43	Idaho	63
43	North Dakota	63
45	Kentucky	62
45	Mississippi	62
47	Kansas	61
48	Massachusetts	51
NA	Maine**	NA
NA	New Hampshire**	NA
	District of Columbia	85

Source: U.S. Department of Transportation, National Highway Traffic Safety Administration
   "Safety Belt Use in 2002" (http://www-nrd.nhtsa.dot.gov/pdf/nrd-30/NCSA/RNotes/2003/809-587.pdf)
*As of December 2002. National estimate is from the National Occupant Protection Use Survey (NOPUS) using a different methodology.
**Not available.

Percent of Passenger Car Occupant Fatalities
Where Victim Used a Seat Belt in 2002
National Percent = 38.1% of Passenger Car Occupant Fatalities*

<u>ALPHA ORDER</u>

RANK	STATE	PERCENT
19	Alabama	38.7
4	Alaska	50.0
34	Arizona	32.3
41	Arkansas	27.9
6	California	47.0
30	Colorado	33.5
27	Connecticut	35.9
29	Delaware	33.7
24	Florida	36.4
18	Georgia	38.9
13	Hawaii	40.0
23	Idaho	36.5
38	Illinois	30.5
11	Indiana	40.8
22	Iowa	37.2
42	Kansas	26.6
26	Kentucky	36.0
39	Louisiana	30.1
15	Maine	39.6
1	Maryland	55.9
48	Massachusetts	24.2
3	Michigan	51.9
16	Minnesota	39.5
44	Mississippi	26.2
42	Missouri	26.6
45	Montana	25.4
46	Nebraska	25.0
21	Nevada	37.9
25	New Hampshire	36.2
9	New Jersey	43.8
27	New Mexico	35.9
8	New York	44.7
10	North Carolina	43.4
49	North Dakota	24.1
20	Ohio	38.0
14	Oklahoma	39.8
2	Oregon	54.1
40	Pennsylvania	28.4
46	Rhode Island	25.0
34	South Carolina	32.3
49	South Dakota	24.1
37	Tennessee	31.9
5	Texas	48.4
12	Utah	40.3
17	Vermont	39.4
34	Virginia	32.3
7	Washington	46.3
33	West Virginia	32.4
30	Wisconsin	33.5
32	Wyoming	32.9

<u>RANK ORDER</u>

RANK	STATE	PERCENT
1	Maryland	55.9
2	Oregon	54.1
3	Michigan	51.9
4	Alaska	50.0
5	Texas	48.4
6	California	47.0
7	Washington	46.3
8	New York	44.7
9	New Jersey	43.8
10	North Carolina	43.4
11	Indiana	40.8
12	Utah	40.3
13	Hawaii	40.0
14	Oklahoma	39.8
15	Maine	39.6
16	Minnesota	39.5
17	Vermont	39.4
18	Georgia	38.9
19	Alabama	38.7
20	Ohio	38.0
21	Nevada	37.9
22	Iowa	37.2
23	Idaho	36.5
24	Florida	36.4
25	New Hampshire	36.2
26	Kentucky	36.0
27	Connecticut	35.9
27	New Mexico	35.9
29	Delaware	33.7
30	Colorado	33.5
30	Wisconsin	33.5
32	Wyoming	32.9
33	West Virginia	32.4
34	Arizona	32.3
34	South Carolina	32.3
34	Virginia	32.3
37	Tennessee	31.9
38	Illinois	30.5
39	Louisiana	30.1
40	Pennsylvania	28.4
41	Arkansas	27.9
42	Kansas	26.6
42	Missouri	26.6
44	Mississippi	26.2
45	Montana	25.4
46	Nebraska	25.0
46	Rhode Island	25.0
48	Massachusetts	24.2
49	North Dakota	24.1
49	South Dakota	24.1
	District of Columbia	41.9

Source: U.S. Department of Transportation, National Highway Safety Administration
"Traffic Safety Facts 2002" (http://www-nrd.nhtsa.dot.gov/pdf/nrd-30/NCSA/TSFAnn/TSF2002Final.pdf)
**Only those fatalities where seat belts are known to have been used are counted.*

Fatalities in Alcohol-Related Crashes in 2002

National Total = 17,419 Fatalities*

ALPHA ORDER

RANK	STATE	FATALITIES	% of USA
15	Alabama	413	2.4%
49	Alaska	35	0.2%
13	Arizona	477	2.7%
28	Arkansas	242	1.4%
2	California	1,612	9.3%
20	Colorado	307	1.8%
35	Connecticut	140	0.8%
43	Delaware	51	0.3%
3	Florida	1,276	7.3%
9	Georgia	529	3.0%
46	Hawaii	50	0.3%
40	Idaho	91	0.5%
5	Illinois	648	3.7%
24	Indiana	269	1.5%
36	Iowa	131	0.8%
29	Kansas	229	1.3%
21	Kentucky	301	1.7%
15	Louisiana	413	2.4%
43	Maine	51	0.3%
25	Maryland	265	1.5%
30	Massachusetts	221	1.3%
11	Michigan	490	2.8%
26	Minnesota	255	1.5%
19	Mississippi	332	1.9%
10	Missouri	525	3.0%
37	Montana	127	0.7%
38	Nebraska	117	0.7%
34	Nevada	171	1.0%
43	New Hampshire	51	0.3%
22	New Jersey	299	1.7%
31	New Mexico	215	1.2%
12	New York	478	2.7%
6	North Carolina	601	3.5%
47	North Dakota	48	0.3%
7	Ohio	562	3.2%
27	Oklahoma	249	1.4%
33	Oregon	179	1.0%
4	Pennsylvania	656	3.8%
48	Rhode Island	46	0.3%
8	South Carolina	551	3.2%
39	South Dakota	92	0.5%
14	Tennessee	471	2.7%
1	Texas	1,745	10.0%
41	Utah	73	0.4%
50	Vermont	27	0.2%
17	Virginia	371	2.1%
23	Washington	298	1.7%
32	West Virginia	180	1.0%
18	Wisconsin	364	2.1%
42	Wyoming	70	0.4%

RANK ORDER

RANK	STATE	FATALITIES	% of USA
1	Texas	1,745	10.0%
2	California	1,612	9.3%
3	Florida	1,276	7.3%
4	Pennsylvania	656	3.8%
5	Illinois	648	3.7%
6	North Carolina	601	3.5%
7	Ohio	562	3.2%
8	South Carolina	551	3.2%
9	Georgia	529	3.0%
10	Missouri	525	3.0%
11	Michigan	490	2.8%
12	New York	478	2.7%
13	Arizona	477	2.7%
14	Tennessee	471	2.7%
15	Alabama	413	2.4%
15	Louisiana	413	2.4%
17	Virginia	371	2.1%
18	Wisconsin	364	2.1%
19	Mississippi	332	1.9%
20	Colorado	307	1.8%
21	Kentucky	301	1.7%
22	New Jersey	299	1.7%
23	Washington	298	1.7%
24	Indiana	269	1.5%
25	Maryland	265	1.5%
26	Minnesota	255	1.5%
27	Oklahoma	249	1.4%
28	Arkansas	242	1.4%
29	Kansas	229	1.3%
30	Massachusetts	221	1.3%
31	New Mexico	215	1.2%
32	West Virginia	180	1.0%
33	Oregon	179	1.0%
34	Nevada	171	1.0%
35	Connecticut	140	0.8%
36	Iowa	131	0.8%
37	Montana	127	0.7%
38	Nebraska	117	0.7%
39	South Dakota	92	0.5%
40	Idaho	91	0.5%
41	Utah	73	0.4%
42	Wyoming	70	0.4%
43	Delaware	51	0.3%
43	Maine	51	0.3%
43	New Hampshire	51	0.3%
46	Hawaii	50	0.3%
47	North Dakota	48	0.3%
48	Rhode Island	46	0.3%
49	Alaska	35	0.2%
50	Vermont	27	0.2%
	District of Columbia	25	0.1%

Source: U.S. Department of Transportation, National Highway Traffic Safety Administration
"Traffic Safety Facts 2002, Alcohol" (http://www-nrd.nhtsa.dot.gov/pdf/nrd-30/NCSA/TSF2002/2002alcfacts.pdf)
*Drivers with Blood Alcohol Content (BAC) of .01 or more. "Legally Drunk" BAC differs from state to state but is often .08 or higher.

Fatalities in Alcohol-Related Crashes
As a Percent of All Highway Fatalities in 2002
National Percent = 41% of Highway Fatalities*

ALPHA ORDER

RANK	STATE	PERCENT
27	Alabama	40
19	Alaska	41
15	Arizona	43
36	Arkansas	38
27	California	40
19	Colorado	41
15	Connecticut	43
19	Delaware	41
19	Florida	41
41	Georgia	35
18	Hawaii	42
43	Idaho	34
10	Illinois	46
43	Indiana	34
47	Iowa	32
11	Kansas	45
46	Kentucky	33
7	Louisiana	47
49	Maine	24
27	Maryland	40
5	Massachusetts	48
36	Michigan	38
33	Minnesota	39
36	Mississippi	38
15	Missouri	43
7	Montana	47
36	Nebraska	38
11	Nevada	45
27	New Hampshire	40
33	New Jersey	39
5	New Mexico	48
48	New York	31
36	North Carolina	38
4	North Dakota	50
27	Ohio	40
43	Oklahoma	34
19	Oregon	41
19	Pennsylvania	41
1	Rhode Island	55
2	South Carolina	52
3	South Dakota	51
27	Tennessee	40
7	Texas	47
50	Utah	22
41	Vermont	35
19	Virginia	41
11	Washington	45
19	West Virginia	41
11	Wisconsin	45
33	Wyoming	39

RANK ORDER

RANK	STATE	PERCENT
1	Rhode Island	55
2	South Carolina	52
3	South Dakota	51
4	North Dakota	50
5	Massachusetts	48
5	New Mexico	48
7	Louisiana	47
7	Montana	47
7	Texas	47
10	Illinois	46
11	Kansas	45
11	Nevada	45
11	Washington	45
11	Wisconsin	45
15	Arizona	43
15	Connecticut	43
15	Missouri	43
18	Hawaii	42
19	Alaska	41
19	Colorado	41
19	Delaware	41
19	Florida	41
19	Oregon	41
19	Pennsylvania	41
19	Virginia	41
19	West Virginia	41
27	Alabama	40
27	California	40
27	Maryland	40
27	New Hampshire	40
27	Ohio	40
27	Tennessee	40
33	Minnesota	39
33	New Jersey	39
33	Wyoming	39
36	Arkansas	38
36	Michigan	38
36	Mississippi	38
36	Nebraska	38
36	North Carolina	38
41	Georgia	35
41	Vermont	35
43	Idaho	34
43	Indiana	34
43	Oklahoma	34
46	Kentucky	33
47	Iowa	32
48	New York	31
49	Maine	24
50	Utah	22
	District of Columbia	52

Source: U.S. Department of Transportation, National Highway Traffic Safety Administration
"Traffic Safety Facts 2002, Alcohol" (http://www-nrd.nhtsa.dot.gov/pdf/nrd-30/NCSA/TSF2002/2002alcfacts.pdf)
*Drivers with Blood Alcohol Content (BAC) of .01 or more. "Legally Drunk" BAC differs from state to state but is often .08 or higher.

Licensed Drivers in 2002

National Total = 194,295,633 Licensed Drivers

<u>ALPHA ORDER</u>

RANK	STATE	DRIVERS	% of USA
19	Alabama	3,577,986	1.8%
48	Alaska	480,295	0.2%
18	Arizona	3,668,326	1.9%
31	Arkansas	1,965,008	1.0%
1	California	22,394,800	11.5%
23	Colorado	3,165,815	1.6%
27	Connecticut	2,672,145	1.4%
45	Delaware	573,021	0.3%
3	Florida	12,744,055	6.6%
9	Georgia	6,012,847	3.1%
42	Hawaii	814,668	0.4%
41	Idaho	907,029	0.5%
6	Illinois	8,033,399	4.1%
15	Indiana	4,221,123	2.2%
30	Iowa	1,992,803	1.0%
32	Kansas	1,935,361	1.0%
26	Kentucky	2,772,674	1.4%
22	Louisiana	3,168,238	1.6%
40	Maine	948,748	0.5%
21	Maryland	3,523,311	1.8%
13	Massachusetts	4,686,416	2.4%
8	Michigan	7,025,357	3.6%
24	Minnesota	2,997,058	1.5%
33	Mississippi	1,861,496	1.0%
17	Missouri	3,931,448	2.0%
44	Montana	694,743	0.4%
37	Nebraska	1,275,206	0.7%
35	Nevada	1,460,903	0.8%
39	New Hampshire	954,910	0.5%
11	New Jersey	5,711,794	2.9%
38	New Mexico	1,243,894	0.6%
4	New York	10,913,850	5.6%
10	North Carolina	5,943,288	3.1%
49	North Dakota	461,090	0.2%
7	Ohio	7,707,870	4.0%
29	Oklahoma	2,324,442	1.2%
28	Oregon	2,563,529	1.3%
5	Pennsylvania	8,323,741	4.3%
43	Rhode Island	720,550	0.4%
25	South Carolina	2,918,957	1.5%
46	South Dakota	546,386	0.3%
16	Tennessee	4,205,933	2.2%
2	Texas	13,184,629	6.8%
34	Utah	1,529,934	0.8%
47	Vermont	529,453	0.3%
12	Virginia	5,158,232	2.7%
14	Washington	4,381,417	2.3%
36	West Virginia	1,325,029	0.7%
20	Wisconsin	3,529,720	1.8%
50	Wyoming	303,357	0.2%

<u>RANK ORDER</u>

RANK	STATE	DRIVERS	% of USA
1	California	22,394,800	11.5%
2	Texas	13,184,629	6.8%
3	Florida	12,744,055	6.6%
4	New York	10,913,850	5.6%
5	Pennsylvania	8,323,741	4.3%
6	Illinois	8,033,399	4.1%
7	Ohio	7,707,870	4.0%
8	Michigan	7,025,357	3.6%
9	Georgia	6,012,847	3.1%
10	North Carolina	5,943,288	3.1%
11	New Jersey	5,711,794	2.9%
12	Virginia	5,158,232	2.7%
13	Massachusetts	4,686,416	2.4%
14	Washington	4,381,417	2.3%
15	Indiana	4,221,123	2.2%
16	Tennessee	4,205,933	2.2%
17	Missouri	3,931,448	2.0%
18	Arizona	3,668,326	1.9%
19	Alabama	3,577,986	1.8%
20	Wisconsin	3,529,720	1.8%
21	Maryland	3,523,311	1.8%
22	Louisiana	3,168,238	1.6%
23	Colorado	3,165,815	1.6%
24	Minnesota	2,997,058	1.5%
25	South Carolina	2,918,957	1.5%
26	Kentucky	2,772,674	1.4%
27	Connecticut	2,672,145	1.4%
28	Oregon	2,563,529	1.3%
29	Oklahoma	2,324,442	1.2%
30	Iowa	1,992,803	1.0%
31	Arkansas	1,965,008	1.0%
32	Kansas	1,935,361	1.0%
33	Mississippi	1,861,496	1.0%
34	Utah	1,529,934	0.8%
35	Nevada	1,460,903	0.8%
36	West Virginia	1,325,029	0.7%
37	Nebraska	1,275,206	0.7%
38	New Mexico	1,243,894	0.6%
39	New Hampshire	954,910	0.5%
40	Maine	948,748	0.5%
41	Idaho	907,029	0.5%
42	Hawaii	814,668	0.4%
43	Rhode Island	720,550	0.4%
44	Montana	694,743	0.4%
45	Delaware	573,021	0.3%
46	South Dakota	546,386	0.3%
47	Vermont	529,453	0.3%
48	Alaska	480,295	0.2%
49	North Dakota	461,090	0.2%
50	Wyoming	303,357	0.2%
	District of Columbia	309,349	0.2%

Source: U.S. Department of Transportation, Federal Highway Administration
"Highway Statistics 2002" (Table DL-1C)

Licensed Drivers per 1,000 Driving Age Population in 2002

National Ratio = 869 Licensed Drivers

<u>ALPHA ORDER</u>

RANK	STATE	RATIO
2	Alabama	1,020
3	Alaska	1,012
30	Arizona	887
9	Arkansas	931
41	California	840
21	Colorado	909
4	Connecticut	996
27	Delaware	896
6	Florida	961
16	Georgia	920
44	Hawaii	830
28	Idaho	894
45	Illinois	828
29	Indiana	890
35	Iowa	857
15	Kansas	921
38	Kentucky	848
14	Louisiana	922
25	Maine	902
43	Maryland	833
18	Massachusetts	914
23	Michigan	904
49	Minnesota	765
40	Mississippi	847
31	Missouri	885
5	Montana	962
8	Nebraska	950
32	Nevada	881
7	New Hampshire	951
36	New Jersey	854
33	New Mexico	880
50	New York	725
17	North Carolina	919
19	North Dakota	910
34	Ohio	869
36	Oklahoma	854
10	Oregon	927
38	Pennsylvania	848
41	Rhode Island	840
26	South Carolina	901
11	South Dakota	926
13	Tennessee	924
47	Texas	807
19	Utah	910
1	Vermont	1,069
24	Virginia	903
11	Washington	926
22	West Virginia	907
46	Wisconsin	827
48	Wyoming	772

<u>RANK ORDER</u>

RANK	STATE	RATIO
1	Vermont	1,069
2	Alabama	1,020
3	Alaska	1,012
4	Connecticut	996
5	Montana	962
6	Florida	961
7	New Hampshire	951
8	Nebraska	950
9	Arkansas	931
10	Oregon	927
11	South Dakota	926
11	Washington	926
13	Tennessee	924
14	Louisiana	922
15	Kansas	921
16	Georgia	920
17	North Carolina	919
18	Massachusetts	914
19	North Dakota	910
19	Utah	910
21	Colorado	909
22	West Virginia	907
23	Michigan	904
24	Virginia	903
25	Maine	902
26	South Carolina	901
27	Delaware	896
28	Idaho	894
29	Indiana	890
30	Arizona	887
31	Missouri	885
32	Nevada	881
33	New Mexico	880
34	Ohio	869
35	Iowa	857
36	New Jersey	854
36	Oklahoma	854
38	Kentucky	848
38	Pennsylvania	848
40	Mississippi	847
41	California	840
41	Rhode Island	840
43	Maryland	833
44	Hawaii	830
45	Illinois	828
46	Wisconsin	827
47	Texas	807
48	Wyoming	772
49	Minnesota	765
50	New York	725
	District of Columbia	659

Source: U.S. Department of Transportation, Federal Highway Administration
"Highway Statistics 2002" (Table DL-1C)

Motor Vehicle Registrations in 2002

National Total = 229,619,979 Motor Vehicles*

ALPHA ORDER

RANK	STATE	VEHICLES	% of USA
19	Alabama	4,427,999	1.9%
48	Alaska	620,415	0.3%
21	Arizona	3,939,581	1.7%
33	Arkansas	1,872,750	0.8%
1	California	29,618,605	12.9%
31	Colorado	2,150,556	0.9%
29	Connecticut	2,914,831	1.3%
47	Delaware	674,143	0.3%
3	Florida	13,963,596	6.1%
9	Georgia	7,647,523	3.3%
43	Hawaii	892,553	0.4%
38	Idaho	1,385,820	0.6%
6	Illinois	9,577,222	4.2%
13	Indiana	5,664,726	2.5%
25	Iowa	3,310,408	1.4%
30	Kansas	2,336,701	1.0%
24	Kentucky	3,600,752	1.6%
23	Louisiana	3,660,324	1.6%
42	Maine	967,583	0.4%
22	Maryland	3,883,925	1.7%
14	Massachusetts	5,406,846	2.4%
8	Michigan	8,533,635	3.7%
18	Minnesota	4,520,314	2.0%
32	Mississippi	1,954,776	0.9%
20	Missouri	4,235,031	1.8%
41	Montana	1,056,143	0.5%
35	Nebraska	1,655,603	0.7%
39	Nevada	1,252,879	0.5%
40	New Hampshire	1,143,231	0.5%
10	New Jersey	6,687,918	2.9%
36	New Mexico	1,538,284	0.7%
5	New York	10,455,697	4.6%
12	North Carolina	6,149,474	2.7%
46	North Dakota	698,424	0.3%
4	Ohio	10,469,719	4.6%
27	Oklahoma	3,070,954	1.3%
28	Oregon	3,069,310	1.3%
7	Pennsylvania	9,524,997	4.1%
45	Rhode Island	775,725	0.3%
26	South Carolina	3,202,102	1.4%
44	South Dakota	813,908	0.4%
16	Tennessee	4,776,520	2.1%
2	Texas	14,664,328	6.4%
34	Utah	1,847,173	0.8%
50	Vermont	537,146	0.2%
11	Virginia	6,272,836	2.7%
15	Washington	5,336,326	2.3%
37	West Virginia	1,462,983	0.6%
17	Wisconsin	4,557,200	2.0%
49	Wyoming	602,935	0.3%

RANK ORDER

RANK	STATE	VEHICLES	% of USA
1	California	29,618,605	12.9%
2	Texas	14,664,328	6.4%
3	Florida	13,963,596	6.1%
4	Ohio	10,469,719	4.6%
5	New York	10,455,697	4.6%
6	Illinois	9,577,222	4.2%
7	Pennsylvania	9,524,997	4.1%
8	Michigan	8,533,635	3.7%
9	Georgia	7,647,523	3.3%
10	New Jersey	6,687,918	2.9%
11	Virginia	6,272,836	2.7%
12	North Carolina	6,149,474	2.7%
13	Indiana	5,664,726	2.5%
14	Massachusetts	5,406,846	2.4%
15	Washington	5,336,326	2.3%
16	Tennessee	4,776,520	2.1%
17	Wisconsin	4,557,200	2.0%
18	Minnesota	4,520,314	2.0%
19	Alabama	4,427,999	1.9%
20	Missouri	4,235,031	1.8%
21	Arizona	3,939,581	1.7%
22	Maryland	3,883,925	1.7%
23	Louisiana	3,660,324	1.6%
24	Kentucky	3,600,752	1.6%
25	Iowa	3,310,408	1.4%
26	South Carolina	3,202,102	1.4%
27	Oklahoma	3,070,954	1.3%
28	Oregon	3,069,310	1.3%
29	Connecticut	2,914,831	1.3%
30	Kansas	2,336,701	1.0%
31	Colorado	2,150,556	0.9%
32	Mississippi	1,954,776	0.9%
33	Arkansas	1,872,750	0.8%
34	Utah	1,847,173	0.8%
35	Nebraska	1,655,603	0.7%
36	New Mexico	1,538,284	0.7%
37	West Virginia	1,462,983	0.6%
38	Idaho	1,385,820	0.6%
39	Nevada	1,252,879	0.5%
40	New Hampshire	1,143,231	0.5%
41	Montana	1,056,143	0.5%
42	Maine	967,583	0.4%
43	Hawaii	892,553	0.4%
44	South Dakota	813,908	0.4%
45	Rhode Island	775,725	0.3%
46	North Dakota	698,424	0.3%
47	Delaware	674,143	0.3%
48	Alaska	620,415	0.3%
49	Wyoming	602,935	0.3%
50	Vermont	537,146	0.2%
	District of Columbia	237,549	0.1%

*Source: U.S. Department of Transportation, Federal Highway Administration
    "Highway Statistics 2002" (Table MV-1)*
Includes automobiles, trucks and buses. Does not include motorcycles.

Motor Vehicles per Driving Age Population in 2002

National Rate = 1.03 Motor Vehicles*

ALPHA ORDER

RANK	STATE	RATE
8	Alabama	1.26
7	Alaska	1.31
38	Arizona	0.95
46	Arkansas	0.89
17	California	1.11
50	Colorado	0.62
24	Connecticut	1.09
29	Delaware	1.05
29	Florida	1.05
12	Georgia	1.17
43	Hawaii	0.91
6	Idaho	1.37
35	Illinois	0.99
10	Indiana	1.19
3	Iowa	1.42
17	Kansas	1.11
20	Kentucky	1.10
28	Louisiana	1.06
41	Maine	0.92
41	Maryland	0.92
29	Massachusetts	1.05
20	Michigan	1.10
13	Minnesota	1.15
46	Mississippi	0.89
38	Missouri	0.95
2	Montana	1.46
9	Nebraska	1.23
48	Nevada	0.76
14	New Hampshire	1.14
33	New Jersey	1.00
24	New Mexico	1.09
49	New York	0.69
38	North Carolina	0.95
4	North Dakota	1.38
11	Ohio	1.18
15	Oklahoma	1.13
17	Oregon	1.11
37	Pennsylvania	0.97
44	Rhode Island	0.90
35	South Carolina	0.99
4	South Dakota	1.38
29	Tennessee	1.05
44	Texas	0.90
20	Utah	1.10
26	Vermont	1.08
20	Virginia	1.10
15	Washington	1.13
33	West Virginia	1.00
27	Wisconsin	1.07
1	Wyoming	1.53

RANK ORDER

RANK	STATE	RATE
1	Wyoming	1.53
2	Montana	1.46
3	Iowa	1.42
4	North Dakota	1.38
4	South Dakota	1.38
6	Idaho	1.37
7	Alaska	1.31
8	Alabama	1.26
9	Nebraska	1.23
10	Indiana	1.19
11	Ohio	1.18
12	Georgia	1.17
13	Minnesota	1.15
14	New Hampshire	1.14
15	Oklahoma	1.13
15	Washington	1.13
17	California	1.11
17	Kansas	1.11
17	Oregon	1.11
20	Kentucky	1.10
20	Michigan	1.10
20	Utah	1.10
20	Virginia	1.10
24	Connecticut	1.09
24	New Mexico	1.09
26	Vermont	1.08
27	Wisconsin	1.07
28	Louisiana	1.06
29	Delaware	1.05
29	Florida	1.05
29	Massachusetts	1.05
29	Tennessee	1.05
33	New Jersey	1.00
33	West Virginia	1.00
35	Illinois	0.99
35	South Carolina	0.99
37	Pennsylvania	0.97
38	Arizona	0.95
38	Missouri	0.95
38	North Carolina	0.95
41	Maine	0.92
41	Maryland	0.92
43	Hawaii	0.91
44	Rhode Island	0.90
44	Texas	0.90
46	Arkansas	0.89
46	Mississippi	0.89
48	Nevada	0.76
49	New York	0.69
50	Colorado	0.62
	District of Columbia	0.51

Source: Morgan Quitno Press using data from U.S. Department of Transportation, Federal Highway Administration
"Highway Statistics 2002" (Table MV-1)
*Persons age 16 and older. Motor Vehicles include automobiles, trucks and buses. Motorcycles are not included.

Automobile Registrations in 2002

National Total = 135,920,677 Automobiles*

<u>ALPHA ORDER</u>

RANK	STATE	AUTOMOBILES	% of USA
27	Alabama	1,801,678	1.3%
49	Alaska	255,217	0.2%
21	Arizona	2,237,596	1.6%
32	Arkansas	960,263	0.7%
1	California	18,449,629	13.6%
33	Colorado	956,817	0.7%
23	Connecticut	2,026,792	1.5%
45	Delaware	416,503	0.3%
2	Florida	8,471,458	6.2%
10	Georgia	4,211,547	3.1%
43	Hawaii	532,348	0.4%
40	Idaho	598,116	0.4%
6	Illinois	6,099,582	4.5%
14	Indiana	3,216,400	2.4%
26	Iowa	1,861,830	1.4%
34	Kansas	843,199	0.6%
22	Kentucky	2,087,841	1.5%
24	Louisiana	1,988,568	1.5%
41	Maine	583,361	0.4%
18	Maryland	2,523,020	1.9%
13	Massachusetts	3,636,333	2.7%
8	Michigan	4,874,315	3.6%
19	Minnesota	2,503,849	1.8%
30	Mississippi	1,136,337	0.8%
20	Missouri	2,481,695	1.8%
44	Montana	466,043	0.3%
35	Nebraska	841,430	0.6%
39	Nevada	650,178	0.5%
38	New Hampshire	681,842	0.5%
9	New Jersey	4,502,809	3.3%
37	New Mexico	715,474	0.5%
3	New York	7,924,325	5.8%
12	North Carolina	3,687,139	2.7%
47	North Dakota	348,075	0.3%
5	Ohio	6,553,274	4.8%
28	Oklahoma	1,621,817	1.2%
29	Oregon	1,559,986	1.1%
7	Pennsylvania	6,072,248	4.5%
42	Rhode Island	538,771	0.4%
25	South Carolina	1,959,711	1.4%
46	South Dakota	389,260	0.3%
16	Tennessee	2,805,063	2.1%
4	Texas	7,808,911	5.7%
31	Utah	968,327	0.7%
48	Vermont	298,388	0.2%
11	Virginia	4,011,475	3.0%
15	Washington	2,979,789	2.2%
36	West Virginia	782,397	0.6%
17	Wisconsin	2,586,648	1.9%
50	Wyoming	220,408	0.2%

<u>RANK ORDER</u>

RANK	STATE	AUTOMOBILES	% of USA
1	California	18,449,629	13.6%
2	Florida	8,471,458	6.2%
3	New York	7,924,325	5.8%
4	Texas	7,808,911	5.7%
5	Ohio	6,553,274	4.8%
6	Illinois	6,099,582	4.5%
7	Pennsylvania	6,072,248	4.5%
8	Michigan	4,874,315	3.6%
9	New Jersey	4,502,809	3.3%
10	Georgia	4,211,547	3.1%
11	Virginia	4,011,475	3.0%
12	North Carolina	3,687,139	2.7%
13	Massachusetts	3,636,333	2.7%
14	Indiana	3,216,400	2.4%
15	Washington	2,979,789	2.2%
16	Tennessee	2,805,063	2.1%
17	Wisconsin	2,586,648	1.9%
18	Maryland	2,523,020	1.9%
19	Minnesota	2,503,849	1.8%
20	Missouri	2,481,695	1.8%
21	Arizona	2,237,596	1.6%
22	Kentucky	2,087,841	1.5%
23	Connecticut	2,026,792	1.5%
24	Louisiana	1,988,568	1.5%
25	South Carolina	1,959,711	1.4%
26	Iowa	1,861,830	1.4%
27	Alabama	1,801,678	1.3%
28	Oklahoma	1,621,817	1.2%
29	Oregon	1,559,986	1.1%
30	Mississippi	1,136,337	0.8%
31	Utah	968,327	0.7%
32	Arkansas	960,263	0.7%
33	Colorado	956,817	0.7%
34	Kansas	843,199	0.6%
35	Nebraska	841,430	0.6%
36	West Virginia	782,397	0.6%
37	New Mexico	715,474	0.5%
38	New Hampshire	681,842	0.5%
39	Nevada	650,178	0.5%
40	Idaho	598,116	0.4%
41	Maine	583,361	0.4%
42	Rhode Island	538,771	0.4%
43	Hawaii	532,348	0.4%
44	Montana	466,043	0.3%
45	Delaware	416,503	0.3%
46	South Dakota	389,260	0.3%
47	North Dakota	348,075	0.3%
48	Vermont	298,388	0.2%
49	Alaska	255,217	0.2%
50	Wyoming	220,408	0.2%
	District of Columbia	192,595	0.1%

Source: U.S. Department of Transportation, Federal Highway Administration
"Highway Statistics 2002" (Table MV-1)
*"Automobiles" formerly included personal passenger vans, minivans and sports-utility vehicles. These now are counted as trucks.

Bus Registrations in 2002

National Total = 760,717 Buses*

ALPHA ORDER

RANK	STATE	BUSES	% of USA
28	Alabama	8,894	1.2%
44	Alaska	2,250	0.3%
34	Arizona	4,728	0.6%
30	Arkansas	7,331	1.0%
3	California	50,322	6.6%
32	Colorado	5,864	0.8%
25	Connecticut	10,382	1.4%
46	Delaware	2,018	0.3%
4	Florida	46,130	6.1%
12	Georgia	19,072	2.5%
33	Hawaii	4,769	0.6%
36	Idaho	3,801	0.5%
14	Illinois	17,991	2.4%
8	Indiana	29,057	3.8%
29	Iowa	8,320	1.1%
35	Kansas	3,886	0.5%
20	Kentucky	13,742	1.8%
11	Louisiana	20,187	2.7%
39	Maine	2,928	0.4%
22	Maryland	11,945	1.6%
24	Massachusetts	11,398	1.5%
9	Michigan	26,329	3.5%
18	Minnesota	15,107	2.0%
27	Mississippi	9,255	1.2%
23	Missouri	11,806	1.6%
41	Montana	2,841	0.4%
31	Nebraska	6,456	0.8%
47	Nevada	1,834	0.2%
48	New Hampshire	1,796	0.2%
10	New Jersey	22,483	3.0%
37	New Mexico	3,545	0.5%
2	New York	58,733	7.7%
7	North Carolina	31,518	4.1%
43	North Dakota	2,438	0.3%
5	Ohio	39,294	5.2%
15	Oklahoma	17,253	2.3%
21	Oregon	13,603	1.8%
6	Pennsylvania	36,515	4.8%
49	Rhode Island	1,769	0.2%
16	South Carolina	17,046	2.2%
42	South Dakota	2,678	0.4%
17	Tennessee	16,948	2.2%
1	Texas	81,999	10.8%
50	Utah	1,273	0.2%
45	Vermont	2,145	0.3%
13	Virginia	18,022	2.4%
26	Washington	9,893	1.3%
38	West Virginia	3,038	0.4%
19	Wisconsin	14,510	1.9%
40	Wyoming	2,869	0.4%

RANK ORDER

RANK	STATE	BUSES	% of USA
1	Texas	81,999	10.8%
2	New York	58,733	7.7%
3	California	50,322	6.6%
4	Florida	46,130	6.1%
5	Ohio	39,294	5.2%
6	Pennsylvania	36,515	4.8%
7	North Carolina	31,518	4.1%
8	Indiana	29,057	3.8%
9	Michigan	26,329	3.5%
10	New Jersey	22,483	3.0%
11	Louisiana	20,187	2.7%
12	Georgia	19,072	2.5%
13	Virginia	18,022	2.4%
14	Illinois	17,991	2.4%
15	Oklahoma	17,253	2.3%
16	South Carolina	17,046	2.2%
17	Tennessee	16,948	2.2%
18	Minnesota	15,107	2.0%
19	Wisconsin	14,510	1.9%
20	Kentucky	13,742	1.8%
21	Oregon	13,603	1.8%
22	Maryland	11,945	1.6%
23	Missouri	11,806	1.6%
24	Massachusetts	11,398	1.5%
25	Connecticut	10,382	1.4%
26	Washington	9,893	1.3%
27	Mississippi	9,255	1.2%
28	Alabama	8,894	1.2%
29	Iowa	8,320	1.1%
30	Arkansas	7,331	1.0%
31	Nebraska	6,456	0.8%
32	Colorado	5,864	0.8%
33	Hawaii	4,769	0.6%
34	Arizona	4,728	0.6%
35	Kansas	3,886	0.5%
36	Idaho	3,801	0.5%
37	New Mexico	3,545	0.5%
38	West Virginia	3,038	0.4%
39	Maine	2,928	0.4%
40	Wyoming	2,869	0.4%
41	Montana	2,841	0.4%
42	South Dakota	2,678	0.4%
43	North Dakota	2,438	0.3%
44	Alaska	2,250	0.3%
45	Vermont	2,145	0.3%
46	Delaware	2,018	0.3%
47	Nevada	1,834	0.2%
48	New Hampshire	1,796	0.2%
49	Rhode Island	1,769	0.2%
50	Utah	1,273	0.2%
	District of Columbia	2,706	0.4%

*Source: U.S. Department of Transportation, Federal Highway Administration
"Highway Statistics 2002" (Table MV-1)*
Includes private, commercial and publicly-owned buses.

Truck Registrations in 2002

National Total = 92,938,585 Trucks*

<u>ALPHA ORDER</u>

RANK	STATE	TRUCKS	% of USA
9	Alabama	2,617,427	2.8%
45	Alaska	362,948	0.4%
21	Arizona	1,697,257	1.8%
31	Arkansas	905,156	1.0%
1	California	11,118,654	12.0%
30	Colorado	1,187,875	1.3%
32	Connecticut	877,657	0.9%
48	Delaware	255,622	0.3%
3	Florida	5,446,008	5.9%
7	Georgia	3,416,904	3.7%
46	Hawaii	355,436	0.4%
37	Idaho	783,903	0.8%
6	Illinois	3,459,649	3.7%
12	Indiana	2,419,269	2.6%
26	Iowa	1,440,258	1.5%
25	Kansas	1,489,616	1.6%
23	Kentucky	1,499,169	1.6%
22	Louisiana	1,651,569	1.8%
43	Maine	381,294	0.4%
28	Maryland	1,348,960	1.5%
19	Massachusetts	1,759,115	1.9%
5	Michigan	3,632,991	3.9%
16	Minnesota	2,001,358	2.2%
35	Mississippi	809,184	0.9%
20	Missouri	1,741,530	1.9%
40	Montana	587,259	0.6%
36	Nebraska	807,717	0.9%
39	Nevada	600,867	0.6%
41	New Hampshire	459,593	0.5%
15	New Jersey	2,162,626	2.3%
34	New Mexico	819,265	0.9%
10	New York	2,472,639	2.7%
11	North Carolina	2,430,817	2.6%
47	North Dakota	347,911	0.4%
4	Ohio	3,877,151	4.2%
27	Oklahoma	1,431,884	1.5%
24	Oregon	1,495,721	1.6%
8	Pennsylvania	3,416,234	3.7%
50	Rhode Island	235,185	0.3%
29	South Carolina	1,225,345	1.3%
42	South Dakota	421,970	0.5%
18	Tennessee	1,954,509	2.1%
2	Texas	6,773,418	7.3%
33	Utah	877,573	0.9%
49	Vermont	236,613	0.3%
14	Virginia	2,243,339	2.4%
13	Washington	2,346,644	2.5%
38	West Virginia	677,548	0.7%
17	Wisconsin	1,956,042	2.1%
44	Wyoming	379,658	0.4%

<u>RANK ORDER</u>

RANK	STATE	TRUCKS	% of USA
1	California	11,118,654	12.0%
2	Texas	6,773,418	7.3%
3	Florida	5,446,008	5.9%
4	Ohio	3,877,151	4.2%
5	Michigan	3,632,991	3.9%
6	Illinois	3,459,649	3.7%
7	Georgia	3,416,904	3.7%
8	Pennsylvania	3,416,234	3.7%
9	Alabama	2,617,427	2.8%
10	New York	2,472,639	2.7%
11	North Carolina	2,430,817	2.6%
12	Indiana	2,419,269	2.6%
13	Washington	2,346,644	2.5%
14	Virginia	2,243,339	2.4%
15	New Jersey	2,162,626	2.3%
16	Minnesota	2,001,358	2.2%
17	Wisconsin	1,956,042	2.1%
18	Tennessee	1,954,509	2.1%
19	Massachusetts	1,759,115	1.9%
20	Missouri	1,741,530	1.9%
21	Arizona	1,697,257	1.8%
22	Louisiana	1,651,569	1.8%
23	Kentucky	1,499,169	1.6%
24	Oregon	1,495,721	1.6%
25	Kansas	1,489,616	1.6%
26	Iowa	1,440,258	1.5%
27	Oklahoma	1,431,884	1.5%
28	Maryland	1,348,960	1.5%
29	South Carolina	1,225,345	1.3%
30	Colorado	1,187,875	1.3%
31	Arkansas	905,156	1.0%
32	Connecticut	877,657	0.9%
33	Utah	877,573	0.9%
34	New Mexico	819,265	0.9%
35	Mississippi	809,184	0.9%
36	Nebraska	807,717	0.9%
37	Idaho	783,903	0.8%
38	West Virginia	677,548	0.7%
39	Nevada	600,867	0.6%
40	Montana	587,259	0.6%
41	New Hampshire	459,593	0.5%
42	South Dakota	421,970	0.5%
43	Maine	381,294	0.4%
44	Wyoming	379,658	0.4%
45	Alaska	362,948	0.4%
46	Hawaii	355,436	0.4%
47	North Dakota	347,911	0.4%
48	Delaware	255,622	0.3%
49	Vermont	236,613	0.3%
50	Rhode Island	235,185	0.3%
	District of Columbia	42,248	0.0%

Source: U.S. Department of Transportation, Federal Highway Administration
   "Highway Statistics 2002" (Table MV-1)
**"Trucks" include personal passenger vans, minivans and sports-utility vehicles. These were formerly classified as "automobiles."*

Motorcycle Registrations in 2002

National Total = 5,004,156 Motorcycles*

<u>ALPHA ORDER</u>

RANK	STATE	MOTORCYCLES	% of USA
26	Alabama	62,010	1.2%
47	Alaska	18,173	0.4%
7	Arizona	219,105	4.4%
36	Arkansas	34,101	0.7%
1	California	535,424	10.7%
50	Colorado	1,201	0.0%
25	Connecticut	62,061	1.2%
49	Delaware	13,820	0.3%
2	Florida	345,490	6.9%
17	Georgia	109,024	2.2%
46	Hawaii	20,584	0.4%
32	Idaho	42,703	0.9%
6	Illinois	232,187	4.6%
13	Indiana	135,552	2.7%
12	Iowa	140,544	2.8%
30	Kansas	53,687	1.1%
31	Kentucky	48,508	1.0%
29	Louisiana	53,935	1.1%
38	Maine	31,021	0.6%
28	Maryland	56,823	1.1%
16	Massachusetts	129,663	2.6%
8	Michigan	204,805	4.1%
10	Minnesota	158,516	3.2%
41	Mississippi	27,037	0.5%
23	Missouri	64,179	1.3%
40	Montana	29,748	0.6%
43	Nebraska	25,349	0.5%
34	Nevada	35,898	0.7%
27	New Hampshire	57,389	1.1%
15	New Jersey	134,034	2.7%
35	New Mexico	34,467	0.7%
11	New York	142,790	2.9%
18	North Carolina	91,063	1.8%
48	North Dakota	17,865	0.4%
3	Ohio	271,112	5.4%
22	Oklahoma	66,838	1.3%
20	Oregon	74,453	1.5%
4	Pennsylvania	249,916	5.0%
45	Rhode Island	23,009	0.5%
24	South Carolina	62,726	1.3%
37	South Dakota	33,935	0.7%
19	Tennessee	84,334	1.7%
5	Texas	234,922	4.7%
33	Utah	41,421	0.8%
42	Vermont	26,527	0.5%
21	Virginia	70,139	1.4%
14	Washington	134,212	2.7%
39	West Virginia	30,868	0.6%
9	Wisconsin	204,732	4.1%
44	Wyoming	24,791	0.5%

<u>RANK ORDER</u>

RANK	STATE	MOTORCYCLES	% of USA
1	California	535,424	10.7%
2	Florida	345,490	6.9%
3	Ohio	271,112	5.4%
4	Pennsylvania	249,916	5.0%
5	Texas	234,922	4.7%
6	Illinois	232,187	4.6%
7	Arizona	219,105	4.4%
8	Michigan	204,805	4.1%
9	Wisconsin	204,732	4.1%
10	Minnesota	158,516	3.2%
11	New York	142,790	2.9%
12	Iowa	140,544	2.8%
13	Indiana	135,552	2.7%
14	Washington	134,212	2.7%
15	New Jersey	134,034	2.7%
16	Massachusetts	129,663	2.6%
17	Georgia	109,024	2.2%
18	North Carolina	91,063	1.8%
19	Tennessee	84,334	1.7%
20	Oregon	74,453	1.5%
21	Virginia	70,139	1.4%
22	Oklahoma	66,838	1.3%
23	Missouri	64,179	1.3%
24	South Carolina	62,726	1.3%
25	Connecticut	62,061	1.2%
26	Alabama	62,010	1.2%
27	New Hampshire	57,389	1.1%
28	Maryland	56,823	1.1%
29	Louisiana	53,935	1.1%
30	Kansas	53,687	1.1%
31	Kentucky	48,508	1.0%
32	Idaho	42,703	0.9%
33	Utah	41,421	0.8%
34	Nevada	35,898	0.7%
35	New Mexico	34,467	0.7%
36	Arkansas	34,101	0.7%
37	South Dakota	33,935	0.7%
38	Maine	31,021	0.6%
39	West Virginia	30,868	0.6%
40	Montana	29,748	0.6%
41	Mississippi	27,037	0.5%
42	Vermont	26,527	0.5%
43	Nebraska	25,349	0.5%
44	Wyoming	24,791	0.5%
45	Rhode Island	23,009	0.5%
46	Hawaii	20,584	0.4%
47	Alaska	18,173	0.4%
48	North Dakota	17,865	0.4%
49	Delaware	13,820	0.3%
50	Colorado	1,201	0.0%
	District of Columbia	1,465	0.0%

Source: Morgan Quitno Press using data from U.S. Department of Transportation, Federal Highway Administration
"Highway Statistics 2002" (Table MV-1)
*Includes private, commercial and publicly-owned motorcycles.

Average Travel Time to Work in 2002

National Average = 24.4 Minutes*

<u>ALPHA ORDER</u>

RANK	STATE	MINUTES
20	Alabama	23.1
43	Alaska	18.3
17	Arizona	23.2
41	Arkansas	19.9
5	California	26.6
20	Colorado	23.1
17	Connecticut	23.2
25	Delaware	22.7
12	Florida	24.8
6	Georgia	26.5
10	Hawaii	25.4
36	Idaho	20.9
4	Illinois	26.7
35	Indiana	21.2
44	Iowa	18.1
45	Kansas	17.7
25	Kentucky	22.7
20	Louisiana	23.1
28	Maine	22.3
2	Maryland	30.0
8	Massachusetts	25.8
27	Michigan	22.4
32	Minnesota	21.7
31	Mississippi	21.9
17	Missouri	23.2
47	Montana	16.7
48	Nebraska	16.1
32	Nevada	21.7
11	New Hampshire	24.9
3	New Jersey	28.3
37	New Mexico	20.6
1	New York	30.8
24	North Carolina	23.0
50	North Dakota	14.8
30	Ohio	22.0
42	Oklahoma	19.8
34	Oregon	21.5
14	Pennsylvania	23.9
29	Rhode Island	22.2
16	South Carolina	23.4
49	South Dakota	15.0
20	Tennessee	23.1
14	Texas	23.9
40	Utah	20.2
37	Vermont	20.6
9	Virginia	25.7
13	Washington	24.4
7	West Virginia	25.9
39	Wisconsin	20.3
46	Wyoming	17.6

<u>RANK ORDER</u>

RANK	STATE	MINUTES
1	New York	30.8
2	Maryland	30.0
3	New Jersey	28.3
4	Illinois	26.7
5	California	26.6
6	Georgia	26.5
7	West Virginia	25.9
8	Massachusetts	25.8
9	Virginia	25.7
10	Hawaii	25.4
11	New Hampshire	24.9
12	Florida	24.8
13	Washington	24.4
14	Pennsylvania	23.9
14	Texas	23.9
16	South Carolina	23.4
17	Arizona	23.2
17	Connecticut	23.2
17	Missouri	23.2
20	Alabama	23.1
20	Colorado	23.1
20	Louisiana	23.1
20	Tennessee	23.1
24	North Carolina	23.0
25	Delaware	22.7
25	Kentucky	22.7
27	Michigan	22.4
28	Maine	22.3
29	Rhode Island	22.2
30	Ohio	22.0
31	Mississippi	21.9
32	Minnesota	21.7
32	Nevada	21.7
34	Oregon	21.5
35	Indiana	21.2
36	Idaho	20.9
37	New Mexico	20.6
37	Vermont	20.6
39	Wisconsin	20.3
40	Utah	20.2
41	Arkansas	19.9
42	Oklahoma	19.8
43	Alaska	18.3
44	Iowa	18.1
45	Kansas	17.7
46	Wyoming	17.6
47	Montana	16.7
48	Nebraska	16.1
49	South Dakota	15.0
50	North Dakota	14.8
	District of Columbia	29.4

Source: U.S. Bureau of the Census
   "2002 American Community Survey"
Workers 16 and older.

Annual Miles per Vehicle in 2002

National Annual Average = 12,437 Miles*

ALPHA ORDER

RANK	STATE	MILES
22	Alabama	12,989
50	Alaska	7,891
20	Arizona	13,030
5	Arkansas	16,062
37	California	10,836
1	Colorado	20,248
38	Connecticut	10,706
19	Delaware	13,165
25	Florida	12,774
15	Georgia	14,164
46	Hawaii	9,956
45	Idaho	10,223
34	Illinois	11,005
24	Indiana	12,803
49	Iowa	9,318
28	Kansas	12,172
21	Kentucky	13,009
30	Louisiana	11,828
6	Maine	15,220
16	Maryland	13,827
47	Massachusetts	9,852
31	Michigan	11,735
29	Minnesota	12,070
2	Mississippi	18,636
4	Missouri	16,095
48	Montana	9,842
32	Nebraska	11,306
13	Nevada	14,340
35	New Hampshire	11,002
41	New Jersey	10,458
11	New Mexico	14,815
26	New York	12,726
7	North Carolina	15,106
39	North Dakota	10,504
43	Ohio	10,302
10	Oklahoma	14,891
33	Oregon	11,266
36	Pennsylvania	10,969
40	Rhode Island	10,496
12	South Carolina	14,768
42	South Dakota	10,442
14	Tennessee	14,284
8	Texas	15,072
18	Utah	13,298
3	Vermont	18,016
27	Virginia	12,347
44	Washington	10,265
17	West Virginia	13,674
23	Wisconsin	12,891
9	Wyoming	14,939

RANK ORDER

RANK	STATE	MILES
1	Colorado	20,248
2	Mississippi	18,636
3	Vermont	18,016
4	Missouri	16,095
5	Arkansas	16,062
6	Maine	15,220
7	North Carolina	15,106
8	Texas	15,072
9	Wyoming	14,939
10	Oklahoma	14,891
11	New Mexico	14,815
12	South Carolina	14,768
13	Nevada	14,340
14	Tennessee	14,284
15	Georgia	14,164
16	Maryland	13,827
17	West Virginia	13,674
18	Utah	13,298
19	Delaware	13,165
20	Arizona	13,030
21	Kentucky	13,009
22	Alabama	12,989
23	Wisconsin	12,891
24	Indiana	12,803
25	Florida	12,774
26	New York	12,726
27	Virginia	12,347
28	Kansas	12,172
29	Minnesota	12,070
30	Louisiana	11,828
31	Michigan	11,735
32	Nebraska	11,306
33	Oregon	11,266
34	Illinois	11,005
35	New Hampshire	11,002
36	Pennsylvania	10,969
37	California	10,836
38	Connecticut	10,706
39	North Dakota	10,504
40	Rhode Island	10,496
41	New Jersey	10,458
42	South Dakota	10,442
43	Ohio	10,302
44	Washington	10,265
45	Idaho	10,223
46	Hawaii	9,956
47	Massachusetts	9,852
48	Montana	9,842
49	Iowa	9,318
50	Alaska	7,891
	District of Columbia	14,932

Source: Morgan Quitno Press using data from U.S. Department of Transportation, Federal Highway Administration
   "Highway Statistics 2002" (Tables MV-1 and VM-2)
*Includes automobiles, trucks, buses and motorcycles.

Average Miles per Gallon in 2002

National Average = 17.0 Miles per Gallon*

<u>ALPHA ORDER</u>

RANK	STATE	MILES PER GALLON
13	Alabama	17.9
50	Alaska	14.1
37	Arizona	15.8
41	Arkansas	15.4
16	California	17.7
24	Colorado	16.9
14	Connecticut	17.8
4	Delaware	18.8
2	Florida	19.7
20	Georgia	17.2
4	Hawaii	18.8
28	Idaho	16.7
30	Illinois	16.4
32	Indiana	16.3
44	Iowa	15.2
11	Kansas	18.1
38	Kentucky	15.7
41	Louisiana	15.4
23	Maine	17.0
14	Maryland	17.8
28	Massachusetts	16.7
24	Michigan	16.9
27	Minnesota	16.8
17	Mississippi	17.5
20	Missouri	17.2
43	Montana	15.3
39	Nebraska	15.5
49	Nevada	14.2
36	New Hampshire	15.9
48	New Jersey	14.5
20	New Mexico	17.2
3	New York	19.6
11	North Carolina	18.1
45	North Dakota	15.1
32	Ohio	16.3
9	Oklahoma	18.2
17	Oregon	17.5
35	Pennsylvania	16.1
8	Rhode Island	18.3
32	South Carolina	16.3
46	South Dakota	14.7
17	Tennessee	17.5
39	Texas	15.5
9	Utah	18.2
1	Vermont	24.1
30	Virginia	16.4
24	Washington	16.9
6	West Virginia	18.7
7	Wisconsin	18.6
47	Wyoming	14.6

<u>RANK ORDER</u>

RANK	STATE	MILES PER GALLON
1	Vermont	24.1
2	Florida	19.7
3	New York	19.6
4	Delaware	18.8
4	Hawaii	18.8
6	West Virginia	18.7
7	Wisconsin	18.6
8	Rhode Island	18.3
9	Oklahoma	18.2
9	Utah	18.2
11	Kansas	18.1
11	North Carolina	18.1
13	Alabama	17.9
14	Connecticut	17.8
14	Maryland	17.8
16	California	17.7
17	Mississippi	17.5
17	Oregon	17.5
17	Tennessee	17.5
20	Georgia	17.2
20	Missouri	17.2
20	New Mexico	17.2
23	Maine	17.0
24	Colorado	16.9
24	Michigan	16.9
24	Washington	16.9
27	Minnesota	16.8
28	Idaho	16.7
28	Massachusetts	16.7
30	Illinois	16.4
30	Virginia	16.4
32	Indiana	16.3
32	Ohio	16.3
32	South Carolina	16.3
35	Pennsylvania	16.1
36	New Hampshire	15.9
37	Arizona	15.8
38	Kentucky	15.7
39	Nebraska	15.5
39	Texas	15.5
41	Arkansas	15.4
41	Louisiana	15.4
43	Montana	15.3
44	Iowa	15.2
45	North Dakota	15.1
46	South Dakota	14.7
47	Wyoming	14.6
48	New Jersey	14.5
49	Nevada	14.2
50	Alaska	14.1

District of Columbia	21.1

Source: Morgan Quitno Press using data from U.S. Department of Transportation, Federal Highway Administration "Highway Statistics 2002"

*Total vehicle-miles for 2002 divided by total highway motor-fuel use. Includes gasoline, gasohol, diesel and other "special fuels."

Railroad Mileage Operated in 2001

National Total = 143,361 Miles of Railroad*

<u>ALPHA ORDER</u>

RANK	STATE	MILES	% of USA
17	Alabama	3,296	2.3%
46	Alaska	482	0.3%
35	Arizona	1,855	1.3%
29	Arkansas	2,607	1.8%
3	California	6,052	4.2%
23	Colorado	2,850	2.0%
44	Connecticut	635	0.4%
48	Delaware	227	0.2%
24	Florida	2,771	1.9%
7	Georgia	4,795	3.3%
50	Hawaii	0	0.0%
37	Idaho	1,642	1.1%
2	Illinois	7,197	5.0%
9	Indiana	4,185	2.9%
11	Iowa	4,091	2.9%
6	Kansas	5,084	3.5%
25	Kentucky	2,760	1.9%
26	Louisiana	2,753	1.9%
39	Maine	1,202	0.8%
43	Maryland	760	0.5%
41	Massachusetts	1,071	0.7%
14	Michigan	3,699	2.6%
8	Minnesota	4,504	3.1%
28	Mississippi	2,613	1.8%
10	Missouri	4,168	2.9%
18	Montana	3,293	2.3%
15	Nebraska	3,480	2.4%
40	Nevada	1,199	0.8%
47	New Hampshire	437	0.3%
42	New Jersey	922	0.6%
33	New Mexico	1,966	1.4%
13	New York	3,788	2.6%
21	North Carolina	3,251	2.3%
12	North Dakota	3,795	2.6%
4	Ohio	5,484	3.8%
19	Oklahoma	3,286	2.3%
32	Oregon	2,334	1.6%
5	Pennsylvania	5,145	3.6%
49	Rhode Island	102	0.1%
31	South Carolina	2,367	1.7%
36	South Dakota	1,768	1.2%
27	Tennessee	2,682	1.9%
1	Texas	10,473	7.3%
38	Utah	1,443	1.0%
45	Vermont	600	0.4%
20	Virginia	3,262	2.3%
22	Washington	3,145	2.2%
30	West Virginia	2,433	1.7%
16	Wisconsin	3,478	2.4%
34	Wyoming	1,904	1.3%

<u>RANK ORDER</u>

RANK	STATE	MILES	% of USA
1	Texas	10,473	7.3%
2	Illinois	7,197	5.0%
3	California	6,052	4.2%
4	Ohio	5,484	3.8%
5	Pennsylvania	5,145	3.6%
6	Kansas	5,084	3.5%
7	Georgia	4,795	3.3%
8	Minnesota	4,504	3.1%
9	Indiana	4,185	2.9%
10	Missouri	4,168	2.9%
11	Iowa	4,091	2.9%
12	North Dakota	3,795	2.6%
13	New York	3,788	2.6%
14	Michigan	3,699	2.6%
15	Nebraska	3,480	2.4%
16	Wisconsin	3,478	2.4%
17	Alabama	3,296	2.3%
18	Montana	3,293	2.3%
19	Oklahoma	3,286	2.3%
20	Virginia	3,262	2.3%
21	North Carolina	3,251	2.3%
22	Washington	3,145	2.2%
23	Colorado	2,850	2.0%
24	Florida	2,771	1.9%
25	Kentucky	2,760	1.9%
26	Louisiana	2,753	1.9%
27	Tennessee	2,682	1.9%
28	Mississippi	2,613	1.8%
29	Arkansas	2,607	1.8%
30	West Virginia	2,433	1.7%
31	South Carolina	2,367	1.7%
32	Oregon	2,334	1.6%
33	New Mexico	1,966	1.4%
34	Wyoming	1,904	1.3%
35	Arizona	1,855	1.3%
36	South Dakota	1,768	1.2%
37	Idaho	1,642	1.1%
38	Utah	1,443	1.0%
39	Maine	1,202	0.8%
40	Nevada	1,199	0.8%
41	Massachusetts	1,071	0.7%
42	New Jersey	922	0.6%
43	Maryland	760	0.5%
44	Connecticut	635	0.4%
45	Vermont	600	0.4%
46	Alaska	482	0.3%
47	New Hampshire	437	0.3%
48	Delaware	227	0.2%
49	Rhode Island	102	0.1%
50	Hawaii	0	0.0%
	District of Columbia	25	0.0%

Source: Association of American Railroads
   "Railroads and States 2001" (http://www.aar.org/AboutTheIndustry/StateInformation.asp)
**Includes Class I and non-Class I miles. Excludes trackage rights. Synonymous with route-miles, so that a mile of single track is counted the same as a mile of double track.*

XVI. SOURCES

ACT, Inc.
500 ACT Drive, P.O. Box 168
Iowa City, IA 52243-0168
319-337-1000
www.act.org

Administration for Children and Families
U.S. Dept. of Health and Human Services
370 L'Enfant Promenade, SW
Washington, DC 20447
202-401-9215
www.acf.dhhs.gov

American Cancer Society, Inc.
1599 Clifton Road, NE
Atlanta, GA 30329-4251
800-227-2345
www.cancer.org

American Dental Association
211 E. Chicago Ave.
Chicago, IL 60611-2678
312-440-2500
www.ada.org

American Hospital Association
One North Franklin
Chicago, IL 60606-3421
312-422-3000
www.aha.org

American Medical Association
515 North State Street
Chicago, IL 60610
800-621-8335
www.ama-assn.org

Association of American Railroads
50 F Street, NW
Washington, DC 20001-1564
202-639-2100
www.aar.org

Bureau of the Census
4700 Silver Hill Road
Suitland, MD 20746
301-457-2800
www.census.gov

Bureau of Economic Analysis
U.S. Department of Commerce
1441 L Street, NW
Washington, DC 20230
202-606-9900
www.bea.doc.gov

Bureau of Justice Statistics
U.S. Department of Justice
810 Seventh St., NW
Washington, DC 20531
202-307-0765
www.ojp.usdoj.gov/bjs/

Bureau of Labor Statistics
Department of Labor
2 Massachusetts Ave., NE.
Washington, DC 20212-0001
202-691-5200
www.bls.gov/iif/

Centers for Disease Control and Prevention
1600 Clifton Road
Atlanta, GA 30333
800-311-3435
www.cdc.gov

Centers for Medicare and Medicaid Services
(Formerly Health Care Financing Administration)
7500 Security Boulevard
Baltimore, MD 21244-1850
877-267-2323
www.cms.gov

College Board
The College Board
45 Columbus Avenue
New York, NY 10023-6992
212-713-8000
www.collegeboard.com

Economic Research Service
U.S. Department of Agriculture
1800 M Street, NW
Washington, DC 20036-5831
202-694-5050
www.ers.usda.gov

Energy Information Administration
1000 Independence Avenue, SW
Washington, DC 20585
202-586-8800
www.eia.doe.gov

Environmental Protection Agency
Rios Ariel Building
1200 Pennsylvania Ave
Washington, DC 20464
202-272-0167
www.epa.gov

Federal Bureau of Investigation
935 Pennsylvania Avenue, NW
Washington, DC 20535-0001
202-324-3000
www.fbi.gov

Federal Election Commission
999 E Street, NW
Washington, DC 20463
800-424-9530
www.fec.gov

Federal Highway Administration
400 7th Street, SW
Washington, DC 20590
202-366-0660
www.fhwa.dot.gov

Federation of Tax Administrators
444 North Capitol St., NW
Ste 348
Washington, DC 20001
202-624-5890
www.taxadmin.org

XVI. SOURCES (continued)

Food and Nutrition Service
U.S. Department of Agriculture
3101 Park Center Drive, Room 926
Alexandria, VA 22302
703-305-2286
www.fns.usda.gov/fns/

General Services Administration
1800 F Street, NW
Washington, DC 20405
202-501-0705
www.gsa.gov

Health Care Financing Administration
See **Centers for Medicare and Medicaid Services**

Internal Revenue Service
U.S. Department of the Treasury
1111 Constitution Avenue, NW
Washington, DC 20224
800-829-1040
www.irs.ustreas.gov

National Agricultural Statistics Service
1400 Independence Ave, SW
Washington, DC 20250
800-727-9540
www.usda.gov/nass

National Assembly of State Arts Agencies
1029 Vermont Ave., NW 2nd Fl
Washington, DC 20005
202-347-6352
www.nasaa-arts.org

National Association of Realtors
430 N. Michigan Ave
Chicago, IL 60611
800-874-6500
www.realtor.org

National Association of State Park Directors
9894 E. Holden Place
Tucson, AZ 85748
520-298-4924
http://naspd.indstate.edu/index.html

National Center for Education Statistics
U.S. Department of Education
1990 K Street, NW
Washington, DC 20006
202-502-7300
http://nces.ed.gov

National Center for Health Statistics
U.S. Department of Health and Human Services
3311 Toledo Road
Hyattsville, MD 20782-2003
301-458-4636
www.cdc.gov/nchswww/

National Conference of State Legislatures
770 E. First Place
Denver, CO 80230
303-346-7700
www.ncsl.org

National Education Association
1201 16th Street, NW
Washington, DC 20036-3290
202-833-4000
www.nea.org

National Highway Traffic Safety Admin.
U.S. Department of Transportation
400 7th Street, SW
Washington, DC 20590
202-366-9550
www.nhtsa.dot.gov

**National Institute on Alcohol Abuse
And Alcoholism**
5635 Fishers Lane, MSC 9304
Bethesda, MD 20892-9304
301-443-9970
www.niaaa.nih.gov/

National Oceanic & Atmospheric Admin.
U.S. Department of Commerce
14th Street & Constitution Ave., NW. Rm 6217
Washington, DC 20230
202-482-6090
www.noaa.gov

National Weather Service
Storm Prediction Center
1313 Halley Circle
Norman, OK 73069
405-579-0771
www.spc.noaa.gov

Social Security Administration
Windsor Park Building
6401 Security Boulevard
Baltimore, MD 21235
800-772-1213 (information)
www.ssa.gov

Taubman Center for State and Local Government
Kennedy School of Government—Harvard University
79 JFK Street
Cambridge MA 02138
617-495-2199
www.ksg.harvard.edu/taubmancenter

Tax Foundation
1900 M Street, NW
Ste 550
Washington, DC 20036
202-464-6200
www.taxfoundation.org

U.S. Department of Defense
The Pentagon
Washington, DC 20301
703-697-5737
www.defenselink.mil

U.S. Department of Veterans Affairs
810 Vermont Avenue, NW
Washington, DC 20420
202-273-5700
www.va.gov

U.S. Geological Survey
12201 Sunrise Valley Drive
Reston, VA 20192
1-888-275-8747
www.usgs.gov

XVII. INDEX

XVII. INDEX (continued)

XVII. INDEX (continued)

XVII. INDEX (continued)

CHAPTER INDEX

Agriculture

Crime & Law Enforcement

Defense

Economy

Education

Employment & Labor

Energy & Environment

Geography

Gov't Finances: Federal

Gov't Finances: State & Local

Health

Households and Housing

Population

Social Welfare

Transportation

HOW TO USE THIS INDEX

Place left thumb on the outer edge of this page. To locate the desired entry, fold back the remaining page edges and align the index edge mark with the appropriate page edge mark.

Other books by Morgan Quitno Press:

- *State Statistical Trends (monthly journal)*
- *Health Care State Rankings 2004 ($54.95)*
- *Crime State Rankings 2004 ($54.95)*
- *City Crime Rankings, 10th Edition ($42.95)*
- *Education State Rankings 2003-2004 ($49.95)*

Call toll free: 1-800-457-0742 or
visit us at www.statestats.com